TAYLOR BRANCH

SIMON & SCHUSTER

PILLAR

America

in the

King Years

1963–65

OF

FIRE

SIMON & SCHUSTER
Rockefeller Center
1230 Avenue of the Americas
New York, NY 10020

Designed by Edith Fowler
Photo research by Natalie Goldstein
Manufactured in the United States of America

10   9   8   7   6   5

Library of Congress Cataloging-in-Publication Data

Branch, Taylor.
  Pillar of fire : America in the King years, 1963–65 /
Taylor Branch.
      p.   cm.
  Includes bibliographical references and index.
  1. Afro-Americans—Civil rights.   2. Civil rights
movements—United States—History—20th century.
3. King, Martin Luther, Jr., 1929–1968.   4. United States
—History—1961–1969.   I. Title.
E185.61.B7915   1998
323.1' 196073—dc21   97-46076   CIP
ISBN 0-684-80819-6

FOR CHRISTY

Contents

Preface to *Pillar of Fire*

THERE WAS NO historical precedent for Birmingham, Alabama, in April and May of 1963, when the power balance of a great nation turned not on clashing armies or global commerce but on the youngest student demonstrators of African descent, down to first- and second-graders. Only the literature of Passover ascribes such impact to the fate of minors, and never before was a country transformed, arguably redeemed, by the active moral witness of schoolchildren.

The miracle of Birmingham might have stood alone as the culmination of a freedom movement grown slowly out of Southern black churches. Yet it was merely the strongest of many tides that crested in the movement's peak years, 1963–65. They challenged, inspired, and confounded America over the meaning of simple words: dignity, equal votes, equal souls. They gripped Malcolm X along with President Johnson, buffeted the watchwords "integration" and "nonviolence," broke bodies and spirits, enlarged freedom.

This is a continuing work, which follows *Parting the Waters,* an account of the King years from 1954 to 1963. To introduce impending elements as well as continuing ones, it begins with five chapters that approach Birmingham from afar, sometimes unconsciously. The characters include Orthodox rabbis, sharecroppers, Muslim prisoners, and a dispirited Vice President, in settings from North America's oldest Christian settlement of St. Augustine, Florida, to its western frontier in Los Angeles. All had reached points of crisis by Birmingham spring, when the young marchers released collateral forces that drew them together. Seekers of the black vote in rural Mississippi, who literally could not move in 1963, rose to dominate the pivotal year of 1964.

I try to employ nomenclature authentic to the historical period. People of African descent are "Negroes" until the prevailing term of self-reference changed, or when characters at the time spoke differently. Muslim mosques appear as "temples" when the members called them so. My mission statement for the trilogy, the last volume of which will be *At Canaan's Edge,* remains expressed by the following words from the preface to *Parting the Waters.*

Almost as color defines vision itself, race shapes the cultural eye—what we do and do not notice, the reach of empathy and the alignment of response. This subliminal force recommends care in choosing a point of view for a history grounded in race. Strictly speaking, this book is not a biography of Martin Luther King, Jr., though he is at its heart.

I have tried to make biography and history reinforce each other by knitting together a number of personal stories along the main seam of an American epoch. Like King himself, this book attempts to rise from an isolated culture into a larger history by speaking more than one language.

My purpose is to write a narrative history of the civil rights movement out of the conviction from which it was made, namely that truth requires a maximum effort to see through the eyes of strangers, foreigners, and enemies. I hope to sustain my thesis that King's life is the best and most important metaphor for American history in the watershed postwar years.

Baltimore, Maryland
November 1997

PART ONE

Birmingham

Tides

1

Islam
in Los Angeles

O N APRIL 27, 1962, Muslims gathered for the Friday evening prayer service at Muhammad's Temple No. 27 in South-Central Los Angeles, east of Culver City and west of Watts. Some two hundred followers of Elijah Muhammad sat in folding metal chairs, separated by sex—the women wearing head coverings and floor-length dresses, generally white, and the men in distinctive dark suits with suspenders and bow ties, their heads closely shaved. Facing them from the podium, a blackboard posed in large letters the thematic question of the Nation of Islam: "WHICH ONE WILL SURVIVE THE WAR OF ARMAGEDDON?" To the left, framed by a cross, an American flag, and a silhouette of a hanging lynch victim, the blackboard offered a grim choice labeled "Christianity, Slavery, Suffering, Death," in pointed contrast to the alternative proclaimed on the right: "Islam, Freedom, Justice, Equality." Thus, explained the quick-witted Minister John X Morris, the Honorable Elijah Muhammad answered one of the central puzzles of all religion—how to reconcile unmerited suffering with the existence of a benevolent God. Allah had permitted the Christian nations to bring Africans into slavery—"chewing on men's bones for three hundred years," as Muhammad put it—to test the will of the victims to reestablish their religious dignity.

Muhammad's Nation of Islam demanded that followers assume full responsibility for their own rehabilitation, and give whites due respect for enterprise if not for morals. "You are the man that is asleep," Elijah Muhammad scolded through his new newspaper, *Muhammad Speaks.* "The white man is wide awake. He is not a dummy by any means. He has built a world. His knowledge and wisdom is now reaching out through space." Even Assistant Minister Arthur X Coleman, who spoke that night, acknowledged the human cost of following the Nation's exacting discipline. His own wife had left him for home back in Tennessee not long after he had thrown all the sweet potatoes and pork products out of their refrigerator to follow the Muslim diet. Although Coleman scoffed at some teachings from the beginning—he told his grandfather he doubted claims that Mr. Muhammad had conversations directly with God—he struggled toward a new identity through an eclectic regimen that included Dale Carnegie public speaking courses, military-style fitness exercises, a program of readings on ancient civilizations, and what amounted to a second job selling Muslim newspapers and "fishing" for prospects on the streets.

The typically rough, streetwise membership of Temple No. 27 included few with any higher education. Among these, Delores X Stokes was a minor celebrity as a lifelong Muslim who had actually seen and talked with Elijah Muhammad himself. Her father, though far too old to serve in World War II, had entered federal prison voluntarily with Muhammad to protest the white man's wars, and then in 1945, when Delores was a girl of ten, had gone to Michigan to establish one of the Nation's first farms, always sending a portion of the crops to feed the membership in the cities. Delores remained frail after a severe case of childhood rickets, with a small soft voice and tentative movements, but she excelled first as a student and then as a strong-willed teacher, married to one of the first college-trained men in the Nation of Islam, Ronald X Stokes of Boston. After their wedding in August of 1960, they had come west to help shore up the Nation's outpost in Los Angeles, both of them working days for the county government but spending many of their off-duty hours at the temple, where Ronald served as secretary. Within the tiny colony of Muslims, the young couple were admired for serene, spiritual qualities that transcended the hard fixation upon vengeance more common among the regular members. Ronald Stokes was taking lessons in Arabic, the better to appreciate the poetry of the Q'uran in its original tongue.

The prayer service went past ten o'clock that Friday, after which fiscal "Lieutenant" William Rogers, a parking lot attendant who aspired to become an accountant, counted cash donations that ran to some $500, mostly in small bills. Men were required to bring cars around to the door as a protective courtesy for women, who supervised children during temple events. Mabel Zeno wondered what was taking her husband, Charles, and their three grade-school children so long. Not knowing they had stopped to buy gasoline for their Ford station wagon, she left Delores Stokes at the women's waiting area and walked to the front entrance, scanning the Broadway traffic. Although most of the congregation had dispersed, Monroe X Jones stayed on to complete a clothing sale. As a delivery driver for S&M Dry Cleaners, he had occasional access to abandoned or discarded items, for which the temple was a good resale outlet because even the poorest Muslim had to dress formally in public. About eleven o'clock that night, he invited Fred X Jingles, who shined shoes at Ward's Shoe Shine Stand in Long Beach, to inspect an old suit with a hole in the pants. Jones had obtained two repair estimates: one for a cheap patch, another for a reweaving job that might cost a few dollars more than the suit itself.

Officers Frank Tomlinson and Stanley Kensic were driving south on Broadway when they passed two Negro males standing behind the opened trunk of a 1954 Buick Special, examining what appeared to be a plastic garment bag. Their first night together as partners was special for both young policemen—the eve of Kensic's wedding and Tomlinson's last shift of the one-year rookie probation. Given their good moods, only an afterthought prompted Kensic to suggest that Tomlinson back up for a burglary sweep. Tomlinson double-parked, turning on the cruiser's flashing lights, and as they exited Kensic asked the two men if they were Black Muslims. "Yes, sir," came the clipped, businesslike response, which matched the intelligence reports passed along lately at roll call about the dangerous new cult. The officers frisked the two suspects for weapons and compared the Buick's tag number with those on the stolen car hot sheet, coming up negative. Before calling in their names to check for outstanding warrants, they asked where the clothes came from. The two Muslims had only begun to tell of the reweave-or-patch choice on the suit when Kensic decided to split them up for individual accounts. According to subsequent conflicting testimony, his approximate words to Jingles were either "Come with me" or "Let's separate these niggers."

The commotion was attracting a small crowd. Roosevelt X Walker, a city garbage worker and escort lieutenant, on post to escort unattended women from the service, ducked inside the temple to call Clarence X Jingles, saying, "Your brother is in trouble," and they ran down Broadway. Officer Kensic later conceded that he detected no belligerence in Fred X Jingles while walking toward the front of the Buick, and certainly no flight or resistance, but Kensic did object to a take-your-hands-off-me attitude, or gestures, which so challenged his sense of command that he swiftly put Jingles into the police hold, twisting his arm behind him and wrapping an elbow around his neck to lift him in the air and fling him facedown across the Buick's hood. Instead of going limp in submission, Jingles surprised Kensic by screaming and writhing. He managed to twist out of the hold and fought upward to get off the hood. Just then, Monroe X Jones bolted from Tomlinson and pulled Kensic off Jingles. A fistfight broke out, and as a stunned Tomlinson ran from the back of the Buick to assist his partner, Roosevelt X Walker raced up with fellow Muslims and grabbed him, too. Tomlinson would retain an indistinct memory of being twirled above their heads like a trophy.

William Tribble, who was driving home from a moonlighting job as a doorman at the nearby Club 54, double-parked near the police cruiser and jumped from his car, alarmed by the sights of a street brawl. Kensic was down, trying to ward off attackers who darted in to hit him before he could get up or draw his gun. When they ignored shouts to leave the officers alone, Tribble ran behind his own car, unlocked the trunk, fumbled for his special deputy's .38, pulled out an old box of cartridges, loaded the gun there in the middle of Broadway, then ran around near the curb behind the Buick and fired a warning shot into the air. Its loud crack silenced the frenzy for an instant before the Muslims, their belligerence loosed by a sense of victory over the police, turned upon the none-too-confident Negro who had once aspired to be a policeman. When Tribble's gun misfired on a second warning shot, they inched toward him as he backed up, his gun trembling visibly.

This became a moment of regret for Tomlinson, who found himself freed on the sidewalk behind the Muslims while their attention was riveted upon Tribble in the street. Training told Tomlinson to stand clear, draw his gun, freeze everyone, and then radio for help, but he pulled out his sap instead and lunged toward the nearest Muslims from behind, aiming to get even for having failed to land a single blow. Just then, however, Tribble fired into the crowd, hitting Clarence Jingles in the side, and Tomlinson joined his adversaries scattering in headlong dives away from the bullet. Monroe X Jones landed on the pavement close to Kensic, who was so dazed that Jones was able to pull Kensic's gun from its holster. Before Tomlinson could jump up with his gun, Jones shot him—the bullet tearing a path from the back of Tomlinson's left shoulder, down his arm, and out through his elbow. Then Jones danced along the curb to face Tribble, and in a wild panic they emptied their guns at each other from a range of some ten feet. When the terrible noise ceased, each man was amazed to find himself still standing. Jones, discovering blood from a gunshot wound in his shoulder, threw Kensic's gun down a sewer and ran blindly through the streets until he stopped exhausted at a phone booth to call his mother for help.

When Officer Paul Kuykendall passed by just after Tribble's frantic departure, the excited looks on the faces of the gathering crowd made him snap into a U-turn and park his Ford Falcon station wagon across from Tomlinson's cruiser, a block south of the temple. A fifteen-year veteran of the Los Angeles Police Department (LAPD)—blue-eyed, burly, and so light-skinned that many of his colleagues did not know he was a Negro—Kuykendall was famous among the Negro officers as the first nonwhite ever to win assignment "on motors," as cruiser patrol was called, back in the early 1950s. For a long time he had patrolled alone, or paired with one of his Negro successors, as the department's policy against interracial partnerships had been reversed only the previous year, in 1961. To protect his ambiguous identity, or escape from it, Kuykendall carried himself as a loner and for a number of years had managed to avoid assignments most likely to make race a blatant issue in daily police work.

Extraordinary events began to conspire against camouflage when the off-duty Kuykendall leaped from his car in civilian clothes, transfixed by the sight of a bloodied police officer weaving unsteadily in the middle of Broadway surrounded by angry Muslims. This was Kensic, whose first shocked thought after the gunfire had been to tackle anyone who might have taken his revolver. Now in a helpless rage, like a baited bear, Kensic went down again. The assailants—among them an athletic teenager named Troy X Augustine—paid no attention to Kuykendall's shouts to desist until he drew his own revolver and fired into the air. The shot refocused all their adrenaline instantly on Kuykendall, who backed them down with the gun until he could get close enough to Kensic to hear that his gun was lost and his partner shot over on the sidewalk. A Negro woman was kneeling there, comforting Tomlinson and wailing about why on earth did anyone shoot a policeman. Kuykendall kept his gun and one eye on the Muslims, who were beginning to melt away, as he backed to the driver's door of Tomlinson's cruiser, reached in for the radio, and sent out the department's most urgent message: officer in trouble.

A moaning Roosevelt Walker was among the first of the fleeing Muslims to reach the temple. He limped through the closer of two entrances and collapsed at the foot of the stairs leading up to private offices above the assembly hall. His cries for help brought Minister John X Morris and other officials hurtling down to find their escort lieutenant bleeding profusely, yelling, "I'm shot!" A stray bullet from the Tribble-Jones exchange had pierced his crotch. Morris shouted for Secretary Ronald Stokes to call an ambulance. Some Muslims began to carry Walker upstairs for comfort; others thought they should take him to the hospital themselves. Walker became stymied cargo halfway up a jammed stairway, with some trying to take him up, others down, and still others bursting in with news from the fight.

A horn blast and loud shouts for Minister John X Morris came from a carload of Muslims who pulled up outside yelling that they had Brother Clarence inside with them, shot, and what should they do? Morris signaled from the window that they should wait, but chaos overtook him before he could find out about the ambulance. The car lurched off, carrying a hysterical debate about whether they should speed home, to the hospital, or back to the temple to await definitive orders from Minister Morris. With the sounds of police sirens rising, Morris pushed his way outside and up the sidewalk to the main entrance—where Mabel Zeno was still waiting for her husband—herding everyone he could into the assembly hall.

Officers Donald Weese and Richard Anderson, in the first cruiser that roared up to the fight scene a block south of the mosque, scarcely slowed down as they caught sight of the two downed uniforms and Kuykendall in the street windmilling them with one arm as he pointed with the other toward the men in Muslim dress who were running for the temple. Some of these were stragglers from the fight; others, like Ronald Stokes, who was hoisting Roosevelt Walker's feet, were spilling out of the office entrance. Anderson yelled for Weese to let him jump out of the cruiser in foot pursuit. This small delay allowed Officers Robert Williams and Robert Reynolds to barrel around them in the second crusier to a screeching, skewed halt north of the temple. Just before then, from the opposite direction, Charles X Zeno pulled up looking for his wife. A small bit of the emergency registered quickly from the faces and sirens, whereupon Zeno told his three sons to wait in the car while he ran to get their mother before there was trouble.

Overtaking several Muslims, Officer Anderson stopped one with his nightstick on the landing at the main entrance and dragged him back down into the sidewalk, yelling for everyone to freeze. Observing this as he converged from the other cruiser, Officer Williams drew his gun and ran past them through one of the big double doors. Behind him, Officer Reynolds started to object that—quite apart from any scruples about search warrants, probable cause, or religious sanctuary—smart tactics called for sealing off the building until help arrived, but by then it was too late, and, on an instinctive flash that even if Williams was an impulsive six-month rookie, he was still his partner, Reynolds lowered his shoulder to follow. He slammed into Charles Zeno with enough momentum to carry both of them through the hallway at an angle into the men's coatroom on the right, grappling in mutual shock, swinging each other by the lapels for leverage while they bounced off walls and crashed into the water cooler, whose glass jug shattered on the floor as the two men landed in a heap. Several other Muslims joined on Zeno's side until they heard the loud voice of Minister Morris saying to leave the officer alone and turned to see Officer Williams holding his gun at Morris's temple. Reynolds freed himself and retrieved his own gun from the floor. Then, overtaken by rage and release, he drove his fist into Zeno's jaw about the time the first shots rang out from the sidewalk.

Officer Weese took up a position at the curb directly in front of the entrance with his gun pointed and his off hand resting at the knee, yelling freeze. From the next of the cruisers now piling rapidly in, Officer Lee Logan came up on the right with his weapons out. The Muslims compressed back upon Officer Anderson, fighting and resisting him as he swung his nightstick to drive them against the exterior wall. One or two of them cried out, "Why? Why?" Then nearly all of them took up the rhythmic Arabic chant *"Allah-u akbar! Allah-u akbar!"* ("God is great! God is great!"), which further unnerved the officers as something unintelligible and voodooish, much as the sudden onslaught of the police undid some of the Muslims, especially William X Rogers, who had carried a morbid fear of guns since being wounded four times in Korea. When Rogers made a dash for the entrance, Weese shot him through the spine.

Following a tiny aftershock of peace came the blur of violence. The younger brother of William Rogers pummeled Officer Logan, who finally threw him a few feet away and opened repeated fire along with Weese, hitting Robert X Rogers four times. As Arthur Coleman dived away from the shots, one of the bullets went through his hip and lodged at the base of his penis. Officer Anderson came out of the crowd to the left in the grip of Ronald Stokes, who was clinging to him as a shield. When Anderson broke free to leave his adversary alone in an open space, Stokes raised both hands toward Weese, who shot him through the heart from about eight feet, then started to reload.

Coleman attracted notice by struggling to stand. Officer Logan tried to cuff him back to submission with the butt handle of his gun, but Coleman seized his wrist and the two men came face-to-face. Logan kneed him in the groin, and even in terror the officer felt sickened by the unexpected warmth of the blood from Coleman's wound. With the gun deadlocked between them, Logan managed to fire a shot into the left side of Coleman's chest less than an inch above the lung. Still, Coleman hung on—his hands wrapped tightly around Logan's, his finger twisted over Logan's on the trigger, each man desperate to push the barrel away.

Just then Officer Kuykendall came running up from the south to put his revolver at Coleman's head. "Let go of the gun!" he ordered, and Coleman yelled, "Are you crazy? He shot me twice!" When Kuykendall threatened to blow his brains out, Coleman told him to go ahead. Then came a frozen moment in front of paralyzed onlookers—three men's heads close together, a black man and a uniformed white officer in a death struggle joined by a man of hidden ties to each side, with Logan's gun trembling back and forth under pressure in their midst. As Coleman slowly wrenched the muzzle around toward Logan, Kuykendall had to decide whether to take one life instantly or risk another by delay. He put away his gun, pulled out his sap, and slammed it again and again to the skull until Coleman finally lost his grip on Logan's gun and slumped to the pavement.

In a skittering aftermath outside, the Long Beach minister, Randolph X Sidle, darted out to smash the water jug from the women's coatroom against the head of Officer Anderson, then melted quickly back among the captives inside. A few moments later—so long after it was over that the suicidal dash seemed to take place in slow motion—Fred X Jingles ran full speed up Broadway from the car that had circled the block indecisively with his wounded brother, screaming at the police, and finally leaped high on Officer Logan's back as though to ride him. Four or five officers from the scores now gathered with shotguns and other heavy weaponry beat

Jingles to the ground and handcuffed him, as they also handcuffed the four shot Muslims lying facedown nearby. Violence lasted longer in the men's coatroom, where there was vomiting from shame or fear, and where some of the victorious officers punished more than a dozen Muslims spread-eagled against the wall. They took turns searching them, screaming at and beating them, kicking them between the legs from behind, and finally, ripping each of their suit jackets from coattail to the neck and each of their trousers from the rear belt line forward through the crotch to the zipper. An episode that had begun over a used suit for Fred X Jingles ended half an hour and much chaotic hatred later with many shredded, torn ones. Mabel Zeno, who had slipped out the back of the mosque with Delores Stokes and was straining against the police lines to recover her sons—still parked in the Ford near all the shooting—saw her husband, Charles, marched out to police wagons in a line of prisoners, dragging his pants at his feet.

A DAY LATER at Central Receiving Hospital, Officer Kensic was startled to receive a visit from LAPD Chief William Parker. Arthur X Coleman, on being bailed out of General Hospital, was no less surprised to find himself facing the pocket camera of the Nation of Islam's national minister, Malcolm X, who had flown in from New York. The opposing leaders swiftly took the public stage from the combatants themselves. Calling Friday night's violence "the most brutal conflict I've seen" in twenty-five years as a Los Angeles policeman, the last twelve as chief, Parker portrayed his men as victims of a savage attack from a group he described as a "hate organization which is dedicated to the destruction of the Caucasian race." Malcolm X, for his part, drew a large crowd to the Statler-Hilton Hotel on the day before the funeral of Ronald Stokes, and he shocked many of the curious reporters with the audacity of his opening words: "Seven innocent, unarmed black men were shot down in cold blood...." He described Chief Parker as a man "intoxicated with power and with his own ego," who had transmitted an obsessive fear of the Muslims to his officers. "The same feelings he harbors towards the Muslims extend to the entire Negro community and probably to the Mexican-Americans as well," said Malcolm, who accused the "white press" of acting as tools of Chief Parker to "suppress the facts" through one-sided stories such as appeared in Los Angeles: "Muslims Shoot, Beat Police in Wild Gunfight."

For Earl Broady, the Malcolm X who appeared unannounced at his office seemed quite different from the daredevil Black Muslim in the news. He spoke with evenhanded precision to reconstruct the chaos and asked for Broady's representation in the criminal trials he felt were sure to come, calculating that the state must prosecute the Muslims in order to ward off civil damage suits. Broady turned Malcolm away more than once, saying he was too busy and too close to Chief Parker. As a policeman himself from 1929 to 1946, before entering law, Broady saw Parker as a reform autocrat in the style of J. Edgar Hoover and gave him credit for modest improvements over the frontier corruptions of the old Raymond Chandler–era LAPD. Broady's wife, a devout Methodist, objected vehemently to the case on the grounds that the Muslims were openly anti-Christian, unlike the worst of his ordinary criminal clients, and Broady himself resented the Nation of Islam, drawn largely from stereotypical lowlifes, as an embarrassment to the hard-earned respectability of middle-class Negroes. The Broadys recently had acquired an imposing white colonnade home in Beverly Hills, where Malcolm X visited when he could not find Broady at the office—calling day after day, always alone with a briefcase, playing on Broady's personal knowledge of the harsh, segregated inner world of the LAPD precincts. His patient appeals, plus the largest retainer offer in Broady's career, finally induced the lawyer to take the case.

Malcolm X helped work a similar transformation among the entire nonwhite population of Los Angeles. As an opening wedge, he brought with him from New York a telegram of support from National Association for the Advancement of Colored People Executive Director Roy Wilkins calling for an investigation of possible police brutality in the Stokes case. Based upon the NAACP's long record of complaints against Parker's department, Wilkins doubted the police version that unarmed Muslims had been uniformly the aggressors against armed officers. "From our knowledge, the Muslims are not brawlers," he said. At first, Wilkins and NAACP leaders in Los Angeles tried to distance themselves from the stigma of the Muslims, saying that the NAACP on principle would defend even the segregationist White Citizens Council against excessive police force, but Malcolm and the city fathers worked from opposite ends to deny the established Negro leaders their safe ground. At a Board of Supervisors leadership meeting on May 8, Negro leaders supported Chief Parker's call for a grand jury campaign to wipe out the Muslims, until large numbers of nonleaders who had jammed into the room hooted them down, yelling that it was the police, not the Muslims, who needed investigation. One supervisor announced that he had not felt such racial tension since the "zoot-suit riots" of 1944–45. Three days later, twenty-five Negro ministers obtained an emergency audience with Chief Parker, but they had scarcely begun their pitch for a cooperative effort to eliminate the Muslims *and* police brutality when Parker stalked out, declaring that he refused to be lectured by anyone who questioned the integrity of his department.

As word spread of this rebuff, the ministers felt compelled to call a mass meeting to steady their course. They secured one of the most prestigious pulpits in the city—that of Rev. J. Raymond Henderson, the old friend and rival of Rev. Martin Luther King, Sr., on Atlanta's Auburn Avenue back in the 1930s, who had migrated to California to build one of the largest congregations in the West—and on Sunday evening, May 13, an overflow crowd of three thousand packed Second Baptist Church. As a non-Christian, Malcolm X was not permitted on the podium, of course, and there was heated discussion among the deacons about whether to admit him at all, but once he was there seated next to the wheelchair of William X Rogers, who was permanently paralyzed from the gunshot wound through his back, and once he rose and asked to speak from the floor after the Pledge of Allegiance and several fervent prayers for God's justice, there was no polite alternative but to allow the exotic Muslim to hold forth from the sanctuary of the Negro Baptists. He spoke for the better part of an hour. A Negro newspaper described him far down in its story as "a brilliant speaker and a studied orator, capable of swaying any audience in the typical manner displayed by Adolf Hitler...." One of Chief Parker's own undercover agents reported that when Reverend Henderson interrupted to chastise Malcolm X for inflammatory raw speech about police conduct, members of Second Baptist led the booing of their own pastor and demanded that Malcolm continue.

The white city fathers threw up an opposing wall of indignation. Mayor Sam Yorty, who had won his office the previous year partly on the strength of Negro votes, after campaigning against Chief Parker's segregated, "Gestapo organization," endorsed his former antagonist "one hundred per cent" over the shootings at the Muslim mosque. He publicly accused the NAACP leaders of consorting with Muslims of known criminal records, such as Malcolm X, and of following a "Communist-inspired" program of "wild and exaggerated charges of police brutality." Together with Chief Parker, Yorty flew to Washington for a publicized conference with Attorney General Robert Kennedy. They described the LAPD's ongoing intelligence operation against the Muslims, and obtained Kennedy's promise of a federal investigation. These consolidating moves sealed off most citizens behind warlike news stories such as appeared in the *Los Angeles Times:* "Muslim Hatred Called Threat to Community—Fanatical Cult Said to Direct Venom at All Whites and Negroes Trying to Oppose It."

At least one political career rose on the recoil of sentiment among minorities. Mervyn Dymally, a schoolteacher from Trinidad and fringe candidate for the California Assembly, complained to the local Muslims that he had been excluded from the mass meeting at Second Baptist, obliged to stand outside in the rain with the overflow crowd while his heavily favored opponent served as emcee. By the next Sunday's mass meeting, Malcolm X had gained not only a position on the podium but considerable influence over the program. He brought on an American Indian speaker and a Mexican-American, urging the more respectable ethnic leaders to "work together with us, and if we Muslims get the white men off our backs, they'll never get on yours." Then he introduced Dymally, whose first words to the crowd—the traditional Muslim greeting in

Arabic, *"As-Salaamu—Alaikum"* ("Peace be upon you")—produced a sharp breath of surprise and then thunderous applause on the swelling inclusion of outcasts.

Dymally explained that although he was a Christian through his mother, he had learned the greeting from his Muslim father in the Indies, and that what spanned these religious differences among them was a reasonable but degrading fear of the Los Angeles police, which the new candidate said he had experienced himself many times on being stopped for interrogation in spite of his middle-class dress and his college degrees. An explosion of wounded sentiment, which allowed the starchiest Negroes to express at least some identification with previously alien Muslims, stretched the narrow bounds of acceptable civic leaders to include new-comers such as Dymally, who, long after reaching the U.S. Congress, traced his miracle victory as the first foreign-born minority member of the California legislature to the emotional chemistry of the second mass meeting.

THE STOKES CASE marked a turning point in the hidden odyssey that surfaced Malcolm X as an enduring phenomenon of race. He saw the shootings as a fundamental crisis in several respects—first as a test of Muhammad's teachings on manhood and truth. Ever since the Montgomery bus boycott of 1955–56, Malcolm had criticized Martin Luther King as a "traitor to the Negro people," disparaging his nonviolence as "this little passive resistance or wait-until-you-change-your mind-and-then-let-me-up philosophy," and he did not hesitate to ridicule a national movement built on sit-ins and Freedom Rides. "Anybody can sit," said Malcolm. "An old woman can sit. A coward can sit.... It takes a man to stand." Always there was an element of swagger in Malcolm's appeal, and at times a bristling, military posture: "... You might see these Negroes who believe in nonviolence and mistake us for one of them and put your hands on us thinking that we're going to turn the other cheek—and we'll put you to death just like that."

Before his first emergency flight to Los Angeles, Malcolm confided to associates that the moment demanded an honest Muslim response and that they should expect to hear of blood flowing. His exacting investigations were conducted as prime research toward the Nation's independent justice in which, at a minimum, sanctioned Muslims would strike one of the most guilty of the LAPD officers. Malcolm carried forward his plans by stealth until strict orders intervened through National Secretary John Ali: no retribution. "Play dead on everything ...," instructed Elijah Muhammad. "Just tell Malcolm to cool his heels."

Malcolm obeyed, but he chafed. When an all-white coroner's jury on May 14 required less than thirty minutes to deliver a ruling of justifiable homicide in the Stokes case, even though Officer Weese bluntly testified that he had shot an unarmed man whose arms were raised because he felt menaced, reporters asked the new public figure in Los Angeles whether he really despaired of getting justice in the courts, and if so, what would he do? "I can only say that I am thankful there is a God in Heaven to give real justice to our people when necessary," Malcolm replied. Pressed to reconcile this otherworldliness with his icy realism, he would only say, "God gives justice in his own way."

Back in New York, the editor of Harlem's *Amsterdam News* observed that Malcolm had lost face by looking passively to the Almighty. The internal strain caused a brief public stir in early June of 1962, when an Air France jetliner crashed near Paris, killing more than one hundred leading white citizens of Atlanta, Georgia. "I got a wire from God today . . . ," Malcolm announced at a Los Angeles rally protesting the first criminal indictments handed down against Muslims in the Stokes case. "Many people have been asking, 'Well, what are you going to do?' And since we know that the man is tracking us down day by day to try and find out what we are going to do, so he'll have some excuse to put us behind his bars, we call on our God. He gets rid of 120 of them in one whop . . . and we hope that every day another plane falls out of the sky." To cheers and applause, he offered tortured consolation. "God knows you are cowards," he said. "God knows you are afraid. God knows that the white man has got you shaking in your boots. So God doesn't leave it up to you to defend yourself."

Mayor Yorty played a police agent's recording of Malcolm's remarks at a press conference. "This shows the distorted type of mind this fiend has," he announced, and the resulting stories—"Warn on 'Mouthing' of Muslim"—became the first news item about Malcolm X to draw national press attention. In Atlanta, where Martin Luther King and Harry Belafonte had just canceled sit-ins against downtown segregation as a conciliatory gesture to the grieving city, reporters asked King what it meant that Malcolm could express joy over the random deaths of white strangers. "If the Muslim leader said that," King carefully replied, "I would certainly disagree with him."

"The Messenger should have done more," Malcolm told a few trusted associates in his own Temple No. 7. "People in the civil rights movement have been brutalized, and we haven't done anything to help them. Now we have our own brothers killed and maimed, and we *still* haven't done anything." Even this tiny, private glimpse of frustration was startling to Muslims trained by Malcolm himself for unswerving homage to Muhammad's edicts. The Nation's quasi-military apparatus under captains and lieutenants, which guarded doctrines against heresy or even "slack talk," also collected revenue by an exacting system of investigations, trials, and sanctions ranging from reprimands to "slap-gantlets," communal shunning, and excommunication. Muhammad required all males to meet a street-hawking sales quota of his newspaper, *Muhammad Speaks,* and to guarantee performance by prepaying allotments of each issue in cash. "Credit will ruin them," he told his officials. "They are just out of the jungles." Sales of the new paper rose nationwide on spectacular coverage of the Stokes case. By the summer of 1962, Muhammad remarked in wonder that $15,000 was now "merely pocket change," and he agreed to pay the astronomical blanket fee of $120,000 to defend his members in Los Angeles.

Late that year, on being introduced for trial preparation at Elijah Muhammad's second home in Phoenix (bought from the estate of blues-man Louis Jordan), Earl Broady and his co-counsel, Loren Miller, confronted a wizened, wheezy old man of sixty-four years—to them a field hand in a fez, plainly ignorant and inarticulate* as he mumbled thanks for helping "my mens." Utterly astonished that Muhammad held any authority over someone of Malcolm X's polished commitment, the lawyers avoided each other's eyes to keep from laughing impolitely at the attendants who constantly uttered obeisance to the "Holy Apostle." To others, however, the humble manner of Elijah Muhammad only confirmed his miracle power to transform thousands of primitive, decayed "lost souls" into Muslims of permanent zeal. Even the gruff, fearsome Captain Joseph, enforcer of discipline at Malcolm's Temple No. 7 in New York, barely managed to keep his teeth from chattering in the Messenger's presence. Joseph automatically found truth in every twist of Muhammad's reaction to the Los Angeles shooting: surely it was suicidal to risk a war of retaliation when the Nation was so weak.

In December of 1962, at preliminary hearings for the Stokes case defendants—Arthur X Coleman, Fred X Jingles, Minister John X Morris, Roosevelt X Walker, Charles X Zeno, and eight other Muslims—Malcolm X sat erectly in the back of the courtroom and then regularly castigated white reporters at sidewalk press conferences for "writing only the prosecution's side of the story." By then, wiretap clerks in Chicago and Phoenix reported hints of Muslim friction to the FBI, which had been maintaining microphone bugs and telephone wiretaps on Elijah Muhammad since 1957. They heard Muhammad fret with lieutenants about "who's to control Malcolm." While still flattering Malcolm in their direct talks as "a modern Paul" with a genius for gaining public notice, Muhammad occasionally signed off abruptly with an edge of warning: "I hope Allah will keep you wise."

Malcolm's one kindred ally within the Muslim hierarchy—destined to succeed where he failed, as quietly as Malcolm's notoriety would be loud—missed the early Stokes ordeal because he had been locked away in the federal prison at Sandstone, Minnesota, since his twenty-eighth birth-

---

* Similarly, prison psychiatrists during World War II had diagnosed Muhammad as a hard case of paranoid dementia with the mental capacity of an eleven-year-old child.

day in 1961. This was Wallace D. Muhammad, who, since being named by and for the founder of the Nation of Islam, W. D. Fard, had been marked as the seventh and most religious of Elijah Muhammad's eight children. Wallace had been born just before Fard, the mysterious silk peddler, disappeared, having fashioned a revolutionary cosmology for thousands of Negro sharecroppers who migrated north for the paved gold of jobs only to crash into the Depression. Elijah Poole of Georgia, humiliated into alcoholism by relief lines, was one of Fard's most enthusiastic aides in a sectarian movement that swept up eight thousand members and registered as a tribal curiosity among a few whites, including one scholar who published in *The American Journal of Sociology* a 1938 article entitled "The Voodoo Cult Among Negro Migrants in Detroit." Though plainly bemused by some of the sectarian peculiarities, sociologist Erdmann Beynon was impressed that "there is no known case of unemployment among these people." He reported that new members applied to Fard for new Arabic names as a first step toward the recovery of lost culture. "They bathed at least once a day and kept their houses scrupulously clean," wrote Beynon, "so that they might put away all marks of the slavery from which the restoration of the original name had set them free."

In the 1950s, when federal prosecutors denied Wallace Muhammad the military draft deferment due legitimate clergy, Chicago lawyers William Ming and Chauncey Eskridge* arranged for him to serve medical duty as a conscientious objector, but Elijah Poole (now Muhammad) unexpectedly rejected the plea bargain with white law. Much against his will, thinking that his father meant to keep him cloistered and useless, Wallace dutifully entered Sandstone, where he taught Islam to inmates in the prison laundry room or on nice days in the baseball bleachers. For the first time he felt responsible for his own thoughts, and although he attracted a large following of Muslim converts, which excited the fears of most prison authorities, the Sandstone warden became so convinced of salutary effects on inmate rehabilitation that he invited Wallace to write an article on the Islamic concept of sacrifice for the 1962 Christmas issue of the prison journal. Muhammad sent the published magazine home to his mother, Clara, who, in spite of her role as the maternal rock of the Nation of Islam, hummed hymns from her Holiness Church upbringing in Georgia. She was proud that he had gained the balance to draw upon the merit in other religions, and Wallace reluctantly thanked his father for the paradoxical, unseen wisdom to build in him the independent strength to contest Muhammad's concocted version of Islam.

This fight was precisely Wallace Muhammad's purpose at the Sandstone release gate on January 10, 1963, but his brother Elijah Jr. upstaged him on the long drive home to Chicago with a shocking report on im-

---

* Who successfully defended Martin Luther King in his Alabama criminal case of 1960.

pending crises within the Nation—threats, thefts, scandals, plots, betrayals, and rampant fears that Malcolm X might usurp the entire structure if the sickly old man died soon, as appeared likely. The continuing aftermath of the Ronald Stokes violence in Los Angeles kept pushing the stakes higher in revenue, publicity, and prestige, and the family members were disappointed to hear that prison made Wallace less rather than more tolerant of material ambition. "The corrupt hypocrites high in the organization would throw people out for smoking a cigarette while they themselves were drinking champagne every night and going to orgies," he later recorded. When it proved difficult to obtain parole permission to visit Phoenix, he wrote his father two long letters of criticism buttressed with citations from the Q'uran.

Turmoil threw Wallace Muhammad together with Malcolm X late in February, when some four thousand Muslims gathered by bus and motorcade for the annual Savior's Day convention in Chicago. As always, speakers chanted the words "the Honorable Elijah Muhammad" as a practiced mantra, but apprehension ran through the submissive crowd because Muhammad himself was absent for the first time, wheezing from asthma at his retreat in Phoenix. Although not a few Muslims believed Muhammad to be immortal, anxiety for him was so intense that cries went up for reassurance from the chosen son, who was observed and hailed upon his return from prison. Wallace refused to speak. Having received no response to his letters of criticism, he was half convinced that his father was avoiding or testing him. Besides, he considered Savior's Day the embodiment of his father's most egregious blasphemy from the 1930s: proclaiming founder W. D. Fard as the Savior Allah incarnate, much as Jesus was called the incarnation of the Christian god. More than once, Wallace had asked how his father could demand worship of a human being—Fard—in light of the Q'uran's clear definition of "one God, the everlasting refuge, who begets not nor is he begotten," and Elijah Muhammad said he would not understand.

Malcolm X, who presided in Muhammad's absence, made excuses for Wallace by prearrangement. Very privately, the two men met during the convention as the two most likely successors—friends but possibly rivals —each of whom threatened the top officials at headquarters. When Wallace disclosed his determination to resist his father's bizarre, unorthodox religious teachings, Malcolm defended Elijah's adaptations such as the assertion that white people were devils by creation, saying they fit the experience of black people closely enough to gain their attention, and Elijah could correct come-on doctrines once the "lost-found" people were ready. In a related complaint, Wallace confessed that several of his own relatives prospered off the Nation without knowing the first thing about Islam. His stories about power struggles over jewelry and real estate touched a nerve, and the two men fell into collusion.

Malcolm X convened a meeting of Elijah Muhammad's family during the February convention in Chicago, at which he carefully announced his intention to mediate solutions for festering problems before they injured the Nation. They were delicate, he said, and included everything from petty personal disputes to gross personal misconduct and disrespect for doctrine. Privately, he told one family member that he just wanted to help —that he had known of shortcomings in Chicago for some time but had been afraid Allah would punish him if he investigated. Family members boycotted a second meeting, however, and the phone wires burned with indignant calls to Phoenix. Wallace's sister Ethel Sharrieff told her father that Malcolm was insinuating there was something wrong with them and "smart" Malcolm must act as parent. Others warned Elijah that Malcolm was maneuvering to divide them, promote himself, and take over the Nation. It was subversive on its face that he called such a meeting without clearance from Elijah. They said Malcolm was using Elijah's Cadillac and making speeches all over the Midwest to promote himself. From Phoenix in mid-March, Elijah told officials to seize the keys to his Cadillac, cancel Malcolm's lectures, and order him back to New York.

Only then did Malcolm broach to Wallace a fourth issue of corruption beyond money, religious distortion, and dishonest exploitation of the Stokes shootings. At Elijah Muhammad's home before Savior's Day, he said, two former secretaries appeared on the lawn with their babies and shouted that they were going to stand there in the cold until Mr. Muhammad comforted his abandoned children. The household had reacted strangely, said Malcolm, who told Wallace he had rebuffed such rumors until the two frightened and shunned women petitioned in person for help. Wallace replied uncomfortably that he would seek out the secretaries, whom he knew personally, and he soon confirmed to Malcolm that he believed their confessions. Elijah had told them that his wife, Clara, was dead to him, like Khadijah, the wife of the original Prophet Muhammad, and likewise Elijah felt divinely sanctioned to seek out virgins to produce good seed.

Wallace Muhammad felt the revelations as a cruel injustice to his spurned mother, and raged against Elijah as an imposing but distant icon. Wallace scarcely knew his father, who had vanished into hiding for seven years after rival heirs to Fard offered a $500 bounty for his death in the 1930s. Although disciples arrived with daily tributes and breathless word of the aspiring Messenger, Wallace saw Elijah only a few times throughout his childhood—most notably in 1942 when he watched his mother and brothers roll the newly arrived fugitive under the bed in a rug, in a vain attempt to evade arresting police officers. Now, as a young man just out of prison, desperate to hang on to something from the bizarre omens of his past, Wallace interpreted the enormity of his father's sins as the price of strength that was implanting a new religion on the continent, allowing people of African descent first to define themselves by their own deity. He steeled himself to face facts, and to recognize that religious births in history tend to spread unseemly trauma over many decades. This became his anthem to Malcolm.

The FBI had known of Elijah Muhammad's bastard children for more than three years, and without much success had tried to generate publicity about them. Late in 1962, the Chicago FBI office began a prolonged campaign known as a counterintelligence program (or COINTELPRO) against the Nation of Islam that by later internal appraisal "was to be, and continues to be, operated on the 'highest possible plane' and would not involve racism, name calling or mud slinging." Agents recruited prominent Negro citizens, including a Chicago judge, to deliver scripted public attacks on the Muslims, but the wiretaps opened, on a lower plane, the chance to exploit the bastard children as the most sensitive, closely held secret within the Nation of Islam. Imaginative FBI agents anonymously composed and sent to Muhammad's inner circle a series of accusing letters laced with two years' accumulation of salacious details. "There was no indication Muhammad's wife or any of his followers made a direct confrontation with him as a result of these letters," concluded the Chicago SAC (Special Agent in Charge). "The wife did come to hate some of the secretaries, but Muhammad continued his activities and probably still is continuing this activity."

During jury selection for the Stokes trial, wiretappers picked up so much "griping within the 'royal family'" that the Chicago FBI office recommended to J. Edgar Hoover that the Nation be left alone to stew without "any disruption tactics in the form of anonymous letters or phone calls." Modestly, Chicago concluded on March 7 that provocation would be superfluous to the "extreme discontent" spreading naturally, "which could cause Malcolm to fall in disfavor with Muhammad." When Malcolm sent Elijah Muhammad letters attempting to justify his Chicago initiatives, officials on tapped lines between Phoenix and Chicago denounced "a nasty letter" full of lies about the family, which was "seeking, prodding, and prying" while pretending to help. One told Muhammad that Malcolm was "an addict to publicity," another that he was "a spoiled child." Elijah sometimes praised Malcolm for meaning well, and for talent "boosting us up" all over the country, but he also ridiculed him as a usurper reaching beyond his depth, a changeling who bowed down to him like a lamb but then went outside and pretended to be a lion.

Muhammad predicted that Malcolm would never have the courage to talk with him in person about the cryptic "problems" described in his letters, but Malcolm did fly to Phoenix in April. Fainthearted in the presence of the Messenger, he made sure to mention the prodigal son Wallace as his cohort in an anguished mission of preventive repair. Should the irrepressible rumors of secretaries with babies prove true, Malcolm said delicately, he and Wallace were collecting precedents of justification from the Q'uran. Elijah nodded evenly, and suggested scriptural citations himself—the infidelity of King David, the debauchery of Noah, the incest of Lot. He betrayed no fear of this exercise. Both he and Malcolm maintained the pose of being helpful to the other through a preliminary test of will.

The unspoken reality was that Malcolm X already had crossed the threshold of defiance in a sect that allowed no initiative at all. He was tinkering with the image of a leader who claimed the very souls of his followers and the power to pronounce ultimate reality for black people. Both men shied from the consequences of the breach—Malcolm from Muhammad's command of the Muslim apparatus, Muhammad from the loss of Malcolm's visibility as the Muslim ambassador—just as outside upheavals crashed upon them from Birmingham and elsewhere.

2

Prophets in Chicago

D URING THE WEEK of Wallace Muhammad's chilled homecoming from Sandstone prison to South Chicago, Martin Luther King was introduced to Rabbi Abraham Heschel on the North Side of the same city. They came from backgrounds as different from each other as was either from the Nation of Islam—King the Baptist of Atlanta, descended from Negro preachers back into chattel slavery, Heschel the Orthodox Jew of Warsaw, descended from dynastic generations of Hasidic rabbis whose names remained luminous in East European Jewry—among them Rabbi Yitzhak of Berdichev, Rabbi Israel of Rizhyn, Heschel's namesake the Apter rebbe, and Rabbi Dov Ber of Mezeritch, successor in the eighteenth century to the founder of Hasidism himself, Rabbi Israel Ba'al Shem, who, wrote Heschel, "banished melancholy from the soul and uncovered the ineffable delight of being a Jew." After Hitler made a vast cemetery of Jewish ghettos from Amsterdam to Kiev, Heschel in one of his books had memorialized his vanished heritage as a culture that measured its history not by wars or material landmarks but "by how much spiritual substance there is in its everyday existence."

The separate paths of Heschel and King converged at the January 1963 Chicago Conference on Religion and Race, an unprecedented ecumenical gathering of nearly one thousand delegates including world-renowned theologians such as Paul Tillich and the established leaders of nearly every religious body in America. In private, there was a fair amount of sharp-eyed professional jockeying among the assembled clergy. Protestants considered themselves on the defensive because their churches housed nearly all those touched by the dispute over racial segregation in the South, where all warring sides claimed inspiration from the same Protestant doctrine. Since the landmark Supreme Court decision out-lawing school segregation almost nine years earlier, only the former Vice President, Richard Nixon, had been able to convene the skittish Protestant denominations to deliver even platitudinous declarations on race, and not a few organizers of the Chicago conference hoped to relieve the embarrassment of that record. For the minority clergy, including Jews and Catholics, race was considered an "opportunity" issue on which leadership could reduce the stigma of inferior numbers or unorthodox belief, and for the Catholics there was also a chance to make membership inroads in new territory by moving more liberally than the entangled Protestants. Some cynics attributed to competitive church arithmetic the voluntary presence in Chicago of twenty-four Catholic bishops—a historic record, more hier-archy than ever assembled for anything other than a strictly Catholic conclave.

It was just as well that most delegates were spared the harsh truth that each keynote speaker was dangerously exposed where he was presumed to be strong—Heschel among rabbis and King among Negro preachers. Long before they knew each other well enough to disclose this, or to reveal the secret missions that preoccupied each of them in Chicago, the two men were drawn to each other by a shared commitment to the lan-guage and experience of the Hebrew prophets. The lasting bond that grew between King and Heschel was among many historical legacies of the ecumenical conference.

Heschel almost did not come. Since 1945, he had been conditioned to accept his private status as an outcast among his colleagues at the Jewish Theological Seminary in New York. The accepted rumor was that he had been hired at least partly as an ornament of piety, so as to blunt criticism of the seminary as a haven for Reconstructionist teachers who held that atheism was an acceptable, even preferred, belief for rabbinical students. Heschel was not permitted to teach courses in Jewish philosophy or theol-ogy, the subjects that had made him famous in Berlin and Frankfurt before he escaped the Nazis, and his elective course on Jewish mysticism was billed almost overtly as a quaint remnant from the speculative era. He bridled at the constraints. Students were startled to hear him say they were being trained for mere synagogue administration in the guise of the rabbinate, as it was possible to complete the seminary curriculum without attending a single class on the Jewish conception of God. "Intellectual evasion is the great sin of contemporary Jewish teaching," Heschel warned. "Urgent problems are shunned, the difficulties of faith are ignored... Jewish thought is sterile. We appeal to Jewish loyalties, we have little to say to the imagination."

Heschel only increased the discomfort of leading rabbis when he began to take his case outside the sealed space of the rabbinate—first through his books and then in public speeches as he grew more adept in the language of his adopted country, acting on his premise that there was healing sustenance within Judaism for gentiles as well as Jews. With his thick accent and striking visage—a kind of elfin patriarch of white beard and twinkling eyes—Heschel had delivered his trademark aphorisms at the Eisenhower White House ("Wisdom is like the sky, belonging to no man, and true learning is the astronomy of the spirit") and more recently at President Kennedy's conference on aging (". . . the cult of youth is idolatry. Abraham is the grand old man, but the legend of Faust is pagan"). Some of his colleagues were proud of Heschel's effort to take Jewish thought out of its protective cocoon, but others considered it dangerous, presumptuous, or demeaning.

By far the most sensitive venture Heschel joined was a quest to reform the ancient teachings of the world Catholic Church—official pronouncements, catechism, textbooks, even religious art—which appeared to exacerbate a hatred of Jews that culminated in the Nazi Holocaust. For his upcoming Vatican Council, Pope John XXIII assigned a study of anti-Semitism in Christianity to a secretariat on non-Christian religions headed by Augustin Cardinal Bea, who, in November of 1961, began consultations so secret that Bea's own staff heard whispers only afterward that a learned rabbi had slipped into Rome. Heschel submitted a private memorandum entitled "On Improving Catholic-Jewish Relations." "There has never been an age which has witnessed so much guilt and distress, agony and terror," he wrote. "At no time has the earth been so soaked with blood; at no time has man been less sensitive to God." He asked Bea to consider four proposals, including a request that the Vatican Council declare by historic vote that the Jews were not a deicide people cursed by God for the murder of Jesus. "It is our understanding that the Church holds the sins of all mankind responsible for the death of Jesus," Heschel added, in one of the delicate statements by which each side advanced an understanding of the other's doctrine, groping for language to reduce contempt without denigrating either religion. The shared goal was to block the path from private disdain to social catastrophe. "Speech has power and few men realize that words do not fade," wrote Heschel. "What starts out as a sound ends in a deed."

Still risking attack from all sides over his clandestine role as a Jewish lobbyist at the Vatican, Heschel did not accept the invitation to Chicago until he consulted Jewish specialists on the peculiar American politics of the race issue. He knew it was the presence of Martin Luther King among the religious hosts that would make the conference worthy of controversial attention, and he wanted to be careful about the mutterings against King that reached him at the Jewish Theological Seminary. Could it be true, asked Heschel, that King was a shallow, hack politician for Negroes, a troublemaker of hidden and perhaps Communist motives who might belong in the jail cells he frequented?

On being assured that King seemed spiritually well grounded in his mission against segregation, Heschel put aside practical equivocation to seize the Chicago Conference on Religion and Race with his opening speech. "Religion and race," he said. "How can the two be uttered together? To act in the spirit of religion is to unite what lies apart, to remember that humanity as a whole is God's beloved child. To act in the spirit of race is to sunder, to slash, to dismember the flesh of living humanity.... Perhaps this Conference should have been called Religion *or* Race. You cannot worship God and at the same time look at a man as if he were a horse." Far from positioning Jews safely as helpful bystanders to an essentially Christian conflict, Heschel declared that the soul of Judaism was at stake and had been so ever since Moses contended with Pharaoh at the "first" summit meeting on religion and race. "The exodus began," said Heschel, "but is far from having been completed. In fact, it was easier for the children of Israel to cross the Red Sea than for a Negro to cross certain university campuses."

To CLOSE the Chicago conference, King brought with him his standard sermon on the complacency of the church. "Eleven o'clock on Sunday morning is still America's most segregated hour," he said, "and the Sunday school is still the most segregated school of the week. The unpardonable sin, thought the poet Milton, was when a man, like Lucifer, so repeatedly says, 'Evil, be thou my good,' so consistently lives a lie, that he loses the capacity to distinguish between good and evil. America's segregated churches come dangerously close to being in that position." Behind his placid exterior, King concealed an impatience with religious institutions that far outran his text. In the past few days he had committed himself consciously to a life-threatening, watershed risk in Birmingham that neither relied nor waited upon the cooperation of his fellow clergymen.

King's resolve to gamble alone was the result of frustrations that had built in phases since the Montgomery bus boycott of 1955–56. After the boycott's strategy of nonviolent withdrawal proved difficult to transplant or expand, he had followed his trained gifts as a pulpit orator to preach hundreds of sermons against segregation in a touring frenzy modeled on the crusades of Rev. Billy Graham, from whom King received quiet encouragement and occasional advice. Through the late 1950s, this conversion approach had brought King the orator's nectar—applause, admiration, and credit for quite a few tearful if temporary changes of heart—but in everyday life Negroes remained a segregated people, invisible or menial specimens except for celebrity aberrations such as King himself. When college students pioneered a fresh tactic of nonviolent confrontation in the sit-ins of 1960 and the Freedom Rides of 1961, King had acknowledged their point that race was too intractable to be repaired by the inspiration of any orator. Only by slow, wrenching concession could someone like King admit that eloquence was weak even when buttressed by rank and education. And although he was honest enough to praise the students' courage, King repeatedly declined the drumbeat summons—"Where is your body?"—by which they made the first test of leadership not statements or seniority but a stark, primitive surrender to public witness.

Instead, King had clung to methods suited to his stature as a prince of the Negro church. While petitioning white leaders for change, he and his allies maneuvered to gain control of the National Baptist Convention. Their dream was to make of this largest voluntary body of Negroes in the world—upward of ten thousand preachers and some five million members —a ready-made civil rights phalanx that upon command could descend upon segregated targets for protest or Christian revival. The prerequirements were seductively in line with ordinary ambitions in church politics, as King's group aimed to establish a base in the isolated world built by their fathers and grandfathers before seeking any new confrontations with white segregationists. Even so, their plans ran into disaster in the person of the incumbent "Negro Pope," Rev. J. H. Jackson. At two national conventions, the usual spectacle of sermons and massed choirs had descended into something more like soccer riots, in which the Jackson forces outshouted, outshoved, and finally, at Kansas City in 1961, outscrimmaged the forces supporting King's civil rights platform to secure physical control of the podium before the police arrived. Victorious, Jackson had accused King of being responsible for murdering one preacher who had been pushed to his death in a brawl, and excommunicated King from the National Baptist Convention. In what amounted to a major schism, some two thousand pastors, including Rev. Gardner Taylor of Brooklyn and Benjamin Mays, president of Morehouse College, resigned with King, but others, including old family friends and eminent preachers such as Adam Clayton Powell, Jr., could not bear to tear away from the one place on the sparse landscape of Negro institutions that had anchored their identities in a national church.

Not until then, stripped of a reform agenda within the Negro church, did King throw himself into the escalating civil disobedience of the movement, most notably in the mass marches to jail at Albany, Georgia, beginning late in 1961. Hard experience there taught him that in any racial conflict large enough to draw the concentrated attention of the press, reporters inevitably would center their stories upon King as the character known to most readers, and generally, the focal issue of their stories would not be the moral worthiness of King's cause but the competitive outcome —who's winning, King or segregation? Thus pitted against the legal and cultural standard of the entire South, King had left Albany in 1962 branded a loser because segregation still stood, and as an ugly bonus he took the festering resentment of overshadowed colleagues. Then, on January 1, 1963—exactly one century after the effective date of Lincoln's Emancipation Proclamation—President Kennedy had dodged the last natural deadline for a scheme that King had pushed upon him privately but insistently for two years: a historic Kennedy proclamation to abolish at least some part of segregation by executive order.

Within days, King summoned his ten closest associates to a private retreat near Savannah, Georgia, to tell them in effect that there was no easy button to push, no executive alliance to be made. All the dignified routes had been closed off. The only paths he saw led either to retreat or forward over the cliff, and, haunted by fear that the integrationist mandate of the Supreme Court's 1954 *Brown* decision and the energy of the Kennedy years soon would dissipate, King disclosed his resolve to take a calculated leap. Wyatt Walker, his chief assistant, presented a blueprint for a staged, nonviolent assault on Birmingham, the symbolic bastion of segregation—a city that combined the plantation attitudes of the surrounding Alabama counties with the bare-knuckled politics of its steel mill economy, personified in both aspects by the local police commissioner, Eugene T. "Bull" Connor.

Instead of avoiding risks, or grumbling about moral obtuseness in the press, King's forces would embrace the public drama of a showdown between King and Bull Connor. Above all, King insisted, he would not again be drawn in as a "fireman" after someone else's campaign had gone awry. He would take the initiative for the first time, seeking to apply all the accumulated movement lessons since the bus boycott. One of these was stealth. King did not invite his father, Daddy King, to Savannah or seek the approval of his board at the Southern Christian Leadership Conference (SCLC), knowing that his dear but long-winded elders would filibuster against the idea with consummate skill. He would lay groundwork in stages, move by fiat, spring surprises. The lesson pressed upon him by the Student Nonviolent Coordinating Committee (SNCC) was that unmerited suffering was required to supplement reason in a selfish world, that in nonviolent wars no less than shooting ones, dramatic risk and suffering were the surest, swiftest messengers for breaking through to guarded or disinterested strangers. King believed, he warned his friends at the retreat, that "some of the people sitting here today will not come back alive from this campaign." When they accepted the plan nevertheless, he left Savannah for the Conference on Religion and Race.

SECRECY ABOUT Birmingham did not relieve King from the normal bombardments of pressure. On the airplane flight into Chicago, Leslie Dunbar of the Southern Regional Council leaned over from the adjacent seat to say gravely that he had an important message from high officials in the government whose identities King probably could guess. Dunbar felt obliged to speak in the evasive spy language of the Cold War. Although it was a painful message for him, as one of King's closest white allies and sponsor of much of the foundation money being funneled into voter registration, Dunbar had reluctantly agreed to warn that certain very high officials in Washington considered some of King's advisers to be Communists, as he well knew, and that they wanted him to get rid of them to protect the cause and everyone's best interests, including King's.

"Yes, yes," King intoned in his deep, rolling preacher's voice, giving no hint of great interest or alarm.

The Kennedy people were having a hard enough time getting the FBI to move against powerful Southern interests on behalf of voter registration workers, Dunbar went on, and it made their task all but impossible as long as the FBI could protest that those workers were infiltrated. King must break off from his New York adviser Stanley Levison completely, as though he were dead—no dealings, meetings, or even phone conversations. Dunbar's contacts in the administration were saying that the movement must be like Caesar's wife, above taint or suspicion.

"Yes, yes," King kept saying, nodding along almost automatically. When Dunbar fell silent, having relayed the main points Robert Kennedy had sent through his chief aide for civil rights, Assistant Attorney General Burke Marshall, King turned at last to reply. "I agree with everything you've said," he told Dunbar. "But I have to weigh other factors, too, before I can shun anybody like that. You see, Leslie, I have a pastoral responsibility."

This perspective ambushed Dunbar, who had been uncomfortable enough urging a blacklist on cold political necessity. Unexpectedly, King made it into an intimately brutal, profane act, leaving Dunbar feeling like an executioner at the confessional. Whereas government security officials considered it a prerogative of office to define national enemies, and to prescribe conduct toward them, King claimed as the democratic ideal a religious standard under which he would shun no one, friend or foe. This was the underlying principle of his nonviolence. Dunbar realized that if King were determined to maintain the hope of human contact even with those segregationists who were beating his nonviolent colleagues with tire chains, surely he would not cut off Stanley Levison, his trusted friend of six years' sacrifice to the movement. Never again did Dunbar raise with King the issue of his alleged Communist associations. He knew that although Robert Kennedy and Burke Marshall shared his misgivings about the secret blacklisting, they defended caution in civil rights on this ground. Subversion politics allowed them to deflect blame through the FBI back into the civil rights movement itself.

King did not know the intensity of the Bureau's institutional animosity. Most of his information about the FBI came from Robert Kennedy and his assistants in the Justice Department—the same people passing messages through Dunbar. Their pitch softened King's perspective on Hoover and missed one of the strongest of the forces driving the FBI bureaucracy against him—a sensitivity to criticism that had sharpened across Hoover's nearly forty years as the Bureau's founding director. In an article of recommendations written for the incoming Kennedy administration, King had included the FBI among the federal agencies that needed racial integration in the workforce (there being no Negro FBI agents except for five liveried members of Hoover's personal staff, including his chauffeur and doorman), and this relatively trivial reference had rocketed up to the Director's office as the first Martin Luther King item to reach Hoover's personal, frowning attention.

In late 1962, asked why he thought the FBI had not arrested some of the local officials who openly had assaulted nonviolent Negroes in and around Albany, Georgia, including one lawyer inside the courthouse, King had speculated that the local FBI agents were Southerners in cultural sympathy with the segregationist officers. Publication of this comment created lasting outrage among the highest officials of the FBI. Hoover authorized his political and public relations emissary, Assistant Director Cartha "Deke" DeLoach, to orchestrate a public rebuttal through press contacts that included the major Negro newspaper chains. Both the *Defender* papers of publisher John H. Sengstacke ("whom we know most favorably," DeLoach boasted to Hoover) and the four *Afro-American* newspapers attacked King for offhand comments that stood out sharply from the customary public praise heaped upon Hoover even by presidents who disliked him, such as Truman and Kennedy.

Early in 1963, FBI agents gathered wiretap intelligence that King invited Stanley Levison down to a summit meeting near Savannah. Neither diligent surveillance nor a canvass of informants gained FBI officials a clue about King's secret purpose—the nonviolent gamble in Birmingham—but they treated the gathering as sinister to the core, sneaky, for one thing, and proof that King ignored FBI instructions not to associate with Levison. On these assumptions, DeLoach added enough malice to draft a summary epitaph for King at FBI headquarters. Charging that King used "deceit, lies and treachery as propaganda to further his own causes," he recommended that the FBI write him off as a "vicious liar," beyond hope and unworthy of contact. "I concur," Hoover scrawled at the bottom of the memo, marking King as an enemy of the Bureau. This was on January 15, King's thirty-fourth birthday, one day after Heschel's opening speech to the Conference on Religion and Race.

Unwitting, King was wary of royal hostility much nearer at hand from the Baptist conqueror, Rev. J. H. Jackson, who was forbidding his loyal pastors to attend the conference. Over the past year, a procession of ecumenical leaders had been turned away from Jackson's enormous Olivet Baptist Church in Chicago, shocked and befuddled that the elected leader of the largest religious body of Negroes could curtly refuse to join the first national, interracial conference, right there in his home city. One prominent Negro scholar among the conference planners was so disgusted with Jackson that he renounced his own Baptist affiliation to become a Presbyterian. The few white clerics who came to meet Jackson could only speculate that he was mired in primitive, otherworldly fundamentalism, but they did not fret over the strange surprise because they already had cooperation from King, the best-known Negro pastor. Jackson's boycott had the ironic effect of building rather than undercutting Martin Luther King's image as the embodiment of the Negro clergy, and because the separation of religious cultures concealed his internal opposition, King was careful to let this one by-product of segregation stand uncorrected in the larger world. Privately, he and his allies had no doubt that Jackson simply refused to recognize any forum tainted by renegades against him. They felt Jackson's hostility as a politically intimate force, so extreme in pettiness as to seem perversely but warmly human.* What King could not yet appreciate was how a distant national icon such as J. Edgar Hoover could hold personal fixations against him every bit as intensely as J. H. Jackson, Daddy King's occasional houseguest since King's childhood. When King arrived in Chicago, the vast FBI was opening secret, unfriendly eyes on him, while "Old Jack" professed a lofty disregard.

DURING THE VOLLEY of tributes to Heschel's speech, William Stringfellow stunned the huge audience with a prepared commentary declaring that white pastors had allowed racial hatred to sink into the American character beyond the reach of religion. "The most practical thing to do now is weep," he advised. The cold resignation of these remarks by a prominent Episcopalian lay author flustered dignitaries on the podium and sent reporters digging to confirm a fresh theme of controversy. They found explosive potential in the advance text of Rev. Will D. Campbell, a theologian born in Mississippi and one of the few white clerics with a long record of advocating racial integration in the South. Campbell warned his colleagues not to assume that Negroes would welcome or wait upon their blessing. "In our generation," he predicted, "white children will be marched into gas chambers by dark-skinned masses, clutching their little toys to their breasts in Auschwitz fashion." What he meant to communicate by hyperbole was that no one could count upon Negroes to maintain the heart-melting courage and forbearance that had so astonished Campbell as a counselor to the Freedom Riders, who integrated interstate bus travel in

---

* Seven years later, after King's death, Jackson would have the Olivet congregation spend upward of $50,000 to seal up the stone doors facing South Parkway and carve out another entrance around the corner, just so that the church address never would be listed on the street to be renamed Dr. Martin Luther King Jr. Drive, after Jackson's nemesis.

1961. On reflection, he had decided that such saintliness should not be expected to endure or always to dominate, and that the average human being must have built up through the long centuries of slavery and humiliation at least as much resentment as, say, the German generation following World War I.

The convention floor at the Edgewater Beach Hotel buzzed over whether Campbell would be allowed to speak this sentence. Some delegates charged him with anti-Semitism for appropriating the imagery of the Holocaust. Privately, Campbell's employers at the National Council of Churches pressed him to delete the sentence so as not to play into the hands of segregationists, arguing that to acknowledge a capacity for evil in Negroes, especially collective evil, was to support the fear upon which segregation was built. Worn down, Campbell substituted a terse warning: "It is too late for us to be here." Under the circumstances, the omission was greeted with immense relief, but clashing apprehensions ran through the delegates. Just as the titled leaders were roused to urgent calls of mobilization—with the conference host, Albert Cardinal Meyer of Chicago, declaring that "our whole future as a nation and as a religious people may be determined by what we do about the race problem in the next few years"—some of the most experienced church activists concluded that religious people had forfeited their chance already.

King changed his advance text, too. His handwritten additions reflected a raw edginess, perhaps born of the melancholy judgment that he had more to lose than to gain by informing even these religious colleagues that he was going into Birmingham without them. "We have listened to eloquent words flowing from the lips of Christian and Jewish statesmen," he said, brushing close to sarcasm. "We have analyzed with painstaking care the broad dimensions and deep complexities of this haunting problem. And now the valley of injustice, with all of its ghettos, economic inequities, and demoralized children of God, stands before us in grim, stark, and colossal dimensions. Will this conference end up like all too many conferences on race?" Words were not enough, he said. From the hardest lessons of his own young career, he cried out for clergymen willing to "make their witness real." Oddly enough, he quoted the lament of celebrated ex-Communist Whittaker Chambers that modern religion had "lost its power to move anyone to die for it." The august Chicago assembly might have buoyed his hopes five years earlier, but now it could not contain his impatience. "One must not only preach a sermon with his voice," King said. "He must preach it with his life."

WHAT BROUGHT KING and Heschel together was a prescription for the dilemma that plagued the Chicago conference. Most of the delegates searched for ways to overcome a stubborn avoidance of race in religious discourse. ("I wonder why I can go to church 52 times a year and not hear one sermon on the practical problems of race relations," said Sargent Shriver, Director of the Peace Corps.) To break such a barrier, nearly all the theologians felt the need for a calming approach that labeled racial prejudice a feeble anachronism, a holdover of premodern irrationality, but this very impulse to soothe and minimize opened them to charges of false engagement from realists such as Stringfellow and Campbell. Yet, the realists' tinge of fatalism reminded Heschel of a ghostly legacy from the Jewish past—the defiant urge to abandon hope of any divine presence in the face of inexplicable calamity. "The greatest heresy is despair," he told Stringfellow in sharp retort, echoing his continuing plea to fellow victims of the Nazis and to the secularized Jews he found in America: "We all died in Auschwitz, yet our faith survived. We knew that to repudiate God would be to continue the holocaust."

As proof that human beings could engage the most deadening crises without falling into either of the classic polar traps—nihilism or blandness —Heschel held up the ideal of the Hebrew prophets. While facing, even welcoming, the destruction of themselves and their own people, the prophets remained suffused with redemptive purpose. Far from soaring off into saccharine self-persuasion, however, they made biting symbols out of daily pains and predicaments. "Moralists of all ages have been eloquent in singing the praises of virtue," wrote Heschel. "The distinction of the prophets was in their remorseless unveiling of injustice and oppression. . . ." Heschel's seminal study of the prophets had just been published in the United States, translated from the original German, and it gained the eager devotion of King and his fellow pastors because they had grown up with Moses and Isaiah in their pulpits. The distinctly molded personality of the Negro preacher, as recognized by W. E. B. Du Bois and memorialized by James Weldon Johnson in God's Trombones, was a cousin to the blazing psychic originals such as Jeremiah and Daniel—marked by passion, vivid images of slavery and deliverance, and arresting combinations of the earthy and sublime. To King and Heschel alike, the prophetic tradition came naturally as a grounding language.

At Chicago, they raised strikingly similar cries. "May the problem of race in America soon make hearts burn," said King, "so that prophets will rise up . . . and cry out as Amos did, 'Let justice roll down like waters, and righteousness like a mighty stream.'" Heschel quoted the same passage from Amos, which he used in his book to illustrate the emotive force in the prophetic conception of justice as contrasted with the arid rationality of the Greek ideal. They both quoted theologian Reinhold Niebuhr, Heschel's personal friend in New York and one of King's primary influences as a seminary student. When King declared that the durable sins of race stressed "the need for prophecy," he did not mean the popular notion of foretelling but the prophecy described by Heschel as "the voice that God has lent to the silent agony," through prophets able and willing to draw upon themselves the excess poison in the world. Their communion on this rich subject was a pleasant surprise to both men, who vowed to see more of each other, and for once King encountered an orator who reached for notes in his register. "Let there be a grain of prophet in every man!" Heschel exclaimed.

After generous applause, the Chicago delegates reacted cautiously to the summons for prophetic witness. Observers wryly noted that the only resolution they approved, an "Appeal to the Conscience of the American People," called for no binding action by any of the participating religious bodies. No doubt many of the clergy had hoped to treat race with an insightful malediction, and were surprised to have the challenge shoved under their own collars. Reports of a contemporary scandal filtered in from a prosperous Chicago suburb, where civic groups blocked the local symphony's invitation to its first Negro performer, a violinist. "We just thought we were not the organization to crusade and pioneer in a controversial subject in the community," said Geneva Palmer, president of the symphony association. "Nothing is integrated in Oak Park, you know." Local ministers intervened, citing the mandate of the national religious conference, only to stimulate round-robin evasion on collateral issues, including a charge that the symphony conductor had pressed the integration because he was Jewish. *Time* magazine ridiculed the entire Chicago conference as another exercise of "doleful hand wringing" by theologians, who "proved themselves still unable to offer much wisdom."

Undaunted, volunteer clergy resolved to continue the mission of the four-day conference by forming permanent local commissions across the country. A groping awkwardness persisted in their work. Intramural differences kept popping up even among the subdivisions of the major white groups, especially Protestants and Jews, and hostile archbishops all but shackled Catholics in Los Angeles and Philadelphia. A Catholic leader of the organizing coalition reported that no city began with even a communicating familiarity between the white and Negro clergy. Approaching such gaps in city after city, he found the bravest of recruits wanting to perceive the task not as a step into the unknown but as a restoration of an imagined past that somehow might "bring sanity back" into race relations. By fits and starts, those chastened and inspired by the Chicago conference placed the issue on the agendas of most of the upcoming church and synagogue conventions. Fledgling local commissions were meeting in thirty states by April, when King sent his first Birmingham volunteers to jail.

3

LBJ in St. Augustine

N<small>O ONE COULD GUESS</small> what bumps lay just ahead—certainly not the Vice President of the United States on a ceremonial visit to prepare for the four hundredth birthday of the nation's oldest city. In the false quiet before the first lasting reverberations rolled in and out of obscure places like St. Augustine, Florida, transforming people of every station, it remained possible to muffle the conflict over legal segregation with a few exertions on behalf of accommodation, and politicians of stature still managed to leave such details to the staff. On March 11 in St. Augustine, Lyndon Johnson waved expansively from the balcony of a restored Spanish mansion to a festive crowd that appreciated what the rare visit of a sitting Vice President meant to a small tourist town of fifteen thousand people. There were no Negro picket signs to mar the occasion—an invisible success Johnson took for granted. While his aide George Reedy broke away to make sure that the other parts of the racial truce were holding up, Johnson's motorcade rolled off to a shrine marking the first permanent outpost of European culture on North American soil.

At Mission Nombre de Dios, the Vice President slipped away briefly from his entourage during a private tour of the chapel. In one darkened alcove, a nervous priest showed him the small wooden casket of the Spanish explorer and *adelantado* Don Pedro Menéndez de Avilés, who had named his new settlement St. Augustine—for the great African Bishop of Hippo, brooding genius of early Christianity, architect of its lasting accord with temporal governance in Rome—whose feast date, marking Augustine's death on August 28 in the year 430, Menéndez was celebrating aboard ship when the Florida coastline at long last appeared.

The *adelantado*'s fleet chaplain said outdoor mass a few days later on September 8, 1565, planting a continuous Christian presence at Nombre de Dios, and Menéndez promptly marched up the coast to exterminate an explorer's colony of French Huguenots, thus renewing the religious wars of the Counter-Reformation on the western side of the Atlantic. From King Philip II of Spain, Menéndez had royal permission to bring five hundred African slaves into the New World, and while no proof survives that Menéndez himself used this license, entries in the mission registry about the Spaniards who stayed on in St. Augustine contain the earliest documentary slave records on the continent—dating more than fifty years before 1619, the commonly accepted beginning of African slavery in the future United States.*

Nearly two centuries after Menéndez, the Spaniards tweaked their British enemies to the north by chartering Fort Mose, the first armed, independent settlement of free blacks in North America, just outside St. Augustine. (Enraged Protestant colonists in South Carolina prescribed, and more than once carried out, the penalty of castration against slaves who tried to escape to refuge in Spanish St. Augustine, and James Oglethorpe, the original governor of colonial Georgia, personally led prolonged, bloody expeditions against Fort Mose as an archevil haven for insurrectionary runaways and papists.) Soon after the British first gained control of Florida in 1763, causing the entire population of Fort Mose to evacuate with the Spaniards to Cuba, an enterprising Scotsman named Andrew Turnbull tried an experiment in the area by importing the largest mass of *white* indentured servants ever assembled in North America, "Turnbull's niggers" as they were called—Greeks, Italians, and some three hundred families from the island of Minorca off the coast of Spain. Before his indigo plantation succumbed to disease and disaster, large numbers of these laborers stole away to asylum in nearby St. Augustine. Their Minorcan descendants were among those on hand to greet Vice President Johnson.

Fortune hid many exotic layers of American antiquity in Florida, which in modern times came to specialize in the sale of dredged swamplands and sunshine dreams. For generations, established St. Augustine families had held or traded franchises on proven tourist attractions. Purists on the city's historical commission struggled valiantly to put disclaimers

---

* Slavery in American territory is generally dated from the sale of "Twenty Negars" from the Dutch ship *Jesus* at the Jamestown, Virginia, colony in August of 1619. The much earlier slave practice in Spanish Florida is almost universally discarded or overlooked, perhaps because it lacks the symbolic clarity of a first shipment, or because even self-conscious chronicles of cultural oppression customarily trace American history through the British settlers, as history's eventual winners.

on the more egregious frauds, such as the Oldest House and the working site of Ponce de León's Fountain of Youth, but facts fell lame before imagination. The Alligator Farm relied upon the sheer atmosphere of the Ancient City, and some historical amusements—most notably Ripley's Believe It Or Not—shook loose to offer daredevil exhibits of tabloid wonder, such as the Calf With Two Heads. In the 1930s, some polls showed Robert Ripley to be the most admired man in America, just ahead of FBI Director Hoover and far above FDR.

Since then, St. Augustine guarded a share of Florida's migrations by promoting buncombe exaggerations on the free enterprise side of tourism, balanced by a rigid uniformity against public controversy. Typically, Archbishop Joseph Hurley preached with genuine horror against the reforms submitted to the new Vatican Council in Rome, especially the proposal that the clergy turn their faces instead of their backs to the congregation during mass. To Hurley, this gesture invited needless popular doubt about the clergy's claim to sovereign, lineal authority direct from Jesus. He and city leaders treated racial matters as unmentionables, whether historical or current, except for the colonnaded downtown square known as the Old Slave Market. As breezily described by buggy drivers, the site fascinated tourists as the relic of a storied past.

The priest who guided Vice President Johnson through the old mission was a historian, in charge of Catholic preparations for the four hundredth birthday of the nation's oldest city, upcoming in 1965. President Kennedy had appointed a federal commission to plan for the Quadricentennial—Johnson was there to swear in its members—and the priest seized his private opportunity to communicate some quieter aspects of a heritage he thought worth reflection: the true dates, the neglected Spanish history in America, the religious toll of seesaw colonial wars, the sacredness of local ground not only to the Vatican but also to the Orthodox Church, which had built a shrine to the first Greek settlement in the Western Hemisphere. To the priest's discomfort, however, Johnson remained silent for a long time before speaking his first words of the tour. "Fifty-five," he said. Somewhat unnerved, the priest noticed that the Vice President was staring at a sign beneath the wooden coffin. He explained that indeed Menéndez the Conqueror had died at that age in 1574, and that some 350 years later Spain had donated the coffin back to the mission he had founded in St. Augustine.

"Fifty-five," Johnson repeated. From his own line of work, the priest recognized a mortality reverie without knowing that Johnson was approaching his own fifty-fifth birthday that August, still haunted by a three-pack-a-day smoking habit and a massive heart attack eight years earlier. Once outside, Johnson snapped back to full energy before an honor guard of Catholic schoolchildren. Instead of waving to them, he insisted on shaking each one's hand, picked up several for hugs and chitchats and ear-pulls, to squeals of delight, and then, just as suddenly tired again, he announced that he was heading to the hotel for a massage and a nap.

IN THE NEGRO neighborhood called Lincolnville, George Reedy spent a day of intense mediation at the home of Mrs. Fannie Fulwood, president of the local NAACP. Threats and chaos were normal to him, but to Fulwood—the humbly upright daughter of a railroad worker, who in her forties kept up an arduous schedule as housemaid for the commanding general at the National Guard armory—excitement had grown almost unbearable since the marathon creation of her letter asking Johnson not to give his approval for $350,000 in federal assistance to celebrate the four hundredth birthday of a city that still excluded Negro citizens by legal segregation. There had been three formal readings of her draft at a board meeting, plus a consultation with a Negro college president to make sure the language was presentable, and when Johnson replied only days ago that "no event in which I will participate in St. Augustine will be segregated," a jolt of hope dissolved into panicky questions. Did Johnson mean that the Fairchild defense plant would have to integrate its workforce before he would visit, or merely that Negroes might accompany him to the plant? Was a visit to a segregated company by private invitation not itself a segregated event? Did the pledge mean that at least one Negro would be added to President Kennedy's all-white Quadricentennial Commission? Was the commission an "event"? What about the "white only" signs downtown—did they make it a segregated event for the Vice President to stroll near the Slave Market?

The implications of Johnson's pledge burned so hotly through the wires that the chief aide to Florida Senator George Smathers soon turned up on Fannie Fulwood's doorstep. Later came George Reedy, a silver-haired ex-socialist from Chicago, long in the service of the ex-segregationist Vice President from Texas. Both talked long hours to please the NAACP delegation, but it seemed that every time either one called contacts in Washington or white St. Augustine, who in turn were checking with other contacts, new semantic obstacles arose. Word once came back that any Negroes who did attend the big banquet for the Vice President must do so as "guests" rather than as paying ticket holders, which raised new questions about whether a social exception broke segregation. Whose guests would they be? What if the Negroes preferred to pay on an equal footing? Negotiations dragged on so long that Fulwood had to duck out to catch up on her cleaning.

These talks themselves marked a drastic leap for the local NAACP, which had stood aloof from the two previous blips of racial protest in town. In 1960, a mob had punished and dispersed a spontaneous student sit-in at Woolworth's that was inspired by the publicity out of Greensboro, North Carolina. Some months later, to dispel the mood of abject failure he found back home on returning from school, a gifted local student named Henry Thomas decided to apply some of the more precise nonviolent techniques he had observed as a freshman at Howard University in Washington. With recruited friends, he synchronized watches for a convergent movement on McCrory's, but Thomas alone showed up at the lunch counter. Worse for him, the manager was amiably puzzled about what this familiar local Negro thought he was doing, then amused when Thomas advised him to call the police. Everyone laughed when Thomas stretched forth his hands to be handcuffed, and the officer, whom he knew, merely waved him along to straighten things out. Finally in jail, Thomas endured a look of mortal disappointment from his mother as she apologized to the desk sergeant, a neighbor, for the inexplicable lapse of decency that had come over the first Thomas ever to reach college. After an extended jailhouse sanity interview by the white family doctor of his childhood, Thomas was released to enduring ridicule from both races.

Since then Dr. Joseph Shelley, the makeshift sanity examiner, had been elected mayor of St. Augustine, and Henry Thomas had become a battered, unsung hero of the 1961 Freedom Rides—other than John Lewis, the only one of the original fourteen Riders to survive both the Alabama ambushes and the medieval privations of Mississippi's Parchman Penitentiary. Left behind in the sticky local fears of Negro St. Augustine, the adults agitated and goaded themselves over their paralysis until one night the pastor of First Baptist Church froze up inside while presiding over an NAACP chapter meeting—remaining dysfunctional, as though struck dumb—and when none of the usual professionals came forward, Roscoe Halyard "volunteered" Fannie Fulwood into the chair. Her credentials were lifelong service and a strong belief in memorials for redress, but Dr. Robert Hayling, as youth adviser of her NAACP chapter, pushed aggressively from behind in keeping with a lesson from Henry Thomas: that it was difficult for confrontation to be taken seriously amid old hometown ties, and that the spark of extraordinary personal challenge was more likely to ignite among strangers. As the new Negro dentist in St. Augustine, Hayling did not see a life's story behind most faces in town. He thought a few picket lines were just the thing to shake these people out of their first-name illusions.

The threat of pickets stirred up the negotiations at Fannie Fulwood's house, opening to Johnson's aide Reedy some of the internal politics on both sides. From New York, Roy Wilkins called to remind his St. Augustine branch that no picketing proposals had been cleared through NAACP channels, which were nearly as centralized and formal as the FBI's, and that pickets could cause an "international incident" owing to the presence of the Spanish ambassador. Loyalists spoke up for Wilkins and the tested chain of command, but Hayling's supporters grumbled about how the NAACP "national boys" were always telling them what to do, posing as the pilots of a finely tuned national policy machine even though the only telephone in their statewide Florida NAACP office had been disconnected many months ago for failure to pay a $159 phone bill. Pickets were simple. All they needed were a handful of brave people, some cardboard, and unobjectionable American messages. What could be wrong with that?

For Reedy, the scandalous threat of Negro pickets actually gained leverage on the white side of town to secure Johnson's most visible pledge of an integrated banquet. When the whites also agreed to hold a special City Commission meeting the very next day on the more lasting segregation issues beyond the banquet, such as the "colored" signs and the all-white city library, Reedy leaned on the NAACP members to give up the pickets for the deal. Almost immediately, he had to shift direction again to offset a wave of trepidation that ran through some of Fulwood's colleagues. Exactly who would be willing to go now that the banquet was more than a bargaining issue? A lack of suitable clothing and other deferential excuses welled up, along with the fear of lost jobs. Some told Reedy of receiving phone threats already. They knew there could be no more sensitive breach of segregation than a banquet at the Ponce de León Hotel, the double-towered Moorish castle built almost on the scale of the Alhambra by Henry Flagler—partner of the original John D. Rockefeller and pioneer tycoon of Florida fantasy. The first Negroes to present themselves there as guests instead of doormen would make themselves as conspicuous as the Ponce itself.

MARTIN LUTHER KING himself would come to St. Augustine for bloody demonstrations in the coming year, but those cataclysms could scarcely match the quiet ripples of intimidation before this banquet. Katherine Twine, an NAACP stalwart who would lead four teams to jail in 1964, took off her best evening dress, unable to go. Her husband, Henry, a postman whom everyone called simply Twine, agreed to escort Fannie Fulwood from the rendezvous point. They mustered only ten volunteers for a motorcade of apprehension to the hotel, where Reedy, true to his promise, met them outside. The Vice President's assistant guided them through the palm gardens and Spanish archways, past the fountains and the staring, bewildered crowds of whites who had come to glimpse the celebrities, and inside safely to dinner beneath the Tojetti ceilings and other fine appointments of Bernard Maybeck's interior design.

Excusing himself from one of the two Negro tables in the vast banquet room, Scott Peek, the Smathers aide, went upstairs in the hotel to find out why the Vice President was late. Johnson, out of sorts since his nap, said he had decided to have his dinner there in the room and come down later for his speech, but Peek protested desperately because of the politics of the situation downstairs. Putting aside the four hundredth birthday of the nation's oldest city, the little town of St. Augustine was important to Florida's two senators—who in turn were important to Johnson and President Kennedy—because local banker Herbert Wolfe was a principal fund-raiser for the whole state, treasurer to Smathers in his campaigns. Wolfe, whom President Kennedy had appointed chairman of the Quadricentennial Commission, was the key to all the concessions wrested from local whites for the occasion; he had leaned on the management of the Ponce for the two Negro tables. Now, Wolfe and both Florida senators were waiting downstairs among the dignitaries.

Everyone had stretched themselves to the breaking point for Johnson and his national policies, said Peek, his temper rising under stress to the point of lecturing the former master of the U.S. Senate. If the guest of honor skipped the dinner, he told Johnson, no one would believe or care that he was tired. He must make an appearance, if only to relieve tension and spare the Negroes the embarrassment of feeling boycotted by the Vice President of the United States. "I'm *eatin'* with 'em!" shouted Peek. "At least you can come." Thus prodded, Johnson roused himself to make an entrance at the banquet, and on his way to the dais he stopped by the Negro tables to shake hands. ("Don't forget us, Mr. Vice President," said Robert Hayling.) Back upstairs after the formalities, Johnson complained over drinks about the hardships of the evening. Smathers ought to fire Peek "for the way he talked to me," he grumbled, but soon he invited Peek to fly back to Washington on his Air Force Jetstar.

The next day's newspapers reviewed the ceremonies in lavish detail, welcoming the plans of both the Spanish and U.S. governments to subsidize the preparations for the four hundredth birthday—"St. Augustine Pledged Restoration Assistance." There was no mention of integration at the banquet, the prior negotiations, nor racial content of any kind. Florida politicians dodged the subject of race even in their private communications; in a follow-up memo to George Reedy, one of the negotiators passed off the conflict by misleading euphemism as "the local problem which existed in St. Augustine." Local white interest evaporated as soon as Johnson took flight. When the nine-person NAACP delegation filed into the City Commission chamber for their appointment the next morning—Fannie Fulwood was absent, being unable to rearrange her work schedule on short notice—they encountered a tape recorder on an empty table. A city employee instructed them to leave recorded complaints for the commissioners, who found themselves unable to attend.

Nonplussed, the Negroes took turns leaning toward the machine. Rev. J. H. McKissick mentioned the "colored" signs still up at the courthouse and the City Yacht Pier, saying it "would make the city a little more democratic not to have such signs." He also petitioned for at least one Negro poll worker during city elections. Clyde Jenkins, a barber, protested the confinement of Negroes to menial jobs in city employment. Robert

Hayling asked for ordinary courtesy at the offices of the water department, the coroner, and other public agencies, objecting that Negro citizens were commonly ignored or humiliated. J. E. Proctor, a carpenter, seconded this point by recalling that when his sister died the other day and his family sought a death certificate, "we had to stand on the outside to give the information they wanted, and I did not think that was fair. It was cold and raining. We are human like everybody else, and try to do right."

Roscoe Halyard raised a grievance about the meeting itself, saying the NAACP delegation had been assured of a talk with the city commissioners "and not with a tape recorder." This opened the wound of immediate disappointment. "We stay too far apart and never come to any understanding," Halyard told the recorder, "because we never come face to face." Others expressed sorrow that Senator Smathers and even Vice President Johnson had been deceived with false promises about the meeting. One man said that if the city commissioners were not concerned, "they should have the fortitude to say so." Otherwise, they should take note of the pleadings, preferably by discussing them in person.

Two months later, Fannie Fulwood would advise President Kennedy by letter that still there was no response to the tape recording, nor fulfillment of the promise to Johnson. "Since St. Augustine is the nation's oldest city," she wrote, "we feel that democracy should have had its inception here, but it isn't even practiced here as late as 1963." President Kennedy did not reply. Not until the pressure of events later in the year did Mayor Shelley respond at all, with the novel objection that biracial dialogue "defeats the very purpose for which it is formed. It polarizes the White race and the Negro race and begins with the assumption there is a difference." By then, Shelley and other white leaders were riding a backwash of resentment against concessions such as the tape-recorded meeting and the integrated banquet. "People on the scene state that the City will not take any further steps," concluded a federal intelligence report circulated in Washington, "and that City officials feel that they went even further than they should have gone to accommodate the Vice President when he was there...."

4

Gamblers in Law

IN THE PIVOTAL MONTH of April 1963, Martin Luther King's lawyer Clarence Jones worked simultaneously on three defining disputes headed for numerous trips to the U.S. Supreme Court: *James v. Powell, Jr., New York Times Co. v. Sullivan,* and *Walker v. City of Birmingham.* A unique background prepared him for the multiple roles. As a son of servants to the Lippincott family of New Jersey, Jones had grown up around his father's chauffeur's uniform, imitating manners of the wellborn. Circumstances forced him as a boy into a series of Catholic foster homes, where he responded to lectures on Demosthenes and the transforming powers of oratory, practicing diction in front of a mirror for endless hours—so long that the words "acronym" and "felicitous" forever bubbled up randomly in his trained ear. By 1956, he acquired a law degree and enough polish to marry a publishing heiress in an interracial wedding of storybook ceremony for New York society, with the bride providing guests from the financial aristocracy and Jones supplying a number of the kitchen workers and musicians from his own family.

On the morning of April 3—as the first nonviolent volunteers were stepping off toward arrest in Birmingham—Jones and lead counsel Charles McKinney put Harleston "Cool Breeze" Patterson on the witness stand in New York. Aside from sporting-life philosophy—"When a gambler gets into trouble, he always loses girlfriends"—Patterson presented testimony on his sullen but faithful protection payments to Esther James from the late 1940s until somebody tried to gun her down from a passing car in 1958. According to Patterson, the police had hauled him in on the assumption that if he hadn't shot at James himself, he must know which gangsters were violently angry over her arbitrary adjustments in the "pad," and while his denials satisfied the detectives, Esther James herself had been certain enough of his complicity to pronounce street judgment on him in Harlem, shouting, "Cool Breeze, you can't take no more numbers in this neighborhood. You are through. You are through. Don't nobody do nothing to Miss James and take numbers!" Since then, Patterson testified, troubles made a wreck of him.

His account did help Jones and McKinney discredit the public image of plaintiff Esther James as a churchly matron. They brought out her prior convictions on such charges as striking neighbors in the head with a hammer, and on cross-examination she dropped her professed innocence about the daily mechanics of the rackets. ("Do I look like a fool to you?" she snapped, when asked how she knew that numbers writers reconvened in hallways after turning in bet slips on each morning's "lead" number.) Still, Cool Breeze Patterson did not testify that he actually saw James pass on the pad money to police. In fact, he shied away from earlier affidavits on this critical link out of the fear that made him a lonely witness: for a racketeer to accuse police officers of accepting his bribes was to bare his own neck, not only to underworld retribution but to the crooked police themselves, who could ruin him by pretending to be honest.

The lawyers were trying to mask the gaps in Patterson's testimony when a secretary slipped into the courtroom with a whispered message that Adam Clayton Powell abruptly had decided not to attend his own trial. This news visibly staggered McKinney and Jones at the defense table; neither they nor Powell's closest aides ever settled on a convincing explanation. Their best guess was that some sort of status phobia kept the grand titan of Congress from appearing in the dock. After the opposing lawyer summoned Powell as *his* witness for effect—just to have the bailiff bellow out the name of the skulking, no-show defendant—jurors needed only four hours to find him guilty of libel damages totaling $211,500. An overjoyed Esther James announced that she would donate an unspecified portion of Powell's restitution to the care of crippled Jewish children.

This judgment put a tenacious clamp of doom on Powell, destined to gnaw its way up his leg in collateral Supreme Court suits over contempt and congressional expulsion while he struggled to avoid paying. Even so, the verdict was scarcely more galling to Powell than the contrasting public acclaim for Martin Luther King's libel case as opposed to his. Like star-crossed twins, Powell and King were being filtered through the courts as well as the press. For three years, the libel cases marched together on the calendar while their reputations split by polar refraction.

King's case rose from a 1960 *New York Times* advertisement placed by friends, including Harry Belafonte and Bayard Rustin. The ad appealed for money to defend King against Alabama's latest indictment, which the text denounced as a transparent effort by "Southern violators of the Constitution" to crush nonviolent dissent against segregation. Alabama officials promptly counterattacked with lawsuits of bizarre contrivance in at least three respects. None of the Alabama plaintiffs was mentioned by name in the ad, and each one—beginning with Montgomery police commissioner L. B. Sullivan—claimed to be dishonored by generic inference. Because there was no accountable "author" of the ad copy, as in normal libel actions, the plaintiffs sued the *Times* itself and four of King's Alabama colleagues whose names appeared in small print at the bottom along with Eleanor Roosevelt, Langston Hughes, Shelley Winters, and some sixty others who "warmly endorse this appeal." Finally, the facts at issue were trivial. Plaintiffs alleged that Negro students actually sang "The Star Spangled Banner" during one demonstration, not "My Country, 'Tis of Thee." Under Alabama law, which gave juries full discretion to decide whether a factual mistake of any kind was defamatory, the first jury granted Sullivan damages of $500,000—the full amount sought and the largest libel judgment in Alabama history. A second jury matched this award, and three suits demanding an additional $2 million were held in abeyance pending outcome of the *Sullivan* appeal.

Powell's case grew from a ten-speech kamikaze crusade in which he exposed on the floor of the U.S. House what amounted to a phone directory of the Harlem underworld. "I hold in my hand photostatic copies" of the regular police protection pad, he announced. "Louis the Gimp [Avitabile], who operates in front of my church, has five drops in Harlem...." Listing names, addresses, and "drop" collection centers for more than a hundred syndicate figures in "both numbers and narcotics," Powell charged that organized crime was "pauperizing Harlem." Because all 212 New York police captains and fifty-nine of sixty inspectors were white, he argued, graft was exported along with crime profits from the Negro districts, which, being poor to begin with, were pinioned, corrupted, and systematically fleeced. He quoted his gun-carrying, addict-gathering assistant at Abyssinian Baptist, Rev. Oberia Dempsey, on the social implications for America's pioneer urban center of migrating Negroes: "We have in our hands the wreck of a generation.... My people will not overcome this evil for 50 years."

When the first salvos drew little interest, Powell outlined the accounting practices on the police side of the rackets. "All pads are due on the first of the month," he told the House. From a typical crime banker's monthly pad of roughly $2,700, he explained the shares apportioned— "borough headquarters, $275.... 23 precinct sergeants at $10"—and named those in charge of distributing payoffs in Harlem. This extreme accusation produced only the quiet resignation of one sergeant ("who lives luxuriously in New Jersey"), whereupon frustration or mad vertigo drove Powell to reiterate the "bag" system of graft intermediaries on New York television—arguably forfeiting libel immunity for congressional speech. Lawyers materialized to file suit on behalf of Esther James, one of those Powell named as a "bag woman," and trapdoors of public scandal finally opened—under Powell himself.

THE U.S. SUPREME COURT agreed to review the *Sullivan* case just before Powell's 1963 trial. Sensitivity and high-stakes conflict had stripped both controversies almost entirely of racial content, but otherwise their public images sharply diverged. Powell's original alarm about crime, corruption, and urban decay sank to an unseemly quarrel in which a powerful member of Congress gratuitously insulted the lowly widow Esther James—described by the *Times* as "a 66-year-old domestic who lives on earnings as a servant and her late husband's railroad pension." By contrast, the Alabama *Sullivan* case refined away its raw origins as a concerted segregationist vendetta ("If you dance, you must pay the fiddler," joked Governor John Patterson, who himself filed one of the libel suits) toward purified legal theory as the century's foremost First Amendment case.

Clarence Jones, Harry Wachtel, and other King lawyers on the *Sullivan* appeal concurred in the suppression of racial aspects. Because the blatant realities were so thoroughly soaked with Alabama's intent to punish Negro protest, they knew that the Justices of the Supreme Court could not grant relief on any argument derived from them without impugning the integrity of Alabama's courts and executive officers from top to bottom, plus those of a dozen other Southern states more or less aligned with Alabama. Strategic realism demanded that the essence of the conflict be finessed entirely, with no racial issues pressed upon the Court. Moreover, the King lawyers welcomed the *Times* as controlling defendant even though the newspaper entered the Alabama cases wholly by commercial accident. (No news reporter created, approved, or even saw the contested appeal as it passed through the *Times* advertising department.) Ironically, this inadvertence helped strip away factual performance and framed the *Sullivan* verdict as a generalized threat to public debate through the nation's premier news journal. Among King's advisers, Stanley Levison especially hailed the approach, saying it fostered emergency coalitions with precisely those groups most needed for the civil rights movement: labor unions, religious groups, press outlets, large corporations—anyone who could imagine being victimized by parochial politics or a runaway jury.

Lawyers for the *New York Times* scarcely associated with counsel for the Negro co-defendants during trial in Alabama, and managed to split off the newspaper for independent appeal. This separation, together with a hostile procedural ruling, gave the State of Alabama a legal opening to seize the property of the four preachers during the litigation. Under court order, sheriffs impounded and sold automobiles belonging to Revs. Fred Shuttlesworth, Ralph Abernathy, and Joseph Lowery. They auctioned off land belonging to Rev. S. S. Seay, Sr., of Montgomery, placed a lien against farmland that Abernathy had inherited jointly with his siblings, and filed motions to discover other assets that might be confiscated to satisfy Sullivan's judgment. (Shuttlesworth and Abernathy moved out of Alabama, in part to escape further expropriations.) When *Times* publisher Arthur Sulzberger privately asked his chief counsel at Lord, Day & Lord whether this procedural trampling could be stopped, the lawyer regretfully replied that the *Times* could not help without compromising the immense tactical advantage of separation from the preachers' case.

Unlike the King side, Adam Clayton Powell exercised neither strategic forbearance nor journalistic appreciation for the *Times,* which he described as "the unfriendliest newspaper in the United States to me." Powell thought the *Times,* as a defendant in the Alabama suit, ought to have granted a fellow libel target at least some high ground of purpose and prerogative. Objectively, both test cases threatened to squelch discussion on vital public issues, and Powell felt deserving of extra motivational credit for taking deliberate, pioneer risk. Subjectively, the stakes were widely perceived as nothing less than freedom in the *Times* case, nothing more than Powell's scoundrelhood in his. When a congressman made a speech castigating him as a spendthrift playboy, the *Times* published a detailed account on the front page, but the paper never addressed the substance of his manifesto on New York corruption—not then or later, after a gambler named Arthur Powers was shot in the head one noon on a Harlem corner before a dozen witnesses, falling a body length from Esther James. Safely but ineffectually back on the House floor, Powell named three assassins and declared that there would be no arrests because the killing was too balled up in the corruption, with Esther James acting as "finger woman" against an intruder "moving into her territory." Racketeers "have all the protection they want," Powell told the House, which helped explain "why half the dope in the United States comes into Harlem."

Powell confounded Machiavellians and idealists alike with his stage-crafted rascalism. "I am against numbers in any form," he cried out at Abyssinian, "but until the day when numbers is wiped out in Harlem—I hate to say this from the pulpit!—I am going to fight for the Negro having the same chance as an Italian!" His defiance of the sober downtown *Times* played well to Harlem voters, just as his entertainments—showgirl wives, smoke rings from trademark cheroots, and explicit, earthy remarks about Jewish gangs, Irish police brass, and paramount loyalty among Negroes—offended editors who denounced him for many shortcomings including "his notably racist attitudes."

Powell's warning was beyond assimilation, in part because no one was ready to hear from a freebooting gadfly that racial callousness could fasten pervasive corruption on sophisticated cities in the North. He was an irritant too far advanced, anticipating elements of Mario Puzo on Mafia culture and Malcolm X on the structural exploitation of Northern Negroes. A decade later, when the image of cities had turned and a New York commission confirmed Detective Frank Serpico's wrenching allegations on the rackets and the pad, the late Powell was a lost casualty of a forerunner's crusade that never registered.

For CLARENCE JONES, it was a short trip over vast emotional distance from the Powell trial to Birmingham jail. In the April 5 edition whose front page announced the triumph of Esther James, the *Times* reported on page sixteen that the "Integration Drive Slows/Sit-ins and a Demonstration Plan Fail to Materialize—Dr. King Takes Lead." Four picketers reached jail on a day when the schedule called for a crescendo of hundreds. To stave off collapse, Fred Shuttlesworth submitted to arrest on April 6, and King personally persuaded three other preachers including his own brother to join him. Since Shuttlesworth miraculously survived the dynamite destruction of his home in 1956, he had marked himself as a possessed soul through a score of arrests and convictions that left trial dates following him in a multilayered jumble; the next Supreme Court session would review among them a criminal conviction from the 1961 Freedom Rides (absurdly, for conspiring to gather a white mob) along with his civil conviction in the *Sullivan* libel case. Shuttlesworth used his apartness as a weapon. He commuted sporadically to Birmingham from his new home in Cincinnati, and when more than three quarters of Birmingham's four hundred Negro preachers voted to discourage any nonviolent showdown in their city, Shuttlesworth had assured King that he alone could head off any backward stampede.

Shuttlesworth was out of jail and back again within six days. Of the maelstrom in Birmingham—lost jobs, court hearings, injunctions, freedom songs and sermons, rumors of political maneuver and abuse in the jail—what reached Clarence Jones in New York was that January's Savannah plan was battered to such weakness that even the master coordinator, Wyatt Walker, felt obliged to put down his clipboard to join Shuttlesworth in jail. Ralph Abernathy went, too, after a running tactical argument on Good Friday, April 12, that was so full of venom and tears that Martin Luther King could not bring himself to render a decision in words and silently reentered the jammed motel wearing crisp denim "jail clothes," resolved to commit a "faith act" over the anguished objections of his father. For Jones, King's arrest meant a month's frenzy crammed into a single weekend of emergency petitions, dragnet searches for bail money, and finally a rare plane flight into the heart of segregated territory.

Alone in the jail corridors, Jones made an extra show of his professional status for hostile guards. Nerves made him concentrate on a long checklist of urgent questions, but King displayed little interest. "I'm writing this letter," he said. Furtively through the bars—because the jail rules allowed no material possessions to prisoners in solitary—King showed Jones a copy of the *Birmingham News* that had been smuggled in on a previous legal visit. All around the margins, meandering from page to page, he was scribbling a passionate response to a small story headlined "White Clergymen Urge Local Negroes to Withdraw from Demonstrations." Led by C. C. J. Carpenter, the Episcopal bishop of Alabama, an ecumenical group of eight religious leaders—all at least mild critics of segregation—had issued a statement calling King's Birmingham campaign "unwise and untimely." They were precisely the sort of clergy who had attended the Chicago conference on the religious demands of race, and yet in crisis they found it prudent to address King's constituents as their own, speaking of him only obliquely as an irritant.

Jones dismissed the clergy statement as a predictable sleight of no consequence. At first, he tried to understand King's preoccupation as a semantic catfight peculiar to theologians, or as a distracted form of therapy for the strains of prison. Over several days, however, as King consumed precious visiting minutes demanding more blank paper to be sneaked in, and giving detailed instructions for stitching together the piecemeal letter —all the while brushing aside desperate practicalities from the outside— Jones began to worry that King was mentally unstable, or worse, that his endless letter amounted to a eulogy for a doomed movement.

King himself regarded his letter as partly cathartic, a venting of emotion "when the cup of endurance runs over." More freely than at the Chicago conference in January, he thundered against anyone "who paternalistically believes he can set the timetable for another man's freedom," and raged against inert spirits of mannered goodness. "Shallow understanding from people of good will is more frustrating than absolute misunderstanding from people of ill will," he wrote. He addressed the eight Birmingham clergy in dozens of voices—begged, scolded, explained, even cooed to them, and conspired icily with them as fellow experts. He showered them with pathos over unmerited sufferings as grand as the martyrdoms of Saint Paul and Socrates and as personal as his own young daughter's tears on learning that colored girls were barred from the Funtown amusement park. On through memorized quotations from Martin Buber, Saint Augustine, Reinhold Niebuhr, and others, his focus sometimes wandered from the Birmingham clergymen altogether as King seemed to plumb within himself for the core reason he submitted to jail.

Invariably, he pulled up hope in paired phrases of secular and religious faith. "We will win our freedom," he wrote, "because the sacred heritage of our nation and the eternal will of God are embodied in our echoing demands." No fewer than five times, he called upon variants of "Constitutional and God-given rights" as the twin footing that grounded his outlook. There was something characteristically American about the notion of divine sanction for democratic values, but King's own struggle against despair pushed beliefs back to the earliest prophets of monotheism. Centuries before Plato, they introduced a deity that shockingly held kings and peasants to the same moral laws and rejected the forceful authority of state violence as evil. Their concept of equal souls anticipated and lifted up the democratic principle of universally equal votes.

To hold the belief in justice among equal souls as the key to religious as well as political conviction seemed at once crazy and noble, wildly improbable and starkly human. In his letter, King called it a daring "extreme." He hailed luminous extremists in a paired roll call that included Jesus on the pure refusal to hate, Jefferson on equal standing in creation, Amos on the rolling waters of justice, and Lincoln on the crucible of democratic commitment: "This nation cannot survive half slave and half free." In warning of new black nationalists—"the best-known being Elijah Muhammad's Muslim movement"—King made sure to point out that the Muslims repudiated not only Christianity and white people but also democratic values. They had "lost faith in America." There was no democracy in the Nation of Islam, just as Elijah Muhammad neither found nor expected any in America. In effect, King offered two convergent paths to understand why he had sought out the Birmingham jail, each in the language of justice. If indeed the long arc of the universe bent toward justice, and the universe proved friendly, history's slow triumph over slaughterhouse evil would be a compelling sign not only of benevolent design behind the cosmos but of a democratic bond in human nature. In King's tradition there were no proofs, only witnesses.

To Americans grown weary of singsong slogans and campaign speeches, it was strange or even blasphemous to put the humdrum workings of democracy on a par with belief in God, but from the slave side of history they were comparable wonders. In the Civil War, when both sides claimed divine blessing, Lincoln's distinctive purpose was to uphold the democratic intuition. From his cell, King did not hesitate to stress the political side of conviction to the Birmingham clergy, or to transcend race as a prophet of redemption to his own persecutors. "One day the South will know," he concluded, "that when these disinherited children of God sat down at lunch counters, they were in reality standing up for what is best in the American dream and for the most sacred values in our Judaeo-Christian heritage, thereby bringing our nation back to those great wells of democracy...."

Outside the jail, the finished letter was typed neatly at a length of twenty pages, then copied and distributed widely by hand and post. Wherever he could, Wyatt Walker added press tips about the daily jail marches in Birmingham, plus human interest details about how King had worked under surveillance and duress in solitary, allowed no personal comforts and certainly no reference materials. Nevertheless, the power of the appeal lay dormant. None of the eight addressees replied. A Quaker journal alone expressed interest in publishing the letter, and no reporter found news in what amounted to a dense sermon on familiar King themes.

Less than three years after journalists absorbed the amazing conclusion that John Kennedy may have won the 1960 presidential election by minor attentions to King's confinement in a Georgia jail, most national news organizations stressed nonpartisan calm as the essential condition for racial progress—much like the clergymen who criticized King. *Time* magazine and the *New York Times,* for instance, blamed King in Birmingham for creating "inflamed tensions" and "tensions that have grown alarmingly." In Birmingham itself, city fathers openly called upon citizens to "ignore what is being attempted." On April 24, with nonviolent veterans crowded around Birmingham television sets in the desperate hope of encouragement, President Kennedy's press conference dwelled upon grand subjects such as nuclear tests and the prospects for war upon Cuba. No one asked about the ongoing jail marches or King's eight days of imprisonment—let alone his letter.

By then Wyatt Walker was preparing ground for retreat, hinting to Burke Marshall that the Birmingham campaign would soon shift to less confrontational voter registration, which Kennedy officials had favored all along. Coverage of King's trial and conviction fell to the back pages, leaving Jones and various teams of lawyers still another landmark Supreme Court case to go with *Sullivan* and *Powell,* testing whether plainly unconstitutional injunctions must be obeyed until vacated by the courts. Historic favor opened and then closed again to King before late 1967, when the Supreme Court in *Walker v. City of Birmingham* would send the author of a world-famous letter back to the Birmingham jail.

5

To Vote in Mississippi: Advance by Retreat

MISSISSIPPI STARTED at the bottom. At least four stages of prior retreat made the active frustrations of Birmingham and St. Augustine comparatively advanced—even enviable. A year earlier, when Bob Moses appealed for refuge at a statewide meeting of NAACP chapter presidents, he brought with him only two teenage recruits and a record of anguish. Moses was not from Mississippi, nor an NAACP member. He was a twenty-seven-year-old New Yorker with a Harvard master's degree in philosophy, who had become an object of wonder since venturing into the southwest timber region around McComb on a solo mission for the Student Nonviolent Coordinating Committee, a youth organization that had grown out of the sit-ins. For trying to escort would-be voters to register, he had been arrested more than once, pummeled by a courthouse mob, and beaten severely near a town square in open daylight by a cousin of the Amite County sheriff. Still bleeding, he walked into the courthouse to file criminal charges, then testified against the cousin, and, until the local prosecutor advised him to flee for his life before a jury brought in the customary verdict of acquittal, continued doggedly to behave as though he possessed the natural rights of a white person. This presumption shocked Mississippi people more than the blood and terror.

John Doar sought out Moses to learn of the violence in Amite County, just as he had introduced himself to Medgar Evers and Vernon Dahmer on a previous clandestine tour of Mississippi—traveling incognito in khakis and boots, knowing enough to be fearful himself even as a high-ranking official of the Justice Department. A Republican from Wisconsin, Doar had been asked to stay on in the Kennedy Justice Department partly because he had pioneered a go-out-and-poke-around-for-yourself approach to civil rights lawsuits, which made him unusual among desk-bound Washington lawyers. With Moses, Doar visited Negro farmers who were afraid to come to registration meetings because of the intangible reality of rural life—ominous messages maids and sharecroppers were hearing—and several were particularly worried about signs of anger on the part of E. H. Hurst, a state representative of local influence, against Herbert Lee, an NAACP farmer who attended Moses' registration meetings. Doar promised to drive out to Lee's farm on his next trip, but he found waiting at his office the next day a message from Moses that Hurst had just shot Lee to death in full public view outside the Liberty cotton gin.

In nearby McComb, while Moses pressed in vain for arrest in the Lee murder, his youthful admirers went to jail from a sit-in that quickly inspired a spontaneous march of more than one hundred high school students. Failing to dissuade them, Moses and other in-gathered SNCC leaders went along as protective support until McComb police plucked them from the line, ran some through gantlets of enraged citizens, and eventually crammed Moses and seventeen others—virtually the entire national leadership of SNCC—into the drunk tank of the Magnolia, Mississippi, jail. They obtained release more than a month later on appeal bonds financed by Harry Belafonte, and Moses soon asked the NAACP county leaders to sponsor a second foray anywhere apart from the skittering violence around McComb. "We had, to put it mildly, got our feet wet," he wrote. "We now knew something of what it took to run a voter registration campaign in Mississippi."

Many NAACP officials saw Moses differently, as a young mystical amateur—he had studied Zen Buddhism on a college sabbatical in Japan—who produced deplorable net results: no new registered Negroes, one NAACP corpse, needless beatings, some legal bills handed to NAACP adults, and an unruly class of damaged children expelled from school. Field Secretary Medgar Evers already had written a relentlessly critical assessment of SNCC's entry into Mississippi, which the national NAACP office circulated in urgent warning against the "continuing problem" of rival civil rights groups. Moses retained a foothold only because of one hardheaded practical farmer. Vernon Dahmer, obsessed by the sufferings of his friend Clyde Kennard, responded to a kindred grit in Moses.

At an NAACP banquet late in 1961, while Moses was in McComb, Medgar Evers broke down during his report on the condition of Kennard—a former paratrooper, both in Germany and Korea—who had been called home from his last year at the University of Chicago to run the farm he bought for his ailing mother outside Hattiesburg. Carefully, Kennard had applied to finish his degree at Southern Mississippi, the only college in the area, but neither sterling character nor extenuating family circumstances excused his effort to become the first Negro openly to attend a white college in Mississippi. Disasters ensued, culminating in his arrest when five bags of stolen chicken feed were discovered one morning in his barn. On the shaky testimony of a single witness that Kennard masterminded the pointless, untimely heist—a transparent frame-up, said Evers—Kennard drew a felony conviction that made him ineligible by law to attend any state college even if he finished seven years' hard labor at Parchman Penitentiary.

This was doubtful, Evers announced, because cancer had invaded Kennard's colon in prison. Evers wept again, then reproached himself furiously for the weakness. Since the Emmett Till lynching of 1955, he had weathered these occasions with the taciturn formality of a man who insisted that his own wife call him "Mr. Evers" at the office, but Evers could not stop saying that hate and fate cut down in Kennard an unassuming peer who outdid him on both flanks—more disciplined and accomplished militarily, warmer and more forgiving in spirit. He gave way a third time. "That's all right, son," called out a woman from the crowd. "We all feel the same way."

None of this was news to Vernon Dahmer (pronounced *"Day*-mer"), the barrel-chested, fifty-three-year-old farmer whose sons had been collecting the eggs from Kennard's chickens every morning in his absence, taking them to Bourne's grocery for sale. The Kennard place was only two miles from Dahmer's farm, and in recent years Dahmer had recruited his neighbor Clyde to run the Youth Council of the Forrest County NAACP chapter. Now Dahmer was left with grim realities. Without Kennard to work the land, eventually his farm and chickens must be put up for sale and someone found to take in Kennard's mother, who would be left without even the egg money.

Dahmer told the Hattiesburg NAACP chapter of his resolve to honor Kennard's sacrifice with a special voter registration meeting. He volunteered to secure his own church, Shady Grove Baptist, but members shrank from public assembly on that issue. The current registrar—Theron Lynd, a hulking young man with thick horn-rimmed glasses, weighing over three hundred pounds—had not allowed a single Negro to register since assuming office in 1959, the year of the Mack Charles Parker lynching at nearby Poplarville. Less than a hundred of Forrest County's eight thousand voting-age Negroes could vote, and intimidation so thoroughly saturated the county that no Negro church or club had opened its doors to the NAACP for years. Dahmer lost his bank credit and all his insurance, after which he survived on his independent financial strength as no other local Negro could do. The moribund local chapter was reduced to one secretary and a handful of old men who met secretly in the Dahmer living room.

Still, Dahmer rose one Sunday from his family pew to argue that

Shady Grove should take the risk for Kennard now that federal men were suing registrar Lynd to put national power behind Negro voting rights. Everybody knew that Justice Department lawyers visited the Dahmer farm more than once to identify potential witnesses—collecting names of qualified Negroes who were rejected and unqualified, even illiterate, whites who routinely voted. Even rejected Negro voters could help the cause now as living evidence, said Dahmer, but to become citizens they must act like citizens.

It was a simple speech, and Dahmer enjoyed considerable respect as a church trustee and by far its largest contributor. His message seemed to sway the congregation until Rev. Ralph Willard, Sr., dean of Forrest County's Negro preachers, declared from the pulpit that politics had no business in God's house. Willard preached forcefully on the wages of sin, then offered a substitute motion that Dahmer be expelled from Shady Grove along with his three closest supporters and all their immediate families. He prevailed in a tally marked by moans and outbursts, whereupon Dahmer led a doleful recessional from a lifelong church home that stood upon land donated by his family. For seeking the right to vote in public elections, he and his supporters lost with their church memberships the only franchise they exercised freely.

This schism at Shady Grove fell within days of the bonded release of SNCC prisoners in Magnolia, some sixty miles west of Hattiesburg. When Moses pleaded for relocation sponsors toward spring of 1962, at a meeting of NAACP chapter presidents, Dahmer came forward to ask about the alleged transformation of the two rough-cut kids, Hollis Watkins and Curtis Hayes. They had been ordinary teenagers—out of high school, out of work, on the edge of trouble—until Watkins, the tenth surviving child of sharecroppers, had peeked boldly into a room to investigate a rumor that Martin Luther King was in McComb, and, coming upon Moses instead, followed his curiosity from long conversations swiftly into classes on voting, nonviolence, and the surge of freedom in the world. On first leaving the farm for likely arrest, Watkins said he was spending the night with a friend lest he shame or enrage his parents, but word came to his cell that his father stood in church to praise his son's courage. From the Magnolia jail, having telescoped generations of unimagined experience into six months, Watkins and his friend Curtis Hayes yearned to restart the cycle by going out alone into new areas, just as Moses had come with nothing to McComb.

Dahmer made up his mind sight unseen. "I'll take them both," he told Moses. "You can send them to Hattiesburg."

NORTH OF HATTIESBURG, meanwhile, Moses fell into uneasy, recuperative alliance with a trio of student leaders from the Nashville movement: Diane Nash, Bernard Lafayette, and James Bevel. From experimental workshops on nonviolence taught since the late 1950s by James Lawson—a Korean War pacifist who studied Gandhian techniques in India—Nashville students became shock troops of the sit-ins and the earliest legends within SNCC. After the original Freedom Riders of May 1961 were so bloodied in Birmingham that they were urged to quit even by Fred Shuttlesworth, it was Diane Nash who sent a fresh wave down from Nashville and then straw-bossed a summer-long procession of witnesses into Mississippi's Parchman Penitentiary.

When the last of some three hundred Freedom Riders obtained release, the Nashville trio stayed on in Mississippi. Stung by observation that local Negroes shunned the Freedom Rides, and had slinked obediently into the colored waiting rooms even as new arrivals were being hauled off to prison, Nash and her two friends brought Martin Luther King into Jackson for a rally and trolled the streets for recruits. They organized the earliest mass demonstrations against segregation in Mississippi—until state authorities shrewdly prosecuted Nash and Bevel for contributing to the delinquency of minors. Convicted, sentenced to two years apiece, they groped for a new start from a tough place, like Moses.

In transition, the three Nashville students released ordinary ambitions for a floating, expanding identity as movement people. Lafayette was the most scholarly of them—slightly built, with just enough of an Asian cast to justify his movement nickname, "Little Gandhi." Lafayette saw himself as a spiritual explorer. After surviving his forty days at Parchman, he accosted idle young Negroes on the streets of the state capital of Jackson with an abrupt question, "Do you want to go downtown and fight some white people?" Of every fifty takers, he hoped to interest two or three in nonviolence.

His sidekick James Bevel was at once more and less conventional. Born in the Mississippi Delta hamlet of Itta Bena, Bevel looked the part of the itinerant Negro preacher—dressed, except for the accent of a white clerical collar, all in black from his shirt and waistcoat down to his high-top Stacey Adams comforts, known as "preacher boots." He also wore a yarmulke in honor of his Jewish heroes, Jesus and the prophets. Bevel's sermons were rockets of energy and imagination. In jail, he was rumored to hear voices in collaboration with God on schemes to "draw the devil out of these white people." Many young colleagues thought his high-fevered ecstasy boiled over into rascalism—at church functions, he thought nothing of asking the pastor if his wife had any good-looking sisters—but Bevel almost welcomed nervous gossip about his wobbly mind. He said Negroes needed to be crazy in order to dream of freedom against the hegemony of white society. For him, the constant task of the movement was to distinguish between creative and self-destructive insanity.

Bevel was the scourge of movement disciplinarians such as Diane Nash, who had been raised Catholic in Chicago amid the Sisters of the

Blessed Sacrament, hoping to become a nun. Ever since Nashville, she had hounded Bevel for wasting his talents. A former beauty contest competitor of classical features—so light-skinned that she easily infiltrated angry white bystanders at lunch counter demonstrations—Nash was renowned as a leader of unattainable purity. Those who had pined for her as the movement spread through Negro colleges could scarcely absorb news from Mississippi that Nash accepted a marriage proposal from Bevel late in 1961, and worse, seemed possessed and even tamed by him. Comparable shock hit the Catholic authorities of Mississippi when a marriage request disclosed that the woman who had been faithfully and uneventfully attending mass at a white parish was Diane Nash the Negro felon and incendiary of the Freedom Rides. Evasive clerics informed her that a Catholic wedding might have been arranged if Bevel were an indifferent rather than an "enthusiastic" Protestant.

With Bernard Lafayette, the newlyweds shared a house of refuge with Bob Moses first in Jackson and then with their common mentor Amzie Moore in the Delta. Sharp differences often put awkward silences between them. Moses quoted the existential philosophy of Albert Camus, shunned publicity, and sought as a teacher to kindle a self-sustaining new passion for the vote. By contrast, the three Nashville students preached confrontational Christianity, shunned politics as corrupt, and sought to prove that nonviolent spectacles could work miracles among victims and oppressors alike. Moses saw them as too self-centered in their yearning for sacrifice, and, without the stability of Negro votes, too ephemeral in effect. They saw Moses as too intellectual for Mississippi farmers and too entangled in ramifications of leadership. As philosopher and moralist, Moses fought leadership's compulsion to dominate the common people even in democratic causes, but he tumbled through doubts that his anti-leadership convictions merely shielded him from inevitable responsibility. There was a haunted aspect to his constant self-examination—to what degree was he morally complicit in the death of Herbert Lee?—with a tone at once dreamy, fated, and cavalier. "After the hunting comes the killing," Moses wrote the SNCC office in Atlanta. "And if we're all dead, I want to be cremated and snuck into the next sun-circling satellite for my last rites...."

They compromised on a practical experiment. Bevel persuaded Moses to manage a congressional primary race in Jackson while he managed another in the Delta, for the first Negroes to run in Mississippi since Reconstruction. The spring campaigns coincided with Diane Nash's first pregnancy, during which one of James Lawson's nonviolent precepts— that oppression requires the participation of the oppressed—turned in her mind until she saw her felony appeals as participation that soothed Mississippi with a false presumption of justice. Accordingly, she withdrew the appeal, activating her two-year sentence. At a bond revocation hearing on April 30, 1962, Judge Russell B. Moore first banged down an additional ten days for contempt when Nash refused to sit in the colored section of the courtroom. Bevel, serving as her lawyer, made a speech to the court, and Nash herself read from an apocalyptic statement on why she chose to give birth behind bars. "This will be a black baby born in Mississippi," she declared before being led off to the Hinds County Jail, "and thus wherever he is born, he will be in prison.... I have searched my soul about this and considered it in prayer. I have reached the conclusion that in the long run, this will be the best thing I can do for my child."

Judge Moore summoned Bevel some days later to recommend insistently a first duty in all his roles—as lay attorney, citizen, husband, and expectant father—to keep Nash *out* of prison, not in it. "You know, son," he said ruefully, "you people are insane."

"Judge Moore, you don't understand Christianity," Bevel replied. "All the early Christians went to jail."

"Maybe so," said the judge. "But they weren't all pregnant and twenty-one." Bevel held his ground during the odd standoff, assuring Moore that Nash would renounce any court-appointed lawyer who tried to reinstate her appeal. Moore eventually ordered her release and simply ignored the uncontested two-year sentence.

Speaking invitations for Nash drifted in from the North, where church groups and readers of the Negro press turned out to hear the young lady who had dared Mississippi to make her give birth in jail. Bernard Lafayette, who spent much of the summer riding buses between fund-raising testimonials, arranged to bring Nash to Detroit for a series of rallies in August. His anxiety over her advanced pregnancy diminished only after he concealed her belly beneath an enormous raincoat to smuggle her without medical approval aboard a flight bound for Albany, Georgia, where Martin Luther King struggled to salvage a prolonged campaign against segregation.

Bevel was already there, exhorting a dwindling supply of volunteers. Like Judge Moore in Mississippi, Albany city fathers found that having King in jail punished them far more than him or his cause. Twice they had expelled King to freedom—once by outright deceit and once by disguised fiat—but they proved quite willing to imprison ordinary, local Negroes in numbers upward of a thousand. As cumulative suffering and economic loss wore down the Albany movement, one of King's new assistants, Rev. Andrew Young, desperately tried to persuade Nash to lead a jail march even after the onset of labor.

When King was compelled to retreat from Albany, Bevel and Nash hitched rides with their infant daughter across Alabama back to Amzie Moore's house in the Mississippi Delta. Bob Moses was starting voter registration again, based from Greenwood, using a new placebo organization called COFO—the Council of Federated Organizations—as a channel for small foundation grants. Like the Montgomery Improvement

Association for the 1965 bus boycott, and several umbrella groups since, COFO allowed civil rights groups to cooperate through a kind of truce office, and the new name also buffered white opposition because it lacked the fiendish stigma of the NAACP. Temporarily, at least, pastors who had been afraid to open their doors to the NAACP might be talked into hosting a COFO workshop.

Bevel returned in time for one of COFO's earliest church gatherings on Monday, August 27, at Williams Chapel Baptist in the tiny hamlet of Ruleville. Preaching from Matthew 16:3, he waved off individual fears of poor sharecroppers along with the presumed advantage of all-powerful Mississippi segregationists who, like the hypocrites denounced in his text, could not "discern the signs of the time." Just as the biblical hypocrites could read the stars in the heavens but not hearts, cried Bevel, the segregationists could run the space program but not see that freedom was sweeping the whole world. In America, freedom meant the vote, and in Sunflower County, where nearly three quarters of the potential voters were unregistered Negroes, the vote meant that meanness and hatred and suffering could be reduced if only the least of these would step into the Indianola courthouse to register.

Among those answering the call for raised hands was Fannie Lou Hamer, the twentieth child of sharecroppers. Short and stout at forty-one, she walked with a limp and was semiliterate in all subjects except biblical wisdom. Hamer had come to see whether this odd Mississippi preacher fit the reputation spreading on the plantations, and having caught Bevel's fire, she showed up that Friday among eighteen volunteers for what amounted to a mass registration attempt and a major word-of-mouth news story. There was no violence at the courthouse, but the Highway Patrol arrested Moses again on his way back to Ruleville. That night, the owner of the Marlow plantation evicted the Hamers from their shack of the past eighteen years, not so much on his own account, he told the Hamers—he could understand why somebody might want to vote—but for the gossip her action instantly stirred against him among the neighbors. Hamer presented herself as a refugee at a registration meeting, never to return home. The hostile climate stifled any sympathy local whites felt for her, and clerks at the welfare office declined even to accept her application for emergency surplus food until Diane Nash fired off a letter to Washington on her behalf, reminding the U.S. Secretary of Agriculture that treatment of Hamer violated the laws under which Sunflower County received nearly all its public relief funds. The new Delta project registered practically no new voters, but reprisals gained recruits one by one.

THE COFO REGISTRATION grants were slow to reach SNCC's tiny Hattiesburg project down in southern Mississippi. After their meager SNCC fund of $100 ran out, Curtis Hayes and Hollis Watkins spent more time earning their keep as farmhands for Vernon Dahmer, where they boarded when no family in town dared to take them in. Long before dawn each morning, Dahmer pounded a meaty fist on two walls of his bedroom to jolt awake sons and SNCC workers on the other side. "Let's go, bulls!" he hollered. They all tumbled out to the fields, and over breakfast several hours later Dahmer regularly pressed Hayes and Watkins for results on the previous day's canvassing—what area are you working, anybody ready to go down to the courthouse, how about the churches, any luck talking with the Negroes who come into the general store? Then Dahmer herded them all back to the fields or the sawmill. Already he had taught his seven-year-old daughter, Bettie, to drive one of the tractors, and while she did get help with the heavy fertilizer bags, he expected her to load the seeds by herself. Dahmer pushed himself and the hands so hard that his son Harold entered the Army that year and was writing home that his older brothers were correct—Army life was easy compared with the regimen at home.

Before the end of the summer, Curtis Hayes decided that he had not conquered his fear of jail for a mission so compromised by farm toil. He drifted back to Jackson just before a rescue letter finally reached Hattiesburg from SNCC headquarters in Atlanta. Unfortunately for Watkins, the long-awaited check was useless to him because it was made out to the departed Hayes. This was the sort of detail that paralyzed an early project for weeks. To request a reissued check by phone was a major logistical undertaking—a budget obstacle, a paranoia drama, and above all a location problem, as SNCC's fledgling new administrators usually were missing somewhere themselves, often in jail.

Staying on alone at the farm, Watkins gradually learned that the Dahmer family's Faulknerian bloodlines wandered across racial boundaries and taboos. Vernon Dahmer's mother, Ellen Kelly, had been one of four light-skinned mulatto daughters born during Reconstruction to a white plantation owner named Kelly, for whom their farm region north of Hattiesburg was named Kelly Settlement. Old man Kelly had no wife or other children, and he honored his mulatto family far beyond accepted custom. In the 1890s, Ellen Kelly caused something of a family crisis by entertaining a marriage proposal from George Dahmer, a most unusual white man —born illegitimately in 1871 to a transient German immigrant and a white woman who, during the chaos and destitution that followed the Civil War in Mississippi, had gone on to marry an ex-slave with whom she produced eight dark-skinned children raised as George Dahmer's younger siblings.

To the ex-Confederate planter Kelly, the problem with George Dahmer as a suitor for his daughter Ellen was not so much his bastard status or the racial confusion of a genetic white man living within Negro culture, but his lack of higher education. Kelly withheld consent until young George Dahmer completed courses at Jackson State, Mississippi's

Reconstruction-built Negro college, but then he blessed the newlyweds with a full share of his estate: forty acres, a cow, two calves, and a feather bed. Although some of the surviving white cousins contested these gifts to Negroes as the folly of a lunatic bachelor, the bequest stood, and in time George and Ellen Dahmer gained possession of additional Kelly acreage.

In December of 1908, four months after Lyndon Johnson was born in the Texas Hill Country, Vernon Dahmer arrived as the eighth of twelve Dahmer children. He may have become the superior farmer of the lot in any case, but competition decreased significantly when three of his five brothers married "out of the race" into white society in the North, one as a church pastor. Not all family members on either side of the color line were aware of the secret. Among Vernon Dahmer's most delicate tasks as an adult was to maintain ties among the witting ones even while engineering an innocent extinction of bonds in the next generation. Life's passages—births, marriages, deaths—posed the most difficult decisions about which distant ones could be notified, and how to do so without risking the fateful curiosity of the unwitting. With time, the simplest family communications across the color barrier became trying and dangerous. On the Negro side, parents faced the crippling issue of whether to acknowledge the possibility that especially light-skinned children might cross over, and if so, whether it was mutually safe and emotionally tolerable to seek the counsel of those who had gone before.

Vernon Dahmer narrowed such dilemmas by choosing successively darker wives. After fathering three sons during the Depression who grew up to look like him and his father, George—that is, by all appearances as white as the governor of Mississippi—he married a darker woman who bore three discernibly Negro sons during the 1940s, and two years after the second wife died, he married Ellie Dahmer in 1952 and produced a son, Dennis, and a daughter, Bettie, his young tractor driver, also clearly of African descent. In public, Dahmer learned to expect different reactions according to which sets of children were in his company. Among strangers, he could pass with his eldest children as a white family so long as Ellie was not along, whereas with her and the younger children he functioned separately across the color line as an ambassador. On Southern highways, he easily picked up food from the first-class "white" side of segregated restaurants if his family remained hidden in the car. Less pleasantly, white strangers who encountered the entire family assumed sometimes that Dahmer was a white boss among servants. Some made collegial remarks to him about his niggers.

Closer to Hattiesburg, where people tended to know one another, the complexities of color shifted. Most local whites considered all the Dahmers respectable for Negroes because of their prosperity and manners, but on some hidden level the children were perceived as less of a threat because of their defining dark skin, whereas Vernon Dahmer attracted a combustible undertone of resentment for "trying to act like a white man." Very few white people had any idea what a strenuous effort Dahmer made to stay in Mississippi and *not* be one of them. Dahmer himself remained wary of irrational traps near the point of acceptance, where some quirk of identity could turn all his industry and attainments against him. In the old days, his father, George, had invoked his lifelong motto—"You don't want to be too big too fast"—against Dahmer's plans to buy a tractor conspicuously beyond the means of most white farmers. A mix of frontier ruggedness and acute racial sensitivity shaped George Dahmer's identity until death claimed his Caucasian body for the country graveyard behind Shady Grove Baptist Church in 1949. (His wife, Ellen Kelly Dahmer, was buried there just after the *Brown* decision of 1954.) Although his traumatic expulsion from Shady Grove made the church alien territory in 1962, Vernon Dahmer took Hollis Watkins by the family plot to explain one of his inherited precautions: never buy vehicles with the fancy new automatic transmissions.

Not until the end of summer did Watkins find a weak spot in Reverend Willard's control of the Negro churches. It was the Methodists, a few of whom insisted that no Baptist ran their affairs. Watkins tugged at this sensitivity, emphasizing that he needed a site not for an NAACP meeting, as Reverend Willard so heatedly charged, but merely to discuss the right to vote, and the first open meeting took place at the tiny St. James CME Church off Mobile Street in downtown Hattiesburg. There was considerable advance controversy, including an incident in which Vernon Dahmer and his sons ran out of their house one night after a phone call and fired rifles into the air just to let potential attackers know they were ready. They refused to discuss the phone call or their interpretations with the baffled Watkins, on the theory that he had more than enough to worry about already as a twenty-year-old expected to run the meeting.

Watkins nearly burst with joy when two dozen people arrived. By way of welcome, he told them that he and Curtis Hayes had sung freedom songs for as few as one person in houses all through Hattiesburg and well out into the surrounding farm counties. Between songs, he talked to them about the new hopes since the sit-ins and the Freedom Rides, about the mechanics of the voting tests, and how he had escorted small groups of two and three into Theron Lynd's office, where the registrar always demanded to know what he was doing in the courthouse. "I turned the question around on him," Watkins announced. "I asked him, 'Am I breaking any law?'" This was daring enough for the first meeting. Before the last song, Vernon Dahmer rose to say they should all pitch in to support this voting work, and a special collection raised money to buy two or three reams of paper for leaflets.

St. James rested awhile. The next step—a "citizenship" meeting advertised in advance—posed greater risk because leaflets would make it impossible to disguise the event as a spontaneous prayer gathering. Eventually, the pastor and female board members arranged to open St. John Methodist Church in Palmer's Crossing, a hamlet on the opposite side of Hattiesburg from Kelly Settlement. Only a dozen people attended. This time, after his songs and testimonials, Hollis Watkins announced that he needed new volunteers to go with him to see Theron Lynd. "Who will meet me tomorrow morning down at the courthouse?" he asked. There was a long stillness before the hand of a visiting country preacher named Rev. L. P. Ponder went up.

Registrar Lynd failed Reverend Ponder and the four people who kept their promise to join Watkins at the registration test: two school bus drivers, a "sanctified" traveling preacher known as Aunt Virja, and a pioneer businesswoman named Victoria Gray. Gray had been a schoolteacher until an Army marriage exposed her to the door-to-door cosmetics industry, with a striking sales uniform of white trimmed in pink, after which she persisted to become Beauty Queen's first franchise entrepreneur in the South. Her brother owned a television repair shop with J. C. Fairley, the new NAACP chapter president, and while Victoria Gray never took part in NAACP work herself, she had heard enough to make sure that St. James was not the only Methodist church willing to hear young Watkins.

When John Doar arrived in Hattiesburg on September 17, 1962, for the latest trial of *United States v. Lynd,* he had no time to get acquainted with Gray or any of the hundred people subpoenaed there sight unseen. He went straight into court as his colleague Robert Owen hurriedly funneled witnesses inside to the stand, alternately white and Negro, for Doar to question off shorthand cover notes. The pell-mell witness selection system was one of many adaptations by the twenty lawyers of the Civil Rights Division, who, already overwhelmed by an avalanche of brutality complaints and a glacial crisis of school litigation, had a dozen voting rights cases in the courts with more than forty others just behind in gestation. Federal law required them to proceed county by county on voting, starting each time anew like Sisyphus. Harold Cox, the federal district judge assigned to *Lynd,* was so ardent a segregationist that he had dismissed the discovery portion of the action unaccountably as "abandoned." To bypass Cox, Doar's lawyers convinced the 5th Circuit Court of Appeals to resurrect the case as though it were lost, and further, to issue a newly invented device called an "injunction pending appeal," which in effect ordered Lynd to register Negroes equitably through interim proceedings. Lynd ignored that order among others, and presiding Judge Cox again scheduled no proceedings on noncompliance. Then, behind a thin facade of normalcy, in further detour before any trial on the merits of voting, a panel of 5th Circuit judges conducted a one-week contempt trial in Cox's place.

Doar had come almost to expect new witnesses to materialize against all practicality, just as he expected daring new acts of resistance from the segregationist powers. For Victoria Gray, a lifelong belief in simple choices and natural turning points calmed nerves through swift, bizarre consequences of raising her hand at St. John Methodist, such as explaining the early success of Beauty Queen to not one but three judges ranked just below the U.S. Supreme Court. Her brother's partner, J. C. Fairley, sat every day in court next to Vernon and Ellie Dahmer, who thought it important to have their young daughter Betty beside them even though the marshals were strict about not letting her sleep.

Late on the third night of the contempt trial, Tally Riddell suffered a heart attack during an interminable meeting of the university trustees in Jackson. Riddell was one of a small minority who favored compliance with the 5th Circuit's order to admit James Meredith to Ole Miss in a sensational marathon case running parallel with *Lynd*. The state's largest newspaper led a chorus of sovereign fervor with headlines such as "On Your Guard—Commies Using Negro as Tool" and "Thousands Said Ready to Fight for Mississippi." At least three Mississippi judges ordered Meredith arrested instead of admitted to college, and the legislature passed what amounted to a bill of attainder making him a criminal ineligible for classes. The three *Lynd* case judges promptly moved from Hattiesburg to New Orleans for emergency hearings on Governor Ross Barnett's contempt in the Meredith case. Doar argued Meredith's side through bristling drama that absorbed full attention in Washington. Even as President Kennedy announced a peaceful resolution on national television, students and beer-cooler vigilantes erupted in an all-night riot that killed three bystanders and wounded 160 U.S. marshals—twenty-eight by gunfire. A bivouac of some 23,000 soldiers safeguarded Meredith's academic debut during the Cuban Missile Crisis in October. Army units searched Ole Miss dormitory rooms at bayonet point on reports that white students were distributing cherry bombs from Mayes Hall.

The trauma of Ole Miss was so severe as to muffle celebration among Negroes in the state. There was no rush of students to follow Meredith, whose battered success made the continued suffering of Clyde Kennard all the more poignant, especially around Hattiesburg. In consultation with Vernon Dahmer and Medgar Evers, J. C. Fairley volunteered to accompany Kennard's mother into Parchman Penitentiary along with *Jet* reporter Larry Still, posing as visitors with the announced purpose of making a family portrait. In addition to a large flash camera, which he knew would be confiscated at the gate, reporter Still carried a small camera taped to his ankle. This was a dangerous mission. For Negroes to infiltrate Parchman for political purposes was to risk joining Kennard rather than helping him. Once they made it out safely, *Jet*'s photographs of the emaciated prisoner contradicted Mississippi's official position that Kennard was a healthy but undeserving thief of chicken feed. Prison authorities transported him under guard to a hospital for medical evaluation, which opened Governor Barnett to two accusations in the supercharged racial politics of Mississippi: that he admitted factual errors alleged by Negro critics, or was guilty of humanitarian sentiment for Kennard. He finessed both problems with a brazen statement that if Kennard was sick, Barnett had not realized it when he authorized a routine hospital visit. Anyway, reported the *Jackson Clarion-Ledger,* "the negro is not nearly so bad off, prison doctors think, as news stories have pictured."

At the Dahmer farm, a runaway yearling calf eclipsed chores and the latest Kennard news late one afternoon. Just as the Dahmers decided with practiced eyes that pursuit was fruitless, and were calculating the loss, Hollis Watkins sprinted headlong into the distant pasture. Hired hands trailed halfheartedly behind, joking that even if Watkins did prove fleet-footed he would not know what to do with a hard-muscled young steer that weighed three times his 140 pounds. Spurred on, Watkins got close enough to fling an arm around the neck and throw the yearling to the earth rodeo-style. By the time the Dahmers arrived, their teasing had a fresh tone of affection.

There was a kind of family loss on both sides when Bob Moses pulled Watkins out of Hattiesburg to the hard-pressed Delta project nearly two hundred miles north. Only seven new Negro voters had registered successfully during the nine-month stay with the Dahmers, adding to the minuscule total of twelve Negroes eligible to vote in the 1960 election. Still, more than fifty had tried, many of them solid witnesses in the federal lawsuit, like Victoria Gray, and the ordeal of Negroes at the courthouse had once attracted network news cameras. The overall record put Hattiesburg ahead of Greenwood, where Watkins withdrew.

BERNARD "LITTLE GANDHI" LAFAYETTE was setting off alone that fall to revive a project in Selma, Alabama, where the Kennedy Justice Department had filed its first original voting suit in April of 1961. He knew Selma mostly as a point on the map at the heart of Alabama's Black Belt. Its chief attraction was that no other SNCC worker wanted to go there since a pioneer had been run out of town the year before, and Lafayette sought to duplicate what Moses had begun alone in Mississippi: gain a toehold in strategic new territory. Less than two hundred of fifteen thousand voting-age Negroes were registered in Selma's Dallas County, and only seventy-five even tried to register during the entire decade since 1952—all rejected, including twenty-eight college graduates. On the wall of their Selma insurance office, Sam and Amelia Boynton posted the names of all seventy-five rejected applicants as an honor roll of the brave.

In Selma, as in Hattiesburg and Greenwood, outside movement workers followed the Justice Department to veteran local stalwarts like Dahmer and the Boyntons, then converged upon the registrar's office from above and below, each side willing to spend months for an applicant or court ruling that amounted to a snowflake in the hand. Into the spring of 1963, there were few hints of looming history at the three sites.

The survivors on the Boynton honor roll were prospective witnesses to Doar and contacts to Lafayette, but with sadly tattered potential. After the *Brown* decision of 1954, a number of prominent Negroes, including professors at Selma University, had followed NAACP instructions to petition for their children to attend the white schools—only to be crushed by retaliation against school budgets, bank loans, and other middle-class vulnerabilities until every name was withdrawn from the petition and the local NAACP disbanded. Even the Boyntons admitted that leading Negroes were fearful, protective, and escapist—more likely to take private flying lessons than visit the courthouse.

Lafayette was marked as a Freedom Rider within hours of his arrival in Selma, and diligent sponsorship of the Boyntons gained no early ground for his voting project. Only one intrepid female schoolteacher agreed to provide boarding. A medical technician named Marie Foster did soon teach nighttime literacy classes, but her lone pupil was a man in his seventies and she knew better than to think that literacy itself could open the voting booth. Foster and her brother, Selma's only Negro dentist, were among those rejected at the courthouse in spite of advanced education. Father Maurice Ouellette, a white Catholic priest who ran a missionary outpost for the Fathers of St. Edmund, allowed workshops in his rooms at considerable risk to the Edmundites. Lafayette started slowly with Bible lessons and freedom songs, but he could not expand beyond a core group of students without access to a mainstream Negro church. His best hope, Tabernacle Baptist, was heavily freighted with history and pulpit politics.

During the era of Franklin Roosevelt, Tabernacle of Selma had been renowned among Negro Baptists, on a par with FDR's Little White House at Warm Springs. Its pastor, Rev. D. V. Jemison, ruled the National Baptist Convention for more than twenty years before J. H. Jackson, hanging on to power by tenacious entrenchment long after the northward migrations reduced Tabernacle to a shell of its former glory. Selma's children remembered how the august Jemison always carried a pocketful of pennies for those who could pass his stern Bible quizzes on street corners, how limousines pulled up to Tabernacle with kinglike preachers from afar and even the local white people treated "Dr. Jemison" with respect. Not a few of the Tabernacle deacons and trustees had swelled through decades of partnership with such a pastor, to the point that they looked down upon his replacement as a shriveling agent of decline.

Rev. L. L. Anderson arrived just as the celebrated bus boycott broke out in Montgomery, fifty miles east of Selma, and several Tabernacle officers promptly claimed the prerogative to decide whether the new pastor should speak on that controversy. Some said Anderson lacked the experience to care for Tabernacle's reputation, others that he belonged at a church nearer his native Ohio. Enmity festered until some of Tabernacle's deacons produced the affidavit of an unmarried woman in Montgomery that Anderson was the father of her child. Anderson denounced the affidavit publicly as a fraud, whereupon some Tabernacle officers tried to get a court order banning him from the pulpit. Finally, one wealthy deacon stood to interrupt a worship service. "That little nigger has got to go," he declared, pointing his finger dramatically at Anderson. "Money talks. He can't stay here."

Facing open rebellion, Anderson went to Montgomery to seek counsel among the pastors gathered during the bus boycott, including Daddy King, who advised a substitute motion for the removal of the rebellious deacons. Under Baptist rules, King pointed out, Anderson required no specific accusations—a generic charge of malfeasance would do. With this strategy at the showdown debate, Anderson's partisans routed deacons led by Deacon N. D. Walker, a physician of grand manner and a rolling bass voice, who had been wealthy among peers even before his daughter married the founder of *Jet* and *Ebony* magazines in Chicago, sealing an alliance deemed worthy of Tabernacle. Walker's threat to leave the congregation backfired unexpectedly, as a number of members shouted that they would feel well rid of him, and Anderson withdrew his removal motion as a gesture of reconciliation. "That will be your mistake," predicted a senior preacher from the bus boycott. "Don't ever stop the folk from kicking tail when they are kicking it for you."

No sooner did Anderson wear down his adversaries than he gave them a fresh line of attack. On an afternoon drive in 1959, his Lincoln collided with another car in an intersection, then careened from one side of the street to the other—killing an elderly pedestrian before it flipped over into a tree. A woeful Anderson testified that the initial collision had knocked him unconscious, but Selma's prosecutors indicted him for murder. Found guilty of manslaughter, he drew a sentence of ten years, and church adversaries cried out that he had brought down unimagined shame upon Tabernacle. The conviction stood until overturned by the U.S. Supreme Court not long before Bernard Lafayette first asked to use Tabernacle for a mass meeting.

Lafayette beseeched Anderson through winter into 1963, playing on his bus boycott connections without success. For eight years, running parallel with the rise of the modern civil rights movement, Anderson had gained stature as a survivor in a luminous pulpit, but he told Lafayette he could do no more because Selma was not as modern as Nashville or Atlanta. The active possibility of being retried on the manslaughter charges still held him vulnerable to whim or conspiracy, Anderson believed, especially when his enemies at Tabernacle boasted of their ties to Selma's white aristocracy.

Stymied in Selma, Lafayette followed Sam Boynton's advice to search for aspiring voters among illiterate yeoman farmers in the surrounding hinterland. He wandered farmhouse doorsteps for a month before receiving surprise invitations in March from a settlement in Wilcox County so remote that it had to be reached by pole ferry across a lake, so inbred that nearly all families were called Petteway. By official record, no Negro had applied for registration for more than fifty years; the county defended itself with this fact, arguing that Negroes did not desire to register. Lafayette first held meetings on nonviolence to introduce the very idea of farmers going to town without their rifles, and after a final purging of fears, at which several volunteers disclosed to relatives where family valuables might be dug up if they did not return, he escorted a solemn procession that drew stares on the streets of Camden. Nonplussed courthouse authorities, eyeing specially alerted Justice Department observers, accepted registration applications from all eight unarmed Petteways. Several signed with an "X."

IN MISSISSIPPI, where Moses conceded that the movement was "powerless to register people in significant numbers anywhere in the state," Hollis Watkins joined twenty or so volunteers determined to maintain a bare presence in the Delta towns—faces in plain sight, making even solitary trips to the courthouse. Five projects centered around Leflore County and its small county seat of Greenwood, stretched across a confluent loop of three meandering rivers—the Yazoo, the Tallahatchie, and the Yalobusha. The White Citizens Councils maintained southwide headquarters in Greenwood, which remained among the world's trading centers for cotton, and Medgar Evers had revoked the local NAACP charter for lack of activity since the Emmett Till lynching. Fear shut Greenwood to the movement so tightly that COFO could not secure an office for five months after a night posse ran them out of a photo studio in August of 1962, and project director Sam Block was obliged to spend more than a few nights in parked cars when host families showed him the door with fearful apologies. Conditions were no better next door in Sunflower County, where it would take more than a year to match the eighteen applicants arrested with Fannie Lou Hamer on the first try.

A dry 1962 harvest left the cotton crop low to the ground, more accessible to mechanical cotton pickers. Sharecroppers earned even less than usual, ate less, and were vulnerable in great masses to displacement. "So that you had a lot of Negro families who were destitute," Moses reported, "who were just rock bottom poor, poverty which you just can't imagine in most parts of the United States...in which the mothers were not able to send their kids to school because they didn't have shoes and they didn't have winter clothes." In Leflore County alone, the nation's surplus food program sustained 22,000 people between growing seasons—

more than 40 percent of the total population, including many Indians and not a few whites, as nearly a third of the whites were tenant farmers. The local role was merely to distribute cheeses and other staples bought by the federal government to support agricultural prices, and no one imagined that two of the nation's poorest counties could or would spurn free food for their own needy, until Leflore and Sunflower counties publicly terminated all food relief in October. Only a minuscule fraction of those hit by the cutoff were Negroes who had tried to register. Nevertheless, in the surly mood after James Meredith's forced integration of Ole Miss, county officials exercised what amounted to a nuclear war option to prove they gave no succor to racial agitators.

As winter hardened, and the counties blamed the ragtag Delta projects for conditions of famine, the COFO workers appealed to Northern support networks for survival donations. Future SNCC leader Ivanhoe Donaldson entered the movement by driving a carload of relief supplies from Michigan State down to Mississippi over Christmas vacation. (He wound up in jail even before reaching Greenwood.) By early 1963, a Chicago group led by crossover comedian Dick Gregory was donating supplies by the ton, and on February 1, Harry Belafonte gathered up sympathy and money for Mississippi at SNCC's first national fund-raising concert, in New York's Carnegie Hall.

Relief trucks pressed heavily against the logistical freeze in Greenwood, as young workers who lacked safe beds and an office suddenly needed storage space for shipments of food. In crisis, COFO secured one room of a dry cleaning plant called the Camel Pressing Shop on McLaurin Street, which held the workers but not much cargo. To break the lockout by the local churches, Hollis Watkins, up from Hattiesburg, shared the lesson of his success with Methodists, and James Bevel finally gained entry through Rev. D. L. Tucker to Turner Chapel AME. Freedom songs spilled from the first tentative church meetings in Greenwood, but the tiny, two-story structure quickly proved too small. Aiming for Wesley Chapel—with its ample basement and central location—Bevel obtained from presiding bishop Charles F. Golden a stiffening order that the pastor and congregation must admit the starving to sanctuary.

Acute hunger transformed the paralyzed COFO project into a refuge of desperate hope. Recipients in the food lines met registration workers hand to hand, eye to eye, and registration workers seized every chance to tell them they were hungry in large part because they were second-class citizens, and that they would remain so until they laid claim to the right to vote. Of the few sharecroppers who began following the COFO staff down to the registrar's office, nearly all were illiterate—better than 80 percent by the estimate of Bob Moses. As such, they were just the opposite of the exemplary, educated registrants that Justice Department lawyers and COFO's own projects normally recruited. The sharecroppers came instead from the great masses being pushed for decades into big cities without education or prospects. ("This is why you have your big problems in Washington and Chicago," Moses soon testified before Congress, "and I don't know whose responsibility it is.")

In the fresh mayhem of the Greenwood COFO office, Moses spent hours discussing a trap within the circular powerlessness of racial subjugation itself: how to gain the vote without literacy, and literacy without the vote. One theoretical remedy was somehow to remove the literacy requirements in favor of universal suffrage, but such ideas touched the rawest nerve of the conflict between race and democracy. "We killed two-month-old Indian babies to take this country," one white voter explained succinctly to the press, "and now they want us to give it away to the niggers." On the literacy side of the trap, against generations of ignorance and segregated, dilapidated Negro schools, COFO workers grasped for small-scale relief from Martin Luther King's new Citizenship Education Program, which offered intensive, one-week adult literacy courses near Savannah and Charleston. James Bevel and Diane Nash petitioned King to open a third citizenship school in the Delta. Nash urgently lobbied for the schools at the Carnegie Hall fund-raiser, but King's administrator, Andrew Young, rejected the plan as unrealistic. "The chances are that you would be closed and the property confiscated in short order," he wrote, "that is, if it wasn't bombed first." Young's worry was hardly far-fetched; he had inherited his program after the Highlander Folk School suffered such a fate in Tennessee. He teased Nash in a postscript over her edgy, possessed mood, which was common among those who left and reentered Mississippi's reality warp. "Diane, you really should have stayed over a day or so in New York so we could have 'done the town,'" Young advised. "Then you'd have had to go back to Mississippi and work hard to get rid of your guilt."

AMONG THOSE who ogled Bob Moses from a distance was June Johnson, who had turned fifteen in December. One of twelve children being raised by a laborer and a maid, young Johnson had heard grown-ups whispering about the mysterious stranger in a tone very similar to the life-and-death gravity with which they had trained the children never to say a word about Emmett Till, even at home. One morning on the way to school, she led a fearful, half-giggling group of her friends up to Moses, walking a street with hands in his pockets, as always. "Are you from Greenwood?" she asked. When he said no, she asked boldly about the rumors that he was a Freedom Rider. Moses only smiled, asked about her family, and offered to carry her books.

After that, Johnson found excuses to sneak near the COFO office on McLaurin Street. "Honey," she told her sister, "I heard that they got some good-looking men up at that place." One afternoon a mischievous friend pushed her headlong into Moses. "What you-all do here?" asked Johnson, recovering from embarrassment. "We hear you-all are troublemakers."

Moses replied that they were having a registration meeting that night, and asked if she might like to see one of the canvassing notebooks that explained why voting was so important. The girls took the notebook and ran, passing it back and forth like contraband. Before June Johnson could hide the notebook under her mattress, one of her sisters obediently informed their mother, Belle Johnson, whose wrath turned the whole house silent. She ordered her daughter to "trot right back down there" with the confiscated book and "don't bring that stuff here no more."

THE DELTA FAMINE worsened until more than six hundred sharecroppers lined up outside Wesley Chapel on February 20, 1963. Cleveland Jordan, an old cotton-row preacher recruited to supervise the food distribution, kept up a running speech about the connection between poverty and voting. "We just mean to register and vote, and we don't mean to fight and we don't mean to run," he said, calling to recipients by name. "We just mean to go to the polls and get our freedom." Kerosene arson struck the Negro section of Greenwood that night, destroying four stores next to the Camel Pressing Shop. When Sam Block told sharecroppers in the relief line that the fire targeted the registration project, Greenwood police arrested him for incendiary public remarks.

Block's quick conviction and six-month sentence galvanized many sharecroppers who had heard him sing freedom songs as they received packets of Spam and cheese. More than 150 Negroes, nearly all from the relief lines, presented themselves at the courthouse on February 25 and 26. They still averted their eyes from white faces out of conditioned inferiority, and only a handful of them managed even to apply for the vote, but these limits only underscored their newfound tenacity. In spite of taunts and shouted threats from bystanders, including their plantation bosses, sharecroppers held their ground on the public sidewalk for two days and vowed to come back. Never before had Mississippi's common Negroes stood in such numbers for the ballot.

Two nights later, a sudden zipper-line of automatic gunfire from a Buick without license plates left thirteen bullets in a COFO car, wounding volunteer driver James Travis in the shoulder and neck as Moses managed to swerve to a halt in a roadside ditch. This attack made Greenwood a small national news item. In the immediate aftershock, COFO leaders decided to reinforce nonviolence against vigilantes by concentrating Mississippi volunteers from outlying projects into Greenwood. They arrived along with important people looking for information. Police at the bus station arrested and manhandled one well-dressed Negro before learning that he was a federal staff investigator for the Civil Rights Commission. From Washington, Attorney General Robert Kennedy himself pushed negotiations to make Leflore County resume the federal food relief, and Medgar Evers reported to his NAACP superiors in New York that he "noticed" a surprising surge of registration activity led by members of Greenwood's defunct NAACP chapter—a portrayal that was almost entirely cosmetic salve for bureaucratic vanities at NAACP headquarters. Pretending to be alarmed, Evers pushed New York for permission to stay ahead of the competition.

Andrew Young reached Greenwood the same day Evers did, bringing a concession to James Bevel and Diane Nash: they could have a walking, substitute literacy school in the person of Annell Ponder, one of three experienced teachers from SCLC's Citizenship Education Program. On March 4, her first night in Greenwood, Ponder heard Bevel and Reverend Tucker urge the board members of Turner Chapel AME to open the church now to her literacy classes, and Ponder herself explained methods that her mentor, Septima Clark, had been developing nearly fifty years since World War I—teaching words from newspapers and the Bible, arithmetic mostly from simple, practical farm measures. With drills from basic civics—how to spell "freedom," the basic duties of a sheriff—Clark needed only an intensive week's retreat to have most former illiterates proudly signing their names, writing letters, and lining up at the courthouse, able and inspired to register. Moreover, she taught the early signs of gifted illiterates, who might be trained quickly to teach *other* illiterates, plus leaders at the next level who might teach other teachers, and so on through a small-scale miracle of compressed evolution. With permission from the skittish Turner Chapel board, her disciple Ponder started the first church-based literacy classes in the Mississippi Delta, two nights a week. Within a month, she enrolled more than 150 sharecroppers in primary classes.

On the other side of Greenwood, white officials ended months of rancorous negotiations with federal representatives who argued that news stories on the willful starvation of disfranchised Negroes were embarrassing to U.S. leadership in the Free World. Leflore County supervisors defended their March 19 settlement as a strategic maneuver to spare Mississippi from an "invasion" of federal bureaucrats, but skeptical voters criticized them for spineless surrender. "Who is going to believe that Leflore County runs its own affairs now?" demanded the *Greenwood Commonwealth*. "This tends to prove that a naked political sword from the Kennedy arsenal in Washington has flashed into Leflore County to encourage the groups of racial agitators now operating here.... The power move by the Federal Government should have been resisted."

Four nights later, arsonists set fire to the COFO office at the Camel Pressing Shop. Curtis Hayes noticed smoke when he drove by about midnight, but he was helpless against the flames. Word of the fire boosted attendance for Annell Ponder's first awards ceremony at the next night's mass meeting. Announcing that eight of twelve students had persisted through rigors of second-level training, she called forward all eight women, including Fannie Lou Hamer, to receive graduation certificates proclaiming them qualified to teach literacy and citizenship. The next evening, March 26, a shotgun blast ripped through the front of the much-admired Greene family—a son had applied to succeed James Meredith as the second Negro at Ole Miss—and nearly two hundred supporters gathered spontaneously outside Wesley Chapel the next morning to sing freedom songs. Bob Moses made occasional remarks from the sidewalk. SNCC's executive director, James Forman—who had rushed from Atlanta to investigate the office fire—suggested a march downtown, but squad cars soon converged on Wesley Chapel and officers with guns drawn waded in to arrest SNCC leaders they could recognize, including Forman, Moses, Willie Peacock, and Lawrence Guyot.

Sudden spasms opened and shut the Greenwood registration movement to the world like a fluttering lens. Dozens of reporters, including a CBS News camera crew, reached Greenwood before the next day, March 28, to observe one hundred Negroes who stood all morning in the registration line outside the courthouse, then marched two abreast toward Wesley Chapel once the registrar closed his office for an extended lunch hour. The orderly spectacle offended crowds of white citizens along the route, many of whom cheered "Sic 'em! Sic 'em!" when officers piled into the line behind police dogs. Negroes scattered in bedlam. Cleveland Jordan half dragged an injured Reverend Tucker in desperate retreat behind a young COFO staff member, Charlie Cobb. President Kennedy saw a photograph of a German shepherd biting Tucker in the next morning's *New York Times,* and sent word that Burke Marshall should do something about it. Medgar Evers earned thunderous ovation with a resettlement donation for an elderly minister evicted because he refused to withdraw his registration application. With Dick Gregory, James Bevel led audacious courthouse marches through barricades of fire trucks. When a week's national attention generated a question about Greenwood at the next White House press conference, President Kennedy said there did appear to be violations of federally protected rights, including the right to vote, but deflected judgment with an announcement that his Justice Department had just filed suit on the issue and "the court must decide."

Later that same day, April 3, John Doar visited Bob Moses and his fellow COFO leaders in the Leflore County jail. The prisoners were overjoyed to be the Justice Department's new clients in a legal action just announced on national television by the President of the United States himself. They had refused bail for eight days to maintain public leverage toward precisely this result, and Moses understood Doar's statutory jargon well enough to know this was a long-awaited "(b) suit." Instead of undertaking to prove by tedious accumulation a "pattern" of voting preference that could be explained only by race, as in the long-standing "(a) suit" against Theron Lynd in Hattiesburg, a (b) suit alleged specific acts of unlawful "intimidation" by local officials against would-be voters. The government's burden of proof was higher in a (b) suit, but the enforcement sanctions were correspondingly greater: criminal injunctions, federal arrest, and in extreme cases court-ordered replacement of offending registrars with federal substitutes.

Guards unexpectedly threw open the jail doors the next morning for the blinking COFO prisoners, who were slow to accept the good news of freedom. All charges dropped. No bail. Free to go. When they observed no tricks, high spirits spilled over into dancing and tears. At long last they felt the decisive intervention of the federal government behind the voting movement, but Moses intuited something amiss. He hung back apprehensively from the celebrations in Negro Greenwood until a wordless exchange of looks with John Doar killed any trace of euphoria that same day.

The moment was no better for Doar. He had made his arguments for the (b) suit inside the Justice Department, but Burke Marshall and Robert Kennedy went against him in a close decision governed less by risk of losing than by fear of winning. A (b) suit victory against Mississippi officials raised for them a "Meredith problem" of contempt on a potentially open-ended scale, causing a vacuum of public order that the U.S. government might be obliged to fill with soldiers and bureaucrats in numbers not seen since Reconstruction. This prospect was so grim that Kennedy and Marshall bargained instead to drop the (b) suit in exchange for release of the COFO leaders. For good measure, the federal government agreed to pay local distribution costs for the surplus food, which allowed county officials to say honestly that not a dime of local tax money supported protesting sharecroppers.

The overnight truce removed the two most inflammatory public conflicts between the federal and Mississippi governments, but Doar faced vigorous dissent from his own staff lawyers. Several of them had pushed to the point of rebellion once before, when the Kennedy Justice Department declined to file (b) suits in response to the forceful repressions that drove Moses from his original McComb project in 1961. This was politics again, the dissenting lawyers argued—a Democratic administration did not want to punish Democratic officeholders—to which Doar replied that in barely two years the administration had turned the South from a bastion of Democratic support into a region where the Kennedy name was heard most often as an epithet, largely because of Robert Kennedy's positions on civil rights. This was hardly a record of pure expediency, said Doar, who argued stoically for loyal duty in the chain of command.

First sight of Moses—only hours out of jail—made Doar swallow his planned explanations, knowing how conscientiously Moses had followed advice to build his work around voting rather than sit-ins, how steadfastly he had relied upon assurances that voting was the firmest ground of national authority in race relations. What the governments saw as a trade-off, the forlorn Moses saw as a catastrophe. Having sacrificed willingly and purposefully toward the goal of federally protected voting rights, he realized that the government surrendered that leverage to reduce public pressure. Worse, the deal punctured a Greenwood movement that had taken a year to build from nothing. It receded swiftly from that April 4, the same day Esther James won her libel judgment against Adam Clayton Powell far away in New York. Reporters evacuated Greenwood within a week, and previous conditions were restored in many respects. Local officials prudently supplied a courtesy bus between Wesley Chapel and the courthouse, so voting applicants could obtain rejections with less public friction.

BEFORE THE LEADERS made their way out of Greenwood by bus and carpool over the weekend of April 12, young June Johnson boldly told Moses that she would run away from home unless he found a way for her to attend SNCC's annual conference. Mesmerized through the upheaval, she fixed upon the notion that in Atlanta she might learn where these movement Negroes came from, and pestered Moses until he agreed to visit her mother. When she tried to sidestep the undertow by insisting that her daughter must have a suitable female chaperone, Johnson soon returned unfazed with Moses and the impeccable Annell Ponder, who offered to keep June in an apartment she retained from her college teaching days. Distress pulled Belle Johnson between the ominous comments she picked up as a maid in the homes of white families and the novel pleas of upstanding strangers on behalf of her headstrong daughter. When she finally relented, an ecstatic June Johnson made her first trip out of Mississippi.

Greenwood supplied sixty of some 350 students who gathered at Gammon Theological Seminary on the campus of Atlanta University. Some veterans from scattered outposts already displayed symptoms of nonviolent combat fatigue. These were heroes made suddenly fragile and young. Intensity spilled in all directions—between self-hatred and messianic pride, utopianism and fresh disillusionment, cynicism and psalms, race as a tissue of irrational fiction or a huge chamber of primary stuff. Remarkably, students wrestled openly with issues that for many generations baffled elders into avoidance. "It's still not clear to my mind, even on the voting issue, that Negroes will gain the vote rapidly enough," Moses told the conference. "The squeeze is always the automation of the cotton crops, the inability of the Negro with his poor education to adapt to new technology, the unwillingness of the white people to train them, and the programs of the Citizens Council to move them out." Against this tide of misery and oppression, there was little solace in the movement's distant goal of voting rights for the tiny minority of educated Negroes. Only a suffrage without slippery qualifications offered hope, said Moses, taking up the slogan of the African anticolonial movements: "one man, one vote." Thinking out loud, he urged the students not to minimize the political cost of this demand to white Southerners, who would face a new electorate in which the controlling, marginal voter would be a Negro unable to read or write. No other Americans faced such a prospect, including those most attached to the image of potbellied, ignorant Southerners.

Moses told the conference that Greenwood had glimpsed a miracle when five hundred sharecroppers tried to register instead of five. "For us that's a big number," he said. "That's a big breakthrough." Nevertheless, he speculated that they needed "not five hundred but five thousand going down." Even then, no one could predict the result nor be sure even where to look for guiding clues—in courtrooms, cotton prices, national news stories, churches full of fresh courage, or in the eyes of white policemen.

Back in Greenwood, Annell Ponder lost no time gathering up applicants for advanced citizenship training from Septima Clark. Belle Johnson flatly refused to allow her daughter June to make another long trip—at least until the end of the school year—but Fannie Lou Hamer signed up for the April workshop. In Hattiesburg, Victoria Gray learned of the teacher classes from Vernon Dahmer, who passed along what he heard from Hollis Watkins. With her brother and J. C. Fairley of the NAACP, Gray recently visited the Clyde Kennard home to gather supporting facts for a clemency petition, only to be stunned by the skeletal visage of Kennard himself in his mother's rocker. Without notice or announcement, Governor Barnett had "indefinitely suspended" his sentence, almost certainly to avoid the minor embarrassment of having Kennard die in state custody. Of all the colliding shocks the visitors absorbed—the joy of unexpected freedom, the horror of a young man eaten with cancer—what transfixed Victoria Gray was his gentle recollections of outrages committed against him. His unnatural lack of bitterness disturbed her to the point that she remarked on it with a hint of criticism. "No, I'm not angry," Kennard replied. "Not anymore. I'm just very, very thankful to be home." Afterward, Gray could not decide whether this was the serenity of approaching death or something else beyond hatred and fear. It reminded her of the strangely clear energy from young Hollis Watkins at her first mass meeting. A nagging attraction sealed her resolve to let Beauty Queen run itself for a week, and when no one else from southern Mississippi would go, she hitched a ride alone north to Greenwood and, with Fannie Lou Hamer, boarded Annell Ponder's bus bound for SCLC's retreat near Savannah.

6

Tremors:
L.A. to Selma

JAMES BEVEL was in Birmingham by then, summoned by Martin Luther King. With Diane Nash and their eight-month-old daughter, Bevel arrived from Greenwood just in time to preach at the April 12 mass meeting in place of King, who had submitted to solitary confinement that afternoon. The carefully planned Birmingham campaign was in crisis. Over the next week, Bevel and Nash pitched in behind King's exacting administrator, Wyatt Walker, who labored to keep pace with chaos on many fronts—lobbying for some hint of public support from the Kennedys, cultivating reporters and distant celebrities, coaxing forward new jail volunteers, weeding out laggards and training the rest in nonviolence for the daily marches toward the forbidden landmarks of segregated commerce.

One of Walker's tactical innovations presented an opportunity uniquely suited to Bevel. Walker demanded punctuality in the daily demonstrations until he noticed while fuming through the inevitable delays that news reporters often lumped Negro bystanders together with actual jail marchers in their crowd estimates. After that, Walker went against his nature to hold up the marches with deliberate tardiness, so that daily stories of growing crowds could disguise the dwindling number willing to accept jail. As the delays stretched past school hours, crowds began to fill with Bevel's preferred recruits—Negro students.

To Bevel, looking past the arrests to the teenagers in the background, the flagging demonstrations already had accomplished the work of many months in the Mississippi Delta, where the bulk of the Negro population was widely dispersed on rural plantations: they had gathered a crowd.

With Nash and student volunteers, he distributed handbills advertising a daily youth meeting at five o'clock, two hours before the regular seven o'clock mass meeting. There he preached on the meaning of the primal events downtown. His crowds grew so rapidly that Andrew Young helped run the youth meetings, and Dorothy Cotton, Young's assistant in the SCLC citizenship program, led the singing. Following his practice in Mississippi, Bevel showed a film—an NBC White Paper on the Nashville student movement of 1960, which featured the stirring, climactic march of four thousand students that had desegregated Nashville's libraries and lunch counters. By April 20, when King and Abernathy bonded out of the Birmingham jail, the youth meeting already surpassed the adult meeting in numbers. By April 23, when reporters again failed to ask President Kennedy about Birmingham at his press conference, the adult mass meeting first packed St. James Baptist Church because the students in a mass stayed over from their own session. By April 26, when the jail march was reduced to a handful, forcing Fred Shuttlesworth to play for time by announcing a massive new phase to begin on May 2, most of the jail volunteers who rose in the mass meeting came from the youth workshops.

King praised the children for their courage but told them to sit down. The Birmingham jail was no place for them. At the nightly strategy sessions, King and the other leaders flailed among themselves to devise a master stroke for May 2 that might hold off the movement's extinction— a hunger strike or perhaps a jail march by Negro preachers in robes. No idea promised to crack the reserve of the outside world. Sensing their exhaustion from the other side, Birmingham's white leaders rallied to the "velvet hammer" policy of firm but nonsensational resistance, and the local newspaper published an article of encouragement entitled "Greenwood Rolled with the Punch—And Won." King's sessions grew more rancorous. They were promising their followers and the national press nothing less than "a nonviolent D-Day" on May 2, but all the thunder of preachers and the honey of massed choirs pulled no more than forty or fifty volunteers from the pews, Wyatt Walker admitted. He bristled at Bevel's claims that the youth meetings were spilling over into another church almost every day. Walker resented Bevel as an upstart, an intruder, and a free spirit who played loose with the chain of command.

Still, Walker was a man of results. Having come into Birmingham with only minority support from the Negro adults of Birmingham, and having delivered mostly suffering and disappointment since then, King and Shuttlesworth already were fending off internal pressures to evacuate gracefully. Backbiters predicted that the outsiders would leave Birmingham Negroes worse off than ever, with segregation hardened by the besieged anger of whites. Worse, Bevel's proposal would leave the best of the next generation with criminal records, not to mention the psychological scars of wide-eyed children dragged into the inferno of a segregated jail. King's host family in Birmingham, John and Deenie Drew of a prominent insurance family, resolved to send their children off to boarding school lest they get caught up in the trouble. Like most of King's strongest supporters, they would have recoiled in horror had they known that Bevel aimed to use not just the older teenagers but also the junior high students on down to "the babies" just out of kindergarten. What dismayed much of the senior staff was not so much that King, smiling and noncommittal, insisted on hearing Bevel out, but that King seemed to respect the "voices" Bevel heard even when they urged him to subvert the damaged authority of Negro Birmingham through its children. "Against your Mama," Bevel told King, "you have a right to make this witness."

When the doors of the Sixteenth Street Baptist Church opened shortly after one o'clock on Thursday, May 2, a line of fifty teenagers emerged two abreast, singing. The waiting police detail hauled them into jail wagons, as usual, and only the youth of the demonstrators distinguished the day until a second line emerged, then a third and many more. Children as young as six years old held their ground until arrested. Amid mounting confusion, police commanders called in school buses for jail transport and sent reinforcements to intercept stray lines that slipped past them toward the downtown business district. On the first day, nearly a thousand marching children converted first the Negro adults. Not a few of the onlookers in Kelly Ingram Park were dismayed to see their own disobedient offspring in the line, and the conflicting emotions of centuries played out on their faces until some finally gave way. One elderly woman ran alongside the arrest line, shouting, "Sing, children, sing!"

With the jails swamped by nightfall, Bull Connor ordered a massed phalanx of officers to disperse rather than arrest any demonstrators King might send the next day—intimidate them, shoo them away. When more than a thousand new children turned out in high-spirited, nonviolent discipline, giving no ground, frustration and hatred erupted under Connor's command. Police dogs tore into the march lines, and high-powered fire hoses knocked children along the pavement like tumbleweed. News photographs of the violence seized millions of distant eyes, shattering inner defenses. In Birmingham, the Negro principal of Parker High School desperately locked the gates from the outside to preserve a semblance of order, but students trampled the chain-link fence to join the demonstrations.

King, preaching at night to a serial mass meeting that spilled from one packed church to another, urged crowds to remember the feel of history among them. He cast aside his innate caution along with criticism and worry over the children in jail, shouting, "Now yesterday was D-Day, and tomorrow will be Double-D Day!" From Shuttlesworth's old pulpit, Bevel cried out in playful hyperbole that they would finish off Birmingham before Tuesday by placing every Negro young and old in jail so that he could be "back in Mississippi, chopping cotton." Bevel did not make his deadline, but nonviolent Negroes did overflow the jails and flood the forbidden downtown streets within a week. By Monday, May 6, the sudden conversion gushed from child to adult until no fewer than 2,500 demonstrators swamped the Birmingham jail, and King welcomed in awe the tangible sensation of history spilling over at frenzied mass meetings of four times that number.

SOMETHING PRIMAL welled up the same day in a Los Angeles courtroom. Defense lawyer Earl Broady faltered while cross-examining Officer Lee Logan about the mayhem at the Muslim Temple No. 27 in April of 1962. "Now this 'male Negro' business, this is significant to you, isn't it?" asked Broady in a whisper, his face suddenly clouded. " 'Male Negroes,' " he repeated. When Logan replied that the term was merely descriptive of the brawlers that violent night, Broady tried to resume his planned examination but stopped again. "You called them niggers while you were in this fight with them, didn't you?" he blurted out.

"I did not," Logan replied.

Broady asked for time to compose himself, but he called for a bench conference as soon as Logan testified that his first sight at the crime scene was "several male Negroes" fighting with officers a block south of the Muslim temple. "Your Honor, I believe these defendants should be referred to exactly the same as if they were Caucasians," said Broady. "This officer wouldn't refer to male Jews. He wouldn't refer to male Irishmen. He wouldn't refer to male Swedes. He wouldn't refer to male Caucasians."

Judge David Coleman hushed stirrings in the courtroom and spoke gently to Broady, whom he had known for years, observing that race was a standard designation in all police reports. "This issue has been made by the defense and not by the People," said the judge, who went on to remind Broady that the defense lawyers had tried to insert a racial standard by objecting, for instance, to the all-white jury. (On that matter, Judge Coleman had assured Broady privately that the all-white jury was probably best because most Negro jurors were too emotional to be objective about such a sensational case.) Broady argued that the drumbeat repetition of generic racial phrases was far from neutral in effect, and spread a blur of prejudicial guilt over all Negroes, including the fourteen Muslims on trial. "This man has said 'male Negroes' eleven times," Broady protested. "We kept an accurate count on it."

Judge Coleman chided Broady for insecurity. "Someday we will get to a period of confidence and respect for ourselves," he said at the bench, "when a reference to us as Negroes, Jews, or anything else ... will not be a matter that disturbs us very much, but it would be in effect something which we are very proud of."

Unable to reply, Broady walked back to the defense table and stood paralyzed for some time. Perversely, the judge's rebuttal struck deep within him. As dean of Negro lawyers in Los Angeles, Broady had spent years believing that to speak and think as a Negro was to confess inferiority, and that to think white was clear and refined. Recently, when business required him to talk with the employer of a criminal defendant, Broady had found himself cringing involuntarily in manner and speech—"yessiring"—to a Beverly Hills neighbor he claimed as a peer. Only then did he begin to admit that he was learning lessons from bootblacks and reformed thieves. For a month now—as long as King had campaigned in Birmingham—up to 250 armed deputies had guarded the courtroom against tinderbox fears of a race riot, and yet only the fourteen Muslim defendants spoke forthrightly of race. They sat in perfect order at the defense table a few rows ahead of Malcolm X, as crisp as their Muslim suits. Each testified with unflinching discipline about degradations—their broken homes, poor educations, and criminal records, their loss of bladder or bowel control after the shootings outside the temple. Broady had come to admire them in spite of their religious hokum, as he saw it, but he could not push race to the surface and hope to win in court.

"Your Honor," he said finally, "...I don't feel I can continue this cross-examination." Broady later minimized his breakdown as a suppressed fit of temper, telling reporters he feared he "might pull a Muslim" if he spoke, but at the defense table he could only bury his face in his hands while his co-counsel gamely took over.

The two sides skittered back and forth on the open mention of race. Prosecutors occasionally slipped in loaded questions: "As a Muslim, Mr. Jones, does the phrase 'kill the white devils' have any significance?" A deputy DA was careful to ask one question of Officer Paul Kuykendall: "Just for the record, are you of the Negro race?" Kuykendall's positive response established that one of the government's police witnesses was a Negro, much to the discomfort of Kuykendall himself. Within the department, he no longer could pass as a white officer. Acid doubt about Kuykendall's moment of hesitation in that night's death struggle between Officer Lee Logan and Muslim Arthur X Coleman—sparing Coleman's life in exchange for even an instant's added danger to Logan—dissolved fraternal trust among police for Kuykendall, while practically no Negroes allowed him offsetting credit for professionalism or humanity. Kuykendall was to remain a morose figure, stranded in a cloud of isolation.

For the defense, Broady did ask teenage defendant Troy X Augustine if he could have used the word "Negro," among others, as recorded in a disputed statement. "No, sir," Augustine replied. Asked why, he said, "Ever since I have found out what Negro means, I stopped calling people that." Broady cut off the testimony before Augustine could explain, however, and a prosecutor made sport of the inconsistency, saying the defense wanted to discuss race some times and not others. Broady could not afford testimony on the meaning of "Negro" because it would open the treacherous subject of Elijah Muhammad's Muslim teachings. Members of the Nation of Islam strictly and exclusively used the term "black" instead of "Negro," the Spanish word for "black," saying it was as absurd for them to ground racial identity in a foreign language* as it would be for white people to call themselves "Blancos."

Most of the testimony re-created the chaotic violence of April 27 as mirror images of primeval savagery, with each side portraying itself as victim. Medical testimony lent some support to the dramatic accounts of police suffering, especially early in the altercation when Tomlinson was shot and Kensic badly beaten. As descriptions moved to the later shootings and reprisals inside the temple, however, officers seemed to have emerged remarkably unscathed from the mass attack. Officer Reynolds had a thumb injury, which defense counsel suggested was the result of his own aggressions. As for the defense, Muslim witnesses consistently denied that they ever saw any fellow Muslim fighting back against the officers. They embraced their wounds and their lack of weapons as the anchor strength of their testimony, discarding Elijah Muhammad's posture of virile self-defense along with his militant sarcasm about the cowardly weakness of the nonviolent movement. Malcolm X coached all the defendants, demanding precision of testimony and a uniform politeness under the most scathing hostility. In the crucible of trial, they displayed an air of acceptance that bordered on forgiveness.

Small wonders took seed in the obscure Muslim trial just as nonviolence seized the emotions of the larger world from Birmingham. King's demonstrators literally carpeted Birmingham's downtown business district that second week of May. Having no place to put them, police officers in their midst shrugged helplessly to the city's business leaders, who were traumatized by the sudden evaporation of normalcy and commerce alike. Nearly two hundred reporters had converged from as far away as Germany and Japan. "We are not sitting idly by," President Kennedy's spokesman announced tersely in Washington. "We just can't say anything." Privately, Kennedy and several members of his Cabinet were calling the heads of corporations with subsidiaries in Birmingham, urging them to enter negotiations with King, and on Friday, May 10, Fred Shuttlesworth announced triumphantly that Birmingham "has reached accord with its conscience." Birmingham's merchants had accepted a schedule for desegregating their

---

* "The average so-called Negro today gets indignant if you call him black in English, will say call me Negro," Malcolm X said in 1963. "And if you ask him what does Negro mean, he will say it means black in Spanish. In other words, don't call me black in English, call me black in Spanish. It makes him sound ridiculous." Because "Negro" originated with the early Spanish and Portuguese slave traders, Muslims considered the term a grotesque legacy of slavery.

dressing rooms and lunch counters—even hiring Negro clerks. "Now this is an *amazing* thing!" King cried out at the mass meeting.

In Los Angeles, Charles X Zeno testified that same Friday about how he had left his sons in the car while he went into the temple to find his wife, Mabel, and how Officer Reynolds crashed through the door into him so that they tumbled pell-mell into the water cooler in the next room. Like other Muslim witnesses, Zeno identified the shreds of the suit he had worn. By the time Earl Broady gave up the witness for cross-examination, deputy DA Howard Kippen was eager to remove the torn coat and trousers from view. "Well, let's take these away so we can see each other," he told Zeno, and then paused. Instead of contesting detailed testimony about vengeful police hysteria, Kippen abruptly reversed course to make use of it. "Now the night of April 27, 1962, at any time did you get angry?" he asked.

"No, sir," Zeno testified.

"You didn't get angry?" Kippen asked, underscoring surprise.

"No, sir."

"You were struck from the back?"

"Yes, sir."

"You were punched in the mouth?"

"Yes, sir."

"Your gums were bleeding, your teeth were bleeding and loose?"

"Yes, sir."

"Your clothes were ripped?"

"Yes, sir."

"You were hit in the groin?"

"Yes, sir."

"You didn't get angry?"

"No, sir."

Broady jumped up to object that Kippen was not allowing the defendant to explain himself—perhaps Zeno meant he was too frightened at the time to be angry—but Kippen had his answer. In summation, he argued that no human being could endure such abuse without getting angry, suggesting that the police deserved the benefit of doubt if the Muslims joined in the violence—or alternatively that the Muslims were inhuman. Either way, they deserved what they got. Only one defendant ever admitted feeling resentment of the rawest humiliation and pain, he scoffed. Prosecutors said the Muslims were too good to be true. By their formulation, the defendants were guilty unless the jury could find them as innocent as the youngest child in Birmingham jail.

BERNARD LAFAYETTE drove to Birmingham to help Bevel and Diane Nash drill young people for the climactic jail marches, but he seldom stayed over. The thunderous breakthrough in Birmingham made him uncomfortable away from his new post some hundred miles to the south, and La-fayette returned to Selma most evenings that week to sit in vigil at tiny, segregated Berwell Infirmary, where a last debilitating stroke did not keep Sam Boynton from proselytizing whenever conscious. "Are you a registered voter?" he called out to strangers walking down his corridor. "I want you to go down and register. A voteless people is a hopeless people."

Boynton expired within hours of the jubilee news from Birmingham, and the coincidence loosed a flood of emotion so powerful that Lafayette canvassed ministers about the fleeting chance to hold Selma's first mass meeting. He half concealed his political purpose by calling it a "Memorial Service for Mr. Boynton and Voter Registration," but no one was fooled. Boynton's own pastor declined to have such a service at First Baptist of Selma, which had shunned controversy since driving off its pastor, Fred Shuttlesworth, a decade earlier, and other pastors refused for fear of having their churches bombed. "They don't feel disposed to build another church," advised Rev. L. L. Anderson of Tabernacle Baptist. "Most of them have their churches paid for." Anderson himself admitted that he could not offer Tabernacle on his own, even as a last resort. "That's too big a thing for one man," he said, but he did preach an impromptu eulogy for Boynton at a business meeting, asking who could deny tribute to such a man. When no deacon objected, Anderson quickly spread word of his commitment. Within hours, a local Negro printer on his own wits refused Lafayette's order for high-quality leaflets. "I understand you call yourself a printer," Anderson thundered at the balky shopowner. "When people bring things to you, your job is just to print them. You are a printer."

Lafayette got his leaflets, but by nightfall the Tabernacle deacons caucused on their own in the boardroom of Selma University. Anderson rushed there with foreboding, knowing the deacons considered Selma University their turf. Many were on the faculty, and D. V. Jemison had doubled as president of the college when he was alive. To Anderson's dismay, the spokesman for the rebellious deacons was the redoubtable Dr. William H. Dinkins, a history professor of pioneering degrees from Brown University among other schools, with a puckish sense of theater to lighten his pomposity. Anderson liked Dinkins and often called upon him spontaneously from the pulpit for a scriptural reference or historical fact, which Dinkins invariably supplied. Father of the woman Anderson hoped to marry, Dinkins had supported him through the schism of 1956, tormenting the Walker faction with learned expositions on the difference between "misfeasance" and "malfeasance." These ties made it painful on both sides for Dinkins to say the deacons canceled any use of Tabernacle for a Boynton memorial. "You are forsaking your friends, pastor," he said. "You are going with strangers." He meant the young Freedom Rider Lafayette, whom Dinkins called "this rabble-rouser who says he's a preacher."

Almost nose to nose, Anderson and Dinkins debated which sin most profaned a house of worship: a purpose tinged with secular politics, or a spirit corrupted by worldly fear. Each man cited the story of Jesus driving money changers from the Temple, drawing opposite lessons on the propriety of the Boynton memorial. The clash of emotions caused a number of deacons to wail and intercede clumsily for peace. One confessed that he had always avoided his friend Boynton in public view downtown, for fear of association with a voting zealot. When religious arguments were exhausted, Anderson pretended to concede. "You built the church," he told the deacons. "You carried the mortar. You stacked the bricks. I don't have a dime in the building, and as a matter of fact I wasn't even born. So I'm not going to take this church." While confident that the members would support him if he went ahead by fiat, Anderson declared, he would defer instead and move the Boynton service outdoors to a strip of land just off church property. He described the boundaries with precise detail and rising excitement. "I'm going to wire it up with loudspeakers," he shouted. "And I'm going to tell the folks that they can't come into Tabernacle because the deacons are afraid! Afraid of the white folks!"

"No, no, brother pastor, don't do that," Dinkins replied. Ambushed, the deacons tried to gauge the mix of bluff and determination in Anderson's face.

None of this internal anguish showed when the crowd of 350 gathered at Tabernacle Baptist on Tuesday evening, May 14. For them, soft organ music and the calming presence of Reverend Anderson in his robes preserved the repose of the sanctuary against a tension that was shockingly external. Glaring red and blue police lights flashed through the stained glass windows. On their car radios, many in attendance had been listening to the angry voice of Governor George Wallace denouncing the presence of U.S. Army troops in Birmingham as "an open invitation to resumption of street rioting by lawless Negro mobs, under the assumption that they will be protected by the federal military forces." For three days, since bombs detonated outside Martin Luther King's motel room, tremors of race spread from Birmingham to Selma and far beyond, rattling bones in Tabernacle.

Sheriff Jim Clark entered the sanctuary with a brace of deputies. The sudden appearance of any white person would have hushed the church, but these armed men, led by the widely feared enforcer of the white supremacy laws, drew an instant crowd of nervous Tabernacle deacons. Clark showed them a court order giving him access to the church to guard against insurrection, explaining it as something like a search warrant. Waving off a humble request that the guns not be displayed in the church, Clark posted his men all around the rear of the curved walnut pews beneath Tabernacle's imposing central dome. One deputy transmitted

Clark's orders by walkie-talkie to some fifty reinforcements posted outside among flashing lights. Angry shouts and the sounds of breaking glass filtered through the walls. Those seated in the pews could not be sure whether the damage to their parked cars came from white bystanders or the law enforcement officers themselves, or both. The threat was as ambiguous as Clark's court order, which could be stretched to mean that the officers were protecting the church against the insurrectionary violence of white segregationists.

For three hours, the gathered Negroes expressed their own double meanings on the edge between heavenly and earthly reward. When hymns and testimonials to Boynton had lifted spirits, Lafayette introduced as featured speaker the man who had assigned him to Selma, SNCC Executive Director James Forman. Although Forman at thirty-four was a few months older than Martin Luther King, he remained a student leader in title and function, and his measured audacity often bowled over audiences who expected the tentative suggestions of youth. Preaching a sermon called "The High Cost of Freedom," Forman said it was good that the white officers were there to deprive them of cheap courage. If they wanted to shout amen to the mission of Sam Boynton, they should do so in front of the sheriff who stood in its way. "Someday they will have to open up that ballot box," said Forman. A crescendo of enthusiasm made a number of elders cringe for the reaction of Sheriff Clark. Among them was the senior minister, who hastened to deliver the closing prayer. "You shouldn't put all of the blame on the white man," he said. "... We've got a lot to do in our own homes and own community before we talk about these other things."

Upon dismissal near midnight, the buzzing crowd exited no further than Tabernacle's front steps before clumping hesitantly at the sight of angry whites strewn along Broad Street, Selma's main thoroughfare. Most prominent were teenagers wielding freshly lathed table legs from a nearby furniture company. Sheriff Clark surprised some of the Negro leaders by shouting for everyone to disperse, but nothing happened. His special deputies mingled among the whites, who stood their ground. As Negroes huddled in panic, fearing arrest if they stayed and attack if they moved, decisive peacemaking authority arrived in the person of the football coach from Selma High School, who jumped from his car and pointed out his current and former players, telling them to go home.

NEITHER THE SELMA mass meeting nor the Muslim trial in Los Angeles competed with the avalanche of movement stories breaking out in city after city. Government statisticians counted 758 racial demonstrations and 14,733 arrests in 186 American muncipalities over the ten weeks following the May 10 Birmingham settlement. Sites quivered separately, unaware of one another or of the converging potential to lift up the right to vote and the raw alienations of cities outside the South. Less than two years later, Malcolm X would speak from a Selma pulpit alongside James Bevel and Fred Shuttlesworth, with Martin Luther King in jail, in a voting movement that made Selma an American landmark.

7

Marx in the White House

THE BLOW LANDED with strange subliminal force. Nearly everyone reacted to the riveting images of dogs biting children, but public commentaries were loath to analyze the phenomenon, and retrospectives on the decisive political tactic were nowhere to be found. Insofar as public figures did comment specifically on children's jail marches, they were critical. "I cannot condone, and you cannot condone, the use of children to these ends," said the mayor of Birmingham, and the *Atlanta Journal* denounced King for "extreme and extremely dangerous tactics." "School children participating in street demonstrations is a dangerous business," Attorney General Kennedy declared more guardedly. "An injured, maimed or dead child is a price that none of us can afford to pay."

Within the civil rights movement itself, there were cascades of thanksgiving but no calls to imitate the winning formula. For the minority voice of the Nation of Islam, a scornful Elijah Muhammad told the *Los Angeles Times* that King was "making a fool of himself," and Malcolm X declared on television "any man who puts his women and children on the front lines is a chump, not a champ." To a radio audience in Washington, Malcolm X brushed aside nonviolent methods. "You can't call it results when someone has bitten your babies and your women and your children," said Malcolm, "and you are to sit down and compromise with them . . . and drink some coffee with some crackers in a cracker restaurant, desegregated lunch counters. Now what kind of advancement is that?"

Still, beneath the silence and disparagement alike, there were signs of a rare, deeper tribute in the form of dumbstruck attachment. More than a month after the first children's march—while ridiculing every premise of nonviolent strategy—Elijah Muhammad devoted the entire front page of his own national newspaper to the photograph of a police dog biting the midriff of a Birmingham youth, paired with an equally large photograph of a white policeman holding a shotgun over the prostrate, handcuffed corpse of Ronald Stokes in Los Angeles. "Grievances of the Two Are the Same," proclaimed a joint headline in *Muhammad Speaks.* President Kennedy saw the Birmingham photograph in the *New York Times* and said it made him sick.

Leaders of every rank groped for responses to a coming flood. Race, so long conceived as a distant element of nature, slow-moving as a bank of rain clouds, suddenly bubbled up everywhere to sweep away the prevailing notion that passion was the enemy rather than the friend of racial goodwill. Where reason had twaddled, a tide of emotion swept forward conviction that segregation was fragile and that human nature contained untapped reserves for improvement. From the first children's march on May 2, the *New York Times* published more stories about race in the next two weeks than during the previous year. Attention spilled from the news to the editorial and features pages, and from there to a rash of projects on racial subjects that within a year published new and reprinted books at the rate of nine per week.

Race issues, declared *U.S. News & World Report,* "have moved out in front in people's thoughts," displacing a lengthy obsession with nuclear arms and the Cold War. The conservative journal *National Review*—while predicting without remorse that Negro hopes for integration were "doomed to founder on the shoals of existing human attitudes"—found "a serious idea" in Elijah Muhammad's doctrines of racial separation and sexual purity. Although notice of Malcolm X had been growing independently from his college lectures and the reverberations of Muslim rallies, the children of Birmingham soon raised him to mainstream recognition as a news counterpoint to Martin Luther King.

Within the federal government, an instant proposal for King to tour Africa as a symbol of peaceful change charged through the new, relatively limber Peace Corps bureaucracy on the weekend of the Birmingham settlement, only to be ambushed two days later by a counterevaluation from Bill Moyers, a deputy to Director Sargent Shriver. "The Peace Corps has won acceptance on its merits and not because it has resorted to political stunts," Moyers wrote confidentially to Shriver. "I even suspect the Africans, at least some of them, will be suspicious, too." Moyers argued that a King trip to Africa represented not only something artificial and dishonest —"political trickery and hypocrisy"—but a breach of faith with the leading Southerners in Congress, who, Moyers said, would be forced by the "political facts of life" to eviscerate the Peace Corps in retaliation. "You have me reeling," replied Shriver, whose travels in Africa convinced him that King was almost universally admired there. Still, he deferred to Moyers on the political costs in Congress, and the plan died in its first week.

President Kennedy himself wobbled above unstable new currents of politics. No sooner did he praise the Birmingham settlement to the world as a *local* initiative than Governor Wallace tried to invoke local segregation laws to nullify it, and local white bombers delivered warning samples of terror. With the historic agreement in danger of being scuttled, President Kennedy met privately in the White House day after day with Army Chief of Staff Earle Wheeler and others, listening to plans to execute troop movements into Alabama for Operation Oak Tree. If he did not use the troops to secure the agreement, President Kennedy told his advisers, defiant segregationists would be emboldened to counterattack behind Wallace, which in turn would spawn more Negro demonstrations and more extraordinary outbursts of sympathy in Northern states. (Two white men chained themselves to the railing of the Ohio legislature, vowing to stay until segregation was abolished.) If he did use the troops, however, Kennedy would let loose the passions of organized force in a charged racial standoff. One likely consequence, he announced gravely to the advisers, was that the leaders of Birmingham "might tear up that paper agreement they made" with the Negro movement. These embattled Southerners, who represented Kennedy's remaining white support in the region, warned that they could not bear to stand with invading Yankee soldiers.

Still another drawback to the use of troops was the prospect of having to do so over and over again in countless segregated jurisdictions, each of which was racially charged, politically tangled, and legally murky in its own distinct mix. Successful or not, integration by bayonet in Alabama would have no legal bearing upon Durham, North Carolina, where a thousand student demonstrators went to jail within a week of the Birmingham settlement. President Kennedy realized that it made no sense to slide toward federally enforced integration agreements without a national standard of law. A bill to outlaw segregation by federal statute promised to resolve a hundred potential Birminghams from El Paso to Baltimore, and the clarity of inescapable tensions drew President Kennedy toward the relief of that single, huge gamble. Yet he hesitated over complications of sovereign appearance. For years, civil rights leaders had been urging just this step. Now that King in particular was buffeted by the unmistakable signs of crossover stardom, and within a week of Birmingham was greeted by motorcades and huge rallies in Cleveland, Los Angeles, and Chicago, hailed before crowds by bellwether politicians such as Chicago mayor Richard Daley, President Kennedy fretted privately that "it will look like he got me to do it." He resolved to cushion the public impact by first receiving delegations of Southern governors and businessmen. "We ought to have him well surrounded," the President told his closest aides in a secretly recorded meeting. "... King is so hot these days that it's like having [Karl] Marx coming to the White House."

Robert Kennedy personally scouted the territory ahead. In contrast to the more detached, cerebral President, he sought to engage primary experience at close quarters, like an explorer. In this crisis, he wanted to gauge the motivations of the Negro demonstrators still popping up in city after city throughout May—what drove them, did they understand politics, how fine was the line between political inspiration and insurrection? When a confidant suggested that the essayist James Baldwin might speak for the seething streets, Robert Kennedy characteristically introduced himself by telephone and on May 24 gathered a chorus of Baldwin's choosing at the Kennedy family apartment in New York. It was a hurried encounter to fit a compressed moment. Harry Belafonte, eyeing guests who ranged from singer Lena Horne to Baldwin's literary agent, wondered why Kennedy did not meet with the civil rights leaders themselves, and could only guess that this was intended to be a freer exchange.

The room grew clammy with tension. Several guests jumped in on the side of racial despair against Kennedy, who answered with barbed questions about where the administration could find levelheaded support for the ordeal of governing. Through groans and clenched teeth, each side wound up laughing at things the other held dear. When a guest suggested that President Kennedy personally escort the next James Meredith into an all-white school, the Attorney General dismissed the idea as ridiculous—ineffective, losing politics, demeaning to the presidency. When Kennedy extolled the labors of FBI agents and Justice Department lawyers such as John Doar, several guests guffawed about them as complicit bystanders.

Kennedy fumed even before a description of the fracas found its way into the *New York Times,* which, by suggesting that the Attorney General had lowered himself to an unseemly shouting match with assorted Negro celebrities, gave a small boost to Baldwin's burgeoning fame at his expense. Kennedy especially resented King's lawyer Clarence Jones for telling him at the end of the meeting, as a soothing gesture, that Jones and King appreciated the administration's private lobbying on behalf of the historic Birmingham settlement. Fatefully, Kennedy marked Jones as a coward for failing to defend him during the heat of the open discussion, and within weeks would order FBI wiretaps on Jones to monitor his work for King. Tumbling between temper and remorse, Kennedy surprised an aide by reflecting that perhaps he would be as bitter as Jones if he had been raised a Negro, then reproached himself as a political albatross to his brother's chances for reelection. Five days after the Baldwin drama, Kennedy hurled his conflicted energies into Vice President Johnson's small corner of the federal bureaucracy—as though some dawdling government committee were concealing an escape route from the pressures of racial politics.

□

ON MAY 29, Johnson convened a public meeting of the President's Committee on Equal Employment Opportunity, of which he served as President Kennedy's designated chairman. He welcomed the members with an acknowledgment that the circumstances were "somewhat unusual" because demonstrations had erupted in "many of our cities" since the last gathering. Just the day before, sit-ins had reached even into Jackson, Mississippi, where white mobs had beaten integrated groups at the Woolworth's lunch counter in full view of news cameras, and there, as elsewhere, observers feared an explosive escalation on both sides. Johnson told his members that he had just come from a meeting with President Kennedy and a number of governors on the urgent need to break down appalling barriers to Negro employment. The governor of New Jersey confessed that builders who agreed to meet integration goals had to import nonunion plasterers from a thousand miles away, because no labor union in New Jersey would admit or train Negro plasterers.

Attorney General Kennedy walked in as Johnson's staff director was reviewing the committee's employment initiatives, including a voluntary corporate program for Negro hiring called Partners for Progress and a hearing process for complaints against government contractors. The President's brother instantly commanded the room, and Kennedy soon interrupted with quiet intensity. "In these companies that you receive complaints about, what is the percentage rate of Negro employment in these companies?" he asked. "Do you have that rate broken down into communities, and also, what their level of jobs are that these people hold?" As the staff director nervously explained the latest report on racial employment by industry and region, Kennedy pressed repeatedly for different breakdowns—by plant, by company, by raw numbers and trends instead of percentages.

Kennedy wanted precision to avoid repeating the calamity just suffered in Birmingham. Pointedly, he said that although the Vice President had "led the fight to insure greater employment for Negroes within government," and had produced national statistics showing "great improvement," the actual, mortifying numbers in Birmingham had proved the leading merchants to be correct that the federal government itself was essentially segregated. Kennedy quoted their words that turned the Justice Department's pressure back on the government itself: " 'Why should we hire Negroes? *You* don't hire Negroes.' " Outside of the post office and the veterans hospital, where menial work was plentiful, Negroes held fewer than twenty of the two thousand federal jobs in Birmingham—less than 1 percent in a city that was 37 percent Negro. The regional disbursing office of the Treasury Department and the Army ordnance plant, among many others, employed no Negroes at any level, and Kennedy conceded that his own Justice Department had done "virtually nothing."

The Attorney General's cross-examination constantly reached beyond fresh statistics that had been compiled by nothing short of wartime bureaucratic mobilization since the crisis earlier in May. "Can I obtain from you immediately the number of employees of United States Steel in Birmingham, and how many Negroes?" he asked. Told yes, Kennedy asked for such data in Gary, Indiana, and from all major employers across the United States. He also asked for a list of all unions and union locals that barred Negroes. The staff director explained that companies were not required to supply information unless they were government contractors, or volunteers in Partners for Progress, and that even then questionnaires must be approved by the Bureau of the Budget, printed by the Government Printing Office, and so on. "How long will that take?" Kennedy asked. "... I ask you, how long will it take?"

By brushing aside answers, speaking in the exaggerated softness of controlled anger, the Attorney General left no doubt that the committee had failed the administration's supreme test of character: the proven ability to act in the world by skillful application of brains and courage, in this case to cut through the morass of segregation. Johnson once tried to deflect part of the blame into the segregated school system by interjecting that of two thousand Birmingham Negroes who had just taken the mandatory civil service examination by emergency roundup, only eighty had passed, and half of these few said they would wait for a federal job outside of Alabama. "It may be, Mr. Attorney General, that deliberate speed is not enough," Johnson said, and suggested that the Justice Department file more school desegregation suits.

For the most part, the Vice President endured the grilling in silence until Kennedy slipped out during one of the statistical elaborations. Then Johnson delivered a sulking monologue on his lack of authority. He read from President Kennedy's order giving him nothing more than the duty to preside over committee meetings—"period and paragraph," he said. "That is the way the Vice President is referred to, not only in the Executive Order but in the Constitution and other things," he added balefully, drawing a laugh. Johnson recited a list of the committee's weaknesses, including the absence of appropriations or permanent staff—everything was borrowed—and the very fact that the Vice President headed the committee. By the time he introduced his guest, Antonio Taylor of New Mexico, to talk about job discrimination against Mexicans and Native Americans in the Southwest, Johnson was openly morose. Part of his motiviation for inviting Taylor, brother of his wife, Lady Bird, was to show a family member how the racial emergency was relieving the enervated despondence of his two years in a powerless office. Instead, Taylor's presence only magnified his humiliation in front of the distinguished public appointees and high representatives of nearly every government agency.

The next morning, May 30, Johnson flew by helicopter to deliver the

Memorial Day address at the Gettysburg battlefield. He berated his staff for setting him up to be lampooned in inevitable comparison with the most famous address in American history—certain to be criticized as a cornpone Southerner if he ducked the subject of racial demonstrations altogether, Johnson complained, or as a clumsy opportunist if he squeezed a racial reference into the patriotic veterans ceremony. After a customary series of conflicting tirades, while emptily demanding that the speech be canceled, Johnson had resolved around his backyard pool to gamble. He would hide from neither race nor Lincoln.

At Gettysburg, Johnson took his leap after only a few paragraphs of traditional Memorial Day oratory. "One hundred years ago, the slave was freed," he said. "One hundred years later, the Negro remains in bondage to the color of his skin. The Negro today asks justice. We do not answer him—we do not answer those who lie beneath this soil—when we reply to the Negro by asking, 'Patience.'" In the next two sentences, Johnson endorsed a theme of Martin Luther King's oratory on the neutrality of time. "It is empty to plead that the solution to the dilemmas of the present rests on the hands of the clock," said Johnson. "The solution is in our hands." Then the Vice President drew a line from Gettysburg to Birmingham, squarely recognizing the crisis thread of American history. "Our nation found its soul in honor on these fields of Gettysburg one hundred years ago," he declared slowly. "We must not lose that soul in dishonor now on the fields of hate."

He continued only another few hundred words. While not as cogent or nearly as poetic as Lincoln, Johnson stuck single-mindedly to his theme that American democracy must rise above the divisions of race to survive. He knew before leaving the platform that his directness had touched a chord in a tough audience—nearly all whites, with the colors of high school bands scattered among martial units ranging from grizzled World War I veterans to the American Legion Drum and Bugle Corps. Johnson's mood swung to euphoria. To the end of his life, his Gettysburg address remained a proud achievement—the speech he would mail as a prized sample of his oratory—but over that Memorial Day weekend, even the editorial praise of newspapers such as the *Washington Post* could not keep him from reverting mysteriously to depression at a rare Saturday work session in the Oval Office.

The subject was civil rights, with Johnson a newcomer. Not once had he been consulted during the James Meredith crisis at Ole Miss the previous fall, even though the administration was desperate for accommodation with Southern politicians Johnson had known for decades, and up through the previous week Johnson had trotted into the large civil rights meetings on short notice, often reading the briefing notes over the shoulder of an aide because no one had bothered to make him a copy. Now, called for the first time into a summit with the Kennedy brothers and two of their closest aides, Ted Sorensen and Burke Marshall, the Vice President wilted. When the President asked what ought to be included in civil rights legislation, Johnson almost sleepily demurred. "I haven't seen it," he said.

"I haven't seen it either," President Kennedy replied. They were exploring what elements, if any, should be included in a desegregation bill —lunch counters, hotels, restaurants, schools, university, private schools. When Johnson did not respond to prodding, Robert Kennedy emphasized that they were dealing with some thirty major demonstrations that week, with no end in sight. "You could make a pretty strong argument that we should end those, and get them off the front page of the paper," he said. "It's bad for the country and bad for the world." With Republicans beginning to introduce their own bills, the Attorney General argued that the administration could not defend having none, but the various agencies of government were at loggerheads over coverage and enforcement, each one trying to deflect responsibility elsewhere. On "something as sensitive" as school integration, President Kennedy himself said it was "better to have the courts making the decisions as much as possible rather than the political branches."

Asked again for an opinion, Johnson replied that he was "not competent to counsel you" on the details. He fell from sheepish whisper to silence, but then started and stopped again like a balky engine until his energies revived on the subject of taking legislation to Congress with suitable resolve. "You've got to recognize first that it's gonna be your people that are gonna be cussing you, the Democrats," he told the President. "Every civil rights bill, nine out of ten people who talk will be Democrats . . . talking about states' rights. And the papers will be reporting on it every day, and the public will be sitting back, kind of sitting on it. And if we do that, then we got to go through with it and *pass* it . . . gotta bear down . . . got to do that, or else yours will be just another gesture."

Johnson fell silent again, allowing speculation that he was wary, resentful, or confused about his sudden rehabilitation among Kennedy's inner council. Overnight, however, he recovered his Gettysburg euphoria for a sustained campaign of private lobbying in the relentless Johnsonian style. What he had been unable to say to the group in the Oval Office, he said to each of them: they were going about civil rights backward. Johnson buttonholed even his personal nemesis, Robert Kennedy, with a capsule of his message, "absolutely poured out his heart" to a Kennedy assistant, and later that same day gained Sorensen's ear. What could not wait, Johnson kept saying, was a defining message from the White House. "We got a little popgun, and I want to pull out the cannon," he said. "The President is the cannon. You let him be on all the TV networks just speaking from his conscience."

Johnson wanted Kennedy to make a Gettysburg speech. He described an imaginary one in San Antonio and another in North Carolina, complete with quotes from Lincoln and a recitation of the Golden Rule. "If he'd make it in Jackson, Mississippi," Johnson told Sorensen, "it would be worth a hell of a lot more than it would in Harlem." He envisioned a patriotic setting with the President in a bank of flags next to an integrated military honor guard. "Then let him reach over and point," Johnson said, working himself up again into rough rehearsal, "and say, 'I have to order these boys into battle, into foxholes carrying that flag. I don't ask them what their name is, whether it's Gomez or Smith, or what color they got, what religion. If I can order them into battle, I've got to make it possible for them to eat and sleep in this country....'"

Johnson said his purpose was to shift the psychology of racial politics. "I know the risks are great and it might cost us the South," he told Sorensen, "but those sorts of states may be lost anyway." As a Southern politician himself, he knew that a national policy of reasoned accommodation could and did encourage resistance. No matter how much private, inward fury the administration poured into administrative changes on behalf of Negroes, a hesitant public attitude signaled to segregationists that the administration feared showdown more than they did. Against segregation, therefore, the normal courtesies of politics could be fatally seductive. Ironically, Johnson argued, the current approach fostered doubts about the administration's commitment among the Southern whites and Negroes alike. "The whites think we're just playing politics to carry New York," he said. "The Negroes feel and they're suspicious that we're just doing what we got to do. Until that's laid to rest, I don't think you're going to have much of a solution."

Even worse, Johnson told Sorensen, the Republicans were "sitting back giggling." While matching or exceeding Kennedy's proposals aimed to please voters in the North, Republicans waited for a "civil war" of demonstrations to erode his Democratic base. "They cut off the South from him and [are going to] blow up the bridge," said Johnson. "That's what they want to do." He argued that Kennedy had "played into the Republicans' hands" by taking an indefinite position between Negroes and the South, and predicted disaster for halfhearted measures. "Every cruel and evil influence in this country, plus all the uninformed, plus all the people that got a wounded air and a persecution complex, are going to be unified against the President. That oughtn't be," he said. Kennedy could "almost make a bigot out of nearly anybody that's against him" by putting the presidency on high moral ground. "If *I* can do it," said Johnson, "... the President can *sure* do it."

Johnson knew politicians were off balance, and that the Kennedy people must find it equally extraordinary to hear him, the oil-state deal-maker added to the ticket expressly to shore up the Democratic white South, urge the White House to take a position to satisfy James Baldwin. ("So the only big problem," Johnson told Sorensen, "is saying to the

Baldwins and to the Kings and to the rest of them, 'We give you a moral commitment. The government is behind you.' ") He asked assurance that he would not read trial stories about how the Vice President was advocating a radical Gettysburg strategy or guaranteeing political success in the South. In return, he promised Robert Kennedy never to mousetrap the administration if the President "put it to them" in Georgia and Mississippi and Texas. "They'll probably boo me off the platform," he told Sorensen, "but I'll be right there with him. I'll be saying it myself if he wants me to."

POLITICAL GROUND shifted under Negro leaders, too. Adam Clayton Powell, chairman of the House Education and Labor Committee, refused White House overtures for help in containing demonstrations because he sensed that the uprising out of Birmingham was too big for normal favors. "I'm not gonna watch the parade pass me by," Powell candidly advised President Kennedy's chief lobbyist, Lawrence O'Brien. "I'm gonna lead it." His humiliation in the Esther James trial a month earlier had emboldened Roy Wilkins to vent criticism in an official NAACP pamphlet entitled ...*Adam...Where Art Thou?: The NAACP and Adam Clayton Powell*, scolding him for playboy whimsy.

Striking back, Powell claimed the wit and audacity to reinvent himself under pressure at the age of fifty-four. On May 17, one week after the settlement in Birmingham, he sketched in his own hand an eighteen-point outline of a new political ideology, scrawling "Re-Cap" at the top of the first page. The first point—"1. So called Negro org. must be *black* led"— sounded a theme of more open racial assertiveness that foreshadowed the black power movement three years later. More immediately, it gave Powell a cudgel of redress against the NAACP. Henceforth, he challenged the NAACP to purge its prominent white board members, belittling Roy Wilkins as the puppet of a white cabal. To answer King and the Southern student movement, Powell criticized the use of children for jail marches: "12. No demonstrators who are not voters (over 21—wearing voting reg. card on lapel when you protest)." More importantly, he pointed out that a law against segregation offered nothing to most American Negroes. ("5. Civil Rights Act Meaningless for ²/₃ outside of the South.")

Another guideline touted his senior leverage: "16. Negroes must follow only those leaders who can sit at the bargaining table and bargain as equals." Still, after Birmingham, Powell was wise enough to realize that he could gain nothing by quibbling with King over credentials. To draw a parade toward himself, he fashioned an insistent new call for racial solidarity: "14. Unashamed preference of black man in politics." Unlike King, who tried to hold nonviolent demonstrators to a strict discipline, and always maintained hope of reconciliation, Powell laid claim to grievances and dignity without reassuring whites or holding Negroes to special standards, just as Powell himself mischievously bent the rules with the most grasping of his House colleagues. After all, American whites had enslaved Africans for centuries—far too long to be excused as an aberrational lapse of character—without much taxing their national self-esteem or their entitlement to full citizenship. With showman's abandon, Powell prescribed for Negroes a similarly forgiving definition of democratic freedom: "17. A new massive involvement with ourselves."

In consciously repackaging himself, Powell aimed toward the black nationalist themes of the Nation of Islam. Powell and Malcolm X began appearing together more frequently, muting their differences to exhort a chorus of racial pride in their respective styles—Powell more saucy and confident, befitting his established fame, Malcolm more biting and original, drawing waves of applause. An edge of competition crept beneath their mutual exchanges of compliments. The notion that a Muslim might unseat the mighty fixture of Abyssinian in Congress was yet too preposterous even for Harlem gossip columns, but Powell's sharp antennae for opposition detected just such a possibility. Malcolm X, who did nurse ambitions in spite of the official Muslim disdain for electoral politics, dared to criticize Powell as a changeling. "It's hard to tell which direction Congressman Powell moves in," he said. "He moves in one direction one minute and another direction another minute." For his part, Powell announced that Malcolm was superfluous to his own leadership in New York. When Elijah Muhammad briefly transferred Malcolm from Harlem to Washington in May, Powell said Malcolm might fill a leadership vacuum among Washington's Negroes whereas Harlem was amply supplied.

Elijah Muhammad himself stirred the Powell-Malcolm rivalry through his control of the Muslim newspaper, *Muhammad Speaks*. Beginning that spring, Muhammad regularly lionized Powell in its pages as the one Negro politician Muslims could trust. Suddenly overlooked were Powell's former deficiencies as a lifelong Christian integrationist and vicemonger who openly flouted Baptist rules of conduct, much less the stricter Muslim regimen. Muhammad put Powell in *Muhammad Speaks* as a black nationalist hero just as he made Malcolm X slowly disappear.

LATE IN APRIL, the *New York Times* declared that the "new assertive mood" of the Black Muslims "lies behind" the prolonged jail campaigns in Greenwood, Mississippi, and Birmingham. This questionable interpretation stretched or even reversed the truth, but the nonviolent uprisings in the South were little more than a news pretext for a groundbreaking exploration into the rumblings of Negro politics in the North. M. S. "Mike" Handler, a senior but low-ranking obituary writer on the city desk, had built a maverick fascination with Malcolm X into a specialty that no other *Times* reporter coveted. Finally, Handler managed to squeeze a profile of black nationalism onto a back page of the *Times*. With gingerly, sober purpose, he introduced the notion that sophisticated Negro thinkers might resent rather than admire whites, and pricked the assumption of superior white values with the anecdote of a well-dressed Negro who thanked a white man for giving him a ride home, saying, " 'It was mighty black of you.' " Handler, like most observers outside the Nation of Islam, responded to Malcolm as a charismatic performer. His article dismissed Elijah Muhammad for lack of interest, accomplishing in print what neither conspiracy nor rumors of death had achieved inside the Nation: "Malcolm X, who is of impressive bearing and is endowed with a shrewd mind, today overshadows Elijah Muhammed [sic]."

Malcolm X called Phoenix to apologize for the *Times* article. He tried to excuse the reference to his overshadowing Elijah Muhammad as the divisive work of white devils, and almost supinely, he vowed to make amends by telling reporters henceforth that he submitted to orders not only from Elijah Muhammad but also from Elijah's family. The sheer cultural weight of the *Times* made its coverage important to Negroes and whites alike, opening up a huge potential audience outside the walls of Muhammad's temples. The media audience was Malcolm's—instant, volatile, and thus utterly different from the small membership that had accepted slow indoctrination into the mystique of Elijah Muhammad.

In May, seeking a quick Muslim reponse to the national trauma from Birmingham, *Life* magazine photographer Gordon Parks attended a karate class inside Malcolm's Temple No. 7 in New York. His most dramatic shot recorded what first appeared to be a blurry canine walking lightly on air around a Fred Astaire–like pirouette, but actually was a formally attired Muslim instructor who "shows how to deal with a live police dog like those used against demonstrating Negroes in Birmingham: grasp its leash, whirl it around in air, and the dog will surely strangle." This image, mixed with homely scenes of Muslim families at prayer, would take most *Life* readers into disorienting new territory, and it was no less a strain for the leadership of the insular racial sect. On May 13, just after King and Shuttlesworth announced the breakthrough settlement, the FBI's Phoenix wiretap picked up Malcolm calling again in panicky apology to say he was doing his best to delay the article until *Life* could include more material on Elijah Muhammad. He promised Elijah to keep knocking down rumors of his retirement, but the Messenger was far from mollified. Word went out of Phoenix that the Nation wanted nothing to do with the *Life* article because it was "being built around Malcolm."

THROUGH *LIFE* and the *Times,* Birmingham helped deliver Malcolm X to greater attention at an awkward moment. He spent May shuttling between New York and the Stokes trial in Los Angeles—one foot sliding toward a future that was dangerous among his own people, the other anchored in the grim realities that had made him a Muslim. On May 20, when President Kennedy was complaining privately in the White House that Martin

Luther King was as "hot" as Karl Marx, Malcolm found himself staring into the drawn revolvers of police officers when he arrived at the Los Angeles temple to address a defense rally for the ongoing Stokes trial. A police spokesman blandly explained the incident the next day as a mix-up growing out of an armed robbery investigation in the temple neighborhood. In fact, the Los Angeles Police Department was locked into a war of nerves. Commanders had instituted a special radio call—"Code 6-M"—to fortify police responses at any scene where Muslims were expected, and intelligence reports painted an alarming picture of Malcolm X as a guerrilla general whose nod at any moment could activate fanatics trained to attack police with their bare hands. Police vigilance followed Malcolm to his usual seat in the courtroom for the opening summation. The tense crowd remained silent until a rhetorical flourish late in the day, when prosecutor Kippen declared, "There is nothing about this case which has, in my opinion at least, racial overtones." Laughter exploded in the courtroom. As Judge Coleman banged his gavel repeatedly for order, the prosecutor said he meant that the case was not racial like "the racial trouble that is going on at this time" elsewhere, meaning the South.

Two days later, senior prosecutor Evan Lewis opened his final argument by telling the jurors they would remember their part in "the Black Muslim Riot Case" if they lived to be a hundred. "And I think you have never heard of such a case as this in your reading of the newspapers in North America since the end of these Indian wars that they have on television all the time. . . . You actually expect to hear it somewhere in a clearing in the jungle in South America." To answer the snickering that had greeted his partner's comment about race, Lewis waded into the subject explicitly for the first time. If any defendants had ever been prosecuted because of race or religion, he said, "they ought to take the American flags out of the courtroom. It just can't be." Any lingering racial trouble was not a matter of hatred or fear but "a matter of communication, actually," and to say otherwise was to malign the city and distort the meaning of the trial. "I don't say that this represents our fine colored community," said Lewis. "And we have a fine one here in Los Angeles." If there were criminals disproportionately among them, "it is not the colored people that live here, that were raised up and grown in Los Angeles. It is probably some people from out of the South, who had had no opportunity, no chance at all. . . ."

By afternoon, prosecutor Lewis addressed a messy flaw in the state's case against its chief target, the local Muslim minister John X Morris. Against the unanimous testimony of both Muslim and police witnesses that Morris remained in or near the Muslim temple on the night of the violence, the indictment charged that Morris not only joined several fights but actually went down the street to shoot Officer Tomlinson. These counts rested on the evidence of William Tribble, the well-meaning motorist who had stopped to fire the first gunshots in a hapless effort to quell the brawl. On the stand, Tribble had misidentified or misdescribed Morris numerous times and otherwise impeached himself as an overly cooperative, confused witness, but prosecutor Lewis rolled out a theory to support what was left of the central charges. "Now, without going into this matter of race at all again," he told the jury, "it is obvious it is easier for a person that is Japanese, for example, to recognize Japanese people, or a Chinaman to recognize Chinese, or a colored person to recognize a colored person. ...I can't tell generally a Chinaman from a Japanese. I can't tell one colored person from another. But if you are used to dealing with colored people, it is different." From there, Lewis made his immediate point that an identification based on common race could make up for glaring deficiencies in evidence. "Mr. Tribble was colored and he said he had seen Mr. Morris before," he declared. "He positively said that Mr. Morris is the man."

Once loosed, racial observations slipped from the prosecutor's tongue with wildly erratic implications. He forthrightly rebutted defense claims that white policemen were routinely abusive to Negroes, for instance, on the ground that such conduct would be too dangerous. "I can't see an officer in that area saying nigger," Lewis told the jury. "He would be beaten up within the first twenty-four hours he was on the job—and I wouldn't blame them—if he called somebody a name like that." As an alternative to this perspective, which brushed close to defense theories of the entire case, Lewis asserted that racial epithets were extinct, anyway. "So many people were so fine in the war, and so many got to know each other, that we just dropped those words," he said. "They were dropped out of the vocabulary." More traditionally, Lewis said that apparent misconduct was extraneous to the case and not racially motivated, coming from "pure meanness" on the part of "one or two officers who were pretty sour." Returning to frontier imagery, he told the jurors that the officers' only alternative that night was to have "thrown their guns down and surrendered and pleaded for mercy."

On May 24, when the Kennedy-Baldwin meeting fell to social disaster in New York and the Stokes case went to the jury, Malcolm X sent a careful letter of concession to Elijah Muhammad in Phoenix, with veiled reminders of his charges. On May 28, Muhammad replied that he had received Malcolm's letter and was pleased that Malcolm had "admitted certain things." He said they should not allow themselves to be divided, and signed off enigmatically by advising Malcolm to "concentrate on the spiritual side." Muhammad's power reversed the burden of Malcom's corruption allegations for an uneasy truce that paralleled the tensions of an astonishingly long Stokes deliberation of nearly three weeks, during which one juror collapsed of a heart attack. The final verdict acquitted three defendants, including Minister John X Morris, which contradicted

Muhammad's doctrine that there could be no justice from "the white man's court." Criminal convictions for the other eleven Muslims mocked his passive response, and the subsequent conduct of jurors was as startling as the defendants' posture of saintly nonviolence during the trial. Nearly half the jury mounted a campaign against their own verdict. Female dissenters —white, mostly suburban—complained to both sets of attorneys that L.A. officials had browbeaten them in the jury room. Six jurors eventually gave Judge Coleman a joint letter of recantation, saying "we do not think justice was done."

The saga of the renegade jurors never caught on as a story in the press or legal issue in the courts of appeal. More than a year after the shootings, the Stokes case remained the leading story in *Muhammad Speaks* and a principal engine of the Nation's financial growth, but Muslims themselves slanted or avoided interpretation. Malcolm X covered his private vexation with blistering rhetoric. "It will take fire to straighten out the white man!" he cried out at a rally protesting the convictions. "Fire from God!" He soon discarded as a lecture prop his giant photograph of the grisly Los Angeles shooting scene, and with few exceptions phased out the Stokes case from his public speeches, as later from his autobiography. The entire episode was at once too vivid and too muddled.

MARTIN LUTHER KING needed no coaching to avoid the subject when he passed through Los Angeles during the last week of the trial. For the most part, he sailed high above the derelict stigma of that courtroom. His national tour earned the movement the astronomical sum of $150,000 in a week—including so much from a single Beverly Hills fund-raiser that a friend said movie stars kept the $45,000 figure out of the newspapers to protect the film industry. Privately, King did welcome what he called "a feeling of nationalism" everywhere, including Los Angeles, where the Stokes case and the amazing church rallies of Malcolm X were too risky to explain across cultural lines. "The Negro element is really aroused," he said.

On May 30, he sent a telegram to the White House requesting a private conference with President Kennedy, underscoring his urgency by listing four available dates the next week. Unlike previous telegrams that had struck a tone of supplicant or petitioner, King pressed himself as a natural claimant for the President's time. His bargaining goal, unstated in the telegram, was remarkably similar to the recommendations being pushed secretly at the time by Vice President Johnson. "We need the President to do crusading work for us," King told his advisers.

To press Kennedy into open alliance, King needed to maintain a balance among a host of movement forces, including hundreds of spontaneous jail marches that were being attributed to his leadership. The demonstrations were nonviolent for the time being, but they activated the natural fears of middle-class Negroes—disorder, indignity, hooliganism— along with competitive worries that King's tactics would eclipse the senior civil rights organizations. National NAACP officers went so far as to order their local leaders to head off "the King forces" across the South. This internecine opposition was neither a secret nor a surprise to King. While pushing for new status with President Kennedy, he knew Roy Wilkins would be pushing in a different direction.

Help came suddenly by way of Jackson, Mississippi. The sit-in of May 28 was tiny—only three students at first, with a handful of supporters later joining—but it cracked the wall of intimidation that had kept the Birmingham aftermath out of Mississippi. The demonstrators clung to the Woolworth's lunch counter, enduring curses, shoves, cigarette burns, showers of sugar and ketchup, a hail of fists, and other churlish, brazen violence that lasted long enough for news stringers to assemble and record the scene for transmission over national wires. By then, distant newspapers were so sensitized to the pattern of chain reaction that the editors of the *Wall Street Journal* took note the very next morning, predicting that "Jackson is in for a siege similar to Birmingham's." Mayor Allen Thompson deputized a thousand special officers. At the Negro mass meetings, only students called for marches. "To our parents we say we wish you'd come along with us," declared a high school junior from the pulpit, "but if you won't, at least don't try to stop us." A few adults joined their runaway demonstrations, including a matronly nurse who jumped into a march line with a huge pocketbook and a look of rapture, shouting, "This is the *biggest* thing I have ever done." On the third day, the students spilled out of their own nonviolent workshops and marched downtown into a phalanx of police. Officers used city garbage trucks to haul away overflow prisoners, and the *New York Times* compressed a day of numbing pathos into a striking page-one headline: "Jackson Police Jail 600 Negro Children."

Medgar Evers groaned under conflicting pressures. He presided over the mass meetings as the accepted leader of the Jackson movement, but he could not join or endorse the jail marches on the direct orders of his NAACP employers in New York. Evers was doubtful of demonstrations, too, but he practically begged Roy Wilkins to reconsider NAACP policy in light of the mass uprising of youth, arguing that he and the NAACP were being left behind while the students transformed all of Negro Mississippi. Secretly—and not for the first time—Evers collaborated by phone with King. He told his New York office that King might come to Jackson if the NAACP avoided command, and the specter of such a coup helped motivate Wilkins to fly to Jackson on the evening of the six hundred arrests. He did not tell his wife, to spare her the worry and himself her objections.

On a few hours' emergency notice, the Justice Department crashed federal observers into Jackson ahead of Wilkins, including John Doar and

Thelton Henderson, the first Negro staff attorney hired by the Civil Rights Division. When Wilkins pulled up the next morning with Medgar Evers, wearing a tan poplin suit, carrying his reading copy of Harper Lee's novel *To Kill a Mockingbird,* tense Jackson police officers arrested Henderson along with his official notepad and most of the other Negroes who crowded anywhere near the picket site outside the downtown Woolworth's. Then they ceremoniously hauled Wilkins off to what he called "the hoosegow," in his first arrest in nearly thirty years. Wilkins bailed out of jail and departed by plane that same evening, leaving behind NAACP lawyers with instructions for a switch from pickets to litigation. He had tried to calm the Jackson movement—the *Times* noted his arrest on a back page— but nothing could diminish the specialized impact on King. From Atlanta, he arranged for a conference call with his New York advisers Clarence Jones and Stanley Levison as Wilkins was flying home. "We've baptized brother Wilkins!" King announced with excitement.

What seized King was the day's precedent for collective strategy: with his body, the national leader of the NAACP had declared that under some circumstances, at least, the NAACP would join in a strategy of nonviolent protest. King worried out loud about the strain of arrest on Wilkins's imperfect health, and discussed the wording of a supporting telegram. When Levison and Jones moved on to normal conference call business, such as the upcoming board meeting, King cut them off. "We are on a breakthrough," he said, "and we need a mass protest." King wanted to think beyond individual movements. "We are ready to go on a national level with our protests," he said. They discussed whether A. Philip Randolph, the venerated founder of the Brotherhood of Sleeping Car Porters union, might enlarge his planned Washington labor rally for jobs into a giant rally for freedom issues. "There is no problem with Phil," said Levison, who volunteered to make inquiries.

King fed off the idea in a rush. If he endorsed a giant rally, Randolph's stature as the unifying senior presence among the quarrelsome civil rights leaders would make it difficult for Wilkins and the NAACP to withhold support, especially now that Wilkins was newly baptized for protest. "Roy will only act under extreme pressure," said King. Now there was an opening to get Wilkins behind a giant national protest that could concentrate, symbolize, and define the spreading energy of local movements before they dissipated or something went wrong. That in turn could push President Kennedy into being a crusader who could move the country and a recalcitrant, fearful Congress. They agreed that it would take a crowd of a hundred thousand to generate enough political force, and that it would take at least until August to mobilize.

By the end of the conference call, King had put such a charge into Levison and Jones that they called each other like teenagers to replay and analyze his words. Jones said it was thrilling to hear King talk that way.

The normally taciturn Levison agreed that "when Martin said what ought to be done and why the possibilities are good, you tingled." In nearly seven years as all-purpose adviser on everything from King's personal taxes to speech themes for his trip to India, Levison normally had pushed King not to underestimate his strength, but now Levison found himself "one step behind" King's appraisal of the historical opening. "He says the hour is now," Jones reminded Levison.

8

Summer Freeze

ON KING'S INSTRUCTION, Jones and Levison made their first contacts about a national march over the Memorial Day weekend, when Vice President Johnson returned from Gettysburg to the turmoil of White House strategy sessions. That Monday, King received a reply to his telegram: the President was too busy to see him. The buffeting of events led President Kennedy to change his terms about a King appointment twice before the end of June.

New outside forces came to bear almost daily. On June 7, the General Board of the National Council of Churches addressed the racial crisis. Nearly all the assembled leaders had attended the conference on religion and had carried out resolutions to form a volunteer Continuing Committee of the Chicago Conference. What was bold and unprecedented in January became shamefully tame in May. The General Assembly of Presbyterians in Des Moines—after narrowly rejecting a subterranean groundswell to invite Martin Luther King from Birmingham to supersede the scheduled speakers—hailed by uproarious acclamation a preacher who challenged the denomination to "put its money where its mouth is" by committing $500,000 to support the civil rights movement. This bugle call from one of its thirty-one constituent bodies prompted the General Board of the National Council, meeting at the historic Riverside Church in New York, to create a professional strike force called the Commission on Religion and Race (CORR). "The world watches to see how we will act," the church leaders declared in a public statement, "whether with courage or with fumbling expediency."

Ironically, CORR's first action was to bypass the leadership of the National Council's own Department of Racial and Cultural Relations, headed by Oscar Lee, who for many years had served as the only Negro on the six-hundred-member professional staff of the National Council.* For all Lee's qualifications, church leaders instinctively sought a white minister to get action. By tradition, race relations was a timid division of the labyrinthine church bureaucracy. A single denomination might take decades to revise its hymnal or redefine a word of its creed, and the National Council was cross-knitted in denominational layers to guard against unintended offense. Church leaders wanted a sharp break from the patterns of Lee's department, which distributed mellifluous brotherhood statements to be read in churches on Race Relations Sunday.

Once Birmingham exposed "the real depth of the evil we face," as one speaker put it to the General Board, epiphanies occurred almost continuously among church people, and the new CORR gathered stories of compressed awakening in "Twenty Days Later," its first, unabashedly transfixed report. "In such a time the Church of Jesus Christ is called upon to put aside every lesser engagement," declared the General Board. On the assumption that racial justice is inherently ecumenical, members voted to pursue an alliance of fellowship with Catholics and Jews. Having picked up already the buzz of preparations for a freedom march, they voted "to assemble in Washington as soon as is strategic." In stark departure from the customary practice, the senior figures of the white Protestant establishment pledged "to *commit* ourselves, as members of the General Board, to engage personally in negotiations, demonstrations, and other direct action in particular situations of racial tension."

Segregationists piled in from the opposite side. On Sunday, June 9, the Citizens Council of Selma, Alabama, posed a question in a large newspaper advertisement: "What Have I Personally Done to *Maintain Segregation?*" The text challenged readers to "probe deeper and decide," and then join the campaign to "prevent sit-ins, mob marches and wholesale Negro voter registration efforts in Selma." That same afternoon, a Trailways bus carried Annell Ponder's group through Alabama on the way home to Greenwood. After a week of advanced teacher classes under Septima Clark at the SCLC citizenship school, the high spirits of the seven Negroes collided with the resentments of Highway Patrolmen and police

---

* Andrew Young became the second Negro staff member in 1957, and worked in the National Council's youth ministry until he went south to direct Martin Luther King's citizenship program in 1961. Oscar Lee, a pioneering Negro graduate of Yale Divinity School (1935), knew nearly all the preachers leading jail marches in the South, and had performed wedding ceremonies for the family of Bob Moses, the student registration leader in Mississippi. Before the Chicago conference in January, it was Lee who had carried on the truncated negotiations with the Negro Baptist leader J. H. Jackson, and who had become so disgusted with Jackson's reactionary views on race that he renounced his Baptist heritage to become a Presbyterian.

at a rest stop in Winona, Mississippi. Everything about Ponder's politely correct leadership training offended the officers—how she led her charges to the white side of the cafe, told the officers it was against the law for them to throw her out, objected to racial epithets, took out a pad to write down their names and tag numbers.

When Ponder did not arrive in Greenwood on the scheduled bus, Hollis Watkins began calling police stations, newspapers, and movement contacts back along the route. This was standard alarm procedure. Evasive answers and other clues converged on Winona, so that a bulletin intruded upon King's six-way midnight conference call about plans for a march on Washington. Andrew Young interjected that he had just received a secondhand report of an arrest in Winona, and that he was trying to get the FBI to investigate. From Greenwood, Lawrence Guyot volunteered to drive over and try to bail them out, but a designated observer soon reported from Winona that Guyot himself had disappeared into the jail. By the next day, a second emergency intruded from far away in Danville, Virginia, where police, instead of ignoring or arresting the daily prayer line outside city hall, attacked with high-powered fire hoses followed by a charge with billy clubs that sent more than forty marchers from the Danville Christian Progressive Association to segregated, substandard Winslow Hospital.

Martin Luther King protested "the beastly conduct of law enforcement officers at Danville" in a telegram to Attorney General Kennedy just as Kennedy, on his own, was pressing the FBI to find out what had happened in Winona. The Attorney General's quick, personal interest in the Winona incident—even before there was solid evidence of foul play—signaled that the government and movement alike were on daily tenterhooks against the live possibility of violence. Kennedy's attention was all the more remarkable because the Winona and Danville reports coincided with an overriding crisis on Tuesday in Alabama, where Deputy Attorney General Nicholas Katzenbach, backed by federal troops, read to the assembled national and international media a proclamation by President Kennedy, and Governor George Wallace, with his own proclamation and an opposing array of state troopers, fulfilled his campaign pledge to stand in the schoolhouse door against the court-ordered admission of the first two Negro students to the University of Alabama. What came off in the end as a carefully staged compromise—with Wallace gaining the spotlight of public resistance in exchange for the registration of the two students quietly off camera—carried the drama of a battlefield showdown because no one could be sure what civilities would survive.

So pervasive was the expectation of official or unofficial attack that peace itself became a focus of news. "There was no violence," the *New York Times* announced of the Katzenbach-Wallace confrontation. In a parallel news departure, the *Times* also placed on its front page ("Dr. King

Denounces President on Rights") an account of an interview in which King called upon President Kennedy to be more visible in leadership and to speak of the morality rather than the politics of race. Perhaps goaded by the subtle change in coverage, President Kennedy decided spontaneously at six o'clock to go on national television that very night at eight with a declaration that he would submit an omnibus bill against segregation. Over the panicky advice of his advisers—who objected that the President had no prepared speech, no time to make preparations in Congress, and above all no reason to magnify his political risks—President Kennedy rushed to unburden himself in the favorable climate of the success in Alabama.

The peaceful Monday did not last long enough. Soon after President Kennedy hurriedly composed a speech in a clatter of aides with swarming television technicians readying his cue—"Come on now, Burke," Kennedy prompted Burke Marshall, "you must have some ideas"—Bernard Lafayette was frightened to observe a white man in a two-toned 1957 Chevrolet parked outside his apartment in Selma. In less than a month since the Boynton memorial mass meeting, Lafayette had been arrested from a moving car and tried, absurdly, for vagrancy, and otherwise targeted in the local newspaper and Klan hate leaflets. So many people had been fired or traumatized after the first meeting that Lafayette only now managed to schedule a second. He was immensely relieved to hear the Chevrolet owner say he only wanted a push for his stalled car. When Lafayette pulled into position and looked down to make sure the two bumpers were not locked or misaligned, a blow to the head knocked him senseless. Bludgeoned twice more, he tried from nonviolent training to make eye contact, and only then realized he was being struck with a gun butt.

Sight of an apartment neighbor rushing to his defense with a shotgun made Lafayette scream, "No, Red, don't shoot!" The white man suddenly fled in the Chevrolet, and Lafayette wound up for the night at Berwell Infirmary being sewed up by Dr. Dinkins, son of Professor Dinkins, the malfeasance expert at Tabernacle Baptist. Treating a battered race victim unnerved the doctor even before Lafayette insisted that he would keep wearing his blood-caked shirt as a badge of commitment to Selma. To change the subject, Dinkins advised Lafayette that he did not consider milk a good source of calcium for healing his injured bones. "Milk is for calves," he said somberly, and offered instead his preferred nostrum of calcium pills made from ground bones. Lafayette tried to make a joke to ease the tension. "If milk is for cows," he replied, "bone pills ought to be for dogs." Dinkins took offense at the levity; Lafayette later took the bone pills faithfully as a goodwill gesture toward one of Selma's leading Negro professionals.

On national television, President Kennedy delivered what the *Times* called "one of the most emotional speeches yet delivered by a President who has often been criticized as too 'cool' and intellectual." Wandering on and off a skeletal text, Kennedy spoke with the fervent directness that Lyndon Johnson had been urging upon him. His words rose from the twin moorings that anchored King's oratory at the junction of religious and democratic sources. "We are confronted primarily with a moral issue," Kennedy told Americans. "It is as old as the Scriptures and is as clear as the American Constitution." For those in the movement, the President's ringing speech was an answered prayer that collided with news from Jackson that a sniper ambushed Medgar Evers that night from a honey-suckle patch, killing him with a rifle shot through the back. Like Kennedy's speech, the murder of Medgar Evers changed the language of race in American mass culture overnight. The killing was called an assassination rather than a lynching, Evers a martyr rather than a random victim—recognized as such with a post-funeral cortege by train to Washington and a family audience of condolence at the White House.

In Birmingham, where he and his colleagues were trying to maintain the May agreement against a persistent backlash, Andrew Young mourned Evers as a conflicted martyr who bled for the NAACP even as he chafed against its patronizing hierarchy, who allowed his love for a cause to sweep him toward death in a battle not of his own choosing. To James Bevel, also in Birmingham, the concurrent hospital reports on his classmate Bernard Lafayette were closer to the throat personally, but he and Young had to push their reeling minds past Selma and Jackson. By Wednesday morning, June 12, a law student newly arrived in Greenwood as a summer volunteer had made it safely in and out of Winona, and her reports supported a string of fearful tips that Annell Ponder's group had been arrested and held incommunicado since Sunday, were beaten savagely while in custody, and that officers had seized Lawrence Guyot for similar treatment when he came to help. The Winona jail seemed to be a flytrap, cordoned off by lynch-fear so thick that Negroes shrank from being seen or asking ques-tions. All measures having failed, including the promised intervention of Attorney General Kennedy, Young and Bevel decided they must drive over to bail out Annell Ponder.

An argument broke out when they tried to borrow Dorothy Cotton's car. She wanted to go, too, saying Annell Ponder was her dear friend and fellow teacher in the citizenship program—Cotton had put her on the bus back to Greenwood. Young vetoed Cotton as nonessential, saying she had no reason to expose herself to this danger, which was not just normal movement danger they preached about in nonviolence classes but some-thing evil that had boiled over all around them—with Medgar, Bernard, Annell, Guyot—random as all their acquaintance and yet near as the next breath. Bevel told Young that guilt was driving Cotton to get beaten up herself. "Andy, we don't need to take this crazy broad," he said. Dangling her keys, Cotton spoke up, "Well, dammit, it's *my* car." She finally jumped in and lurched off down the street, forcing Young and Bevel to trot after her to make a truce. Overwrought, Cotton soon swerved off an Alabama highway to avoid crashing into a large trailer truck, and on the shoulder she collapsed with Young and Bevel into a cleansing hysteria of jokes that even on this forlorn mission, headed into Mississippi instead of away from it, they might die any moment of a fluke that had nothing to do with civil rights.

In Winona, expelled from the city jail to wait outside for the sheriff, Cotton read her copy of Kahlil Gibran's *The Prophet* as nonchalantly as she could, while Bevel and Young tried to maintain their composure. Under pregnant daytime scrutiny, their delicate task was to look purposeful but not impatient, important but not so conspicuous as to incite attack. A stroke of luck arrived with a long-distance call for the sheriff just as they were ushered in. Overhearing the caller's name, Young remarked that he knew this Wiley Branton, head of the Voter Education Project in Atlanta. He spoke to the jailers as though Branton were white—not as his friend whose organization sponsored drives to register Negro voters across the South—and thus insinuated himself as a telephone intermediary in the matter of the troublesome prisoners. Young "talked colored" to Branton, like a flunky eager to do the bidding of an eminent lawyer whose contacts among Southern senators, newsmen, and other notables all wanted to make sure that proper bail procedures were followed, so as not to give ammunition to the liberals. Branton played along through what was destined to become a merry reminiscence after Young obtained the bonded release of all prisoners that afternoon.

Three of them—Guyot, Ponder, and Fannie Lou Hamer—were a mess of untreated injuries such as broken teeth and back bruises crusted over with leather-hard skin, in part from systematic, chorelike pummeling with blackjacks. A fourth, June Johnson, was beaten less severely. She arrived in Greenwood as a ghostly curiosity, but the whole family fell silent under the baleful look of Belle Johnson, who grudgingly had acquiesced in another citizenship trip once the school year ended. The sum total of adult commentary on June Johnson's puffy face and bloody dress came from grandmother Johnson, a migrant farmworker, who pointed an accusing finger at her daughter Belle and shouted, "I hold *you* responsible!" She said June was just a baby. The mother kept everything inside. Never in her life would she ask her daughter what happened inside the Winona jail.

AMONG THE REPORTS that reached King on a speech trip in New York came word of a second telegram from the White House. This time President Kennedy took the initiative to invite King for a visit. King sent an eager acceptance hard upon his letter praising Kennedy's televised speech, but he changed his mind by lunchtime. In the interim, a flurry of adviser calls established that King, instead of joining President Kennedy for a political meeting, was to be one of some three hundred religious leaders herded into the East Room of the White House for a pep talk on racial issues. "Deeply regret that I had overlooked an important longstanding commitment when I accepted...," King wired the President disingenuously. He closed with a pointed reminder of what he sought: "Thank you very kindly, and I hope we will be able to talk privately in the not too distant future."

For President Kennedy, who took for granted the ritual importance of status jockeying among politicians, the lesson here was that a neophyte young Negro was no pushover. King's lifelong experience in the elite Negro Baptist clergy had schooled him in the game. Politics, like preaching funerals, required a certain amount of callousness, and movement politics all the more so because regular travel across racial barriers intensified the personal toll. As King left New York for the Medgar Evers funeral, trustees of Lovett School in Atlanta voted to bar all Negro applicants, which ratified and ostensibly depersonalized an earlier ad hoc decision to reject young Martin III from first grade. A muffled debate was under way in Atlanta about how much the decision did or did not reflect the influence of Episcopal authorities with which Lovett was affiliated by charter. In Jackson, Roy Wilkins bristled with anger that King claimed Medgar Evers as a nonviolent crusader, and speakers sniped at King during the funeral itself as a usurper of the NAACP's rightful glory. Hailed as inspiration, reviled as accomplice, King slipped from the funeral just before John Doar of the Justice Department stepped alone between a breakaway youth demonstration and mass of police, snatching a truce from the brink of violence.

On no other subject did critics on both sides dismiss a President more quickly as tyrant or pygmy, and nowhere else did the high claims of government trip more awkwardly over stubborn, unpolished human nature. In Washington, Senator Richard Russell of Georgia vowed on June 12 to fight any civil rights law as a step toward Communism, and conceded only that the President's message "may intimidate a few weak-kneed people [who] have no business in positions of power." A summit that day at the White House locked in polar standoff, with former President Eisenhower supporting action only in the one area—voting rights—that Kennedy planned to leave out of his proposed legislation. Eisenhower promptly went out to make a rousing partisan speech about the urgency of defeating Kennedy in the next year's election, just as a new report found off-base segregation against Negro soldiers so stubbornly pervasive that Kennedy's own commission publicly endorsed the ultimate sanction of closing military installations. Racial politics threatened the core of Kennedy's Democratic support in Northern cities, where labor unions overwhelmingly excluded Negroes. Between the death and burial of Evers, a large annex to Harlem Hospital ceased in mid-construction over the disputed use of segregated unions under public contract. In Philadelphia, the arrival of the first handful of Negro plumbers at a school construction site under a tentative agreement set off clashes between angry white workers, Negro pickets, and police, leaving thirty-nine people injured.

In St. Augustine, Florida, where local leaders had waited several months without a response to their tape-recorded petition to the city commissioners, NAACP president Fannie Fulwood again lamented the approach of a segregated Quadricentennial, in spite of hopes that had soared during Vice President Johnson's visit, and youth adviser Robert Hayling announced that without some sign of progress he could no longer contain the desire of students to march like the children of Birmingham. This gained a meeting on June 16, after which NAACP leaders complained that the chief of police aggressively pronounced the word "Negro" as *"nigger"* while reading to them—as his preferred alternative to dialogue —from conspiratorial magazine articles on subversive influences behind integration. While fruitless and humiliating to the Negroes, the session itself offended anonymous Klan callers who promised retaliation upon the NAACP, and Hayling erupted two days later under threat of ambush. "I and others have armed and we will shoot first and ask questions later," he told a reporter. "We are not going to die like Medgar Evers."

These two sentences cracked a news barrier of color. Hayling, who had obtained no publicity before and since the Lyndon Johnson visit, became an instant sensation in radio reports that Negroes were arming for racial violence. NAACP officials, who would have bristled against a public statement of *non*violence as a policy capitulation to King, repudiated Hayling's statement of self-defense as a provocation to whites. Contacts in the Florida NAACP told the FBI they were working to muzzle Hayling, and that "racial feelings amongst the Negroes were well under control [with] no Muslim or other violent influence. . . ." Whites already were stirred to militance. An investigator from the Florida governor's office reported that St. Augustine policemen received orders to shoot any Negro protesters who might interfere with traffic. Less officially, hotblooded teenagers buzzed the streets of the Lincolnville neighborhood to exchange taunts with Negro residents; one carload of four fired a shotgun into Hayling's garage, wounding two members of his NAACP Youth Council.

ON TUESDAY, JUNE 18, the day of Hayling's outburst in Florida, a Medgar Evers memorial registration mass meeting swelled to capacity some ninety miles north of Jackson in tiny Itta Bena, which was visible off the highway as a grove of trees and a water tower rising from the vast flatness of Delta plantations near Greenwood. Some 150 Negroes, mostly plantation sharecroppers, were packed into the little brick Hopewell Missionary Baptist Church, singing, when someone ran in with word that there was a bomb under the raised skirts of the church, which sat a few feet off the ground on brick pilings. An intrepid scout soon came back to announce proudly, "Well, that has been taken care of," but with the singing stopped, cars could be heard driving by at high speed, and an acrid gas began to seep upward between cracks in the floorboards.

Some shouted that it was fire, or smoke bombs, or tear gas, and someone said they had heard the local doctor might have some sort of canisters stored in his office. Thuds could be heard as cars zoomed by—mostly whites, came the reports, but some Negroes, too, sharecroppers beholden to their bosses. Stalwart elders gathered at the pulpit—among them two part-time preachers and James Bevel's father—but they deferred to the young project leader, William McGee, a pin boy at the Greenwood bowling lanes until he had discovered a speaking voice in the movement meetings and then grown so swiftly as an apprentice to Sam Block, the senior youth apprentice to Bob Moses in Greenwood, that McGee had been farmed out as an independent movement colonizer in Itta Bena, canvassing its dirt roads, sneaking onto plantations, attracting mostly teenage girls with movement songs and tales of the vote, and through the girls dampening fear in would-be boyfriends. Now, as the ushers supervised a piecemeal evacuation, McGee tried to fortify morale by leading songs until the fumes choked them off and a Reverend Strong grabbed his arm, saying, "You can't stay in here."

Outside, McGee was astonished to find most of the crowd huddled together, dodging cars and projectiles, awaiting his plans. Against his own impulse to run for safety, McGee improvised a processional along the few short blocks to the town hall, several times jumping for cover in a roadside ditch. Ed Weber, the town marshal who doubled as deputy sheriff, showed no interest in a verbal petition for police protection against the vigilantes still hotrodding within earshot, and instead supervised the arrest of all those who stood with McGee. After short-order trials the next morning, fifty-eight veterans of the Hopewell Church meetings went off to the Leflore County prison farm, where the women shelled peas and the men used swingblades to cut roadside grass under guard.

News that weekend stunned both sides of nearby Greenwood, where FBI agents swooped in to arrest a local white man, Byron de la Beckwith. Mainstream white Mississippi first cringed in avoidance. A bizarre local newspaper story, "Californian Is Charged with Murder of Medgar Evers," painted Beckwith as a California drifter even though he had lived in Mississippi since 1925, was related to several of the Delta's pioneer families, and for years had felt at home enough among high-church Episcopalians to circulate letters on "God's laws of segregation" as a kind of lay theologian* for white supremacy. For those defending the respectability of segregation, there was a cold chill to the first revelations—photographs of the scoped deer rifle left in the honeysuckle, traceable to Beckwith by fingerprints and otherwise—but a compartmentalized empathy rallied. Newspapers described Beckwith as "weary." Leading politicians offered to assist his defense, playing to the strong expectation that no jury would convict him on any set of facts.

A sharp foreboding jabbed movement leaders across town: if a local white-collar man could shoot Medgar Evers in Jackson, what might happen to simple country folk in places like Itta Bena, some ten miles "out in the rural," where semifeudal peonage still domesticated Negroes to segregation? Only the courage of such extremely vulnerable people could chasten Greenwood, where the Winona victims had returned not long after Bob Moses was arrested again. Emergency caucuses resolved that if the Greenwood movement was too poor to obtain bail for the Itta Bena prisoners, and too weak to replace them out at Hopewell Baptist, it must honor their purpose. After immense labors of recruitment, some two hundred Negroes presented themselves at the Leflore County courthouse on June 25. With tempers rising in opposition, Greenwood authorities abandoned their truce policy of peacefully rejecting Negro applicants. That same morning, the city council passed an ordinance requiring citizens to vacate courthouse property on request—a measure aimed at Negroes who made great efforts to come to town from outlying farms—and at noon officers arrested the recognizable leaders. In five-minute summary trials, nine of them, including Hollis Watkins and Lawrence Guyot, drew identical sentences of six months and a $500 fine.

They received a mixed reception from the Itta Bena prisoners at the Leflore County prison farm that afternoon. Already there had been grumbling against William McGee over his assurances that the movement vigilantly looked after its own, as in Winona, and that James Forman or Martin Luther King himself would bail them out if necessary. Instead, after a week of silence, their most likely rescuers turned up as fellow prisoners. Fights broke out. Some exclaimed that whites would extend

---

* "I have sworn to practice and maintain segregation in the Episcopal Church in Mississippi, and I am not alone," Beckwith wrote in an open letter published by the *Jackson Daily News* in 1956. His purpose was to arouse Episcopalians against a young priest in Cleveland, Mississippi. "It should be the painful duty of the Right Rev. Bishop Duncan M. Gray to publicly rebuke his son, and all other priests in the Diocese of Mississippi preaching integration," Beckwith declared. Denouncing what he saw as an attempt by false clergy to "maliciously defy the laws of God" and "crucify the white race on the black cross of the NAACP," Beckwith prescribed that "each priest found guilty of advocating integration must be immediately stripped of all robes and vestments...." He committed himself to the dirty work of crusading zeal: "Let's get red-hot on the subject—if the race mixers don't resign and leave, I say, throw them out bodily, if necessary."

their sentences at a whim. Others resented random insults, bad food, or pessimists for loss of faith. The nine Greenwood leaders faced special harassments on the road gang, where motorists recognized them, joined the guards for overlording gossip, followed the prison truck, and went so far as to point guns at them in sporting menace. As soon as they protested with a hunger strike, a truck hauled them away to an unknown fate, leaving the Itta Bena prisoners more lost than ever.

KING RECEIVED his third White House telegram of the month on June 19. Medgar Evers was buried at Arlington Cemetery that morning, and Secretary of State Dean Rusk sent a cable urging every embassy and consular post in the world to defend the United States against the global convulsion of bad publicity about race relations. President Kennedy, as promised, sent Congress his proposed omnibus legislation against segregation, then granted King his long-desired invitation for a parley. Appointments Secretary Kenneth O'Donnell confirmed it by evening telegram that coupled the private appointment to a hastily arranged gathering of prominent supporters such as Walter Reuther, president of the United Auto Workers. "We assume," O'Donnell wired King, "that since you will be meeting that day with the President that you will be in attendance...." King submitted without comment to Kennedy's last protective subtleties—first scheduling him on a slow-news Saturday, then camouflaging the private meeting with a larger one packaged for attention.

For all his tempered realism, King went to the summit unprepared for a serial bushwhacking that left him chuckling in disbelief. First Burke Marshall, then Robert Kennedy, and finally President Kennedy himself gravely insisted that King must tend to advisers tainted by Communism; specifically, he must agree to banish Stanley Levison from all contact with the movement. Tenaciously, they turned each of King's objections on its head. His personal devotion to Levison only showed Levison to be more dangerously skilled as a deceiver, and the evidence of subversion was withheld only because it was too important for ordinary eyes. The more sinister the picture of Levison—President Kennedy called him a top Kremlin agent—the more far-fetched and warped became the entire conversation for King. When he could not bring himself to jettison his friend outright, and Kennedy would discuss no other subject until he did, the meeting drifted to stalemate.

Like King, President Kennedy was cutting loose from historical norms. To touch the splendor of his standing among nations, he could step from the King meeting into a helicopter on his way to speak for the entire Free World from Germany *("Ich bin ein Berliner"),* but he gained no respite at home. To suit elements in Congress, he weakened or reversed executive actions against segregation—canceling, for instance, a long-awaited order banning white-only work crews in federally assisted road projects.* Robert Kennedy offered publicly to soften the bill's integration requirements—suggesting that hotels and restaurants beneath a certain size might be exempted—only to be denounced by a chorus of integration supporters. Whereas nobody in Congress had been interested in civil rights before Birmingham, the Attorney General privately complained, now suddenly they swamped the administration with destructively intense passion—both from the impractical liberals, as he saw them, with their "sort of death wish, really wanting to go down in flames," and from the cunning, flint-hearted obstructionists. House Majority Leader Carl Albert told President Kennedy in June that civil rights was "overwhelming the whole program." Congress floundered without predictable votes or political discipline, he said, and the President ruefully agreed. "Civil rights did it...," Kennedy lamented. "I mean, it's just in everything. I mean, this has become everything."

King himself escaped the glamorous pinch at the White House to soar briefly again in Detroit, where some 125,000 people pushed downtown along Woodward Avenue with such enthusiastic force that King and the mayor could only lock arms at the front of the surging mass, their feet lifted off the ground. Motown Records, then a fledgling company aimed at crossover rock and roll, issued a record of the rally entitled *The Great March to Freedom,* featuring King's address on race and the American Dream. At his next stop, however, a jeering crowd of Negroes pelted King with eggs outside a church in Harlem. Neither the glory of the march nor the humiliation of the egg attack made much news, coming outside the established drama of his confrontations in the South. "The incident was attributed to the Black Muslims," noted the *Chicago Defender* in a blurb. King skirmished briefly with Malcolm X over the meaning of the egg attack, and kept to himself a telegram in which a Harlem minister confessed that his Baptist church members—not the Muslims—"did this unbecomming [sic] thing to you."†

---

* The reprieve for segregated road construction was a concession to private lobbying by politicians, principally from Louisiana. The President's briefing papers stressed the need for secrecy: "Of course, the less that is said about this in the newspapers, the better off everyone will be."

† "They said their [sic] was innocent human beings being bit by dogs[,] slapped by men[,] knocked down with water hose[s,] and raped in the jail[,] and you was against them fighting back and protecting those innocent people," wrote Rev. James Early, Sr. Malcolm X announced in Harlem that Muslims had not attacked King or anyone else, being trained strictly for self-defense, but he warmly endorsed the scorn of the egg throwers. "I think any effort by anyone to tell the people of Harlem to love their enemy or turn the other cheek will produce violence," he said. "They think it comes from the lips of a traitor.... If white men have the right to defend themselves against attack, the black people have that right also." In reply to Malcolm, King stated loftily that the "growing bitterness" fomented by a Muslim minority "gives me greater responsibility to help get rid of conditions that created such misguided and bitter individuals."

Away from the cheers of Detroit and the boos of Harlem, King debated with some of his advisers the Kennedy administration's demand that he purge others. Could Kennedy really believe they were Kremlin agents, or was the President forced to play along with Hoover? Was this dispute really about the puny remnant of American Communism, or was Kennedy putting King through a painful test of submission, like Abraham's near sacrifice of Isaac? Harry Belafonte and Clarence Jones warned that to accept the government's monstrous definition of Stanley Levison would not remove the taint of subversion but spread it instead on the evidence of King's own tacit confession, and it was naive to think otherwise.

Pragmatists around King replied that the Kennedys were trying to balance a government among power politicians, not moral theorists, and that Levison's head was a small price to pay for ending segregation. No one on either side volunteered to tell Levison, who was handling King's book project on Birmingham among a dozen assignments, selflessly efficient as always, briefly unaware that his colleagues had withdrawn to squirm about his fate.

ELEMENTS WERE ALIGNED from the White House down to the lowliest movement enclave—each one teetering, overheated, and stalled in a kind of vapor lock. In Mississippi, the prisoners from Leflore County endured the crudest, most literal confinement. Along with eight others snatched away from the county prison, including four women, all nine of the Greenwood leaders wound up in notorious Parchman Penitentiary, a timeless fusion of prison and antebellum plantation with cell blocks and guard towers dotting forty-seven square miles of rich Delta cropland.* Normally sullen guards greeted them expressly as recalcitrants to be broken, saying, "You're going to pay me." Shorn of hair from head to foot, every patch of stubble slathered with a bluish delousing grease, they were marked apart from other inmates—the thirteen males crammed into cell number seven of the death house built around Mississippi's gas chamber, with seven sleeping on the floor and one on the toilet. From there, guards shuffled them in more or less random punishment between isolation cells and the sweatbox, six feet square without lights or windows, vented only by a crack under the door.

As the weeks of July dragged by, the prisoners fell into illness and disorientation, so that they half believed the guards who said they were taking Lawrence Guyot and Hollis Watkins away to kill them. In a blink, Guyot and Watkins found themselves alive in a courthouse telling what

---

* Parchman was built during the governorship of Greenwood's James K. Vardaman, who won office in 1903 on the slogan "A Vote for Vardaman Is a Vote for White Supremacy." Famously vulgar, Vardaman composed verse the previous year to lampoon President Theodore Roosevelt for receiving Negro guests: "The coons smelt as loud as a musk rat's nest/ And Teddy licked his chops/And said it smelt the best."

they remembered of the Winona incident to friendly Justice Department lawyers who had filed three novel actions to restrain the Mississippi officers after the stationhouse beatings, but who only nodded to hysterical accounts from the prison-borrowed witnesses of horrible outrages since then. The lawyers, already bleary under voting and school cases, had been battered also by the escalating protest and reprisal since May—John Doar's infant son went nameless for six weeks while Doar tended emergencies across the South—so that in another blink Watkins and Guyot were back in the Parchman death house, as though nothing had happened.

What gnawed at them most was a cold suspicion that the movement itself did not care enough to contact or rescue them, and was letting them slide to oblivion because they were ordinary Mississippi Negroes who lacked the middle-class connections of Annell Ponder in Winona. The thought punctured memories of jail triumph and transforming brotherhood since Bob Moses had drawn them into the registration movement. For Hollis Watkins, somehow it was the heroic memory of catching the runaway yearling at the Dahmer farm that turned to dust; he beat back the thought by singing movement songs even when the punishment came to be hanging in handcuffs* from a horizontal bar of his cell door. A guard informally sentenced Douglas MacArthur Cotton to stretch beneath the handcuffs for forty-eight hours but took pity on him after three. Willie Carnell hung sleepless for a full thirty hours. Watkins and others lost track of how long they hung, but all of them, still singing or not, eventually gave way to helplessness and let their wastes fall down their prison-issue trouser legs.

---

*Evidence of widespread handcuff-hanging and similar abuse at Parchman would be central to *Gates v. Collier,* a landmark prison reform case of 1972.

9

Cavalry:
Lowenstein and the Church

O F MANY NEWCOMERS swept into the maelstrom of Birmingham spring, one democratic adventurer brought pertinent experience in facing such helplessness. In 1959, after a stint as a young foreign policy aide to Senator Hubert Humphrey, Allard Lowenstein had trekked across the Kalahari Desert into South-West Africa [now Namibia] on a private mission that blended comic spy bungling with tear-choking epiphany. Escaping just ahead of the South African secret police, Lowenstein broke a ten-year global news blackout. "We will not soon forget the stories of arbitrary arrest and police brutality which are the daily bread of the African people," he testified at a special hearing of the United Nations, "nor the prisoners in their red-striped clothes working in a private home in Keetmanshoop...." He said all the member nations bore a heavy responsibility for assigning the U.N. trusteeship to neighboring South Africa, which had sealed off the South-West under a colonial regimen more degrading even than its own notorious apartheid. No African had finished high school —more starved than reached fifth grade—and yet Lowenstein met noble chiefs and Christian pacifists among the sufferers. Because the South Africans ruthlessly blocked contact with the outside world, he had pledged "to take the story and the message of the non-European peoples of South-West Africa to this forum, and to the people of the world beyond the deserts and the seas."

Lowenstein scarcely had delivered his testimony when the domestic sit-in movement made a startling political force of his chosen constituency —students—in North Carolina, where he had finished college in 1949.

Within a month of the first sit-in, he undertook a fact-finding tour of Southern campuses and then another tour to spread the word at Northern schools, including Yale, where he had completed law school in 1954. On the road, Lowenstein was formally introduced as a founder and third president (1950–51) of the National Student Association, popularly known to admirers and detractors alike as the "world's oldest student activist." By 1960, several North Carolina citizens had complained to the FBI about Lowenstein's agitation against segregation, alleging that he was a Communist or at least an agnostic whose "teachings and philosophies followed the communist line."

No sooner did FBI officials file away these vague charges than the State Department mandated a more thorough investigation of Lowenstein's machinations overseas. Since boyhood in the 1930s, when he had plotted the heartache of Spanish Republican defeats on maps in his New York bedroom, Lowenstein had held dear among his far-flung passions the goal of a democratic Spain. After President Kennedy's U.N. ambassador Adlai Stevenson twice visited the dictator Francisco Franco, both times snubbing leaders of the democratic opposition, "an energetic young American writer and teacher... called at the Embassy... to register his personal dissatisfaction," as a State Department report archly put it. Lowenstein introduced himself with a copy of the new book he had written about his mission to South-West Africa, *Brutal Mandate,* boasting of its foreword by Eleanor Roosevelt. His rumpled appearance and blunt, evangelical eloquence scandalized diplomats who listened for two days as Lowenstein "made it clear from the outset that he... found it difficult to even talk with Embassy personnel as he was so deeply engaged in activities directly contrary to US policies, namely, in personally trying to overthrow the Franco regime as soon as possible."

Investigating FBI agents mostly chased the zigzag trail of a dervish. By the time they traced him to a job near San Francisco in the spring of 1962, perturbed administrators of Stanford University advised that they were taking steps already to dismiss Lowenstein for "stirring up" the students on countless issues other than the Spanish dictatorship. A privileged tradition of high-WASP insulation had prevailed at Stanford, where President J. Wallace Sterling discouraged political speakers as troublesome, and Professor James T. Watkins IV modeled the study of government on Stanford's dominant Greek fraternity system. According to biographer William Chafe, Lowenstein single-handedly bowled over campus culture in less than a full academic year as assistant dean. He moved into Stern Hall, a dormitory scorned as the "turkey house," and so electrified students with his public forums on world citizenship that Stern Hall became the hub of Stanford life, its misfits suddenly attractive, even socially compelling, to the point that an eccentric Jewish graduate student miraculously defeated fraternity candidates in the next campus election for student president—"We can't fight [injustice] with a drink in one hand and a deck of cards in the other"—becoming the first of five successive Lowenstein protégés elected long after Lowenstein himself left Stanford to pollinate elsewhere.

"Last week was perhaps the single most exciting week at Stanford," the student president wrote Lowenstein, describing three complementary events of May 1963: Rabbi Abraham Heschel's lectures on humanity's search for meaning,* James Baldwin's address on race, and a giant Stanford rally in support of the Negro children attacked on the streets of Birmingham. "The whole campus seemed to come alive all at once," the student president observed. By then, Lowenstein was across the country in Raleigh, North Carolina, clinging to another teaching job as a base for his excursions. With an acquaintance from Africa, he was refused restaurant service at the most prestigious hotel in North Carolina, the Sir Walter, creating a small racial incident that drew a puff of criticism from the State Department, which charged that the demonstration had been "staged" by Lowenstein inasmuch as he failed to identify his companion, the Liberian ambassador to the United Nations, as a diplomat immune from the segregation laws, thus embarrassing the hotel.

Lowenstein characteristically disappeared in the midst of the campaign. One of his many protégés sent a running press summary on the Raleigh crisis to New York and "this extra one to Cal. in case you're still in the West." A delegated strategist, guessing that Lowenstein was at Yale, complained that he had decamped just before "the hostile peak." While conceding his point that the Raleigh movement was at its usual "bickering, falling apart stage," she insisted that the students had overcome numbing pressure and fear through a long vigil at the hotel when "they got themselves thrown out on their heads with their hands still clasped around their knees, and Gloria got slapped around inside. Now I don't know what you want from these kids, Al.... In the past they've looked to you, and they've taken your advice and they were willing to follow you to Sir Walter or the middle of the street or wherever you said go, but now you've left them, and it's not fair for you to say they don't have the guts to continue what you started." Hers was a common reaction to Lowenstein: enthralled, dependent, activated, resentful. To FBI officials still on the Spain investigation, Lowenstein had all the earmarks of a bizarre subversive, but more than a few battered activists suspected he was some sort of covert government agent.

---

* "Awe is more than an emotion," Heschel told the Stanford students. "It is a way of understanding, insight into a meaning greater than ourselves. The beginning of awe is wonder, and the beginning of wisdom is awe.... Man may forfeit his sense of the ineffable. To be alive is a commonplace; the sense of radical amazement is gone.... Deprived of the ability to praise, modern man is forced to look for entertainment; entertainment is becoming compulsory."

□

LOWENSTEIN VANISHED southward with the multilayered preoccupations of his correspondence: with Albert Luthuli of South Africa, whose receipt of the 1960 Nobel Peace Prize Lowenstein had attended as an aide ("Dear Chief: It is always hard to write you a letter because one has the feeling that it will be seen by many eyes..."), with an airline that maintained a ticket office in a segregated hotel space ("Dear Sir: I thought you would want to know that the Sir Walter Hotel in Raleigh has refused to remove its color bar..."), and with the idol of his daydreams, actress Katharine Hepburn ("Dear Miss Hepburn, I hope you'll not think me too presumptuous to leave a copy of this book here for you. Mrs. Roosevelt mentioned once..."). Pulled by the chilling mystique of the Medgar Evers assassination, Lowenstein drove alone to Mississippi to make personal acquaintance with the movement figures in the news. He managed to eat three meals with James Meredith, and on July 4 introduced himself to a suggested contact at Tougaloo College outside Jackson.

Lowenstein's picture of Mississippi began to dissolve with first sight of the young white minister's face, which was caved in on the left side, covered with fresh bandages and an eye patch. Over the past six weeks, Rev. Edwin King had hurtled literally and figuratively into collision with Mississippi. From a ministers' vigil protesting the violent repression of the May 28 sit-ins, he had been hauled away from the Jackson courthouse to jail, still praying. Bailed out by Medgar Evers, he stood trial on May 31 at the annual meeting of his Mississippi Methodist Conference, which voted to bar him from all church posts in the state. Since then he had been stalked after attempts to integrate white worship services with Medgar Evers, in Evers's last demonstrations*—marked so publicly as a traitor that police officers barreled into a private home to seize him in dragnet arrests following the Evers funeral. Someone loosened the lug nuts on his tires, and when a marauding car sideswiped him and a companion into a head-on collision June 18, few in the Mississippi movement believed the wreck was an accident.

For all this—left weak, sickened with fear, facing reconstructive surgery—King insisted to Lowenstein that he felt relatively fortunate. The vote against him in the Methodist Conference had been close, 89–85, and even the segregationist local newspaper acknowledged some weeping confessions among the Methodist clergy during the debate. A number of the delegates seemed to believe that Edwin King had been lured astray temporarily by his Northern religious training at Boston University, where

---

* Two days before he was shot, Medgar Evers and a small group of worshippers were turned away from Galloway Church in Jackson. To protest segregation within his own church, Dr. W. B. Selah resigned his pulpit of eighteen years, making public an internal conflict that consumed Mississippi's largest Methodist congregation.

he had been captivated by the Negro pacifist James Lawson, mentor of the Nashville student movement. On summer break in 1961, King had visited Lawson and other Freedom Riders imprisoned at Parchman Penitentiary, smuggling to them gift books by Gandhi concealed within Billy Graham jacket covers. That mission of mercy had faded already into a comparatively innocent memory, as movement people no longer dared visit Parchman.

Lowenstein seemed to know everybody and to soak up the personal details of the movement leadership struggles as though he had heard them before. On guidance from Edwin King, he followed the trail of leadership northward into the Delta, visiting NAACP state president Aaron Henry in Clarksdale just after the stealthy departure of Martin Luther King himself. White authorities had Clarksdale under such tight clamp that the hunted minister withdrew behind a safety telegram ("...I am at present in the heart of the Mississippi Delta under injunction..."), and Lowenstein followed him into an atmosphere that might have been Keetmanshoop or Sharpeville, where all eyes followed any strange car or person, police camped outside Aaron Henry's pharmacy, and the local court order forbade even private meetings on the topic of integration. Then he walked into a Greenwood SNCC meeting as a startling white face—"I'm Al Lowenstein," he said. "Go ahead with what you were saying"—and saw for himself the transformed activists who had made national news the previous spring. Food shipments still trickled into Greenwood along with a few celebrities—folk singers Bob Dylan and Josh White had performed privately a few days earlier. The Greenwood movement was gamely "holding out," in Lowenstein's judgment, but all the passion and outside support were bottled up tightly in the Negro part of town.

Lowenstein extended his journey until finally he located Bob Moses in Jackson. Moses remembered him from a lecture on Africa at Lowenstein's high school alma mater, New York's Horace Mann, where Moses taught math in 1959. Mississippi flooded them again with images of South Africa, and Moses confessed the paralysis of the movement candidly, in part because Lowenstein so readily grasped the situation by analogy. On voting, Moses said, SNCC researchers may have found one small glint of promise in an obscure law that allowed unregistered voters to cast provisional ballots on claim of being unlawfully disfranchised. (Ironically, the provision had been designed to recover the voting rights of white ex-Confederates.) Still, such a tactic required Negroes to face white authorities at the ballot box, and under the current crackdown this meant enduring terror or jail without positive result. Lowenstein recalled that many Africans withdrew into formal mourning on election days in South Africa. Of course, he went on, mourning was appropriate there because voting by Africans was explicitly prohibited by law. In Mississippi, where Negro voting was permitted in theory, he figured that the equivalent gesture would be the massive display by Negroes of homemade, meaning-less ballots.

From this seed grew the Freedom Vote of 1963—a mock election parallel to the official Mississippi governor's race. There would be no small resistance to the indignity of a "pretend" vote for Negroes, but Moses and Lowenstein saw the advantage of theater where reality was closed off from hope. By withdrawing into make-believe, they could reduce the threat from whites and thereby regain breathing space to organize shadow voters for a first taste of citizenship—choosing candidates, hearing speeches, marking and counting ballots—and from the hunger of that exercise they could fashion a new appeal for help "beyond the deserts and the seas," as Lowenstein had said of South-West Africa, meaning in this case outside Mississippi. The two New York intellectuals, a quiet Negro philosopher from Harvard and a bombastic Jewish globetrotter from Yale, approached Mississippi by analogy with underground agitation in surreal South Africa, coming together much as Lowenstein had described in his book: "Across the chasm between white and nonwhite politics leap or limp or sneak a handful of hardy idealists and intriguers, themselves split half a dozen ways and doubtless bearing in their midst the usual contingent of govern-ment agents."

Lowenstein popped up from Mississippi with a breathless report to a national student congress while fielding skirmish bulletins from the Ra-leigh movement ("Dear Al, Bad news! The Western Lanes Bowling Alley went and resegregated on us again."). Within a few weeks, he passed through the Stanford campus with a stemwinding speech called "Missis-sippi: A Foreign Country in Our Midst?," describing an alien culture in which "you can't picket, you can't vote, you can't boycott effectively, can't mount mass protest of any kind, and can't reach the mass media." To escape this dead end, he told the assembled students, "we've come up with two ideas": the mock election and another plan "still being toyed with" for a "massive assistance campaign from outside Mississippi next summer." The second notion developed into the Freedom Summer project of 1964, which brought among other fateful results the first sizable integration experience among movement activists themselves.

THESE BLUEPRINTS offered no immediate benefit to the Greenwood and Itta Bena prisoners languishing through a second month of isolation in Mississippi prisons. Their rescue fell indirectly to an unlikely explorer trailing just behind Lowenstein. In Robert Spike, the new head of its Commission on Religion and Race, the National Council of Churches deliberately selected a novice. Trained in social justice theology at Union Theological Seminary and elsewhere, Spike had distinguished himself as pastor of a new "outreach" church in Greenwich Village, but his published work revealed practically no interest in racial questions until May of 1963, when he reviewed James Baldwin's *The Fire Next Time* in a church journal. Behind his fastidious exterior of tie clasps and three-piece suits, Spike gained a reputation as a subtle manipulator of church bureaucracy, and national leaders of the white Protestant clergy promptly showed how much they valued maverick qualities. On July 4, only six days after naming Spike as the founding executive of the CORR, Rev. Eugene Carson Blake led a dozen clergy and some 270 laypersons to jail protesting segregation at the Gwynn Oak Amusement Park outside Baltimore.* The *New York Times* placed a large photograph of Blake's arrest on its front page, and Spike lost no time plunging after his eminent boss. Even before assuming his CORR duties on July 15, he tracked down Andrew Young in Savannah about the time Lowenstein reached Clarksdale.

Martin Luther King had sent Young into Savannah after the arrest of local leader Hosea Williams. Within a year, King would bring Williams close on his staff at SCLC, calling him affectionately "my wild man, my Castro," but in 1963 Williams was still a full-time chemist for the Agriculture Department, testing pyrethrum and other pesticides as a pioneer Negro scientist in federal service. As the local youth council adviser, and regional supervisor for voter registration, Williams had used his super-abundant energy to build his candidacy for a Georgia seat on the NAACP national board, until Roy Wilkins sought him out before the 1962 convention and told him with characteristic directness that Williams simply was not board material. Family background was a mark against him. His mother had died in childbirth after running away from a school for the blind, having concealed her pregnancy by another blind student, and Hosea Williams had lived twenty-eight years as an orphan before stumbling upon his birth father, "Blind Willie" Wiggins, quite by accident in Florida. Waifish country flaws poked through his deportment. He refused then and later to drink coffee, having been raised to believe it would turn his skin darker, and he broke into uncontrollable tears when called unsuitable for the board. "I am very emotional," he told Wilkins.

Hosea Williams had always been volatile—some said it stemmed from head wounds received in Germany with an all-Negro unit of the 41st Infantry—but he was also irrepressible, and he refused to rest until he could complain of his NAACP treatment to Martin Luther King, who laughed, telling Williams not to worry too much because the national Baptists had expelled King himself as unfit. This celebrity confession endeared King to Williams, who vowed to redouble his efforts as the most prolific recruiter of students for King's new citizenship schools near Savannah. He became like a son to the venerable teacher Septima Clark, whose practice of asking her most stammering adult pupils to speak out loud of

---

* Twenty-five years later, film director John Waters adapted the Gwynn Oak controversy into a whimsical romance called *Hairspray*.

what was inside them led Williams to develop his tongue for nonviolence. King saw evidence of his powers on his occasional visits to Savannah's historic Negro pulpits such as First African Baptist, founded by the legendary slave preacher Andrew Bryan in 1788. No one soon forgot the gasp of astonishment when the local seaport gangster "Big Lester" Hankerson accepted nonviolence by marching down the aisle of First African to surrender both of his trademark .38-caliber pistols to a collection table in front of Martin Luther King. This was in response to preaching by Williams, just after the Birmingham breakthrough in May.

Sometimes wearing his chemist's lab coat, Williams went downtown near the docks to Wright Square and climbed upon Tomochichi's Rock, a monument marked in honor of the Yamacraw chief who surrendered Indian land to the original English settlers. At first, his sermons drew crowds of curious whites and the passing notice of Willie Bolden, a uniformed bellhop at the Manger Hotel. When the managers locked the doors against the well-drilled Negro teenagers who sought restaurant service, Bolden listened more intently from his post on the hotel porch, but he stayed aloof until sometime after Williams brought Martin Luther King to speak at his pool hall, with King in his conspicuous silk necktie gamely playing billiards against some of the beer-swilling longshoremen. Bolden eventually sought out Williams to volunteer for a surreptitious scheme: he unlocked the hotel doors from the inside just before hordes of young demonstrators arrived to fan out through the lobby for a sit-in that landed dozens of them in jail. Hotel managers fired Bolden for the betrayal. Williams asked him to explain at a mass meeting why he had cut loose from his established life, and Bolden himself became a stand-in leader after police arrested Williams on July 8.

By then, more than five hundred Savannah Negroes had gone to jail, and the port city bounced through the news alongside Birmingham and Danville. Since Williams himself had not demonstrated, nor even publicly advocated disobedience of the segregation laws, authorities resorted to an obscure Civil War ordinance that allowed white citizens, by sworn affidavit, to command the indefinite imprisonment of any suspicious character who threatened the peace. The twentieth century's first application of this emergency law—designed to stop the hemorrhage of runaway slaves by locking away possible facilitators—provoked a protest march that led to another hundred arrests. When the Savannah movement raised the money to free Williams under the required "good behavior" bond, eleven white citizens stepped forward to swear out additional warrants against him, and the blind local judge, Victor Mulling, ruled that Williams must remain in jail until each bond was guaranteed by a separate piece of property, to be held at risk as long as twenty years.

From a church convention in Denver, incoming CORR director Spike landed in Savannah just as two thousand Negroes marched to free Hosea

Williams from open-ended incarceration. There were street clashes, rock battles, gunshots, Klan attacks, and seventy more Negroes arrested—"Two Negroes Shot in Savannah Riot," announced the *New York Times*—and local white church leaders were grateful to Spike for introducing them to Andrew Young as a Negro with whom they could discuss matters rationally. Menaced by potential violence from every quarter, the pastors made contacts for Young with equally worried local officials, but no whites felt comfortable at large meetings across the color line.

Spike went alone with Andrew Young, who explained undercurrents within Negro Savannah. The local NAACP had denounced the Hosea Williams demonstrations as lawless incitements to strife, and the last four churches had closed their doors to movement meetings, in spite of an organized campaign by church women to withhold tithes and offerings until they opened. Frozen out, the movement was holding mass meetings at the Flamingo Club, a nightspot favored by "Sloppy," the local numbers game operator. Spike followed Young into the underworld with trepidation, only to be assaulted by the thunderous rhythms of a mass meeting. Song leader Carolyn Barker—a Septima Clark trainee who was teaching her own father in a citizenship literacy class—presided in solos over a foot-stomping, hand-clapping, call-and-response chorus that spilled from one spiritual to another, most memorably for Spike, "Oh, Freedom." When music spent the crowd, Spike was further surprised to hear Andrew Young introduce an unfamiliar preacher in overalls and a yarmulke. "It was largely the work that James Bevel did with the students of Birmingham," Young announced, "that turned this whole nation out!" Not only did the articulate, credentialed Young defer to the country youth, Spike observed, he presented Bevel to the Flamingo audience as the one "who has given his life to freeing you people and my people and me, 'cause I'm not free."

Bevel scolded the crowd for exaggerating their afflictions. "You think these white folks over here know how to beat up Negroes?" he asked mischievously, beginning a litany on truly "mean" atrocities in Alabama and Mississippi. "When I hear of white people shooting up Negroes," he cried, "well, I know that's part of their tradition. They have always shot up people, and in fact most of their heroes are somebody who have killed up a lot of people." What disturbed Bevel was "only what Negroes do." They could see from the newspapers that a few Negro rock throwers turned a nonviolent march into a "riot," he said, which meant that both whites *and* Negroes wanted an "excuse" to turn away from the movement. "More Negroes get killed fighting on Saturday night than in the nonviolent movement," said Bevel. "... We didn't come here to hurt the mayor or the city. We didn't come here to destroy anybody's business. We came here to teach men how to live and love black folks. I'm proud to be a black man. ... So I don't want you to be beating up white folks and throwing at them —and you become worse than they are."

As Bevel preached the crowd into a singing frenzy, assistants circulated with buckets to collect anything that could be a weapon, even nail files and scissors. Streetwise leaders such as Willie Bolden called to the seaport's tougher elements by name, coaxing them to check in the bucket their heavy items such as knives and brass knuckles. By then, the white visitor Spike realized that they were gearing up for precisely what the leaders across town had been saying all day was impossibly dangerous, a street march at night. Savannah's atmosphere had been tense enough in the abstract, but Spike found himself enveloped in a fear that he could taste and touch. "This is the first time in my life," he recalled, "that I experienced this to be a physical fact and not just a figure of speech." The crowd filed from the Flamingo Club into the darkness for another march marred by sporadic attack and eventually mass arrest that included Andrew Young's first trip to jail, marking another step in his transition from church executive to movement leader. Spike, struggling two weeks later to convey the impact of the mass meeting to his colleagues back in New York, reached for the starriest images in history. "I had the strongest feeling that I was in Egypt on the night of the Passover," he reported. "... Or it could have been in the catacombs of Rome in the first century, or in the Warsaw ghetto twenty-five years ago, or in Sharpsville [sic], South Africa, not so very long ago."

SPIKE EXTENDED his scouting trip into Clarksdale, Mississippi, where state NAACP president Aaron Henry still sought the modest goal of a biracial committee. When the first group of white emissaries from CORR was promptly served with the same injunction that had restricted Martin Luther King, the clergymen left the state in wounded bewilderment, unaccustomed to treatment as presumed outlaws. By telephone, they negotiated with skittish local ministers who first made and then canceled plans to discuss the Christian view of integration across the state line in Memphis. These talks convinced Spike's group to abandon thoughts of demonstrating in Mississippi on the bleak realization that any public display would doom their hopes of becoming goodwill mediators. Instead, Spike and the CORR delegation returned to Clarksdale at noon on Thursday, August 8, for an integrated worship service, after which they filed out to call privately on local pastors. Even this purpose was thwarted on the sidewalk as inflammatory. "There was constant police surveillance," he reported to colleagues in New York. "All members of the group were served with the same injunction the first group had received, and a young white student was seized by the police in retaliation against us. The emotion and tension of the occasion are hard to describe."

The Northern ministers retreated a second time. Some found it difficult to let go of the presumption that the unschooled Negro movement must have erred somehow from faulty tactics, impure motives, poor manners, or garbled communication, harder still to accept that repression in Mississippi went so far as to anticipate and forbid expressions of conscience by white pastors. The only concession that came easily from local authorities was bail for the arrested student, which facilitated the clergy's quick departure. From this, the CORR delegation began to comprehend the movement's crushing burden of leaving people behind in jail. On learning from Aaron Henry that large numbers of movement people had disappeared from Itta Bena and Greenwood nearly two months earlier in June, Spike helped convince the United Church of Christ that a $10,000 bail grant was a wise departure for its Board of Homeland Ministries.

An offer to become CORR's first lawyer came to Jack Pratt, a new graduate of Columbia Law School, on a Long Island beach where he sunbathed pending the results of his bar examination. In the mid-1950s, distraught over the sudden death of his mother, Pratt had studied theology at Union Seminary, where he had come to know Spike and others destined for the national council's new venture, and now in August, within a week of Spike's proposition, Pratt visited Mississippi long enough to despair of finding professional help from any Mississippi counsel or bonding company. Back in New York, with a volunteer partner from the eminent Shearman & Sterling firm, he talked officials of a New York casualty company into writing bonds for CORR and agreed to minimize publicity about the company's Mississippi branch by calling it "Company X" wherever possible. With duly authorized bond applications, Pratt rushed back to Mississippi to discover that most of the information about nearly sixty lost prisoners was incorrect—names, ages, spellings, plantation addresses, trial dates, sentences. He bounced between court clerks, sheriffs, notaries, and the COFO office in Greenwood, guided by telephone advice from names new to him, such as Wiley Branton and James Forman.

On the morning of August 16, with acceptably amended bonds, Pratt finally led a four-car motorcade some two miles inside the main gate at Parchman Penitentiary to the death house. During delays for verification of papers, angry voices could be heard threatening to shoot the prisoners, but four guards with shotguns eventually marched thirteen blinking figures down the dusty road. When they approached Pratt's waiting caravan, one of the tower guards aimed his rifle so convincingly that the Negro drivers dived for cover under their cars. Pratt instinctively raised his arm. "Put that gun down!" he shouted. "I am an officer of the court!" This textbook command seemed to perplex those with shotguns or rifles, who froze until the warden arrived.

The ex-prisoners broke silence just outside the main gate, singing movement songs on the highway all the way back to a welcoming celebration at the Greenwood COFO office. Sam Block and Curtis Hayes presided along with Stokely Carmichael, a lanky, liquid-eyed Howard University student who swapped stories about the Parchman guards from his stretch there as a Freedom Rider in 1961. As was his habit, Carmichael subdued demons of fear beneath cooing, mocking bravado, telling the normally rotund Lawrence Guyot—now haggard and virtually unrecognizable after losing nearly a hundred pounds—that he looked much better skinny. The dashing heroics of the young white lawyer who had faced down old Charlie the tower guard drew admiring laughter, but Pratt already realized that his chirpy naïveté was gone. Trembling now, in a hurry to leave Mississippi, he went to gather up the other bond papers and present them after nightfall at the Leflore County Work Farm, where jail superintendent Arterbery greeted him with deputies, shotguns, and barking dogs, reinforced by several police squad cars.

Trouble came this time not so much from the guards as from the forty-four prisoners themselves, who were reluctant to accept release into the custody of a white stranger after dark. Called from their cells, the male prisoners pressed themselves around the walls of the jail entrance until the seventeen female prisoners appeared hesitantly at the top of the rickety staircase from the upper cell block. All the prisoners, including Itta Bena leader William McGee, deferred wordlessly to two frail women well into their seventies. They questioned Pratt, pondered his story and perhaps his accent, then announced a decision. "Praise God!" one of them called out. "The church has come and set us free!"

10

Mirrors
in Black and White

Hollis Watkins did not attend the great march itself. After the long bus trip to Washington, he joined Bob Moses and Curtis Hayes on a lonely picket line outside the Justice Department with offbeat placards—"Even the Federal Government Is a White Man." Sight of them was a curiosity even for most of the arriving, early-bird marchers, while for Watkins this first trip to the capital and its monuments had the quality of a space journey. As in the Parchman death house, he led freedom songs in a clear, ringing tenor that made him a beacon of high morale for fellow prisoners and marchers alike, giving no hint that he was fighting a sense of being abandoned in prison by some of the same SNCC brethren who, in the chaos of last-minute infighting over the agenda for the march, protested that they were neglected in suffering and militancy by the higher Negroes bent on placating white people, especially the Kennedy administration. Telling himself that some things were best left unsaid, Watkins followed his SNCC friends into march headquarters at the Statler-Hilton Hotel to catch a glimpse of the magnetic sideshow in the mezzanine, where Malcolm X smiled, sparred, and bantered with a constant stream of spellbound onlookers—a phantom in flesh, a picket against the picketers.

Malcolm was not supposed to be there. Elijah Muhammad instructed his followers to avoid politics entirely—never to vote, march, petition, or otherwise implicate themselves in a system doomed to certain apocalypse —and Malcolm faithfully heaped invective on the foolish Negroes who wanted to "integrate into a burning house." To an audience in Virginia on August 22, he dutifully recited the Nation's racial cosmology according to

Muhammad. "The black man is the original man," Malcolm declared. "The white man was dormant in the seed of the black. Yacob, a scientist ... grafted out the white race from the black race and formed Abraham. When Yacob made the weaker race of whites, he knew they'd exist six thousand years. They are referred to in the Bible as devils.... In the last four hundred years they'd have in their clutches the lost tribes of God. At the end of that period there would be the coming of the son of man, Master Fard. His coming has given Elijah Muhammad the gospel of truth." Malcolm denounced integration as contrary to the laws of nature, and branded the hopes of the march a naive deceit. "The whites will never accept the so-called Negroes and will always be hypocrites," he said.

Still, Malcolm came alone to Washington a few days later, speaking neither of Yakub nor his private conflict in the Nation of Islam. Instead, he held court for passing demonstrators, mostly students, including Hollis Watkins, James Forman, and SNCC's newly elected chairman, John Lewis, who was consumed by an offstage controversy over the advance text of his speech to the Lincoln Memorial crowd. Malcolm relished his encounters with the movement students—their tentative, slack-jawed approach, their garrulous relief when the forbidding Muslim turned out to be full of smiles, taking them seriously. When Lewis stopped by the mezzanine again after delivering his address on national television and then meeting with President Kennedy, Malcolm congratulated him for an excellent speech. He offered the nonviolent Christians gentle criticism instead of firebrand ridicule. "I am not condemning or criticizing the march," he said, "but it won't solve the problems of black people."

THE MARCH ITSELF reduced Malcolm X and Hollis Watkins to faceless dots in the crowd. Like other formative experiences of the mass communications era—the coronation of Britain's Queen Elizabeth in 1953, the presidential conventions, the dramas of astronauts rocketing from launchpad to splashdown—the Freedom March commanded national attention by preempting regularly scheduled television programs. Broadcast networks voluntarily surrendered their revenues, and gathered their most important news correspondents to preside over a transcendent ritual of American identity. As the first ceremony of such magnitude ever initiated and dominated by Negroes, the march also was the first to have its nature wholly misperceived in advance.

Dominant expectations ran from paternal apprehension to dread. On *Meet the Press,* television reporters grilled Roy Wilkins and Martin Luther King about widespread foreboding that "it would be impossible to bring more than 100,000 militant Negroes into Washington without incidents and possibly rioting." In a preview article, *Life* magazine declared that the capital was suffering "its worst case of invasion jitters since the First Battle of Bull Run." President Kennedy's advance man, Jerry Bruno, positioned himself to cut the power to the public address system if rally speeches proved incendiary. The Pentagon readied nineteen thousand troops in the suburbs; the city banned all sales of alcoholic beverages; hospitals made room for riot casualties by postponing elective surgery. More than 80 percent of the day's business revenue would be lost to closed and empty stores. Although D.C. Stadium stood nearly four miles from the Lincoln Memorial rally site, Major League Baseball* canceled in advance two night games between the Minnesota Twins and the last-place Senators. With nearly 1,700 extra correspondents supplementing the Washington press corps, the march drew a media assembly bigger than the Kennedy inauguration two years earlier. By way of advance scorn, a U.S. representative submitted for the *Congressional Record* the testimonial letter of a satisfied Virginia Negro who shunned the march† altogether.

Not all the apprehension was racial in origin. Washington was an insular city, slow to accept a new communications fact that the natural audience for political rallies was public opinion back home. Many Washingtonians, including politicians who supported civil disobedience in the South, assumed that the purpose of any demonstration must be some sort of mob coercion against them, like the Bonus Marchers of 1932. The Senate, with no pending business, stayed in session primarily to put on an unperturbed face of normalcy. Representatives ordered a quorum call at the exact moment the rally began at the Lincoln Memorial, so as to publish the names of some 340 members who were dutifully attending to the Railroad Arbitration Bill and the formalities of Save Your Vision Week.

The March on Washington earned the capital letters of a landmark event by the end of the afternoon. Beyond the record-breaking numbers —upward of a quarter million—and the stunning good order that turned all the riot troops and plasma reserves into stockpiles of paranoia, the march made history with dignified high spirits. News outlets gushed over scenes of harmony—"White legs and Negro legs dangle together in the reflecting pool"—and Roy Wilkins congratulated Negroes for passing what amounted to a character test: "I'm so proud of my people." Police recorded only four march-related arrests, all of white people: one Nazi, two violent hecklers, and a health insurance computer‡ who drove to work

---

* By comparison, the National Football League would play its full schedule of games on the weekend of the Kennedy assassination. To guard against potentially riotous anger toward the murder site, the league did require public address announcers to identify one team only as "the Cowboys," forbidding mention of the word "Dallas."

† But for slavery, Zeak Crumpton purportedly wrote, "I would walk around in my bare feet with a metal ring in my nose. On holidays we would feast on elephants' toes, roasted grasshoppers, and the milk of a coconut. I get on my knees each night and thank God for permitting my ancestors to come to America as slaves." The *Richmond Times-Dispatch* published the letter with an editorial saluting Crumpton as "a credit to his race."

‡ In 1963, a dozen years before the dawn of the microcomputer industry, the word "computer" popularly referred not to a machine but to a person who made computations.

with a loaded shotgun. The outcome so embarrassed predictions that march organizer Bayard Rustin gained credit as a fresh wizard of social engineering, whose command of scheduling and portable toilets had worked a miracle on the races. Overnight, Rustin became if not a household name at least a quotable and respectable source for racial journalism, his former defects as a vagabond ex-Communist homosexual henceforth overlooked or forgiven.

A sense of relief raised the goodwill of the march into heights of inspiration, as millions of television viewers, including President Kennedy, heard a complete King speech for the first and last time that day. The occasion introduced King's everyday pulpit rhetoric as a national hymn. Despair wrestled deep in his voice against belief in democratic justice, producing his distinctive orator's passion, but the passion itself went to the core of the American heritage. From his reassurance of a common political ideal, the address spilled over into fresh cultural optimism. Although King's peroration invited polyglot America—"*all* God's children, black men and white men, Jews and Gentiles, Protestants and Catholics"—to join in a spiritual song of African origin, most observers pictured integration in reverse as a journey made comfortable by the ability of Negroes to behave like white people. *Life*'s review issue on the march, with Bayard Rustin on the cover and a text evoking "beatific calm" instead of Bull Run, presented a signature couple marching in crisp matching overalls, captioned "Negro Gothic ... reminiscent of famous Grant Wood painting."

TELEVISION STILL was a youthful medium, transmitting black-and-white programs except for the few such as *Bonanza* and Johnny Carson's new *Tonight Show*—specially marked in newspaper listings with a "(c)" for color —and some executives expressed moral misgivings about the generalized projection of sensate luxury. "Beer drinkers especially seem to live in a world of huge delight ... flashing smiles, toothy grins, and eyes popping with pleasure," observed an advertising director who warned colleagues that "fun, status symbolism, and sex in their current usage are suspect, and should be watched." Against lingering inhibition, a strong faction of network management believed that the industry was poised for an explosion of revenue in the maturing postwar economy. The key to competitive domination lay in network news programs—or so ran working theory since tandem hosts David Brinkley and Chet Huntley achieved a national popularity at the 1956 political conventions that carried over from their nightly news show to NBC's prime-time programs.

On the Monday following the march, rival CBS launched a calculated comeback by doubling regular news coverage with television's first half-hour newscast, featuring news-anchor Walter Cronkite. Two years in the making, the plan aimed to build the prestige of the Cronkite program toward the political conventions in the 1964 presidential election year. For the premiere, President Kennedy granted Cronkite an exclusive interview that opened with the President's concession that civil rights had cost him heavily in a number of states crucial to reelection, especially in the South,* and ended with a discussion of what President Kennedy called "a very important struggle" against a Communist-led insurgency in Vietnam, where forty-seven American soldiers had been killed. Reviewers called the Kennedy interview "leisurely." While some critics welcomed the extra time for thoughtful or amusing "soft" stories (and complimented in particular Cronkite's segment on Japanese singers trying to master the English diction of "With a Little Bit of Luck" in the Tokyo production of *My Fair Lady*), others doubted that CBS could fill a thirty-minute report every night.

NBC waited a week to match Cronkite† with an expanded version of the Huntley-Brinkley news. The network gambled heavily against the President Kennedy and Cronkite debut with a three-hour special on the race issue, entitled *American Revolution '63*. The entire program aired without commercial interruption, as regular sponsors declined to be associated with controversy, and the network itself showed signs of reluctance. Producers allowed no mention of segregated churches, or church activity on either side, for instance, and, to avoid hazarding any structural concept, they adopted the odd contrivance of segments presented alphabetically by the names of cities. An opening on protests in Albany, Georgia, gave way to a flashback on pre–Civil War abolitionists in Amherst, Massachusetts.

In rare lapses from professional aloofness, NBC narrators revealed the tension of a great personal leap, like trembling knees at a wedding. "There comes a time, there even comes a moment, in the affairs of men when they sense that their lives are being altered forever," began correspondent Frank McGee. "...We are experiencing a revolution." McGee told viewers that he had first sensed it years earlier as a local news director during the Montgomery bus boycott,‡ and other voices cited the culminating impact of televised violence against children: "The outrage in Birmingham, the sparks from this fell on every state in the Union."

Among numerous segregationists filmed expressly for the special, Governor Ross Barnett of Mississippi argued that the national turmoil was a sinister illusion created by television itself. "You are witnessing one more chapter in what has been termed the television revolution," Barnett

---

* "We are trying to do something much more difficult than any other country has ever done," President Kennedy told Cronkite, reacting to criticisms of the administration's policies on race. "A good many people who have advised us so generously abroad have no comprehension of what a difficult task it is that faces the American people in the '60s."
† ABC stayed with a fifteen-minute program until 1967.
‡ Montgomery "was not an evil city," McGee said, speaking over footage of the boycott. "We didn't realize Negroes demanding better treatment could no longer be treated as teenagers demanding to stay out after 9:30."

declared. On the NBC screen, he introduced a pregnant new ideology rooted in the assertion that the news media were driven by a secret racial agenda, saying that the past year's coverage "publicized and dramatized the race issue far beyond its relative importance," and that this deliberate media bias served as "a smoke screen to hide the biggest power grab in American history." Barnett concluded that "the real goal of the conspiracy is the concentration of all effective power in the central government in Washington."

The NBC documentary answered Barnett indirectly with a segment on Madison Avenue. "Outside this building there were pickets last week," a correspondent soberly disclosed over previously unused footage in which NAACP pickets complained that Negroes were excluded not only from television and radio ads, and thus from consumer fantasy, but also from news and entertainment programs. Each of the three networks had hired its first Negro correspondent within the past year; most major newspapers had no Negro reporters at all; even the educational broadcast channels, which favored civil rights by reputation, employed less than 1 percent Negro talent; the first and only televised entertainment shows featuring Negroes had been the stereotype comedies *Beulah* and *Amos 'n' Andy,* both canceled at the end of the Korean War.

When the alphabet came to Montana, Chet Huntley told viewers that the schools in his home state had been integrated with the few Montanans of color. Half of NBC's dominant news team, Huntley was a formidable presence as a Western, conservative balance to the more urbane David Brinkley—a kind of real-life model for the rugged "Marlboro Man" of cigarette advertising. His stoic delivery accented a startling departure into reflection. "We were a frontier people," he said, "or at least our fathers were, and the tradition of judging each man by his merits had by no means died out. Still, in an odd kind of way, the Negro was outside our tradition, a thing apart. In a sense we never really saw him, not the way we saw our friends. We never looked with honesty at Negroes the way we examined the anatomy of a grasshopper, say, or speculated on the after-hours life of our teacher. We looked, but we had been told what to see." Over old footage of lynchings, Negroes eating watermelons, cross burnings by the Klan, and black faces conniving in minstrel shows, Huntley's voice recalled images of separation. "What we were really showing, of course, was ourselves," he said.

Newsweek magazine published "The Negro in America," a special issue before the March on Washington. "Who are these revolutionaries? What do they want?" asked the editors, adding that the answers "lie in a world as remote and as unfamiliar to most white Americans as the far side of the moon—the dark side." An ambitious *Newsweek* poll showed Martin Luther King with a favorable national rating of 88 percent among Negroes, above 68 percent for Roy Wilkins, 51 percent for Adam Clayton Powell, and 15 percent for Elijah Muhammad. More than 40 percent said they did not recognize Malcolm X or the Muslims by name. A majority of Negroes would fight violently before giving up, said the report, but a larger majority preferred moderate, nonviolent methods "to join the white man," and were determined to gain "dishwashers and clothes driers as well as human rights." *Newsweek* concluded that Negroes "are playing to win. They think they can."

An avalanche of mail led to a second special issue, "What the White Man Thinks of the Negro Revolt," in which editors asked, "How much equality is the white man willing to grant the Negro?" About 80 percent of whites, including 60 percent of Southerners, said they believed Negroes were unfairly treated and deserved equal rights, but most preferred things to be put right without personal contact on their part. "We don't hate niggers," a California woman told the poll-taker. "We just don't want them near us." According to the poll, 85 percent of whites believed Negroes laughed a lot, 70 percent that Negroes had loose morals and a different smell, half that Negroes possessed inferior intelligence. In a special section, "What Science Says," experts evaluated claims that a smaller Negro cranium meant less intelligence. Some anthropologists pointed out that such specious logic would make Eskimos smarter than white people, given the relative sizes of the average brain pan. A psychiatrist explained the allegedly large Negro sex drive as a bittersweet function of poverty. "When Negroes start moving up into the middle class," he said, "they begin to experience the same kind of impairments of potency." Overall, *Newsweek* found that "the 1964 election would be a Kennedy landslide except for the racial problem." The largest disparity in the combined polls concerned the pace of integration: 3 percent of Negroes but 74 percent of whites said, "Negroes are moving too fast."

RUNNING STORIES lasted months in the back pages, such as the Americus, Georgia, death case. For refusing a police order to stop singing at a street corner freedom rally in August, four SNCC workers had been charged under a dusty racial insurrection law that provided for a death sentence upon conviction. Just as important to the local prosecutors, who said they were fed up with demonstrations, the capital offense allowed indefinite pretrial incarceration without bail. The transcript of a telephone conversation about prison conditions in Americus was read to "a shocked and silent audience" at the annual convention of the National Student Association in Indiana, where Al Lowenstein was recruiting student help for the Mississippi freedom vote. Georgia officials tenaciously held the four in jail from August until November, when successive legal forays by lawyers, including the new church troubleshooter, Jack Pratt, finally won their freedom on bond.

In mid-July, Robert Hayling had deployed his NAACP Youth Council on small picket lines outside segregated lunch counters in St. Augustine. A local judge, Charles Mathis, ordered seven demonstrators younger than seventeen held at the county jail, there being no youth detention facilities in the area. After five days, during which Hayling rallied outside the jail to protest cruel treatment, Judge Mathis offered to release the seven prisoners if their parents signed a probationary guarantee of nonparticipation in racial protest until the juveniles reached the age of twenty-one. Four families refused, whereupon Judge Mathis bound two boys and two girls over to jail indefinitely, pending transfer to state reform schools. In desperate attempts to draw attention to the case, Hayling placed calls to reporters, NAACP superiors, the Justice Department, and to the FBI office in Jacksonville, which reported that he "seemed emotionally upset, rambled, and on occasions talked incoherently." According to the wire from Jacksonville to headquarters, Hayling was "admonished vehemently" for suggesting on the phone that local FBI agents were lax in protecting the rights of the four juveniles.

A small newspaper in nearby Daytona Beach expressed outrage over the "totalitarian" conduct of Judge Mathis, likening his order to Fidel Castro's practice of sending children to Moscow for indoctrination. "Florida is going to get a black eye over this case," predicted the *Morning Journal,* but most newspapers took the disappearance more calmly. A correspondent for the *New York Times* passed through a week later and reported that St. Augustine "drowses today under the hot Florida sun, unstirred by the marching feet of the Negroes...." The *Times* found the summer tourist season in full swing—"horses drawing old-fashioned carriages clop down the street"—and a prevailing view that "the whole racial problem" was manageable and best left ignored. "The townspeople...do not regard it as anything serious," said the *Times* dispatch, which mentioned the disposal of the four Negro teenagers as something new under Florida law.

The St. Augustine students were destined to remain locked up until December, their appeals sometimes lost as the criminal and child welfare systems tried to unload jurisdiction on each other. Among local Negroes, however, the high reputations of the four families lifted controversy over responsibility for their suffering. As with the children of Birmingham, blame first fell on adult movement leaders for ruining the records of model students, but the callousness of white authorities slowly converted many who realized that four teenagers were about to lose their fall school term as well as their freedom. Resentment and inspiration welled up on Labor Day into St. Augustine's first large-scale demonstration, with more than a hundred adults carrying integration placards to the Old Slave Market. Police cut short the imitation March on Washington by sweeping in to arrest twenty-seven protesters, including Hayling.

Two Sundays later, on September 15, dynamite obliterated the exterior stone staircase and tore a large hole in the eastern face of the Sixteenth Street Baptist Church in Birmingham, freezing the sanctuary clock at 10:22. A concussion of flying bricks and glass destroyed a bathroom inside the staircase wall, where four adolescent girls were preparing to lead the annual Youth Day worship service at eleven, wearing white for the special occasion. Seconds later, a dazed man emerged clutching a dress shoe from the foot of his eleven-year-old granddaughter, one of four mangled corpses in the rubble. His sobbing hysteria spread around the world before nightfall. The Communist oracle *Izvestia* of Moscow raised a common cry with the Vatican newspaper in Rome, which bemoaned a "massacre of the innocents."

A *New York Times* reporter kept busy that day making a list of twenty previous bombings in "Bombingham" since the destruction of Fred Shuttlesworth's home in December of 1956—all unsolved and all against movement homes or sanctuaries, including three at Shuttlesworth's former church. Those farther from the scene made numb gestures with Birmingham in mind. Mercer University of Macon became the first Southern Baptist college to admit Negroes.* In New York, the American Civil Liberties Union announced plans to intervene on the side of Shuttlesworth and the *New York Times* in the Sullivan libel case, which the U.S. Supreme Court agreed to review in the fall term of 1963; at stake, said the lawyers, was Alabama's claim to repressive power "even more drastic than that imposed by the Alien and Sedition Act of 1798." In Nashville, white Baptist leaders drafted a resolution of sympathy for the stricken congregation at Sixteenth Street—saying "we join you in mourning your dead" and "encourage our people to contribute toward restoration of your building"—but the executive committee of the Southern Baptist Convention rejected the expression and managed for thirty years to seal records of its fitful consideration.

"I know I speak on behalf of all Americans in expressing a deep sense of outrage and grief," announced President Kennedy, who sent Burke Marshall of the Justice Department into a city on the verge of open racial warfare. A Negro boy had been killed already, shot off his bicycle by a white Eagle Scout who could not explain his sniper's reflex, and so many guns were brandished on street corners that federal officers refused to escort Marshall into Negro neighborhoods. The funerals produced the largest interracial collections of clergy in Birmingham history, but no city officials attended. Images of the bombing were so starkly black and white —of young black girls in white murdered by unfathomable evil, almost

---

* Enrolled the day after the Birmingham church bombing, Sam Jerry Oni waited three years before trying to attend the Tattnall Square Baptist Church, just off campus. Deacons repulsed Oni with force on September 26, 1966, and the congregation voted that same day to fire all three of its ministers who tried to welcome Oni, an African educated at Baptist mission schools in his native Ghana.

certainly in white skin—that they cut beneath intimate defenses. As in May, when bombings punctured the jubilation of the children's break-through, the church terror caused many Birmingham Negroes to seethe against Martin Luther King. Lashing out, King himself blamed "the apathy and complacency of many Negroes who...will not engage in creative protest to get rid of this evil." On the other side, a white lawyer made himself a lifetime pariah from Birmingham by blaming every citizen who took discreet comfort in segregation, saying, "We all did it," but Mayor Albert Boutwell stoutly insisted, "We are all victims." In his statement to the nation, President Kennedy carefully pledged the full power of the federal government to the "detection" of those responsible, rather than to conviction or trial.

DIANE NASH and James Bevel heard the news in Williamston, North Caro-lina, where they were assisting one of the most unusual of the satellite movements that had grown large since Birmingham. White divinity stu-dents from the New England chapter of King's SCLC migrated south for demonstrations with their teachers, such as Harvard theologian Harvey Cox and Yale chaplain William Sloane Coffin, and Clarence Jones had recruited as their volunteer counsel Charles McKinney of New York, Adam Clayton Powell's principal lawyer in his libel trial. McKinney, who proudly traced his lineage back through eight generations of Northern free Negroes, developed a jailworthy devotion for the local leader, Golden Frinks, a nightclub owner of uncertain grammar and insightful charisma. As a tactician of theatrical flair, soon to release a flock of live chickens in the state legislature to protest the tabling of a desegregation bill, Frinks welcomed Bevel and Nash to his home as kindred spirits.

Retreating into a spare bedroom, Bevel and Nash raged in sorrow through Sunday afternoon. To answer the Birmingham crime with deeds of equal magnitude, their first impulse was to become vigilantes—to iden-tify, stalk, and kill the bombers in the place of corrupted white justice. Bevel believed it could be done; he knew that the identities of lynchers tended to become more or less an open secret. In wild caroms of mood, Nash and Bevel swung from a "Black Muslim" option to a grand alterna-tive as pioneers in nonviolence: to combine voter registration work in Mississippi with the tactics of Birmingham direct action, including the children's marches. They would raise a nonviolent army across the entire state of Alabama to converge upon Montgomery and settle for nothing less than the enfranchisement of every adult Negro in Alabama. By Mon-day night they were possessed to propose the latter plan to movement leaders gathering for the funerals. Leaving their one-year-old daughter behind with Bevel, who stayed to help Golden Frinks, Nash set off alone by bus.

She reached Birmingham on Tuesday afternoon in time to hear Fred

Shuttlesworth preach the funeral of Carole Robertson, after which Nash pushed her way through cordons of mourners and preachers' helpers to outline the concept for him. For a second time—as with her declaration that the Freedom Rides must be renewed—Nash put Shuttlesworth in the rare state of being ambushed by a posture more audacious than his. With Ralph Abernathy, Shuttlesworth already had advocated a bold march to Montgomery to place a funeral wreath at the Alabama statehouse, but Nash's proposal swept far past symbolic gestures. When Shuttlesworth asked her to reduce the plan to writing for presentation to Martin Luther King, Nash found a typewriter and wrote late into the night, setting down guidelines of military zeal and organization: "...Marching and drills in command and coordination of battle groups....Instruction in jail know-how; cooperation or non-cooperation with jail procedures and trial.... Group morale while imprisoned....Drill in dealing with fire hoses, dogs, tear gas, cattle prods, police brutality, etc....Practice in blocking runways, train tracks, etc...." She proposed to begin with Birmingham students straight from the funerals, fanning out across Alabama for recruitment and training toward the goal of laying siege to Governor Wallace's state government—"severing communication from state capitol bldg. and from city of Montgomery" with lay-ins, call-ins, park-ins, and a sea of nonviolent bodies. "This is an army," Nash concluded. "Develop a flag and an insignia or pin or button."

Carrying her finished proposal, Nash heard King preach the next day over the open caskets of the three remaining victims. "There is an amazing democracy about death," said King, who urged mourners to take from hard reality—"as hard as crucible steel"—a comfort in the message left behind. "History has proven over and over again that unmerited suffering is redemptive," he said. "The innocent blood of these little girls may well serve as the redemptive force that will bring new light to this dark city.... We must not lose faith in our white brothers. Somehow we must believe that the most misguided among them can learn to respect the dignity and worth of all human personality."

When the service ended, and King pulled away with the motorcade toward the burial sites, Nash was left behind among a crowd of several thousand that walked a short way after the last hearse, then stopped and spontaneously sang "We Shall Overcome." Although there were numerous leaders among them—including Bob Moses, who had brought a busload of movement veterans from Greenwood—the clinging mass of people spilled aimlessly in one direction after another, never marching more than two or three blocks before confronting a blockade of white policemen. Alarmed, seeing that the crowd and the police were in no mood to tolerate each other, Nash tried to push her way through to head off the march, only to find herself behind a constantly shifting front. Freedom songs mixed with the sporadic sound of rocks and soft drink bottles lobbed toward police lines. Nash shouted that this was not the way—no demonstration could succeed without organization and clear purpose. Coming upon Rev. Ed King of Tougaloo, still wearing heavy bandages in recuperation from his facial surgery, she begged him to help her control the swirling crowd, which eventually subsided.

That evening Nash pushed her way into King's room at the Gaston Motel, where a wake competed with phone threats and rumors of a visit to the White House. She seized time to distribute her plan for laying nonviolent siege against Montgomery, which King received politely at best. Some waved off the proposal as inflammatory and apocalyptic—not to mention an abrupt shift out of Birmingham. Nash insisted that the first duty of movement leaders was to offer a constructive outlet for people burning with nonviolent spirit. When she lost the general attention of the room, Nash began to advocate the plan one-on-one, distributing copies, accusing the preachers of being too eager to rush off to Washington. The young Negro staff lawyer for the Justice Department, Thelton Henderson, would forward a copy by mail to Washington officials, who received it like a hand grenade. Burke Marshall called the document's attitude "revolutionary."

ON THE WEDNESDAY of the Birmingham funeral, Robert Hayling decided that he must not let the evening's Ku Klux Klan rally go unchallenged in St. Augustine, Florida—not after the church bombing, and not after authorities had so brutally repressed the first local rally for racial democracy. He called local television stations to urge coverage of the Klan event. More boldly, he proposed to NAACP friends that they scout the Klan rally themselves to prove that Negroes no longer were afraid of the invisible empire. Most contacts feared that Hayling had taken leave of his sanity. A few volunteered but soon made excuses. The postman Henry Twine later insisted that he had been waiting at the designated pickup spot, but Hayling managed to collect only three NAACP stalwarts, including Clyde Jenkins, the barber. The four of them drove slowly toward the rally site in a wooded field off the highway, behind a bowling alley. Hayling stopped indecisively, then turned onto a dirt road—either to sneak toward the rally by an indirect approach, or, as some in the car hysterically recommended, to turn around for a hasty retreat. A car pulled up behind while they hesitated, and one man with a shotgun jumped out to freeze them under guard. Finding a telltale NAACP sticker on Hayling's windshield, he and his cohorts smashed the car windows and marched their captives off through the field toward the rally.

A crowd of three hundred had gathered sometime earlier for the ceremonial burning of a twenty-foot cross, plus the featured address by a traveling celebrity Klansman, Rev. Connie Lynch of California, founder of the National States Rights Party. Lynch had arrived in his custom coral

Cadillac, wearing his trademark string tie. In his rhythmic, brickbat oratory, perfected during twenty years in sectarian pulpits, he declared that a resurgent Klan was on the move to destroy a worldwide conspiracy of Negroes and Jews. "Some of you say, 'But Jesus was a Jew,'" he said, feigning a religious qualm. "That just goes to show you how these cotton-picking, half-witted preachers have fooled you. Jesus wasn't no Jew. He was a white man!"

Similarly, Lynch dismissed squeamishness about the Birmingham church bombing, saying the four young girls had been "old enough to have venereal diseases" and were no more human or innocent than rattlesnakes. "So I kill 'em all," he shouted, "and if it's four less niggers tonight, then good for whoever planted the bomb. We're all better off." On local politics, Lynch denounced Robert Hayling as a "burr-headed bastard of a dentist," and challenged the Klavern to "kill him before sunup." The crowd was fairly well spent, growing bored with follow-up speakers and Klan announcements when an electrifying cry of "Niggers! Niggers!" went up in the darkness at the perimeter. Lynch scrambled to retrieve a rifle from his Cadillac, and the audience bristled with lesser weapons by the time sentries led the four captives to the platform.

Poked with knives, menaced with guns, Hayling and his three companions stood miserably at the center. When one of them claimed to have gotten lost on a fishing trip, the crowd hooted at transparent panic. When a search of wallets identified Hayling as "the nigger who wants to be king," cries of murderous bravado rose against one of the very Negroes whose death had been proposed and applauded moments earlier. A Congregationalist minister, who had sneaked in to study the Klan, subdued his repulsion with the thought that so precise a delivery of quarry must have been staged. The Klansmen circled and swaggered, but eventually their threatening gestures lapsed into empty, self-conscious inhibition against attacking helpless people, Negroes or not. A lull of surreal confusion set in until women of the Klan prodded the hesitant enforcers with graphic shrieks of encouragement. Uncertainly at first, men darted in to tear away pieces of shirt, then struck with fists, chains, and assorted clubs. Sight of blood turned theater to reality for the horrified Congregationalist minister, who repressed urges to intervene for fear that the slightest betrayal of sympathy would draw hostility upon himself. He worked his way slowly to the rear, he reported, "then sauntered casually towards my automobile ... kicking aimlessly in the sand as I walked along."

A shotgun blast from an overexcited Klansman briefly scattered the attackers, diverting them long enough that sheriff's deputies came upon the Negroes alive in a heap. Abrasions, concussions, and broken teeth sent all four to the hospital, but authorities interpreted events steadily against the victims. The earliest FBI teletypes reported that "Negroes were discovered by Klansmen approaching meeting area from woods, resulting in fight between Negroes and Klansmen." Taking professed evenhandedness a step further, county authorities prosecuted the four Negroes as well as four of the armed men found standing over them. All charges against the Klansmen would be dismissed on November 4, but a jury convicted Hayling of criminal assault. Judge Marvin Grier, mindful of Hayling's wounds and the absence of injuries to Klansmen, limited the punishment to a hundred-dollar fine.

NOT A WORD of the St. Augustine Klan beating intruded upon the September 19 summit meeting at which President Kennedy received King, Fred Shuttlesworth, and five Negro leaders of Birmingham. Rev. J. L. Ware took the lead. A conservative senior minister, who had resisted King's spring campaign, Ware let loose an unguarded torrent of despair about Birmingham authorities who refused to carry out the spring settlement or even meet with Negroes. Ware said troopers had aimed guns and insults at him on his own property. "People are frightened," he told the President. "... Some of them won't even go to church during the day services. The police are *brutal.* ..." President Kennedy interrupted to ask, "What's the hope in Birmingham?" When Ware, taken aback by the President's irritation, said he thought U.S. troops might be the only answer, Kennedy pressed the issue with snappish finality—"What is the *long-range* hope for Birmingham?"—and King stepped in quickly to retreat. "I still have faith in the vast possibilities of Birmingham," he said. "There are many white people of good will in Birmingham. They need help."

The volatile standoff recurred four days later in mirror form, this time with a delegation of white leaders from Birmingham. When the President implored them to hire at least one Negro policeman, the mayor's assistant replied that a third of the Birmingham officers would quit rather than serve in an integrated force. They answered Kennedy's pleadings with theories that the four girls accidentally may have set off a cache of dynamite stored in the church basement, and with rumors that the FBI had spirited the janitor out of town to hide Negro complicity in the crime. When a vice president of the local telephone company accused President Kennedy of giving comfort to King's meddling ways, Kennedy emphasized the greater menace of SNCC. He disclosed alarming intelligence about the Bevel-Nash campaign to paralyze Alabama, warning that SNCC "has got an investment in violence."

"Who is heading up SNCC?" asked the telephone executive.

"Well, this fellow Lewis," replied Kennedy.

"They're sons of bitches, I'll tell you that," said another Birmingham guest.

"Oh, they are," agreed Kennedy. "They're gonna get tougher. They're gonna be tough." Someone jumped in to say that SNCC students protested segregation at "the airports and the libraries and the buses, and everything else. That's a real militant group."

If the President slandered SNCC purposefully, to make concessions to King seem more palatable, the ploy failed with all the others. When he proposed that they undertake "even a public relations action . . . anything that gives a hook that suggests that the prospects are better," the white leaders replied that such actions would only encourage the Negro demonstrators. Their backs up—"we came here, sir, with big chips on our shoulder"—they rejected all hints that they were not doing more than enough already. Kennedy backed away from their prickly distemper, as the Negro delegation had backed away from his. He sent two retired Army officers—General Kenneth Royall, Truman's Secretary of the Army, and Colonel Earl "Red" Blaik, coach of legendary West Point football teams—to Birmingham as nonbinding mediators. King dutifully predicted that the two presidential emissaries "will help a great deal," but within days he regretted his trust. Kennedy explicitly ruled out federal intervention, and his negotiators disappeared into private, segegated meetings in Birmingham. To avoid controversy, they issued no public statements or recommendations. Movement critics ridiculed King for allowing the Kennedys to palm off the national crisis of the church bombing on a football coach.

King despaired. After nearly three years, his relationship with President Kennedy had run out of room. Although the movement needed federal intervention more than ever, realism told King he could not pressure President Kennedy an inch further. Brooding, he took the young Justice Department lawyer Thelton Henderson privately aside. "I'm concerned about having you in my meetings," King said, taking pains to say he liked Henderson personally* and accepted his duty to report what he heard to Robert Kennedy. King said something worse was eating at him lately. "I'm worried that the Kennedys only want to know in advance if we're going to do something," he told Henderson. "Then they act to stop us. But they don't act when the whites do something. They just let us take another beating."

King explored the idea of mounting a new campaign elsewhere, but held back for fear that a fresh start would be taken as an anticlimax, or an admission of failure in Birmingham. Meanwhile, SNCC chairman John Lewis led carloads of students directly from the Birmingham funeral to join systematic daily demonstrations at Selma, Bernard Lafayette's voting project. Some three hundred people went to jail there within two weeks,

---

* James Bevel had been teasing Henderson for months about how much danger he was willing to face as an ordinary Negro before invoking his official status. Arrested three times since the Roy Wilkins demonstration in June, Henderson had endured a cutting blow to the hand and one trip to a Mississippi jail, where vomit on the cell floor made him pull out his Justice Department credentials.

including Lewis himself and the embattled Rev. L. L. Anderson, whose arrest sent another shudder through the upstanding members of Tabernacle Baptist.

By then King was in Richmond, suffering through SCLC's annual convention. Several ministers in his inner circle endorsed variations of the Bevel-Nash mass siege as a desperate gamble to save nonviolence, but harsher voices said nonviolence was dead beyond revival—the fifth casualty of the church bombing. Wyatt Walker huffily resigned as King's chief of staff for lack of a threefold salary increase. Adam Clayton Powell flatly told the Richmond convention that the civil rights bill would not pass the Congress, then offered King a consolation job in his pulpit at Abyssinian.

On September 27, King closed the convention with an address of abject confession. "I was naive enough to believe that proof of good faith would emerge," he said of his support for the Kennedy emissaries to Birmingham. "Today we are faced with the midnight of oppression which we had believed to be the dawn of redemption," he told the convention. "We must deal with today. . . . We are faced with an extreme situation, and therefore our remedies must be extreme." Yet King found himself helpless to propose remedies. He found a way to make everyone an accomplice to the church bombing—from Governor Wallace to his own movement followers—but still he renounced no one. Instead, he exhorted listeners to bridge rather than exploit gulfs of separation. He retold the story of Lazarus and Dives, and preached from his blend of sources: Jesus on loving one's enemies, Reinhold Niebuhr on justice, Abraham Lincoln on the ideal of common citizenship. King quoted Lincoln's reply to a vengeance-starved Unionist who resented his stubborn refusal to call the Confederates enemies: "Do I not destroy my enemies when I make them my friends?" He wobbled on a sensitive spot, desperate to move but stuck in melancholy, confessing that his leadership was "standing still, doing nothing, going nowhere."

11

Against All Enemies

King's aversion to "enemy-ism" isolated him in politics, especially crisis politics. Leaders routinely molded support against a villain, and for most politicians a skillfully cultivated foe could become a source of advantage, energy, idealism, even comfort. Enemies of many kinds dominated the Kennedy presidency: foreign and domestic, mythological and real, racial and military, overt and clandestine. The partisan question—whether a Democratic President could reduce the historic estrangement of Negroes without making fatal enemies of Southern whites—remained secondary to the national passions of the Cold War, but by the fall of 1963 the two were closely intertwined.

Kennedy had won his office as a modern champion against Cold War enemies, pledging to redress a "missile gap" created by Republican laxity in the face of ominous Soviet advances. During the 1950s, the United States and Soviet Union had magnified their mutual hostility through telescopes of fear. American intelligence agencies had predicted that the Soviet Union would possess one hundred operational nuclear missiles by 1958, but they found zero instead. By then, however, the first Sputnik space launch in 1957 frightened Americans into believing that the Soviets were leaping ahead in military science, and nationwide alarm carried the estimated threat upward rather than down. President Eisenhower remarked that it was militarily "fantastic," "crazy," and "unconscionable" for the United States to have built some five thousand weapons averaging a hundred times the power of the Hiroshima bomb, be cranking out two more thermonuclear bombs every calendar day, and still push for more.

Yet the respected commander of D-Day resigned himself as "only one person," helpless against the tide of arms.

At his first press briefing as President Kennedy's incoming Secretary of Defense, Robert McNamara had disclosed that the celebrated missile gap did not exist after all. He retracted the statement under sharp public attack, and privately offered Kennedy his resignation. Remarkably, McNamara survived to swiftly remove Eisenhower's internal brakes on the development of strategic weapons—expanding the sea-based nuclear fleet from six to forty-one Polaris submarines, raising the land-based missile program from forty to more than a thousand. Drastic buildup suited an era in which President Kennedy, shaken by a contentious Vienna summit meeting with Soviet leader Nikita Khrushchev in 1961, addressed the nation frankly on the risks of general war. "Those families which are not hit in a nuclear blast can still be saved," he told American viewers.

Invisible within the gargantuan labors of the arms race grew future realities as diverse as the computer revolution and the scourge of plutonium,* but President Kennedy already perceived a few unintended consequences. When the Cuban Missile Crisis of October 1962 suspended the posturing for a fortnight of common dread, decision-makers shared white knuckles with the least political of citizens. (Etched into the memory of Vice President Johnson's secretary were normally demure college students who openly wailed along dormitory hallways that the end of the world was about to leave them forever virgins.) Khrushchev's sudden retreat gave them a second breath, and White House crisis managers drew contradictory lessons: that weakness "invites Soviet transgression" while strength risks panic. They retained a blurry psychological legacy of power and helplessness, righteousness and guilt. A new breed of war theorist factored miscue and mistrust into enemy-proof doctrines such as the "balance of terror," but terror did not lend itself easily to balance. Spurred on by the Missile Crisis, the United States committed in 1963 to a "triad" standard of deterrence by which each of three strategic arms—bombers, land missiles, and submarine missiles—must be able to answer nuclear attack with an independent retaliation more than sufficient to obliterate the Soviet Union, calculated at the equivalent of twenty thousand Hiroshima explosions apiece.

All that year, while feeding the tiger, President Kennedy tried to step gingerly off its back. Over the objections of critics who saw folly and danger in communication between doomsday enemies, he arranged for the

---

* The frontier electronics demanded by two massive anti-Soviet programs—the Minuteman missile and the mission to the moon—created a takeoff market for the microchip, and in effect produced the computer revolution as a "spinoff." Far less happily, the arms race also spun off mountains of plutonium waste so toxic and indestructible that experts hatched Aesopian schemes to rocket the stuff into the sun, bury it in salt caverns, or pay Indians and pauper countries to store it.

first direct phone lines between Washington and the Kremlin. Technicians were installing the new "hot line" during the March on Washington. More ambitiously, Kennedy negotiated with Khrushchev the first Limited Test Ban Treaty against nuclear tests in the earth's atmosphere, and urged Americans "to use whatever time remains" to reduce the chance of a nuclear exchange that "could wipe out more than 300 million Americans, Europeans, and Russians...." Seeking treaty ratification in the Senate, where early mail ran overwhelmingly against it, the President courted the endorsement of former President Eisenhower. Although the general favored the treaty and far broader ones, he also resented the ongoing Kennedy arms buildup as a slur against his defense record, his military judgment, even his patriotism. Eisenhower generally remained neutral, and in fact expressed mild reservations about the treaty, which obliged the Kennedy administration to bargain for support with promises of extra weapons and underground bomb tests.

It complicated vexations between the two presidents that Kennedy simultaneously sought a kind word from Eisenhower about the pending civil rights bill. He sent a mutual friend, Rev. Eugene Carson Blake, to visit Ike at his Gettysburg farm in hopes that the eminent churchman might appeal to Eisenhower's religious side. The Birmingham church bombing intervened, and when Blake reported Eisenhower's noncommittal response back to the White House, it was Kennedy's turn to tack grumpily against his own private views. He said the Republicans stood to gain no matter what they did on civil rights, and would behave just sincerely enough to push Kennedy over the cliff of his exposure. "The Republicans have a great temptation to think they're never gonna get very far with the Negroes anyway," Kennedy told a nonplussed Blake, "so they might as well play the white game in the South."

BENEATH PUBLIC OPINION, which teetered over fault lines of race and nuclear terror, rare tremors shook the national security agencies. These secret arms of government had extended dramatically against Cold War threats deemed too ruthless to be checked by democratic methods. Because they actively specialized in enemies, assimilating layers of intrigue that would be unseemly or inconsistent in public, the security agencies contained the rawest passions within the government.

In the Justice Department, for instance, Attorney General Kennedy and FBI Director J. Edgar Hoover feuded over the basic agenda for nearly three years. Kennedy argued that the real domestic enemy should be organized crime rather than Communist infiltration, which he said "couldn't be more feeble or less of a threat." Hoover argued that criminal syndicates were a myth—"baloney," he called talk of a Mafia—whereas American Communists remained dangerous far beyond their numbers, as "rigidly disciplined fanatics unalterably committed to bring this free nation under the yoke of international communism." Like Hoover, Kennedy was an ardent anti-Communist, but it galled him that for every FBI agent targeted against organized crime, Hoover maintained nearly one hundred agents on various "Red Squad" details against alleged and potential subversives. In September of 1963, Kennedy arranged televised hearings at which a contract killer named Joseph Valachi took a stunned national audience inside the unknown realm of godfathers and underbosses. Because of Valachi, Kennedy claimed, "the FBI changed their whole concept of crime in the United States."

An irritated J. Edgar Hoover minimized the Valachi hearings. His Bureau skillfully wielded the intelligence mission in its own defense, and by accepted folk rumor, high officials all over Washington were paralyzed by what Hoover held against them in his files. Such fear was strength in itself, but Hoover bound presidents to the FBI with a more complex entanglement of respect, complicity, gratitude, and dependence. When FBI agents discovered that Kennedy's CIA had enlisted three prominent gangsters in plots to assassinate Fidel Castro, Hoover presented the information confidentially to President Kennedy and the Attorney General, as a warning that this bizarre national secret might be compromised by leaks or incompetence. He did not need to say that the bungled scheme made fools of his rivals in the CIA, or point out that this classified government partnership with Mafia bosses humiliated the very argument Robert Kennedy pressed on his FBI about the priority of underworld prosecutions.

Similarly, Hoover advised President Kennedy to break from a mistress he shared with one of three gangster leaders of the official plots against Castro, Chicago godfather Sam Giancana, in order to curtail multiple avenues for blackmail against the White House. Shortly before the March on Washington, a private warning from Hoover enabled Robert Kennedy to spirit out of the country another of President Kennedy's mistresses, an East German woman named Ellen Rometsch. Political threat lingered after Rometsch, who offered Republicans the only politically and socially acceptable path toward a White House sex scandal: tracking a fugitive seductress from behind the Iron Curtain, then demanding to know what national secrets might have been compromised. Averting such disaster fell to Robert Kennedy, who carried a heavy load for his brother's illicit pursuits, and by October the Attorney General was obliged to beg assistance from Hoover. He asked the FBI Director to warn the Senate leaders that if they opened the Rometsch matter to hurt the administration, related smut from FBI intelligence files about Rometsch and her friends inevitably would discredit the entire U.S. government, including senators of both parties.

This was sordid business—gangster-spy assassination plots, molls and Mata Haris in the President's bed, blackmail between branches of government—all beyond the era's capacity for cynical imagination. Hoover was a patient, gifted bureaucrat—knowing everything, appearing to initiate nothing. When FBI intelligence lines picked up these and other reflections of seaminess in government, Hoover cleaned up the language into neutral "Bureau-speak" and passed it along as a dutiful public servant. Moreover, in spite of his active scorn for Robert Kennedy, Hoover would keep these secrets until his death, leaving behind corrosive revelations for later years. The Attorney General had reason to be grateful. For all his griping about Hoover's senile fits of "good days and bad days," his old-fashioned, segregationist ways, and his penchant for surrounding harmless old Marxists with legions of informants, Kennedy could hardly argue that Hoover's FBI dragged down ethical standards in the secret parts of the government. Hoover absorbed power mostly from the lapses of others, and the FBI's compulsion to know everything was useful to Kennedy as well as the Bureau. By wary accommodation, Kennedy and Hoover moved in September toward installing wiretaps on Martin Luther King.

FROM SAIGON, on the same day late in August that the FBI marked King internally as "the most dangerous Negro of the future in this nation," U.S. Ambassador Henry Cabot Lodge declared war on an American ally overseas. "We are launched on a course from which there is no respectable turning back: the overthrow of the Diem government," Lodge cabled Washington. Spearheading a dominant faction within the Kennedy administration, Lodge considered President Ngo Dinh Diem of South Vietnam too despotic to mobilize effective warfare against insurgents favorable to North Vietnam. All through September and October, Lodge plotted intimately against Diem along a tightrope of coup and betrayal, often exchanging multiple cables with Washington on a single day. Deadly intrigue consumed top foreign policy officials far more than their visible duties, while Hoover maneuvered against King on a parallel track.

In the first week of September, Hoover ordered his technicians to scout the ground ahead by making sure that wiretaps could be operated without detection on King's home and his SCLC offices in Atlanta and New York. While they were working, Ambassador Lodge worried that the South Vietnamese leader might become more resentful of his foreign allies than of his North Vietnamese enemies, in which case Diem might strike a unification deal with the Communists and ask the Americans to vacate his country. "This is obviously the only trump card he has got and it is obviously of the highest importance," Lodge cabled Washington. "It is also obvious to me that we must not leave. But the question of finding a proper basis for remaining is at first blush not simple." On September 16, the day after the Birmingham church bombing, the FBI's intelligence division recommended not only an expanded program of wiretaps but also a campaign of covert, extralegal FBI warfare against the civil rights movement. Assistant Director William Sullivan urged the plan upon Hoover as a justifiable war measure for a nation "engaged in a form of social revolution."

Pangs of faith and treachery crossed at many levels on Monday, October 7. Most publicly, President Kennedy assembled dignitaries at the White House to witness the formal signing of the newly ratified nuclear test ban treaty. "If this treaty fails, it will not be our doing," Kennedy declared, "and even if it fails, we shall not regret that we have made this clear and honorable national commitment." From the ceremony, Kennedy withdrew to intensive consultations over the Nhu family (President Diem and his brother Ngo Dinh Nhu, who ran the South Vietnamese secret police). The latest cable from Ambassador Lodge warned that "we cannot remove the Nhus by non-violent means against their will." Over the weekend, American secret agents had met with Vietnamese generals planning a coup, and four of the crisscrossing reports mentioned assassination of the Nhus among the contingent details. These contacts were all the more sensitive because a number of administration officials still believed that fidelity to the ten-year alliance with President Diem offered the only chance of victory in the war. White House instructions required explorations for a successful coup to be "totally secure and fully deniable." A few blocks away at the Justice Department, an emissary hand-delivered Hoover's written request for authorization to wiretap King at his Atlanta home and office. Attorney General Kennedy hesitated before a decision of such gravity.

King himself was speaking at a mass meeting in Birmingham, where he once again disguised the movement's paralysis with high-spirited rallies. "If the conditions that brought on the dynamiting and the death of four beautiful little girls are not changed," King cried, "we will put on our walking shoes and demonstrate all over town." In Selma, October 7 was Freedom Day, modeled on the upcoming Freedom Vote in Mississippi. SNCC leaders invited celebrities and national reporters to witness what might happen on one of the two days each month when citizens were permitted to register. All through the morning, writer James Baldwin, comedian Dick Gregory, two Justice Department lawyers, four FBI agents, SNCC leader James Forman, a dozen reporters, and several photographers observed a line of 350 Negro applicants stretching backward through the doors, down the exterior steps of the green stone courthouse and along the sidewalk, closely monitored by a parallel line of nearly a hundred state police, sheriff's deputies, and hastily recruited armed civilians known as the posse.

About five minutes before noon in Selma, a stir among the deputies interrupted what amounted to a motionless vigil, and Sheriff Jim Clark sent officers across the street to arrest two young Negroes who appeared on the steps of the Federal Building behind the observers, holding cardboard placards: "Register to Vote" and "Register Now for Freedom Now."

The mutual siege resumed almost silently until two o'clock, when a SNCC volunteer handed his wallet to Forman in a traditional act of jail readiness, and with a friend crossed the street toward the lines. At the curb, the volunteer tried to tell the applicants that no law prevented them from leaving for water or bathroom relief, but he realized from the frozen responses—and especially from a fearful woman who whispered desperately, "You can't talk to us"—that it was taking all the applicants' concentrated strength just to stand all day under the glare of the officers. When volunteers tried to step around the police line to offer sandwiches, converging officers clubbed them to the ground and dragged them along the street toward jail.

Only a handful of Negroes was permitted to apply for registration by the close of courthouse business. James Baldwin publicly called Selma "one of the worst places I ever saw." Justice Department lawyer Thelton Henderson muttered, "I've become jaded." Henderson was upset that after more than two years of federal litigation over Selma, which had resulted only the previous week in another injunction requiring fair treatment, Sheriff Clark could so brazenly turn the protective order on its head by forbidding rest, food, and friendly human contact as "interference" with would-be Negro voters. Henderson's partner, a senior white attorney, talked of resigning after Washington disallowed the lawsuits to enjoin police violence in the voting line and illegal arrests on federal property.

Others welcomed Freedom Day as an unexpected miracle. "Nothing like this ever happened to Selma," exclaimed a seventy-three-year-old World War I veteran at the mass meeting that night. Like James Forman, he was jubilant that the reborn courage of the May mass meeting had moved outdoors and lasted all day. That night, Amelia Boynton reached Martin Luther King with an excited appeal for his personal support. Across town, whites expressed equal amazement that such things came to pass in the town where Alabama's Citizens Councils had been founded. "I never thought it would happen in Selma," declared a Citizens Council official. "But I tell you this. We are not going to give in."

On Thursday, October 10, the sandwich volunteers were tried and convicted in Selma on charges of criminal provocation. In New York, the United Nations passed a resolution—with the United States abstaining— urging South Africa to call off the Rivonia Treason Trial of eleven political prisoners* charged with plotting against the apartheid government, and from Saigon, highly classified cables warned Washington of reciprocal threats in Vietnam. "For Diem and Nhu even to be thinking of my assassination is so unbelievably idiotic that a reasonable person would reject it out of hand," wired Ambassador Lodge. As a precaution, Lodge reported, he was sending a message to the South Vietnamese leaders that in the

---

* Including African National Congress leaders Nelson Mandela and Walter Sisulu.

event of his death, "American retaliation will be prompt and awful beyond description."

The arrival that afternoon of Soviet Foreign Minister Andrei Gromyko was a comparatively cheerful event for the White House. President Kennedy introduced the departing Russians to the next scheduled visitors, who arrived with the Attorney General. Before Colonel Blaik and General Royall could settle in for an off-the-record discussion of Birmingham, the President's two young children bounded into the Oval Office ahead of an embarrassed White House nurse. They chased each other in giggling circles, and Uncle Robert allowed himself to be tackled playfully to the carpet. A trailing White House photographer took a picture of John Kennedy, Jr., then nearly three years old, crawling through a secret compartment of the Ulysses Grant antique desk before President Kennedy ended the amusement with a clap and a wave for the nurse. He was pleased to hear that his two emissaries had been received well in Birmingham, and had helped contain explosive tensions for three weeks since the church bombing. Before Blaik could introduce more difficult, substantive choices in Birmingham, beyond what he resented as his partner's "bland, p.r. approach," Kennedy took several interrupting phone calls from Defense Secretary McNamara about flashpoint confrontations with the Soviets along the East German autobahn. Backing off from the President's troubles, Blaik mentioned a bumper sticker he and Royall had seen in Birmingham: "Kennedy for King—Goldwater for President." The slogan briefly puzzled the quick-witted President, who was fond of royalty, until he realized that the hostile Birmingham driver meant to relegate him to Martin Luther King and the Negroes while putting Republican Barry Goldwater in the White House. Kennedy laughed uproariously along with his brother. He and Blaik fell to talking football, and eventually they decided to postpone the promised report on Birmingham.

The Attorney General could not so easily put off J. Edgar Hoover. That same afternoon he reviewed his turmoil over the King wiretap request with Courtney Evans, his FBI liaison officer. There was nothing more risky, he said. Any leak would undermine the government by destroying credibility among Negroes and millions of whites coming to view King as a figure of democratic conscience. Worse, it would touch off fiercer resistance in Congress and the South by sanctioning the belief that civil rights was infected with the Communist enemy. On the other hand, Kennedy needed leverage precisely because of King's swelling influence since Birmingham and the march. Wiretaps would help the administration tack against King when necessary, even if they supplied nothing more than accurate foreknowledge of his moves. Kennedy told Evans that a wiretap was the most likely method to prove ties between King and the Communist party, if there were any, although two years of blanket coverage on King's presumed Communist channel, Levison, had turned up nothing Soviet or spylike. Still, once the question was framed as one of knowing or not knowing, the Attorney General leaned toward reliance upon Hoover. Emphasizing "the delicacy of this particular matter," as Evans reported to the Bureau, Kennedy signed the wiretap request.

The undertow of the October 10 wiretap decision registered within a week, as Hoover's FBI completed and disseminated throughout the government a monograph describing Martin Luther King as "an unprincipled man" who "is knowingly, willingly, and regularly taking guidance from communists." Horrified when he found out, Robert Kennedy personally demanded that Hoover retrieve all copies before politically ruinous accusations leaked out of the State Department or Pentagon. Hoover was only too glad to comply—by Kennedy's later account he even suggested that the FBI take responsibility for the recall—because the King paper had served notice already that the FBI was freshly independent in security matters. If challenged within the government, or in Congress, Hoover could justify practically any attack on the civil rights movement by pointing to Robert Kennedy's trophy signature on the King wiretap authorization. Moreover, the signature severely reduced Kennedy's ability to influence the FBI's overall priorities, and it undercut his unique leverage as the President's brother—especially since Robert Kennedy still needed favors from the FBI intelligence files to protect the President through the first Senate hearings in the Bobby Baker investigation, where the Ellen Rometsch affair threatened to erupt.

Hoover moved to consolidate his advantage by forwarding a request to place wiretaps on all four telephone lines at King's SCLC office in Atlanta. Robert Kennedy, while "still vacillating...still uncertain in his own mind," signed it on October 21, just as Andrew Young, in King's private world, glumly recommended that SCLC pull out of the South altogether to register voters in the North. A few days later, the FBI obtained Kennedy's permission for wiretaps on Bayard Rustin, too. Still shaken by Hoover's King monograph, the Attorney General could say variously that he was humoring the FBI, hedging political bets, or taking extra security precautions, but in reality the King wiretap severely eroded his control over the FBI. For King, who did not yet know, the wiretap was a permanent addition to his enemy load. Whatever shape the movement might take, from grounded ship to rolling hymn, henceforth he must push forward not merely through hulking reluctance but the FBI's more or less unfettered hostility.

12

Frontiers on Edge:
The Last Month

KING SUFFERED enemy trouble over an automobile ride. In Birmingham on October 15, he and several preachers had stalled in the parking lot at the Gaston Motel just as Thelton Henderson of the Justice Department by chance pulled in to retire. (As a Negro, Henderson shared the Gaston Motel with the movement, while the white government lawyers stayed elsewhere.) King explained hurriedly that he was late, as usual, between a mass meeting at New Pilgrim Baptist Church and a promise to Amelia Boynton that he would speak still later that night down in Selma. Henderson lent the King party his rental car for the trip. Three days later, Governor Wallace accused the Kennedy administration of abetting subversion against Alabama law by serving as King's chauffeur.

Alabama members of Congress demanded to know whether a prevaricating Justice Department was in cahoots with King. A month after the church bombing, with that criminal investigation at standstill or worse,[*] state investigators swarmed over car rental records with a contrasting thrill of the hunt. Two state grand juries collected testimony about what Judge James Hare of Selma called "men high in the circles of Federal Government maliciously lying," and U.S. courts of appeal would be drawn into state claims that the car ride charges ought to disqualify the Justice De-

---

[*] Both Burke Marshall and J. Edgar Hoover privately reported to Attorney General Kennedy that Alabama officials effectively sabotaged the federal investigation. The church bombing case remained dormant for fourteen years, until Alabama convicted Klansman Robert Chambliss in 1977. He died in prison.

partment's other work in Alabama, such as the marathon voting rights suits in Selma. A disheartened King lamented "so much fuss," as he put it, over the "rather insignificant matter" of the car ride. With racial politics so highly charged that murders were treated like car rides, and car rides like murder, he resisted pleas for the big Nash-Bevel campaign on voting rights.

In Mississippi, shortly after announcing the Freedom Vote campaign on October 14, Bob Moses convinced a reluctant Rev. Edwin King, chaplain of Tougaloo College, that no other white candidate was available to run for lieutenant governor with NAACP chairman Aaron Henry on what became Mississippi's first integrated ticket of the century. With his right cheek still bandaged from injuries in June, which marked him as a survivor of demonstrations with Medgar Evers, King appeared alongside Aaron Henry at Negro mass meetings.

Once fully committed, with candidates and a goal of "getting 200,000 Negroes to vote in a mock election which will act as a trigger for a stepped-up registration drive," campaign manager Moses wrote out what amounted to a formal recruitment charter for Al Lowenstein as chairman of the "Aaron Henry for Governor" advisory committee, and Lowenstein pulled off a firebell tour of college campuses to call in nearly a hundred student volunteers, mostly from Yale and Stanford. He obtained large contributions from a New York philanthropist and from UAW president Walter Reuther, among others, and alerted his far-flung network of contacts. ("Dear Al," wrote Frank Porter Graham, retired president of the University of North Carolina, "I am sending this check for $50 in case you or any of the Yale students need bail again.") On his return to Mississippi, Lowenstein was arrested twice the same day in Clarksdale—once while riding with Aaron Henry from a campaign rally, later when trying to walk from a parked car to his hotel. "We all go through the most unpleasant harassment," Lowenstein wrote his family in New York, "much worse than what South Africa used to be, though South Africa has gone ahead recently."

Many students arrived with Ivy League confidence and missionary enthusiasm. "Any white Northerner who's had the good fortune to achieve even an average education in the North is going to be, just by virtue of this fact, so much more talented than the Negro leadership in the movement in the South, that in *one day*, he can make a significant contribution," one history major declared in a recruiting speech. The most presumptuous recruiter could not have expected the vigilant notice that adult Mississippi gave students on leave from premed courses and literature seminars. The first volunteer to reach Yazoo City drove straight to a prearranged meeting with three Negro leaders, where police called within half an hour to announce that they had the building surrounded, and the local leaders, deciding that the Freedom Vote was too dangerous, delivered the student for police escort outside the city limits. Five days later, on October 28, the first carload of Yale volunteers completed the thirty-hour drive to Hattiesburg just after midnight and collapsed at an assigned home in a Negro neighborhood, only to be dragged from bed to jail early the next morning. "My experiences here in two days of field work have bordered on the unbelievable," wrote one of the students to his senator in Washington. Shortly after posting his letter, the student was beaten by an irate white taxi driver who saw him canvassing for Freedom Votes, and Hattiesburg police arrested the student again, this time for assault.

Similar reports from across Mississippi put the Stanford University campus into what the student editor called "a whirlwind." At a spontaneous rally on October 28, some three hundred students volunteered as reinforcements, and an early busload pulled out for Mississippi before the Hattiesburg police chief called the *Stanford Daily* that evening to warn of $500 fines and six-month sentences awaiting "any white agitator" who disturbed his town. This message pitched campus leaders again into a late-night strategy session, at which they decided to divert their energies from recruiting to fund-raising. A hefty collection left for Mississippi by the next morning, when Lowenstein was grasping for positive developments. "Norman Thomas, bless his heart, is coming down Thursday," he wrote of Thomas—the seventy-nine-year-old patrician socialist and six-time candidate for President—"Most astonishing and cheering of all is that Stanford has sent $4,300.00!!—which is making all the difference in the world."

Young white volunteers who reached Mississippi tumbled through flattery, terror, and awe. A philosophy major from Stanford found that Negroes in the college town of Oxford were too afraid to talk with him under the gaze of the police cruiser that trailed slowly behind. He soon "decided to confine my activities to the telephone." A Yale volunteer, in shock from the moment a Delta policeman greeted him with a drawn pistol, retreated to stealthy canvassing on the rural plantations, where sharecroppers were conditioned to avert their glance from his face and agree automatically with anything he said. The volunteer figured to collect more votes if he "cut the palaver" about the meaning of the Henry-King candidacy and simply instructed the sharecroppers to mark the Freedom Ballots, which worked efficiently until a Negro SNCC worker admonished him to treat the sharecroppers with full respect. Through the ensuing discussion, the Yale volunteer recalled that he and the SNCC worker "spent a decade together in thirty-six hours."

Not all the two hundred recorded cases of intimidation targeted the highly visible white volunteers. When police detained Bob Moses at the Rankin County airport, a squad car followed the four SNCC workers who retrieved him, pulled them over at a gasoline station near Jackson, and a patrolman accosted them as "NAACP niggers" stirring up trouble. Charlie

Cobb pointed out that they were not NAACP—"We're SNCC," he said —but the correction infuriated the officer enough to spread-eagle Ivanhoe Donaldson for interrogation while his partner held the others under guard. Several times he struck Donaldson's knuckles with the butt of his revolver for unsatisfactory answers, and put the barrel against Donaldson's head while working himself up and down in fitful rage about "killing you right here and right now," until his partner said it was not the place. Donaldson, who had been arrested two weeks earlier in Selma, and again since then in Greenwood, collapsed in the back seat upon release. Eventually he began to recover through gallows humor, congratulating Cobb's panicky efforts to educate the officers on basic differences between civil rights organizations. "That was gonna cool them right off," he teased.

Lowenstein, when not attending mass meetings or bail crises, bombarded the long-distance wires with appeals for political help. One contact in the House of Representatives reported that he had carried out instructions to petition Senator Wayne Morse only to find that "Morse was on the phone with you when I called." Norman Thomas did keep his promise to fly in from New York to speak at a rally for the three-week Freedom Vote campaign. Attackers rammed a car in his caravan as it left the site, and the novelty of Thomas exhorting a crowd of Negroes on Halloween night in Greenwood helped capture nationwide press interest. "A drive to get votes that are not legally cast for candidates who are not on the ballot began in Mississippi Saturday," the *Washington Post* wryly reported.

Most of the 85,000 ballots finally collected for the mock election were signed and delivered at church meetings, or at hideaway polling places such as Vernon Dahmer's store in Hattiesburg. At an emotional rally for Aaron Henry and Edwin King on the last night in Jackson, Moses quietly praised the movement workers for sounding hope in a crushed silence. "The measure of freedom has now been heard in every part of Mississippi because you took it there," he said. "There may be towns where you got only one or two votes, but the people there have heard . . . the whisper of freedom is spreading."

Lowenstein also spoke, emphasizing the national significance of the event. "This is the first time in America it was necessary to campaign underground," he said. The presence and the suffering of the white students had encouraged many Freedom Voters as a marvel, but Lowenstein himself considered the students more valuable as antennae for the outside world. At the victory rally, network reporters jostled for interviews with the sons and daughters of leading American families. The history major who had recruited them for superior education begged the reporters to interview the local Negroes instead, already ashamed of his prior arrogance. At a homecoming press conference on the Stanford campus, photographers took pictures of wounds, and reporters pressed for shocking details. ("Well, besides being shot at once, I was hit on the head once by a policeman standing outside of a church," one student replied.) The impact of the Freedom Vote volunteers began to spread not only through the press but more directly within campus culture, as curious Yale students jammed the law auditorium to hear from returning volunteers. An open forum on their reminiscences captivated many future activists while putting others off. A writer from the *Yale Daily News* made fun of the clash between Jacobin passion and the cocktail sherry atmosphere, observing tartly that Mississippi hardships seemed to create "a bond stronger than the Whiffenpoofs."

BEFORE DAWN on Friday, November 1, secret cables alerted the White House that South Vietnamese generals were launching their coup against President Diem's government. Rebel units knocked out regular communication lines in Saigon, but the coup plotters maintained contact with Ambassador Lodge over a direct wire installed between their officers' club and the U.S. embassy. During the early fighting, before Kennedy's breakfast, Lodge confidently advised that he had invited the Vietnamese generals over to legitimize their anticipated victory, and Kennedy, always sensitive to the risks of U.S. complicity, sent Lodge instructions to make sure that the coup leaders "will not call on you in [a] large group, thus giving false impression they were reporting to headquarters." Some hours later, the Vietnamese generals gave a hideously different show of independence by murdering Diem and his brother Nhu in the back of a troop carrier after they had surrendered unarmed from refuge in a Catholic church, then hacking up the bodies with machetes and clumsily announcing that the prisoners had committed suicide.

The brutality of regicide in unfamiliar foreign lands was sport for some wags across the sea—"No Nhus is good news." Ambassador Lodge boasted privately to Kennedy that "the ground in which the coup seed grew into a robust plant was prepared by us," and some of the future's harshest critics of the American war in Vietnam hailed the coup as a messy but decisive improvement for the larger war against Communism. Still, the grisly murders shook President Kennedy as something closer to an underworld hit on two brothers running an allied family. For months, consumed by the difficulty of controlling the plot while avoiding the appearance of responsibility, his government had created a policy world of deniability, contingency planning, and a clean change of government. The mutilated corpses ripped away artifice, animating the mountain of secret cables—evasion, remorse, and bloody determination, like speeches from *Macbeth*.

A quieter drama interrupted President Kennedy's coup watch. When he had returned to the White House from the morning mass for All Saints' Day, when the fate of Diem was still undetermined, Robert Kennedy called about a troublesome letter from Senator Richard Russell of Georgia, asking whether or not Martin Luther King was a Communist. The President was fully up to speed on the matter, having worked well into the previous evening with the Attorney General and Burke Marshall, preparing three alternative replies for Robert Kennedy's signature. Between a first draft that artfully dodged Russell's question altogether, and a third draft that described Martin Luther King in some detail as a man clinging to Communist influences, Kennedy had selected a middle version portraying King as provisionally clean, dusted off under the prodding of the adminstration and the vigilant watch of the FBI. Now, however, the Attorney General called to say that J. Edgar Hoover objected to the use of the FBI as covering authority.

President Kennedy asked his brother to read the FBI's amended three-page draft over the telephone. If it was rare for a sub-Cabinet officer like Hoover to force reconsideration of communications already cleared by a President, and rarer still for a President to edit mail personally in the midst of a foreign crisis, the arcane gravity of the issue proved overriding. There was desperate hurry because Senator Russell had written to FBI Director Hoover more than three months earlier, on July 27. Since then, after Hoover promptly informed Russell that he was referring questions about King and Communism to the Attorney General, Robert Kennedy had procrastinated all through the March on Washington and the long ordeal over the King wiretap. Russell was demanding an answer on behalf of a constituent, and any day might denounce the administration for inexcusable neglect or incompetence. Three more times that day, the Attorney General called the White House to read new versions of the letter to President Kennedy, who had his national security team in the Cabinet Room with incoming flashes from Saigon. Three more times President Kennedy rejected the drafts.

Part of the dilemma turned on the cosmetics of ego,* but the heart of it was raw politics. President Kennedy needed the FBI's protective cover to tell Senator Russell that while the FBI was monitoring super-secret national security concerns, the administration still could vouch for the overall integrity of the civil rights cause. If stripped of the FBI qualification, the Robert Kennedy letter " 'clears' King," as FBI headquarters noted ominously of the first draft. For President Kennedy, this was a suicide ledge. Unqualified endorsement of King and the movement would cut off a line of retreat from the civil rights bill. It would put him directly at odds with Hoover, and repudiate—in writing—the very justification the

---

* Robert Kennedy proposed to tell Senator Russell that "some time ago" the administration had ordered the FBI to intensify its guard against subversion within civil rights groups, but Hoover rejected the sentence. "We didn't need to be told to intensify our efforts," headquarters sniffed. "We had already done so."

Attorney General had just embraced—in writing—for the politically explosive wiretap order on Martin Luther King as an enemy suspect.

The alternative course proved no better. Whenever Robert Kennedy himself adopted any part of the accusations against King that had been attributed to the FBI, the letter to Russell sounded as though the administration had ferreted out subversive information and was notifying the most respected and powerful of the Southerners fighting the civil rights bill. Unlike FBI intelligence, the Attorney General's conclusions could not be stamped secret. They would be read on the floor of the Senate, and no amount of tinkering could render them less than a major political statement. In effect, Hoover held a dagger through King to Kennedy without risking the Bureau's name or reputation, much the way Lodge had maneuvered the Vietnamese generals to turn on President Diem.

President Kennedy finally scrapped the revisions altogether. Without Hoover's cooperation, he could devise no way to finesse the Communist issue in writing, and therefore he directed Robert Kennedy to send Deputy Attorney General Nicholas Katzenbach to answer Senator Russell that very afternoon in person. Hauled in for urgent briefings on how to explain the delay and the unorthodox channels without hiding or revealing too much, Katzenbach was told to draw on his personal rapport. FBI liaison Courtney Evans went along to make sure he did not unwittingly disclose any of the national security incantations about Stanley Levison that Hoover had refused to transmit on paper.

Alone with the sudden callers in his Senate office, Richard Russell quickly seemed to grow bored. What came across to the senator was not so much the words of Katzenbach's rehearsed circumlocution as the acute discomfort of two tightly wound government officials. He interrupted to put them at ease, saying he pressed the letter only because any senator deserved the courtesy of a timely reply. As a Georgian acquainted with many Negro preachers like King and his father, Daddy King, Russell said, he already knew for himself that King was not a Communist, and wouldn't make a Senate speech about such suspicions, anyway. Katzenbach was beaming with stunned relief as Russell made jokes about how serious he had looked on television confronting George Wallace. Ever the courtly Southener, Russell spoke distastefully of Wallace as a showboating demagogue whose self-defeating crusade against Communism among Negroes would injure the segregationist cause. "You and I are a mile apart on civil rights," he told Katzenbach as he escorted his visitors to the door, "but I'll tell you I'm a hundred miles away from George Wallace."

Courtney Evans took news of the anticlimactic resolution back to FBI headquarters. Senator Russell's lack of interest in the subversive angle raised a significant barrier to FBI advocacy on race relations, but Russell had not criticized the Bureau, either, and Evans knew to stress the positive lesson that Robert Kennedy's paranoid mishandling had allowed the whole inquiry to be "magnified into proportions finally reached." J. Edgar Hoover declared procedural victory: "This shows wisdom of FBI *prompt* handling of our Congressional mail."

At the Justice Department, Katzenbach delivered a mission report of complete success. Senator Russell was satisfied; in fact, he turned out to be a "pretty good fellow" about not "hitting below the belt" on Communism. This good news arrived about six o'clock on Friday evening, just as a cable from Ambassador Lodge informed the White House that President Diem and his brother were surrendering on promise of safe conduct out of Vietnam.

ON NOVEMBER 5, Burke Marshall included a sketch of St. Augustine, Florida, among his status reports for Robert Kennedy. "In summary," he began, "the situation has been quite bad. There has been shooting, beatings, and one killing." Since the Klan rally in September, carloads of joyriding whites had careened through Lincolnville almost nightly, firing shotguns, until one white teenager was killed by return fire. (When hit, the victim blew a hole in his own car by reflex action of his trigger finger.) Then, especially after Rev. Connie Lynch addressed a post-funeral Klan meeting, sniper fire intensified to the point that city police tried to impose a children's curfew on Halloween night. Meanwhile, the four young Negro picketers remained incarcerated since July as wards of the state. Although the national office of the NAACP was moving carefully to expel Robert Hayling for unauthorized demonstrations, a number of formerly staid Negro leaders vowed to stick with him as a hero of fortitude.* Angry white leaders held firm against biracial meetings, let alone integration of the 1965 Quadricentennial, and the Klan threatened to assume active control of St. Augustine. "I do not see what we can do," Marshall advised Kennedy, "unless you want me to explore the situation through political channels."

In Mississippi, racial forebodings shook the foundations of elective politics. Democrat Paul Johnson, elected governor of Mississippi on November 5, denounced the very existence of partisan competition in a state where white Republicans were said to be scarcer than polar bears. "Kill the threat of the 'two-party' system!" exclaimed his campaign literature, which warned that "a vicious two-party political system" would "divide the conservative white men and women of Mississippi into two political camps and thereby place the balance of power in the hands of the negro minority." Johnson urged Mississippi voters to "bury Republicanism for another 100 years," and his courthouse regulars did their part at the polls.

---

* Because Hayling "was the prime mover in the desegregation campaign," the NAACP's director of branches instructed Florida to get rid of him "carefully and slowly," taking care "not to be accused of making him the scapegoat."

"They are treating my workers like niggers," protested the Republican gubernatorial candidate, Reubel Phillips, a fresh ex-Democrat who proclaimed that only Republicans could save Mississippi from race-mixing Kennedy Democrats. No Republican had bothered to run for governor since 1947, but Phillips multiplied that token showing by a factor of thirty, gaining more than 40 percent of the official vote.

In the North, Malcolm X bluntly accused the entire country of adopting Mississippi's raw preference for white supremacy. "Your democracy is nothing but hypocrisy where black people are concerned," he told a white college audience in New York on November 7. He asserted that most of the 22 million former slaves were damaged—repugnant to themselves, to civilized standards, and to whites alike. "We know what's wrong with you, and we know what's wrong with us, and we try to look at both objectively," he said. To rebuild themselves, he argued, the former slaves first must ignore sweet words and their own defensive pride. They must accept the harsh reality that whites treated them as vassals whether in the segregated South or sophisticated North, no better than imperial Romans might administer a conquered population of Nubians or Gauls.

A few weeks earlier, Elijah Muhammad had removed Malcolm from his secondary assignment post at Temple No. 4 in Washington. His replacement there—a Ph.D. mathematician hailed as the first certified intellectual among the largely self-taught ministers in the Nation of Islam—noticed that the Chicago officials dropped surprisingly barbed comments about Malcolm's independence and love of publicity. Malcolm, for his part, found that the Nation of Islam had consolidated its control of Temple No. 7 during his absence. National Secretary John Ali and other Chicago officials dealt directly with Captain Joseph, and often visited New York to monitor Malcolm's sermons. Captain Joseph took his old mentor aside to say his words no longer sent chills up his spine, to which Malcolm replied that perhaps Joseph was not spiritual enough to hear. "Could be," Joseph replied, "but I can't dig you no more." Malcolm confided nothing of the breach to his devoted assistant ministers, but they noticed fewer references to the guiding wisdom of Elijah Muhammad.

"You may take offense at what I'm saying," Malcolm told the bristling crowd at City College of New York, "but how in the world can you take offense when I say democracy brought the Negro in this country to the level he's on, when it was democracy that has made us a slave?" Over gasps and a few catcalls, he pushed his thesis that the brute divisions of race were far stronger than the kinships of democracy. "It was people who advocate democracy who sold us like cotton and cows from one plantation to another," said Malcolm. "It was people who advocate democracy who had black people lynched from one end of this country to another, and it is people who today represent themselves as defenders of democracy that let a government that represents itself as a democracy continue to deceive and exploit the so-called rights of black people in this country. All the hell our people have ever caught in this country, they have caught it in the name of democracy."

FOR THIRTY YEARS, since leaving Union Theological Seminary during the Depression, Myles Horton had made a life's work of experiments in racial democracy. With the long-standing support of sponsors including Eleanor Roosevelt, Walter Reuther, Norman Thomas, and his former theology teacher Reinhold Niebuhr, Horton had run camps for interracial dialogue in the mountains of Tennessee, where he had known Rosa Parks before the Montgomery bus boycott, recruited Septima Clark as a citizenship teacher, and in tandem with Clark conducted weekend retreats that helped convert students like James Bevel into movement leaders. Beginning on Monday, November 11, 1963, Horton presided over a week-long workshop in Greenville, Mississippi, for more than seventy young veterans of the Freedom Vote campaign. Initial topics ranged from the movement's moral responsibility for reprisals to techniques for enlisting barbers and beauticians in a registration campaign. By the weekend, focus shifted to a sparse, three-item agenda: "a. Role of whites b. Summer project c. Federal involvement." Many of those present first learned of the tentative plan to expand the Freedom Vote drastically the following summer, with white college students, up to two thousand of them. The idea loosened a flood of pent-up controversy. Many of the staff—particularly the Negro college students from outside Mississippi, such as Charlie Cobb and Ivanhoe Donaldson, and some of the original state field workers, such as Hollis Watkins and Curtis Hayes—considered the white volunteers more trouble than they were worth, arrogant and yet naive, so clueless about cultural subtleties that they posed a constant danger to themselves and anyone around them.

Past midnight on Friday, as recorded by SNCC adviser and historian Howard Zinn, they debated political necessity against personal reservations, and vice versa. For some, the rub was how much they resented the natural command of arriving white Freedom Workers, for others how much they admired their skills, for still others how much they resented admiring them. "I think one way and act another," said one. "It's not rational." William McGee of Itta Bena supported integrationist whites however flawed as a stunning revelation to the backward areas, "that makes the people from Mississippi understand better." Others replied that using whites as rescuers only reinforced the inner inferiority of Mississippi Negroes.

A straw vote late Friday went against having a summer project for white volunteers at all. On Saturday, Bob Moses arrived late to speak up for Lawrence Guyot and Fannie Lou Hamer on the other side. "If we're trying to break down the barrier of segregation," said Hamer, "we can't segregate ourselves." To the rejoinder that *something* in America ought to be led by Negroes, Moses expressed a tellingly complex hope for the movement, saying he always thought "the one thing we can do for the country that no one else can do is to be above the race issue." Under his sway, a second straw vote went in favor of the summer project, but the issue was deferred in hopes of later consensus, and the exhausted participants joined hands to sing "We Shall Overcome."

Outside pressures prolonged indecision. Moses received summary notice from Wiley Branton that the Voter Education Project was terminating voter registration grants to Mississippi for lack of concrete results. Although the sudden loss of subsistence grants pushed COFO to seek federal assistance, SNCC leaders also perceived signs that the Kennedy administration was turning against intervention in the South, which, if true, undercut the political rationale for the summer project. James Forman, suspecting correctly that Robert Kennedy had an unseen hand in the publication of a sweeping, two-part *Life* magazine article on race by Theodore H. White, assigned a Harvard honors student to analyze the contents at SNCC's Thanksgiving meeting in Washington.

White, whose best-selling *The Making of the President 1960* established a new romance for superpower politics, began his *Life* series with a lurid overview of big-city demographics in an era when "Negroes, bursting out of inhuman, crowded slums, fleeing the smell and the rats and the noise and cackle, like flood waters under pressure, squirt and spill over adjacent neighborhoods." By the 1980s—"almost tomorrow in the eyes of history" —White predicted that seven of America's ten largest cities would have Negro majorities. Given that cities since Jerusalem and ancient Athens had been the cradle of Western civilization, he asked, "what kind of metropolitan civilization will we have?"

In his second installment, White graded civil rights organizations beginning with "thoughtful" mainstays and fringe militants that "find a simple joy in what can be done by mischief." Out beyond "still more sinister groups" such as the Communists, he described the "more serious penetration by unidentified elements made in SNCC—the Student Non-Violent Coordinating Committee." Twice, he asserted, "agents of this group tried to convert a peaceful march into a violent *putsch* on government offices," and SNCC students had created "one of the most chilling documents this writer has seen recently." What White called "violent *putsch*" attempts actually were the Medgar Evers funeral march and the aimless demonstration Diane Nash helped contain in Birmingham. The "chilling document" was the Bevel-Nash right-to-vote blueprint, which was destined to make history from Selma in 1965. Forman's young analyst easily identified factual distortions, but concluded that White's larger purpose was to create a deplorable image of movement students—"lunatics and aliens," the series called them.

New racial images flooded the news media in November, a sure sign of identities in flux. *Jet* reported that high school students in Ohio nearly rioted when a vice principal referred to them as "black" instead of "Negro" students on the intercom. A Chicago professor called for massive reeducation of Southern whites as the necessary remedy. In Virginia, a Baptist convention adopted a resolution commending fellow clergy for "not leading too rapidly or pushing too far beyond the understanding of those who follow." *U.S. News & World Report* published a special section on intermarriage in which one of seven experts identified miscegenation as the "goal of the Negro pressure groups."

From Birmingham, Robert Kennedy's confidant at the *Birmingham News* sent word that the Justice Department's usefulness "has just about been brought to an end anywhere in this state" as a result of the Thelton Henderson scandal. Although Burke Marshall had fired Henderson and publicly apologized to Alabama, editor E. L. "Red" Holland advised, a feeling lingered "on the part of some who are not uninformed that Rev. King is in fact, and has been, used explicitly by Justice as a kind of agent." Holland said the few whites favoring negotiation were reduced to tremulous bravado. "I talked with one of the three most prominent ministers in Birmingham only yesterday," he wrote. "Oh, we will have to show courage—courage, he said. I have kin in his congregation. He has been told that if one Negro is ever allowed to cross the front doorstep, the majority of the monied members will leave and go to Canterbury in Mountain Brook. And they mean it. His courage personally I do not doubt. That it will register, no.... I assume this letter will be destroyed, of course."

PRESIDENT KENNEDY flew south to Florida on November 18. In Miami Beach, wearing a dapper bow tie, he delivered a foreign policy speech criticizing military coups and tyranny in Cuba, blending in language of social justice. "It is impossible to have real progress as long as millions are shut out from opportunity and others forgiven obligations," he told the Inter-American Press Association. "In my own country, we have prepared legislation and mobilized the strength of the Federal Government to insure to American Negroes and all other minorities access to the benefits of American society. Others must also do the same for the landless campesino, the underprivileged slum dweller, the oppressed Indian. Privilege is not easily yielded up...."

Bands, bunting, and cheering crowds marked his motorcade routes past early Christmas decorations, as Kennedy—the first President ever to visit Tampa—sought business support from the Florida Chamber of Commerce. Profits were up, taxes down, and the gross national product had risen from $500 billion to $600 billion in the three Kennedy years, he said, and yet many businessmen feared socialism and bankruptcy, pointing to a national debt ceiling just then raised from $309 billion to $315 billion.

Kennedy defended his $11 billion deficit as an aberration smaller than Eisenhower's 1958 deficit, and pointed out that the postwar federal government had shrunk relative to the states and the total economy. "While the Federal net debt was growing less than 20 percent in these years, total corporate debt—not my debt, *your* debt—was growing by nearly 200 percent, and the total indebtedness of private individuals rose by 300 percent," he said, then flashed a Kennedy smile. "So who is the most cautious fiscal manager? You, gentlemen, or us?"

While pushing on that same day through an airport rally, a speech to steelworkers, a military review, and a campaign address at a baseball park, Kennedy did manage to duck with two Secret Service agents into a holding room for a quiet interval with Father Michael Gannon, the historian-priest who had guided Vice President Johnson through St. Augustine's Catholic mission in March. Gannon made his nervous pitch for a presidential visit in connection with the four hundredth birthday of the Oldest City, surprised that Kennedy's hair had a more reddish tint than he picked up on television. He presented a gift photograph of the oldest surviving European record in the Western Hemisphere—the first page of the St. Augustine Parish Registers, dated 1595—and, encouraged by Kennedy's enlivened interest in its survival, showed the President an assortment of drawings, maps, and models for the Quadricentennial celebration, which would include a giant, two-hundred-foot cross on the site where *adelantado* Menéndez had planted his mission in 1565. President Kennedy promised to keep in touch as he moved off. "What is your name again?" he asked.

ON NOVEMBER 19, Martin Luther King and Rabbi Abraham Heschel appeared together at the annual convention of the United Synagogue of America, in Kiamesha Lake, New York. Since their introduction ten months earlier in Chicago, King had written his letter from the Birmingham jail, delivered hundreds of orations, including his "I Have a Dream" speech and the funeral address in Birmingham, and acquired among the mass of Americans a searing but selective fame. When not making news in a confrontational march, he easily could disappear into the Catskills to nurture private ties, commending the nineteen conservative rabbis who, before the marches of children, had solemnly walked into a Birmingham mass meeting as surprise reinforcements from United Synagogue's spring meeting.

Heschel introduced King to the convention as a prophet, saying, "The prophets' great contribution of humanity was the discovery of the evil of indifference. One may be decent and sinister, pious and sinful." With his salute, Heschel also reminded King of the prophet's burden: "Mere knowledge or belief is too feeble to be a cure of man's hostility to man, man's tendency to fratricide. The only remedy is *personal sacrifice,* to abandon, to eject what seems dear, even plausible, like prejudice, for the sake of a greater truth, to do more than I am ready to understand for the sake of God. Required is a breakthrough, *a leap of action.*"

From Heschel, King accepted the convention's Solomon Schecter Award. "Freedom is not some lavish dish that the federal government will pass out on a silver platter while the Negro merely furnishes the appetite," he said. "If freedom is to be a reality, the Negro must be willing to suffer and to sacrifice and to work for it." In addition to his standard themes, King urged the delegates to rise up against the prevailing wisdom "that we will probably not get a civil rights bill in this session of Congress." They must agitate for passage with reminders "that our nation is in danger of destroying its soul over this very issue." King praised Heschel for following the prophets' example of speaking the harshest truths to the closest kin— in this case for saying that even Jews managed indifference to slow spiritual liquidation under Communism. King added a passage on the plight of Soviet Jews to his address the next day at the annual convention of Reform Jews in Chicago.

On his way there, King stopped over at Idlewild (now John F. Kennedy) Airport in New York to meet Clarence Jones and Stanley Levison about the Birmingham book project. King's planned account of the seminal campaign had been plagued not only by buffeting historical aftershocks— Medgar Evers, the civil rights bill, the March on Washington, the church bombing—but also by the loss of Stanley Levison as his practiced intermediary with ghostwriters, book editors, and business agents. Painfully, Levison had broken off his long association with King that fall. Bowing to the edicts of Hoover and the Kennedys, he had banished himself in order to spare his friend the awful choice between principled resistance and threatened damage to the national movement. ("I'm not going to let Martin make that decision," Levison said.) Since then, unable to tell normal contacts of the spy blackmail, Levison had made awkward excuses—that he had handed the arrangements to Clarence Jones during his vacation, for instance, and was reluctant to take them back for fear of hurting Jones's feelings. Finally, with the book under threat of being scuttled, the wiretaps heard Levison confide uncomfortably to a friend, "You know, I'm, I'm not going to be seeing him [King], but I have to finish off this book thing that was started."

Fully alerted by the installation early in November of the six wiretaps on King himself, FBI agents overheard the advance logistics in time to be posted from the Idlewild gate to the meeting room at the Intercontinental Hotel, on lookout when King met Levison and Clarence Jones. "Notwithstanding trying circumstances, both from a climatic and security standpoint," headquarters later boasted, "our New York agents were able to secure a photograph of the aforementioned three individuals." Oblivious to the substance of King's business, Hoover sent the photograph to Robert Kennedy as vindicating fruit of the King wiretaps—and as potential evidence in a criminal spy trial.

As King headed for Chicago, Heschel flew from Idlewild to Rome for emergency intercession with Cardinal Bea at the Vatican. Word had leaked into the *New York Times* a month earlier of Bea's long-standing consultations with Jewish leaders before November 18, when the Vatican Council formally opened debate on the 399-word schema entitled "The Relation of Catholics to Non-Christians and Especially the Jews." In a jolting departure from the hushed pomp of two thousand church fathers in spectacular raiments, three Patriarchs denounced the schema as a political surrender to Israel, and Ernesto Cardinal Ruffini—Archbishop of Palermo, Sicily, spokesman for the entrenched Vatican bureaucracy—accused Cardinal Bea of heresy, saying the integrity of the faith forbade "giving honorable mention" to Jews. When Bea rose to address the crisis himself the next day, November 19, bishops in St. Peter's Basilica applauded before he spoke a word.

The historic Vatican Council—first since 1870, thirteenth of the millennium—seethed with conspiracy and emotional intrigue by the time Heschel arrived. Mysterious couriers delivered to every delegate a crudely anti-Semitic monograph. Pope Paul VI was rumored—accurately, as it turned out—to be planning a year's postponement of the entire Jewish question, moving to bury public acrimony with a stunning announcement that in January he would become the first Pontiff since the original Apostle Peter to set foot in the Holy Land.

Heschel took action most directly against an amendment that conditioned Bea's entire reform upon the eventual acceptance of Christianity by Jews. "As your Eminence knows," he wrote Bea, "such an implication would deeply hurt the sensitivity of the Jewish people. The enemies of the Church will spare no effort in maintaining that the whole document is intended to bring about the end of the Jewish faith." With this letter, Heschel managed at last to gain a private evening audience with the besieged cardinal. Bea's staff urged Heschel not to panic. The Church would defeat the offending amendment, they predicted, but delay might well be prudent. Bishops from Africa and South Asia, who had almost no exposure to Jews, thought the schema should be perfected as part of a larger statement on non-Christian religions. Cardinal Bea himself counseled patience. "What is put off is not put away," he said.

A bullet interrupted. While escorting Rabbi Heschel back across the Tiber River to his hotel, one of Bea's aides was struck by an inscription in the Piazza Cavour: "The light shining in the darkness." Another fixed upon the eerie hush among even the boisterous young people on the streets of Rome, whose whispers about a faraway murder in Dallas told of changes let loose in the world.

PART TWO

New Worlds Passing

13

Grief

REPORTERS from the press bus banged through the double doors of the Dallas Trade Mart, desperate to know why the motorcade had left them. Finding no clues in the blank stares of the two thousand waiting guests at the presidential fund-raiser, one of them called the New York Hearst office and shouted "Parkland Hospital" in a tone that drove them all back through the banquet hall. The *Herald-Tribune* correspondent bowled over a waiter carrying a tray of vegetable dishes and ran on without a backward glance. One observer retained a surreal perception of fear and awe "moving across that crowd like a wind over a wheatfield." It registered with such clarity that the luncheon companion of Federal District Judge Sarah Hughes cried tears of apprehension even before a rumor of gunshots reached their table.

Outside the hospital, a disembodied radio voice announced, "The President of the United States is dead—I repeat..." just as Tom Wicker of the *New York Times* ran by Lyndon Johnson's limousine convertible, parked askew. Not far away, a hovering cloud of Secret Service agents shoved Johnson at a trot into three unmarked police cars and lurched off for the airport amid clashing orders about how to avoid follow-up assassins. Some agents shouted for more speed through the red lights, others for fewer sirens and motorcycle escorts so as not to attract attention. The Johnsons boarded *Air Force One* just ahead of Judge Hughes, who administered the presidential oath barely two hours after the rifle shots, and the jet roared off for Washington above a carload of reporters giving chase.

Lady Bird Johnson summoned the will to ask gently whether she might help Jacqueline Kennedy change clothes from her pink suit flecked with blood, one glove and one stocking thickly smeared. The new widow declined with a glint of ferocity—"I want them to see what they have done to Jack," she said—then lapsed toward stoic remove. That night from his vice president's office, Johnson exchanged phone calls with world leaders and confidants. "Just ah, think, think, think," he urged Supreme Court Justice Arthur Goldberg, pleading for advice to "unite the country to maintain and preserve our system in the world because I, if it starts falling to pieces . . . why we could deteriorate pretty quick."

Before dawn on Saturday, November 23, President Kennedy's body arrived at the White House from overnight autopsy at the Naval Medical Center, and was placed under military honor guard in the East Room. Sargent Shriver sent home to retrieve a small carved wooden crucifix that a Benedictine priest had given him and his wife, Eunice, Kennedy's sister, as a wedding present. He laid the crucifix at a corner of the casket and placed a portable prie-dieu, or kneeling frame, beneath it on the floor. All was prepared—the corpse's waxen face sealed from view on orders of Robert Kennedy—before the new president and his wife arrived among dignitaries to pay respects in whispered bewilderment.

As Johnson's first business caller that morning, J. Edgar Hoover attempted to correct panicky errors of the previous day, when he had reported the murder weapon as a Winchester and a Secret Service agent among the victims. By now, FBI teams had traced the Mannlicher-Carcano rifle found in the Texas School Book Depository from the manufacturer through a Chicago sporting goods dealer to a mail order buyer under the name A.J. Hidell, whose receiving post office box in Dallas had been rented by Lee H. Oswald, the suspect under custody. Agents were rushing ballistics and fingerprints among a thousand details, but even Hoover confessed perplexity when Johnson asked about intelligence reports that suspect Oswald, a former expatriate to the Soviet Union, had visited the Soviet embassy in Mexico City two months earlier. "That's one angle that's very confusing," Hoover told Johnson.

By one later survey, the average American adult watched ten hours of television news uninterrupted by commercials that Saturday—a pounding, repetitive mix of helpless mystery and bonding drama. That evening, long after former President Eisenhower and the senior members of the Cabinet, economist Walter Heller took his brief turn in the solemn procession of visitors who heard the new president ask their help through the emergency. Johnson also begged patience, saying he was not as quickwitted or sophisticated as his predecessor, but Heller noticed, after he reported how many points the stock market had dropped on assassination day, that Johnson calculated the loss at 3 percent before he could. Heller informed Johnson that he had given President Kennedy a status report about the economy only four days earlier on November 19. He omitted anecdotal details that would be maudlin during the wake—how toddler John Kennedy, Jr., had forced Heller and the stiff National Security Adviser McGeorge Bundy to eat imaginary slices of cherry-vanilla pie off his plastic tea set, serving so many that Heller said, "I have to talk to your daddy first," and how Kennedy had pilloried bankers with a rakish term that the reserved Heller euphemistically recorded as "his favorite expression."

For Heller, who chaired the new Council of Economic Advisers, it was a risky, impulsive leap even to mention his esoteric poverty workshops on an occasion that cried out for brief solace. Since spring, when President Kennedy had proposed his controversial plan to lower tax rates, Heller's economists had pushed for a poverty initiative to offset the tax cut, whose benefits would flow disproportionately to wealthy citizens. And since June, when Kennedy had introduced his civil rights legislation, the economists had recommended a different balance based on the prevailing image of poor people as white hillbillies and migrant workers. "Having mounted a dramatic program for one disadvantaged group [the Negroes]," Heller told President Kennedy, it seemed "both equitable and politically attractive" to offer a program "specifically designed to aid other disadvantaged groups." To Johnson, Heller acknowledged that Kennedy had qualified his interest in poverty with an instruction to "make sure that we're doing something* for the middle-income man in the suburbs," and he only slightly exaggerated his presidential mandate to keep formulating an "attack on poverty."

This was more than enough for Johnson. "That's my kind of program," he said with enthusiasm. Heller had been processing the unfinished program under sleepy trial titles such as "Human Conservation and Development," but now Johnson said to "push ahead full-tilt." The President often recalled that as a young teacher in 1928 he had watched hungry Mexican children chew discarded grapefruit rinds behind his schoolhouse at Cotulla, Texas† —that their poverty had gnawed at him more than his own, and that his proudest moment as a young congressman was in 1939, when his dam project and his federal cooperative had lit up 90 percent of the farms in the Texas Hill Country with their first electricity for water pumps and radios and washing machines, lifting aeons of toil from hardscrabble people. That was the purpose of government, he told Heller. To make his point physically, as was his habit, Johnson forcefully shut the door

---

* Earlier in November, unbeknownst to Heller, strategists for the 1964 campaign had warned President Kennedy that a commitment against poverty would gain him no votes among poor people, who were for him already, and that the election would be decided in the new suburbs.

† "[The children] never seemed to know why people disliked them," Johnson would declare in his voting rights speech of March 1965. "...Somehow you never forget what poverty and hatred can do when you see its scars on the hopeful face of a young child."

that Heller had opened to leave, then grabbed the arm of the nonplussed economist to announce up close that he was a Roosevelt New Dealer at heart.

The next morning, Sunday, November 24, as Blackjack the riderless funeral horse escorted the casket to public viewing in the Capitol Rotunda, Johnson attended services at St. Mark's Episcopal Church nearby on Capitol Hill. The Rev. Bill Baxter urged his congregation not to forget that the shock of the assassination had dissolved the callous, selfish divisions of ordinary life, revealing them as insignificant against the shared bonds beneath. Visibly moved, Johnson covered his face with his handkerchief during the hymn "America the Beautiful." Afterward, he walked spontaneously into the parish hall to shake hands, seeming to find relief in the contact. His Secret Service detail, already agitated by this first public outing since Dallas, roughly challenged more than a few churchgoers and practically dragged Johnson into his car minutes before a voice cried out on the street: "Jesus Christ, they've shot Oswald." Millions of NBC viewers had just witnessed the first murder ever broadcast on live television.

Ambassador Henry Cabot Lodge, who had flown back from Vietnam to meet with President Kennedy, met instead with Johnson and his top foreign policy leaders three hours after church. He began by flatly denying that the United States had been involved in the coup three weeks earlier against President Diem, but his evident satisfaction indicated otherwise. Pointing to photographs of joyful crowds in Saigon, Lodge described the coup as a success that promised a favorable settlement with North Vietnam. He said his mission was pushing on all fronts—military, diplomatic, even religious—with Lodge now bound for Rome to reassure Pope Paul VI that the United States understood the political risk of losing the Catholic president Diem in Buddhist Vietnam, and was fully alive to "dangers of an anti-Christian move." In recounting the coup, Lodge offered a veiled reference to the phone call in which Diem first asked urgently about the U.S. knowledge of and response to the military revolt, and reported his crisp reply that Diem should leave his country in prompt surrender. "Lodge said that we were in no way responsible for the death of Diem and [his brother] Nhu," CIA Director John McCone recorded in his minutes, "that had they followed his advice, they would be alive today."

While Defense Secretary McNamara, among others, objected that Lodge was overly optimistic about Vietnam, Johnson was merely formal and cool toward Lodge. The ambassador's boastful report did nothing to relieve his misgivings about the murder of Diem—a man he had praised in 1961 as "the Churchill of Asia," whose portrait hung on a wall of the Johnson home. To confidants, Johnson soon confessed a vague fear that the Kennedy assassination was retribution for American plotting against Diem. "We had a hand in killing him," he remarked to Senator Hubert Humphrey. "Now it's happening here." Nor did Lodge improve the phantom chill that swirled through Johnson's early spy reports on Oswald, the Russians, and Cuba. Although Lodge did not work for the CIA, Johnson associated him with an unfavorable image of CIA officials as mediocre dissemblers from overbred patrician families. ("Whenever those rich people have a son they can't trust with the family brokerage," Johnson once grumbled, "they ship him down to the CIA.") Still, at his first foreign policy meeting, Johnson only hinted at his suspicions. A lot of people were upset about the overthrow of Diem, he told the assembled advisers, but nothing could be done about it now. He instructed Lodge to eliminate the meddlesome backbiting and hidden agendas within the American mission. With that, photographers were admitted and a bland press statement was distributed to the effect that Johnson was adopting the Kennedy course in Vietnam.

Within an hour of President Kennedy's burial on Monday, as television networks returned to afternoon soap operas after three days and nights of stupefying news, Johnson called Kennedy's chief congressional lobbyist, Larry O'Brien, and said, "I need you a lot more than he did." It was an awkward moment for O'Brien, who replied that another time might be better because he was grieving with Kennedy's chief of staff, Kenneth O'Donnell, an Irish politician who had been close to the slain president and remained undone. Johnson disregarded the plea for privacy and said he needed O'Donnell, too, and that he admired the whole staff. "I don't expect you to love me as much as you did him," he told O'Brien, "but I expect you will after we've been around awhile." When O'Brien responded, "Right, Mr. President," Johnson pressed forward with questions about upcoming votes in the Senate.

By the end of a long working day, Johnson had rearranged billions in the upcoming budget and reversed Kennedy's intention to push the civil rights bill to a vote before the tax bill. His late evening phone calls included one of thanks to Martin Luther King for public statements urging calm. King managed to squeeze in a few encouraging words that the new law would be "one of the greatest tributes" to Kennedy's memory, and the two virtual strangers spoke with a glancing intimacy common to the crisis. (King: "Regards to the family." Johnson: "Thank you so much, Martin.") Still later that night, Johnson complained to Kennedy's chief speechwriter, Theodore Sorensen, about the crush of ceremonial duty—"all these ambassadors . . . I bet I saw twenty of them this afternoon . . . I mean heads of state, [French President Charles] de Gaulle and [Canadian Prime Minister Lester] Pearson and all this crowd . . . then they're running fifteen more on me tomorrow. . . ." Johnson tried to tell Sorensen gently that he planned to use other drafts than Sorensen's for his first major speech. "Well, anyway, you liked Galbraith," Sorensen said glumly, referring to a draft that Johnson had solicited from Harvard economist John Kenneth Galbraith. All the next day and night, Johnson snatched time to sift phrases from contributors ranging from U.N. Ambassador Adlai Stevenson to his former Senate aide from Texas, Horace "Buzz" Busby, author of his Gettysburg speech.

On Wednesday, the day before Thanksgiving, Johnson delivered to a joint session of Congress an address that won acclaim as a nearly perfect first step to lead the nation out of its stupor. A *New York Times* critic noted the reassuring thread of Kennedy themes and even some trademark rhetorical devices such as the parallel inversion of phrases, as in Johnson's "We will demonstrate anew that the strong can be just and the just can be strong." Still, the emotional core of the speech would have been too earnestly moral for Kennedy's taste. Johnson urged the country "not to turn about and linger over this evil moment." He expressly joined the unknowable motive for the murder with the knowable hatreds of race, and drew from them jointly the healing, historical purpose of passing the civil rights bill. "We have talked long enough in this country about equal rights," he said. "We have talked for a hundred years or more." An audience conditioned for shock by the nightmare weekend embraced his colloquial, earthy style—his slow Texas twang and Southernisms ("... as I did in 19 and 57 and again in 19 and 60 ..."), his unabashed recital of "America the Beautiful," and sentimental gestures such as placing Zephyr Wright, the Johnson family cook, prominently in the House gallery. ("Heavens to Betsy," she told reporters, "I don't give my age out.") Many tearful members of Congress interrupted him with applause—thirty-four times, by Johnson's count—most heartily when he denounced "hate and evil and violence" and, near the end, when he echoed Lincoln at Gettysburg: "So let us here highly resolve that John Fitzgerald Kennedy did not live—or die—in vain."

"As soon as Lyndon Johnson finished his speech before Congress, twenty million of us unpacked," quipped comedian Dick Gregory, who, after submitting to the breakthrough year's jail campaigns in Greenwood, Birmingham, Chicago, and Selma, expressed relief that Negroes did not see Lyndon Johnson emerge in the White House as a cowhide segregationist. From North Carolina, Professor Al Lowenstein scribbled one of several thousand viewer responses. "Like everyone else I was shattered by the bullet," he wrote Johnson. "Your speech to Congress today started the long pull back together, for me and countless others...." As was his habit, Lowenstein wrote on whatever scrap was at hand—in this case on stationery from the Castellana Hilton in Madrid, Spain, a souvenir of his quixotic campaign against the Franco dictatorship.

In Washington, movement workers arrived by bus and caravan at Howard University for a Thanksgiving SNCC conference. Two U.S. representatives of Lowenstein's acquaintance had agreed to sponsor a public forum on the political meaning of the Mississippi mock election earlier that month, but the assassination wiped out the planned agenda. To a crowd of onlookers and movement veterans, a nervous volunteer delivered his assigned press analysis of the current *Life* series, saying it painted SNCC students as putschists and troublemakers worse than Communists. A proposal to march to the fresh Kennedy grave site for a vigil of respect was voted down as hypocritical given the movement's estrangement from the federal government.

Bob Moses quietly told the conference that the white people of the country had not yet grasped or decided the deeper questions of freedom, that beneath the national swoon of remorse over Kennedy and violence there remained a hard shell of disbelief about the blanket repression of voting rights in the Deep South and what it portended for racial politics elsewhere. The hotly debated summer project was designed as a tactic to force that awareness upon the country. Meanwhile, he said, movement volunteers remained shock troops struggling every day in every town with "the problem of overcoming fear." Small delegations of volunteers fanned out to labor unions and government offices in the capital, seeking ears for their message, while those at Howard aroused movement spirit through marathon freedom songs. Fannie Lou Hamer, the lifelong sharecropper who had discovered an immense voice since her jail beating in Winona, took the lead in "Go, Tell It on the Mountain." Over rhythmic hand-clapping, Willie Peacock of Greenwood alternated between storytelling exhortation and improvised verses for the slave spiritual "Wade in the Water": "Well, if you don't believe that I've been to hell/just follow me down to the county jail/Wade in the water. . . ."

Toward the end of the conference, the Rev. Robert Stone of New York approached Moses to ask whether the organized clergy might help combat the fear in Mississippi. Stone, a Union Seminary graduate and Freedom Rider, had joined the new Presbyterian Commission on Religion and Race in October—his most vivid memory since was crawling on hands and knees in search of stray shards of stained glass outside Sixteenth Street Baptist Church. Moses told Stone that never in history had Mississippi authorities tolerated a voting rights picket line, and perhaps the prestige of the Northern clergy might help break that barrier. Seeing no chance yet in the Delta, Moses sent Stone to the new SNCC project manager in Hattiesburg, Lawrence Guyot.

From the other side of the vast political chasm, White House officials looked also to the church as a catalyst on civil rights. Over the Thanksgiving weekend, Lawrence O'Brien wrote President Johnson that the civil rights bill would never even reach the House floor for a vote unless they could break the months-long stranglehold of the House Rules Committee. To do that, Republican votes must be marshaled for one of two rare parliamentary maneuvers—a discharge petition signed by a majority of the entire House, or a politically sensitive committee revolt against the segregationist Rules Committee chairman, Rep. Howard Smith of Virginia.

To succeed either way required an effective channel to reach opposition Republicans, many of whom represented nearly all-white districts in the Midwest and Plains states, where the problems of segregation were unfamiliar. "The Negro groups as such don't have the broad spread strength to get this done," O'Brien wrote Johnson as he prepared for a meeting with the NAACP's Roy Wilkins, "but Wilkins should be urged to press the religious leaders...."

President Johnson was practicing his own parallel lobbying strategy on selected callers. "Say to the Republicans, 'You're either for civil rights or your not, you're either the party of Lincoln or you ain't,'" he exhorted. He hoped to dislodge the bill from committee with public arguments that Republicans of conscience must vote at least for consideration by the full House. "I believe that we can dramatize it enough that we can wreck them," he told Rep. Richard Bolling. "God almighty," he said of the obstructionists, "I don't see how California and Chicago can stand up against civil rights."

While laying the groundwork, Johnson maneuvered to contain the seepage of public trust since Dallas. With J. Edgar Hoover, he pretended to be against calls for a national commission of inquiry, which he said "would be very bad and put [the controversy] right in the White House." Such a commission would be a "regular circus," Hoover agreed,* but Johnson carefully told congressional leaders that Hoover's true goal was to head off any independent review of the FBI investigation. Among dozens of orchestrated calls on the Friday after Thanksgiving, Johnson warned Senator Richard Russell of Georgia about the likelihood of multiple, runaway investigations. He hinted to Russell that assassination hearings in the House would be disorderly, unproductive, and careless with legitimate national secrets, and that the state murder investigations in Texas would only exacerbate sectional mistrust, especially since Oswald had been killed while in Texas custody. As he approached his purpose, Johnson ladled compliments over his former mentor in the Senate, going so far as to say that "the country would be in a hell of a lot better shape" if Russell were president instead. Russell scoffed, "I'll be dead in another two or three years," and Johnson, in sounding out names for the proposed relief of a single national commission, passed breezily over the various Justices of the Supreme Court as unlikely to serve. He asked Russell what judge might be appropriate "if I didn't get the Chief."

Five hours later, Johnson called Russell again with a statement naming the members of the assassination commission, reading them swiftly.

---

* When Johnson asked Hoover to help him resist the *Washington Post*'s press campaign for a commission, Hoover begged off, saying, "I don't have much influence with the *Post,* because I frankly don't read it. I view it like the *Daily Worker."* Johnson, who was much friendlier with the *Post*'s leadership than he was with Hoover, dryly replied, "You told me that once before," and signed off.

The old senator fairly howled when he heard his own name just after that of Chief Justice Earl Warren. "I couldn't serve on it with Chief Justice Warren," he gasped. "I don't like that man. I don't have any confidence in him." Johnson roared right back, dismissing the courtly Southerner's contempt for the architect of the *Brown* decision. Racial feelings were trivial compared with assassination rumors that involved Castro and Khrushchev and might spill into what Johnson called "a war that could kill forty million Americans in an hour." "You're my man on that commission, and you're going to do it, and don't tell me what you can do and what you can't," he shouted. "Because I can't arrest you, and I'm not going to put the FBI on you, but you're goddammed sure going to serve, I'll tell you that, and [mutual friend Judge] A. W. Moursund is here and he wants to tell you how much all of us love you."

Johnson soon took the phone again to swear that he had cleared these names with Russell in the earlier call. "You did not," Russell complained. "...Mr. President, please now." Johnson told him it was too late anyway: "I gave the announcement. It is already in the papers...." For the next half hour, he dragged Russell along a swerving roller coaster of tweaks ("I'm not afraid to put your intelligence up against Warren's"), blandishments ("Well, of course you don't like Warren, but you will before this is over with"), bluster ("Well, you're damned sure going to be at my command!"), and endearments so nakedly primal ("Nobody ever has been more to me than you have, Dick, except my mother.... I haven't got any daddy, and you're going to be it...") that even the fuming Russell laughed helplessly.

Having employed a similar bombardment, in person, to bowl over Chief Justice Warren's initial refusal to serve, Johnson mollified FBI Director Hoover with a steady application of flattery. His deferential questions stimulated Hoover's clipped, authoritative updates on the investigations, which invariably led to diversions of personal animus. Hoover insistently referred to the shady nightclub owner who killed Oswald, Jack Ruby, as "Rubenstein," for instance, and denounced Ruby's defense counsel, Melvin Belli, as "a West Coast lawyer somewhat like the Edward Bennett Williams* type and almost as much of a shyster." In discussing security improvements, Johnson asked if it were true that Hoover had a bulletproof limousine, and Hoover proudly replied that he had four of them, including one stored in California for his horseracing vacations. He recommended that President Johnson acquire half that many armored cars himself—one for the White House and one for his Texas ranch.

Hoover did not challenge the President's assertion that an independent inquiry was the only way to prevent wildcat investigations, but he

---

* A Washington defense lawyer, Williams had earned prominence—and Hoover's lasting enmity—in large part by pioneering tactics designed to fight prosecutions through forced disclosure of politically sensitive government conduct, such as illegal wiretaps.

took it as a personal affront that the FBI's conclusions would not suffice. He described the Warren Commission to his staff as "the proposed group they are trying to get to study my report," and as insurance against the unwelcome scrutiny he ordered headquarters to stockpile all information —no matter how far-fetched—that might deflect blame back into the White House. "In Florida and on Cape Cod, Mr. Kennedy often jumped behind the wheel of an automobile and drove off," an assistant director reported in a list of security defects. "He has been characterized by the Secret Service as a notoriously poor driver who drove through red lights and took many unnecessary chances."

IN ATLANTA, Martin Luther King preached on Thanksgiving morning to his own congregation at Ebenezer Baptist. To Paul Good, an ABC television reporter who stopped by out of curiosity to witness his first Negro church service, the opening of the sermon was formal, even pedantic, and King's passing reference to the cataclysm of the assassination seemed devoid of warmth or comfort. Making no effort to address the grief that saturated nearly all conversation, King astonished Good by preaching instead on slavery.

King had identified with Kennedy as a leader—studied his skills in public speaking, assumed the code name "JFK" in Birmingham, and consistently tried to understand the political pressures pushing Kennedy away from the movement. Moreover, King long since had braced himself for the martyr's fate that had come so unexpectedly to Kennedy, and friends still weighed his risks by direct comparison. "If they hated him, you know they love you less," warned his mentor, Benjamin Mays, president of Morehouse College. King associated with Kennedy so strongly, in fact, that he was wounded when the Kennedy family had not invited him to the funeral mass. On his own initiative, King had stood unattended and unnoticed among the sidewalk crowds that watched the cortege pass by.

Adding to his sense of invisible companionship, King was suffering through a bad phase of his contentious relationship with Robert Kennedy. In a particularly galling outgrowth of the 1962 campaign in Albany, Georgia, federal prosecutors who had ignored pleas to punish or prevent flagrant violence against local movement leaders managed instead to indict nine of those leaders on federal conspiracy charges. Recently, King had gone to the extreme of personally asking the Justice Department to review the indictments, only to have Deputy Attorney General Nicholas Katzenbach turn him down, and a post-assassination letter from the Attorney General defended as racially impartial the prosecution of people King considered heroes. "I trust that the within information will satisfy your concern," Robert Kennedy advised.

At Ebenezer, concealed disappointment canceled tribute so thoroughly that King did not mention the new president or the impact of the assassination on civil rights. Good, who was passing through Atlanta from emergency assignments in Dallas, was marking King off as a hollow speaker when the sermon moved from a slow introductory cadence through a biblical text from Kings about the wisdom of seeing beyond tribulation. "Is it well?" King intoned, quoting a barren woman's exchange with the prophet Elijah. "No, it is not too well, but thank God it is as well as it is." To summon up the chronic travail of what he called "midnight in human relations," King looked swiftly past "the events of last week," then back beyond the Birmingham church bombing and the murder of Medgar Evers to common ground between the Bible and the experience of Africans in America. Good recorded his surprise that King could use such an occasion to dwell on bondage, "a dead historical issue for me," and yet he felt King's sermon "gathering emotional momentum with remembrance of slavery."

"And let nobody fool you," King declared. "They try to romanticize slavery with all the magnolia trees and what have you." The congregation laughed. By now King was preaching at a trot, with his companion Ralph Abernathy among those urging him on in rhythmic response. "Slavery was a low, dirty, evil thing," said King. (Yes) "Men and women chained to ships like beasts. It is a terrible thing to uproot someone from their family, land, and culture." (True) "They knew the rawhide whip of the overseer. Sizzling heat. Long rows of cotton." (Preach on) "They had their songs to give them consolation, because they knew how dark it was." King recited the titles and familiar lyrics of several slave spirituals, evoking the grind of previous centuries before abruptly yanking the congregation into the present. "We've broken loose from the Egypt of slavery!" he cried.

They were moving, said King, commencing a series of illustrations that fused their experience with those of the biblical prophets. "Caleb and Joshua have come back with a minority report," he said. "They are saying we *can* possess the land." (True) "Thank God, it is as well as it is." (Come on now) "Atlanta is a better city today than it was three years ago." King roamed in words over mountaintops toward the promised land: "We can say, 'God of our weary years/God of our silent tears/Thou who hast brought us thus far on the way....'" In a cry of full possession, he recited the entire final stanza of James Weldon Johnson's hymn of Negro pilgrimage. The congregation recited along with him, and the Kennedy assassination was not so much missing from King's sermon as swallowed up already within a cultural heritage unbroken from slavery. Although much of the service was utterly foreign to him, Good responded to a universal comfort beneath the novelty, to a leveling passion that made an ancient companion of mortal suffering and milked hope from the blues. Almost immediately, Good resolved to ask ABC to transfer him to the South from his current base in Mexico City, becoming neither the first nor last visitor so swiftly redirected by exposure to a mass meeting.

□

AT A THANKSGIVING RALLY in Queens, New York, Malcolm X endorsed a shopping boycott against merchants along Jamaica Avenue who refused to hire Negroes. His appeal violated Elijah Muhammad's ban against secular activism in the white world, but such a tiny, old-fashioned rebellion was lost among larger confrontations in the South. Similarly, when Malcolm first repeated statements that the slain President Kennedy had been no better than a "prison warden" to American black people—a "fox" distinguishable from the hateful "wolf" George Wallace only by his wily smile —the usual "white devil" doctrines failed to register upon the traumatized outside world. Malcolm remained sealed within the Nation's sectarian isolation. From Chicago, Elijah Muhammad sent out written orders forbidding all his ministers to make public comments on the Kennedy assassination, and on Sunday, December 1, he pointedly reminded Malcolm of the restriction before an afternoon rally. Doubly warned, Malcolm for the first time wrote out in advance the text of an entire speech, entitled "God's Judgment on White America," which he read verbatim from the podium at the Manhattan Center. He accused President Kennedy of cowardice and all manner of devilment, as usual, but conditioned submission stopped him just short of the trigger words until someone in the audience asked explicitly about the assassination.

Malcolm—remarking out loud that reporters were baiting him for an expression of glee, knowing also that National Secretary John Ali, one of his chief antagonists, was there from Chicago to witness any disobedience—stepped consciously over the precipice. He described the Kennedy murder as a case of "the chickens coming home to roost." White Americans had spread stealthy, controlling force against darker peoples at home and abroad, he said, citing Patrice Lumumba of the Congo and Diem of Vietnam among foreign leaders victimized by official American intrigue. These were the chickens that had come home to make the wife of an American head of state a widow, he said, and when the crowd of nearly seven hundred whistled and howled—amazed above all, said one delighted observer, that Malcolm "had the nerve to say it," true or not—he pushed rebellion a notch higher by adding that as an old farm boy himself, "chickens coming home to roost never did make me sad, they've always made me glad."

The next morning's *New York Times* recognized Malcolm X as a fresh threat in American race relations. Mike Handler, the night editor who had made a hobby of observing Malcolm, got an unsigned article into the paper as a full-fledged news story, and the *Times* promptly assigned one of its frontline reporters to replace Handler for a follow-up story about Malcolm and the "speech in which he mocked the assassination of President Kennedy." Malcolm was fully prepared to defend himself before a broad population of shocked, hostile readers—not only whites newly introduced to him and the Nation but to the majority of Negroes who followed the mainstream white news. Even without knowing of President Johnson's private remorse over Diem, or his fears of plots by and against Castro of Cuba, Malcolm argued from history that the "climate of hatred" so widely blamed for the assassination was anything but marginal to American society. This was the gauntlet of an aspiring prophet—telling a nation that a revered leader had been struck down by righteous punishment instead of villainy, choosing words that might sink in like those of the biblical prophets Nathan, Amos, and Jeremiah, before the speaker was stoned to death.

On the day after the New York speech, Elijah Muhammad summoned Malcolm to Chicago under escort by John Ali and imposed a discipline of public silence. Shrewdly, Muhammad also instructed his officials to announce the punishment in telegrams to all the news outlets that had reported Malcolm's scandalous comments. As a result, Malcolm was flooded with press inquiries when he returned to New York. Having counted on the Nation's cloistered removal from the white world to give him space on the flank of the civil rights movement, Malcolm discovered instead that Muhammad had used his notoriety in the white press to undercut him.

Shaken, Malcolm X called Muhammad at his winter home in Phoenix to ask whether the Messenger really intended for all these news organizations to know of the Nation's internal business. Muhammad said he did, whereupon Malcolm asked whether the terms of his punishment permitted him to answer demands for a response to the press. Muhammad authorized him to say only that he submitted, no more. He forced Malcolm to choose between his Muslim identity and his ambition to move out into the larger world. Stranded, Malcolm submitted, and Muhammad soothed him with his approval. "I think it is good for the whole entire community," he said, meaning that Muslim converts would take strength from the humble example of the famous disciple who for so long had drummed into them acceptance of Muhammad's semidivine will as the requirement of miraculous rebirth. Malcolm replied that the punishment had helped him already.

Public dispute over the chicken speech marked the debut of a Muslim presence in American politics. After nearly thirty-five years' gestation among urban refugees, the Nation of Islam attracted national attention through Malcolm's piercing oratory, with Elijah Muhammad in counterpoint as an exotic, wizened old man of pale Asiatic complexion beneath an embroidered fez, seeming to defend President Kennedy. "The nation still mourns the loss of our President," Muhammad declared in his public statement on Malcolm's suspension, and he placed a commemorative photograph of President Kennedy on the cover of the next *Muhammad Speaks*. To reporters who asked whether he was softening his former teaching that all whites were devils, especially presidents, Muhammad said Kennedy deserved respect as head of a sovereign nation. When an editor from Los Angeles asked why he had decreed no punishment for Malcolm's earlier statement welcoming the plane crash that killed white Georgians after the Stokes riot, Muhammad replied that "my work is in accordance with God's plan." To CORE's James Farmer, who promised to tell President Johnson that most Negroes welcomed Muhammad's rebuke of Malcolm, Muhammad minimized the action as "just a little spanking." His enigmatic answers underscored his claim to arbitrary authority. The *New York Times* referred to him as "the ruler" of the Black Muslims, the popular term for the Nation of Islam.

Rumors of an impending split within the Nation surfaced almost immediately, but they suggested to most readers that the universal grip of the Kennedy tragedy had put even this bizarre anti-white group into leadership quarrels. Few within the Nation itself suspected that the sect was nearing fission. As soon as Malcolm submitted, Elijah Muhammad privately extended the speaking ban from public events to closed Muslim services, including those at Malcolm's base in Harlem. He also dispatched letters to Captain Joseph and several key "laborers" in New York, detailing exactly how he wanted Temple No. 7 to be run during Malcolm's suspension; they were to block him physically if he tried to address his congregation. Muhammad's ambush deprived Malcolm of administrative retreat into Harlem as well as his free public voice—all under cloak of Muslim orthodoxy—and a panicked Malcolm tested a defense in kind. From the Q'uran's accounts of Noah and King David of Israel, among others, he fashioned parables about how a prophet's concubines should be justified as wives and his bastard offspring raised above worldly scandal to fulfillment of purpose. On Saturday, December 7, he secured Elijah Muhammad's permission to bring specific substitute ministers to teach in his place at Temple No. 7—beginning with Minister Louis X of Boston and Minister Lonnie X Cross of Washington. On the surface, Malcolm presented his parables to them as a vigilantly orthodox precaution against rumors about Muhammad, the better to defend him, but in reality he was sounding out allies for a counterattack.

THAT SAME SATURDAY in Washington, Lyndon Johnson held his first news conference. While acknowledging that he had not yet slept in the White House, as Jacqueline Kennedy and her children were just then vacating the living quarters, he described the job as old. "I feel like I have already been here a year," he remarked somberly of his two weeks in office. Beyond conveying a sense of calm, Johnson stressed a theme of frugality, announcing that Secretary of Defense McNamara had pledged to eliminate 25,000 civilian jobs at the Pentagon, then reciting in detail his efforts to submit in January a federal budget of less than $100 billion. Sound-money Senate conservatives had extracted that limit from him, refusing to accept the Kennedy tax reduction without spending cuts to keep the budget in balance, but Johnson soon would add his own economizing by prowling the White House at night, dousing unnecessary lights. "I don't want to waste a dime," he told the reporters. ("I've never agreed," he privately told economist Walter Heller, "that you had to prove you're liberal by showin' how much money you could throw away.... I'm a kind of a Harold Ickes liberal.")

Immediately after the press conference, Johnson and Senator Russell of Georgia resumed their quarrelsome banter by telephone. "You destroyed me," Russell complained, "putting me on this [Warren] commission."

"You told me at least a hundred times that you were ruined," scoffed Johnson.

"No, this is the first time," Russell insisted.

He was calling, Johnson confided, because American military missions were "short of ammunition" both in Vietnam and Korea. To fix that, he wanted to route the supplies through the Pentagon budget, which Russell controlled in the Senate, rather than through the controversial foreign aid package. Russell bowed to patriotic duty. "I tried my best to keep them from going into Laos and Vietnam," he said, recalling their emergency trip together as congressional leaders to the "last meeting we had under Eisenhower before we went in" to replace the crumbling French army in 1954. "Said we'd never get out," Russell reminded Johnson. "Be there fifty years from now."

Johnson steered Russell back to current military decisions, then invited his old friend to "come and sit in the warm water" of the White House pool. He ignored Russell's objections ("I've got this shortwinded business, I can't breathe"), sent a presidential car to fetch him from the Senate, and, by impulse or design, cut short the pleasantries to give notice of his determination on the civil rights bill. "I'm not going to cavil and I'm not going to compromise," he told Russell, almost nose-to-nose. "I'm going to pass it just as it is, Dick, and if you get in my way I'm going to run you down. I just want you to know that, because I care about you."

Russell returned fair notice. "Mr. President, you may be right," he said. "But if you do run over me, it will not only cost you the South, it will cost you the election." He warned that the Democratic party never had, and never would, win national elections if it split openly with the South on the race issue. Having staked their ground, the two men returned quickly to more congenial subjects in the White House pool, paddling naked.

Through December, Johnson revived and redefined other political associations that stretched back to his first days in Washington in the 1930s. He made peace with James Rowe, a former clerk to Justice Oliver Wendell Holmes who as a White House aide had facilitated young Congressman Johnson's early appointments with President Franklin Roosevelt. Johnson and Lady Bird had made some lasting friendships with prominent young couples of the New Deal—Rowe's wife, Libby, still called Johnson "Uncle Lyndon" for kindnesses to her daughter—but more than a few bumps dotted the tumultuous decades since. In March of 1949, Rowe had objected to the overt racialism of Johnson's maiden speech to the U.S. Senate—a "we of the South . . . we cannot legislate love" defense of the filibuster rules—and they had argued again in 1954, when Rowe, despite his partisan distaste for Secretary of State John Foster Dulles, sent Johnson an apocalyptic letter warning that if he and Senator Russell did not allow the Republicans to stop Communism in Indochina, "there won't be any Senate, and what is vastly more important to me, there won't be any little Rowes either." They had patched that up, too, but in 1960 Rowe kept pushing candidate Johnson to display more of the broad passion that had made him a favorite of the New Dealers—to become more than a strictly Southern balance for the Kennedy ticket—and Johnson raged in such towering insecurity that Rowe finally denounced him to his face as a "Mogul emperor." They maintained an angry silence for three years before Johnson summoned Rowe to the Oval Office, where each insisted that the silly feud was his own fault until Johnson pulled rank, saying, "Damn it, can't you be content to be the first man the thirty-sixth President of the United States has apologized to?"

While Rowe was a useful contact, having matured into a powerfully connected Washington lawyer, Johnson also reached out to New Dealers whose enduring activism made them politically marginal, even dangerous. He invited to the White House Arthur "Tex" Goldschmidt, who had moved his poverty work from FDR's Interior Department, where he and Abe Fortas had helped Johnson electrify the Texas Hill Country, to the United Nations, where he worked on international plans to develop Vietnam's Mekong River Delta. Johnson also called his hero and New Deal boss from 1935–37, Aubrey Williams, head of FDR's National Youth Administration, but he did not extend a White House invitation. Williams was a political casualty of the race issue. Since the Senate had rejected his nomination by Roosevelt to head the Rural Electrification Administration, largely because he paid racially equal wages for NYA youth jobs, Williams had associated openly with Negroes, refusing to mask himself with guile or hypocrisy. A segregationist boycott destroyed the *Southern Farmer,* a newspaper he owned in Alabama, after which Williams maintained a threadbare retirement, occasionally offering to post bond money for arrested Negro demonstrators. Shortly before the Kennedy assassination, a raiding party of Louisiana police had confiscated records of the Southern Conference Education Fund (SCEF), claiming that Williams and the other integrationists who ran it—among them Fred Shuttlesworth and Myles Horton of the Highlander Center—were tools of Communism. Even as president of the United States, Johnson could not rescue his former chief from persecution, but he could say he was sorry to learn that Williams was in failing health, and reminisce about the energy of their old NYA motto —"Put them to work!"

IN CONTRAST with President Johnson, Martin Luther King faced a variety of torments for the slightest acquaintance with Aubrey Williams. Soon after King protested the Louisiana raid to Attorney General Kennedy as an illegal "continuation of effort to intimidate and harass civil rights organizations," the Louisiana Committee on Un-American Activities began to disseminate samples from the truckload of records seized. As usual, neither directives from Moscow nor Communist confessions were found, but gossipy criticisms within the civil rights movement did sow dissension among King's own supporters. When a batch of purloined letters reached Clarence Jones in New York, he recommended that King "sever any and all relationships, if any exist, with Aubrey Williams," so offended was Jones to read the white liberals complaining privately among themselves that King was pompous, indecisive, and perpetually late. ("King is playing a crafty game," Williams had written in 1960, criticizing King's reluctance to break with the NAACP in support of the early sit-ins.)

Unlike Jones, who admitted to King "a shortcoming in my character that I do not possess a larger degree of love and forgiveness," King defended Williams against smears and petty resentments. "Now interestingly enough," King told a graduate student who interviewed him at his home, "in the picture that they have of me at Highlander, I'm sitting next to Aubrey Williams, whose only crime is that he's a white man from Alabama saying Negroes ought to have a square deal." King referred to the photograph of himself at Highlander's twenty-fifth anniversary celebration in 1957, which had become infamous—popping up on highway billboards labeled "King at Communist Training School"—since Governors Ross Barnett and George Wallace had displayed blown-up reproductions as the central exhibit of their congressional testimony that the civil rights bill was the pawn of an alien conspiracy.

"Yeah, yeah, that's right," King told the graduate student, "That's Aubrey.... This has been used over and over again." King described the pitfalls of trying to answer emotionally loaded propaganda about Highlander. "I haven't done anything but give a speech there," he said, "but the minute I go to arguing about I wasn't 'trained' there, it looks like I'm trying to say there's something wrong with the school." The state of Tennessee had destroyed Highlander because it "brought Negroes and whites together in a way they would have never been brought together ... they live together," King said, adding that from fearful hysteria about integration, Highlander "suffered what many white liberals suffer in the South, the Communist tag ... SCEF has suffered the same thing."

It came as a surprise to King that President Johnson never mentioned the Communist issue at their meeting early in December, not even as a hazard of domestic politics. The omission was a stark contrast with President Kennedy's exclusive preoccupation at King's White House meeting in June—and more than a welcome relief from the vulgar Nazi signs picketing the visit outside the gates: "Down with Martin Luther Coon," "I Wants to See Dee President Too!" Like others, King found the new president to be a nonstop talker who consumed nearly all their forty-three minutes in the Oval Office working through the mechanics of his plan to get the civil rights bill out of the House Rules Committee before Christmas. The careening, folksy President, taking a phone call on the lobbying effort from David McDonald, president of the steelworkers' union, said, "Well, here's Dr. King that's talking to me about it right now," and impulsively handed the phone to King. Afterward, King praised Johnson to reporters as an advocate of equal rights, but warnings still sounded from elsewhere in the government, including an obscure newspaper report that the grieving Attorney General Kennedy soon must decide whether to expose the "Red ties" of a Negro leader "known by the FBI to be linked with a Soviet agent in a massive drive to register Negro voters throughout the country." This was worrisome if true—"horrifying," said King.

During the Johnson transition, King was off balance on a host of matters great and small. With the SCLC fund-raising office in disarray because of staff turnover, he once again was compelled to cancel telephone credit cards in the face of huge unpaid bills. His lawyers were locked in revolving negotiations with mismatched partners—including the steadfast, bureaucratic NAACP Legal Defense Fund against the impetuous free-lancer William Kunstler—over control, expenses, and public rhetoric for a large backlog of movement cases. A dentist who treated gospel star Mahalia Jackson after a joint appearance with King was pressing for a large fee against SCLC's claim that he had rendered complimentary service. Wyatt Walker, who had handled dentists as well as grand administrative strategy for King since 1960, was quitting for lack of a pay raise in proportion to the triumph of Birmingham, and in disgust over King's tolerance for the freewheeling visions of James Bevel. To replace Walker, King was torn between strong personalities at polar extremes: the temperamental genius Bayard Rustin, who had become a public figure since the March on Washington, and the reflective church administrator Andrew Young.

Young himself was torn by the upheavals of the previous year. "I really have been struggling along just content to survive since the summer," he wrote King. Young had spent frustrating months riding circuit among demonstrations across the South, fitfully spurring them on and throttling them down. "We are trying to free people when we are also enslaved by lack of background under a segregated upbringing," he concluded. "All of the emotional problems, lethargy, misguided enthusiasm and impetuosity which we have to face comes from our being Southern Negroes. It takes time to overcome these ills [which] keep us tearing each other apart...." Young felt the special weight of criticism from SCLC's literacy teacher, Septima Clark, who scolded the preachers in King's executive circle for chasing drama and applause to the neglect of unglamorous work with plain people. She warned of "smoldering hate" within the movement itself, especially among young activists who had broken through their fears of jail.

For King, the conflicting pressures converged on the worth of large-scale demonstrations. Under heavy pressure from an anxious publisher, King labored to craft a durable interpretation of the Birmingham campaign. What he first portrayed as a focused attack on local conditions had broadened across the summer into a contagious national optimism, which imploded after the church bombing and dissipated again after Dallas. "This book," Stanley Levison remarked on the telephone, "always seems to be in the shadow of tragic deaths." FBI wiretappers heard Levison tell friends that although he would not be seeing King anymore, "I've got to finish off this book thing that was started." As the trusted liaison between King's literary agent, Joan Daves, the publisher, New American Library, and the editors hired to work on the manuscript, Levison managed to coordinate revisions "to interpret the direction of change," while still crippled by the ban against direct communications with King. "This is now much closer to what Martin means to say," Levison would tell Joan Daves of a draft early in 1964, "and says it the way he would say it."

The blurred meaning of Birmingham confronted King nearly every day with summons to demonstrations somewhere in the South, including Birmingham. His dilemma was elevated to national and even international urgency: President Johnson told him that any new street agitation would jeopardize the historic opportunity in Congress, but experience told him to keep pushing, as did steady streams of newcomers. On December 15, at what the *New York Times* called "the first major civil rights demonstration in the South since President Kennedy's assassination," King emerged under heavy guard by Atlanta police to address a crowd of four thousand under freezing drizzle at a downtown park. He described segregation as a "glaring reality" in his home city, and warned that the local movement was losing faith in prolonged negotiations. "We feel that we are the conscience of America and its troubled souls," King declared. "...Let us go out united and inspired by the words of our slave foreparents, 'Walk together, children, doncha get weary.'"

King held back when the rally triggered sustained, small-scale demonstrations in Atlanta. For seeking service at a local Toddle House restaurant, SNCC Chairman John Lewis went to jail for the twenty-seventh time since 1960, following two white women so transfixed by their first arrest that they impulsively told the booking officer they were Negroes. Almost daily into winter, robed Klansmen and angry lunchtime crowds squared off with integrated pickets outside segregated restaurants—notably Leb's, a kosher delicatessen whose owner pummeled integrationists from his door —in ugly scenes that mortified Atlanta's image-conscious city leaders. By straddling the conflict, King strained close ties on both sides. Technically, he honored his unwritten pledge not to join or launch demonstrations in his home city, which disillusioned some student demonstrators suffering through a long skirmish of low visibility. He supported their courage, however, by appearing at street vigils outside the jail, which showed up the more conciliatory Negro leadership, including his own father. (Reporter Paul Good made it back from Mexico City in time to see Daddy King hounded from the pulpit at a mass meeting.)

With cracks and uncertainties looming from the Oval Office down through the Birmingham book revisions into his own staff and family, King arranged to gather twenty advisers at a church-owned retreat in North Carolina. They would set movement goals for 1964 in what King called "a where do we go from here discussion." King commissioned a staff report on whether Stanley Levison's coerced withdrawal from the movement might be ended under the new administration. He set a retreat date of January 6, then postponed it for two weeks on notice from Clarence Jones that King, Jones, and most of the other conferees were to be in Washington that day for oral arguments before the U.S. Supreme Court in their three-year-old case, *New York Times v. Sullivan.*

AT THE FEDERAL BUILDING in Oxford, Mississippi, prosecutors under John Doar presented their case that December against the five Mississippi officers charged with civil rights violations from the jailhouse beatings in Winona the previous June. On the witness stand, an FBI agent explained the physical evidence, such as photographs of the bloodstained shirt worn by the youngest victim, June Johnson. Two Negro prisoners—one of them retrieved from Parchman by court order—told the jury that they had taken over the heavy cudgeling of the civil rights workers under duress, intimidated by the Winona police chief and bribed with a pint of corn whiskey. Along with SNCC's senior adviser, Ella Baker, Septima Clark sat daily among the courtroom spectators, keeping watch over her former citizenship students and her assistant teacher, Annell Ponder, who testified that she was not yet "completely over" the terror. Defense lawyers challenged her testimony as the sort of lies taught at the "Communist training school," Highlander, where the citizenship classes originated. "Your name has not been called," Septima Clark wrote Myles Horton in mid-trial, "but the school as the sponsor was mentioned many times. One man sitting in front of me said, 'I know Russia had something to do with it.'"

As expected, the federal jury needed only an hour's deliberation to acquit all five defendants—the Montgomery County sheriff, a Highway

Patrol officer, the Winona police chief, and two police officers. Some observers consoled themselves with the hope that the extraordinary effort by the Justice Department at least might sound a warning against heinous abuse, while Mississippi COFO leader Aaron Henry expressed a practical worry about retaliation against the two friendly witnesses still in confinement. (As a thin tissue of protection, Henry recruited preachers for prison visits.) In the courtroom itself, the two grand old women of the movement counseled the beating victims to rise above their resentment. "You can be bigger than this," Clark told Lawrence Guyot, who complained bitterly that his tormentors had won with lies and coarse racial insults. Like Clark, Ella Baker had a way of reducing oppression to a childish retardation. "Look beyond this foolishness," she advised. "Don't let it stop you."

Back at his new COFO assignment in Hattiesburg, Guyot presented to local leaders his plan for a Freedom Day modeled on the October event in Selma. He argued that voting rights would remain null throughout Mississippi so long as the local registrar, Theron Lynd, successfully defied the Justice Department's marathon lawsuit against him. With Lynd's most recent contempt citation on appeal before the U.S. Supreme Court, and with the local movement paralyzed in the meantime by threat of imprisonment, Guyot proposed a one-day demonstration dramatic enough that it might push the U.S. government to enforce one of its decrees against Lynd, so that cowed local Negroes could "see his ass put in jail." To supplement the jail-weary movement veterans, Guyot planned to recruit not only celebrities but also volunteer clergy, mostly white, from the North. ("I think there will be roughly 25 preachers in all," his church liaison soon confided, "though not all of them will picket, i.e., go to jail.")

Local scrutiny of Guyot's plan fell largely to the yeoman farmer Vernon Dahmer, who had lost his own church and his friend Clyde Kennard to the voting rights movement. "Are you strong enough for this?" Dahmer asked Guyot. "Do you know what these folks around here are capable of doing?" With Dahmer's blessing, recruitment went forward quietly beneath the larger debate over a statewide program for the summer. At a COFO meeting in mid-December, the plan rejected in November was reintroduced first as a grandiose scheme to import 100,000 college students into Mississippi, then pared all the way down to one hundred. "You're going to get a lot of folks killed!" shouted Willie Peacock when the vote carried, prompting another reconsideration. A number of delegates were reluctant to pursue the question in the absence of Bob Moses, who was away in New York, which prompted a stinging accusation that the self-consciously independent movement people were in fact captives of one leader. "I'm not attacking Moses," said Guyot, who supported the summer project. "I'm mad because nobody's challenging Moses." Another speaker voiced private doubts about "the Bob Moses mystique—we've operated as though the very word of God was being spoken."

Moses only enhanced his moral authority by trying to reduce or escape its burden. When the Mississippi debate resumed after Christmas, at a SNCC meeting in Atlanta, he was reluctant to speak to the issue at all, saying it was too divisive within the movement and too fraught with responsibility for him to disclose an opinion either way. His doubts about the propriety of charismatic leadership within a democratic movement were a hallmark of SNCC culture generally, at odds with Martin Luther King and other leaders who actively cultivated techniques of command. Like King's SCLC, SNCC veterans did contend privately over the Cold War issue of red-baiting—whether the inclusion on principle of alleged subversives was worth the price of being tarred by association*—and they worried that a spectacular failure could destroy their organization, but SNCC's bias against hierarchy combined with the intense introspection of Moses to accent a personal, purgative quality in its debates. Among the roughly fifty SNCC leaders gathered in Atlanta, abstraction mingled with confessions about "bossism" of nearly every kind. To diagnose ongoing SNCC troubles around Albany, Georgia, some attributed an "image of failure" to the nebulous local goal of "freeing men's minds," others to limitations of the mass meeting approach, and still others to project director Charles Sherrod's use of white staff workers.

On the awkward issue of racial tensions within the movement, speakers rose to say that the movement did not know how to utilize white staff people, or that whites required more supervision because of their erratic psychological passage through a predominantly Negro movement. ("Some of the whites in SNCC are among the strongest advocates of black nationalism," said one white staff member. "This is a necessary step.... It is fruitless for all the whites in SNCC to try to be Negro.") Whether viewed as growing pains or warning signs, apprehensions about whites in the movement saturated the looming decision about the Mississippi summer proposal "pushed by Al Lowenstein," as Moses told the Atlanta meeting, to "pour in thousands of students and force a showdown between local and federal governments in an election year." Nearly all those students would be raw white recruits, entering a state where movement veterans could not so much as carry a sign in public without being snatched away to hang from cell bars at Parchman. By unanimous exhaustion, as usual, the Atlanta meeting adopted Marion Barry's vague resolution that SNCC "intends to obtain" universal suffrage in Mississippi in 1964, "using as many people as necessary." Details were left to a "final showdown" debate scheduled for late January in Hattiesburg, after Guyot's Freedom Day.

---

* "We have to be practical," Moses told SNCC's Executive Committee at the December 1963 meeting in Atlanta, pointing out that SNCC already accepted various political restrictions attached to voter registration grants.

14

High Councils

Early on Monday, December 23, as swaths of black crepe were removed from the chandeliers of the White House state rooms and flags nationwide were raised from half staff to close the month of official mourning for President Kennedy, seven top FBI officials gathered in the office of Fred Baumgardner, section chief, Internal Security [Division Five], for an all-day conference "aimed at neutralizing King as an effective Negro leader." Robert Nichols, one of two Atlanta agents flown to Washington for the occasion, arrived with some misgivings about his extraordinary new wiretap operation. Unlike other wiretap monitor lines, which ran from the telephone company to the Atlanta FBI office, the King tap monitors were wired into a phony engineering company that Nichols had been ordered to set up as a front, complete with a made-up name, a leased suite at the new downtown Peach Tree Towers, and rented office furniture. These stealthy arrangements made the taps more difficult to trace to the FBI, and already had prompted gossip among the Atlanta agents that Director Hoover must be operating without the required legal authorization from Attorney General Kennedy.

Assistant Director William Sullivan reassured the Atlanta agents that headquarters possessed signed wiretap orders for each installation. The documents left Robert Kennedy a figurehead in no position to supervise or restrict the FBI's pursuit of King, and Bureau officials, in restoring traditional direct channels to the White House, were free to disclose fruits of the unknown surveillance to the new administration as they saw fit. This was heady stuff for the Atlanta agents. (Afterward, Sullivan sent a memo to Hoover's office stating that "the men from the field expressed their appreciation for the opportunity of being brought into the Seat of Government...[and] were both enthusiastic about the case....") Still, they would have preferred to hear that the King investigation was headed toward arrest or resolution, as criminal cases were the coin of respect among field agents. Agent Nichols in particular felt that his entire Bureau career had been trapped in Cold War loyalty investigations. No agents in Atlanta wanted to be part of his King detail, because they knew it was all sedentary paperwork and waiting—deciphering intercepted conversations, trying to fathom the personal dynamics of a separate world, writing reports. Agents on the lowly bad check squad, who at least got out to chase suspects, resisted transfer into security work as clerk duty.

The agenda for the headquarters conference of December 23 included a few virile options, such as recruiting inside informants or "placing a good-looking female plant in King's office," but Assistant Director Sullivan ruled out the Bureau's standard technique of multiple, dragnet interviews to elicit cooperation. In fact, he strictly forbade all interviews, along with visits to "show the badge" and other actions that might disclose the FBI's interest in King. His operational summary repeated five times a first requirement that the operation must avoid "embarrassment to the Bureau." Practically, such secrecy constrained the FBI to gather information by surreptitious, technical methods such as wiretaps, and to use the results covertly. Wiretaps conferred a special tactical advantage: by overhearing King's travel plans on the telephone, FBI eavesdroppers gained advance knowledge necessary to have electronic transmitters (popularly called "bugs," known in FBI parlance as "misurs," short for "microphone surveillance") implanted in the walls of King's hotel room before he arrived. The conference adopted plans to let the first step—wiretaps on telephones— facilitate the more intrusive second step of bugs placed to intercept all sounds within a private space. The resulting peek at intimate, unguarded moments promised more gossip than evidence, information better suited to personal attack than courtroom prosecution. "We are most interested in exposing him in some manner or another in order to discredit him," declared the preconference agenda.

For Agent Nichols and his primary King wiretap crew of fifteen recruits, it remained a disappointment that headquarters essentially restricted them to stenographic duties—long hours of tedium interrupted by disputes over how to distinguish one muffled voice from another over earphones. As consolation, they developed a kibitzer's interest in King's world, along with a proprietary stake in its importance. After only two months' eavesdropping, many of the wiretap crew took it for granted that King was the most significant American orator of the century. As they monitored the running debate over the departure of Wyatt Walker, some endorsed King's repeated assertion that money was the root of evil, while others argued for the fine distinction that not money itself but "the love of money" corrupted, which Walker used to legitimize his demand for a salary increase.

At a deeper level, however, the wiretap squad adopted the headquarters view that a fundamental defect made King the most subtle and dangerous of Communist allies—the sort who did not believe in the immediate threat of the Communist subversion. As a field agent, Robert Nichols did not pretend to understand the intellectual nuance marshaled by Assistant Director Sullivan, the Bureau's senior expert on Communism, but he picked up enough to stress one intercepted remark by King that he "pretty much agreed with Hegel" on dialectics in history, which Nichols knew was a tenet of German philosophy that had led to Marxism. At the December FBI conference, this was the ready explanation for King's shocking association with Stanley Levison against the explicit personal order of the President of the United States, and it became a standard theme of the wiretap shop that King was making the racial situation more uncomfortable than necessary. Atlanta's limited role was to funnel intelligence ammunition to headquarters under two most desirable headings: money and sex. Section Chief Baumgardner quoted the suspicion of an Alabama representative that "so-called civil rights organizations... could be a front for a full-grown racket." On that premise, the conference resolved to enlist the quiet cooperation of the IRS to investigate King and his financial supporters for tax avoidance or unbecoming extravagance. As to sex, headquarters aimed to follow up the wiretap indications that King liked to pursue women after hours on the road. Assistant Director Sullivan closed his report on the December meeting with confident determination: "We will, at the proper time when it can be done without embarrassment to the Bureau, expose King as an immoral opportunist who is not a sincere person but is exploiting the racial situation for personal gain."

Like every other successful FBI executive, Sullivan accurately read Director Hoover's moods. Less than a week later, when King appeared on the cover of *Time* magazine as "Man of the Year," praised editorially for the historic Birmingham breakthrough* that made him "the unchallenged voice of the Negro people—and the disquieting conscience of the whites," Hoover circulated at headquarters his own reaction: "They had to dig deep in the garbage for this one." Animosity toward King gained free rein in FBI policy up to the restraining edge of "embarrassment to the Bureau," as was evident a few days later when a crude letter of multiple assassination threats reached headquarters from St. Petersburg, Florida. "We here to get Martin Luthr King and Wilkson [Roy Wilkins] and Mayr [Ivan] Allen [of Atlanta]," said the letter. "We wont miss no. Two more in Washington to get Bob Kenedy and 2 nigers, then Johnson if he push integratin.

---

* After 1963, *Time* proclaimed, "the Negro will never again be where or what he was."

We plege not fail or die. We not fail no." In the midst of the standard full-scale trace alert on possible danger to President Johnson, the FBI extended notification to the lesser targets mentioned—except for King. In his newfound assertiveness after the Kennedy assassination, Director Hoover suspended official courtesies that smacked of FBI solicitude for King's welfare, and declared him specifically unfit to receive death warnings. On these instructions, the Atlanta FBI office notified only the local police, but complications arose when Roy Wilkins asked to have a copy of the threat letter for his personal files. If "Wilkson" saw King's name listed before his, natural conversation between them might reveal that King remained in the dark, excluded by an edict Hoover did not care to explain. To avoid such risk, Hoover's office ordered New York officials to "diplomatically decline" the request for the copy, and suggested several pretentious excuses to mollify Wilkins.

KNOWING NOTHING of the FBI's extraordinary war council against King, President Johnson left Washington to spend Christmas and New Year's at his Texas ranch. A small army of federal workers already had transformed the 1890 farmhouse and surrounding buildings into a presidential command post, complete with coding equipment for secure communications, radar saucers for air security, and perimeter searchlights for the assassination-haunted Secret Service. Johnson himself was a gadget person, but he preferred earthier uses: high-powered showerheads, special blades to cut thick steaks into the shape of Texas, an amphibious jeep that he loved to drive into his lake by "mistake" with unwitting passengers, and, mounted on his Lincoln touring convertible, a horn whose sounds stimulated the mating instincts of nearby cattle, producing sights that mortified those whom Johnson gleefully called "citified" guests.

Never was Johnson's domain more thoroughly overrun than these holidays, when he postponed Christmas dinner with twenty-odd relatives, including Aunt Josefa and Cousin Oriole, to take fifty of the regular beat reporters on a tour of the main house. The *New York Times* published on the front page a photograph of the President astride his horse, Lady B, and another of him speaking from an outdoor rostrum mounted on a bale of hay. Five Greyhound busloads of supplementary reporters covered the arrival of West German Chancellor Ludwig Erhard for the first state barbecue, with entertainment by classical pianist Van Cliburn. Erhard was followed closely by the Joint Chiefs and most of the Cabinet. Johnson handed out souvenir ashtrays and offered cigarettes from displays artfully swirled in hospitality bowls.

Stress showed more privately. Whenever Mrs. Johnson saw the President reaching for a cigarette, she matched his actions ostentatiously to achieve a silent standoff—having learned that her own threat to take up smoking if he returned to the habit yielded more effect, and less abuse, than verbal correction. The smallest criticisms could agitate Johnson for weeks, as when he noticed that *Jet* magazine mistakenly said he had refused to be photographed with Martin Luther King. He retrieved prints to prove otherwise, then pleaded with the Urban League's Whitney Young to make *Jet* "quit cuttin' us up sayin' we hate the nigras." In his Christmas call to Roy Wilkins, Johnson protested in such unconsolable distress—"I had my picture made with every damn one of 'em!"—that his shortness of breath moved Wilkins to interject repeatedly, "Please take care of yourself."

The new president also labored painfully to gain acceptance from aides who had been close to President Kennedy. Having courted Kennedy's chief speechwriter, Theodore Sorensen—"I've done as much as I can and have any pride and self-respect left," he complained to a friend—Johnson commandeered him to the ranch for the holidays. Sorensen arrived with his three young sons and a vacant look, having lost not only a president but also a wife from whom he had recently separated. He remained polite but pinched as Johnson aggressively befriended him with compliments, Stetson hats, cowboy adventures, and overly close attention so transparently misguided that the household help winced for both men.

Poignant discomforts carried over to the marathon poverty caucus in the rustic guest house, a green frame structure set in a pasture where white-faced Hereford cattle grazed. With Bill Moyers and economist Walter Heller, among others, Sorensen brainstormed Johnson's charge to design a dramatic but practical legislative attack. The money people argued for something "experimental," meaning visibly new but cheap, while the political people argued for something to spread among the competing bureaucracies that claimed expertise in health, education, and job training. As paper cups and crumpled scratch sheets piled up on the table, Johnson reacted to various proposals including one to create a trial "one-stop" poverty center in Washington's Union Station, envisioned as a synergetic beehive for experts and the needy alike. Horace Busby made the mistake of speaking up from his wall seat to ask how all the poor people would get there to seek jobs, and where would they park? This comment drew a withering look from President Johnson, who promptly summoned Busby outside for a scolding. "Why did you say that?" he demanded. "Don't you realize these are Kennedy's people?" Johnson's pride in Texas gave way to fear that yokelism within his camp would drive away the Ivy League holdovers who lent a sophisticated image to his government.

Hypersensitive and erratic, President Johnson attended a reception in part to make up with Busby. Alumni from the University of Texas were honoring Busby, the wartime editor of *The Daily Texan,* now a celebrity as special assistant to the President, with a party at an off-campus faculty retreat called the Forty Acres Club, a short helicopter ride from the LBJ Ranch. Like the university itself, the club had been locked in an icy, three-year standoff over segregation, with the politically connected regents maintaining an arcane fallback line since court-ordered integration. Restrictions banned some two hundred Negro students from all varsity sports and leading roles in campus theater, for instance, and a prolonged faculty boycott failed to breach strict segregation at Forty Acres. As Vice President, Johnson had hosted dinners to encourage some of the embattled professors, but these intercessions were trivial compared with the simple gesture of escorting Gerri Whittington to the Busby reception on New Year's Eve. Throughout the formal and informal salutes due the new president, faculty members pretended not to stare at the White House secretary on his arm. No one mentioned to Johnson that Whittington shattered precedent as the first Negro ever admitted to the premises. Managers at Forty Acres soon began accepting reservations for mixed tables, saying "the President of the United States integrated us on New Year's Eve," and other university practices began to fall in line as though one step through the glass partition pretty much settled the entire race issue.

ELIJAH MUHAMMAD struck on New Year's Eve. From Phoenix, he called one by one Captain Joseph and the principal ministers whom Malcolm X had been recruiting with cryptic "parables" about sexually corrupted prophets. All of them had warned of incipient revolt by Malcolm, but Muhammad guarded forcefully against double dealing. The parables were nothing but "rotten stuff," he said, ridiculing Malcolm's claim to be his loyal agent preparing to defend the Nation if the devil's propaganda should spread. "What kind of fool would I be to go out to tell him to tell people something like that on me?" Muhammad demanded. No, Malcolm was a renegade. "I saw that in him a long time ago," said Muhammad, "and I didn't think he would be able to stand any joy at all." He vowed to remove Malcolm. "I'm going to strip him of everything," he told Minister Louis X of Boston. He warned the ministers not to let Malcolm's fame seduce them into rebellion, saying that "all of Malcolm's speeches at the colleges did not make one convert and he did not make many where he went outside of Harlem." Converts were the cement of the Nation; submission was its saving doctrine. Muhammad advised each of the ministers to judge very carefully between "Allah and his Messenger" on the one hand and "this person," Malcolm X, "to see which one you would rather get along with."

All the ministers swore loyalty to Muhammad and pleaded with him to disregard rumors to the contrary. Minister Louis X told Muhammad that Lonnie X of Washington, the prized new Ph.D. mathematician among the ministers, was "all torn up" over Malcolm's disclosures "and just can't figure it out in his own mind." When Louis volunteered to help the Messenger secure Malcolm's territory in New York, Muhammad replied that he would take up the question of succession when Malcolm was "completely off the list." Meanwhile, ministers should spread word that the Messenger would "not have any mercy" on those taking Malcolm's side. "Any laborer or minister who takes any of this poison shall be removed at once," Muhammad warned Minister Isaiah X of Baltimore. "I will not let a man like that mess me up with twenty million people."

Muhammad allowed his notice to reverberate for two days before calling Malcolm X. "I cannot understand why you took this poison and spread it out and told them it was poison," he said. "... If you love Allah, you must love me as the Messenger of Allah." Malcolm defended himself halfheartedly, then confessed that he had lost much of his drive since the previous February in Chicago, when Wallace Muhammad had confirmed rumors of extra children in his father's household. Muhammad chastised Malcolm. "You should have put out this fire when you and Wallace found it in Chicago," he said, "rather than to start it up in other places." Malcolm, on a conference call joined by two of his principal enemies on the financial corruption issue—National Secretary John Ali and Supreme Captain Raymond Sharrieff—plus FBI clerks listening in over wiretaps, prayed that Allah would forgive him.

Elijah Muhammad scrambled to contain the talk loosed already. To an assistant who reported that Muhammad's wife, Clara, was upset that he had bought maternity clothes for his secretaries, Muhammad admitted the purchases but said they "did not prove anything." Through intermediaries, he supervised treacherous negotiations with his secretaries Evelyn and Lucille, the latter being "in the nest" expecting her third child by Muhammad. The women, already bitter that the Nation provided only $100 per month for each child, were holding out for $8,000 in relocation expenses instead of $5,000, arguing that they would have to move all the way to Hawaii to become safely isolated. Muhammad ordered the transfer done "even if they move to the Fiji Islands." On another front, he told Captain Joseph to assume complete control of Temple No. 7 in New York, and specifically not to allow Malcolm to select the guest ministers any longer. Muhammad also ordered his aides to tell Wallace Muhammad that Malcolm had blamed him as the instigator—"Let my son know that," he said—and then he summoned both men to summary court in Phoenix on January 6: "I'm not through with Malcolm yet."

Wallace Muhammad managed to avoid the stacked hearing on the excuse that his parole officer would not let him leave Chicago. Malcolm appeared in Phoenix, and said little when Muhammad extended his ninety-day suspension indefinitely, contingent on what he called the strength of Malcolm's faith. As a first test, Muhammad ordered Malcolm to retract in person everything he had said. Malcolm sent an emergency request that Ministers Lonnie X of Washington and Isaiah X of Baltimore meet his return flight at a layover in Washington. At the airport, he told them he had lied about the Honorable Elijah Muhammad and was undertaking a mission of penance. Pacing the floor, he struck both his colleagues as agitated to the point of incoherence. As he rushed off to catch his next airplane, Malcolm promised to contact them soon about how this mistake had occurred, and what it meant, but he disappeared instead. Minister Lonnie X never saw him again.

Back in New York, Malcolm X recorded a statement about the multiple allegations of corruption against Chicago—personal and financial— plus charges of religious hypocrisy and charlatanism, saying some members from the Muhammad family had not bothered to learn the most basic facts about Islam. By mail, Malcolm presented the tape as a loyal fulfillment of the instruction to submit every trouble to the Messenger, but the tone and content shocked Muhammad. Each detailed "confession" from Malcolm carried the double edge of accusation, and the very enthusiasm of his humility had an undertow of threat. At first, Muhammad fretted to an aide about the Nation's changeling: "Sometimes he speaks nice and good, and other times he is altogether different." Then in quick succession arrived another tape and a letter in which Malcolm charged that the other ministers were ridiculing him in hopes of usurping his job, and warned that he would do all in his power to stop them. Muhammad interpreted the lurching communications as a sign of desperation. "When a man is falling," he said, "he reaches for everything that he thinks will support him."

On January 14, Malcolm escaped into an airport hotel room to spend seven secluded hours with a magazine writer named Alex Haley. The two made an oddly matched team. In 1939, Haley's father, a stern professor, had been so disappointed with his dreamy, lackadaisical son's failing French grade in college that he had enlisted young Alex as a U.S. Coast Guard seaman. Lonely and adrift aboard ship, the younger Haley had developed a thriving business as the ghostwriter of individually tailored personal letters for less literate white shipmates, mostly Cyrano-style love entreaties to girlfriends on shore. Twenty years later, cushioned by his Coast Guard pension, Haley had turned his literary hobby into a second career as one of the few Negro freelance magazine writers. *Reader's Digest* hired him to write an article vilifying Elijah Muhammad in 1960, which positioned Haley three years later to interview Malcolm X for *Playboy* magazine. From that assignment slowly grew their collaboration on Malcolm's autobiography.

Once Haley had learned that Malcolm did not trust tape recorders, he sat patiently at his typewriter while Malcolm brooded across the gulf between them. Eventually, the ex-con Muslim sectarian and the mild-mannered writer established a working relationship based in part on common interests such as a love of Shakespeare. As Malcolm gradually disclosed his life, he maintained a disciplined reverence for Muhammad in private speech, so that Haley had no inkling of the explosive schism building between Malcolm and Chicago. Malcolm walled it off except for one or two classical allusions that he scribbled on a notepad: "You have not converted a man because you have silenced him—John Viscount Morley."

From the airport session, Malcolm flew to Miami with his pregnant wife, Betty, and their three daughters. It was their first family trip in six years of marriage. The Miami FBI office picked up the strange informant report that a Malcolm X party was met and escorted to their hotel by the flamboyant young boxer Cassius Clay, known as the "Louisville Lip," who was training for a February bout against heavyweight champion Sonny Liston. FBI analysts—perhaps more informed on the raw internal politics of the Nation than all but a handful of its leaders—were so skeptical of the unlikely pairing that the Miami office did not report the tip to FBI headquarters until five days later on January 21, when confirming informants reported that Cassius Clay flew with Malcolm to New York for a Temple No. 7 dinner at the Rockland Palace. Malcolm honored his banishment by declining to attend, but Clay teased the crowd of better than four thousand with the Muslim greeting and rejoined Malcolm for the return flight to Miami. Both the Miami and New York FBI offices rushed the puzzling news to headquarters by air telegram.

POPE PAUL VI dominated world news during the first week of 1964 with his three-day pilgrimage—the first papal trip of any kind taken by airplane, and first papal visit to the Holy Land since the original Apostle Peter left Palestine for Rome in the first century. The Pope uttered the Muslim greeting on arrival in Amman, Jordan, and throngs surrounded his motorcade on its path down to Emir Abdullah Bridge, where Paul VI stood in silent vigil overlooking the Jordan River while the young Jordanian King Hussein piloted a security helicopter overhead. Inside the Damascus Gate to the Old City of Jerusalem, ecstatic worshippers were compressed so tightly in the narrow streets that several Jordanian police were trampled and the Pope's entourage briefly panicked for fear of being crushed.

On January 5, among private audiences for some of the visiting dignitaries who attended his historic mass at Nazareth, Pope Paul received Sargent Shriver, the director of the American Peace Corps, who delivered a goodwill letter from President Johnson. Though awed by the occasion, Shriver asked for a papal blessing upon the wooden crucifix he had supplied when President Kennedy's body lay in state, and Paul VI invited Shriver to accompany him back to Jerusalem, where that night he was to greet the Orthodox Patriarch Athenagoras of Constantinople. In their twenty-nine-minute summit on the Mount of Olives—the first of its kind since an abortive meeting in 1431 between Pope Eugenius IV and Patriarch Joseph II—Paul VI and Athenagoras pledged to end the mutual excommunication that had divided the church into East and West since 1054.

With Shriver in the background stood the Greek Archbishop Iakovos of New York, the Patriarch's deputy for the Western Hemisphere, who had served for some years as a kind of secret agent of reconciliation for the Orthodox Church, working at the Vatican on a track parallel to that of Rabbi Abraham Heschel for the Jews. In 1965, Iakovos and Heschel would join as the two ranking clergy to march alongside Martin Luther King under threat of death in Selma, but for the moment, most observers struggled to acquaint themselves with the ancient religious separations between the leaders of half a billion white Christians.

As Shriver continued his courier's journey around the globe delivering presidential letters to the King of Nepal and other world rulers, he took with him ecumenical inspiration on the grandest scale. To Muslim audiences in the Holy Land, Pope Paul had quoted the Apostle Peter, who in turn was quoting the Psalmist King David: "He that would love life and see good days, let him keep his tongue from evil and seek peace and pursue it." Religious politics seethed beneath the biblical words. Although Pope Paul was careful never to speak the word "Israel" or otherwise recognize the Jewish state in ceremonies with Israeli leaders, his visit inflamed anti-Israeli sentiments. At a closed conference in February, bishops representing the Christian minorities of the Middle East joined with theological supremacists in Rome to strip the long-proposed statement of fraternal truce with Jews and Judaism from the fall agenda of the Vatican Council.

ON JANUARY 6, as Pope Paul VI returned to Rome and Malcolm X submitted to summary court in Phoenix, Martin Luther King took a reserved seat at the U.S. Supreme Court for oral argument in the *Sullivan* case. He arrived among celebrities conscious of a historic occasion that commanded the attendance of three former U.S. Attorneys General and featured opening remarks warning the Court of constitutional dangers "not confronted since the early days of the Republic." From the bench, Justice Arthur Goldberg discreetly sent down his copy of *Stride Toward Freedom,* King's book about the Montgomery bus boycott, with a note requesting an autograph.

On the appointed day, the Court never reached the portion of the *Sullivan* case closest to King. Having divided the appeal into two halves, the Justices consumed extra time with the arguments for and against the co-appellant *New York Times,* which Alabama courts had found guilty of libel for publishing the original 1960 advertisement seeking funds to defend King. The Justices held over the "Negro half" of the case, the libel judgments against King's four ministerial colleagues: Ralph Abernathy, Joseph Lowery, S. S. Seay, and Fred Shuttlesworth. This overnight delay, while a letdown, gave King an opportunity to meet with all his side's lawyers that afternoon at the Washington office of William Rogers, Eisenhower's second attorney general, whom Harry Wachtel had recruited for the oral argument.

Now and then for the rest of King's life, Wachtel was to be called Stanley Levison's "twin" by Negroes of the inner circle, who quipped that the only white advisers close to King were interchangeable Jewish lawyers from New York—you could not tell them apart, went the joke, which extended to a sporting confusion between their wives, Bea Levison and Lucy Wachtel. A relative newcomer, having first met King in 1962, Wachtel was a powerful corporate lawyer longing to recover some of the idealism of his days as a student radical in the 1930s. With Clarence Jones, he had drafted appellate briefs in the *Sullivan* case and incorporated for King's projects in nonviolence a tax-exempt conduit called the Gandhi Society. Brash and aggressive, Wachtel pushed himself forward as a partial replacement for Levison during the latter's grudging withdrawal. Although he lacked the monkish Levison's writing skills and long-established personal bond with King, Wachtel brought complementary talents as a successful practicing lawyer with connections in high places. From previous business dealings, he called Rogers by his first name, Bill, when he introduced the highly prized counsel to King.

Before the assembled team of lawyers, Wachtel opened with a harsh appraisal of the day's performance by the eminent Herbert Wechsler, chief counsel for the *New York Times.* While it was true, he wryly conceded, that Wechsler once gave him his lowest grade in law school, Wachtel insisted that his former teacher made a timid presentation to the Justices. To insulate the *Times* from its controversial Negro co-appellants, Wechsler had pictured the contested advertising copy as a theoretical test of press freedom. Even there, said Wachtel, Wechsler had offered the Court several paths to overturn the verdict short of upholding an absolute First Amendment right to attack public officials—a "balancing test," for instance, between the libel rights of public officials and the protection of vigorous political debate. Moreover, Wechsler argued that the retracting apology published in the *Times,* as demanded by the governor of Alabama, ought to protect the newspaper from the suit brought over the same material by Sullivan, a city commissioner in Montgomery. Wachtel thought these defensive arguments betrayed a lack of confidence.

William Rogers took issue with Wachtel, saying he had found Wechsler too bold for his taste, not too timid. Only Justices Hugo Black and William O. Douglas were likely to vote for a pure First Amendment reversal, said Rogers. The other seven Justices wanted to preserve at least some legal recourse for public figures who claimed to be libeled, and Rogers would have preferred Wechsler to aim his argument more at the middle ground where the deciding votes were likely to be, which was also where Rogers felt most comfortable. His comments prompted Martin Luther King to stand up. "I agree with you," he told Rogers, interrupting the debate. "Just because I'm out there in public, I don't want people to say and print anything they want about me and be protected." King's words startled several of the lawyers who assumed he would hold a doctrinaire position, and were slow to realize how much he identified with the targets of press vilification. Threats and slander being almost daily fare for him, King respected in principle the claims of his sworn enemies to fair legal redress. He could scarcely imagine a reversible world in which he and all his colleagues could secure through the courts gigantic punitive judgments against any segregationist who declared that civil rights threatened the American way of life.

Before the Justices that day, Wechsler had described the overall situation with a word rarely used in formal law: "fantastic." Rulings up through the Alabama Supreme Court held that the truth of a public statement could be invalidated by the most trivial factual error, such as the misstatement in the *Times* ad about the number of times King had been arrested as of 1960. From there, under presumption of libel, Alabama law allowed juries first to recognize as victims parties never mentioned by name, such as Sullivan (a Montgomery police commissioner who claimed damage from the ad's generic complaints against segregation), and from there to award punitive civil damages as the jury saw fit—$500,000 to Sullivan, the largest judgment of its kind in Alabama history, a thousand times the statutory maximum for criminal libel.

Race was the driving explanation, but William Rogers was no more eager than Herbert Wechsler to ask the Supreme Court to find that Alabama judges and juries systematically subverted plain justice to segregation. The notion undermined the working presumption of the entire legal system. Thinking it wise to finesse the issue instead, Rogers advised King's lawyers that there were too many racial references in their petitions for the four ministers. This was a legal judgment, and he did not mention the converging political pressures on him as a prominent national Republican. A number of his friends in the Senate were annoyed with Rogers for taking part in a case that could embroil the national party on the losing side of sectional politics.

The lawyers concurred in Rogers's strategy for the following day. For all their complaints, they were happy to have their fortunes tied to the *New York Times.* Had Sullivan and the other Alabama plaintiffs chosen to sue the four Negro ministers alone, or together with a lesser newspaper, the clients might well be ruined already. What was burned into the clients themselves by life's lesson, Rogers and the other lawyers could appreciate by comparing the public indifference to partial enforcements of the *Sullivan* judgment thus far in Alabama—the seizure of Shuttlesworth's car, the confiscation for auction of family land in Abernathy's name—with coverage of the historic threat to the *Times.* Wechsler had minced no words with the Justices in calling the *Sullivan* judgment "a death penalty for any newspaper if multiplied," and multiplication was running apace. Libel judgments seeking some $300 million in damages were pending in Southern courts, including four others from the ad at issue in *Sullivan*. With national crisis emanating from such huge institutional stakes, William Rogers settled on a plan to give the Court technical arguments for the four preachers and concede the defining ground of the case to the *Times*.

FROM THE LONG strategy session at the Rogers law firm, King returned on the night of January 6 to the Willard Hotel, near the White House, where with small drills, wires, and the cooperation of hotel management, FBI "sound men" had installed microphone bugs in his room. Monitoring technicians in the suite next door fed the reception into a large tape recorder, which so far had picked up four reels of informal conversation between two women. With King's return, the bugs recorded the shedding of Supreme Court decorum into a party with clinking glasses. In the midst of an eventual eleven reels and fourteen hours of party babble, with jokes about scared Negro preachers and stiff white bosses, arrived sounds of courtship and sex with distinctive verbal accompaniment. At its height, Bureau technicians heard King's distinctive voice ring out above others with pulsating abandon, saying "I'm fucking for God!" and "I'm not a Negro tonight!" Soon after the cries subsided, a businesslike attendant was heard rapping at the doorway, saying it was time to go.*

By morning, word of this first top secret microphone surveillance sent a jolt of triumph through commanding echelons at FBI headquarters. After the first of many agents and officials verified King's voice, the Intelligence Division prepared a "highlights" tape and an eight-page written synopsis for Director Hoover, who exclaimed, "This will destroy the burrhead!" Although his dreaded files had accumulated a fair number of couplings in Washington hotel rooms, nearly all represented scandalous frailty that was familiar and controlling, almost reassuring, to the spymaster. Here, beyond the bare evidence of extramarital sex, what fixated the FBI Director was a separate culture of exuberant, profane, theatrical release, whose sounds battered his microphones. "King is a 'tom cat' with obsessive, degenerate sexual urges," Hoover scribbled on a memo. Detailed instructions went down overnight to the wiretap hub in Atlanta ("It is believed that the submissions from your office should be on a daily or near daily basis..."). The next day, January 8, Assistant Director Sullivan recorded fresh resolve "to take [King] off his pedestal and to reduce him completely in influence," while a team of his intelligence specialists worked to ap-

---

* The author did not hear the bugging tapes from the Willard. These quotations, together with the one on page 250, are from interviews with three FBI officials of varying rank and outlook who did hear them. The eavesdroppers' shards presented here are the blackmail version of King, which FBI officials put into historical effect with a host of subsequent reports and oral briefings designed to ruin him.

Partly in reaction to the FBI's intrusive, hostile characterization, King's admirers have responded with anguish and outright denial over the subject of his extramarital affairs.

proach the Internal Revenue Service on a hunch that "recent income tax returns of King might well reveal information which could assist the Bureau in its efforts to discredit King or neutralize his effectiveness."

FOR KING, January 7 brought the renewed calm of the Supreme Court chamber, where William Rogers stressed to the Justices that the four Negro appellants were mere bystanders, their names having been added without their knowledge or approval to the list of supporters published in the offending ad, and that only a hangman's court could condemn them as libelous authors on such evidence. "If this judgment is permitted to stand," said Rogers, "it will be a mild forerunner of what will follow." After his co-counsel Samuel Pierce argued for reversal on the ground that an all-white jury and strictly segregated courtrooms had denied the four ministers a fair trial, friends of the appeal gathered for a large farewell luncheon at the Washington Hotel. King thanked the lawyers and supporting organizations for nearly four years' work since the Eisenhower administration and the early sit-ins, when the movement had been an obscure speck to Washington. Back then, King told Rogers, he never dreamed that Ike's attorney general would be defending them before the Supreme Court.

The *Sullivan* case itself disappeared behind the closed doors of the Court, where over the next nine weeks the nine Justices would bargain over an extraordinary nine drafts of landmark law. Justice William Brennan carried the burden of crafting a decision that would favor the *Times* and the Negro appellants—thereby stopping the blatant use of state libel laws to defend segregation—yet do so without exacerbating sectional tensions. Elaborating on a suggestion from Herbert Wechsler's oral argument, Brennan essentially transposed *Sullivan* two centuries backward to the dawn of the American republic, when the Federalist Congress had enacted the Sedition Law of 1798 to punish political opponents as criminals. "Although the Sedition Law was never tested in this Court," wrote Justice Brennan, "the attack upon its validity has carried the day in the court of history." The dramatic analogy served the double purpose of stepping into a buffered past, free of overt racial consideration, while addressing a fundamental American conflict at parallel depths of democratic theory. Brennan quoted Jefferson's stated reasons for pardoning all convictions under the Sedition Act: "I considered, and now consider, that law to be a nullity, as absolute and as palpable as if Congress had ordered us to fall down and worship a golden image."

Through Brennan's negotiated language, the Supreme Court unanimously subjected state libel laws to constitutional scrutiny for the first time, holding that First Amendment protection of political debate imposed a new, higher standard of proof in libel actions brought by public figures.

At the White House two weeks after John F. Kennedy's assassination, the new President, Lyndon Johnson, warned his Senate mentor, Richard Russell of Georgia, that "if you get in my way" on the civil rights bill, "I'm going to run you down." *(Yoichi R. Okamoto, LBJ Library Collection)*

At a Harlem rally, Malcolm X with a photo of Muslims shot down and handcuffed by police officers on a Los Angeles sidewalk on April 27, 1962. *(UPI/Corbis-Bettmann)*

Hattiesburg Freedom Day, January 22, 1964. Police officers in formation *(above)*. Fannie Lou Hamer in picket line outside the Forrest County, Mississippi, courthouse *(left)*. Bob Moses under arrest *(below)*. *(Three photos: © Danny Lyon, Magnum Photos)*

Vice President Johnson addressing workers at a defense plant in St. Augustine, Florida, March 1963. *(Florida Times Union, © 1997 Florida Publishing Company)*

Police Chief Virgil Stuart observing pickets near the columns of the Old Slave Market in St. Augustine, May 30, 1964. *(AP/Wide World Photos)*

St. Augustine movement leader Robert Hayling at a press conference, June 10, 1964. *(UPI/Corbis-Bettmann)*

Mary Peabody of Massachusetts under arrest by Sheriff L. O. Davis in St. Augustine, March 31, 1964.

Martin Luther King encouraging young pickets in St. Augustine, June 10, 1964.

Segregationist J. B. Stoner *(with microphone)* at a rally in St. Augustine, June 19, 1964.
(Three photos: AP/Wide World Photos)

King and Ralph Abernathy jailed in St. Augustine, June 11, 1964.
(UPI/Corbis-Bettmann)

Police breaking up a demonstration on St. Augustine beach, June 1964.
(AP/Wide World Photos)

Andrew Young with an injured demonstrator after a night march in St. Augustine, June 25, 1964.
(AP/Wide World Photos)

ABOVE LEFT: SCLC organizer James Bevel.

ABOVE RIGHT: Robert Spike, director of the Commission on Religion and Race, National Council of Churches. *(Two photos: General Board of Global Ministries/The Estate of Ken Thompson)*

LEFT: SNCC leader Diane Nash. *(AP/Wide World Photos)*

LOWER LEFT: King adviser and lawyer Clarence Jones. *(UPI/Corbis-Bettmann)*

BELOW: Movement leaders Hosea Williams, King, and Bernard Lafayette. *(AP/Wide World Photos)*

King with his lawyer Harry Wachtel. (Newsday, *courtesy of Harry Wachtel*)

King with actor and movement supporter Harry Belafonte. (© *Charles Moore, Black Star*)

King receiving an award from Rabbi Abraham Heschel *(right)*, professor at the Jewish Theological Seminary, and George Maislen, president of the United Synagogue of America, November 19, 1963. *(AP/Wide World Photos)*

King and Malcolm X shake hands in a Capitol corridor during the Senate filibuster of the civil rights bill, March 26, 1964. *(AP/Wide World Photos)*

New heavyweight champion Cassius Clay, soon to become Muhammad Ali *(seated, right),* posing for Malcolm X during their interval of friendship, February 26, 1964. *(Bob Gomel, Life Magazine © Time Warner Inc.)*

Malcolm X *(at podium),* Louis X (Louis Farrakhan), James Shabazz, Elijah Muhammad, Wallace Muhammad *(seated behind Elijah),* and Clara Muhammad *(seated, right)* at a Nation of Islam convention in Chicago. *(Frank Scherschel, Life Magazine © Time Inc.)*

A Nation of Islam martial instructor exhibiting self-defense tactics against police dogs, in contrast with non-violent demonstrators attacked in Birmingham, May 1963. *(© Gordon Parks)*

Alabama governor George Wallace campaigning for President in Indiana, September 1964. *(AP/Wide World Photos)*

A Wallace rally in rural Georgia, July 1964. *(© Matt Herron/Take Stock)*

National Guard soldiers arrest SNCC photographer Clifford Vaughs and demonstrators before the Wallace campaign reaches Cambridge, Maryland, May 1964.
(© Danny Lyon, Magnum Photos)

Segregationist billboard in Alabama showing Aubrey Williams *(seated, left of King)* and Rosa Parks *(seated, far left)* at the Highlander Folk School in Tennessee.
(UPI/Corbis-Bettmann)

President Johnson after signing the Civil Rights Act, July 2, 1964. *(UPI/Corbis-Bettmann)*

Future Georgia governor Lester Maddox *(with pistol)* chasing away a would-be customer in defiance of the civil rights law, July 1964. *(Courtesy of the Atlanta History Center)*

Movement activists Reverend Edwin King and Allard Lowenstein before Mississippi Freedom Summer. *(© Matt Herron/Take Stock)*

SNCC staffer Hollis Watkins giving instruction to summer volunteers at Oxford, Ohio, June 1964.

James Forman of SNCC *(holding pipe)* at a nonviolence training session with volunteers, including Andrew Goodman *(in dark T-shirt)*, Oxford, Ohio, June 1964. *(Two photos: © Steve Schapiro/Black Star)*

SNCC leader Bob Moses at Oxford, Ohio, June 1964. *(© Tamio Wakayama)*

FBI executives J. Edgar Hoover, Cartha "Deke" DeLoach, and Clyde Tolson greeted by Mayor Allen Thompson at the Jackson, Mississippi, airport, July 10, 1964.

Rabbi Arthur Lelyveld after being attacked with summer volunteers in Hattiesburg, Mississippi, July 10, 1964.
(Two photos: UPI/Corbis-Bettmann)

King in Philadelphia, Mississippi, in July 1964, a month after the disappearance of three civil rights workers. *(UPI/Corbis-Bettmann)*

Touring Mississippi, King talks with a Greenwood family, July 21, 1964. *(AP/Wide World Photos)*

President and Mrs. Johnson at a Kentucky home, on tour to support the 1964 anti-poverty bill. *(© Walter Bennett/Time Magazine)*

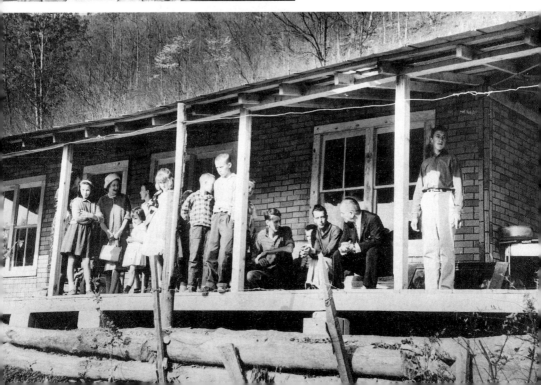

Civil rights leaders Bayard Rustin, Jack Greenberg, Whitney Young, James Farmer, Roy Wilkins, Martin Luther King, John Lewis, A. Philip Randolph, and Courtland Cox at a New York summit meeting, July 29, 1964. *(AP/Wide World Photos)*

Bodies of three missing civil rights workers—Andrew Goodman, James Chaney, and Michael Schwerner—uncovered from an earthen dam by FBI agents *(standing, left)* near Philadelphia, Mississippi, August 4, 1964. *(UPI/Corbis-Bettmann)*

Bob Moses at a memorial service on the ruins of Mount Zion Baptist Church, near Philadelphia, Mississippi, August 16, 1964. *(© Tamio Wakayama)*

MFDP leader Victoria Gray of Hattiesburg, upholding a banner for the right to vote at the Democratic National Convention in Atlantic City, New Jersey, August 1964.
(© George Ballis/Take Stock)

MFDP lawyer Joseph Rauh *(left)* before the Democratic Convention's Credentials Committee, August 22, 1964.

MFDP delegate Fannie Lou Hamer testifying before the Credentials Committee, August 22, 1964.
(Two photos: UPI/Corbis-Bettmann)

TOP: MFDP vigil outside Atlantic City's Convention Hall, August 25, 1964. *(AP/Wide World Photos)*

ABOVE: King at an MFDP rally on the Atlantic City boardwalk, with memorial posters for Goodman, Chaney, and Schwerner, August 1964. *(UPI/Corbis-Bettmann)*

RIGHT: Bob Moses in Atlantic City, August 1964. *(© George Ballis/Take Stock)*

King with National Council of Churches lawyer Jack Pratt in Atlantic City, August 1964.
(Courtesy of Jack Pratt)

MFDP delegate Fannie Lou Hamer singing at a rally on the Atlantic City boardwalk with Emory Harris, Stokely Carmichael *(wearing hat)*, Sam Block, Eleanor Holmes, and Ella Baker. *(© George Ballis/Take Stock)*

Jacqueline Kennedy shaking hands with Hubert Humphrey at a reception for Atlantic City delegates, with Averell Harriman, Lady Bird Johnson, and Robert Kennedy.
(J. Dominis/Life Magazine © Time Inc.)

Fred Berger, Douglas Wynn, and C. R. Holladay, besieged by reporters as the only three Mississippi regulars willing to take delegate seats under the Atlantic City compromise at the Democratic National Convention, August 1964. *(AP/Wide World Photos)*

MFDP delegates sitting in for possession of Mississippi's vacated delegate seats on the convention floor, August 1964. *(© George Ballis/Take Stock)*

President Johnson in the fall 1964 campaign with New York senatorial nominee
Robert Kennedy. *(Francis Miller, Life Magazine © 1964 Time Inc.)*

King campaigning for President Johnson in Baltimore, October 31, 1964, with
Bernard Lee *(glasses)*, Bayard Rustin, and Walter Fauntroy *(front passenger)*.
(© Leonard Freed/Magnum Photos)

King's Nobel Prize delegation. *Front row, beginning second from left:* Ralph and Juanita Abernathy, Coretta Scott and Martin Luther King, Jr., Alberta and Martin Luther King, Sr. *(Courtesy of A. Philip Randolph Institute)*

King leaving truce talk with FBI Director J. Edgar Hoover on December 1, 1964, with Walter Fauntroy *(rear, right)* and Andrew Young *(holding door).* *(UPI/Corbis-Bettmann)*

Four sons view ruins of their home after a Klan arson attack killed their father, Mississippi voting rights activist Vernon Dahmer, January 1966.
(Courtesy of Vernon Dahmer, Jr.)

After ten years in waiting, Wallace Muhammad assumes leadership of the Nation of Islam upon the death of his father, Elijah *(rear photo)*, February 26, 1975.
(AP/Wide World Photos)

The Johnson family preparing to leave the White House for inauguration ceremonies, January 20, 1965.
(Yoichi R. Okamoto, LBJ Library Collection)

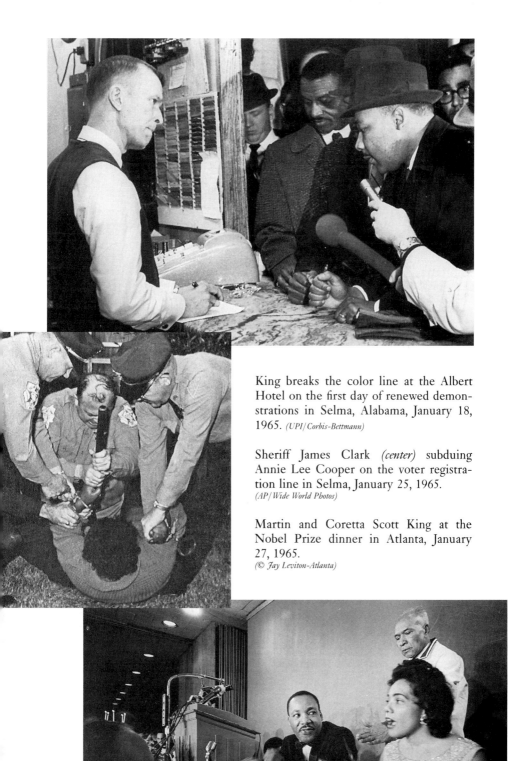

King breaks the color line at the Albert Hotel on the first day of renewed demonstrations in Selma, Alabama, January 18, 1965. *(UPI/Corbis-Bettmann)*

Sheriff James Clark *(center)* subduing Annie Lee Cooper on the voter registration line in Selma, January 25, 1965. *(AP/Wide World Photos)*

Martin and Coretta Scott King at the Nobel Prize dinner in Atlanta, January 27, 1965.
(© Jay Leviton-Atlanta)

SCLC organizer C. T. Vivian praying at the Selma courthouse before his arrest with a line of aspiring voters by Sheriff James Clark *(center)*, February 5, 1965.
(AP/Wide World Photos)

King at a mass meeting upon his release from jail in Selma, February 5, 1965, with Fred Shuttlesworth, Andrew Young, Juanita Abernathy, and Coretta Scott King. *(UPI/Corbis-Bettmann)*

Arrested young people are marched into a Selma jail compound during right-to-vote demonstrations, February 6, 1965. *(AP/Wide World Photos)*

Beyond falsity and defamation, henceforth plaintiffs must also prove that an alleged attack was delivered with " 'actual malice'—that is, with knowledge that it was false or with reckless disregard of whether it was false or not." The decision overturned the Alabama judgments, and barred similar ones, because even Commissioner Sullivan never alleged that the four unwitting civil rights leaders or the advertising employees of the *Times* had concocted malicious falsehoods themselves. This practical result was all but lost among broader implications of the "actual malice" test, which opened a new field of constitutional law with sweeping effects for every news organization, officeholder, and public figure in the country. By casting the decision as unfinished business from the Jeffersonian era, Justice Brennan raised attention permanently above its origins in concerted racial repression. "The case of the individual petitioners requires little discussion," he wrote for the Court, and the *Abernathy et al.* portion of *Sullivan* disappeared beneath the legacy of the *Times.** In later years, wondering what could have prompted the Montgomery police commissioner to sue over the innocuous *Times* advertisement, Brennan's biographer could only speculate that Sullivan "was apparently a man of some thin skin."

WHILE THE JUSTICES labored to submerge racial passions in constitutional law, FBI executives debated whether to offer a summary of the sensational Willard Hotel recordings to the Attorney General. If they did, warned Assistant Director Sullivan, the impulsive Robert Kennedy might well "reprimand" Martin Luther King for illicit behavior, which could shock King into reform or greater discretion. Either way, Sullivan wrote Hoover, King's reaction likely would deprive the Bureau of opportunities to develop "any more such information by the means employed." The prospect of fruitless bugs was enough to make up Hoover's mind. "No," he wrote Sullivan. "A copy need *not* be given A.G." Hoover had been ignoring the Attorney General since November 22 anyway, and he used the Willard coup instead to restore his accustomed direct line to the White House. On January 14, the day before King's thirty-fifth birthday, Hoover arranged a private peek at the Willard transcripts for President Johnson and his chief of staff, Walter Jenkins. Deke DeLoach, the Director's carefully chosen emissary, had known both men since his service as FBI liaison with Congress, and he returned to headquarters satisfied that Johnson and Jenkins were duly impressed.

DeLoach had scarcely delivered his report when President Johnson

---

* The metaphorical cleansing of *Sullivan* anticipated and very likely facilitated the literal disappearance of the minority oral argument from archival records. Before 1968, the Supreme Court transcribed official recordings of historic proceedings, but never of case No. 40, *Abernathy et al. v. Sullivan.* When the Court Library destroyed the tape itself in the 1980s, the January 7, 1964, arguments were permanently lost.

—rudely and mysteriously, from the FBI point of view—confounded hopes that he would recoil from political association with King. To the contrary, White House aides informed reporters that Johnson personally had requested that King, Wilkins, Farmer, and Whitney Young visit him on Saturday, January 18. The invitation itself turned out to be the first in a string of positive surprises for King and the other leaders. Instead of pressuring them to accept weakening amendments to the pending civil rights bill, Johnson assured them of his determination to secure passage "without a word or a comma changed." Far from accepting their gloomy vote counts or fears of further delay, he predicted that the bill would be out of the Rules Committee and through the entire House before the Lincoln's Birthday recess. Incredibly, Johnson was ahead of the civil rights leaders on their own legislation, and most unexpectedly of all, he looked past it to the "war against poverty" announced in his January 8 State of the Union message. Johnson sought their cooperation as full citizens rather than specialists confined to race. When he authorized them to say that publicly, they assumed the grandly vague language of fellow statesmen, telling reporters outside the White House of their "lengthy and fruitful discussion with the President on vital issues concerning our nation."

King put questions about Johnson's aggressive strategy to the score of advisers who gathered the following Monday, January 20, for his Black Mountain retreat near Asheville, North Carolina. Could Johnson make the war on poverty a serious historical force, or was this a mirage caused by the emotional dislocation of Kennedy's assassination? Could the movement safely plan for issues beyond the end of legal segregation, or might an agenda of economic oppression and recompense be a political trap? Johnson's vision raised immediate practical implications for the book about Birmingham that King was rushing to print. In the manuscript as it stood, King recalled an anecdote from his 1959 trip to India, when he had asked how Prime Minister Nehru justified the new national program of job and education preferences for members of the untouchable caste—was it not discrimination?—and Nehru had replied, "Well, that may be, but it is our way of atoning for the centuries of injustices we have inflicted upon these people." Toward the end of his book, King introduced a similar proposal of national redress for the cumulative effects of American slavery and segregation. Now at Black Mountain, he asked whether this provocative idea had been overtaken by the Johnson approach to poverty. To separate race from the question of poverty was to forfeit powerful historical arguments that might bring home to Americans the dire conditions among great masses of maids, day laborers, and semiliterate ex-farmers. But to focus on Negro poverty alone was to invite questions about why the movement ignored the white poor. After extensive debate at Black Mountain, King accepted advice to straddle the issue. He retained historical arguments on the economic burden of race, and proposals for advantage modeled on the GI Bill for veterans of the world wars, but he revised the concept to make it more compatible with Johnson's. In the final book manuscript, his "Negro Bill of Rights" became a "Bill of Rights for the Disadvantaged."

Harry Wachtel was watching the tape recorder. As enthralled as he was to be included with his wife in three days of softball games and mountain resort picnics, and to meet a half dozen King associates new to him, including historians Vincent Harding and Lawrence Reddick— Reddick had been in India with King for his talks with Nehru—and nonviolent strategist James Lawson, the former mentor to the Nashville student movement, Wachtel privately warned King to assume that government agents were infiltrating his Southern Christian Leadership Conference. He shuddered to think what hostile authorities might do with recorded proof that Bayard Rustin predicted political revolt from the structural decay of an economy losing forty thousand blue-collar jobs each week to automation, or with speculations by King that some sectors might need to be socialized to rescue the chronically unemployed. Such things could be political dynamite, Wachtel told King, who finally agreed to have the recordings destroyed.

As instructed, Clarence Jones had brought to North Carolina Stanley Levison's candid appraisal of his own danger to King. Levison sent word that he had broken off with Albert "Doc" Blumberg and other Communist party officials some years earlier—in fact, Jones told King confidentially, Levison said they had accused him of forgetting that for decades Communists had advocated and tried to practice racial equality. Levison had a theory that an old personal adversary was feeding false information about him to the FBI or CIA, but he could not be sure. Whatever the cause, Levison assumed that the recent, welcome relief from high-pressure government loyalty purges may be only temporary. He proposed to keep his distance from King, helping the movement by proxy through Jones. Ironically, for a branded Communist, Levison was caught up in marketing plans for King's forthcoming book. Through his publishing contacts, he pushed for higher advertising budgets and a strategy aimed at hardcover trade sales rather than the "religious" specialty stores, and he hoped for a cover review in the *New York Times Book Review*. Levison also was engaged in a winter-long struggle to hire more efficient personnel and clean up the mailing lists in New York toward the goal, he told Jones, of making the SCLC fund-raising office run like a business.

The written questions King posed to the Black Mountain assembly were deceptively simple. "What are SCLC's basic aims and purposes?" he asked. After nearly a decade in the backwater, the nonviolent movement had flooded over walls of resistance since Birmingham. Now that King was on the cover of *Time*,* the focus of the Supreme Court, and a guest at the White House, he asked his advisers for "a critical evaluation of nonviolent direct action in 1963." Exactly what was different, what the same? "Should we have massive demonstrations in 1964?" he asked. Or should they lobby for the civil rights bill and prepare for the presidential election? Should SCLC remain a consortium of preachers in the South or become a national membership organization?

As always, discussion of the alternatives was an outwardly polite reflection of ferocious infighting. Those who favored a national member-ship organization were prepared to escalate the contained rivalry to com-petitive warfare with Roy Wilkins and the NAACP. Wyatt Walker wanted to target Atlanta for demonstrations on the scale of Birmingham, but James Bevel, who still pushed with his wife, Diane Nash, for a voting rights campaign in Alabama, argued that Walker's imperious manner had alien-ated student demonstrators from King, and that SCLC would never grow until it got rid of him. Walker, who was contemplating a higher paying job in New York, sought to retain a supervisory role over Northern expansion, especially if Bayard Rustin replaced him. Cleveland Robinson, a New York labor leader in King's confidence, flatly called Rustin a self-promoting manipulator unfit to be dogcatcher, while Rustin, for his part, insisted that he report directly to King. Rustin himself was in transition, his credentials never stronger. He was just then closing down his March on Washington office, having written a widely discussed article saying the movement should graduate from a strategy of protest to one of politics. When King cautiously offered to hire him, provided SCLC could avoid the "trouble" of 1960—a veiled reference to the ostracism mounted then by King's fellow Baptist preachers against Rustin as a homosexual—Rustin held out for firmer protection. "If the boys can run you once," he told King at Black Mountain, "they can run you again."

Into the muddle of internal conflict came steady reminders that King's essential message was all too clear to some people wherever he went, South and North. Answering a telephone page at the North Carolina airport, Wyatt Walker heard an anonymous female caller hope that an airplane bomb would rid Asheville of King. Authorities dismissed the threat as a prank and allowed passengers to board, but later called the plane back from the runway for evacuation and search. Piedmont Airlines

---

* The recognition, which so outraged J. Edgar Hoover, nonetheless pricked King's ego with a "Man of the Year" essay that called him a humorless, unlikely, unimposing leader. "Whatever his greatness," said *Time*, "it was thrust upon him." Most painful to King, the essay ridiculed some of his worst youthful metaphors—segregation as "the adultery of an illicit intercourse between injustice and immorality," which "cannot be cured by the Vase-line of gradualism." Over wiretapped phone lines, Stanley Levison described the heavily qualified praise as a "typical hatchet job." King mentioned no complaints in his letter of thanks to *Time* founder Henry Luce.

flight 45 departed for Atlanta three hours late on January 22. Four days later, a "Mr. Adams" called the Denver, Colorado, fire department to warn that a bomb would destroy the Macedonia Baptist Church during King's morning sermon. Military demolition units searched the Montview Boulevard Presbyterian Church before another King sermon the same afternoon. Three days later, the Milwaukee police department concluded that four different callers had warned the *Milwaukee Journal* and other local offices of a bomb set to blow up the civic auditorium during King's rally. As usual, King urged that the threats be disregarded so as not to sow terror in the audience, and local papers played down news of the threats as alarmist embarrassments. Milwaukee police, having assured King that FBI demolition experts were alerted, had no more idea than he did that the FBI saw the bomb commotion as an irritating distraction from the serious business of intercepting King's sex life. In cables to headquarters, agents worried that the extra security details posted around King at Milwaukee's Schroeder Hotel would deflate interest in women, thereby wasting the microphones planted in his room. Director Hoover followed the surveillance debate closely enough to write down a prediction that King would misbehave no matter what. His Milwaukee FBI office, perhaps dreading to contradict the Director, took an apologetic tone in the next morning's bug report: "No activities of interest developed."

15

Hattiesburg Freedom Day

DURING KING's North Carolina retreat, veterans and newcomers converged in Mississippi for the Hattiesburg Freedom Day. Recruitment of prestigious clergy from the North had not gone smoothly since Robert Stone, the ex–Freedom Rider minister from the Bronx, had volunteered his support to Bob Moses during SNCC's Thanksgiving meeting in Washington. Stone's proposal met resistance where he least expected it—from Robert Spike, leader of the new Commission on Religion and Race at the National Council of Churches. In the "God Box," as church bureaucrats called the National Council's massive New York office building near Union Seminary and Riverside Church, Spike was famous for his zealous summons to active church witness. Summoned to the White House in December, with four executives of the National Council, Spike had received President Johnson's personal plea that they guide their actions by what would help the civil rights bill through Congress. Spike knew that the incoming governor of Mississippi was from Hattiesburg and would not welcome the blot of an ugly pastors' demonstration in his hometown just after his festive inauguration. To give Governor Paul Johnson the benefit, Spike declined to have his commission sponsor Freedom Day or seek jail volunteers from its affiliated Protestant denominations. The most he would do was to lend his overworked staff counsel to help arrange bail for Stone's Presbyterians, who had no lawyer. When Governor Johnson strained in his inaugural address toward what passed for racial moderation in Mississippi —"I would say to you that you and I are a part of this world. Whether we like it or not, what happens here through no fault of ours affects us"—Spike sent him a telegram of encouragement from New York.

Left on their own, Stone and his two colleagues on the Presbyterian commission divided their national phone directory into thirds and canvassed fellow clergy. To their dismay, even the most sympathetic contacts were put off by an emergency invitation to pay their way down to a small town in Mississippi to be abused or worse and then pay their way out of jail and back home. The few who were positively inclined wondered how to explain their departure from normal life, and eventually the commissioners pleaded with the heads of the major Presbyterian agencies to set a desperately needed example. This was the idea of Dr. Gayraud Wilmore, a Negro theologian hired from Pfister Theological Seminary to head the three-man commission staff, but Wilmore was reduced to little hope by the time he approached the pink-cheeked, silver-haired John Coventry Smith, who, as secretary of the Commission on Ecumenical Mission and Relations, headed the bureaucracy that supervised 1,300 Presbyterian missionaries worldwide. Unaccountably to Wilmore and Stone, who considered him a piece of soft furniture at ecclesiastical conferences, Smith reached back to the pluck of his experience as a World War II missionary imprisoned in Japan. "I have people who can keep the office going without me," Smith said. "That's what they're paid for. I will go to Hattiesburg."

Smith's name put a jolt of adrenaline through Presbyterian phone lines, but Stone and Wilmore still had received more maybes and devotionals than firm commitments when they journeyed ahead to Mississippi. They left behind the third member of the new Presbyterian commission, Rev. Metz Rollins—a tall, slender Negro with a cavernous bass preaching voice, best known for televised pictures of him beaten bloody on Easter Sunday in Nashville during the first wave of demonstrations after the 1963 Birmingham breakthrough—to escort John Coventry Smith from New York to Hattiesburg as the ranking standard bearer for the Northern church. Into the final mass meeting on the evening of January 21, others appeared one by one until fifty-one white faces and clerical collars dotted St. Paul's AME Church. Presbyterians numbered more than thirty, with reinforcements including ten Episcopalians, two rabbis, and Professor Gibson Winter of the University of Chicago Divinity School. A crowd of four hundred jammed the sanctuary, and an overflow of half that many outside gave the ministers a warm tribute mixed with disbelief, as though a company of strange volunteers had turned up for a parachute mission before D-Day. One movement veteran marveled that Hattiesburg's previous attendance record for mass meetings was twenty-seven.

Reporters and movement leaders also concentrated in Hattiesburg. Ella Baker arrived from New York in time to give a speech that evening, as did James Forman, who led a SNCC caravan from Atlanta. Aaron

Henry, the state chairman of COFO and the NAACP, had been arrested when his familiar car entered town that afternoon, but he posted bail in time for the meeting. Amzie Moore, who four years earlier had sold Bob Moses on the idea of recruiting students for voter registration, drove down from the Delta along with Fannie Lou Hamer, Hollis Watkins, and many others. The doelike Annell Ponder, Martin Luther King's representative in Mississippi, praised Victoria Gray for her swift development from Hattiesburg's first citizenship student to its teacher of teachers. Jack Pratt, the church lawyer on loan from Robert Spike, reviewed from the pulpit the long trail of lawsuits against the local registrar, Theron Lynd, whose defiance of contempt orders, recently left standing by the U.S. Supreme Court, now posed a delicate problem for the federal government—how to punish Lynd for contempt without setting a politically uncomfortable precedent in the contempt case against former governor Ross Barnett, still pending from James Meredith's integration of Ole Miss in 1962. "We're here to prod the Justice Department a bit," Pratt told the crowd.

The largest ovation came toward midnight when Lawrence Guyot summed up the agenda. In the past few months, since being assaulted with Hamer and Ponder in the Winona jail and bailed out of Parchman by Pratt, Guyot had worked toward Freedom Day as the Hattiesburg project director for Hattiesburg, assigned by Moses. He raised his arm for silence and pronounced two words, "Immanuel Kant." After a dramatic pause, Guyot continued: "Immanuel Kant asks, do you exist? Kant says every speck of earth must be treated as important." Among the Northerners, John Coventry Smith was surprised to hear a college-aged Negro make such connections to an audience largely of maids and laborers, some holding babies—so much so that Smith wrote down one of Guyot's sentences ("Redemption is an experience that recreates only those who wish to be redeemed") and later complimented him for making a theological statement. Guyot moved from philosophical thoughts to practical warnings about the morning picket line. Volunteers should conceal money in their shoes and bring toothbrushes for jail, but avoid pencils and anything else that might be construed as a weapon. He suggested some nonviolent techniques to reduce injury from police nightsticks, or from beatings by angry white bystanders if police gave them leeway. Whatever happened would be over quickly, Guyot said, because no civil rights demonstration lasted more than fifteen minutes in Mississippi. These ominous prospects collided with the inspiration of speeches and freedom songs, so that Rabbi Andre Ungar of New Jersey closed his anguished benediction with a forthright plea for "the guts to march."

Only Pratt and the white reporters, under cover of professional neutrality, could lodge safely for the night in white hotels. Since no Negro hotels existed in Hattiesburg, and no white homeowners offered hospitality, the visitors scattered into Negro neighborhoods. John Coventry Smith drew celebrity housing at the Vernon Dahmer farm in Kelly Settlement. Daisy Harris, who had been wrestling with an urge to take Victoria Gray's citizenship class, agreed to provide a bed for two white preachers and wound up with four. Until the mass meeting, her first, Harris had understood that they were coming in to start some new kind of Montgomery bus boycott; afterward, she squeezed the preachers into the beds of three young sons whom she stacked elsewhere. In the chaos of her own home, Victoria Gray announced a last bathroom call before she turned out the lights, warning that anyone who groped toward relief in the dark surely would step on an occupied pallet. Still later, when SNCC historian Howard Zinn discovered someone asleep in his assigned cot at the downtown freedom office, behind J. C. Fairley's television repair shop, he wandered off into the predawn with an interracial group of strays. Zinn soon awakened on a mattress, listening through the walls to the full-throated morning prayer of the woman who had taken them in: "Oh, Lord Jesus, oh let things go well today, Jesus. Oh, make them see, Jesus."

A COLD MORNING rain was pelting Main Street on Tuesday, January 22, when a phalanx of riot-trained auxiliary police marched into sight three abreast—some in yellow slickers, all with helmets, truncheons, and conspicuously holstered guns—and halted on military command in front of the newly formed picket line at the Forrest County courthouse. Some eighty pickets stoically refused a series of bullhorn orders to disperse. Intermingled, the visiting clergy and movement stalwarts braced to absorb a charge, while a hundred white spectators across the street waited expectantly to ogle, cringe, or cheer. After some minutes of standoff, one of the bystanders asked what was going on, and a troubled voice replied from the police formation, "Well, we got to protect the niggers that want to vote."

Few people heard this comment, and even those who did notice the police line turn sullenly from the pickets toward the bystanders were confused at first, figuring a ploy. Guyot stared as though the police unit had levitated. When it dawned on Jack Pratt that an assured mass arrest was turning into the first state-protected civil rights demonstration in the history of Mississippi, his reflex reaction was terror that he and other jubilant sympathizers on the far side of the street would become targets of the vengeful betrayal that swept through the segregationist crowd all around them. Some Negro observers who had held back, fearing arrest, suddenly decided they would be safer among the pickets, and a darting few became a stream of crossovers to augment the lines. Others were inspired to go beyond the pickets to take their first voting tests in the courthouse, where Registrar Lynd was accepting applications one at a time in a calculated stall. Daisy Harris asked James Forman to escort her past the police and the pickets, but her legs went limp as Forman half carried her to the courthouse side. Forman pressed Sheriff Bud Gray about why he permitted only four Negro registrants at a time inside the courthouse, where whites roamed freely, making others like Daisy Harris line up outside in the rain.

With city prosecutors and other Hattiesburg officials who had jurisdiction over the sidewalks, Sheriff Gray had reached a difficult decision not to arrest the pickets. The prevailing thought was to spare the "Hub City"—home of the University of Southern Mississippi and Camp Shelby, the second largest Army camp in the nation, as well as the new governor —a "black eye" of publicity for arresting prominent white preachers, especially now, with Theron Lynd so exposed in defiance of the Supreme Court. The surprise stance of the city fathers frustrated the efforts of SNCC's communications office in Atlanta, headed by Julian Bond, which by diligent promotion of impending drama had drawn to Hattiesburg a large contingent of reporters and network camera crews. For them, even an unprecedented picket line was a dull story. "In such situations, blood and guts are news," candidly observed the *New York Times* correspondent on the scene, "and there is no blood and guts."

Having won the press battle, the city fathers had to endure the rest of the day when hopes proved unfounded that the demonstrators would retire rather than stand in the soaking rain. Officers harassed the swelling lines of pickets and would-be voters. By late morning, annoyance focused on Bob Moses, the young New Yorker widely recognized among Mississippi officials as responsible for much of the Negro voting agitation over the past three years. Moses, ordered to vacate the area, withdrew for consultations but quickly reappeared with a small sign—"Register to Vote"—which made him the "lone picket" among the observers across Main Street. As Moses prepared to escort an aspiring registrant to the courthouse, police officer John Quincy Adams moved to place him under arrest for breach of the peace, whereupon Moses publicly announced that he was making a citizen's arrest of Officer Adams instead, for violation of Section 242, Title 18 of the U.S. Code. By prearrangement, SNCC chairman John Lewis urgently summoned nearby FBI agents to assist Moses in his declared enforcement of the federal criminal statute forbidding state interference with the lawful exercise of voting rights. When the Bureau agents stood passive, merely adding the request to their written notes on the day's events, Adams and two reinforcements hustled Moses off to jail.

By their theater of dueling arrests, Moses and Lewis acted out the enforcement of elementary voting rights that the movement so desperately wanted from Washington, and at times had been promised. Their point was too technical for news and was lost on most of the Northern clergy, who did their best to keep marching. Like the movement itself, they experienced epiphanies and wild mood swings. The whole world seemed to have changed, then nothing at all. To rise above hostility and fatigue, a chorus of pickets formed on the courthouse steps behind the sidewalk lines and sang movement songs through the afternoon rush hour. Swaying along on her gimpy hip, Fannie Lou Hamer belted out the solo lines of "Which Side Are You On?" In memoirs written nearly twenty years later, John Coventry Smith would remember the patriotic lyric "My Country 'Tis of Thee" as anything but corny: "Try to sing 'America' under these circumstances and you begin to understand what a revolutionary song it is."

Freedom Day turned into the siege of Hattiesburg. Having gained an unexpected toehold on the right of public petition, the movement participants vowed to maintain the picket line indefinitely. They marched again all the next day, then gathered for the evening trial of Bob Moses in municipal court, where presiding judge Mildred Norris smoked from a long cigarette holder and fanned herself with one of the picket signs seized as evidence: a photograph of small dark children above the caption "Give Them a Future in Mississippi." Observing the Northern clergy and Mississippi Negroes scattered without regard to racial custom, Judge Norris ordered marshals to segregate the courtroom, but she relented to general astonishment after defense counsel Pratt asked for a recess. Allowing Hattiesburg's first judicial integration, "provided you do not create a disturbance," the judge promptly imposed a guilty verdict and sent Moses back to jail under a sentence of sixty days.

Other judges quickly restored segregated courtrooms, and the siege retained a touch of surrealism. Something boyish and perplexed about his boast, "My dog's so mean he'd bite another police officer," produced howling laughter rather than terror for Officer J. Q. Adams along the picket lines. The county attorney snappishly interpreted a fruit basket meant for prisoner Moses as a slur on the quality of Southern jail food. Sheriff Gray shared convivial meals with white opponents during truce hours, and more than once honored Jack Pratt and companions with a "little taste" of vintage bootleg whiskey from the confiscated stocks that had supplied Governor Johnson's inauguration. On Saturday, January 26, a deranged Negro prophetess leaped around the perimeter of the picket line, shouting, "Preachers gone astray! Preachers gone astray!" Neither side claimed her. By then, after five days on the sidewalks, John Coventry Smith had cut slits in his shoes to relieve swollen feet, and regular hecklers were calling him "grandpa nigger" with a trace of comforting familiarity.

ON SUNDAY, the first batch of replacement clergy arrived in Hattiesburg, summoned by emergency phone barrage from new territories in Colorado, Illinois, and Missouri. Nine of them were arrested the following week, but they handed an unbroken line to twenty-one third-week successors. Home reports of the forerunner clergy spread enough inspiration to keep up the logistical miracle of a perpetual picket line, supplied from distant pulpits. In response, local officials soon arrested Guyot on charges that his speeches corrupted minors, fired Victoria Gray's husband from his job at the city waterworks, along with several others recognized on the picket lines, then aimed new discouragements at the visiting clergy. The city obtained a restraining order against Moses and the religious groups, and in April the state legislature would seek to relieve Hattiesburg with a law against picketing near public buildings, under which sixty pickets went to jail. Still, the defendants bailed out to maintain a continuous presence at the courthouse, while the federal appellate courts disposed of the laws, and pickets marched on through spring into summer, the pilgrim clergy in week-long shifts.

Their tenacity gained little public notice, in part because Hattiesburg never became a major news story in 1964, but the waves swept quietly through the church world into politics. Beyond their contributions in Hattiesburg itself, the new veterans brought home powerful tales. "You asked what the point of it is," a Presbyterian from rural Illinois wrote his two sons. "I think the point is that this is much like Germany at the beginning of Hitler's rise—fear, police intimidation, and summary arrests. I don't want you, or any other kids, to grow up in America in those circumstances." By strategic coincidence, the Northern Protestants were strongest precisely where the fate of the national civil rights bill would be decided—in the Midwest and Mountain States—where civil rights groups and labor unions were scarce and the race issue least familiar. There was no better catalyst for dormant church influence than the astonished personal accounts of Mississippi, delivered by respected ministers to congregations, colleagues, and members of Congress back home in Iowa or Minnesota.

Robert Spike saw these possibilities. Only six months into his new job at the National Council, he pitched them both to the White House and to Bob Moses. For Moses, it was Spike's shrewd vision on the potential combinations of movement experience and conventional politics that made him trust Spike's reservations about Hattiesburg. Spike had thought a one-day jailing was too great a risk for too little gain, that the Presbyterians alone might jeopardize his work to mobilize all the ecumenical churches. Once Hattiesburg became a conveyor belt of transformed and transforming church lobbyists, Spike modified his approach to religious administration. "Never ask in advance" became his motto to the staff for moving any church bureaucracy into racial controversy.

One such step for Spike was the proposed Freedom Summer in Mississippi. In Hattiesburg, the gathered movement leaders resumed debate on this larger issue after picket hours on January 24, with Moses still in jail. Speaking for SNCC headquarters in Atlanta, James Forman complained that the number of students sought for the Mississippi summer project had fluctuated crazily with every meeting: from five thousand in November down to a mere one hundred in December, now back up to one thousand. Ella Baker said plans were galloping in opposite directions. The National Council of Churches already hoped to establish a permanent civil rights ministry in the Delta, for instance, but movement workers there had just informed Baker that they opposed having any Northern whites at all. Some told her it would be impossible to house integrationist whites safely anywhere in the Delta, let alone associate with them in public. Others objected that articulate whites would dominate their projects, still others that white students would approach backward Mississippi as a piece of "sociological research."

McArthur Cotton, who had hung by his handcuffs from Parchman cell bars the previous August, expressed a note of pragmatism. Although he agreed with critics who saw the summer project as haphazard, manipulative, and poorly defined, Cotton said he would wind up doing "all I can" for an influx of Northern volunteers. The movement was messy anyway, said Cotton, and everybody knew that recruitment was going on in the North while they argued. This was true. Not only was Al Lowenstein barnstorming college campuses in search of summer volunteers, but more whites were headed south to join the permanent movement staff. That very week in January, young New Yorkers Michael and Rita Schwerner were opening a CORE community center in Meridian.*

Against impassioned, protective argument that the Mississippi movement should remain local, and should avoid schemes aimed toward publicity or national politics, leaders already were looking beyond the summer project to the national political conventions. Rev. Edwin King had submitted a week earlier the first draft of "Plans for Action at Democratic National Convention." Toward the strategic, educational goal of challenging Mississippi's regular delegates as segregationist, and therefore illegitimate, King recommended forming alliances with supportive civil rights groups nationwide. "They could also advise us on the possibilities for civil disobedience," the report concluded, "not against the convention itself (which would probably not win us any friends) but against the Mississippi delegation—lying in front of their hotel rooms, etc. Bob Moses is trying to get such a group together, we understand."

Moses himself bailed out of the Hattiesburg jail the following week. On Friday, January 31, Guyot swapped places with him to begin a six-month sentence on his conviction for influencing children with movement speeches, and that night Moses kept silent through another marathon

---

* "We have an office and one broken down typewriter," Rita Schwerner advised a contact in a January 23 letter appealing for file cabinets and a mimeograph machine, plus books, paper, and pencils for her Freedom School classes. "We have big ambitions and we know it," wrote Schwerner, "but with the help of people all over the country who believe in freedom, we know we can succeed."

Her husband, Michael, a social worker two years out of Cornell, had first submitted to civil rights arrest the previous July 4 at a Baltimore amusement park, along with Rev. Eugene Carson Blake of the National Council of Churches. Two months later, the Birmingham church bombing had moved the Schwerners to apply together for long-term assignment in the South.

argument about the summer project for 1964. Against pleas of emergency and exhaustion, he refused to use his influence to end the bickering. Once, in a mass meeting, Moses had risen to point out that the congregation had just applauded with equal enthusiasm two rousing speeches advocating opposite courses. They must think about consistency as they claimed the rights of free citizens, he had said before sitting down. In the Hattiesburg strategy sessions, Moses withheld his recommendations even from those who knew of his farsighted contingency plans. By withdrawal, he dramatized his conviction that the movement should draw leadership from the people rather than impose it from above. He waited steadfastly for consensus. Paradoxically, his self-effacing reluctance enlarged his mystique and the hunger of people to follow him.

THE STALEMATE carried over to the morning of February 1, when COFO state chairman Aaron Henry called from Clarksdale with news that yanked Moses out of Hattiesburg. He drove alone west across southern Mississippi through McComb into Amite County, reproaching himself for losing track of Louis Allen since his warning letter to John Doar ("They are after him in Amite...") more than a year earlier, after Deputy Sheriff Daniel Jones had broken Allen's jaw with a flashlight. A struggling, independent logger of forty-four, Allen had witnessed the event that snuffed out the first SNCC Mississippi project in 1961. Bravely, or naively, Allen had told the FBI and other federal investigators that he saw state representative E. H. Hurst execute by point-blank gunfire on a public street a farmer named Herbert Lee, one of the few Amite County Negroes to express support for Moses' voting classes, and that he had been pressured to say otherwise. Now, after this fatal shooting, white reporters from McComb carefully reported local legend that the victim Allen had been the " 'tip-off man' for the integration-minded Justice Department."

Moses had anticipated what grieving relatives told him. The great swell of the national movement that lifted and obsessed Moses all through 1963 had touched even neglected Amite County, where white fears of Negro domination flared around Louis Allen. Although there was no realistic chance then or later for the Lee murder case to be reopened, Allen heard that he was marked for worse than a broken jaw. He had tried more than once to leave Mississippi, which fed the rumor of a plot to secure his testimony from a safe remove. A matching panic took hold of Negroes, to the point that one of Moses' old contacts admitted he had jumped into a roadside ditch when a white man's car approached, just to avoid being seen with Allen. Finally, on a promise of free lodging with one of his brothers, Allen bought a railroad ticket to Milwaukee for the morning of February 1. To overcome the handicap of his second-grade education in a new city without jobs for loggers, he took the risk of asking former white employers for work recommendations, knowing the requests would spread word of his renewed plans to migrate. A mill owner for whom Allen worked seven years said he could not take the chance of helping a suspected Communist.

Elizabeth Allen told Moses her husband had cried through the day before his departure, doubting that he could survive in Milwaukee or hope to send for his family. He had made one last appeal—for a local employer to write a letter vouching that he could drive a bulldozer—then drove home after supper and saw the ambush coming just when he started to open his farm gate at the highway. Allen dived headlong back under his pickup, whose motor was still running, and scrambled toward the rear. His feet were beneath the front bumper when the killer crouched low enough to aim a shotgun under the chassis. The first shot tore off Allen's forehead from his left hairline; the second ripped through his neck and blew out the left front tire. The truck ran out of gas and the battery died before young Henry Allen discovered his father's body.

Moses arrived just after the former deputy Daniel Jones, recently elected high sheriff, stood at the murder site to tell reporters that while there were no suspects he had ruled out voting agitation as a motive. Ordered to investigate a suspected political murder, FBI Director Hoover issued his hold-our-nose instruction reserved for unpleasant civil rights cases: "Advise All Persons Interviewed [That] Investigation Is At Specific Request [of] AAG [Assistant Attorney General] Burke Marshall." By adopting the rationale of Sheriff Jones, if not his word, the Bureau concluded within hours that there was no basis for investigation of a federal crime, inasmuch as "the victim is not a registered voter, has never been active in voter registration activities, and there has been no voter registration activity in Amite County in the past two or three years." No charge would be brought in the Allen murder case.

Anticipating this result, Moses drove out of the Allen gate on Sunday, February 2, past one reporter who recognized him as "the mainspring in the McComb racial turmoil of 1961." Back in Hattiesburg, Moses threw his influence behind the summer project. For him, shell-shocked reality overrode lingering scruples about importing masses of white volunteers. It prevailed over staff resentment that whites would intimidate movement Negroes, and over moral reservations about using young whites as sensational guinea pigs to force federal intervention. It also overrode in Moses a philosophic unwillingness to cut off debate by fiat or personal authority. "We can't protect our own people," he gravely announced. From then on, the summer project became merely a question of details.

A few days later, the distinguished Yale poet and author Robert Penn Warren sought out Moses in Mississippi for an interview. Across more than thirty years—since writing his equivocal essay on segregation, "The Briar Patch," in a manifesto of Southern literary figures who defended agrarian values against Northern materialism—Warren had remained preoccupied with race. He found a reflective companion in Moses, who said he had been rereading Albert Camus in the Hattiesburg jail. Moses was drawn to the French existentialist's challenge of refusing to be a victim without becoming an executioner. "It's the importance to struggle…" he told Warren, "and at the same time if it's possible, you try to eke out some corner of love or some glimpse of happiness within. And that's what I think more than anything else conquers the bitterness." When Warren asked him whether the movement could hope to attain such a standard, Moses confessed that it was hard for Negroes who had absorbed hatred all their lives "not to let all of that out on the white staff." Without disclosing to Warren his decision to go forward with Freedom Summer, Moses described a recent staff meeting at which a Mississippi colleague erupted with "a whole series of really racial statements of hatred.… And we sort of all just sat there. The white students were, in this case, now made the victims."

After three weeks on the Hattiesburg picket lines, the Presbyterian organizer Robert Stone decided to return home temporarily in order to keep up the recruitment of clergy. Vernon Dahmer invited him to dinner before he left for New York, and Stone took the chance to get acquainted with the largely invisible presence always described to him as the buttress, refuge, and final court of disputes for the Hattiesburg movement. Stone hazarded a guess that evening about the delicate mystery of Dahmer's own voting status. Although local whites pointed to him as the sort of upstanding Negro who had voted for years, the most informed movement people could remember only his escorting other Negroes to the courthouse. No one knew for certain that Dahmer registered or voted himself.

Dahmer replied evasively, discouraging further inquiry. "They'd let me vote," he told Stone. "They'd let half a dozen Negroes vote here in this county. But I don't want to do it when they let me. So I don't do it."

16

Ambush

IN WASHINGTON on January 31, as the House solemnly opened final debate on the civil rights bill, Sargent Shriver kept an appointment to brief President Johnson about his month-long trip around the world. Focusing on the moment in Jerusalem when Pope Paul VI had blessed his wooden cross from the Kennedy casket, Shriver said he still had to keep pinching himself to comprehend that an American born on a Maryland farm could stand there with the Pontiff on the soil of reborn Israel, in the presence of the Eastern Patriarch.

"Well, Sarge, that's really wonderful," Johnson interrupted. He spared Shriver his satirical views on Vatican ceremony,* but abruptly shifted ground. "Let's go for a walk," he said, leading outside through the Rose Garden to the driveway of the White House South Lawn. The President announced on the way that he wanted Shriver to launch his new war on poverty.

Shriver replied nervously that he remembered reading in Pakistan or somewhere that Johnson had mentioned poverty in a speech, but he was sure the President could find someone better qualified. Besides, he was more than occupied as Director of the Peace Corps. Johnson said Shriver could run the Peace Corps and poverty at the same time, and Shriver

---

* Since enduring as vice president what for him was the terminal boredom of Pope John XXIII's funeral the previous June, Johnson often caricatured the drone of the Gregorian chant and the fog of liturgical incense in mimicry that incorporated his version of Indian peace pipe ritual.

escaped with a promise to consider the flattering proposal. Not knowing Johnson, he assumed the next move was his.

The next day, Saturday, February 1, a White House operator startled Shriver at home, and Johnson's voice came on the line: "I'm gonna announce your appointment at the press conference."

"What press conference?" asked Shriver.

"This afternoon," said Johnson.

"Oh God," whispered Shriver, who began sputtering that he knew nothing about poverty. Johnson brushed him off. "You can't let me down," he said, "so the quicker we get it behind us the better." Shriver in full panic waved silently for his family to prompt him with excuses. "Could you just say that you've asked me to study this?" he suggested to Johnson, who said, "No, hell no." When Shriver begged politely for time—"I must say that I would prefer it if I had forty-eight hours"—he got back a resounding preview of the morning headlines: "You're Mister Poverty."

"You got the responsibility," Johnson told him. "You've got the authority. You got the power. You got the money. Now, you may not have the glands."

"The glands?" asked Shriver.

"Yeah," said the President.

"I've got plenty of glands," said Shriver.

Johnson mischievously observed that Shriver's Peace Corps was overmanaged anyway, with 1,100 administrators for ten thousand volunteers overseas. "There's not a Kennedy compound that's got a babysitter per ten," he said, "and you've got it in the Peace Corps." This comment reduced Shriver to temporary silence, whereupon Johnson signed off: "Good luck to you. And happy landing." The President fended off a last frantic call for reprieve, which Shriver insisted be put through in the midst of a Cabinet Room briefing on test performances of the Redeye and Walleye missiles, then announced the appointment from the White House movie theater. Hours later, he explained to Shriver that haste was necessary to quell violent opposition within government departments to the choice of an untested outsider.

The poverty program scrambled forward by improvisation from the next day, when miscellaneous experts overran Shriver's home at his invitation. Frank Mankiewicz, who called his boss for reassurance about the newspaper stories and was summoned instead to the first meeting, wound up working six months on poverty before returning to his Peace Corps assignment in Peru. Adam Yarmolinsky, an assistant to Defense Secretary McNamara who had been present when Shriver interrupted the missile briefing, took just as long to get back to the Pentagon. They were among those jammed into Shriver's living room to hear a presentation by Walter Heller and budget director Kermit Gordon.

"It will never fly," Shriver bluntly commented during a break. He conceded some advantages to the "community action" model, as modified since the Christmas skull sessions at the LBJ Ranch. To break through to pockets of "hard-core" poverty, community action advocates wanted the poor themselves to present blueprints for improvement to a lean new poverty agency that would behave more like a research foundation than a traditional government department. Small and experimental, this bottom-up approach carried the flair of innovation, like Shriver's own Peace Corps.

Still, Shriver thought the community action idea fell short of his marching orders to conquer poverty itself. As critics in the room quickly pointed out, the community action proposal lacked even a clear definition of poverty and its causes. By contrast, the jockeying government departments brought statistics and hard experience to bureaucratic politics, with public works agencies eager to fight poverty through public works, housing agencies through housing. To Assistant Secretary of Labor Daniel P. Moynihan, the root of poverty was lack of opportunity, and his department stood ready to run massive jobs programs. To Wilbur Cohen, Assistant Secretary of Health, Education, and Welfare, poverty was disability, and his department pushed programs for training, literacy, and basic nutrition. Shriver, always mindful of what he could sell to Congress, searched for ways to turn bureaucratic conflict to his advantage—perhaps in a war fought "on many fronts." He called in scholars, old schoolmates, bureaucrats, campaign veterans, anyone he thought might be smart enough to "get a handle on poverty." Ideas ran from space program tie-ins back to flat taxes. With his workday stretched at both ends, Shriver scheduled breakfasts, pre-breakfasts, even walking interviews on the way to buy his newspaper. When Hyman Bookbinder called from the Eleanor Roosevelt Memorial Foundation in New York to ask if he could help, Shriver replied, "How soon can you be here?" Bookbinder found himself working with Mankiewicz and Yarmolinsky off corners of desks in temporary offices at an abandoned court building, carrying files under their arms and queueing up for scarce telephones.

POLITICAL SUSPICION complicated the poverty debate. Many saw Johnson as either rescuing or usurping a Kennedy idea, and Shriver as a loyal Kennedy in-law or sellout to Johnson. When Shriver first tilted against community action, Kennedy partisans mistakenly assumed him to be acting on orders from President Johnson, who was considered too much of a hack politician to favor a novel approach. Community action had an avant-garde quality stressed by intellectuals in new, euphemistically named poverty fields—"juvenile delinquency," and "gray areas" of urban decay. Some of them looked to Attorney General Robert Kennedy for rearguard action to champion community action.

Kennedy scarcely noticed. Since Christmas, he no longer gave way to the mordant despair of earlier remarks—"Been to any good funerals lately?"—but he remained wounded and withdrawn, staring over his desk in solitary trances that no one dared interrupt with business. Kennedy read tragic poetry and wrote notes to himself: "The innocent suffer—how can that be possible and God be just." Privately, he referred to President Johnson as "the new fellow," and lost most feeling for politics except for occasional torments over lost power.

Late in January, shortly after returning from a diplomatic trip to Indonesia, Kennedy was ambushed by House members angry that the United States Information Agency was distributing a film on civil rights featuring King's "I Have a Dream" speech. They said J. Edgar Hoover had disclosed to them in off-the-record testimony that King was a Communist philanderer, and worse, that Kennedy had prevented the FBI from distributing warnings about King. This set off a tense, three-week spitting match between Kennedy's office and Hoover's, with each side accusing the other of leaks, bad faith, or carelessness about subversion.

Like litigants, principals from both sides dictated memoranda on meetings and phone calls. "I pointed out that anything the AG had said had been cleared with the FBI," recorded Kennedy's press secretary. "I told Deke [DeLoach] that our record in this matter could withstand any scrutiny." The FBI took a more aggressive stance, pressing its advantage now that Kennedy no longer had family in the White House. "[Burke] Marshall is a liar," wrote Hoover, who circulated this exact charge by memo twice more before the end of February. To Kennedy himself, Hoover rambled on February 5 through veiled warnings about coddling King, then switched abruptly to feigned worries about the general spread of sleazy rumors, all couched as friendly advice: "I stated just like that woman we had in here last week who retracted all the statements she had made about sexual relations with the former President, with him the Attorney General, and everybody else, that there were only two Senators she stuck to, but we had gotten her under oath and she had retracted her statements. I stated some private detective had recorded her statements and was selling it for $500 a copy.... I said people who listen to the recording, which is a vile recording, get a salacious pleasure out of it and then repeat it until it builds up. I stated it rolls like a snowball. I said it is an outrage to the people involved, but Washington is filled with gossip. The Attorney General stated he thought if we all just work closely together that is the best thing, and I agreed." Kennedy talked of leaving office soon, absorbed himself in memorials for the slain president, and resisted the advice of friends who tried to revive his zest for politics. "The hurt that others feel can be only a shadow of your own feelings," wrote Assistant Secretary of State Fred Dutton, who gently coaxed Kennedy toward a long-range idea of "giving much fuller expression to your concern for younger people...

fuller harnessing of your potential impact with the rising generation (over half of the people on this globe are under 26)...."

INTERNATIONAL YOUTH landed in New York on Friday, February 7, at John F. Kennedy Airport, newly renamed for Kennedy's brother. Astonished reporters watched a throng of teenage girls dive into the street to fight over a cigarette butt that Paul McCartney had flicked from his limousine, the winner emerging bloody but enthralled with her trophy. Two nights later, 75 million television viewers witnessed the sustained scream that all but drowned out the Beatles' American debut on *The Ed Sullivan Show*. Few of these could assimilate the flat pronouncement by the London *Sunday Times* music critic that John Lennon and Paul McCartney were "the greatest composers since Beethoven," but the blast of youth hysteria itself seized national attention.

The Beatles rode a tidal wave of numbers. A million more Americans would celebrate their seventeenth birthday in 1964 than in 1963, and behind them the postwar baby boom stacked more than a million "extra" children in each year's age cohort down to the cradle. The number of teenagers, which actually had declined all through the 1940s and stagnated in the 1950s, was about to double to twenty million by 1970. Anticipating what he called "the buyingest age group in history," Ford general manager Lee Iacocca was rolling off the assembly lines for April introduction the first expressly designed youth mobile, the Mustang—affordable but sporty and full of energy, seat belts still optional. Marketing followed suit in industries ranging from cosmetics and soft drinks to politics.

Within their own idiom, the Beatles were a compounded crossover of race traveling back and forth over the Atlantic Ocean. Rock music, one of many jazz offspring, had adapted the distinctive, evangelical abandon of Negro gospel—essentially by lightening its message from religion to romance and pointing its fervor toward youth. Ever since 1952, when Clyde McPhatter and the Dominoes had recorded "Have Mercy, Baby," substituting the word "baby" for the "Lord" of their own gospel standard —and certainly since 1955, when blind pianist Ray Charles changed the gospel lyrics of "I Got a Saviour" to "I Got a Woman"—the formula had registered with certified hits across the racial divide.

The Beatles brought crossover music back to America* with a wallop of clean energy, free of assassination gloom, and white teenagers swooned like Pentecostals at a great awakening. "Beatlemania" swept from February's news the contemporary campaign to ban the song "Louie Louie" by

---

* During their obscurity in Liverpool, the early Beatles made imitative "cover" recordings not only of gospel-bred crossovers Chuck Berry and Little Richard but of more obscure pioneers such as Arthur Alexander ("Anna").

the Kingsmen. (The lyrics were indecipherable, said Indiana Governor Matthew Welsh, but he knew the song was pornographic because his "ears tingled.") Harvard sociologist David Riesman told *U.S. News & World Report* that the four Beatles, "although unkempt in one way, are very 'kempt' in another...it's very safe for a young girl to admire these Englishmen."

On the spearhead of what would become a "British invasion," the Beatles put the careers of American originators into prolonged decline. They bowled over even Sam Cooke, son of a prominent "holy roller" preacher in Chicago, precocious star of gospel's premier group, the Soul Stirrers, until he crossed over into white rock with his 1957 hit, "You Send Me." Cooke had bridged audiences from backwoods church revivals to New York's posh Copacabana Club, with compositions ranging from party pop ("Twistin' the Night Away") to sugar-coated segregation ("Chain Gang"). In 1962, his childhood friend Lou Rawls, formerly of gospel's Pilgrim Travelers, sang background vocals on his soulful hit "Bring It on Home to Me," and by the end of 1963, amazed that "a white boy" like Bob Dylan could have written "Blowin' in the Wind," Cooke wrote a song inspired by road life amid freedom marches and church bombings. With simple lyrics about trees bending beside river currents, he invited his huge cross racial audience into a song of prophecy.

Future critics would uphold "A Change Is Gonna Come" as the outpouring of Sam Cooke's accumulated artistry, but he had the misfortune to perform his new release on national television the same Friday the Beatles arrived at the Plaza Hotel with "I Want to Hold Your Hand." Not yet fully aware how completely their acclaim swamped him and his song, Cooke flew south to visit the Miami training camp of his friend Cassius Clay, who still boastfully ignored ten-to-one odds that the heavyweight champion would crush him. Uncannily, the Beatles followed Cooke to Miami, too, and climbed into the ring with Clay to promote each other in front of the chortling press. "You guys ain't as dumb as you look!" Clay shouted to the Beatles. "No, but you are," replied John Lennon in his deadpan put-on, and Clay pantomimed as mighty Tarzan standing over four pretended knockout victims.

IN MISSISSIPPI, Byron de la Beckwith stood trial for shooting Medgar Evers in the back. The defendant regularly entered the Jackson courtroom with a swagger and a smile in spite of the evidence against him: his fingerprint on the murder rifle, his ownership of the telescopic sight. He acknowledged making the statements offered to establish motive, such as his courthouse speech ("I believe in segregation like I believe in God") and his letter to the National Rifle Association ("For the next fifteen years we in Mississippi will have to do a lot of shooting to protect our wives and children from bad niggers and sorry white folk.") Beckwith took his flamboyant gamesmanship so far as to refuse an alibi and to toy with taking credit for the deed. From jail, he submitted to an outdoor magazine a droll allegory under the heading, "Shooting at Night in Summertime for Varmints."

His confident predictions of acquittal were so widely shared that supporters scheduled a victory dinner in his honor and the widow, Myrlie Evers, prepared an advance statement of protest against the verdict, but the jury returned on Friday, February 7, deadlocked seven to five for Beckwith. Reporters wrote of shock that some Mississippi jurors held out for conviction of a white man for murdering a Negro integrationist; the correspondent for the *Saturday Evening Post* called the mistrial "a victory for the law." At a mass meeting that night, Bob Moses tried to calm celebrations by reminding his listeners that the recent ex-governor Ross Barnett had strolled publicly into the courtroom to shake Beckwith's hand during jury deliberations. Two nights later, Moses introduced the itinerant Al Lowenstein to tell COFO's statewide convention of ambitious plans for a summer project. As a sobering indicator of fear, some COFO delegates proposed that farmers be allowed to use assumed names even on the "Freedom Registration" rolls within the movement.

SEVEN NEGROES were summoned, but none chosen, for the Beckwith jury. Throughout considerable controversy over the all-white panel, Mississippi's legally required exclusion of women from the ninety-five prospective jurors escaped notice as common practice, especially in capital cases. National assumptions about gender rested comfortably apart from the furor over racial identity and citizenship, which accounted for the amused bewilderment that greeted Virginia Rep. Howard Smith's proposal to add the word "sex" to the civil rights bill. "Now I am very serious about this amendment," Smith told his colleagues on February 8, a rare Saturday session in Washington toward the end of the nonstop debate. On the floor of the House, Smith read a letter—"to show you how some of the ladies feel about discrimination against them"—he claimed to have received from a Nebraska woman upset about the nation's "surplus of spinsters." He explained through interruptions of howling laughter her tart demand that Congress equalize the sexual ratio in the population, and recited her indignant charge that "instead of assisting these poor unfortunate females in obtaining their 'right' to happiness, the Government has on several occasions engaged in wars which killed off a large number of eligible males."

Judiciary Committee chairman Emanuel Celler of New York, floor manager of the civil rights bill, rose to oppose the amendment as unnecessary because of the "delightful accord" that had prevailed in his own household for fifty years. "I usually have the last two words," he told Smith, "and those words are, 'Yes, dear.' " The House leaders engaged in a tongue-in-cheek duel of henpecked witticism. Celler found it "anomalous that two men of our age should be on opposite sides of this question."

"I'm sure we are not," said Smith.

"As long as there is a little levity here," said Celler, "let me repeat what I heard some years ago, which runs as follows: 'Lives there a man with hide so tough/Who says, 'Two sexes are not enough.' "

Eleven of the twelve female representatives stood indignantly to challenge the jocular mood. Had there been any doubt that "women were a second class sex, the laughter would have proved it," Martha Griffiths of Michigan told the House. She demanded respect for the amendment on its own merits—not as a Southern ploy to kill the civil rights bill. Technically, Smith's amendment applied to the declaration and enforcement sections of Title VII, which outlawed racial discrimination in employment, but Griffiths accused Congress of exploiting women over Negroes in many other respects since the Civil War. "Your great-grandfathers were willing as prisoners of their own prejudice to permit ex-slaves to vote, but not their own wives ..." she declared in a blistering, overwrought speech. "Mr. Chairman, a vote against this amendment today by a white man is a vote against his wife, or his widow, or his daughter, or his sister."

Republican Katherine St. George of New York rushed immediately to her support, saying that women, too, had been treated as chattels, and were not even mentioned in the Constitution. "We do not want special privilege," she exclaimed. "We do not need special privilege. We outlast you. We outlive you. We nag you to death. So why should we want special privileges? I believe that we can hold our own. We are entitled to this little crumb of equality. The addition of that little, terrifying word, 's-e-x,' will not hurt this legislation in any way."

Embolded, Southern opponents of civil rights stampeded in earnest for passage. "Unless this amendment is adopted," cried George Andrews of Alabama, "the white woman of this country would be drastically discriminated against in favor of a Negro woman!" A Georgian gallantly observed that no Southern gentleman could vote to leave women deprived of employment rights guaranteed to Negroes. Mendel Rivers of South Carolina agreed, saying, "I know this Congress will not be party to such an evil."

By then, legislative historians would record, "pandemonium reigned on the floor." Merriment turned to nervous titters, faces flushed, and panic spread among the marshaled forces of civil rights. Deputy Attorney General Nicholas Katzenbach had warned that chairman Smith might try a desperate ambush of this sort once the bill was wrested from his Rules Committee to the floor, but no one had anticipated that the segregationist Smith could bait the trap with a clear up-or-down vote on female rights. Unexpectedly, Smith's goading and Celler's condescension aroused a storm. Male representatives did not want to speak against the surprise amendment for fear of seeming anti-woman, or anti-white, and the Johnson administration prevailed upon only one female loyalist to speak for the opposition. Rep. Edith Green of Oregon—lamenting that "after I leave the floor today, I shall be called an 'Uncle Tom,' or perhaps 'Aunt Jane' "—told the House she did "not believe this is the time or place for this amendment." It was a difficult decision for her, having watched only recently a female editor being led up the fire escape through the back door of the all-male National Press Club. "I hear more jokes about women in politics than about women in any other field," said Green. Nevertheless, she said, for every slight to women, "there has been ten times, maybe a hundred times, as much humiliation for the Negro woman, for the Negro man and the Negro child, yes, and for the Negro baby who is born into a world of discrimination."

Off the floor, administration lobbyists scrambled to remind representatives of the hard parliamentary realities ahead in the filibuster graveyard of the Senate. President Johnson vociferously opposed even the slightest amendment to the civil rights bill, saying the bill must survive the two chambers in identical form. Otherwise, the dominant Southern chairmen would bury the legislation in an inter-house conference committee. A hundred arguments tugged at the coat sleeves of the representatives who lined up to vote. "We've won! We've won!" shrieked a jubilant supporter of the National Woman's Party as Smith's amendment gained approval, 168–133. For this startling breach of decorum, attendants hauled her bodily from the House gallery.

Only a short weekend determined the impact of the surprise amendment to the civil rights bill. Constitutional expert Alexander Bickel scolded the House for what he called "the apples-and-bananas fallacy . . . burdening with the regulation of bananas an agency already sufficiently overwhelmed with the problem of apples," but other observers dismissed the change in the lighthearted spirit of the Smith-Celler colloquy. The *Washington Post* quipped that the vote made it "pretty plain . . . who's head of the House up there on the Hill." *Newsweek* dedicated the amendment to May Craig, "the frilly-bonneted Maine reporter seen so often on TV." Serious implications did not register, and powerful industries that advertised and regimented employment as much or more by sex as by race—female stewardesses, male pilots, legions of low-paid telephone operators, secretaries, and nurses—were not inclined to stand publicly against the tide of racial reform.

"Smith outsmarted himself," said a Michigan Republican in the House. "At this point there was no way you could sink the bill." On Monday night, February 10, with the gavel banging for order and bedlam threatening in the corridors, the full House voted by roll call on final passage of H.R. 7152, the omnibus civil rights act of 1964—ten titles of which outlawed segregation in schools, public accommodations, and federally assisted programs, while one title outlawed both racial and sexual discrimination in employment. When the tally rolled to decisive approval, 290–130, floor manager Emanuel Celler nearly collapsed with joy over what he called the zenith of his forty-one years in Congress. "I sort of feel like I climbed Mount Everest," he said.

President Johnson jubilantly worked telephones from the White House. "I'm proud of you," he told Majority Leader Carl Albert, who gamely replied that "we stayed put" even though he feared Oklahoma voters "may take me out" over the bill. ("You should see the telegrams I got from home today," Albert told Johnson. "Gosh, they were awful.") Johnson rushed on to consult advisers about whether to praise Albert by name in public statements—"You reckon he wants to be congratulated?" —and about tactical pressures for the Senate. Recognizing that Southern senators were stalling civil rights behind the tax-cut bill—sabotaging tax negotiators until "they couldn't pee a drop"—Johnson instantly proposed to Robert Kennedy and Nicholas Katzenbach that they flip the Senate calendar ahead to civil rights "and then let these tax boys wonder whether we're gonna let the tax bill get through or not." Katzenbach chuckled respectfully at Johnson's giddy schemes. "Whatever you want," Johnson told Kennedy, "I'll be for."

Celebrations erupted that night among an unusual combination of lobbyists. To Robert Spike of the Commission on Religion and Race, plus the hordes of church letter-writers and ministerial visitors supervised by his new Washington coordinator, James Hamilton, the most gratifying positive votes came from fifty-four of fifty-five representatives from Ohio, Indiana, and Illinois, and from eight of the twelve upper plains states Republicans. Jane O'Grady of the garment workers union had stayed up all Sunday night baking Equality Cookies, embossed with an equal sign, which her cadre of volunteers shared with allied message runners, mimeograph operators, and phone managers.

The two chief civil rights lobbyists did not get any cookies. A thirteen-year-old boy banged at a door of the House Gallery with the news that President Johnson was calling lawyer Joseph Rauh and NAACP representative Clarence Mitchell at their temporary office in the Congressional Hotel. Mitchell and Rauh ran anxiously to a pay phone, unaccustomed to emergency calls from the White House. Both of them had spent careers opposing Johnson as a Texas senator, and a Johnson partisan actually had decked Rauh as a liberal intruder outside the LBJ suite at the Democratic convention in 1960. Now Johnson bellowed at them as civil rights commander: "Why are you still there? You fellows get on over to the Senate and get busy."

17

Spreading Poisons

NIGHT RIDERS shot the Hayling bulldog late on Valentine's evening, and within a month, by the patchwork circuitry of the movement era, the plight of St. Augustine engaged theologians throughout New England. In December, the parents of the four juveniles incarcerated since the July sit-ins had capitulated to Judge Charles Mathis of St. Augustine, offering pledges that their children would forgo demonstrations and obey a nine o'clock curfew until adulthood, as the judge required. Even so, Mathis refused to release the youths for Christmas, with a hard determination that stifled protest and celebration over the four young heroes. Fannie Fulwood did not refer to them in January when she gained audience with the city commissioners. Still seeking a biracial committee, she gave them assurance that Hayling had resigned his NAACP post and would not be a participant, but her surrender, like that of the parents, did not go far enough for them. The commissioners wanted to know why Mrs. Fulwood had not retracted her written complaints to Washington about segregation in the upcoming Quadricentennial, which they felt endangered the city's hoped-for $350,000 federal subsidy. They rejected her petitions, and expressed confidence that racial friction would take care of itself now that Hayling was out of the leadership.

Vigilantes found harsher ways to take care of aspiring Negroes. They firebombed a car owned by Charles Brunson, a deaf-mute employed at the Florida School for the Deaf and Blind (alma mater of Ray Charles), while Brunson and his wife were attending a parents meeting. On Friday night, February 7, they burned the home of Bungum Roberson, another parent who had volunteered for the first year of court-ordered school integration at Fullerwood Elementary School. By the following Friday, when small-town St. Augustine buzzed with rumors about likely targets, Hayling stood guard against something more serious than cross burnings in his yard. At midnight, just after calls confirmed that a gasoline-soaked tire had ignited the car and garage of Rev. J. H. McKissick, pastor of First Baptist, warnings that Hayling's dental office was next sent him racing to protect his livelihood. In his absence, a fusillade tore into his home at 1:25 A.M. Four shotgun blasts destroyed windows and furniture, and deer rifles penetrated the walls. Mrs. Hayling and two daughters escaped injury, but a .30-caliber bullet killed their bulldog in the front hallway.

An enraged Hayling moved his family to safety in Cocoa Beach, then told confidants in St. Augustine that it was time to put in the phone call to Martin Luther King. He had resisted taking this step, because nonviolent preachers were not to his taste as an Air Force veteran and freethinker, scornful of religion. Still, seeing no better alternative, he managed to locate King on speaking tour in California. King had followed St. Augustine among a hundred other simmering movements in 1963, and now said he wanted to help, but he could not see Hayling until his next trip to Florida three weeks later. When Hayling pressed the emergency, King steered him to Rev. C. K. Steele, president of King's Florida affiliates. Steele had developed influential contacts in his home town of Tallahassee, the state capital, since leading a bus boycott there in 1956, and he used them to arrange an audience for Hayling and himself with an aide to Governor Farris Bryant. The aide promised to look into Klan violence around St. Augustine.

Hayling flew at his own expense to New York, and tried without success to patch up his feud with NAACP headquarters. Then he talked his way into the Washington office of Assistant Attorney General Burke Marshall, who assured him that the federal government was monitoring St. Augustine. Hayling complained that no one made inquiries at his home since the shooting—not the police nor the FBI—and that the only individuals who had been punished for the September Klan beatings were the victims. He called the White House to remind the President of the promises he made in St. Augustine the previous spring, and got through to an aide who was familiar with the NAACP correspondence about the Quadricentennial, but not with any promises made by the former Vice President. Everywhere, Hayling lamented, he ran into double talk. "This is my last swing," he told a reporter for the Negro weekly, *Jet*, pronouncing himself on the verge of giving up the search for allies.

Although none of these appeals reached the President, a bizarre coincidence drew Johnson's attention to the threat of violence in St. Augustine. On the night of February 25, the President convened his security advisers in the White House family quarters to address intelligence warnings that Cuban kamikaze pilots planned to assassinate him two days later in Florida, by crashing small airplanes into *Air Force One* or his transport helicopter. FBI Director Hoover counseled the utmost caution, especially in light of swirling rumors that Cuban agents may have been involved in the murder of President Kennedy three months earlier. Secretary of State Rusk and other Cabinet officers debated how to protect Johnson without jeopardizing intelligence sources or letting on that the government was rattled. General Maxwell Taylor, Chairman of the Joint Chiefs, developed plans for Air Force fighters to scramble from the Florida bases where the President would land and take off. After the meeting, Johnson fussed privately to Defense Secretary McNamara that "cops and robbers" excesses could consume the whole budget, and that the ever-growing Air Force protection squadrons, which were bound to be noticed, would be "indefensible politically."* McNamara conspired with him to hide the squadrons at extremely high altitudes, saying he did not think jet escorts would be "worth a damn" against propeller-driven kamikazes, anyway.

On February 27, President Johnson flew into a compounded security crisis near Jacksonville, Florida. With military and civilian units primed for air attack on his life, one dynamite explosion derailed thirty-two railroad cars in St. Augustine, and a second blast struck fifteen miles to the west—halfway between St. Augustine and Johnson's helicopter destination at Palatka, where he dedicated excavations for the ill-fated Cross-Florida Canal. The two bombs severed rail lines along the coast, blowing freight cars across highway arteries and snarling automobile traffic. Presidential guards dreaded a third bomb that never came.

That night, President Johnson angrily pounded the lectern at a Democratic fund-raiser in the Fontainebleau Hotel on Miami Beach. "This criminal action must stop now!" he shouted, and announced that he had ordered J. Edgar Hoover by telephone to send "one of the greatest inspectors" into St. Augustine. His outburst startled the assembled guests and reporters, who, unaware of the kamikaze threats, frowned at what seemed an extreme, unpresidential reaction to yet another bombing in the year-old labor strike against the Florida East Coast Railway. By then, Hoover already had dispatched FBI inspector Joseph Sullivan with a team of thirty FBI agents to lead a massive federal-state investigation of the ongoing war between the railroad unions—angry over company refusal to pay a ten-cent-per-hour wage increase prescribed by arbitration—and the combative, eccentric railroad president, Edward Ball of St. Augustine, a DuPont heir known for his nightly toast over a glass of bourbon: "Confu-

---

* "If they ask you what are they doin' up there," Johnson explained to McNamara, "and you say, they're ceremonial, they'll say well here's a guy who cuts out lights in the White House…but he's got a big escort. If you say, it's to protect his life, they say Godamighty, what's happened?"

sion to the enemy." Within three weeks, Sullivan's team would arrest union sympathizers on sabotage charges.

Hayling, for his part, watched federal agents swarm over St. Augustine just as he had hoped, but could only regret that they had no mandate to investigate the violent defense of segregation. On March 6, he led a small caravan from St. Augustine to Orlando for the Florida meeting of the Southern Christian Leadership Conference, only to find that King had canceled his appointment with them to join a freedom march of ten thousand at the Kentucky State Capitol in Frankfort. In his place, they met with the SCLC director of affiliates, Rev. C. T. Vivian, a pioneer of the Freedom Rides who had served with James Lawson as a mentor to the Nashville student movement. Vivian promptly visited St. Augustine himself, but he further disappointed the Hayling delegation with word that SCLC would not adopt a group with so little local support. The Negro pastors of their city were passive and afraid, he said, and much of the NAACP leadership seemed to agree with segregationists that Hayling was too abrasive. Until they could build up their own movement, Vivian could offer only what he had provided Golden Frinks of North Carolina the previous fall: an appeal to King's friends in the New England clergy. He offered to help recruit seminarians for demonstrations over spring break.

For Hayling, the prospect of student pilgrims was an enormous letdown from dreams of rescue by Dr. King, let alone from his hopes for FBI protection. He derided the scheme as futile, but his NAACP remnant asked Vivian to recognize them as a new SCLC chapter. On March 11, before they could get their SCLC stationery printed, Hayling composed a letter to King's only affiliate in the North. "Spring Vacation is a time when college students from all over the nation head south to the sunny beaches of Florida," he began, then exhorted students to stop short of Daytona Beach at the end of March and join the "struggle for human rights in St. Augustine."

Hayling's letter and a host of phone calls placed the plight of St. Augustine before the small network of clergy and theologians running the Massachusetts SCLC chapter. Its president, Rev. Virgil Wood, had served until recently on the SCLC board from his home church in Lynchburg, Virginia. Of all his campaigns, the violent police repressions in Danville the previous June still haunted Wood, who had survived one terrifying march when nearly fifty of his cohorts were hospitalized, he believed, only by maintaining a desperate contact with his captor. ("I got his eyes and wouldn't let his eyes go," he told movement veterans.) Shortly afterward, Wood had proposed that he relocate his family to establish new SCLC chapters in the North. He sensed in his colleagues a suspicion that he was shell-shocked and battle-weary, deserting them for self-preservation, which he knew to be partly true, and therefore he was supremely grateful to Daddy King for declaring gruffly that he thought Wood's Northern expansion was a fine move for SCLC, whether it offended Roy Wilkins or not.

Wood had obtained employment as director of the Blue Hill Christian Center, an experimental parish in the Negro slums of Boston sponsored by his former seminary, the prestigious Andover-Newton. Blue Hill ran a tutoring center, a shelter, a "mothers' club" nursery for working parents, and a street ministry featuring a radio worship hour at noon on Saturdays. After the March on Washington, Wood and former classmates had recruited fifteen Boston clergy to go south in the first of several waves supporting Golden Frinks and his Spontaneous Movement Youth Choir in Williamston, North Carolina. Now, three weeks before Easter, the staff and volunteers of Massachusetts SCLC solicited a second line of recruits for Hayling in St. Augustine. *"This is not a vacation,"* they stressed in the application form mailed to seminaries and college chaplains in New England. "... Students should previously secure a source of bail...." Professor Harvey Cox of Andover-Newton wrote a capsule history of the struggle to end segregation in St. Augustine before its Quadricentennial.

With James Breeden, Paul Chapman, and other core clergy from Wood's SCLC chapter, Cox approached three prominent Episcopal bishops about escorting the student demonstrators to Florida. The bishops declined to go when they could not coax a courtesy invitation from their counterpart bishop in Florida. Their deference to church protocol produced grumbling within their own households, and the wives of the SCLC clergy obtained substitute commitments from the wives of all three bishops. "If you never see me again, look out for your father," said Esther Burgess, wife of the first elected Negro bishop in the history of mainstream American churches, to her children. One of her companions, Mary Peabody—a Boston Brahmin of highest pedigree, daughter-in-law of the founder of Groton School, wife of Bishop Malcolm Peabody, mother of Massachusetts Governor Endicott Peabody—caused a small stir from the moment she made her way down to the Blue Hill Christian storefront for hurry-up training as a nonviolent witness.

As IN FLORIDA, white vigilantes of Mississippi mobilized in shadows cast by their political leaders. To preserve a unified white vote, Governor Paul Johnson sponsored bills to bar electoral machinery and political opportunity from the negligible Republican party of Mississippi. The legislature authorized two hundred new state troopers with special powers to control racial disturbance, and in February, seeking to deter any summer "invasion" by Northern students, Jackson's Mayor Allen Thompson gathered his heavily reinforced police battalion—including a riot squad in gas masks, with a fresh arsenal of two hundred shotguns and a new, custom-built armored wagon called "Thompson's Tank"—to pose in parade-ground formation for news cameras. "There will be no unlawful marching and peaceful picketing," he told *Newsweek* as he described the city's emergency preparations to hold as many as 25,000 prisoners.

Almost simultaneously, on February 15, two hundred men met secretly in Brookhaven to create the White Knights of the Ku Klux Klan as a more disciplined, commando-style splinter group from the parent Klan. With theological language that protested earthly corruption ("Selfishness is the festive queen among humankind, and multitudes forget honor, justice, love and Almighty God, and every Christian principle in order to do homage to her"), Samuel Bowers of Laurel summoned Klan converts to a purifying war against Satanism as manifested in the Communist yoke of civil rights. "We are men who humbly submit to the Will of Almighty God, and who beseech Him for Guidance in our works," each new member pledged at initiation, "but who will not under any circumstances see the Nation and its Constitution destroyed without violent, Physical resistance...."

Bowers, a charismatic with a knack for clandestine warfare, orchestrated random night attacks that quickly frightened the Negro movment. ("We are being deluged," Bob Moses wrote Al Lowenstein. "There have been five killings in S.W. Miss. in the last 3 months. Klan activity—3 whippings, scattered shootings, 180 cross burnings.") In April, the Mississippi White Knights were strong enough to send a statewide recruiting message by burning crosses in more than sixty counties on a single night, and secret membership mushroomed toward ten thousand by the end of May.

The Mississippi State Sovereignty Commission worked an intermediate ground between press conferences and cross burnings. A state agency, funded by the legislature to defend white supremacy after the *Brown* decision, the commission responded in February to a complaint from the mayor of Ruleville that Fannie Lou Hamer was distributing food and clothing on condition that destitute families try to register to vote. Commission operatives consulted the state attorney general about bringing bribery charges against her. They determined that the donated relief supplies came from Cambridge, Massachusetts, and traced the names of freight companies and suppliers. From the Sunflower County registrar at Indianola, they obtained descriptions and license plate numbers of those escorting Hamer's applicants. Because few of the applicants were successful, and no more truckloads from Cambridge were expected through the winter, the commission decided with the Ruleville mayor "not to give this group of agitators any type of publicity for the time being; however, their activities are going to be under close surveillance."

Sovereignty Commission investigators also moved steadfastly to curtail Tougaloo College, which was one of the state's few havens for integrationists. From faculty and student informants, commission director Erle Johnston compiled "a list of the trustees and sources of revenue for the school," and then, with Governor Johnson and legislative chairmen, presented a blunt proposal to institutional supporters as far away as New York. If Tougaloo president Daniel Beittel and Chaplain Edwin King were fired summarily, Johnston informed Wesley Hotchkiss of the United Church of Christ, "we are in a position to guarantee . . . that no punitive action will be taken by the Mississippi Legislature. . . ." Otherwise, he added, the state would revoke the Tougaloo charter or remove accreditation for its graduates to teach in public schools. Tougaloo held out for Chaplain King's faculty status, but President Beittel submitted to forced resignation in April. Johnston expressed optimism that carefully applied threats could stamp out agitation elsewhere. "We have put into action a plan for Rust College similar to the plan we used at Tougaloo College," he advised Governor Johnson.

A SLOW TIDE of crisis spread pressures and counterpressures to odd places at great remove. The Sovereignty Commission expanded from Mississippi into Washington, D.C., to underwrite the principal lobby against civil rights legislation in partnership with newspaper publisher William Loeb of New Hampshire. As chairman of the Coordinating Committee for Fundamental American Freedoms, Inc., Loeb opposed the "Socialists' omnibus bill" through paid advertisements in two hundred newspapers, while in his home state he trumpeted two parallel crusades. Determined to keep New Hampshire free of statewide income or sales taxes, Loeb sought to create by ballot initiative the first legal state gambling lottery of the twentieth century. "Don't Forget to Vote FOR the Sweepstakes," he urged voters from the front page of his *Manchester Union Leader*. He also campaigned tirelessly for Senator Barry Goldwater in the nation's first presidential primary, warning New Hampshire voters of a nefarious plot by civil rights forces to make sure that "the Negro will gain the upper hand and be strong enough to take over every government office in this country." On a claim to have discovered Negro-authored hate leaflets "rolling into the Granite State," the *Union Leader* reprinted dubious texts that rallied the minuscule Negro population of New Hampshire (about three people per thousand) against Goldwater as "the choice and champion of the white man."

On Thursday, March 5, Loeb hosted a Goldwater rally at the Manchester armory. "ROAR APPROVAL OF BARRY," the *Union Leader* proclaimed. Senator Goldwater denounced Washington's "failure of leadership," and actor Ronald Reagan, presented as "The Gipper," appeared on a film screen. "A democracy cannot exist as a permanent form of government," said Reagan, who told the Manchester crowd that he was citing the eighteenth-century historian Fraser Tydler. "It can only exist until the voters discover that they can vote themselves favors out of the public treasury," Reagan declared. "From that moment on, the majority always votes for the candidate promising the most benefits from the public treasury, with the result, the democracy always collapses over a loose fiscal policy, always to be followed by a dictatorship." While the film likeness of Reagan recommended Goldwater as America's best chance to avert such a calamity, Reagan remained at home in California, pondering a career move to politics. He supported a statewide ballot initiative called Proposition 14, which sought to repeal California's Rumford Fair Housing Act of 1963.

Although Proposition 14 would become a harbinger of national backlash against civil rights, and of California as a bellwether in citizen politics, it was overlooked at the time as a subplot of the election year. The success of the civil rights movement swept nearly all perception of race into the framework of Southern segregation, whose fate was hanging on a threatened filibuster in the U.S. Senate. When King urged California audiences to protect their fair housing law from Proposition 14—"Every citizen must rise up and save it!" he told a rally at the Los Angeles Palladium—his alarms were confined to the Negro press. Supporters of Proposition 14 defined their initiative as a matter of homeowners' freedom rather than the right to exclude Negroes in real estate, as King described it.

In Northern campaigns, early signs of white resentment were dismissed as illusion. Until he verified the flattering reports by personal inspection on March 6, George Wallace doubted that a political novice from Oshkosh had on her own initiative recruited a slate of pledged delegates and collected enough signatures to enter him—the arch-segregationist governor of Alabama—as a candidate for president in the liberal state of Wisconsin. When Wallace announced his challenge to President Johnson in Wisconsin's April 7 Democratic primary, reporters downplayed the story.

Leading thinkers did not know what to make of civil rights protests close at hand, where there was no legal segregation. "The Negroes are starting a boycott in NYC this morning," theologian Reinhold Niebuhr wrote privately on the February day when nearly half a million children stayed home from New York public schools as unfit for learning. "I think they are overplaying their hands. The poor things have wretched schools in Harlem.... They think that a massive desegregation will raise the level of their schools, but that will require transportation of negro and white children.... Human nature is not that good...." Socialist leader Norman Thomas, who had risked his own safety during the Mississippi Freedom Vote, complained that public disturbance in the North "alienates the friends we have got to win and hold."

When a wiretap alerted the FBI that Bayard Rustin, an adviser to the one-day boycott, planned to attend a U.N. reception honoring a Soviet writer, Vadim Sobko, who had been invited to America by pacifists, FBI headquarters moved swiftly. From Washington, Assistant Director De-Loach planted a story on the front page of the *New York Daily News:*

"Boycott Chief Soviets' Guest." The ambushed Rustin gamely predicted that "the Negro people will pay no more attention to this than they do when Adlai Stevenson has lunch at the Soviet Mission," but FBI officials boasted that "Rustin is now at the very least a controversial figure." Not only were puzzled readers—many wondering why New York Negroes would punish their own children—susceptible to suggestion that the school boycott might be a Soviet Communist plot, but private recriminations among Negro leaders opened ground for follow-up operations. Privy to the telephone backbiting over Rustin's conduct, FBI wiretappers detected "a tremendous opportunity to cause Roy Wilkins and the NAACP to attack Rustin."

Like the Mississippi Sovereignty Commission, the FBI's clandestine political arm (called COINTELPRO, for "counter-intelligence program") adopted the premise that the civil rights movement was a disguised arm of Communist conspiracy. COINTELPRO grew into active use just as the actual threat of Cold War subversion diminished, expanding into new territory against the connective alliances of the civil rights movement. As Northern clergy mobilized against Mississippi segregation, the Bureau carefully combed security files for "Communist Party domination or control" of the twenty-one incoming officers at the National Council of Churches, including the Hattiesburg Freedom Day marcher, John Coventry Smith.

COINTELPRO specialists intervened to weaken some racial forces to which the Bureau itself assigned no pretext of Communist influence. To "widen the rift between [Elijah] Muhammad and [Malcolm X] Little and possibly result in Little's expulsion from the NOI [Nation of Islam]," FBI headquarters drafted an anonymous news story about "war within the ranks of the Muslims' empire," based on the infighting gleaned from wiretaps. In February, DeLoach and his assistants fed directly into the *Chicago Defender,* the nation's largest Negro newspaper, a provocative text that described Malcolm's suspension after his Kennedy assassination statement as a public cover for a factional battle in which Malcolm, attacked by his colleagues as a "religious fanatic and a hard-to-control true revolutionary," countercharged that luxury had corrupted the Muhammad family from the Nation's strict moral code. The story was close enough to the truth to give FBI authors the satisfaction of learning by wiretap that Elijah Muhammad's advisers considered it a leak by Malcolm X. "All the papers have it," they fumed.

FROM THE FBI point of view, harassment of Malcolm X or Bayard Rustin was routine background business compared with the political warfare against Martin Luther King, who played an unwitting central role in the triangular struggles among Hoover, President Johnson, and Robert Kennedy. In a state of political crisis on the evening of February 17, Johnson's chief of staff, Walter Jenkins, and his young assistant, Bill Moyers, summoned Assistant Director DeLoach. He arrived at the White House just ahead of a night courier who delivered the Justice Department's voluminous King file. Burke Marshall, Jenkins explained gravely to DeLoach, had dispatched the file to them with a warning that the FBI was trying to leak derogatory stories about King, which could destroy the civil rights bill in Congress. Marshall said he wanted the White House to know the full extent of the FBI's intelligence effort against King, but Jenkins suspected that Robert Kennedy had put Marshall up to it for an ulterior motive. He confided to DeLoach his theory that the Attorney General, "who desperately wants to become Vice President," aimed to establish a record that he had notified Johnson fully "about King's communistic background." Moyers, as DeLoach later told Hoover, expressed a more sinister interpretation: Kennedy himself planned to leak anti-King stories, framed with the accusing suggestion that President Johnson kept up "political footsie" with King even after learning of his flawed character.

This was intrigue of Shakespearean dimensions. It played on the fears, jealousies, and clashing ambitions of Johnson and Kennedy after the assassination, with the White House itself teetering over control of explosive racial secrets. The very fact that Jenkins consulted DeLoach signaled that the Johnson White House favored the FBI on such treacherous ground, leaning toward alliance with Hoover against Kennedy rather than vice versa. DeLoach pressed the Bureau's advantage by arguing to Jenkins and Moyers that Robert Kennedy—not Johnson—was politically vulnerable over the King files. Kennedy had "shielded King for a long time," he said, and had also signed the secret wiretap order. DeLoach persuaded Jenkins to reject the King files as a political land mine and ship them overnight back to the Justice Department.

Hoover restored his cherished direct line to the White House in large part by cultivating President Johnson's personal resentment of Robert Kennedy. He shored up the common bond of two senior statesmen breaking from a humiliating dominance by the same younger man, and chafed meanwhile against nominal superiors in the Kennedy Justice Department as the burden of a foul vendetta. "Katzenbach did his dirt against us before the Warren Commission,"* the Director wrote on one of DeLoach's memos, " + now Marshall is trying to poison the W.H. [White House] about FBI." Hoover sent Johnson a stream of secret messages through DeLoach that Kennedy was plotting against him, too. Johnson fired two White House aides on the strength of FBI intelligence that they were

---

* Deputy Attorney General Nicholas Katzenbach re-earned Hoover's enmity in February by insisting that he provide the Warren Commission with unpolished records about the Kennedy assassination. Some of them, such as reports indicating the Bureau had excised Lee Harvey Oswald's name from the address book of a Dallas FBI agent, became grist for later generations of conspiracy theorists.

working undercover for Kennedy, and Hoover followed up with ominous reports that Kennedy's prosecutors were concocting investigations to embarrass Johnson.

Kennedy worries preoccupied Johnson all through February. When he tried to arrange a job for Theodore Sorensen through producer Darryl Zanuck, and Sorensen resisted a condition that he be available to help Johnson through the 1964 campaign, the President gave way to suspicions that Sorensen was plotting to help Kennedy run against him instead. He joked balefully about surrendering the White House to accept the Hollywood job himself. "We'll let Bobby and them take over," he told his New York adviser Ed Weisl. "And let 'em run against a Republican and let a Republican beat 'em." On another front, Johnson personally supervised investigations of Paul Corbin, an irrepressible Kennedy loyalist said to be promoting a Kennedy-for-President write-in vote for the New Hampshire primary. Just after House passage of the civil rights bill, he confronted Kennedy with plans to fire Corbin from the Democratic National Committee, and the Attorney General objected with emotion that Corbin should be given a fair hearing. Kenneth O'Donnell, still in the White House, offered Johnson "my two bits" on the crisis: "First, this fella [Corbin] is absolutely no good, and I can say on the other hand, Bob's got a complete blind spot on him." The President rallied his forces against Kennedy's attachment to Corbin, saying "it's gonna be a problem and it's gonna be serious."

For Martin Luther King, the Johnson transition sent a misleading message about FBI attitudes. Relieved of the persistent pressures and veiled warnings of the past three years, he had reason to hope that he was escaping Cold War suspicion, but it was Hoover instead who was getting free of political constraint. Almost daily, an FBI blow landed somewhere in the country against the oblivious King, who searched for a revised movement strategy. On March 4, as he flew to Alabama for a statewide SCLC meeting, the Bureau's top officials learned to their horror that Marquette University had offered him an honorary doctorate. This was "shocking indeed," recorded an FBI supervisor, especially coming from "the same institution which honored the Director with such a Degree in 1950." Headquarters instructed Milwaukee agents to approach reliable contacts at Marquette with a confidential sample of the Bureau's worst allegations about King's private life and "communistic connections."

King, who knew of the proposed honor from Marquette, addressed conflicting pressures in Montgomery. "We have not lost sight of the fact that nonviolence was born in Alabama," he told two hundred SCLC associates. He pictured a bold new campaign variously as statewide or concentrated, run from Montgomery if not from Birmingham, directed against stubborn segregation or possibly for the right to vote. Drawbacks plagued each option. A return to the "unfinished business" of Birmingham would advertise the trauma still there six months after the unsolved church bombing,* not to mention white backsliding from the terms of King's landmark settlement. Against the impassioned advocacy of James and Diane Bevel, on the other hand, critics objected that it was foolish to launch a drive for voting rights while Congress was debating segregation.

Undecided, King broke away for the Freedom March in Frankfort and then speech travels to Atlanta, Connecticut, New York, and back to Kentucky. He learned on the run that Marquette had dropped its honorary degree because of commencement conflicts with his June schedule—but not that FBI headquarters bestowed a special commendation upon the agent who engineered the Marquette "impasse," or that the Bureau was blocking another honorary degree at Springfield College. Massachusetts Senator Leverett Saltonstall, DeLoach reported to headquarters, was deeply shaken by the derogatory briefing on King he received in strictest confidence, and "said if it were not for the integrity of the FBI he would disbelieve such facts."

On March 6, DeLoach reluctantly met with Robert Kennedy's press secretary, Edwin Guthman, who blurted out grievances accumulated over the past four months. He charged that President Kennedy's body had not yet cooled before Hoover and the FBI began circumventing the Justice Department to deal directly with the Johnson White House. Not only were Bureau people shunning the Department, Guthman said, but Kennedy was picking up stories of political collusion between Hoover and Johnson against him. He said the Kennedy people deserved better, especially in light of the Attorney General's public record of defending Director Hoover. "I made no comment to this obvious lie," DeLoach told headquarters in a report that stressed scorn for Guthman's "entire line of chatter."

On DeLoach's recommendation, Hoover took the Guthman peace feeler straight to the White House as fresh evidence of conspiratorial leaks from presidential holdovers loyal to Robert Kennedy. After lunch on the following Monday, March 9, Hoover and DeLoach accepted President Johnson's invitation to paddle around with him and Walter Jenkins in the White House pool. The President asked Hoover for a confidential evaluation of actress Janet Leigh, a possible nominee as ambassador to Finland. (Three days later, the Director called Johnson to report that Leigh was "absolutely clean... one of the finest, cleanest persons out in Hollywood ... a fine mother.") Johnson showed no distaste for the recent batch of weekly reports on Martin Luther King's sex life and phone calls, including the latest, rather mundane bulletin about King's second thoughts on hiring Bayard Rustin, and he pushed Hoover to report on Paul Corbin and other

---

* Two white teenagers, who confessed to the whimsical snipering of young Virgil Ware from his bicycle on the afternoon of the church bombing, received suspended sentences early in March.

connections to Robert Kennedy that might pose political danger. Like Hoover, Johnson worried obsessively about press criticism, which gave the Director an opening to present his Bureau as politically loyal detective agency. That afternoon, hours after hearing Johnson decry as slander a current news report that he planned to lower the military draft age to seventeen, Hoover called Johnson from headquarters to identify Sargent Shriver as the Bureau's chief suspect in the leak.

Still, Hoover the master bureaucrat was more than shrewd enough to read signals about Johnson's limits. From the President's expressed hopes for passage of the civil rights bill in the Senate, where debate opened that same Monday, Hoover knew to refuse Rep. Howard Smith and other Southern committee chairmen permission to attack Martin Luther King with FBI material circulating on Capitol Hill. "I do *not* want anything on King given to Smith or anyone else at this time," Hoover instructed DeLoach,* knowing that any controversy would mark the Bureau as the source. Similarly, Hoover recognized a test when Johnson interrupted their pool conversation with a monologue on his forthcoming poverty program. The President asked the Director to read and review the advance recommendations of the new Shriver task force, a request so foreign to Hoover's taste that he was unsure whether Johnson intended it as an idle remark or a hint to temper his criticism of Shriver. DeLoach treated the unpleasant chore as a straightforward test of loyalty, and drafted for Hoover an enthusiastic appraisal of the anti-poverty blueprint. On his own, DeLoach thanked President Johnson for social courtesies with the flattery that served well in Hoover's FBI: "The informality, yet quiet dignity you possess, never ceases to inspire me."

MARTIN LUTHER KING spent the Monday of Hoover's White House luncheon at home in Atlanta, reflecting on recent history. He did his best to shut out dramatic news—the Supreme Court's announcement that morning of its historic reversal in *New York Times v. Sullivan,* and published reports that U.S. District Judge Harold Cox referred in court to would-be Mississippi voters as "a bunch of niggers . . . acting like a bunch of chimpanzees"—and withdrew for hours to record one of the first oral histories for the contemplated Kennedy presidential library. On assurance of confidentiality until his death, King surprised the interviewer by stating that he had not found much difference between Kennedy and Richard Nixon during the 1960 campaign. Senator Kennedy, said King, struck him as "so concerned about being President of the United States that he would

---

* "I told Judge Smith also that despite our desire to see this scoundrel [King] exposed, it would be out of the question for us to furnish him information and then his expecting us to back it up later on," DeLoach wrote obediently to headquarters in his own Runyonesque syntax. "I told Judge Smith that this would disrupt certain operations which appeared to be more important than an exposure of King from a communistic standpoint."

compromise basic principles." Abandoning his customary detachment, King lapsed into a reminiscence on his surprise night ride to state prison before the election. "They had me chained all the way down there, and, you know, the chains about my legs," he said. "They kind of tied my legs to, they had something in the floor where the chains were attached, and I guess it's a method they use when they transport real criminals, so it would be no way for me to escape. And I was handcuffed."

He recalled from the standpoint of a helpless prisoner an event that analysts had identified as a turning point of national politics. "I had known Nixon longer," he said. "He had been supposedly close to me, and he would call me frequently about things, getting, seeking my advice. And yet when this moment came, it was like he had never heard of me, you see." Of the contrasting phone call by John Kennedy, King tried to talk himself into a generous reading. "And I would like to feel, I really feel this, that he made the call because he was concerned," he told the recorder. "He had come to know me as a person then. He had come to know more about this problem. Harris [Wofford] and others had really been talking with him about it." Those briefings must have opened Kennedy to King's personal and racial burdens, he reasoned, and yet he realized that candidate Kennedy had pondered the risk of a friendly gesture toward a Negro leader. "And there's nothing wrong with it," he said of political calculation. From his habitual effort to project himself into the mind-set of a white leader, King managed to find clues of genuine sympathy in Senator Kennedy's phone call to Coretta. "That's the other thing," he said. "He didn't *know* it was politically sound."

Throughout his interview, King generally admitted that political frictions remained far stronger than personal bonds or shared conviction. He recalled the Kennedys' stinging rebukes over his conduct during the Freedom Rides, his Albany jail marches ("They were very, very upset about that"), and the Birmingham campaign. He said events changed President Kennedy rather than vice versa. If made public, his account would have been received both as a slur on President Kennedy's reputation and a confession of King's wounded self. By ingrained training, King normally adjusted his sharp inner divisions—a sturdy dignity at war with enraging exclusion, which the scholar Du Bois had called the "twoness" of race— toward a middle ground that he could present to whites and Negroes alike. "I really think we saw two Kennedys, a Kennedy the first two years and another Kennedy emerging in 1963," he told the interviewer more than once. The Kennedy who had vacillated over his "razor-thin edge" from the 1960 election changed after Birmingham into one who addressed race as a moral issue of national survival. "At this point," said King, "he went through what Lincoln went through."

King never mentioned the FBI, even in his confidential oral history. The Bureau was remote to his awareness, and neither King nor Hoover realized that Robert Kennedy just then was discarding his own conditioned advice that the hypersensitive Hoover must be coddled and assuaged, or at least let alone. In the second installment of *his* oral history, Kennedy described the Director as a creature of delusion and excess. "He's rather a psycho," said Kennedy, who told stories of FBI bureaucrats so attuned to Hoover's whims that they tied store-bought grapes to a bare arbor outside his vacation villa rather than tell the Director that the crop was not in season. What made the FBI "a very dangerous organization," Kennedy told the tape recorder, was not active blackmail so much as artfully managed intelligence—"so much information on so many people that doesn't leak out." Kennedy let slip that Hoover had paid no attention to him since his brother's assassination, but then, as though to salvage even a negative respect for himself as Attorney General, he allowed that the FBI Director was engaged "in every way that he can think of to cause difficulty for me."

King did not yet perceive FBI animosity so near, but Hoover's agents kept the SCLC office under physical surveillance throughout the day of his oral history interview. Forewarned by New York wiretaps, agents had spotted Stanley Levison among arriving train passengers in Atlanta and followed him to King. From an intercept on King's home phone, headquarters learned that Levison slept over there that night. Assorted wiretaps outlined for FBI officials the range of troubles that made King send for Levison—among them SCLC's crippling debt, King's indecision over staff replacements, and prolonged frustration over choice of a renewed public campaign. King was toying with the notion of a personal hunger strike to support the civil rights bill, but Levison warned that senators would let him starve to death rather than curtail their filibuster.

As usual, Levison was most indispensable as a crisis manager among New York publishers. He labored over publishing conflicts and marketing plans for King's much-revised book about Birmingham, scheduled for publication in May. In the text, they carefully omitted the FBI's name from suggested improvements in the fight against Klan violence, having learned that the Director resented even positive encouragements that associated the Bureau with imperfections. This precautionary silence only goaded headquarters into deeper suspicion. "It, of course, cannot be positively determined what he has in mind," wrote an intelligence supervisor, "but this could be a backhanded way of taking a slap at the Bureau."

King and Hoover looked at each other through opposite ends of a powerful telescope. To King, Hoover was a distant speck of white authority, hostile and yet necessary to hopes for justice in the South, whereas Hoover closely examined King's magnified pores. Two weekends earlier, when King had returned from Hawaii by way of the Hyatt House motel in Los Angeles, FBI technicians had obtained a second bonanza of microphone surveillance recordings: twenty-one reels of tape. From a Western trip that had receded already for King into a blur of speeches, dinners, airports, road parties, and assorted details—plans to open a West Coast SCLC office, notes from his secretary that she had not cried this time during his absence, and that the incoming president of Union Theological Seminary in New York was holding open the offer of a professorship for King—FBI technicians boiled down what the bugs had picked up while King was watching television in his motel room. Hoover fastened upon one sentence of lewd political blasphemy.

On Tuesday, March 10, the day after King's oral history in Atlanta and Hoover's White House luncheon, New Hampshire voters went to the polls in the first presidential primary. Hoover, freshly secure in his position, and confident that Robert Kennedy could not and would not make effective protest to Johnson, ordered Assistant Director Courtney Evans to take a top secret report that morning to the Attorney General. Since the assassination, Hoover had reduced Evans—Kennedy's chosen FBI liaison —to the status of cipher without duties, marked in the Bureau for dismissal. The delivery itself was a reminder of the bustling glory days when Kennedy labored to control Hoover by voluminous two-way communication strictly through Evans, and the content carried a crueler, gratuitous sting. After the usual warnings that disclosure would jeopardize vital national security secrets—the motel room bugs—Kennedy read that Martin Luther King, while watching a televised rerun of the Kennedy funeral, had sneered obscenely at the famous moment of mourning when Jacqueline Kennedy knelt prayerfully with her children against the late President's coffin. "Look at her," the agents heard King say. "Sucking him off one last time."

Hoover, professing to be sickened by what headquarters called "vilification of the late President and his wife," safely skewered three nemeses at once. Using King's unguarded rage,* which pierced his own reputation along with the national reverence for the dead Kennedy, Hoover aimed a dart for the eye of the surviving brother, the Attorney General, who returned the memo to Evans with a terse, vacant comment that it was very helpful. Kennedy sent King a standard letter of "deep personal appreciation" for his candid oral history about President Kennedy's life.

---

* The circumstances of King's outburst remain obscure, and its causes are too personal for the scope of this history, but at least a sliver of hidden fury was traceable to the Birmingham church bombing. King felt the losses there as deeply as most Americans felt the tragedy of Dallas, and he was angry at President Kennedy for getting away with an empty show of Federal response, behind a retired football coach (see page 144).

18

The Creation of Muhammad Ali

ALCOLM X bolted upright in his car when he heard Elijah Muhammad's raspy voice say on Harlem radio station WWRL that the name Clay lacked "divine meaning." Over a nationwide hookup of Negro stations, the Messenger announced: "Muhammad Ali is what I will give to him, as long as he believes in Allah and follows me."

"That's political!" exclaimed Malcolm. "That's a political move! He did it to prevent him from coming with me." Only that afternoon, Malcolm had taken liberties with the Nation's formal admission procedure to introduce the new heavyweight champion as Cassius X Clay, explaining to a U.N. press conference that the "X" stood for an identity lost to slavery. Now Elijah trumped Malcolm by exercising his prerogative to choose and bestow a "completed" Islamic holy name. To aspirants within the Nation of Islam, the award signified life's supreme achievement, reached so far by few of the most steadfastly devout pioneer Muslims from the 1930s. Malcolm's passengers knew that their troubled mentor was under punishment, and as insiders they were realistic enough to accept that the Honorable Elijah Muhammad could make a celebrity exception for the boxer. Still, the open disrespect in Malcolm's outburst was disorienting, and reduced them to awkward silence.

This was late evening on March 6—the Friday when Robert Hayling drove across Florida to appeal for Martin Luther King's help in St. Augustine. Malcolm wheeled around on St. Nicholas Avenue and headed back toward his home in Queens, hoping in vain to reach the champion before the news swept him off his feet. ("I am honored," the new Muhammad Ali told reporters who found him at his New York hotel.) When a police car intercepted Malcolm on the Triborough Bridge, he pointed confidently to a Bible as proof that he was in a hurry to preach a religious message. Malcolm and each of his assistant ministers always traveled with a Judeo-Christian Bible on the dashboard for just such emergencies, but for once neither the prop nor Malcolm's impressive ministerial diction staved off a speeding ticket.

Ten days earlier, Malcolm had retreated overnight from Miami to placate the frightened, irascible boxing promoter Bill MacDonald, who, rightly fearing that Clay's mismatched, half-sold title fight stood to lose money, confronted the challenger with rumors of his connections to unpatriotic, anti-white Muslims. "Don't start hitting me with the Constitution!" MacDonald shouted at Clay's representatives. "This is the South." With hints of the truth already seeping into the news, MacDonald briefly canceled the fight for fear that Clay's open association with the notorious Malcolm X would ruin him. To revive the bout in crisis, Malcolm left town on MacDonald's reluctant agreement that he could return for the actual event on February 25.

In a straw poll, all but three of fifty-eight ringside reporters anticipated a swift knockout by the ferocious champion, Sonny Liston, who had flattened his previous three opponents in the first round. Mindful of the weak box office and lackluster competition, editors of the *New York Times* sent a feature writer rather than a sports reporter to Miami, with instructions to learn in advance where Clay might be sent for hospital repairs. Instead, Clay's jubilant leaps and his manic, trademark shouts that he was the greatest and prettiest clashed with stony disbelief—even charges of fraud—when Liston did not answer the bell for the seventh round, and shock soon spilled beyond the world of boxing. The new champion spurned a lavish victory party at the Fontainebleau Hotel to disappear that night across Biscayne Bay into Negro Miami, telling confidants he wanted to spare reporters the "heart attack" of discovering that his idea of celebration was to retreat into Malcolm X's motel room for vanilla ice cream and Muslim prayer. (Informants soon told the FBI that Malcolm hosted singer Sam Cooke and pro football star Jim Brown, too, stirring fears that the Muslims were infiltrating black entertainment as a whole.) The next morning, after stuffing cotton into his doorbell to ward off those who had tracked him there by daybreak, Clay did appear for a tumultuous press conference, newly subdued and accompanied by Malcolm X. As he made his way through the crowd to leave, someone blurted out the accusing question: "Are you a card-carrying member of the Black Muslims?"

"Card-carrying? What does that mean?" Clay replied. His comments, while generally friendly to world Islam ("Followers of Allah are the sweetest people in the world. They don't carry knives"), were evasive enough to contain the story another day ("Muslim Story Irks Cassius").

Outside the Chicago Coliseum that afternoon, a long line of Muslims and a few white reporters stretched along South Wabash Avenue for the strict security search to gain entry to the annual Savior's Day convention. Malcolm X, who had presided the previous year, was conspicuously absent and unmentioned under edict of silence. In his place, Louis X of Boston introduced a procession of ministers for speeches of tribute to the Honorable Elijah Muhammad: James X of Newark gave thanks for being lifted from the gutter, Lonnie X of Washington for lessons of congruity between life, Islam, and mathematics. Minister Louis "whipped the crowd of 4,000 into hysteria in preparation for Mr. Muhammad's speech," according to Mike Handler's eyewitness account in the back pages of the *New York Times,* and the appearance of the frail Muhammad in his velvet fez touched off bedlam. "I have been given the keys to heaven," he declared in an asthmatic wheeze, and he electrified his audience by announcing that Cassius Clay indeed was his follower. Together with Allah, said Muhammad, he had caused the young boxer to win the world crown because of his Muslim faith.

Muhammad's statement was on the news wires before reporters in Miami found champion Clay at breakfast with Malcolm X on Thursday, two mornings after the fight. Flushed into the open, Clay used one of Malcolm's animal metaphors to speak glowingly of his conversion. "A rooster crows only when it sees the light," he said. "Put him in the dark and he'll never crow. I have seen the light and I'm crowing." All day long, his words stunned the sportswriters like blows to the solar plexus, knocking them from traditional pugilist banter on bums and heroes. Malcolm X interrupted to defend Clay,* and the champion himself tried to deflect indignant questions about anti-white religion by stressing his preference for racial separation and his deep personal fear of the civil rights movement. "I don't want to be blown up," he said. "I don't want to be washed down sewers. I just want to be happy with my own kind." Flustered sportswriters insisted that Clay was ruining himself, and predicted correctly that boxing would move to revoke his title.

Malcolm returned to New York on the wave of Clay's triumph, only to collide with Captain Joseph on his homecoming from the Chicago convention. On the last day of February, the two old colleagues were careful to discuss their differences privately in a car. Joseph objected to a fresh story in the *New York Times,* "Malcolm X's Role Dividing Muslims," saying that Malcolm could not hope for reinstatement while he expressed disloyalty to Elijah Muhammad. They argued over motivation and respon-

---

* Clay "will mean more to his people than any athlete before him," said Malcolm. "He's more than Jackie Robinson was, because Robinson is the white man's hero. But Cassius is the black man's hero. Do you know why? Because the white press wanted him to lose. They wanted him to lose because he is a Muslim. You notice nobody cares about the religion of other athletes."

sibility. Joseph did not contest Malcolm's facts, conceding that the minister of meticulous "homework" might be correct in his charges of corruption, but, as a soldier, Joseph demanded that Malcolm sacrifice to help their leader. "Now's the time to stand with the man," he said, insisting that the Nation was nothing without Muhammad.

"Aw, man, the Nation is finished," Malcolm replied. "You can forget about it."

Captain Joseph glared at his former teacher, but said politely, "I don't agree with you."

Within a day or two, Lukman X, a distraught member of Malcolm's Temple No. 7 came to him with news that Captain Joseph had ordered him to wire Malcolm's car with a bomb. Lukman confessed the plot instead. Malcolm knew that Lukman, who claimed to have fought with Fidel Castro in the Cuban revolution, had the background in demolitions for the assignment, but he also knew that it made him suspect as a possible police agent. If Malcolm believed Lukman, did Joseph really intend to kill him, or could he have assumed that Lukman would inform Malcolm? Was the order a warning, or a test to see whether Malcolm would report the threat to his despised superiors in Chicago, as required by the Nation's rules?

The new heavyweight champion checked into Harlem's Hotel Theresa on Sunday afternoon, March 1, and went straight into private conference there with Malcolm X. Although he arrived grandly in a chauffeur-driven Cadillac, Clay complained bitterly that he had been barred from restaurants and restrooms during his two-day drive (being afraid of airplanes) from Miami through the segregated South. He later composed some playful verse about his humiliation: "Man, it was really a letdown drag/For all those miles I had to eat out of a bag." Malcolm tried to soften the naive Clay's introduction to hidden dangers within the authoritarian sect, and suggested that it might be possible to fight against segregation and still preserve the independence of Muslim culture. Overnight, he leaked word to the Negro press that Clay might join him on such a course, which went against Elijah Muhammad's teaching of aloofness from a doomed white world.

Crowds mobbed them on a night stroll through Times Square. "Malcolm X got more requests for his autograph than I did," a beaming Clay told reporters. "He's the greatest." Malcolm took Clay to look for a permanent home on Long Island, near his in Queens. On Wednesday, when Malcolm guided Clay on a tour of the United Nations, admiring dignitaries and employees swept past security guards to engulf them. Clay pronounced himself champion not only of the United States but of the whole world, including Africa and the globe's 750 million Muslims. Malcolm X fielded questions about American race relations. Reporters said the two of them caused the greatest buzz in U.N. hallways since Soviet Premier Nikita Khrushchev had pounded his shoe against capitalism in 1960.

The whirlwind association of Malcolm X with Cassius Clay, while muffled generally in the press, drew the wrath of Elijah Muhammad. From his winter home in Phoenix, he sharply contradicted reports that Malcolm's suspension was nearly over, as Malcolm implied breezily in his public appearances. "I'm holding him down until he proves he can keep his mouth shut," Muhammad told Captain Joseph. He scoffed at the rumors that Malcolm planned to create a new organization, saying he never could finance one—not with his proposed African imports company or the "many little things going on up his sleeve." Muhammad prescribed a gentler approach to the young heavyweight champion: Joseph should inform Clay that the Nation would supply another Muslim escort in Malcolm's place. This proved a difficult assignment, and when Malcolm took Clay to the United Nations a second time on Friday, March 6, announcing there that he was granting Clay his "X," Elijah Muhammad intervened with a statement recorded over the telephone to Chicago for broadcast that same night. He renamed Clay "Muhammad" after the original prophet of Islam and himself, and "Ali" after a commanding general of the Third Caliphate.

This radio announcement, which so jolted Malcolm X, was only one of several blows that weekend. Elijah Muhammad extended his suspension indefinitely in a scolding formal letter, and he sent Minister Louis X of Boston, who had been showcased in Chicago as Malcolm's replacement, to teach on Sunday at New York Temple No. 7. Nearly a thousand turned out to hear him, and Captain Joseph reported that he and other captains rousted large congregations elsewhere that stood to give Elijah Muhammad emphatic vows of allegiance "regardless of circumstances."

Malcolm called reporters that same Sunday to announce that he was leaving the Nation of Islam. While professing loyalty to the teaching of Elijah Muhammad, he said he needed greater political freedom "to cooperate in local civil rights actions in the South and elsewhere." He asserted that the nonviolent civil rights movement had run its course. "There can be no revolution without bloodshed," Malcolm told reporters, "and it is nonsense to describe the civil rights movement in America as a revolution."

THE EXIT STATEMENT made crossover headlines on Monday, March 9, putting Malcolm X for the first time on page one of the *New York Times,* alongside the news from Washington—"Debate on Civil Rights Bill Opening in Senate Today." He reclaimed his public voice just as heightened sensitivity fragmented racial news. "Now It's a Negro Drive for Segregation," announced one of the national news magazines, suggesting that Negroes might be changing their minds about the civil rights bill. Malcolm tried to explain himself to those left hostile or captivated, sincerely or disingenuously confused, by introduction to his novel doctrines. "See, the mistake that the whites make, especially the white liberals, they throw that at me as if I am against integration," he told a New York television audience. "My contention is that *America* is against integration. But they're hypocrites. They pose as being for integration while they practice segregation."

Malcolm suffered the sharpest, most immediate rebukes from those who best understood his language. Although he publicly urged all Muslims, including the new heavyweight champion, to remain loyal to Elijah Muhammad, he ran afoul of Muhammad's teaching that Islam required absolute submission to him. "You don't just walk away from the sect of Islam as a deviater or hypocrite," Muhammad told a reporter who called him in Phoenix, "and someone weep and cry over it." In a fury, Muhammad called Captain Joseph with orders that Malcolm "must give up everything he has that belongs to Islam," including his house.

Told that week of the wrathful notices being prepared inside the New York temple, Malcolm drafted a contorted defense. He presented Muhammad and himself as common victims of evil conspiracy by middlemen—Captain Joseph, Raymond Sharrieff, and National Secretary John Ali—and went so far as to describe his resignation as an act of loyal sacrifice. In order to "preserve the faith your followers have in you and the Nation of Islam," he told Muhammad in a two-page telegram, Malcolm had assumed blame for scandal and corruption that rightly belonged to the conspirators. "You are still my leader and teacher," he wrote, "even though those around you won't let me be one of your active followers or helpers."

Captain Joseph led a grim delegation to Malcolm's house in Elmhurst, bearing a notarized letter dated Tuesday, March 10. Glumly, but without protest, Malcolm surrendered some of the temple valuables, including papers of incorporation and securities from the Nation's national treasury, but he balked at the demand that he vacate his premises. During the ensuing argument, some of Joseph's subordinates were visibly conflicted by personal sympathy for Malcolm as their fallen mentor. Maceo X Owens, the temple secretary who had prepared the letter of notice, had insisted on one conciliatory sentence: "If you continue to use the Nation's name on your car, then the Mosque will have to take possession of the car, which we do not want to do because this car is your personal property." Owens felt that Malcolm had left the title in the Nation's name to set an example of fealty, but when Malcolm pressed a similar claim for the house, Joseph insisted that the Nation would sue if necessary.

Being stripped swiftly of defenses, Malcolm fought back through white newspapers. On Thursday morning, March 12, he took a tiny entourage and a stack of printed handouts to a jammed press conference at the

Tapestry Suite of the Park Sheraton Hotel in midtown Manhattan. His purpose was "to clarify my own position in the struggle," he told reporters, in a statement nevertheless littered with mixed signals. While he was creating a new Muslim Mosque Inc. as a base for his followers, Malcolm said he did not want to compete with his teacher, Elijah Muhammad. Moreover, recognizing that most people might be put off by Islam, he promised to make room at his mosque for secular members. He wanted to find common ground with civil rights leaders for what promised to be an explosive year ("As of this minute, I've forgotten everything bad that the other leaders have said about me," he announced with a broad smile, "and I pray that they can also forget the many bad things I've said about them"), but he rejected their goal of integration along with their prevailing tactic of nonviolence. "It is criminal to teach a man not to defend himself when he is the constant victim of brutal attacks," he asserted. Citing Birmingham and Danville among ugly spectacles of unpunished violence the previous year, Malcolm called for mobile rifle clubs to defend the life and property of Negroes wherever the authorities failed.

Malcolm's words about armed defense jumped above the muddle of sectarian politics. "His Theme Now Is Violence," warned *U.S. News & World Report.* "The Ominous Malcolm X Exits from the Muslims," said *Life.* In a scalding editorial, the *New York Times* called Malcolm an "embittered racist" and an "irresponsible demagogue" who threatened the precarious chance for integration. The *Times* tried to dismiss him as an unfit subject—"Malcolm X will not deceive Negroes in New York or elsewhere"—but its news pages reported the stir of controversy: "Negroes Ponder Malcolm's Move"/"Dr. King Urges Nonviolence." King and the established leaders sounded ponderous against Malcolm's avenging swagger. "It is regrettable that Malcolm X has publicly confessed to so negative and desperate a course of action," King said in a statement released during his next trip through New York. "I must honestly say that this new turn of events is not so much an indictment against him as it is against a society whose ills in race relations are so deep-rooted that it produces a Malcolm X."

Whether they stirred fascination or contempt, papers of all kinds approached Malcolm X carefully across the divide of race. The *Pittsburgh Courier* and *New York Times* alike treated his troubles with the Nation of Islam as a conventional power struggle over spoils of succession. Only baseball pioneer Jackie Robinson tried to see in Malcolm the schisms of a newborn religion colliding with the intermingled love and war of the movement era. Disparaged by Malcolm as a tool of the white man, Robinson struck back at a vulnerable spot. "Whom do you think you are kidding, Malcolm, when you say that Negro leaders ought to be 'thankful' that you were not personally present in Birmingham or Mississippi?" Robinson asked in his newspaper column. Against Malcolm's provocative implication that he would have been—and still might become—a prowl-ing wolf of retribution, Robinson threw up his past performance. "I think you would have done exactly what you did after your own Muslim broth-ers were shot and killed in Los Angeles," he wrote. "You left it to the law to take its course."

Robinson charged, and Malcolm X cheerfully agreed, that the emerg-ing public sensation was largely a creation of the white press. "White colleges flood him with speaking engagement offers," Robinson com-plained. "You can count on one hand Negro colleges which have invited him, if there are any." Some Negro newspapers reported with gleeful irony that Georgia Senator Richard Russell emerged as the first major public figure to defend the Black Muslims and to oblige the heavyweight champion by using the name "Muhammad Ali" in public. Russell praised Ali for the courage to criticize integration in the face of humiliation and insult ("He will never be invited to the White House"), and castigated fellow senators for holding hearings on his fitness for the ring. Mischie-vously, he used the taunts being thrown at Southerners—"so intolerant, so narrow-minded, so bigoted"—to chastise the World Boxing Association for efforts to strip Ali of his title, observing tartly that boxing routinely embraced low-life criminals of "no religion at all."

Most white papers left these volatile comments unmentioned, pre-serving Russell as a statesman of decorum, just as they avoided notice of the Racial Relocation Commission. On March 16, in his second major speech of the civil rights debate, Russell proposed an amendment that would resettle families massively until racial proportions were equalized among the fifty states. Alabama would export 637,263 Negroes, while California and Alaska would import 776,445 and 16,976 respectively, ac-cording to a large map Russell placed in the rear of the Senate chamber. "I have grappled with this problem and studied it, to the very best of my ability, over a long period of years..." he declared. "I favor inflicting on New York City, the city of Chicago, and other cities the same condition proposed to be inflicted by this bill on the people of the community of Winder, Georgia, where I live." Russell defended his amendment against objections that it was preposterously unconstitutional and impractical, like schemes for a separate black nation. "I was never more serious in all my life," he assured the Senate.

TWO QUICK-WITTED FBI agents slipped into Malcolm's Tapestry Suite press conference on March 12, disguised as journalists. For the record, they asked pointed questions about revolution and civil war ("I don't think I'm dumb enough to advocate armed revolt," Malcolm replied), but their primary mission, for which they later received commendation from FBI headquarters, was to photograph the Muslim entourage under pretext of news. The New York FBI office knew already that Muslims willing to associate openly with Malcolm were scarce. Of twenty-two faces surreptitiously photographed at the press conference, Bureau agents identified only four as known Muslims—three bodyguards and James 67X (the sixty-seventh "James" granted the Nation's "X"), who had served as a lieutenant under Captain Joseph.

Those absent were more significant. Less than a week after deferring to Malcolm at the United Nations, the heavyweight champion recoiled from mentioning his name. "You just don't buck Mr. Muhammad and get away with it," Muhammad Ali told a startled Alex Haley. "I don't want to talk about [Malcolm] no more." Elijah Muhammad had sent a high-ranking delegation from Chicago to envelop Ali with a new identity, total business management, and the promise of a readymade wife to be selected from the Messenger's eligible granddaughters. Malcolm, deprived of Ali's public glamour, also found himself without visible support from fellow ministers in the Nation of Islam. None of his four trusted assistants stood with him at the break.

Pressure fell heavily on the ministers as second-level opinion leaders, and Captain Joseph prodded the New York assistants to denounce Malcolm from the temple rostrum as a hypocrite. To protect himself, Malcolm campaigned to undo years of resolute indoctrination from his own mouth. The assistants had been inclined to see his suspension as the result of friction with Captain Joseph—the soldier grown resentful of the minister's overbearing independence, the minister annoyed by Joseph's ties to Chicago as guarantor of the revenue stream. It did not occur to them that scandalous, deadly grievance ran directly to the august Elijah Muhammad, whom none of the assistants had ever met in person, until Malcolm began taking them one by one to the hideaway attic of his home to sample detailed "insurance" tapes about sexual and financial corruption.

For Assistant Minister Benjamin 2X, the precisely dictated revelations caused prolonged dizziness and sharp pangs of nausea, recalling the impact six years earlier of Malcolm's lecture on the sewer-like digestive tract of the pig. Benjamin had discovered himself physically unable to put pork into his mouth at dinners with friends, and had returned to Temple No. 7 for Malcolm's history lecture on Egypt and the land of Ur. Thunderstruck to hear that Africans had been something other than potboiling savages with bones in their noses, he persevered through ten rejected applications to gain his 2X from Elijah Muhammad. Malcolm had invited Benjamin to join the Wednesday evening public speaking class, where he not only conquered a childhood stutter but devoured books beyond the voluminous reading list, beginning with *The Story of the Moors in Spain* by Stanley Lane Poole and *The Crusades* by Harold Lamb. Possessed, Benjamin had worn out library cards at the Manhattan public library on Fifth Avenue. He copied scholarly articles and prepared class reports on shortwave radio broadcasts from mainland China. He quit his job as a shipping clerk for

Vanguard Records and hired out as a live-in doorman, enabling him to study feverishly at his post.

At the end of 1958, Malcolm sent Benjamin out into Harlem with three props: a stepladder, a Bible, and a banner depicting the choice between the American and Islamic flags. He climbed the ladder to preach at the corner of Seventh Avenue and 125th Street, in front of the Chock Full 'O Nuts store where Jackie Robinson worked as a coffee spokesman. Like his contemporaries who passed the test as "ladder men" to become Muslim ministers, Benjamin eventually drew large crowds of "mentally dead" Negroes with spirited sermons asserting that he could answer any question from the Honorable Elijah Muhammad's complete body of knowledge. Malcolm sometimes observed from the fringe. "Never repeat anything you hear me say unless you confirm that it's true," he instructed sharply, and he maintained an exacting, hidden distance from his assistants even as they founded new mosques together. Through sectarian study, they developed a more priestly version of the discipline that Captain Joseph instilled with martial drills and enforced quotas for newspaper sales.

Against Malcolm's secret revelations, Captain Joseph assured Elijah Muhammad that he was maintaining Benjamin 2X as a spy within Malcolm's camp at the Hotel Theresa. He conceded that Malcolm maintained counterspies, but boasted that even in his strongholds Malcolm attracted only the "weak ones" looking for an excuse to smoke cigarettes and vent their petty complaints. Elsewhere, Muhammad's officials felt secure enough to banish any Muslim associated with Malcolm X, and the FBI wiretaps picked up only one fence-sitting minister brazen enough to fight back. "As far as being a leader, they can have that," he shouted over the phone to Chicago on March 17. "As far as coming to the temple, they can have that, too. But when they start saying, 'don't you come by here looking for no money,' they gonna be in trouble! Do you hear me?" The renegade demanded his regular cut of the newspaper sales and refused to be treated like an innocent to the Nation's secrets. "You ain't dealing with no baby or with no faithful believer," he growled. "I used to be a faithful believer. I'm just here now trying to get understanding.... I'm one of the ones threatening to kill people, beat up brothers for throwing the paper [*Muhammad Speaks*] in the trash."

On March 18, Malcolm X lectured again at Harvard University, where he fended off questions about violent revolution by stating that America recognized upheaval and suffering "only when the white man himself bleeds a little." Two professors argued dryly that the notoriously poor record of third-party movements in American politics weighed heavily against his agenda of black nationalism. Immediately after the lecture, and again a few days later, Malcolm ventured into the Boston ghetto to keep clandestine appointments at the Original Pastry Shop and other

Muslim spots along Blue Hill Avenue. He recruited there among pre-screened favorites from the first congregation he had founded for Elijah Muhammad, Temple No. 11, likening his desperate mission at times to the Christian Apostle Paul's fateful journey to confront Caesar in Rome.

From Phoenix, where word of the Boston soundings reached him overnight, Elijah Muhammad denounced "that no-good, long-legged Malcolm." He told Minister Louis X of Boston and other officials that the Nation must make examples of the bad ones and cut the heads off hypocrites. Muhammad told John Ali and Captain Joseph that if the courts could not stop Malcolm from slandering his private life, then the Nation must "tell ours" to do so. He ordered them to file eviction papers for Malcolm's house.

Malcolm X, while not privy to what was being said in the opposing camp, recognized that his protégé Louis X made a convincing show of loyalty to Elijah Muhammad and that the shifting Muslim conspiracies crackled with potential violence. Returning from Boston to New York, he called reporters with accusations so sensational that only Harlem's *Amsterdam News* picked them up for the Saturday, March 21, edition: "Malcolm X Tells of Death Threat." The story burned as a silent fuse in the regular Sunday evening service at Temple No. 7. Assistant Minister Benjamin 2X gripped his chair on the rostrum while Assistant Minister Henry X repeated the prescribed banishments on Malcolm X. For the third week, Henry X read from the *New York Times* article on Malcolm as the wedge of schism. He cried out that the Nation must shun slack talk from Malcolm the hypocrite, lest it destroy the faith that was raising them all from the gutter.

"Excuse me, brother minister, may I say a word real quick?" Benjamin 2X interrupted. He rose as mildly and routinely as possible, leaving Henry no choice but to surrender the microphone. The entire congregation fell silent. Benjamin temporized with metaphorical remarks about two planes sitting in a hangar, one about to take off, and Captain Joseph nodded ominously to his squadrons before Benjamin pulled out the *Amsterdam News.*

"Are you going to say it in the name of Allah?" Joseph called out loudly from the floor.

The question froze Benjamin at the microphone. To say yes was to begin the obedient litany about the Honorable Elijah Muhammad as His Messenger; to say no was to confess heresy in advance. Benjamin hesitantly tried to compromise, beginning, "As a Muslim . . ."

Captain Joseph bellowed his question again. His troops took it up as a chant, but opponents answered with shouts of, "Let him speak!" As some members gasped in horror, Benjamin shouted a question over the sound system: "If I can believe the *New York Times,* which is the devil's newspaper, and what it said about Minister Malcolm, then can I believe what the *Amsterdam News,* which is a black newspaper, said about Captain Joseph sending Lukman to Malcolm's house to put a bomb in his car?"

Joseph's security detail converged on the rostrum, enabling Henry X to snatch back the microphone. "If you're not going to say it in the name of Allah," he told Benjamin over the booming speakers, "then you're not going to say it at all!" He kept repeating this above the bedlam. Benjamin yelled that Malcolm only wanted a chance to bring his case before the members, and more than two hundred listeners—about a third of the attendance—stalked out of the temple behind him.

Captain Joseph, while counting Benjamin 2X as the first minister to break to Malcolm's side, assured Elijah Muhammad that Temple No. 7 had foiled the attempted coup. Most of those who left were merely put off by the chaos, he said, but he did complain that things were happening too fast for outsiders to keep up. The loyal members of Temple No. 7 were being harassed mistakenly on the street as followers of Malcolm X, for instance—mostly by young white police officers whose hostility had been roused by recent publicity about the strange association of Muslims with championship boxing. The previous Friday night at Madison Square Garden, when fans had showered the new heavyweight champion with angry boos instead of the customary tribute, resentment seemed triggered by his demand to be introduced as Muhammad Ali instead of Cassius Clay, as Garden management insisted was his rightful name.

With strange new Muslim influences bouncing between sports and civil rights news, Malcolm's internal struggle confused the FBI's intelligence experts as well as the public. When J. Edgar Hoover ordered his Chicago office to make up its mind whether Malcolm X was or was not independent of Elijah Muhammad, the agent in charge of Chicago replied that the wiretaps themselves were contradictory. "As the Bureau can imagine, these conversations are extremely difficult to monitor and are even more difficult to make sense from and to intelligently record," he cabled FBI headquarters on March 25. "Muhammad, at his best, is very difficult to understand." Some reports ascribed to Malcolm about forty converts from Temple No. 7 ("five or six of them had guns"), some twenty-six, and others next to none. The Chicago agent was clearer that Elijah Muhammad would disdain Malcolm's request to defend himself before assembled peers within the Nation. "I do not have a court," Muhammad declared on his wiretapped phone. "I *am* the court."

19

Shaky Pulpits

DURING THE PRELUDE to an evening service on March 22 in Jackson, Mississippi—far from the chaotic split inside Temple No. 7—twenty-four young boys and girls were seated in front pews as prospective new members when an integrated group of five slipped quietly through a side door of Galloway Memorial United Methodist Church, a grand white structure of fluted columns ("the Cathedral of Mississippi Methodism") across from the state Capitol. Alarmed ushers trotted down the aisles to intercept them, and, hoping to minimize commotion in the sanctuary, took the visitors silently by the arms toward the exit. "I am from India," cried out Madabusi Savrithri, a diminutive new Ph.D. from Syracuse University and interim professor at Tougaloo. When the ushers shoved more firmly to remove her, Savrithri asked in protest what they would think if their women or their missionaries were manhandled on a visit to India.

Galloway's new pastor, Rev. W. J. Cunningham, worried especially that this latest expulsion took place in front of his impressionable young church candidates on Palm Sunday. He had walked into race trouble the previous fall, knowing that his predecessor had resigned over the congregation's explicit enforcement of segregated services. ("It is not un-Christian that we prefer to remain an all-white congregation," the official board resolved by a vote of 184–13.) Warning that he would not preach segregation, Cunningham reached an understanding with determined church elders to cover their differences within a reconciling Christian purpose. He never mentioned integration from the Galloway pulpit—to the point of avoiding inflammatory words such as "brotherhood"—but conflict burrowed into his ministry. While lawyers and politicians helped fend off abstract questions, such as whether trespass charges against integrated worshippers rested on church or state initiative,* Cunningham had to decide whether to laugh when his ushers jokingly dubbed themselves "The Color Guard." Every tangible presence—a Negro seeking communion, a furtive huddle of elders, a motion about race in some committee —produced what Cunningham would recall in his memoirs as "tension so thick you could pick it up with your hands..." and "so high you could scrape it off the ceiling."

For Reverend Edwin and Jeannette King, tension at Galloway Memorial had become a familiar experience over the nine months since King had been stripped of Methodist credentials and had run for lieutenant governor on the integrated Freedom Ticket. On Palm Sunday, escaping this time with physical eviction instead of arrest, they pushed on to a second rejection at St. Luke's Methodist. With numerous prior convictions trailing behind in appellate courts, the Kings discussed between them signs of a cumulative emotional toll, called "burnout" in movement slang. Idealism was wearing thin as a substitute for normality, especially after March 15, when the public announcement of Freedom Summer aroused little response.

As with Allard Lowenstein the previous summer, Edwin King grasped for hope in the quixotic schemes of pilgrim visitors. On cue from Bob Moses, who cherished dreams of acquiring a "Freedom Radio" station for the movement, he joined a media reformer in a dangerous gamble. Everett Parker, a professor at Yale Divinity School and part-time producer of educational television shows, brought to the United Church of Christ a specialty in broadcast law and religion. For thirty years, since his 1935 dissertation on the original Federal Communications Act (back when stations banned all advertisement during family listening hours between seven and eleven o'clock, and when NBC introduced the National Radio Pulpit as the first network program) Parker had published rearguard legal studies against rampant commercialism that obliterated, in his opinion, the public trust concept of the law. At the request of Andrew Young, his former colleague at the UCC in New York, Parker had undertaken to shame the Birmingham television stations into fairer coverage of the 1963 civil rights movement, and in early March of 1964, he activated at Tougaloo College the first stage of his revolutionary scheme.

Trained volunteers stealthily moved batteries of television sets, reel-to-reel recorders, and Parker-designed log books into designated monitor-

---

* In *Bette Poole et al. v. Ross R. Barnett et al.,* church lawyer Jack Pratt pressed for specificity on the legal basis for the Jackson "kneel-in" convictions. A church-based, "private club" complaint of trespass would put segregated congregations in conflict with national denominations, framing the religious question starkly posed by Bette Poole on her arrest at the church door: "But what would Jesus do?" A state-based complaint, on the other hand, raised constitutional issues about political rules for religious worship.

ing homes, where primary and secondary teams matched sound recordings to formularized observations of all 7,186 minutes of the program week on Jackson television stations. The tabulated results showed, for instance, that the NBC affiliate WLBT never referred to any Negro civic event during an aggregate fifteen minutes and fifty-five seconds of public service announcements, never showed a Negro congregation in church services nor a Negro face on local shows, including *Romper Room, Today in Jackson,* and *Teen Tempo.* This was the accepted landscape of television almost everywhere, but the survey also logged the occasional use of the epithet "nigger" by two of the station's political commentators, and counted sixteen enthusiastic promotions for the segregationist literature at the White Citizens Council bookstore inside the WLBT station, run by its manager.

Parker and allied lawyers prepared a petition for the FCC to block license renewal on ground that the hostile, systematic exclusion by WLBT of nearly half the viewing audience (Negroes) violated legal obligation to broadcast in the public interest. Precedent had evolved so heavily against such a claim that the FCC allowed complaints only from rival broadcasters, and recognized no standing for public representatives to contest a license on any basis. Perpetual renewal had turned the free, three-year public license into permanent property that could be trafficked and inherited confidently, like peerages of fantastic value. (The small-market WLBT license was worth about $12 million to the Dallas-based insurance company that owned it.) On this structure rested many postwar American fortunes, including a small one for President Johnson's family in Texas, and Parker fully realized that any wisp of challenge would draw the concerted wrath of broadcast powers everywhere.

Mississippi's NAACP counsel advised state chairman Aaron Henry to avoid Parker's WLBT petition for fear of signing his own death warrant. Henry signed anyway, on the slim chance that the meticulous documentation might ameliorate news coverage of the movement. From such a beginning, even Parker could not imagine a twenty-year legal odyssey that would shake the foundations of broadcast regulation and make Aaron Henry himself the millionaire chairman and largest shareholder of WLBT. Rev. R. L. T. Smith, whose congressional campaign Bob Moses had managed in 1962, held fast as the second petitioner, but Tougaloo College dropped out when officials learned of a bill in the Mississippi legislature to revoke its charter. In a futile effort to save college president Daniel Beittel's job, Edwin King stepped forward as a substitute white petitioner, signing as campus chaplain of the United Church of Christ at Tougaloo. For King, the risk of media persecution seemed remote and superfluous. He was more than consoled by the upcoming visit of celebrity ministers that Easter Sunday, with their promise to relieve King and his wife of integrated witness in Jackson's mainstream churches.

□

In Washington, President Johnson gathered 150 leading ministers from the Southern Baptist Convention for a brief reception in the White House Rose Garden on Wednesday, March 25. He permitted no reporters, recorders, or cameras, and began his informal remarks with a string of jokes about Baptists baptizing each other in the White House pool ("I wish you could have seen Billy Graham and Bill Moyers in that pool together the other day"). To underscore his own Baptist heritage, Johnson read to the ministers a yellowed 1857 letter he kept on his office wall in which the patriarch of Texas, General Sam Houston, had commiserated with his pastor, Johnson's own great-grandfather Baines, over the miserly church contributions of most members. ("They ought to know that paper currency will not pass in heaven," Houston wrote.) Johnson told his audience that his frontier ancestor, Rev. George Washington Baines, Sr., had been selected to deliver the annual sermon to the Southern Baptist Convention of his day. "If that doesn't make him orthodox," he added with a twinkle, "nothing will."

The President allowed that since the trauma of the Kennedy assassination he had caught himself reciting forgotten childhood prayers learned on his mother's knee. "The occupant of the world's most powerful office, like the most private citizen, has nowhere to go for help but up," he said. He professed humility in their realm ("I am not a theologian. I am not a philosopher"), and ventured the opinion of "just a public servant" that there was hope for the nation "only if the separation of church and state does not mean the divorce of spiritual values from secular affairs." Johnson defined that political line with an eloquence pleasing to his guests. "The principle, the identity of private morality and public conscience, is as deeply rooted in our tradition and Constitution as the principle of legal separation," he declared. "Washington in his first inaugural said that the roots of national policy lay in private morality. Lincoln proclaimed as a national faith that right makes might. Surely this is so."

Then abruptly Johnson dropped the folksy banter and supplication. Saying "no group of Christians has a greater responsibility in civil rights than Southern Baptists," he cut through the usual bromides like a brimstone preacher grasping sinners by the throat. "Your people are part of the power structure in many communities of our land," he said. "The leaders of states and cities and towns are in *your* congregations, and they sit on *your* boards. Their attitudes are confirmed or changed by the sermons you preach and by the lessons you write and by the examples that you set."

Johnson challenged the South's leading white ministers to become suffering prophets in keeping with the Baptist struggle for religious liberty, guided by compassion, not conformity, and "unafraid of the consequences." Warning against "voices crying peace, peace, peace, when there is no peace," he summoned them to answer "with truth and with action. Help us pass this civil rights bill. . . . Let the acts of everyone, in government and out, let all that we do proclaim that righteousness does exalt the nation. Thank you."

Word spread so rapidly that Martin Luther King issued a statement that evening, before the next day's newspapers, praising Johnson's "eloquent and passionate" plea to white Baptists. King was in Washington to attend a climactic session of the Senate debate, and on Thursday he looked down from the visitors' gallery on Senator Russell's racial relocation map, still standing on exhibit. Southerners, breaking off their warmup filibuster, yielded at last for the procedural vote to take up the bill, after which Senator Wayne Morse of Oregon stirred the chamber by moving to send it back to committee for hearings, as required by Senate practice. Well aware that Judiciary chairman James Eastland of Mississippi had killed all but one of 121 civil rights measures over the past decade, Morse foresaw still greater peril in cutting corners. To shut off debate by the required two-thirds vote—and thereby gain final passage over the real, mortal filibuster looming ahead—he declared that supporters must court senators who opposed cloture on principle, plus powerful chairmen with their own reasons not to bypass any committee, and also with Senate traditionalists who were loath to base historic legislation on the reports or hasty amendments of the House. Majority Leader Mike Mansfield, who had favored Morse's course as painful but prudent, now rose to announce that he had changed his mind. Even if Chairman Eastland did not manage to suffocate or disfigure the bill in committee, Mansfield pointed out that the ordeal of calling it up as pending business would start all over again. He moved to table Morse's motion and keep the bill before the Senate. After a dramatic afternoon debate, in which Republican leader Everett Dirksen joined Morse and the Southern senators in opposition, Mansfield prevailed by a vote of 50–34, and the Senate adjourned for a brief Easter recess.

"We shall now begin to fight the war," vowed Richard Russell. Off the Senate floor, he and other senators fielded questions about whether supporters could find the seventeen additional votes necessary for cloture. A small cloud of reporters gathered around Martin Luther King as he moved from the visitors' gallery to a nearby conference room, where, on a sofa off toward the rear, the unmistakable figure of Malcolm X took a seat.

No one, including the two leaders, acknowledged the bizarre joint presence. Although thoughts of Malcolm X had been gnawing at King of late—not so much over philosophical differences as public jibes about "my being soft* and my talking about love and the white man all the time and...my being a sort of polished Uncle Tom"—the press conference

---

* In a March 18 interview with Robert Penn Warren, King dwelled on the lingering affront of being pelted with eggs by Malcolm's followers the previous summer, of his efforts "to get my mind off of myself and feeling sorry for myself and feeling rejected," and of frustration that Malcolm called nonviolence submissive. "I'm talking about a very strong force," he insisted, "where you stand up with all your might against an evil system, and you're not a coward, you are resisting, but you come to see that tactically as well as morally it is better to be nonviolent."

ostensibly proceeded as though Malcolm were not there. King announced that he had discussed the bill's prospects with sponsors including Senator Hubert Humphrey, and had met with movement colleagues about contingency plans for demonstrations. "If there is a prolonged filibuster, it will be necessary to engage in a creative direct action program to dramatize the blatant injustice to Negroes," he said, predicting a "dark night of social disruption" if the bill failed. He answered the usual range of questions about whether nonviolence contributed to violence, and whether Negroes would stop agitating if they got the bill. "Oh, no, we will not be content," he replied, ". . . until we have absolute and full freedom." Even in the best case, there would be summer demonstrations to test compliance with the new law.

When King finished and made his way from the conference room in the midst of reporters, Malcolm left by a separate door. Guided by Benjamin 2X, he placed himself directly in King's path along the corridor.

"Well, Malcolm, good to see you," said King as he grasped the outstretched hand.

"Good to see you," Malcolm replied.

Wire service photographers called for them to hold their clasp. With his tourist camera, Benjamin 2X excitedly snapped a full roll of film as Malcolm chatted with King in the halls of the U.S. Senate, hinting that he might join an integration march.

"Now you're going to get investigated," quipped Malcolm in a parting jest. He assumed incorrectly that federal investigators had gone easier on King as a respectable Christian.

News portraits of Malcolm towering over King appeared the following day in a number of second-tier newspapers. Both men smiled jovially in the Associated Press version, or looked sober for UPI. One white paper warned that King's pose "could wave the red flag of Black Muslimism in front of those opposing or uncertain about the civil rights bill." King stood firm to rebukes for association with an anti-white, anti-integrationist symbol. "I would go so far as to say that I would gladly shake hands with Governors Wallace and Barnett and greet them with a kind smile," he replied to a critic from Savannah. "This would in no way be indicative of my sharing their segregationist views."

The meaning of the handshake was more complicated on Malcolm's side. He told some reporters that the Senate debate was a useless "con game," but to others he called on the Senate to pass the House bill "exactly as it is, with no changes." In a striking echo of King after the bus boycott, he went so far as to model his role on Billy Graham's independent crusades, saying he hoped to spread the gospel of black nationalism without offending any political or religious organization.

Unlike King in the 1950s, Malcolm did not have several years to resolve his approach, and he could not wait for an equivalent of the student sit-in movement to demonstrate the value of public sacrifice beyond rhetoric. On the day he sought out King for a handshake in the Senate, his brother held a press conference in Chicago by order of Elijah Muhammad. In trembling but dutiful submission, Minister Philbert X of Lansing read a statement drafted for him by national secretary John Ali, denouncing Malcolm as a devious schemer, hypocrite to Islam, and a traitor comparable to Judas, Brutus, and Benedict Arnold. "My brother Malcolm will do anything and say anything to gain mention and his picture in news coverage," warned Philbert.

Malcolm said privately that Philbert wept over the emotional cost of blind submission to the Messenger, but he knew better than to appeal for reconsideration. Instead, he ridiculed Philbert as the only minister in the Nation of Islam "with no congregation," called him "dumb enough to allow someone to put a script in his hand," and dismissed him as beneath reply. "My brother was unknown, you know," Malcolm said on Chicago television. "Until he allowed himself to be used in this attack against me, you never heard of him."

A third brother, Minister Wilfred X of Temple No. 1 in Detroit, concurred in Philbert's anathema after Elijah Muhammad himself telephoned to declare that he would not tolerate "what happened in 1935"—meaning the family schism that had paralyzed the Nation after Elijah's own brother opposed his divine claims. This time Muhammad wielded allegiance sharp enough to slice away family ties. At his order, officers from Temple No. 7 served court papers on March 31, seeking Malcolm's eviction from his house. The senior minister of the Nation told readers of *Muhammad Speaks* that Malcolm could not believe in Islam—"If he did, he would be afraid for his future." Minister Louis X of Boston, billed as the "Minister Who Knew Him Best," prepared a three-part series on "Malcolm's Treachery, Defection." Most graphically, at the suggestion of Captain Joseph, the cartoonist for *Muhammad Speaks* illustrated the April 10 story about Philbert's denunciation with a drawing of Malcolm's severed head growing devil's horns as it bounced toward a gravestone reserved for traitors.

With money borrowed hastily from his half-sister in Boston, Malcolm took flight three days later on a one-way ticket to Cairo, saying he hoped to "get spiritual strength" in Mecca. He left his lawyer, Percy Sutton, to arrange postponement of the eviction hearing until his unspecified return. James 67X and Benjamin 2X remained behind as caretakers among a loose assortment of Muslim rebels, clamoring ideologues, and untutored new fans who thrilled or shuddered over Malcolm X.

FROM HEBRON, ILLINOIS, Rev. Robert Beech rode the *Spirit of New Orleans* southward on his own uncharted journey. Although he had rejected the emotional appeals of several returning Presbyterian ministers to join the revolving picket line in Hattiesburg, Beech was haunted during preparations for Easter by their argument that white ministers in clerical collars dampened the likelihood of violence against Mississippi Negroes. His eight-member board of sessions had divided sharply over his sudden request to attend a trial extension of the Hattiesburg Freedom Day in Greenwood on March 25. Some lay elders grumbled that it was irresponsible to ask leave on such short notice, especially during Holy Week, others that a Northern Presbyterian had no business in the South. Supporters reflected more positively that their young minister had a teddy bear quality that indeed might soothe racial passions. Since Beech admitted that he could not fully explain his impulse even to himself, but felt strongly enough to leave behind a newborn third son, the session deferred to him.

Traveling alone, Beech stepped mistakenly off the Illinois Central in Grenada instead of Greenwood. When he managed to reach the Greenwood SNCC office on Avenue N, movement workers scarcely took notice of him in the crush of Freedom Day alarms. A policeman had kicked Miss Dorothy Huggins on the picket line, and the owner of Short Tire and Oil Co. had informed George Davis that he could no longer drive a truck there because police photographs of him on the picket line had been displayed at a meeting of the White Citizens Council. Someone handed newcomer Beech a sheaf of leaflets promoting the evening mass meeting, and his anticipation gave way to shock—first when Negroes turned him away from their doors without accepting his leaflet, then when police arrested him on a dusty street less than two hours after he arrived in Greenwood.

At the station, Beech endured fingerprinting, minor manhandling, and menacing talk of littering and other charges before he heard himself snap: "Hey you! I want a receipt for every single item you just got from my pockets." This outburst led to discussion with the police chief himself, and soon, at the whispered urging of a brassy Greenwood girl from a nearby cell, to Beech's suggestion that his new friend the chief might as well release the others, too. He left with ten Negroes arrested earlier that day, including SNCC veteran Willie Peacock, but what he remembered most vividly on the train back to Illinois were the eyes of the Negroes afraid to look at him, much less take a leaflet—images of faces and bodies turning away from his friendliest pastoral smile. When Beech called New York to volunteer for what he called a "long-term commitment to this stuff," Rev. Gayraud Wilmore of the Presbyterian Commission on Religion and Race offered the only available position, as the first resident coordinator of the Hattiesburg Ministers Project. Picket lines would be in the eighteenth continuous week around the Forrest County courthouse by the time Beech could disengage from his two pulpits and move south in May.

ON MARCH 29, seven white theology professors and two Mississippi Negroes approached Capitol Street Methodist Church of Jackson for the

Easter morning service. "That's far enough—no end runs," announced the spokesman for a line of ushers interposed on the front steps. A standoff ensued. "I guess you'll have to arrest us," concluded Rev. Van Bogard Dunn, dean of Methodist Theological School in Ohio. While being led away toward a sentence of six months' jail and a $500 fine, Dunn got the commanding officer to say that police would have taken no action without the explicit request of the church ushers. The reply was legal grist for Jack Pratt of the National Council of Churches, who planned to argue on appeal from paragraph 2026 of the Methodist Church *Discipline* that no Methodist church could ban interracial worship on legitimate religious grounds.

Outside Galloway Methodist Church, ten blocks away from Capitol Street, two bishops in distinctive clerical garb drew a sizable crowd. Leaving ushers to hold them at bay, the church's board chairman hurried off to seek the counsel of pastor W. J. Cunningham, who recommended that the segregation policy be relaxed on his authority. When Cunningham explained that Methodists could not dream of refusing worship to sitting bishops of their own denomination, even if one was a Negro, Galloway leaders melted away in sullen disagreement. They held fast against the bishops—James K. Mathews of Boston and Charles Golden* of Nashville —who left behind the gloomier of two prepared statements. ("Easter is an occasion for entirely new attitudes and fresh beginnings.... If we are not admitted, we shall feel no ill will toward those who may feel compelled to turn us away.")

Over the next several months, the Easter incident consolidated resentment against Cunningham and bishops of the national church. "They were wrong to come here," the board chairman aggressively complained. Some five hundred members withdrew to form independent Methodist churches free of integrationist doctrine, and those left behind voted to rescind Galloway's entire World Service budget of $6,700 in order to shut off the tiny portion that passed through the National Council of Churches. Edwin King, in a one-paragraph addendum to his FCC petition against segregationist television, swore that although the networks reported Jackson's Easter demonstrations as national news, "WLBT made no mention of these events."

IN ATLANTA, Al Lowenstein spent much of Easter Sunday talking impatiently on one pay telephone while guarding another, anticipating go-ahead instructions that never came. An enthusiastic mediator, fresh from consultations with his NAACP contacts in Mississippi, he had flown in at

---

* Golden, as regional bishop for the segregated Central (Negro) Conference of the United Methodist Church, had been instrumental in opening the first Mississippi churches to movement meetings two years earlier in Hattiesburg and the Delta.

the request of Bob Moses to exhort the SNCC Executive Committee to set aside recurrent misgivings about the Mississippi summer project. Moses, on learning that SNCC Executive Director James Forman nursed an overriding suspicion of Lowenstein from old political battles inside the National Student Association, had parked Lowenstein at the airport until he could smooth over the invitation privately. He told Forman that SNCC owed an audience to the Mississippi movement's chief outside catalyst and recruiter of college volunteers, but Forman opposed hearing Lowenstein with unexpected vehemence, warning that he and others would strenuously object if the invitation were pressed openly in the meeting. Embarrassed, Moses backed down to avoid poisonous new divisions over a planned unity speech. He was swept into the contentious session for hours, stranding Lowenstein at his airport phone station.

Lowenstein was becoming a branded prototype of the isolated white liberal. His name acquired in movement circles a volatile symbolism that would eclipse biographical fact, somewhat like Malcolm X for the larger society. From the tangle of cultural and ideological resentments ahead came preview struggles over control. In February, three weeks before Moses publicly announced any plans for Freedom Summer, a Lowenstein protégé told the *Harvard Crimson* that he would be moving south to assume personal command of "more than a thousand" student volunteers in Mississippi. ("I apologize in advance if this story is premature or in any way embarrassing," he wrote Lowenstein.) By then, Lowenstein's Stanford group already had pushed ahead with fund-raising committees, campus-wide meetings, faculty advisers (theologian Robert McAfee Brown, historian Otis Pease), and even a "secretariat." The energetic student editor wrote Lowenstein that "on Monday we will break the whole thing in the *Daily*," and, in spite of their best intentions, the Stanford students bruised sensibilities in Mississippi by organizing publicity on Western campuses around an April speaking tour by Martin Luther King—reasoning that King would interest college students who knew nothing of SNCC or COFO.

The Easter meeting launched the SNCC leaders into new conflict between conventional and movement politics. Moses frankly sought power alliances in a letter to twenty supporters ranging from Ella Baker to actor Marlon Brando: "It is our conviction that only a massive effort by the country backed by the full power of the President can offer some hope for even minimal change in Mississippi." SNCC leaders vacillated over how to obtain an audience to tell President Johnson that "responsibility rests with him, and him alone." If they petitioned jointly with the titular leaders of COFO—King, Farmer, Roy Wilkins—they might be ignored among national figures more congenial to Johnson. One alternative—asking unaffiliated dignitaries to sponsor their request—proved ineffective and awkward when James Baldwin and Reinhold Niebuhr thought they were being asked to join a White House meeting themselves. To finesse hard rules of political access, SNCC leaders reluctantly asked King as a favor to let Mississippi Negroes do the talking once he got them into Johnson's presence.

In Lowenstein's absence, SNCC leaders debated poaching charges against other civil rights groups. CORE had issued a press statement making the entire summer project sound like a CORE initiative, and traditional Negro newspapers blithely advertised the summer showdown as an NAACP registration drive. In response, Moses gently reprimanded CORE's James Farmer, and aggressive student voices pushed "to project SNCC's image or else we'll be continually overridden." In Atlanta, they resolved to fight back by quietly seeking the organizational allegiance of individual summer volunteers as "SNCC people," beyond the COFO cause. Having disdained the promotional emphasis of other civil rights groups, they sought targeted publicity as the key to fund-raising at the volume necessary to float the summer project. Proposals to hire fund-raisers met opposition on the ground that professionals "don't think the same way we do and get money in a different way." The trick was to gain the benefit of commerical skill without losing the moral identity of SNCC's experience in Mississippi.

Holding fast on one controversial issue, SNCC leaders confirmed in Atlanta that the summer project would accept help from anyone willing to brave movement service in Mississippi. They welcomed the National Lawyers Guild, a venerable leftist society that did not exclude Communists and former Communists, even though every one of SNCC's allies vehemently objected. On King's behalf, Andrew Young promptly advised that it was a losing game to fight the "red issue" and segregation at once, especially in Mississippi. Gloster Current of the NAACP called SNCC "naive" to think the guild was acceptable. CORE's chief counsel took his worries to the FBI in Washington, reporting that the students were too young to remember from the 1930s and 1940s that the slightest Communist presence was invisibly corrupting. Jack Greenberg of the NAACP Legal Defense Fund threatened to pull his lawyers out of Mississippi rather than work with the guild. Jack Pratt seconded Greenberg for the National Council of Churches, and his boss, Robert Spike, warned Moses against SNCC's "deliberate link" with guild lawyers. The church objection weighed heavily on Moses, because Spike had followed up the Presbyterian work in Hattiesburg with the first institutional commitment to the summer project: a pledge from his Commission on Religion and Race to finance all training and transportation of summer volunteers.

Lowenstein campaigned against the guild, too, in a way that would be remembered long after the broader opposition was forgotten. Something about Lowenstein mirrored the internal tensions within the student movement. Moving between separate worlds easily—too easily for many students—he was part big shot and part itinerant waif. Lowenstein would materialize out of nowhere, argue all night, and nap on the floor like a fresh recruit for the sit-ins, all the while dispatching messages to personal friends in Congress. Lowenstein wanted to debate not merely the substance of decisions but how they were made. Rather than deferring as an outsider to peer consensus, he pressed for votes and rules of representation to match SNCC's goals for Mississippi. He wanted to know why the approval of the summer project remained tentative but the welcome of the Lawyers Guild seemed final. He wanted to know how the wishes of several thousand Mississippi NAACP members were to be counted against those of a few hundred SNCC workers and followers. To objections that sharecroppers like Fannie Lou Hamer represented a moral and political transformation far beyond their present numbers, Lowenstein argued that COFO needed a working bridge between politics and ideology. If the SNCC workers of Mississippi could not find common language with the middle-class Negroes who had supported Medgar Evers, how could they hope to reach an understanding with President Johnson?

These were sensitive questions. Rebuffed in Atlanta, Lowenstein peppered SNCC with so many questions on the terms of political cooperation that Moses finally asked an assistant to fend off his calls. Lowenstein knew SNCC well enough to cite the one cardinal rule of its informal brotherhood: that the movement should respect the wishes of those willing to put themselves on the line. Students had built the movement on this standard, breaking through traditional authority, but now embattled pioneers wanted summer volunteers to face the risks of Mississippi while submitting to them as entitled experts. Lowenstein believed the movement should treat the summer volunteers as partners. To run the summer project, he proposed a joint policy board composed of students and Mississippi workers, headed by Yale chaplain William Sloane Coffin. It infuriated him to hear that while the SNCC leaders refused to exclude guild lawyers on principle and necessity, they could bar him from meetings and exclude the volunteers themselves from their councils.

Over the two chaotic months of preparation that remained, Lowenstein tried to protect the summer project from public attacks, sometimes against his own sympathies. When the NAACP's Roy Wilkins threatened to denounce COFO as infiltrated by the National Lawyers Guild, Lowenstein hurried to New York to pacify him with the traditional argument that defendants had a right to counsel of their choice, Communist or not. He delivered more speeches about Mississippi as a historic crucible of American democracy. "My roommates were positively awed, and they don't awe easily," wrote an admiring correspondent from Yale. At Queens College, Lowenstein inspired New York students to apply for Mississippi assignment—including one senior, Andrew Goodman, who was completing a term paper on the startling racial controversies emerging from the

Nation of Islam*—and a Stanford speech rallied even those students to whom Lowenstein had confided his stinging criticisms of SNCC as immature and undemocratic. He confined his public doubts to cryptic remarks —"militancy should not be confused with effectiveness"—but close contacts knew he felt troubled and betrayed. His acolytes included campus politicians who by nature were acutely conscious of student rights on everything from cafeteria quality to constitutional expression, and some of them looked past Lowenstein's barnstorming enthusiasm to pick up his cautions about going blindly into alien Mississippi. "It is fundamental to our role in this that we insure the student voice and perspective in policy formulation," a worried student body president wrote Lowenstein.

To SNCC leaders still struggling with fundamental strategy, Lowenstein represented two opposing nightmares about the Mississippi summer project. A newly calculating, political faction feared that his recruits would bowl over a fledgling movement by numbers and cultural connections, while those who embraced the conscience of the "beloved community" shrank from the implications of using prominent white volunteers as bait for federal intervention. If the daughter of a U.S. senator were arrested, who would decide when to post bail—her family or the Mississippi movement? If she were jailed with Mississippi Negroes, must they be released as a group? How would the safety and comfort of the prisoners be weighed against the political value of continued confinement?

Nervous applicants and their parents bombarded COFO headquarters with hundreds of related questions, receiving mostly evasive replies. A Stanford organizer complained that COFO planners remained about "as communicative as a colony of Trappist monks." Moses, firmly resolved that control must be retained within the Mississippi movement, lacked the means to supply definitive answers even if he had them. As late as early May, he acknowledged that SNCC could not feed even the few permanent workers who were supposed to be processing volunteer applications. Only $10,000 had been raised for the project against a minimum budget of $800,000, and the toilet in the Jackson Freedom House remained clogged for want of $5 cash to pay a plumber. Moses sometimes despaired of going forward at all.

Hearing that Moses was giving up, Lowenstein discontinued his campus recruiting in May. SNCC workers rallied to the project as a leap of faith, and even those who still opposed the summer project recoiled from the notion that Lowenstein might call it off. Some saw Lowenstein as folding for selfish reasons, while others suspected that he had been plotting

---

* "While it is somewhat of a fantasy to believe that all white men are devils," Goodman wrote, "it is true that the white man (and by this I mean Christian civilization in general) has proved himself to be the most depraved devil imaginable in his attitudes towards the Negro race.... The historical contempt that the white race held for the Negroes has created a group of rootless degraded people."

sabotage all along. Lowenstein railed against mixed signals, and battled personal rejection by maneuvering with more frenetic stealth than ever—showing up on the fringe of meetings, drawing confidants aside while looking past everyone else. The few whites already working with SNCC in Mississippi mistrusted him as a manipulator.

As deadlines approached, Lowenstein became as evasive about his own plans as COFO leaders were about the inner workings of the summer project. Admirers who still called him the "human syllogism" grew mystified by his hints that he might not be in harness with Bob Moses. "I admit it took me four readings to discover I still didn't know what was happening after getting your letter," confessed one correspondent. Another bewildered, aspiring volunteer wrote: "Where will you be this summer if not in Mississippi?...Where are you going to be for the next few months so I can catch you some time? Won't you be in Miss. at all?"

In the end, Lowenstein fled not only Mississippi but the United States. Before retreating to Europe and the ferment of his original childhood cause—restoring democracy to Franco's Spain—he asked some volunteers to withdraw from the summer project, too, arguing that COFO was forfeiting its chance to develop a historic biracial coalition. Dennis Sweeney, one of his most ardent student followers, was among those trapped between warring passions. But for Lowenstein, he never would have left Stanford to work on the Mississippi Freedom Vote the previous fall; having gone, he could not stay away from fears and inspirations of melting purity. Sweeney decided to return to Mississippi without the approval of his mentor. Lowenstein, characteristically, first resented the choice as a personal defection, then helped arrange a foundation grant to finance it. Sweeney was destined to become one of the movement's most extreme psychological casualties—he would assassinate Lowenstein in 1980—but for now he shrugged off the conflict. "Please let me know what you're doing next year when you decide," Sweeney wrote as he left for Mississippi. "I may join you."

20

Mary Peabody
Meets the Klan

ABOARD AN EVENING FLIGHT from Boston on March 29, still wearing their church dresses and Easter hats, there arrived four distinguished reinforcements known mainly for their marital connections to three Episcopal bishops and to H. S. Payson Rowe, a socially prominent insurance executive with John Hancock. They were greeted at the Jacksonville airport by a man of slightly oversized head and superabundant energy—Hosea Williams of Savannah, who, since capturing publicity the previous year with his jail marches and his daily sermons atop Tomochichi's Rock, had volunteered his way into trial duty on Martin Luther King's SCLC staff. Williams briefed the arriving matrons on the drive south to St. Augustine. In less than a week, he had battled the equally temperamental local leader Robert Hayling about the discipline of nonviolence while preparing white New England college students for coordinated demonstrations over spring break. Integrated groups had been turned away from most of the white churches that morning, he reported to his passengers, and nearly seventy people had been jailed in the opening sit-ins.

Not all the passengers shared Williams's excitement over what he called the early signs of a bona fide movement. In particular, Mary Peabody, wife of Bishop Malcolm Peabody, replied that while she had enjoyed the nonviolent training at the Blue Hill Christian Center, she did not think they would need it once they got a chance to explain themselves to local authorities. "I do not believe they will deny me the pleasure of lunch with my Negro friend," she said pleasantly.

Hosea Williams turned from the steering wheel. Although he knew

Dr. King had entrusted him with a maximum celebrity in the mother of the Massachusetts governor, he felt compelled to prepare her for reality. "Mrs. Peabody," he said finally, "these folk will deny Jesus." His comment stifled discussion in the car. The women remarked that if it could be true, there would be little common ground for discussion.

In St. Augustine, they made a grand entrance upon the mass meeting at Zion Baptist Church, where the wife of a Yale divinity professor told of being surrounded by angry-looking men that day while handing out leaflets to tourists—how the terror had lifted from her face with such mysterious clarity that her assailants left her alone. The chaplains of Smith College and Amherst were present, along with nearly a hundred students from Harvard, Mount Holyoke, Brown, and schools as far north as Gorham Teachers College in Maine. All of them joined Hayling's local stalwarts the next morning for nonviolent workshops at the Elk's Rest Lodge in the center of Lincolnville. From there, the four senior arrivals went off to test segregation against the perfume of chivalry.

Downtown near the Old Slave Market, Esther Burgess made sure that the fruit cup at McCartney's lunch counter was fresh rather than canned, and her three companions ordered a breakfast of pancakes. When their dishes arrived, Mary Peabody congratulated the waitress. "How nice it is that you serve colored people here," she said.

"We don't," the puzzled waitress replied.

"Well, Mrs. Burgess is colored," Peabody observed, whereupon the waitress retreated from view. A premonition made Burgess hastily consume her fruit cup before a store manager arrived to study the four faces at his lunch counter. Settling before Burgess, whose skin was light enough to pass, he asked whether she considered herself a Negro. She did.

Evicted, the four women walked on to other designated sites. Peabody decided that she had declared victory too early, and devised new strategies, but advance blockades materialized at every entrance. The women eventually gave up on the assumption that someone had spread a warning, perhaps identifying them by Peabody's distinctive red hat crowned with a double tier of sequins.

Back at Elk's Rest Lodge, Hosea Williams asked if they would join the afternoon corps of jail volunteers. Burgess stepped forward, and late that afternoon seven companions escorted her first to the Monson Motor Lodge—where the manager intercepted them with an offer of outdoor service near the kitchen. "But that's insulting," protested Mary Peabody, speaking for the delegation.

"You and I will never live to see the day when people will be forced to take others into their hearts," the manager declared.

"Where is your heart?" Peabody inquired, but she moved on when the manager held his ground.

The group managed to reach a table in the empty bar of the Ponce de Léon Motor Lodge, and when Sheriff L. O. Davis entered with a brace of police officers and two German shepherds, Peabody refused to leave until he retrieved and read for her the exact language of Florida's "undesirable guest" statute. None of the unflattering definitions applied to her party, she remarked, but Peabody and two of her Boston friends retreated politely before Sheriff Davis's stern choice of immediate departure or jail. The other five stayed on to face arrest: Hayling, two chaplains, a Pembroke student, and Esther Burgess, who, trembling, was placed with one of the police dogs in the back seat of a squad car. A Boston reporter called out to her, asking whether her husband, Bishop John Burgess, would approve of her course. "I have a higher loyalty to God," she called back.

Sealed off from the hymns of public encouragement in the mass meeting, a leadership crisis was flashing from the back room at Elk's Rest Lodge to the sponsoring officers of the New England SCLC chapter. It superseded even the concurrent plague of hit-and-run violence against the spring prayer vigil in Williamston, North Carolina, their chapter's adopted project. (On Easter, segregationists had beaten their colleague Paul Chapman outside the local Espiscopal church, smashed the windshield of Lois Chapman's car, and hospitalized a visiting Massachusetts student with blows from a baseball bat.) From Boston, Virgil Wood and James Breeden contacted William Sloane Coffin at Yale, where he was on standby alert, and dispatched him to St. Augustine with the sole objective of talking Mary Peabody into jail, grandmother of seven or not.

BEFORE COFFIN ARRIVED in St. Augustine the next day, March 31, Peabody tried to attend the morning communion service at Trinity Episcopal Church, a prestigious congregation across the Slave Market plaza from the cathedral. She found the doors locked and Sheriff Davis standing guard outside along with the rector, Rev. Charles Seymour, who explained that the vestry considered her attendance a demonstration rather than worship, and therefore had canceled the service to protect life and property. Seymour invited Peabody into the church anteroom to hear his vestrymen defend the cancellation vote on the ground that their Florida bishop had interceded with her husband, bishop of the Massachusetts diocese, to argue by phone that his wife's purpose would damage comity within the national church. For more than an hour, Peabody tried to justify her theology against their charges of meddling.

Meanwhile, Hosea Williams drilled more than 150 teenagers who skipped school that day to conduct a climactic march, honoring their four friends who had been locked away for the entire fall semester. As in Savannah, Williams preached ecstatically on nonviolence as a glorious kind of militant perfection, and he placed a large collection bucket up front to gather up knives, rocks, and rulers—anything the most hostile segregationist might construe as weapons. Willie Bolden, the former Savannah bellhop who had bonded himself to Williams in a new movement life, walked up and down the aisles coaxing students to surrender even pens and pencils before they marched off in double file down the sidewalks to the Old Slave Market. There they sang hymns, including an up-tempo "We Shall Overcome," then marched before bystanders through the downtown streets to the majestic Ponce de Léon Hotel, through its doors and on into the enormous dining room where Vice President Johnson had spoken the previous year. The hall having emptied on word of their approach, the marchers sat down and waited alone in good order—careful not to wrinkle the white linen or touch the crystal—until Sheriff Davis and his men surrounded them with cattle prod "persuaders" and the full squad of fifteen police dogs. After quiet consultations between student leaders and the few white New England volunteers with them, the marchers decided that they could not submit to arrest there without inevitable muss to the place settings. They passed the word to stand up in unison, push back their chairs, and file outside to be arrested in the driveway.

News of the impeccable student witness was relayed to Elk's Rest about the time Mary Peabody returned from Trinity Church. William Sloane Coffin had arrived there along with Robert Hayling, who had paid a cash bond out of the county prison. In private, asking permission to speak straightforwardly, Coffin told Peabody that the arrest of Esther Burgess from her group sent a demoralizing message to the local integration movement: the Negro alone suffered, while her white friends accepted a privileged escape. Peabody confessed that her experience thus far had strained her belief in persuasive dialogue, especially since some of the Trinity vestrymen had refused to shake her hand. "I think I'd better call my son," she sighed. Within minutes, she informed Governor Peabody of her predicament, worrying out loud that her controversial deeds might injure his political career. His encouraging response brought mist to her eyes. "Thank you, Endicott," she signed off. "You're a wonderful fellow."

Florence Rowe decided that she could not go through with the arrest, but Hester Campbell determined to stick with Peabody. With a Harvard divinity professor making a third white volunteer, Hayling scoured Elk's Rest for Negroes willing to fill out an integrated arrest group. He found no takers, the remaining adults intimidated and the supply of teenagers depleted by the morning march. Before offering to go back himself, Hayling ventured into a nearby kitchen where the humblest women supporters were cooking chicken and cornbread snacks for the evening mass meeting. He begged them not to let Peabody's important gesture go to waste, and painted images of glory, asking whether they ever dreamed of going to jail with a governor's mother. Finally, Georgia Reed, a diminutive home seamstress crippled by polio, who walked laboriously on heavy canes, spoke up with powerful effect. Her example inspired four of her fellow cooks. Drivers excitedly sprang up to rush the five women home and help them change into their best outfits for the occasion.

During these midday preparations, phone lines continued to hum between Florida and Massachusetts as politicians took over from the worried bishops. Governor Peabody warned Florida Governor Farris Bryant of his mother's intentions, and Bryant promised to protect her from serious harm. Governor Bryant still thought Peabody did not quite grasp the acute political sensitivity of what Bryant called "the civil rights thing." He was having similar trouble getting Walter Jenkins and other White House aides to understand why Florida's elected officials were refusing to serve as delegates to the upcoming Democratic convention. To Bryant, these racial matters required a sixth sense that was essentially Southern. He advised Mayor Shelley and other St. Augustine leaders not to arrest Mary Peabody at all, no matter how incensed they were with her. Jail was exactly what she wanted, he warned, and they should let her sit in at restaurants or motels until she got tired and went home—all night if necessary. With everything seemingly agreed to, it exasperated Governor Bryant all the more to learn that his St. Augustine friends got their backs up within minutes and arrested the Peabody group. Their stubbornness left Bryant feeling more victimized than the prisoners.

Inside St. Johns County jail, the newly arrived Georgia Reed and the four volunteer cooks spread word that the governor's mother was being fingerprinted and booked behind them. Nearly two hundred demonstrators filled the segregated jail to double its capacity, with sixty-five Negro men jammed into one large cell for sixteen, and fifty-seven Negro women in a smaller cell with only four beds. When Peabody appeared in the hallway, and paused to speak with Esther Burgess on her way to a cell for white female prisoners, a hush fell over the incarcerated Negro women. By social standing and seniority, most of them looked to Katherine Twine to say something. Going to jail had more than healed the year's humiliation since she had backed out of the Lyndon Johnson dinner the previous Easter, letting her husband attend without her. This time, Twine the postman had to stay home to protect his federal job. The sight of Peabody through the cell bars—"every inch the Boston blueblood," according to one arrest story, wearing sensible shoes and what the *New York Times* called "a muted pink suit"—reduced Katherine Twine to momentary awe. All she could say was, "You look just like Miss Eleanor Roosevelt."

"We are cousins," Peabody replied.

Fifty reporters clamored outside for jail interviews. Within two hours of the booking, their news bulletins stimulated demands for briefings by the Justice Department and the FBI from U.S. senators concerned about Peabody's welfare, and St. Augustine sprang up instantly among the leading national news stories, alongside the death watch for a comatose General Douglas MacArthur and reports of a United States–favored military coup in Brazil. The *New York Times* noted that Senator Hubert Humphrey formally commenced final debate on the civil rights bill with a speech of three hours and twenty-six minutes, opening with the Golden Rule quotation from St. Matthew ("Do unto others..."), and the *Times* placed on its front page a large photograph of Mary Peabody in custody, flanked by Sheriff Davis with a cattle prod in his hands and a cigar in his mouth.

In Washington, during an unseasonably late snowstorm, CBS television news pledged that its correspondent Roger Mudd would report nightly for the duration of the Senate filibuster from an outdoor perch on the Capitol steps. Emissaries from Walter Cronkite, Mudd's colleague, guaranteed Mrs. Peabody an appearance on the nightly news if she would bail out in time to film a network interview at a Jacksonville studio. She declined, sending word that she preferred to stay in jail with her new friends.

AMONG THOSE most shocked by the news from St. Augustine was the church lawyer Jack Pratt, who as a seminary student had reported to the celebrity prisoner's husband, Bishop Malcolm Peabody. With the permission of his CORR employer Robert Spike, Pratt flew south the next morning, April 1, and reached the jail just as it bulged with eighty-eight new demonstrators, pushing the week's total to nearly three hundred. Aside from seventy marching teenagers, the new arrivals included Chaplain William Sloane Coffin and Yale professor Jacques Bossiere, who delivered to Mrs. Peabody a reading copy of *L'Etranger* by Albert Camus, in French. At a crowded cell block press conference, Peabody mortified Sheriff Davis and amused the reporters with the comment that she had enjoyed her breakfast of hominy grits even though obliged to eat with her fingers. Davis, who made a show of his hospitality toward Peabody, hastened to fetch proper utensils and offer an apology. Later, while Pratt advised his client to downplay her chipper camaraderie with Sheriff Davis, in view of his sharply contrasting treatment of Negro prisoners, a visitor introduced himself as another Peabody. "I understand you're representing my mother," said Rev. George Peabody of New York. "What are your qualifications?"

Pratt himself felt the sheriff's meaner side. Well past midnight, on the concurring authority of local judge Charles Mathis, Sheriff Davis refused to release any civil rights prisoners without stiff cash bonds ranging from $200 to upward of $2,000. He thought the whites might as well stay in jail—"These bums will all be back here for holding hands with niggers," he said coldly—and he avoided discussion of the Negroes altogether. Pratt, with fellow itinerant counsel William Kunstler, pointed out that these extreme bail restrictions would buttress their petition to remove all the cases from state to federal court. Civil rights lawyers had developed the removal petition as a standard tactic, relying on a Reconstruction statute designed to protect former slaves from the vengeance of ex-Confederate judges.

Impressed, Sheriff Davis relented to approve a few standard, discounted release bonds written by a surety company, but by the next morning—after Peabody's second night in jail, with five prisoners sleeping on the floor even in the white women's cell—Davis again blocked all releases. His deputies tried to confine the lawyers in order to forestall their protest in court, to the point of shoving Kunstler and Pratt headlong across the waiting room. With the help of an early-bird reporter who investigated the commotion, the lawyers talked their way out to attend the emergency removal hearing in Jacksonville.

U.S. District Court Judge Bryan Simpson, a tall, white-haired Truman appointee known for his laconic habit of whittling on the bench, rebuffed the argument that civil rights defendants could not obtain a fair trial in state courts. "Somebody goes and sticks their head in a noose and then complains that the rope burns their neck," he told Kunstler and Pratt, "I don't see how they have a great deal to complain about, as long as fundamental due process is accorded in the trial procedures." Simpson also brushed aside testimony about police dogs and crowded cells, saying he was not about to second-guess or restrict the performance of local officers. Yet he did display a protective interest during the testimony of the fifteen-year-old prisoner, Annie Ruth Evans, sternly admonishing lawyers for the State of Florida that they must abide by that week's new Supreme Court ruling, which required counsel to address Negro witnesses by courtesy titles instead of first names. The Florida lawyers stumbled so painfully over the words "Miss Evans," that it seemed to awaken a cautionary balance in Judge Simpson. While he formally remanded all three hundred cases back to Judge Mathis in St. Augustine, Simpson extracted a promise that local prosecutors would delay trial and punishment at least until May, affording Kunstler and Pratt time to pursue removal to federal jurisdiction on appeal.

This glimmer of judicial sympathy was more than enough to sustain a small celebration back in the St. John's County jail. Mary Peabody bailed out to address a mass meeting that night at First Baptist, where she praised the courage of St. Augustine's movement. "I feel as if a wall were crumbling," she said. Pratt accompanied her on the flight back to Boston the next morning, to be greeted by Governor Peabody, Bishop Peabody, Rev. Virgil Wood, Rev. James Breeden, a phalanx of reporters, and a full motorcade of Massachusetts law enforcement. Martin Luther King sent a public telegram to the governor—"I have been so deeply inspired by your mother's creative witness in Florida"—and "Grandmother Peabody," as a fresh national celebrity, soon extolled the promise of St. Augustine on NBC's *Today* show.

☐

ADRENALINE SUBSIDED from Elk's Rest as soon as Peabody and the spring break volunteers returned to New England, and press observers focused on the harsh fact that segregation still stood. "Protesters Fail in St. Augustine," declared the front page of the *New York Times.* Rest and bail jitters preoccupied the fresh veterans, so much that a frustrated Hosea Williams could not coax new jail volunteers from the mass meetings. King withdrew him temporarily after Williams publicly scolded local Negroes for undermining their own movement.

Local whites rallied to the offensive through April, beginning with a forceful statement of personal belief by Mayor Shelley. "I consider myself a segregationist," he told reporters. "God segregated the races, as far as I'm concerned, when he made them a different color." Yet Shelley also insisted that because his city lacked official segregation ordinances, the trespassing demonstrators must have some malicious ulterior purpose. In a rebuttal appearance on the *Today* show, Shelley argued that his city had enjoyed racial harmony before it was targeted by outsiders. Florida newspapers embraced his defense in headlines: "Mrs. Peabody's Act Seen Harmful to All."

A reelection drive by Sheriff L. O. Davis became the most visible campaign of the spring Democratic primary. He wore a gun openly for the first time in his long career, saying he intended to protect himself from the likes of Hosea Williams, and told friends the daily tensions were worse even than the grisly case of the mangled pieces from forty-odd bodies that had washed up on local beaches two decades earlier, which he had attributed in the wartime hush to Nazi submarine attacks on offshore merchant vessels. Davis campaigned aggressively to secure white support. He told Negro audiences in Lincolnville that he did not seek or want their votes, using the epithet "nigger" to drive home his meaning. A vote count well above 70 percent made Sheriff Davis a significant new political force after the May 5 primary. Bristling confidently against the threat of renewed demonstrations, he deputized a volunteer militia and gave known Klan leaders the run of his office.

A quieter state of emergency gripped St. Augustine's leading citizens, many of whom generally avoided the new white militiamen as uncouth drunkards and roughnecks. Answering his doorbell on a Sunday afternoon, the owner of the local Ford dealership was dumbstruck to face one of his lowliest employees, who had ventured into the prime neighborhood not to the back door—and not in a desperate quest to secure a salary advance—but to say with aplomb that he was there for a social visit, just to talk.

"Who do you want to visit?" asked the incredulous Ford dealer.

"You."

Horrified, the dealer fired the man summarily, and soon thereafter also fired Negro foreman Bungum Roberson, the pioneer parent of local school integration, on the assumption that Roberson was helping Robert Hayling pump brotherhood fantasies of primitive religion into every tranquil corner of society.

At Trinity Episcopal Church, the Ford dealer followed the guidance of the most learned Sunday School teacher, Dr. Hardgrove Norris, who buttressed his conservative theological teachings with arcane tidbits from anti-Communist literature. Knowing the names of three elderly women who had once served as nominal owners of the Communist *Daily Worker,* for instance, Dr. Norris held that Mary Peabody fit an established pattern of old ladies as conspiratorial "catspaws" for the Communist party. With A. H. "Hoopie" Tebeault, editor of St. Augustine's newspaper, Norris in May pushed a resolution through the vestry to shut off church contributions to the Episcopal diocese until it withdrew from the National Council of Churches. He detected socialist tendencies in the sermons of Rev. Charles Seymour, Trinity's rector since 1949. Seymour, in a rare public hint of conflict within white churches, told a television interviewer that "any or all of us ministers may be leaving town soon at the request of our constituents."

FROM HIS SPEECH-MAKING tours, King sent a succession of scouts to evaluate prospects in St. Augustine. His traveling aide Bernard Lee reported that adult leaders were thin and badly organized. Another King representative recommended a grand campaign to achieve negotiations with white officials while rebuilding the movement by door-to-door canvass. The city rejected negotiations, however, and all but a few Negro adults shied away from Hayling's leadership. Some NAACP stalwarts, such as Fannie Fulwood, never missed a Hayling mass meeting but refrained from demonstration as unwise. Others feared Klan violence and job reprisal, or were swayed by whites who demonized Hayling, and a few succumbed to partisan rivalries. Internal NAACP reports speculated with transparent satisfaction that "King is now having to back down from his endorsement of Dr. Hayling in order to save face."

The St. Augustine project faltered for lack of a sponsoring minister within King's councils. During their two-day annual meeting in mid-April, the SCLC board members scarcely mentioned even the high-profile alternatives for renewed demonstrations in Birmingham and Danville, or a march on the U.S. Capitol to break the Senate filibuster. James Bevel lobbied for his Alabama voting crusade—to achieve historic redress for the Birmingham church bombing, he reminded King—and also to repair the national image of nonviolence after a rash of wildcat "brinksmanship" protests, which were feeding a white backlash. Board members knew, however, that Bevel would get nowhere while feuding so intensely with SCLC's executive director, Wyatt Walker. They relegated his Alabama plan to hallway caucuses along with other touchy matters, such as SCLC's empty treasury and columnist Joseph Alsop's public charge that King was harboring Communists.

Gathered at the Bibleway Church of Washington, D.C., the SCLC board members conducted business sessions through the usual exchange of collegial sermons, in a kind of pulpit variation on the baronial customs of Congress. One preacher dramatically summoned King to undertake a public fast against the Senate filibuster. Another hailed the previous year as a vindication for SCLC's model of crossover leadership from churches into politics, and a third proposed an SCLC expansion drive targeted through the Baptist ministerial associations. Wyatt Walker closed his lengthy review of four years' service with final notice that he was quitting effective June 15. For nearly nine months, since his first resignation in September, Walker had postponed departure while he secured another job. Out of respect for King, he only hinted at grievances over what he saw as chronic forgiveness toward aimless or insubordinate free spirits, particularly James Bevel. Walker maintained with philosophical resignation that King was losing touch with practical standards to the point of appearing scruffy at the edges—no longer so fastidious about new suits and silk ties, even a trifle indifferent about a frayed collar. In a farewell address of fiery pulpit oratory, Walker recalled the triumph of Birmingham with such impact that Ralph Abernathy rose to declare that Walker was indispensable, and begged him to withdraw his resignation. Daddy King headed off a stampede of acclamation with booming declarations that Walker deserved to make up his own mind, and interceded with a prayer of adjournment that assigned Walker's fate to heaven.

In mid-May, Wyatt Walker agreed to reconnoiter St. Augustine as his last official task at SCLC. He sketched a battle plan remarkably similar to his original blueprint for Birmingham. While favoring action campaigns over barnstorming, Walker warned King that "our operation appears to be raggedy." He saw no stabilizing base among the Negro preachers of St. Augustine, and Hayling's legions of teenagers triggered the same authoritarian anxiety about childish disorder that made Walker so resentful of SNCC students. "There is a danger that our demonstrations will keep or assume the character of a minstrel show," he wrote. The only advantages he perceived in St. Augustine were the vulnerability of its tourist-based economy and the unique, symbolic potential of segregation in the nation's oldest city.

King, who recognized drawbacks to every option, also weighed reminders from the past about the distorting perspective of his traveling engagements. For all the daily excitement of large crowds and police escorts, often with a buzz over rumored threats or a newly broken color barrier, these occasions were no more than thimbles of conversion that evaporated in reality, while civil rights eruptions made hard news in dozens of cities. Yet again, he had to decide whether to tear himself from the inertia of sermons, and whether another leap toward suffering would fortify the nonviolent message or merely aggravate the opposition. Eight years after the Montgomery bus boycott, his familiar dilemma touched the rudder of national politics.

21

Wrestling with Legends

TIME AND AMBITION dimmed President Johnson's image as the healing caretaker of the Kennedy legacy. When Kennedy's press secretary tried to resign in March to run for the Senate in California, Johnson refused to accept the news from Pierre Salinger himself or any of his aides until one secretary told him that Salinger was leaving that very day. Johnson then called the hospital where George Reedy was confined to lose the excess of his 285 pounds, and yanked him back to the White House within the hour as Salinger's emergency replacement. Reedy, a scholarly man whose hospital reading included works by theologian Paul Tillich and a historical tome on the Irish famine (the better to appreciate his diet, he joked), noticed that the President was absorbed in a book, *The Rich Nations and the Poor Nations*, by the British economist Barbara Ward. For the first time in Reedy's long acquaintance, Johnson avidly reread and quoted a work of nonfiction. The book's resolutely positive outlook on prosperity* and its moral call to global statesmanship gripped Johnson as an approach that unified his idea of foreign policy with his intended crusade against domestic poverty. He struck up ongoing conversations with Ward, to the point of having Air Force jets transport her from Europe to Washington.

Reedy tried to introduce public themes for an emerging presidency just as White House reporters began to discover Johnson as an independent

---

* "Now that we are 'in orbit,'" wrote Ward of the Western nations, "our own wealth can multiply by compound interest because we are already wealthy...we now face thirty to forty years of world-building on a scale never known in human history...."

personality. Early in April, *Time* portrayed the President as a madcap cowboy who drove terrified correspondents over the bare hills of his Texas ranch at speeds above eighty miles per hour, dodging his livestock and bellowing nonstop yarns while sloshing Pearl beer from a paper cup. Johnson protested the account as a stinging departure from the respectful coverage through the transition since Dallas. Journalists were remarking already on his sensitivity to criticism, speculating that he was paranoid because of his lack of Kennedy charm.

In private, Johnson exhibited his mercurial temperament. He put Sargent Shriver into uncontrollable titters with a sunny, spontaneous description of Bill Moyers at the LBJ Ranch, "going around with a prayer in his eyes and a doleful look, and wishing that you were here, and got a glass of sweet milk in each hand." Johnson also excoriated Moyers and Reedy in front of others and told secretaries their outfits or hairdos were ugly. He berated the legendary Secret Service agent Rufus Youngblood, hero of Dallas, with threats to fire "the whole damned Secret Service" and to puncture the tires of escort limousines. "Your damn Secret Service stays right up behind me every trip," he growled at chief James Rowley. "...When I'm driving and I stop in a hurry, they're liable to hit my bumper and break my neck."

Only with fellow politicians did Johnson maintain an even keel of professional understanding. When he told freshman senator Robert Byrd of West Virginia that Byrd's stand against civil rights would ruin his presidency, and the wounded Byrd protested, Johnson teased that he didn't expect Byrd's vote but hoped he would not fight cloture too hard. "I might make you stay at home and nurse me, and give me a thermometer," said Johnson. "I'm gonna be so sick, and I'm gonna have to have somebody put cold packs on my head." On the other hand, Johnson knew not to banter when Senator Fulbright expressed anguish about opposing the same bill. "It is a kind of embarrassing thing for me, as you know," said Fulbright. "Goddamn it, I'm never very enthusiastic...."

"I know," said the President. "I know. I know it."

"Jesus Christ, I'm really over a barrel on this thing," said Fulbright. "I wish to hell I could vote with you. You know that."

"I know that," said Johnson. "I know it."

The President abhorred the press but consumed as many as fifteen newspapers each day, raged against the authors of the smallest unfavorable reference and yet looked hungrily to the same reporters for ways to present himself more favorably. He absorbed James Reston's private recommendation that he try "something new in Presidential TV" by taking the press with him to visit the country's problems rather than receiving them passively in the White House. An approving aide observed that Reston's proposal would "permit your genuine personality to have its full impact on the public...." When Eric Sevareid of CBS suggested that Johnson needed to develop his own slogan, like FDR's New Deal or Kennedy's New Frontier, the President seized upon the ideas.

On April 22, towing an expectant press corps behind *Air Force One*, Johnson flew off to open the New York World's Fair against the threat of massive civil rights protests. Met by five thousand police and Pinkerton guards who reinforced his Secret Service security detail, Johnson reacted far more charitably to what few pickets actually turned up near his speaker's platform ("I felt sorry for them") than did national news outlets, one of which denounced the "wild-eyed, hare-brained, crackpot scheme" of "about 25 seedy, sleazy Congress of Racial Equality demonstrators, some of them appearing to be white beatniks." Calling them rude and fanatic —"bearded and untidy, the seats of their pants muddied from sitting on the soggy ground"—the *New York Times* rebuked hecklers for insulting the President and for spoiling the $1 billion fair, which the *Times* promoted unabashedly in news columns as a "glittering mirror of national opulence." Mayor Robert Wagner issued a statement of shame over the protests. The fanfare of wounded civic pride overlooked gaping faults within the fair itself, which, boycotted for gaudy, gouging commercialism by nearly all the nations that normally sponsored pavilions at international expositions, was destined to close the next year in debt and neglect, abandoned as a rusting hulk.

President Johnson predicted much better. Just as the most fantastic forecasts of the 1939 World's Fair had fallen short of feats since the Depression—satellite communications, eradicated diseases, atomic power, push-button kitchens—so the next generation would surpass his expectation of a society without bigotry, destitution, or war. "I prophesy peace," he declared, and beyond that a promised land within the next generation. Scarcely pausing, Johnson flew back to Washington, invited the presidents of nine railroads up to his family room that afternoon, settled a debilitating strike that dated back to the Eisenhower administration, and ordered a spontaneous motorcade to announce the good news from a nearby television station. On the way home, exhausted reporters learned that Johnson had just decided to take them on an unscheduled tour of Appalachian poverty. After a formal press conference and a journey to Chicago the next day, the full presidential retinue was up before dawn to gallop by nightfall through the coal mining regions of five states.

Announced as a surprise speaker, Johnson waded through the tumult of 250,000 people who materialized along the streets of Pittsburgh, grasping their hands long after his own fingers started bleeding. Hours later, in the stillness of the hills near Inez, Kentucky, the entourage of dignitaries and reporters watched Johnson "hunker down" on the porch of a tarpaper hovel with Tom Fletcher, an out-of-work miner who talked softly of raising his eight children on a $400 annual income and why his teenagers had not finished fourth grade. Helicoptering on through Kentucky into West

Virginia, Johnson strayed from his improvised itinerary into poverty so authentic that some in his party gagged from the acrid smell of open sewage and permanently unwashed bodies. He once veered off unwittingly into the parlor of a functioning backwoods bordello; panicky aides extricated him in time to preserve what became Johnson's uproarious tales about his presidential sense of direction.

Always, Johnson talked of poverty as the nation's enemy. He said he kept a photograph of his birth shack over his bed in the White House, and seemed to draw inspiration from the staggering contrasts of his own experience. Mentioning his favorite author Barbara Ward, Johnson tried out the phrase "great society" to evoke a nation of humane grandeur, in which "no child will ever have to say in any territory where that flag flies, 'This is not my day to eat.'" Back in Washington before midnight, reporters expressed awe over his "breathtaking, nerve-shaking, totally implausible" pace. *Time* more than made up for the embarrassment of the Pearl beer incident by publishing a cover story on Johnson as a Texas whirlwind with "no ceiling on his energy, no limit to his endurance, no issue or individual to whom he would not offer a hayseed's aphorism or a statesman's advice.... No man in the White House has ever moved faster."

MARTIN LUTHER KING whirled simultaneously in his own orbit from Washington to Atlanta to New York, back to Atlanta and on to a tour of California, raising money and preaching against segregation. Against pressure from his fellow heads of civil rights groups, he declined to sign their joint manifesto against the World's Fair "stall-in." Instead, on April 21, King explained himself in a conflicted letter of self-examination. He agreed that unruly demonstrations such as the "stall-in" were unwise, King wrote in a joint letter to Roy Wilkins and the others, and he certainly shared their alarm about political backlash against the movement. (The *New York Times*, stunned since Governor George Wallace won a third of the primary vote in Wisconsin,* had just published a special page with a chart of the nationwide spread of protest, warning of "hostile white reaction.") Still, King advised that he was "just as hesitant" about joining the manifesto's "outright condemnation." "Which is worse," he asked, "a 'Stall-In' at the World's Fair or a 'Stall-In' in the United States Senate? The former merely ties up the traffic of a single city. But the latter seeks to tie up the traffic of history, and endanger the psychological lives of twenty million people." While acknowledging the criticial need for political allies, King refused to discard nonviolence at the first sign of opposition

---

* On April 8, beneath an overarching banner headline, "Civil Rights—A Grim Day," the *Boston Globe* published companion stories about the Wallace vote in Wisconsin and the death in Cleveland of a white Presbyterian minister, Bruce Klunder, who was crushed by a bulldozer during a sit-in against construction of segregated schools.

in the North. "I hear a lot of talk these days about our direct action program alienating former friends," he wrote. "I would rather feel that they are bringing to the surface many latent prejudices which were always there."

King still wanted to hire Bayard Rustin to replace Wyatt Walker as SCLC's executive director, but incompatibilities between Rustin and King's staff had compounded delays on both sides. Some warned King that Rustin's prestige as organizer of the March on Washington could not erase the political vulnerability of his private life as a homosexual former Communist—especially now, during the Senate filibuster, with opponents of the civil rights bill looking for ammunition. Beyond that, some of Rustin's own advocates raised a new issue from the murkiest recesses of left-wing politics. King's New York advisers worried that Rustin was becoming too close to the sectarian Shachtmanites, a tiny band of socialists who followed the exotic, sixty-year-old theorist Max Shachtman.

A Communist prodigy of Polish birth, transplanted to the Bronx, Shachtman still brandished the romantic authority of one who had known world revolutionaries back to Zinoviev in 1925. Leon Trotsky himself, while being hunted down by agents of Josef Stalin, had included Shachtman among the trusted few who shared his exile in Turkey, then in Mexico —Shachtman with a German pistol strapped to his leg. Shachtman had served after Trotsky's 1940 assassination as an executor of the Trotsky literary estate, even though he rejected the Trotskyite "line" that the Soviet Union was a defective workers' state, corrupted by Stalin. Declaring the Soviet empire a totalitarian perversion beyond repair, and therefore his mortal enemy, Shachtman fiercely opposed the Soviets and their American Communist "lackeys" throughout the 1940s and 1950s. While his socialist disciples never numbered more than several hundred, Shachtman's dialectical workshops at times included influential writers such as Michael Harrington and Irving Howe, plus Albert Shanker of the United Federation of Teachers among many labor officials. Intellectually, what linked their obsessive polemics with Karl Marx and the nineteenth-century utopians was Shachtman's unswerving belief that a "correct" diagnosis of history could cure the world's ills. By the early 1960s, the long arc of Shachtmanite heroes inched all the way over to the gruff AFL-CIO boss George Meany —perceived as a patriotic, militantly anti-Communist "purification" of Lenin. Radiating from Manhattan, this arcane line of thought took hold within the neoconservative movement that became popular a decade later.

Early complaints reached Martin Luther King that Rustin was behaving strangely—pushing hard for the SCLC job, then disappearing mysteriously for days. Rustin himself said he was thinking fondly of a steady income after three decades as a vagabond radical, but King's three New York lawyers reported that Rustin was making his transition in step with the Shachtmanites, who were rumored to be searching out positions close to organized labor. Harry Wachtel, the corporate lawyer who had worked with Clarence Jones on the *Sullivan* case, picked up the political gossip, and Stanley Levison told Jones that Rustin was letting personal favorites among the Shachtmanites put ideas into his head. Wachtel, who admired Rustin, initially quibbled with Levison; in fact his first thought was that Levison might be "operating" with American Communists again, which would explain his hostility to Shachtmanite adversaries. Levison insisted from years of friendship that Rustin was surrendering his trademark independence to the Shachtmanite caucus, which he said moved in concert like a swarm of bees. Ironically, Levison was obliged to send his analysis indirectly through Jones, because Levison had submitted to the painful banishment demanded by the Kennedy administration and J. Edgar Hoover. Filtered warnings reached King by phone during his travels. Coming on top of the vexing personal feuds that clouded the Rustin matter already —not to mention the aversion to homosexuality from preachers on the SCLC board—these obscure intrigues exasperated King as a sign that enemy-thinking was infecting his own camp. "You're doing the same thing to Bayard that Hoover did to us about Stanley!" he complained to Clarence Jones.

A competing alarm intruded just then from the underground politics of J. Edgar Hoover. Joseph Alsop's syndicated column of April 15 asserted that Communist agents "are beginning to infiltrate certain sectors of the Negro civil rights movement." Alsop reported that King was "still accepting Communist collaboration and even Communist advice"—ignoring official government notifications as well as his own promises to sever contacts with one "genuine Communist article" and another "key figure in the covert apparatus of the Communist Party." Alsop's tone mixed the hush of FBI secrets with scolding disbelief that King could be so blind to manipulation.

This single press item shattered respite on the subversion issue. Like other observers who knew Joseph Alsop as a famous journalist—distant cousin to the Roosevelts and oracle for Washington's most powerful anti-Communist Democrats—King took the column as a message directly from the Johnson administration. Because the column revived arguments that the civil rights movement was Communist-inspired, King assumed the administration was testing a line of retreat from the Senate filibuster, with him as the scapegoat. This interpretation so distressed King that he resisted the urgent counsel of Clarence Jones that he must refute Alsop publicly or face accusations of confession by silence. Given the reality that no answer would matter much if Johnson had indeed turned against the movement, King instead sent Walter Fauntroy, a young SCLC board member based in Washington, to ask Burke Marshall whether some misunderstanding might have caused the Alsop attack.

Much to the disgust of the FBI wiretappers who overheard, Fauntroy reported back that Marshall had listened sympathetically. When Fauntroy explained that the few contacts between King and Stanley Levison were emergencies related to special projects such as King's book on Birmingham, Marshall implied that the Alsop column was an unfair exaggeration based on an irresponsible leak of FBI information.

A follow-up press attack landed before anyone could digest the Marshall meeting. "Hoover Says Reds Exploit Negroes/Asserts Party Infiltrates Rights Drive," reported the *Times* on opening day of the World's Fair, April 22. Hoover's words—that through "vitally important" Communist influence, "large masses are caused to lose perspective on the issues involved and, without realizing it, succumb to the party's propaganda lures"—were three months old. They made headlines, anyway, and King had no way of knowing that Hoover, blocked by Robert Kennedy from issuing a fresh statement through Justice Department channels, had asked friends in the House to release his secret testimony from the previous January. Nor did King know what leverage Hoover possessed over Joseph Alsop. The Director retained in his confidential files what he called "the Alsop case" of 1957, when male KGB agents had seduced and photographed Alsop during a visit to Moscow. For seven years since, Alsop had gamely persevered through real and imagined reminders that his homosexual entrapment could break the surface of public scandal. Hoover carefully disseminated the records to high government officials; periodic mailings of the graphic Moscow photographs shocked Alsop's colleagues in the press. Nevertheless, the Alsop secret would hold for two decades beyond disclosure of the Martin Luther King wiretap.*

King embraced the assumption that the FBI was the direct source for both press attacks, which relieved his greater fear that the President himself was peddling classified smears. All through the night of the *Times* article, King pushed his advisers by phone to craft a public response that would isolate the FBI as responsible. The next morning, some fifty reporters and a few interspersed FBI agents greeted him in San Francisco for a boisterous airport press conference that more than lived up to advance billing: "Rev. King's Icy Fury," reported the *San Francisco Examiner.*

FBI agents bypassed teletype channels as too slow and dictated the King statement across the country by phone line into headquarters. Barely an hour after King's plane landed in California, intelligence chief William Sullivan circulated a scandalized bulletin. "King mentioned the Director by name," he reported, "... and challenged the Director if he had any real

---

* The later historical record opened a tangle of irony beneath this jousting on sex and subversion. Hoover, reported the *Times* in 1964, charged that Soviet spies used "revolting" sexual entrapments to blackmail unnamed Americans. Alsop, without mentioning his own vulnerabilities, or his reliance on FBI spy information, warned readers that Communists were taking advantage of "Rev. King's political innocence." He entitled his column "An Unhappy Secret."

evidence, to come forth with it." Worse, Sullivan noted, King had invoked the words of Robert Kennedy against the FBI position on Communists in the racial movement, and had charged Hoover with stiffening resistance to the civil rights bill. Still worse, if possible, King impeached not only Hoover's motives but also the Bureau's sacrosanct reputation in law enforcement. "It would be encouraging to us," King declared, "if Mr. Hoover and the FBI would be as diligent in apprehending those responsible for bombing churches and killing little children, as they are in seeking out alleged communist infiltration in the civil rights movement."

Hoover prudently declined to take up the frontal assault on King's chosen ground. (President Johnson himself had prodded Hoover about why the Bureau had solved none of the racial bombing cases, especially those in Birmingham, and Hoover, in a confidential "My dear Mr. President" letter earlier that month, sidestepped one direct inquiry with a cloud of statistics—"we have utilized a peak of 231 Agents....") Assistant Director Sullivan let Hoover's charges of Communism stand in public while he channeled the Bureau's efforts into guerrilla tactics. That afternoon, while King delivered a speech at Stanford University, Sullivan placed an emergency call to the Bureau's best "sound man" in San Francisco, who swiftly arranged microphone bugs in Sacramento—where King was to meet with California Governor Edmund (Pat) Brown—and the following two nights in Los Angeles. These installations would glean no embarrassments the Bureau could use, but wiretaps did confirm that King had broken through Hoover's intimidation as the rare adversary who refused to be bullied. "I want to hit him hard," King said. "He made me hot, and I wanted to get him."

Bob Moses arrived at Stanford on April 24 to address an audience about a fifth the size of King's the day before, composed mostly of students whose interest in Mississippi had been planted by Al Lowenstein. Those stirred by the classical oratory of Lowenstein and King witnessed the stark contrast of Moses speaking in quiet soliloquy, following his own thoughts with what one listener recorded as "the rhythms of man crossing a stream, hopping from rock to rock." Reviewing the four years since SNCC students first went to Mississippi, Moses paid tribute to the unexpected teaching of sharecroppers. "If we have any anchor at all," he said, "...if there's any reason why we can skip around from the bottom of Mississippi to the top of the skyscrapers in Manhattan and still maintain some kind of internal sense of balance, I think a lot of it has to do with those people, and the fact that they have their own sense of balance." The farmers gave Moses a sense "that you had hit rock bottom, that you had some base that you could work with and that you could build on." For a long time it had been impossible to communicate the promise or terror of Mississippi because those outside "really didn't know and didn't have any way of understanding," he went on, but with the cumulative pounding of distant news, "and finally after Birmingham, the country came alive." A vocabulary was emerging for national questions "much deeper than civil rights," said Moses—automation, schools, the nature of cities—questions that affect "our whole international affairs" and "go to the very root of our society.... It just happens that the civil rights question is at the spearhead of all of these." No one recognized the signs because they fell upon Negroes, he said, "but when the Negroes take to acts of terror, they will know about it. The country will know about it." Preconditions of breakdown "exist already," he said. "They exist within the cities....

"Seventy percent of the Negro youth in Philadelphia are unemployed," he said. "It's a fantastic figure. It affects white people when they organize gangs and start hitting and shooting and fighting each other, and then maybe turn their violence into the street and attack property, which probably belongs to white people." Because Negro literacy had always been a political threat to the white South—"if you teach people who want to read and write, then they're going to want to begin to govern themselves"—heavy migration from Southern plantations—"every year there are 10 percent fewer jobs"—had delivered up two generations of refugees who were largely useless to the modern world. Their claim on the future clashed with the World's Fair's dazzling model of slumless cities for the year 2000, with plant-filled glass buildings connected by whizzing elevated sidewalks encased in tubes. "The deep irony of that really hasn't reached out across the country," said Moses. "All everyone was concerned with was, 'Don't mess up our World's Fair.' Whose World's Fair?"

Moses drew his Stanford audience into some of SNCC's internal arguments. "There are deep moral problems that are connected already with the summer project," he said, and mentioned Herbert Lee, "who was killed that summer [in 1961], was killed just as surely because we went in there to organize as rain comes from the clouds. If we hadn't gone in there, he wouldn't have been killed." Moses confessed that nonviolence could not insulate its believers from blood responsibility, nor answer "whether those people who are enslaved, in order to get their freedom, have to become executioners and participate in acts of terror and death, and what sense they do participate in it." He was posing those questions now to an auditoriumful of recruits—potential replacements for Lee. "We're back in that same kind of dilemma," he said, his voice trailing off, "which can be put maybe not very precisely in terms of victims and executioners, and maybe not very philosophically, but still, when you come to deal with it personally, it rests very heavy." Several seconds later, realizing that the speaker had lapsed into silence, some four hundred students rose for a standing ovation that lasted several minutes.

Moses returned to Mississippi, where only a handful turned up on April 26 for the founding convention of the Freedom Democratic Party.

"All the colored folks in the state should be here," fumed Tony Gray as he surveyed the cavernous Masonic Temple in Jackson. His wife, Victoria, still running her Beauty Queen business in Hattiesburg, had announced her candidacy for the U.S. Senate less than two years after responding to Hollis Watkins at her first mass meeting. Fannie Lou Hamer was running for Congress from the Delta. An exhausted Lawrence Guyot, disappointed over the lack of support for these pioneers, collapsed after the convention. Moses withdrew in depression. The Kentucky college secured as a training site by Robert Spike's CORR suddenly backed out on complaints from its trustees, and the very idea of volunteers, trained or untrained, still overwhelmed many who prepared to receive them. "It is unbelievably absurd to think that 2,000 bright and eager youth are coming down here to help," wrote a Mississippi staff worker. "And what in the name of God can they help with? . . . Please forgive me for this. I am too afraid."

22

Filibusters

By Monday, April 27, the Senate debate acquired recognition as a marathon. The CBS graphics department bestowed a logo on Roger Mudd's five-a-day special reports from the Capitol steps: a superimposed clock showing the continuous days and hours of a filibuster that stretched into its eighth week. That morning, representing seventy-five cooperating seminaries, an interfaith trio of religious students—one Protestant, one Catholic, one Jew—entered the eighth day of vigil at the Lincoln Memorial, resolved to pray around the clock in shifts until the civil rights bill passed. The next night, upward of five thousand religious leaders from across the country gathered at Washington's Georgetown University for what the *New York Times* called an ecumenical rally "unparalleled in the annals of worldwide religion." The musical director of Howard University led a consortium of college choirs through the spiritual "Done Made My Vow," plus selections from Mendelssohn's *Elijah,* and Eugene Carson Blake concluded the speeches with an assault on the notion that the equal treatment provisions of the civil rights bill would violate the Thirteenth Amendment as a reverse "enslavement" of white people, especially business owners required to serve Negro customers. "How can any Christian or Jew sit still when such an immoral argument is voiced?" cried Blake. "Where in the Holy Bible, in Old Testament or New, can one find one single passage to support the rights of property as against the rights of men?...Have we learned nothing since the day Amos thundered against those who, for profit, degraded men?"

President Johnson, finding himself without available advisers that night—"I turn around and the whole damn shop's gone"—hounded White House phone operators until they tracked down Bill Moyers in New York. "By God, you took off," he complained. Johnson brushed off excuses that he had cleared the night's absence for Moyers long ago—"Oh, I never heard of it," he snorted. "You got me in a weak moment."—to say he had no decent draft for a speech to religious leaders the next day. He firmly suggested that Moyers either steal a Gideon Bible from his hotel room or "go buy you a Bible, and I'll pay for it," and search on the flight home for "some good quotations on equality and we're all God's children." Moyers promised to be back by midnight.

On April 29, more than a hundred visiting clergy fanned out to lobby the Senate, and Oscar Lee preached the first in a long series of daily Capitol prayer rallies, after which President Johnson received Blake, Spike, Archbishop Patrick O'Boyle, Rabbi Uri Miller, and nearly two hundred other religious leaders at the White House. "From the time of the ancient Hebrew prophets and the dispersal of the money changers," he told them, "men of God have taught us that social problems are moral problems on a huge scale. They have demonstrated that a religion which did not struggle to remove oppression from the world of men would not be able to create the world of spirit." Johnson eulogized the abolitionist preachers of the previous century, saying they had endured the scourge of burned churches and ostracism to lift the country out of slavery. "Today, as we meet here," he declared, "again the problem of racial wrongs and racial hatreds is the central moral problem of this Republic." Quoting Abraham, in one of the Bible's first pleadings against tribal division, Johnson called for an end to strife "between you and me, and between my herdmen and your herdmen, because we are brothers." He challenged the clergy "to reawaken the conscience of your beloved land." This, he said, "is your job as prophets in our time."

Despite his passionate sermons, Johnson received more attention that week for lifting his twin beagles, Him and Her, by their ears on the White House lawn.* Beneath public uproar over animal cruelty that lasted beyond May, a number of religious bodies nearly split apart at their national conventions. When Northern Presbyterians elected Rev. Edler Hawkins as their first Negro executive, dissenting elders renewed a drive to remove the church from integrationist politics. Southern Baptists voted down a statement of support for "laws designed to guarantee the legal rights of Negroes." Southern Presbyterians rejected proposals to form a race commission and require open church membership, but they did invite

---

* Stung by the protests of kennel clubs and humane societies, Johnson explained ear-pulling as friendly stimulation—"If you ever follow dogs, you like to hear them yelp"—which only provoked the publisher of *Dog World* to charge that the President could not distinguish a healthy bark from a howl of pain.

Rev. Henry Russell, brother of Georgia Senator Richard Russell, to relax segregation policies voluntarily before his Memphis congregation hosted the 1965 convention.

In Pittsburgh, national representatives of ten million Methodists contended over a proposal to abolish their Central Jurisdiction. Created in the 1939 compromise that reunited Methodists from their schism over slavery, the Central Jurisdiction governed Negro congregations only, in a geographical misnomer that masked ecclesiastical segregation. The previous Methodist assembly of 1960 had rejected integration guidelines in favor of the traditional rule that Negro churches could transfer into regular jurisdictions only by mutual consent. ("I would like to remind the General Conference," an Alabama delegate had shouted, "that Jesus Himself never set a specific target date for the coming of the Kingdom!") Four years later, the tumultuous Pittsburgh assembly did set an integration goal of 1968 but retained the voluntary absorption method. A slim majority held that more aggressive plans would divide the church again—orphaning Negro bishops and congregations, driving white Methodists into Baptist havens of local control. Rev. James Lawson wept openly among the defeated reformers on the floor of the assembly—more dismayed by his straddling church than by any of his persecutions as Gandhian resister or nonviolent tutor to the student movement. Shortly after midnight on May 2, Lawson and Edwin King of Mississippi joined a prayer vigil that swelled overnight until more than a thousand marched around the Pittsburgh Civic Arena, outnumbering the delegates inside. A Chicago divinity student carried a charred cross that the Klan had burned on the Tougaloo campus.

Deep crosscurrents churned partisan politics, too. On May 1, Senator Russell told colleagues he hoped to keep the Senate filibuster going long enough for George Wallace's presidential campaign to light warning fires for politicians behind Northern lines. Events favored his strategy a few days later when the Alabama governor obtained nearly 30 percent of the vote in Indiana's Democratic primary. A *New York Times* editorial acknowledged that Wallace's surprise strength earlier in Wisconsin may have been no fluke, and that "grassroots resistance to effective civil rights legislation is disturbingly widespread." Wallace himself claimed the satisfaction of a redeemed pariah. "We have shaken the eyeteeth of every liberal in the country!" he boasted. Wallace developed a stump speech that courted resentment of "sweeping federal encroachment" by "pointy-headed bureaucrats," tyrannical judges, and "tax, tax, spend, spend," politicians—all supported by what he called "the ultra-liberal controlled press." He downplayed the race issue except to poke fun at hypocrisy outside the South. In Boston, he chortled over the discovery that a crusading anti-Wallace television station employed no Negroes at any level. "Anybody here from Philadelphia?" he cried at another campaign stop. "You know, they can't even have night football games any more because of the trouble between the races.... Now, whoever heard of such a thing?" Of the nation's capital in Washington, he quipped that "they are building a new [Theodore Roosevelt Memorial] bridge over the Potomac for all the white liberals fleeing to Virginia."

Senator Russell looked for help not only from segregationists in the North but also from Republican forays into the solid Democratic South. Against the interests of his own national party, he appealed to the Republican dream of becoming competitive in Southern elections, telling Northern senators that to do so they must support or at least tolerate the civil rights filibuster. When Republican leader Everett Dirksen hinted instead that he might vote to shut off the filibuster if the Johnson forces would consider some seventy amendments he intended to offer, Russell was not deceived by the howls of Senate liberals who, fearing delay and paralyzing incompatibilities with the House bill, resisted the offer. Like Hubert Humphrey, his chief opponent in the Senate debate, Russell knew that the civil rights bill had no chance without Dirksen's Republicans. The voluble Humphrey, who later joked that he flattered and wooed Dirksen as ardently as he had courted his own wife, Muriel—"Oh, I was shameless"—took joy from the first murmurs of Republican cooperation, and Russell was correspondingly downcast. He soon rose on the floor of the Senate to castigate Dirksen for having "killed off a rapidly growing Republican Party in the South, at least so far as his party's prospects in the presidential campaign are concerned."

Fixed upon the task of derailing a civil rights bill sponsored by the renegade Texas Democrat in the White House, Russell needed a visible shift in sectional and racial alignments as old as the major parties themselves. Instead, there were only embryonic signs. For the upcoming national convention, Tennessee Democrats selected the first Negro delegates in their party's history; newspapers reported that the intrepid COFO summer project would challenge the unbroken record of all-white Democratic delegations in Mississippi. More dramatic changes on the Republican side remained almost invisible because of the party's minuscule Southern presence. In Georgia, where candidate Barry Goldwater had trouble drawing crowds to fill even barber shops, his newly organized supporters took over the tiny state convention, electing all but two of the delegates to the Republican national convention, and in the process they evicted the caretaker Negroes of the old Black and Tan coalition. "The Negro has been read out of the Republican party of Georgia here today," a Goldwater spokesman announced frankly on May 2, as the new Georgia Republicans broke tradition by celebrating with an all-white dinner. Bitterly disappointed, Daddy King and his generation of lifelong Republicans soon became a discarded remnant from the Party of Lincoln.

□

ON MAY 2, anniversary of the first great children's jail march in Birmingham the previous year, King joined Fred Shuttlesworth to preach the funeral of William Shortridge, the prickly but dependable former treasurer of the Birmingham movement. "There was no guile in his mouth," Shuttlesworth told mourners in a bittersweet eulogy. "...Mr. Shortridge was a sick man ever since I knew him, but he did much more being sick than most men I know being well. I pray God that He would afflict many more men with a sickness like that." King followed with a distracted, more somber tribute, quoting Shakespeare's Horatio on the death of Hamlet, and then flew on short notice to Nashville. Students—supported by C. T. Vivian and numerous white religious leaders, including the renowned Vanderbilt Bible scholar Walter Harrelson—had picketed segregated restaurants through a week marked by a hundred arrests and numerous violent attacks, mostly by spectators. SNCC Chairman John Lewis, face bruised and lips split open from blows that morning, escorted King into a mass meeting at Fisk University.

Back in the Ebenezer pulpit the next day, King preached in his deepest bass register at slow cadence, which often signaled a troubled mood. Modifying his standard sermon on the parable of the Good Samaritan—"Who Is My Neighbor?"—he projected three distinct philosophies upon those who had encountered the waylaid traveler on the road to Jericho. "Everybody within the sound of my voice today lives by one of these three philosophies," King told his congregation. Beginning with the robber—"whoever robbed that man had a philosophy"—he offered examples of predatory behavior ranging from ancient slavery and modern colonialism to street crime. Preachers were not immune, King said acidly, saying he had just heard a prominent fellow minister sell his members "a real blessing" of rebaptism for $10 apiece, offering each one a drop of the genuine holy water the preacher had brought back from the Sea of Galilee. "Out of that bottle of water, I can imagine that he got himself a good ten thousand dollars," King declared with a fury that carried through a dozen repetitions of the robber's philosophy: "What is thine is MINE! And if you don't give it to me, I'll take it from you."

He began more gently with a second outlook—"What is mine is mine, what is thine is thine"—saying that the priest and Levite in the story may have had good reason to bypass the waylaid man on the Jericho road. To indict their cautious self-preservation, King recited other Bible stories, including his favorite parable of the rich man Dives, who went to hell for no overt crime. Wealth itself did not condemn Dives, King told his congregation. "I can assure you," he said, "if there is a hell there will be plenty of poor folks in it." What undid Dives was failure to bridge the gulf that divided him from humanity, including the beggar Lazarus at his gate. Dives "never saw Lazarus even though he passed him every day," said

King, who went on to scold worshippers "here this morning" for withholding their talents from those in need.

King proceeded to what he identified as the "third philosophy," that of the Samaritan who stopped to help the victim. This merciful stranger "of another race" proved that "a man's back is never straighter than when he bends it to lift fallen humanity," he said. King summoned up an assortment of models, including Albert Schweitzer and Peace Corps volunteers, plus students, rabbis, preachers, and other movement volunteers "willing to go to jail, willing to be on picket lines, willing to be beaten and persecuted for righteousness' sake. They know somehow, 'what is mine is thine....'" Their philosophy "says in substance that all humanity is tied together," King told the Ebenezer congregation, warning that neither predators nor bystanders could be healthy so long as misery, famine, plague, and hatred scavenged millions on the globe. "For you can *catch* these diseases, you know," he said wryly, and some of the gloom lifted from his tone. "He who lives by this philosophy lives in the kingdom NOW!" King cried, and "not in some distant day." This was "the kingdom within," which rose from the sordid world "in a *great act* and a noble destiny." It was the witness of Jesus, "who said in his own life, 'what is mine is thine, I'll give it to you, you don't have to beg me for it.' This is why the cross is more than some meaningless drama taking place on the stage of history. In a real sense, it is a telescope through which we look out into the long vista of eternity and see the love of God breaking forth in the night.... It is God saying, 'I will reach out and bridge the gulf that separates me from you.' ... And may this morning in some way we grasp this idea.... We open the doors of the church now...."

Off for another week's travel, King returned by way of Cincinnati after a speech on Friday, May 8. He just missed President Johnson, whose huge entourage had landed in Georgia on another whirlwind poverty tour from Ohio down through Tennessee. Atlanta's Mayor Ivan Allen presented Johnson with a gift of two newborn tiger cubs, named Lyndon and Lady Bird. With the notable exception of Richard Russell, Georgia's major politicians attended a Friday breakfast sponsored by the state legislature, where they applauded not only the President's homespun recollections of "my Georgia ancestors," including Sheriff Jesse Johnson of nearby Henry County, and his invitation to join the "quest for a great society," but also his straightforward appeal to pass the civil rights bill. "Justice also means justice among the races," said Johnson, who reminded his audience that Americans "are a very small minority living in a world of 3 billion people, where we are outnumbered 17 to 1, and no one of us is fully free until all of us are free."

Cheering crowds lined every block of the route to the Atlanta airport so thickly that they held Johnson's motorcade to walking speed for fifteen miles. At a noon rally in the poultry center of Gainesville, Georgia, Rep.

Phil Landrum hailed Johnson as "the finest President the United States of America has ever had," and a beaming Johnson kept asking if anyone had ever seen anything like the enthusiasm of the forty thousand people—roughly equal to the entire town population—who turned out to see him in Franklin D. Roosevelt Park. The *New York Times* saluted the "public triumph" of Johnson's bold speeches in the South.

On returning to Washington late that Friday afternoon, Johnson called his political director Lawrence O'Brien still giddy from the crowds. "I need two new hands!" he moaned happily. "My right one's chewed up. ...I made sixteen speeches and we had a million people. That's a minimum. I think it's two million, but the goddamn mean Republicans gave us a million. Today we looked up there and just as far as you could see.... Old Herman Talmadge got up after I made two civil rights speeches that he was present at, and said, 'I just want to say that I have never seen as many people anywhere.'..." Then Johnson summoned reporters to the White House Rose Garden for an announcement on J. Edgar Hoover's tenure at the FBI. As expected, he used the occasion of Hoover's fortieth anniversary at the FBI to heap praise upon the first and only Director as "a household word ... a hero to millions of decent citizens and an anathema to evil men." Confounding speculation that he might replace Hoover when he turned seventy on New Year's Day, the President told Hoover he had "just now signed an Executive Order exempting you from compulsory retirement for an indefinite period of time." The advance retention of Hoover—at Johnson's pleasure—kept reporters off balance with a display of the poverty crusader as crafty power politician.

MARTIN LUTHER KING trailed Johnson to Washington for an appearance on the Sunday television talk show *Face the Nation*. Before leaving Atlanta, he spent much of Saturday with a rare and welcome overnight visitor from Boston. The kindly, gnomish Harold DeWolf positively doted on King as a former graduate student who had become famous in the service of theology. Since supervising King's doctoral studies at Boston University a decade earlier, DeWolf had fallen somewhat out of touch during two year-long sabbaticals to Africa, where his son had been a Methodist missionary, but he welcomed King's occasional post-midnight phone calls and the greetings of the King children, who called him "Uncle Harold." After catching up, DeWolf promised to contact King's new SCLC representative in New England, Virgil Wood, and offered "to place my less than youthful and rugged body on the line" in Alabama that summer, if King needed him for the Bevel-Nash voting campaign.

Significantly, DeWolf also offered Boston University as a depository for King's burgeoning personal papers. Death threats and hate mail alone overflowed boxes in King's basement and office, as did speaking invitations, and DeWolf urged King to place his accumulating correspondence in a special division of the Boston University library that housed historic collections. Flattered but undecided, King replied that he had always intended to leave his papers to Morehouse, his alma mater in Atlanta. He confessed doubt, however, that any Negro institution in the South could afford to maintain a permanent research library—based partly on years of baleful notices that Morehouse was on the verge of insolvency. King worried also about the political vulnerability of the college, as manifested in an awkward point of personal contention with his family mentor, Benjamin Mays.

In spite of pleas from Daddy King, a thirty-year trustee, Morehouse President Mays had refused for several years to put the younger King's name forward as a candidate for the Morehouse board. His pained explanation to both Kings was that some board members, both Negro and white, resisted King as a poor role model because he had gone to jail so often, or as a controversial figure who would hurt Morehouse fund-raising among large donors. Therefore, Mays said, he avoided the issue to spare the grave public embarrassment of having King elected by anything less than a unanimous vote. While King tried to be understanding—he admired Mays and appreciated the toll upon him of perpetual begging for college funds —his keen nose for rationalization made the board policy seem weak and insulting. King hesitated, sending Mays a thousand-dollar donation from a *Life* magazine article fee. (The unsolicited gift "amazes me," Mays wrote King. "I wish your loyalty and devotion to Morehouse were contagious. . . .") As for DeWolf, King asked for time to evaluate Boston University's offer. Rushing off to Washington after his daughter Yoki's ballet recital on Saturday night, May 9, he left his old professor to preach for him the next morning at Ebenezer.

Reporters on *Face the Nation* pressed King to admit that public opinion had turned against nonviolent demonstrations, but they also reminded him that he had promised to mount "massive" demonstrations in 1964, especially if a Senate filibuster endangered the civil rights bill. "Where is the direct action?" prodded Paul Niven of CBS. Why the delay? King responded that signs of a backlash confirmed race as "a national problem," and he worried that the Republicans might turn into a new "white man's party," which he said would be "tragic for the Republican party as well as tragic for the nation." He maintained that demonstrations still could "mobilize the forces of good will," and cited polls showing heavy majority support for the civil rights bill, but he equivocated about a time or place. In fact, King seemed relieved to hear questions about the newspaper reports that he coddled Communists. "I am very happy that this question came up," he replied, calling it "unfortunate that such a great man as Mr. Hoover allowed himself to aid and abet the racists. . . ."

The comments about Hoover worsened animosities already stewing deep within the government. On Friday, fortified by President Johnson's affirmation of Hoover, Deke DeLoach had pushed for Justice Department clearance of a new public warning about Communism in the civil rights movement. He and the department's press secretary, Edwin Guthman, dueled again over semantics, with DeLoach calling fact what Guthman defined as gratuitous speculation. When Guthman proposed to add a balancing statement that any Communist infiltration of the movement "should not distract us from the fact that discrimination does exist," DeLoach refused on the ground that Director Hoover never stooped to "philosophize." After King reprimanded Hoover on national television on Sunday, the clearance negotiations escalated to a catfight. DeLoach accused the Justice Department of trying to "suppress" Hoover's national security warning. Guthman, after emergency consultations with Burke Marshall and Supreme Court Justice Byron White, among others, decided to fight back by imitating DeLoach's tactic of constructing a bureaucratic "fact base" from his own memos on every significant conversation. Accordingly, Guthman quickly sent the FBI a "memcon" (memorandum of conversation) emphasizing his side of the clearance debate, which left DeLoach howling with indignation. "Obviously, Guthman is skeptical of the solidity of his position," DeLoach wrote in his own memcon, "and consequently desires to make himself look as good as possible in the record...." Meanwhile, Robert Kennedy sent Hoover what amounted to a forlorn peace feeler on May 12: "In the past few months I have not had the pleasure of associating with you as closely as formerly." Within a week, Guthman and DeLoach would agree to suspend further clearance talks as pointless.

FOR PRESIDENT JOHNSON, the FBI squabble remained among background matters finessed or contained through May. In Congress, Johnson weathered the annual ritual of raising the authorized national debt ceiling—this time just above $312 billion, before a mandated rollback to $309 billion would have halted government payments. He also resisted Rep. Jamie Whitten's nettlesome demand that the Pentagon compensate Mississippi, rather than vice versa, for military operations supporting James Meredith's right to integrate the state university in 1962. (Whitten pressed claims for damaged runways and trampled grass, plus the cost of relocating a football game after the Army "usurped" latrines at Ole Miss.) More delicately, Johnson steered a course in the House between seniority rights and festering resentment against Adam Clayton Powell, who, shortly after his first criminal contempt citation for refusal to pay assessed libel damages to Esther James, agreed to let the popular white Southerner, Rep. Phil Landrum, sponsor the revised anti-poverty legislation. As compensation for his support in the upcoming election, Powell presented the Johnson campaign with what Lawrence O'Brien privately called "a laundry list a yard long." "Christ," O'Brien told Johnson, "all he wants is for the federal goverment to finance the [proposed] Hotel 2400 [in New York], to wipe out the $47,000 indebtedness to Internal Revenue, to get that judge to drop any threats of arrest, and a few other things." O'Brien assured the President that he and Louis Martin, the Democratic Party's expert on minority affairs, would bargain carefully with Powell, outside the White House.

In foreign affairs, Johnson coped with whispers that he was not sophisticated enough to understand fundamental changes in the world order, such as the controversial evidence of enmity between Communist China and the Soviet Union. With Mao Tse-tung calling Soviet Premier Khrushchev a bourgeois traitor "even more stupid than the Americans," and Khrushchev calling Mao a rotting Trotskyite—two world leaders opened doubts to the accepted theory that Communists were distinctive by nature, synchronized in ideological harness and immune to ordinary human divisions. Over lingering fears that the quarrel was a Communist ruse, *Time* recognized "The Communist Split" in a careful cover story advising that Americans, who "for many years underestimated the importance of the split, should not now overestimate it." As president, Johnson offered guarded hope for dealing with Communists. When India's Prime Minister Jawaharlal Nehru died that month, he called upon world powers to negotiate for peace in the void left by the preeminent Cold War neutralist.

At the end of his first half year in the White House, the *New York Times* declared that "Mr. Johnson has left an indelible imprint on American political lore." In a glowing profile of a president who "stood high in all the popularity polls, dominated the national political outlook, and was heavily favored to win the election," the *Times* questioned Johnson's mastery only in regard to the lingering dangers of Vietnam and race relations: "the two major problems that disturbed the last year of Mr. Kennedy's life."

News stories almost invariably referred to Vietnam as a nasty little war in a far-off place. Six American soldiers were killed there in April, raising the cumulative U.S. death toll since 1961 to 220. "Opposing forces are known as Viet Cong," advised a war primer in *U.S. News & World Report*, which noted that the Vietnamese Communists had defeated a French army of nearly half a million soldiers. "French generals, however, misunderstood the nature of the conflict," said the article, emphasizing that Americans must learn to build political support among Vietnamese peasants in the midst of guerrilla combat. As a harbinger of ground-level difficulties for Americans in telling friend from foe, an April 1964 television special discovered a U.S. soldier who pinned to his hat a peculiar but handy Vietnam slogan, "Sorry About That." The strategic imperative was clearer in the abstract, especially to U.S. officials who saw the southern part of Vietnam as a tripwire of global war. "Loss of this area would be a catastrophe," proclaimed Ambassador Henry Cabot Lodge, "and would make a lot of Americans think that we'd better resign from the human race, so to speak, and fall back on a fortress America and gird ourselves for a fight with guided missiles."

Lodge spoke with the weight of an established Republican presidential candidate, having defeated Barry Goldwater in the New Hampshire primary despite his handicap as an undeclared write-in candidate. From his post in Saigon, Lodge had campaigned instead for the war partnership with South Vietnam—touring the provinces with Defense Secretary McNamara that March, jointly holding aloft the arm of the anointed General Nguyen Khanh, who had overthrown the generals who overthrew President Diem in the November coup. After Vietcong demolition teams nearly assassinated McNamara on his next visit in May, he and Lodge curtailed American-style gestures of public solidarity to conduct their field inspections under bulletproof cloaks. By then, the CIA had secretly reported a "tide of deterioration" against the South Vietnamese allies, and the wispy North Vietnamese president, Ho Chi Minh, likened the United States to a fox with its hind legs caught in a trap, who "by still trying to jump around is doing his best to get his front legs caught as well."

Lodge, facing a new coup against Khanh (there would be four more regimes that year), favored dispensing altogether with the troublesome formality of a South Vietnamese government so that the United States might assume more efficient direct command, but this idea horrified even the supremely confident McNamara as reckless and shortsighted. He and Lodge compromised on a package of military assistance that promised to stave off immediate disaster. The President put their recommendation far more positively in his formal request to Congress on May 18, saying the $125 million increase would enable the new Khanh government to "mount a successful campaign against the Communists."

Johnson confronted apprehensions about Vietnam in dozens of secret conversations through May. Senator Mansfield's written proposal to "neutralize" South Vietnam by international agreement was "just milquetoast as it can be, he's got no spine at all," he complained to National Security Adviser McGeorge Bundy. "But," came his next word, "this is a terrible thing we're getting ready to do," and Johnson pressed Bundy for specific actions to stop the drift toward losing the war.

"Well, I think that we really need to use some target folder work, Mr. President, that shows precisely what we do and don't mean here," Bundy replied. "And the main object is to kill as few people as possible while creating an environment in which the incentive to react is as low as possible. But I can't say to you this is a small matter."

Johnson sought more soulful advice from his intimate friend and civil rights antagonist Senator Russell, chairman of the Armed Services Committee. "What do you think of this Vietnam thing?" he asked. "I'd like to hear you talk a little bit."

Russell made baleful jokes about how bad the situation looked to him. "It's a mess," he said, "and it's going to get worse." His best idea, which he outlined three times, was to engineer a new South Vietnamese government by coup, "and get some fella in there that said they wished the hell that we would get out. Then that would give us a good excuse for getting out." When Johnson asked about strategic loss of Vietnam, Russell scoffed, "It isn't important a damn bit. . . .

"I don't know, sir, you'd better get some brains from somewhere," advised Russell, who said he found the administration's foreign policy leaders somewhat opinionated, perhaps because they had been "kicked around" on Asia already. Russell seconded Johnson's confidential charge ("I don't want this repeated to anybody") that Ambassador Lodge was "one of our big problems out there, Dick . . . he ain't worth a damn," saying that he had found Lodge ineffective since joint service in World War II. "He thinks that he's dealing with barbarian tribes out there, and that he's the emperor and he's going to tell them what to do," Russell said. "And there's no doubt that, in my mind, that he had old Diem killed out there."

Johnson and Russell also were agreed on fears that overpopulated China would enter any ground war against the United States in Vietnam. ("We'd do them a favor every time we killed a coolie," said Russell, "and when one of our people got killed, it would be a loss.") Johnson said his military and security advisers were pretty well agreed that the Chinese would not intervene, "and in any event, that we haven't got much choice, that we are treaty bound, that we are there . . . and that we've just got to prepare for the worst."

Within the internal consensus to "show some power and force," Johnson praised McNamara as a "pretty flexible fellow" who "thought he was biding his time and that we could get by until November. But these politicians got to raising hell . . . Lodge, Nixon, [New York Governor Nelson] Rockefeller, Goldwater all say move, [and] Eisenhower." They were advocating air campaigns to stop the enemy while minimizing American casualties.

"Oh, hell, it ain't worth a hoot," said Russell. "That's just impossible." He told war stories of dropping "millions and millions and millions of pounds of bombs day and night," blowing whole mountains down over roads and railbeds only to find them operating again the next morning. "We never could actually interdict the lines of communication in Korea," said Russell, "although we had absolute control of the seas and the air. . . . And you ain't gonna stop these people either."

"Well, they'd impeach a president that would run out, wouldn't they?" Johnson asked. He said he always pictured one particular sergeant from his White House detail. "When I think about making this decision," he told Russell, "and sending that father of six in there, and what the hell are we going to get out of his doing it, it makes the chills run up my back."

"It does me, too," said Russell.

"I just haven't got the nerve to do it," said Johnson. "But I don't see any other way out of it."

"It's one of those things, heads I win, tails you lose," said Russell. "... We're in the quicksands up to our neck, and I just don't know what the hell to do about it."

"I love you," said Johnson, "and I'll be calling you."

ON MAY 11, the day of the foiled terrorist attack on McNamara in Saigon, Governor Wallace of Alabama took his presidential campaign to the small Maryland town of Cambridge, where a proclamation of martial law had throttled sporadic rallies against local segregation for nearly a year. When SNCC's Gloria Richardson defiantly led a line of marchers from the Negro Elks Hall through Cambridge toward Wallace's campaign event— hoping to protest what she considered a rally *for* segregation, and to dramatize its sharply contrasting official protection—nearly five hundred state troopers and National Guard soldiers massed along Race Street to block and disperse them. Through the next several nights, as Wallace completed a hasty, ten-speech campaign elsewhere, soldiers wearing bipodal gas masks returned to the same spot to arrest, tear-gas, and skirmish with demonstrators, including seven Catholic priests and SNCC Freedom Rider Stokely Carmichael.

Over the same span in nearby Washington, the civil rights bill surpassed the longevity record for Senate filibusters on any subject, eclipsing an 1846 debate on British occupation rights in territorial Oregon. With President Johnson holding firm, the U.S. Senate transacted no other official business for a tenth consecutive week, although security officers did clear a large tourist buildup from the Senate steps by removing Roger Mudd and his CBS cameras to a more secluded outdoor location. On Tuesday, May 19, as the rotating trio of divinity students approached 750 hours of continuous prayer at the Lincoln Memorial, Governor Wallace won 43 percent of the Democratic vote in the Maryland presidential primary. Elated, Wallace instantly regretted his decision to run a token campaign in only three states. ("I wish I had entered California," he sighed.) Elsewhere, the Maryland result registered as a third Wallace nightmare. "Most distressing of all," declared a *Times* editorial, "is the fact that an actual majority of the white voters apparently cast their ballots for him." In a rare sign of alarm, the front page of the august newspaper projected an oddly comforting nuance into the motives of Wallace supporters: "Maryland's Vote Held Anti-Negro/Wallace's Showing Is Viewed as Protest over Militancy, Not over Rights Bill."

Undaunted, President Johnson gazed beyond the millennium. At the University of Michigan on May 22—exactly six months since the Kennedy assassination—he challenged a giant commencement audience of eighty thousand to "help build a society where the demands of morality, and the needs of the spirit, can be realized in the life of the Nation." The entire urban United States must be rebuilt over the next forty years, he said, because "our society will never be great until our cities are great." He also set out to restore what he called the "natural splendor" of the American landscape. "Today that beauty is in danger," said Johnson. "The water we drink, the food we eat, the very air that we breathe, are threatened with pollution." Beyond that, he vowed to expand and reform outmoded education. "Nearly 54 million—more than one-quarter of all Americans—have not even finished high school," he declared. "...So we must give every child a place to sit and a teacher to learn from. Poverty must not be a bar to learning, and learning must offer an escape from poverty." He summoned up the will and imagination of Michigan youth to "advance the quality of our American civilization," and thereby refute "those timid souls who say this battle cannot be won, that we are condemned to a soulless wealth."

On the presidential jet back to Washington, Johnson glowed with satisfaction. After twenty test runs over the past month, he had adopted his own signature slogan by raising "Great Society" into capital letters ten times in a single speech, and now with a Scotch highball he bounded rearward to sound out the reaction in the press compartment. Reporters noted that the speech received "a hell of a reception." One of them respectfully announced that he had counted twenty-seven interruptions for applause.

"No, no," Johnson insisted. "There were twenty-nine."

23

Pilgrims and
Empty Pitchers

O N THE DAY before Johnson's Michigan speech, Malcolm X returned to New York from his five-week journey abroad. The most conspicuous changes in him were religious: his new Sunni Muslim name—El-Hajj Malik El-Shabazz—his African walking stick, and his reddish goatee after the fashion of orthodox pilgrims to Mecca. To the few who had followed him out of the Nation of Islam, where facial hair remained strictly forbidden, these features gave Malcolm an exotic cast, like a desert nomad from his favorite film, *Lawrence of Arabia*.

His new message was no less bizarre to the fifty reporters who mixed uncomfortably with spellbound Muslims, turning a welcoming reception into an impromptu press conference. "Incredible!" Mike Handler kept muttering to himself as he furiously scribbled notes in the airport's Skyline Room. Handler's story two weeks earlier in the *New York Times*—"Malcolm X Pleased by Whites' Attitude on Trip to Mecca"—had touched off a buzz among journalists and Muslims alike. The homecoming generated further headlines, such as "Malcolm Rejects Race Separation," and corollary reports about his revised opinions on Judaism. (Instead of lumping Jews together with devil whites, as before, Malcolm declared that "we can learn much from American Jews." He recommended a cultural and psychological Pan-African migration, rather than a physical one, modeled on the Jewish bond with historic Israel.*) Editors generally relegated these follow-up stories to small corners of back pages.

There was calculated naïeveté behind the newsworthy letters Malcolm had sent home to Handler, James Farmer, and many others, announcing his discovery that true Islam included "pilgrims from all over the world . . . *of all colors,* from blue-eyed blonds to black-skinned Africans." The letters allowed him to rise above the Nation's "white devil" doctrines without admitting that he had known of white Muslims for many years, and even discussed them in public, or that he had joined in what amounted to the Nation's pulpit trade secret—propagating theological black supremacy as a shock attraction for primitive "lost-found" Negroes who would not otherwise entertain Islamic ideas. Malcolm's revelation gambit succeeded in spite of its flimsy plausibility. While most Americans did not know or care whether he would revamp his religious philosophy on sighting a white Muslim, many seized upon what the *Times* called his "new, positive insights on race relations."

The religious surface of the new Malcolm was incidental to nearly everyone but Malcolm himself, whose claims of "spiritual rebirth" carried his distinctively naked candor. He had fled the country alone in April under repeated threat of death, marked as an apostate. Making his way through Jedda, Saudi Arabia, to complete the *hajj* pilgrimage as prescribed by the Q'uran, Malcolm found himself snatched from the masses passing through a checkpoint toward Mecca, then detained as a questionable Muslim because he carried an American passport and bungled the ritual Arabic. Uncomprehending, clad only in the prescribed pair of white towels— the *Izar* around the waist and the *Rida* over the left shoulder—he was confined through the day and night in a crowded dormitory among people who spoke no English. "I never had felt more alone, and helpless, since I was a baby," he recalled. He began to copy the prayers and prostrations of his neighbors.

Coming upon a strange-looking telephone in the holding compound, Malcolm recalled that he had brought one Saudi Arabian phone number belonging to the son of an Islamic author, who turned out not only to speak English but to open the hospitality of his relation by marriage, the Saudi Crown Prince Faisal. From this third-hand contact, Malcolm found himself catapulted upward with a royal interpreter through the *hajj* court, which accepted him as an authentic Muslim, and into a state limousine for an escorted drive to Mecca. Seven times he marched around the stone *kaa'ba*—venerated as the holy shrine created by the first prophet Abraham,

---

* The "new" Malcolm's Jewish interests were not always speculative and weighty. In Harlem, tickled by one of the first multicultural advertising posters, he asked a friend to snap a picture of him next to the young black poster boy—"You don't have to be Jewish to love Levy's"—who looked at a slice of kosher rye bread with a smile of delight that matched Malcolm's.

in submission to the merciful God who spared his son from willing sacrifice—and he joined ecstatic multitudes who prayed for six solid hours on the spot where the prophet Muhammad is said to have preached his last sermon.

Completion of the *hajj* briefly lifted the siege of Malcolm's life. As dictated to Alex Haley, descriptions of the journey would sustain an interval of delight through more than forty pages of his autobiography. The hunted Malcolm gloried in safe adventure, and the daredevil outsider unabashedly relished attentions due a touring head of state—"Chinese Ambassador and Mrs. Huang Hua gave a state dinner in my honor...a small motorcade of *five Ambassadors* arrived to see me off!" In Ghana, he snapped photographs of the library, gardens, and summer home of the late W. E. B. Du Bois, excitedly collecting evidence to contrast the honor Du Bois received in Africa with the scorn and criminal prosecution from his native United States.

Hailed as a world citizen, and oracle of boldness, Malcolm bumped into new regions of politics. African Marxists pressed him to see race as a component of the class struggle, against writer Julian Mayfield's argument that Karl Marx was a shield for selfish white control. African presidents were intrigued by Malcolm's proposal to redefine American race practice as a violation of fundamental human rights, and to haul the United States before the United Nations for sanctions, but even the powerful Ghanaian president, Kwame Nkrumah, shied away from the idea publicly for fear of offending the U.S. government.

On his last night in Accra, Ghana, Malcolm ran into Muhammad Ali outside the Ambassador Hotel. After an awkward pause, the new heavyweight champion rebuffed Malcolm's greeting and turned away with an entourage led by his business manager, Elijah Muhammad's son Herbert. Though hurt by this snub only three months after their shared triumph over Sonny Liston, Malcolm knew better than to try to pry Ali's young mind from sealed captivity within the Nation of Islam. He merely hinted at the gigantic beckoning world of *hajj* Islam. "Because a billion of our people in Africa, Arabia, and Asia love you blindly," he wired Ali the next day, "you must now be forever aware of your tremendous responsibilities to them." (Ali dismissed the advice by joking to reporters that he had come to the Muslim world to find four wives: one to shine his shoes, one to feed him grapes, one to rub olive oil on his muscles, and one named Peaches. He ridiculed Malcolm to reporters as a loony in a "funny white robe.... Man, he's gone. He's gone so far out.... Nobody listens to that Malcolm any more.")

Upon his tumultuous homecoming to New York, Malcolm X presented orthodox Islam as the reconciling link between his new ideal of brotherhood and his continuing indictment of white America. "America needs to understand Islam," he declared, "because this is the one religion that erases from its society the race problem." On another occasion he said, "True Islam removes racism," and within days he flatly evangelized those he had scorned as devils: "The American whites should adopt the Islam religion." These religious appeals lasted no longer than candles in the hurricane of attention to Malcolm's recantation as applied to white people generically, and specifically to Americans. From the first question in the Skyline Room—"Do we correctly understand that you now do not think that all whites are evil?"—reporters swarmed over his newsworthy mix of forgiveness and vengeance. Calls from journalists intruded on the intense dictation sessions for his autobiography, to the point that Alex Haley once pacified a *Life* correspondent by placing the phone receiver near enough to pick up some of what Malcolm was telling an interviewer from ABC.

Among those Malcolm received personally at Harlem's Theresa Hotel was the Yale author Robert Penn Warren, collecting material for his forthcoming book, *Who Speaks for the Negro?* Like other writers, Warren did not bother with distinctions between world Islam and the Nation of Islam, which outsiders called the Black Muslims, but he burrowed into cross-racial psychology. "I begin by asking if the Negro's sense of a lack of identity is the key for the appeal of the Black Muslim religion," he reported. Malcolm X briskly agreed but then distinguished between a cultural void and a sense of religion. "The two must be separated," he said.

Like an attorney at the bar of history, Warren cross-examined Malcolm as a stand-in witness for all Negroes living and dead—probing the far limits of guilt and grievance, asking to what degree they were individual or collective, empirical or attitudinal, inherited or created anew. Occasionally, a plaintive tone crept into the diagnostic questions. "Can any person of white blood—even one—be considered guiltless?" Warren asked. Taken aback, Malcolm denied the validity of "blood damnation" on a religious basis but observed that it would be difficult to filter out the actual "criminal oppression of the American Negro."

"Let's take an extreme case," pressed Warren. He postulated that "a white child of three or four—an age below decisions or responsibility—is facing death before an oncoming truck." Did such a child bear guilt for the oppression of Negroes?

Malcolm X turned the question around. "The only way you can determine that," he replied, "is to take a Negro child who is only four years old. Can he escape—though he's only four years old—can he escape the stigma of segregation?"

Warren tried another tack. "Let's put the Negro child in front of the truck," he supposed, "and put a white man there who leaps, risks his own life, to save the child."

However noble the deed, Malcolm replied, "that same man would have to toss that child back into discrimination, segregation."

"But what is your attitude toward his moral nature?" asked Warren.

"I'm not even interested in his moral nature," said Malcolm. "Until the problem is solved, we're not interested in anybody's moral nature."

Malcolm's refusal to open a door for individual absolution deeply affected Warren, who, for all his introspections since the 1920s on the American experience of race, still craved the possibility of simple innocence. "There is something of that little white girl in all of us," he wrote. "Everybody wants to be loved....But Malcolm X, even now, will have none of this. That stony face breaks into the merciless, glittering leer, and there is not anything, not a thing, you—if you are white—can do, and somewhere deep down in you that little girl is ready to burst into tears."

Warren sizzled with fury on the written page. He transformed Malcolm three times into a looming vision of evil itself—as vivid as his quoted passages from Joseph Conrad, and also, unintentionally, as cartoonish as a fairy-tale villain. Warren described what he saw: Malcolm's "pale, dull yellowish face that had seemed so veiled, so stony, as though beyond all feeling, had flashed into its merciless, leering life—the sudden wolfish grin, the pale pink lips drawn hard back to show the strong teeth, the unveiled glitter of the eyes beyond the lenses, giving the sense that the lenses were only part of a clever disguise, that the eyes need no help, that they suddenly see everything."

"I MUST BE HONEST," Malcolm told Alex Haley, admitting that he found no one in America to share his rush of inspiration since the *hajj*. He alone could make an appeal to the United Nations sound exciting—the idea struck most who heard it as diversionary or anemic—and even the Muslims who clamored around his hotel headquarters were largely deaf to ideas from Mecca. His lieutenant James 67X seethed against Malcolm's revised teaching on white people, because he wanted only to purify Elijah Muhammad's doctrine from sexual and financial corruption. Some refugees from the Nation looked for Malcolm to duplicate Captain Joseph's enforcement of moral order—three-day fasts, rigid sobriety, strict separation of the sexes—while allowing them to freelance in politics. Others reveled in the new freedom to have a date without approval from their Muslim captain, or to smoke a cigarette, but expected to serve in a Malcolm X militia that would show Martin Luther King how to strike fear in segregationists. Either way, James 67X despaired of establishing security or discipline while overrun by reporters, glamour-seekers, curious students, gangsters, religious sectarians, and a wide assortment of secular radicals—many white, nearly all non-Muslim. For Benjamin 2X, the thrill of serving as interim spokesman gave way to aimlessness. Malcolm's caretakers struggled over the content of an interim program, and those attending one meeting puzzled over an introductory presentation on yoga.

Malcolm quickly abandoned his floundering disciples again. In Chi-

cago on May 23—only two days after returning from abroad—he headlined a public debate in the Civic Opera House before a racially mixed
audience of nearly two thousand, and appeared with celebrities on columnist Irv Kupcinet's television show. He ridiculed the suggestion that Americans need only follow the example of bridge expert Oswald Jacoby, who
proudly claimed not to have noticed that one of his card-playing partners
was a Negro. He shocked polite optimists by disdaining American history
since the first colonial landings as an exercise in "your white nationalism,
which you call democracy." When he lapsed from confrontation to a hum-
bler description of his isolation in Mecca—"I was worried because I
couldn't communicate"—his television hosts cut to their next guest, film
star Olivia de Havilland.

A new public face partly emerged in Chicago. Malcolm refined his
scorn for the civil rights bill by arguing that it mistakenly assumed a
foundation of basic human rights. "I very much doubt that you can make
a citizen out of anyone you don't regard as a human being," he said.
Instead of defending racial separation, Malcolm presented integration and
separation as alternative methods to gain what Negroes "really want—
recognition and respect as human beings." Caught reverting to Elijah
Muhammad's separationist metaphor of white America as a sinking ship,
he confessed in debate that he was not sure how to find a floating log for
escape in mid-ocean, or where he might hope to sail one. Most notably,
Malcolm seldom mentioned the Nation of Islam—omitting both his veiled
criticisms and his habitual mantra of tribute to "the Honorable Elijah
Muhammad." His purpose was to demonstrate a fearless independent
drawing power in Muhammad's home city, and from there to sound out
the terms of separation from the Nation. He offered to quit fighting the
eviction suit and give up his home as part of a comprehensive agreement.
"I want to settle the situation quietly, privately, and peacefully," he told
the Negro press.

Malcolm's mission collided with a hostility that had intensified rather
than cooled while he was abroad. From Los Angeles, where thirteen Muslims remained on criminal appeal from the Stokes trial, the temple captain
informed Chicago of the prevailing rage against Malcolm's reported "conversion" from the Nation's teachings on white devils. Supreme Captain
Raymond Sharrieff replied that Malcolm's mind had been turned from
true Islam, and that "if Allah pleases him to live, he will come back
crawling." To stamp out Malcolm as the personification of a whole cluster
of heresies, Elijah Muhammad himself told not only his followers but
his printers and other non-Muslim contractors to have no dealings with
Malcolm. He ordered his temples to retrieve into active membership all
those Muslims being shunned on "time-out" suspension for infractions of
his rules. This defensive measure insulated from recruitment all those
Elijah called "the weak ones"—Muslims with a continuing hunger for

sectarian reinforcement in every aspect of daily life, from diet and entertainment to belief, but lacking complete submission. However, the amnesty
also removed ostracism as a principal tool of discipline. In its place, the
Nation further adapted the quasi-military regimen that Elijah Muhammad
first had instituted to train his Fruit of Islam for self-defense against
white devils. Specialized enforcement squads, expanded since the Stokes
violence to collect revenue quotas on newspaper sales, now expanded
again on the captains' orders to inflict corporal punishment and intimidation upon dissenters from Elijah Muhammad.

Malcolm verified personally in Chicago that Wallace Muhammad,
the one friend he knew to be committed to the reform of the Nation
toward *hajj* Islam, lived under siege within his own family. Young
Chicago Muslims, including Wallace's nephew Hassan Sharrieff, carried
guns to protect Wallace from threat of attacks. Earlier in May, when
Wallace had told a delegation of troubled Muslims from his former
temple the truth about his father's deviations as he knew them, a
running war of fistfights and ambushes broke out in Philadelphia
between those who could and those who could not accept their report.
Similar battles loomed in cities where Malcolm's personal following
among Muslims was strongest—New York, Chicago, Boston, and Los
Angeles. From Boston, Minister Louis X continued to excoriate Malcolm
for his "evil and vicious attack on the Messenger," branding him a
renegade false prophet who was "trying to lure us into following him."
Writing in *Muhammad Speaks,* Louis called down upon his former teacher
the cursed lament of the biblical Cain: "Everyone that sees me shall
slay me."

Against this torrent of dogma from the Nation, Wallace Muhammad
cautiously explored the idea of forming an embryonic community of
American-born *hajj* Muslims by leading a secession that would be parallel
to Malcolm's, only quieter. But Wallace warned Malcolm from harrowing
experience in Chicago that his family was resolved to wipe out Muslim
opposition. This left Malcolm and Wallace all but helpless—branded enemies by a war chorus of former colleagues and loved ones, while cut off
from whites, Negro Christians, and the Muslims abroad. Their isolation
from the Nation galled them because they understood it so clearly. Exaggerations once designed to uproot white control had become tools to bury
Negro minds again. Small corruptions—the semidivinity of Elijah as the
Messenger, the forced extraction of revenue—slipped from doctrine to
convenience to self-protection, until the Nation's leaders preyed upon the
blind loyalty they demanded. Malcolm retreated to New York. Sometimes
he counseled peace toward Muslims who repeated the Nation's formularized threats against him, saying they were not in control of their own
thoughts. Under pressure, he also exploded with agonized regret. "We had

the best organization the black man's ever had," he snapped, adding what was for him a rare and profane epithet: *"Niggers* ruined it!"

Malcolm seized a moment of calm to look through his Africa photographs as treasures of a vanished dream. "You know," he said wistfully to Benjamin 2X, "if it wasn't for you all here in this country, I would have stayed there, in Ethiopia." While he could not accept a permanent exile for survival, he swiftly let go of any hope that he could begin a "reform" denomination of American Islam peaceably. The bellicose Nation offered Malcolm X only the exit of surrender. He could crawl, renouncing any claim to speak as a Muslim, and work the fringes of the civil rights movement with a wholly secular message, essentially bluffing vigilante action. Malcolm gagged on this option. In exchange for suppressing or repudiating his own *hajj* beliefs, he would gain not even a guarantee of safety. Stripped of Muslim company and defenders, he would remain an admitted apostate to the Nation and, for its army of robots, an irresistible object lesson.

He decided instead to fight from the inside. Cornered and disorganized, having lost ground by absenting himself in the vain hope of a truce, Malcolm saw only a desperate chance to puncture the mystique of Elijah Muhammad by publicly denouncing him. His strategy amounted to stirring up a nest of honeybees while shouting that their queen was defective.

Malcolm knew better than to move tentatively. By the first of June, less than two weeks after his return, he dispatched Jamex 67X to locate the two women encamped near Elijah Muhammad's home in Phoenix, Arizona, where they were begging for family support. Operating as Malcolm's spy behind enemy lines, James implored Evelyn Williams and Lucille Karriem to sign notarized affidavits for what they had confirmed to Malcolm and Wallace Muhammad—that Elijah had impregnated them and four others who worked as his secretaries, then humiliated them before the membership of the Nation as harlots and tramps. The women allowed photographs of themselves and their children to be taken, but wavered between resentment and fear, whereupon James put them on the telephone to New York. "Mister Muhammad will be brought to justice," Malcolm X assured Lucille Karriem, who was expecting her third child by the Messenger, "and if you and Evelyn speak up, Allah will reward you."

Government surveillance lagged just behind. FBI intelligence experts, having noticed months earlier that Malcolm no longer showed up on their Nation of Islam wiretaps, had gained Robert Kennedy's approval for the first intercept on Malcolm X himself at the Elmhurst home he still occupied under threat of eviction. Technicians finished the June 3 installation just in time to overhear the first barrage of battle communications. Malcolm told a friend that he was "a trapeze artist" trying to leap into public view with the Muhammad sex scandal before the Nation could kill him.

He told an ally in Los Angeles that the Nation's temples were "pumping these brothers with poison and trying to get a shot at me." One confidant reported that newspaper editors were afraid to print stories about scandals involving Elijah Muhammad and told of hearing an official of the Nation say that Malcolm, "being black in America," could never protect himself. "Well, we'll see," replied Malcolm. While railing against the press—its insatiable interest in rhetoric about hatred and violence against whites, as contrasted with what he called a "blackout" on his Africa trip and his deadly dispute with the Nation—Malcolm vowed to break through. "I know how to do it," he said. "With Allah's help, I'll do it." Of Elijah Muhammad he said, "the only way to end this is to expose him," and he called New York police to report an attempt on his life.

FBI SUPERVISORS shrugged off Malcolm's alarms as "just another effort... to obtain publicity," and refrained from notifying other federal agencies or local police departments. Here and elsewhere across a vast range of secrets, government officials made use of selective and idiosyncratic interpretations. During his exclusive June 4 interview with author William Manchester on the Kennedy assassination, J. Edgar Hoover minimized the FBI's record of contact with Lee Harvey Oswald, including its relatively benign prior assessment of Oswald as a kookish nonspy, then abruptly preempted any suggestion of corresponding lenience toward Soviet Premier Nikita Khrushchev. With his aide Deke DeLoach looking on, Hoover expounded on the nature of Khrushchev's "very cold and evil mind" to the nonplussed author. "The Director told Manchester that he had always felt it better to kick individuals like Khrushchev on the shins once in a while rather than to boot-lick them," DeLoach wrote in his memcon. "The Director explained that Khrushchev was basically an oriental, and that individuals opposing orientals usually lost face in the oriental's opinion when fear or trepidation was shown."

Under Hoover's orders, the FBI's intelligence division had just completed a security review of the National Council of Churches that assigned its leaders to a category similar to Oswald's—shady and suspect, but not "under Communist Party domination or control." In sharp contrast, officials at the Justice Department were portraying the National Council leaders as stabilizing heroes at the forefront of an approaching racial confrontation in the South. From John Doar up through Burke Marshall to Nicholas Katzenbach and Attorney General Kennedy, and from there over to the White House, memos warned of a buildup in Klan terrorism against Negroes, especially in Mississippi. For political balance, Katzenbach described the student leaders planning Freedom Summer as hotheads and provocateurs at the opposite extreme, and praised the adult church leaders under Robert Spike for trying to "turn the students who will be in Mississippi to some sort of useful and productive activity."

The motive behind this careful posturing was to enlist and assist President Johnson in the delicate task of maneuvering Hoover's FBI toward greater vigilance and protection for civil rights workers. Burke Marshall, who undertook a brief trip to Mississippi so that he could pretend to discover the looming emergency for himself, gave Robert Kennedy a briefing paper drafted consciously "to avoid as much as possible any appearance of criticism of the Bureau's handling of specific investigations." The collaborators from the Justice Department recommended that Kennedy ask Johnson to describe the ominous Klan conspiracies to Hoover as a threat analogous to the Communist menace, cajoling the Director to fight it with the spy tactics that had proved so "spectacularly efficient" against the American Communist party.

On June 4, meeting alone with President Johnson as White House reporters speculated furiously about deals being made for the Democratic campaign ticket, Robert Kennedy outlined the Mississippi dilemma. He said that Mississippi police and sheriffs were believed to instigate criminal violence, "or at the very least to tolerate it," and he impressed Johnson with his command of details: a recent upsurge of some forty racially motivated arrests, beatings, and bombings in a climate of impugnity for segregationist violence, with Byron de la Beckwith recently freed after his second mistrial for killing Medgar Evers and state officials rallying citizens against a pending "invasion" by integrationist college students.

Kennedy found Johnson consumed by real Communist threats, not mirages meant to influence Hoover. Secretary McNamara had just delivered a gloomy report from the new American commander in Vietnam, General William Westmoreland, and Ambassador Lodge was coming home from Saigon to pursue the Republican presidential nomination. Johnson described his frustrations so strongly that Robert Kennedy did not press his risky and complex strategy for mobilizing the FBI in Mississippi. Instead, Kennedy volunteered to replace Lodge personally in Saigon as coordinator of the American war effort, acknowledging later to Johnson in a handwritten note that Vietnam "is obviously the most important problem facing the United States."

THE FBI steered its own course on race relations for another three weeks. From the Atlanta wiretaps, agents had learned in advance that Martin Luther King would be returning to California for six days of speeches and fund-raising at the end of May. Headquarters ordered the San Francisco office to prepare bugs for King's room at the Sheraton Palace Hotel. Wiretaps also alerted the FBI to negotiations for King to rent a summer beach cottage near St. Augustine, Florida, where he addressed a mass meeting on the night of May 26. Inside a packed First Baptist Church, where some children held banners reading, "Let Freedom Ring with Dr. Hay-ling," King exhorted a crowd that cheered every gesture and cue of his long-awaited appearance: "You are proving to be the creative spiritual anvils that will wear out many a physical hammer." By call and response of shouted acclamation, King extracted promises of steadfast nonviolence through hardships—stonings, arrests, attacks by police dog. "If they *shoot* at you," he cried, "will you *still* remain nonviolent?"

The next day, on his way to California, King stopped off in New York to address the NAACP Legal Defense Fund. Through wiretaps on Clarence Jones and Bayard Rustin, FBI analysts confirmed that King was meeting occasionally with a new advisory board called his Research Committee, formed largely at the initiative of corporate lawyer Harry Wachtel. Some members of his board joked that it took nearly a dozen senior men to replace the wisdom King missed from his nightly phone conversations with Stanley Levison. Others tended to fret over the greater consequences of rash mistakes now that King was a force near the center of national politics. Bayard Rustin urged King to avoid the advance publicity over the Freedom Summer in Mississippi, arguing that unstructured and immature SNCC leadership threatened to undermine political alliances. Wachtel and Clarence Jones thought King's nonviolent philosophy was growing stale and insipid to Northern tastes, endangering financial contributions. They wanted something dramatic—an advance since Birmingham—but they also worried about any gamble that might belittle King or backfire in violence before the civil rights bill passed.

King feinted in several directions but stopped short of engagement. Segregation "is so deeply rooted in the entire nation," he told the *New York Times,* "that I will have to give more attention to the struggle in the North." He also pledged to return South with a nonviolent army, and left Andrew Young behind in St. Augustine as his designated spokesman—much to the disgust of Hosea Williams. From experience in Savannah, Williams considered Young a well-bred conciliator by nature. Without knowing of King's actual instructions to dampen the local demonstrations below any flashpoint of mass jailing, he guessed that if King really wanted a nonviolent uprising, he would have chosen one of his marching lieutenants such as C. T. Vivian, who led a peaceful march of four hundred through St. Augustine after King's speech on May 26.

The next night, while addressing a mass meeting of twice that number at St. Mary's Baptist Church, Williams rebelled against letting all that carefully cultivated courage dissipate again. Outside the church, Andrew Young endorsed the prudence of King's orders even before gathering reports of white hoodlums sighted near the Old Slave Market with clubs and a few guns. One adolescent boy had been seen on the doorstep of a grocery store, calmly cleaning a shotgun of nearly his own length. As Young made his way inside with plans to call the turnout a victory and dismiss it safely for the night, Williams ambushed him from the pulpit.

"Here is Reverend Andrew Young, down from Atlanta!" he shouted to the crowd, pointing his finger. "Who is going to lead this march?"

Young drew Williams off to the side of the sanctuary. "Hosea, there must be five hundred Klansmen down there in that slave market," he said under his breath. "If we go down there, we'll get killed."

"We've got to go, Andy," said Williams. "We've got to go."

"*Why* have we got to go?" whispered Young.

Williams threw up his arms as though Young had agreed. "I want the prettiest girl in this church," he cried out, "to march up front with the Reverend Andrew Young!"

Young extracted one condition: the march downtown would be a silent one, without any morale-building songs or chants that might provoke hostile whites. Passing one-story homes through Lincolnville, those in the long double column did receive awkward calls of recognition and encouragement from thick clusters of bystanders that dwindled to nothing as Cordova Street neared the business district. At the King Street intersection, Police Chief Virgil Stuart halted the line to announce that "serious trouble" was lurking just around the corner in the darkness. Stuart firmly advised retreat and cut off Young's explanation. "I'm not gonna argue with you at all," he said, adding that his officers could not protect the marchers a step further.

Withdrawing to a nearby parking lot, Young gathered the marchers for a short speech about the choice they all faced. "And so tonight we have to decide whether to stand back and give in to fear," Young said, "or whether we really mean the words that we sing, 'Before I'd be a slave, I'd be buried in my grave, and go home to my Lord and be free.'" Young tried a joke or two to lighten the suffocating mood, then offered a long prayer for guidance ("... We come before Thee like empty pitchers before full fountains, confessing our doubts.... We ask you this evening for courage. ... Give us the strength of the prophets of old ... but we would also pray, dear Father, for those who would stand between us and our freedom ..."). When he called for those willing to go forward, nearly everyone in the giant circle assented by clasping hands through a hymn. Among press observers, Paul Good of ABC television noted a weeping middle-aged man who kept saying, "Oh, these beautiful people." At the center of the circle, Willie Bolden found himself staring at tears streaming down the cheeks of Andrew Young, which gave Bolden pangs for having assumed that he would need to goad the aloof movement executive into the leap ahead.

"May we march," Young said simply.

Three hundred fifty people in long double rows silently crossed King Street and turned toward the old cathedral, almost touching figures obscured behind trees and lampposts. Exposed, now that Chief Stuart had evacuated the area with his officers, C. T. Vivian flinched at the first loud toll of the Trinity Episcopal church bell, striking eleven o'clock, and others behind him and Young shrank inwardly from intermittent sounds, including the dull clang of a crowbar dropped on pavement. As the marchers passed the Old Slave Market, however, and turned back up King Street by Trinity Episcopal without suffering more than epithets, terror thawed to jitters of disbelief and brightened all the way to euphoria as they reached Lincolnville safely. Young theorized that the spectacle of Negro columns had paralyzed the Klan ambushers with temporary awe, but others shouted of Daniel's deliverance from a den of lions.

The march rekindled the spirit of the Mary Peabody campaign two months earlier. Enthusiasm carried through Thursday, May 28, when the frail polio cripple Georgia Reed volunteered to renew sit-ins at tourist motels, leading fifteen local Negroes back to jail under Florida's "undesirable guest" laws, and the mass meeting that night spilled over at ten o'clock into another one-mile march downtown from St. Paul's AME. Stimulated by the previous night's drama, television reporters imported camera crews, and nearly 250 whites amassed to defend the Old Slave Market. The head of the double column made it around the perimeter and back near the return on Cordova Street, where, the path obstructed, Andrew Young tried an evasive move by calling out loudly for prayer. Spittle, jeers, and rebel yells rained down from surrounding hecklers, but no violence erupted until press photographers tried to capture the scene with flashbulbs and television spotlights, and attackers darted in to smash the equipment. A man with a bicycle chain flayed open the neck of NBC cameraman Irving Gans, sending him to Flagler Hospital. Associated Press photographer James Kerlin was kicked and beaten to the ground, losing his cameras. Flying arms snatched a tape recorder from correspondent Paul Good, whose cameraman crawled through swirling legs in an unsuccessful attempt to escape with his newsfilm.

As Harry Boyte snapped photographs of the melee while crying out for officers to stop it, a deputy sheriff recognized him as the white man who had been introducing himself as Martin Luther King's newest SCLC staff member. By his own subsequent testimony in federal court, the deputy charged behind a German shepherd, shouting, "There's that nigger lover!" Bowled over and entangled in the leash, Boyte spun on the ground as the dog bit his leg and ripped his jacket. Reporters helped Boyte to his feet while the crowd diverted to destroy his camera. By then Negroes were dodging blows in full flight, with officers escorting or shooing them toward Lincolnville. A marcher named Clifford Eubanks was clubbed unconscious by an assailant who emerged from behind a hedge. Most others escaped serious injury, one story reported, "although some teen-age girls were weeping with fright."

Sheriff Davis and Chief Stuart interrupted the soaring hymns of thanksgiving and recovery at St. Paul's AME to summon Andrew Young outside. "We are declaring martial law," Stuart announced, meaning that the authorities would block further demonstrations. Long past midnight, after strategy sessions in which Young decided to challenge the edict in court, Harry Boyte picked up his college-age son, who had taken a bus to see the civil rights movement for himself. Boyte's apprehensions grew as a car followed closely behind from the bus station to his parking space at the Holiday Inn. He sent his son scurrying to the room with the key, and ducked on the front seat just before a shotgun blast tore through his windshields back to front. The Boytes sought refuge the next morning in the empty beach cottage rented for Dr. King, only to discover that bushwhackers had fired more than a dozen rifle shots through its windows during the night, shattering furniture and breakables inside.

BULLETINS REACHED King the next day before a rally in the San Francisco Cow Palace. To answer press suggestions of movement weakness—the *New York Times* detected a "loss of momentum" after the "Rout of Marchers" in St. Augustine—King pledged to "continue our efforts there through songs and prayers and not rifles and bullets." On another tack, he defended peaceful renewed demonstrations to critics who saw them as inflammatory rather than strong. "We cannot in good conscience postpone our nonviolent thrust merely because violence has erupted against us," he wired President Johnson on Saturday, May 29, before addressing an audience of eleven thousand in San Diego. That weekend, he called Burke Marshall and White House aide Lee White to seek emergency federal protection. From a Klan rally in St. Augustine, reports already buzzed of roving night patrols vowing to "hang a Negro," and an explicit death threat against King was relayed to him Sunday in Los Angeles just as pressures ruptured along another tangent. Coretta King complained bitterly from home about his constant and prolonged abandonments, after which the couple exploded over the phone line in mutual recrimination—each accusing the other of compounding rather than soothing the unbearable strains of movement life.

Within days, FBI agents offered Florida officials a copy of the wiretap recording. They were tempted by the chance that King might agree to withdraw from St. Augustine rather than risk publicity about his nasty family quarrel, but gave up the idea of confronting King for fear of an uproar over the wiretaps themselves. Harassments remained safely covert. Only hours before the rifle ambush against King's beach cottage, the Jacksonville FBI office had asked permission to bug the premises, and anonymous tipsters had publicized its exact location through the local press.

For federal and state officials alike, the desire to avoid the St. Augustine conflict overrode notions to suppress or resolve it. Governor Bryant of Florida boasted to the White House that he had placed state forces on protective alert so subtly as to keep the public unaware. Hoover plucked from his desk a memo noting press claims that the FBI would investigate violence "against King and other Negroes," and countered with a written instruction: "Be certain that we do not yield on our basic stand against doing guard duty." On hearing that White House assistant Lee White had promised publicly to "keep an eye on" violations of Negro rights through the FBI in Florida, Hoover asked his aides, "What do we know about Lee White?" To Hoover, White's statement implied FBI sympathy for St. Augustine protesters, which earned a full FBI file search for derogatory information about President Johnson's top civil rights aide.

Johnson, in the midst of a political call with Florida's Senator George Smathers on June 1, mentioned that he was catching "unshirted hell" on St. Augustine, with demands for federal intervention and "reports that they're shootin' into King's white man's house down there...and trouble like that." Smathers, with the caveat, "I hope I'm still maintaining some of my objectivity," replied that the shooting episodes were "a damn plant," most likely engineered by King's people because King was conveniently uninjured. "King is, naturally he loves the headlines," Smathers told the President, "and I think it would be very bad if the federal government did anything more than confer with Bryant." On June 5, Robert Kennedy's personal emissary reported from St. Augustine that the city was too volatile for overt mediation, let alone enforcement initiatives. "Discussions should be begun to buy time," he recommended, hoping for the federal courts to step forward.

That night in St. Augustine, Martin Luther King addressed a mass meeting. "I want to commend you for the beauty (Yes!) and the dignity and the courage (Yes, Lord!) with which you carried out demonstrations last week," he cried to an audience mostly of women fanning themselves in the pews. He praised them as "heroes of St. Augustine" before withdrawing to hear arguments over tactics to sustain the local movement.

With marches forcibly bottled up within Negro neighborhoods, and the supply of volunteers depleted by heavy fines and intimidating police blockades, King's colleagues considered an unlikely prospect from the U.S. District Court. In open hearings that week, Judge Bryan Simpson had asked for a courtesy moratorium on sit-ins and even tiny, lawful outdoor rallies, pending his decision in lawsuits seeking protection for demonstrations. Ordinarily, King's strategists might reject such a request as surrender, especially from a judge who had ruled consistently against them, but Andrew Young and his lawyers discerned subtle signs of conversion on the bench. Simpson ceased his whittling, for instance, when Georgia Reed testified in homespun detail about the new "chicken coop" outside the county jail, and how Sheriff Davis jammed fainting male and female prisoners together into the unshaded pen through the heat of the June days with only a shallow hole in the ground for a common toilet. (Davis testified that the coop was a bonus exercise yard for integrationist prisoners.)

From the bench, Judge Simpson himself questioned the logic of the state's position that only curfews and bans could protect Negroes from bloodshed, given the refusal of Sheriff Davis and Chief Stuart to say the opposing white crowds had been armed, hostile, or dangerous. "They were just a bunch of kids," Stuart insisted on the witness stand. When Davis, under court order, read a list of his 169 supplementary deputies, Simpson bolted upright at the name "Holsted Manucy," saying, "Why that man's a convicted felon in this court!" From a 1959 moonshine trial, the judge recognized "Hoss" Manucy as a rough-cut pig farmer and leader of the thousand-member Ancient City Hunting Club. Simpson asked whether the Hunting Club was a parallel Ku Klux Klan for Catholic St. Augustine, technically separate because the Klan proscribed Catholics along with Jews and Negroes, and did not seem satisfied with Sheriff Davis's bland denials. From these hints of judicial favor, movement leaders decided to accept Simpson's truce request in spite of the risk that he would rule against them or smother them with delay.

King left St. Augustine to deliver the baccalaureate address two days later at Wesleyan University in Connecticut, taking Coretta with him to calm the recent marital discord. They passed together through surreal acclaim. A young girl on campus amused King by asking persistently why he was not at least vice president of the United States. A well-meaning visitor called at the door of his faculty guest home with a pet Great Dane, causing a fright and then permanent banter between King and his traveling aide Bernard Lee over who had recoiled more ignominiously. In his college address, King spoke of a "long and difficult wilderness" between the Red Sea of liberation and the Promised Land of democracy. By the afternoon commencement, when Sargent Shriver exhorted Wesleyan graduates to help enact the Johnson poverty legislation,* King had moved on to New York as the first gentile to receive an honorary degree from the Jewish Theological Seminary, sponsored by Rabbi Heschel.

---

* A seasoned optimist, Shriver omitted discouraging facts from his speech, such as the current balance of exactly $67 in his government account for preparing the national war on poverty.

24

Brushfires

THAT SAME NIGHT, Sunday, June 7, arsonists set fire to the St. Augustine beach cottage for the second time since the May 28 fusillade. King and his new Research Committee were discussing movement strategy in a New York hotel room, and nearby, Malcolm X was working the telephone to spread the story of Elijah Muhammad's sins, calling Muslim women for the most part, hoping they would use their networks to verify his accusations that Muhammad seduced at least five of his secretaries, plus his own niece. Malcolm told them that Muslim men were factionalized to the brink of gang war, and complained that Captain Joseph's men had swarmed angrily upon a street corner discussion just the day before in Harlem, with Malcolm's sympathizers escaping only when one of them pulled a shotgun from the trunk of a car. The Nation of Islam was threatening bloodshed in the hope of eliminating him before he could establish the ugly truth, Malcolm told one telephone confidant on a wiretapped telephone line.

"You think the Messenger is that ruthless?" she asked.

"Any man," Malcolm replied, "who will go to bed with his brother's daughter and then turn and make five other women pregnant, and then accuse all these women of committing adultery, is a ruthless man."

At the Audubon Ballroom later that Sunday night, Malcolm departed from his speech about the *hajj* and his hopes for the United Nations to tell 450 listeners about the concubines. "The Nation would even murder to keep this quiet," he said. Word of his public revelation flashed across Harlem into the regular service at Temple No. 7, where loyalist members stayed late to hear lieutenants declare war in a closed emergency session.

At 9:08 the next morning, Malcolm's wife, Betty, received the first of many anonymous phone messages: "Just tell him he's as good as dead." Before noon, without mentioning the threat, Malcolm patiently unfolded the scandal to CBS correspondent Mike Wallace, who, saying he was still digesting news reports of Malcolm's revised philosophy on white people, had some trouble adjusting to an avalanche of internal Muslim gossip. Nevertheless, on hearing that the story was being offered to other journalists, Wallace rushed him into a studio that day to film the allegations in meticulous detail. For verification, Malcolm produced the written and recorded statements of several accusing mistresses. He alerted friends to watch Wallace's New York news show the next day, saying that quick publicity could drain the potential for intra-Muslim violence in many cities.

IN WASHINGTON, at the National Theater on Pennsylvania Avenue, Bob Moses introduced witnesses for a citizens' hearing on Mississippi that lasted through Monday, June 8. "It cannot be stated too many times," declared an invitation to members of Congress, "that our basic goal is to obtain Federal preventative action *before* any more names are added to the list of civil rights martyrs." Lawrence Guyot testified about labors to maintain Mississippi's first picket line since the Hattiesburg Freedom Day in January, and a halting Elizabeth Allen told how her husband, Louis, had tried to survive after witnessing the daylight murder of pioneer registration worker Herbert Lee. ("That is why [Louis] went to Jackson when the police broke his jawbone," she said. "He asked the FBI for protection, and they tell him different ones would help him, because he has a fear in himself. They took his credit from him. He had stood good in Mississippi, but after he tried to raise himself, and he, a man that wasn't just anything, they took his credit from him and which he got killed the 31st of January....") Hartman Turnbow testified about the retributions against him as the first Holmes County Negro of the century to present himself as a voter ("I attempted to register, and they bombed my house and shot in it.... So every little thing they can get on me, they still do"), and Fannie Lou Hamer told of her troubles in the movement since being beaten a year earlier in the Winona jail. "Not only have I been harassed by the police," Hamer said, "I had a call from the telephone operator after I qualified to run as congresswoman. She told me, 'Fannie Lou, honey, you are having a lot of different callers on your telephone. I want to know do you have any outsiders in your house? You called somebody today in Texas. Who was you calling, and where are you going? You had a mighty big bill.'"

While the hearing was under way in Washington, five young SNCC workers piled into a car and headed from Greenwood to Atlanta for the final staff meeting before Freedom Summer. They included Hamer's campaign manager, Charles McLaurin, and Sam Block, who had accompanied Hartman Turnbow to the Holmes County courthouse. A Highway Patrol officer stopped them outside Starkville, Mississippi, and, upon discovering campaign leaflets for Fannie Lou Hamer in the trunk, transported the prisoners to the Lowndes County jail for a night of interrogation and violence, with each slapped by fist or blackjack until he admitted that he was a nigger rather than a Negro. Released the next morning on payment of assorted fines, the Greenwood contingent made it safely through Alabama to the Atlanta office of Dr. James D. Palmer for treatment before they brought their bruises into the basement of Frazier's Lounge.

Some thirty SNCC workers converged there with tales and emergencies from several states, but Mississippi eclipsed the others. Reports filtered in of another beating the previous day outside McComb, where a roadside posse had ambushed three white magazine writers researching local plans for Freedom Summer. Arriving with Moses from Washington, James Forman reported that orchestrated plans for a White House audience had dwindled to hopes for a congressional hearing and finally, at great sacrifice, to a self-generated production at National Theater, and that while novelist Joseph Heller and other sponsors were sending President Johnson a renewed petition for help, SNCC's apprehensions went generally unregarded. Roy Wilkins was candidly criticizing the Mississippi summer project as pointless suffering that might embarrass President Johnson, said Forman, and corrosive doubt was spreading within SNCC itself. Staff members from the state headquarters in Jackson had reached Atlanta wincing over the fresh counsel of a jail volunteer from India who told them gently they lived too much in the present, without history or plans of long scope, vacillating unstably between suicidal hopelessness and an expectation of fixing Mississippi right away. "Oh, but you are all so American," said the wizened companion of Gandhi, who measured his own jail time in years instead of weeks.

James Forman told the SNCC gathering that he had watched Martin Luther King defend student initiatives to skeptical senior colleagues from the national civil rights leadership. King had praised the Mississippi summer project as "the most creative idea in the movement," Forman reported. His generous tone surprised listeners accustomed to Forman's trademark competitive edge toward King, but he could not dispel tensions that ran much deeper than the usual organizational rivalries.

On June 9, beginning a three-day marathon at Frazier's Lounge, complaints erupted that SNCC had lost the intimate kinship of the sit-ins and Freedom Rides. "There used to be a bond among us," lamented Marion Barry. Others replied that SNCC was no longer a student movement, that the staff had grown fivefold in the past year, and that SNCC needed adult political discipline to replace its naive dormitory methods.

When Prathia Hall rose to say that these arguments glossed over unspoken doubts about nonviolence and the compatability of blacks and whites in the movement, Charles McLaurin disclosed that Negroes around Greenwood were collecting arms to defend themselves during the summer project. Willie Peacock, another of those just released from the Lowndes County jail, confessed that he had brought guns into the Greenwood SNCC office. Hollis Watkins said that most supporting farmers kept guns in their houses; the SNCC staff had been able to create a covering atmosphere of nonviolence around movement activities, he added, but no more. Young SNCC workers blurted out that the Mississippi staff was "totally demoralized" just days before the first eager hordes of college volunteers were to present themselves for duty.

Prathia Hall rose again. "No one can be rational about death," she said. "What is happening now is that for the first time as a staff we are coming to grips with the fact that this may be *it.*" All their fears and heartache were valid, she cried out, but no matter how primal the urge to strike back or how pure the grievance, violence could gain nothing. "If you kill an attacker outside the window, you lose your home anyway," she said, "because the townsmen will come to the defense of the attacker and take everything from you." In a fit of Freedom Ride spirit, Hall declared her purpose to "bring our blood to the White House door. If we die here, it's the whole society which has pulled the trigger by its silence."

Ruby Doris Smith chastised Hall and others for pretending to be surprised. "There is no one in this room who thought of this project as not involving bloodshed," she said with fierce determination, but then Smith, too, was wrenched in the other direction. "What does it mean to say we will bring our blood to the doorstep of the White House?" she asked. "Let's face it. When the four children were killed in the church bombing in Birmingham last year, there were no thousands of volunteers to take their place." Lawrence Guyot, brushing close to his own private wounds, said they could not blame all the silence on the outside world, as no movement friends had rallied on behalf of him and Hollis Watkins and Willie Peacock and the others chained inside Parchman Penitentiary the previous summer. Still, Guyot argued against taking up arms. "Don't you see?" he shouted. "They'll shoot us quicker if we're armed!"

Debate broke loose from the usual factional and personal alignments. Purists berated themselves for leading lambs to slaughter, while more worldly strategists spoke up for the hard practical merit of nonviolence. "To the extent that we think of our own lives, we are politically immobilized," said Courtland Cox. Robert Moses proposed to focus upon what he called "the controllable things." They might not persuade Negro farmers to stray too far from their rifles, he said, and segregationists would pick their own victims, but the movement itself could resolve that neither staff nor summer volunteers would carry guns. Weary sighs of acclamation eventually drowned out quibbles, and Moses later sent Stokely Carmichael to rid the Greenwood SNCC office of weapons.

ON JUNE 9, Malcolm X was devastated to learn that Mike Wallace had broadcast on television only his premonition of murder—"I am probably a dead man already"—without any of his careful accusations. Wallace vaguely told viewers that Malcolm felt endangered because he possessed "certain information" about Elijah Muhammad. Malcolm, concluding that the legal departments of all three networks had vetoed airing the sex charges for fear of libel suits, then set out to obtain formal paternity complaints by the mistresses. He hoped that courtroom documents would provide enough protective cover for news outlets, and that the stories in turn would relieve sectarian hostilities building in the Muslim world.

Six Muslims were jailed and two hospitalized after a brawl outside the Philadelphia mosque on Monday. Seven young men went to the extreme of seeking refuge in the Chicago FBI office after beatings, claiming that Supreme Captain Raymond Sharrieff's enforcement squads were lumping together dues delinquents with potential dissenters as "hypocrite" followers of Malcolm. In Chicago, FBI wiretaps picked up reverberations among the women of Elijah Muhammad's extended household. Wallace Muhammad's wife unburdened herself to her mother-in-law, Elijah's wife, Clara, saying that Wallace's own brother had brought squads to their home threatening to kill him. Wallace's sister Ethel, wife of Raymond Sharrieff, promptly denounced her for upsetting her mother with talk of "that junk," while another sister bemoaned the hurtful intrigues within the family. "If we don't stop clowning," she said, "I am going to be ashamed of being a Muslim."

IN ATLANTA, Andrew Young took much of June 9 to compose a searching personal letter about "the direction which my life should take." Young sought pastoral counsel from Truman Douglass and Wesley Hotchkiss, two senior officials of the United Church of Christ who, in parallel roles with the National Council of Churches, had created historic initiatives for Mississippi. Aside from underwriting the training of Freedom Summer volunteers, the council had just voted formally to recruit and pay clergy for a long-term interracial project called the Delta Ministry. Young expressed gratitude for interest in him as its potential first director, but he wrestled in his letter with two other choices: staying on as administrator of the Citizenship Education Program, or succeeding Wyatt Walker as Martin Luther King's chief assistant. Mindful of his privileged legacy from the missionary Congregationalists who had educated his forebears since the Civil War, he wrote Douglass and Hotchkiss that he keenly felt the "guilt that I incurred as I watched those so educated filling their own coffers, with little concern for the needs of their less fortunate brethren." With apologies for restless imprecision ("At times my passion for these problems gets the best of my ability to communicate"), Young groped for an administrative role to join the nonviolent street masses with "talented tenth" church bureaucrats. "I have considered myself a link between these movements," he wrote.

Young was diverted from such thoughts by news of court rulings in Florida. That same day, June 9, Judge Bryan Simpson terminated the ban on marches in St. Augustine and proscribed some of the county's customized punishments for civil rights prisoners, such as the chicken coop, concrete sweatboxes, miniature padded cell, and the thirtyfold bail increase for misdemeanor charges. "More than cruel and unusual punishment is shown," Simpson wrote. "Here is exposed, in its raw ugliness, studied and cynical brutality, deliberately contrived to break men physically and mentally." Because the judge made his orders instantly effective, Robert Hayling and Hosea Williams considered it a jubilant duty to march forthwith that very night.

Their pleas for support rang north into the Atlanta headquarters of SCLC, which had been embroiled all day over a crisis from Alabama. In Tuscaloosa, home of the state university, police first had blocked an anti-segregation march by forcing some five hundred marchers to retreat back inside the First African Baptist Church, and later, deciding to force them outside again for arrest, hurled tear gas and sprayed fire hoses through the church windows. The Tuscaloosa jail gained ninety-two Negro prisoners, including SCLC's field representative for Alabama, Rev. T. Y. Rogers, and a volatile new siege held against pressures from both sides. By triage, King dispatched James Bevel to rally the nonviolent movement in Tuscaloosa, then turned to events in Florida.

Meanwhile in Washington, President Johnson took a phone call shortly after noon from Attorney General Kennedy, who had "heard of this incident of last night." The first two U.S. reconnaissance jets had been shot down over northern Laos. On secret, crisis recommendations that "unless we showed some strength and made some kind of reply, it would be very bad for us," he told Kennedy, Johnson had tried to knock out the anti-aircraft batteries with surgical air strikes, which failed because of bad weather. ("It shows us that we can't rely too much on airpower," he said.) Kennedy expressed worry that "the Chinese will probably talk about it, and the Russians will probably talk about it," which would break secrecy about the shadow conflict in Laos behind the undeclared war in Vietnam. Johnson managed to avoid news reports. He spent the afternoon notifying congressional leaders confidentially, saying he did not want to make "too big a deal of it" with a White House briefing. "If they'll just quit advancing," he told Senator Mansfield, "why then we can get out." Mansfield pleaded for a public explanation of the administration's Asia policy, and

Secretary McNamara agreed Tuesday evening in a postmortem on the immediate crisis. "If we're gonna stay in there," he told Johnson, "if we're going to go particularly up the escalating chain, we're gonna have to educate the people, Mr. President. And we haven't done so yet. I'm not sure now is exactly the right time."

"No," said Johnson. "And I think if you start doing it, they're gonna be hollerin', 'You're warmongers.'"

"That's right," said McNamara. "I completely agree with you."

In Atlanta, meeting across town from SNCC's ongoing debate about the Mississippi project, the SCLC staff argued all Tuesday afternoon about how King might honor his pledge to return to St. Augustine. What Daddy King heard about two specific threats against his son alarmed him enough to call Burke Marshall in the Justice Department with pleas for protection. Marshall called Lee White in the White House, who called Florida's Governor Bryant. SCLC sent a telegram to Attorney General Kennedy charging that the federal government was ignoring racial strife in St. Augustine. From New York, Clarence Jones orchestrated supporting messages from James Baldwin and others calculated to gain attention. Wyatt Walker called the Jacksonville FBI office only to be advised that threats against King were not a federal matter and should be referred to Sheriff Davis. Late on Tuesday afternoon, yielding to a chorus of worry that he was rushing into a death trap, King told reporters that he had postponed his flight until the next morning. With C. T. Vivian, Andrew Young raced off to the airport in his place, leaving behind a handwritten note on a copy of his fresh request for career guidance: "Dr. King—this is the letter I wrote...."

Young's journey coincided with Senator Robert Byrd's last-stand address on the civil rights bill in Washington. Observers noted that the energetic West Virginian took the Senate floor at 7:38 P.M. for the final scheduled speech before a test vote on shutting off debate. Determined not to yield the filibuster while breath remained, he read into the record the entire text of the Magna Carta signed in June of 1215—"749 years ago next Monday." Byrd traced American doctrines of constitutional liberty to historic roots in Anglo-Saxon character and specifically to the property rights British nobles had forced upon King John at Runnymede, then declared that the civil rights bill fatally undermined this foundation. From time to time, friendly senators rose for colloquies that allowed Byrd to rest his voice without endangering his parliamentary right to the floor. Senator Russell opined that the bill would guarantee the commercial destruction of white people "when it comes to employment, when it comes to promotion, when it comes to being laid off in times of economic distress," by ensuring that "the average garden variety type of American has no chance whatever." To prompting questions from Senator Strom Thurmond about a future in which "a woman of one race is required to give a massage to a woman of another race against her wishes," Byrd readily agreed that the bill imposed a new form of slavery by federal mandate.

In St. Augustine, Andrew Young walked again into a river of enthusiasm and a command invitation from Hosea Williams. Within minutes of his arrival at a tumultuous mass meeting, he was heading a double-column march of three hundred out of St. Mary's Baptist Church downtown to the steps of the Old Slave Market. Aggressive but isolated calls of "nigger" sustained an eerie tension until one man broke from the wall of white hecklers to strike Young across the mouth, knocking him to the pavement. Curiosity seemed to check war fever for a moment, as the crowd watched Young rise slowly to his feet and resume the march across the plaza. The hecklers proceeded to St. George Street a block away, and then to the corner of Cordova. At both standoffs, the attacker darted in to knock Young down with a blackjack, and at Cordova he stood over him delivering kicks until Willie Bolden threw himself down over Young, cradling his head in his stomach, absorbing blows on his back. Another attacker singled out one of the few whites marching with Young—Boston University chaplain Will England, who had returned two months after accompanying Mrs. Peabody to jail—and beat him to the ground. "The thud of the kicks were [sic] punctuated with groans from the victim," reported an account in the local Jacksonville newspaper. "Then a slender Negro boy, about twelve, broke from the ranks of the halted marchers and threw his body over the chaplain. The assailant turned and slouched away slowly. Policemen attempted no arrests...." Half a dozen other marchers needed hospital treatment before the columns reached the safety of St. Mary's, from which a battered Andrew Young later emerged. "Despite what happened, we are going to continue protesting unjust discrimination," he told reporters, shrugging when asked about prospects for federal protection.

BY THE NEXT MORNING, June 10, as Martin Luther King left Atlanta for St. Augustine, Senator Byrd was turning to religious themes after speaking all through the night. "I have attempted to reach some understanding as to the Scriptural basis upon which we are implored to enact the proposed legislation..." he declared to a Senate gallery brimming with people and anticipation. "I find none." Noting that the King James translation of the Bible had been published in the same year colonial Virginia first imported slaves (1619), Byrd listed accepted giants of theology and evangelism who had made little or no mention of race ever since. It would be preposterous to find a clear religious imperative in civil rights after all this time, he argued, because doing so would impeach the leading American divines as knaves or hypocrites. "Shall responsible men and women be persuaded that throughout the religious history of this country, they failed to preach the truth?" Byrd inquired, adding that if so, "I might say to Christians that Christ died in vain."

To support his point, Byrd expounded on the biblical "curse of Noah" and quoted the law of Leviticus against letting "thy cattle gender with a diverse kind." Citing the parable of vineyard laborers, he said Jesus not only condoned employment discrimination but endorsed a property holder's right "to do what I will with mine own." He found authority in the book of First Peter for a hierarchy of kinds, "even in heaven," and went on to dismiss Jefferson's doctrine of equal creation as extraneous *obiter dictum* from "the verbiage of the Declaration of Independence." Byrd recited the parable of the ten virgins from the book of Matthew to justify a society stratified by attainments and inherited features. "If all men are created equal," he asked the Senate, "how could five of the virgins have been wise and five foolish?"

The exhausted senator pressed through segregationist interpretations of Luke and Paul, pausing only to thank his chief opponent for a gift of red roses "from the garden of Mrs. Humphrey." After conceding a superficial relevance to civil rights in the Good Samaritan parable and Jesus' command to love neighbors as oneself, Byrd thundered his response: "But the Scriptural admonition does not say that we may not *choose* our neighbor! ...It does not admonish that we shall not build a wall betwixt us and our neighbor." With a final flourish from Daniel Webster's eulogy for George Washington, he yielded the floor after fourteen hours and thirteen minutes —the longest speech of the longest filibuster in Senate history.* The Senate secretary then called the roll on the petition for cloture, and one by one, relayed from the hushed chamber through Roger Mudd's live outdoor broadcast, the suspenseful tally grew. Californian Clair Engle, hospitalized and unable to walk or speak for months after two surgeries for brain cancer, was wheeled unexpectedly into the Senate long enough to record an aye vote by pointing to his eye.

In Massachusetts, handed a note ten minutes after the roll call, President Johnson interrupted his commencement address to announce simply that "we voted cloture in the Senate today by a vote of 71 to 29." No further explanation was needed to elicit a standing ovation in the Holy Cross College football stadium, led by Governor Endicott Peabody. Johnson flew home to a rubdown before grim war bulletins from Vietnam were delivered, and was huddled over them that evening with adviser McGeorge Bundy when Attorney General Robert Kennedy poked his head in the office. "Hello, hero," said Johnson, in tribute to Kennedy's hard work toward cloture.

"Wasn't that good?" Kennedy replied, and the President whisked him off to daughter Lynda Bird's hamburger party in honor of young Presidential Scholars. Under red-striped tents on the White House South Lawn,

---

* Lasting 534 hours, the 1964 filibuster filled 63,000 pages of the *Congressional Record* with an estimated ten million words.

they joined a host of attending celebrities, all of whom (except for J. Edgar Hoover) celebrated the day as buoyant supporters of civil rights: among them choreographers George Balanchine and Martha Graham, poets Ogden Nash and Gwendolyn Brooks, baseball star Stan Musial, folk singers the Kingston Trio, conductor Leonard Bernstein, actor Sidney Poitier, and writers Philip Roth, Katherine Anne Porter, Robert Penn Warren, and Harper Lee. Before retiring, Johnson conferred with congressional leaders on his foreign aid bill, and instructed Lee White to respond to wire stories about King's plight in St. Augustine. "Open up some communication down there," he said. ". . . Then call the governor, too. . . . Get Burke Marshall on it. Let's watch it now."

On Thursday, even while complaining to his staff that Robert Kennedy was planting political stories against him, Johnson called the Attorney General to say that his follow-up note on Vietnam was "the nicest thing that's happened to me since I've been here."

"Oh, that's very nice," said Kennedy.

"And you're a great, great guy, or you wouldn't write that kind of letter," said Johnson.

Johnson also reached across the passions of the cloture debate, asking Richard Russell to "do a little heavy thinking for me" about Asia.

"Well," said Russell, "we're just like a damn cow over a fence out there in Vietnam."

Johnson bemoaned his dilemma in earnest: "A. W. Moursund said to me last night, said, 'Goddamn, there's not anything destroy you as quick as pullin' out and pullin' up and runnin', 'cause America wants by God prestige and power, and they don't want.' I said, 'Yeah, but I don't want to keep—' "

"That's what he said?" Russell interrupted.

" 'I don't want to kill these folks,' " Johnson continued. "He said, 'I don't give a damn.' Said, 'They didn't want to kill 'em in Korea,' but said, 'if you don't stand up for America, there's nothing that a fella in Johnson City or Georgia or any other place, they'll forgive you for everything except being weak.' "

"Well, there's a lot in that," said Russell. "A whole lot in that."

The President sighed, wandered through other subjects, then congratulated Russell for gallantry in defeat on the cloture vote. "Bob Byrd just stood to the last, didn't he?" he said.

"Yeah, he sure did," said Russell. ". . . He's tough as hell."

"He's a good little boy," said Johnson.

AT HIS MASS MEETING Wednesday night in St. Augustine, Martin Luther King recognized the "magnificent drama taking place on the stage of American history." He praised as its vanguard "all of these persons back with us who have been in jail, I think about ten days"—Georgia Reed and others just released under Judge Simpson's bail reduction. After beckoning them to stand in the church, "so that we can see them and give them a great hand for their courage and their dedicated witness in this city," King preached on what he called the dignity and discipline of those who had marched with Andrew Young the previous night. "And we go on with a faith that unearned suffering is redemptive," he said. "Now we face the moment of great decision. Now we face the moment when we must put on our walking shoes and get ready to make a definite witness."

King withdrew to debate the complications of that decision. He and his aides realized that the conflict in St. Augustine was a footnote to the national legislation against segregation, and they wanted to avoid an upheaval that might jeopardize the measure on the edge of victory. (While the filibuster was broken, the Senate version differed from the House version, and numerous pitfalls littered the path toward final approval of identical bills, suitable to become law.) Parallel to Johnson's tricky course between the House and Senate, King tried to keep the nonviolent movement healthy without feeding the incipient white backlash. Privately, at his urging, Johnson officials pushed the St. Augustine officials for small concessions—such as a biracial commission—that might allow King to withdraw. Without a truce, they argued, St. Augustine was about to repeat the 40 percent loss in tourist business that had followed Mrs. Peabody's arrest in April. The White House brokered messages between King, Judge Simpson, and Florida politicians. "The Governor said that he would talk to the Mayor about the possibility of calling a meeting," Lee White reported to Johnson.

When St. Augustine held fast, King felt obliged to keep faith with the local jailgoers and with the national movement that had created the civil rights bill in the first place. To do nothing was to risk charges of collapse from the same people who accused the movement of provocation. Despite growing Klan violence, King's hopes for state or federal protection were slim. He was not privy to the vituperative hate mail that greeted Judge Simpson's order restoring Negro demonstration rights,* but he knew from impeachment rumors and overt pressures that Simpson had stretched judicial help to the limit. Therefore, by logic familiar from the low point in Birmingham the previous spring, the battered local movement must expose itself to further punishment, and King resolved to submit himself

---

* One writer put Simpson on notice that "we are not going to stand by and let TRASH like old KING and his bunch of GOATS punch us in the nose, and we are not going to be slaves to them." A dentist asked "how does it feel to be an agent of the police state?" More polite letters complained that Negro demonstrations disturbed social harmony, and a few praised Simpson's courage, but most assailed him crudely: "You S.O.B., If I were a man I'd beat you to a pulp.... I hear rumblings of removing you somehow, and it's gaining momentum fast. Don't wait for that, just drop dead and save the expense so the whites can have equal rights again."

to jail. Personalized threats and his demolished beach cottage recommended that he get there by a short, unannounced route, in the daytime.

At 12:22 on June 11, along with Ralph Abernathy, Chaplain Will England, and two others, King presented himself for lunch at the Monson Motor Lodge, a motel favored by visiting journalists. Several dozen reporters gathered behind in a tight semicircle, jostling for notes and photographs as owner James Brock confronted King's group outside the entrance. "We can't serve you here," he told King. "We're not integrated." King said he would wait. When Abernathy asked about a sign welcoming tourists, Brock explained that exceptions to segregation were reserved for Negro servants of white patrons, who could take meals from the service area. King asked Brock if he could understand "the humiliation our people go through."

A waiting customer called out from the back of the crowd, asking whether Brock was open for business. Told yes, the burly man pushed his way through, shoved Abernathy into King, then threw King roughly to the side of the door. "Black bastard," he said on his way inside.

Brock told King it would ruin his white business if he accepted Negroes. He appealed for consideration of his own hardship as a local citizen of prominent obligations—a Rotarian, head of the Community Chest, president of the Florida Hotel and Motel Association. "I ask you on behalf of myself, my wife, and our two children," he told King, "to leave." As he turned to face news cameras, Brock added, "I would like to invite my many friends throughout the country to visit Monson's. We expect to remain segregated."

Chief Stuart and Sheriff Davis arrived to end the dialogue with arrests for breach of peace, conspiracy, and trespass with malicious intent, among other charges. Eight volunteers, including a white woman, stepped forward on Davis's announcement that he would accommodate anyone who wanted to join King in jail. A Negro teenager changed his mind when asked pointedly by Stuart if he were sure.

A rumor swept through Lincolnville that Klansmen dressed as women were training to assassinate King, and a fantasy report came back from the white side of town that a squadron of seventy-five Black Muslim snipers was already deployed to fire from rooftops near Lincolnville. (The latter took hold as accepted fact. "Had it not been for the white police," a leading radio station reported of an aborted Klan parade, "veteran observers say that no white would have gotten out alive.") In the placid daylight hours, city work crews removed the brick borders from public flower beds near the Slave Market, so they could no longer be heaved during night marches.

Police officials told the FBI they wanted to move King out of St. Augustine to avoid a jailhouse lynching. "Medgar Evers was just a two-bit local philanthropist, and now he's a martyr," editor "Hoopie" Tebeault explained. "We don't want that to happen here." Handcuffed, placed inches from a German shepherd guard dog in the back seat of Sheriff Davis's car,

King was removed from the county jail the next day for grand jury questioning, then returned when the paperwork was not complete for his transfer to Jacksonville.

Messages on everything from local gossip to long-range trends in national politics reached King's cell. Historian Lawrence Reddick, King's friend and first biographer, was submitting to his New York Research Committee a sober analysis of the George Wallace campaign. He discerned from its stunning success that while Northern whites had sympathized with the Negro movement against crude Southern brutality, many privately favored "the principle of racial separation." Reddick warned King confidentially that a voting majority "can be mobilized by the anti-Negro camp on an appeal that is reasonable and correlated with other long-time, deep-seated desires and irritations.... Many an individual in our society feels overwhelmed by gigantic forces." If George Wallace himself could refine such a message from hateful segregation,* Reddick reasoned, other national politicians surely would follow. "This also may be part of the secret of Goldwater's support," he wrote. Reddick advised that the movement should forswear any claim to racial preferences or compensatory treatment, no matter how justified by history. "Equality is the principle that permeates the American ideology (despite exceptions here and there)," he concluded. "... We cannot win without allies. We cannot win with the majority of Americans apprehensive of our advances."

King, knowing he could not stay in jail long, grasped for ways to maintain the spirit of the St. Augustine movement. His goal was to hold on through the anticipated ordeals, with an eye on the civil rights bill and a finger on the pulse of nonviolence. Already, he had urged national celebrities to bring their witness to the mass meetings in St. Augustine, but none agreed to come. (Actor Marlon Brando sent King a telegram of regret on account of his bleeding ulcer and "great personal strife.") King eventually came down to those who had answered his most desperate calls the previous two years, from Albany and Birmingham. "Dear Sy," he wrote, "I am dictating this letter from the St. Augustine City Jail." Andrew Young had brought King word that Rabbi Israel Dresner—a Freedom Rider from 1961, who had brought King to preach at his New Jersey synagogue after the Chicago Conference on Religion and Race—was about to attend a convention of reform rabbis in the Catskills. "Perhaps if this letter could be read to your brethren next week, it might be considered a 'call' to St. Augustine," King wrote Dresner. "I would imagine that some 30 or so rabbis would make a tremendous impact on this community and the nation. We would hope that some would be prepared to submit to arrest."

---

* One contemporary magazine writer offered a similar distillation of Wallace's campaign oratory: "He gave every hearer a chance to transmute a latent hostility toward the Negro into a hostility toward big government. The technique was effective."

PART THREE

Freedom Summer

25

Jail Marches

ON FRIDAY, JUNE 12, with King in jail, Hosea Williams presented himself for arrest in order to cajole fifty-five reluctant recruits to join the daily restaurant sit-ins. With local volunteers running low, the St. Augustine movement welcomed a busload of temporary reinforcements who arrived that day from Birmingham, and Williams announced on his way to jail that other buses would arrive from Albany, Georgia, and Williamston, North Carolina. A crowd of nearly two hundred mustered for an early evening rally at the Slave Market, guarded precariously by a ring of police officers. No sooner did the Negroes retreat than a larger crowd of hecklers seeped into the plaza for a boisterous counterrally featuring the white opposition's imported talent. "We're not gonna be put in chains by no civil rights bill now or any other time!" shouted J. B. Stoner. "There's nothing in the Constitution that gives Congress the authority to tell us we've got to eat with niggers!"

A whiff of legend about Stoner helped him command the enthusiasm of the segregationist crowd. He had turned up after spectacular racial violence for years, as police suspect in conspiracies from the 1958 bombing of Atlanta's Temple Beth-El to the Birmingham church bombing the previous September, and as defender of his friend Byron de la Beckwith in the Medgar Evers murder. Until his conviction more than a decade later on an old charge—blowing up part of Fred Shuttlesworth's church and parsonage—Stoner would carry the Klansman's presumed immunity from restraint by any jury.

Almost alone among whites of the 1950s, Stoner had studied the

Nation of Islam with the taunting respect of an opposing sectarian. "You need to learn more about that evil genius, Elijah Muhammad, or you will never stop him and his niggers from taking over your city," he had warned the New York police commissioner in 1959, offering to lend specially trained warriors from his Christian Knights of the Ku Klux Klan. Stoner claimed to have been called into Klan leadership in 1942, at the age of seventeen, and had specialized in anti-Jewish polemics as founder of the Stoner Anti-Jewish Party out of Chattanooga. Like his friend and fellow stump speaker, Rev. Connie Lynch, and Sam Bowers of the new White Knights Klan in Mississippi, he championed the sectarian doctrines of Dr. Wesley Swift, a California fundamentalist who managed to repackage the historical Jesus as an Aryan instead of a Jew—and Anglo-Saxons as the Chosen People of the Bible—by tracing strange, previously unknown migrations of the Ten Lost Tribes of Israel through Bethlehem and the Caucasus into Northern Europe. Evolving years later into Aryan Nations, Swift's Christian Identity movements would inspire white supremacy groups for the remainder of the twentieth century.

That Friday in St. Augustine, Stoner waved a Confederate flag behind an imposing wall of bodyguards. His discourse on the Founding Fathers—"When they said that all men were created equal, they weren't talking about niggers..."—drew only sporadic cheers from an audience that was easily bored, dressed in beach clothes on a balmy night, but Stoner struck home with coarser talk. "The coons have been parading around St. Augustine for a long time!" he shouted, and proposed to get even by marching through the darkest streets of Lincolnville with flags, weapons, and scraps of Klan regalia. His dare provoked a crescendo of war whoops. "Under no circumstances should you panic," Stoner advised. "If some nigger calls you a bad name, pay no attention because what a nigger says doesn't matter anyhow."

Flanked by Chief Stuart and Sheriff Davis, who had assembled a protective escort of armed officers, Stoner led a double column of two hundred segregationists and some thirty trailing reporters out of the Slave Market, behind accommodating Negro "scouts." Stoner walked with a slight limp from childhood polio. When the march entered Lincolnville, which lacked street lamps, police flashlight beams scanned wary faces and crowded front porches on both sides of the narrow streets. Near the point of greatest apprehension, a rowdy nightclub called Big Daddy's Blue Goose Bar, Negro residents ambushed the semi-martial cavalcade with repeated choruses of Andrew Young's favorite hymn for mass meetings, "I Love Everybody, I Love Everybody in My Heart." Faltering at first, the orchestrated welcome grew stronger once its effect on the grim invaders registered clearly. Stoner called for a strong white marching song to drown out the fraternal mush from Negro residents, but there was confusion down the long columns about what selection fit the moment. The whites half-heartedly settled on "She'll Be Comin' 'Round the Mountain."

At the Slave Market on Saturday, Stoner raised very little enthusiasm for a second march into Lincolnville, while Andrew Young found only fifteen jail volunteers, including eight local juveniles and three visiting whites from the North. In bigger news, Florida Senator George Smathers made public his offer to raise the necessary bail money if Martin Luther King would promise to leave Florida. "I respect you as a man working in behalf of your race," Smathers wired King at the Duval County jail, "but willful violation of laws, no matter how unjust they may seem to each of us at the time...does serious harm to our form of government and the image of the United States of America." King declined the offer, but he did post his own bond late Saturday. From Washington, Lee White told King's staff that the White House had no record of Johnson's trip to St. Augustine the previous year, nor of promises by the former vice president to secure a "dialogue" between the races.

Just before the Sunday commencement service at Springfield College in Massachusetts, where King delivered his Rip Van Winkle sermon about how too many Americans were sleeping through a great social revolution, two churches in St. Augustine summoned police to arrest a Yale student from Little Rock along with six other aspiring worshippers in mixed groups. On Monday, Yale President Kingman Brewster introduced King, saying, "The gratitude of people everywhere and of generations of Americans yet unborn will echo our admiration," and ten thousand people determined the headlines for Yale's 263rd commencement with two prolonged, standing ovations when King received his honorary Doctor of Laws.

IN NEW YORK, Clarence Jones decided not to tell King about the evening of his secret introduction to Malcolm X. Harry Belafonte declined to attend, saying he thought some of the invited celebrities were too hotheaded to trust with such an explosive, newsworthy encounter, but Jones, holding himself out with slight exaggeration as King's authorized spokesman, ventured with novelist John Killens to actor Sidney Poitier's home. Malcolm captivated Jones with his vision of a worldwide human rights campaign to make U.S. racial practices a test case at the United Nations, like South African apartheid and persecution of Soviet Jews, but Jones was obliged to conceal his excitement from colleagues in the Southern movement. He knew that King—stretched to the breaking point by the demands of nonviolence—would be pained to learn that his New York lawyer was drawn to a nascent alternative behind a Black Muslim.

Like King, Malcolm X was tumbling through his own extremes between punishment and acclaim, glamour and despair. He arrived at Poitier's from a weekend recruiting trip among disaffected Muslims from Muhammad's Temple No. 11 in Boston, where he had made his pitch for six hours on Friday over the airwaves of two radio talk shows. Afternoon host Paul Benzaquin announced that his guest arrived at station WEEI under police escort, following an anonymous warning to police dispatchers that Malcolm would be "bumped off" if he appeared. Malcolm told listeners of the "real reasons" for his split with the Nation of Islam, reciting his accusations about Elijah Muhammad's bastard children. Among the on-air callers was a confused Muslim who asked whether Malcolm still considered Elijah Muhammad the Messenger of Allah. Malcolm said no, citing Wallace Muhammad and officials in Mecca, adding that the Nation was guilty of idolatry under Islam for deifying Elijah Muhammad. Late that night, Malcolm amplified his charges. He had discovered, he told host Jerry Williams over station WMEX, that Minister Louis X of Boston had learned of Muhammad's infidelities long before he did.

On Saturday, June 13, Malcolm interrupted his Boston trip to attend the Poitier rendezvous in suburban New York. He called the tentative coalition of black luminaries his "brain trust," through which he would develop a new national agenda somewhere beyond civil rights. To them he displayed only a residual buzz of danger from the Nation's intrigues, but alone again, shortly after midnight, Malcolm tuned in Boston's WMEX to hear guest Louis X denying all his accusations from the previous night. Malcolm dialed into busy signals until he got through to the Jerry Williams show, then challenged Minister Louis to meet him at the station and hear the facts repeated "to your face." Louis X replied that he would need the permission of the Honorable Elijah Muhammad.

Malcolm still saw Louis X as his devoted protégé who had closely studied his mannerisms at the lectern, down to the smallest hand gestures. ("Tell Minister Louis to stop imitating me!" he had ordered some months earlier.) While appreciating the pressures that bound Louis X tightly to the Nation against him, Malcolm retained some confidence that he could win him back. He did not know that Elijah Muhammad had summoned Louis across the country that week to hear only "a few words, but it should be done in person." Returning swiftly from Phoenix to Boston, Louis reported to Muhammad that Malcolm was still in town "going right after the whole thing." The FBI wiretap in Phoenix recorded Louis's cryptic question—asking whether it was "wise to go after it with the body"—and Muhammad's reply that he was not in a position to answer because he did not fully understand all the circumstances. With an air of disinterest, Muhammad told Louis X that while he cared nothing about a dog barking, the dog was "very silly to bark in everyone's house."

On Sunday afternoon in the Roxbury section of Boston, jammed into a room of her home that Malcolm's half-sister Ella Collins had converted into a kindergarten, more than a hundred people turned crestfallen when

Benjamin 2X arrived as the substitute speaker. They had come to hear Malcolm, drawn by his electric revelations and his promotional announcements on radio. Benjamin could offer only a few definitive statements about Malcolm's evolving public stance—that he no longer advocated a return to Africa, and now favored a leadership congress of black organizations rather than the Nation of Islam's "monarchy" structure. Every other idea and detail was in flux.

Although many disaffected Muslims in the room still admired Malcolm X as the minister who had converted them, bitter experience left them wary of blind commitment a second time. Most were rebels against the Nation's bareknuckled debt collections. Not long after Temple No. 11 members battered one delinquent member in Franklin Park, and placed a warning noose around another's neck at the edge of the Charles River, a number of members had signed a letter vowing to retaliate against Louis X if there was further violence. Captain Clarence X promptly announced that the temple would answer the slightest harm to the minister by killing the signers of the letter along with their children and "some of their parents." Some frightened Muslims traced corruption to Chicago and the hoodlum past of Captain Clarence X; others blamed Minister Louis himself for sermons that ignited holy wrath by contrasting the infinite gifts of the Dear Holy Apostle Elijah Muhammad with the skulking ingratitude of the slackers listed by name on a temple blackboard.

Since Malcolm's suspension, the Nation had relied more than ever on fear. Temple investigators, still authorized to enter Muslim homes at any hour to confiscate cigarette butts and forbidden pork, now prowled also for heretical complaints and suspicious friends. They lumped dissenters together with deadbeats as "hypocrites," the Nation's term for traitors to Elijah. Against all this, a dozen leading defectors—including Aubrey Barnette, a graduate of Boston University and cousin of the slain Los Angeles secretary, Ronald Stokes—looked to Malcolm X for a "positive program" to redeem the sacrifice of their youth to Islam. In the kindergarten room, they waited stoically for many more specific answers about discipline and purpose than Benjamin 2X could provide.

THE CHASE BEGAN as Benjamin 2X rode back to the Boston airport in a Cadillac late Sunday afternoon, reminiscing with Goulbourne X Busby about Army service in Korea and Japan. A white Lincoln pulled alongside, tried to run them off Massachusetts Avenue in tandem with a 1955 Chevrolet, then commenced high-speed pursuit on and off expressways and even sidewalks. The Chevrolet managed to get ahead of the Cadillac and skidded to a stop across both lanes inside the Callahan Tunnel. The Lincoln did likewise from behind, and as traffic piled up in each direction, Temple No. 11 Muslims, led by one of its lieutenants, jumped out of the chase cars with pistols, shouting, "You ain't leaving here!" Some inside the trapped Cadillac shouted hysterically that Malcolm X was not among them. Goulbourne X grabbed a shotgun from beneath the seat to hold attackers at bay. A passenger screamed as Malcolm's nephew Rodnell Collins lurched the Cadillac backward and forward into the blockading cars until he rammed the Chevrolet far enough aside to squeeze by. The mangled cars resumed the chase all the way to Logan Airport, where Benjamin's frantic party—despite honking the horn and abandoning the Cadillac in the taxi lane—failed to attract any police notice until they ran through the Mohawk Airlines concourse out onto the airstrip and back inside to another ticket counter, waving the shotgun. "It was here the Massachusetts State Police arrested them," an investigative report dryly noted, "for which they all thanked Allah."

On Monday, when Martin Luther King was at Yale, Benjamin 2X returned with his tale and his bail bond papers to find Malcolm X under siege by New York Muslims, having delivered his bastardy speech again the previous night to four hundred listeners at Harlem's Audubon Ballroom. Wiretappers overheard Malcolm challenge one threatening caller to bring his rifle around to the house "and talk some stuff." New York police received so many corroborating reports that thirty-two officers escorted Malcolm and his eight Muslim bodyguards into Queens that morning for Malcolm's hearing on the eviction petition brought by Temple No. 7. Testifying for the plaintiffs, Captain Joseph defined the Fruit of Islam as an organization "just like the Boy Scouts." He smiled from the witness stand as he broke courtroom tension with one of Malcolm's own laugh lines, deflecting suggestions by Malcolm's lawyer that the Nation was built on intimidation.

That night from Boston, Minister Louis X reported to Elijah Muhammad that he would not sink so low as to debate Malcolm in person, having "cut him to pieces" on the radio. He said he had rebuffed Malcolm's private pleas for help by answering that if Malcolm's life was on the line, he had put it there himself. Louis X assured Muhammad that newspapers would not print Malcolm's "inside story of the Nation" without proof in court, and Malcolm tacitly accepted the point when he testified the next morning in Queens. He approached what he called a "very private" complaint several times but backed away in favor of his technical defenses— that Muhammad had promised him the house, that in any case he was being removed improperly from the ministry. Finally, after Judge Maurice Wahl showed little interest in the Nation's internal arrangements, Malcolm blurted, "I found out that he had nine children by six different girls."

To Malcolm's disappointment, the imprimatur of courtroom testimony gained little public notice for his allegations. White newspapers ignored what for them were hearsay sex charges from a squalid and inscrutable race schism, and instead found plenty of news in predictions of boomerang violence. "There is no people in the United States more able to carry out this threat than the Black Muslims," reported the *New York Herald Tribune*, quoting Malcolm: "I know. I taught them myself." Leading Negro papers headlined the gangland hostility—"Muslim Factions at War"—while reporting merely that Malcolm attacked Elijah Muhammad's character. A few, such as the *Philadelphia Tribune*, did break the sex barrier —"Says Muhammad Brought Stork to Six Teens/Claims Two Local Lasses from Gtn. [Germantown] Are Among Them"—but the voltage from Malcolm's revelations surged mostly within the Muslim world. Before nightfall in Chicago, Wallace Muhammad ventured out of hiding to see his mother, Clara, who confessed that she had learned of what she called her husband's "troubles." Lonely and distraught, she begged her favorite son to stop associating with Malcolm's terrible poison and confide in "the big man," Elijah. Wallace tried to comfort her while insisting that he was not afraid to have his money cut off again, and would not shrink from the next threat. In New York, meanwhile, police made six arrests to stop a street rumble between Muslims carrying rifles, and Malcolm X found the telephone dead at the house he had lost that day in court. (Judge Wahl allowed him a grace period of several months to vacate.) An impostor had ordered the phone company to disconnect the line, saying Malcolm would be going away for a long time.

KING WAS BACK in St. Augustine. Former baseball star Jackie Robinson had received a tumultuous response the night before in King's absence, and had been moved to invite several of the youngest movement heroes to be guests at his summer camp in Connecticut. Of fifty-one demonstrators who went to jail from restaurant sit-ins that Tuesday, June 16, the majority were visitors from the Williamston, North Carolina, movement, led by Sarah Small and Golden Frinks. King's staff, running short on bail money and volunteers, labored to sustain morale on celebrity appearances and low-budget sacrifice in the hope of reaching at least a minimal settlement with city officials. A camera crew from Miami caught glimpses of busy preparations in and around the Elk's Rest Lodge: working the telephones, C. T. Vivian excitedly confirmed the pending arrival of the rabbis from Atlantic City, and checked on the besieged church in Tuscaloosa. "How is Bevel?" he asked. "How long has he been out of jail?" Nearby, drilling sit-in volunteers in groups of four and five, Andrew Young worried about whether the rabbis would need to return north to their synagogues for Friday night services. Willie Bolden gave a workshop lecture on the need for "jail discipline," saying catfights and quarrels hurt the movement. Robert Hayling—just back from a mission to Washington with Henry Twine, where they petitioned Burke Marshall and others for federal assistance— asked a Yale journalism major whether he had remembered to recruit local help for the daily movement newsletter.

"No, but I'm working on that," the student replied.

"Have you even tried to have some of the young people write an article or two?" Hayling pressed.

"Yeah, I have," said the Yale student, busy over his papers, "but actually they just aren't experienced enough to handle this sort of thing, and that's why I'm doing it myself now."

King himself kept apart for small meetings. Having abandoned the rented beach cottage, he was staying at the Lincolnville home of a registered nurse named Janie Jones, teasing her about why she and the other "high Negro Catholics" from the segregated parish of St. Benedict the Moor could not bring themselves to go to jail. With Bernard Lee sleeping on the couch, King shared the guest room with Ralph Abernathy, who occupied himself during daytime lulls by eating figs off a tree in the yard. In the afternoon, calling as one of the journalists who carried feelers back and forth across the racial divide, ABC correspondent Paul Good sat on the screened porch to discuss King's minimum truce condition of a biracial committee, which prominent white businessmen tentatively favored and Mayor Joseph Shelley adamantly opposed. When Good suggested that whites would be more inclined to accept biracial dialogue if Negroes agreed in advance to exclude movement activists—especially Hayling—King's disgust cut through his forbearance. "This is the old story we find every place," he said. "They never want to deal with the local man who began the movement, because invariably he is a true leader and a dynamic force in the community. What it really means is that they don't want to deal with anybody they can't control. We went through this in Birmingham with Fred Shuttlesworth."

That evening, Chaplain Will England told a cheering crowd at First Baptist that he had lost twenty pounds fasting in jail since his arrest the previous Thursday with King. From the pulpit, King walked a fine line between disengagement and commitment in St. Augustine. He prepared the audience for a settlement within a few days, saying his attention was required elsewhere, but he embraced their purpose. "Thank you very kindly my dear friends and fellow jail mates," he said. "For I do see some of my fellow jail mates here tonight." He told them their goal of a democratic St. Augustine was both theirs and universal, then preached on the tension between nobility and lonely submission. "Jesus has made it clear that he who is greatest among you shall be your servant," he declared. (Yes sir!) "And we have been servants to a great theory and a great idea. We have allowed the idea of nonviolence to work *through* us (Yes!), and to move out into the community and transform dark yesterdays into bright tomorrows. This is greatness. Greatness is found in the *power* of one soul. So with your soul force, you have done something for the community, and you have done something for the nation . . . that can serve as I have said as a purifying prelude for this hot, sweltering summer that we face ahead."

After the meeting, three hundred Negroes and seven whites marched behind Fred Shuttlesworth to the Slave Market and back.

In Washington, President Johnson buzzed an assistant to ask, "How is St. Augustine?" Lee White answered that "Governor Bryant said he was going to maintain law and order," that a settlement was possible, and that "at the moment, it seems to be in perfect control."

"Is King satisfied with our reply, and our talking to the governor?" asked Johnson. "His man [Wyatt Walker] I noticed is over...raising hell with Burke Marshall."

White explained that Walker was lobbying about unfulfilled promises of biracial negotiations allegedly made during Johnson's visit in 1963, which neither Marshall nor White knew about. Johnson then briefed White from memory, saying everything had been settled. The St. Augustine leaders "didn't agree to integrate the town, or to change a thing, or to sweeping reform," he told White. "They just agreed that they'd let Negroes come for the first time to the hotel to eat at the dinner I spoke to, and that they would talk to 'em about what their demands were."

"And both those things took place?" said White.

"And both those things took place," confirmed the President.

White said he was delighted to hear this, because King's people were trying to "push way beyond" the prior agreement.

IN AN OHIO AUDITORIUM that night, the first two hundred volunteers-in-training watched a CBS television documentary entitled *Mississippi and the Fifteenth Amendment.* For three days, the assembled volunteers and movement veterans from Mississippi had encountered each other awkwardly, with whites quoting James Baldwin and Negroes singing jail hymns with Fannie Lou Hamer. Bob Moses had welcomed the college students as instruments of national mobilization—"getting the country involved through yourselves"—but grizzled SNCC members eyed them warily as privileged waifs, perhaps too naive to survive Mississippi. Drills in nonviolence swerved between frozen timidity and hostile excess. Some volunteers were awestruck by the moral bondedness of the movement ("I met those SNCC people and my mouth fell open"); others felt excluded by cliquish veterans "who looked down on us for not having been through what they had." A few volunteers were shaken by their first sight of Rev. Edwin King's scarred, sunken cheek, but others seemed to view Mississippi as a kind of fantasy.

Tension rose as the Mississippi SNCC staff watched volunteers snicker at televised images of the obese Forrest County registrar Theron Lynd drawling on about contented Negroes. In spite of themselves, the students laughed also at the simplicity of rural Negroes who vowed to brave buckshot for the vote in order to get a street paved. Hollis Watkins could not bear it. Two years earlier in Hattiesburg, he had overcome his own fears to help the CBS crew shoot this film footage of the implacable Lynd, who remained a frustration to the U.S. Department of Justice and a tormentor to Negroes as intrepid as Vernon Dahmer. The rage of Watkins and other veterans in turn scalded the Northern volunteers. "Six of the staff members got up and walked out of the movie because it was so real to them while we laughed because it was so completely foreign to us," one of them wrote home. "... We were afraid the whole movement was going to fall apart...." Arguments spilled from confrontation to tears over what could and could not be helped, and how to protect each other in Mississippi across immense cultural gaps.

Far to the south, that same Tuesday night, an advance attack blurred the line between fear and understanding. In the woods outside the hamlet of Longdale, Mississippi, between Meridian and Philadelphia, ten stewards of Mount Zion AME Church finished their regular business meeting. As a point of decorum, the AME Methodists distinguished themselves from impatient Baptists by deferring nonspiritual matters—including dispersement of the visiting preacher's fee—from Sunday until a weekly accounting on Tuesday night. That done, the stewards locked the church and drove away as usual, but ran into roadblocks a hundred yards in both directions. At one end, perhaps because the stewards had their young children with them in the cars, armed Klan interrogators reluctantly accepted word that Mount Zion harbored no white plotters, but frightened answers only seemed to infuriate the ambushers at the other end. "Where are your guards?" they shouted, clinging to an assumption that something military was going on in preparation for the summer "invasion." Cries of liar turned into slaps and several beatings. One Klansman reached inside the cab of a pickup to break Georgia Rush's collarbone with the butt of a pistol, after others had dragged Rush's son from the driver's seat. Nearby, Beatrice Cole ran screaming, "Lord have mercy, don't let them kill my husband," around her car to a place in the road where a circle of men was stomping her prostrate husband, Roosevelt "Bud" Cole. She asked permission to pray and fell to the ground crying out the words of a Methodist hymn that came to her, "Father, I stretch my hands to Thee, I stretch my hands to Thee, no other help I know," until someone said to let him live and the Klansmen withdrew to torch Mount Zion Church with gasoline. Cole took her bleeding husband back to their farm with a broken jaw and spinal injuries, but did not dare take him to a hospital before daylight.

The attack on Mount Zion jolted those in Ohio with a message far stronger than any lecture. The volunteers knew or quickly learned that James Chaney and Mickey Schwerner, two CORE staff members then present at the Oxford training sessions, had asked Mount Zion to host a Freedom School, and that the tiny congregation had agreed to do so with trepidations and second thoughts. Merely for these intentions, it seemed, the hand-built church was destroyed. This news, coming only three days after the latest written appeal by Bob Moses,* spurred another COFO press release calling for federal protection and a flurry of orchestrated letters to Washington officials from volunteers and their families. Most of the pressure fell upon the President's exasperated civil rights aide, Lee White. "Although on the surface it is nearly incredible that those people who are voluntarily sticking their head into the lion's mouth would ask for somebody to come down and shoot the lion," he wrote President Johnson on June 17, "we now have a request for the parents group to meet with you and their insistence on Federal protection 'before a tragic incident takes place.'"

In the shock of the Wednesday morning news, James Lawson addressed the Ohio trainees on the nonviolent philosophy that had guided most of the student movements since the Nashville sit-ins of 1960. Stokely Carmichael, designated project director for the Delta, disputed him by attacking deliberate self-sacrifice as an unnatural philosophy. Dramatized suffering by Negroes was no longer novel to reporters, nor moving to a jaded public, Carmichael argued, though he supported nonprovocation policies such as barring guns from COFO locations.

Remarks by church lawyer Jack Pratt, Bayard Rustin, and others also precipitated conflict. When John Doar warned that the Justice Department would not be able to prevent or punish most crimes against volunteers, James Forman denounced the cowardice and treachery of the federal government. Doar sidestepped what was for him a painful distinction between political and legal limits on federal power. Enduring some jeers, he told Forman that he simply did not want to mislead civil rights workers by overpromising again, as after the Freedom Rides in 1961, and Bob Moses intervened to support Doar's candor. He urged volunteers not to think of Washington as omnipotent, nor as an enemy withholding some magic solution, and later expressed worry that no students had dropped out of training by Wednesday. Something about Moses reassured even those he pushed to confront danger. "He is more or less the Jesus of the whole project," one volunteer wrote home, "not because he asks to be, but because of everyone's reaction to him. (I forgot to say, he's a Negro.)"

By Friday, Moses told the first groups heading south that Mississippi, like race, could not be discovered in the abstract. Whether terrified by nightmares or giddy with invincibility, volunteers knew from the ardent attentions of reporters that they were sensors for a national exploration into Mississippi. One carload noted with amused bravado that a CBS crew had wired their Corvette for the drive to Mississippi to "record our pro-

---

* "We are asking that the Federal Government move before the fact this summer," Moses wrote the President on June 14. "I hope this is not asking too much of our country."

found thoughts as we went into battle...." On buses, press-savvy volunteers realized that *Look* magazine was sifting them "for the ideal naive Northern middle-class white girl," and that *Life* was focusing its coverage on Greenwood. Heading south, asking his parents to "keep your eyes open" for him on television, a Harvard student summarized the week of training: "The workshops were very helpful—getting us used to hearing nigger and white nigger without flinching and so forth. Also how to keep together when getting beaten so that they can't get you one at a time, and all of that jazz."

IN ST. AUGUSTINE, sixteen Reform rabbis and lay administrator Albert Vorspan converged upon First Baptist Church for the mass meeting on Wednesday night, June 17. Martin Luther King announced their entrance to an enthusiastic crowd, then invited Rabbi Israel "Sy" Dresner to speak from the pulpit. Dresner, as the only Reform volunteer with experience at such events, astonished his colleagues with call-and-response preaching that evoked a tumultuous response. Carried away, he retained his customary long-windedness beyond the endurance of several rabbis who, wilting from fatigue in the Florida heat, discreetly chanted *"genug"*—Yiddish for "enough already." They all followed Shuttlesworth and Andrew Young on a long march beyond the Slave Market, then dispersed for the night in Negro homes as King debated strategy with his staff. Hosea Williams suffered a ribbing when he refused for once to lead one of his own wild schemes to maintain public momentum at low cost, by trying to integrate a swimming pool. Williams admitted that he could not swim.

On Thursday, Fred Shuttlesworth and C. T. Vivian led the rabbis and some fifty supporters downtown to the Monson Motor Lodge, where owner James Brock blocked the restaurant door at 12:40 P.M. Normally a bookish and controlled businessman (who routinely showed reporters an office adding machine with his precise tabulation of integrationists arrested at Monson's, standing thus far at 239), Brock lost his temper when the rabbis knelt to pray over his refusal to serve their party. One by one, he shoved the rabbis toward arresting officers until 12:47 P.M., according to reporters and FBI observers, when shouted alarms sent the whole mass of spectators on the run to find two white civil rights workers holding room keys in the pool, saying that as registered motel guests they had a right to invite their five Negro friends to swim. While Florida State Police strained to hold back onlookers enraged by the sight of intermingled wet bodies, Brock poured two gallons of muriatic acid into the pool, screaming that he would burn them out. (This was a scare tactic, as the cleaning acid was relatively harmless.) "Hold me, baby, I'm scared," said a Negro female who dog-paddled beneath shouted threats to shoot, stone, or drown them. Finally, Officer Henry Billitz removed his shoes and jumped in fully clothed to haul them out. An AP photograph captured his leap in midair for the front pages of many newspapers, including the *Miami Herald* and the *New York Times.* By previous order of Governor Farris Bryant, state officers assumed custody of prisoners under the near-riot conditions, but an overwrought local deputy reached over and around a trooper to pummel one arrested swimmer most of the way from the pool to a State Police cruiser.

King watched the two-pronged demonstration of rabbis and swimmers from a waterfront park across the street. He and Brock were falling from opposite ends of a spinning log. At a press conference the previous day, Brock and State Senator Verle Pope had hinted vaguely at white concessions ("a study of the legitimate problems of this community by responsible, local, law abiding citizens") behind a screen of wounded victimization ("we find ourselves beset by outside forces"). King had responded positively, saying he hoped to move on soon to a voting project in Alabama—only to hear that a special grand jury sensed new weakness in him and was holding out for better terms. Stiffening, King had gone forward with Wednesday demonstrations. Now, the enraged Brock, feeling betrayed on both flanks for his moderation, drained and refilled his pool to purify it of integration. He posted guards and hoisted a Confederate flag over his motel.

Late that Thursday afternoon, a deputy sheriff served King with the grand jury's formal presentment: "...Racial harmony has existed in the past.... This Grand Jury now calls upon Dr. Martin Luther King and all others to demonstrate their good faith by removing their influences from this community for a period of 30 days." King promptly wrote a press response on the back of the legal papers, rejecting "not only an impractical request, but an immoral one. It is asking the Negro community to give all, and the white community to give nothing." He reversed the order of the grand jury's minimum terms with an offer to leave St. Augustine for thirty days if a biracial committee were established first.

In convention that evening at the Ambassador Hotel in Atlantic City, the president of the Central Conference of American Rabbis announced the imprisonment of the volunteer delegation to St. Augustine and extended "our prayers and best wishes and our sense of gratitude." At the St. Johns County jail, parched and miserable after sun-drenched hours in the outdoor "chicken coop," the prisoners refused an order to come inside to segregated cells. While guards fetched Sheriff Davis, the rabbis formed a protective circle around Shuttlesworth and Vivian, vowing to stand on their constitutional right to remain together with the Negro clergy. Shuttlesworth laughed, saying they did not understand jails, but the rabbis held firm through booming threats and pointed guns until Sheriff Davis had a Negro teenager hauled from the cell block and shocked in front of them with a cattle prod, causing her to scream and shrivel to the floor like an autumn leaf. Then they parted to let the Negro prisoners separate, and marveled when Shuttlesworth veered toward Sheriff Davis to say, "I love you, brother."

The rabbis talked until dawn about what had brought them from eight different states to such a place. They told of supportive or puzzled congregations, or of blunt warnings from synagogue boards not to cause scandal or neglect their regular duties. Some said they were stung that local Jews avoided them; others confessed a creeping taste for sanctimony among the righteous few. One by one, with Rabbi Eugene Borowitz taking notes on the back of a leaflet about the Ku Klux Klan, each man spoke, and then they composed a lengthy common testament: "... We shall not forget the people with whom we drove, prayed, marched, slept, ate, demonstrated and were arrested. How little we know of these people and their struggle.... How many a Torah reading, Passover celebration, prayer book text and sermonic effort has come to mind in these hours.... These words were first written at 3:00 a.m. in the sweltering heat of a sleepless night, by the light of the one naked bulb hanging in the corridor outside our small cell." On Friday, most of the rabbis refused their first jail food—small jars of Gerber's Baby Food merrily offered as a "special meal"—and bailed out to fly home for the Sabbath.

FOR THE MOST PART, movement news trailed on the back pages along with notice that Nelson Mandela and six other black leaders had received life sentences on June 12 for treason against apartheid in South Africa, and were shipped off to lime pits on Robben Island. However, headlines did trumpet stories with a movement subtext. Governor William Scranton of Pennsylvania "stunned the nation" by announcing a "stop-Goldwater" candidacy barely a month before the Republican convention. On Monday, June 15, in a decision the *New York Times* called as significant as the *Brown* cases on school segregation, the U.S. Supreme Court required states to apportion their legislative districts to equalize the weight of each citizen's vote, undercutting the preserved advantage of rural areas. On Tuesday, Southerners kept the Senate in session past midnight for a record thirty-four roll call votes on futile amendments to the civil rights bill, with speeches of exhausted defiance that a team of congressional historians likened to "death scene arias of an interminable opera...."

On Wednesday, Senator Goldwater flew to a farm outside Gettysburg to seek the blessing of Dwight Eisenhower for his own vote on the bill. Afterward, fuming that Eisenhower gave him no better than a noncommittal response, the candidate returned to find his Senate office besieged by politicians awaiting the result, including the young chairmen of fledgling Republican parties in Mississippi and Alabama. Goldwater, on the counsel of his legal advisers,* stressed constitutional rather than moral or political arguments in his catalytic announcement on the Senate floor, opposing the civil rights bill as a "threat to the very essence of our basic system" and a "usurpation of such power... which 50 sovereign states have reserved for themselves." While renouncing segregation personally, he voted with five other Republicans and twenty-one Democrats against the decisive majority of seventy-three fellow senators on Friday, June 19—exactly one year after President Kennedy sent his original version of an omnibus civil rights bill to Congress.

J. Edgar Hoover reacted to the Senate vote with bitter foreboding, seasoned by bureaucratic caution. In strictest secrecy, he retrieved copies of FBI surveillance photographs showing Martin Luther King together with Stanley Levison, on the remote chance that a leak against King and the bill might become worth exposing the Bureau's hand. Hoover disallowed—"because of the occupations of the individuals using the office"—a detailed plan to bug Harry Wachtel's law office when King met there with his New York advisers on June 22, but he encouraged vigilant surveillance by safer methods. Teams of New York agents followed Clarence Jones in the hope of observing scandalous political activity, while the Director himself supervised an overhaul of selected files at headquarters. Finding the boilerplate description of Bayard Rustin too tame, he called for revision based on "the most pertinent and adverse information concerning him from a subversive standpoint." Hoover decreed that allegations be updated if they sounded too old, and that "the term 'noncommunist' not be used."

President Johnson declared that the civil rights bill "goes further to invest the rights of man with the protection of law than any legislation in this century." He hailed the Senate vote before a San Francisco crowd of thirty thousand, and continued triumphant motorcades through Los Angeles on Saturday, pausing long enough to make calls about two senators, Edward Kennedy and Birch Bayh, whose private plane had crashed after adjournment Friday night, killing the pilot.†

Johnson's polls showed him favored to become the first Democrat to carry California since Truman in 1948, and his buoyant speeches against poverty and racial injustice ("I have come to California to ask you to throw off your doubts about America") attracted what one reporter called "wealthy industrialists, ranchers, and other generally conservative types not recently to be found at California Democratic Party dinners." His

---

* William Rehnquist, Phoenix attorney and future Chief Justice, and Robert Bork, Yale law professor and future Supreme Court nominee.

† "Well, he's got a lot of broken bones," Robert Kennedy told the President of his severely injured brother, "and his back is in bad shape, but he's not paralyzed...."

evening fund-raiser at the Ambassador Hotel overflowed with large donors until it displaced the long-scheduled bar mitzvah party of young Lyle Peskin from the Embassy Room. Hotel officials hastily moved the Peskins to a substitute location, and the President himself dropped by after midnight to make amends.

The President already had determined his strategy for the last legislative mile on civil rights. To avoid revisiting the quicksand of the Senate, he resolved to have the House accept the Senate-passed version intact, first by bowling over Howard Smith of the House Rules Committee to forestall the slightest amendment. Johnson immediately called House Republican Leader Charles Halleck to push for assistance. "Y'all want civil rights as much as we do," he said. "I believe it's a nonpartisan bill. I don't think it's a Johnson bill."

"No, no, no, we're not gonna get a goddamn thing," sputtered Halleck, who protested that Johnson was using popular sentiment to swindle Republicans. "I don't know what the hell the Senate's put in there," he said. "That means we ought to kind of take a little look at it."

"Well, maybe you ought to," said the President. Pretending simply to be helpful, he asked, "Well, you wouldn't want to go to your convention without a civil rights bill, would you?"

"... Now wait just a minute," said Halleck. "If I had my way, I'd let you folks be fussin' with that goddamn thing before *your* convention instead of ours."

When Johnson said he would like to have a rule permitting a vote on his poverty bill, too, before the House recessed for the Republican convention, Halleck sputtered again. "No, no," he said. "Now wait a minute. I'll give you a rule in due time, but don't press me."

"I'm not pressing you," Johnson innocently replied.

"Goddamn it, Mr. President," shouted Halleck.

"I'm not pressing you," said the President, who opined over chuckles that he was just an "old Senate hand" and "an old House hand," and an "old Halleck man," too.

"All right, you're a Halleck man," groused Halleck.

"Give me a little rule up there in the morning...," said Johnson, still chuckling.

"Mr. President, Jesus Christ," said Halleck.

"I'll call you this week," said Johnson.

From California, Johnson urged Roy Wilkins and Whitney Young to channel the energy of Senate celebration right back into the House. Looking ahead, he asked for suggestions on federal appointments and ideas about how to keep the South calm once the bill was signed. "I'm just afraid of what's gonna happen this summer, like [what] I saw yesterday at St. Augustine," he told Wilkins Friday. He said his goal was compliance, not enforcement. "If they'll observe the law," he said, "then we won't have to take pistols and enforce it."

The President did not call Martin Luther King, with whom he lacked the comfortable rapport of a parliamentary commander, anyway, in part because of the controversy in St. Augustine. With the rabbis departing there, the two sides rallied to opposite moods over the Senate vote Friday —King praising a "dawning of new hope" while J. B. Stoner predicted race war to a thousand whites at the Slave Market, saying "niggers want to integrate because they want our white women."

ON SATURDAY AFTERNOON, the St. Augustine movement tried a new tactic designed to keep up demonstrations while avoiding both the tinderbox of the Slave Market and the costly burdens of jail. Thirty Negroes and four white supporters waded into the Atlantic Ocean off a beach that tradition restricted for whites. From a circle of onlookers, enraged by word that officials could not make trespass arrests on public property, lone vigilantes broke ranks to assault unresisting waders. Police first arrested attackers and victims in pairs, which attracted swarms of segregationists intent upon getting in their licks before police cleared away the Negroes. Dorothy Cotton, SCLC's deputy director of citizenship classes, was among those slugged to their knees in the surf, forcing State Police officers to intervene with nightsticks to drive off attackers from the wounded. This rescue struck the segregationists as betrayal, curdling their resentment against the police themselves. "I can't understand why any white citizen would want to protect niggers against white people," explained Hoss Manucy, who had summoned and deployed most of the posse over his gun club's two-way radio network.

The fearful prospect of open conflict between police and white civilians caused Governor Farris Bryant to proclaim within hours an executive order suppressing all nighttime assembly in St. Augustine. This edict further ensnarled white leaders in conflict. U.S. District Judge Bryan Simpson summoned the governor of Florida to show cause why he should not be jailed for contempt of Simpson's June 9 court order in the Andrew Young case, which protected the right to demonstrate.

Passing through St. Augustine the next morning, a Florida motorist came upon a Sunday scene of children in miniature Klan robes on the fringe of a public rally, repeating exhortations about firing every coon and baboon in town. "We saw niggers coming out of the Episcopal church this morning," J. B. Stoner called out over his bullhorn. "The preacher there has gone against his congregation in allowing niggers to attend services." The visitor wrote down his impressions of "a charged atmosphere such as I had never felt before." Lines of black and white marchers passed each other grimly downtown, as though observing a fragile cease-fire in the midst of motorcycles and police vehicles bristling with hardware.

By then Martin Luther King was entering Chicago's Soldier Field in the back of an open-air limousine. He drew a standing ovation from an interracial turnout that fell below expectations, owing to persistent rain, but still generated crowd estimates running upward from 55,000. After James Farmer and James Forman, King delivered a keynote address on the civil rights bill as "a step in a thousand-mile journey." He challenged Negroes to "make full and constructive use of the freedom we now possess," in order to compete with whites after more than three centuries of oppression, and he welcomed the interracial alliance especially to fight the corrosion of long-range unemployment. Automation, said King, was eliminating 45,000 jobs per week.

The Soldier Field rally was predominantly a local event, scarcely noticed outside Chicago on June 21—a Sunday when Jim Bunning of the Philadelphia Phillies, father of seven, pitched the eighth perfect game in major league history against an expansion team called the Mets in New York, and when dictator "Papa Doc" Duvalier of Haiti proclaimed himself President for Life. Even so, the clamoring Chicago press conferences highlighted for King the paradoxical contrasts of his communication. Just off a flight from St. Augustine, where fear prevented any white leader from deigning to talk with him even on the telephone,* he watched tens of thousands at the Chicago rally sign pledges to work personally toward seven major goals of human rights. Desperate for help in Florida, King awakened his former professor Harold DeWolf well after midnight that weekend with reminders of his standing offer to volunteer in crisis. On King's assurance that modest theological hides might somehow make a difference, DeWolf recruited a carload of Boston professors for the thousand-mile drive to St. Augustine.

---

* Through a buffer of two subordinates, Archbishop Joseph Hurley had just turned aside King's latest entreaty for mediation on grounds that the local diocese was fully engaged already: "The Catholic church in Saint Augustine has used its influence consistently to achieve equal justice under law.... We have taught the lesson of justice and fraternity not only in words but also by example."

26

Bogue Chitto Swamp

AT THE COFO CENTER in Meridian, Mississippi, Louise Hermey of Drew University followed the first rule of her communications training on her first day as a summer volunteer: she called the Jackson COFO headquarters to report that an expedition had failed to return by the appointed check-in time of four o'clock Sunday afternoon. Advised to wait an hour in case of unexpected delay, she called back at five and was told to activate the search procedure. Hermey steeled herself to make inquiries at the local jails from the master phone list, and called places where the group might have turned up safely. Movement veteran Sam Block, who turned up instead, volunteered to check the city jail. About ten o'clock, Hermey called Mary King in the Atlanta SNCC office.

Fellow volunteer Edna Perkins, a nineteen-year-old student at Bryn Mawr College, sat down near Hermey's phone desk to write her first letter home, trying to explain why "we're all sitting here in the office being quietly nervous as hell": "This morning Mickey, who's the project director, and Chaney, a local staff member, and Andy, who's a volunteer, all went out to one of the rougher rural counties to see about a church that was burned down a few days ago.... No word from them of any kind. We've had people out looking for them and they haven't found anything.... They said that Meridian was an easy town." The new community center above Fiedler's pharmacy was nestled within a cluster of businesses—the E. F. Young Hotel, hair care and insurance companies, Beal's Cafe—that extended toward the heart of white downtown, a rare and wispy beacon of progress for all of Negro Mississippi. Confidence collapsed as the hours wore on. Hoodlums menaced a mixed group that went out for coffee, and young Negro boys outside wrote down the license numbers of slowly passing cars. "Still no word from the missing people," wrote Perkins. "It must be 11 by now.... Nothing to do but play pingpong or read and wait for the phone to ring. I've been reading *All Quiet on the Western Front...*."

In Atlanta, Mary King "felt a prickly sensation," knowing that most of the movement people experienced enough to understand a delay of seven hours were still in Ohio for the training sessions. She called the Mississippi jails, posing as a reporter from the *Atlanta Constitution.* She called the FBI office in New Orleans—there were none in Mississippi—and helped the Jackson and Meridian COFO offices track down the few resident FBI agents posted in nearby Mississippi towns. By then Hermey and the others had located a Justice Department lawyer passing through Meridian on assignment. After midnight, desperate to find someone who appreciated why the alarm could not wait until morning, Mary King called John Doar at home in Washington. With a cringe, she awakened the parents of volunteer Andrew Goodman in New York and notified Mickey Schwerner's wife in Ohio. Only yesterday, when Rita Schwerner stayed behind there to help with the second week's training, her husband, Mickey, had made the long drive to Meridian in a station wagon with James Chaney and six volunteers, including Louise Hermey, Edna Perkins, and Goodman.

Calls spread through emergency networks before dawn—from Mary King to *New York Times* reporter Claude Sitton in Jackson after 2:00 A.M.; to John Doar again at three o'clock and again at six; to hospitals and highway patrol offices; at three o'clock to CORE chairman James Farmer, sleeping at home after the Soldier Field rally, and from Farmer to contacts ranging from the FBI's Deke DeLoach to comedian Dick Gregory; to the Schwerner parents and to a Mississippi preacher who was comforting James Chaney's mother, Fannie Lee; from the Goodmans to lawyers and the homes of New York senators and representatives; at first light to the county jails once more.

At Peabody Hall in Ohio, on the campus of the Western College for Women, Bob Moses greeted three hundred new volunteers on Monday morning with a meditative speech. "We've had discussions all winter about race hatred," he said. "There is an analogy to *The Plague,* by Camus. The country isn't willing yet to admit it has the plague, but it pervades the whole society." Staff people soon interrupted to huddle with him, after which Moses stared for some time at his feet. "Yesterday morning, three of our people left Meridian, Mississippi to investigate a church bombing in Neshoba County," he announced. "They haven't come back, and we haven't had any word from them."

Rita Schwerner appeared on the stage to organize a telegram campaign to members of Congress. She erased a map of Mississippi from the blackboard to write in large letters the names of her young husband and the two other missing workers. The fresh trainees could tell something was terribly amiss beneath the veneer of exaggerated composure. "It suddenly became clear that she, Moses, and others on the staff had been up all the night before," wrote one volunteer. During the scramble to write telegrams, Moses slipped out of the auditorium to sit alone on a small porch outside the college cafeteria. What had prompted his disclosure to the trainees was a report from Jackson that the jailer in Neshoba County now acknowledged having the three missing workers in cells there until sometime the previous evening. Moses drifted into solitary apprehension, not wanting to disclose his interpretation to Rita Schwerner. He sat on the porch for nearly six hours. Those who knew him best approached tentatively with hugs of consolation. "You are not responsible for this," Victoria Gray whispered.

Theologian Vincent Harding and Jesse Morris of SNCC quietly urged the staff to carry on with volunteer training, despite frantic calls from parents who wanted their sons and daughters sent home. From Mississippi, Edwin King passed along word from one white sympathizer in Neshoba County, an ostracized Methodist like himself, that Sheriff Lawrence Rainey was rumored to have beaten the three civil rights workers while they were under his custody. Shortly before noon, James Farmer got through to President Johnson's assistant Lee White with a request for help. Someone else alerted the patrician socialist Norman Thomas, who at 12:17 dispatched a terse emergency wire from New York to Al Lowenstein in Europe: "Developments COFO seem to some parents and me to make your return imperative since you recruited students."

Meanwhile, a civic-minded local woman named Florence Mars stopped by to ask the editor of the *Neshoba Democrat* if it could be true that Klansmen had burned the nearby Mount Zion AME Church the previous Tuesday night, as reported in her out-of-state newspaper. The editor replied that he was withholding the story as untrustworthy, because he was finding Negro members who were so deeply troubled by the idea of civil rights work at Mount Zion that they might have destroyed their own church in protest. Crazy things were happening, he told the skeptical Mars, informing her of the fresh kidnapping rumors that could be no more than a fund-raising hoax.

By mid-afternoon, the first two national reporters arrived at the Neshoba County jail, just after the local FBI agent finished initial interviews there and set out for Longdale to verify from Beatrice Cole and other Mount Zion victims that Mickey Schwerner indeed had tried to visit them the day before. Sheriff Rainey and his deputy, Cecil Price, repeated for the reporters their story that they had held the three civil rights workers for six hours after a speeding arrest and then released them safely about ten-thirty. "If they're missing," said Rainey, "they just hid somewhere trying to get a lot of publicity out of it, I figure."

A menacing crowd accosted the journalists in the courthouse rotunda outside the sheriff's office, led by an insurance executive who bluntly promised violence against the lying, mongrelized Northern press. Claude Sitton of the *New York Times* managed to duck into the Turner Furniture Store across the street. Introducing himself and his companion, Karl Fleming of *Newsweek,* Sitton begged the proprietor to explain to the men threatening to kill them outside that they were not agitators but Southerners themselves, just doing their jobs. He said his managing editor in New York had advised him to stop in the family furniture store if he ever got in trouble, which he definitely was now.

The uncle of Turner Catledge, managing editor of the *New York Times,* studied Sitton and the angry noises from the sidewalk. "I'll tell you what," he said. "If that mob gets you and Mr. Fleming down in the street and is kicking the hell out of you, I wouldn't participate in that. On the other hand, I wouldn't lift one damn finger to help you." He urged Sitton to leave town as the crowd instructed.

In Washington, John Doar went to the White House that afternoon as one of four chosen recipients of the President's Award for Distinguished Civilian Service. After a ceremonial handshake and a word of praise from President Johnson—who hailed his "basic contribution to our democracy as a vigorous champion of equal voting rights," and did not fail to point out that he was a Republican—Doar returned to the barrage of Mississippi phone calls at the Justice Department. At 5:20, he informed Mary King in Atlanta that the Mississippi Highway Patrol had put out an all-points alert, then reviewed with Burke Marshall the case for doing more. Although there was as yet no direct evidence of any federal crime, and although the tangible hostility of Neshoba County could not be the basis of federal policy any more than Sheriff Rainey's nasty language and bulging chaw of tobacco, they could cite objective reports of recent Klan violence at Mount Zion. Doar vouched for the meticulous training of the civil rights workers as an indication that they would not willingly remain out of touch. At 5:48 P.M., Marshall reached Robert Kennedy at a hospital in Massachusetts, where his brother Edward was under care for his broken back, and at 6:20 the Justice Department announced Kennedy's order for a full federal kidnap investigation under the 1936 "Lindbergh Law." FBI headquarters sent New Orleans agents overnight into Neshoba County.

Off a flight from St. Augustine, ABC correspondent Paul Good walked into rumored hard news that superseded his assigned general feature on the arrival of summer volunteers. Late into the night, his proposal to divert a film crew into Neshoba County ran into heated opposition from network producers who argued that missing people could not be filmed for television. He raced with his crew the next day across Mississippi to Meridian, up to the Neshoba County jail, and out to the ruins of Mount Zion AME, where he filmed his report near a gravestone that read, "Just Sleaping."

CLAUDE SITTON's front-page story—"3 in Rights Drive Reported Missing"—appeared in the *Times* on Tuesday, June 23. A delegation of New York representatives escorted the Goodman parents, Carolyn and Robert, and Nathan Schwerner, father of Mickey, to press Burke Marshall, Nicholas Katzenbach, and Robert Kennedy for an expanded investigation, then moved on to appointments on Capitol Hill. President Joachim Prinz of the American Jewish Congress urged President Johnson to assume personal command of the search; others pushed for spotter planes and Navy helicopters.

Johnson stuck to his breakneck schedule—a congressional breakfast on legislation, a political meeting with the governor of Nevada, a speech on public safety, an audience for the visiting Prime Minister of Turkey, a ceremony transferring Army land to New Jersey, quick photographs, a recording session for USIA about Denmark, and the latest round of Vietnam huddles so intense that Johnson shouted out a command to a secretary—"Tell [McGeorge] Bundy to come on in. I'm going to the bathroom, but come on in anyway." Late Tuesday morning, Johnson told an impromptu press conference that he was sending General Maxwell Taylor, Chairman of the Joint Chiefs of Staff, to replace Ambassador Lodge in South Vietnam. Signaling military resolve with such an illustrious choice, he refused to guess whether Lodge was coming home to run against him. To a question about "those three kids that disappeared in Mississippi," Johnson replied that FBI searchers "have substantially augmented their personnel in the last few hours," but that he had heard no search reports since breakfast.

Attorney General Kennedy, informed that President Johnson was filming a statement on Vietnam, left word in mid-afternoon that the President might want to issue a statement of personal sympathy for the families ("I think it's the human equation that's damn important for everything"), and recommended presidential calls to put pressure on Mississippi investigators. Johnson tried to return the call twenty minutes later, when Kennedy had departed to film an announcement that he would not run for a New York Senate seat in the fall, and promptly reached Katzenbach and Marshall instead. Both supported Kennedy's impression of genuine crisis, and Katzenbach guessed it was "probably" a Klan murder.

"How old are these kids?" asked Johnson.

"Twenty and twenty-four and twenty-two," replied Katzenbach. He and Marshall suggested that Johnson not see the families, which would set a precedent for presidential audiences in missing persons cases, but they supported the idea of discreet pressure on Mississippi. Anything public in a civil rights case, they warned, would make it politically ruinous for state officials to cooperate.

Within minutes, the President was interrupting his own warm-up phone chatter about how much a dry Texas rancher envied the ample rainfall on Senator James Eastland's Delta plantation. "Jim, we got three kids missing down there," he said. "What can I do about it?" Eastland was ready with several reasons "why I don't think there's a damn thing to it," beginning with local geography. He said the alleged disappearance took place in Neshoba County "right next to John Stennis's home county," where there was no Klan chapter nor even a Citizens Council. "There's no organized white man in that area," said Eastland, "so that's why I think it's a publicity stunt." While expressions of White House concern were unnecessary, he conceded that they could not hurt and eventually offered to pass along encouragement to Governor Paul Johnson.

The President pounced. "You just do that," he said, "and I'll say I've communicated with the proper people."

News from Mississippi swamp scavengers intervened before Eastland could relay the governor's reply. Hours earlier, local FBI agent John Proctor had roared at high speeds over the thirty-eight miles from Meridian to the Choctaw Reservation outside Philadelphia to hear what the superintendent would not say over the telephone: Indians had come upon a smoldering Ford Fairlane in a thicket about eighty feet off the highway, just past the bridge over Bogue Chitto Creek, and they admitted stealing the hubcaps if that was important. As soon as Proctor rounded up agents to find the burned-out hulk, and saw that its license tag matched the CORE-owned station wagon driven by Mickey Schwerner, he drove to the nearest farmhouse, introduced himself as an insurance salesman, asked to borrow a telephone to avoid being overheard on police radio, and sent a coded message through New Orleans to FBI headquarters: car found, no bodies. Obeying orders to deliver updates every fifteen minutes, Proctor was returning from his second or third trip to the farmhouse, his insurance ruse wearing thin, when he was astonished to see FBI Major Case Inspector Joseph Sullivan supervising the grid search of the surrounding Bogue Chitto Swamp.

Since completing his railroad sabotage cases in St. Augustine that spring, Sullivan had reviewed the stalled church-bomb murder investigation in Birmingham and happened to be in the Memphis FBI office the previous night to overhear the mobilizing orders to Mississippi. By rank and reputation, the FBI agents on the scene instantly deferred to the sphinx-like Sullivan—bald, pin-striped, and imposing—when Sheriff Rainey and Deputy Price pulled up with a fleet of Mississippi sirens. Sullivan blocked them on the swamp path, denying access to the car until FBI technicians could secure evidence. After a standoff in which the formidable Rainey first hotly denied that any federal agent could keep him from a crime scene in his own jurisdiction, the state forces withdrew, and Sullivan muttered his trademark phrase about not being there to make anybody's hit parade.

FBI Director Hoover insisted that he speak with the President at 4:05 P.M., six minutes after Johnson's call to Senator Eastland. "I wanted you to know that we have found the car," he announced, adding that "we can't tell whether anybody's in there in view of the intense heat." Hoover regretted his dramatic, precautionary hedge about the bodies as soon as the President questioned him intently about why agents could not get close enough to look in the windows for telltale signs of burned bones or belt buckles. "You mean the car is still burning?" asked Johnson. In five more phone calls over the next four hours, Hoover introduced new exaggerations—"the entire inside of the car is melted into molten metal"—behind an adjusted, "offhand presumption" that the car was empty.

Senator Eastland called back in the midst of these updates to report that Governor Johnson wanted the President to send an impartial observer to examine evidence of civil rights fraud. Mississippi investigators had established that the COFO people had reported the three boys missing *in advance*, said Eastland, and the governor "expects 'em to turn up... claiming that somebody has whipped 'em, when he doesn't believe a word of it."

Johnson cagily heard him out. "Okay, now here's the problem, Jim," he said. "Hoover just called me one minute ago...." Senator Eastland groaned to hear of the burned car, but quickly recovered his aplomb. "The governor says if you'll send some impartial man down here," he emphasized, "that you'll get the surprise of your life.... There's no violence, no friction of any kind."

Within an hour, Johnson had the Goodmans and Nathan Schwerner brought from Capitol Hill to Lee White's office and then into the Oval Office, where he informed them of the ominous discovery.* He called Defense Secretary McNamara in their presence, so they could hear his order that helicopters, Navy divers—"every facility of the department"—be made available to search for the missing sons. Word of these commitments was posted in the Jackson COFO headquarters within thirty minutes of the delegation's emotional departure from the White House. Bob Moses turned on a cafeteria microphone during supper in Ohio. "The car has been found outside Philadelphia," he announced starkly. "It's been badly burned. There is no news of the three boys."

Well into Tuesday night, Johnson conferred at the White House

---

* While waiting for the parents, the President turned to his closest aide, Walter Jenkins. "You better comb your hair, Walter," he said. "Looks like you been sleepin' on it. Run in my office right quick there. Put some water on it. You're worse than George Reedy these days."

with Robert Kennedy, Nicholas Katzenbach, and Burke Marshall on how, assuming the worst, to keep this gruesome triple murder from going unsolved, like the Birmingham church bombing, or from multiplying into similar crimes over the summer. Seeing little hope for initiative by Mississippi authorities, they discussed how to maneuver the FBI into the only state where Director Hoover steadfastly refused to open a full-fledged FBI office. Kennedy reviewed his exasperation that Hoover managed to fulfill the letter of every assignment and yet do only what he wanted, and Katzenbach remarked that Hoover seemed to respond at times to flattery. Both Kennedy and Marshall observed that Hoover liked spy intrigue more than law enforcement, which he seemed to regard as drudgery.

President Johnson summarized the problem as a delicate manipulation of three distinct sovereignties: Mississippi, the United States, and his old friend J. Edgar Hoover. Perceiving a need for flattery with a sting, he fixed upon the opening for an "impartial observer," reasoning that Governor Johnson could not now withdraw his invitation, and he proposed to send the retired CIA director Allen Dulles. The idea at first seemed silly to the Justice Department officials, but Johnson explained how much Hoover hated Dulles, having wanted to be CIA director himself, and told tales about Hoover's sputtering mortification that Dulles already sat on the Warren Commission, positioned to protect the CIA at the expense of his beloved FBI. Dulles was the perfect motivational tool for the mission, reasoned the President, because Hoover would not passively endure hints of criticism or competition from his rival.

Johnson initiated his plan with a swift display of semi-exhibitionist phone work. "We got the ox in a ditch, and we need a little help," he told Dulles, and talked him into an emergency assignment as presidential emissary, leaving the next day. He sealed the mission by explaining it to Hoover as Governor Johnson's idea, and to Governor Johnson as a mild, cooperative response. Burke Marshall, meanwhile, left to instruct John Doar to collect overnight reading for Dulles on the Mississippi Klan. Lady Bird Johnson patiently received her husband for supper after eleven o'clock, and the departing Justice Department officials, while variously uncomfortable with Johnson by background and taste, could not help marveling upon their first exposure to his style—an adroit, relentlessly unabashed application of raw personal chemistry to politics.

PHOTOGRAPHS OF the charred station wagon circled the globe before a frantic Wednesday morning when Robert Kennedy postponed a scheduled journey to Poland, packed off John Doar and Burke Marshall as last-minute escorts for Allen Dulles to Mississippi, then received Myrlie Evers on the first anniversary of her husband's burial in Washington. Kennedy and Evers emerged with Roy Wilkins to behold a dignified march of nearly two thousand NAACP convention delegates outside the Justice Department.

Kennedy welcomed placards of prayer and outrage over Mississippi, eliciting cries of amazement that the Attorney General himself seemed to be joining a demonstration to spur federal resolve.

Students threw up less congenial picket lines at other federal buildings—more than a hundred people in Boston and nearly seven hundred in New York, where a card was delivered in the morning mail to the stricken Goodman apartment, postmarked Sunday and written in the hand of the missing Andrew: "I have arrived safely in Meridian, Mississippi. This is a wonderful town and the weather is fine."

In Chicago, officers around the U.S. Attorney's office used a tarpaulin to screen from photographers an all-day sit-in that led finally to the arrest of SNCC's Bernard Lafayette, Charles McDew, Curtis Hayes, and Marion Barry.

In Ohio, church leader Robert Spike successfully implored Bob Moses to discourage an incipient SNCC demonstration in Washington, warning that some rattled nerves there already were inclined to interpret the entire summer project as a plot to embarrass the Johnson administration. As an alternative, Moses took a delegation of volunteers immediately to the capital for private meetings to conserve a tide of support against an undertow of doubt. To refute worries that SNCC might have created Klan terror, they recited a long list of persecutions that predated the first thought of the summer project, and they parried criticism that faulted their motives as symbiotic to the Klan's. ("It is a dreadful thing to say, but it needs saying," wrote Joseph Alsop. "The organizers who sent these young people into Mississippi must have wanted, even hoped for, martyrs ... [which] is not exactly admirable either.")

Moses then joined the converging rush to Mississippi behind SNCC chairman John Lewis of Atlanta and Dick Gregory of Chicago, who followed James Farmer of New York in a caravan of movement cars from Meridian past a roadblock at the Neshoba County line and on to an unproductive interview with Sheriff Rainey in Philadelphia. More than fifty state troopers pushed milling crowds off the courthouse square to stare from store windows at the temerity of such Negroes.

Journalists covered the dramatic arrival of Allen Dulles in Jackson late that Wednesday, while Rita Schwerner, slight and intense, slipped from Ohio into the E. F. Young Hotel in Meridian. She issued a public statement, written on airline stationery: "Why can't the FBI do something about cases of violence against voter registration workers...." At the Meridian airport, FBI Inspector Sullivan absorbed what for him was a major surprise when Assistant FBI Director Alex Rosen emerged from a government jet among the evidence technicians he had summoned from Washington. Known somewhat derisively within the FBI as "Hoover's token Jew," a consummate bureaucrat said to have confined himself within headquarters for many years, Rosen explained that only hours ago, when Director Hoover tried to assure President Johnson that he had a top FBI official supervising the Mississippi search from Washington, Johnson had barked, "Send him down there, too!" Rosen said he knew better than to pull rank in a field investigation, being out of his element, and he further mollified Sullivan with sage internal advice: always hold back at least one juicy detail from the daily flow of reports to headquarters, so as not to be caught empty-handed when Hoover demanded something extra.

In Washington, President Johnson called the FBI Director late Wednesday about reports that Hoover's man Deke DeLoach was upset over the Dulles mission. When Hoover mentioned press rumors that Dulles would "take over the investigation" in Mississippi, Johnson declared repeatedly that Dulles "wasn't going to spy or be an investigator of any kind," and he launched a soothing monologue that reduced Hoover to grunts of assent. "Now I felt like if the governor asked me to send an impartial observer, and I didn't send it," said Johnson, "I'd be in bad shape later on if I had to do something."

"Certainly would," said Hoover.

"...I haven't got a better friend in this government than you," said the President. "...Ain't nobody gonna take our thirty-year friendship and mess it up one bit....God bless you."

On Thursday in Jackson, Dulles blandly told reporters that his visit had nothing to do with the Neshoba County investigation, which was "in the very able hands of authorities here." He received the private entreaties of Bob Moses and other civil rights leaders. He talked separately with Governor Johnson about how FBI Director Hoover might help isolate bad elements within the Klan, and nodded politely at intelligence briefings on Communist infiltration of the civil rights movement. Speaking as one spy to another, leaders of the Mississippi Sovereignty Commission told Dulles that the missing civil rights workers were still being sighted here and there, most reliably in Alabama. By their analysis, the burned-out car had been left suspiciously near the edge of Bogue Chitto Swamp, as though intended to be found quickly, and there was something odd about the multitude of carefully placed phone calls out of COFO since Sunday—something paranoid or worse, consistent with a reverse conspiracy.

Dulles left Jackson before the huge Thursday night campaign rally at which George Wallace denounced both national parties and "the manipulations of a soulless state." Above the hearty cheers of ten thousand supporters, Governor Johnson seconded Wallace's proclamation that the South's 112 electoral votes were the fulcrum of national power, shouting, "It's time the white people of our various states started bloc voting!"

In Ohio, Bayard Rustin met with long silences as he dissected the psychology of nonviolence for the second-week volunteers. They may not be able to say so, he argued, but their whole purpose in Mississippi was to love their enemies in the special sense of bearing witness to a redeeming, common nature with the most bestial Klansman and with Senator James Eastland, the most callous defender of segregation—"to take power from those who misuse it, at which point they can become human, too." Many of the trainees watched the national news after Rustin's lecture. "Then it happened...," one wrote home of a special report on CBS television. "...Walter Cronkite told how the whole country was watching Mississippi." James Forman and other familiar speakers from the Ohio training sessions appeared on the screen along with Senator Eastland himself, who declared that Negroes were perfectly free to vote. News film showed U.S. sailors, mindful of swamp snakes, poking through Bogue Chitto for the three missing workers on orders of President Johnson, and when the audio portion took up the movement anthem "We Shall Overcome," the volunteers in Ohio joined hands to sing along with the broadcast. "Stunned, I walked out alone into the night," wrote the correspondent. "Life was beautiful. It was perfect. These people were me, and I was them."

Against the void of the disappearance, the most ordinary news from Mississippi seemed charged to the trainees in Ohio. Detailed reports filtered north of baths in backyard tubs using water heated over a fire, of heart-stopping trips to mail letters in town under the heavy gaze of white eyes, and of vivid sensory overload where "you feel the heat, breathe the dust, smell the outhouses, hear the kids and the chickens." Already there were debates about whether the white volunteers should patronize segregated restaurants, and a daily ration of sketchy "incident" reports shaped the middle ground of expectation for the second wave. On Thursday morning, Ron Ridenhour turned up shell-shocked in Jackson with notice that he and two other volunteers had been arrested Tuesday out of their host's home in Moss Point, on the Gulf coast south of Hattiesburg, after which Ridenhour knew only that he had been moved to a different county for what he called mental torture culminating in the jailer's solemn announcement that one of the co-workers had been found sawed in half. (A *New York Times* reporter established that the co-worker had retreated homeward in one piece.)

Thursday afternoon, in tiny Itta Bena, an armed posse hijacked two volunteers from a railroad track where they and project director William McGee were walking with registration leaflets. McGee took refuge in Hopewell Church, where the smoke bomb raid a year earlier had touched off the summer-long incarceration at Parchman, and his phone alarms spread rapidly to nearby Greenwood and down to Bob Moses and John Doar in Jackson, interrupting their attentions to the Dulles mission. From Greenwood, sensitive to runaway regret over slow reactions the previous Sunday in Meridian, movement supporters flocked to Itta Bena and located the hijackers calmly holding their prey under shotgun at a gasoline station, waiting to ship them out on the next bus. Safe but undone, saying he had been warned graphically how he would "disappear" like the boys in Philadelphia if he stayed, one of the volunteers persuaded William McGee to drive him as far north as St. Louis before dawn.

THURSDAY NIGHT, not long after the CBS report on the Bogue Chitto search, two SNCC leaders carefully made their way eastward from Greenville across Mississippi. Although Stokely Carmichael at twenty-two was only a year older than Charles Cobb, they were movement veterans, seasoned enough to undertake a dangerous clandestine initiative *into* Neshoba County, hoping to elicit clues about the disappearance from local Negroes. Before dark, they had stopped on the way to remonstrate over a mysterious decree that had thwarted one small outpost of the summer project all week. The mayor of Hollandale confirmed that it was indeed forbidden for any white volunteer to live with or otherwise "molest" local Negroes, and that only local citizens could appeal an unwritten ordinance to that effect —"that's the law, and that's that"—whereupon Carmichael and Cobb continued on Highway 12 until transportation problems, as usual, undermined their precautions.

First, they had to stop briefly under a streetlight to repair engine trouble, which attracted the suspicion of a white pedestrian and soon the police. Second, while the automobile registration papers had no mention of SNCC ownership, Carmichael had misplaced his letter of permission from the stand-in owner, which landed him in the Durant city jail for investigation of car theft. After several car and luggage searches, officers located civil rights literature that Carmichael had taken pains to conceal, which brought conspicuously armed civilians to the jail by midnight. Released, Cobb found himself pleading to stay in his cell. Refused, ordered to leave, he locked himself in the car just outside the jail. Movement logic told him that his best chance was to stay put, positioned at least to holler in the town square. His imagination circled all night on fear and adrenaline, wondering whether Mickey Schwerner had faced the same predicament.

Their safe emergence from Durant was among the Friday morning bulletins that raced to Jackson—along with confirmation that both the Ridenhour and Itta Bena alarms were resolving into mere scares. In Washington, with President Johnson and Justice Department officials looking on hopefully, Allen Dulles called J. Edgar Hoover at midday from the Oval Office. Following the carefully prepared script, he reported that all the leaders of Mississippi had spoken highly to him of the FBI. For Hoover's sake, Dulles promised to use his family influence with the National Council of Churches to curtail funding for the incendiary summer project, and he sympathized with Hoover's complaint that the volunteers were irritating Mississippi white people, first by living in colored homes and second by indoctrinating colored people to vote. Then Dulles outlined his recommendation to the President that Hoover "ought to review the number of agents" in Mississippi. "I realize it's difficult for you," he said, but state officials would not enforce the law without "somebody looking over their shoulder a bit, and I think you're the only fellow that can do it."

Hoover gave ground, but suggested that U.S. marshals would be better than FBI agents for the "superhuman task." When he praised the marshals as "symbols of authority," who could deter civil rights violations, Dulles realized that his influence had crested. Motioning for help, he fended off Hoover with hasty excuses—"I'm in the President's office now, and I think he wants this office"—and gave up the telephone.

"Edgar?" said President Johnson. "... What he is sayin' there in substance is we want to . . . avoid the marshal thing and the troops thing. . . . I'd rather you send another fifteen people or twenty people."

Hoover improvised a fallback idea. If the marshals handled deterrence, and the Justice Department concurred, he suggested that the Bureau could make a show of aggressive civil rights arrests in "Teenie Weenie," as he mistakenly called Itta Bena.

Johnson, winking at Nicholas Katzenbach, said he would make sure Katzenbach would authorize the arrests, but he parried Hoover's idea about sending in the U.S. marshals. Only the Bureau was respected enough to frustrate integrationist schemes for military occupation, he said, and cajoled Hoover until the Director agreed with the Dulles recommendations. "You get your men in there now," urged the President in a rush. He said the White House would announce that "we've asked for additional men, and you're gonna send 'em."

"Yes, that's right," Hoover replied.

By nightfall, there were celebrations in Mississippi over miraculous reports that FBI agents had arrested three of the previous day's shotgun-toting vigilantes from Itta Bena. "You dig it," wrote a giddy Harvard volunteer from Greenwood. "They are in a Southern jail!" Editors of the *Times* received news from "that horror-ridden state" swiftly enough to make Saturday editions in New York, praising these FBI arrests as "the first sign anywhere in Mississippi of effective action to uphold the upholders of the Constitution."

Bob Moses dampened optimism that whipped through the Ohio training center. So did John Doar, who had arrived to address the second-week volunteers before they embarked for Mississippi. The volunteers saw the arrests as recognition of federal authority that had been there all along —in Section 3052 of Title 18, and elsewhere, according to the COFO handouts—and by logistical extension ought to generate FBI protectors throughout Mississippi. Doar regretted that the world of civil rights did not yield to logic. From the day's maelstrom of phone consultations within the government, he saw Itta Bena as a feint in the contorted maneuvers over the federal presence in the state. Doar was hearing that Hoover was on the verge of surrender, which might produce the first permanent FBI offices in Mississippi, but he knew better than to guarantee the outcome. He only repeated his warning from the previous week, that the volunteers should count on zero federal protection, and endured a greater volley of protest now that the violations were no longer hypothetical.

Moses defended Doar again. Later Friday night, to hushed volunteers with their bags packed, he began farewell remarks with symbols from literature, wondering if the volunteers had read any of the "Ring" novels by J. R. R. Tolkien on the weariness of constant attention to good and evil. After a long pause, he said abruptly, "The kids are dead."

Moses explored readiness for other deaths: "I justify myself because I'm taking risks myself, and I'm not asking people to do things I'm not willing to do. . . . If for any reason you're hesitant about what you're getting into, it's better for you to leave." He nearly begged them to go home, recorded one volunteer, and closed with a special plea to those going forward in the second wave, most of whom had trained as teachers to open the experimental Freedom Schools. "Be patient with the kids and with Mississippi," he said. "Because there is a distinction between being slow and being stupid. And the kids in Mississippi are very, very . . . very slow."

Moses withdrew to compose statements for the next day: a ringing defense of the summer project* and a passionate request that untrained sympathizers stay out of Mississippi. The volunteers started a slow movement song, "They say that freedom is a constant struggle." Boarding buses, they rolled south from Ohio in the darkness so that they, like Louise Hermey and Andrew Goodman the week before, could be dropped off at appointed stations in Mississippi before sundown on Saturday. By then, FBI Inspector Sullivan extended the systematic search of Neshoba County with grappling hooks and a small armada of skiffs to drag a fifty-mile stretch of the Pearl River.

---

* ". . . We are fully committed to continuing the Summer Project. This does not mean that we will attempt to provoke the state. . . . We are specifically avoiding any demonstrations for integrated facilities, as we do not feel the state is ready to permit such activity at this time. All workers, staff and Summer Volunteers alike, are pledged to non-violence in all situations."

27

Beachheads

On HIS WAY to receive Greek Premier George Papandreou before lunch on Thursday, June 25, President Johnson encountered Lee White outside his office with a message that Martin Luther King wanted him on the telephone. Johnson waved off the call. "Tell him I've sent eight helicopters down there this morning," he instructed White. "And two hundred marines." Running late to a prebriefing from Dean Acheson and McGeorge Bundy on how to get Papandreou to calm chronic Turkish-Greek violence on the island of Cyprus, Johnson told White to tell King that he already had "made available every facility of the federal government and the Defense Department."

White lacked the time or nerve to say that King was not calling about Mississippi but St. Augustine, where he was caught in his own trap of violence. Segregationists, held back from demonstrators by a thin line of State Police, directed their fury all week against others, including the national press. Troopers rescued John Herbers of the *Times* from one mob, after which Herbers moved on to Mississippi in time to earn a byline for chasing down the missing companion of volunteer Ron Ridenhour. When a Danish photographer created a small international stir by complaining to his embassy of a Klan beating on a St. Augustine beach, Halstead "Hoss" Manucy's vigilante deputies retaliated by offering "protection" only to reporters who ostracized the Dane. A UPI reporter told FBI agents that he had been forced to match what his ABC competitors were paying Manucy for safety during demonstrations.

More disappointing for King, beyond the dwindling press corps huddled behind Manucy's lines, were settlement negotiations that kept stalling. On his instructions, the quartet of Boston University professors checked into the Monson Motor Lodge under assumed names, having exchanged Harold DeWolf's Massachusetts vehicle for a local rental with Florida license plates. While three of them tried to establish cover identities as tourists—with church historian Neil Richardson posed as an archaeologist, hoping to examine artifacts from the Spanish period—Harold DeWolf looked for an isolated pay telephone. From a booth, he arranged clandestine meetings to receive truce terms from white business leaders, and only then did he make contact with Negroes, slip across no-man's-land to meet a series of Lincolnville couriers ending with Andrew Young, and finally come upon the sight of six-year-old Martin Luther King III playing with his father at the home of Janie Jones.

Movement leaders unanimously rejected the offer DeWolf presented; King kept saying that while he did not want to humiliate anybody, he needed at least the pledge of a biracial committee in order to leave town in good conscience. Before DeWolf could return to white leaders to seek better terms, however, State Senator Verle Pope refused to see him again, pleading threats against his home for selling out to Negroes. Night riders had thrown six concrete blocks through the windows of his insurance business, and Pope said he no longer could subject his family to such danger. His withdrawal on Thursday morning left DeWolf dangling with a frayed disguise. Reporters at the Monson debated whether he was an odd-looking FBI agent or a suicidal fool. King remained convinced that the hard-pressed white business leaders wanted to settle as badly as he did. Seeking a federal mediator to break the barrier of a small town under siege, he placed a call directly to President Johnson—only to have Lee White put him off with word that the President was doing everything he could.

Two hours later, at 2:30 on Thursday afternoon, the most intrepid of the movement demonstrators mobilized from Elk's Rest Lodge for the second wade-in of the day. A newcomer among them, Rev. Elizabeth Miller, was more apprehensive than most because segregationists only yesterday had broken the nose of the sole white female in the line. Like the rabbis the week before, Reverend Miller had answered an appeal to her religious assembly—the American Baptist Convention of Valley Forge, where she headed the Division of Christian Social Concern.* Close behind Fred Shuttlesworth and C. T. Vivian, Miller joined double columns of forty marching down the broad low-tide beach inside a protective corridor of assorted state and local officers that funneled them into the water. They halted knee-deep before an opposing crowd of nearly a hundred

---

* "I felt that we could not say no to Dr. King after we had applauded him and had given him the Dahlberg Peace Award at our convention," she told reporters.

segregationists stretched across the mouth of the funnel. From a shower of epithets, Miller heard obscene guesses by white women about the nature of her company with the Negro demonstrators.

An officer with a bullhorn warned that anyone who interfered with the integrated swimmers would be arrested. This new policy superseded the previous practice of jailing nonviolent victims while releasing their attackers, which had allowed the white opposition to grow more rowdy under tacit license. Segregationists growled with disbelief at the change. Several of them closed in to knock Shuttlesworth and a visiting Episcopal minister off their feet. Rev. Walter Hampshire of New Jersey called out for prayer, which soon made Reverend Miller all the more conspicuous behind him as one of the few demonstrators who, wearing street clothes instead of bathing dress, declined to kneel in the Atlantic. Three white women darted from the beach through the line of officers to bowl Miller over and then pummel her, one with a rubber-thong sandal, touching off a general assault. Demonstrators threw themselves over those fallen in the water. Several segregationists resisted when troopers waded in to make arrests— one so fiercely that troopers clubbed him. The unexpected sight of a bleeding white fighter triggered sympathy, then rage against the Florida officers. "They didn't beat the niggers!" shrieked one woman. Conflicted local deputies switched sides and loudly protested—reported an FBI observer—that "blows struck by the state officers were unnecessary." Some of them came to the aid of segregationists, whereupon fights erupted among the officers themselves. As combatants were pulling themselves apart and away, Reverend Miller remembered enough nonviolent training to dumbfound one of her recent attackers by returning her sandal.

About five hundred segregationists rallied first that night at the Old Slave Market, drawn by outrage over treatment of whites on the beach. The four Boston University professors stepped gingerly among them, curious to observe their first demonstration now that their clandestine negotiations were in stalemate. Arriving fresh from a mass meeting at St. Paul's, where a foot-stomping rendition of "When the Saints Go Marching In" greeted King's entrance to speak, the professors came to a plaza decorated with a banner of King's face over a raccoon's body, captioned "Martin Luther Coon/And All His Little Coons/Are Going Down." Harold De-Wolf was startled to find himself standing near Manucy, which he discovered by overhearing a press interview in which Manucy proclaimed with easygoing frankness that his business was "raisin' pigs and shootin' niggers." From the platform, J. B. Stoner stirred the crowd's indignation against the all-white state troopers for their betrayal that afternoon, urging segregationists to write down the badge number of any officer who interfered. When he introduced a featured speaker "bigger than the FBI and all the niggers in St. Augustine," Rev. Connie Lynch acknowledged applause, showing off his speaking vest made from a Confederate flag.

Still fondly remembered by local Klansmen for his rousing speeches the previous September, Lynch vowed to liberate any arrested segregationists "one way or another." To the silent astonishment of DeWolf and his fellow theologians, he worked the crowd into righteous frenzy over what he called the divine mission of 140 million American white people. "Let me tell you that God's with the white man in this struggle for racial purity!" he cried. "This is law ordained that came out of the heavens!" He liberally quoted the Bible: "Remember the words of Jesus Christ, who said, 'You can't love two masters.' You love the one ... and you HATE the other!"

Suddenly, Lynch pointed over the crowd to a stirring across Cathedral Plaza to the rear. "There they come!" he shouted. "The niggers are coming now!" His audience turned upon Fred Shuttlesworth's nightly march from the mass meeting up King Street and back. The attackers pushed nearly two hundred of Governor Bryant's assorted special detail—troopers, wildlife officers, liquor agents—back hard upon the double column. The demonstrators, mostly teenagers paired boy and girl, knelt to cover their heads. There was a pause, during which one Florida reporter remembered hearing the click of traffic signals, followed by an ignition of guttural cries. Rocks, city trash cans, and other missiles rained down on Negroes and officers alike. One trooper fell, shot through the arm with a zip gun. Some officers melted away, leaving gaps for assault by fists and clubs; others rousted Shuttlesworth and his columns through an opening back to the west along Cathedral Street.

The retreat stalled at the far end of the plaza, hemmed in. Crowds closed on state troopers who held five captured attackers in custody, then chanted, "Turn 'em loose!" When the cowed officers released their prisoners to stand aside, roars of approval dissolved restraints on the surging mob. Nineteen immobile Negro bodies soon lay in clumps on the pavement; chaos drowned out the sirens of arriving ambulances. Demonstrators broke ranks to flee zigzag through gantlets. Harold DeWolf, too frightened to move or speak, saw in front of him what became an indelible slow-motion memory of a Negro girl slugged to the ground, a foot drawn back, and a boy draping himself over her head in time to absorb the kick. Homer Bigart compressed the scene into one sentence for the morning *New York Times:* "A number of Negro women had their clothes torn off while they were being clawed and beaten by screaming terrorists."

Newsweek correspondent Marshall Frady was trampled while trying to help a wounded girl hiding in shrubbery. Fred Shuttlesworth picked up another young girl who had knocked herself out running headlong into a parking meter; in a lapse of his nonviolence, he brandished a fist to hold follow-up attackers at bay. A few demonstrators fought back aggressively, sending three whites to the hospital. Officers arrested violent Negroes when they could. Some local police blended into the mob, or lent billy clubs to friends, and Sheriff Davis later conceded in court that he had used his bullhorn in the waning moments to invite whites back for a "march through niggertown" the following night. What limited casualties to roughly a quarter of the 180 demonstrators, an FBI observer concluded, was that the mob after a time "seemed primarily interested in preventing officers from making arrests." Sensing this, the most dutiful of the state troopers single-mindedly herded stragglers back to Lincolnville. Trotting at the front, Rev. Elizabeth Miller learned to recognize outbursts of sporadic violence by the bark of police dogs and the sudden flashes of television lights trailing behind.

King preached to the wounded and rescued back at St. Paul's, then placed telephone appeals. "This is the worst night we've ever had," he told Clarence Jones in New York. He said forty people were beaten badly enough to need treatment—more trauma than the Freedom Rides, bigger hospital bills than Birmingham—in bedlam that was "getting tough on nonviolence." Only demonstrators were being arrested, he complained bitterly, adding that "the Klan is making a showdown down here and the federal government has not done a thing!" King scrambled with Jones to plan a telegram campaign demanding federal mediation—possibly federal troops to stop a "reign of terror"—but reality overtook him within minutes. He conceded to Jones that President Johnson was preoccupied already with the presidential campaign and the death watch in Mississippi. Even in the aftershock of the Florida rampage, King broke away to call the Goodman parents about their missing son. He did call Burke Marshall at the Justice Department, begging for federal intervention, but he did not criticize Marshall's noncommittal response too harshly—in part because just then he was encouraging Marshall to push the civil rights bill through the last mile of its journey through the Congress.

For all its passion and historical resonance, small-town St. Augustine had no chance to capture attention that was running off to Mississippi by Thursday night, when Allen Dulles returned from Jackson. King tried literally to muffle the conflict. As a unilateral gesture of conciliation, he sent District Judge Bryan Simpson a pledge that any further night demonstrations would observe "a total absence of hand-clapping or shouting."

The contest continued in Simpson's chambers, especially after secret, out-of-town truce talks, cobbled together by the Boston professors, broke down again. Conflicting lobbies from Washington and Florida bombarded Judge Simpson as he heard testimony about Governor Bryant's emergency ban on demonstrations. Mayor Shelley, who rejected a biracial committee as a humiliating concession to Martin Luther King, supported the Bryant order as a means of shutting down the Negro movement, but Judge Simpson poked at Governor Bryant's claim that his ban was a last resort against anarchy. Pressed for precise testimony on the source of violent acts, state witnesses could neither acknowledge misbehavior by segregationists nor verify accusations against movement supporters. The commander of the state troopers said he had "heard people say that the Negroes are importing bombs." If the demonstrators themselves created a threat, Simpson asked from the bench, why had police made only three arrests for assault? Shown photographs of guns and riot clubs in abundance, Simpson demanded to see the weapons themselves, which eventually elicited from Sheriff Davis an admission that the armaments had been returned to "anti-demonstrators." Simpson forced police witnesses to concede that only two weapons had been seized from Negroes anywhere in St. Augustine over the previous month, neither of them positively connected with the movement marches. By approaching the movement's version of truth—that segregationist authority was complicit in mob coercion—Judge Simpson wedged himself tightly between constitutional law and politics. Without a settlement, he had to accept the ban or hold the governor of Florida in contempt of his order protecting the movement's right of assembly. Farris Bryant, who managed a shaky defiance through the weekend, dared Judge Simpson to put him in jail.

IN HARLEM, Malcolm X and Elijah Muhammad scheduled competing rallies that Sunday, June 28, in their first head-to-head test of strength. Hours before the first event, a jittery Malcolm X called Wallace Muhammad in Chicago, and Wallace candidly reported that he had twice fended off ambush by his father's enforcers. He considered Malcolm to be in greater danger still. "You have to be very careful," he warned. Malcolm hinted at staggering possibilities being discussed secretly—even an alliance with Martin Luther King for voter registration—and assured his friend that many Muslims "very faithful to Islam" looked to Wallace the son, instead of his father, Elijah, in religious matters. Malcolm predicted that Elijah Muhammad would cancel his rally at the last minute rather than face a skeptical New York crowd that was accustomed to Malcolm's oratory. When Wallace gently told him otherwise, he insisted that Elijah would only embarrass himself in public. "He'll look bad," said Malcolm.

Full mobilization of the Nation proved him wrong. From distant cities, convoys of women in white robes and men wearing "We Are with Muhammad" armbands filled the Harlem Armory with nearly eight thousand people, which would put Elijah Muhammad on the front page of the *New York Times.* Security forces dumped two sympathizers of Malcolm X on the sidewalk outside, beaten senseless. The crowd cheered new heavyweight champion Muhammad Ali, then roared when tiny Elijah Muhammad emerged from a moving cocoon of stern bodyguards. "I will not beg 22 million people to accept me as their leader," he declared, claiming divine communion in his plan to separate the race from the scorn and oppression of white slavemasters. "I am the key to every one of you," he said. "I'm not something of myself, I'm something of God."

After his speech, Elijah Muhammad vanished by motorcade to the airport without acknowledging controversy or the defector Malcolm X, who attracted a crowd roughly a tenth of his to the Audubon Ballroom that night. Outdone for once as a speaking attraction in Harlem, Malcolm challenged Elijah—"if he is the leader of the Muslims and a leader of our people"—to end his sectarian withdrawal and engage the world boldly. "Lead us against our enemies," he said in his address. "Don't lead us against each other." Elijah Muhammad smirked over Malcolm's small crowd as an undisciplined mix of residual Muslims, curiosity seekers, and self-centered intellectuals—"a lot of those fishes and freaks from Greenwich Village," reported one of his spies. Among the new faces at the Audubon, King's lawyer Clarence Jones commended Malcolm's statement of principles to literary friends. He went so far as to offer Malcolm legal advice and staff work to disseminate his message, parallel to his services for King.

All day Monday, FBI surveillance teams followed Clarence Jones through the Manhattan business district, recording his movements in the hope of discovering an overtly Communist deed ("7:08 P.M. Jones left the Post Office and returned to 165 Broadway stopping in route for a hot dog"). The agents acted on Director Hoover's worry about the impending civil rights bill, while Jones struggled to reconcile a fresh enthusiasm for Malcolm with his commitment to King. Although he had promised to "feel out" King about an accommodation, Jones could not bring himself even to mention Malcolm's name to King on the telephone. Instead, he promised to help prepare King's testimony for the upcoming Republican National Convention in San Francisco.

Malcolm, for his part, chafed that only ninety members of the Audubon audience registered interest in his new Organization of Afro-American Unity, the secular initiative he had designed to bypass the negligible appeal of Islam. He publicly offered vigilante assistance to suffering integrationists. "We will creep into Florida and Mississippi like Jesus," he announced. Malcolm wired King in St. Augustine on Tuesday: "If the federal government will not send troops to your aid, just say the word and we will immediately dispatch some of our brothers there to organize self-defense units among our people, and the Ku Klux Klan will then receive a taste of its own medicine. The day of turning the other cheek to those brute beasts is over."

Elijah Muhammad laughed when he learned of Malcolm's telegrams. "He doesn't have anyone to send," he scoffed, driving home his point that Malcolm mesmerized fans but commanded no unquestioning soldiers. "He's no general, he's a fool," Muhammad told one adviser. "He is dying a little at a time," he told another, predicting that Malcolm and his children "will be out in the bread lines soon."

□

IN ST. AUGUSTINE, where some whites already imagined Black Muslim snipers deployed on rooftops, Governor Bryant devised a blustering gambit to escape his own fearful predicament. Battered all weekend between choices leading variously toward insurrection, voter revolt, or humiliating punishment for contempt of Judge Simpson's federal court, he summoned reporters late Tuesday afternoon to announce that he had prevailed upon four distinguished local citizens to mediate the crisis in St. Augustine. He said he was withholding the names temporarily so that his state-appointed biracial committee could meet securely without harassment. When Mayor Shelley called to protest this surrender to Negro demands, Bryant swore him to secrecy before disclosing that the biracial committee did not exist; his announcement was a ruse to keep Judge Simpson at bay and get Martin Luther King out of town.

An avalanche of press attention demanded response in St. Augustine, where King detected no sign of truce. Connie Lynch was rallying segregationists again at the Slave Market. No Negro leader verified receiving an invitation to membership on a biracial committee. King himself had surrendered and made bond earlier that day on fresh criminal charges of corrupting Negro youth. Nevertheless, he decided to embrace even the appearance of concession by the governor of Florida as a "first step that at least opens the channels of communication." He announced that the movement would suspend protest for two weeks to allow the unnamed committee to pursue a settlement. Looking up from his hastily composed statement, he told a mass meeting that the historic civil rights law would buttress their cause in the interim. "If things go as they are expected to go," he said carefully, "the President of our great nation will sign this bill Saturday." Then King began to preach about struggle and commitment. "And for God's sake let us not be satisfied until the total problem is solved," he cried. "A few days ago I was in a community ... and the newspaper came out with an editorial saying, 'When will Martin Luther King and the Negroes be satisfied?' ... We will not be satisfied until all of God's children can walk the streets of St. Augustine, Florida, with a sense of dignity and self-respect. We will not be satisfied until the walls of segregation in St. Augustine, Florida, have been finally crushed.... We will not be satisfied until justice rolls down like waters...."

Wednesday morning brought the first of July and a one-day lull of quiet foreboding to St. Augustine, where the Episcopal bishop of Florida convened a hushed private audience within the walls of Trinity Church. "Outside influences have created upsetting upheavals within normal patterns of life," Bishop Hamilton West declared in an opening bow to feelings of trampled resentment. Then he rebuked the assembled vestrymen for turning "certain persons" away from worship services by locking church doors, and for abusing racially mixed groups with "obscene or unseemly language." Rejecting the 9–1 vote by which the vestry sought the resignation of their pastor, Rev. Charles Seymour, Bishop West closed with a prayer that "the love of God will claim each vestryman for Himself."

Historian David Colburn later recorded that West's unexpectedly forceful statement threw the vestrymen into shock. One of them argued that even the forthcoming civil rights bill exempted churches from mandated integration. Another complained of excruciating social exposure, warning that because many outsiders did not know how fiercely Trinity resisted integrated services, "people will think we're trying to get the Negroes in." One vestryman apologized for the policy of defining all Negro visitors as "demonstrators," which allowed Trinity to practice segregation behind a claim of welcome to "worshippers" of all races. ("We are using the demonstrator bit as a cover-up," he confessed.) Vestryman Hoopie Tebeault, owner of the local newspaper, asked squarely whether Trinity officials "must enforce entrance of Negroes to the church," and wrestled out loud with his choice to be "an American or an Episcopalian." Tebeault confronted Bishop West: "Must we provoke you to excommunicate?"

"Either that or be converted," replied Bishop West. He held firm against dissenting interpretations of Scripture, prompting Tebeault to resign formally from the national Episcopal Church. Two leading vestrymen joined him before a rush to adjournment halted the exodus. Reverend Seymour, who stood trembling and mute through the confrontation, would accept transfer out of Florida by the end of the summer.

THAT SAME WEDNESDAY, two advisers sent letters of caution to the White House. From the Justice Department, Deputy Attorney General Nicholas Katzenbach warned President Johnson against the popular clamor for federal intervention in Mississippi. "If they [Mississippi authorities] encourage violence or abdicate responsibility for law enforcement functions," he wrote, "violence on a substantial scale is virtually certain to occur and the possibility of maintaining order by any means short of the use of federal troops becomes negligible." Citing his harrowing experiences protecting the Freedom Riders and later James Meredith at Ole Miss, Katzenbach reminded Johnson that the U.S. government employed only six hundred deputy marshals and that drafting these scattered civilians for makeshift interventions presented dangers "more practical than legal." *

From his sickbed, dying of cancer, Aubrey Williams scrawled a "Dear

---

* On the legal front, Katzenbach did not dispute the published contention of law professors that the "breakdown" of justice in Mississippi justified federal intervention under 10 U.S.C. 331–34. He did argue that the June 26 FBI arrests in Itta Bena were legal only because the white assailants had loudly announced their desire to punish Negro voters—a rare, almost cinematic, declaration of intent that met the Supreme Court's absurdly restrictive test of federal jurisdiction from the *Screws* case.

Lyndon" letter to his rambunctious protégé of the New Deal era. He instructed the President that if he received the letter and did not find it "worth answering, do *not* send me one of those synthetic letters that some body signs for you.

> What I want to say—and I feel sure I speak for the great majority of the American people—for Godsake don't get us bogged down in a hopeless *mess* in South East Asia. [John Foster] Dulles made as many mistakes as any one man in our history. Agree to a conference and get out. It must be costing us 2 million dollars a day. That is a lot of money.
>
> Will you let me give you one more piece of advice. All men want *individual freedom.* It may take time for them to work it out, but one of the great things about Franklin D. Roosevelt was *poise.* He knew human nature and had the courage to give it a chance.
>
> I hope you get to see this. Still devotedly,

Johnson soon defended his Asia policy as "the correct one" in a letter assuring his old mentor he "would never reply to you synthetically." Before then, he called to congratulate Florida Senator George Smathers on the St. Augustine settlement, and Smathers partly confessed placing sole responsibility for a biracial committee on "poor ol' Herb Wolfe, who's got no business undertaking it because of his age. He's got Parkinson's disease, anyway, but he finally agreed. We begged him." Toward the close of business on Wednesday evening, Johnson stopped by the desk of his secretary, Juanita Roberts—a gruff, savvy chain-smoker whose desk was perpetually clouded in haze from Viceroy cigarettes—to pick up an early draft of the remarks Bill Moyers had prepared for Thursday's signing of the historic civil rights legislation. The President rushed off by motorcade to a reception for the President of Costa Rica, then back to the White House for a private screening of the new Hollywood film *Night of the Iguana.*

ALL SEMBLANCE of peace within the tiny Muslim world shattered on Thursday, July 2, when Evelyn Williams and Lucille Rosary filed paternity suits against Elijah Muhammad in Los Angeles. Malcolm X escaped knife-wielding assailants outside his home even before the suits made the news. "Things are pretty hot for me, you know," he told his mass meeting. "I'm trying to stay alive, you understand. I may sound like I'm cracking, but I'm facting." Officials at FBI headquarters dismissed his speech as "merely another effort on the part of Malcolm Little to obtain publicity," although the Bureau's own wiretaps picked up the gangland intrigue. They over-heard the Los Angeles plaintiffs stand up to threats from Elijah Muhammad's lieutenants—"she didn't want to hear from any of them about any of their mess," recorded a note-taking agent—then frankly confess terror to Malcolm: "she feels that they don't have a chance and will all be killed." A caller warned Malcolm that orders had gone out in Chicago to kill him in New York, and an FBI contact reported that one of Muhammad's sons had sent members to get him in Detroit.

In Chicago, two of Malcolm's allies within Elijah Muhammad's own family made parallel accusations against the Nation of Islam. Within a week of the Los Angeles filing, young Hassan Sharrieff testified in open court that "Grandpa" Elijah's enforcers savagely beat Muslims of independent mind or pocketbook. Sharrieff explained his defection to reporters as a quest for true Islamic faith: "Uncle Wallace told me that conscience is the soft whisper of God in man." Like Sharrieff, Wallace Muhammad rushed to the police and FBI for protection. "I know they are fanatics and will kill you," he said of his relatives running the Nation. Wallace composed a manifesto about his lifelong odyssey between chosenness and dissent within the Nation of Islam. "Often I would imagine being in the presence of the Saviour, God, who wrote my name on the wall behind the door before I was born," he recalled. "This my parents, my brothers and two sisters told me as far back as I am able to remember." His manifesto sought to preserve something religious from predatory corruptions. "I beg all of you to face the facts," he exhorted Muslims. "Your hopes of keeping my father's system of lies standing is like a man who hopes to eat the same portion of food that was eaten and digested by him yesterday...."*

To generate maximum publicity for the charges against Elijah Muhammad, Malcolm X recruited a press-savvy counsel who had guided the Sinatra family through the sensational kidnapping ordeal of Frank Sinatra, Jr., the previous December. Wearing her wide black sombrero, Gladys Towles Root held press conferences with the plaintiff mistresses and bastard children at her side, achieving wildly mixed coverage. The *Chicago Defender* announced the actions in gigantic Pearl Harbor typeface: "DENY PATERNITY SUITS AGAINST ELIJAH MUHAMMAD." Some Negro papers blatantly favored the Nation of Islam—"False Charges Filed Against Muhammad" (Chicago), "Negro Prostitutes Accuse 67-Year Old Muslim Leader" (Los Angeles)—and one went so far as to allege that Wallace Muhammad opposed his father out of temporary insanity, having been "injected with medicines of unknown origin while incarcerated." Many others ignored the Muslim tempest as a distraction from the historic awakening in civil rights. A general silence from the white press infuriated Malcolm X, who complained bitterly that reporters had promised him coverage if he provided legal shelter from libel charges.

---

* To the *Chicago Defender,* John Ali denied the accusation of corruption and violence as "just charges ... allegations ... lies."

For Malcolm's purpose, the paternity suits generated more danger than relief. On July 9, he flew to Egypt by way of London on a one-way ticket. Saying he expected to be gone a short time, he stayed overseas a majority of his remaining days. The *Pittsburgh Courier* announced his departure with banner headlines: "Malcolm X Flees for Life; Accuses Muslims of Sordid Sex Misconduct." White newspapers noted only the surface itinerary of a newsworthy extremist: "Malcolm X Flys to African Parley." From Cairo, the *Times* reported that Malcolm "said he intended to acquaint African heads of state 'with the true plight of America's Negroes.'" Malcolm himself skimmed over the baffling conflict of his sectarian life. His autobiography used only eight words to describe the seven weeks of revelation and betrayal since his *hajj* trip to Mecca: "After a while in America, I returned abroad."

28

Testing Freedom

PRESIDENT JOHNSON swore in General Maxwell Taylor as his new ambassador to South Vietnam about the time the Muslim paternity suits were filed in Los Angeles, but the national stage on July 2 belonged to the Congress, where resistance to the civil rights bill collapsed that morning. "In a few minutes you will vote on this montrous instrument of oppression upon all of the American people," declared Representative Howard Smith as he yielded the floor effort to delay or amend the Senate-passed version. At 2:05 P.M., Majority Leader Carl Albert called into Johnson's Cabinet meeting with word that "we are past the danger point" on final roll call. The President briefly channeled his excitement into the political debate of the moment, betting that Dwight Eisenhower would not support the longshot anti-Goldwater candidate, William Scranton. Then he excused himself to eat lemon cake at a seventeenth-birthday celebration for his daughter Luci, freeing the White House staff to make logistical preparations for him to sign the civil rights bill before dark.

Johnson had resolved not to wait the two days until July 4th. Rushing to strike a note of national relief before independence festivities, he entered the East Room of the White House at 6:45 P.M. to face television cameras and a host of dignitaries. Robert Kennedy sat next to Senator Everett Dirksen in the front row, near Lady Bird Johnson. Martin Luther King sat next to AFL-CIO president George Meany in the second row, in front of Secretary of State Dean Rusk and a few seats over from J. Edgar Hoover.

The President introduced the finished legislation before him as a legacy of the American Revolution. "One hundred and eighty-eight years ago this week a small band of valiant men began a long struggle for freedom," he said, adding that the founding Americans "knew that freedom would be secure only if each generation fought to renew and enlarge its meaning. From the minutemen at Concord to the soldiers in Viet-Nam, each generation has been equal to that trust." Alongside this war metaphor, Johnson claimed footing for the new civil rights law in the moral universe: "...those who are equal before God shall now also be equal in the polling booths, in the classrooms, in the factories, and in hotels, restaurants, movie theaters, and other places that provide service to the public."

Johnson completed a brief national address—"My fellow citizens, we have come now to a time of testing. We must not fail. Let us close the springs of racial poison"—then used seventy-two ceremonial pens to sign H.R. 7152 into law. With his Justice Department officials and eight Negro leaders (including Rosa Parks and James Forman), Johnson withdrew to the Cabinet Room to argue for restraint in the uncertain new world of enforcement. The leaders resolved to curtail street demonstrations, calling them unnecessary and potentially "self-defeating" in the election year. Before the movement leaders emerged—solemn and yet giddy in triumph —the "time of testing" commenced outside. The owner of the Heart of Atlanta motel had filed suit within the hour, challenging as unconstitutional the fresh requirement that he accommodate Negro customers. Also in Atlanta, a diminutive restaurateur repulsed the first Negro arrivals at the Pickrick, his popular fried chicken house, in a public confrontation that made him instantly a symbol of white resistance. Lester Maddox would build himself into the next governor of Georgia as a peppery ingenue of segregation, maintaining then and later that his stand had nothing to do with racial hostility or caste.*

Most Southern politicians urged at least a grudging compliance. "As long as it is there, it must be obeyed," declared Senator Richard Russell of Georgia, and Senator Allen Ellender of Louisiana announced that "the laws enacted by Congress must be respected." Over the next several months, visible public separations broke down across the South in count-less pioneer dramas—often mutually and meticulously prearranged to control discomforts on all sides. The generally peaceful sectional adjust-ment became a comforting theme of national news, seasoned by flamboyant exceptions like Lester Maddox and by apprehension over deeper applica-tions of the law. Police in Tuscaloosa, Alabama, rescued Hollywood actor

---

* Maddox recalled the pivotal incident in his 1975 memoir: "The photographs of Lester Maddox and his son, armed with pistol and pick handle in defense of what was theirs, were widely circulated, and everywhere the liberal press made me out a racist and bigot and rabble-rouser. I knew then, just as I know now, that I was trying to protect not only the rights of Lester Maddox, but of every citizen, including the three men I chased off my property...."

Jack Palance and his family from the local movie theater after a mob stormed the box office on a false rumor that Palance had escorted a Negro inside. Mississippi Governor Paul Johnson held a morose news conference on the night of July 2. Predicting that rapid enforcement of the new law "could cause a great deal of civil strife," he advised the state's business leaders not to obey it. The governor bristled when reporters asked about the three civil rights workers then missing eleven days from Neshoba County—"I have no reason to believe that these people have been killed" —and warned that the whole issue would bring "a very bad reaction against Lyndon Johnson."

SNCC CHAIRMAN JOHN LEWIS arrived at summer project headquarters in Greenwood for the voter registration canvass on Friday, July 3, when jubilee optimism about the movement's destiny caused one local woman to address the courthouse registrar Martha Lamb by her first name. ("Guess *she* will never pass until Mrs. Lamb is ousted," a summer volunteer candidly wrote home.) In private, Lewis joined the staff debate over an unusually stern dictum from Bob Moses that the summer project would engage in no testing whatsoever of the new law. Against conventional assumptions and a tide of enthusiasm, Moses clung to movement policy that sit-ins for integrated hamburgers or library cards were not worth the cost of repression in a state inflamed already over the summer project's very presence. White Greenwood mooted the most tempting target by closing public swimming pools for both races.

Dissenters grumbled that Moses was too cerebral in his relentless focus on long-range political work. Word reached Greenwood of rejoicing that the tough business owners of faraway St. Augustine, Florida, had voted unanimously to accept Negro customers. In Albany, Georgia, where King had cut losses in his desegregation campaign two years earlier, Rev. Samuel Wells blessed the first integrated meals all across town, in celebration unspoiled by a salted milkshake at the Krystal or even his own arrest at the suburban Victory Club restaurant. A blue-ribbon NAACP delegation from New York made national headlines by integrating two of Jackson, Mississippi's, premier hotels—the Heidelburg and the King Edward.* For an SCLC conference in Birmingham, the city that had arrested him on the street fifteen months earlier, Martin Luther King with three dozen colleagues checked into a polite welcome at the Parliament House. "White folks act like they intend to do right by this Civil Rights Bill," Andrew Young wrote in a burst of optimism.

---

* Jackson's Robert E. Lee Hotel posted a sign on the front door: "Closed in Despair— Civil Rights Bill Unconstitutional." As a private club, the management invited the entire Mississippi legislature to board without charge during a special session called to convert the state school system into segregated clubs, which proved impractical.

In crisis meetings, young colleagues reminded Moses that SNCC owed its original allure in Mississippi to the direct action of the 1961 Freedom Riders, who had rolled into Parchman Penitentiary to take their beatings and abuse for integrated bus travel. Freedom Rider Stokely Carmichael felt torn between the fear-conquering bravado of demonstrations and his respect for Moses, who had appointed him project director for the Delta counties. Carmichael's movement persona was built on carefree jests in the face of danger—"I don't worry about a gun pointing at me unless the guy is shaking," he quipped. "If he's scared, I'm scared"—and he nearly wept to hear himself counseling volunteers for once to back down and postpone challenges to segregation in public places even now, with the new law behind them. To crestfallen faces, and worries that SNCC might lose its vanguard reputation, Carmichael could only argue at mass meetings that no Negro in Greenwood would dare go against segregation without the full and considered support of the local movement.

Silas McGhee was not there to hear Carmichael. A year out of high school, independent-minded at twenty-one, he agreed with the argument of his civics teacher that any civil rights law was superfluous to the Bill of Rights and the Fourteenth Amendment. Still, having avoided the movement meetings, he walked on July 5 from his family farm in Browning three miles on foot to the downtown Crystal Grill, only to find it closed. Disappointed, he decided not to waste his solitary effort and walked instead to the Sunday matinee at the Leflore Theater.

Sight of him drove the nervous attendant to confer with the manager, who eventually resolved to sell McGhee a ticket. His presence in the darkened theater soon attracted hecklers, ear flickers, snack spillers, and hard brawlers before McGhee fled to refuge in the manager's office. When he finally convinced hostile police officers that he was not part of a conspiracy, they took him home in a cruiser. His delivery by police brought together the McGhee family in alarm. To his brothers, who demanded to know why he had gone off alone, Silas replied, "Well, you wasn't nowhere around when I decided to go. I just went." To his mother, Laura, who wanted to know whether the trauma was worth it, he replied, "No, mother, I don't even like [movie comedian] Jerry Lewis." Although Silas McGhee was far from comfortable as a movement representative, his trip to the Leflore Theater made him such a word-of-mouth sensation in the Mississippi Delta that Aaron Henry invited him to address an NAACP function in Clarksdale by midweek. In Greenwood, Stokely Carmichael and Sam Block recruited the new celebrity. While praising his example, they discouraged such tests in accord with the summer project's painful restraint.

JOHN LEWIS moved eastward to Selma, Alabama. Since the Freedom Day march the previous October, the small local movement there had operated clandestinely from fragile sanctuary provided by Father Maurice Ouellet's

Catholic mission. Literacy teachers, registration workers, and a few itinerant SNCC staff workers—successors to Bernard Lafayette—carefully
avoided cross-racial contact or association with one another in public, and
they solicited outside help with the utmost discretion. ("Would appreciate
any mail in plain envelopes," wrote director Mary Varela of the Selma
Literacy Project to Andrew Young at SCLC.) On Saturday, July 4, four
fresh literacy volunteers from Northern colleges, who had chosen Selma
over Freedom Summer in Mississippi, broke free of established caution to
celebrate the new civil rights law at the segregated Thirsty Boy Drive-In
Restaurant. Sirens quickly converged, and Sheriff Jim Clark of Dallas
County introduced himself with a cattle prod to the back of Silas Norman,
brother of aspiring opera singer Jessye Norman.

With the four literacy workers hauled away to jail, their car impounded, sympathy crowds overflowed that afternoon from the Negro
balconies to the white downstairs seats of Selma's two movie theaters. This
breach of segregation in turn prompted a rallying alarm among whites
("There's niggers in the Wilby!"), and Sheriff Clark closed both theaters
after chasing the Negroes outside. When the commotion generated a
packed church for a Sunday night mass meeting at the AME Zion Hall, a
posse of fifty special deputies invaded behind tear gas and billy clubs to
disperse what Sheriff Clark called a riot. It was then that John Lewis
arrived.

On Monday morning, July 6, Lewis led seventy aspiring voters to the
courthouse on a designated day for registration. Sheriff Clark's deputies
herded them into a back alley out of sight, chased off reporters and twenty
marchers who changed their minds, then placed Lewis and fifty holdouts
under arrest. "The Negroes were marched five blocks to jail," reported the
New York Times. "Repeatedly jolted by the cattle prods, they responded
with 'freedom songs.'" Rev. Ralph Abernathy drove down from the Birmingham SCLC conference on Tuesday to pledge Martin Luther King's
full support at what would be the last mass meeting in Selma for nearly
six months. On a complaint signed by Sheriff Clark, Judge James A. Hare
issued an injunction banning any "assembly of three persons or more in a
public place" under the sponsorship of SNCC, SCLC, or any of forty-one
specified movement leaders including John Lewis, Amelia Boynton, Rev.
L. L. Anderson, Mary Varela, Silas Norman, and literacy teacher Marie
Foster. The movement's brief spurt of visible optimism fell back beneath
unbroken segregation. "New Law Hoax, Fraud, Says Governor Wallace,"
declared Selma's leading newspaper, which highlighted Wallace's new rhetorical theme that "liberalism is destroying democracy in the United
States."

From Boston, Harold DeWolf wrote Martin Luther King on July 3
that he had stopped off to lobby the White House staff on his way home.
He found that Lee White and other Johnson aides were working to develop

the biracial committee for St. Augustine regardless of its beginnings as a trick, and he saw the positive adaptation of local business as a sign that "one of the main objectives of the whole freedom movement in St. Augustine seems mostly accomplished." Back in Florida, however, the opposition took the initiative to spoil any afterglow about the new law. The St. Augustine Klan marched on the night of July 4, and the next day, unsatisfied after chasing away what few Negroes approached restaurants, one squad of segregationists ambushed families fishing off a bridge on Sunday afternoon—lashing a group of six with bicycle chains, cutting one young man badly enough to require forty stitches in his back, then lurching toward another who jumped to safety in Matanzas Bay. Not until Thursday did testers dare to appear downtown, and when James Brock kept his word to serve them, Hoss Manucy threw up picket lines outside the Monson Motor Lodge with Confederate flags and signs reading, "Niggers Ate Here." Within a week, Lee White advised President Johnson that most of the complying businesses in St. Augustine had resegregated, "claiming that they were afraid."

DOWN IN HATTIESBURG, Lawrence Guyot devised a unique way of emphasizing that the Freedom Summer projects should stick to themselves and leave segregated public places alone: a festive 4th of July picnic. After noon that Saturday (because Vernon Dahmer still demanded a full morning's work on holidays), the entire four hundred acres of Dahmer's farm became party ground for nearly two hundred movement workers, including the last few Freedom School teachers off the bus from a training course in Memphis. Northern volunteers who came steeped in mental preparation for terror and destitution walked instead into a celebration of fellowship—hayrides, games, music, a massive fish fry, and watermelons so abundant that Mississippians simply cracked them open to scoop out the sweet red meat with their hands. Some newcomers pitched in with joyful relief, while others hung back. Stanley Zibulsky of New York assumed his host Vernon Dahmer was a white man before learning otherwise, which scrambled his indoctrination about what was safe in Mississippi. Shaking hands, picking cautiously at what to him was a strange new fried fish called mullet, he stared blankly at the day's one incident of panic among movement veterans, when daredevil SNCC worker Doug Harris drove the hayride tractor outside the invisible refuge line of Dahmer property. Zibulsky slept on Victoria Gray's floor for his first night in Mississippi, eyeing a nearby sentry with a shotgun, so locked in fear that his bowels refused to move for the next thirteen days.

Hattiesburg's Freedom Schools, planned for about one hundred teenagers, overflowed on Monday with more than six hundred students ranging in age from eight to eighty-two, partly on the success of Victoria Gray's prior recruitments for Septima Clark's SCLC citizenship schools. The rush confounded the nervous summer volunteers, many of whom were classroom teachers experienced in traditional instruction. One of them wondered how to teach movement history when not a single student had heard of the *Brown* decision. Richard Kelly of Chicago and Paula Pace, daughter of Truman's Secretary of the Army, scrambled to keep ahead of their own assigned readings on African history. A course in basic civics faltered when the word "mayor" was understood as "mare," and the youngest students of a Jewish volunteer would not listen until they could feel his head for the devil's horns that their preacher had assured them lay under his yarmulke.

The question, "Where do roads come from?"—which was meant to introduce the practicalities of citizenship and voting—evoked instead a one-word answer, "God," and then a lengthy detour through theology. Discussion on any subject broke down walls, however, and some teachers abandoned lectures for song, theater, testimonial, and debate. One class used a Volkswagen bus to simulate tests of a white-only restaurant, with improvisations followed by critiques about how realistically Negro boys could play police officers, or whether personal trust in the summer volunteers was stable enough for them to play "roles" as segregationists. Meeting outdoors in the summer heat, other teachers rigged up a phonograph to play recitations of poetry by Countee Cullen, Margaret Walker, and Langston Hughes, which stimulated an outpouring of commentary and spontaneous verse. Volunteer Barrington Parker III, the austere son of a pioneer Negro judge, broke down in tribute to the untrained folk poets in his class, saying their expression "has so much more depth than what passes for culture in our society."

Menacing cars occasionally glided by the five Hattiesburg Freedom Schools, and there were daily reports of incidents. In Moss Point, sixty miles to the southeast on the Gulf coast, Lawrence Guyot was addressing a voter registration rally on opening Monday, July 6, when shots rang out and young Jessie Mae Stallworth fell wounded by a sniper. ("I saw a woman lying on the ground clutching her stomach," wrote a summer volunteer. "She was so still and looked like a statue with a tranquil smile on her face.") Some sixty miles west of Hattiesburg, eight specially trained volunteers established the first movement presence in McComb since the Herbert Lee murder of 1961,* and night riders bombed the group Freedom House on the night of July 8, knocking project leader Curtis Hayes unconscious and leaving Stanford volunteer Dennis Sweeney with a concussion. That same Wednesday in Hattiesburg, sheriff's deputies arrested Rev. Robert Beech on a technical charge that one of his small personal checks,

---

* With clear trepidation, Robert Moses told a July 5 news conference that the dispatch of summer workers into the McComb region resolved a long-deferred choice between ignoring the Negroes there or "sharing their terror with them."

though good for payment, had been "uncovered" briefly during its clearing process.

From a makeshift barracks in the back of J. C. Fairley's television repair shop, with floor mattresses and a hose-rigged shower, Beech supervised the pilgrim clergy who had maintained a continuous weekly rotation since the Hattiesburg Freedom Day in January. On Friday, July 10, segregationists ambushed one of Beech's volunteers with fists and a lead pipe as he walked with voter registration canvassers toward lunch at a Negro church. Arthur Lelyveld, the fifty-one-year-old rabbi of Fairmount Temple in Cleveland, fled bleeding along a railroad track only to be intercepted a second time when the attackers doubled back in their truck. Lelyveld wound up hospitalized along with two summer volunteers from Stanford, one with a broken arm. The assailants later drew suspended sentences and a fine, with local white newspapers emphasizing that they lived outside Hattiesburg in Collins, across the county line.

In southern Mississippi, the spiral of persecution and summer projects continued to rise without tests of the new civil rights law. The McComb project survived to open a Freedom School with thirty-five students, which grew in spite of the destruction of Mount Zion Hill Baptist and two other Negro churches within a week. ("75 students on the lawn in front of the second church bombed in two days, while the children play in the ruins," recorded a volunteer. "Everywhere there is enthusiasm....") Volunteer Dennis Sweeney, along with a visiting white minister from the National Council of Churches, tried to make contact with white McComb, but he succeeded only in ripping out the social roots of the one local couple who agreed apprehensively to listen. Neighbors from a local militia called Help, Inc. surrounded the home of Malva and "Red" Heffner to abort their fleeting introduction to Sweeney on July 17, then stalked and harassed the Heffners, poisoned Falstaff, their dachshund, and orchestrated such a merciless ostracism that the Heffners abandoned their Mississippi home for good on September 5. By then, Red had fallen from 1963 Lincoln Life Salesman of the Year nearly to bankruptcy, and Malva already had lost more than her prestige as the daughter of the governor's old law partner and mother of the reigning Miss Mississippi. "When I'd go downtown," she lamented, "people I had known all my life would treat me like I had leprosy."

North of McComb in Greenwood, where Red Heffner had grown up a classmate of arch-segregationist Byron de la Beckwith, Stokely Carmichael reenacted his latest arrest for the mass meeting of July 15. "I said, 'That's right, niggers don't do nothin' but gamble and drink wine, but who taught us how?'" he declared impishly, recalling how he had preempted the word "nigger" to neutralize the sting of an arresting officer's insults. He convulsed his audience with laughter, exhorting and emboldening them to join Greenwood's fourth Freedom Day the next morning, but then suddenly turned somber about the dangers. "Now I don't want any funny business here!" he shouted. One by one, names were called out of those assigned to the voter registration picket line, so they could make preparations for jail. Carmichael teased eager newcomers who welcomed the task as an honor—"*I* ain't goin'," he said—but when tension actually gave way to outrage and inspiration at the courthouse the next day, movement leaders joined an improvised call to fill the jails. Greenwood police tore up "One Man/One Vote" signs as they hauled away 111 pickets, including Carmichael and thirteen summer volunteers.

Silas McGhee watched the Freedom Day drama from across the street, still pondering his quirky notion to sit through a movie at the Leflore Theater. He was recognizable enough in a small town for three Klansmen to surprise him on his solitary walk home and abduct him at gunpoint in their truck. Vowing to teach him a lesson, they surrounded him with shovels and a two-by-four inside a construction shed. In blind panic, McGhee tackled one of them, who grabbed his ankle and shouted, "Hit him in the head!" to the other two. They clubbed McGhee until he stomped his way loose with his free foot and ran all the way back downtown to the elevator of a temporary FBI office on Washington Street, where he collapsed. Agents followed his lead to arrest the three Klansmen under the new civil rights law—the first such case in Mississippi—and the new Silas McGhee incident became an extra rallying tale that night at the Greenwood Elks Hall.

Excitement died down into a staff meeting that wrestled toward morning over what to do now, with precious manpower locked up and a further diversion of time and effort required to arrange bail. (It would take six days.) "James Bevel, the wonderful reverend who wears a skull cap . . . was there," a mesmerized volunteer wrote home. "He is King's right hand man, and is 10 times as good." Bevel reminded the staff of COFO policy that jail marches in Mississippi amounted to aimless self-punishment— "just run up your bail a few thousand dollars"—and he managed to make retreat sound audacious. They should take their dilemma directly to the people, he said, and urge them to keep supporters out of jail to work hard on the summer projects. "Bevel came up with the best thing I have heard for a long time," the volunteer concluded.

MARTIN LUTHER KING returned to St. Augustine that same night of July 16, and recalled his departure seventeen days earlier with a tinge of regret. "The businessmen said before we left that they would comply with the civil rights bill and we were very happy about this," he told a mass meeting. "It represented a degree of progress, and I said to myself maybe St. Augustine is coming to terms with its conscience." He called the subsequent record a trail of violent setbacks and mixed results. Three days earlier, when postman Henry Twine tried to discuss integration with the manager of the Palms Motor Lodge, near the Fountain of Youth, a small mob of shirtless young men surrounded Twine's car and beat him through the window, straining to drag him outside while Twine crooked his elbow around the steering wheel to resist.* Chicago Bears football star "Galloping" Willie Galimore, Lincolnville's most treasured native son, achieved unpublicized, luxury integration by checking into a suite at the Ponce de León Hotel. Beyond the reach of Klan picketers, he celebrated with room service champagne for his friends.†

At the Monson Motor Lodge, owner James Brock was refusing all Negroes. ("Don't look back," he warned a group of testers on July 16. "There are four Klansmen in a truck passing now.") By resegregating, Brock obtained a truce agreement from Hoss Manucy, but out-of-state Klansmen firebombed the Monson anyway, and U.S. Judge Bryan Simpson soon ordered Brock to integrate again regardless of threats. At Pappy's Seafood Restaurant, angry white customers fell upon a team of four testers. "One of the Negro integrators ran from Pappy's into the woods," FBI agents wired headquarters, "and was missing for about two hours until located by the Florida Highway Patrol."

King sent SCLC lawyers back into Judge Simpson's court for relief under the new law. He expressed hope for continued negotiations, but promised renewed marches under Hosea Williams if necessary. "We have gone too far to turn back," he said. Even so, King's attention was fixed upon national politics. He told his St. Augustine crowds how much he would cherish the pen President Johnson gave him on July 2. "It was a great moment," said King. "It was like standing amid a new Emancipation experience ... something like the signing of the Emancipation Proclamation by Abraham Lincoln." But he perceived one historical turning point to be imperiled by another, and most of his remarks in St. Augustine addressed the nomination that very day of Senator Barry Goldwater. "While not himself a racist, Mr. Goldwater articulates a philosophy which gives aid and comfort to the racist," King declared. "His candidacy and philosophy will serve as an umbrella under which extremists of all stripes will stand."

TREMORS SHOOK American politics along the color line. King had come to St. Augustine from the Republican National Convention in California, where he reviewed for the platform committee "profound and revolution-

---

* When Twine recovered enough to try again, tensely divided observers watched him take a seat in the Palms restaurant. Managers tried to compromise by bringing Twine his order in a sack for takeout, whereupon several of the Negro cooks threw down their aprons and stalked off the job, one saying, "That ain't no trash out there."
† Later that July, Galimore died in an automobile crash near the Bears' summer training camp.

ary changes" since his testimony before the same committee four years earlier. He warned Republicans of "national disaster and discord" if either political party backed away from the bipartisan affirmation of the freedom movement: "It would be a tragedy and an irony of history if the Party of Lincoln should now, some 100 years after the Proclamation of Emancipation, omit from its platform a strong declaration of commitment to the enforcement of all sections of the civil rights bill." King made two further points. He urged Republicans to support effective protections against terror for those who sought to exercise fundamental rights such as voting, and he proposed as a "test for the next decade" a Bill of Rights for the Disadvantaged, comparable to the GI Bill, designed to help the poor of all races overcome the combined weight of bigotry and automation.

FBI agents again bugged King's hotel room that week, and officials at headquarters recommended adding four new wiretaps to the three already installed at his office. Director Hoover, yielding to the elaborate cajolements from the White House, flew aboard President Johnson's jet to open a permanent FBI mission in Mississippi. He arrived on July 10 to a legend's frenzied press reception, at which he complimented Mississippians on their generally low crime rate and described the new FBI presence as a small administrative adjustment. While he and state officials agreed privately to undertake limited cooperation against Klan-sponsored violence, they publicly danced a minuet of friendship without mentioning racial discord. Jackson Mayor Allen Thompson welcomed Hoover effusively, saying, "I'm mighty glad you're here!" and Governor Johnson tried to make him feel at home by pointing out the motto ("Dieu et les Dames"—God and the Ladies) of Hoover's old college fraternity, Kappa Alpha, painted on the Capitol ceiling. When a reporter asked about the summer project, local newspapers headlined Hoover's pinched statement that his Bureau "most certainly does not and will not give protection to civil rights workers." The *Jackson Clarion-Ledger* noted with approval that "Hoover would not criticize statements of Gov. Johnson that the state should refuse to comply with the new Civil Rights Law."

For all the Director's skillful accommodation, it did not escape notice that he spent the night of July 10 at the Sun 'n Sand, one of the few Jackson motels to accept integration, or that he frankly agreed with a reporter's suggestion that the three missing civil rights workers must be presumed dead after three weeks. These small contradictions of segregationist conceit confirmed for wary Mississippians Hoover's unmistakable purpose. His FBI deployment merely fueled "the wild 'to-do' the government is making out of the disappearance of three civil rights workers," complained the *Meridian Star*, which blamed President Johnson for trying to "prove to COFO that he is their devoted slave." A state senator denounced renewed federal "occupation" as a "calculated insult," and resentful commentators urged citizens to shun FBI investigators with protective silence. "With so many FBI agents sleuthing in our state," wrote one, "we should keep our eyes open and our mouths shut."

FBI officials passed their first test when the Director noticed nothing flimsy or fake about the FBI's new Mississippi headquarters, which he had ordered created on Tuesday. By Friday, having labored frantically around the clock as Roy Moore, the freshly assigned Special Agent in Charge, shouted, "Money is no object!" teams of agents had leased and furnished two stories of Jackson's First Federal Building well enough to pass as a fully functional state headquarters for dedication by Hoover, despite empty files and dummy walls hiding bare concrete. FBI Inspector Joseph Sullivan then delivered a status report on his search for the Neshoba County victims, which earned a nod from Hoover but a subsequent reproach from Washington aides for unwanted detail when the Director needed his sleep. The same aides decided not to wake Hoover that night when several callers promised to shoot their former hero the next morning as a traitor to states' rights. Instead, the aides quietly reinforced the guard detail that whisked Hoover from the Sun 'n Sand to the airport. "Hoover Leaves State/Negro Church Burned," announced the Saturday *Clarion-Ledger,* but Mississippi's ninth church loss of the summer was a footnote to weekend chaos ahead. Before Hoover landed in Washington, his office logged three emergency calls from Walter Jenkins and another from Lyndon Johnson about a predawn bushwhacking in Georgia.

OF THE MANY Army Reserve officers who completed two-week summer training about midnight Friday at Fort Benning, three friends—all Negroes unsure of finding safe overnight lodging—decided to drive straight through to homes in Washington. They made it as far as Highway 172 near Colbert, Georgia, when a car pulled alongside their 1959 Chevrolet. From a range of three to four feet, two .12-gauge shotgun blasts obliterated both windows on the driver's side. One missed Lieutenant Colonel John Howard as it tore through a suitcase into Army uniforms on hangers at the far side of the rear seat. In the front, Major Charles Brown snapped awake to find his friend Lieutenant Colonel Lemuel Penn slumped over the steering wheel beside him, dead of massive wounds to the neck and head. When Brown managed to bring the careening Chevrolet to a stop, and noticed through heavy fog that the attack vehicle ahead seemed to be doubling back, he and Howard moved Penn's body aside to retreat at such high speeds that they ran off the road down an embankment, turning the Chevrolet on its side.

Bulletins greeted Hoover at an afternoon flight layover in New York. His orders summoned Assistant Director Joseph Casper from vacation in Myrtle Beach, and Casper commandeered reinforcements from Newark, New York, and Washington into Georgia for instant Saturday travel and all-night interviews, which boiled down to a day-after report for the White House about five "good suspects" from the Athens, Georgia, Klan. Agents had already spread word that "a substantial payment will be made by the Bureau for good information," and were dragging the Broad River with a magnet in hopes of recovering shotguns. "Press vigorously," instructed Hoover on Penn case memos.

Hoover called President Johnson on Sunday, by which time superseding alarms were sounding out of Natchez, Mississippi. In the Old River, a bayou formed by the shifting Mississippi, fisherman James Bowles had discovered the badly decomposed lower body of a young Negro male, his legs tied together. Armies of reporters converged there and also upon Meridian a hundred miles east, on the chance that this might be James Chaney. "FIND HEADLESS BODY IN MISS.," screamed the *Chicago Defender*.

On Monday, when President Johnson called Robert Kennedy for suggestions on the Penn investigation in Georgia (saying, "That was a dastardly thing, wasn't it?"), the Attorney General deflated his hopes for a breakthrough in Mississippi. "Evidently it's not any of the three," said Kennedy, but he confessed that his information did not come from the FBI. In fact, Kennedy asked the President to "give us a hand with the Bureau ... because most of the stuff now we get we read in the papers. For instance, the body, we just, hell, we don't know." Within minutes, before Johnson could check with Hoover, White House aides rushed in with television reports that search teams had found a second floating torso in the Pearl River, tentatively identified as Chaney.

"No, that's not correct," Hoover told the President. "The second body has just been found, within the last hour.... It looks like we've got another case." Before Hoover signed off, Johnson squeezed in Kennedy's request that he ask Hoover to dictate for the President a basic diary of his Mississippi trip—and send a copy to the Attorney General. In Mississippi, forensics experts identified neither body as James Chaney, and the disappearance seven weeks earlier of Charles Moore and Henry Dee,* both nineteen, began to register as a phantom event that had been unreported to the civil rights movement or authorities. FBI agents eventually arrested —though state officials declined to prosecute—two Franklin County Klansmen who confessed kidnapping Moore and Dee off the streets of Meadville, beating them to death on a far-fetched suspicion of Black Muslim conspiracy, then sinking their bodies weighted to a Jeep motor block.

Later on Monday, Inspector Sullivan imported Navy frogmen to

---

* A waterlogged notice found in a jeans pocket helped identify Charles Moore as one of several hundred students expelled on May 20 for protesting social restrictions at no-nonsense Alcorn A&M. Killers seized him on his way home.

scour for Schwerner, Chaney, and Goodman in case killers were using the Old River bayou as an all-purpose disposal area. For emergency manpower and equipment, he found himself jostling across two states with Atlanta SAC Joseph Ponder, who was running the FBI's investigation of the Lemuel Penn murder. In Washington, meanwhile, an exchange of letters set a tone of governmental calm. Hoover assured the White House that he had opened "a fully staffed FBI field office in Mississippi...without the rancor and bitterness of a Federal 'take over,'" and Johnson replied that it was a "great solace to lean on an old friend [for] such delicate assignments."

29

The Cow Palace Revolt

Republicans opened their national convention in the San Francisco Cow Palace that same Monday, July 13. All three television networks covered the four-day national pageant more or less continuously, anticipating an abrupt regional and ideological shift of power toward Senator Goldwater's Western conservatives from the long-dominant Eastern business interests. There was little suspense beyond a slight possibility that Dwight Eisenhower, the only Republican president of the past thirty years, might throw his transcendent influence publicly against Goldwater. Eisenhower was known to resent Goldwater for calling his administration a "dime store New Deal," and privately he had threatened to renounce the Goldwater forces for reckless exploitation on civil rights, saying that if Republicans "begin to count on the 'white backlash,' we will have a big civil war." Rumors of a decisive Eisenhower statement quickened when his brother Milton delivered a passionate nominating address on behalf of William Scranton, the surviving alternative to Goldwater, but Eisenhower remained neutral to the end. He could not bring himself to split his party in support of Scranton, a sure loser to Goldwater, and he had never been comfortable speaking about racial harmony, anyway.

In his speech to the convention on Tuesday night, Eisenhower himself stirred the passions for which he blamed Goldwater. "Let us not be guilty of maudlin sympathy for the criminal...roaming the streets with switchblade knife," he declared. The Cow Palace came alive with roars of approval. ("The phrase 'switchblade knife' means 'Negro' to the average white American," explained a dismayed Roy Wilkins in a newspaper column entitled "Ike Struck Lowest Blow." Wilkins could only hope that a speechwriter had inserted the sentence without Eisenhower's knowledge.) Eisenhower evoked still greater emotion when he attacked the press, urging his audience to "particularly scorn the divisive efforts of those outside our family, including sensation-seeking columnists and commentators, because ... these are people who couldn't care less about the good of our party." This time the delegates responded with standing cheers, many shaking angry fists at the reporters' booths around the Cow Palace.

Campaign historian Theodore White described the release of pent-up anger as a turning point for the convention, if not for the role and reputation of the American press. Before then, White contrasted the "well-dressed and well-mannered Goldwater delegates" favorably with "civil rightsers" marching and picketing outside the Cow Palace,* but the Eisenhower speech opened the convention itself to confrontation. Goldwater delegates and the spectator galleries showered New York Governor Nelson Rockefeller with catcalls and boos when he tried to speak against extremism. Hostilities erupted on the convention floor. Afterward, neither the triumphant Goldwater conservatives nor the defeated Rockefeller-Scranton liberals smoothed their raging antagonism in the interest of party unity. "Hell, I don't want to talk to that son-of-a-bitch," Goldwater growled when Rockefeller called him to concede the nomination. *Life* magazine bemoaned the "ugly tone" of the entire convention.† The *New York Times* called it a "disaster" for both the United States and the Republicans, saying the Goldwater nomination could "reduce a once great party to the status of an ugly, angry, frustrated faction."

On the morning after his acceptance speech, Senator Goldwater sought an audience with General Eisenhower, who was straying again toward rebellion over Goldwater's chief applause line, "Extremism in the defense of liberty is no vice." Echoing a widespread public outcry, Eisenhower demanded to know how Goldwater could see "extremism" as good politics when it smacked of kooks. More personally, he told Goldwater that the slogan reminded him of right-wing zealots who had called Eisenhower himself "a conscious agent of the communists" in the White House, which was "utter tommyrot." Goldwater stammered through several unsuccessful replies before trying a D-Day analogy. What he meant was that patriotism required sacrifice, said Goldwater, and that General Eisenhower had been the ultimate "extremist" for liberty when he sent the Allied troops across the English Channel against Hitler. This interpretation transformed Eisenhower's mood. "By golly, that makes real sense," he said with a smile of

* "... girls with dank blond hair, parading in dirty blue jeans; college boys in sweat shirts and Beatle haircuts; shaggy and unkempt intellectuals; bearded Negro men and chanting Negro women."
† "It was a gathering of the utterly comfortable, come together to protest that they should be having it better ... angry even in victory."

relief that nearly matched Goldwater's. Still, this close call within the Republican bosom shook the new presidential candidate, who resolved never to repeat his signature phrase during the campaign.

NEWSWEEK PRONOUNCED the San Francisco convention "stunningly total— and unconditional ... an authentic party revolution, born of deep-seated frustration with the existing order, executed by a new breed of pros with a ruthless skill." Other mainstream outlets speculated about Eisenhower, the rejection of Wall Street Republicans, or Goldwater's poor prospects against Lyndon Johnson, but their excitements were mild beside the acute distress of Negro publications. "GOP Convention Spurns Negroes," cried the *Cleveland Call and Post.* "Negro Delegates to GOP Convention Suffer Week of Humiliation," headlined the Associated Negro Press newswire. "The Great Purge of Negroes," announced *Jet.* "GOP Negroes Washed Away by the Goldwater Ocean," said the *Chicago Defender.* Their focus was less on the Goldwater nomination itself than on the institutional rejection of cherished Republican fixtures such as George W. Lee of Memphis, delegate to every GOP convention since 1940, who had "seconded the nomination of Robert A. Taft" in 1952. The San Francisco convention, sweeping aside Lee's credentials claim that he and two hundred "regular" Negro Republicans had been railroaded out of the Shelby County caucus, seated "lily-white" delegations in Tennessee and every other Southern state "for the first time since Reconstruction Days," reported the *Pittsburgh Courier,* noting that the caucus of Southern Republicans, "to add insult to injury," named its hotel headquarters Fort Sumter. Southern Republicans re-formed as a homogeneous group. Of the region's 375 convention delegates, all were white and at least 366 supported Goldwater.

Minority observers mourned the loss of Republican stalwarts far beyond the sinecures* and patronage posts of the South. In "Cal. GOP/ White Man's Party," the *California Eagle* of Los Angeles protested a seldom-mentioned fact about Goldwater's victory over Rockefeller in the decisive June 2 primary: it gained convention seats and control of party machinery for a slate of eighty-six California delegates that "by deliberate choice" was exclusively white. Nationwide, by slating no Negro candidates and defeating most opposing tickets, Goldwater strategists whittled the number of Negro delegates to a minuscule fourteen of 1,308, roughly one per hundred, in what newspapers called the fewest "ever to be certified to a Republican convention."

At the Cow Palace, the rolling invective that startled television viewers fell personally upon this tiny remnant. The *Cleveland Call and Post* reported that George Fleming of New Jersey ran from the hall in tears,

---

* "The Georgia delegation," recalled a Cleveland paper, "for many years was headed by the first Negro national committeeman in either party, Henry Lincoln Johnson."

saying Negro delegates "had been shoved, pushed, spat on, and cursed with a liberal sprinkling of racial epithets." George Young, labor secretary of Pennsylvania, complained that Goldwater delegates harassed him to the point of setting his suit jacket on fire with a cigarette. Baseball legend Jackie Robinson summarized his "unbelievable hours" as an observer on the convention floor: "I now believe I know how it felt to be a Jew in Hitler's Germany."

The *Chicago Defender* raised the Nazi analogy to a blaring headline: "GOP Convention, 1964 Recalls Germany, 1933." Editor John H. Sengstacke eulogized the lost tradition reaching back to the armies of Grant and Sherman: "The Grand Old Party, which fought against slavery, which kept the flame of hope burning on the altar of freedom ... which sustained the faith of the Negro people ... is gasping its last breath in the Cow Palace." In the South, where Negro Republicans could imagine no substitute haven among Democrats, editors and owners of the few Negro newspapers writhed under the assault to their Republican identity. *Atlanta Daily World* owner C. A. Scott first denied the Cow Palace revolution ("Scranton on the Move"), then mitigated its effect ("stands to reason ... that the party as a whole will not be carried too far from traditional Republican principles"), then pretended it was good ("... may have a stimulating effect on the development of a real two-party system in the South"), and finally called upon the scalded, soul-torn Old Guard to "hold the fort" no matter what. He praised the Negro delegates for deciding not to walk out of the Cow Palace in abject resignation. They had endured only a "graphic demonstration" of what Democrats—"the party of Bilbo, Eastland, Thurmond, Barnett, Wallace"—inflicted regularly through the past half century, wrote Scott, concluding solemnly that it was "useless for a Negro today to think he solves the race issue in politics by jumping from one major party to the other."

WHITE VOTERS could jump, too, in numbers of far greater impact. "I think we just gave the South to the Republicans," President Johnson told his staff on the way to his Texas ranch after signing the civil rights bill. Aides debated his words in strictest confidence. One alarmist feared that Johnson could lose the election solely on the race issue. Others thought Johnson was hoping he could win even if he lost the entire South. There was precedent for white Southern Democrats voting Republican on presidential ballots—Eisenhower and Nixon had cracked through to win a few Southern states—but it was daunting for any Democrat to contemplate the terrible math of running against rather than with the full weight of the traditional "solid South."

Only hindsight suggested that Johnson had glimpsed a more dramatic, permanent change. Bill Moyers recalled Johnson saying that he had delivered the South to Republicans "for your lifetime and mine," which would turn the whole structure of politics on a fulcrum of color. In their direst visions, after the Goldwater convention followed hard upon the civil rights bill, neither established experts nor shell-shocked Negro Republicans anticipated a wholesale switch of party identification down to the roots of congressional and local offices. Historic affiliations were too well fixed, with Republicans more united behind Negro rights than Democrats. In Congress, fully 80 percent of House Republicans and 82 percent of GOP senators had just voted *for* the civil rights bill, with Democrats lagging behind because of their entrenched segregationist wing. In precincts and state conventions, Republicans everywhere were organized in part around the glorious memory of Emancipation, which was precisely what had reduced them to near extinction among Southerners. For generations, none but the occasional eccentric Republican had bothered to contest elections for Southern statehouses, legislatures, or courthouse jobs. Of forty-one U.S. representatives from the core Deep South states of Georgia, Alabama, Mississippi, Louisiana, and South Carolina, Republicans in 1964 numbered zero.

The century's first handful of promising Deep South Republican candidates arrived at the San Francisco convention hopeful of novel success in the fall elections. One of them, James D. Martin of Alabama, met alone with Senator Goldwater on the roof of the Mark Hopkins Hotel to propose George Wallace's hastily conceived terms for a campaign alliance. Wallace wanted a public reward—veto power over Supreme Court nominees, or, shockingly, a place on the Republican ticket as Goldwater's running mate—in exchange for his agreement not to run as an independent presidential candidate, which likely would doom Goldwater in Southern states. Goldwater declined, knowing he had more to lose than to gain, saying Wallace after all was still a Democrat. Martin returned to circulate on the Cow Palace floor with his message that Republicans should rise above crude racial appeals to larger issues such as federal heavy-handedness, which he called "Bobby Kennedy tearing around like a predator at the constitution of Mississippi and the registration laws of Alabama." Wallace himself formally withdrew from the presidential race three days after the Republican convention, leaving behind a tacit endorsement of Goldwater and a claim that he had changed the language of political debate. "Today we hear more states' rights talk than we have heard in the last quarter century...," he told *Face the Nation* interviewers on July 19. "...The American people are sick and tired of columnists and TV dudes who...try to slant and distort and malign and brainwash this country."

Only four years earlier, when advocates of civil rights had received a congenial welcome at the Republican convention in Chicago, Negro delegates had walked out of the *Democratic* convention in protest of Kennedy concessions to Southern segregationists. Now Negro leaders of both parties recoiled from the concerted hostility of the Cow Palace Republicans, which they could only hope was an aberrational coup traceable to Goldwa-ter, disconnected from both old tradition and new racial progress. Martin Luther King and others denounced the Republican ticket on its first official day and nearly every day thereafter. With a peculiar mix of vehemence and care, King took pains to stop short of partisan endorsement, saying he was more against Goldwater than for Johnson, hoping that a sound enough defeat for Goldwater might restrain both parties from political white flight.

30

King in Mississippi

KING PRESIDED over contentious staff debates about SCLC's next initiative. Hosea Williams wanted to fight on in St. Augustine, where he had made a movement name for himself with night marches and bombastic courage. James Bevel, beginning an intense rivalry with the upstart Williams, dismissed St. Augustine as a "waste of time" without new political purpose, and ridiculed Williams for bullheaded leadership—"niggers getting people killed so they can get their picture in the newspaper." Williams debunked Bevel's reputation as the visionary of Birmingham, saying everybody knew he was crazy, and he accused Bevel of harboring grandiose ambitions against King's supreme role. To impose a temporary truce, King and others accepted a distilled essence of each warring criticism—that the St. Augustine movement was indeed stale, and that the Bevel-Nash plan for a massive voting rights campaign in Alabama was premature, especially now that SCLC's Alabama affiliates were immersed in tests of the new civil rights law.

Andrew Young, while leaning toward Bevel, favored an interval for repair of personal distress and administrative disorder. His new organizational chart for SCLC contained thirty-five boxes with crisscrossing lines of authority, and Young was defending himself from Septima Clark's scolding reminders that he had neglected the citizenship classes for the buzz of excitement around King. ("There were many days when I thought I might be on the verge of cracking up," he wrote Clark on July 20. "I know I had too much on me, but there seemed to be no way of getting around it.") Still, Young argued that King could not refuse the most dangerous of the new diversions being pressed upon him: an invitation from Bob Moses to tour COFO's embattled summer projects. This idea kindled another ferocious dispute. Some aides protested that the movement could not offer King as the premium bull's-eye to Mississippi Klansmen who were killing civil rights workers already; others shouted that the movement could not shrink from violence. King himself raged against the choice, and when his own staff members denied his claim to "a normal life," he stalked bitterly but briefly from a late-night retreat in St. Augustine.

At midday on Tuesday, July 21, Attorney General Kennedy called the White House with notice that King was on his way to address the evening's mass meeting in Greenwood. He said Mississippi authorities, while refusing to supply police escort, recommended that King not try to spend the night in the Delta. "It's a ticklish problem," Kennedy told President Johnson, "because if he gets killed, it creates all kinds of problems." He laughed nervously. "Uh, just being dead, but also a lot of other kind of problems."

The President suggested that Kennedy have the FBI guard King, which produced an awkward silence. "Well, it's difficult...uh they're not, uh, I suppose," Kennedy sputtered, then blurted out his most galling complication: "I have no dealings with the FBI anymore." His frustration veered into bitter accusation. "I understand that he sends, you know, all kinds of reports over to you," said Kennedy, "but *about* me."

"What are you talking about?" asked the President.

Kennedy hesitated and then complained—accurately—that Hoover was painting him as a traitor to Johnson. "Well, I just understand he's got me planning and plotting," said Kennedy, "...plotting the overthrow of the government." He added wryly, "Leading a coup."

"No, that's in error," the President replied. His flat, innocent denial led to a dead-end pause, after which Kennedy proposed getting back to the issue of King in Greenwood. When Johnson volunteered to arrange FBI protection himself, Kennedy fought tense chuckles over the absurd mix of treachery, helplessness, and polite manners. "I hate to ask you to be dealing with somebody that's working over in the Department of Justice," he said. "That's not a very satisfactory situation." The President joined briefly in the tickles before both men recovered to unspoken truce. "The other thing, Mr. President, is New York," said Kennedy. He wanted the FBI to investigate reports that Communist groups were fomenting the recent disturbances in Harlem.

President Johnson promptly called Director Hoover with orders to treat the Harlem troubles with regional balance—just as seriously as the Klan crimes in Georgia and Mississippi. "Maybe you can put a quietus on that Muslim X and all that stuff," he suggested vaguely of Malcolm X. "I think the Communists are in charge of it." The President introduced "another problem" without reference to the Attorney General, which would have been inherently inflammatory to Hoover, saying he had word that Martin Luther King was on his way to Greenwood.

The Director was prepared. "I understand someone there's threatening they're gonna kill him," he replied.

"Yeah," said Johnson. He thought it "the best part of wisdom in the national interest" to make sure "we don't find another burning car." He said it would be a good idea for "someone" to be "in front and in back of him when he goes in." On the next pass, he added that there "ought to be an FBI man in front and behind to observe," and finally he said King should have an escort of FBI agents "in front and behind."

Hoover got the point. Although there was suspicion in headquarters that King himself had planted assassination rumors through Burke Marshall in order to manipulate the FBI, Hoover threw the FBI into temporary high-speed reverse on two policies: his publicly announced stance against protecting civil rights workers and his special policy of aloofness about threats to King. He sent Assistant Director Alex Rosen back to Mississippi and ordered the leader of the New Orleans FBI office to command an emergency expedition of Louisiana agents.

INSPECTOR SULLIVAN was excused from the first day of the "King special," because he and his agents were combing Neshoba County by car and helicopter on the guidance of a young witness with a cardboard box over his head. The search was the culmination of a tip from local white women about the sufferings of Mrs. Fannie Jones, who showed agents a long letter from her son Wilmer about his May 30 arrest on suspicion of asking a white female store clerk for a date. The letter described how Sheriff Rainey and his deputy, Cecil Price, had slapped him around in the cell, cut off his scraggly new high school graduation goatee with a pocketknife, and finally released him around midnight to armed abduction by four Klansmen waiting outside the jail. Located and retrieved from his permanent hiding place in Chicago, terrified of reprisal against himself or his family, Wilmer Jones looked through holes in the cardboard to lead FBI agents through a tentative search for an isolated spot where the Klansmen had threatened to kill him if he did not confess lewd intentions toward the salesclerk. The caravan attracted intense curiosity and so many accurate whispers about his identity that Jones threw off the stifling disguise before the end of the day. Sullivan reconcentrated his ongoing search for the three MIBURN bodies around what the four kidnappers called "the place," according to Jones's letter—an abandoned well near a weather-beaten shack, through a barbed-wire gate. Even if that site yielded nothing, as proved the case, Sullivan hoped to rattle potential witnesses with graphic advertisement of FBI interest in "jailhouse giveaway" conspiracies, which was the working theory about how Chaney, Schwerner, and Goodman had been murdered exactly one month before.

King knew nothing of FBI wiretaps, Neshoba County investigations, or secret presidential orders for his safety. Aboard his flight from Atlanta, he flipped through news magazines like a business tourist while his traveling assistant Bernard Lee read Du Bois's classic, *The Souls of Black Folk*. A well-dressed young passenger across the aisle recognized King. "I happen to be a Christian," he repeated several times, asking with a polite edge whether King thought he advocated "the same love Jesus taught" even though King's methods "incite one man against another." King replied that nonviolence aimed at a "love that is strong, so that you love your fellow men enough to lead them to justice." He asked whether his questioner thought segregation was Christian. "I was anticipating that," the passenger warily replied, adding that he was less resolved on the large issue than on his hunch that King's methods were "causing more harm than good." King asked what methods the passenger suggested, which eventually elicited an opinion that the new civil rights law was harmful, too, and would "just carry on the trend toward federal dictatorship." When he expressed his inclination to vote for Goldwater, they lightened the stakes by sparring over presidential election odds until the passenger moved to another seat. King returned to his magazines, shaking his head. "Such a young man, too," he said to Bernard Lee, who scarcely had noticed. "These are the people who are rallying to Goldwater."

At the Jackson airport, blinking into bright sun at the foot of the outdoor stairway, King looked lost when reporters converged to ask about riots in New York and rumors that Goldwater might agree to set aside the race issue in the presidential campaign. "I'm here on a twofold visit," King declared. "First I'm here to demonstrate the absolute support of the Southern Christian Leadership Conference for this summer project, this COFO project. Uh, secondly, I am here to...support the tremendous quest for the right to vote on the part of the people of the State of Mississippi in the midst of bombings, murders, and many other difficult experiences...." Roy Moore, SAC of the new Mississippi FBI office, identified himself from the crowd, and when King's connecting flight landed a few hours later in Greenwood, an FBI escort mobilized for the drive into town.

The 111 prisoners arrested on Greenwood Freedom Day were emerging from jail, foul-smelling and haggard from a six-day hunger strike, and some of them briefly mistook the commotion downtown as a welcoming ceremony for them. Unfamiliar reporters prowled with clipboards and camera equipment, wrote volunteer Sally Belfrage, who noticed that "for Negroes there hardly seemed to be anyone who wasn't rushing around looking for King, cooking for King, talking of King as if they couldn't find him, and thinking of him if there was no one to talk to." The famous visitor turned up here and there at the heart of a swirling entourage. "Gentlemen, I will be brief," he told customers at the Van Pool Room.

Dorothy Cotton, James Bevel, Andrew Young, and C. T. Vivian went ahead with runners to summon patrons from the Red Rooster Club and the Savoy Cafe to hear King, standing on a bench, tell them that "Mississippi has treated the Negro as if he is a thing instead of a person. Above all things they have denied us the right to vote. We have got to show the world we are determined to be free." *Times* reporter John Herbers recorded that "most residents appeared to be astonished by Dr. King."

There were two fervent mass meetings that night. An airplane overflew the Negro neighborhoods to drop Ku Klux Klan hate leaflets denouncing the "Riot King." In the churches, Ralph Abernathy raised $1,288 with an appeal for everyone to give COFO "the price of a good fifth of Scotch," and the crowds received King's speeches with what volunteer Belfrage called "searing love." She marveled at the crowd's mass adulation from the fringe where some staff workers shouted "De Lawd!" with the mocking undertone that was becoming a private signature of SNCC. Resentment of King festered among young movement veterans who disapproved of his royal style or criticized him for harvesting attention that was built on their long sacrifice. They took the conspicuous FBI detail as evidence of a double standard.

The next morning, while FBI SAC Roy Moore posted agents on King's flight from Greenwood to Jackson, James Eastland interrupted Senate debate on President Johnson's poverty bill with a speech charging first that King was corrupted by Communists, second that the summer project was, too, and third that integrationists with such glaring character defects were not above concocting the Neshoba County murders as a hoax. "Many people in our state assert that there is just as much evidence, as of today, that they are voluntarily missing as there is that they have been abducted," the senator declared. He challenged critics to produce hard proof of a crime, and defended Mississippi voters as victims rather than perpetrators of bigotry. "They do not seek racial violence," he said. "They do not want it. There is a conspiracy to thrust violence upon them."

King rejected Eastland's claims of subversion, saying there were "about as many Communists in this freedom struggle as there are Eskimos in Florida." As for the charge of self-abduction in Neshoba County, King told reporters that he could only hope the FBI would pursue the case with the same dedication and technical wizardry it had employed "some years ago" to prove that an airplane crash near Denver was homicidal insurance fraud. King's comments, which reflected what he had picked up in Mississippi about the 1955 case for which SAC Roy Moore was best known, were broadcast by Walter Cronkite on the Wednesday network news—then instantly and sourly noted at FBI headquarters as a criticism of the Bureau. Roy Moore himself stayed up past midnight on the logistics of King's FBI protection. Early the next morning, Atlanta agents monitoring the wiretap on King's home phone overheard an ABC News correspondent warning

Coretta King of news tips that her husband would be assassinated that day in Mississippi. Flash bulletins about the call briefly detached Atlanta SAC Joseph Ponder from his Lemuel Penn investigation to address the thorny question of how to verify and respond to the information without compromising the secrecy of the King wiretap. In Mississippi, Moore buttressed the protective detail with "all available manpower as necessary."

For King himself the threats were old and the FBI escorts a welcome novelty. Inspired by Greenwood, he told a large rally at the Jackson Masonic Temple about his 1957 visit to Africa for independence ceremonies in the new nation of Ghana, recalling how much it impressed him to see that "all of those leaders who are now in the cabinet and in Parliament are men who went to prison. In other words, I'm saying to you my friends that often the path to freedom will carry you through prison." King's homage to sacrifice received a tepid response from the relatively prosperous "city" crowd of Jackson Negroes, who preferred to hear less about jail. "Yes, in a real sense, we are the conscience of America," King persisted. "We are its troubled souls, and we will continue to insist that right be done because both God's will and the sacred heritage of our nation speak through our echoing demands."

King's message, while too fiery for Jackson and too theatrical for Greenwood SNCC workers, was a rare fit for Bob Moses. Just before King's arrival, Moses had circulated an "EMERGENCY MEMORANDUM" about the summer project's political ambition to unseat Mississippi's regular, all-white delegation at the Democratic National Convention in Atlantic City. Sounding an alarm that movement workers "are not aware of the massive job which remains" to create an alternative party organization called the Mississippi Freedom Democratic Party (MFDP)— democratic in the sense of open to all persons, and Democratic in the sense of loyal to President Johnson—Moses urgently demanded that supporters "*must* devote all their time to organizing for the convention challenge." The required groundwork, which amounted to precinct canvassing for a hypothetical political party, ran against the summer project's emotional tides of cathartic inspiration, survival, cultural epiphany, and tests of bravado at the courthouse. Some strategists opposed the entire venture as a quixotic diversion into conventional politics for a summer project that was overwhelmed and nearly spent, but Moses prevailed. With his allies, he saw the shortfall in political preparation as yet another reason no worker could be spared to go to jail over an integrated meal or movie. To make up ground in a desperate hurry, Moses looked to Martin Luther King for raw celebrity leadership on the traditional model, as opposed to the patient, low-key cultivation SNCC had pioneered in Mississippi.

KING MET MOSES at Tougaloo College on Thursday, July 23, the morning of the wiretapped prediction of his murder. They discussed a host of tactical questions, including the prudence and design of demonstrations in Atlantic City to dramatize the plight of Mississippi. Al Lowenstein, back from Europe, stayed away from the meeting because of the controversy about his overbearing manner, but his traveling speeches and agitations remained fixed on what he called "my obsession with Mississippi." By telephone, Lowenstein peppered the Tougaloo agenda with suggestions ranging from public relations ("Praise the civil rights act and then proceed to talk about all our needs that it doesn't meet") to the selection of challenge delegates ("Must be clear that the delegation is in control of its own decisions..."). Of the hasty preparations for the MFDP's own founding state convention, he had forwarded advice from Los Angeles: "Create an atmosphere of representation with placards for all counties. Invitations would go to all prominent Democrats we can think of, even though they can't come...."

King, as had promised, made tape-recorded radio spots urging support for the Freedom Democratic Party. He promised to continue speaking of the MFDP challenge as a national test ("America needs at least one party which is free of racism..."), and discussed with Moses a coordinated strategy of negotiation, lobbying, and demonstrations for the late-August Democratic convention. On Friday, his fourth day in Mississippi, King appeared on television to explain the elementary facts of the MFDP. "What is it?" asked the moderator. "Why is it? How does it work and who can join?" Officials of Jackson's WJTV parried intense viewer criticism of King's appearance by citing a legal obligation to sell airtime to Negroes, but in truth they sold nothing and yielded instead to the faint new risk of catastrophic loss. Acutely aware of the ongoing, church-sponsored petition to strip the crosstown NBC affiliate WLBT of its FCC broadcast license, WJTV's management produced King's panel show as an exhibit of fairness, which observers later recognized as the "first Negro political television program in Mississippi history."

From the station, King drove eastward in a caravan of more than twenty cars belonging mostly to news correspondents and the FBI. He took extra time at one highway rest stop to snack on a pickled pig's foot from a large display jar on the counter of a rural store. Abernathy and others joined him to gnaw through one foot after another, leaning forward to keep from dripping on their suits, while they enjoyed the queasy abstention of Andrew Young. "Come on, Andy," prompted King, who often teased his companion for "high white" refinements and limited cultural range.

Additional FBI units from Inspector Joe Sullivan guided them into Neshoba County, leapfrogging ahead to cover highway intersections all the way to the small town of Philadelphia. Of the local citizens who stared grimly at the arriving procession, Sheriff Lawrence Rainey and Judge Leonard Warren promptly wrote letters demanding to know how the FBI reconciled the presence of "20 to 24 agents" around King with Director Hoover's public disavowal of protective duty for civil rights workers. ("We believe that the protection of King could have been adequately handled by state and local law enforcement officers," Sheriff Rainey wrote Hoover.) The inconsistency squeezed Hoover's assistants, who could neither disclose President Johnson's explicit order nor ignore Sullivan's reports that Judge Warren and Sheriff Rainey were themselves among more than a dozen people being investigated in the triple disappearance. Eventually, headquarters resolved simply to ignore the letters. Hoover, who often stressed the more salacious angles in his investigative reports, told President Johnson that Bureau agents identified "a long line of Negro women with whom [one of many suspects] has had sexual relations."

King received a lukewarm reception even in Philadelphia's Negro neighborhoods. There was no organized turnout or church sanctuary for a meeting, and advance criers rounded up no more than fifteen hesitant listeners at street stops and grocery stores on a roving tour. On spreading word that King had challenged a young hustler in a pool hall, more than fifty drifted in to watch the famous preacher playfully lose a game of billiards. Reporter Paul Good winced at the "cornpone evangelism" of Ralph Abernathy's worshipful introductions of King, whose big words and florid metaphors seemed to leave his audience cold until he spoke of fear. King said he had no doubt that the three missing civil rights workers were long since murdered from the jail down the street, or that everyone there lived with reasons to be afraid. "But if we are gonna be free as a people we've got to shed ourselves of fear, and we've got to say to those who oppose us with violence that you can't stop us by bombing a church," he said. "You can't stop us by shooting at us. You can't stop us by brutalizing us, because we're gonna keep on keeping on until we're free." These words stirred a response, after which King explained why they should tell their friends and family to register with the Freedom Democratic Party. He said on the walk through Philadelphia that he drew strength from the faces of people who remained human through such visible suffering.

The caravan reassembled for a drive ten miles into the countryside, where King and SNCC chairman John Lewis spoke briefly over the ruins of Mount Zion Church. In late afternoon, when most reporters had dropped away to file their stories, King drank iced tea in the Cole farmhouse nearby, listening to reports on the Klan ambush and arson five weeks earlier. Bud Cole, nearing sixty years old and still recovering from injuries, did not say much as usual, but Beatrice Cole recalled the exact hymns for mercy that had welled up in her during her husband's awful beating. She had King and his party singing prayerfully along, then howling with laughter at her folksy account of the other thing that had seized her mind—a panicky uncertainty about which of two pocketbooks she had brought to the church that night. One was filled with Mount Zion church literature, she said, the other with MFDP leaflets, and she had been petrified that the Klansmen surely would kill them all if they found the leaflets. Fortunately, it did not occur to the attackers that she, rather than the male church trustees, might be Mickey Schwerner's prime contact at Mount Zion.

AT ROUGHLY the same hour in Washington, legions of reporters strained to find out what was transpiring at the White House, where President Johnson and Senator Goldwater met alone for sixteen minutes to discuss ground rules for the presidential campaign. There had been press reports all week that the two sides were jockeying over a "gentlemen's pact" to exclude the race issue from active contention. Johnson and Goldwater complimented each other as American patriots above all differences, and agreed to avoid emotional appeals that might exacerbate national divisions in troubled times—on both civil rights *and* the military conflict in Vietnam. The President later expressed relief that the Republican candidate did not use the White House as a "launching pad" for campaign attacks. Instead, a bemused Johnson told Nicholas Katzenbach in confidence that Goldwater talked about how much he wanted to fly one of the new military aircraft, "and got on about it like a kid on a toy."

In Mississippi, King made it safely to a late rally in Meridian that Friday and then to rooms at the E. F. Young Hotel, where he and his travelers stripped to boxer shorts in the humid night heat and sipped beer as they swapped stories of the long day. On Saturday, he flew home to Atlanta only to be summoned promptly to a festering crisis in New York City.

The summer project proceeded without King. Two more churches in McComb had been arsoned during his visit, and on Sunday in Greenwood Silas McGhee decided to return to the Leflore Theater for the fourth or fifth try of the month, this time with his brother Jake. They made it safely through the feature presentation of *The Carpetbaggers,* starring George Peppard, but an angry crowd of two hundred blocked their exit—"cursing and hollering and carrying on," said Silas—daring them to leave.

Young Greenwood whites clogged traffic from the theater back past the courthouse onto the Yazoo River bridge. From the theater lobby, the McGhees called three Negro taxi companies, which refused to run the blockade, then the police and the local SNCC office. From there, calls for help established that while local FBI agents and most of the Greenwood police department had reached the lobby, the police refused to escort the McGhees through the hostile crowd and the FBI agents insisted their job was to observe. Telephone appeals spread to distant journalists, members of Congress, and to FBI offices in Memphis and Jackson, where agents dodged questions about how the Bureau could lavish protection on Martin Luther King and then leave the McGhees to a mob. ("I'm not going to go into that," one agent replied.) When two SNCC rescue cars pushed through to the theater entrance about ten o'clock, confusion about which was the decoy slowed the McGhees' escape so that both absorbed blows, and one attacker threw a Coke bottle through the car window, cutting both brothers—especially Silas—with shards of exploding glass.

The blockade promptly relocated to Leflore County Hospital, where the McGhees received emergency treatment. There were fewer cars but more guns by midnight, when Corporal Clarence McGhee, a strapping paratrooper on home leave, darted in to rescue his younger brothers but could not get back out. A call to his commander at Fort Campbell, Kentucky, was among the host of appeals going out on the hospital pay telephones. From Washington, John Doar advised movement callers not to alienate FBI agents, but recrimination ran high on all sides, along with mutterings against President Johnson. Summer volunteers made notes: "Now (12:40 Atlanta) hospital doors are locked. SNCCs are inside. There are 3 FBIs . . . and highway patrols are back and forth in front."

After Sheriff George Smith finally escorted the hostages home early on Monday, popular support for the courageous McGhees made project leaders reluctantly undertake a lawsuit on their behalf, and bubbling resentment about helplessness and passive law enforcement made them schedule a mass meeting on nonviolence, at which Clarence McGhee spoke for the doubters: "When a man fights back, he is not attacked." These detours, plus voluminous incident reports and affidavits, dragged the Greenwood summer project further from the single-minded purpose Bob Moses desired. Still, Greenwood workers managed to assemble the county convention of the MFDP at Friendship Baptist Church that same Monday night. Stokely Carmichael delivered the keynote address, and Laura McGhee, mother of the McGhee boys, was one of eight delegates elected to represent Leflore County at the MFDP's first state convention in Jackson.

31

Riot Politics

KING SPENT MONDAY, July 27, in a crossfire of mediation between Harlem and New York's City Hall. There, far removed from the rural culture of segregated Mississippi, one small incident had flashed into a ten-day crisis of national proportions, exposing political nerves connected through the movement years. Analysts blamed a host of causes, including a school board that assigned citywide summer remedial classes to a school on Manhattan's wealthy Upper East Side. A crusty building superintendent exchanged daily criticisms with the passing traffic of unfamiliar teenagers, to the point that he turned his cleaning hose on one unruly group and yelled, "You dirty niggers! I'll wash the black off you!" When a swarm of students drove him into retreat with bottles and trash can lids, an off-duty police lieutenant responded to the commotion and shot to death a fifteen-year-old boy on the sidewalk of 76th Street. Many of the nearly eight hundred summer students in the vicinity gathered around the body in rage, so that it took police reinforcements several hours to clear the neighborhood.

White House aides exchanged fretful memos the next day. Hypersensitive to the northward spread of racial conflict, they worried that "a great deal of the Negro leadership simply does not understand the political facts of life.... They are not sophisticated enough to understand the theory of the backlash...." This was before New York CORE workers organized three hundred student pickets outside the Robert Wagner School with signs reading "Stop Killer Cops," and well before large crowds gathered outside the Levy and Delaney Funeral Home in Harlem, where James Powell's corpse lay. From the first rocks and bottles hurled down upon police cordons, and the first police gunshots to drive away rooftop attackers, pitched battles and sporadic looting spread through the weekend from Harlem into Brooklyn's Bedford-Stuyvesant area. When Bayard Rustin pleaded for calm through a bullhorn, street battlers booed him as an Uncle Tom. "I am prepared to be a Tom if that's the only way I can save women and children from being shot down in the street!" Rustin shouted. "And if you're not willing to do the same, you're fools!" Hooted down, Rustin retreated by escorting a bloodied teenager to the hospital. James Farmer of CORE fared no better when he tried to tell another angry crowd that they were only feeding police violence, not redressing it. "We don't wanna hear *that* shit!" jeered a heckler.

By the daylight lull on Monday, July 20—with fifteen people shot, two hundred arrested, a dozen police officers and more than a hundred civilians injured (mostly by rocks and nightsticks, respectively)—secret consulations had engaged the highest staff echelon at the White House. If Johnson did not respond, aides warned, voters would wonder why he showed such interest in Mississippi and Georgia but not New York, when "too many people up there are 'scared.'" Bill Moyers recommended "Sending Bourke [sic] Marshall up (he knows most of the Negroes in NYC)," but Johnson decided instead to announce that he had sent in the FBI. Privately, at the same time he ordered him to keep King alive in Mississippi, Johnson confided to Hoover that he had recruited former New York prosecutor Thomas E. Dewey to be a surprise public "sponsor" of the Bureau's future report. Dewey, the Republican presidential nominee in 1944 and 1948, offered bipartisan cover for findings on a treacherous issue, and he fit Johnson's pattern of maneuvering Hoover behind prestigious figureheads.

Plunging into the backroom politics, Hoover called New York Governor Nelson Rockefeller at the Wyoming ranch where he was recuperating from his bitter defeat at the Republican convention. They agreed at first that "left-wing labor groups" seemed to be behind the New York riots, but Rockefeller disclosed that underhanded Goldwater partisans had taunted him with predictions of embarrassing race riots in his state, and therefore may have fomented rebellion. Hoover relayed Rockefeller's suspicions to President Johnson, with assurances that the FBI would look for conspiracy by Communists *and* right-wing extremists. On the burning issue of police conduct in the death of James Powell, he talked his way out of a Justice Department request "to investigate the police lieutenant who killed the colored boy the other night"—as Hoover put it in his personal files—because he did not want to burden the New York police commissioner "by harassing his officers when he is doing everything he can to control them...."*

---

* The Bureau's sole initiative in the case was to cull from private records the victim's confessions to social workers that he liked to fight, skip school, and "get high on whiskey" —a portrait that contrasted sharply with *Jet* magazine's eulogy for "Little Jimmy," as a "quiet youth" who worked in a neighborhood store and volunteered for summer school.

No sooner did the street conflict subside in New York City than a similar one broke out in Rochester, New York, then shortly thereafter in three New Jersey cities, and by summer's end in four more Northern settings, including isolated Negro areas in Oregon and New Hampshire. In each case, a street arrest triggered escalating hostility. At the White House, Walter Jenkins told the FBI's Deke DeLoach that the uprisings were the "Achilles heel" of the Johnson administration. Theodore White, in both his book and an award-winning CBS documentary on the 1964 campaign, highlighted them as a stab of danger not only to Johnson but to the future "strategy of domestic tranquility," exhorting the nation "to ask itself, in agony of conscience, what kind of civilization is being bred in its great and changing cities."

More than any other mainstream interpreter, White saw in the riots an awakening to race as a national rather than sectional concern. "Starkly put," he wrote, "the gross fact is that the great cities of America are becoming Negro cities."* He perceived that the passing storm of riots would change the meaning of the new political term, "backlash." Introduced the previous year among economists predicting a fierce racial competition for diminishing blue-collar jobs, the word had been transformed by the spring successes of George Wallace into a phenomenon among white voters, and now its reference began to shift toward a pathology among city Negroes. White himself recoiled from "not only a physical terror in those streets where the decent are prey for the savages, but an intellectual terror which condemns as Uncle Toms or traitors all who try to participate in the general community or lead the way to better life." As a New Yorker, he was as much perplexed as startled by riots so close: "Why had the Negroes chosen to disrupt New York first.... No city had made a greater effort to include Negroes in its community life—or succeeded better." In an echo of traditional segregationist argument, he assumed that the uprisings were at once mindless and contrived. Rabble-rousers, White concluded, preyed on "adolescent troops whose moral restraint had been entirely eaten away by dramatic producers and eloquent intellectuals on television, who somehow persuaded them that revenge for Mississippi and Alabama could be taken by looting and violence in the cities of the North."

FBI investigators labored to identify any network of rabble-rousers. The New York office proposed Malcolm X as a likely architect—noting

---

* Noting that Washington, D.C., was then the only major city with a nonwhite majority, White projected that by 1990—"almost tomorrow in the eyes of history—these trends, *if unchanged,* will give America a civilization in which seven of her ten largest cities (all except New York, Los Angeles and Houston) will have Negro majorities; and the civilization in this country will be one of metropolitan clusters with Negroes congested in turmoil in the central cities and whites defending their ramparts in the suburbs.... Something has got to give."

that some rampaging crowds had shouted, "We want Malcolm X!"—but theory stumbled on the fact that Malcolm had left the country well in advance. Wiretap intercepts of his few calls home from Africa, including the following excerpt from July 31, hardly suggested an active mastermind of insurrection:

MALCOLM: Has there been anything in the papers about me being in Cairo?
ANSWER: Yes, in several papers, and when they mention you on tv they say that you are in Cairo.... And also that you're coming back Saturday.... Are you coming back Saturday?
MALCOLM: Answer my questions first. Have things cooled down yet?
ANSWER: Yes, they have simmered down. Martin Luther King has been meeting with the Mayor, and all of the leaders are mad at him.

While collecting examples of numerous radicals who "took advantage" of riot conditions, FBI analysts backed away from the assertion that anyone had prior knowledge or exerted control anywhere—let alone across nine scattered cities.

On the law enforcement side, FBI agents did discover a pattern of erratic response: "a 'don't get involved' attitude on the part of many officers" in the early stages, with occasional orders simply to ignore looters, followed by abrupt reversal into military-style suppression. This tendency—a natural hazard of all-white or nearly all-white police forces confronting novel disorder in minority areas—seemed only to exacerbate violence in both phases. To criticize unprofessional conduct would be risky to the FBI itself, supervisors realized, because some police commanders who had been trained at the FBI Academy proved "as incompetent as other police officers to cope with the riot." When they warned J. Edgar Hoover of inevitable attempts "to wrongly discredit and smear FBI-trained officers," Hoover responded with orders to "lay the facts on the line irrespective of the consequences."

Hoover thought better, however, or his legendary command wilted for once as the FBI bureaucracy processed its confidential riot report. There was talk of staging a general White House conference on law enforcement at which the police issue could be surfaced discreetly, but Deke DeLoach could find no acceptable way to exclude two big-city chiefs (Orlando Wilson of Chicago and William Parker of Los Angeles) whom Hoover detested as his rare, outspoken critics. FBI authors would pull back to safety by September, praising police performance except for a hint of passivity that they excused as the result of political interference: "...where there is an outside civilian review board, the restraint of the police was so great that effective action against the rioters appeared to be impossible." Omitting the fact that such a board existed in only one of the nine riot cities, the Bureau detected a "general feeling" among commanders that they would be "pilloried by civilians unfamiliar with the necesssities of mob control or even ordinary police actions and may lose their posts and their pensions."

The Bureau's draft would be sanitized again in political screenings at the White House, where top aides objected that use of the word "Negro" three times on one page was "overdoing it." Dewey told Hoover he did not care whether the report lamented a "moral breakdown" or merely a "breakdown" in cities, and Hoover told Walter Jenkins that he would not make an issue of "nitpicking" his investigation. When President Johnson decreed that the finished product be issued from the Justice Department in Hoover's name—not Dewey's—Justice Department officials discerned that the FBI had developed the entire project on a back channel to the White House. They were "greatly perturbed," DeLoach noted with satisfaction, and Hoover ordered that the Justice Department be furnished only the report itself without any of the accompanying political communications. "Nothing at all should be said about Dewey, etc.," he admonished.

The document, released on Saturday, September 26, raised to art form the language of a disapproving, omniscient shrug. "For some reason," declared the overview, "there suddenly occurred a rupture of the cords that normally bind people to decent conduct and respect for law and the rights of their fellow citizens.... A common characteristic of the riots was a senseless attack on all constituted authority without purpose or object." The Sunday *New York Times* stacked its front page with headlines: "F.B.I. Says Riots Had No Pattern or Single Leader/Tells President They Were Not Basically Racial, but Attacks on Authority/Finds Some Reds Active." Mayors and police chiefs endorsed "the broad conclusions," and Roy Wilkins was pleasantly surprised that the FBI not only downplayed race and conspiracy but "cleared the civil rights movement completely." A thin tissue of universal relief survived intact, largely because the Warren Commission made public its voluminous report on the Kennedy assassination that same Sunday, burying the riot question under fresh memories of national trauma.

THIS MARKED the second time in three months that Kennedy news helped sweep aside unwelcome controversy. On the last Monday of July, as King arrived in New York, President Johnson invited Attorney General Robert Kennedy to the White House that Wednesday to discuss his political future. A political buzz on the intervening day followed Kennedy to New York, where competing rumors had him making or not making deals with President Johnson, reconsidering or confirming his decision not to run for New York's Senate seat in the fall. On Johnson's side, there was a flurry of consultation about Kennedy's larger ambitions and how he might react to a host of scripted rejections. After Kenneth O'Donnell warned Johnson of "a big blowup" in the Democratic party if he did not select Kennedy as his running mate, National Security Adviser McGeorge Bundy predicted that the risk of schism depended largely on how Johnson handled the face-to-face meeting. Like O'Donnell and Robert McNamara (other intermediaries close to Kennedy), Bundy confirmed that the Attorney General wanted to be vice president, but he thought the threats of open revolt may be a bluff. "My judgment is that when he looks that one in the eye," Bundy told Johnson, "it's going to be so destructive to him and his brother's memory that he won't do it."

The President, in spite of approval ratings near 70 percent in the polls, complained of vulnerability and isolation. He fretted that nearly all top officials in his government, like most delegates to the upcoming Democratic convention, were Kennedy holdovers,* and said that the race issue wiped out his chief source of political strength from 1960. "If I can't offer the ticket the South, I haven't really got anything to offer," he lamented. "I don't have any standing in Chicago . . . or Iowa or Los Angeles or New York City." Johnson woke up nights in fear that Kennedy could seize *his* job at the convention, on a political tide of Camelot emotion, and he confessed corresponding personal insecurity. "When this fella looks at me, he looks at me like he's gonna look a hole through me, like I'm a spy or something," the President told his Texas protégé, Governor John Connally. And yet, above the skittering suspicions, the President and the Attorney General cooperated on government business. They talked congenially, for instance, about ideas to move beyond riot control and reach unemployed young people with jobs.

Kennedy's political energy had markedly revived in recent weeks with his brother Edward's steady recovery from plane-crash injuries and his own triumphant tour of Poland and Germany. In Berlin, the Attorney General had drawn a Caesar's crowds, reprised his late brother's "Ich bin ein Berliner" speech, and publicly confronted the undertow since Dallas —vowing to rise from the stubborn grip of resignation "that with him there died idealism and hope and what was clean and best in all of us." National polls consistently showed Kennedy as the most popular choice for Johnson's running mate. On the fallback option of a Senate race, he took soundings among New York leaders on the depth of voter resistance to him as a transplanted Bostonian. His private polls showed that he stood a better chance to defeat the incumbent Republican Senator Kenneth Keating than either of the aspiring Democrats, U.N. ambassador Adlai Stevenson and New York mayor Robert Wagner.

Mayor Wagner, having cut short his vacation on the Spanish island of

* "I have Jack Valenti, who nobody knows, and Bill Moyers, and Walter [Jenkins]," Johnson said privately. "That's my team here. The rest of them are their people."

Majorca, spent more than six hours on Tuesday in stalemated negotiations with King over the aftermath of the Harlem riots. Wagner looked for King to control what his assistant called "the undermuck of Harlem," but he wanted an advance commitment that King would not criticize New York's handling of the crisis. Some of Harlem's established leaders, such as Harlem Unity Council president Livingston Wingate, invited King to help boost their leverage in City Hall, then diverted attention from their own weakness by branding King an interloping Uncle Tom. "Wingate of course double-crossed Martin," complained Bayard Rustin, who shuttled between the parties. Rustin told the Harlem leaders that King was unsophisticated and averse to conflict, while telling King that the leaders were "crackpots." He said the Harlem street radicals were "dangerous dogs who will lash out at anything," but he also said any settlement must meet their legitimate demands.

By Wednesday, July 29, Mayor Wagner agreed to petition President Johnson for funds to create jobs and "eradicate slums" in New York, on the theory that the contagion of violence had spread partly on economic desperation. His talks with King deadlocked permanently, however, on the volatile question of the original shooting on East 76th Street. King supported the demand of the Harlem leaders that the police lieutenant be suspended, or at least placed on administrative leave, but city leaders refused on the ground that such actions would convey doubt about the officer's conduct, which implied the need for an investigation and inevitably would build pressure toward something beyond the police department's internal review. After four fruitless rounds of talks, King issued a public statement of unusually sharp personal tone, drafted by Bayard Rustin, in which he attacked New York police commissioner Michael Murphy as "utterly unresponsive to either the demands or the aspirations of the Negro people." Murphy, charged King, had "obstructed establishment of a Public Review Board to investigate charges of police brutality."

King's comments eventually added a nettle to his trail of pending legal actions, in the form of a slander suit filed against him and other prominent Negroes by Roy M. Cohn, the tenacious former counsel to Senator Joseph McCarthy. He faced more immediate problems on July 29 as the swing vote at a summit meeting of civil rights leaders called by Roy Wilkins. The NAACP executive, after strategy talks with President Johnson, had gathered his peers to New York with a telegram that mixed the direst apprehensions with his customary parlor-game metaphors, warning of "violent and futile disorder . . . if we do not play our hand coolly and intelligently."

With Whitney Young of the Urban League, Wilkins proposed that the leaders declare a nationwide moratorium on marches and demonstrations until the fall election. The idea touched off rancorous debate. John Lewis of SNCC objected that because the NAACP and the Urban League seldom engaged in protest anyway, the proposed talk of "a major change of tactics" falsely claimed joint credit for past sacrifice while choking off the signature discipline of activist groups such as CORE and SNCC. More substantively, Lewis and James Farmer of CORE argued that a publicly announced moratorium would lump nonviolent witness together with riots under a vague heading of "Negro trouble," which implicitly accepted the segregationist charge. Against this argument, Wilkins stressed the overriding importance of dampening racial disturbances—which wags called "Goldwater rallies"—to secure Johnson's election and with it a kind of national ratification for the new civil rights law. Rustin and A. Philip Randolph generally agreed with Wilkins, while King found merit on both sides. He helped modify the posture on demonstrations from a ban to a "broad curtailment, if not total moratorium," but Wilkins announced the leadership pact with strong emphasis on his original language. When Lewis and Farmer issued correcting statements, the *Times* proclaimed "Negro Leaders Split" and quoted the stinging judgment of Malcolm X from Cairo, Egypt, that the summit leaders "have sold themselves out and become campaign managers to the Negro community for Lyndon Johnson."

AT THE HOUR of the Wilkins summit in New York, Robert Kennedy found himself listening in the Oval Office as President Johnson read a careful memorandum on reasons "it would be unwise for our party in this election to select you as the vice presidential nominee." Facing Goldwater, Johnson explained, the campaign would be vulnerable in the border states and Midwest, where the Attorney General would only weaken the Democratic ticket. Kennedy gracefully acquiesced, saying, "I think I could have been of help to you." Johnson digressed from the formal reading to praise Kennedy as a likely president and to offer a choice of jobs to broaden his political experience. Kennedy, as he had signaled through Bundy, asked whom Johnson would choose in his place, and Johnson, as he had planned with Clark Clifford and other counselors, responded that he had made no selection.* Kennedy recommended Nicholas Katzenbach to succeed him as Attorney General, then asked how Johnson planned to reveal the decision to eliminate him from the ticket. Johnson replied that he would leave the manner of public announcement to the Attorney General. Kennedy asked time to think about it.

There was a flicker of private relief on both sides. Clark Clifford privately congratulated Johnson for "courage and forthrightness," saying,

---

* Johnson knew that Kennedy did not like the front-runner and eventual nominee, Senator Hubert Humphrey, because he had run against John Kennedy in the presidential primaries of 1960. Also, Johnson's advisers warned that advance notice would give disappointed contenders time to rally against any choice.

"This is the kind of president that I want." McGeorge Bundy reported that Kennedy came from the Oval Office into his without rancor, in a relatively cheerful mood. "This is quite hopeful, really quite hopeful," Bundy told Johnson. "I think you must have handled it grade A, because I wasn't so sure." By late afternoon, however, Bundy said Kennedy sounded "edgier." That evening, Kennedy declined suggestions from both Bundy and Robert McNamara that he simply announce, or ask Johnson to announce, that he wished to remove his name from consideration. It was not true, Kennedy told them, and it would make him seem fickle to those with whom he had discussed seeking national office.

By the next afternoon, keeping public silence through intense speculation in the capital, the President pressed Kenneth O'Donnell of his White House staff about what the Attorney General wanted said for the record. "Any preferences or choices?" asked Johnson.

"No, no," said O'Donnell.

"Well, does he prefer that I announce it instead of him?" asked Johnson.

"I think he does, Mr. President," said O'Donnell. "He just sort of feels that it's rather arrogant of him to announce that he's decided not to allow himself to be a candidate." O'Donnell endorsed a cosmetic proposal to eliminate all Cabinet-rank officials from consideration, so as "not to cause a furor by singling him out," and the news statement followed later that afternoon of July 30. The transparently concocted rationale served Johnson's more lasting desire to conceal a personal obsession with Robert Kennedy.

Resentments crackled over contending versions of the hidden power struggle. Johnson was said to entertain reporters with theatrical imitations of Kennedy's disappointment in the showdown, recalling "his Adam's Apple going up and down like a yo-yo." The Attorney General was said to consider McGeorge Bundy a traitor to the Kennedy legacy, and to relish Johnson's anguish over how to jettison him without offending millions of voters devoted to him as its namesake. Oracles of Washington perceived a Shakespearean breach between the rival camps. Kennedy loyalists saw Johnson as a transparent manipulator; Johnsonians considered Kennedy an unelected prince not yet forty, whose partisans treasured his mordant jokes about riding off to form their own country.

When Mayor Wagner arrived from New York a few days later, the capital fairly hummed with the gossip of jilted sovereigns and mutually exaggerated slights. Wagner's Senate ambitions gained no advantage, however, because the President insisted that both Wagner and Adlai Stevenson withdraw from the Democratic race in favor of Kennedy. Johnson's paranoid side believed that the LBJ national ticket would be safer if Kennedy were focused upon a Senate race. His sentimental side believed that Kennedy would benefit from seeking and holding elective office. His practical side knew that Kennedy had the best chance to win the New York seat for the Democrats.

Sitting with the Johnsons on the Truman balcony at the White House, Wagner reviewed his effort to bridge deeper chasms in his own city. He said he had imported Martin Luther King because of his "emotional hold" over New York Negroes, but that even King was no match for seething hostility to police. When Lady Bird Johnson remarked that to her as an outsider, the proposed civilian review board seemed to offer a workable bridge between police and community standards, Wagner politely dismissed the idea. The first step toward civilian review, he said, would make the morale of New York police "drop to zero overnight."

32

Crime, War,
and Freedom School

I N GEORGIA, a task force of eighty-three FBI agents eventually pressed the investigation into the July 11 murder of Lemuel Penn by means of an unorthodox ploy: a birthday gift to the Klan. As Director J. Edgar Hoover reported to President Johnson, agents had discovered a locally notorious pattern of everyday brutality inside the Athens Klan Klavern 244, escalating from the purchase on March 6 of three double-barreled shotguns and a Smith & Wesson pistol at a local pawnshop. The next night, about twenty robed members tested vigilante resolve on the nearest Negro at hand, James Potts, a forty-nine-year-old laborer at an automobile garage that served the klavern as an after-hours headquarters. On the outskirts of Athens, they whipped Potts for his unsatisfactory "general attitude," including guarded indications that he might welcome the pending civil rights bill. A few days later, after Potts tried bravely but unsuccessfully to press charges, Klansman Howard Sims led assailants more boldly against an anti-segregation sit-in at the Varsity Drive-In, a famous precursor of fast-food restaurants, where Sims bludgeoned the head of one demonstrator with the Smith & Wesson. He was arrested and the four shotguns confiscated from his seconds, but the police chief released Sims and two days later returned the shotguns to Herbert Guest, owner of the Klan's garage hangout on Hancock Street.

In July, on reviewing these and more recent attacks, FBI agents working the Penn case learned from Clarke County officials that prosecutions had been declined because the evidence seemed "sketchy," and Solicitor D. M. Pollock frankly allowed that community standards precluded conviction anyway, especially after Klansman Sims cleverly adopted a standard alibi that he attacked Negroes only because he "thought" they were about to attack white police officers. Through spring, armed Klan patrols had grown rowdier on weekend nights, roaming from the Guest Garage in cars boldly marked "KKK" as an unofficial but avowedly enthusiastic police auxiliary against Negroes deemed troublesome or out of place. By June the Klan patrols were firing their weapons for effect, not only on lonely country roads but in Athens near the campus of the University of Georgia. On Saturday night, June 20, shots were fired over the heads of downtown Negro pedestrians at 11:30 P.M. and again at 12:20 A.M. At 12:50 A.M., a random blast through the rear window of an apartment building embedded shotgun pellets in the faces of two teenagers, after which Police Chief Edward Hardy hauled scared witnesses directly to the Guest Garage to identify the two KKK patrol cars and four well-known shooters on their expected return.

Herbert Guest paid a hundred-dollar fine for disorderly conduct, and more serious penalties loomed during the few days when one hospitalized victim lost his eyesight, but charges lapsed in time for vigorous marauding over the Independence Day weekend. At a racecar speedway outside Atlanta, attending a giant 4th of July rally that featured the Grand Dragon of the Georgia Klan and presidential candidate George Wallace, several members of Klavern 244 were detained briefly for pummeling civil rights pickets with metal chairs, but they returned to Athens in time for the Saturday night exercise of harassing Negro motorists who passed Guest's garage. One carload of Negroes, chased by a KKK patrol car with brandished weapons, jumped out to seek refuge in Bob Walker's Drive-In Restaurant, where the waitress, hearing that a Klan posse was right behind, inquired, "Well, what did you run in *here* for?" Assistant Police Chief James Hansen later confirmed to FBI agents that he rescued the refugees by sending Howard Sims and the KKK patrol after another carload of Negroes on a tip that the license tag looked suspicious. Later that same night, the Klan patrol pulled up behind a police officer giving highway directions to out-of-state Negroes. The officer, cowed but resentful of swaggering civilians, confided to FBI agents that Klansmen Howard Sims and Cecil Myers had superseded him with a conspicuous display of their pistols, ordering the Negroes back to New Jersey.

Night riding expanded from weekends to work nights. The FBI task force confirmed reports that on Monday night, July 6—not far from the spot outside Athens where Lemuel Penn would be ambushed four nights later—a Negro named Benny Johnson had been run over by a passing freight train and swiftly buried without so much as a death certificate, nor attention to the train engineer's statement that Johnson lay motionless on the tracks, nor investigation of reports by local Negroes that Johnson had been shot to death earlier that night. No sooner did the FBI arrange to have Johnson's body exhumed than reports surfaced of another body simi-larly discarded two years earlier. The two railroad cases appeared to have in common visits to a powerfully protected mistress, however, and the investigators set them aside from the Penn killing, especially after one Klansman disclosed that the KKK patrol had been engaged elsewhere that night of July 6. Outside Winder, Georgia, near Athens, night riders from Klavern 244 had chased down, harassed, and beaten a lone Negro pedes-trian with sticks before Howard Sims went beyond the established routine by pulling out his shotgun to fire at the victim as he fled into a field. By the time FBI agents identified the anonymous pedestrian as Melvin Reed, and confirmed the Klan informant's tale, agents from the Charlotte, North Carolina, FBI office were examining more than fifty small dents in an automobile belonging to a salesman from the Afro-American Life Insur-ance Company. On the night before the Lemuel Penn murder, the sales-man had reported, highwaymen pulled alongside just after he passed through Athens with his wife and two children on their way home from a family vacation, blasting away without warning until he escaped at high speed.

FBI technicians matched the car dents with Number 4 shotgun pel-lets, and Georgia search teams recovered the inner wadding of shotgun cartridges from the highway. When agents verified the salesman's reports that he knew no one in Athens, had not stopped there, and had never taken part in any civil rights activity, FBI investigators interpreted the Penn murder within a pattern of random attacks upon isolated Negroes, and settled upon the patrol from Klavern 244 as conspicuous chief sus-pects. As they blanketed Clarke County with offers of reward money, they pestered the Klansmen almost hourly for interviews, though with little success. Many members of the klavern were functionally illiterate—garage owner Herbert Guest had finished only the first grade—but they were clever enough to keep silent, spurning the FBI agents so as not to entrap each other in conflicting alibis.

At the end of July, without hard evidence to show for nearly thirteen thousand man-hours of intense work, agents from the huge FBI detail searched for ways to exploit signs of mistrust within the Klan families. Several of the wives, resenting the Klan patrol for long nights of abandon-ment, were reported to suspect that the hush about important absences camouflaged wild binges or assorted infidelities. One wife took to bed sick with worry. Suddenly, on Friday night, July 31, two FBI agents knocked at the door of the Guest Garage not with the usual gruff questions but a frosted white cake and well wishes on the occasion of Herbert Guest's thirty-seventh birthday. Their swift departure left the recipients stunned. Herbert's wife, Blanche, refused to let anyone eat of it for fear of being poisoned. She froze the cake in wax paper, and Klan families frequently removed the curious totem from the refrigerator to debate the meaning of significant details: several pink candles, one red one. Meanwhile, FBI agents encouraged rumors that they knew everything through well-paid informants.

THAT WEEKEND into August, Inspector Joseph Sullivan's agents loosed a whirlwind of gossip in the small town of Philadelphia, Mississippi. A banker let it be known that FBI agents said they were planning to arrest Deputy Sheriff Cecil Price, but a courthouse secretary shared contrary reports that two agents were offering Price a reward of $1 million for information about the three missing civil rights workers. Some people heard that FBI agents visited Constable Clayton Livingston with the promise of "enough money to last him the rest of his life." Others passed word that agents were threatening to ruin reputable citizens for involvement in the lucrative moonshine trade, still others that FBI payments in the range of $30,000 were being dangled before Sheriff Lawrence Rainey, several civilian Klansmen, and at least one judge.

In marked contrast with the Herbert Guest birthday cake, Sullivan's Mississippi rumor blitz was designed not to stimulate the flow of information but to conceal the identity of one informant who had talked already. For $30,000, contingent upon positive identification, Sullivan had just bought precise information that the three bodies lay beneath a fresh earthen dam on the Olen Burrage farm, about five miles southwest of Philadelphia. In Washington, President Johnson confided to a caller on August 1 that "they think they know where ... the boys in Mississippi are buried," and high officials at FBI headquarters were fretting in advance about how to conceal "our modus operandi," fearing that the cash purchase of evidence would be embarrassing "in a case such as this involving the Bureau's prestige." In Mississippi, Sullivan focused on securing practical results. By scouting the remote forest property, he mapped the location and access routes to the sizable dam—547 feet long, twelve to twenty feet high, with a maximum base width of twenty feet. On Sunday, August 2, he arranged to secure a search warrant, and, through SAC Roy Moore in Jackson, hired out-of-town earthmoving equipment to meet him Tuesday morning at a blind rendezvous spot.

HALF THE GLOBE AWAY, after a voyage from Japan, Navy Captain John Herrick initiated the first spy cruise off the coast of North Vietnam. Aboard the specially equipped destroyer *Maddox,* patrolling unfamiliar waters dotted with islands, Herrick and shipmates were acutely aware of their exposure at the far edge of American war policy. Officially, they knew nothing of nearby commando raids inside North Vietnam, but in reality they monitored the raids by advance coordination so that the on-board electronics for the new intelligence mission, code-named DESOTO, could track the location and response of North Vietnam's shoreline defense communications. The raids themselves were doubly secret. If discovered at all, the acts of covert warfare were to be passed off as independent actions by South Vietnamese allies, although the entire OPLAN 34A commando program was named, funded, and controlled from Washington, then supervised in action by undercover Americans called "hired personnel."

Through nine months of disorder since the death of President Ngo Dinh Diem in November, U.S. officials had stretched many layers of secrecy to reconcile the ongoing claim of noncombatant support status with the impulse to assert direct command. Secretary of State Rusk speculated in a recent classified cable that "a pervasive infusion of Americans" might be the only way to seize South Vietnamese leaders "by the scruff of the neck and insist that they put aside all bickering and lesser differences." At the insistence of General Maxwell Taylor, the new ambassador in Saigon, the South Vietnamese government was being remodeled after the U.S. National Security Council, and coup leader General Nguyen Khanh already was protesting, as summarized by Pentagon analysts in their idiom, that "the Vietnamese had some difficulty in adjusting their ministerial organization to the requirements of meshing with the U.S. mission subdivisions."

For Captain Herrick, plotting a zigzag course along the remote north coast in the Gulf of Tonkin, there was instinctive alarm when the first light of Sunday, August 2, presented the strange spectacle of several hundred North Vietnamese junks massed at sea. Herrick steered clear on the assumption that the fishing boats might associate the *Maddox* with the OPLAN 34A raiders and be armed for retaliation. That afternoon, three North Vietnamese PT boats emerged from behind Hon Me island, which commandos had bombarded with cannon fire over the weekend. Faced with swarming attack vessels that seemed to care little for the fine points of maritime neutrality, Herrick retreated swiftly for open sea to protect the secrecy of the DESOTO mission. Much to his surprise, the high-speed PT boats doggedly pursued the *Maddox* some twenty-five miles offshore, where they opened fire with torpedoes that missed and machine guns that fared poorly against the U.S. destroyer's heavier 5-inch cannon. Herrick's distress signal scrambled pilots from the nearby carrier *Ticonderoga*—"This is no drill," announced the startled intercom dispatcher. "I repeat. This is no drill."—and four strafing Crusader warplanes repulsed the North Vietnamese attack within twenty minutes. They sank one PT boat and disabled the other two, which sputtered back to port near the Red River delta.

In Washington, exactly twelve time zones behind Vietnam on the clock, aides rushed a crisis report into President Johnson's bedroom before dawn, and the government's top security officials debated their concerted response through most of Sunday. One surface fact stood clear: the United

States must treat the incident as an unprovoked attack upon a flagship in international waters. U.S. leaders genuinely puzzled over what could have motivated the North Vietnamese to break from covert hostilities to open naval combat, where the American military advantage was most pronounced. The one-sided result—zero American casualties, no material damage to the *Maddox*—allowed President Johnson to act with restraint on his hunch that an isolated North Vietnamese commander may have attacked without authority. He ordered the *Maddox* to resume its mission with a second destroyer at escort, issued stern notes of warning against repeat violations, and, in his first use of the Kennedy "hot line" to Moscow, advised Soviet Premier Nikita Khrushchev to instruct his North Vietnamese allies on the rules of engagement.

In overnight cables from Saigon, Ambassador Maxwell Taylor objected to the policy as too weak, stating that the lack of robust military retaliation would deflate America's worldwide prestige by signaling "that the U.S. flinches from direct confrontation with the North Vietnamese." Independently, the President received warnings on the political side from his Texas friend Robert Anderson, Eisenhower's former Treasury secretary, who called to report on his efforts to form a Citizens for Johnson campaign committee. Wary of Goldwater, Anderson urged the President to "make it look like a very firm stand" on the previous day's gunboat battle. "You're gonna be running against a man, who's a wild man," said Anderson, "and if he can show any lack of firmness...this fella's gonna play all the angles."

Johnson replied that the American response had been superior, especially since he thought the North Vietnamese were trying to stop the secret commando attacks. "What happened was, we had been playin' around up there," he told Anderson, "and they came out, gave us a warning, and we knocked hell out of them."

"That's the best thing in the world you can do," said Anderson, but he recommended "a little emphasis" on the firmness, because Goldwater might say, " 'I would have knocked them off the moon.' "

A few minutes later, Johnson discussed with Defense Secretary McNamara alarming rumors that Jacqueline Kennedy would return from Italy to make her first public appearance since the assassination at the Democratic convention, which might set off an emotional stampede to nominate Robert Kennedy. McNamara said he did not believe she wanted to, and hoped she would stay away, then turned to plans to brief congressional leaders on the Tonkin Gulf incidents. The President, citing Anderson, instructed him to "be firm as hell without saying something dangerous."

At McNamara's suggestion, President Johnson clarified his course late Monday morning. Gathering the press corps into his office without notice, he explained that Navy commanders were to meet any renewed threat off the coast of North Vietnam "not only with the objective of driving off the attack force but of destroying them." Five minutes later, having dismissed the reporters with the makings for dramatic headlines, the President resumed a deliberately tranquil White House schedule: a bill signing on land transfers in Minnesota, a statement of national hopes for the International Hydrological Decade, and a speech to the editors of America's foreign language newspapers, who made him an honorary member of the Chinese Historical Society and gave him an autographed copy of the Hungarian weekly, *Az Ember.*

IN FLORIDA, nine male clergy maintained their own tenuous calm as they answered an unexpected summons. One by one, rabbis and Protestant ministers converged from distant home states at the Tallahassee airport where their ecumenical bus journey, inspired by the original Freedom Rides, had ended with arrest in 1961. Some defendants had nursed hopes of being spared even after the U.S. Supreme Court sent their appeal back to the Florida courts for jurisdictional review. They doubted that Florida authorities wanted to jail religious leaders on a dusty conviction now outdated by law—for seeking an interracial meal at the airport cafe—but on Monday, August 3, Judge John Rudd sent them off to the doggedly segregated Leon County jail for sixty days.

Stanford professor Robert McAfee Brown, an author and theologian of national reputation, trimmed the grass edge of Tallahassee roadways with a hoe, while AME Rev. John Collier of Newark stacked bricks on the Negro work crew. In the Negro cell block, drunks and thieves among the regular prisoners treated Collier and two fellow preachers shyly as celebrity heroes, whereas white inmates more often reviled the six strange clergy in their midst. One irate convict set fire to the mattress of Rabbi Martin Freedman. Outside, a defense lawyer tracked down the nearest federal judge, G. Harrold Carswell, who rebuffed a petition for writ of habeas corpus with an invitation to check back with him in a month. Inside, the Protestants used their allotted phone calls to talk with their wives; one of the rabbis notified a White House office of his intention to refuse all food behind bars.

TOP OFFICIALS in Washington were preoccupied Tuesday morning with warnings of renewed battle near the South China Sea. It was night in Asia, and Secretary McNamara warned the President that "this ship could be attacked tonight." When Johnson expressed a wish to have targets "already picked out" for retaliation if there were a second incident, McNamara said he and McGeorge Bundy were doing precisely that for the midday security meeting, so that the United States could "move against North Vietnam in the event this attack takes place in the next six to nine hours." An hour later, McNamara notified the President of a message that Captain Herrick had sighted "two unidentified vessels and three unidentified prop aircraft."

Naval commanders, having rejected a proposal to ease back on new OPLAN 34A commando attacks on Monday, denied Herrick's request to monitor them from safer waters, and ordered him instead to hold a tight legal course near the coast and to treat North Vietnamese vessels "as belligerents from first detection." On radar and intelligence warnings of a trap, Herrick put the *Maddox* and *C. Turner Joy* into evasive maneuvers heading toward the Chinese island of Hainan. His radio alarms, which scrambled warplanes this time from the *Constellation* as well as *Ticonderoga*, chronicled a naval engagement until nearly noon on Tuesday, Washington time. At 1:27 P.M., shortly after President Johnson dispatched his top security officials to prepare retaliatory airstrikes against the North Vietnamese mainland, Herrick flashed a message of second thoughts: "...many reported contacts and torpedoes fired appear doubtful. Freak weather effects on radar and overeager sonar men may have accounted for many reports. No actual visual sightings by *Maddox*." This caution, from a commander whose men had blasted on-screen blips from a moonless dark fog of ocean squalls and fifteen-foot swells, landed in the back channels of an American capital already surging toward the afternoon news deadlines on adrenaline and rumors of war. From the Pacific command in Hawaii, Admiral Ulysses Sharp reassured colleagues that the aggression was real and Herrick's misgivings a mirage, not vice versa. Herrick concurred an hour later, before dawn in the gulf, in a strangely worded message that reverified the North Vietnamese attack with a tinge of endorsement: "Certain that original ambush was bona-fide."

It was mid-afternoon Tuesday in Neshoba County, Mississippi. The air temperature broiled at 106 degrees as sudden swarms of blowflies caused the Caterpillar dragline operator to cease excavations in the Olen Burrage dam. Teams of FBI agents dug the fourteen-foot-deep pit in short shifts, some puffing strong cigars to dilute the cloud of decay. With handheld garden tools, they carefully chipped impacted clay from what became two hours later the unearthed sculpture of a shirtless man pitched facedown behind outstretched arms, like a diver. The agents wrapped the hands in plastic bags, and one of them extracted from the left rear pocket a billfold containing Mickey Schwerner's draft card. By cryptic code, prearranged to thwart eavesdropping Mississippi authorities, Inspector Sullivan soon notified FBI headquarters of the discovery. "We've uncapped one oil well," he said.

During the hours of painstaking exhumation, which soon revealed a second form partially beneath the first, President Johnson reconvened his

National Security Council. Robert McNamara detailed the military options for swift retaliation against North Vietnam, and addressed the unnerving contradictions in the morning battle reports. Under questioning from McNamara himself, distant theater commanders, including Admiral Sharp, had conceded a "slight possibility" that the American crews only imagined themselves under fire; pilots returning to Tonkin Gulf carriers reported no sight of vessels other than the two U.S. destroyers. Secure transpacific calls were routed through the Pentagon to McNamara at the White House for vigorous cross-examination on remedial facts. Within days, for bracing proof that at least the *first* reported attack had been real, McNamara would retrieve to his office the sole 50-caliber shell fragment recovered Sunday from the deck of the *Maddox,* and President Johnson would lament that on Tuesday "those dumb stupid sailors were just shooting at flying fish."*

Innocent of doubt, while news outlets compiled dramatic secondhand accounts of the day's battle,† sixteen congressional leaders gathered in the White House Cabinet Room to answer North Vietnam's disregard for the warning Johnson laid down so publicly the day before. Flanked by McNamara, Rusk, McGeorge Bundy, the Joint Chiefs of Staff, and CIA Director John McCone, the President greeted them at 6:45 P.M. with a stern reminder on the dangers of loose lips. Reporters were trailing every congressional movement or consultation, he noted ominously, and any disclosure of military developments put vulnerable soldiers more at risk. "Some of our boys are floating around in the water," said Johnson.

"I did not tell a damn person," protested House Republican leader Charles Halleck. Maybe not, Johnson replied, but crisis information was "on both tickers anyway." In response to briefings under pledge of secrecy, House Speaker John McCormack declared that the United States must meet the deliberate act of war by North Vietnam. Secretary McNamara rebutted one representative who quibbled that the ammunition on board the *Maddox* and *C. Turner Joy* had not been "powerful enough to do the job." Senate Majority Leader Mike Mansfield worried out loud that North Vietnam, though a "third-rate state" of marginal interest to any of the great powers, was so determined that it might cost "a lot of lives to mow them down." Otherwise, leaders from both political parties rallied when

---

* Three decades later, the prevailing judgment of historian Stanley Karnow and others held that the Tuesday attack never happened.
† *Newsweek:* "The U.S. ships blazed out salvo after salvo of shells. Torpedoes whipped by, some only 100 feet from the destroyers' beams. A [North Vietnamese] PT boat burst into flames and sank. More U.S. jets swooped in.... For more than three hours the battle continued in the turbulent seas. Another PT boat exploded...." *Life:* "There was now plenty for the radar-directed guns to shoot at. The *Maddox* and the *Joy* were throwing everything they had."

Johnson—saying, "I think I know what the reaction would be if we tucked our tails"—proposed limited airstrikes against North Vietnam. Three senators thought the word "limited" sounded too mild.

Final authorization for airstrikes flashed from Washington to carriers in the Tonkin Gulf at 7:22 P.M., and at 8:01 Walter Jenkins interrupted the congressional war council with word from Deke DeLoach that Sullivan's FBI team had just located all three disappeared bodies in Mississippi. To hear advance word from the President on the twin crises, frenzied relays of telephone and radio locators fetched two men ashore from vacation fishing trips: Mississippi Governor Paul Johnson to a dock at Ocean Springs on the Gulf of Mexico, and Republican nominee Barry Goldwater to the Balboa Bay Club in Newport Beach, California. That done, the President preempted the three television networks at 11:34 P.M. He stressed forbearance—"We still seek no wider war"—and the solemn responsibility of ordering "even limited military action by forces whose strength is as vast and as awesome as those of the United States." CBS correspondent Dan Rather concluded that Johnson's address on his first foreign policy crisis climaxed "a day of tension here at the White House."

NAVY PILOT Everett Alvarez, shot down at tree altitude during one of sixty-four authorized bombing sorties over North Vietnam, survived a fractured back to become the first POW and first officially acknowledged casualty of the looming American war. In Meridian, Mississippi, folksinger Pete Seeger used movement songs to calm panic over the grim discovery at the Burrage dam, urging the nightly mass meeting to let mortal awareness lift up the inner force of the words. By contrast, angry vindication whipped through the mass meeting in Greenwood, which bristled against assorted foes and Uncle Toms who had doubted the movement. "From now on," shouted Stokely Carmichael, "we're gonna check on niggers who ain't doin' right." Informed by COFO staff that local Negroes were agitating for armed self-defense, Carmichael gravely replied, "We can only control them by joining them." He went off to notify Bob Moses by telephone of a policy change on nonviolence, only to return somewhat subdued with word that the staff should stick with the summer project. In Neshoba County, definitive evidence of murder obliged Sullivan's FBI agents to share criminal jurisdiction with prime suspects such as Deputy Sheriff Cecil Price. At 1:14 A.M. Washington time, after lending a hand with the body bags under close scrutiny, Price escorted a hearse caravan from the Burrage farm to Jackson for autopsies.

Stokely Carmichael went to jail on Wednesday as a compromise between rebellion and the summer project's enveloping restraint. He joined Silas McGhee and others bent on claiming rights to eat lunch in a Greenwood cafe, but the cathartic demonstration displaced the movement's quieter political work and aroused hostility. Mobs guarded defiantly segregated facilities including the former town swimming pool—now operated by the local Kiwanis Club to dodge the civil rights law—and authorities cut electric power to the city grid that supplied COFO headquarters. Staff members holed up behind nonviolent sentries. "We had to call Washington to have our lights turned on," wrote volunteer Sally Belfrage.

At the first of several memorial services for the three murder victims, Bob Moses held aloft a Mississippi newspaper with a large headline from President Johnson's toughening clarification on Monday—"Lyndon Gives Navy Shoot-to-Kill Order." He asked how a country that declined to protect civil rights workers from clear and evil designs could galvanize so readily to do violence in Asia. It seemed to him partly a matter of vision. The country was largely blind to the movement's reality until it perceived Mississippi through the eyes of summer volunteers. Through whose eyes did it see Vietnam? Moses circled with questions: was the freedom their three friends died for in Mississippi the same freedom the United States was fighting for in Vietnam?

ON THURSDAY, AUGUST 6—a week after the delivery of the FBI birthday cake—James Lackey, manager of a gasoline station in Athens, Georgia, conceded that he had fudged some details of his whereabouts on the night of the Lemuel Penn murder. He and Cecil Myers indeed had intended to be home from Klan patrol by midnight, as they promised when dropping Cecil's wife, Ruth, and her three sons off at the Lackey home after supper, but in fact they did not return until dawn. "I raised the roof," Lackey's wife, Loretta, told FBI agents in a separate statement, "asking where they had been all night... & why they hadn't called." The only answer she got was a cocked pistol in her face from a testy Cecil Myers—"I've killed one. Two won't make no difference," she quoted him—and his refusal to apologize had festered between the families ever since.

Shortly after James Lackey admitted driving for Myers and Howard Sims—"Sims and Myers kept insisting that I follow the car from Washington... I had no idea that they would really shoot the Negro"—Herbert Guest claimed a more passive role, saying he had been present when the Klan trio had departed from the Guest Garage after unknown quarry and had questioned them following their return about whether they had used his shotgun. Thursday night, on the arrest of Myers, Sims, Lackey, and Guest as conspirators, Georgia Governor Carl Sanders issued a telling statement of balanced regret: "Further, if they are held responsible, I want to extend my sympathy to their families, the same as I did to that of the murdered man, because it will be those families who will have to bear the burden of this nonsensible act."

At FBI headquarters, Deke DeLoach and his supervisors shared satisfaction that "for the second successive evening a Bureau accomplishment highlighted all newscasts." The Penn case attracted a tiny fraction of the news attention to Mississippi's triple murder, but public relations machinery made sure to arrange "exclusive credit to the FBI" and "prominent mention" of Director J. Edgar Hoover himself. Supervisors compiled imposing statistics to describe the feats of the Penn task force: 50,611 investigative miles driven by Bureau vehicles, 4,307 clerical hours worked, of which 1,372 were overtime. Meanwhile, other FBI officials searched diligently for ways to circumvent the Supreme Court's crippling *Screws* precedent,* which all but blocked federal jurisdiction in civil rights cases by requiring proof of "a specific intent to deprive a person of a federal right." Review of the Penn case confessions yielded ordinary gutter sentiments— "I am going to kill me a nigger"—far beneath the *Screws* standard of an expressly anti-constitutional motive. The prospect of a halfhearted or aborted state prosecution was so vexing that President Johnson himself made futile suggestions about how to construe the Penn murder as a federal crime. "I think a soldier in uniform ought to have something to do with it," he said. "Doesn't it?"

In Mississippi, on the advice of a chagrined John Doar at the Justice Department, Moses had posted emergency notice to every COFO office that summer workers must think quickly and clearly to give potential attackers a "*Screws* warning" at the first instant of violence, saying, "I want to inform you that I am here working on voter registration." This farfetched legal prescription would lay groundwork for U.S. redress. "If you're gutsy," Moses continued, "you can add something like, 'You should know that this is protected by federal law.' Carry on."

ON AUGUST 6, the day of the Lemuel Penn arrests in Georgia, the Mississippi Freedom Democratic Party held its founding statewide convention. Mostly by bus, a crowd upward of two thousand gathered at Jackson's Masonic Temple. The hall was decorated in humble imitation of the national political conventions. Hand-lettered placards grouped the elected delegates by county: Neshoba, Sunflower, Forrest, Leflore. At center stage, beneath an American flag and a banner reading "Freedom Democratic Party," speakers welcomed a gathering predominantly of sharecroppers who ate sandwiches from paper bags, advanced their dream of voting with formal roll calls, and answered the chilling loss of three colleagues who lay in the morgue with the spirited conviction of a mass meeting. "Until the killing of a black mother's son becomes as important as the killing of a white mother's son," one speaker cried out, "we who believe in freedom cannot rest."

* During World War II, the Court overturned the federal conviction of a Georgia sheriff named Claude Screws, who methodically had beaten to death a handcuffed Negro prisoner in his custody, on the ground that his deed, while "a shocking and revolting episode in law enforcement," lacked a distinct, provable motive that applied to federal rather than state crime.

Heat wilted everyone in the hall. COFO chairman Aaron Henry wiped his face with a handkerchief on the platform near Rev. Edwin King, who stirred the air with a church-issue hand fan. In shirtsleeves and his trademark bow tie, Washington attorney Joseph Rauh explained his "magic numbers" for achieving a practical miracle at the Democratic National Convention two weeks hence. "Eleven and eight!" he shouted. Under party rules, eleven votes (10 percent) from the 108-member Credentials Committee could send a minority report to the convention floor recommending that the Freedom Democrats be seated instead of, or alongside, the regular Mississippi Democrats, and a petition from eight states could secure a roll call vote. Rauh envisioned a stark moral and logical choice posed on national television in the glare of widespread revulsion against racial brutality in Mississippi. Democratic delegates would be loath to support the all-white delegation over the Freedom Democrats, he predicted, especially since the regular Democrats, including Governor Johnson and the state legislature itself, were endorsing the Republican nominee because of his stance against the civil rights bill. "When you have two [delegations] that claim to represent the regular party, you take the *loyal* one," Rauh declared, surveying a Masonic Temple unanimous for Lyndon Johnson. "There's not a Goldwater fan in the house!"

"Bob Moses didn't seem so confident," one volunteer in attendance wrote home. "President Johnson is afraid he will lose the whole South if he seats the FDP." One Sunflower County delegate rose from the floor to ask exactly what the Freedom Democrats would do way up in New Jersey, where most had never ventured. "As things stand right now," Aaron Henry candidly replied, "we don't know what the hell we're going to do when we get to Atlantic City."

In a plaid suit jacket, removing her dark glasses to speak, Ella Baker alone seemed in command as she compressed the lessons of thirty years' activism into a keynote address. She declared the new party "open to *all* the people who wish to subscribe to its principles ... even the son of the planter on whose plantation you work." To exercise the vote was a serious matter, and beyond courage they would need knowledge of history plus the good sense to detect phoniness in their leaders and themselves. "Now this is not the kind of a keynote speech perhaps you like," said Baker, "but I'm not trying to make you feel good." At night after work, "instead of spending our time at the television and radio," she said they all needed to be studying the world around them. She urged them to read W. J. Cash's classic political study, *The Mind of the South.* "Young men and women want some meaning in their lives," said Baker. "Big cars do not give meaning. Place in the power structure does not give meaning."

In the audience, correspondent Paul Good marveled that Baker's summons to civic duty earned thunderous ovations. The crowd erupted into a prolonged demonstration of dancing and weaving to a succession of freedom songs—"Go Tell It on the Mountain," "This Little Light of Mine." "This was probably the most soul-felt march ever to occur in a political convention," a volunteer wrote home. Another volunteer, transfixed by the sight of county placards bobbing above heads and arms, observed that "all of us here are pretty emotional about the names of the counties." Labels that normally headed the daily toll of affliction, she added, for once "meant people who work 14 hours a day from sun-up to sun-down picking cotton, and live in homes with no plumbing and no paint, were casting ballots to send a delegation to Atlantic City."

Strong sentiments masked some conflicts and caused others. Charles Evers refused to observe even a moment of the historic convention, taking refuge in his office upstairs at the Masonic Temple. Like his slain brother Medgar, he partly shared the resentment of his NAACP employers toward the upstart young people and their untried tactics such as the "pretender" political party. In reply, organizers of the summer project pushed slates of freedom delegates that excluded most NAACP candidates as too "middle-class" to represent Mississippi Negroes. "Misunderstanding" over fund-raising memorials briefly divided partisans of SNCC, which claimed martyr Andrew Goodman, from CORE, which had employed Schwerner and Chaney.

Outside the hall, shrill public disputes continued over the meaning of the three murders. Some agents of the state government hinted that the precise information about the location of the grave site indicated the FBI's complicity in the crime, while others drew comfort from reports that the still-secret autopsies showed no signs of beatings—as though proof of swift execution by gunshot might somehow deflect suspicion from the Mississippi Klan.

Church lawyer Jack Pratt pitched into the propaganda war. On Thursday and Friday—a year after bursting naively into Parchman Penitentiary to rescue forgotten Leflore County prisoners—he arranged and observed a follow-up autopsy on behalf of the Chaney family, then persuaded pathologist David Spain to render his conclusion in nontechnical language: "...I have never witnessed bones so severely shattered, except in tremendously high-speed accidents such as airplane crashes." Although later evidence would show that the bone damage had been caused by a bulldozer during burial, Pratt's efforts reversed the *New York Times* news headings overnight, from "No Evidence of Beating...learned authoritatively," to "Chaney Was Given a Brutal Beating."

Hastily—once the mortuary segregation laws were invoked to block family desires for joint permanent burial in Mississippi—the remains of James Chaney were transported from the second autopsy in Jackson home to Meridian for reinterment alone before dark on Friday. Then silent marches wound through town from four churches to converge upon the tiny, wood-framed First Union Baptist. ("The police held up traffic at stoplights," a volunteer wrote home, "and of all the white people watching, only one girl heckled.") There, under the bright lights of television news, one architect of the summer project delivered a volcanic eulogy. CORE's David Dennis had promised his national office a calming and hopeful message, but on sight of the victim's broken young brother—"little Ben Chaney here, and the others like him in the audience"—he snapped.

Dennis gripped the broad pulpit draped with white cloth. "I bury," he started, then winced, eyes closed. "Not bury. Sorry. But I *blame* the people in Washington, D.C., and on down...." He decried "the living dead we have right in our midst, not only in Mississippi but throughout the nation." His voice became a whispered shriek: "See, I *know* what's gonna happen! I feel it *deep* in my heart. When they find the people who killed those guys in Neshoba County, they've got to come down to the state of Mississippi and have a jury of all their cousins, their aunts, their uncles. I know what they're gonna say—not guilty... I'm *tired* of that!" Overwrought, Dennis waved spread fingers to and from his chest. "I'm not going to stand here and ask anyone not to be angry, not to be bitter tonight!" he shouted. "... We've got to stand up. The best way we can remember James Chaney is to demand our rights.... If you go back home and sit down and take what these white men in Mississippi are doing to us ... then God damn your souls!" Tears choked off further words, and the crowd answered with moans.

Bob Moses snapped differently. He lost himself to what a kindred observer called the "blessed chaos" of a Freedom School convention that same Friday and Saturday in Meridian. While it was impossible yet to know the future miracles among the youth delegates from across Mississippi, such as the fourth-grade sisters destined to become a law professor and a Fulbright scholar, no gloom could withstand the energy of the recitals, displays, and caucuses on public business. The student assembly took as its call a variation on the Declaration of Independence* composed by the Freedom School at St. John's United Methodist in Hattiesburg— the church of Victoria Gray, now a Freedom Party candidate for the U.S. House of Representatives—then formed eight committees to create a "youth platform" for the Freedom Democratic Party. An education caucus proposed thirteen planks: "4. That the school year consist of nine (9) consecutive months.... 13. That teacher brutality be eliminated." Others returned with recommendations that were variously general ("Negroes appointed to the police force in large numbers"), specialized ("Cotton

---

* "In this course of human events, it has become necessary for the Negro people to break away from the customs which have made it very difficult for the Negro to get his God-given rights. We, as citizens of Mississippi, do hereby state...."

planting allotments to be made on the basis of family size"), and clairvoyant ("We oppose nuclear testing in residential areas").*

In plenary session, the Freedom School delegates eventually voted down as "too socialistic" a plank calling for land reform, and replaced, in the foreign policy section, a targeted boycott of Fidel Castro's Cuba with a more general call: "The United States should stop supporting dictatorships in other countries...." For Moses, specifics counted little next to the pulsating debate itself, with haggles over procedure and the meaning of words. It rolled back primal fear not only in the students but the volunteer teachers—Stanley Zibulsky, the New Yorker petrified when he arrived at Vernon Dahmer's farm in July, was among many hoping to stay on in Mississippi past the summer. Debate released crippled imaginations into soaring, unpredictable flight, as Freedom School students who newly measured the world by their notions also undertook to decorate COFO offices with original art. They carried Moses beyond shock or the revelry of a ragtime funeral. "It was the single time in my life that I have seen Bob the happiest," said a fellow observer at the Freedom School convention. "He just ate it up."

---

* This plank protested evacuations set for October 22, when the Atomic Energy Commission detonated a 5-kiloton underground device near Hattiesburg. Stronger than expected blast effects lifted the surface of the earth ten inches and rolled detectable tremors as far away as Finland. Shortly after this first—and last—nuclear test east of the Mississippi, New York's Port Authority abandoned plans to clear ground for a new airport with visionary applications of atomic force.

33

White House Etiquette

In Washington, President Johnson stirred his own whirlwinds behind two historic bills that converged in Congress that same Friday, August 7. Working the telephone mercilessly toward the critical votes, he spurred a harried operator to find targeted legislators: "I want to talk to him, honey, wherever he is...whether he's on the floor, if he's got a red tie on, or if he's barefoot. And I also want Senator Smathers—get him even if he's in a beer house."

To "resist further aggression," and to assist South Vietnam "in defense of its freedom," the Tonkin Gulf Resolution authorized the President to use "all necessary measures," including military force. For Johnson, the nearly unanimous vote—416–0 in the House, 88–2 in the Senate—fixed a national claim for the United States as the aggrieved party in Southeast Asia, and also neutralized Vietnam as a presidential campaign issue by depriving Senator Goldwater of political ground to press for bolder attack. Johnson congratulated Rusk and McNamara for harnessing an instant wave of public enthusiasm, but he told them secretly that he "did not wish to escalate just because the public liked what happened...." Instead, he wanted to use the reprieve to seek methods of "maximum results and minimum danger" before weakness in South Vietnam presented another crisis. Already, while grandly inspecting the war "front" in a jeep under camouflage of ferns, General Nguyen Khanh had seized upon the American airstrikes as a pretext for imposing a state of siege to stifle his political opposition. He enjoyed little support among Vietnamese in or out of his army, warned Ambassador Taylor, who predicted that "Khanh has a 50/50 chance of lasting out the year."

In the second pivotal vote, final House passage of Johnson's War on Poverty hinged on the fate of a political hostage. More than a score of powerful Southern Democrats were demanding the ouster of Adam Yarmolinsky, Sargent Shriver's deputy director on the poverty task force. While they complained formally of Yarmolinsky's "suspect" background among Russian-speaking New York intellectuals—his father had translated Tolstoy and Dostoevsky for the Modern Library—their real grievance traced to his service at the Pentagon, where, as special counsel to Secretary McNamara, Yarmolinsky had spearheaded orders putting segregated rental quarters off limits to military personnel. This made him a bellwether symbol of controversy, especially for politicians sensitive to partisan upheaval in the South. With Goldwater sentiment running high among traditional Democrats, stalwart House segregationists treated the poverty proposal as another civil rights bill—picturing integrated job training programs, newfangled Head Start classes, perhaps even federal grants to the NAACP, with "nothing to stop them," cried the theatrical Representative Howard Smith of Virginia, "from establishing a nudist colony in your community." Against almost unanimous Republican opposition in the House, Johnson had begged poverty votes from a losing position for two weeks, one by one, saying, "This is my blood. This is it." He focused mostly on Southern Democrats. "We've bled 'em to death and we've wrung their arms," he told union leader Walter Reuther, "and twisted 'em and bought 'em and everything else." Needing 218 votes to win, he had reached late Wednesday night the "magic 200" level of promised votes, and was teetering near the brink on Friday when two unwelcome controversies intervened from the South. In the afternoon, working with Attorney General Kennedy, the President delivered a scripted phone message to Louisiana Governor John McKeithen—urging state forces to protect Monday's first court-ordered integration in St. Helena Parish, saying "it is my duty to enforce those orders if they don't." Shortly after this ordeal, Johnson reacted sharply to news coverage of the previous day's MFDP convention. "Joe Rauh was on television just raising hell . . . on the Freedom Party," he complained to Bill Moyers. "Now that's gonna ruin us if you do that . . . because you run all the border states out." More immediately, Johnson knew that such issues only emboldened moderate Democrats—those looking for a safe way to support the poverty bill so dear to their President—to demand the head of Yarmolinsky as proof to their constituents that they could curtail interference in racial customs.

Shriver squirmed through a showdown meeting in Speaker McCormack's office, protesting that only President Johnson could hire and fire executive employees. "That isn't going to satisfy those people," McCormack replied. From a phone in the hallway, Shriver pleaded with Bill

Moyers and President Johnson to spare him the awful choice, only to be told that he must take care of the matter himself. Shriver hedged miserably. He told the holdout Democrats that he would not positively recommend Yarmolinsky for a job, which they accepted as a guaranteed purge. Their swing votes established the War on Poverty on the night of the Tonkin Gulf Resolution, and Shriver returned from Capitol Hill to face Yarmolinsky. "Well, we've just thrown you to the wolves," he said, "and this is the worst day in my life."

Johnson endured final torments when Minority Leader Halleck refused to dispense with the archaic requirement that the House vote on an "embossed" copy of the poverty bill, which meant a night's delay. The President exploded with rage on learning that several Texas representatives "really had the gall" to say they would stay over in Washington for the Saturday vote only if the administration supplied government planes to fly them home afterward. Early the next morning, Secretary McNamara called with threats from a different quarter. Because CIA Director McCone had disclosed too much to congressional leaders about the secret commando raids on North Vietnam, he warned, Johnson might face questions at his Saturday press conference on whether the United States had provoked the Gulf of Tonkin incident. "This is a very delicate subject," McNamara told the President. He said he and McGeorge Bundy had prepared careful contingent replies, because, while Johnson could not admit that the raids took place, "neither should you get in a position of denying it." The North Vietnamese already had requested international inspection of the island targets, said McNamara, "and it would be very unfortunate if they developed proof that you in effect have misstated the case."

The President survived the day on both fronts. His poverty bill survived, 226–184, and he laughed when Walter Jenkins reported that Halleck's formality allowed some straddling members to record a vote each way. Johnson sailed through the press conference at the LBJ Ranch without challenge on the Gulf of Tonkin, but there were questions about the reported sacrifice of Yarmolinsky from the poverty task force. Johnson cut them off by tersely denying that Yarmolinsky had ever left the Pentagon: "No, your thoughts are wrong. . . . He never left."

A worried Joseph Califano, who in fact had replaced Yarmolinsky months earlier at the Department of Defense, privately asked Secretary McNamara how Johnson could hope to lie so brazenly in public. McNamara replied that Califano was missing the larger point that power is not for the squeamish, and that the greater good as defined by the President superseded all personal concerns. "None of us is important," he told Califano. "Everyone's expendable."

IN TALLAHASSEE, the nine clergy celebrated their release with an integrated breakfast Friday morning at the airport cafe where they had been arrested as Freedom Riders. ("Service—3 Years Later," a newsphoto caption noted wryly.) Groggy and light-headed from fasting since Monday while lawyers scrambled to free them on bond, the former prisoners were immensely relieved to learn that jail rumors of outright war in Asia were exaggerated. They absorbed the headlines radiating from their lost week—Tonkin Gulf, Mississippi, War on Poverty—and shared what details they could glean on their own. Rev. Robert Stone learned that a judge in Hattiesburg was just then setting free with suspended sentences the two admitted pipe-beaters of Rabbi Arthur Lelyveld of Cleveland—one of the religious pickets Stone had been recruiting weekly since the original Hattiesburg Freedom Day in January—and that Lelyveld would deliver the principal eulogy for Andrew Goodman on Sunday in New York. Israel Dresner of New Jersey—one of the rabbis who had answered Martin Luther King's jail summons to St. Augustine in June—missed word that King had returned there, just across Florida, because King had drawn less notice than the jailing of the Tallahassee prisoners themselves.

King floundered in backwater behind two breaking waves. He praised Judge Bryan Simpson for ordering seventeen segregated or resegregated public businesses to comply with the civil rights law, saying, "Now the citizens of St. Augustine have an opportunity to live together in peace and harmony." Hours later, however, the St. Johns County grand jury undercut Simpson by releasing a new presentment that rebuked King and the federal government alike as outsiders. In a reluctant concession to the St. Augustine movement, the grand jury established a biracial commission that never met because its white members promptly resigned. King reverted to critical lament, telling another audience that the presentment was "out of line with the mood of the age," but he saw no timely role for his protest methods now that rival government powers were in conflict over racial standards. Judge Simpson already was displacing him as a focus of resentment and death threats. (St. Augustine mayor Joseph Shelley, who publicly accused Simpson of being "bought and paid for by Lyndon Johnson," joined civic leaders from Trinity Episcopal church in a protracted but fruitless campaign to have the judge impeached as a federal tyrant.) Along with Jackie Robinson and Yale Chaplain William Sloane Coffin, King offered encouragements to the local movement, which in turn supported Judge Simpson through the painful aftermath of the summer's clashes at the Slave Market. Robert Hayling, who lost his dental business to the point of bankruptcy, struggled with bouts of depression and letdown, feeling abandoned by King. "On the surface, conditions have quieted down considerably," he wrote in a newsletter with Henry Twine, "but a closer look reveals the same old trouble and discord seething underneath."

Swamped also by larger news, King made phone calls from St. Augustine about Johnson and the primeval drama in Mississippi. Both these tides—one becoming a colossal popular force in the White House, the other awakening millions of Americans to the meaning of the civil rights movement—were heading toward the Democratic convention in Atlantic City. Bayard Rustin reminded King that he foresaw a "terrific squabble" there between friendly forces, with Johnson and Mississippi's Freedom Democrats each expecting King to control the other. King told Rustin he was thinking of an extreme middle course: a public fast through the convention, honoring his commitment to the Mississippi movement without undue public disruption.

From St. Augustine, King called his lawyer Clarence Jones about drafting an article for him to temper a strain of "thinking now prevalent" in the movement: that by ratcheting up militancy in nonviolent protest, "you can somehow capture political power." He returned to Atlanta long enough to ransack home and office for a lost passport, growing desperate enough to ask Harold DeWolf to search for it through the truckload of personal papers just shipped in boxes to Boston University. He asked for a meeting with President Johnson by telegram, tended church business on the side—arranging a guest pulpit appearance for Ralph Abernathy— then rushed to New York in time for newsmaking services on Sunday, August 9. To overflow crowds that backed up into the streets outside the separate funerals of Andrew Goodman and Mickey Schwerner, loudspeakers carried the voices of David Dennis, James Farmer, Arthur Lelyveld, and John Lewis.

From his pulpit at Abyssinian Baptist, Adam Clayton Powell scolded King by name as an interloper during the recent riots—"...no leader outside of Harlem should come into this town and tell us what to do..." —while King himself reprised one of his standard sermons, "A Knock at Midnight," a few blocks away at Riverside Church: "The church must be reminded that it is not the master or the servant of the state, but rather the conscience of the state." At the "midnight" of personal or national crisis, King preached, the prophetic voice must raise hope of a just morning, as slaves once sang, "I'm so glad that trouble don't last always."

After a speech on Monday at Amherst College in Massachusetts, King returned for long strategy meetings with his New York Research Committee. The imposing site—usually the library of Wachtel's Madison Avenue law firm—suggested that King's public business had outgrown the old days when the now-banished Stanley Levison had supplied most of King's worldly advice from his head. Members debated far-ranging choices before King as a nonviolent leader of religious credentials—approving with reservations a proposed *Playboy* interview with King,* to be published among photographs of nude models, while painfully reprimanding one of

---

* *Playboy* interviewer Alex Haley—whose book subject, Malcolm X, remained overseas— sweetened the magazine's offer with his own admiration. If King would sit for an interview, Haley promised to donate his entire writing fee to SCLC.

their own number, Clarence Jones, for telling a reporter that King might cooperate one day with Malcolm X. In an atmosphere of shifting internal politics for King's favor, the latter subject opened blistering contentions about loyalty and free expression, but the overriding issue of the time was the political crisis ahead in Atlantic City. King told the Research Committee on Tuesday of his request for a personal audience with President Johnson.

Bayard Rustin undertook to run political interference at the White House. Getting through to a secretary in the office of Johnson aide Jack Valenti, he vouched for himself with details behind the telegram. "Mr. Rustin told me very confidentially that Dr. King's family needs him," the secretary recorded, "and they want to know what he is going to be doing." Her memo circulated that night to Walter Jenkins among other top assistants, and Lee White called Rustin the next day to scout King's purpose. When King himself later called White from the New York World's Fair, where he was keeping a promise to spend a rare day with Coretta and their children, White told him that secrecy would be essential to any White House talks on the sensitive subject of the Mississippi Freedom Democrats. King agreed, but White recommended that Johnson duck him anyway. "If it looks like a secret meeting and is discovered, there are all sorts of implications that might be drawn," he warned the President. "If he comes through the front door, it is simply an unnecessary affront to a large number of people at this particular time."

The awkward minuet continued through the week, with Rustin presenting himself as friend to each side. He told White that he detected "a sense of distress" in King, and perhaps in King's other advisers, over an impression that Johnson did not want to offend white voters by meeting with King. When White countered that Johnson was eager to see King under proper conditions, Rustin tried to present King as a reasonable professional with constituent worries of his own, namely, that civil rights supporters would bridle at the White House "moratorium" on demonstrations unless assured that their issues were being addressed. Somewhere in Rustin's fraternal incantation, however, White identified a nefarious intent: "...King has made it so crystal clear that what he really wants is the publicity of meeting with you," he wrote the President. On instructions from Johnson, White put King off with polite schedule regrets.

The President worked feverishly in advance to avoid a convention debate over the MFDP. He rejected as ludicrous the idea of seating both delegations. "We'd have more damn wars than you ever saw," he told UAW president Walter Reuther. "Who's gonna haul the [state] banner in demonstrations?" He told Senator Humphrey that "if we mess with the group of Negroes ... we will lose fifteen states without even campaigning." He instructed his political friend James Rowe to identify and target every MFDP supporter on the convention's Credentials Committee. Saying he did not want to be "panicky or desperate," he told Roy Wilkins that "the cause you fought for all your life is likely to be reversed and go right down the drain if you don't... find some possible solution." Wilkins apologized for the pressures, saying the NAACP was "in the Mississippi project just by being almost on a letterhead, you might say." The President understood that political survival in the NAACP required Wilkins to support the MFDP, and shared Wilkins's self-serving slurs against King as a security risk.* He disparaged the MFDP delegation as the artificial creation of "questionable people that met here in a Washington hotel," and said the FBI reports on them were "shocking." On the other hand, the President told Reuther, the convention would prefer the MFDP to the all-white Mississippi delegation in a roll call vote, and if such an openly destructive choice could not be avoided, "I ain't much good as your leader."

The President confessed to Reuther some guilt about his facade of high government duty. "The country is going to hell while I'm talking about the Freedom Party in Mississippi," he said. Lee White continued to stall the appointment request by Martin Luther King. "I did not detect any anger or annoyance or other sign of trouble in his voice," he reported. "But I also did not detect any regret or apology for having said he would call and then failing to do so." When King, having located his wayward passport, left on Friday, August 14, for a speaking tour in Holland and West Germany, White expressed hope that a long trip might solve the problem by delay. "He won't be gone through the convention," Johnson sourly predicted. "He'll be back here on your doorstep."

THAT FRIDAY MORNING, after the final session of summer classes, volunteer teacher Sandra Adickes gave in to six students who clamored to act upon what they had learned at her Priest Creek Freedom School. She escorted five girls and eleven-year-old Curtis Ducksworth to the downtown Hattiesburg Library, where group leader Jamilla Stokes explained their wish to apply for children's library cards. Eyes rolled in dismay, and a distraught supervisor whispered urgently that such a thoughtless request could backfire against readers throughout the city. Sure enough, on the hasty instruction of Mayor Claude Pittman, Police Chief Hugh Herring arrived twenty minutes later to close the library for an unscheduled inventory, then joined a gathering crowd that trailed Adickes and her resolute charges down Main Street to a hushed standoff over the integration barrier at the S. H. Kress & Co. lunchroom—with the manager claiming to fear imminent mob action by nearly a hundred frowning patrons. A waitress unhappily notified the Freedom School table of management's improvised fallback policy, saying, "We have to serve the colored, but we are not going to serve

---

* "The motivation of King, of course, is well known to yourself," Wilkins told Johnson. "You know some of the forces behind him."

the whites who come in with them." When the students chose to leave rather than eat without their teacher, police herded the group into an alley and nipped any chance of another stop on the Freedom School excursion by arresting Adickes for vagrancy. The criminal charge did not last long, but the Kress Company of New York and Hattiesburg officials would defend themselves through civil litigation all the way to the U.S. Supreme Court* six years later on complex twists pertaining to the status of "a Caucasian in the company of Negroes," arguing successfully that they did nothing to mistreat Adickes under federal law.

Hours after the Adickes arrest, two of the world's premier entertainers stepped from a small charter plane on a dark airstrip near Greenwood. Harry Belafonte, who clutched a black satchel, had recruited Sidney Poitier for the mission with banter—saying, "They might think twice about killing *two* big niggers"—but levity fell away at the sight of their Mississippi reception. Night bugs swirled around an outdoor light bulb dangling over a latched gate and a dirt road that led outward through wooded fields. SNCC leader James Forman drew aside several staff members to talk logistics over walkie-talkies, leaving the two arrivals with lead driver Willie Blue and two waiting cars that had been sanded for night travel—every inch of chrome or paint finish stripped to military dullness. Young Blue wore a big straw hat and a cast on an arm that he allowed had been broken in jail. When the convoy moved out through the gate, Belafonte expressed relief at a signal of headlights shining from a distant line of cars. "That's the Klan," Forman corrected him, and silence gripped the passengers through a swerving chase over back roads. Only one of the pursuing vehicles got closer than a threatening pass, and each time Willie Blue managed to interpose the SNCC escort car to absorb the ramming blow. The movie stars retained the image of a heavy piece of lumber strapped to the attacker's front bumper.

They escaped at a trot into jubilee bedlam at the Elks Hall, where Idella Craft achieved local fame by lowering herself from the balcony to drape her arms around Belafonte's neck. Bob Zellner, one of the few white SNCC veterans, led the freedom songs, and Bob Moses delivered the welcome to a crowd that gasped with amazement, unfazed for once by the massed headlight flashes outside or the drone of the Klan leaflet drops overhead. Not even Martin Luther King had turned out Greenwood's Negro schoolteachers in any number, but the veneer of show business rendered vulnerable prestige jobs safe or madly unimportant. Some had journeyed far to see the film *Lilies of the Field,* and everyone had seen or

---

* In *Adickes v. S. H. Kress & Co.* (1970), Justice John Harlan delivered the prevailing opinion that lower federal courts had erred in summarily dismissing the Adickes complaint, and remanded the case to Mississippi for further proceedings, which Adickes chose not to pursue.

knew about the Academy Awards show on television that spring when Poitier broke the color line for Best Actor. "I am thirty-seven years old," Poitier told the Greenwood crowd. "I have been a lonely man all my life ...because I have not found love, but this room is *overflowing* with it."

Belafonte sang his signature song, "Banana Boat (Day-O)," with its sing-along choruses known to everyone, including the Klansmen posted outdoors. After a short speech about years of private dedication to the movement, he held up the black satchel to climactic cheers. Everyone knew there was money inside—Forman talked of "manna" gathered by Belafonte on emergency request, and Moses of a saving lifeline for the summer project—but it was well understood that the details were best left unsaid. Privately, Belafonte told Forman he had raised $10,000 beyond the $60,000 cash in the satchel, and that the extra money was reserved to finance a post-summer getaway trip as his own prescribed therapy for the cumulative "battle fatigue" of movement leaders.

Gunshots cracked the windshield of a staff car parked outside COFO headquarters later that night. Inside, Poitier and Belafonte overheard two-way radio dispatches about a volunteer being followed in Tallahatchie County. They were spared background grumbling about their special beds and all-night sentries (COFO staff workers pointedly reminded Forman that he had criticized Martin Luther King for accepting celebrity treatment in Greenwood), but neither visitor slept much. Poitier did calisthentics on the floor.

Saturday night, in the afterglow of the Belafonte mission, a farewell party for departing volunteers offered free tunafish salad until a cracking noise emptied Lula's Restaurant into a steady rainstorm. Shouts led just outside to a familiar parked car with a freshly shattered driver's side window, and Silas McGhee tumbled toward the pavement when someone opened the door. With Bob Zellner and others ripping off their shirts to bandage a gunshot wound below his left temple, a COFO caravan transported McGhee—still conscious—to the Leflore County Hospital. Segregationists arrived to resume the perimeter blockade from the theater incident three weeks earlier. When Zellner grabbed a gurney and wheeled McGhee past the emergency room standoff over segregation, fearful hospital staff tried to block him for failure to wear a shirt. When a nurse tried to administer a sedative during the paralysis of doctors and administrators, McGhee himself reared up and refused any shots until a Negro doctor arrived. A Negro doctor finally arranged ambulance transport to Jackson for a midnight operation to remove a bullet that had broken through McGhee's upper jawbone on a slightly downward path—he had been leaning against the window, dozing through the rain on volunteer taxi duty—to lodge behind his nose near the throat. Sunday morning, having relieved breathing by tracheostomy, the medical team expressed confidence that McGhee would survive.

The shooting put the Greenwood movement into a spasm of firsts—first daytime mass meeting, first attempted youth march against riot police, first stampede of newcomers armed with revolvers to guard Lula's and many rumored follow-up targets. Volunteer Sally Belfrage nervously ducked home to hide one confiscated pistol under her bed, only to behold a shiny weapon out handy on the sink near the kitchen table where her host family was busily staying calm together, shelling peas. Both Silas McGhee's brothers were in jail by Sunday night, but Moses, Forman, Stokely Carmichael, and other leaders withdrew from Greenwood and parallel crises elsewhere: a beating in Laurel, a bombing in Natchez, a Saturday night raid in McComb.

Moses balanced his footing on charred brick ruins to address a memorial service under blue sky at Mount Zion Baptist in Neshoba County—exactly two months after the June 16 burning—then drove to a three-day COFO summit meeting at Tougaloo College. With Belafonte's cash delivery, they could extend a presence beyond the summer to reassure new followers, many of whom knew nothing of the original timetable and expressed fear that the movement was shutting down in the face of violence. The COFO leaders wrestled with a host of consequent decisions such as which skeletal projects to keep, where to find volunteers during the school year, how to balance Freedom Schools with regular Mississippi classes, what levels of violence to anticipate, and whether they could muster enough support for training and security. They also resolved to send the entire MFDP delegation to Atlantic City immediately—in advance of the next week's Democratic convention—to buttress their claim to seats representing Mississippi.

Returning to New York from Europe, Martin Luther King maneuvered toward Atlantic City on a tandem course. On Monday, Rustin renewed by telegram King's urgent request to meet with President Johnson. On Tuesday, Lee White said the meeting was set for Wednesday morning and tried to breeze over a few White House stipulations: first, that King's audience would be "broadened" to include other civil rights leaders such as Roy Wilkins and A. Philip Randolph, and also that the session was to be entirely off the record. King's second, Bayard Rustin, tried to make sure that he would be among those invited, saying he could help the White House prevent trouble from the boisterous young people of Mississippi. When denied an invitation, Rustin reported to King that President Johnson was up to something fishy. King, for his part, perceived signs reminiscent of a White House move in June of 1963, when President Kennedy had sandwiched a crowd around him as a means of controlling the political agenda.

The King and Johnson camps skirmished through telephone intermediaries. Johnson had the advantage of better sources. Bill Moyers heard from his clergyman friend Robert Spike, head of the national Commission on Religion and Race, that civil rights leaders were preparing for demonstrations in Atlantic City because they anticipated no White House concessions to the Mississippi freedom delegation. "He says the chances of serious violence are high," Moyers wrote President Johnson—leaving ambiguous whether mayhem would arise from previously nonviolent movement Negroes or Klan sympathizers in New Jersey. Either prospect posed ruin for a presidential campaign.

Beyond volunteer sources, the White House enjoyed spy intelligence from the FBI, which, under the "roving" wiretap order signed the previous October, placed a temporary intercept on King's guest home in New York. There and over the tap on Bayard Rustin's phone, Bureau technicians overheard King's camp forecast accurately that Johnson, secure of the pro-Negro vote already, would act to preserve hope of reconciling now or later with the Democratic white South. King and his allies labored to make the President explain on the public record why he preferred a segregated, pro-Goldwater delegation to the suffering, loyal MFDP, but King's interest in the White House meeting faded with every indication that Johnson's entire purpose was to avoid mentioning or hearing about Mississippi. Through Tuesday night into Wednesday, King debated whether to skip the session rather than allow Johnson to finesse his purpose. High-speed summaries of these conversations reached FBI headquarters, where Deke DeLoach filtered out most of King's substantive reasoning to portray him as insolent and headstrong, yet subservient to advisers. "Deke's information is that if King did show," Lee White advised President Johnson, ". . . he was instructed to 'speak up to the President.'"

President Johnson burst into the gathering of civil rights leaders, minus King, with a declaration that he would consider no political matters related to the convention, followed by a monologue on his plans and achievements that exhausted the fifty-nine minutes until his next engagement. The Johnson assistants who had disparaged King for a self-promotional desire to meet the President found cheekiness in his last-minute notice of "regret that I am unable to attend." King, for his part, tried to circumvent Johnson's control of the White House agenda. Affecting an offhand desire "to communicate my views on subjects which might come under discussion," he filled three telegram pages on precisely the one subject he correctly assumed would be off limits. In his own name, King presented Johnson with four arguments why he should seat the MFDP delegates, ranging from gritty politics and moral choice to civic abstraction: "Number three, pressures of metropolitan existence require some firm evidence the democratic process can prevail in the United States[,] and that persons deprived of representation at the state level can receive redress of grievances before some national body."

Lee White notified President Johnson of King's rapid maneuver before the other Negro leaders left the secret meeting ("The attached telegram from King was received here at 11:23...”), warning of FBI intelligence that King's friends wanted him to release the telegram to the press. At noon, George Reedy called the President for guidance on press rumors about a telegram, saying King's “whole life's work would be ruined if the Mississippi delegation were seated.” Johnson's staff threw together contingency plans for muting a major news break, or “beating King to the punch,” with a White House announcement that the Mississippi question rested properly before the Democratic convention. King backed away from a direct statement or release to the press, however, and the two sides accepted a preliminary standoff heading into Atlantic City.

Mortified FBI officials were battling their own peculiar crisis. The front page of the Wednesday morning *Atlanta Constitution* revealed the FBI's gift of a birthday cake to murder suspect Herbert Guest. FBI field agents dodged as best they could internal inquiries about why they had undertaken—without approval from headquarters—a ploy that raised wild suspicions of fraternization and exposed the Bureau to public ridicule.

Elected MFDP delegates from all parts of Mississippi were converging upon Tougaloo College, where Bob Moses ended the three-day staff conference with a Wednesday announcement that COFO had decided to extend or replace roughly two hundred of seven hundred summer volunteers. Moses acknowledged to reporters that the summer project was better known for a running tally of arrests (250) and beatings (fifty-two) than its negligible increase in registered Negro voters, but he claimed success for the political goal of opening Mississippi to the rudiments of common citizenship. A visiting *New York Times* correspondent described siege conditions that night in Philadelphia, Mississippi, where a select group of ten interracial volunteers dared to open a project office in territory still traumatized by the triple murders of June. Deputy Sheriff Cecil Price served eviction notices and a court summons for trespassing; one of the more polite phone messages announced, “The end is tonight,” and carloads of conspicuously armed whites prowled outside as the rattled volunteers lying on bedrolls contemplated whether to resist attack. “We decided to remain nonviolent to the death,” a white graduate student from Princeton told the *Times*. In the morning, his colleague Ralph Featherstone, a Negro teacher from New Jersey, drove a bookmobile into the rural areas toward Meridian, where churches burned that night and the next. The bookmobile canvass was COFO's prescribed regimen until Freedom School classes could be opened after the September cotton was picked.

On Thursday morning, August 20, President Johnson addressed a ceremonial crowd in the White House flower garden. “For so long as man has lived on this earth, poverty has been his curse,” he said in a voice husky with his own memories, adding that the first great nation was willing and able "to make a commitment to eradicate poverty among its people. ... The days of the dole in our country are numbered." First to Adam Clayton Powell, then to scores of legislators and guests (including, discreetly in the back, the sacrificial scapegoat Adam Yarmolinsky), Johnson dispensed pens used in signing into law the $947 million Economic Opportunity Act. Between ceremonies for two other new laws that day—a defense appropriation more than fifty times larger than the proposed War on Poverty, and a securities reform bill—reporters trailed on walks behind an energized President who fished from his pocket one astonishing preelection opinion poll after another: Johnson running ahead of Goldwater 67–32 in Wisconsin, 70–30 in New York, 77–23 in Republican Maine.

At Tougaloo College, where buses were loading with MFDP delegates, many of whom never before had left Mississippi, a radio reporter from the destination state of New Jersey interviewed Stokely Carmichael about the summer project. Carmichael stressed the travail of registration work in Tallahatchie County, and reviewed his own intermittent movement service since entering Mississippi and Parchman Penitentiary in 1961 as a twenty-year-old Freedom Rider. When the reporter asked about the bullet holes in the car he had parked, Carmichael explained that his vehicle was well known in the Delta's Second District, where he was project director. He pointed out windshield damage from potshots during the Friday night Belafonte-Poitier visit, then the driver's side hole from the bullet that hit Silas McGhee.

"Were they aiming for Silas himself," the reporter asked in awe, "or do you think they thought it was you in the car, knowing your car?"

"That's hard to say," Carmichael replied. His explanation echoed the mentoring tone of Bob Moses behind his own insouciant bravado: "If they were aiming for Silas—and I know that they want Silas McGhee very badly because he's one of the local youth who just wouldn't tolerate any of their nonsense—then I wouldn't feel bad. But if they were aiming for me because it was my car, and Silas took the shot, then that's something I have to deal with. And I'm not sure. Now, they've chased my car several times and shot at it before. It's very hard for me to say."

34

A Dog in the Manger:
The Atlantic City Compromise

ATLANTIC CITY, marooned by the spread of convenient air travel to warmer resorts, was suffering slow reduction from splendor to relic. Home to the Miss America Beauty Pageant, and still the storied setting for the board game Monopoly—Marvin Gardens, Reading Railroad, Boardwalk —the aging queen of seashore destinations hosted a great storm of Democrats also in transition. At a preconvention hearing on Friday, August 21, George Wallace hotly denounced national Democratic leaders as revolutionaries who "would sell the birthright of our nation" to install "an alien philosophy of government." Having arranged by recent state law to expunge President Johnson and his running mate from Alabama ballots in November, so that Wallace himself could allocate "Democratic" votes in the Electoral College (eventually to Goldwater), Wallace notified convention leaders that he cared little whether or not they unseated his Alabama delegation over this supercession of the party's nominees. "I'm not here to beg," he declared. Wallace demanded that national Democrats repeal the civil rights law, and foretold otherwise an "uprising" on par with the revolt against Reconstruction. Against an excess of "central authority, given free reign by this very party," he promised a conservative movement to "take charge of one of the parties in the next four years."

Busloads of Mississippi Freedom Democrats were arriving at the Gem Motel on Pacific Avenue, an address tarnished enough to welcome late-booking stragglers who ate from cracker boxes and slept four to a room. One national correspondent who watched them disembark for a spirited mass meeting described "a hymn-singing group of dedicated men and women who feel as though they had temporarily escaped from a Mississippi prison and who think they may be jailed when they get back home." They matched Wallace in fervor, towing behind them as an exhibit of democratic devotion a burned-out replica of Mickey Schwerner's station wagon. On the long ride north, they had reviewed legalistic primers on why the regular Democrats in their state had forfeited legitimacy ("IV. B. 2. There was not a single Negro at the State Convention"), and they soon deployed in best Sunday dress as folk lobbyists among the incoming delegations. Summer volunteer Dennis Sweeney escorted MFDP representatives to search out delegates from his home state of Oregon. SNCC staff member Charles Cobb, architect of the summer Freedom Schools, wangled meetings with Massachusetts delegates who reflected the cautious sympathy of Governor Endicott Peabody, son of "Mother Peabody" from the spring crusade to St. Augustine.

With Victoria Gray of Hattiesburg, Fannie Lou Hamer had flown ahead to tell her story before a panel of historians at New York's Town Hall. She reached Atlantic City for Saturday morning breakfast with a delegate targeted as a swing vote in the Mississippi dispute. Vera Canson of Sacramento, one of two Californians and seven Negroes assigned to the Credentials Committee, absorbed a preview of Hamer's testimony in open torment. California Democrats had resolved during the summer project to support the MFDP challenge, but Governor Pat Brown expressed second thoughts about the resolution before leaving to see President Johnson that afternoon. Canson was moved by Hamer and yet mindful of larger pressures on her role; what was just for Mississippi might not be wise for the national party.

Reports on scores of wavering Democrats bombarded MFDP counsel Joseph Rauh just before his presentation to the Credentials Committee. When an NBC correspondent rushed in to shout, "Joe, they've screwed you!" Rauh replied, "My god, already?" before learning that convention managers were preparing a room too small for television. Rauh's strategy needed cameras—not so much to win initial votes as to fix an impression of Mississippi that would last through the chaotic politics of a national convention.

His protest percolated secretly by telephone into the Oval Office. "This is a helluva thing to be taking up with you," confessed Walter Jenkins to the President, "but I'm kind of scared to be making a decision by myself." He said the prepared room was big enough only for one pool camera, and that "the television people are raising hell" for separate ones. Johnson backed the single camera to minimize attention for party disputes, saying they needed to accommodate only the rival delegations. Jenkins then explained that the site was expressly chosen to hold only the testifying witnesses, and that "Joe Rauh is raising hell" over the exclusion of his MFDP clients. Conceding the point on merit, Jenkins fretted with the President over the potential theatrics of white and Negro Mississippians intermingled in a larger space. "Rauh will storm the room," Johnson feared.

Jenkins had Democratic officials, including party chairman John Bailey, holding on other lines, "kind of shook up" by Rauh's arguments about the arduous journey of the MFDP challengers from Mississippi and how "it will be awful hard to get 'em to accept any compromise if you don't even let 'em see what's going on." After a half hour's anguish over several calls, the President authorized Rauh to have the ballroom and the cameras. "I don't give a damn if he puts on a little show," he said, "as long as he just don't wreck us." Setting a pattern for the week, Johnson ordered confidants to deny flatly his involvement in Atlantic City matters large or small. "I never heard of it," declared the President. "... My name's Joe Glutz, and you haven't talked down here."

ON SATURDAY AFTERNOON, the MFDP challengers filed into seats directly across from the opposing Mississippi regulars. "We have only an hour to tell you a story of tragedy and terror in Mississippi," Rauh began. He faced the Credentials Committee as a comfortable peer, owning one of its 110 votes himself as a delegate from the District of Columbia. To counter the notion that Mississippi's regular Democrats were "legal," he emphasized the freewheeling independence of American political parties and addressed the committee as a jury of political choice. (His printed brief for the MFDP cheerfully quoted a statement by Mississippi's Democratic chairman that the convention "could seat a dozen dead dodos brought there in silver caskets and nobody could do anything about it.") Rauh summoned a hurried parade of witnesses to support his assertion that MFDP delegates were not only deserving and loyal but "willing to die" for the party's cause. Aaron Henry told of wholesale persecution over the right to vote, and accused party regulars of tending an airtight white supremacy that confined Mississippi to a garrison at the bottom rank of states ("On them is the blood and responsibility..."). Rev. Edwin King followed with firsthand accounts of white Mississippians ("...over one hundred ministers and college teachers have been forced to leave the state. ...I have been imprisoned. I have been been beaten..."), after which former governor David Lawrence of Pennsylvania asked delicately from the chair for more on party procedures and less on the state's "general life." Rauh objected that the regular party's everyday terror was "what I want the credentials committee to hear."

He called Fannie Lou Hamer, who limped forward on her polio-damaged left hip to place her purse on the witness table as attendants pinned a microphone to her cotton dress. Hamer launched her story: "It was the 31st of August in 1962 that eighteen of us traveled twenty-six miles to the county courthouse in Indianola to try to register to try to become first-class citizens. We was met in Indianola by Mississippi men, highway patrolmens...the bus driver was charged that day with driving a bus the wrong color...." She told in four sentences how her attempt started earthquakes by nightfall.

> My husband came and said the plantation owner was raising cain because I had tried to register, and before he quit talking the plantation owner came, and said, "Fannie Lou, do you know—did Pap tell you what I said?"
> I said, "Yes, sir."
> He said, "I mean that," he said. "If you don't go down and withdraw your registration, you will have to leave."

She stared straight at the bank of Credentials Committee delegates, flouting norms of polished authority with her unlettered grammar. Words that first seemed a masquerade of Aesop rose toward the spare cadence of a biblical text, packing abstract force into stories of household strife.

> And I addressed him and told him and said, "I didn't try to register for you. I tried to register for myself." I had to leave that same night.
> On the 10th of September, 1962, sixteen bullets was fired into the home of Mr. and Mrs. Robert Tucker for me. That same night two girls were shot in Ruleville, Mississippi. Also Mr. Joe McDonald's house was shot in.
> And in June, the 9th, 1963, I had attended a voter-registration workshop, was returning back to Mississippi. Ten of us was traveling by the Continental Trailway bus. When we got to Winona...

She recalled the Winona incident from the first commotion ("I stepped off the bus to see what was happening") to the steadily approaching dread in jail. "I began to hear the sounds of licks and screams," Hamer testified. "...I was carried out of that cell into another cell where they had two Negro prisoners. The State Highway Patrolman ordered the first Negro to take the blackjack." Then, near the end of her allotted eight minutes, Hamer vanished from television screens. "We will return to this scene in Atlantic City," said correspondent Edwin Newman from a control desk, "but now we switch to the White House and NBC's Robert Goralski."

President Johnson was hosting thirty Democratic governors. Four strays—McKeithen of Louisiana, Orval Faubus of Arkansas, Johnson of Mississippi, and Wallace of Alabama—boycotted the sendoff to Atlantic City, and McKeithen, who had just resigned as head of the Louisiana delegation, was calling for a general walkout if the convention unseated regulars from sister states. On this issue, the nationally televised Mississippi hearing sounded a fire bell beneath the Washington conference, which Governor John Connally of Texas described to reporters as "a very enjoyable and very delightful meeting." President Johnson mounted a diversion with the cooperation of news outlets massed on alert for revelation of his vice presidential choice. He stepped before White House correspondents, with several governors in tow, and stretched the moment with small news and a sympathetic reference to Connally—still suffering from rifle wounds inflicted in the Dallas motorcade—noting that "on this day nine months ago at very nearly this same hour in the afternoon, the duties of this office were thrust upon me by a terrible moment in our national history." The President ducked questions and withdrew to the governors' conclave in the East Room, leaving reporters with material for unrequited headlines: "Johnson Still Silent About Running Mate."

Knocked off camera, the Atlantic City hearing concluded with four more MFDP witnesses. After Rita Schwerner, for whom a section of spectators stood in silent tribute, Rauh called the national leaders James Farmer of CORE and Roy Wilkins of the NAACP, then King for a summary exhortation. "I say to you that any party in the world should be proud to have a delegation such as this seated in their midst," said King. "For it is in these saints in ordinary walks of life that the true spirit of democracy finds its most profound and abiding expression." With a glance to the Mississippi regulars at the opposite table, he bemoaned a state party that since the last Democratic convention had forced the dispatch of twenty thousand troops before it yielded "a single Negro into a state university," and was "already pledged to defy the candidate and platform of this great national body." King testified that Mississippi was "no mean issue" in world affairs—not "for all the disfranchised millions of this earth, whether they be in Mississippi or Alabama, behind the Iron Curtain, floundering in the mire of South African apartheid, or freedom-seeking persons in Cuba who have now gone three years without election. Recognition of the Freedom Democratic Party would say to them that somewhere in this world there is a nation that cares about justice. . . ."

Then came the regular Mississippi Democrats for their hour, with mountains of evidence on standard election practice and their cries to be spared "a political cross." If the convention seated ragtag "rump" challengers in place of the "lawful delegation," declared State Senator E. K. Collins, "the party in Mississippi certainly will die." Soon after, Chairman Lawrence finished all pending cases except Alabama and Mississippi, which he deferred because the politicking yielded no settlement strong enough to prevent an unseemly floor fight.

At 6:15 P.M., when Martin Luther King limped out of the hearing on a recently sprained ankle, surveillance agents radioed an SOS that yanked

FBI technicians out of Room 1923 at the Claridge Hotel on Indiana Avenue, after they had wiretapped the two telephones but before they could install microphone bugs in the walls reserved for King. In the room directly below, SAC Leo Clark of the Bureau's Atlantic City office had arranged a satellite branch of the hideaway command center in the old Post Office, where, with J. Edgar Hoover's reluctant approval ("Lyndon is way out of line"), Assistant Director Deke DeLoach had thrown together a "special squad" of twenty-seven agents, a radio operator, two stenographers, and assorted informants. Secretly, apart from FBI security liaison with the Secret Service or local law enforcement, DeLoach pushed his squad on a mission to insure that nothing could occur in Atlantic City "to embarrass the President," reporting personally to Walter Jenkins and Bill Moyers at the Pageant Motel.

One agent with a mobile radio was permanently assigned to Jenkins. Several undercover agents posed as reporters on credentials supplied by NBC News, while others monitored wiretaps on the Atlantic Avenue storefront rented for the MFDP. Agents already knew that Bayard Rustin was telling King his sprained ankle was "the most fortunate thing to ever happen to you," because it gave King an excuse to hobble out of town on crutches before President Johnson exerted his power. When he did, Rustin was predicting, many delegates professing support for the Mississippi challenge would "fall by the wayside."

Euphoria reigned for the moment among MFDP supporters. *Jet* reporter Larry Still described a tumultuous moving swarm around Fannie Lou Hamer, who "wiped the tears from her round, streaked face and sighed, 'I felt just like I was telling it from the mountain. That's why I like that song *Go Tell It on the Mountain.* I feel like I'm talking to the world.'" Indignant to learn that President Johnson had cut into her airtime, she was denouncing a plot when voices at the Gem Motel called out that television was showing film clips from the end of her testimony.

> After the first Negro had beat until he was exhausted, the State Highway Patrolman ordered the second Negro to take the blackjack. The second Negro began to beat and I began to work my feet, and the State Highway Patrolman ordered the first Negro who had beat to set on my feet to keep me from working my feet. I began to scream and one white man got up and began to beat me in my head and tell me to hush. One white man—my dress had worked up high, he walked over and pulled my dress down—and he pulled my dress back, back up.
>
> I was in jail when Medgar Evers was murdered.
>
> All of this is on account we want to register, to become first-class citizens, and if the Freedom Democratic Party is not seated now, I question America....

Evening news broadcasts delivered Hamer to larger audiences than Johnson had preempted in the afternoon. Atlantic City's Western Union office reported 416 night telegrams supporting the MFDP, against only one for the regulars, and Rauh claimed that his "knockout" witnesses "won the Boardwalk." Observing that President Johnson knew above all else how to count votes, he relished the bargaining ahead. "We won't take any of those second-rate compromises," Rauh told reporters Saturday night.

Rauh did not disguise the compromise he preferred. Fully half the twenty-six major credentials contests cited in his written brief—dating back to 1836—had been settled by the simple formula of splitting the prize. His most treasured example was the Texas case of 1944, when New Deal loyalists, including young Congressman Lyndon Johnson, challenged the dominant Texas regulars over their refusal to endorse Franklin Roosevelt's wartime reelection. Johnson had denounced the regular delegation as "Republicans who posed as Democrats" in an effort to "sabotage democracy," and the convention had seated the rival Texans with half votes apiece.

None of the precedent cases turned on racial imagery, however, which made the face of Fannie Lou Hamer doubly sensitive to Democrats on both sides. She gave the MFDP cause a moral urgency far above the esoteric record of warring local factions, but she also presented a daunting new symbol for the majority party of any state. "The thing is out of hand now!" Senator James Eastland squawked to President Johnson Saturday night. From his home in Mississippi, where he watched proceedings on television, Eastland despaired of selling the President's offer to seat the all-white delegation in exchange for some veneer of party loyalty. (A mild statement of *intention* to support the Democratic nominees would do, said the President, even if they knew they would back Goldwater.) Eastland told Johnson that "to be perfectly frank," the Mississippi party had nearly endorsed Goldwater already and that most delegates had not wanted to go to Atlantic City in the first place. The President objected that "poor 'ol Mississippi" was making it impossible for him to help his friends. "People oughtn't to want to come and stay all night with you if they're gonna bomb your house while they're there," he said, and joked with an edge about shutting off the cotton subsidy program. Even so, the best Eastland could secure was a vague promise from Governor Paul Johnson not to bring official "reprisals" against any Mississippi delegates who accepted the convention's terms.

On Sunday afternoon, Walter Jenkins notified the President that Chairman Lawrence of the Credentials Committee was about to entertain votes on a motion offensive to both sides: strong enough to make the South walk out, weak enough for Rauh to take a minority report to the convention floor. "I thought he was gonna procrastinate," objected the President, after which Lawrence postponed the issue again. He appointed Minnesota attorney general Walter Mondale to head a five-delegate Mississippi sub-committee charged to resolve matters before Monday night's opening gavel, and from seclusion, communicating with dozens of roving caucuses, Mondale's group bickered to exhausted recess toward dawn.

At midnight Sunday, a hundred supporters of the Mississippi movement set up a circular picket line outside Convention Hall, pledged to keep a perpetual vigil until the MFDP was seated. James Forman, Stokely Carmichael, and others huddled in the center with their walkie-talkies to orchestrate messages of song and silence among numbers that grew above three hundred the next day, when dignitaries began to drop by with speeches of encouragement. Among pickets still adjusting from the summer project to the neon lights of Atlantic City, many were further disoriented by Monday's influx of 5,260 delegates and alternates who arrived for the main event festooned in political buttons and patriotic colors, often topped with LBJ souvenir cowboy hats. Bound for receptions, caucuses, lobster feasts around open beach fires, and parties given to eight hundred guests at a time in the Ventnor villa rented by hostess Perle Mesta, the delegates and observers swallowed up the Mississippi vigil among other spectacles along the jammed boardwalk pier, such as Dixie Blandy, the flagpole sitter, and a daredevil lady who plunged on horseback from a high tower into a vat of water.

On Monday morning, Democratic leaders had no better strategy than permanent delay—hoping the Mississippi question would "get lost in the business of the convention" behind a proposed statement from the Mondale subcommittee that the issues were "complex." Walter Reuther praised the notion to Johnson as "your original idea," but Johnson foresaw an impatient walkout spreading to eight or ten states. Into this White House quandary arrived a fresh telegram from Martin Luther King. "In the last few days," King wired from Atlantic City, "the charged atmosphere of the convention has left the impression that only you are in a position to make clear the Democratic Party's position.... Members of the Credentials Committee have made clear their wishes to follow you...."

The President sought the advice of Richard Russell, who, like most prominent Southern Democrats, was staying home from the convention. Johnson complained that King had been pushing him to take a public position—"trying to get me in it every way he can"—and feared a plot. If King could force him to defend the white delegation, then the civil rights forces would have "an excuse to say I turned on the Negro," and Robert Kennedy could swoop in to say Johnson was unfit for the Democratic nomination because he coddled Mississippi segregationists. "I think this is Bobby's trap," the President confided.

Russell tried to calm his friend. He thought King at worst might "increase the backlash a little bit" and cut a million votes or so off Johnson's victory margin. While he recommended that the President not dignify King's wire with an answer, Russell said Johnson was not the first politician to be rattled by King's political moves. "For example, in Atlanta, he can scare the hell out of [Mayor] Ivan Allen any time he wants to," said Russell, "and rightly so ... from a political standpoint."

No words could cure Johnson's fears of racial emotion in combination with the Kennedy myth. He had already arranged to postpone until safely past the close of convention business two much anticipated events—a film tribute to the slain president, and Jacqueline Kennedy's appearance at a marathon reception to shake the hand of each Democratic delegate. To guard against schemes to set loose floods of mourning that might sweep away normal arrangements, including his nomination, Johnson tasked Deke DeLoach and his undercover FBI squad to mount surveillance of Kennedy, their nominal boss, in tandem with King and the Negro challengers.

On Monday, FBI agents circulated reports on a press interview in which Kennedy promised an unspecified statement on Tuesday, noting suspiciously that he "refused to elaborate" on its nature. Kennedy turned out merely to be teasing a Senate endorsement from Mayor Wagner of New York, but agents hinted that his Senate plans could disguise a presidential coup by spontaneous "draft" in Atlantic City. When Kennedy paid a courtesy visit to the delegation from West Virginia, a pivotal state for his brother's nomination in 1960, observers sensed political electricity that made "applause hit like thunder." Meanwhile, on Hoover's orders, analysts dissected Sunday's *Washington Post* story on Kennedy's tenure as attorney general, which, because of a passage saying Kennedy had reformed some entrenched attitudes at the FBI, headquarters scornfully dismissed as "obviously another attempt by the Department to claim credit for FBI achievements in organized crime and civil rights, at the same time making a snide attack on Mr. Hoover and the Bureau—for political purposes."

The President's worries were no secret to those who saw him regularly. On learning of Robert Kennedy's discreet withdrawal that Monday as a Massachusetts delegate—the better to qualify as a candidate in New York—a secretary handed Johnson a note that borrowed Kennedy tactics for the Mississippi dilemma: suppose one or more of the loyal white regulars "got a virus," and then chose Freedom Democrats as ad hoc substitutes (the way Kennedy had designated his sister-in-law Joan to substitute for him in the Massachusetts delegation)? By this scenario, Negro delegates would break the Mississippi color line by personal invitation rather than by the imposed dictum of the convention. President Johnson thought enough of the idea to make several calls to Atlantic City, but Walter Jenkins found no support in Southern delegations for Negro company. Besides, the few Mississippi regulars who might volunteer to withdraw were precisely the ones Johnson wanted to showcase for future conventions. He threw the crumpled note into his trash can.

In Atlantic City, reporters noticed Martin Luther King and Senator Hubert Humphrey push separately through mid-Monday crowds into the Pageant Motel, known as the "convention White House." Safely removed to a quiet suite with Bob Moses and some dozen MFDP negotiators, Humphrey passionately advocated the convention's three-part settlement offer. First, as a condition of being seated, each Mississippi regular delegate must pledge support for the Democratic candidate and the party's pro–civil rights platform, which most were expected to refuse. (The Credentials Committee had just voted to require a similar pledge from the Alabama delegation.) Second, the formal call to future conventions would give notice of disqualification for segregationist creed or practice, and third, the freedom delegation would be welcome in Atlantic City as nonvoting guests. To objections that MFDP delegates should have at least those seats vacated by disloyal regulars, Humphrey swerved uncomfortably from alleged deficiencies in the MFDP's selection process to direct personal appeal. He said the President was testing them all in the battle against Goldwater. Without revealing his direct and indirect orders from the White House,* Humphrey said he was given to understand that his own chance to be nominated for vice president depended on his ability to prevent floor fights over Mississippi, which in turn demanded superhuman forbearance from the Freedom Democrats. He pleaded with them to stop pushing for seats.

Fannie Lou Hamer confessed awe of Humphrey before shaming him like a disappointed mother. "Senator Humphrey, I been praying about you, and I been thinking about you, and you're a good man," she said. "The trouble is, you're afraid to do what you know is right." In tears, Humphrey protested that his commitment to civil rights was long-standing. Hamer cried, too, saying she was going to pray further over him. Rauh and others, including Allard Lowenstein among the MFDP legal advisers, made peacemaking suggestions until Humphrey objected to the presence of Rep. Edith Green of Oregon, who was fighting White House direction on the Credentials Committee. She took offense, which allowed the stalemate to break up on procedural jealousies.

Humphrey sneaked away with Walter Jenkins to report his frustration. "I walked into the lion's den," he told the President. "I listened patiently. I argued fervently. I used up all the heartstrings that I had." Johnson put Clark Clifford on an extension phone to listen. Walter Jenkins said Edith Green claimed a surplus of ten votes to force a floor fight on her plan to split the Mississippi votes. He said some members of the committee were

---

* Johnson had put Humphrey's challenge succinctly to Walter Reuther on August 17: "You better talk to Hubert Humphrey, because I'm telling you that he's got no future in this party at all if this big war comes off here, and the South walks out, and we all get in a hell of a mess."

growing restive because of hair appointments and other pressing needs. Johnson wondered if they realized that they might have to hold up the entire convention to avoid a roll call.

Down the elevator and through the lobby, the negotiators pushed into a throng of reporters that merged with an incoming crowd around Credentials Committee chairman David Lawrence. Thrown together in the center, Lawrence and Joseph Rauh parried each other's questions about that night's opening session ("What do you want to do?" "Well, what do *you* want to do?"), until snickering from the cameramen prompted Rauh to pat his briefcase and say that if Lawrence went before the whole convention with the current offer to Mississippi, he had the votes to bring the MFDP alternative to the floor. If so, Lawrence replied, the Credentials Committee would put off its decision yet another day. Rather than call attention to the Mississippi delinquency, he would open the convention without certifying any delegates at all.

Lawrence broke away to deal with troubles over Alabama. Only thirteen of fifty-one Alabama delegates and alternates appeared before him to sign pledges of personal support for the Democratic ticket. These tokens of unity—required to console the national party for George Wallace's blatant apostasy—so offended the unsigned delegates that they shoved their way through credentials checkpoints for the opening session Monday night, past guards specially alerted to prevent their entry. None other than Bull Connor of Birmingham led the crashers into the Convention Hall seats reserved for Alabama, where fratricidal resentments broke out. Some of the signers tried to evict the nonsigners, while others wanted to retract their own loyalty pledges. "This is as embarrassing as all hell," mourned one Alabaman; another shouted, "I hope the whole damn state goes Republican!"

Nearby in giant Convention Hall, the Mississippi section remained empty. Convention officials provided the contending delegations with spectator tickets for the balcony, pending settlement of the credentials dispute, but most of the regulars stayed in their hotel. (In his hotel lobby, informed by veteran political reporter Bill Minor that E. W. Steptoe sent regards from the MFDP delegation, an Amite County regular replied with a jovial edge that Steptoe was alive only because "he owes me $400 and I wouldn't let anybody kill him.") Outside Convention Hall, MFDP delegates walked the singing picket line while Joseph Rauh and allied delegates frantically shored up support for a credentials floor vote, beating back one panic that Rauh had lost control of his own District of Columbia delegation.

MONDAY EVENING, the President betrayed little of his depressed mood when James Reston pressed him for an off-the-record hint about his vice presidential choice. Reston argued that the *Times* needed a head start to prepare stories on the right man "so that it looks right in the libraries twenty years from now." Johnson denied that he had chosen Humphrey or anyone else, and pretended to be out of touch: "How is the convention going?... The platform, is it out yet?... I haven't seen it." Offhandedly, he asked whether it made any difference "what happens on the Mississippi thing," and Reston replied that it was of minor interest next to the vice presidency. "I don't really have the impression that it's all that important," he said. "Nobody's got a temperature about it around here except a few people like Rauh, who, you know, he's always got a sweat about this question."

Johnson, huddled with Clark Clifford and Abe Fortas, privately mourned his inability to prevent a party-splitting roll call on Mississippi. "They are just distressed beyond words," he said candidly when UAW president Walter Reuther called from Michigan a few minutes after Reston. Johnson raged against those who would expose his powerlessness. "I think the Negro is going back to Reconstruction," he told Reuther. "... They're gonna set themselves back a hundred years...." Reuther agreed. Alarmed, he said he had a charter plane standing by, and promised to break away from his own emergency—negotiations on strike deadline for 550,000 automobile workers—and fly into Atlantic City before dawn.

Retiring to their White House bedroom, Lyndon and Lady Bird Johnson watched the Monday night ceremonies while eating dinner off trays with houseguests John and Elaine Steinbeck.* They saw nothing but praise for Johnson. Senator John Pastore of Rhode Island lifted Convention Hall repeatedly to standing cheers with a keynote speech of partisan passion (*Life* called it "Full Fiery Throttle"), which raised speculation about Pastore himself as a new long shot for vice president. Still, Johnson remained lost in his own worries. Groping for a defensible public stance on the imminent Mississippi roll call, he asked his companions how he could justify resistance to the Freedom Democrats. "I am not going to bend to emotionalism," his wife coached him to say. "I don't want this convention to do so either. The election is not worth that." Jack Valenti drafted similar language: "It isn't a matter of what our emotions want, it is a matter of what the law demands."

The President ignored Tuesday morning's headlines from the convention ("Unbroken Harmony," reported the *Times* front page). When party chairman John Bailey tried to congratulate him for the "good start" in Atlantic City, Johnson glumly predicted that the Mississippi roll call must come that night and that "every one of those big states will have to

---

* Johnson had sent a plane to fetch the Steinbecks from their home on Long Island. The novelist had developed a private bond with the President since volunteering to design for him an aura of personal folklore, which he defined as a "vernacular of the spirit.... Lincoln breathed it, Kennedy exuded it.... LBJ exudes little of it, although I think he would like to."

go with the Negroes." Bailey confirmed that his native New England delegations would likely vote three to one for the MFDP minority report ("they don't like Mississippi"). Johnson said the victorious Negro coalition was digging its own grave. "I think they're bigger than the President this morning," he told Bailey, "and I think it's just water on Goldwater's paddle."

He disclosed a new plan that morning to his Texas rancher friend, Judge A. W. Moursund. When George Reedy called for instructions before the midday press briefing, Johnson read to him from a statement in progress—the first one drafted by his own hand in twenty years—announcing his intention not to run.* He told Reedy the convention could nominate "a new and fresh fellow." His voice trailed off.

Reedy let the silence hang. "This would throw the nation in quite an uproar, sir," he said quietly.

The President called Walter Jenkins in Atlantic City. "If anybody's entitled to know, you are," he said. He repeated his suspicion that the MFDP was "born in the Justice Department" as a creature of Robert Kennedy. "I don't believe there'll be many attacks on the orders I issued on Tonkin Gulf if I'm not a candidate," said Johnson. He tearfully described fears of a breakdown. "I don't want to be in this place like Wilson," he said, "and I do not believe I can physically and mentally carry the responsibilities of the bomb and the world and the nigras and the South and so forth."† When Jenkins gently doubted he would go through with it, the President insisted that he would—sometime after his foreign policy lunch with McNamara and Rusk.

Lady Bird Johnson endured all through Tuesday the depressed side of her husband's distemper—wide-eyed silence under the covers for naps, shades drawn from the daylight. "I do not remember hours I ever found harder," she would write in her memoirs, and at the time she wrote out for him her anguished appeal: "Beloved—You are as brave a man as Harry Truman—or FDR—or Lincoln. You can go on to find some peace, some achievement amidst all the pain. . . . To step out now would be wrong for your country, and I see nothing but a lonely wasteland for your future. Your friends would be frozen in embarrassed silence and your enemies jeering. . . . I know it's only *your* choice. . . . I love you always, Bird."

EVERYONE ELSE prepared blindly for the decisive crunch in Atlantic City. DeLoach delivered Tuesday morning intelligence on Martin Luther King's last-minute lobbying schedule. The FBI wiretaps picked up frantic consul-

---

* ". . . The times require leadership about which there is no doubt and a voice that men of all parties, sections, and color can follow. I have learned after trying very hard that I am not that voice or that leader. Therefore. . . ."

† Johnson referred to President Woodrow Wilson, who suffered a debilitating stroke in 1920, toward the end of his second term.

tations with MFDP workers who wanted King to call the governors of New Hampshire, Alaska, and Hawaii, among others, plus Mayor Richard Daley of Chicago, and who arranged for King to address the full New York and California caucuses. DeLoach also reported signs that White House counterpressure against the MFDP was effective: wiretaps overheard a delegate from Washington state apologize to King, saying "people who were previously friendly are getting harder to find."

At a midday mass meeting, exhausted MFDP partisans rallied for a last push before the evening session. Above snappish arguments rose general agreement to hold out for their fallback position of shared seats with the regulars. Joseph Rauh, charged to bargain for nothing less, was intercepted outside the Credentials Committee with a peremptory message to call Walter Reuther. "The convention has decided," Reuther told him sharply. He disclosed two new concessions: Aaron Henry and Edwin King of the MFDP would be seated as voting delegates at large, and the party would establish a special commission to enforce nondiscrimination standards for the 1968 convention. Reuther emphasized that Johnson was holding out for a basic party loyalty oath for Mississippi as well as Alabama; no delegate could vote without signing one. "This is a tremendous victory," he said. "I want you to go in there and accept it." If he refused, Reuther promised to terminate Rauh's employment as Washington counsel for the United Auto Workers.

To reporters who clamored around his Convention Hall pay phone, Rauh lied that the caller had been "a pretty girl." He entered the committee room, verified that Reuther's new compromise was on the table, then began to agitate for a recess so that he could consult his MFDP clients. Their leaders were tucked away in the bedroom of Hubert Humphrey's suite at the Pageant Motel, where Reuther concentrated his argument on Martin Luther King. "Your funding is on the line," he said sharply. "The kind of money you got from us in Birmingham is there again for Mississippi, but you've got to help us and we've got to help Johnson."

King deferred to Moses, Aaron Henry, and Edwin King, who huddled across the bed from Humphrey and Bayard Rustin. Their skeptical questions about the overall fairness of the compromise raised resentments on its fine points. The two proposed at-large delegates, for instance, would raise the official number of convention seats from 2,316 to 2,318. Humphrey defended this as an extraordinary concession to the Freedom Democrats, on par with expanding the size of Congress, but it also guaranteed that MFDP delegates would sit outside the Mississippi section and, technically, represent no one in Mississippi. Moses bridled when Reuther complained that Negroes who got the vote often misused it to elect irresponsible people.

Edwin King suggested that if there must be only two at-large delegates, he would withdraw in favor of one of the many farmworkers and nonprofessionals. Bayard Rustin guessed that the administration would accept substitutions, but Senator Humphrey cut short an exploration of ways to rotate or subdivide the two votes by ruling out Fannie Lou Hamer. "The President will not allow that illiterate woman to speak from the floor of the convention," he said. Moses objected to her exclusion as racist and autocratic, whereupon Humphrey jumped in to mollify him, saying the standard was not his but Johnson's, and he was sure the President only meant that Hamer spoke too emotionally to help the party.

While the Humphrey negotiations dragged on at the motel, Rauh filibustered inside the closed meeting of the Credentials Committee. His supporters stammered under insistent questioning about whether the proposed compromise wiped out the need for a minority report. Rauh himself hedged, praising the concessions while pleading for a fair chance to ask his MFDP clients whether they would accept. He finally persuaded subcommittee chairman Walter Mondale to arrange a brief recess, but aides near the chair vetoed the delay. A chant of "Vote! Vote!" gathered speed like a downhill train until Governor Lawrence moved the LBJ compromise to approval by the Credentials Committee. Thunderous acclamation drowned out requests for a tally along with scattered shouts of "no" from MFDP holdouts. Celebrations bolted to the corridors on adjournment.

Across Boardwalk at the Pageant Motel, frantic knocks and cries of "It's over!" pulled the negotiators from the Humphrey bedroom to behold the commotion around the suite's television set, on which Mondale was presenting the Mississippi compromise to reporters as a finished deal. "You cheated!" shrieked Moses, whirling to accuse Humphrey and Reuther of sham talks as a diversionary trick. The MFDP leaders stalked out with King to their meeting place in the basement of Union Temple Baptist, and the remnant that converged there from the Credentials Committee walked into pandemonium. Questions flew about a "fix," whose most treacherous and paralyzing effect seemed to be a cascading rumor that the MFDP had accepted the compromise already. There was talk of setups, especially against negotiating brokers such as Rauh, who recalled that Moses flinched from the trapdoor settlement as from "a white man hitting him with a whip."

Rauh protested that he and the core delegates had *not* agreed to surrender and the vote was *not* unanimous—even Governor Lawrence admitted hearing "no" votes he declined to count—but he conceded that Johnson may have annihilated their prospects for a better deal. Rauh's anguish moved several MFDP members to say they should give in to the compromise, whereupon Moses, according to one surprised summer volunteer, "actually raised his voice and interrupted their speeches." He said they should snap out of defeatist postmortem talk. At his urging, the MFDP delegates voted to reject the committee's offer while they still had an hour or two to scrounge up votes for a minority report to the full convention.

Rauh reluctantly agreed to fight on. Eight of the required eleven Credentials Committee delegates were present in the church and still willing to hold against the pressure. They included Rauh's stalwart Washington colleague Gladys Duncan, wife of baritone Todd Duncan (Gershwin's original Porgy on Broadway). Still, signatures had vanished from the large states of New York, California, and Michigan, and MFDP leverage vaporized from a power base reduced to delegates from Guam and the Panama Canal Zone.

THE UNEXPECTED BREAKTHROUGH revived President Johnson until he heard from the two leading moderates who had been rallying Southerners for him at the convention. Together, governors Carl Sanders of Georgia and John Connally of Texas called Tuesday afternoon to warn of "a wholesale walkout from the South." Sanders himself threatened to leave, and take the Georgia delegation with him. Johnson, having despaired for a month that Humphrey and Reuther could prevent a roll call for the MFDP, recoiled from sudden ambush on the other flank. Exasperated, he demanded to know how the MFDP's two "symbolic" at-large delegates could hurt anybody when they did not reduce the vote of the all-white delegation. "Mississippi's got every vote they ever had," said the President. "Georgia's got every vote they ever had. And we're not gonna *have* any votes to begin with!"

"I'm telling you because you want me to tell you the truth," Sanders declared. "It looks like we're turning the Democratic party over to the nigras. . . ." Martin Luther King was deciding who could be a delegate, he said. "It's gonna cut our throats from ear to ear."

Johnson argued that the MFDP really deserved representation in Mississippi itself. "Pistols kept 'em out," he said heatedly. "These people went in and begged to go into the conventions. They've got half the population, and they won't let 'em. They lock 'em out."

"They're not registered," Sanders insisted.

Johnson's temper fell into quiet pronouncement. "You and I just can't survive our political modern life," he said, "with these goddamn fellas down there that are eatin' 'em for breakfast every morning. They have got to quit that. And they got to let 'em vote, and let 'em shave, and let 'em eat, and things like that. And they don't do it."

Connally took up for Sanders with less passion, given the President's agitation. Johnson pleaded with him not to let the South walk out—not to say, "I'm gonna be a dog in the manger." He said that meant to have everything—all their votes—and then also "bark if somebody across the hall gets a couple."

The President urged Walter Jenkins in Atlantic City to resist the "dog in the manger attitude," which became his rallying cry. By early evening, convention aides told him the South was now the threat. Mississippi's state chairman praised his regular delegates for walking out on the compromise, and Governor Paul Johnson went on television to proclaim liberation from the bond that had kept his state purely Democratic since Lincoln and Reconstruction: "Mississippi's debt to the national party is now paid in full."

On the convention podium, Governor Lawrence and Senator Pastore banged the credentials report to adoption, and finality released energy from all sides of the conflict. Joe Rauh shed tears as he marched dutifully to the podium to return unused the at-large delegate credentials issued for Aaron Henry and Edwin King. As much as he wished his clients would accept them as a victory, he longed more for the lost trust of Bob Moses. Most MFDP supporters recaptured the fervor of Freedom Summer from a rejection all too reminiscent of Mississippi. Their Boardwalk vigil escalated swiftly to a protest more like the Hattiesburg picket line, and lobbying gave way to daring demonstrations.

Prominent Democrats such as Senator Wayne Morse of Oregon and ex-governor Mennen Williams of Michigan boasted of helping to smuggle MFDP members onto the convention floor to claim Mississippi seats as rightfully theirs. "I made about four or five trips in and out—it was really exciting," observed one summer volunteer who relayed entry badges illicitly with a fake press pass and a Young Citizens for Johnson disguise. "I felt like Mata Hari and the French Resistance and the Underground Railroad all rolled into one." Nearly two dozen MFDP delegates made it past security into the Mississippi section, which prompted the precious few oath-signing regulars there to flee.

There were only three of them, trying to incubate a loyal presence with the encouragement of President Johnson,* and their evacuation sorely distressed Johnson's floor commanders. Walter Jenkins called the President to report that delegates could not get into Convention Hall because of riots and demonstrations outside. White House aide Marvin Watson angrily ordered the MFDP sit-ins dragged from the Mississippi section; Jenkins countermanded him for fear that a televised eviction would be worse than the sit-in. Demonstrators, asked why they were making such a scene, asked in reply why network interviewers made no corresponding uproar over banned whites who had crashed the Alabama section again.

---

* Johnson reached one of the three before the commotion on the convention floor that night. "You're a patriot," he told Doug Wynn of Greenville, a family friend. "... This is history and you'll always be proud of this." Within days, the President would be asking the Justice Department to protect the nonwalkouts from Klan death threats on their return to Mississippi.

Moses waved off the suggestion that he spurned a fair compromise. "We are here for the people and the people want to represent themselves," he told NBC's John Chancellor. "They don't want symbolic token votes."

Press Secretary George Reedy hesitantly answered a summons to the presidential quarters when the convention broadcasts signed off about midnight Tuesday. From considerable experience, he hoped the morning's resignation vow was forgotten, but he found Johnson in renewed despair over the threat of demonstrations and Southern walkouts. "By God, I'm gonna go up there and quit," said Johnson. "Fuck 'em all."

Reedy slathered on reassurances, lumbering after Johnson on one of his hyperkinetic walks around the White House South Lawn. He said the President did not need to go to Atlantic City until Thursday, once he was nominated and the convention safely in his pocket. He pleaded with Johnson not to hand the country to Goldwater. Johnson merely said that he was having trouble with his withdrawal statement and ordered Reedy to draft it. When Reedy refused, the President flayed him as an incompetent, disloyal tormentor. Reedy ended the ordeal only by promising to write something, but the predawn resignation he typed out was his own.

ON WEDNESDAY MORNING, the MFDP delegation regathered amidst second thoughts about the compromise and rumors that the administration might relax some of the insulting details. Rauh told his friend Senator Humphrey that "the dumb bastards on your side—and I'm sure it wasn't you, Hubert —chose our two people instead of letting them choose their own two people." Humphrey dragged himself back to work, saying he was so battered that "I honestly don't care too much anymore" about Johnson's test for vice president, and Rauh joined a phalanx of speakers at Union Temple Baptist. He urged the delegates to reconsider the compromise, as did Senator Morse and Aaron Henry. Bayard Rustin argued that they must broaden their outlook from moral protest to political alliance, during which Mendy Samstein of SNCC jumped up to shout, "You're a traitor, Bayard!" In an atmosphere charged with rebellion, James Forman eyed Al Lowenstein to make sure he did not dare speak for the pragmatism of experts. Church lawyer Jack Pratt did endorse the compromise, saying rejectionists were failing to disclose its many side promises—federal hearings, training programs, interventions long sought—but a cold reception made him wander off to get drunk in a bar.

Martin Luther King delivered a speech of formal neutrality. "I am not going to counsel you to accept or reject," he said. "That is your decision." He balanced a denunciation of Johnson's remote-control mistreatment against the leavening hope for political progress, airing his conflicted private advice: "So, being a Negro leader, I want you to take this, but if I were a Mississippi Negro, I would vote against it." The delegates gave King generous applause on both sides. Some were still pinching themselves that all the big shots were worked up over their decision, and some shared the distaste of the student movement for King's straddling.

Bob Moses swayed nearly all of them against the compromise. "We're not here to bring politics to our morality," he said, "but to bring morality to our politics." One admirer said, "Moses could have been Socrates or Aristotle.... I mean he tore King up." When the outsiders departed after the speeches, a few MFDP delegates ventured praise of the compromise as "getting somewhere," but the larger voices—especially Victoria Gray, Annie Devine, and Fannie Lou Hamer—scorned it as a paltry temptation. Gray said people back home were counting on them to bring back gains deep enough and fair enough to hold against conditions in Mississippi. "When they got through talking and hoopin' and hollerin' and tellin' me what a shame it was for me to do that," recalled an old man from Issaquena County, "I hushed right then." The delegates voted again to reject the Democratic offer. "We didn't come all this way for no two seats," said Hamer.

Meanwhile, Walter Reuther left for Washington to deliver a report in the West Hallway outside President Johnson's bedroom. No record survives of their eighty minutes alone, nor of Johnson's initial state of mind after serial crises, but Reuther's bracing news included an agreement by Martin Luther King to carry on a specialized LBJ campaign tour among Negroes. His morning reports accented the positive. There was no residual chance for a roll call on Mississippi. The *Washington Post* predicted that the "vast bulk" of Southern delegates would stay on, and praised Johnson as the invisible wizard who helped the Democratic party "finally rid itself of the divisive civil rights issue which has plagued every national convention beginning with 1948."

The President buzzed for his press secretary after Reuther departed, but Reedy, cringing with his own undelivered resignation, ducked three calls before learning that Johnson was racing forward again. The President summoned Humphrey and Senator Thomas Dodd of Connecticut by private jet from Atlantic City, then took off for a spontaneous midday walk with his beagles, Him and Her, and sixty trailing reporters. He sent the exhausted dogs to their kennel after four breakneck laps around the White House driveway—about a mile—then herded the reporters through eleven more laps without dispensing a vice presidential announcement. Other reporters followed the two senators around the Washington Monument and other tourist sites in a Johnson-mandated holding pattern.

"One of them must now at last be chosen to stand within a heartbeat of the presidency," campaign historian Theodore White recorded of the contenders' late afternoon arrival in a single limousine. Johnson privately consoled Dodd as his decoy, extracted pledges of loyalty from Humphrey, and called Humphrey's wife, Muriel, under bond of secrecy. "We're going to nominate your boy," he said. His abrupt order scrambled the entire presidential entourage for Atlantic City a day ahead of schedule. Reedy, who had released White House reporters to evening cocktails, relieved that Johnson had abandoned his mad fits about quitting that night, recalled them to sudden departure. He replaced for safety reasons an inebriated member of the press pool who nearly walked into a helicopter blade.

Johnson announced Humphrey within hours, in person, to a pleasantly astonished convention that swept them jointly to nomination. The nominees returned to give acceptance speeches at the closing session Thursday night, when Robert Kennedy's speech in Convention Hall indeed broke the dam, as Johnson had feared. An unbroken wave of applause lasted fully twenty-two minutes when Kennedy introduced the film about his brother with Shakespeare's tribute to Romeo: "When he shall die/Take him and cut him out in little stars/And he will make the face of heaven so fine/That all the world will be in love with night/And pay no worship to the garish sun." Johnson by then could welcome, even absorb, some of the outpouring as the secure successor to President Kennedy. "Party and nation both now gaze in wonder at the huge man," wrote Theodore White for the CBS election special. "Yet no man but he knows all the measure of the huge distance he has come."

Private dramas continued in the background. George Reedy endured embarrassing bureaucratic torment after a colleague retrieved the unused letter of resignation from his White House desk and leaked it to reporters. Reedy strongly suspected aides to his agile rival Bill Moyers, but he could only say he was "puzzled" by news stories painting him as an idiot who "quit because Mr. Johnson had ignored his advice not to go to Atlantic City." Any hint of the truth would have scandalized voters over a manic, unstable President. "I don't want to louse things up," he told Johnson morosely.

Deke DeLoach applied successfully for Director Hoover to bestow secret letters of commendation upon the agents of his Special Squad, highlighting their undercover work to "make major changes in controlling admissions into the Convention Hall and thereby preclude infiltration of the illegal Mississippi Freedom Democratic Party (MFDP) delegates in large numbers into the space reserved for the regular Mississippi delegates." Agents posing as reporters had broadcast warnings to agents posing as security guards, who helped strip the chairs from the Mississippi section and block entrances to the empty rows.

Bob Moses and six others stood vigil in an aisle through the Kennedy tribute Thursday night, wearing black neck placards embossed with JFK's silhouette and his exhortation, "Ask not what your country...." Moses was among many who already felt Atlantic City a bitter turning point for the Mississippi movement, if not for all of American politics. Outside, Fannie Lou Hamer led farewell choruses of "We Shall Overcome," and fireworks from President Johnson's gigantic fifty-sixth birthday celebration illuminated the whole Boardwalk, including portraits of Mississippi martyrs held aloft.

President Johnson left the convention giddy with energy, having conquered political and mortal anxieties on a birthday never reached by most Johnson men. Racing from a helicopter to *Air Force One*, with the Humphreys as guests, he veered across the airfield toward a crowded security fence to lift *Washington Post* publisher Katharine Graham happily off the ground. "We're going to Texas and we want you with us," Johnson announced as he swept her aboard without regard for the luggage and corporate jet she left behind. All the trappings of government flew from Atlantic City to the LBJ Ranch, where on Friday the President whirled among the vistas, gadgets, and livestock of his domain. He dressed Senator Humphrey in an LBJ-sized ranch outfit—"I looked ridiculous and I felt ridiculous as I smiled wanly from under a cowboy hat," Humphrey recalled—and abruptly commandeered six other guests, including Katharine Graham, to visit two venerable kinfolk in a ramshackle house down the road. "Cousin Oriole, wake up!" shouted Johnson, banging on the screened porch where he sank into a nap as soon as he got homecoming hugs. To his party, seated near the sleeping President, Aunt Jessie Hatcher recalled that even as a small boy young Lyndon sat in the front and held the reins on donkey rides. "He still does," quipped Humphrey.

Cousin Oriole Bailey told them that in order to get her chores done back in the old days she had staked toddler Lyndon outside in the dusty yard, where he played to the end of the tether rope and pulled on it to go farther.

35

"We see the giants . . ."

A HANDFUL OF NATIONAL CORRESPONDENTS proceeded directly from the crush of Atlantic City to the hot Snopesian stillness of Danielsville, Georgia (pop. 362), for the Lemuel Penn murder trial. Reporter Paul Good counted twenty-three Coca-Cola signs hanging from buildings around the courthouse lawn, where a historical marker noted the first use of surgical ether by local-born physician Crawford Long in 1842. An uncovered staircase rose along the exterior wall into an unlit courtroom balcony strictly segregated for Negroes, but the judge otherwise ran an informal trial to the point of praising from the bench the lunch dishes that the women's club had thrown together for the week's occasion.

When prosecutors presented a string of FBI witnesses on the conspicuous vigilante rampage by Klavern 244, a defense lawyer casually scoffed, "There's no crime in Georgia against intimidating colored people." Garage owner Herbert Guest, whom the state grand jury had declined to indict, testified that he had lost all memory of his sworn statement. Loretta Lackey sat mute on the stand, refusing instruction to speak, but she could not endure testimony by a defense psychiatrist that impeached her husband's confession as the delusion of a subnormal "paranoid personality" who had turned against his friends, possibly out of anxiety over a misshapen head. In the hallway she cried out, "Doctor, does that mean my husband is crazy?"

The defense case, which consumed less than two hours on Friday, September 4, portrayed not only the defendants but the entire region as victims of big shots such as the bushwhacked Lieutenant Colonel Penn and his companions. "I wasn't no officer," summarized the lead defense lawyer. "Officers have a pretty good deal, we all know that." In a peroration —"my mind is boiling"—his co-counsel exhorted the jurors to stand against "the untold resources of the federal government" and its "howling mob" of preying carpetbaggers that had swarmed down from FBI head-quarters under instructions, "Don't come back until you bring us white meat!" The jury recessed to a truck stop for Friday evening supper and then acquitted the defendants Cecil Myers and Howard Sims eighty-seven minutes later. Humiliated state authorities aborted the separate murder trial scheduled for Lackey. To a local judge who complained that the FBI's wasted prosecution "cost my good county several hundred dollars" and had brought down hostile suggestions that it be "wiped off the map" from as far away as Yokohama, Japan,* J. Edgar Hoover replied that the FBI had merely assisted a prosecution handled by Georgians.

FBI officials "telephonically advised" FBI headquarters of exact de-velopments: 8:45 P.M., jury back from supper; 10:12 P.M., verdict returned. Director Hoover regularly ordered notices on the Penn trial sent to Walter Jenkins at the White House. Earlier on September 4—his first full day on the job following the resignation of Robert Kennedy—Acting Attorney General Nicholas Katzenbach wrote President Johnson that creation of a new federal grand jury in Mississippi was "certain to raise speculation" that the FBI had solved the Neshoba County triple murder. "This is not so," Katzenbach emphatically warned. The grand jury was merely a tool for Inspector Joe Sullivan in his investigation into "a conspiracy on the part of law enforcement officials and others," he wrote. The cautionary note was aimed at Johnson himself, because the eager President had pub-licly forecast imminent success in the Mississippi case.

In Atlanta that same Friday, Martin Luther King interrupted his glancing home life—and his campaign for a personal audience with Pope Paul VI two weeks hence—to take a phone call from the Miami training camp of heavyweight champion Muhammad Ali. It was Chauncey Esk-ridge, the urbane Chicago lawyer who, while working for King since the narrow escape of his Alabama income tax trial in 1960, had also repre-sented Elijah Muhammad through several unpopular religious freedom cases, including the draft imprisonment of his son Wallace and a lawsuit for the right to buy Nation of Islam poster ads on Chicago public transit vehicles. Through Muhammad, Eskridge was working to dislodge and replace the syndicate of Louisville businessmen who had managed the career of the pre-Muslim Cassius Clay. When he introduced his two famous clients by telephone, King congratulated the young boxer on his

---

* "These letters... have *not* been appreciated," wrote Judge H. C. Echols, who added his criticism of FBI methods: "Personally I thought your agents had no right to give Mr. Guest a birthday cake...."

recent marriage and Ali invited King to his rematch against Sonny Liston. By the FBI wiretap log, Ali then assured King that he "is keeping up with MLK, that MLK is his brother, and [Ali is] with him 100 but can't take any chances." The buoyant Ali urged King to "take care of himself" and "watch out for them whities."

Nearly five years later, from a Texas courtroom, this passing courtesy call opened a crack to vast chambers of subterranean history. With Ali then stripped of the heavyweight title for refusing to fight in the Vietnam War, and his appeals lawyers questioning whether FBI wiretaps might have tainted the government's criminal prosecution of Ali, FBI witness R. R. Nichols testified that the September 4 call had been captured on a wiretap that Nichols supervised on King himself. This marked the first official acknowledgment of FBI operations against King or the movement. Instantly, Hoover launched a crossfire of public denial. He branded columnist Carl Rowan a "racist" for writing truthfully that the Bureau bugged King's hotel rooms and "shadowed [him] right up to the time he was slain." He blamed the late Robert Kennedy for initiating—and King for deserving —any unspecified surveillance, and banished Special Agent Nichols for his slip of candor to silence in the Oklahoma City FBI office. By these and other scattershot intimidations, the Director tamed public speculation on the sensational topic without further breach of secrecy. Not until 1975, three years after Hoover himself was dead, did congressional investigations begin to uncover in retrospect the outlines of the FBI's covert crusade.

In Atlanta, as King chatted with Muhammad Ali, members of the SNCC Executive Committee opened debate on a new course after Atlantic City. Young SNCC veterans saw the Democratic convention as a "watershed" or "end of innocence," after which "things could never be the same." Now that the Democrats had deflected the rare chance to align a major political party openly with the movement, Bob Moses forlornly predicted, national politics would submerge the race question into other issues—order, urban adjustment, world affairs—where its democratic clarity would recede. "Well, I'll give fifty years for this to work itself out," he sighed. Some students expressed shock that Atlantic City had snuffed out their eager expectations—"it never occurred to us that our delegation would be turned down"—while others claimed to have known all along that the power brokers would undercut their cause. Nearly all leaders bristled against the Johnson compromise. Even the steadfast chairman John Lewis called it a blow to the movement's long-standing strategy of seeking redress from the federal government. Charles Sherrod of the southwest Georgia SNCC project railed against the constant pressure on the movement to curtail just claims in order to beat Goldwater, or comfort those who fretted about riots. "Who holds the power?" he wrote. "Let *them* be responsible.... We are a country of racists with the racist heritage, a racist economy, a racist language, a racist religion, a racist philosophy of living, and we need a naked confrontation with ourselves."

This was the unifying passion of telescoped history. Having begun in 1960 as a campus-based clearinghouse for the sit-ins, with one paid staff member during its first year, SNCC had grown after the Freedom Rides to a cadre of sixteen ex-students through 1962, then from seventy by the end of 1963 to 144 far-flung field organizers by the end of Freedom Summer, all on subsistence wages. With expansion outrunning both the identity and structure of the original SNCC family, the September debates tested ideas of purity against ambition. Some wanted to hire professional fund-raisers to maintain a temporarily bountiful treasury—$165,000 in one New York account alone. Others, shunning "hired guns," wanted to keep relying on the Friends of SNCC support groups that had sprung up in Northern cities. James Forman said the support groups could be rewarded with inside reports on SNCC operations, but Moses argued that "the problem is deeper than that." Mindful of the philosophical split with Al Lowenstein over the summer project, he asked, "What is our responsibility to Friends of SNCC?" In return for the money and volunteers they sent south, did the support offices deserve representation in SNCC decisions? Could they mount their own SNCC demonstrations in, say, Los Angeles or Boston?

Divisions tended toward a Moses faction and a Forman faction. Each one advocated discipline against glamour. Moses wanted to step back from all that Atlantic City represented—press conferences, lobbying, clamoring for Washington's attention—to the "normal" movement work of Freedom Schools and registration drives in communities of hard-core oppression, where personal risk sorted out matters of control. Forman wanted to weed out self-starting romantics to forge SNCC in an unabashed quest for power. To organize around the experience of certain oppression, he would reject the untrustworthy alliances of Atlantic City along with proposals to give voting privileges within SNCC to new, "unproven" staff. There were pressing applications from more than a hundred summer volunteers who said staff wages would allow them to forgo college for the school year.

Ironically, the most immediate choice in Atlanta was glamorous to all sides: the selection of ten SNCC guests for the Belafonte trip to Africa. Forman announced tentatively that John Lewis was going, along with Julian Bond and Ruby Doris Smith of SNCC headquarters in Atlanta, plus Bob and Dona Moses of the Mississippi project, Don Harris of Georgia, Prathia Hall of Alabama, and perhaps Forman himself. Moses objected to the privilege but was overruled. Marion Barry proposed that Matthew Jones be added as a representative of the Freedom Singers; Bill Hansen of the Arkansas project was included to integrate the delegation by race.

When grumbles erupted against the choices, Forman explained that the idea was to choose a cross section of leadership. Some objected that list was weighted with sophisticates and French speakers suited to the language of Guinea, contradicting SNCC's vehement protests in Atlantic City over the arbitrary exclusion of unlettered sharecroppers like Fannie Lou Hamer. They hooted down the excuse that Hamer lived too far in the backwoods to obtain her yellow fever shots and travel documents on short notice, whereupon she was hustled into an extra spot. Caretakers stepped forward to manage a host of deferred issues—a South-wide summer program for 1965, troubled projects, missing staff cars, business options to buy a building, the fall election and the MFDP, how to get a fellow staff member named Randolph Battle out of the Albany jail. Despite the misgivings of Moses and others about leaving SNCC on the blade of change, the delegation of eleven flew to Guinea by way of Senegal on September 11.

Awed themselves by Mother Africa, her companions were fondly amused by Hamer's wide-eyed exclamations over the miraculous sightings of black-skinned people in positions of authority: a pilot, customs clerk, protocol officer, bank teller, television correspondent. The delegation was scarcely in sight of Villa Silla, an elegant seacoast compound that had belonged to French governors before independence in 1958, when invitations came to a dinner at the presidential palace, and Hamer had just withdrawn to her cottage when President Sékou Touré's car pulled up for an unannounced visit beforehand.

Moses, Forman, and Julie Belafonte conversed in French while Harry Belafonte rushed off to summon Hamer, who shouted through the door that he must be joking. "I'm having a bath!" cried Hamer. "I'm definitely not ready to meet no president." Rattled for once, she dressed in time to limp into the welcoming arms of Touré's white African robes. She received his ritual kiss on each cheek, which amazed her more to see bestowed also upon men, and then broke happily into tears during conversation in another language. Imagine that, she told Belafonte. Having lived in Mississippi with no dream of meeting a president, then begged vainly to see one in Atlantic City, she was dumbstruck that this exotic head of state brought personal greetings before she could get out of the bathtub her first day in Africa.

All through September, the American guests received banquets of fish around a huge table overlooking the African side of the Atlantic Ocean, with Belafonte presiding like a king. Forman's executive side found the group unwieldy for political briefings—"I realized on this trip," he wrote, "that three is the maximum number of people for a delegation that seeks to hold serious, intensive discussion"—but the others relaxed with fine wines and Scotch fetched by servants. Ruby Doris Smith alone consented to be braided in cornrows like Guinean women; Hamer refused the strange custom, being particular about her hair. On outings, they noticed grinding barefoot poverty as well as clothes and art forms of exuberant color, and one Guinean tempered their rhapsodies on ancestral brotherhood with a boastful claim that his great-grandfather "sold about three million of you." Transformed, yet reminded how American they remained, all but two went home early because of telephoned alarms of impending rupture within SNCC.

Don Harris, who had relatives working for an American oil company in Ghana, stayed on another ten weeks to escort John Lewis on a SNCC-style tour, alternating between red-carpet press conferences and pallets on floors. Arriving in Lusaka "with 1 pound ($2.81) between us," they witnessed the tumultuous independence ceremony of the new Zambia ("a woman broke from the stands, ran onto the field, and embraced Dr. Kaunda's knees..."), then managed from there to sample not only Ethiopia for the thirty-second annual coronation of Emperor Haile Selassie but also scattered hideouts of South African guerrillas or starry-eyed students—"debating the practicality of various kinds of daggers, learning where the best women on the continent were, and joking about the kind of white man that angered us most...." They trailed in every country the "fantastic impressions" left by Malcolm X over the past four months, and bumped into the Muslim exile himself at the New Stanley Hotel in Nairobi, Kenya. Malcolm entranced them for nearly two days in a friendly fireworks of ideas and his electrifying sense of danger. "Always sit with your back against the wall," he advised, "so you can look out and see who is watching you." By way of Cairo and Paris, where Lewis visited the cabaret of Adam Clayton Powell's ex-wife, jazz pianist Hazel Scott, they reached Atlanta in November with a plan to create an international division within SNCC.

ON SEPTEMBER 11, when the Belafonte group had embarked for Africa, Martin Luther King departed for Germany shortly after a press conference at Boston University on the deposit of his personal papers. He offered only hints of disappointment over the ambivalence of his mentor Benjamin Mays at Morehouse, explaining that he had favored Boston because his postgraduate alma mater was "desirous enough of having these papers to give them the kind of attention that I think they will need...." News-hungry Boston reporters quickly baffled King by asking to hear the fabled recordings of his phone conversations with the Kennedy brothers. These questions were based on the erroneous inference that King—not the Kennedys—had controlled the eavesdropping vaguely suggested in news accounts of the Freedom Rides and the Meredith crisis at Ole Miss, and King could only say he recalled no such Kennedy intercepts in his collection. "Now there are certainly letters," he added, to a noticeable deflation of interest. The reporters asked repeatedly about the extent of the white backlash, Communist or Black Muslim influence in riots, and whether King favored a "change of tactics on the part of the Negro perhaps to be less aggressive." His replies were diplomatic—"Well, I don't think we can afford to be less aggressive.... Now it may be necessary to change tactics here and there.... I still feel that nonviolence is the most potent weapon available to oppressed people..."—but King did startle those who wondered why "Southern Negroes were actually brought to Boston because of allegations about our school system." He predicted expansion of the nonviolent movement because "racial injustice does exist in the North in a serious way."

With Ralph Abernathy, King flew to a German cultural festival at the invitation of West Berlin mayor Willy Brandt. On Sunday, September 13, again having mislaid his passport, he passed through the Berlin Wall on celebrity recognition to preach at Marienkirche in Communist East Berlin. From this austere city, from which Adolf Hitler had ruled Nazi Germany less than twenty years before, he sketched a biblical analogy about Israel's quest. Americans were climbing from "Egypt" at long last through the "wilderness" of segregation, King said—"For the first time we stand on the mountain"—and he surveyed historic choice from an imaginary perch. "As we look back into the wilderness, we see our brethren who have borne the burdens of slavery and segregation much too long," he said. "Many have not had the opportunity to get an education.... Many are hungry and physically undernourished.... Many bear on their souls the scars of bitterness and hatred, seared there by the crowded slum conditions, police brutality, and the exploitation they experienced on the rural southern plantations. Still others lack self-confidence and courage to compete in this new land, and they wallow in drunkenness and despair."

Looking ahead, King pictured intimidations in the "promised land" of interracial freedom, just as biblical spies once told Moses they felt "like grasshoppers" among the natives of Canaan. "We see the giants," he said. "We see massive urban societies, dominated by well-entrenched political machines that see new voters as a threat to their power. We see automation ... slum landlords ... and poverty far worse than the wilderness conditions we have just left behind." Then, quoting to the East German audience the movement hymn "Ain't Gonna Let Nobody Turn Me Around," he preached. "We will learn to confront these demons just as we have those in the past," he concluded, "and we shall overcome."

King stayed on to receive an honorary degree from the Theological Seminary of Berlin, unaware of the fury stirred within the FBI over his pending request to visit the Pope in Rome. "It would be shocking indeed for such an unscrupulous character as King to receive an audience with the Pope," wrote an intelligence officer, warned two weeks earlier by the wiretaps on King's telephones. FBI officials remixed the sabotage formula "we previously used in preventing King's receiving an honorary degree from Marquette University"—and piped it this time into the Vatican. At Hoover's instruction, Assistant Director John Malone visited Francis Cardinal Spellman of New York with the FBI's dossier on "the unsavory nature of King's character, both from a subversive and moral standpoint," warning that the slightest sign of papal favor might even boost King toward a Nobel Prize.

Malone followed two orders: to "stress of course the confidential nature of our briefing so that the Bureau would not be drawn into the picture," and to make sure Spellman reached the Vatican directly, so that if he did not, the Bureau could use "other channels." Afterward, reporting success, Malone notified headquarters that "the Cardinal was most pleased and gratified that the Director thought enough of him to take him into his confidence and to rely upon him to handle such a delicate matter." Not only did Spellman telephone the Pontiff's Secretary of State, Cardinal Cicognani, but he assured Malone that he would be in Rome personally to "further insure that the Pope is not placed in an embarrassing position through any contact with King."

Spellman did proceed to Rome among two thousand bishops who gathered for the third plenary session of the Vatican Council, and by coincidence, Rabbi Abraham Heschel slipped into Rome also to seek the Pope's ear on a mission as secret as Malone's but of mirror purpose, parallel to King's, to rally ecumenical hope against divisions of faith and tribe. Since the second-year conclave had recessed the previous November, putting off a proposed statement of fraternal reconciliation with Judaism, traditional elements within the Church had "drastically watered down" Augustin Cardinal Bea's historic text, according to information leaked to the *New York Times*. Behind closed doors, by scriptural exegesis and political maneuver, they first omitted the retraction of pre-Holocaust Church teachings that Jews were accursed as a "deicide people," and by September they inserted a "conversion clause" that three times expressed "with immovable faith" an expected "reunion of the Jewish people with the Church...."

Heschel reacted to the rumored alterations with vivid dismay: "I am ready to go to Auschwitz any time, if faced with the alternative of conversion or death." Simultaneously, he upheld the lasting promise of the Vatican Council designed by the late Pope John XXIII: "We ardently pray that this great blessing may not vanish." Only with trepidation did Heschel seek to lobby Pope Paul VI on Church doctrine, as few ranking Catholics and practically no Protestants ever did. For an Orthodox Jew the idea invited backfire on all sides—with conspiracists charging already that Zionist moles were bribing the Vatican for pardon in the death of Jesus, and Jewish leaders* of all three branches sealing themselves off from "Christian concerns." Against entreaties that he not go, Heschel arranged a small measure of protection from Rabbi Louis Finkelstein of his seminary, then ventured alone on September 14 to plead face-to-face with

---

* In the *Times*, Orthodox Rabbi Joseph Soloveitchik rejected talk of kinship with "any other faith community as 'brethren' ": "Rabbi Says Faiths Are Not Related."

Pope Paul VI, who ceremoniously scratched what he said was the conversion clause from the parchment before him.

The third plenary session resumed titanic struggle *"mostly* with words," a council participant recorded, "nevertheless, it was a war with all its wickedness." Bishops from Muslim countries predicted pogroms against their Christian minorities if the Church moderated traditional antipathy toward Jews. Scandal sheets circulated in Rome. When Cardinal Cicognani stunned the council by announcing—ostensibly for the Pope—that the draft was withdrawn again from consideration, Bea's European allies fought back with a heart-wrenching letter of appeal to Paul VI, beginning *"Magno cum dolore"* [With great sorrow], and eventually substituted for the conversion clause a balanced prayer that "all peoples will address the Lord in a single voice and 'serve Him shoulder to shoulder.' " While falling short of final passage, Bea's signal revision of Church teaching on Judaism survived on the voting schedule for the concluding plenary in 1965. Anti-reform headlines bitterly lamented its escape from the brink of extinction: "Who Crucified Christ? The Vatican in the Year 1964."

Rabbi Heschel had hastened back to New York in time for Yom Kippur observance through sundown of September 16, the same day the Atlanta SCLC office announced that Pope Paul would receive Martin Luther King before King left Europe. The news struck hard at FBI headquarters, where supervisors ordered an emergency review "to determine if there possibly could have been a slip-up." Aides to Cardinal Spellman retransmitted the FBI's warning to the aged Cicognani, whose career in the Vatican labyrinth matched Hoover's longevity at the FBI, but Paul VI greeted King in the library of the Apostolic Palace for twenty-five minutes on Friday evening, September 18, during the Vatican Council deliberations. King happily emerged to brush aside press suggestions that his overwhelmingly Protestant followers back home might disapprove of his contact with a pope. He described the Pontiff as well informed on the American civil rights movement and optimistic about peaceful compliance with the new law. Surely it meant "new days ahead," King joked, when a pope met "a fellow with the name of Martin Luther." Reports of the harmonious occasion moved Hoover to write his galled reaction to a news clip in Washington: "I am amazed that the Pope gave an audience to such a degenerate."

EXTRALEGAL SURVEILLANCE against King became so securely routine that Bureau supervisors took license with the required internal paperwork. To bug the eighth annual SCLC convention at the end of September, they first cited a need to monitor the subversive influence of Harry Wachtel, on what historian David Garrow later called "a new and transparently disingenuous concern" about two unverified informant reports that Wachtel and his wife had been leftists in the 1940s. Wachtel offered convenient symmetry as the substitute Stanley Levison: in reality, as King's New York adviser, and on paper, as the all-purpose justification for FBI surveillance. When Wachtel dropped plans to attend the convention, clerks rushed to fill the gap with an old comment in the files that King's father might be a Communist. Atlanta agents who knew Daddy King winced at using such casual nonsense, which came from an antagonistic Bureau source, but it sufficed as bureaucratic cover for the bug order.

King returned from Rome by way of stops in Spain and England, jotting down scores of staff reminders and "executive orders" for the upcoming convention of some five hundred SCLC delegates. C. T. Vivian was to notify Aaron Henry that he would receive the Rosa Parks Award, make sure Parks attended as an honored guest, and "get program printed." Andrew Young was to "send letter in my name" reminding all SCLC board members to bring the expected contribution of $50 as the price of their often pontifical remarks. King himself issued the usual crackdown restrictions against runaway travel expenses and staff telephone calls, saying costs had swelled even beyond the year's receipts of $626,000. He departed in haste from a Research Committee meeting in New York, leaving behind a suit jacket in his room at the Ritz Hotel, preached for Fred Shuttlesworth in Cincinnati, begged off one engagement with a plea of exhaustion, and on September 28 arrived for his convention in Savannah, Georgia. King checked into one of fifty rooms reserved at the Manger Hotel, where, only a year earlier, Hosea Williams had recruited bellboy Willie Bolden to full-time movement work during demonstrations against the city's rigid color line.

While participants celebrated their generally cordial reception through Savannah's debut in mass integration, FBI cables praised the "extremely cooperative and reliable" hotel management for confidential favors, including the assignment of King to Room 902, directly beneath the rented monitoring station from which Bureau technicians had just dropped three bugging devices in the walls. Neither these intercepts nor the well-placed physical surveillance agents yielded any derogatory information on King through the week-long convention, and the only positive moment for the Bureau was a security relief that a segregationist bomb threat targeted not the Manger Hotel but an SCLC banquet being addressed by King and Jackie Robinson at the nearby DeSoto, sparing the microphone clerks in Room 1002 from being flushed out during bomb search evacuation.

Closer to convention business, Chauncey Eskridge established a trust agreement for the new Southern Christian Leadership Foundation, which created essentially a Chicago-based alternative to New York's nearly defunct Gandhi Society in the competition among King's lawyers to obtain a permanent tax exemption for charitable fund-raising. Also, lionizers of Wyatt Walker joked that it took King no fewer than four promoted assistants to replace him: James Bevel, Andrew Young, Randolph Blackwell, and Hosea Williams. Daddy King, on hearing an oral report to the SCLC board that his son might be a candidate for the Nobel Peace Prize, jumped up to propose that the remarks be printed for public distribution.

To five hundred delegates on October 1, King explored what he called "profound and revolutionary changes" since SCLC's shell-shocked 1963 convention in the wake of the Birmingham church bombing. He tried to describe a trembling center, from which legal segregation was being vanquished and new meanings of freedom were spilling abroad. His formal address reprised sweeping Exodus themes: "It is true that, by and large, we have left the dusty soils of Egypt...." Pairing Jeffersonian foundations with prophetic ones, as usual, he reached for high-flown images of the American Revolution: "We will have our Valley Forges and summer soldiers, and even Benedict Arnolds...."

On finding that state powers were making "surprisingly reasonable plans to comply with the civil rights bill," for instance, King said he had pulled back from systematic demonstrations to test public accommodations in Alabama. With the South in orderly retreat from public laws on race, King foresaw that the signature tactic of nonviolent witness would become less effective there for lack of resistance, and told his Savannah audience that the movement must learn to adapt. "When we are idle," he observed, "the white majority very quickly forgets the injustices which started our movement," but poorly designed initiatives such as the World's Fair stall-in only backfire politically. He reviewed the traumatic experience in St. Augustine as a transitional campaign "to again remind the nation" of the need for the civil rights bill, and admitted little success beyond that purpose: "We were able to proclaim a relative victory...."

At the heart of his message—aside from SCLC program descriptions and budget figures—King interpreted three signal events from a year of spreading upheaval: the triple murder in Mississippi, the riots in Northern cities, and the ongoing presidential campaign. He saw in the dramatic publicity about Freedom Summer a national recognition that political inequality went much deeper than segregated schools and lunch counters, to mortal issues of voting by color. "Our next campaign was to have been in Alabama," he said, "[where] it would take 135 years to register ten thousand Negroes under the existing voting regulation." He sketched the Bevel-Nash plan for large-scale nonviolent war to gain the franchise, which had grown out of Birmingham, then frankly confessed distractions. Saying he had dispatched Bevel and other SCLC staff to test nonviolent methods in Rochester, Philadelphia, and other riot-torn Northern cities— "The results were spectacular"—King told the Savannah convention that SCLC was wrestling with an imperative to expand nationwide. The stakes were high, the consequences far-reaching but unknown. Such a move risked intensified petty rivalry with the NAACP. On a larger scale, it threatened to turn Northern economic support into opposition, and invited reappraisal of an issue known almost entirely by association with the South.

King contemplated the riots together with the new War on Poverty as a second storm of the floodtide year. "The struggle for rights is at bottom a struggle for opportunities," he said. "... The Negro is not seeking charity. He does not want to languish on welfare rolls any more than the next man." Endorsing Johnson's crusade, King said the plan was sound politically—roughly 80 percent of its beneficiaries would be white—and relatively modest in cost, with an annual budget ($927 million) little more than half the after-tax profits ($1.7 billion) just announced for the first six months of 1964 by the three leading car companies alone. Before Congress gave Shriver the first dollar, however, King warned the Savannah convention of a subliminal national politics already at work to obscure such facts. "By appealing to deep-rooted prejudice," he said, "it suggests that the War on Poverty is solely to aid the colored poor, that it is just part of the civil rights issue. . . .

"We understand what motivates this mischief," King added. He addressed the implications of a message begun by George Wallace that translated racial politics into expressions of contempt for government itself. To King, the underlying change in presidential politics was primary among the forces he saw crowding into the great year of realization in civil rights—more important even than the voting questions raised by Freedom Summer or the nationalization of race by the economics of urban riots. He analyzed the presidential year without a single mention of Johnson, the tragedy of Dallas, or any Kennedy, and made no reference to the Atlantic City convention or Mississippi's Freedom Democrats. Instead, he concentrated entirely on the meaning of the Republican convention in San Francisco. "The Republican Party took a giant stride away from its Lincoln tradition," King said. He worried not so much about Goldwater the candidate, whom he described as merely a "best man" at the marriage of white racial appeal with conservative economic values. "A cold fear touched the hearts of twenty million Negroes," he said, alarmed at what he called the capture of a national party built on civil rights—against the peak strength of bipartisan unity for civil rights—by "the counter forces to Negro liberation."

King urged his Savannah audience not to panic. "We are on the move, and the burning of our churches will not deter us," he cried. "The bombing of our homes will not dissuade us. The beating and killing of our young people will not divert us. The wanton release of their known murderers will not discourage us. We are on the move now. . . ." He preached a full rhythmic litany on marching that paused near ancient Jericho for a word of caution. There were "no broad highways" or "quick solutions" ahead, and "it would be irresponsible" to say there were. "Instead, the course we must follow lies through a maze of interrelated demands and counter demands, hopes and aspirations, fears and hatreds," King said. "But difficult and painful as it is, such a course must be charted." He resumed his oratorical march with a reminiscence on "the wondrous signs of our time," calling out names and fond descriptions from the movement's "nonviolent army" since the Montgomery bus boycott. "The patter of their feet as they walked through Jim Crow barriers in the great stride toward freedom is the thunder of the marching men of Joshua," he concluded. "And the world rocks beneath their tread. My people, my people, listen, listen, the battle is in our hands."

36

Movements Unbound

THE JOHNSON-GOLDWATER CAMPAIGN marked an era of transition in classical grand style. The Hollywood spectacle *Cleopatra* ended a first run of sixty-three weeks, giving way to relatively restrained epic movies such as *Becket* and *Dr. Strangelove.* Americans embraced two new Italian films starring Sophia Loren and Marcello Mastroianni, the zany British comedy of Peter Sellers, and an offbeat Beatles picture called *A Hard Day's Night.* The Beatles themselves—gently dismissed by *The New Yorker* as "a benign infection, perhaps incurable"—started their first American concert tour in the San Francisco Cow Palace a month after the Goldwater convention, and caused adoring youth riots eastward into September. In New York, the Russian-born French master Marc Chagall installed stained-glass peace figures at the United Nations. In San Diego, the McDonald's Corporation prepared a public stock offering to market fifteen-cent hamburgers to mobile baby boomers. Air Force safety experts completed tests on a new "steerable parachute" that opened up the future sport of skydiving, and Detroit engineers secretly designed a front-wheel-drive model to eliminate the "bothersome hump" along the floorboard of American cars.

The presidential race never wavered from preview handicapping as an epochal mismatch. On the night of Labor Day, for the holiday start of the fall campaign, the Johnson forces premiered to an estimated fifty million network viewers a stark thirty-second drama of a girl counting the petals on a daisy, one by one to ten, then holding the visual as her angelic voice transformed into the ominous, virile announcer of the nuclear countdown, backward down from ten. At zero, her picture dissolved into the thermonuclear mushroom cloud, out of which came a pronouncement by Lyndon Johnson: "These are the stakes—to make a world in which all of God's children can live, or to go into the dark. We must either love each other, or we must die." The screen went black to a tag line, "Vote for President Johnson on November 3," then back to the "Monday Night at the Movies" presentation of *David and Bathsheba,* starring Gregory Peck and Susan Hayward.

The "daisy girl" ad transformed political speech. Far beyond Nixon's celebrated stubble in the debates of 1960, which revealed a magnified effect of pictures over synchronized words, this commercial demonstrated the vast potential of crafted celluloid to shape image apart from language. Campaign debate would evolve swiftly into a specialized branch of advertising, its nature and cost driven by the thirty-second television spot. Agitated callers instantly lit up telephone switchboards over the daisy spot. Broadcasters freely exhibited the footage as news, marveling at its power to evoke doomsday menace around Goldwater without so much as mentioning his name. Johnson's managers instinctively canceled all further bookings as "overkill," a word borrowed from the creation of real atomic bombs.

Goldwater would spend 40 percent more than Johnson on television —often in long "position paper" addresses that only reinforced the impression he tried to combat. In a paid, half-hour broadcast, Goldwater dismayed some of his own strategists by using grim phrases such as "nuclear destruction" and "holocaust" almost once per minute, suggesting preoccupation, and his dull assurances of respect for atomic weapons never matched the spicy swagger of comments about "lobbing one into the men's room at the Kremlin." Newspapers lined up with solemn editorials— "The President and the Bomb"—pronouncing Goldwater more eager than trustworthy.

Goldwater treated some subjects with far greater public ease than critics and admirers alike. He relished tales of his grandfather "Big Mike" Goldwasser of Konin, who had fled Poland during the Revolution of 1848 to build a pioneer Jewish family on the Western frontier, of growing up bicultural in the home of his bar-mitzvahed father, Baron, and his poker-playing Episcopalian mother, Josephine. Nevertheless, his status as the first presidential candidate of direct Jewish ancestry remained almost universally unmentionable on any account—whether as a proud outpost for the American Dream, beyond Kennedy's much-discussed Catholicism, or pundit's quarry for signs of overcompensation (as in his praise for the Wehrmacht), or even as an item of note.

Senator Goldwater and his press coverage shared a more equal discomfort about race, the year's uncorked well. From Springfield, Illinois, rubbing the nose of Lincoln's bust in the Republican nominee's traditional supplication for good luck, he accused Democrats of fostering disorder and predatory crime, but confined his racial message to innuendo: "Every wife and mother, yes every woman and girl, knows what I mean, knows what I'm talking about." He endorsed the segregationist charge that the new civil rights law was a cause rather than a cure for injustice—"... the more the federal government has attempted to legislate morality, the more it actually has incited hatred and violence"—but he forthrightly renounced segregation as a personal creed. On a September tour of the South, Goldwater praised states' rights and Southern accents while attacking every facet of "the central government": Supreme Court "dictates," imposed Social Security numbers, new proposals "to tell you what to print on the front of your cigarette pack." Yet he came off as stiff, cheerful, and academic, emphasizing constitutional concepts rather than harangue, which took the edge off his all-white crowds heading into South Carolina.

From the White House, planning a whistle-stop train tour to hold the South against Goldwater, Lady Bird Johnson applied the experience of three decades to canvass the Democratic leaders, but politics strained old ties. When she specified a request that Senator Byrd of Virginia meet her train in public support, her diary recorded, "an invisible silken curtain fell across his voice." Of the many like Byrd who avoided the Johnsons through campaign season, the First Lady noted that Richard Russell, "the dearest of them all," said nothing of civil rights differences or anything else unpleasant, and in fact discreetly sent aides to guide the tour through Georgia. South Carolina's senior senator and governor bravely volunteered to ride the whole way, bringing "two daughters who were mighty good hard-working Democrats," but junior senator Strom Thurmond regretted that he faced "a really basic decision."

Thurmond was at once a bellwether and maverick of Southern Democratic politics. Six years older than President Johnson, he had been born to the only state where Negroes ever constituted a voting majority, in the year 1902, when South Carolina rejected its last Republican officeholders by a purge of Negro voters. His life mirrored the century—childhood when the region enacted Jim Crow laws so comprehensive as to outlaw fraternal orders whose bylaws in theory might compel interracial members to address one another as "brother"; an elected career from the late 1920s, just before Democratic hegemony produced 98 percent of the South Carolina vote for FDR; governor in time to volunteer as the 1948 Dixiecrat nominee in protest of World War II's integrationist effects on the Democratic White House; to Washington by historic write-in campaign in the year of the *Brown* decision. Thurmond was a gifted and attentive politician —reputed to have dispensed a political kindness to nearly every constituent family—with a knack for distinguishing clarity on the race issue. In his plea against final passage of the civil rights bill in June, he told Senate colleagues that it "will make a Czar of the President of the United States and a Rasputin of the Attorney General."

Barry Goldwater had courted Thurmond secretly since then, not merely to endorse him for president across partisan lines but to "go all the way and change parties." On September 16, Thurmond accomplished the switch in a statewide television address of slashing boldness. "The Democratic Party has abandoned the people . . . ," he declared in the first of twenty-two bullet-like paragraphs on his former party as consummate evil: "The Democratic Party has invaded the private lives of people . . . has succored and assisted our Communist enemies . . . worships at the throne of power and materialism . . . has protected the Supreme Court in a reign of judicial tyranny." Thurmond proclaimed the November election a fulcrum of the ages: "The party of our fathers is dead. Those who took its name are engaged in another Reconstruction. . . ." Should Democrats prevail, he warned, "freedom as we have known it in this country is doomed."

Thurmond welcomed the Republican nominee the next day wearing a distinctive new lapel pin—a GOP gold elephant sporting tiny, Goldwater-style horned-rim glasses—hosted a Goldwater rally with Louisiana segregationist Leander Perez, and pledged to campaign actively through the fall. South Carolina Democrats stammered in shock. Although most fellow officeholders shared Thurmond's opposition to Lyndon Johnson as a turncoat semi-Southerner, none followed his leap from established identity and power to a minority Republican party that remained a dirty word at home, and a voting bloc for civil rights in Washington. Publicly silent, Mendel Rivers and other Democratic chairmen privately marveled that Thurmond left no room for retreat in case Goldwater turned out to be a fluke. The *New York Times* minimized the switch as a desperate union of two discredited species, Dixiecrats and "lily white" Republicans, and the South Carolina Democratic chairman questioned Thurmond's "moral right" to keep a Senate seat granted by Democratic voters in a Democratic primary. Incorrectly, the chairman said Goldwater could not win a state that even Eisenhower had failed to carry, and predicted that the "violence" of Thurmond's attack on their heritage would reunite South Carolina Democrats.

IN HOLMES COUNTY, MISSISSIPPI, Hollis Watkins claimed that discipline pulled his area through the summer project relatively unscathed. Having first rebuffed Stokely Carmichael's plan to appoint a "greenhorn" college Negro above him as county director, Watkins had laid down strict rules to his twenty-three summer volunteers on the night of their arrival: no drinking, no dating of locals, no bravado experiments or interracial street appearances, no displays of argumentative skill to rebut local segregationists. He promptly shipped out one volunteer who insisted on her right to hold hands in public, and constantly emphasized his prior experience in Greenwood—where only a year earlier he had been snatched off the streets to hang from the bars of the Parchman death house—and before that in his native Pike County.

All summer, especially after specially trained volunteers opened a Pike County project in early July, Watkins passed along stories of chronic Klan violence around McComb. When three Freedom School churches were burned there in a single week, his personal knowledge of the victims made vivid object lessons for volunteers who considered schoolwork too tame. Watkins confined his Holmes County volunteers in seven fledgling Freedom Schools until he could tell which ones respected unseen dangers. Of these he approved a few for the hazards of outdoor registration canvass, including Mario Savio, a philosophy student who conquered a pronounced stutter and a tendency to overthink.

Savio returned to the University of California for the fall term. Other California students stayed on in Mississippi for the extension projects financed by the Belafonte rescue, and those in McComb suffered an undiminished vigilante rampage. The home of a COFO supporter was bombed at the end of August; McComb police, finding that the handyman victim had been repairing a volunteer's car in the yard, arrested him for unlicensed commerce. On September 2, Klansmen publicly beat a registration volunteer in the streets of McComb. On September 5, Stanford volunteer Dennis Sweeney presided as the distraught Red Heffner family told the local press they were surrendering their home to relentless persecution. Bombs struck three Negro sites in McComb on September 7 and a preacher's home two days later. That night, project director Jesse Harris wrote a pleading letter to Burke Marshall at the Justice Department: "... our situation has become critical...."

In Berkeley, California, Mario Savio highlighted emergency news from McComb at a line of outdoor information tables, among students holding forth on parallel causes. A year earlier, shortly after the Berkeley Jaycees canceled the annual Festival of Football Queens to block the first Negro student among the parade escorts, Malcolm X had delivered a biting speech on the limits of precocious activists who saw the race problem as existing only in far-off Mississippi. Since then, students had mobilized against Proposition 14, the pending ballot initiative to repeal California's new fair housing law, while allied groups protested the racial agenda of Goldwater delegates at the Republican convention in nearby San Francisco, and still others in September picketed the *Oakland Tribune*. Owned by former U.S. senator William Knowland, state chairman of the Goldwater campaign and leading supporter of Proposition 14, the *Tribune* portrayed the student pickets as nettlesome, immature, and very likely infiltrated by Communists. Investigators from the *Tribune* notified university administrators of property records showing that the area reserved for student information tables—a twenty-six-foot-wide brick strip between the sidewalk and a campus gate on Bancroft Way—was owned by the university, not the city, and the administrators claimed the power and duty to banish the tables effective September 21.

□

IN MCCOMB, late on the night of September 20, four Klansmen threw fourteen sticks of dynamite onto a porch, shattering the front rooms. "People grab whatever clothing they can find and run into the streets," Dennis Sweeney wrote in a volunteer dispatch. "...It's Mama [Mrs. Alyene] Quin's house. It couldn't be worse. Everybody loves Mama Quin. She owns a popular cafe." By the time rescuers pulled two young Quin children from beds beneath a collapsed ceiling—one with a punctured eardrum, the other with minor bruises—a second, more powerful bomb destroyed Society Hill Baptist, where C. C. Bryant was deacon. Bryant had been the only adult willing to sponsor SNCC's original registration project in Mississippi, from which Bob Moses retreated in 1961 with Hollis Watkins and Curtis Hayes as teenage disciples. The Quin Cafe had been their refuge.

AT BERKELEY, student pickets of every description protested the closing of the Bancroft Strip the next morning: pacifists, religious clubs, civil rights groups, the YMCA, Youth for Goldwater. After a stalemate of some days over shifting issues, such as where the classroom started and stopped, several groups deliberately set up their information tables in the Bancroft Strip as before. Academic deans summoned five of them for peremptory discipline, whereupon nearly five hundred students signed a spontaneous petition of solidarity—"We have jointly manned the tables"—and marched into the administration building for the summary hearing at which the five, plus Savio and two others who organized the petition, were suspended. On the steps of Sproul Hall, when a professsor warned against "the continued, and I fear willful, breaking and violation of regulations," a voice from the boisterous crowd shouted, "You have stated that the university must withstand the outside pressure. I maintain that the university is walking *hand in hand* with the outside pressure!" Cheers went up, along with cries of "Let Savio speak!"

In the tradition of Bob Moses, Savio entranced his peers with a meandering discourse on the distinction between legal and political neutrality. By banning the tables and solicitations, and insisting that off-campus speakers be regulated well in advance, he said, the Regents were stifling speech behind claims of law. "Let's say, for example—and this touches me very deeply—let's say that in McComb, Mississippi, some children are killed in the bombing of a church.... Let's say we have someone who's come up from Mississippi and wanted to speak here and he had to wait.... And everybody will have completely forgotten about those little children because, you know, when you're black and in Mississippi, nobody gives a damn...."

"Now the issue is free speech," Savio declared. He called restricted speech a symptom of larger anti-democratic jitters, saying "after that Tonkin Bay incident," both presidential candidates quickly agreed that "Vietnam is not an issue in the campaign." Therefore, voting Berkeley students "can't choose on what kind of foreign policy we want," he argued, and it was only one step from there to matters of nuclear survival. "Now note—extremely important—the University of California is directly involved in making newer and better atom bombs," he said. "Whether this is good or bad, don't you think . . . in the spirit of political neutrality . . . there should be some democratic control?"

Students caucused all night on the suspensions. Even while the Berkeley story remained confined to the campus newspaper, the *Daily Californian,* ramifications spread nationally within the movement from Savio's desire to be identified by his affiliation as "Chair, UC Campus Friends of SNCC." At a summit meeting in Oakland, Friends of SNCC chapters that ardently supported Savio nevertheless questioned "official" use of the SNCC name as a touchy subject at the Atlanta headquarters, especially since the Atlantic City convention. The chairman of a Bay area confederation, himself a summer volunteer, argued that "wildcat" projects obscured SNCC's purpose, and that Friends of SNCC chapters must confine themselves to fund-raising for the Southern movement. Savio reluctantly agreed to curtail free speech about his own motivating identity.

QUESTIONS OF CONTROL were more tender than ever since a notoriously failed New York truce meeting of civil rights organizations on September 18. Host Robert Spike of the National Council of Churches had scarcely finished his opening call for goodwill after Atlantic City—"let us try to avoid raking the coals of the past"—before Gloster Current of the NAACP attacked Mississippi SNCC workers in general as hotheaded "johnny-come-latelies" and Bob Moses in particular as a mumbling slacker who left "a very bad impression" on members of the NAACP Executive Board.

Backed by Andrew Young of SCLC, Spike pleaded again for peace to "eliminate the suspicion that exists among us," but sniping erupted anyway. One SNCC representative protested a "diatribe against Bob and SNCC," another invited the New York executives to relieve their snobbishness by attending a "low level meeting" with the common people of Mississippi. "I don't want to listen to [Pike County farmer E. W.] Steptoe," Current indignantly replied. "We need a high level meeting to cut away the underbrush." John Morsell, assistant director of the NAACP, defended his traditional hierarchy with a fond assurance well suited to Hoover's FBI: "We are bureaucratic. Many memos get to our desks and have to wait for our decisions."

A clergyman from the National Council of Churches remarked on an "air of unreality" about the discussion, and Al Lowenstein stepped across the gulf with a procedural approach "to maximize cooperation" on

Mississippi. "Right now decision making is metaphysical . . . ," he said. "We need structured democracy, not amorphous democracy." SNCC leaders resented Lowenstein's criticism in part for its maddening grain of truth. Internally, political ambition tore at their informal traditions of brotherhood consent, with young veterans and newcomers alike pulling SNCC's name in many directions. Apprehensions worried SNCC's caretakers enough to summon Moses and James Forman home early from Africa.

Spike's clergy pushed hard as neutral facilitators for the disparate civil rights groups. Within forty hours of McComb's September 20 bombings, they transported Alyene Quin and two fellow victims from Mississippi to the Justice Department for a meeting with Burke Marshall, John Doar, and Lee White. Matti Dillon told them her husband, Willie, had been in jail since their home was bombed September 2, hauled off on the preposterous charge of running an illegal auto garage "when he doesn't even have a garage." Ora Bryant told how her home had been bombed two months before her Society Hill Baptist Church, and Quin said she and her children had no place to stay in McComb: "Everyone's afraid to have me in their house now." On behalf of the three women, Spike and other church officials "argued strenuously"—as Lee White put it in a memo—that the President himself should receive the three women to signal encouragement and resolve against the Klan siege. Johnson's advisers saw "no political benefit" in such an audience, saying that "as serious and as moving as the problem is in McComb, this is not the right time to use the President for this purpose." Vowing to stay in Washington as long as necessary to get through, the redoubtable McComb women changed minds in the White House overnight. They met with columnist Drew Pearson, who adopted their cause. At a press conference, Alyene Quin dismissed public statements by the Pike County sheriff that she and other Negroes must be bombing their own homes: "Do you think I would work eleven years to keep a house and then plant a bomb under it while two of my children were in it?"

Presbyterian leader Eugene Carson Blake, Spike's chairman at the Commission on Religion and Race, told reporters that "nothing in the history of Christianity is comparable to the mass desecration of the houses of God in Mississippi." Events built news pressure more than words. There were two more bombings on September 23, and McComb police jailed twenty-five movement supporters, including volunteer Dennis Sweeney, under a catchall new "criminal syndicalism" statute designed expressly against the summer project.

By Thursday morning, September 24, Lee White was preparing President Johnson for a brief addition to his schedule. "They are coming through the basement entrance and will leave the same way," White advised, "although obviously they will tell the press about their visit here." The three McComb women spent several minutes with Johnson at one o'clock, just after Chief Justice Earl Warren and his six commissioners formally delivered an advance copy of their report on the Kennedy assassination. Shrewdly, perhaps with background coaching from the Justice Department, the McComb-CORR delegation generated news stories proposing that President Johnson send Allen Dulles back to Mississippi: "New Dulles Mission Urged." Mindful of his goading effect upon J. Edgar Hoover after the triple murders of June, McComb advocates pictured the ex-CIA director moving from his completed duties on the Warren Commission to investigate the "national shame" of unsolved Mississippi bombings.

THIS TIME Johnson officials decided that Hoover was not the primary obstacle. Like the summer project itself, the new Jackson FBI office had trouble covering territory in southwest Mississippi, where fear was so pervasive that even stalwart segregationists felt the chill of Klan violence. A bomb went off in the yard of the Natchez mayor on a rumor that he favored hiring Negro workers at a new shopping center, and in Vicksburg, after a bomb demolished the COFO Freedom House, Mayor John Holland issued a written statement denying any slightest common bond with its occupants: "I never said they were good kids, or anything complementary [sic]...." To Mississippi FBI chief Roy Moore, already swamped under eight hundred cases a month, the Southwest was a low-priority area. Having been made to stick to his internal working conditions—that he would accept only agents motivated to volunteer for Mississippi,* not the usual draftees from FBI headquarters—Moore distributed arriving agents by triage. The Southwest got few, and federal sources instead planted threats of martial law that surfaced in a McComb newspaper on September 25.

Full-scale skirmishes were overwhelming Moore's major theater of operations in Neshoba County. All that week, on leads developed by the FBI task force under Inspector Joe Sullivan, Justice Department attorneys began hauling one hundred subpoenaed witnesses before a U.S. grand jury in Biloxi, whereupon a state grand jury in Neshoba County instantly called most of the same witnesses to ask what they were telling the feds. The two grand juries dueled. Judge O. H. Barnett introduced to the state grand jury as its investigative leader "the most courageous sheriff in all America, Lawrence Rainey," whom Sullivan considered a prime suspect in the triple murders.

FBI officials first thought Judge Barnett was the brother of former governor Ross Barnett, then discovered they were cousins. Whether or not the judge presumed too much political accord with J. Edgar Hoover, he

---

* Moore's volunteers for Mississippi came disproportionately out of the New York FBI office, where agents wished to escape the notoriously clumsy supervision of Assistant Director John "Cement Head" Malone.

underestimated the FBI's territorial instinct by demanding to know leads and sources that Hoover zealously guarded even from his employers in the Justice Department. When Judge Barnett wired Hoover to instruct not only Joe Sullivan and Roy Moore but "all of your agents that have information regarding the death of three civil rights workers ... to appear in person at the county courthouse ... Monday, September 28, 1964," Hoover resisted behind the authority of Acting Attorney General Katzenbach. On Friday, Katzenbach wired formal orders to Moore that all FBI agents must refuse to testify, and lawyers scrambled over the weekend to quash the state subpoenas and implement an eight-point contingency plan against possible attempts to jail FBI agents.

With even armed federal agents under such stress, the few local whites sympathetic to the investigation begged not to be called before the federal grand jury. Klan cars were said to follow suspected witnesses on the highway to Biloxi, and there were rumors that Negroes were paying turncoats to lie about Mississippi. Sullivan cajoled witnesses to confirm for the grand jury basic information about the Klan reputations of Rainey and his deputies, then sometimes changed his mind and persuaded attorneys *not* to call witnesses who might suffer beyond the value of their testimony. One advantage for Sullivan was that the agents of his task force, having held their ground through multiple conversations with much of the hostile population, were developing two informants inside the White Knights of the Ku Klux Klan.

Roy Mitchell, a rookie agent relegated mostly to errand duties, had first reported something odd in the taunts of one garrulous young policeman. Officer Wallace Miller, known in Meridian for impishly flashing the secret Klan sign in news photos, turned out to have pangs over the deadly violence, which ruined his zest for belonging to the Klan. Despite Sullivan's security worries over the combination of an inexperienced handler and a notoriously bumbling informant—"If Wallace Miller walked across a farm with only one cow pie on forty acres, he would step in it"—their conversations had yielded profiles of fellow Klansmen, including nearly a dozen who were said to have gathered at the Long Horn Drive-In that June Sunday night after a posse alarm from the Neshoba klavern, in the next county. Inside the FBI task force, Sullivan prodded his veterans well into September for being outdone by a young street agent, until two of them broke through on what recruiters called the lucky hundredth pitch.

"I've been expecting you," said Delmar Dennis, a part-time Methodist minister and chaplain to the Klan.

When Dennis agreed to risk his life for an informant's fee of a hundred dollars a week, FBI agents John Martin and Tom Van Riper took forty pages of notes at their first briefing session. Dennis confirmed Wallace Miller's knowledge of orders within the White Knights that marked Mickey Schwerner as a special target, and he described firsthand the sight of Klan member Alton Wayne Roberts returning breathless with bloody knuckles from the ambush and arson at Beatrice Cole's Mount Zion Church on June 16. Both Dennis and Miller were in place for a summit meeting of the White Knights on Sunday, September 27, when armed Klansmen with radios patrolled the perimeter of a factory outside Meridian, and Imperial Wizard Sam Bowers quoted the Book of Romans to ordain that any "fourth-degree sanctions"—as the White Knights referred to murder—be accomplished by compartmentalized command "without malice," in the spirit of Christian soldiers. The FBI task force had the informants' reports on his speech before midnight. They were hearsay, and stopped well short of direct evidence in the triple murders, but they gave the agents a new veneer of omniscience in psychological warfare. "Once we had Miller and Dennis providing a pool of information," Sullivan later recalled, "we were pretty hard to beat."

ON ITS PUBLIC RELEASE that same Sunday, the *New York Times* massed typesetters to reproduce the Warren Commission report overnight for a forty-eight-page special, which James Reston introduced as "the greatest repository of Presidential political history, drama and fiction since the murder of Mr. Lincoln...." Each clue raised "a whole new catalogue of mysteries," he observed, and he pronounced the Kennedy assassination "so involved in the complicated and elemental conflicts of the age that many vital questions remain, and the philosophers, novelists, and dramatists will have to take it from here."

The emotional impact of the Warren report buried the previous day's FBI report on race riots in the North, in which Hoover's Bureau groped toward the Black Muslims as scapegoats, just as Philadelphia riot police in multiple platoon strength had stormed what they thought was the national citadel of Black Muslims only to find a man who had been riding the streets with an NAACP leader to urge calm. The *Times* stressed the lone captive's alien resonance and exotic names—Abyssinia Hayes, aka Shakkyh Muhammad—calling him "an apostate from the Black Muslims who now leads a cult of his own."

The actual violence among seedling Muslims was precise, confined, and nearly invisible—far removed from the interracial fears of the riots. The Nation of Islam sealed its hold on core believers with attacks that lumped together "rebel" doubters and temple debtors with "hypocrite" followers of Malcolm X. In Los Angeles, firebombs struck one of the few Negro newspapers that commented on such internal conflict. Private enforcements escalated in most major cities. Captain Clarence X led a squad from Temple No. 11 in Boston that blocked traffic as it dragged ex-secretary Aubrey Barnette and a companion from their car and stomped them on a Sunday afternoon—fracturing Barnette's ankle, two ribs, and a vertebra. From his nonviolent training center, SCLC's Rev. Virgil Wood ran behind the rush of sirens up Blue Hill Avenue into a milling crowd, where he heard that the bloodied figure on a stretcher was a Boston University graduate who had gotten mixed up with the Black Muslims. Barnette felt the attack as a brutal lesson for those tempted to follow him out of the temple, as well as a warning that he should not testify against Muslim defendants in the car-chase ambush of June 14, when Malcolm's aide Benjamin 2X had fled into Logan Airport. Only three years after he and his cousin Ronald Stokes proudly served as Elijah Muhammad's first college-educated temple secretaries, Barnette had lost his cousin to police violence in the sensational LAPD shootout of 1962, then his own savings and religious beliefs to corruption within the Nation. Still bitter about the Nation's exploitation of the Stokes family,* Barnette resolved to press criminal charges against the thirteen attackers he remembered.

Earlier in September, at an improvised program for the disoriented remnant of Malcolm's followers, twenty-two people had heard Benjamin 2X read a letter in which Malcolm grandly volunteered to raise an expedition army of ten thousand Harlemites to drive white mercenaries out of the African Congo. Collateral events just then were shutting down the wiretap on Malcolm's phone lines, as the U.S. Departments of Justice and State—upset that the overseas traveler reportedly was urging African heads of state to "take the issue of racialism in the United States before the United Nations as a threat to world peace"—asked the FBI to discontinue any practice that could taint criminal prosecution if and when Malcolm returned to the United States.† The Bureau's ongoing Chicago wiretaps did pick up acid remarks by Elijah Muhammad that Malcolm was staying in Africa because he "does not have a hundred people in all the United States." The Arabs, scoffed Muhammad, were "laughing at him and not committing themselves."

Muhammad minimized the parallel defections of his youngest sons Wallace and Akbar, the latter of whom was studying orthodox Islam at Cario's Al-Azhar University. "Other messengers, like Moses and King David, have had trouble with their sons," he said. Akbar remained in Egypt with Malcolm, but Wallace openly challenged what he described as his father's determination "to be the strongest black man on the face of the earth." Two hundred Muslims from several cities answered his call to Philadelphia's Venango Ballroom on Sunday, September 27. In Malcolm's absence, his wife, Betty X, came with Benjamin 2X from New York, and

---

* "Now the Black Muslims say they're supportive, they're looking out for each other," Barnette said in a 1965 interview. "But when Ronald Stokes was killed, no support was given.... His child had to live in the home of my aunt, who is a Christian, for one year. Not a Muslim from Boston came to visit that child...."
† In its closing intercept, the FBI recorded a phone notice from an unknown foreign cleric who pronounced Malcolm an orthodox Muslim qualified to "spread Islam among the Afro-Americans."

Abyssinia Hayes arrived in a flowing white robe. They heard Wallace say he had come out of prison determined to teach no more lies, and solemnly announce that Muslims should forget everything Elijah Muhammad had taught them about Islam. He instructed them to stop applying for and using "X" names, for openers, although they could adopt African or Arab ones through the courts. By claiming authority to supersede the Nation of Islam, Wallace knowingly launched the active opposition that had brought his father's sectarians swarming against Malcolm. All that protected him, other than his lingering status as the troublesome but designated heir in Elijah's "royal" family, was Wallace's reputation for straightforward candor about religion. He was perceived to be both genuine and dangerously weak. Wallace told the Venango audience that he abhorred violence, and therefore could not work wholly in concert with Malcolm because of his "violent image."

Betty X rose from the floor to object that her husband had committed no crimes or retaliations against anyone. Wallace carefully replied that while he admired Malcolm for defying the Nation's gangsters, and did not consider him to be violent by nature or performance, Malcolm nevertheless cultivated an aura of violence that could not be reconciled with true Islam or with the black man's crusade against bigotry.

ONCE AGAIN, race served as the hidden midwife for far-flung, mysterious upheaval. It was, as Lincoln said in his own more terrible era, "somehow, the cause." In early September, when sitting governor Endicott Peabody unexpectedly lost the Democratic primary in Massachusetts, pundits variously blamed his stiff manner and his mother's arrest in St. Augustine, which either upstaged him as a hero or associated him with unpopular meddling. Opinion polls showed that heavy majorities in New York were deeply attached to the civil rights bill while also resentful of the civil rights movement for having "gone too far," with a front-page *Times* survey story quoting whites bitter that Negroes expected "everything on a silver platter."

President Johnson ventured north for his first major campaign trip into an unyielding sea of admirers that swallowed up his motorcade on the streets of Providence, Rhode Island. It was September 28—publication day for the Warren Commission report—and the near hysteria of the crowds alarmed Secret Service agents even before one of the overheated limousines exploded into flame, but an oblivious Johnson pulled as many as fifteen pedestrians at once into the convertible to share the overflow glory. A record one million people hailed him in person through the six New England states before dawn on Tuesday the twenty-ninth, and he ended with a hospital visit to young Edward Kennedy, still recuperating from his June plane crash. Johnson scarcely noticed his own hands bleeding from a press of flesh that left his White House touring car, the *Queen Mary*, with assorted dents and a buckled roof.

That Thursday morning, October 1, Berkeley students protested the shutdown of the Bancroft Strip by setting up a token three information tables on the steps of Sproul Hall. Jack Weinberg of CORE distributed literature on Chaney and Schwerner, the two CORE staff members murdered in Mississippi, but he refused to identify himself to an assistant dean, who decided to have Weinberg arrested. Rather than walk him through the gathering crowd, the arresting lieutenant summoned a squad car onto the broad plaza in front of Sproul Hall, but as Weinberg debated campus authorities through the window, students by the score sat all around the car, singing "We Shall Not Be Moved," impervious to the revved engine and commands to make way.

Sight of the captured vehicle astonished Mario Savio on his arrival for a scheduled noon rally. Reinforcements of press and police ringed an expanding perimeter as Savio waded through to the center and stood on the roof of the squad car to be heard. Over the intermittent crackling of the police radio, he explained the arrest of Weinberg with a parable from Herodotus. His speech made the roof a platform for serial speakers from all sides, uncertain what to do next, and the student body president implored Savio to join him for negotiations with campus officials. "All right," shouted Savio, "but I want it understood that until this person in this car is placed, you know, *out* of arrest, nobody will move from here!" The car, with Weinberg in it, remained trapped all afternoon and through the night. Students massed in numbers great enough to detach sit-in expeditions of five hundred.

A world away, Minister Louis X was reporting by phone to Elijah Muhammad on trial testimony in Boston. While repeating that his members had been provoked by the "hypocrite" Aubrey Barnette and his companion on Blue Hill Avenue, Louis X noted the day's medical evidence on fractures and ruptured kidneys, plus eyewitnesses that "the Muslims pulled a car in front of them and pulled them out from the car and beat them." The judge was an "original," he added—the Nation's term for black—and had remarked so favorably on the prosecution thus far that Louis X asked whether it might be wise to offer a guilty plea to lesser charges. Muhammad emphatically vetoed the suggestion on the ground that renegades were a threat to worship in the Nation. "They needed a severe beating and should have been killed," he declared, telling Louis X he would rather his members serve time than pay a nickel for the medical bills of hypocrites. Accordingly, nine defendants, including Captain Clarence X, stood fast through trial to eventual conviction in January.

Elsewhere on Thursday, the FBI's Deke DeLoach took a bulletin to the White House about McComb, Mississippi, where attention had concentrated in the week since President Johnson received its delegation of three women. The local white editor hazarded his first oblique community warning—"bombings cause tension"—which earned a firebomb through his office window and a burned cross in his yard. (An anonymous caller offered the editor a pinch of chivalrous regret about the burned cross, saying the Klan would not have struck that particular night "had we known of your mother's death.")

On Wednesday, Acting Attorney General Katzenbach reported confidentially to the President that McComb's "local officials are publicly claiming that Negroes are bombing their own homes, and responded to the latest bombings by making a number of arrests of Negroes." Four Episcopal ministers from the National Council of Churches made news that day over McComb's refusal to allow visits with twenty-four jailed Negroes, including eight minors, and Governor Johnson ventured his first public doubt on the self-terror theory, saying, "Some were bombings by white people." Historian John Dittmer later discounted any chance that President Johnson would have sent martial law troops before an election, but state officials used a torrent of such rumors to spur the emergency response DeLoach tracked on Thursday: the FBI and highway patrol jointly arrested off McComb's streets three Klansmen who more or less admitted their klavern bombed weekly by drawing Negro names from a hat, and confiscated their automobile arsenal of one pistol, four high-powered rifles, eight wooden clubs, "a black leatherette hood and apron," brass knuckles, an explosives box, and a deputy sheriff's badge.

Hours after his annual address to the SCLC convention, Martin Luther King announced this news in Savannah to a Thursday evening mass rally of fifteen hundred inside Saint Paul CME Church, plus several hundred overflows standing outside in the rain. He praised the three arrests in McComb as an "indication that the nonviolent movement by its relentless exposure has finally penetrated the closed society of Mississippi."

In Jackson, television station WLBT* was reporting that the bomb charges filed against the three McComb Klansmen carried "a possible death penalty," but Mississippi judge William Watkins soon released the

---

* Lawyers for the station submitted transcripts of the McComb broadcasts as evidence of fair (or reformed) racial coverage, in rebuttal of the FCC license challenge prepared in March of 1964 by researchers from the National Council of Churches. The case would consume the balance of the decade. Judge Warren Burger—in his last decision before becoming U.S. Chief Justice—revoked WLBT's license in a landmark 1969 decision that established procedural rights for consumers and minorities in broadcast license awards. Ownership of the former WLBT-TV devolved to a consortium that included NAACP chairman Aaron Henry.

three—and eight others who similarly pleaded guilty—to probation on suspended sentences, telling the defendants from the bench that because they were "unduly provoked" by outsiders of "low morality and unhygienic," he had decided "to make your punishment light, and I hope you appreciate it." Like the bombings themselves, his action both revealed and broke down Mississippi's isolation. In a rare public attack on a conservative jurist, J. Edgar Hoover denounced Watkins for "blindness and indifference to outrageous acts." When McComb police arrested thirteen COFO workers the day of the Watkins sentencing—on charges of sharing meals in the McComb Freedom House without a food license—syndicated columnist Drew Pearson sent bond money from Washington, and the *Stanford Daily* in California headlined two bail releases of McComb volunteer Dennis Sweeney over four days. Oliver Emmerich, the embattled local newspaper editor, published a revolutionary "Statement of Principles" in which 650 citizens of McComb endorsed "equal treatment under the law."

In Biloxi, Inspector Sullivan's task force obtained sealed indictments from the grand jury at three o'clock Friday afternoon, October 2, and Justice Department lawyers generated national headlines suggesting imminent results in the triple murder case: "Judge Orders Secrecy on Identity Pending Arrests in Mississippi Deaths."

In California, negotiations were consuming a second day with CORE's Jack Weinberg still unmoved from the squad car at the center of a giant demonstration on the Sproul Hall plaza. Sheer numbers of exuberant young people magnified the event on the Berkeley campus, where enrollment was just shy of 30,000.* A campus dean had solicited the aid of fraternity students, and all Thursday night huge throngs of demonstrators and anti-demonstrators gathered from dormitories, pubs, and athletic halls to cheer competitively for the rights of Weinberg or the police car, with volatile scrums on the fringes. Choruses of "We Shall Overcome" echoed against derisive renditions of the Disney television jingle "M-I-C-K-E-Y M-O-U-S-E." Late Friday, marching reinforcements from the California Highway Patrol raised police strength to five hundred. Some demonstrators melted away and others tensely passed conduct instructions for arrest ("remove sharp objects from pockets..."), before University President Clark Kerr signed a six-point truce agreement at 7:20 P.M. "Let us agree by acclamation to accept this document!" Savio cried ten minutes later. "I ask you to rise quietly and with dignity, and go home." Beneath him, Weinberg submitted to arrest after thirty-two unbroken hours under the now-flattened car roof, and some four thousand students dispersed

---

* One of every ten American students lived in California, which became the country's most populous state in 1964. Nationally, the first baby boom cohort left high school that year in numbers bulging one million more than in 1963.

from an event that began to shift the student movement out of the Negro South.

On Saturday morning, FBI agents arrested Sheriff Lawrence Rainey, Deputy Sheriff Cecil Price, and three other Neshoba County officers on assorted charges of beating Negroes in their custody. Although newspapers with a hint of pique noted that the accusations concerned "Violence Not Linked to Triple Murder," the jailing of such powerful local figures achieved the desired psychological effect within the besieged White Knights klaverns. Informants reported that several overwrought conspirators took flight beyond the region, where FBI agents enjoyed a rare advantage over the tight-knit Klan in tracking them down. They traced one to Louisiana and located Jimmy Jordan in the Mississippi coastal town of Gulfport, where he headed on Monday, October 5. Agents John Martin and Tom Van Riper found the thirty-eight-year-old Jordan a jumble of contradictions—fatalistic, saying he expected to have been caught long ago, yet remorseless, fitfully defiant of Klan retribution and the FBI alike. When three long, tantalyzing sessions yielded no breakthrough, John Proctor petitioned Inspector Sullivan for a crack at Jordan, one of Meridian's binge-drinking drifters. "I know that son of a bitch," said the agent who had found the burning COFO car in June. "If he did this, I can make him talk."

INQUIRIES CLOSED on the enormity of Freedom Summer. While FBI agents pressed Klansmen for facts about its first night, movement participants sifted the aftermath. First in Atlanta, then in Hattiesburg and at a retreat in the town of Waveland not far from Jordan's hideaway in Gulfport, the veterans and inheritors of the student Freedom Rides debated the issues that had brought their leaders home early from Africa: "affiliations, the black-white problem, who should be on staff, who should not," and "Why do we organize . . . how are decisions made?" Some argued that the movement could not afford to sink into critical reflection, saying, "After the election, win or lose, the forces behind Goldwater will gain strength," or, "Well, shit on your personal feelings!" Others protested executive tyranny ("Who made that decision?"), pleaded moral exhaustion ("I have begun to split up"), or vented frustrations of youth snatched from campus life to the edge of martyrdom: "One reason guys fight on projects is [they] feel others are using the girls they are bitching about during the day." The internal contest was widely defined as a struggle between the power "hard-liners" of Forman and the "floater" existentialists of Moses, but Moses sat silent, refusing to use his own personal influence to rebut the power faction. A student took the floor with a silent pantomime of SNCC's characteristic hand gestures, which earned applause for anguished expression and snickers for burned-out absurdity. Dov Green, one of many SNCC poets, composed a wry stanza on the crisis:

Moses is drinking.
And Forman's in bed.
Now the whole world is thinking
That SNCC has gone red.
Well, we've lost our picket lines,
FDP has gone right,
We're all showing signs
Of losing this fight.
N double A's a-gambling
That our next breath will be our last.
Now the whole world is crumbling
And I'm sitting on mah ass.

"We've got to stop being Muslims during the day and integrationists at night," declared a staff worker in Hattiesburg. "Rivals are not enemies," warned another. One memo writer focused upon governance within SNCC: "If we assign a quota on whites, or even eliminate 'them' entirely, what will we prove?" Another asked whether "we really believe what the white man tells us, that the Negro is really too stupid to vote. You know there are some Negroes in SNCC who believe that." A movement conceived in biracial sacrifice toward voting rights warred over the internal franchise. Dissenters asked why Freedom School teachers of both races were not invited to the deliberations at all, and a prophetic paper, written anonymously for fear of ridicule, raised by racial analogy an intercutting issue of gender: "Assumptions of male superiority are as widespread and deep-rooted and every much as crippling to the woman as the assumptions of white supremacy are to the Negro."

Student shock troops who had helped punch their stupefied country out of segregation confronted the perennial snares of democratic practice. If binding popular rule carried inside SNCC, it threatened to swamp the Negro pioneers with white votes, and all of the veterans with newer faces ("The new people are naive ... I cannot really be honest with them ..."). Voting came to suggest either dead rules and parliamentary tricks, which made Atlantic City loom as decisive betrayal, or classical "mobocracy" in the form of Mississippi's broadly representative white rule. "I was sure that we were closer to the truth than anyone else," wrote a staff member from Atlanta headquarters. Privately Dennis Sweeney and others took up a curdling slogan about the ballot itself—"the best way to keep someone a slave is to give him the vote and call him free"—while still declaring in public that elected authority must "be made to come forward with some sort of answer to all of this."

During the October emergency meeting in Atlanta, controversy spread from the rare—some said unprecedented—demand for a binding vote on whether to grant voting status to post-summer volunteers. It was rejected as smacking of bourgeois liberalism, which "tried to give equal weight to all shades of opinion when there were two hundred people in a room." In a harbinger of future decades, insiders glossed over racial implications to develop the word "liberal" as an epithet for shallow understanding and preoccupation with democratic norms. Al Lowenstein emerged as the prototype bad liberal only a year after bringing some of the original ideas for the summer project to Mississippi from South Africa. Bayard Rustin, Joseph Rauh, and Roy Wilkins joined Lowenstein in categories of scorn that shaved kinship into smaller circles of trusted allies—radicals, pacifists, nationalists, Marxists. Paradoxically, social forces on the brink of militant explosion reverted to preoccupation with enemies and niches. SNCC's Waveland meeting, wrote James Forman, "finally broke down on the question of firing people." About that time, asked whether Mississippi had reached a "pre-revolutionary situation," Bob Moses told a Stanford audience that any revolution most likely would break out in the North instead, where "the cities are our jungles."

In Gulfport, FBI agent Proctor patiently visited Jimmy Jordan every few days through October. Jordan neither disputed nor confirmed reports that he had talked to friends about "shooting a nigger." Full of hardship, he expressed feelings of abandonment against the Klan, which Proctor cultivated on the FBI's tavern tab. The agent kept up his matter-of-fact warning that one day he would bring an arrest warrant, and when Jordan began to mention the likelihood of doing some prison time, Proctor assured him that the Bureau could arrange for him beforehand to visit his dying father in Georgia.

Jordan's confession, and another soon to follow, looked back through the eyes of astonished Klansmen into the heart of the Mississippi movement at the peak of its conviction, only four months earlier. From word that Neshoba County had locked up the White Knights target known as "Goatee"—Mickey Schwerner—with two civil rights friends who "needed their asses tore up," there had been furtive recruitments at homes and parking lots, errands for sandwiches and protective gloves, plus logistical mix-ups in the rendezvous between Jordan's Meridian Klansmen and the Philadelphia klavern of Billy Posey, whose 1955 Chevrolet broke down with carburetor trouble in the night caravan that overtook the newly released civil rights workers. Deputy Sheriff Cecil Price took them to the isolated Rock Cut Road in his cruiser, with Jordan riding shotgun.

Of a thousand details to the hasty lynching, such as securing a spare key to the bulldozer, only Schwerner's last words confounded the Klansmen themselves. Jordan and others preserved them verbatim for agents who passed them to Inspector Sullivan as indelible signs. The Klansmen heard nothing fearful or defiant, nor anything practical to escape the moment of terror, but they could not forget the spark of supremely disciplined faith that reached across the last human barrier. Alton Wayne Roberts exploded past more hesitant Klansmen to yank Schwerner from the cruiser next to a ditch. He jammed a pistol into his ribs and screamed from a face of animal hatred, "Are you that nigger lover?" Schwerner had an instant to reply, "Sir, I know just how you feel."

PART FOUR

"Lord, Make Me Pure —but Not Yet"

—St. Augustine,
The Confessions

37

Landslide

THE MIRACLE CARDINALS, who overtook the collapsed Philadelphia Phillies in the last twelve days of the season, represented the National League partly by adapting to integration and speed, with a team built around Bob Gibson's fastball and two fleet outfielders, Lou Brock and Curt Flood. They were World Series underdogs to the New York Yankees of Mickey Mantle, Roger Maris, and Whitey Ford, whose corporate management stood on its astonishing record—thirteen pennants and nine championships since 1949—to resist Negro players beyond their pioneer Elston Howard, as an unnecessary risk to the patronage of white ballpark customers.* Neither adverse odds nor racial subtext mattered to St. Louis fans, who welcomed the surprise gift of fall pageantry on Wednesday, October 7, cheering Dixieland bands that marched in the Busch Stadium outfield. The crowd howled with delight when a goofy reserve player named Bob Uecker impulsively caught pregame fly balls in the throat of a borrowed tuba, then roared when the blithe and limber Cardinals unexpectedly thumped the Yankees in the first game, 9–5.

That evening in Washington, Walter Jenkins stood in for President Johnson at an office-warming cocktail party given by the editors of *Newsweek*. He departed alone on foot to the nearby YMCA, where at 8:35 P.M. police officers accosted him in a basement pay toilet together with an elderly resident of the U.S. Soldiers Home. Jenkins quietly submitted to

---

* "I don't want you sneaking around down any back alleys and signing any niggers," Yankees president George Weiss instructed scouts into the 1960s.

his second stakeout arrest from this rendezvous spot on the charge of "disorderly conduct (pervert)," giving his true name and occupation. Booked and fingerprinted, he obtained release on $50 forfeit bond and returned to work past midnight at the White House, very likely in catatonic denial.

Unaware for days, President Johnson campaigned obsessively right into Barry Goldwater's hometown of Phoenix, where more than once he abruptly halted the entire presidential motorcade, seized a bullhorn, and "verbally caressed" a handful of gawking pedestrians. On October 9, he rode *Air Force One* through stops at Louisville and Nashville, then in New Orleans walked half a mile down track number two to greet the incoming *Lady Bird Special* at Union Station. A predominantly Negro crowd cheered him to the obvious discomfort of straddling Democrats such as Louisiana governor John McKeithen, who tacitly supported Goldwater behind a stated posture of "nonparticipation, but just short of being neutral." As toastmaster, Congressman Hale Boggs of Louisiana tried to smother the palpable tension among nearly two thousand influential donors that night by embracing the Johnsons as kindred Southerners. He praised Lady Bird as one who "knows the sound of the wind in the pines and the song of the mockingbird in the morning." The President himself, with a nod to Senator Russell Long at the dais, reminisced beyond his text about hearing the controversial speeches of Long's father, Huey, during the early Depression. "I thought he had a heart for the people," said Johnson, playing on fond local memory of Huey the Kingfish as a champion of schoolbooks, roads, and other instruments of common opportunity. He played further to the regional sense of victimization by national economic powers since the Civil War. "And all these years they have kept their foot on our necks by appealing to our animosities, and dividing us," he said.

"Whatever your views are," Johnson added with a significant pause, "we have a Constitution and a Bill of Rights, and we have the law of the land. And two-thirds of the Democrats in the Senate voted for it, and three-fourths of the Republicans. I signed it, and I am going to enforce it, and I am going to observe it...."

Having hushed his audience in the coded language of Southern politics, without mentioning the new civil rights law by name, Johnson pushed on. "I am not going to let them build up the hate and try to buy my people by appealing to their prejudice," he vowed, and leaned forward to tell "you folks" a tale of deathbed lamentation over a wasted political career. Johnson recalled how an old senator—"whose name I won't call"—once beseeched Speaker Sam Rayburn for encouragement to make just one speech toward the common good of his despoiled state. "'I feel like I have one in me!'" Johnson quoted the senator. "'The poor old state, they haven't heard a Democratic speech in thirty years. All they ever hear at election time is, Nigger! Nigger! Nigger!'"

"The audience gasped," recorded one historian. An eyewitness called the shock in the Jung Hotel banquet hall "a physical thing—surprise, awe—ears heard what they plainly could not hear." A president of the United States had shouted the word three times, in a context that at once revealed and rejected a racial core of politics. The initial grudging and scattered applause grew into an ovation that lasted fully seven minutes, but the next day the reporters lacked the nerve to quote him exactly. From *Jet* magazine to the *New Orleans Times-Picayune*, the President's climactic phrase was rendered "Negro! Negro! Negro!" The *New York Times* dodged the word choice by omitting the passage altogether, and book accounts later modified it to "Nigra! Nigra! Nigra!" It was not until Johnson wrote his memoirs that the word "nigger" was put into the mouth of a president of the United States. *The Vantage Point* was famously selective about war and race—without a word, for instance, about the MFDP challenge at the Democratic convention—but Johnson claimed the raw truth of New Orleans as another Gettysburg moment.

His boldness did gain sympathy in news outlets that shied away from the actual words. "Johnson Hits at Hatred as Southern Vote Bait," proclaimed the *Atlanta Journal*, and White House aides privately reported a wave of "respect and admiration" within a previously skeptical traveling press corps. While many reporters remained "tired and negative" about quirks such as "your interest in the polls," Horace Busby advised Johnson, "the New Orleans (Negro, Negro, Negro) speech captured them.... Thus, overnight, they are speaking of you—as once of FDR—as 'the master,' 'the champ.'"

Johnson's campaign rose on extraordinary national tides, lifted by fear and remorse that converged from the Kennedy assassination, threats of nuclear war, and from incidents of bared racial hatred. William Stringfellow, who at the 1963 Chicago conference had advised religious leaders to "weep" over lost hope for racial justice, now collected signatures from seven hundred Episcopal bishops and priests protesting Goldwater's "transparent exploitation of racism." Republican newspapers rallied to Johnson, most notably New York's *Herald Tribune*, which had been founded in 1840 expressly to oppose Democrats. "Travail and torment go into those simple words," the *Herald Tribune* editors wrote of their groundbreaking endorsement, which the *New York Times* quoted as front-page news, "...but we find ourself as Americans, even as Republicans, with no other acceptable choice."

In a series of confidential October reports, campaign manager Lawrence O'Brien predicted that Johnson would win a landslide "without too much difficulty," and conceded only Alabama and Mississippi to Goldwater. Nevertheless, he identified the undivided Negro vote as a tricky new valve in political mechanics. "It is becoming more and more apparent to me that we need to make a special effort to get out the vote in Negro precincts," O'Brien wrote Johnson, after campaign inspections revealed practically no working relations among Democratic politicians to turn out the vote across racial lines. Separate political structures were axiomatic in the South—"Dependence upon the Negro vote is a new experience.... Before this year they never had encouraged the Negro to vote—or particularly wanted him to vote"—but prevailed elsewhere, too. In New York, Adam Clayton Powell was still bargaining for his promise to deliver constituent votes, demanding intervention to fend off the Esther James judgment. Democrats, lacking a unified political apparatus, labored to invent "safe" public appeals for the Negro vote, and O'Brien's state-by-state reports on resistance alarmed Johnson about party realignment in future elections.

Democrats pursued vital Negro turnout with some care. "Obviously," O'Brien advised Johnson, "we must see this is done by passing the word without fanfare to avoid further backlash." Pressure fell upon Martin Luther King to mount specialized campaign tours designed to generate Negro votes for Johnson while minimizing spillover pressures on local white candidates. King held out for assurance that Roy Wilkins and Whitney Young would pull their share of the load, signaling Johnson that he could not look to King at the ballot box and still ascribe prime Negro leadership to more comfortable patronage figures. Besides, King told aides, campaigning alone would make it "look like Johnson has me in his pocket."

On his own grueling schedule to raise money for SCLC, King delivered four speeches in three East Coast cities over the weekend of Sunday, October 11, then two speeches on Monday in St. Louis before collapsing at home of viral fever and exhaustion. Dr. Asa Yancey, the first Negro staff physician licensed at St. Joseph Infirmary, managed to admit King on Tuesday for overdue bed rest. Yancey delivered a lecture on the medical need to abandon fried chicken and lose twenty pounds, then prescribed sleeping pills that left King groggy Wednesday morning when Coretta King called to say he had been chosen for the Nobel Peace Prize. Until security barriers were improvised, photographers overran the hospital on its first day of integration to shoot the next day's front-page pictures of King propped up in bed.

An early *Jet* reporter noticed as bedside reading *The Prize*, a celebrated novel about international intrigue behind the Nobel awards. The book confirmed King's awareness that he was being considered, but its plot scarcely prepared him for domestic repercussions ahead. In a vain attempt to head off what he rightly feared would be contending claims among dear ones to shares of the bounty, King instructed his assistant Bernard Lee to issue an unequivocal statement that he would donate to the movement "every penny" of the $54,600 gift accompanying the Nobel Prize. Within hours, hints reached King that the prize had dissolved the political objections that had kept him off the board of Morehouse College. Roman

Catholic Archbishop Paul Hallinan appeared in person to celebrate the news, kneeling with dramatic humility to ask King for a reciprocal blessing. King chuckled over reports of disgusted reactions from Bull Connor, who said the Nobel committee was "scraping the bottom of the barrel," and from St. Augustine police chief Virgil Stuart, who called his selection "the biggest joke of the year." Incoming wires of congratulation filled boxes. Duke Ellington, who had composed *King Fit the Battle of Alabam'* in tribute to the Birmingham demonstrations of 1963, hailed the announcement as "a beautiful bright shining light of hope," and Robert Kennedy called King's "richly deserved" honor a global inspiration for "the greatest of American ideals."

Kennedy received the news while campaigning in New York with President Johnson, whose telegram warmly commending King would be delayed two days because of hysteria over Walter Jenkins. By late afternoon, press inquiries about Jenkins's YMCA arrest the week before put him into George Washington Hospital under heavy sedation. Johnson's legal advisers Abe Fortas and Clark Clifford pleaded privately with news editors to withhold the ruinous story until facts were tested. Jenkins in turn pleaded with the lawyers not to tell the President, sadly insisting that he could remember little of his arrests. With an early evening statement that "the White House is desperately trying to suppress a major news story affecting the national security," Republican national chairman Dean Burch prodded the Jenkins scandal onto the UPI news wire at 8:09 P.M. A tearful George Reedy soon confirmed to reporters in New York that his friend Jenkins—upstanding Catholic, father of six, Johnson's closest aide since 1939—had been hospitalized for "extreme fatigue," and at 10:15 there was a follow-up announcement that Jenkins had resigned.

From Washington, Lady Bird Johnson issued an independent statement of personal sympathy that night: "My heart is aching. . . ." President Johnson doggedly continued his speeches in New York: "And if Lincoln abolished slavery, let us abolish poverty. . . ." Privately, he insisted from then on that the Jenkins tragedy was a Goldwater plot to steal the election. He had the Pentagon retrieve Jenkins's spotless personnel file from an Air Force Reserve unit commanded by Barry Goldwater, and he ordered his lawyers and the FBI's Deke DeLoach to run down suspicions, including a wild hunch that the waiters for the October 7 *Newsweek* party had been Republican operatives trained to use mind-altering drugs.

Inside FBI headquarters, confronting the coincidence of two men hospitalized on the same day—one dropped from the White House into scalding humiliation, the other raised from servile inheritance to a pedestal of global honor—J. Edgar Hoover mobilized his bureau. He sent Walter Jenkins a bouquet of get-well flowers with a card marked "J. Edgar Hoover & Associates," and he denounced the new Nobel laureate to those same associates as "top alley cat," pushing them to generate against King the kind of publicity that had struck Jenkins. Only a tiny portion of the crusade surfaced in public. When William Loeb, James Kilpatrick, and other prominent conservatives complained that the flower gesture betrayed Hoover's own bedrock principles by coddling a homosexual security risk, the Director claimed to have sent the Jenkins bouquet before realizing the nature of his affliction. This fabrication helped insulate Hoover from suggestions of bias when the FBI "cleared" Jenkins—"No Evidence Is Uncovered That Ex-Presidential Aide Compromised Nation," blared the *Times* headline—only a week later. To prove a national security negative so swiftly was a feat of convenient service to Johnson, especially since investigating agents secretly pursued a host of extraneous political angles, such as whether any of Barry Goldwater's aides had homosexual tendencies.

Johnson and Hoover vouched for each other in crisis. Johnson needed Hoover's national authority to shield his campaign from charges of immorality mixed with spy danger; Hoover needed Johnson to overlook his failure to warn of Walter Jenkins's arrest records on file for years at the FBI. With the help of a complacent press, Hoover also managed brazenly to criticize the local police and Secret Service for laxity about Jenkins, and to advertise the FBI's sensitive distance from tawdry gossip—all while secretly bombarding officials from the White House, Justice Department, United Nations, and even embassies overseas with nasty interpretations of King's sexual habits (which the cover note to Hubert Humphrey called "His Personal Conduct"). The contrasting forbearance toward Walter Jenkins was scarcely sentimental. To protect Johnson, FBI agents unsuccessfully pressured doctors to explain Jenkins's YMCA conduct not as "voluntary" homosexuality but the result of a "mysterious disease which causes disintegration of the brain." What guided the FBI through both cases was acute sensitivity to vanities of power at Hoover's level and above.

KING EMERGED from St. Joseph Infirmary into a world engulfed by the news of Thursday, October 15: a coup led by Leonid Brezhnev that toppled Soviet premier Nikita Khrushchev, a change of British government, China's first successful nuclear bomb test—with background stories featuring South Vietnam's execution of a seventeen-year-old who had tried to assassinate Defense Secretary McNamara the previous May, plus the Game Seven victory of the St. Louis Cardinals in spite of Mickey Mantle's eighteenth and final World Series home run. Against statements by leading journals such as the *New York Times* that the Jenkins scandal was "bound to be seriously detrimental to President Johnson's campaign," the embarrassment never registered among voters at large, but the threat erased King's qualms about campaigning nonstop for Johnson.

Louis Martin, a publisher of Negro newspapers and the Democratic National Committee's expert on minority politics since 1944, designed for

King a specialized tour that created what amounted to ticker tape parades visible and audible mostly to Negroes. Martin put King on the back of a flatbed truck that attracted tumultuous crowds to more than twenty neighborhood street corners in Chicago, beginning October 21, and he sent a roaring motorcade through churches and playgrounds of Negro Cleveland. By careful prearrangement, King preached the urgency of voting without saying Johnson's name. "You know who to vote for!" cried King. "Don't you?" His aides shouted "All the way," omitting the last two words of Johnson's slogan, "with LBJ." The thin veneer of neutrality, which suited King's desire to avoid long-term partisan commitment, helped Louis Martin and Lawrence O'Brien harvest targeted voters behind a bland message. The tour received only sporadic external notice, usually in small stories of crossover interest—as when Chicago's Catholic Interracial Council presented King with its John F. Kennedy Award in race relations, or a convention of white evangelicals denounced him as a false Christian.

So strong was word-of-mouth excitement that when a scheduling mix-up pulled the motorcade briefly to curbside in a Negro area of Cleveland, the enterprising principal of Addison Junior High School rushed out to knock on the window and ask King to address her students. Over heated staff objections about the folly of wasting precious time on nonvoters, King followed the principal inside to stand at a hallway corner as students and teachers spilled from stairwells and classrooms to sit packed along both corridors. There he delivered a spontaneous, commencement-style homily. "All of us have the privilege of living in one of the most significant periods of human history," King said. "You're at the age now where you will have to make some great decisions...and I want to say particularly to the Negro students here that doors of opportunity are opening now that were not opened to your mothers and fathers. The great challenge facing you is to be ready to enter those doors." He encouraged students to look beyond their skills for worthy goals in the larger society, and recalled how children had come out of jails in Birmingham to canvass their elders with such effect that the registration of adult Negro voters doubled in three months. "The students did this," said King. "This is what you can do."

He told the Addison students that they would be called upon to give their own answers to the hardest questions that philosophers had asked "over and over again" on the nature of evil and the highest good. "I think I have the answer, my friends," said King. "The highest good is love, and he who loves has somehow discovered the meaning of life and the reality. ... Start now keeping love at the center of your life, and start now keeping nonviolence....I believe firmly that America will be a better nation. I believe firmly that Negroes and white people will be able to live together as brothers....And so I ask you to work hard, study hard, to make the right decision and join us in the movement for freedom."

By the time King reached Los Angeles a week before the election, tour commitments piled up beyond endurance and quarrels festered over the disposition of the Nobel Prize money. Abernathy's wife, Juanita, supported Coretta King's compromise position—that $20,000 of the windfall be set aside toward the education of the King children—if only as an opening wedge for the argument that half the money belonged to the Abernathys anyway, as equal movement partners since Montgomery. Bickering so distracted King that he dropped out of several campaign stops, pleading exhaustion. At Cal State, Los Angeles, facing an impatient crowd, officials announced, "Dr. King can't come today, but here is Jack Pratt." The embarrassed church lawyer from the stand-in advance team introduced Ralph Abernathy with glowing praise, but the crowd's disappointment yielded only slight applause for his salty speech that likened Goldwater to prison fare of bread and water. Abernathy ignored whispers and notes that it was illegal to make partisan remarks on a public campus, then stalked from the rostrum.

King wrote notes to himself on the margins of speech outlines: "Proposition 14 is sinful...." He implored California voters to reject the constitutional ballot initiative that would repeal not only a new statewide fair housing law (the 1963 Rumford Act) but all local ordinances limiting "the right of any person ... to decline to sell, lease, or rent [real estate] property to such persons as he, in his absolute discretion, chooses." All through 1964, against prevailing support for the civil rights bill, the campaign for Proposition 14 had gained spreading recognition as a worrisome countertrend. "This is a strange year in which to push for even greater segregation," declared a perplexed *New York Times* editorial.

King's tour reached Los Angeles on the same day Ronald Reagan emerged as the Goldwater campaign's surrogate spokesman. Goldwater, although desperate for something to jolt the adverse election odds, had repudiated just before it was broadcast his own political documentary *Choice,* calling it "a racist film" and a "dirty movie" that blended scenes of drunken youth and violence with racial demonstrations. In a hurry to find a substitute for the slotted half hour on national television, some of his managers wanted to repeat Goldwater's conversation with former President Eisenhower, and others pushed to air the popular stump speech of the movie actor who was heading California Citizens for Goldwater. The candidate bridled at the tacit concession, and he would always dissemble jealously about how and why Reagan came to represent him at his defining hour in history, but Reagan did fill in for Goldwater on October 27. In his nationwide NBC speech, which *Time* called "the one bright spot in a dismal campaign," Reagan finessed the drawbacks of the *Choice* documentary by omitting direct commentary on race. Instead, he evoked stirring themes of liberty embattled ("Should Moses have told the children of Israel to live in slavery rather than dare the wilderness? ... You and I have a rendezvous with destiny."), and defined freedom's enemy almost interchangeably as totalitarian foreign enemies and the American government itself. "A perversion has taken place," he said. "Our natural unalienable rights are now presumed to be a dispensation of government." Reagan denounced the welfare state, foreign appeasement, and "the schemes of do-gooders" as a creeping threat, saying, "We are faced with the most evil enemy mankind has known in his long climb from the swamp to the stars." Some commentators called his debut the best political oratory since William Jennings Bryan's "Cross of Gold" speech in 1896. Hundreds of local committees rushed to broadcast the film, and the Goldwater campaign bought a repeat national telecast for Saturday night, October 31.

The King tour rolled back through Chicago and Detroit to Baltimore's Faith Baptist Church, where he focused on the nominee's pinched definition of the public space among citizens. "Brother Goldwater has presented me with such a dilemma," he said. "Never before has a presidential candidate taken a stand against the prophetic insights of the ages." From the back of a truck, with Bayard Rustin as sideman on the bullhorn, he urged waving admirers on the streets to vote. Mayor Theodore McKeldin built unusual press interest by joining King's overflow stop at the Masonic temple on Eutaw Street. "My father followed Theodore Roosevelt into the Republican Party," McKeldin announced, "but his son will leave that party for once at this time." Like a candidate himself, King escaped the ensuing bedlam into an open-air motorcade that pushed through jostling, festive crowds dotted with Negro children in Halloween costumes. Bystanders leaned over the car and stretched to clasp his hand.

The next day, November 1, King reached home in Atlanta just ahead of the DNC's Louis Martin, who brought news of a campaign crisis: the sudden appearance in several cities of at least 1.4 million leaflets advocating a write-in vote for Martin Luther King as president. There were published reports (leading to one criminal indictment) that Goldwater officials were buying and distributing the material. Martin had no trouble persuading King to take action; on his way back to the Atlanta airport, Martin heard radio reports that King already had scheduled an emergency press conference at which he disavowed the leaflets and warned of a "venomous" plot to induce Negroes to waste their votes.

In New York, an "emergency committee" of religious leaders—among them Paul Tillich, the Trappist monk and author Thomas Merton, Abraham Heschel, Reinhold Niebuhr, and Gardner Taylor—issued an appeal against scandalmongering in the Walter Jenkins case, chiding those who would "cater to the prurient curiosity" about personal morals in order to "obscure fateful moral issues related to public life."

President Johnson defended the clergy from Goldwater's charges of partisan meddling, in the midst of free-swinging oratory that propelled his campaign home to Texas. As a young boy, he told a final crowd on the Capitol steps in Austin, "I first learned that government is not an enemy of the people. It is the people." And as a young New Dealer in the Depression, he recalled, "I learned that poverty and ignorance are the only basic weaknesses of a free society, and that both of them are only bad habits." Secluded with Lady Bird and half a dozen friends, Johnson reacted to the first election returns of November 3 with a single outburst: "God, I hate for it to be over, because the hell starts then." Before dawn—with a landslide victory assured but helicopters grounded by storm winds and roads closed by floods on the Pedernales River—he hazarded the short jet flight to his ranch.

Johnson overwhelmed Goldwater by nearly sixteen million votes and a popular majority unmatched in history,* with Goldwater carrying only five Deep South states and his home state of Arizona (by half a percentage point). The Democrats also picked up two Senate seats, including one in New York for Robert Kennedy, and forty-eight House seats in previously Republican districts. Support for civil rights was the keenest predictor of outcome: no representative who had voted for the 1964 bill was defeated from either party, while fully half the Northern members who had opposed the bill met rejection at the polls. Likewise, much to Johnson's satisfaction, anti-civil-rights Republicans fell heavily in Texas— losing the only two Republican House seats in a delegation of twenty-three, along with the challenge of George Bush to incumbent senator Ralph Yarborough.

The Republican minority fractured internally. Moderates blamed Goldwater for abandoning the Party of Lincoln, and were blamed in turn for abandoning the party nominee. Those who would survive, like Nixon, were left to pick a course through the ruins.

Based on Johnson's stunning 96 percent Negro majority, strategists from all quarters projected the presumptive Negro Democrat—an inversion of history—as a new fact of politics. "To the Negro," said one, "Goldwater shot Lincoln in the head as surely as John Wilkes Booth." Against a solid racial minority that accounted for Johnson's large victory margins in Virginia and elsewhere, analysts detected no countervailing shift from the Democratic base. "White Backlash Doesn't Develop," announced the *Times*. "Backlash proved only a flick," agreed historian Eric Goldman, and the *Washington Post* projected Southern defections to Goldwater as a "one-shot affair" like the 1948 Dixiecrat revolt, notwithstanding the election of the first ten House Republicans since Reconstruction in four Goldwater states: Georgia, Mississippi, South Carolina, and Alabama.

A warning sign was buried beneath election reviews. California voters embraced both Johnson and a constitutional right to segregated neighbor-

---

* His 61 percent of the national vote exceeded Roosevelt's record of 60.8 percent in 1936, as well as Richard Nixon's future mark of 60.7 percent (1972), for the remainder of the twentieth century.

hoods, as promoted by Ronald Reagan and the real estate industry. Proposition 14 carried California nearly two to one, winning fifty-seven of fifty-eight counties and nearly half a million votes more than Johnson. With its enforcement stayed, pending years of judicial review, and headed toward Supreme Court nullification in what the Justice Department called "the most important civil rights case of the decade," the political import of Proposition 14 remained an asterisk to national election trends, as peculiar to California as the Goldwater spasm to the South.

Not for the first time, the long-range racial determination of white voters was overlooked by the prevailing interpretations on a higher plane. It was inconceivable then, and later muted, that partisan realignment and commanding national leadership were being spawned in opposition to racial progress. (Reagan had opposed the 1964 civil rights law, and would oppose the Voting Rights Act of 1965). Contemporary analysts tried to bury the Goldwater option. Walter Lippmann called the Johnson victory "indisputable proof that the voters are in the center." Eisenhower biographer Robert Donovan worried that Goldwater conservatives would make Republicans "a minority party indefinitely." Two respected political scientists warned of outright extinction, predicting that persistent Goldwaterism would bring "an end to a competitive two-party system." A slow incoming tide was mistaken for an ebbing ripple.

PRESIDENT JOHNSON welcomed the imminent reward of an 89th Congress in which the Democrats would control better than two thirds of each chamber: 68 of 100 in the Senate, 295 of 435 in the House. From his ranch through most of November, he orchestrated twenty-two brainstorming task forces on "problems likely to arise by the year 2000." Bill Moyers informed selected officials that Johnson wanted to emphasize conservation, education, and cities—"straightening out urban problems." On instructions to avoid civil rights and foreign policy, the meetings explored ideas to overhaul the mining laws, eliminate agricultural subsidies, require "an exhaust cleaning device" in cars, study the major causes of death, and establish labeling standards for consumer products. There were schemes for "regional smashing plants" to cut down on automobile junkyards, and for assorted tax credits to specified industries. "I kicked this one pretty good," recorded one participant, noting general agreement that "water pollution will be a tough one." The task forces concentrated in detail on two of Johnson's known ambitions: to establish federal aid to education and insured medical care for the elderly.

On the day after the election, King told the *New York Times* that with the campaign moratorium now expired, he intended to renew demonstrations "based around the right to vote" in Alabama or Mississippi, where, in spite of sacrifices through the movement years, only 21 percent and 6 percent of eligible Negroes were registered, respectively. A week later, at a planning retreat in Birmingham, Wyatt Walker's replacement, Randolph Blackwell, introduced an SCLC organization chart of thirty-four boxes arrayed from "Board of Directors" at the top down to "Citizenship School Teachers" at the bottom, connected by a maze of solid and dotted lines. King invited ideas to take the movement into "a new era" under general guidelines: "...never reach the point of building SCLC by tearing down another organization...remain nonviolent, Christian, accentuating the positive.... To redeem the soul of America, we must bear a cross in the South...[and] consider in these two days the staggering population shift [to] northern and western cities, Negroes are left there ill equipped...still hovering in slums...."

Responses ranged from logistical minutiae—that King aide Bernard Lee should "carry pocket tape recorder when traveling with the President" —and syrupy prescriptions for dialogue on "the ontological need of each person," to Andrew Young's observation that, "We change history through finding the one thing that can capture the imagination of the world. History moves in leaps and bounds."

In the tactical sessions, James Bevel pressed the advantage of an established plan with a dual purpose. For more than a year, since the bombing deaths at Sixteenth Street Baptist (just across Kelly Ingram Park from the current retreat), Bevel and his wife, Diane Nash, had developed their "nonviolent army" blueprint to secure the right to vote throughout Alabama. In his holdover role as chief integration officer, heading the box marked "Direct Action" on the SCLC organization chart, Bevel noted that white leaders at one of the "hard core" voting targets had defied the new civil rights law by outlawing integration checks and even mass meetings. Accordingly, Bevel proposed Selma as "an effective testing ground" for a mass movement building from civil rights to voting rights, and Amelia Boynton, who still kept the honor roll of voter applicants on the wall of her Selma office, seconded him with a personal appeal for help.

King also suffered a bombardment of proposals for the Nobel Prize ceremonies on December 10. His initial preference for a small accompanying delegation of six swelled to a planeload, mostly of prominent friends able and eager to pay their way to help greet the King of Norway. Advisers maneuvered behind King's name. Through contacts in England, Bayard Rustin sought an audience for King with British prime minister Harold Wilson on the London stopover, saying he preferred "it not appear as though this is King's idea," and pushed to intercede with "certain elements" that reportedly were urging the Archbishop of Canterbury to shun King as a Baptist. With Harry Wachtel, Rustin conceived of a U.N. reception for King as a "real head of state deal," seeking personal attendance by President Kwame Nkrumah of Ghana, Johnson, and even Soviet chairman Leonid Brezhnev. (They decided King was too busy to meet with the President of Brazil.) Rustin drafted telegrams appointing himself to handle

Nobel Prize details, and arranged for the pacifist leader A. J. Muste to send out a fund-raising appeal to cover Rustin's expenses abroad. On receiving this letter, Stanley Levison complained to Clarence Jones that Rustin was taking advantage of Muste as well as King. Still, Levison returned a small donation in order to dampen petty disputes among old friends, saying his reply to the appeal was sure to "loom large" in Rustin's subsequent judgments about "who befriended him and who is trying to cut him down."

There was no such collegial understanding at FBI headquarters, where wiretaps funneled reports on the grandiose fits within King's inner circle. Eugene Patterson, the editor of the *Atlanta Constitution,* received a dose of its hostility when an agent appeared in his office to disclose that King was about to take a Caribbean vacation in the company of a mistress. The agent suggested that since the *Constitution* was portraying King in Nobel Prize coverage as a Christian leader, the paper owed its readers a photograph of the lovers on their departure from Miami. Patterson admitted to surprise as the agent, a man he knew from Lutheran church councils, offered to station *Constitution* photographers at the airport. In two days of aggressive lobbying, the agent pushed for a cooperative ambush on condition of absolute anonymity for the FBI—forbidding any mention of the Bureau, even the vaguest suggestions of verifying FBI information. Patterson rejected what he called "peephole journalism."

King left his Birmingham meeting to preach twice on Sunday, November 15. "Evil," he told his congregation at Ebenezer, "carries the seed of its own destruction." He recalled watching the splendor of the British Empire give way to independent Ghana in 1957. He said that societies built on war were headed for doom, which was one of the reasons he "couldn't vote for Mr. Goldwater." America's power and wealth "have made us an arrogant nation," King warned—not just white people but now Negroes within reach of a share. "I'm disturbed about the Negro," he said, adding that no worldly success could calm a troubled spirit. "When you know God, you can stand up amid tension and tribulation and yet smile in the process," he said. "When you know God, you go on livin' anyhow. Nothin's gonna stop you, 'cause you know that God is watching in your heart."

King flew that afternoon to New York's Abyssinian Baptist, where he pursued a competitive preachers' truce offstage. Adam Clayton Powell, having belittled the nonviolent movement as well as the civil rights bill, now tacitly acknowledged Nobel Prize stature, while King paid homage to Powell as a besieged titan. He mediated an arrangement for his former aide Wyatt Walker to fill the coveted Abyssinian pulpit during involuntary absences soon to begin for Powell, who was resolved to dodge New York arrest warrants and contempt citations building from the Esther James case. At King's request, Powell endorsed the big-church guest collection of $1,844.80 to SCLC before taking King along to his hideaway home on the Caribbean island of Bimini. By then, the Lutheran FBI agent in Atlanta had informed the *Constitution* that there would be no King girlfriend at the Miami airport after all, which more than ever perplexed Patterson about the Bureau's haphazard vendetta. Hidden intelligence sources, meanwhile, overheard King tell a friend on his way to Bimini that C. T. Vivian was already in Alabama scouting the political terrain. The Miami FBI office flashed a coded radio warning to headquarters that King had approved tiny Selma as the "site of renewed SCLC activity beginning about first of January."

ON THE FOLLOWING DAY, Wednesday, November 18, Hoover gave a rare press briefing—his first in many years, the first ever with exclusively female reporters—to a maverick offshoot of the Women's National Press Club. Because women were barred (until 1971) from membership in the National Press Club, pioneers had formed the WNPC, and because most members of the Women's National Press Club specialized in traditional ladies' features on family or fashion, the Hoover interview fell to an informal club called the McLendon Press Group, founded by Texas reporter Sarah McLendon. Some members, including one soon to be fired for saying she expected no hard news, shied away from the anticipated spy lecture as so much "male shadowboxing," but eighteen reporters filed into the imposing Director's office furnished with a new silver coffee urn and lamp fixtures in the shape of pistols.

Hoover talked nearly three times his allotted hour. When his monologue on FBI history slowed toward possible questions, he called for the FBI annual report and read excerpts with biting asides. Concerning the section on civil rights enforcement, he commented that the jury's acquittal in the Lemuel Penn case was "absolutely outrageous," and sharply criticized the judge who had suspended sentences in the McComb bombings. He expressed frustration that "in spite of some remarkable success in civil rights cases, some detractors alleged the FBI has done nothing in this field." Hoover indignantly recalled Martin Luther King's complaints about FBI performance in Albany, Georgia, during 1962, which the Director attributed to a misguided belief that FBI agents were native Southerners. "In view of King's attitude and his continued criticism of the FBI on this point," said Hoover, "I consider King to be the most notorious liar in the country."

Deke DeLoach, fearing a public relations disaster, passed Hoover several notes suggesting that the "liar" comment be placed off the record along with Hoover's assertions that King was "one of the lowest characters in the country" and "controlled" by Communist advisers, but Hoover rebuffed any notion of retraction. "The girls," DeLoach would testify eleven years later, "could hardly wait to leave to get to the telephone." No such story had been broken by female journalists alone, and more than a few male news staffs tried to mask their secondhand accounts of the women's interview behind an original emphasis. ("Hoover Assails Warren Findings," announced the *New York Times*, and the *Washington Post* head-lined his "Blast at Police Corruption.") Nevertheless, the "notorious liar" charge exploded above such distractions.

Vacationing in Bimini with King, Andrew Young knew something big had struck when helicopters chartered by reporters began landing. In New York, the first radio bulletins about the "notorious liar" statement broke up a research committee meeting on plans for the Nobel Prize trip. Harry Wachtel drafted a caustic emergency reply for King: "...While I resent the personal attack on my integrity, I will not allow Mr. Hoover to blur the real issue...." FBI wiretaps intercepted Bayard Rustin's suggestion that Wachtel "drop the part about King being resentful, because King is not resentful," along with their stern advice that King should say nothing before consulting them. On Bimini, however, the onslaught of reporters forced King to compose his own brief statement for a press conference at the Big Game Fisherman's Lodge:

I cannot conceive of Mr. Hoover making a statement like this without being under extreme pressure. He has apparently faltered under the awesome burden, complexities and responsibilities of his office. Therefore, I cannot engage in a public debate with him. I have nothing but sympathy for this man who has served his country so well.

In Washington, Acting Attorney General Nicholas Katzenbach walked into Hoover's office. "I couldn't be more unhappy," the Director declared before Katzenbach said a word. "Never should have done it. Never should have seen all those women reporters. DeLoach got me into it." In a preemptive monologue, Hoover said he of course had to tell the truth about King once DeLoach trapped him into a foolish predicament. A despairing Katzenbach went directly to the White House, where the major civil rights leaders loudly complained about Hoover's intrusion into their much anticipated post-election meeting with President Johnson. Roy Wilkins, King's severest private critic among them, announced that Johnson listened without response as "we solidly backed Dr. King."

From New York, before they decided that King's restraint had been wise after all, Wachtel and Rustin peppered SCLC contacts with messages that King's "nothing but sympathy" posture signaled dangerous weakness. On Thursday, King compromised with a telegram to Hoover that melded his own wounded tone—"What motivated such an irresponsible accusa-tion is a mystery to me"—with his advisers' call for strong rebuttal. He had never ascribed shortcomings "merely to the presence of Southerners in the FBI," King wired, but he had "sincerely questioned" the Bureau's effectiveness in racial investigations, "particularly where bombings and brutalities against Negroes are at issue."

Inside the FBI, agents and officials massed behind Hoover as though it were King who had initiated the attack. By late Thursday night, the Atlanta office compiled a review of all past dealings since "the freedom rides in the summer of sixty [sic]," under counterpoint headings—"King States," answered by "Facts"—to buttress Hoover's charge that King was a liar. Each FBI rebuttal, while at least slightly off point, bristled with grievance. Of King's statement that there had been no arrests in the Birmingham church bombing among many notorious cases, the brief responded that interference by Alabama had hampered the Bureau's "most intensive type of investigation which is still vigorously continuing." Of King's statement that he had always cooperated with Bureau investigations, including those targeting the movement, headquarters charged that on July 22, 1961, "King kept the Agent waiting for one hour past the appointed time and stated he was behind in his paper work and had completed some of it before admitting the Agent."

One-way intercepts allowed headquarters to make the worst of rattled private opinions. Wiretaps picked up King telling C. T. Vivian that Hoover "is old and getting senile." Bureau supervisors pounced on wiretap intelligence that Rustin and Wachtel wanted King to seek Hoover's replacement, calling such behavior "further evidence" of subversion "in line with a long-held communist objective, to launch a campaign to oust the Director as head of the FBI." Hoover scrawled a response on Friday's memo recommending that he neither dignify King's telegram with a reply nor justify his own conduct further:

O.K. But I don't understand why we are unable to get the true facts before the public. We can't even get our accomplishments published. We are never taking the aggressive, but allow lies to remain unanswered.

"Being handled—11/20/64," DeLoach wrote next to Hoover's comment. Propaganda operations expanded clandestinely to more reporters, to religious groups, and to civic leaders. Agents rushed the first new batch of anti-King material to other government agencies by Sunday, the first anniversary of the Kennedy assassination, and assembled even before then a "highlight" recording of bugged sex groans and party jokes, together with a contrived anonymous letter calling King "a great liability for all of us Negroes." The letter to King warned that "your end is approaching," and concluded, "You are done. There is but one way out for you. You better take it before your filthy, abnormal fraudulent self is bared to the nation." FBI specialists combined the highlight recording with the letter, and moved what became known as the suicide package at a lightning pace for government work on a weekend—through bureaucratic approval, technical selection, composition, air shipment via courier, and finally mail drop to King from Miami (in order to camouflage its Washington origin) —all by Saturday night, November 21.

AT FBI HEADQUARTERS on Monday, Inspector Joe Sullivan entered the fray from another battle zone. Twenty Mississippi agents had just patrolled the successful integration of restaurants and hotels by traveling NAACP squads in "racially torn" McComb, which made national news, and Greenwood prosecutors declined for the fourth and last time to go to trial in the 1963 highway ambush on Bob Moses, deflating FBI teams that had matched a bullet from the neck of SNCC worker Jimmy Travis with a machine gun belonging to one of two confessed suspects. In Jackson, the new FBI field office processed cases based on nearly two hundred reported intimidations growing out of COFO's second election day Freedom Vote, including that of a Stanford student who was beaten senseless and urinated upon by a circle of attackers in Marks.

Sullivan's abrupt emergence from "the field," on matters called too sensitive for coded teletype, created expectations of a major break in the Chaney-Goodman-Schwerner case. Rumors buzzed the corridors that his elite squadron was answering the Klan's gutter warfare with its own untraceable terror. There was admiring talk of nighttime FBI raids to shove condom-wrapped shotgun shells into the rectums of hostile Klansmen, daring them to complain, and of Mafia informants secretly imported to extract information by old-fashioned torture. Sullivan deflected the rumors. He told Assistant Director Alex Rosen of threats and insults to Mississippi sources as well as agents, and recommended that federal or state charges be lodged to bring endangered witnesses to official shelter. When Rosen and his executive council declined, saying they needed at least one corroborating witness for the James Jordan confession, Sullivan pulled from his pocket the freshly signed November 20 confession of Klansman Horace Doyle Barnette. Like Jordan, Barnette had fled Mississippi, and agents pursuing the fearful ones had tracked him to Springhill, Louisiana. From the jailhouse handoff to bulldozer burial, his statement matched Jordan's account of the murder conspiracy by some two dozen White Knights out of two county klaverns, and established Schwerner's last words—"Sir, I know just how you feel." It contained a host of details down to Barnette's own minimized role: "I only put Chaney's foot in the car."

Inside the FBI, triumph nearly burst the seams of secrecy, indecision, and crosscutting political warfare. Hoover picked that moment to expand upon his "notorious liar" remark. In a Tuesday evening address to a thousand dinner guests at Chicago's Loyola medical school, he denounced "pressure groups that would crush the rights of others under heel" and zealots who "think with their emotions, seldom with reason." He spoke off his text in staccato fury: "They have no compunction in carping, lying, and exaggerating with the fiercest passion, spearheaded at times by Communists and moral degenerates." Negro publications in particular interpreted the second volley as proof of an intentional, all-out attack upon King, and King was forced to broaden his own war council. With the utmost reluctance, he invited Harry Wachtel to the "trilogy" meeting at the Barbizon Hotel of New York.

Advisers gathered somberly in King's room on Wednesday night, November 25, with the returned vacationers Abernathy, Bernard Lee, and Andrew Young in pajamas to receive the New Yorkers: Clarence Jones, Bayard Rustin, noted psychologist Kenneth Clark, labor leader Cleveland Robinson, and Wachtel. Was Hoover acting for Johnson or not? What did Hoover know? What did he want? Why an attack now, and why on an issue so remote as the hometowns of FBI agents in Albany, Georgia? Hunches and secrets about the FBI were reviewed, such as the hushed notice to King from President Kennedy himself that the movement was under close surveillance. Even so, it had been commonly believed that local police did most of the dirty work, and that the FBI remained traditional and grumpy but basically honest. Now, with paranoia running on rumors that even Johnson could not control Hoover's bureau, King sought advice on whether to fight or negotiate a truce.

"Trilogy" emerged from the meeting as shorthand for the three arenas of vulnerability in surveillance politics: money, loyalty, and sex. The most devastating of the three was presumed to be money corruption—slush funds, tax fraud, hidden wealth, charities fleeced for private gain—but here King said he was happy to prove himself innocent again as in his 1960 trial, no matter how much snooping the FBI did. As for the protracted struggle over the taint of Communism, the prevailing view was that the movement had behaved too defensively already. Rather than retreat further, King talked of restoring his friendship with Stanley Levison. On the matter of his private life, however, King conceded vaguely that there were "things that could be exploited." He was squeamish about revealing himself to his white friend Wachtel, and privately enlisted his aides to keep the admission from filtering back to Levison, but the puzzling emergency drove King to seek Wachtel's judgment about Hoover.

Wachtel offered advice from his experience in the corporate world. He saw Hoover as an entrenched chief executive who had sounded off impulsively and now needed a face-saving escape. "If you were one of my clients," Wachtel told King, he would recommend that he arrange a meeting at which Hoover could vent his criticism over King's lifestyle, and then "maybe you and he can issue a statement that you've had a fruitful discussion." This proposal aroused a chorus of dissent from the other advisers, who saw Hoover as an enemy who gave no quarter. They cited the day's late-breaking news: formal release by FBI headquarters of its detailed rebuttal to King's telegram, with a vindicating claim that the Bureau "has developed information identifying those responsible" for the Mississippi triple murder. Wachtel argued that this sensational and clearly improper announcement, which diverted a major criminal investigation outside judicial channels into a public feud, showed how badly Hoover needed a way out of his dispute with King. The others argued the opposite, that the statement proved Hoover would subordinate official duty to his vendetta.

King withdrew undecided from the Barbizon. Over the Thanksgiving weekend, a blind memorandum informed Director Hoover that headquarters had inventoried from six bugging operations in six scattered field offices more than fifty reels of "Highly Sensitive Coverage" on King. Over the relatively calm voice of DeLoach, who thought comprehensive transcription of the recorded arsenal could be postponed because of the "tremendous amount of work," Hoover decreed that "it should be done *now* while it is fresh in the minds of the specially trained agents." That same Friday, November 27, DeLoach held a showdown with his occasional contact Roy Wilkins, and as Wilkins tried to insulate the NAACP and kindred groups from Hoover's wrath, DeLoach rattled his antlers. "I interrupted Wilkins at this point," he reported to headquarters. "I told him that the Director, of course, did not have in mind the destruction of the civil rights movement as a whole...[but] if King wanted war we certainly would give it to him."

Wilkins pressed DeLoach to refrain from using the power of the FBI to expose King, fearing collateral damage to all Negro groups, and DeLoach pressed in return for collective action by Negro leaders to force King into retirement as "president of Morehouse College or something." ("I told him," DeLoach reported, "that the monkey was on his back....") From the Wilkins meeting, headquarters capitalized with two instant strokes: a "My dear Mr. President" letter in which Hoover told Johnson how "Wilkins admitted that he had criticized me unjustly," and a more devious plan to exclude Ralph Bunche and other Negroes of government status from any anti-King cabal, "as they might feel a duty to advise the White House...."

Years later, a number of prominent correspondents acknowledged being pitched by DeLoach and his staff with anti-King briefings on sex and skullduggery. From pay phones and self-conscious trysts, reporters at the time circulated tidbits among government and movement sources, massaging reactions toward an attributable story, and Attorney General Katzenbach himself undertook to trace the Thanksgiving rumors. He called in Ben Bradlee of *Newsweek,* who refused on principle to name

DeLoach as his source, and DeLoach, who flatly denied that the FBI leaked anything. This dead-end matched Katzenbach's experience in the Justice Department. In order to investigate leaks, he could call only upon the FBI, and FBI reports always categorically defended the Bureau itself.* Katzenbach tried to broker a screened confrontation between Bradlee the anonymous accuser and DeLoach the indignant accused, which both declined. Frustrated and angry, Katzenbach took the extraordinary step of presenting his alarm directly to President Johnson on Saturday, November 28, at the LBJ Ranch in Texas. With Burke Marshall, Katzenbach put forward his conviction that the FBI was peddling anti-King poison all over Washington and beyond, that DeLoach was lying about it with brazen impunity, that Hoover was out of touch, bordering on senile, and that the circus of impropriety was especially dangerous now because of breaks in the Mississippi murder case.

For the second time in the ten-day crisis, Johnson listened impassively and promised to look into the matter. He weighed the Hoover-King issue on the scale of national politics, where it registered with surprising balance. Mass polls favored Hoover three to one over King, while a smaller sample of letters to the White House favored King two to one. Johnson assumed a high posture during his thirty-fourth presidential news conference that Saturday, saying that both King and Hoover "have exercised their freedom of speech on occasions," and vowing to make sure that friction "would not degenerate into a battle of personalities." After comments on Cabinet changes and the chances of war with China, Johnson answered a question about the safety of Hoover's job by referring reporters to an earlier statement of support. Thus he muted any FBI crisis with a calibrated message that did not offer the Director a renewed endorsement but declined to reevaluate his status. This was balm enough for Hoover, who on Monday, November 30, sent letters to key supporters bidding good riddance to "the alleged reports of my being replaced as Director of the FBI."

Johnson's private calculation on whether to fire Hoover was direct: "I'd rather have him inside the tent pissing out than outside pissing in." This quip reflected Johnson's estimate of their relative standing in the press. Like other presidents since Calvin Coolidge, who had first appointed the FBI director, Johnson instinctively chose to side with Hoover against reporters rather than with reporters against Hoover. He ordered his staff to warn the FBI that Bradlee of *Newsweek* was not a reliable outlet for confidential information, which of course betrayed Katzenbach's brief and

---

* "Their defense is always that it must have come from somebody in your office," Katzenbach wryly stated in a 1969 oral history. "... You get back thirty seconds later: they made a complete full field investigation [and] it was not leaked by anybody in the FBI. [laughter] And they had positive evidence that it was not. But of course they run that whole operation there."

sent Hoover only the subtlest notice that the President was personally aware of his scurrilous "battle of personalities."

When the next issue of *Newsweek* suggested that Johnson was "disenchanted" with Hoover and might fire him, the President gave Bill Moyers a personal response for Bradlee: "Fuck you." These measures sprang from Johnson's unsparing view of a captive press that regarded Hoover as an impenetrable source—not a target—for scandal. Not in Johnson's lifetime would revelations reach print about the whispering smear that had spread through subofficial Washington. Many reporters resented the heavy-handed FBI, or were proud of resisting ugly stories about King so long as the Bureau refused to stand behind them, but it scarcely occurred to any of them that they could or should write from firsthand evidence the facts about FBI habits far beneath constitutional grade. "If I had seriously proposed exposing the FBI," recalled James McCartney of the *Chicago Daily News*, "it wouldn't have stood a chance of getting into print."

ON NOVEMBER 30, CORE leader James Farmer reached King at the Chicago home of Judge Archibald Carey, speaking urgently of "a matter of life and death" that could not wait nor be discussed safely on the telephone, and King agreed to meet Farmer that night on a stopover in the New York airport. Farmer's contacts had supplied dire reports that the FBI "goods" on King included embezzled funds in Swiss bank accounts, and that Roy Wilkins had said, "Let them hang him." Mistrust was eating at movement alliances. Farmer did not tell King that FBI sources had sent him assurances of safety for the other leaders—"It's just King we gotta get" —but he did get King's blessing to keep a secret meeting with DeLoach, scheduled in the back of a moving limousine for mutual security. As Farmer tested the rumors, saying, "You've got to level with me, so we can find out what we can do," King asserted innocence on money and Communism but straddled warily on marital fidelity. "When a man travels like you and I do," he said, "there are bound to be women." King did not tell Farmer of a planned truce meeting with J. Edgar Hoover that was being arranged by Judge Carey.

Archibald Carey was a special authority on mending relations with the FBI. Although long established as a pillar of South Side Chicago— judge, banker, twice-elected city alderman, AME pastor, and renowned orator (his "Let freedom ring!" address to the 1952 Republican National Convention inspired a refrain in King's "I Have a Dream" speech)—he had been branded since a 1953 field investigation as "a highly controversial colored lawyer" whose FBI file contained "voluminous information of a subversive nature." Reports catalogued speeches to blacklisted groups such as Paul Robeson rallies, and charged that Carey "associated with known or suspected communist sympathizers." Nevertheless, without defiance or recanting, Carey revived his patriotic rating with a courtier's gift for flattery. Beginning with a 1957 headquarters tour in the company of baseball magnate Branch Rickey, he asked to meet Director Hoover, then to introduce his niece on a later trip, and soon to bring his grand-niece Liberty. By 1960, DeLoach had chastised headquarters with a note that "the Director was considerably embarrassed over the failure of our photographer in Chicago to take pictures of the Director and Dr. Carey's sister." In his correspondence with Hoover, Carey exercised a flair for the well-chosen compliment,* and Hoover in return posted word that he invited Carey to call "any time the Bureau or I could be of service to him, officially or personally." At least once, Hoover put his own Bureau car and driver at Carey's disposal for a day.

King knew his FBI mediator was no starry-eyed fool. Part of Carey's FBI cultivation was an accommodation to power in the long tradition of popes without armies. Having learned the FBI culture well enough to prod its officials confidentially on the lack of Negro agents, without triggering their defenses, Carey now translated King's Hoover troubles into the language of church princes. Perhaps because the more easygoing King did not have an autocrat's temperament, he consistently provoked alarm in those who did, including Hoover, J. H. Jackson, and to a lesser degree Adam Clayton Powell. King should talk to Hoover about mundane things, Carey advised, not big issues. If he could not bring himself to soothe the Director with apologetic gestures, he should listen on FBI turf. Carey briefed King on Hoover's office manners, phobias, and preferred small talk. Most important, he used his private telephone numbers and cultivated rapport to request the parley, and Hoover, with encouragement from Attorney General Katzenbach, agreed to receive King on Tuesday afternoon, December 1.

DeLoach handled the last-minute preparations with Andrew Young. "I interrupted Dr. Young again at this point," DeLoach advised colleagues by bulletin, "and told him that it was useless for them to request a 'peace meeting' with us as long as the crusade of defamation against Mr. Hoover and the FBI was to be carried on by Reverend King and his organization." Such bully talk—added to what was assumed to be the psychological crush of the suicide package, which had been mailed to King ten days earlier—led FBI officials to expect a more pulverized man than the one who posed for photographers in the crowded hallway near Hoover's office.

The confrontation turned into a nervous but mannerly chat. King pointedly deferred to Abernathy for a comment about the great privilege of meeting the Director, then commended the Bureau's progress in civil rights cases. He disavowed any personal criticism of the Director and

---

* "The added touch of the group photograph was just so nice of you," Carey wrote Hoover in 1959. In 1960: "I cannot tell you how pleased I was to note that both Houses of Congress joined in voting you a full pay, whenever you may retire."

reaffirmed his opposition to Communism. This prompted Hoover to observe that "Communists move in when the trouble starts," and from there he consumed most of the hour in a review of cases back to the 1920s. Along the way, the Director said it was wrong that a shoeshine boy he met in Miami could get no better job with a Howard University degree, and explained that the Bureau had few Negro agents for the same reason Notre Dame lacked Negro football players—"their grades are never high enough."

In Mississippi, Hoover declared, the Bureau had "put the fear of God in the Ku Klux Klan" and would soon bring suspects to trial on excellent evidence in the Neshoba County triple murder, though he could not guarantee conviction. He closed with a piece of advice: Negro leaders should concentrate on getting their people registered to vote. King flinched, amazed by Hoover's presumption, but said only that he intended to renew precisely that effort soon in Selma, where he feared "a great potential for violence." With Hoover's permission, he told waiting reporters that the discussion had been "very friendly, very amicable," and that he especially welcomed notice of impending action in the Mississippi triple murder.

At that time, inside the Mississippi governor's mansion, Inspector Sullivan and SAC Roy Moore were negotiating intensely over whether to bring state or federal charges in the Neshoba County case. Each side invited the other to go first. The Mississippi attorney general presented ten legal impediments to successful prosecution, including the fact that under Mississippi law only the county coroner was empowered to arrest a sheriff, and that "a Klansman judge is unlikely to disqualify himself or to eliminate Klan members" from jury service. A supervising prosecutor objected vehemently that Washington wanted a state trial but did not trust local officials to preview the confessions in detail. Sullivan pressed Burke Marshall's argument that even a perfunctory state trial on murder charges would be a positive step for the whole country, although he and Justice Department prosecutors felt that a federal trial on weaker civil rights charges offered the only slight chance for conviction.

Governor Paul Johnson pitched two fresh items from Washington: first, Director Hoover had answered a telegram from King with word that the FBI had identified the Neshoba County killers, and now King had brought from Hoover a pronouncement of forthcoming action. To Mississippians, said the governor, this pattern "indicated that King was calling the shots," and any official who said a kind or dutiful word about state prosecution would be seen as King's stooge. Teletypes rocketed back to Washington, and Burke Marshall observed that only President Johnson himself might have the influence to push the governor forward. With rumors flying, and suspects feared to be plotting flight or revenge, Katzenbach and Marshall made a command decision to proceed on federal warrants.

Fifty of Sullivan's agents fanned out before dawn on Friday, December 4, to arrest nineteen of twenty-one targeted suspects in Neshoba and Lauderdale counties. Sheriff Lawrence Rainey and Deputy Cecil Price, who were said to be out looking for a moonshine still, surrendered later in the morning. Crowds gathered on the square in Philadelphia to watch a parade of their handcuffed neighbors, and a few hotheads chased news photographers with knives. "In a small town like this," a young secretary told reporters, "you are either related to the people involved or they are friends of your friends." The vice president of Citizens Bank saw the dragnet as bitter proof that "the whole country is taking orders from Martin Luther King."

News flashes for that Saturday's world headlines reached King at John F. Kennedy Airport. Unable to say no, he had allowed his traveling party to grow to twenty-six people, for a dozen assigned seats at the Nobel Prize ceremony—the men leaving first with King, the women (plus Daddy King) on a second flight with Coretta. Before takeoff for London, King issued a hurried statement on the news from Mississippi. "I must commend the Federal Bureau of Investigation for the work they have done in uncovering the perpetrators of this dastardly act," he said. "It renews again my faith in democracy."

Senator-elect Robert Kennedy was nearby in the Carlyle Hotel, recording under a veil of lifetime secrecy a lengthy installment of oral history about his late brother. Burke Marshall helped him refine his earlier reflections on the FBI as "a very dangerous organization." On race, Kennedy painted Hoover as a figure of ingrained white supremacy, who casually stated that "Negroes' brains are twenty percent smaller than white people's," but he carefully refuted "general criticism... that the FBI doesn't do anything in civil rights." While Hoover had been reluctant to take risks, and especially to offend powerful Southerners in Congress, Kennedy said "that was true of the government as a whole." Now, he added, "the whole country and the whole government have changed," and Hoover was too professional a bureaucrat to be fundamentally out of step.

Kennedy placed in the secret record what he had learned of the "notorious liar" summit meeting only three days earlier. King came in extremely vulnerable, said Kennedy, and "what I understand from Hoover's account that he's given to the FBI offices around the country is that he told him that he was a Marxist and he told him that he was involved in sexual orgies... and said that he wasn't going to take any lip or any opposition from anybody like that... and gave him a lecture for an hour. ... I believe that was the reason why Martin Luther King was so mild when he left the meeting." Afterward, Kennedy added, the FBI picked up a phone call in which King expressed anguished amazement that Hoover knew all his secrets. None of this had happened. Kennedy presented as privileged truth Hoover's fantasy version of his face-to-face conquest.* It revealed the lingering spell of Kennedy's own intimidation by Hoover. Of his relations as attorney general with King himself, Kennedy remarked matter-of-factly, "I never really had any conversations with him over the period other than what he should be doing in connection with the Communists."

---

* In 1970, after King's death, *Time* published Hoover's tough-guy account of the 1964 meeting: "I said, 'Mr. King'—I never called him reverend—'stop right there. You're lying.'"

38

Nobel Prize

MALCOLM X RETURNED to the United States on November 24, just before King's summit meeting at the Barbizon Hotel. Shivering in the clothes he had packed for a summer trip, he stepped off a flight from Paris to greet sixty assorted admirers, reporters, and undercover FBI agents. At an airport press conference, he replied "no comment" when asked why he had called Elijah Muhammad a "religious faker" in Cairo, and he ducked other questions about internal conflict—explaining later that he would have "felt foolish coming back to this country and getting into a little two-bit argument...."

Malcolm spoke instead of global politics, making good his confident remarks over wiretapped lines that he was "coming back loaded" with larger connections and perspective. He told reporters that he had traveled the African continent for nearly five months to be received by seven heads of state and scores of ministers who had welcomed him with "open minds, open hearts, and open doors." He had gained authority to dispense fifteen scholarships for study at Islam University in Saudi Arabia, and the World Muslim Council had assigned a learned Sudanese imam, Sheikh Ahmed Hassoun, to tutor him in Sunni Islam. Malcolm did flick his fiery tongue about a rebellion in the Congo, which was drawing scandalized headlines (*New York Times:* "Congolese Forced American Officials to Eat U.S. Flag"). Only when white people got hurt did Americans notice the Congo, he charged, adding that "Congolese have been killed year after year" by puppet regimes and United States–backed mercenaries. "President Johnson is responsible for what happens in the Congo," he said, and America "is getting what she asked for."

He left the airport for brief personal reunions with his wife and four young daughters, including a baby he had scarcely seen before his trip. Days earlier, Malcolm's estranged brother Philbert X had arranged the release of their mother from her commitment since 1939 at a Kalamazoo asylum. Louise Little had not recognized Malcolm when he visited her in 1952, shortly after his own release from prison, and her faculties were scarcely improved now when Malcolm rushed to see her in Detroit. He rejoiced quietly over her freedom, and her remaining teeth, then returned to war alarms in New York. Far from cooled by Malcolm's prolonged absence, Elijah Muhammad raged privately against Malcolm's potential to join with Elijah's renegade son Wallace, supported by new Saudi money. Muhammad ordered Captain Joseph to warn at a press conference that Malcolm "stands alone . . . and we shall see how successful he will be."

Earlier in November, soldiers from New York's Temple No. 7 had beaten to death on the street a former member named Kenneth X Morton, who had rejected sectarian discipline for reasons loosely inspired by Malcolm. On November 30, six days after his return, an FBI informant inside Washington's Temple No. 4 reported a general announcement to the Fruit of Islam that Malcolm was to be attacked on sight. That same day, on learning that Malcolm was going abroad again, Director Hoover cabled the FBI's London attaché to monitor his appearances in England.

To British audiences in the industrial cities of Sheffield and Manchester, Malcolm attacked the veneer of racial progress in America. "No matter how many bills pass," he said, "black people in that country, where I'm from still—our lives are not worth two cents." At Oxford University, he debated Member of Parliament Humphry Berkeley on television, defending Goldwater's motto on extremism in defense of liberty. He bristled at Berkeley's accusation that his extremism fit the separatist mold of South African apartheid, but earned a standing ovation with his insistence that black people must discard "this wishy-washy love thine enemy approach." In the British press, blurbs about Malcolm trailed beneath accolades for Martin Luther King, in England on his way to Nobel ceremonies. While King was feted on the BBC, or met with Commonwealth intellectuals such as the radical scholar C. L. R. James, Malcolm offered his trademark barbs. On December 5, he told a London radio audience that King's nonviolence was "bankrupt," having been tried and abandoned by Nelson Mandela in South Africa. He said he was a man of peace, but "never could accept a peace prize in the middle of a war."

On Sunday, December 6, while King preached to an overflow crowd in London—the first non-Anglican ever allowed in the pulpit of St. Paul's Cathedral—Malcolm X returned to New York. FBI surveillance agents watched diplomatic limousines whisk him from the airport, and traced their license plates to the new African nation of Tanzania. The next day, Supreme Captain Raymond Sharrieff marked his return with an open telegram to the press: "Mr. Malcolm, we hereby officially warn you that the Nation of Islam shall no longer tolerate your scandalizing the name of our leader. . . ." Malcolm recognized the source. "That was Elijah Muhammad's wire," he said. "Raymond Sharrieff has no words of his own." In *Muhammad Speaks,* Minister Louis X of Boston called Malcolm the agent of defections, including that of Muhammad's youngest son, Akbar. "Malcolm shall not escape," he wrote. Daring the "international hobo" to come home and "face the music," Louis X invited his former mentor to picture his head "on the sidewalk," and *Muhammad Speaks* reprinted among its "Top Stories of '64" the cartoon of Malcolm's severed head bouncing down a road toward the tombstone of traitors.

On Wednesday, December 9, Malcolm won acquittal in traffic court on his speeding ticket from nine months earlier (the day he had heard Elijah Muhammad rename Cassius Clay on the radio). Outside the courtroom, he denounced Premier Moise Tshombe of the Congo and called Martin Luther King "a friend of mine and one of the foremost leaders of Negroes in their fight for recognition as human beings." Shortly afterward, at a seminar sponsored by HARYOU-ACT, the new Harlem anti-poverty agency, the program was delayed because no one wanted to sit next to Malcolm for a brief platform ceremony on 137th Street. Gregory Sims of Harlem's new Domestic Peace Corps said the "word is out" that Malcolm could be gunned down any minute.

King flew from London to Oslo on December 8. Norway's King Olav V sent for him and Coretta the next afternoon, and received them in private audience at the Royal Palace. There was considerable tension within the King group, which had swelled to thirty people. One family friend, who had talked her way into the traveling party with a lighthearted offer to serve as a dressing-aide for glittering occasions, grumbled that Coretta was far too exacting, and the Abernathys made known that Juanita deserved a lady-in-waiting to match. That evening, at a U.S. embassy dinner in honor of King, Bayard Rustin searched out CIA official Robert Porter among the hosts, then brashly advertised his hunch that Porter would know about Oslo's hidden nightlife. "At least five other men . . . ," Porter recorded, "wanted to know where to find the Norwegian girls." Porter described Rustin to Washington as "erratic, utterly cynical, and a born showman," whose "theme for the evening was that everyone was 'depraved' and 'selfish.' " When the tipsy Rustin caused a scene with his pronouncement that two thirds of his traveling companions were "merely using Dr. King," Porter wrote, friends excused him as a good man who was "overly tired."

Rustin stayed up Wednesday night drafting suggestions for the first of King's two Nobel Prize speeches, the five-minute acceptance statement for the next day's medal ceremony. In the end, however, King worked almost entirely from his own handwritten draft, which he fed to typist Dora McDonald after minor editing. His opening declaration accepted the Prize for Peace on behalf of a movement he called far from triumphant. "I am mindful that only yesterday in Birmingham, Alabama, our children, crying out for brotherhood, were answered with fire hoses, snarling dogs and even death," King wrote. "I am mindful that only yesterday in Philadelphia, Mississippi, young people seeking to secure the right to vote were brutalized and murdered." After deleting a third "only yesterday" sentence about more than forty churches destroyed in Mississippi alone, he posed a question: "Therefore, I must ask why this prize is awarded to a movement which is beleaguered and committed to unrelenting struggle, to a movement which has not won the very peace and brotherhood which is the essence of the Nobel Prize."

King would answer that he interpreted the prize as recognition for applied nonviolence itself, which he declared "a powerful moral force" and "answer to the crucial political and moral questions of our time—the need to overcome oppression and violence without resorting to violence and oppression." He adopted three short inserts in the handwriting of Andrew Young, and directed Young to modify a credo sentence: "I believe that unarmed truth and unconditional love will have the final word in reality," sharpening a blander faith in "truth, beauty and goodness." He struggled also with the required gray tailcoat and striped trousers, and quipped that he would never again submit to high formal wear.

Outside the Grand Hotel, officers directed King and Coretta to the limousine with Nobel Committee chairman Gunnar Jahn, and others to the line of cars waiting behind a press barricade. Ralph and Juanita Abernathy requested to ride along in car number one, which pitted them against the Norwegian protocol chief. An argument ensued, with the Abernathys insisting that they always rode with the Kings and the protocol chief standing firm with her calligraphied manifest. Abernathy appealed to King, who stood frozen with embarrassment, then tried to push his way past the security officers. From behind, Bernard Lee and Dora McDonald pleaded with Abernathy that there were plenty of limousines in the motorcade. By the time the Abernathys were removed to their assigned car, Andrew Young and Bernard Lee refused to ride with them. They walked the short distance to the ceremony through the December cold, talking over anew the mystery of King's attachment to Abernathy.

Upon the entrance of King Olav and Crown Prince Harald, all rose in the packed hall at Oslo University, and photographers from world outlets recorded King's receipt of the gold Nobel medallion on a platform decorated with one thousand imported carnations. Reporters interrupted the receptions afterward with news from a preliminary hearing that day in Mississippi at which a federal magistrate shocked the Justice Department by refusing a routine motion to send charges in the triple murder to a grand jury—and instead freed the nineteen alleged conspirators. A visibly distressed King called for a protest boycott of Mississippi products, mentioning Baldwin pianos made in Greenwood. "We had hoped that there could be an indictment at least," he told a press conference. "I must say that I didn't expect a conviction."

King joined spontaneous freedom songs that drew applause in the hotel lobby, and was moved by eloquent words from his mother, Mama King, but he had to keep up a show of alarm when Juanita Abernathy swooned to the floor during dinner and was rushed to the hospital for two days. Some in King's inner circle observed that the incident conveniently thrust her into the limelight. King confessed to his Chicago lawyer, Chauncey Eskridge, a gnawing worry that his own agents in Birmingham still held some $240,000 in SCLC-guaranteed cash bonds from the children's arrests nineteen months earlier.* He complained to Harry Wachtel of large international phone bills being run up from Oslo on SCLC's tab, but preferred to absorb the debt quietly than to risk friction with his friends. During rounds of toasts, which drained a case of champagne that night, Wachtel, Septima Clark, and others marveled at King's gracious ability to deflect praise with kind words all around—and also at the compulsion of the speakers to discuss themselves. Daddy King reviewed his odyssey since teenage migration to Atlanta "smelling like a mule," then raised his glass. "I want to offer a toast," he said, "to God!" Nonplussed revelers embraced the "toast to God" as the inspiration of a teetotaling novice, with amused recognition that Daddy King did not easily toast another mortal, including his beloved son.

King returned the next evening to deliver his formal Nobel lecture at Oslo University, where a standing-room crowd included several hundred students carrying Viking torches. Again he used his own handwritten draft with few modifications. He omitted sentences scribbled in his margins, such as "war is the most extreme externalization of an inner violence of the spirit," and inserted several less abstract ideas suggested by Rustin and Wachtel, including a paragraph welcoming the defeat of Goldwater in the American election. From Gandhi's India through post-colonial Africa to the American South, said King, "the freedom movement is spreading the widest liberation in human history," and he recommended the discipline of nonviolence "for study and for serious experimentation in every field of human conflict, by no means excluding the relations between nations."

He had added sections on poverty and war to his reflections on racial oppression. "All that I have said," King concluded, "boils down to the point of affirming that mankind's survival is dependent upon man's ability

---

* Eskridge promptly wrote NAACP lawyer Jack Greenberg on King's behalf: "Will you help relieve his mind of this pressing problem?"

to solve the problems of racial injustice, poverty and war; the solution of these problems is in turn dependent upon man squaring his moral progress with his scientific process, and learning the practical art of living in harmony." Proclaiming new opportunity for "the shirtless and barefoot people" and hope for "a dark confused world," King pronounced the era "a great time to be alive. Therefore, I am not yet discouraged about the future." He had inserted the word "yet" between the lines of his handwritten draft as a late change.

Members of the King entourage overran the Grand Hotel after hours. Before Wachtel retired with the "squares," he heard Rustin first turn up his nose at plans to search out Norwegian prostitutes, then say with a twinkle that he was off to cruise the nightlife himself. Rustin returned before dawn in time to intervene with hotel security officers who had been summoned by complaints about loud foot traffic of naked or nearly naked people through the corridors. King's brother A. D. King fled into Martin and Coretta's room. Officers chased men who said they were chasing women who had stolen money or personal property, and caught up with prostitutes who said they had been promised Martin Luther King himself in exchange for favors to his unscrupulous associates.

King continued with a small group to Stockholm, where he met the famed sociologists Gunnar and Alva Myrdal, and danced in public with Coretta in a rare, somewhat controversial exhibition for a Baptist preacher, then on to Paris, where he took his parents to a soul food restaurant on Rue Clauzel owned by a Morehouse graduate, and stayed behind when the others visited the Lido nightclub. "Only Martin's family and close staff members knew how depressed he was during the entire Nobel trip," Coretta disclosed privately some years later. "... He was worried about the rumors, and he was worried about what black people might think. He always worried about that." Andrew Young traced his mood more narrowly to disappointment over the childish jealousy from Abernathy: "Ralph's estrangement was much more worrisome to Martin than anything he thought J. Edgar Hoover might do."

WHILE KING WAS ABROAD, Defense Secretary McNamara drew President Johnson aside after a Vietnam strategy session with Ambassador Maxwell Taylor. "It would be impossible for Max to talk to these people," warned McNamara, of White House reporters waiting nearby, "without leaving the impression that the situation is going to hell." Accordingly, Taylor slipped through a rear exit and returned to Saigon. In meetings between December 7 and 10, he carried out instructions to demand that South Vietnamese military factions unite behind their civilian government in exchange for approval by President Johnson of a morale-building secret bombing campaign against North Vietnamese targets in Laos.

On December 10, Bill Moyers addressed the lingering scandal threat of Adam Yarmolinsky, the former Pentagon official who had been dismissed as the price of Southern support for the poverty bill. *"Esquire* Magazine and the *Saturday Evening Post* are both planning stories which will make this a kind of 'Dreyfus' case," warned Moyers, who reminded the President that he had promised to "help Yarmolinsky at the right time."* Johnson chose to risk the publicity rather than a confirmation dispute over a Yarmolinsky appointment.

In California, more than a thousand members of Berkeley's Academic Senate met in crisis. A photograph on the front page of the December 8 *New York Times* showed campus police dragging Mario Savio from the stage upon his first words to a university assembly; nearly eight hundred students had been arrested at sit-ins protesting the reinstatement of restrictions on political speech. "We are told that the mob is waiting outside!" shouted a professor of cell biology. Against an appeal by philosopher Louis Feuer, who recalled how Nazi students "helped destroy freedom and democracy in the universities of central Europe," the faculty voted to support the basic principles of what was now known as the Free Speech Movement, but the university Regents stood firm against an inchoate public image of unruly youth. Across the country, the *New York Times* reported that "Berkeley Protest Becomes a Ritual" and noted that "beards and long hair and guitars were much in evidence along the corridors of Sproul Hall. At least one young man came in barefoot."

In Washington on the night of December 10, Jack Warner of Warner Brothers Studios agreed to pay J. Edgar Hoover $75,000, plus $500 per episode, to film a television series called *The F.B.I.* Hoover's negotiator, Deke DeLoach, who had made it his urgent priority to reverse public relations damage from the "notorious liar" incident, faithfully extracted a host of "image" stipulations for the show—among them that the lead FBI character (based on Inspector Joe Sullivan) would always button his coat, never use informants, and always subdue the villain with a single, nonfatal shot—but DeLoach himself grew weary of Hoover's ever-expanding list of forbidden sponsors: alcohol, lingerie, makeup, footwear, and all bathroom products. The series would enjoy a nine-year run on ABC.

In Los Angeles, not until the afternoon of December 11 did anyone connect the undignified corpse—found in a cheap Watts motel the previous night, clad in a raincoat and one shoe—to the celebrity-red Ferrari parked outside with a copy of *Muhammad Speaks* on the seat. Police routinely accepted statements that the Negro victim was a foiled kidnapper-rapist, and dispatched the body unclaimed to the morgue before entertainment reporters descended upon the LAPD's 77th Precinct

---

* "I remember the conversation well," added Moyers, "because you had just arrived at the Ranch at midnight, your time, and called me. I was having dinner at a restaurant and talked from a phone booth. I felt you were doing the right and honorable thing...."

station with doubts that Sam Cooke died a low-life criminal. Too late, their investigations established it more likely that Cooke, convinced the motel was in cahoots with the prostitute who ran off with several thousand dollars and his clothes, had accused the female desk clerk, who shot him. These clarifications offered modest relief to Cooke's towering reputation or comfort to the five thousand disbelieving fans who gathered at the Chicago funeral, where Billy Preston played an organ prelude and Lou Rawls performed "Just a Closer Walk with Thee." Ray Charles turned up unexpectedly, and was guided down the aisle of Mount Sinai Baptist Church to sing "Angels Watching over Me." The death of Sam Cooke remained a sensational tragedy in the Negro press, but elsewhere it was a bigger story that an Illinois schoolgirl claimed to possess the cremated, post-operative tonsil of Beatles drummer Ringo Starr.

In Saigon, Maxwell Taylor dressed down four South Vietnamese officers who had just arrested military rivals and leaders of the civilian government. "I told you all clearly at General Westmoreland's dinner that we Americans were tired of coups," the ambassador said sternly. "Apparently I wasted my words. Maybe this is because something is wrong with my French.... Now you have made a real mess. We cannot carry you forever if you do things like this." The assembled Young Turks, who included future rulers Nguyen Cao Ky and Nguyen Van Thieu, seethed with humiliation. Their commander, General Khanh, threatened to have Taylor expelled as a colonialist; Taylor countered that Khanh should go into exile. "Generals acting greatly offended by my disapproval of their recent actions," the ambassador cabled President Johnson before Christmas.

HOME BEFORE KING, Bayard Rustin and Harry Wachtel plotted how they might induce President Johnson to invite King aboard *Air Force One* after their meeting on December 18, then "drop him off" in Atlanta on his way to the LBJ Ranch. Rustin also told friends of the prostitute chases in Oslo, boasting that he had thought quickly enough to warn that any arrest would bring down shame on Norway for allowing its criminals to pester King's friends. The calls gave FBI wiretappers "the first indication we have had that President Johnson may see King," and Hoover wrote "Expedite" on paperwork to send the White House a secret bulletin.

Another FBI wiretap picked up a distress call on December 15 between Clarence Jones and Stanley Levison. Neither had gone to Oslo, but they had heard the wild stories. Jones's wife, Ann, who idolized King, could not accept that he would allow such antics around him. When Jones tried to excuse the behavior as harmless sport, she confirmed first that he was neither offended nor surprised, then suddenly realized that her husband had been an accomplice to similar events—including some in their own home. "I never want to see Martin again," said Ann Jones. Clarence

Jones would consider the shock of the Oslo reports a precipitating factor in his divorce, and perhaps even in his ex-wife's untimely death from alcohol depression. At the time he called Levison, who said he knew how much the news had upset the Jones household. They made plans to talk in person, and FBI surveillance agents followed Jones from a distance.

King arrived from Paris to a whirlwind on December 17. Mayor Robert Wagner presented him with New York's Medallion of Honor at a ceremony that overflowed the City Council chamber in lower Manhattan. An enterprising reporter discovered that King was carrying the Nobel Prize check for 273,000 Swedish kroner in his left inside coat pocket, and counted four floodlights, nineteen microphones, and "14 motion picture and television cameras" at the afternoon press conference in the midtown Waldorf-Astoria. King said he was "greatly humbled" on the Oslo trip to hear that many countries beset by ethnic violence looked to the American freedom movement "with a certain amount of hope," and he announced his intention to support the MFDP's expected challenge to the seating of all five Mississippi representatives at the opening of the 89th Congress on January 4.* After an evening reception in his honor at the Waldorf, featuring Vice President–elect Hubert Humphrey, King completed the day's uptown trek with a tumultuous night rally at Harlem's 369th Artillery Armory, on 142nd Street.

Rally organizer Cleveland Robinson, King's friend, who served as New York City's commissioner of human rights, claimed a crowd of ten thousand in the armory. Police said eight thousand. Governor Rockefeller joined Mayor Wagner on the speaker's platform. Andrew Young went down into the crowd to sit briefly with Malcolm X. In his speech, King first returned the Harlem tribute by thanking movement colleagues from "old Sister Pollard" of the bus boycott to "my great abiding friend and a great leader in his own right, Ralph Abernathy." He wrestled out loud with pressures to grasp sweet renown in the larger world. For ten days he had been "talking with kings and queens, meeting and talking with prime ministers of nations," King said. "That isn't the usual pattern of my life, to have people saying nice things about me. Oh, this is a marvelous mountaintop. I wish I could stay here tonight. But the valley calls me."

Six days earlier in Oslo, addressing what he called "man's ethical infantilism," King had used the Greek myth of Ulysses to illustrate his belief that it was better to overcome the siren music of evil by listening to the melodies of Orpheus than by stuffing wax into one's ears. Now he preached in the Harlem armory on his favorite biblical parable of the rich man Dives, condemned because he never noticed the humble beggar

---

* To buttress the contention that the recent elections excluded Negro voters illegally, King recited the 1870 statute that readmitted Mississippi to the Union on condition that Negro residents of age be allowed to vote freely unless they were "convicts or insane."

Lazarus outside his door. King did not mention his resolve to go straight to Selma, but six times he tore himself from the mountain. "Oh, there are some humble people down in the valley!" he cried, in his distinctive mix of despair and inspiration. ". . . I go back with a faith that the wheels of the gods grind slowly but exceedingly fine," he said. "I go back with a faith that you shall reap what you sow. With that faith, I go back to the valley."

He stopped off at the White House on the way, transported Friday afternoon in Governor Rockefeller's private plane. On the other end, aides briefed President Johnson to steer King off three politically troublesome courses: his criticism of the triple murder prosecution, his support for unseating the five incumbent Mississippi congressmen, and the "statements he made abroad about an economic blockade of South Africa and a perhaps unfortunate linkage of Mississippi and South Africa."* Johnson chose instead to emphasize their common agenda. To illustrate the Texas roots of his new poverty program, he showed King and Coretta the family heirloom letter to his Grandfather Baines from Texas hero Sam Houston in 1857 (". . . paper currency will not pass in heaven. It must be the coin . . . from an honest heart") and promised to send them a copy. The President said he had signed the new civil rights law and Justice Tom Clark had "rounded up nine votes" to uphold it, and he made a point of having Clark's son Ramsey, an assistant attorney general, nearby for introduction as yet another Texan in the fight. "Now what's Georgia doing?" the President asked King. "You ought to get back down there and get them to work."

When King pushed for legislation to secure Negro voting rights in the South, Johnson embraced that goal for his administration but deflected it beyond 1965. He did attend to social courtesies by walking to a satellite office to retrieve Ralph and Juanita Abernathy, along with Andrew Young and Walter Fauntroy, for a handshake and a brief return to the Oval Office. Then he was off to light the national Christmas tree, and the Kings flew to Atlanta for the Nobel homecoming.

THAT SUNDAY AFTERNOON, December 20, Malcolm X first encountered Fannie Lou Hamer at a small, integrated church rally in New York. SNCC's Freedom Singers performed movement songs, including a tribute to Vice President Oginga Odinga of the newly independent Kenya, and Hamer asked the audience why the United States could intervene to protect white settlers in the Congo but not Mississippi Negroes who sought the ballot. She told her story of the Winona jail beatings, which was

---

* On the Nobel trip, King called for the removal of foreign troops from the Congo and for the imposition of international economic sanctions on South Africa. The South African government, meanwhile, was resisting the introduction of television for fear that Western programming would undermine apartheid society.

new to Malcolm. He soon gained the floor to speak. "When I listened to Mrs. Hamer," he said, "a black woman—could be my mother, my sister, my daughter—describe what they had done to her in Mississippi, I asked myself how in the world can we ever expect to be respected as *men* when we know that we will allow something like that to be done to our women and we do nothing about it?" He belittled a nonviolent response. "The language they were speaking to Mrs. Hamer...," he declared, "was the language of a brute, the language of someone who has no sense of morality, who absolutely ignores law.... Let's learn his language. If his language is with a shotgun, get a shotgun... a rifle, get a rifle... a rope, get a rope.... Speak his language. There's nothing wrong with that. If something was wrong with that language, the federal government would have stopped the cracker from speaking it to you and me."

Malcolm half apologized. "I know I'm in the church," he said. "I probably shouldn't be talking like this, but Jesus himself was ready to turn the synagogue inside out and upside down when things weren't going right." Malcolm said America measured champions—except for Negroes—by their willingness to fight when provoked. "Your own Patrick Henry said 'liberty or death,'" he told whites in the audience, "and George Washington got the cannons out, and all the rest of them that you taught me to worship as my heroes, they were fighters....

"But now," said Malcolm, "when the time comes for *our* freedom, you want... somebody who's nonviolent and forgiving and peaceful and long-suffering. I don't go for that. I say a black man's freedom is as valuable as a white man's freedom." He called for an American Mau Mau, modeled on Kenya's feared warriors, to go as vigilantes where the government refused to secure justice. He took it as a sign that the nonviolent SNCC Freedom Singers sang a song about Odinga of Kenya, saying violence worked there for the Mau Mau. "He's not humble. He's not nonviolent," Malcolm said of Odinga. "But he's free."

Malcolm presented Hamer and the Freedom Singers to his own rally that night at the Audubon Ballroom in Harlem. There he elaborated on the Mau Mau formula with a story, almost certainly apocryphal, of a Mau Mau leader who asked three hundred followers how many were willing to kill for freedom, and when fifty stepped forward, ordered them first to kill the other 250. "I go for that," said Malcolm, but he recognized that the suggested purge of assimilationist "Uncle Toms" applied more aptly to the Nation's internecine wars than to likely vengeance against white authorities in Winona or elsewhere. He also predicted, accurately, that his Mau Mau comments to the church audience would dominate the next day's news.*

* "Malcolm Favors a Mau Mau in U.S.," headlined the *Times*, which observed that he had reportedly "renounced black racism and had embraced the brotherhood of man, but his

Facing representatives of the nonviolent movement, Malcolm hedged. "If you're going to get yourself a .45 and start singing 'We Shall Overcome,' I'm with you," he told Hamer at the Audubon. But a few days later, he subordinated all questions of method to the goal. "I'm not interested in either ballots or bullets," he said. "I'm interested in freedom.... If Negroes can get freedom nonviolently, good. But that's a dream. Even King calls it a dream."

In Atlanta, King was debating how to cooperate with the controversial MFDP congressional challenge. He knew most members of the House would scarcely welcome a vote to bar their Mississippi colleagues. Moreover, he retained bruised memories of being scorned by movement students for having the high-level connections they now wanted to borrow, and he was aware that SNCC and MFDP were virtually paralyzed with dissension since Atlantic City. Bob Moses was opposing the challenge as a surrender to "glamour" politics (VIPs, lobbyists, and lawyers) and withdrew from deliberations; Hollis Watkins and other young SNCC veterans went back to college courses. On December 21, as MFDP chairman Lawrence Guyot announced in Jackson that an insolvent Mississippi movement was awaiting a promised donation from King, Clarence Jones told King that leaders of the congressional challenge were wary that he would "steal the show." Still, Jones urged, the petitions were sound and creative. On December 24, when Rep. William Ryan revealed that seventeen co-sponsors would offer a preliminary resolution for Mississippi members to "stand aside" pending review of election credentials, King agreed to send House members a letter of support. The novel challenge, he wrote, addressed "the root cause of Mississippi injustices—the total denial of the right to vote on account of race."

In Boston, Leon 4X Ameer took refuge on December 25 in the Sherry Biltmore Hotel. Ameer had served the Nation of Islam as a trained pugilist, assigned as bodyguard to heavyweight champion Muhammad Ali until he had defected to Malcolm. "It was he," Malcolm said publicly, "who heard Elijah Muhammad, Jr.," tell enforcement squads "that I should have been killed, that my tongue should have been put in an envelope and mailed back to Chicago by now." Marked as Malcolm's agent, lured to the hotel lobby with a pretext call from a French reporter seeking the inside story, Ameer stepped off the elevator into an ambush by Captain Clarence X and three subordinates from Muhammad's Temple No. 11. An armed detective arrested the four attackers before severe damage was done, but a follow-up squad broke into Ameer's hotel room that same Christmas night and left him battered, brain-damaged, and unconscious in the bathtub, to be discovered by the morning housekeepers.

words yesterday bristled with militancy." News coverage readily embraced Malcolm's sensational—yet traditional—assumption that brotherhood and militancy are at odds.

At year's end, the *New York Times* reported on its front page that influential Atlantans were agitating against a January dinner planned to honor the local Nobel Prize winner. Integrated social gatherings remained controversial in many cities,* but this exposure stung Atlanta's boosterish civic pride. The *Times* story forced the *Atlanta Constitution* to publish its first acknowledgment of controversy that had been stewing in high circles since the announcement of King's award in October. Anonymous business leaders grumbled that King was picketing a local pen factory over segregated labor practices. Former mayor William Hartsfield answered that he would "certainly hate to see my town held up as a city which refused to honor a Nobel Prize winner," and other supporters offered statements of pinched or brave hospitality. Ralph McGill, the *Constitution*'s outspoken publisher and one of four sponsors behind the King tribute, deflected his own newspaper's questions with a formal "no comment."

King himself, tired of being the honored leper at a forced celebration, told family that he did not care whether or not Atlanta pulled off the testimonial, and the FBI wiretaps on his home picked up no comments on the subject. They revealed King to be depressed instead about the lingering effects of the Oslo trip. Ralph Abernathy was refusing to go to Selma. He did not see the need for a new movement there, and in fact was instructing the SCLC staff not to disturb any of his numerous relatives in the Alabama counties nearby. When publicity about the Nobel banquet erupted from the *New York Times* article on December 29, wiretaps overheard Coretta King worrying about King's depressed mental state and the fight with Abernathy, seeking advice from Andrew Young about how to relieve pressure on her husband.

Late Monday night, December 28, a New York FBI agent took notes on a talk-show appearance by Malcolm X: "He said he considered himself a true Muslim who believed in brotherhood of all people, whereas NOI [Nation of Islam] Muslims do not believe in brotherhood of anyone but Negroes. When asked why he preaches that Negroes should take arms to protect themselves, Malcolm said that just because he believes in brotherhood does not mean that he should not protect himself."

On Tuesday, Malcolm went by train to Philadelphia, where he told a group of black reporters they were "almost as bad" as the white press about distorting news from Africa. Philadelphia FBI agents fielded a report that Malcolm would be shot that night. He took ten bodyguards to tell an audience of thirty that he was forming an alliance with Elijah Muhammad's son Wallace. Outside the Sheraton Hotel that night, a dozen members of the Nation's Temple No. 12 jumped from cars and brawled through

---

* Atlanta had recently canceled its annual goodwill dinner for Georgia legislators because Mayor Ivan Allen could not prevail upon the Commerce Club, which he served as president, to relax its segregation rules for the first Negro state senator.

the entourage, knocking three to the ground before two Philadelphia detectives drove them off. Malcolm called home when he reached radio station WDAS. "Be careful," he told his wife. "Keep those things near the door, and don't let anyone in until I get there." The detectives posted officers with shotguns outside the studio for his midnight appearance on the Joe Rainey talk show.

Two days later, on New Year's Eve in Harlem, Malcolm X received a delegation of thirty-seven young people from McComb, Mississippi. Northern supporters had raised funds to bring members of the summer project's extraordinary Freedom School to New York for a broadening tour, which included a stop by the Hotel Theresa to visit the man with ferocious reputation and X for a last name. Malcolm talked to them at first of civics. "This generation, especially of our people, has a burden," he told them. "... The most important thing that we can learn to do today is think for ourselves." He ranged at length over World War II history and the importance of Africa, until exchanges on the summer siege in McComb distracted him. "Excuse me for raising my voice," said Malcolm, "but this thing, you know, gets me upset. Imagine that. A country that's supposed to be a democracy, supposed to be for freedom, and ... they want to draft you and put you in the Army and send you to Saigon to fight for them, and then you've got to turn around and all night long discuss how you're going to just get a right to register and vote without being murdered. Why, it's the most hypocritical government since the world began!"

He told the Mississippi students that their elders in civil rights organizations had failed them—failed to protect them, failed to stand with them, failed to respond vigorously to the murders of Chaney, Schwerner, and Goodman. "That's what split the Muslim movement," said Malcolm. Almost offhandedly, he stretched a link from the McComb students, heirs to the first rural foray by Bob Moses in 1961, to his own troubled quest for stand-up sectarian vigilantes in Los Angeles. "Some of our brothers got hurt, and nothing was done about it," said Malcolm. "And those of us who wanted to do something about it were kept from doing something about it. So we split."

39

To the Valley:
The Downward King

O
N A SATURDAY MORNING drive from Atlanta to Selma, King mollified his sullen and reluctant companion with ruminations on the line of succession. He told Ralph Abernathy that President Johnson had worried out loud about dying in office before Hubert Humphrey became vice president on January 20, because until then a vacated presidency would fall first to the failing House Speaker, John McCormack, and second to the frail Senate elder, Carl Hayden. He recalled that Johnson had explored various remedies. "If he had sense enough to do it, *I* should have sense enough to do it," King added, saying he wanted to make formal arrangements for Abernathy to succeed him as SCLC president. Abernathy scoffed and protested, short of refusal. He said he had no ambition beyond shared leadership, and figured to be killed along with King anyway, but he did accept the argument that no one else stood a chance to hold together the contentious personalities on the staff. King said he had not expected to live through his summer trip to Mississippi. As he and Abernathy traded raucous snippets of imaginary orations for each other's funeral, a common amusement among SCLC preachers, King parlayed the White House analogy into a promise from Abernathy to accept formal designation as his heir.

Spirits were improved by the time King and Abernathy pulled into the driveway of their Selma hosts, Sullivan and Jean Jackson. The Atlantans made a show of inspecting their joint quarters in the guest room, and the Jacksons made a fuss over King's new Norwegian wristwatch. The four friends shared many ties. Jean Jackson's great-aunt, Ethel Dinkins,* had been Coretta King's childhood music teacher; her best friend had married Ralph Abernathy's college roommate, Rev. Howard Creecy, and she had grown up with Juanita Abernathy. Her husband, Sullivan—"Sully" to King and Abernathy—had testified with Sam Boynton at the 1958 federal hearings on the exclusion of professional Negroes from the Selma voting roles. Since then, chastened by hostile and enduring reaction from local white people, Jackson had confined himself to dentistry and a supporting role in politics, playing straight man for the running jokes of movement preachers. His sister and dental hygienist, Marie Foster, ran the tiny literacy and citizenship classes in Selma, funneling students to Septima Clark's SCLC workshops near Savannah. Foster worked in the Dallas County Voters League with Margaret Moore, the intrepid schoolteacher who had offered lodging to the lone SNCC registration worker, Bernard "Little Gandhi" Lafayette, in 1962.

Andrew Young moved into the guest room of Amelia Boynton, who lived across the street from the Jacksons. On this Saturday, January 2, a concerted movement was scheduled at last to take up two distinct appeals that had ripened from the Birmingham church bombing sixteen months earlier. One was the grand strategic plan for a "nonviolent army" to win minority voting rights throughout Alabama, which Diane Nash Bevel and James Bevel had proposed as a monument of justice to the four murdered girls. The other was a plaintive local request from Amelia Boynton about Dunn's Rest Home for the aged. For attending the first Selma Freedom Day, three weeks after the church bombing, two Dunn's employees had been fired, photographed (to warn prospective employers), and roughed up so badly that sympathetic colleagues walked off jobs paying $18 per week. The result was that "forty colored ladies of Selma...cannot get employment in their hometown," Boynton had written Martin Luther King. "We need your help very much, and we are asking that your organization please give us ONE HIGH POWERED SEWING MACHINE." Boynton and the Dallas County Voters League undertook to sustain the former Dunn's attendants as home seamstresses.

The first step in January tested the most basic power to move. There had been no regular Monday meetings of the Voters League for six months, under Judge James Hare's sweeping injunction that forbade discussion of racial issues at any gathering of "three or more persons." The blatantly unconstitutional order remained in effect during leisurely review by the federal courts, but King's scouts in Selma saw a crack in the wall. Like Birmingham two years earlier, Selma's local government was in

---

* Sister of Professor William Dinkins, the church malfeasance expert during the pulpit wars of Rev. L. L. Anderson at Selma's Tabernacle Baptist Church.

factional transition. In October, the first mayor from outside the agrarian gentry—Joe Smitherman, a young refrigerator salesman without college education—had assumed office as a moderate, image-conscious segregationist, pledged to seek industrial jobs to replace farm belt losses. Smitherman had installed a police and fire chief, Wilson Baker, who had narrowly lost an election to the reigning sheriff, Jim Clark, and the Smitherman-Baker town crowd advocated the polite, jail-'em-with-kindness approach that had stymied Martin Luther King in Albany, Georgia.* They claimed jurisdication within the Selma town limits against the county hard-liners of Sheriff Clark, who had enforced Judge Hare's meeting ban everywhere —to the point of breaking up a strategy session in the Negro Elks Hall of enlisted men from nearby Clark Air Base. Hushed negotiations addressed details down to the control of Selma sidewalks outside Sheriff Clark's domain in the Dallas County courthouse, where aspiring voters must attempt to register. In a small story on New Year's Day—"Dr. King Due to Head Alabama Vote Drive"—the *New York Times* had reported that Wilson Baker considered the Hare injunction to be suspended in Selma during legal challenge by the U.S. Department of Justice. King's campaign, noted the *Times,* "is expected to last about six months."

For King and Abernathy, the first promising break was agreement by several leading churches to house a forbidden mass meeting—not just Tabernacle Baptist, where the embattled Rev. L. L. Anderson rallied the deacons, but also First Baptist and Brown Chapel AME. Their congregations had divined that the ruling segregationists across town were divided enough to make the gamble worthwhile—so confirmed Jean Jackson for her Brown Chapel and Sullivan Jackson for First Baptist, where he and Amelia Boynton belonged. They also delivered a flash report from the interracial listening posts: Sheriff Clark was expected to spend the weekend in Miami, where the national champion Crimson Tide football team —pride of Alabamans, including many fans of archrival Auburn—lost Friday night's Orange Bowl to the Texas Longhorns, 21–17, despite the heroics of the Alabama quarterback, Joe Namath. This news offered hope that Clark would not be rushing home to blockade or tear up a church in front of the reporters who followed King.

Later, after elaborate grooming and goodbyes at the Jackson home, King and Abernathy made an entrance to the imposing, double-towered Brown Chapel, where a standing, cheering crowd of seven hundred heard King decisively challenge Judge Hare's injunction with a reprise of his 1957 "Give Us the Ballot" speech on the Washington Mall. "Today marks

---

* "Segregation was not an issue, because everybody was a segregationist," Smitherman recalled. "...I tried to make a deal with" black leaders to pave their streets if they would oppose King's campaign. "...We did what we thought was a good job trying to defuse it and keep him out of here."

the beginning of a determined, organized, mobilized campaign to get the right to vote everywhere in Alabama," he declared. "If we are refused, we will appeal to Governor George Wallace. If he refuses to listen, we will appeal to the legislature. If *they* don't listen, we will appeal to the conscience of the Congress.... We must be ready to march. We must be ready to go to jail by the thousands.... Our cry to the state of Alabama is a simple one. Give us the ballot!" When the thunder died down on his departure, James Bevel asked volunteers to sign on for work in the movement.

TWO DAYS LATER in Washington, a pilgrimage of some five hundred Mississippians arrived in a convoy of Trailways buses, tattered farm vehicles, and straggling hitchhikers. Although rules did not permit them to carry signs or lobby inside the Capitol, they stood in silent vigil along the underground corridors between office buildings and the House floor, where the representatives-elect passed by to open the 89th Congress. During a standoff at the front door, as Capitol police blocked the three MFDP challengers —Victoria Gray, Annie Devine, and Fannie Lou Hamer—a member of the Nazi Party slipped by into the House chamber and ducked aside to paint himself in blackface with burnt cork. He burst in upon astonished lawmakers, dancing a jig and shouting, "I'se de Mississippi delegation! I wants to be seated!" before police hauled him away to pay a fine of $19.

With order restored, ceremonies proceeded until Speaker McCormack called for the swearing in of Thomas Abernethy from Mississippi's First District, whereupon Rep. William Ryan of New York called out an objection. More than fifty representatives-elect cried out for the Speaker to recognize Ryan, which he did. In the ensuing parliamentary crisis, House leaders countered with a move to seat the five Mississippi representatives on condition of a full House investigation. Rep. James Roosevelt of California, son of FDR, urged colleagues to hold out for vacating the contested seats during the inquiry, saying Mississippi elections manifestly excluded Negro voters. Rep. Edith Green of Oregon demanded and won a roll call vote. The bipartisan leadership prevailed,* 276–149, and the Mississippians were sworn in provisionally, but MFDP supporters deliriously celebrated the day's accomplishments. Not only had they won a hearing, but more than a third of the House had supported them in a straw vote before they marshaled their evidence on Mississippi voting practices. "Back to work!" cried Lawrence Guyot at a victory rally.

The commotion in the Capitol was a minor issue at the background press briefing before President Johnson's State of the Union address. A White House reporter asked whether the President had any specific action

---

* The new Minority Leader, Gerald Ford, survived his first legislative test after defeating incumbent Charles Halleck in the Republican caucus.

in mind for the general endorsement of voting rights in his advance speech draft. Bill Moyers replied carefully. He knew Johnson wanted voting reform, and had long wished the *Brown* decision had been grounded in the right to vote rather than in school integration. He also knew that John Doar, Burke Marshall's replacement in the Civil Rights Division, sought new legal tools after five nearly fruitless years in county-by-county litigation.* On the other hand, Acting Attorney General Nicholas Katzenbach wanted time to absorb the shocks of the 1964 law, and there were two obvious drawbacks to the constitutional amendment favored by Justice Department lawyers: the Southern states could block ratification, and the Fifteenth Amendment already guaranteed minority voting rights. Therefore, Moyers said, the administration planned "to do something." He emphasized Johnson's more specific urgency to send five legislative packages to Congress even before the January 20 inauguration, beginning with health and education, and to define a Great Society concept he knew was "corrupted in certain circles." Outside critics viewed it as "a Communist five-year plan," said Moyers, while some bureaucrats perceived merely an excuse "to raise postal rates."

For America, which he defined that night in his address as "the first continental union of democracy in the history of man," Johnson proposed "a new quest for union" beyond 1965, a century removed from 1865 and the Civil War's "terrible test of blood and fire." The next day, Tuesday, January 5, White House officials basked in the impact of a record 75 million viewers, nearly triple the estimated audience for the 1964 State of the Union address. In Atlanta, a stricken Coretta King called her husband home that day, having routinely opened a piece of SCLC's haphazard, accumulated mail. She had assumed that the reel of tape was another of King's road speeches, which admiring collectors often recorded and mailed to Atlanta, until she read the accompanying letter from the FBI's November 21 suicide package. She was accustomed to written threats, but this one conveyed the chill of an anonymous purported Negro spouting hatred mixed with flowery phrases: "You are finished.... Satan could not do more. What incredible evilness...." With apprehension, she played the tape.

King himself listened to the tape three times before Abernathy was rushed in on summons. For his inner circle—Abernathy, Andrew Young, Joseph Lowery, Bernard Lee—King played the tape over and over. They examined the wrapping and Miami postmark for clues. They analyzed the muffled contents as a familiar mixture of seductions, sex cries, and raunchy, Amos 'n' Andy–style hotel banter,† which seemed chosen for its power to

---

* The litigation method was failing, Doar advised the Justice Department from Selma, although it had been "tried harder here than anywhere else in the South."
† Andrew Young remembered hearing King tease Abernathy about his consuming desire to give the really big speech—saying Abernathy needed first to become president of something, then suggesting he form the National Association for the Advancement of

cause public humiliation. King heard at least three different background settings, which he accurately took to mean the sender had access to hotel bugs in scattered places. The group interpretation was unanimous: the package came from Hoover's FBI, with a letter demanding that King commit suicide before Oslo or be exposed with the "highlights" tape.

They were too rattled to reflect on the tactical ironies—that Hoover, assuming King would have opened the package before their December summit meeting, must have been undone by King's calm demeanor that day, or that Hoover could not have counted on the extra sting of discovery by Coretta. Nor did they realize how quickly the Bureau could catch up with the delayed impact of the hostile message. Wiretaps provided enough advance notice for headquarters to have the New York office install bugs at the Park Sheraton before King and his advisers checked in for an emergency meeting over the weekend of Friday, January 8. Although King now worried about spies and microphones to the point of whispering, the surveillances rewarded headquarters with signs of his anguish. "They are out to break me," King said. He raged against Hoover, but he also reproached himself that the tapes were a sign of his own failure.

King kept word of the suicide package from Harry Wachtel. His minimal disclosures to Wachtel before the Barbizon meeting had been painful enough, and on the flight to Oslo he had solemnly promised to give up any affairs. There was too much at stake, he had told Wachtel, especially since the frightful warnings that Hoover's spying might injure the movement. Now King did not have the heart to revisit the issue over the explicit, sexually focused revelation of the suicide package. He sought legal advice more comfortably from Chicago lawyer Chauncey Eskridge, with whom he had once shared a lover, knowing Eskridge was toughened in such matters by his work for Elijah Muhammad.

In Wachtel's presence, the Research Committee discussed the Selma campaign, and King abruptly announced his desire to restore a working relationship with Stanley Levison. The banishment was wrong, he insisted. He had submitted because President Kennedy and his Justice Department had repeatedly called it the price of the civil rights bill, which was now law, and President Johnson had never mentioned the preposterous spy charges. King wanted Levison back. Wachtel urged caution on behalf of the surprised advisers. His advice, for which he later felt foolish, was that King should be slow to upset the FBI now that Wachtel's summit strategy had patched up relations with Hoover.

Wachtel volunteered to assess the dangers of King's proposal directly with Levison, who had been a decisive voice for his sacrificial banishment. King left New York to deliver two Sunday speeches in Massachusetts.

Eating Chicken. King led guffawing preachers as they "cracked on Ralph" with ridiculous ideas for his organization.

When Harvard's Memorial Church filled long in advance, technicians wired remote speakers into nearby Saunders Theater, which also overflowed. Some of those who applauded King's work in the South were nonplussed by his announcement that he would return in the spring to address racial problems of the Boston area.

On Monday, Abernathy and Andrew Young threw themselves against the FBI's wall of innocence. They had asked on Friday to see Hoover, but settled for DeLoach and his assistant. Unaware that surveillances had forewarned DeLoach of their strategy, they demanded candor about scandalmongering and smear campaigns—only to hear an obliging DeLoach draw them out on their "trilogy" attacks over Communism, money, and sex. They danced around the rumors themselves; DeLoach shrugged off their attempts to focus on the source, saying that the FBI had no interest in King's private life or finances. When Andrew Young pointed to signs of malicious, orchestrated leaks from the government, DeLoach assured him that "there were no leaks from the FBI [and] that the Director ran a tight organization...." King's aides left fuming about being patronized. DeLoach's written report, as summarized by historian David Garrow, "gloated to his superiors that he had tried to make the talk as unpleasant and embarrassing as possible...."

That day in Baltimore, King spoke at Johns Hopkins on the obsolescence of war, and news elsewhere trailed scattered clashes around the movement. Leaked stories, which disclosed the existence of a second Klan confession in the Mississippi triple murder (without mention of Doyle Barnette's name), framed hopes in the Justice Department to revive the federal prosecution. A federal grand jury indicted three Greenwood plumbers for beating Silas McGhee the previous July 16. In Los Angeles, two former secretaries failed to appear for a hearing in their paternity suit against Elijah Muhammad, which was a disaster for the survival scheme long constructed by Malcolm X. He had no doubt the women were petrified, as the Nation's enforcements were rippling everywhere. A few days earlier, two lieutenants from Temple No. 7 had carried out instructions from Captain Joseph to tell Benjamin Brown, a New York prison guard, that he could not teach independent, nonpolitical Islam, even with an homage photograph of Elijah Muhammad posted on his window. Unsatisfied by his response, they shot Brown in the back with a rifle. On January 15, the New York FBI office closed an update about Malcolm with a note that he was using a new alias, "M. Khalil," for hotel registration.

IN SELMA, beneath the fanfare of announcements about King's anticipated return, staff members passed out leaflets for recruits. By Thursday, January 7, the response justified separate night workshops in each of the city's five election wards, and James Bevel stunned the fifty or so participants at the Ward IV session by shooing the sheriff's deputies out of Brown Chapel.

On Friday, at the first Selma youth rally, Bevel showed his well-traveled copy of the NBC documentary on the Nashville sit-ins of 1960, and Hosea Williams sent two hundred students home with provocative questions. "If you can't vote, then you're not free," he told them. "And if you ain't free, children, then you're a slave." Eight-year-old children went home to ask their parents whether they were slaves.

By Tuesday, January 12, the first block captains were elected at nightly training sessions of up to a hundred people in each ward. From a downtown storefront, Diane Nash Bevel began to compile maps of voting-age Negroes by street address, tending the daily fears and afflictions of returning canvassers. Staff members worked the wards in pairs—one from SCLC and one from SNCC. The tandem approach was approved by Bernard Lafayette, who had flown in from Chicago to promote coopera-tion. Well remembered as SNCC's pioneer organizer in Selma, Lafayette retained ties that predated and also bridged frictions between SNCC students and SCLC preachers. Together with Bevel and SNCC chairman John Lewis, he recommended that SNCC strengthen its Selma project. They recruited Silas Norman, the literacy volunteer from the previous summer, to join the SNCC staff as project director. They made Terry Shaw, one of the intrepid high school students who had canvassed for Lafayette in 1962, a co-coordinator in Ward III.

Hungry for manpower, both SNCC and SCLC pitched their self-selected young newcomers into Selma. Charles Fager, a white journalist from Colorado, had moved from curiosity, which drew him to Atlanta, to absorption, after he attended his first mass meeting in December on the Scripto pen strike, then to awe, after he conducted an interview with Septima Clark. In January he joined SCLC's Selma staff. Fay Bellamy, a Negro from Pennsylvania who had searched intermittently for "the movement" since the Birmingham church bombing, made connections to the Atlanta SNCC office independently of Frank Soracco, a twenty-nine-year-old white schoolteacher who drove his Volkswagen from California. Assigned to Selma, both wound up at the SCLC-SNCC joint morning staff meetings, the all-day canvasses, mass meetings, and integrated night socials at the Chicken Shack. "Things are starting to move here organiza-tion wise," Soracco wrote his parents near Sacramento. "It has been calm because the city wants it that way.... Two guys tear gassed our house. No one was home. They got 6 mos.—unheard of 6 mos. ago.... Few things I miss—good food, or place to cook it, clean sheets, friendly girl or two. These here are friendly, but most of their dads would skin them alive if they were around with a white man."

On Thursday, January 14, cheers greeted King's entrance to the mass meeting at First Baptist and then drowned out his shouted pledge to "be coming back again and again and again until...." He declared that the planned campaign called for parallel registration drives in ten surrounding rural counties, and he announced a triple challenge for Monday. They would march through Selma to the courthouse, he said. They would send volunteers to apply for white-only city jobs, and teams would make the first attempts to integrate Selma's hotels and restaurants under the civil rights law. "You see," said King, "I am trying to get over to you that Monday will be Freedom Day.... If we march by the hundreds, we will make it clear to the nation that we are determined to vote." He emphasized the need to "desegregate our minds" and "remove the shackles of fear." He said they would help the white people, too, "whether they realize it or not."

President Johnson called King on Friday, with greetings on his thirty-sixth birthday and requests for recommendation on several pending appointments. In Selma, recruitments intensified over the weekend. Ward captains were asked to speak at mass meetings, and block captains to stand. In Ward V, forty teenagers unexpectedly skipped Friday night's Hudson High School basketball game to petition the staff for roles on Freedom Day, and James Orange, who had moved from the 1963 Birmingham children's marches to the SCLC staff under James Bevel, was assigned to devise a program for "students that refuse to remain in school." Meanwhile, Andrew Young and others continued negotiations with police chief Wilson Baker about what could be done peacefully.

Baker, who confessed that he had petitioned the Justice Department to keep King out of Selma—"begging on my knees for my community"—quoted Scripture on the tests of life, having once considered the Lutheran ministry. While tacitly acknowledging vigilante pressures on the white side of town, he told Young and his own officers that the Selma police would enforce the law as professionals. Staff minutes on the movement side recorded worry about poor organization for Freedom Day. In Ward II, block captains were asked to stretch final recruitments by an extra half block apiece, to cover shortages. In Ward III, on the other hand, "Mrs. Anderson has so many block captains and workers that she is going to help Mrs. Blevins in her block, which is in Ward V."

THE FIRST SKIRMISH began with a Monday morning song service of three hundred, roughly half of them high school students. King led a mid-morning march out of Brown Chapel one block south on Sylvan Street into a police blockade at Selma Avenue. Wilson Baker gave notice of the pedestrian traffic laws, and warned that he would arrest the entire column for violating parade ordinances unless they divided into clumps of five or fewer at intervals of at least ten feet. In compliance, the segmented column marched one more block, turned west on Alabama Avenue, then walked five short blocks to Broad Street, Selma's main thoroughfare, and across toward the Dallas County courthouse on the right.

Those waiting outside included Sheriff Clark, his deputies, his volunteer segregationist "posse," scores of Selma bystanders, some sixty reporters, and Commander George Lincoln Rockwell of the American Nazi Party. In the standoff, while Baker transferred jurisdiction to Clark, Rockwell accosted King as a Communist and challenged him to debate. King agreeably offered Rockwell fifteen minutes to address the mass meeting that night, plus directions to First Baptist. That settled, Sheriff Clark's deputies herded the Negroes into the Lauderdale Street side entrance, past the registrar's office and outside again down into a secluded back alley. Reporters, quarantined by the posse on Alabama Avenue, saw King when he emerged to pursue the day's secondary goal of integrating Selma's public accommodations. Seven of eight tested restaurants served integrated groups that day, and King broke the color bar at the celebrated, antebellum Hotel Albert, named for Queen Victoria's husband but modeled after the Doge's Palace in Venice. Once registered, beneath grand carved arches in the foyer, he tried to break the tension of the milling crowd by addressing the white supremacists he had met at the courthouse. "You're still going to be with us tonight?" he asked.

"No, but I'd like to see you a minute," said James Robinson, of J. B. Stoner's National States Rights Party. When King approached, Robinson slugged him once in the face, knocking him to the floor, and kicked him once in the groin before A. D. King and Wilson Baker pulled Robinson away. (At the flash of violence, reporter Paul Good observed one excited white woman jump on a chair for a better view, shouting, "Get him! Get him!") Baker arrested Robinson. Stunned, King went off to rooms at the Albert with nine fellow guests, including Fred Shuttlesworth. He soon made light of the attack, but there was serious consternation in the Justice Department over the day's twenty-odd FBI monitoring reports indicating that King actually had invited firebrand American Nazis into an all-Negro mass meeting. When Rockwell appeared that night outside First Baptist Church with a small entourage, Selma police blocked the entrance. One of his followers objected, shouting, "Commander! Commander!"

"Commander, hell," growled Wilson Baker. "I'm the commander here, and your asses are going to jail." He arrested Rockwell and two Nazis, including the man who had appeared in minstrel blackface in the House chamber two weeks earlier, along with a J. B. Stoner ally from Birmingham. Stoner himself addressed a small rally that night outside Selma. Rockwell agreed to leave town the next day in exchange for dropped charges.

There was tension that first night of integration at the Hotel Albert. Judge Hare was furious that his injunction had been disregarded, and the Selma newspaper reported "rumblings of discontent that the sheriff and his force were displeased with police handling of the crowds." The city attorney ordered Baker to arrest Negroes when they marched from the church on Tuesday—not to support Judge Hare, he claimed, but to protect them from Sheriff Clark. "And charge 'em with what?" demanded Baker, who resisted being provoked to make illegal arrests in order to forestall something worse.

Movement leaders called on Tuesday for fifty jail volunteers willing to refuse an expected order to confine themselves in the back alley. When they held at proper intervals along Alabama Avenue, awaiting their turn in the registrar's office, Clark ordered their arrest. Deputies first hauled away SCLC's Hosea Williams and SNCC chairman John Lewis. The sheriff did not use his conspicuous cattle prod or nightstick, but he became agitated enough to seize Amelia Boynton by the neck of her dress coat and shove her roughly down the sidewalk in front of the assembled photographers. After that, deputies used the sharp jolt of cattle prods to herd the line back toward the county jail. In the noise and stumbling, teacher Margaret Moore stayed close to third-grader Sheyann Webb. "Don't be scared...," she told her. "Just stay close. Don't let go of my hand."

"It was no surprise to me," a triumphant James Bevel shouted at the Tuesday night meeting, that Selma authorities simply opened jail doors to free Sheyann Webb and several of the adult prisoners. "You see my contention is simply this," he said. "... The moment people want freedom bad enough to pay for it, they can get it. Y'all don't believe that." He predicted the movement would win the right to vote, "probably this year," and challenged the audience to prepare for hard responsibilities. "We could get the Negroes registered," shouted Bevel, "and then the white folks buy the votes for a pint of liquor!" Ralph Abernathy jumped up to propose Jim Clark as an honorary member of the Dallas County Voters League, now that the photograph of him manhandling Amelia Boynton was on the news wires.

Wilson Baker conceded the same point from the opposite side, denouncing Clark to reporters as "out of control." Selma's newspaper conceded that the remaining fifty movement prisoners were held under "Charges Named Later." If Clark had simply allowed the protesters to stand there unmolested one more day, Baker firmly believed, the frustrated registration drive would have moved elsewhere. King took an intermediate position between morale and results. Clark's oppression did raise spirits; more than two hundred marched to arrest on Wednesday in three waves, the first led by Rev. L. L. Anderson of Tabernacle Baptist. However, the movement also needed practical victories, and the hard reality was that not a single Negro who stood all day in the courthouse alley so much as *applied* for admission to the voting rolls, as the registrars managed to be occupied with others.

THAT WEDNESDAY, January 20, for the inauguration of President Johnson, 1.2 million people gathered on the Washington Mall, a mark that would stand above all capital occasions for at least three decades. The multitude was roughly four times the turnout for the March on Washington, and sixty times the frostbitten crowd of twenty thousand that had braved President Kennedy's inaugural address four years earlier. A White House briefer hailed "the first Inauguration where every operation was integrated from the church to the ballroom," and racial breakthroughs were absorbed in a landslide breadth of public optimism. Leontyne Price sang "America the Beautiful" at the formal swearing-in on the East Capitol steps. Roy Wilkins and CORE lawyer Floyd McKissick were among a dozen civil rights figures who took honored turns in President Johnson's reviewing stand for the inaugural parade. Bayard Rustin attended one of the gala balls, as did many leaders of the MFDP's ongoing congressional challenge: Fannie Lou Hamer, Edwin King, Victoria Gray, Aaron Henry, E. W. Steptoe, Annie Devine, and the irrepressible arson-and-ambush survivor Hartman Turnbow, who declared his ambition to dance with the Mississippi governor's wife. *Jet* reported King to be "conspicuously absent from all the inaugural ceremonies," in spite of invitations and Johnson's telegram encouraging him and Coretta to attend. "Informed sources" told the magazine that "the President was concerned about the arrest of 200 Negroes in Dr. Martin L. King Jr.'s voter registration drive in Selma."

With celebrations ended, President Johnson convened on Friday morning the first confidential working session of his full term. He told congressional leaders that the nation's worst problem was Vietnam, which he "wrestles with all the time, day and night." While the President did not describe the situation quite as gravely as Ambassador Taylor's secret summary earlier in January,* he did say it was not safe for the United States to mount air operations while dependent wives and children remained posted in Vietnam, targets for retaliation. Secretary of State Rusk disclosed that U.S. allies considered South Vietnam too politically unstable to risk helping. In reaction, Senator Russell Long of Louisiana advocated bombing North Vietnam, and Senator Everett Dirksen wanted to yank home the dependents of a "pampered" military mission. "Why do we have to send all our civilization to war?" he asked.

AFTER CLASSES in Selma, students raced to spread news that the first teacher was sighted at all-Negro Clark Elementary School, holding her toothbrush silently aloft as a badge of resolve. Inside, educators arrived in their best dress to review elaborate preparations and voted to release a few hardship colleagues from signed pledges on the carefully preserved scroll. The remaining 110 formed two abreast and exited the school in a solemn procession of teachers, thirty feet apart, past awed neighbors and clumps of students. Never before in the movement had there been a demonstration by the most vulnerable class of Negro professionals, all

---

* "We are faced here with a seriously deteriorating situation characterized by political turmoil, irresponsibility, and division.... We are likely soon to face ... installation of a hostile government which will ask us to leave.... There is a comparatively short time fuse ... we are presently on a losing track...."

of whom owed jobs to white politicians—not in Nashville, Jackson, St. Augustine, or Birmingham at its peak. Some were inspired by the example of Margaret Moore or the pep talks of their elected leader, Rev. F. D. Reese. Others were ashamed to teach civics when they could not vote themselves, or could no longer bear to scold absentee pupils who braved jail and taunted them as slaves.

FBI agents recorded that the head of the line reached the front steps of the courthouse at 3:24 P.M. Friday, January 22. School board president Edgar Stewart, a former FBI agent, confronted Reese there with word that the registrar's office was closed and that the teachers' written request to register after class had been denied. While Stewart and Reese politely debated whether it would injure or improve school relations for one or more teachers to walk past the closed office as a testament of desire to vote, Sheriff Clark muttered that the teachers were making a "plaything" of the courthouse. "You have one minute to get off these steps!" he told Reese. Clark led deputies with nightsticks in shoving the teachers down the concrete steps to the sidewalk. He then vanished into the courthouse, whereupon "Big Lester" Hankerson—the former seaport gangster who had surrendered his pistols to King in Savannah—supervised the teachers in collecting themselves and ascending the steps again in good order.

Twice more they returned after Sheriff Clark pushed them down the steps. The third time, with the sheriff threatening to arrest the whole group and the teachers clutching their toothbrush jail kits, a Selma lawyer pulled Clark inside the courthouse for precautionary consultations on what it might mean to incarcerate 95 percent of the Negro schoolteachers. The sheriff emerged more incensed than ever, and once more battered the line down the steps. Andrew Young stepped in to call a halt, saying their point was made, and the double column re-formed to march back up Alabama Avenue.

When they turned onto Sylvan Street, the FBI observers recorded, "three hundred Negro children and teenagers gave the returning marchers an ovation." Reese paraded his jubilant lines straight into Brown Chapel, down to the pulpit and around the perimeter aisles, as inrushing crowds began a spontaneous youth rally with the song "This Little Light of Mine." Teachers pinched themselves to prove they had gone through with it. Children hugged classroom taskmasters they had scorned as windbags. Movement veterans openly wept. Martin Luther King arrived to preach the first of two emotional tributes in two different churches that night, and Reese declared that if the teachers were not afraid to march for the right to vote, *nobody* should be afraid. The morticians began planning their own march to the courthouse. So did the barbers.

MALCOLM X, back from a speaking trip to Canada, fought off a Friday night ambush by three members of the Nation outside his home in New

York. On Sunday, he delivered a lecture about the lost cultural identity of Africans in America, partly by analogy with "lost sheep" and "dry bones" stories in the Bible. During the collection, he confirmed to a questioner that he had reacted strongly to a television news clip of the attack on Martin Luther King at Selma's Hotel Albert. "I saw the man knock him in his mouth," said Malcolm. "Well, that hurt me, I'll tell you, because I'm black and he's black—I don't care how dumb he is." He read a telegram he had dispatched to Nazi commander Rockwell, warning that he was "no longer held in check by Elijah Muhammad's separationist Black Muslim movement," and that he would arrange "maximum physical retaliation" upon anyone who attempted "harm to Reverend King or any other black Americans who are only attempting to enjoy their rights...."

"You and I will not get anywhere by standing on the sidelines, saying they're doing it wrong," Malcolm told his audience. After twelve years of "condemning everybody walking, and at no time were we permitted to get involved," he proclaimed freedom from artificial constraint: "Okay, I say let's get involved, but let's get involved all the way." He announced a general program to win voting rights by threat of execution. "Anyone who stops you from trying to register and vote is breaking the law," he said. "You can waste him. Yes, you can waste him, and there's nothing he can do about it." However, Malcolm perceived fresh obstacles in the way of actions or tactical experiments. On finances, he announced that the night's collection fell $15 short of the nightly rental due for the Audubon Ballroom. More ominously, he said, organizations trained for violence "will turn all of their anger against each other...." This was his own plight. "A very bad situation has set in and deteriorated to the point," said Malcolm, "where you have black people trying to kill black people."

OVER THE WEEKEND, when the death of Sir Winston Churchill dominated world news, U.S. District Judge Daniel Thomas of Mobile issued a court order in reponse to a lawsuit filed by Amelia Boynton and other Selma plaintiffs. The judge ruled that neither side in the voting rights conflict was behaving "in an orderly and effective manner," but his remedy offended all parties. Denouncing him as a "segregationist judge," James Bevel cited his exacting new requirement that applicants line up in the back alley toward Lauderdale Street, as Sheriff Clark desired, and he emphasized the new order's evasive silence on the core issues of pace and fairness in the registration process itself. On the other hand, Dallas County authorities felt betrayed by Thomas's legal finding of "unnecessary arrests" and his detailed rules to guarantee peaceful assembly. James Hare, the courtly but amiable local judge who freely exhibited his distinctive hobby—tracing local Negroes back to the bloodlines of specific tribes in Africa, so as to gauge genetic propensities for trouble or domestication—reacted testily to correction by his judicial friend from neighboring Autauga County. "I don't care what Judge Thomas ordered," Hare told visitors. "If there are any demonstrations in front of this courthouse . . . I have ordered the sheriff to put them in jail." Sheriff Clark bounced miserably between conflicting superiors in the political order. "Y'all don't treat me right," he told Judge Thomas.

By Monday morning, January 25, when Martin Luther King led 250 people down Alabama Avenue to the courthouse, prevailing local sentiment shifted in favor of Sheriff Clark against outside interference. Clark halted the long double column. Under the new rules from Judge Thomas —which specified that one hundred applicants be assigned numbered places in the alley toward Lauderdale—he requested that Chief Baker clear the city sidewalks of "demonstrators" in excess of the one hundred. When SNCC workers contested this interpretation, Baker ordered one dragged off to jail in the first such arrest by city police. Some of those behind stepped out for a better view of the commotion, which prompted Sheriff Clark to walk briskly down the line pushing strays back behind an imaginary half width of the sidewalk.

He ran into trouble from Annie Lee Cooper, one of the two women fired from Dunn's Rest Home for trying to register on Selma's first Freedom Day. Cooper told Clark not to twist her arm, then staggered him with several roundhouse blows. Hefty and berserk, she more than held her own for a time against officers who rushed to Clark's aid—"I probably hit those other deputies, too," she said later—and photographers arrived to shoot the moment when three deputies held her down for Clark to club her with his nightstick. Anger flashed among her compatriots in the line, but march leaders restrained them as officers hauled Cooper to jail in double handcuffs. "Don't bother with it!" shouted King.

That night, in the first mass meeting at Tabernacle Baptist Church since the Sam Boynton memorial service of 1963, speakers ardently fought the day's gloom. "They are not just running around harassing people for the fun of it," said James Bevel, who warned that opponents were trying to do two things: "discourage us" and "make discipline break down." Justified or not, any speck of Negro violence hurt the movement because "then they don't talk about the registration drive," said Bevel. ". . . We want the world to know they ain't registering nobody!" Reverend Anderson presented the incident as both a shortfall in nonviolent devotion and a communal sacrifice by Cooper, who "took a beating today for you and for me." He coaxed an offering from the crowd with a vivid description of her whipping—"If *that* doesn't make you want to give five dollars, you're not worth a dime"—then presented Martin Luther King.

King preached for nearly an hour. He exhorted the audience to remember that Selma was the "proving ground" for a larger movement that would spread through Alabama and beyond. He played to their mirth over opinion surveys showing that race problems had ended with the civil rights bill. He tried to present the day's setbacks as proof that the opposition was desperate, then speculated on the twin effects of guilt. "I have a psychological theory," he said, that guilt has "a constructive angle, and that is, it causes you to repent, makes you penitent . . . and mend your evil," but also makes you "drown the guilt by engaging more in the very act that brought on the guilt. That's what's happening to some of our white brothers." They would revert to compulsive hatred "to try to provoke violence in us," he predicted, and urged Tabernacle listeners to resist with love.

"I'm not talking about emotional bosh," said King. In a reprise of his early sermons, he described the semantic differences between the three Greek words for love, illustrating romantic *eros* with soaring recitals of poetry by Poe and Shakespeare that titillated, impressed, and finally delighted the crowd into punctuating shouts of approval. ("You know," King said impishly, "I can remember this because I used to quote it to my wife when we were courting. That's *eros.*") Setting aside also the friendship devotion of *philios,* he preached on *agape* as the heart of nonviolence. "Theologians would say that it is the love of God operating in the human heart," he declared. ". . . You love every man because God loves him. . . . I think this is what Jesus meant when he said Love your enemies. . . . Love is understanding, creative, redemptive goodwill for all men."

King recalled stories of the movement's darkest hours. "It's still midnight in Selma," he said, but they would persevere no less than their slave forebears who had absorbed to their bones the despairing question "Is there no balm in Gilead?" from the Bible. "They did an *amazing* thing," cried King. "They looked back across the centuries and took Jeremiah's question mark and straightened it. . . . In one of their great spirituals, they could sing, 'There IS a balm in Gilead, to make the wounded whole. . . .' " He preached to climax from the song.

Then Anderson brought on Ralph Abernathy, who pronounced himself dissatisfied that only half the crowd stood for his entrance. "I don't believe in half doing anything . . . not even for myself," he scolded. "Now when I come, you don't have to stand up . . . but if you're going to stand up, stand up! So everybody stand up!" As usual, Abernathy galloped straight for earthy relief. "You may as well get ready and fasten your seatbelts," he said. ". . . They are against us. They are against us because we are black. They are against us because they don't want us to vote." He acted out a dialogue between a grizzled sharecropper and a plantation owner shocked to be called by his first name after the Freedom Riders came through Mississippi. "No, I am not sick," Abernathy's sharecropper said finally. "They have told us, John, that I'm just as good as you, and you are just as good as I am. So I want you to know, and I want you to tell Ann, that from now on it isn't gonna be any 'Mr. John' and 'Miss Ann.' In fact, it's not gonna be 'Miss' anything. It's not even gonna be Mississippi. It's just gonna be plain old 'Sippi'!"

Abernathy's comic delivery had the church howling with laughter as he called for them to send a message to Sheriff Clark and Wilson Baker that "the Negroes are not afraid." He paused curiously to tap the tiny police microphone attached to the pulpit: "This is the doohickey?" He examined the device, then leaned over to address it intimately. "And I want *you,* doohickey, to tell 'em...." A cascade of guffaws drowned him out. "You go places we can't go!" shouted Abernathy. "And will you tell the good white folk of Selma, Alabama, that we are not afraid?"

Abernathy complained about having to walk downtown in supervised pairs. "Now doohickey, this is not right," he said archly, and he described how "the man" had separated him from Dr. King that day. "And then they *put* me," he cried, rising to prissy indignation, "beside somebody I didn't even *want* to walk beside." Abernathy mined an orator's gold with his prop. He made friends with it ("Now little doohickey, I *hope* these few words will find you well"), engaged it in raucous inquiry about whether "some of the people in Selma are backward and dumb," and finally shared his messenger with the crowd. "They have a rumor out that only a few Negroes want to be free," he declared. "And we are *all* gonna talk to this doohickey tonight. You see, we've got to let 'em know.... Now before we'll be slaves we'll be what? *Talk* to the doohickey!"

SCLC's Charles Fager witnessed this mass meeting, a month after his first. "People held their sides and wiped their eyes," he wrote. "They had never seen anything like it." Police discontinued church microphones as not worth the embarrassment, but Wilson Baker ordered the arrest of thirty "excess" registration applicants on Tuesday.

KING LEFT SELMA for Atlanta, where prospects for his Nobel Prize dinner had lurched back and forth in a hushed civic opera. Addressing reluctant business executives caucused at the all-white Piedmont Driving Club, Coca-Cola president Paul Austin had declared, "Fellas, the boss wants this dinner." He referred to Coca-Cola chairman Robert Woodruff, who was generally revered and obeyed as Atlanta's "Mr. Anonymous Donor," and publisher Ralph McGill of the *Atlanta Constitution* confidentially praised Woodruff for recognizing that "he has to sell Coca-Cola all over the world." Still, ticket sales stalled. When Granger Hansell, an attorney for the *Constitution,* criticized his friend McGill for sponsoring the dinner, McGill tried to deflect suggestions of abnormal interest. "I don't agree with everything about Dr. King," he wrote, and he denied another correspondent's suspicion of frequent contact: "I have seen [King] only three times and then casually."

An executive of First National Bank organized a rare revolt within Atlanta's business leadership, urging friends to make sure Atlanta "ain't having no dinner for no nigger," but this effort backfired with the December 29 *New York Times* account of resistance to the King tribute. The city's most prominent banker, Mills Lane, circulated word that he was not the story's unidentified "banker." The *Constitution*'s lawyer, Granger Hansell, changed his mind about buying tickets, and such sales were a hopeful breakthrough for the novel coalition behind the drive: McGill, Benjamin Mays of Morehouse, Rabbi Jacob Rothschild of Atlanta's Temple, and Archbishop Paul Hallinan (who had sponsored King's visit with the Pope), with an interracial workforce mostly of women. "We'd keep meeting down in this basement of this church," said Helen Bullard, Mayor Ivan Allen's political strategist. Allen confessed bitterness about the temporizing of his fellow patricians about the banquet. "Most of you will be out of town or sick, and you'll send someone to represent you," he acidly told one group. "Don't let it worry you, though. The mayor will be there."

FBI officials worked surreptitiously against the tribute. When Ralph McGill attended the Johnson-Humphrey inauguration on January 20, Assistant Director William Sullivan made another clandestine plea for the *Constitution* to brand Martin Luther King a degenerate. Sullivan reported with almost certain distortion that McGill agreed with the FBI position in every respect—". . . regrets greatly that a banquet is being given in King's honor . . . believes that the very best thing that could happen would be to have King step completely out of the movement and out of public life. . . ." In a further Machiavellian twist, headquarters sent a dispatch to the White House that presented the FBI as the passive recipient of an anti-King diatribe on McGill's initiative. McGill "would have liked to convey this message to the President in person," Hoover wrote on January 22, the day the teachers marched in Selma, but he "asked that his views be transmitted to the President by the FBI."

In Atlanta, ticket sales to whites remained slow until the NBC *Nightly News* broadcast a preview of the dinner as a test of Atlanta's reputation for flagship optimism in the South. The evening's image flickered from stigma to pioneer bravery, and rumors of scarce tickets caused a stampede. A vice president of First National Bank ordered twenty tickets. Some latecomers tried to buy entire reserved tables to guard against interracial seating, only to be told of a free-mix policy to discourage enclaves. Even so, swamped organizers sold 1,463 tickets—two hundred above capacity for the Dinkler Plaza Hotel ballroom—and turned away nearly four hundred more at the door on Wednesday evening, January 27.

The night's challenge switched from numbers to nerves. Arriving guests kept watch over their shoulders. "We could get shot, bombed, whatever," recalled Sam Massell, a future mayor of Atlanta. There were fears of Klan demonstrators outside and social disaster inside, until the meal broke tension at mixed tables. "You know how when Southerners have good manners," said the beaming Helen Bullard, "they *really* have good manners." Ralph McGill saluted King as one who "helped us all to realize the power in our Judaeo-Christian heritage, resident but unused," and who "saw clearly . . . that a studied and sane solution could only be brought to bear by committed and disciplined persons." Euphoria took hold through songs and toasts. Mama King kept saying to herself, "To think that this could happen in our lifetime!" Rabbi Rothschild presented King with an engraved Steuben bowl, and King lifted the crowd to standing applause with variations on his Nobel homecoming speech: "I must return to the valley." He did not mention Selma.

"Dear Boss," wrote an immensely relieved Mayor Allen to Coca-Cola chairman Woodruff, enclosing a positive editorial from Philadelphia as "the type of comment that I think we received over most of the country." For King, the Nobel interval lasted only until the next night's staff review concluded that the Alabama voting rights campaign was stalled. They had the beginnings of a movement, but all their labors had opened the registrar's office to a mere fifty-seven Negro applicants in January, all of whom were rejected. King agreed with staff recommendations to step up pressures, as in Birmingham two years earlier, and resolved to go to jail Monday in Selma.

40

Saigon, Audubon, and Selma

HUYNH THI YEN PHI, a seventeen-year-old Buddhist girl, died by self-immolation on the seventh day of renewed hunger strikes against the anti-Buddhist South Vietnamese military. Within hours, Vietnamese officers overthrew their floundering civilian government in favor of General Nguyen Khanh, carrying out the coup threat that had so infuriated Ambassador Maxwell Taylor in December. Bulletins on these violent disorders flashed across the international date line on January 27, the Wednesday of King's banquet in Atlanta, and landed on the front page of the same day's *New York Times* along with a reaction speech by Richard Nixon. "We are losing the war in Vietnam," declared the former Vice President, who predicted that "we will be thrown out in a matter of months" unless the United States adopted a strategy to "end the war in Vietnam by winning it." Nixon prescribed a vigorous application of naval and air power to "quarantine" the battle zone.

America's three top national security officials brought a grim Wednesday morning assessment to the White House residence, where President Johnson, a week after his inauguration, was recuperating from one of his chronic bouts with fever and chills. (Lady Bird Johnson's diary recorded that her husband had "sweated down two or three pair of pajamas" Tuesday, his first night home from the hospital.) Defense Secretary Robert McNamara and National Security Adviser McGeorge Bundy handed Johnson what McNamara later called "a short but explosive" joint memorandum, warning that "our current policy can lead only to disastrous defeat." On that much they agreed with Nixon, but they dismissed as political pabulum his statement that boats and bombs could deliver victory without significant American casualties. Their hope was that U.S. bombing of North Vietnam might rally a unified fighting spirit in South Vietnam.

Secretary of State Rusk narrowly disagreed. He opposed the bombing as a misguided reward for bad behavior by the unstable South Vietnamese government, saying the move would likely draw Americans into greater military responsibility. In December, U.S. policy had promised such bombing explicitly, contingent upon long-demanded reforms, but now Bundy and McNamara proposed to put the bombing first. The South Vietnamese "see the enormous power of the United States withheld," their memo stated, "and they get little sense of firm and active U.S. policy. They feel that we are unwilling to take serious risks." As Rusk argued for the advisory status quo because "the consequences of both escalation and withdrawal are so bad," they argued for bombing to stave off expulsion from South Vietnam "in humiliating circumstances."

President Johnson heard an hour's debate on his "fork-in-the-road" options, then promptly dispatched Bundy to Vietnam for close-hand inspection. Bundy plunged into a cauldron of political intrigue. The Buddhist demonstrations were the most severe since those preceding the coup against President Diem in 1963. Ambassador Taylor explored ways to overthrow the coupmaker, General Khanh, on intelligence that Khanh was sounding out truce prospects with the Vietnamese Communists. Bundy tried to restrain Taylor, saying Khanh was "still the best hope" for stability, but subordinate generals, led by Nguyen Van Thieu and Nguyen Cao Ky, were plotting against their chief on the strength of the American disfavor. "The current situation among non-Communist forces," Bundy cabled the President from Vietnam on February 4, "gives all the appearances of a civil war within a civil war." Taylor, warned by Senator Robert Kennedy of rumored schemes in Washington to make him the scapegoat for American failure, replied to Kennedy: "No good general should ever get himself in such a situation, but here I am—looking more and more like General Custer."

MALCOLM X flew to Los Angeles on Thursday, January 28, in hopes of reviving the paternity suits against Elijah Muhammad. Gladys Root, the lawyer he had retained the previous year, told him her two balky plaintiffs were at once intimidated by and dependent upon the Nation. They moved from house to house, dodging threats—a bomb had gone off nearby—and yet they still lived off informal child support payments from the Muslim treasury. Malcolm volunteered to support them in open court with testimony that Muhammad had cynically scorned and banished the mothers of his illegitimate children, and asked anxiously whether Root might have told anyone of his visit. He said hostile Muslims were following him already. "If these cases aren't hurried, I'll never be alive," he told her.

Fearing a stakeout, Malcolm had Evelyn Williams and Lucille Rosary spirited through Los Angeles to meet him at the Statler Hilton Hotel—only to discover Minister John X, Captain Edward X, and a dozen men from Temple No. 27 deployed through the lobby. Malcolm's party bluffed its way into his room, where he tried to calm the plaintiffs. The two former secretaries slipped out well past midnight, and Malcolm X called his ally Wallace Muhammad in Chicago with an urgent request to meet the next day. Wallace opposed the idea as too dangerous. Because he supported the paternity suit against his own father, in part to punish the emotional cruelties inflicted upon his mother, Clara Muhammad, Wallace himself was skirting retribution. With the Nation inflamed against Malcolm and him as leading "hypocrites," Wallace doubted that it was wise for them to associate on the Nation's home turf in Chicago.

Malcolm made a run for the airport on Friday morning with two carloads of Muslims in pursuit. "They had gotten so insane," he said later, "that they chased me right down the Hollywood Freeway in broad daylight." Malcolm pointed a cane out the window as though it were a rifle. He had spurned any thought of asking Chief William Parker or the LAPD for protection, because of mutual hostilities that overrode even this emergency, but he did rush to airport security officers with a plea for help. While they hid him, one of his escorts ventured out with officers and identified Muslim soldiers posted along the concourse—including Robert 20X Buice and other defendants from the Ronald Stokes shooting of 1962, whom Malcolm had stood by ever since. Security officers escorted Malcolm X surreptitiously through the basement baggage room. Once he boarded by way of a hidden stairwell, unobserved from the concourse, airport officials emptied the plane for a bomb search, and TWA flight 26 left for Chicago two hours late. The local FBI had time to place an informant into the adjacent seat, to whom Malcolm straightforwardly explained his dilemma. "Malcolm declared that the teaching of Islam in the NOI [Nation of Islam] is becoming less and less, and that it is becoming a hate organization," stated the post-flight surveillance report. "... He remarked that if 200 people were guarding him, they will still try to kill him because they are so devoted to Elijah Muhammad they would jump into fire if he ordered it."

At Chicago's O'Hare Airport, waiting to meet Malcolm's flight, Assistant Attorney General Richard Friedman and an associate were surprised by the sudden appearance of six officers from the intelligence unit of the Chicago police department, who had been alerted to the commotion in Los Angeles. The two groups exchanged enough about their respective missions to join forces, and when they had safely removed their quarry to a hideaway suite in the downtown Sherman House, Malcolm arranged a clandestine meeting with the reluctant Wallace Muhammad. He explained to Wallace that the two lawyers were defending the State of Illinois in the federal lawsuit filed by an inmate named Thomas X Cooper, who, since conversion to the Nation of Islam while serving consecutive one-hundred-year sentences for two murders, had been suing for the right to practice religion inside Stateville Prison at Joliet. Malcolm was bargaining over his potential testimony as a surprise state witness. He wanted protection. He wanted a safe forum to prove his own case against Elijah Muhammad. In return, he would support the Illinois position that Cooper deserved no rights of worship because Elijah's Nation was a bogus religion.

Negotiations consumed ten hours over three days, with Malcolm moving in fits between the lawyers and Wallace Muhammad, who felt betrayed. Wallace said Malcolm's purpose had changed from reform to destruction. Malcolm replied that he and Wallace had been trying to get into court for a year to expose Elijah; this was their chance. They could build Islam without the Nation. Wallace replied that Malcolm himself had come to Islam through the Nation's racial furies, and warned against a trapdoor bargain with Illinois authorities that had confined Cooper to isolation cells since 1957—forbidding him to receive Islamic material by mail, meet with a Muslim chaplain, or even read the Q'uran. The Illinois lawyers, for their part, said Malcolm's desperate plight proved that the Nation was a cult of riot-prone, racist fanatics. They could not understand why Malcolm so valued the opinion of the reserved and unknown Wallace.

On Saturday, January 30, Malcolm broke away to tape a television interview on *Kup's Show*. The host, Chicago columnist Irv Kupcinet, remarked that Malcolm seemed to have changed from the "stormy individual" of previous appearances, who "hated all whites, you said."

"I've gotten older," said Malcolm. He answered questions about hatred in race relations and his abandonment of "white devil" theories, saying that while no one could use him as a tool against Elijah Muhammad, he would never shrink from the truth. "To have gotten weak for a woman is one thing," said Malcolm. "It is human, and it is natural. But after getting weak and completely destroying her reputation, to do nothing whatsoever to protect her as a woman, then he is not a man. And to commit murder and to see followers line up to kill each other and to mutilate each other, then this is not a man."

Kupcinet asked whether Malcolm wished to apologize for insisting in the past that the Nation practiced true Islam.

"No, I won't apologize, Kup, for this reason," Malcolm replied. "You see, I don't think the burden is upon any black man in this society to apologize for any stand that he takes.... Most of us are attracted to things extreme, primarily because of the extreme negative condition that we live in."

Malcolm departed the studios of WBKB-TV in an unmarked police car with two detectives and the two Illinois lawyers. A van swerved to the curb across their path. Two bow-tied Muslims jumped out, and a dozen others converged before the six Chicago policemen from the trail car ran up with drawn pistols to disperse them. The lawyers directed the officers to let them go, intent on resuming talks with Malcolm X, and were soon astonished that the attackers regrouped to chase the official convoy through the streets of Chicago.

Malcolm left for New York on Sunday. The lawyers believed they had his commitment to return for their February 22 trial date.* Malcolm promised Wallace Muhammad that he made no such deal. Two nights later, by the count of an FBI report, "nine or ten members" of Captain Joseph's enforcement squad confronted with rifles a like number of Malcolm's escorts outside the *New York Daily News* Building, separated by "a large number of New York City police officers." The next day, Malcolm escaped into the Deep South for the first time in nearly five years. Newspapers reported his destination variously as Tuskegee, Montgomery, and Selma.

Elijah Muhammad also was maneuvering into Alabama through his lawyer, Chauncey Eskridge, who had won from the U.S. Supreme Court an order for the pending trial on the prison rights of Thomas X Cooper. He sent Eskridge secretly to visit his other client, Martin Luther King, in Selma, with instructions to propose a summit meeting. King was a "hard working man," Muhammad told Eskridge, but he "just needs to be put on the right track" by someone old enough to "show him the rough and smooth spots." Muhammad wanted to make news with King before Malcolm did. He offered to pay King's way to Phoenix or Chicago if he was short of cash. Any meeting of the two—even a handshake introduction— would be a "bombshell" upon the white devils, he told Eskridge, like the conversion of Muhammad Ali.

NEWS FROM SELMA forced Eskridge to cancel his trip. King rallied volunteers in two mass meetings Sunday night, and on Monday morning, February 1, told an assembly at Brown Chapel that nearly seven hundred people were leaving another church to launch the first Freedom Day in Perry County, thereby expanding the movement to a neighboring courthouse. "I think this is most significant," said King, "and it reveals that we are going all out." He announced that Selma's young people were gathered in a third church nearby, preparing to follow the adult march with one of their own. "Even though they cannot vote, they have a right to make their witness," King declared, "...that they are determined to be freed through their parents." He called forward Reverend Reese among the local leaders, and summoned Bevel to give "final instructions" about how to march together

---

* *Cooper v. Pate* would result in a mixed decision. Cooper won the right to attend Muslim services and receive some religious mail. Illinois won the right to keep him segregated from non-Muslim prisoners.

this time in continuous rows. "So we are about to move now," King shouted above a crescendo of clapping and freedom songs.

"At approximately 10:42," recorded FBI observers, King led "a group of Negroes, estimated at two hundred sixty four," out of Brown Chapel and down the middle of a deserted Sylvan Street, in a tactic designed to ensure arrest by Wilson Baker instead of the hot-tempered Sheriff Clark. Baker intercepted the line half a block away. Hoarse with laryngitis, he asked King to break up into small groups as before, and retreated when King insisted that the parade ordinance should not interfere with the right of petition. Two blocks later, Baker placed the entire line under arrest. He permitted a kneeling prayer, herded the prisoners upstairs to intake cells at the City Hall building, then tried to send King and Ralph Abernathy away. Their unexpected reemergence from the building attracted reporters who puzzled over a King arrest story that seemed to be fizzling. "And he said we could not come in," King told them with a shrug. "They were full and we could come back." Within minutes, when the potential embarrassment of the sidewalk press conference exceeded his desire not to have King in his jail, Baker sent officers to retrieve the last two prisoners.

Cheers erupted when they passed through the gray metal door into a ninety-foot-long holding tank. King and Abernathy made their way around the perimeter catwalk, listening to sad stories and alibis from the prisoners in cells along the exterior walls, shaking hands through the bars. Among those newly arrested, SCLC staff member Charles Fager heard King suggest a "Quaker-type meeting" rather than a speech by himself. Abernathy read from Psalm 27 in his pocket Bible ("The Lord is my light and my salvation; whom shall I fear?"), and speakers held forth between freedom songs. Jailers soon transferred the recognizable leaders, including King, to smaller cells downstairs, and then King was summoned to Baker's office along with young SNCC staff member Frank Soracco.

Baker said he was worried about the schoolchildren, as Sheriff Clark had just arrested nearly five hundred of them. Most were being released to parents pending trial, but some were being bused to a state prison farm. Baker appealed to King to protect the children by sending them back to school where they belonged. Burly and amiable, Baker quoted scripture, snacked incessantly, and offered them nips from his office stock of bourbon. When King made friendly conversation but declined the suggestion, saying the young people must be part of an overall settlement, Baker returned him and Soracco, who had barely spoken, to a cell.

Only six months after attending a California school forum on Mississippi, Soracco found himself across from King inside a Selma jail. After two weeks in daily demonstrations, he had learned to tape thick newspapers inside his pant legs to reduce the bite of cattle prods and winter chill. He was known for having been spared on one previous arrest by an accident. As county deputies had closed in upon him and a SNCC companion inside the jailhouse elevator, their cattle prods ignited a book of matches in the companion's back pocket, causing a ruckus that spoiled their intent. Soracco ate the jail meals as King fasted for two days. King seemed preoccupied, and refused to leave when Wilson Baker enticed him to do so, but advised Soracco to go. "You're not going to do any good in here," King told him.

Front-page headlines in the *New York Times* were keeping count: "Dr. King and 770 Others Seized" on Monday, and "520 More Seized" on Tuesday after more marches led by Hosea Williams. Five hundred students went to jail Wednesday morning at the Perry County courthouse in Marion (pop. 3,800), thirty miles northwest of Selma, after an Alabama state trooper told SCLC's James Orange, "Sing one more freedom song and you are under arrest." Sheriff Clark hauled away three hundred more in Selma on orders from Judge Hare, prompting Wilson Baker to try to make light of dragnet fever among his hard-line rivals in the county government. "The sheriff is in charge of the courthouse," Baker told reporters, "... but if any of [the prisoners] try to escape, we're going to let them."

King was settled with Abernathy in an eight-foot cell. Before a visit from Andrew Young on Wednesday, writing on Waldorf-Astoria stationery left over from the Nobel Prize homecoming in New York, he composed a dozen political directives "to keep national attention focused on Selma." On word that local leaders were asking Alabama congressmen to investigate conditions in Selma, King instructed Young to jump on the idea by publicly inviting a broader congressional task force. "By all means don't let them get the offensive," he wrote. Young emerged from jail in a hurry. He assigned directive number five ("Keep some activity alive every day this week") to Bernard Lafayette, who was in town from Chicago. On number three, Young called Clarence Jones and others to clarify the President's responsibility to enforce voting rights under the Fifteenth Amendment.

Before the end of the day, Lee White advised President Johnson that Young was relaying three requests from King: that Johnson send an emissary to Selma, make a statement of support for voting rights in Alabama, and take legislative and executive steps to secure those rights. White reminded the President that Justice Department lawyers were consulting Judge Daniel Thomas over a new order that might speed Negro registration, and recommended that Johnson have him deflect Young with a reply that the administration was taking appropriate steps already. "An alternative which King will probably find unsatisfactory," White advised, "would be to refer the call to the Attorney General."

SNCC staff member Prathia Hall arrived late at the nightly strategy session Wednesday in Selma. She reported that two hundred parents had gone to jail in Marion to protest the arrest of five hundred children earlier in the day, and that unlike Selma, where most youth prisoners were quickly released on bail or truancy orders, Perry County had stuffed several hundred young prisoners into a fifty-by-sixteen-foot stockade. Hall said that pastor J. T. Johnson and movement leader Albert Turner had wept in the mass meeting over brutal conditions: prisoners crammed on bare concrete, provided water in "number 3 tubs" from which they were obliged to drink "like cattle or with their hands." Disputes broke out among the Selma staff over whether to address these sufferings or fill the jails still more.

Fay Bellamy and Silas Norman missed the stormy meeting for their own private mission to Tuskegee Institute, some seventy-five miles east of Selma on Highway 80. With three thousand students squeezed into the aisles and window casements of Warren Logan Hall, they heard Malcolm X lecture on racial imagery in international relations. If the United States only spent "some of its time getting peace, freedom, and justice for Negroes," said Malcolm, it would "win the whole world with freedom." Afterward, Bellamy and Norman pushed their way through to introduce themselves, and Bellamy inquired about a mutual acquaintance. "How is Viola?" she asked. "What is she doing?"

"She's not doing anything," Malcolm replied. "She *ought* to be down here in the South doing work like you." This response greatly pleased Bellamy and Norman, who were well aware that Malcolm had disparaged civil rights organizations. They were emboldened to invite him to visit their movement the next day, and soon talked their way into rooms near Malcolm's at the Tuskegee guest house.

Startled FBI agents observed Malcolm X arrive in Selma at 9:47 the next morning. He disappeared into the pastor's study at Brown Chapel, where reporters were soon banging on the door. They eventually gained admittance for a brief press conference at which the first question was, "Why are you here today?" followed by, "Are you in agreement with Dr. King's nonviolence?" and "Are you saying that nonviolence ought to be abandoned in Selma?"

Malcolm artfully dodged. When the reporters left, a spokesman followed them to announce nervously that Malcolm would not be addressing the crowd now swelling in the sanctuary to launch the morning demonstration. This decision caused protracted staff debate in the pastor's study. Norman defended SNCC's invitation to Malcolm. Bellamy said he would make light bulbs go off in young people's heads. Andrew Young and others objected that more than light bulbs might go off in volatile Selma. When they pressed Malcolm on what he would say about nonviolence, he replied that he reserved the right to stomp on the toe of anyone who stomped on his first. Bernard Lafayette objected that a toe-stomping war in America would ruin Negroes and enlighten no one, but said he trusted the audience to see that for themselves. Some proposed limitations on what might safely be said, which prompted Malcolm to observe that "nobody puts words in my mouth." He smiled, seeming to relish how much his presence panicked the SCLC executives. They decided to cushion his remarks by slotting him between their two best nonviolent speakers, Fred Shuttlesworth and James Bevel, then sent for Coretta King and Juanita Abernathy, who were in Selma to visit their husbands, as emergency peacemakers for any incitements.

In his speech, Malcolm ranged from the Congo to slavery's lingering caste distinctions between house servants and field servants. "I'm a field Negro," said Malcolm. "...If the master won't treat me right and he's sick, I'll tell the doctor to go the other way." Still, he offered no tactical advice for the Selma movement. "I'm not intending to try and stir you up and make you do something that you wouldn't have done anyway," he said, to applause and a chorus of laughter.

"I pray that God will bless you in everything that you do," he continued. "I pray that you will grow intellectually, so that you can understand the problems of the world and where you fit into that world picture. And I pray that all the fear that has ever been in your heart will be taken out." When he finished, Malcolm retreated to the church office during a debate on what his presence threatened or promised for Selma. Diane Nash Bevel came to sit with him, expressly to apologize for local ministers who were denouncing him as a traitor to nonviolence. She told him she found nothing in his remarks that undermined or demeaned her own commitment. Those who practiced nonviolent discipline never demanded it of others, she said, and many of the ministers did not understand nonviolence themselves. Soon after, Malcolm told Coretta King that he had hoped to visit her husband and assure him that he meant to aid rather than hinder his cause, but he had to rush off to a conference in London. An FBI observer recorded that a car bearing Malcolm X drove away at 12:40 P.M. for the Montgomery airport, less than three hours after arriving in Selma.

Not all the day's events reached King quickly in jail, where he was still writing directives and random thoughts ("Segregation is the invention of a god gone mad"). Wilson Baker raised the pressure of isolation by refusing visits that day by Coretta and Shuttlesworth. King's writings reflected no notice of Malcolm's visit to Selma, nor any awareness that President Johnson at a late morning press conference had overruled his protective aides to make precisely the announcement King requested. ("I should like to say that all Americans should be indignant when one American is denied the right to vote," Johnson declared for the next day's headlines. "...The basic problem in Selma is the slow pace of voting registration for Negroes....") On the other hand, Baker made sure King did learn of Judge Thomas's latest federal decree, which at midday formally suspended a version of the Alabama literacy test, ordered Selma to take at least one hundred applications per registration day, and guaranteed that all applications received by June 1 would be processed before July. This new ruling threw movement aides into new consternation. They canceled afternoon demonstrations to study it, having suspended morning ones in the tempest over Malcolm X. Jailers presented the moratorium to King as confirmation of an effective settlement.

Cut off in his cell, King was skeptical. He wrote instructions for Andrew Young to "call Jack tonight" with a request that the head of the NAACP's Legal Defense Fund, Jack Greenberg, come to Selma to evaluate the Thomas order. "Also please don't be too soft," he wrote. "It was a mistake not to march today. In a crisis we must have a sense of drama. Don't let Baker control our movement." His notes ranged from grand strategy to deadlines for the church bulletin that would specify Sunday's preacher at Ebenezer. Other nagging worries remained off the page. There was an audit that week in which IRS agents hoped to make King pay gift tax on speaking fees he routinely endorsed to SCLC.* He was embroiled in a dispute between the national teachers' unions, because Bayard Rustin had signed King's name to ads supporting Albert Shanker's American Federation of Teachers. Above all else King hated jail, which revived his bouts of self-reproach and depression. He decided to post bond the next afternoon.

On Friday morning in Selma, when Rev. C. T. Vivian led a march to test the effect of the new Thomas order, Sheriff Clark arrested the line of seventy-four people on Judge Hare's ruling that since the registration office was not open, the vigil was a nuisance in contempt of his court. At noon, when a second march of 450 young people met the same fate, an exasperated Wilson Baker promised discipline against an officer who had hurried the arrest line by firing his revolver. Meanwhile, local officials refused new petitions for the county to open the registration office more often than every other Monday.

At 1:12 P.M., King emerged blinking with Abernathy from the Selma jail. One enthusiastic welcomer left a smudge of lipstick on his heavily stubbled cheek, but six members of King's own Research Committee expressed dismay by telephone over his decision to post bond. Meeting just then at Harry Wachtel's office on Madison Avenue, they pointed to the ad published that morning in the *New York Times:* "...THIS IS SELMA, ALABAMA. THERE ARE MORE NEGROES IN JAIL WITH ME THAN THERE ARE ON THE VOTING ROLLS...." Committee members, already peeved to have had no chance to improve what they saw as a knockoff of the famous Birmingham letter, said King's untimely exit spoiled its impact. Similarly, they said, the fifteen members of Congress whom they had mobilized into Selma for a dramatic afternoon jail visit

---

* Unknown to King and his managers, the new in-house accountant they relied upon to contest this audit was an FBI informant, James Harrison. Bureau officials, needing to preserve their only live source planted inside SCLC, overlooked his minor embezzlement of SCLC funds, and Harrison, as revealed by historian David Garrow, would remain until 1971 a paid informant of modest use to the FBI.

were milling around instead in the chaos of King's homecoming at Amelia Boynton's house, their mission overshadowed. The advisers said a man in King's position could not come out of jail for nothing.

"Why not?" asked Andrew Young from Selma, pleading that King was depressed and needed freedom like anybody else. Nevertheless, the Selma camp was convinced that King must make a statement of purpose coming out—just as he had done going in. Otherwise he would look aimless, or observers might conclude that he accepted the Thomas ruling. They lit on the idea of saying that King had come out of the Selma jail to meet with President Johnson. Young called a press conference for three o'clock at Brown Chapel. Wachtel volunteered to notify the White House.

By the time Lee White returned Wachtel's calls to ask whether it was too late to stop the announcement, Wachtel said that the Selma news was being cranked already into tomorrow's front-page headlines: "Dr. King to Seek New Voting Law/Freed Integrationist Will Fly to Capital Monday." White responded with a tempered version of Johnson's furious response. "Where the hell does he get off inviting himself to the White House?" Johnson had shouted at White, who told Wachtel that they now faced a "lousy situation" caused by "grandstanding" on the part of King. Wachtel gamely defended the initiative as legitimate politics, and plunged into grueling negotiations that went on all weekend. White said Johnson expected to be tied up all day Monday in the National Security Council, which Wachtel resisted as an excuse until he heard the news bulletins about Vietnam. He told Clarence Jones over an FBI wiretap that while he hated to see such a crisis, at least it meant that Lee White might not be lying.

At his press briefing on Saturday, February 6, Press Secretary George Reedy made front-page news by disclosing the administration's intent to offer a "strong recommendation" for voting rights legislation before the end of 1965. He straddled questions about whether President Johnson would accommodate or refuse King on Monday, when alarms reached the White House in mid-afternoon (before dawn Sunday, Vietnam time) of a disaster near the mountain village of Pleiku. Guerrillas had overrun Camp Hollowell, a fortified barracks of U.S. Army Special Forces, killing eight, wounding more than a hundred, and destroying ten aircraft on the ground. The shock of a strike on Americans galvanized official Washington, and President Johnson convened the 545th meeting of the National Security Council at 7:45 P.M. that evening. From Saigon, over secure phone lines, Taylor and Bundy were recommending retaliatory bombing raids. McNamara distributed contingency orders for 120 planes to hit four installations in North Vietnam. When polled by President Johnson in the Cabinet Room, all grimly concurred except for Senate Majority Leader Mike Mansfield, who said that the local population in South Vietnam "is not behind us, else the Viet Cong could not have carried out their surprise attack." The President overrode Mansfield behind a consensus that the United States could not sit still for such treatment.

Journalists compiled an hourly "chronology of the crisis" on Sunday —not only in Washington, where President Johnson ordered the evacuation of all two thousand U.S. dependents from Saigon, and McNamara delivered a crisp briefing on the airstrikes with a map and pointer, but also in South Vietnam, where Bundy, described by the *New York Times* correspondent as "hatless, tense and pale," flew by helicopter to visit the devastation at Pleiku and to a field hospital that lacked enough beds for the incoming wounded, including a gravely injured West Point major who told Bundy, "That's the breaks."

Aboard *Air Force One,* heading home from his fatefully timed mission, Bundy solidified the resolve of the "fork-in-the-road" memo ten days earlier. He wrote a memorandum recommending an air and naval campaign of *"sustained reprisal* against the North," not limited to specific incidents such as Tonkin Gulf. "We emphasize that our primary target in advocating a reprisal policy is the improvement of the situation in *South* Vietnam," he wrote, explaining: attacks on the North would depress morale of Vietcong guerrillas in the South ("This is the strong opinion of CIA Saigon"), and raise morale of South Vietnamese allies behind U.S. initiative. "We have the whip hand in reprisals as we do not in other fields," Bundy argued. Still, he confessed doubt as to whether sustained reprisal could prevent Communist victory. "What we can say," he concluded, "is that even if it fails, the policy will be worth it." His flight reached Washington in time for Bundy to give President Johnson the report before he went to bed Sunday night.

MARTIN LUTHER KING was in Atlanta. He had rushed to catch up with his lost week in Alabama—first speaking in Marion to encourage the new movement there, which was battered, then meeting late into the night with leaders of the movement in Selma, which was tired. He had dispatched Andrew Young and James Bevel to see if they could open a supporting front in nearby Lowndes County, made hasty arrangements to throw together a registration march in Montgomery, and then gone home to preach at Ebenezer. All the while, Harry Wachtel was reporting that the Pleiku crisis had stirred the Johnson White House into a "hornet's nest" over his public quest for an appointment. The most Wachtel could wheedle from Lee White was an offer that if King would settle for Vice President Humphrey on Tuesday, the President might "spontaneously" invite him by for a chat—provided that King kept the plan strictly secret. White insisted that Johnson would renege upon the first hint of advance publicity. King first held out for Monday, pleading commitments in Montgomery on Tuesday, but backed down when aides streamlined his schedule with charter flights. Wachtel and Clarence Jones negotiated a press release on the

Humphrey appointment, which King released late Sunday from Atlanta. Unbeknownst to them, White was recommending that Johnson not see King at all.

On Monday, in Selma, James Bevel led fifty volunteers into the courthouse to confront a symbol of the new procedures established under the Thomas court order: an "appearance book" on a hallway table outside the registration office. Victor Atkins, chairman of the Board of Registrars, informed him that while the office was closed that week, aspiring voters could guarantee a future place in line by signing the appearance book at any time. After Bevel objected that the Thomas order was a sham reform, marchers filed by the appearance book without signing, and followed Bevel outside to form a line of silent vigil. There were three visiting whites among them, two Unitarian ministers from Boston and a Catholic theologian from New York. Some marchers held signs calling for more registration days. Sheriff Clark came outside "shaking with anger," observed the *New York Times* correspondent, that these people would spurn the county's concession. "You're making a mockery of justice!" Clark shouted at Bevel, jabbing him backward down the courthouse steps with his billy club. A deputy attacked Ivanhoe Donaldson at the rear of the line. When the marchers refused to disperse, Clark hauled all fifty upstairs so that Judge Hare could impose five-day contempt sentences for disturbing his courtroom. The local *Times-Journal*, in its first notice of violence against demonstrators, reported that "Bevel was roughed up somewhat" and that others on the way to the county jail "were jabbed by deputies carrying electric cattle prods."

At a Monday night rally in Montgomery, King urged citizens to join him "by the thousands" for a mass voter registration Tuesday morning, but fewer than two hundred showed up to march out of his former church home on Dexter Avenue. The meager turnout was embarrassing, although King knew that infighting had long since withered the local spirit of the bus boycott. Hosea Williams tried to convince reporters that his own poor staff work was to blame. At a press conference, running late for his midday charter flight, King conceded the existence of voter apathy among Negroes, then rushed off with Bernard Lee, Andrew Young, and James Forman of SNCC. In Washington, they gathered late Tuesday afternoon with Harry Wachtel and a swelling entourage in Vice President Humphrey's office, where Attorney General Katzenbach and his staff lawyers joined the discussion on what kind of legislation might break down political barriers to Negro registration in the South. Former MFDP counsel Joseph Rauh submitted a rough draft of a bill. Lee White arrived from the White House next door, having informed President Johnson that King had kept silent as promised. As time passed, White parried anxious looks from Wachtel about whether Johnson would honor his reciprocal pledge.

The President was in a crisis briefing, the first of a series that would bring members of Congress in groups of thirty or so almost daily. Undersecretary of State George Ball, substituting for Dean Rusk, who was ill, described the Vietnam conflict against the sweep of Chinese history. "We can't forget that during the first thousand years of the Christian era, Southeast Asia consisted of vassal states of China," he said, adding that in the present century the dominant geopolitical force in Asia combined a Communist revolution at its "raw, primitive, expansionist state" with the "imperial drive of a proud, arrogant, gifted people." Unless the drive could be "checked in South Vietnam," Ball warned, "sooner or later there will be an overrunning of the whole of Southeast Asia by Red China," with a corresponding withdrawal of American power that would shake confidence from New Delhi and Tokyo to Berlin. "And in the long run," Ball concluded, "the stakes here are very simply the question of the expansion of Communist power both from Peiping and from Moscow. And I think that our options are very limited."

President Johnson followed by introducing McGeorge Bundy as a witness fresh from his transpacific return. Bundy conceded a strong adverse tide while insisting that "the situation is by no means finished business." To the positive headlines from his public comments the previous day ("Bundy Gives an Optimistic Report on Vietnam"), he added a report from the battle zone. "I met no American and no Vietnamese who did not think that the will and power and determination of the United States itself were perhaps the most important variable of all in this effort," he said. Bundy emphasized that McNamara and he had made their crucial Vietnam recommendations before Pleiku. President Johnson resisted congressional entreaties to arouse the public against the Vietnamese adversaries, for fear of a war stampede.

In Humphrey's office, secretaries at last interrupted with word that the President was calling. Humphrey took the telephone briefly and then excused himself to answer a summons to the White House, triggering panic in those who were aware of the scripted plan. Lee White chased after Humphrey, who had simply forgotten, and the Vice President returned to invite the entire group along to see the historic rooms outside the Oval Office. President Johnson emerged for handshakes, then whisked King and Lee White away to discuss politics. Ten minutes later, King did not give waiting reporters the statement drafted for him by the White House ("We all appreciate the heavy demands on the President's time . . ."), but neither did he disclose Johnson's comments. Choosing a middle course, he spoke about his own suggestions for a voting rights bill, and shaped front-page news by referring to the President's commitment to take action.

THAT TUESDAY, February 9, French security officials detained Malcolm X on arrival at Orly International Airport and expelled him two hours later as an "undesirable." They announced that his scheduled lecture at the

Salle de la Mutualité in Paris might "trouble the public order." Malcolm arrived seething in London, protesting that French authorities "would not even let me contact the American embassy." He expressed shock to be branded an outcast abroad, where he had enjoyed refuge from close dangers at home.

The next day, Malcolm delivered a furious lecture to a packed hall at the London School of Economics. He attacked as "absolutely unnoticed" the clandestine warfare waged by Western powers in Africa for colonial and neocolonial regimes—"American planes with American bombs being piloted by American-trained pilots, dropping American bombs on black people...." He said the United States was paying salaries to puppet presidents and employing mercenaries from apartheid South Africa. "Which means," he added with sarcasm, "that I come from a country that is busily sending the Peace Corps to Nigeria while sending hired killers to the Congo." The student crowd laughed. They applauded when he said that an independent Congo might topple Portuguese colonies in Angola and Mozambique, and bring pressure even against the white bastion of South Africa. They cheered when he predicted the demise of Ian Smith's unpopular white supremacist government, which was defying Britain's grant of independence to the colony of Southern Rhodesia (now Zimbabwe). "And you can't win in the Congo," said Malcolm. "If you can't win in South Vietnam, you can't win in the Congo."

He paused to scattered snickers. "You think you can win in South Vietnam?" he asked. "... The French were deeply entrenched in Vietnam for a hundred years or so. They had the best weapons of warfare, a highly mechanized army, everything that you would need. And the guerrillas came out of the rice paddies with nothing but sneakers on and a rifle and a bowl of rice—nothing but gym shoes, tennis shoes.... They ran the French out of there. And if the French were deeply entrenched and couldn't stay there, how do you think someone else is going to stay there who is not even there yet?" Guffaws over the shoe image competed with catcalls ("Shut up!") and derisive comments about the flat presumption that English-speaking superpowers would fare no better than the French.

Malcolm turned his lecture inside out on the consuming subject of hatred. A conqueror's image of Africa had infected 100 million people of African descent in the West, he said, "and in hating that image, we ended up hating ourselves without even realizing it." He teased Britain for producing the common Jamaican immigrant "running around here trying to outdo the Englishman with his Englishness." He scoffed at affected innocence. "Some whites have the audacity to refer to me as a hate teacher...," he said. "In America, they have taught us to hate ourselves. To hate our skin, hate our hair, hate our features, hate our blood, hate what we are. Why, Uncle Sam is a master hate teacher, so much so that he makes somebody think he's teaching love when he's teaching hate. When you make a man hate himself, why, you've *really* got it going." The audience erupted in laughter.

By FBI count, 161 students filed out of Brown Chapel for Selma's Wednesday afternoon march, walking silently in small groups to comply with the city parade ordinance. Once safely past Wilson Baker to the courthouse sidewalk, they pulled from their clothing small signs ranging from "Let Our Parents Vote" to "Jim Clark Is a Cracker." Sheriff Clark, under community pressure to try smothering the protest with nonreaction, permitted the group to stand unmolested, but he waved up two yellow buses to strategic spots that concealed the pickets from reporters stationed across Alabama Avenue. His obvious sensitivity prompted the students to detach roughly half their number around the corner to the Lauderdale Street sidewalk. Clark countered by moving one of the buses to block sight of them, which excited press interest in what the Selma paper called "a ludicrous game of 'hide the demonstrators.' " The sheriff withdrew to confer with legal advisers in the courthouse.

Clark emerged at 2:54 P.M. with a new plan. "Move out!" he shouted to the students, and his deputies herded them eastward in single file down the middle of Alabama Avenue. They crossed Broad Street and passed the City Hall jails. When students asked where they were going, deputies called out, "You wanted to march, didn't you?" At Sylvan Street, instead of left toward Brown Chapel, Sheriff Clark turned the line right at a trot, down to a road that ran out of town along the bend of the Alabama River. Some deputies applied billy clubs and cattle prods to move the students along, while others brought up cars so that Clark and the others could ride alongside the flanks at a pace stepped up to a full-blown run past the Cosby-Carmichael gravel pit.

At a creek bridge two miles up River Road, Clark posted a rear guard to block press photographers and private vehicles. Ahead, clumps of students began bolting into fields where pursuit was difficult. Some stopped to vomit. At a federal hearing on whether Sheriff Clark had violated the injunction to keep constitutional order around the courthouse, Letha Mae Stover would testify that she fell out and told a deputy that it would do no good to keep punching her in the back. The whole line of students was collapsed or dispersed within a mile of the creek bridge, and Clark returned to announce with a wink that he had been marching the students under truancy arrest six miles to the Fraternal Order of Police Lodge, his jails being full, when they "escaped."

There were overflow mass meetings Wednesday night, at which Silas Norman vowed to rise up against Sheriff Clark's cattle drives for children, and King reported firsthand that Selma already made President Johnson "aware of our groans...aware of our yearnings." Then, in a midnight strategy session at the Torch Motel, SNCC leaders challenged King's pained recommendation to drop Bevel's boycott of the appearance book. King called it a small positive step. Ivanhoe Donaldson called it an empty promise from the federal courts, objecting that ordinary citizens still had to walk past cattle prods to get into the courthouse. King said the movement needed relief from adverse press about the boycott, such as the AP story "Negroes Don't Know What They Want." SNCC leader Courtland Cox said the appearance book offered no hope to illiterate Negroes who could not sign it. When King and Andrew Young advocated resting Selma with dramatic moves into other counties, "in order to get a registration bill passed," arguments broke out over who should speak for local people in strategic decisions. L. L. Anderson and F. D. Reese, the only Selma speakers recorded in the minutes, complained of efforts to exclude them because they were preachers.

Before dawn, the SNCC caucus voted to end the boycott of the appearance book after all, saying they wanted every chance to gain enough votes to drive Sheriff Clark from office. King left for Montgomery to catch an early morning flight for fund-raising speeches in Michigan. He called Clarence Jones from the road, asking for speech drafts against what he called a "deterioration" in Negro-Jewish relations, and vented himself on the growing animosity of SNCC leaders. He told Jones it was the same as Albany in 1962, when they charged that he skimmed publicity off their groundwork. The most hostile ones were those who spent the least time in Selma, he said. They were irrational, and had "no sense of political timing." Whereas he bit his tongue, King complained, they were carrying their bitterness to an eager market in the press.* Jones calmed him by volunteering to ask Harry Belafonte to moderate another truce meeting.

Conflicting passions fell hardest upon Diane Nash Bevel. Her husband was running a fever inside the county jail. Prisoners sent word that his outspokenness and shaved head made him a special target for deputies who had hosed down his cell in the February cold. She had supported Bevel's boycott of the appearance book at the Torch Motel, worrying out loud about setting a precedent for rural counties of high illiteracy, but she endured looks from friends who knew how openly Bevel was flouting their marriage. He excused serial rascalism behind a bluster of nonviolent theory. Hatred and violence sprang from the want of love, Bevel preached. He claimed that he gave and received abundant energy by resolving these "contradictions" in his bed. Unabashed, he seduced more than one movement wife while her spouse, his bosom colleague, was in jail.

The forced march of children compounded strains across town. Judge Hare's pressure to resume mass arrests collided with growing opinion that

---

* A *Washington Post* essay that week featured youth charges that King "tries to solve racial problems in a 'hit-and-run' fashion...too often settles for tokenism...goes to jail but doesn't stay very long...is too inflexible...."

polite segregation worked better than cattle prods, and a passionate editorial urged citizens to restrain senseless hard-liners "playing to a worldwide audience."* Wilson Baker, who had smuggled SNCC workers beyond the creek barrier to retrieve injured students, saying, "I'm human, too," threatened to arrest Clark himself if he lost his temper again. However, Baker warned that he would kill any students who dared to disturb Mrs. Baker by picketing near his home.

On Thursday morning, when movement spirits rallied behind a student march four times larger than Wednesday's, Nash desperately tried to rescue Bevel after a doctor at the jail diagnosed his fever as viral pneumonia. She called reporters and badgered Selma officials until she secured his transfer to segregated Berwell Infirmary, where she and Bernard Lafayette were stunned to find Bevel shackled to a hospital bed with a sheriff's deputy guarding the door. Now she hounded the Justice Department by phone, as during the Freedom Rides of 1961, and secured letters that the shackles violated hospital procedures even for murderers. Her crusade pushed Sheriff Clark into a concession before dawn on Friday. He ordered the irons removed, then collapsed early that morning of chest pains, later diagnosed as exhaustion. The front page of Saturday's *New York Times* featured a photograph of SCLC worker Richard Boone in a Bevel-style skullcap outside the white hospital, Vaughn Memorial, with movement students kneeling in prayer for Clark's recovery. "Thus ended," reported the *Times*, "the fourth week of street demonstrations protesting barriers against Negro voting in Alabama."

FOR TWO DAYS in Atlanta, Bob Moses again refused pleas to address SNCC's future course. Some 250 staff members, nearly half from Mississippi, had gathered in the old chapel pews of Gammon Theological Seminary for freedom songs mixed with often raucous debates among ardent newcomers and weary or jail-damaged veterans, with more than a little drinking in the wings. Ella Baker announced that someone had stolen valuables from her satchel. John Lewis and the leadership first pushed through a statement of identity: that henceforth the basic unit of SNCC would be the paid staff member, superseding the campus-based coordinating committees from the sit-ins. Structurally, this meant that SNCC could be governed by majority vote instead of brotherhood consensus, which favored the ambitions of James Forman and others to build a disciplined political "field machine." Forman hailed the decision as a "working-class victory" over dreamy self-sacrifice. Most of the field staff sprang from the poor of the South, which made the focused constituency a runaway hit with all SNCC's factions—"floaters" and religious purists, as well as

---

* "We are on the brink of a decision," declared editors of the *Selma Times-Journal*, "as important a decision as ever faced the citizens of this or any city."

Forman's "hard-liners." Speakers championed them in language destined to spread across the political spectrum. They castigated liberals as treacherous or naive, and rejected as misguided SNCC's history of appeals to a just national purpose in the federal government.

Jesse Morris, a staff worker from Mississippi, formally proposed that the governing executive committee be restricted to black Southerners without a college education, which touched off six hours of heated argument late Friday night, February 12. Forman called the debate "stormy, even traumatic, and at times totally confusing." Some ridiculed SNCC for limiting its own franchise; others shouted that SNCC should make good on rhetoric about giving local people the power to be free. Fannie Lou Hamer questioned the deeper meanings of prestructured votes, saying, "I just don't understand." Several hours into the fracas, Morris brought forward a dozen newcomers from Mississippi, saying he had bolstered their courage with whiskey to prove that unlettered people could speak effectively before large groups. The qualifications issue remained unresolved when Moses at last stepped forward.

"I have a message for you," he said quietly. "I have changed my name. I will no longer be known as Bob Moses." These words caused an electrified hush in the chapel.

He said they should go back to the Morris proposal, which highlighted their direction. "If you want to keep a man a slave, then give him the vote and tell him he's free," said Moses. "If you vote for that executive committee and don't stay here to work out the programs, then don't tell me you're free." It might take five months or five years, he said, but they would not give the time. The real program would be left as usual to the dominant officers and dialecticians, the very people whom the enshrined but intimidated field staff could not address without the fortification of alcohol.

"I am drunk," said Moses. Though he clearly was not, he acted out stumbles and slurs while delivering a poetic reverie on symbols of power and spirit in a democratic movement. Moses said people in SNCC faced so many paradoxes to keep hold of themselves in a whole world gone mad like Mississippi, which feared nonviolence as murder and excused murder as order. He talked of growing up in Harlem under family stress so severe they had to call an ambulance for his mother, and recalled hearing his father scream at the doctors, "She's not crazy! She's not crazy! *You're* the ones who're crazy!" He said years later they had picked up his father, raving on the street that he was the actor Gary Cooper, and had taken him to Bellevue Hospital for extended psychiatric treatment. He told stories of his father loving the whole family very much.

Moses looked up. "I want you to eat and drink," he said. He solemnly passed around a block of cheese and a jug of wine. Wordless, some pretended to drink after the jug was empty. "Some of you need to leave," said Moses. They were becoming creatures of the media, contending for power, and to avoid all that he was adopting his mother's maiden name. "From now on, I am Bob Parris," he said, "and I will no longer speak to white people."

He left the chapel before anyone could respond. "Did he mean it?" someone whispered. Interpretations ranged from sacramental cleansing and mental breakdown to staged parody. Some thought he was abdicating his name and place because of the suffering he felt he left too close in his wake. Others thought it was brilliant, and ran off to see whether he would answer to Parris. The former Bob Moses never attended another SNCC meeting.

MALCOLM X returned home late Saturday from eight days in Europe. A neighbor called in a fire alarm at 2:46 A.M. the next morning, February 14, saying that noises of breaking glass awakened her to flames in the house across the driveway. The first Queens fire truck arrived at 2:50 A.M. to find Malcolm on the front sidewalk with a .25-caliber pistol, having hustled barefoot in underwear out the back door with his pregnant wife and four daughters, aged six months to six years. In the cold, four-year-old Qubilah complained of tear holes in her pajamas. Nearly an hour later, Malcolm returned inside with fire inspectors to retrieve a few clothes and his "insurance" tape recordings from the attic. He deposited his family with friends and caught an early morning flight to Detroit.

He was intent on keeping his schedule, in part because he needed the speaking fees. FBI sources reported that his Detroit hosts summoned doctors with sedatives that made Malcolm sleep most of Sunday, and observed him receive backstage a bonus collection of $200 to help replace smoke-damaged clothes. In daily speeches that week, he made passing references to his desperate plight—hotly denouncing conspiracy theories that he had firebombed his own home,* and wishing out loud for a truce. ("Elijah Muhammad could stop the whole thing tomorrow, just by raising his hand," he declared. "Really, he could.") However, Malcolm curtailed public remarks about an internecine war too obscure for his audiences, and delivered instead sweeping statements of credo. "I have to straighten out my own position, which is clear...," he said. "I don't believe in any form of discrimination or segregation. I believe in Islam. I am a Muslim. And there's nothing wrong with being a Muslim.... Those of you who are Christians probably believe in the same God." He lectured on racialism he found pervasive, from congressional committees and judges to commanders "dropping bombs on dark-skinned people" in Asia, and by contrast he belittled the celebrated new civil rights law that left the federal

---

* Before his death decades later, while still insisting that Malcolm deserved punishment for defying Elijah Muhammad, Captain Joseph conceded that Malcolm had nothing to do with setting the fire. "I *know* he didn't," Joseph declared. "I'll say that much."

government still powerless to protect Negroes seeking the right to vote in Alabama. "Think of this," shouted Malcolm. "Those school children shouldn't have to march." He advocated world recognition and perspective for a race problem "so complex that it was impossible for Uncle Sam to solve it himself."

Over the weekend in Selma, secret talks at the Hotel Albert produced a deal whereby Wilson Baker granted a parade permit for Monday the fifteenth—the second and last courthouse registration day of the month— and movement leaders in return agreed to confine their ranks to voting-age adults. The permit secured a record turnout of some fifteen hundred, stretched nearly ten blocks from the courthouse on Lauderdale Street. More than four hundred of these signed the appearance book for a future place in the registration line; ninety of those with early numbers completed applications to register. After classes, Selma's Negro schoolteachers marched to the end of the line. Thirty laborers filed in behind them in uniforms reading, "Henry Brick Company." Eight hundred students paraded by in salute.

Reporters followed when King broke away to the neighboring county seat of Camden, where he walked along a line of seventy aspiring registrants from Gee's Bend—mostly Petteways, from the extended rural clan that had first tried to register with Bernard Lafayette in 1963. Asked how they were faring, Monroe Petteway told King, "I filled out the form like I have three times before, but I can't get nobody to vouch for me." Under Alabama law, a new voter had to obtain a signed reference from one current voter in the county, and there were no registered voters among the Negro majority in Wilcox County. King led observers across the courthouse lawn to ask Sheriff P. C. "Lummy" Jenkins whether he would vouch for Monroe Petteway, and Jenkins replied that doing so would not "look right" for him in local politics. King's roving party drove back to Selma by way of Marion, where "about 150 Negroes were so inspired by Dr. King's visit that they refused to leave the courthouse at the end of the day," reported the *New York Times.* Deputies shoved them out with nightsticks after dark.

When the registration board closed the appearance book for lunch on Tuesday, C. T. Vivian tried to lead a line of Negroes inside the courthouse to seek shelter from the rain. Sheriff Clark blocked him with a row of deputies who shoved the line down the steps Vivian kept climbing, preaching defiantly, until one of them slugged him in the mouth. They hauled him away, bleeding. By the time King tried to visit Vivian that afternoon at Good Samaritan Hospital, he had been treated and removed to the county jail. Nuns crowded around King in the white habits of the Sisters of Saint Joseph, eager to pose one by one for pictures. King tried to visit Vivian in the county jail, but was refused. That night, over vehement security objections from the staff, he addressed a voting rally in the rural wilderness of Gee's Bend. There were late-night arguments about why no one could find a church in Lowndes County willing to host a mass meeting.

Tensions rose on both sides. Segregationist sentiment shifted against the spectacle of authorized Negro marches, while movement leaders chafed over the negligible return in actual registered voters for so much effort. The Citizens Council published a full-page ad comparing the Communist party's racial equality platform of 1928 with the Civil Rights Act of 1964, ending, "The similarity will certainly shock you." Editors of the *Selma Times-Journal,* who had upbraided Sheriff Clark for violence, warned in a front-page editorial that the tolerant attitudes of the past month— "the ultimate expression of good faith by our white citizens"—were at risk because "outside forces" and "showmen" under King had pushed "all sound-thinking citizens perilously near the breaking point." King, meanwhile, took ill with a fever. Chicago's *Daily Defender* ran a banner headline: "Virus Fells King." An FBI wiretap picked up Ralph Abernathy borrowing $500 from Harry Wachtel, saying King was sick and "completely broke." On his way to Atlanta for home rest, King stopped by the Wednesday night mass meeting at Brown Chapel. "Selma *still* isn't right!" he cried, in a speech reporters called his strongest to date. "We must engage in broader civil disobedience to bring the attention of the nation on Dallas County," King declared. "It may well be we might have to march out of this church at night...."*

At a strategy meeting of white people that night in Marion, irate sentiment prevailed to the extent that two substantial citizens were shouted down and physically assaulted for suggesting negotiations with local demonstrators. Perry County officials called upon Alabama state troopers for reinforcements, and sheriff's deputies arrested SCLC project leader James Orange Thursday morning for contributing to the delinquency of young marchers. In response, Albert Turner of the Perry County Voters League urgently sought a big-name movement speaker from Selma to build the crowd for an evening mass meeting. He requested C. T. Vivian, whom Judge Thomas had just ordered released. Vivian replied that he could not risk jail again, being on weekend duty in King's absence, but he finally agreed to drive over for a quick sermon. His audience overflowed Mount Zion Baptist, a small clapboard church off Marion's courthouse square. The much-discussed plan was to walk to the jail less than a block away, sing a freedom song for the incarcerated James Orange, and disperse.

---

* FBI headquarters was preparing for distribution among intelligence agencies the next day a jaundiced interpretation of recent wiretaps: "The naked boldness of King's egotism is vividly reflected in his pronouncements about the movement needing a leader (obviously King himself)." Director Hoover wrote on the report, "Also to Watson," meaning that a copy should go to the new White House security aide, Marvin Watson.

It was a quick but dangerous venture in view of the darkness. Network news correspondents told their crews to return film cameras to their cars, so as not to provoke the hostile crowds milling outside. C. T. Vivian, who slipped out a rear door into a waiting car, noticed on the drive to Selma a number of flashing police lights speed by in the opposite direction.

At 9:30 P.M., Albert Turner and Rev. James Dobynes of Marion led four hundred people two abreast from Mount Zion. They proceeded less than half a block before halting at a blockade of state troopers and other law enforcement officers. Over a bullhorn, Police Chief T. O. Harris ordered the marchers to disperse or return to the church. When Reverend Dobynes knelt to pray before retreat, a state trooper struck him in the head with a club and two others dragged him by the feet toward jail. Reporters, confined across the square, heard struggles in the darkness. Network news correspondents instantly sent crews to retrieve cameras, but bystanders clubbed down NBC's Richard Valeriani with a severe head wound before they returned. Bystanders also beat two UPI photographers, destroyed their cameras, and sprayed the lenses of arriving film crews with black aerosol paint. No photographs survived. Streetlights went dark, and *New York Times* correspondent John Herbers reported by ear: "Negroes could be heard screaming and loud whacks rang through the square."

Only the first quarter of the march line had left the church. Those who fled back inside collided at the door with those rushing outside to see the commotion. Panic drove the ones trapped outside to flee toward buildings behind the church. Fifty state troopers overtook many of them, including eighty-two-year-old Cager Lee, who stumbled bleeding into Mack's Cafe to find his daughter Viola and grandson Jimmy Lee. In utter chaos, some troopers chased two dozen marchers into the cafe while ten others pushed inside to chase them out. They expelled one crippled customer unharmed, overturned tables, smashed lights, dishes, customers, and marchers. The cafe owner saw troopers attack Cager Lee again in the kitchen. For trying to pull them off, Viola Jackson was beaten to the floor. Her son Jimmy Lee Jackson lunged to protect her. One trooper threw him against a cigarette machine, another shot him twice in the stomach, and then they cudgeled him back outside toward the bus station, where he collapsed. Jackson was the only gunshot victim among ten Negroes who were hospitalized. Several others lay injured in jail, including George Baker, an SCLC volunteer from Illinois. Reporters on the Marion square were surprised to come upon Sheriff Clark among the officers imported from other counties. He quipped that things had been too quiet for him in Selma.

King wired Attorney General Katzenbach from Atlanta late that night: "This situation can only encourage chaos and savagery in the name of law enforcement unless dealt with immediately." Katzenbach replied the next morning that an FBI investigation was under way. At the White

House, Press Secretary Reedy mildly told reporters that the President was keeping informed. The *Alabama Journal* of Montgomery reacted more intensely, calling the Marion attack "a nightmare of State Police stupidity and brutality." In Marion, all-day church services offered prayers for the recovery of Jimmy Lee Jackson—a twenty-six-year-old pulpwood worker, high school graduate, youngest deacon at Saint James Baptist Church, who had applied for the vote five times without success. In Selma, where Jackson was under treatment at Good Samaritan, Hosea Williams collected all potential weapons down to pocket combs and preached a congregation at Brown Chapel into a frenzy for a Friday night march on the courthouse. Wilson Baker stopped him on the church steps to warn that troopers and hotheads and assorted posses were spoiling for night violence downtown. He argued for postponement to protect the town and the marchers themselves, but Williams—glassy-eyed—shouted that he had given himself over to march. Baker had him arrested instead, to the relief of some terrified movement people standing uncertainly behind.

ADAM CLAYTON POWELL had the misfortune to pick that Thursday, February 18, to launch an update of his 1960 speeches on police corruption in the New York rackets—"naming the places and the numbers," asking why "police officers can receive $3,000 per drop in Harlem every month and to whom does it go." Having just lost an appeal to the Supreme Court of the $210,000 Esther James libel judgment, he asked the House of Representatives to "forget about Mississippi for a while." His legal predicament guaranteed more press but no more respectful attention, and Powell was swamped by bigger news from Vietnam to Harlem.

Minority Leader Everett Dirksen set the tone that day for the first bruising Senate debate about Vietnam. On behalf of President Johnson, he rebuked Senator Frank Church of Idaho as a "sunshine patriot" for a lengthy address in which Church, citing a lack of strategic interest or political support in "these former colonial regions," had argued for negotiated withdrawal. ("As the beat of the war drums intensifies, and passions rise on both sides," said Church, "I recognize that negotiation becomes more difficult.") Dirksen bemoaned "a chorus of despair sung to the tune of a dirge of defeat." He said he was "grieved but not surprised" to hear in the Senate chamber, "which echoes with the courageous words of brave men now gone, the opinion that we cannot win...." George Smathers of Florida among other senators rose to support him. "To negotiate in South Vietnam while Communist aggression is spreading...," Dirksen declared, "is like a man trying to paint his front porch while his house is on fire."

At the White House, President Johnson was hosting another congressional briefing on Vietnam. As usual, he spoke convincingly of his personal worry over the safety of each American pilot in the recent air retaliations. ("I stay awake all during the night to see whether my planes come back or not.") When asked, "what's necessary to win that war," Johnson told them confidentially of his consultations on Wednesday with former President Eisenhower. "I asked him how he settled Korea," he said, and repeated Eisenhower's response that he had forced the North Koreans to bargain by aerial punishment. "There are no sanctuaries," Johnson said, affecting Eisenhower. "I am going to bomb wherever I damn please. And we been spending a lot of money on bombs for a number of years, and there is no use of having them if you don't use them." Johnson said the air attacks would be fitting, they would be measured, they would be adequate. He said that if the other side would pull back, he would withdraw U.S. forces "tomorrow morning," as quickly as he had evacuated dependents the previous week. Until then, his course would be fixed by guerrilla attacks at Pleiku and since. "I decided if they were going to get real rough and tough and come into white men's barracks and start picking out our own units in our own compounds in our own billets," he said, "those men had no business with the women and children around. I'd better get them on home, because this is going to be choose up and the winner take it. And that's what we've done."

Under general orders approved February 13, long-range bombers and carrier supports were converging upon the South China Sea. On Friday the nineteenth, one day before the regimen of sustained reprisals was scheduled to begin, South Vietnamese army units arrested General Nguyen Khanh in another coup. The unwelcome news and giant headlines ("Khanh Is Deposed") intruded upon a White House ceremony at which Johnson announced that Head Start, a preschool experiment, would begin hurriedly that summer as the first initiative of his War on Poverty. He swiftly approved Ambassador Taylor's cabled recommendation that airstrikes be postponed "in view of the disturbed situation in Saigon." Saigon plots and counterplots carried into the next week what Taylor secretly called a "condition of virtual non-government," rendering impossible any concurring go-ahead from South Vietnamese allies. On Thursday, February 25, Ambassador Taylor put Khanh on an airplane into exile, securing replacement leaders who would last until June. Final bomb clearance began promptly the next day under the code name ROLLING THUNDER, taken from the theme hymn of the Billy Graham revival crusades. By the time the air war ended after eight years, divided almost evenly between Presidents Johnson and Nixon, "the United States had dropped on North Vietnam, an area the size of Texas, triple the bomb tonnage dropped on Europe, Asia and Africa during World War II," according to Vietnam historian Stanley Karnow.

Also, on Friday, February 26, the President ordered the first two American combat battalions to South Vietnam. The military request for ground protection around the Danang air base had been pending four days. On the Monday it arrived, at the height of reported pandemonium in Saigon, Johnson dictated aboard the White House helicopter a candid draft response to questions about his spiritual life: "Now I pray several times a day, but I don't seem to get any answer."

"THE AIR was heavy," Captain Joseph said later. One of his soldiers said the Harlem temple felt the fury of the Chicago hierarchy over its prolonged failure to get rid of the hypocrite. One of his lieutenants said many distant captains and security officials rolled into New York over the last weekend before the Nation's annual Chicago convention. National Secretary John Ali checked into the Americana Hotel on Friday the nineteenth. Ranking ministers added presence. Minister Louis X of Boston presided at the Newark Mosque No. 25, and Newark Minister James Shabazz anchored No. 7 in Harlem.

Malcolm X knew of the pressures to expunge all blemishes before the convention. He made and canceled trips, applied for a gun permit, called a Thursday press conference to decry a blurred circle of enemies, including the French government. He laughed when a friend advised him to call the police. On a Thursday evening radio show, Malcolm complained that "when I jump out and say that somebody is trying to kill me, the implication is given that I'm trying to do some publicity seeking, or that I'm just making these stories up." On Friday, Malcolm told *Life* photographer Gordon Parks that he had been a "zombie" in the Nation. "It's a time for martyrs now," he told Parks, "and if I'm to be one, it will be in the cause of brotherhood."

On Saturday night, a secretary and four members from the Newark Temple No. 25 bought tickets to a dance at the Audubon Ballroom in Harlem, paying special attention this time to the windows and exits. They returned together in a Cadillac across the George Washington Bridge for Malcolm's announced Sunday afternoon rally, and, being from Newark, passed unrecognized by the ushers and bodyguards who had defected with Malcolm out of Temple No. 7 in New York. All five counted their lives as nothing beside the saving power of Elijah Muhammad. The driver sat toward the rear of the four hundred folding chairs, which were more than half filled. The secretary sat in the front near his three gunmen.

Malcolm X paced backstage. He had changed his mind and asked Betty to hasten from temporary lodgings on Staten Island with their daughters. He berated associates for allowing order to slip away. The guest speakers were not there. The promised platform was not ready. He rejected the comforting touch of his aged Islamic tutor, Sheik Hassoun, and angrily threw everyone out of the dressing room. Benjamin 2X managed a warm-up speech about mischarted history, telling how Columbus thought his voyage landed in China, then brought Malcolm on stage to prolonged applause.

As the crowd answered the Islamic greeting, the Newark driver tossed a smoke bomb and jumped up to accost a pretended thief. "Get your hand out of my pocket!" he shouted. Heads turned to the diversion. "Hold it!" said Malcolm. The three gunmen crouched forward within fifteen feet of the stage. "Hold it!" shouted Malcolm. One of two deafening shotgun blasts ended his life, and extra pistol shots were lost in shock that turned to guttural screams and the crash of chairs thrown at the escapees. Witnesses seized only one of the five assassins, Talmadge X Hayer, in a doorway leading out to 166th Street.

KING ISSUED a statement from Atlanta: "I am deeply saddened and appalled to learn of the brutal assassination of Malcolm X." On Monday in Selma, he and L. L. Anderson joined arms with seventy-two-year-old Elizabeth Hill to lead a march of the elderly that added 205 names to some two thousand already on the appearance book. He visited Jimmy Lee Jackson at Good Samaritan, drove to address the stalwarts at Mount Zion in Marion, and returned to find the mass meeting at Brown Chapel surrounded by state troopers. Twenty of them circled King's car, asking why their colleagues were unwelcome in the church sanctuary. King replied that movement meetings were open to everyone—he would look into it. The confrontation attracted reporters on the run. State investigator Bob Godwin demanded to know why King was critical of troopers and Alabama law. "That is another matter," said King. "I intend to be critical of the troopers and the Alabama laws."

Attorney General Katzenbach called King personally that night to warn against night marches or trips to Marion. He disclosed that the Justice Department considered authentic a report that two men still intended to kill him, after failing to get a clear shot during his visit to Marion the previous Monday. King told reporters that the call, but not the threat, was highly unusual. At a Citizens Council rally in Selma that night, former Governor Ross Barnett of Mississippi shouted that white people faced "absolute extinction of all we hold dear unless we are victorious." Over the private objection of city officials, local citizens welcomed the uninvited but dramatic arrival of the state troopers. Their blood was up, as the onslaught at Marion aroused rather than shamed prevailing white sentiment. Selma's newspaper embraced the news from distant Harlem with warlike headlines that dwarfed those ever applied to local demonstrations: "Followers of Malcolm X Said Planning Revenge."

Colonel Al Lingo, head of the Alabama state troopers, served an arrest warrant upon Jimmy Lee Jackson in his hospital bed Tuesday, and the Alabama Senate formally denounced "baseless and irresponsible" charges of dereliction by his men in the Marion incident. Lingo, scourge of the Alabama civil rights movement since Birmingham in 1963, deployed seventy-five troopers in Selma with the announced purpose of enforcing a new edict from Governor Wallace that banned night demonstrations throughout Alabama. The *New York Times* reported as front-page news the tense scene in which Wilson Baker turned back a "twilight march" before it reached troopers and bystanders massed at the courthouse. King announced that lawyers would contest the ban on night marches, as in St. Augustine, and that the movement planned a "motorcade" to petition Governor Wallace directly. Some staff members fanned out to seek support in new counties, and King flew west for four days of fund-raising.

He walked into a press conference Wednesday morning at the Los Angeles airport. Was Elijah Muhammad's life in danger? What exactly did Attorney General Katzenbach say about death threats on King? Were they from Black Muslims or white segregationists? Did he suspect an international conspiracy? Was King encouraged that thirty-one Republicans jointly chided the Johnson administration for stalling on a voting rights proposal? What would become of nonviolence if "something should happen" to him? Representatives of the city and county proclaimed successive Martin Luther King days, and there were huge police escorts because of FBI reports that the Christian Nationalist State Army vowed to kill him that night at the Hollywood Palladium. The next day, on confirmation of dynamite thefts by fugitives affiliated with the group, bomb squads joined one hundred LAPD officers guarding a theater on Sunset Boulevard, where King attended a fund-raiser screening of *The Greatest Story Ever Told.*

Under close examination on a television interview show, King said that nonviolence was generally a leadership discipline for conduct on public issues, and that he would defend his family from attack in their home. For this comment, the front page of the local Negro newspaper excoriated him as "the biggest hypocrite alive," saying King only half accepted the "manhood" of Malcolm X and "excluded his loved ones from dangers that he constantly imposes upon his followers." By contrast, the *New York Times* dismissed Malcolm's life as "pitifully wasted" because of his "ruthless and fanatical belief in violence," and declared from a survey of correspondents that the world was indifferent to his murder. ("In Poland there was no noticeable reaction of any kind.") In Los Angeles, King preached against the contagion of violence to crowds that swamped Temple Israel and spilled in thousands from Liberty Baptist Church through the parking lot and out among PA speakers strung along McKinley Avenue.

James Bevel returned to Selma from Lowndes County late Thursday. He had made tiny inroads in the rural areas—and found a place that would host King there on Monday—but the fear was thick. Three days later, Rev. Lorenzo Harrison would burst into Brown Chapel, sobbing that his own deacons had run him out of Lowndes County on orders from the local Klan. At home, Bevel learned from his wife that stomach infections had reduced Jimmy Lee Jackson's condition to grave, a week after the shooting in Marion, but this night Diane Bevel was wound also to the breaking point over Bevel's philandering. He hit her in the face. Their marriage cracked toward its end four years later, and Bevel wound up evicted to the streets outside their rented room at the Torch Motel.

Jackson died at 8:10 A.M. Friday morning, February 26. Among the mourners in the afternoon, Bevel walked with Bernard Lafayette to a wood-frame house by a creek in a wooded field outside Marion. The two of them sat in the kitchen with the immediate survivors—grandfather Cager Lee, mother Viola, and Jackson's sister, Emma. They were pitiful sights, all three still bandaged from the rampage at Mack's Cafe. On behalf of the movement, Bevel forced himself to ask what they thought should be done about the marches. The family said they should keep going. When Bevel asked whether they could stand to go on the next one, Cager Lee replied, "Oh, yeah."

Bevel left dissolved in tears, asking if Lafayette could walk with him the fifty-four miles to Montgomery. He said he had a lot on his mind, and the long walk would give the movement time to develop a message. Back at Brown Chapel in Selma, Bevel took the pulpit that night in the mass meeting. "I tell you, the death of that man is pushing me kind of hard," he said, to a response of moans. He pulled up two texts from the Bible. The first was Acts 12:2–3, in which King Herod, after killing James the brother of John and seeing a positive effect, arrested Peter also. "I'm not worried about James anymore!" Bevel shouted. James was Jimmy Lee, who had found release, but Bevel worried out loud about all the Peters remaining to be "cowed and coerced and beaten and even murdered."

He expounded on Esther 4:8, in which Mordecai warned Esther of an order to destroy the Jews, and charged her to go to the king and "make request before him for her people." He preached that the king now was Governor Wallace, who ran the state troopers and kept Negroes from voting. "I must go see the king!" he cried, and soon brought the whole church to its feet vowing to go on foot as in the Bible. "Be prepared to walk to Montgomery! shouted Bevel. "Be prepared to sleep on the highway!"

Diane Nash threw herself behind the plan. Bevel called her his Esther. Beyond the strains of their tempestuous marriage, they retained their life's pledge to honor the four girls killed in Birmingham. There were 500,000 nonregistered Negro voters in Alabama, nearly 80 percent of the state's voting-age population. Five million across the South.

From Los Angeles, Martin Luther King sent a telegram of condolence to Saturday's Malcolm X funeral. He flew to Alabama on Monday to lead a tiny march of twelve at the Lowndes County courthouse—the first Negroes to seek registration in sixty years—then on Tuesday to Howard University in Washington, where he revised his Nobel Prize sermon to oppose the escalating war in Vietnam.

On Wednesday, March 3, King returned to preach the funeral in Marion, making handwritten insertions about Jimmy Lee Jackson on the text of his eulogy from the Birmingham church bombing. Once again he summoned up conviction that "love will conquer hate" through justice. He approved the march on Montgomery to begin on Sunday. He said from Brown Chapel, "We will bring a voting bill into being on the streets of Selma."

Epilogue
1965–97

ON FRIDAY, February 26, 1965, Wallace Muhammad appeared in dramatic submission before the Nation of Islam's Chicago convention. He did not justify or endorse Malcolm's death, as Malcolm's own brothers were required to do publicly. He did not repeat vows of holy war upon heretics who doubted the infallibility of Elijah Muhammad, as did the presiding minister, Louis X of Boston, who incited loyal attackers from the crowd of two thousand upon a "spy" journalist he discerned from the rostrum ("Put the light on him!"). Wallace Muhammad in a short speech begged reinstatement—"I judged my father when I should have let God do it." The convention cheered him as the prodigal, anointed son. He was obedient. But because he considered the Nation to be blasphemous and corrupt, and refused to teach its concoction of Islam, Elijah Muhammad consigned him to unpaid obscurity. Wallace worked as a baker, welder, painter, and rug cleaner, and labored with nephew Hassan Sharrieff in a Campbell Soup factory.

In death, Malcolm X disappeared briefly. Doubleday canceled the forthcoming autobiography, and roughly a dozen New York firms declined the project before it landed at Grove Press, to be published in October 1965. *New York Times* critic Eliot Fremont-Smith praised it as eloquent testament that Malcolm "understood, perhaps more profoundly than any other Negro leader, the full, shocking extent of America's psychological destruction of its Negroes." The book, published just after the Watts riots of August, spoke to puzzlement about why Negroes outside the South might be so angry. On college campuses, where the Vietnam War was

inspiring replicas of the civil rights movement, Malcolm presented a life
that did not flinch from martyrdom. By glossing over his consuming struggles with the Nation of Islam,* the book's account of Malcolm's last two
years magnified the allure of an unfinished myth. Trotskyites, pan-
Africans, and urban guerrillas rushed to claim him. *The Autobiography* would
be translated into fifteen languages and sell three million copies by 1992,
when a Hollywood film helped seal Malcolm's "X" as an international
symbol of race, youth, and fearless passage.

Police seized two New York Muslims as accomplices of Talmadge X
Hayer. Other than suitable profiles as intimidating "enforcer" types—
Norman 3X Butler was already awaiting trial for the January 6 shooting of
a "defector" from the Nation—their most salient contribution to the official version of the conspiracy was numerical. The arrested trio matched
the number of reported gunmen at the scene, which calmed public fears
of loose killers and insurrectionary warfare.

At the trial, Hayer admitted guilt and swore that the other two had
nothing to do with the crime, but prosecutors discredited his statement by
noting that all three defendants also denied being Muslims (which fore-
closed any chain of inquiry that might implicate Elijah Muhammad). Judge
Charles Marks sentenced the three to life terms on April 14, 1966, and
while the outside world lapsed into conspiracy theories or disinterest,
Muslim factions spent decades in mutual recrimination over the transparent frame-up. Malcolm's people acknowledged complicity in convicting
the two "stand-in" assassins, who, both being lieutenants under Captain
Joseph, were as familiar to them as deadly movie stars and never could
have gone unchallenged to the Audubon front rows. Benjamin 2X and
others countered that the Nation could free them by coming forward with
the true killers.

Unchecked, sectarian enforcements for the Nation of Islam evolved
into freelance gangsterism. The same Muslim soldiers who collected dues
payments and newspaper quotas for Chicago also fled into mosques after
bank robberies. Police wrecked the Newark Temple No. 25 after a chase.
In 1968, FBI propagandists mailed anonymous warnings that the members
of New York No. 7 alone were being "swindled" annually of some
$800,000. The Nation acquired among other holdings a bank, a Learjet,
five mansions for the "royal family," and a $100,000 jeweled fez for Elijah
Muhammad. In his final years, Nation officials battled renegade enforcers
as well as dissidents. Intruders filched $23,000 cash off the person of
Supreme Captain Raymond Sharrieff, and bushwhackers winged him on
Chicago streets in 1971. The next year four gunmen from what Boston

---

* In an influential essay that recognized him as an original thinker of the age, journalist
I. F. Stone passed along as revelation that Malcolm had been "shocked when former
secretaries of Elijah Muhammad filed paternity suits against the prophet."

police called a "Black Muslim execution squad" killed Hakim Jamal, a critic of Elijah Muhammad and director of the Malcolm X Foundation. In January of 1973, assassins from the Nation's Philadelphia mosque entered a Washington home in the absence of breakaway Muslim leader Hamaas Abdul-Khaalis and shot his wife and daughter in the head, executed two sons and a follower, and drowned three infants in a tub and sink.

James X Price, one of those assassins, turned state's evidence and secretly agreed to testify against seven others who would be convicted. On the eve of his trial testimony, Minister Louis X—now transferred from Boston and renamed Farrakhan by Elijah Muhammad—delivered a fiery radio broadcast from his post at New York's flagship Temple No. 7: "Let this be a warning to those of you who would be used as an instrument of a wicked government against our rise. . . . Though Elijah Muhammad is a merciful man . . . there are younger men and women who have no forgiveness in them for traitors and stool pigeons. And they will execute you, as soon as your identity is known." Price refused to testify the next day, and hanged himself instead. Later in 1973, after the murder of Minister James Shabazz during a bloody war among factions out of Newark Temple No. 25, Farrakhan broadcast a similar pronouncement. "Cut off their heads," he said. "Roll it down the street and make the world know that the murderer of a Muslim must be murdered."

In 1974, after a hiatus of nine years, Elijah Muhammad allowed his son Wallace to resume teaching. His adversaries within the Chicago headquarters confiscated tapes of his sermons, eager to prove he was deviating again from the Nation's dogma into Islamic scripture, but the old man said inexplicably, "My son's got it right." When Elijah died in 1975, delegations arrived in limousines to find Wallace, the chosen heir, living like a hermit, with a rope tying shut his broken refrigerator door. The next day, February 26, 1975, the ministers swore fealty to the new Supreme Minister on the first day of the national convention, as did Muhammad Ali. "I was born for this mission," declared Wallace Muhammad.

Wallace cloaked himself in the authority of his father, who many Muslims still believed could never die, and suspended the onerous weekly sales quota of three hundred newspaper copies per male. He dismissed Supreme Captain Raymond Sharrieff, capped ministers' salaries at $300 per week, and abolished the Fruit of Islam altogether as a "punch your teeth out" abomination. He survived plots by entrenched officials who accused him of crying "crocodile tears" over his father. Within a year he renamed New York No. 7 for his former ally, Malcolm, saying, "What we should see in Malcolm is a turn for the Nation of Islam from fear and isolation to openness, courage." By 1977, Wallace Muhammad dismantled the Nation's corporate empire, confessed the scandals that Malcolm was killed to hide, and openly renounced his father's claim to divinity. He extracted some purpose from every error and ordeal. "If he hadn't hurt me," Wallace said of his father, "I don't know if I really would have come to Allah like I did."

In Los Angeles, Assistant Minister Randolph X Sidle stalked out of Temple No. 27 "with fire in my ears." He had long since served his prison time from the chaos of the Ronald Stokes shooting,* but he and many veteran Muslims could not abide Wallace's changes, especially the required acceptance of whites in the mosque and the recognition of Elijah's flaws. Sidle was among the first to join when Louis Farrakhan broke away to reconstruct the Nation of Islam by placing himself in Elijah Muhammad's deified seat—living in Elijah's former home, reviving his sectarian doctrines along with the martial arts Fruit of Islam, who hawked bean pies and a Farrakhan-era newspaper, *The Final Call.* To fuse the new Nation with the old one, Farrakhan went so far as to hire several of the deceased Messenger's extra "wives," along with some of the thirteen offspring by these former secretaries. Their lawsuits entangled probate on the Muhammad estate for twelve years, until 1987.

Among the old guard, Captain Joseph could not accept Farrakhan's Nation. He steeled himself to set aside his antipathy for Malcolm X, gave up his powers as a captain for a regular job, and studied Islam under Wallace Muhammad. So did the former Arthur X Coleman, who walked with a cane from wounds in the Stokes shooting, as well as all three men who were in prison for the murder of Malcolm. In 1977, with the support of Muhammad, the former Talmadge Hayer filed affidavits naming his four Muslim accomplices from the Newark mosque, but New York authorities declined to revisit the slipshod case. The two stand-ins served another decade with Hayer.

With Farrakhan defending the memory of Elijah Muhammad, divided partisans briefly threatened to revive the heresy wars of 1964. This time each side claimed the mantle of the previous victim. Beginning in 1984, Farrakhan aggressively insulted American Jews and accused white America of gaping racism, earning for himself public outrage greater than Malcolm ever had, along with mirror notoriety for the ability to provoke it. Comparisons with Malcolm, however, reminded some that Farrakhan had called Malcolm a traitor as well as a mentor. By 1992, he publicly denied involvement in the murder, though he stood by his invectives that preceded it. "Nothing that I wrote or said yesterday do I disagree with today," he declared. In January of 1995, Malcolm's daughter Qubilah was charged with trying to have Farrakhan killed in revenge. Farrakhan and Malcolm's widow declared a truce on the stage of Harlem's Apollo Theater in May.

---

* After criminal appeals, those convicted had entered nine different California prisons on March 8, 1965, the day after Selma's "Bloody Sunday" march. Judge David Coleman suspended all jail time on William X Rogers, who remained in a wheelchair, and on Monroe X Jones for his "recent behavior and attitude." Jones, who shot Officer Tomlinson during the incident, had left the Muslims.

Two years later, Qubilah's young son Malcolm Shabazz set a home fire that killed the widow, his grandmother Betty Shabazz.

Twenty years before, when his rival broke ominously away in 1977, Wallace Muhammad said the word "Farrakhan" came from Arabic roots meaning "one who bares his teeth," and advised followers not to become excited or hostile over the display. He predicted that the new Nation would be forever crippled by supremacist ideas suitable only for bait. "They shut themselves out by their own philosophy," said Muhammad, "and the racists know and encourage it." And most Americans were afraid to study the causes of racial injustice, he preached later, "because they know it leads to religion." The soul of Islam forbids racial images of the divine, he said wryly, and "not even the Muslims have tried it."

Wallace Muhammad was often vague and disorganized. He taught in rambling aphorisms ("The person wrapped up in himself makes a nasty little bundle"), and was forever changing names. He dropped Wallace for the Islamic Warith, changed the spelling of his surname from Muhammad to Mohammed, and called his decentralized community the Muslim American Society. Nevertheless, by the early 1990s, published estimates of Muslims in the United States ranged from five to eight million. Slightly more than half of these—at least three million—were immigrants from Pakistan, Indonesia, Arab countries, and Europe, and the remainder were nearly all black Americans affiliated with his Sunni Islam. Farrakhan's sectarian Nation, like Elijah's in the 1960s, stabilized at ten thousand members, which represented a declining speck of American-born Muslims, roughly one of every two hundred.

Away from the glare on Farrakhan, Imam Warith Deen Mohammed represented American Muslims in Mecca at the council that debated the 1990 Gulf War. At home, his precarious ministry stretched from prisons and fledgling mosques to universities, still menaced by the stigmas of race and foreign novelty. His goal was to win a foothold for Islam with African-Americans as full founding partners, which would lead historians eventually to recognize Malcolm for his most overlooked quality: religion. Beyond that, Mohammed preached an ecumenical "line of purity" among Judaism, Christianity, and Islam, and dreamed that American Muslims could begin to rescue Islam's democratic spirit from its autocratic history, just as the earliest Americans helped reform an Old World of kings and inquisitions. Into his sixties, the former Wallace Muhammad's life already spanned a "voodoo" cult, fantastic legends, bloodcurdling zealotry, enduring devotion, and potboiling dynastic strife—what he called a typical religious birth in history. "All of us," said Captain Joseph, shortly before his death in 1993, "paid a price to establish Islam in America."

CAGER LEE OF MARION, ALABAMA, stepped up to one of the federal voting registrars who opened doors in nine counties on August 20, 1965, and

Justice Department officials asked movement photographers to share their pictures of Jimmy Lee Jackson's frail grandfather, holding up his voting card. All 1,144 applicants that Friday were successful under the Voting Rights Act of 1965, which President Johnson had signed in the Capitol exactly two weeks earlier. Its Section 4 suspended all discretionary voting restrictions in seven Southern states. The powerful new law broke decades of impediment and heartache. In Mississippi, black registration jumped from 7 to 60 percent within two years.

Hollis Watkins drove from Greenwood to Hattiesburg to visit the Dahmer family in the fall. Less than four years earlier, when he and Curtis Hayes had been dispatched there as student emissaries from Bob Moses, churches had been afraid even to allow talk of voting rights, and now the Dahmer farm was a beehive of movement people. Negroes everywhere in Forrest County were getting voting cards. Vernon Dahmer himself secured his first one, saying it was all right now that everyone else could. Four Dahmer sons were away in military service, but Bettie, the ten-year-old tractor driver, and Dennis, thirteen, were old enough to tease Watkins about chasing down the yearling calf.

At year's end, Vernon Dahmer and J. C. Fairley went to see Sheriff Bud Gray about one remaining obstacle. Dahmer was so busy with it that there were unopened Christmas presents stacked in his room on Saturday night, January 8, when he placed a notice on local radio that Sheriff Gray had signed out one of the poll-tax receipt books to him, as the county regularly did for the Jaycees and downtown stores during citizenship drives. Although the poll tax was on the verge of being voided nationwide as unconstitutional, registered Mississippians would need a poll-tax receipt to obtain a ballot through the 1966 elections, and Dahmer encouraged citizens to stop by his general store in Kelly Settlement. He could collect their poll taxes for the county, sparing them a trip to the courthouse, and he offered to pay the $2 fee for hardship cases so they could vote.

Preachers repeated his announcement from Negro pulpits Sunday morning, and shortly after two o'clock that night, shotguns and pistols blew out windows along the front of the farmhouse. As the Dahmers ran from their bed to scoop up Bettie from her nearby room, some attackers threw torches and open bottles of gasoline inside, while others kept up the fusillade. Inside, the Dahmers ran into walls of flame at every door. "Jewel!" shouted Dahmer to his wife. "Get the children out while I hold them off!" He grabbed his shotgun from the closet. Firing from window to window through the smoke, he aimed at masked figures behind trees and at a Pontiac in the front yard, beyond which he could see his general store also in flames. Harold, an older son on Army leave, retrieved Dennis and pushed the family out a back window where the ground sloped downward a story below. Dahmer kept shooting in retreat from the fire, then jumped himself. He and young Bettie were badly burned about the hands and face. As cars roared off in the front, Harold helped the family stumble through the woods for help. The house and store burned to the ground, leaving two chimneys.

FBI Agent J. L. Martin arrived at Forrest General Hospital an hour later to interview the five Dahmers. He knew the family, having arranged transfer to Hattiesburg in 1965 to escape twelve years of bureaucratic torment under John Malone in the New York office. Martin went before dawn to the charred crime scene, where officers discovered a pistol that had been dropped in the chaos, and a Ford on the road nearby with two tires flattened by shotgun pellets. The Ford was registered to a Klansman from Laurel, Mississippi, in neighboring Jones County. Its abandonment led to an argument among the White Knights about whether it was more humiliating to have been disabled by Dahmer or by friendly fire between attack groups.

J. C. Fairley reached the hospital before daybreak. Reverend Robert Beech, still with the Ministers Project two years after Hattiesburg Freedom Day, arrived later in the morning from out of town. Vernon Dahmer described the attack from his hospital bed, his bandaged arms raised by pulleys. "They finally got me," he told Fairley, and said he was worried about his daughter Bettie, heavily sedated in the same room with skin burns more severe than his. "I think I made a mistake," Dahmer told Beech, reminding him that he had always said it was unwise to be too far out front. The visitors departed. Dahmer went to sleep, then swiftly into cardiac crisis and death at 3:45 P.M. Doctors explained that he suffocated because hot smoke and acrid fumes had seared too much lung tissue.

Hattiesburg Negroes nearly rioted at the courthouse. Some local whites banded to rebuild the family properties, but one woman advised the newspaper that charity should be reserved for needier families. "Since the Negroes have equal rights now," wrote Mrs. J. V. Sanford, "it's about time they started looking out for their own." Some of Dahmer's white siblings were moved to break the color line for the funeral; others stayed away. Roy Wilkins claimed Dahmer's memory for a fundraising drive, which revived family and movement quarrels over the NAACP's fidelity to Dahmer. ("There has been no effort by NAACP to exploit the Dahmers in any way," Director of Branches Gloster Current would write to Reverend Beech.) Attorney General Katzenbach announced on the Monday that many officials in the Justice Department had known Dahmer personally and admired his work in "the highest kind of citizenship." President Johnson sent a telegram. That week in Jackson, the all-white Mississippi legislature continued debate on emergency bills designed to neutralize the Voting Rights Act. Floor speeches analyzed the potential vote of "a certain group" by euphemism, wary of new federal sanctions against racial gerrymandering, but some members from safe districts breeched the understanding to protest sacrificial adjustments. "We all know the Negro situation was the main factor," a Chicasaw County representative declared on Thursday, January 13, 1966.*

The Dahmer criminal investigation folded into the two protracted murder cases from the 1964 Freedom Summer: the Chaney-Goodman-Schwerner murders and the Lemuel Penn highway ambush in Georgia. Roy Moore, the FBI's SAC for Mississippi, summoned agents to occupy a block of Hattiesburg motel rooms beginning the night of January 10. They swarmed over Klansmen of the White Knights, who were believed to be active even while under indictment in the Neshoba County murders, concentrating on a Jones County klavern in nearby Laurel, hometown of Imperial Wizard Sam Bowers. By February, suspects were threatening each other as likely informants, and issuing public manifestos of innocence ("I am very sorry about the bombing of the Damer [sic] nigger"), which protested "the brutality of these men with the FBI." A klavern official confessed the plot on March 2, stating in part that he was troubled because Imperial Wizard Bowers had violated an agreement not to send Jones County men elsewhere without his sign-off. This confesson led to a second, which was withdrawn under Klan duress, then to a third.

On the afternoon of March 28, 1966, the Justice Department authorized SAC Moore to arrest and file federal charges against Imperial Wizard Bowers and thirteen members of the Jones County White Knights. The timing was significant. That morning, the Supreme Court had reinstated federal indictments in the Lemuel Penn and Neshoba County murders, a year after U.S. district judges William Bootle and Harold Cox had vacated them as unconstitutional applications of powers reserved to the states. An FBI memo recorded that John Doar was "quite enthusiastic" about the decision, which rehabilitated the civil rights statute for the Dahmer prosecution as well as the two earlier ones.

The Penn case reached trial first, after further delays. Lawyers separated defendant James Lackey on grounds that he had repudiated his 1964 confession, then removed defendant Herbert Guest on arguments related to the lack of federal registration for his shotgun. Both defendants won acquittal at a trial apart from the alleged shooters, Howard Sims and Cecil Myers. In the interim, family violence produced an urgent FBI cable on May 5: "Sims went to Athens hospital where wife employed in nursery and shot her in the face with a pistol. Preliminary report indicates wife will survive. Athens PD presently attempting to apprehend Sims, said to have departed hospital in his car containing a number of firearms." In July,

---

* Thirteen state election laws of 1966 would carve the Delta's Second Congressional District into three majority white districts, submerge the looming black vote in redrawn local boundaries, and substitute strategically placed "at large" races for district school boards and county representatives.

nearly two years after the random ambush of Lt. Colonel Penn on a Georgia highway, a federal jury in Athens convicted Sims and Myers of civil rights conspiracy. They began serving the maximum ten-year sentence upon the exhaustion of appeals in 1968.

In Mississippi, the Dahmer and Neshoba County cases languished into 1967, largely on new defense claims that the indictments were legally invalid for lack of black people on federal grand juries in Mississippi. Prosecutors managed to obtain proper indictments by February. Meanwhile, the White Knights expanded the targets of violence. A bomb destroyed Jackson's Temple Beth Israel synagogue in September. Weeks later, beginning on October 9, Justice Department lawyers at long last prosecuted seventeen alleged conspirators for the Neshoba County murders of 1964.

Cecil Price was confident enough of the outcome to be running for sheriff against one of his fellow defendants, but the mood of the Meridian courtroom tightened dramatically on first sight of prosecution witness Delmar Dennis, Province Titan of the White Knights, who testified that he had spent the past three years working both for Imperial Wizard Sam Bowers and for the FBI. Doar admitted in his closing argument on October 18 that he had tried very few criminal cases and was there because of his commitment and the office he held, "to speak directly and frankly to you about the reason for the extraordinary effort the federal government undertook to solve this crime...." In the end, Doar adapted words from the Gettysburg Address. "What I say, what the other lawyers say here today ... will soon be forgotten," he told the jurors, "but what you twelve people do here today will long be remembered."

The jury stayed out two days, once sending a message that it was deadlocked, before the foreman returned a verdict on October 20 of not guilty for seven defendants, including Sheriff Rainey, deadlock on three, and guilty for Deputy Sheriff Price, Imperial Wizard Bowers, Alton Wayne Roberts, and four others. Authorities declared the seven convictions to be the first by any Mississippi jury against Klansmen for race crimes.

Judge Cox released the convicted men pending appeal. Violence continued. In November, bombs damaged the parsonage next to Saint Paul's Church in Laurel (where opera singer Leontyne Price had belonged as a child) and the home of the Beth Israel rabbi in Jackson. On December 20, a constable who spot-checked a parked car in the small town of Collins came upon Imperial Wizard Bowers and a twenty-one-year-old unknown named Thomas Tarrants, with a .45-caliber machine gun. Tarrants, a solo bomber for the White Knights, disappeared upon release, and Bowers headed to trial for the murder of Vernon Dahmer, where Delmar Dennis would testify. FBI agents renewed investigative pressure, and a supplementary confession of Billy Roy Pitts—the Klansman who had dropped his pistol on the Dahmer property—brought one of four shocks in the demise of White Knights terror in 1968. Pitts verified the identity of the Pontiac driver as Charles Wilson, president of the Laurel Jaycees, owner of an investment firm and a company that manufactured artificial limbs. Shortly after Wilson received Laurel's Distinguished Service Award in January of 1968, his arrest made stunning news for Mississippi: a prominent citizen charged as the alleged shotgunner on a Klan murder squad.

Also in January, a Forrest County grand jury indicted eleven Dahmer suspects on state arson and murder charges, and all-white juries later handed down murder convictions at three trials. The defendants, including Charles Wilson, received life sentences that were upheld on appeal—another first for Mississippi. Feelings about the trials ran so high in Hattiesburg that local prosecutor James Dukes and his brother, an FBI agent, walked to a downtown Klan hangout and "called out" threatening Klansmen to fight or show chicken in front of a noontime street crowd. This was their crest. In May of 1968, a jury deadlocked 11–1 for conviction of Sam Bowers, after defense witnesses accused the FBI of supplying state witness Billy Roy Pitts with Hollywood starlets. Bowers survived a second mistrial, 10–2, then another. Local headlines turned against the prosecution witnesses: "Pitts 'Sings Again' in Dahmer Slaying." Hung juries became the rule. One defense lawyer claimed that FBI agent Martin had secretly poisoned Dahmer at the hospital on orders from LBJ.

White Knights terror centered upon Meridian, in apparent retaliation for convictions there in the triple murder. Klansmen burned a store run by FBI informant Wallace Miller in February of 1968, arsoned two black churches, and in May bombed the largest Meridian synagogue. On June 28, 1968, police and FBI agents surprised two Klan bombers at the home of a prominent Jewish target in Meridian. A shootout gravely wounded Thomas Tarrants, the young Klan bomber who had been arrested with Sam Bowers, and killed his companion of more than one previous mission, Kathy Ainsworth. An investigation convinced authorities that Ainsworth, an elementary school teacher in Jackson, had hidden a Klan life from her family, and the death of a respectable female on a White Knights murder team was a third shock for Mississippi. The fourth would remain a secret until 1970, when reporter Jack Nelson of the *Los Angeles Times* disclosed that Jewish groups, working through FBI agents, had paid $30,000 for a precise warning before the bomb attempt in Meridian—to Klansman Alton Wayne Roberts, who was free on appeal of his own conviction in the Chaney-Goodman-Schwerner murders.

Klan bombers and prosecutors collapsed, leaving behind a five-year toll by FBI reckoning of nine murders connected to the White Knights of the Ku Klux Klan, plus seventy-five church burnings and at least three hundred bombings and assaults. Trials died out in the Dahmer case after a federal jury deadlocked on ten conspiracy defendants in 1969. Charles Wilson served a year at Parchman Penitentiary before receiving a series of gubernatorial leaves in 1970–71, then a grant of work-release to his home in 1972 from Governor William Waller, who had defended him in one of his trials. Waller commuted Wilson's life sentence to time served in 1976. The two others sentenced to life in the Dahmer case were paroled in 1978.

Sam Bowers and Alton Wayne Roberts surrendered with the five others convicted in the Chaney-Goodman-Schwerner case, and served six years before receiving mandatory parole in 1976. Bowers returned to Laurel as a reclusive theologian of racial purity. "When a priest sees the heretic," he said in a rare 1994 interview, "he can do only one thing: he eliminates him." Upon the conviction that year of Byron de la Beckwith for the murder of Medgar Evers, three decades after Beckwith's previous mistrial in 1964, Ellie Dahmer petitioned Forrest County prosecutors to reopen cases against Bowers and other indictees who were either mistried or never yet tried for Vernon Dahmer's murder.

IN 1976, Bob Moses returned from Africa after a decade in exile. After his last SNCC meeting in February of 1965, as Bob Parris, he had drifted from Mississippi into Alabama following the marches from Selma to Montgomery, when Martin Luther King had brought Abraham Heschel down to stay with him at Sully Jackson's madhouse in Selma, with James Bevel sleeping in a bathtub and James Forman under the dining room table, and the rabbi surviving a garlanded march beside King, saying, "I felt like I was praying with my feet." Sometimes movement friends came across Parris on rural farms, drinking corn whiskey out of a fruit jar, thinking about the war in Southeast Asia. He attended the first organized protest on April 17, 1965. "Use Mississippi not as a moral lightning rod," he told a crowd of fifteen thousand at the Washington monument, "but if you use it at all, use it as your looking glass." Likening Vietnam to Mississippi, he held up a news photo announcing the capture of a Communist rebel in Vietnam. "Now I looked at that picture," he told a May rally in Berkeley, "and what I saw was a little colored boy standing against a wire fence with a big huge white Marine with a gun in his back. But what I knew was that the people in this country saw a Communist rebel. And that we travel in different realities."

Parris sought out Al Lowenstein. Although relations between them were still strained from Freedom Summer, and movement radicals increasingly scorned Lowenstein as a red-baiting white liberal, the two men shared a feeling of helplessness about the war, as they had two years earlier about Mississippi. Lowenstein brought Parris to a summer conference of anti-war activists in New York. Where Lowenstein saw the root of the Vietnam conflict as a national hatred for Communist China, and advocated a reappraisal of foreign policy, Parris held to the language of nonviolence. Over the summer of 1965, he approached a number of national religious leaders who supported the civil rights movement, only to be told that black people should not jeopardize hard-earned gains by speaking out on Vietnam. Parris received such advice as an affront. "I got angry," he recalled twenty years later. "Well, I didn't rant and rave."

On August 9, 1965, three days after President Johnson signed the Voting Rights Act, Parris led a march on the U.S. Capitol to "declare peace" in Vietnam. Uniformed American Nazis splattered red paint on him, pacifist Dave Dellinger, and radical professor Staughton Lynd, who had supervised the Freedom Schools in Mississippi. Then Parris accepted an invitation to Ghana for a conference of African nations, and stayed on through the autumn. The following spring, Parris helped organize a conference in New Orleans called "Roots," on the meaning of African heritage. He could not bring himself to visit the Dahmers in Hattiesburg after the firebombing, but he did go to see Amzie Moore in the Delta. Moore had become an official in the federal War on Poverty. His house buzzed with movement people working in Head Start. The MFDP was running candidates that summer, and the new SNCC chairman, Stokely Carmichael, proclaimed a doctrine of black power on a march through Mississippi. Parris, feeling invisible, decided it was safe to become Moses again. His marriage collapsed, partly over his obsession with Vietnam, just before he received a military induction notice.

At thirty-one, beyond legal draft age, Moses interpreted the order as punishment for his statements against the war. He fled underground to Canada in August of 1966, speaking French, living under the assumed name Robinson through a hard winter into 1967. He worked odd jobs as a janitor, telephone salesman, and night watchman. Eventually, he obtained a Canadian identity card and found refuge with a West Indian family, adopted by the children as "Uncle Bob" Williams. By early 1968, still fearing capture, Moses applied for a Canadian passport under which he might reach safer exile in Africa, by way of England. As he waited, news bulletins announced that the FBI was screening Canadian passport files for the fugitive assassin of Martin Luther King. An "Eric Galt"—then a "George Sneyd"—was said to be arranging a Canadian identity for escape, possibly to Rhodesia. Moses panicked, fearing that the manhunt would expose his fraudulent passport papers. He stayed in hiding well after James Earl Ray was arrested in London.

When he reached Tanzania that summer, Moses turned in his false passport to the Tanzanian government, which granted him tacit asylum under his own name. He married Janet Jemmott, a SNCC worker he had met during Freedom Summer, and they had four children while teaching math and English, respectively, in a Tanzanian village school. Moses avoided the family he had left behind. Some among them feared he was dead until he sent home an African cane when he learned of his father's death in 1970. Had he contacted his father, Moses told himself, the FBI would have harassed the older man. Joe Rauh locating Moses by rumor, sent a letter to him in care of the American embassy in Tanzania. Before he died, Rauh wrote, he wanted to convince Moses that he had never betrayed him or the MFDP in Atlantic City. Moses did not reply. He worried that Rauh's letter might alert the embassy.

After the Vietnam War ended, the Moses-Jemmott family returned to the United States and settled under the Jimmy Carter draft amnesty in Cambridge, Massachusetts. Janet Jemmott went to medical school and became a pediatrician. Moses taught high school and went back to graduate school at Harvard. He seemed disconnected from his past, even fearful of it. Some friends counted him among the many "movement casualties," haunted or damaged to varying degrees. He avoided SNCC reunions at which some of the survivors came to terms. Diane Nash told her peers at one of them how, to her own amazement, the late 1960s had swept away her belief in nonviolence. "I felt that way for a few years until I noticed that I hadn't killed anybody," she said. "I hadn't been to the rifle range. I hadn't blown up anything, and truly, I had done very little...." Nash had disengaged under cover of words, perhaps the better to raise children as a single mother.

In 1982, Moses returned to Mississippi for the first time in sixteen years, to attend Amzie Moore's funeral. He made a brief speech. He began to give interviews, and sometimes he asked for documents about himself as though discovering another person. He developed a new way of teaching algebra that blended in Freedom School methods. By the 1990s, his Algebra Project operated in school districts across the country. Moses spent more and more time in Mississippi, having recovered his past. Mastering first-year algebra is an equivalent of the right to vote in the 1960s, he said. It provides hope in the modern world.

In Selma, Martin Luther King confronted furies ahead. In order to win the vote, movement spirits in many small places would have to lift politics into history. Beyond the vote lay Vietnam, which would spoil the celebrations of freedoms that had been set in train over the past two years. King's inner course was fixed downward toward the sanitation workers of Memphis. It was his course, but it was getting lonely. Neither King nor the movement could turn America into a mass meeting, but for three more years they could look to a distant one, at Canaan's edge.

Acknowledgments

MY EDITOR, Alice Mayhew, has inspired, nurtured, and driven this project for fifteen years of her remarkable career. I am grateful to her foremost among the many people at Simon & Schuster who helped produce this book. Most of them made contributions out of an author's sight, but I want to thank by name those standing closest through the whirlwind of production: Roger Labrie, Lydia Buechler, and Fred Chase, along with Kerri Kennedy, Victoria Meyer, Emily Remes, Liz Stein, and Lisa Weisman. Natalie Goldstein diligently tracked down photographs for this book as well as the previous one. I thank Carolyn Reidy for the warm support of the company, and for her formative suggestion that we had enough material to publish a second volume.

My family and I appreciate two generous foundations, Lyndhurst of Chattanooga and MacArthur of Chicago, for grants that allowed me to broaden my research and helped to sustain us. The Ford Foundation provided a research grant in 1993–94, which made possible the excellent library and computer work of Susanne Trowbridge. Jennifer Bard, Frank Drumwright, and Tracy Wallace offered short-term research assistance, as did my mother, Jane Branch. Jonah Edelman conducted a skillful research mission in Los Angeles.

This volume rests on the source foundation begun for *Parting the Waters*. I acknowledge those people and institutions again here, without repeating all the names. Among the employees of the libraries and archives cited in the notes for this volume, I am especially indebted to the following: Linda Evans, Archie Motley, Ralph Pugh, and Corey Seeman of the Chicago Historical Society; Ginger Cain and Ellen Nemhauser of the Robert W. Woodruff Library at Emory University in Atlanta; Kelly Baker, Kirk E. Cromer, Armaria Fleming, Emil Moschella, Helen Ann Near, and Robert Opher of the FBI's Records Management Division in Washington; Robert Colasacco and Sharon Laist of the Ford Foundation Archives in New York; Keven

Proffitt of the American Jewish Archives in Cincinnati; Helen Ritter of the American Jewish Committee in New York; Claudia Anderson, Michael Gillette, Regina Greenwell, Linda Hanson, Tina Houston, Mary Knill, and Harry Middleton of the Lyndon B. Johnson Library in Austin; Susan D'Entremont of the John F. Kennedy Library in Boston; Iris Bethea, Bruce Keys, Cynthia Lewis, and Diana Ware of the King Library and Archives in Atlanta; Philip Runkel of the Marquette University Archives in Milwaukee; Dan Den Bleyker of the Mississippi Department of Archives and History in Jackson; Judy Edelhoff, Mary Roonan, and Steven D. Tilly of the National Archives in Washington; Richard Shrader and John White of the Southern Historical Collection at the University of North Carolina in Chapel Hill; Martin Harris, Pat Priest, Worth McDonald, and Barry Sherman of the Peabody Awards Film Collection at the University of Georgia in Athens; Kristin Gleeson of the Presbyterian Office of History in Philadelphia; Diana Edwards, Page Edwards, and David Nolan of the St. Augustine Historical Society; Howard Dodson, James Turner, Berlina Robinson, and Mary Yearwood of the Schomburg Center for Research in Black Culture in New York; Clayborne Carson of the Martin Luther King, Jr., Papers Project at Stanford University; Kathy Borkowski and Harold Miller of the State Historical Society of Wisconsin in Madison.

Among the authors whose pioneering works inform these pages, I owe a special debt to Steven Barboza, Seth Cagin and Philip Dray, David Colburn, David Garrow, Peter Goldman, and Elizabeth Sutherland. Of the firsthand memoirs, I found special value in those by Charles Fager and Paul Good, along with the book of childhood recollection by Sheyann Webb and Rachel West.

Pillar of Fire relies heavily on interviews with those who made, observed, and studied this history. I am grateful to them for sharing their time and knowledge. For advice and encouragement beyond the contributions cited in the notes, I extend thanks to the following people: Ikhlas Bilal, David Chalmers, Jack Chatfield, Connie Curry, Jonathan Demme, Jed Dietz, Lawrence Elswit, Michael V. Gannon, Charles Guggenheim, Lawrence and Monica Guyot, Henry Hampton, Lawrence Hanks, Abdul Karim Hasan, Gerald Horne, Pam Horowitz, Martha Hunt Huie, Ray Jenkins, Teresa Johanson, June Johnson, Vernon Jordan, Benjamin Karim, Stetson Kennedy, Shira Lander, Lawrence W. Lichty, Arthur Magida, Charles Marsh, Richard I. McKinney, Julia McMillan, Michael Middleton, Michael Miller, Peggy Obrecht, Gerald O'Grady, Becky Okrent, Bruce Perry, Anna Hamilton Phelan, Frank M. Reid, Ray Rickman, Phil Alden Robinson, Ed Saxon, Joel and Myrna Schwartz, Ronald Shaheed, Joe Sinsheimer, Jack Sisson, Frank and Sandy Soracco, Henry Thomas, and Jerry Thornbery.

During nine years' work on this volume, I have leaned heavily at times on a few special friends, including Harry Belafonte, Agieb Bilal, Julian Bond, Marian Wright Edelman, and Dan Okrent. Christy and I have watched our children, Macy and Franklin, pass from lower school to the brink of college. They have brought us joy that surpasses for me even the absorbing wonder of the King years.

Abbreviations
Used in Source Notes

ANP	Associated Negro Press, Claude A. Barnett Papers, Chicago Historical Society
A/AR	Anne Romaine Oral History Collection, King Library and Archives, the Martin Luther King, Jr., Center for Nonviolent Social Change, Inc., Atlanta
A/AT	Papers of Arthur Thomas, King Library and Archives
A/CS	Papers of Charles Sherrod, King Library and Archives
A/JF	Papers of James Forman, King Library and Archives
A/KP	Papers of Dr. Martin Luther King, Jr., King Library and Archives
A/KS	Martin Luther King, Jr., Speech Collection, King Library and Archives
A/MFDP	Papers of the Mississippi Freedom Democratic Party, King Library and Archives
A/OH	Oral History Collection, King Library and Archives
A/SC	Southern Christian Leadership Conference Records, King Library and Archives
A/SN	Papers of the Student Nonviolent Coordinating Committee, King Library and Archives
AAP	Private Papers of Archie E. Allen, Santa Barbara, California
AC	*Atlanta Constitution*
ADW	*Atlanta Daily World*
AFF	Ford Foundation Archives, New York City
AJ	*Atlanta Journal*
AJA	American Jewish Archives, Cincinnati, Ohio
AJC	Archives of the American Jewish Committee, New York City
APR	Papers of A. Philip Randolph, Library of Congress
BIR	Archives Division, Birmingham Public Library
BIR/AB	Papers of Albert E. Boutwell, Birmingham Public Library
BIR/BC	Papers of Eugene T. "Bull" Connor, Birmingham Public Library
BIR/C	Papers of Bishop C. C. J. Carpenter, Birmingham Public Library
BN	*Birmingham News*
BTT	Buice trial transcript, *People of the State of California v. Robert Louis Buice et al.,* Los Angeles County Superior Court Case No. 266717 (1963)
BUK	Papers of Martin Luther King, Jr., Special Collections Department, Mugar Library, Boston University
BW	*Birmingham World*
CD	*Chicago Defender*
CDD	*Chicago Daily Defender*
CHS	Archives and Manuscripts Division, Chicago Historical Society
CORE	Papers of the Congress of Racial Equality, Library of Congress
CRDP/OH	Oral History Collection, Civil Rights Documentation Project, Moorland-Spingarn Research Center, Howard University
CU/OH	Oral History Collection, Columbia University Library
EU	Robert W. Woodruff Library, Emory University
FAC	FBI File No. 77-59135 (Archibald James Carey, Jr.)

FACP	FBI File No. 100-51230 (Adam Clayton Powell, Jr.)
FAL	FBI File No. 105-10368 (Allard K. Lowenstein)
FBNH	FBI File No. 100-448006 (COINTELPRO, Black Nationalist/Hate Groups)
FCNL	FBI File No. 100-449698 (COINTELPRO, New Left)
FCT	FBI File No. 67-9524 (Clyde Tolson Office Files)
FDCA	FBI File No. 44-12831 (Election Laws, Dallas County, Alabama)
FEM	FBI File No. 105-24822 (Elijah Muhammad)
FER	FBI File No. 105-122316 (Ellen Rometach)
FHOC	FBI J. Edgar Hoover Official and Confidential File
FJ	FBI File No. 100-407018 (Clarence Jones)
FJNY	FBI File No. 100-73250 (Clarence Jones, New York Office)
FK	FBI File No. 100-106670 (Martin Luther King, Jr.)
FL	FBI File No. 100-392452 (Stanley Levison)
FLNY	FBI File No. 100-111180 (Stanley Levison, New York Office)
FLP	FBI File No. 44-25873 (PENVIC, Lemuel Penn Murder Case)
FMB	FBI File No. 44-25706 (MIBURN, Chaney-Goodman-Schwerner Murder Case)
FMX	FBI File No. 100-399321 (Malcolm X)
FMXNY	FBI File No. 105-8999 (Malcolm X, New York Office)
FNCC	FBI File No. 100-5086 (National Council of Churches)
FNR	FBI File No. 62-72612 (Nelson A. Rockefeller)
FR	FBI File No. 100-158790 (Bayard Rustin)
FRFK	FBI File No. 77-51387 (Robert F. Kennedy)
FRW	FBI File No. 62-78270 (Roy Wilkins)
FSA	FBI File No. 157-6-63 (St. Augustine, Florida)
FSC	FBI File No. 100-438794 (Southern Christian Leadership Conference)
FSN	FBI File No. 100-439190 (Student Nonviolent Coordinating Committee)
HOH	Oral History Collection, Harry Lasker Library, Highlander Research and Education Center, New Market, Tennessee
JFK	John F. Kennedy Library, Boston
LBJ	Lyndon Baines Johnson Library, Austin, Texas
LAHD	*Los Angeles Herald-Dispatch*
LAHE	*Los Angeles Herald-Examiner*
LAT	*Los Angeles Times*
Legat	FBI abbreviation for Legal Attaché
LHM	Letterhead Memorandum (FBI term designating reports for external distribution)
LOC	Library of Congress
MA	*Montgomery Advertiser*
MC	*Michigan Chronicle*
MDAH	Mississippi Department of Archives and History, Jackson, Mississippi
MOB	Museum of Broadcasting, New York City
MS	*Muhammad Speaks*
MSSC	Records of the Mississippi State Sovereignty Commission, University of Southern Mississippi, Hattiesburg
NA	National Archives, Washington, D.C.
NAACP	Papers of the National Association for the Advancement of Colored People, Library of Congress
NCC	National Council of Churches
NCCIJ	Papers of the National Catholic Conference for Interracial Justice, Marquette University Archives, Milwaukee, Wisconsin
NR	Not Recorded (for serials in FBI files)
NT	*Nashville Tennessean*
NYAN	*New York Amsterdam News*
NYT	*New York Times*
OH	Oral History
PC	*Pittsburgh Courier*
PDD	President's Daily Diary, LBJ Library, Austin, Texas
PEA	Film Collection, Peabody Awards Committee, University of Georgia
POH	Presbyterian Office of History, Philadelphia
PPP	Public Papers of the Presidents
PRA	Pacifica Radio Archive, Los Angeles
RAC	Rockefeller Archive Center, North Tarrytown, New York
RN	Papers of Reinhold Niebuhr, Library of Congress
RS	Files of the Chicago Police Department Red Squad
SAC	Special Agent in Charge (FBI term for the head of a city or state FBI office)
SAHS	St. Augustine Historical Society, St. Augustine, Florida
SCRBC	Schomburg Center for Research in Black Culture, New York City
SHSW	State Historical Society of Wisconsin, Madison, Wisconsin
SKP	Martin Luther King, Jr., Papers Project, Stanford University
STJ	*Selma Times-Journal*
SUARC	Stanford University Archive of Recorded Sound
TOU	Lillian Pierce Benbow Special Collections, Tougaloo College, Tougaloo, Mississippi

UAB	University of Alabama in Birmingham, Oral History Research Office
UF	University of Florida, Gainesville
UNC	Southern Historical Collection, William Round Wilson Library, University of North Carolina at Chapel Hill
WP	*Washington Post*
WS	*Washington Star*

Notes

1. ISLAM IN LOS ANGELES

3 Muslims gathered: Sources for the April 27 conflict include specific documents and interviews cited, plus BTT, generally the Buice trial transcript, *People of the State of California v. Robert Louis Buice, et al.*, Los Angeles County Superior Court Case No. 266717, copy supplied courtesy of Judge Earl Broady.

3 "chewing on men's bones": Elijah Muhammad recording, *The Time of Judgment*, Vol. 2, as transcribed in SAC, Chicago, to Director, FBI, Aug. 14, 1966, p. 12, FEM-NR.

3 "You are the man": MS, Oct.-Nov. 1961, p. 6.

4 sweet potatoes and pork: Int. Nuri Salaam (Arthur Coleman), April 10, 1991.

4 case of childhood rickets: Int. Delores Jardan (Delores Stokes), Feb. 7, 1992.

4 counted cash donations: Testimony of William Rogers, p. 2207ff, BTT.

5 first night together as partners: Int. Stanley Kensic by Jonah Edelman, June 27, 1991; int. Frank Tomlinson, Oct. 15, 1991; BTT, p. 3ff.

5 words to Jingles: BTT, pp. 156–59, 1207, 1261.

5 "Your brother is in trouble": Int. Clarence Jingles by Jonah Edelman, June 21, 1991.

5 facedown across the Buick's hood: Testimony of Fred Jingles, Monroe Jones, Stanley Kensic, and Frank Tomlinson, BTT, *passim*. Also int. Frank Tomlinson, Oct. 15, 1991: Tomlinson recalled first noticing something amiss when he saw Kensic and Jingles wrestling on the hood of the Buick.

5 twirled above their heads: Int. Frank Tomlinson, Oct. 15, 1991.

6 Tribble ran behind: Tribble testimony, BTT, p. 223ff.

6 inched toward him: Int. Karim Muhammad (Troy Augustine) by Jonah Edelman, June 14, 1991.

6 regret for Tomlinson: Int. Frank Tomlinson, Oct. 15, 1991.

6 Jones shot him: Int. Earl Broady, Nov. 4, 1990, and March 25, 1991. Also int. Clarence Jingles by Jonah Edelman, June 21, 1991.

6 emptied their guns: Int. Clarence Jingles by Jonah Edelman, June 21, 1991.

6 call his mother for help: BTT, pp. 1106–7, 1262–63.

6 Kuykendall passed by: BTT, p. 338ff.

6 famous among the Negro officers: Int. Jesse Brewer, June 13, 1991; int. Samuel Hunter, Feb. 6, 1992.

7 Extraordinary events began: Testimony by Kensic, Kuykendall, Tomlinson, Fred Jingles, Clarence Jingles, and Kuykendall, BTT.

7 Officers Donald Weese and Richard Anderson: Weese and Anderson testimony, BTT, pp. 419ff, 509ff.

8 Officer Reynolds started to object: Int. Robert Reynolds, Oct. 11 and 16, 1991.

8 fist into Zeno's jaw: Ibid. Also Reynolds testimony, p. 874, Zeno testimony, p. 1381, Williams testimony, p. 1059, BTT.

8 "Why? Why?": Anderson testimony, BTT, p. 429.

8 unnerved the officers: Ibid. Also int. Robert Reynolds, Oct. 11 and 16, 1991.

9   morbid fear of guns: "I had been shot four times in Korea when I was in the United States Army, and, you know, every time I see a gun I automatically start running for a safe place to go." William Rogers testimony, BTT, p. 2217.

9   Arthur Coleman dived away: Int. Nuri Salaam (Arthur Coleman), April 10, 1991.

9   Stokes raised both hands: Testimony of Horace Christmon (bystander), p. 1903ff, Weese testimony, p. 595ff, BTT; *California Eagle,* May 3, 1962, p. 1.

9   Logan kneed him in the groin: Logan testimony, p. 703ff, Coleman testimony, p. 2018ff, BTT.

9   "Are you crazy?": Int. Nuri Salaam (Arthur Coleman), April 10, 1991.

9   Kuykendall had to decide: Ibid. Also Kuykendall testimony, pp. 359ff, 497ff, BTT.

9   Sidle, darted out: Int. Wazir Muhammad (Randolph Sidle), March 27, 1991.

9   high on Officer Logan's back: Logan testimony, pp. 706ff, 749ff, Fred Jingles testimony, p. 1216ff, Frank Bielman testimony, p. 767ff, BTT.

10   ripping each of their suit jackets: BTT, *passim.*

10   Kensic was startled: Int. Stanley Kensic by Jonah Edelman, June 27, 1991.

10   facing the pocket camera: Int. Nuri Salaam (Arthur Coleman), April 10, 1991.

10   "the most brutal conflict": LAT, May 2, 1962.

10   "Seven innocent, unarmed": LAHD, May 10, 1962, cited in FBI New York office report dated Nov. 16, 1962, p. 17, FMX-52. Also LAT, May 5, 1962, p. 1.

10   "The same feelings he harbors": *California Eagle,* May 10, 1962, p. 1.

10   "Muslims Shoot, Beat Police in Wild Gunfight": LAT, April 28, 1962, p. 1.

10   Earl Broady: Int. Earl Broady, Nov. 4, 1990, and March 25, 1991. Also LAT, June 9, 1992, p. A28.

11   support from National Association for the Advancement of Colored People Executive Director: LAT, May 5, 1962, p. 1; *Washington Afro-American,* May 8, 1962, pp. 1, 2.

11   long record of complaints: In addition to specific brutality complaints, the NAACP often had called for investigation of charges that Chief Parker was autocratic and insensitive to minority interests. In 1959, for instance, a Negro member of the Police Commission had resigned, publicly stating that Parker had refused for years to provide the most elementary information about Negro manpower in the LAPD and instead had been abusive toward the commission member, calling him a liar and throwing him out of his office. In 1960, Parker had touched off a minor scandal with tape-recorded remarks attributing crime among Mexican-Americans in Los Angeles to the fact that "some of these people were not too far removed from the wild tribes of the inner mountains of Mexico." See e.g. LAT, June 19, 1959, LAT Feb. 3, 1960.

11   "From our knowledge": LAT, May 9, 1962, p. 1.

11   Board of Supervisors leadership meeting: Ibid.

11   "zoot-suit riots": *Los Angeles Sentinel,* May 10, 1962, p. 1.

11   Parker stalked out: *Los Angeles Sentinel,* May 17, 1962, p. 1.

11   the old friend: Branch, *Parting,* pp. 53, 242–43.

12   "a brilliant speaker": LAHD, May 14 and 17, 1962.

12   Parker's own undercover: Int. Sam Hunter, Feb. 6, 1992.

12   strength of Negro votes: Int. Earl Broady, March 25, 1991; int. Mervyn Dymally, May 31, 1991; int. Jesse Brewer by Jonah Edelman, June 19, 1991; int. Sam Hunter, Feb. 6, 1992; int. Michael Middleton, July 14, 1991.

12   "Gestapo organization": LAT, June 9, 1961.

12   "one hundred per cent": PC, May 19, 1962, p. 4.

12   "wild and exaggerated charges": *California Eagle,* May 17, 1962.

12   LAPD's ongoing intelligence: NYAN, May 12, 1962, p. 1.

12   obtained Kennedy's promise: LAT, May 19, 1962, p. 1, May 20, p. 1, May 22, p. 22.

12   "Muslim Hatred Called": LAT, May 7, 1962, p. 2. Also "Muslim Trouble Rises in California Prisons," LAT, May 20, 1962.

12   "work together with us": LAHD, May 24, 1962, p. 1.

13   traced his miracle victory: Int. Mervyn Dymally, May 31, 1991.

13   The Stokes case marked a turning point: LAT, Feb. 22, 1965, p. 12; int. Benjamin Karim, March 19, 1991; int. Yusuf Shah (Captain Joseph), Oct. 17, 1991; int. Abdulalim Shabazz, March 14, 1991.

13   "traitor to the Negro people": NY FBI report of April 30, 1958, FMX-21, p. 14.

13   "this little passive resistance": Cone, *Martin and Malcolm,* p. 407.

13   "Anybody can sit": Perry, *Malcolm: A Life,* p. 282.

13   "You might see these Negroes": Goldman, *Death and Life,* p. 96.

13   Malcolm confided to associates: Int. Benjamin Karim, March 19, 1991.

13   National Secretary John Ali: Int. Yusuf Shah (Captain Joseph), Oct. 17, 1991. Also MS, June 1962, p. 2. (That issue of MS also contains an article written from Soledad prison by future Black Panther leader Eldridge Cleaver entitled "As Crinkly as Yours, Brother," in which Cleaver attacked the African-American hair and skin care industry for upholding a white "standard of beauty.")

13   "Play dead on everything": Wiretap transcript of May 23, 1962, FMXNY-2956.

14   "I can only say": MS, July 1962, p. 4.

14   "God gives justice": LAHD, May 17, 1962, cited in NY FBI report, Nov. 16, 1962, FMX-52, p. 18.

14   Malcolm had lost face: Goldman, *Death and Life,* pp. 98–100.

14   Air France jetliner: AC, June 3, 1962, p. 1.

14   "I got a wire from God today": NY FBI report of Nov. 16, 1962, FMX-52, pp. 21–22.

14   "This shows the distorted": LAT, June 7, 1962, p. 1; LAHE, June 7, 1962, p. A24.

14   just canceled sit-ins: Branch, *Parting,* pp. 590–93.

14   "If the Muslim leader": LAT, June 16, 1962, p. 11.

14   "The Messenger should have done more": Int. Benjamin Karim, March 19, 1991; Perry, *Malcolm: A Life,* p. 337.

14   quasi-military apparatus: Int. Benjamin Karim, March 11 and Aug. 31, 1991; Perry, *Malcolm: A Life,* pp. 213–25; Clegg, *An Original Man,* pp. 103–5.

15   "Credit will ruin them": Wiretap transcript of Nov. 14, 1961, FMXNY-2584.

15   "merely pocket change": Wiretap transcript of June 28, 1962, FMXNY-2999.

15   blanket fee of $120,000: Int. Earl Broady, March 25, 1991.

15   bluesman Louis Jordan: Perry, *Malcolm: A Life,* p. 52; FBI surveillance documents for the Phoenix residence begin Sept. 8, 1961, FHOC-24; Clegg, *An Original Man,* p. 159.

15   fn paranoid dementia: SAC, Detroit, to JEH, Aug. 9, 1957, FEM-25; Clegg, *An Original Man,* pp. 95–96.

15   "my mens": Int. Earl Broady, March 25, 1991.

15   teeth from chattering: Int. Yusuf Shah (Captain Joseph), Oct. 17, 1991.

15   "writing only the prosecution's side": MS, Dec. 30, 1962, p. 3.

15   maintaining microphone bugs: JEH to the AG, Dec. 31, 1956, FEM-14; JEH to SAC, Chicago, Jan. 2, 1957, FEM-14; SAC, Chicago, to JEH, Oct. 30, 1959, FEM-56x; Powers, *Secrecy and Power,* pp. 312–52. Oddly, but perhaps significantly, J. Edgar Hoover placed this sensitive surveillance paperwork, known in the FBI as "June mail," in his Official and Confidential file on Martin Luther King, FHOC-24. This may reflect a simple association in his own mind of the two black leaders, or the more subtle purpose of reinforcing precedents for such surveillance. The Muhammad and King paperwork is similar in the use of detail important to the FBI, such as its addition of the phrase "any address to which he may move" to language on the target location. The Bureau relied upon this phrase to justify installing an unlimited number of short-term wiretaps even in hotel rooms without having to ask for further authorization from the Attorney General.

15   "who's to control Malcolm": Wiretap transcript of May 23, 1962, FMXNY-2956.

15   "a modern Paul": Wiretap transcript of Jan. 12, 1963, FMXNY-3326.

16   This was Wallace D. Muhammad: Sources on Warith Deen Mohammed (Wallace D. Muhammad) include int. W. D. Mohammed, Nov. 14, 1991; int. Agieb Bilal, Nov. 6, 1990; int. Benjamin Karim, March 11, March 19, and Aug. 31, 1991; int. Yusuf Shah (Captain Joseph), Oct. 17, 1991; public statement of Wallace D. Muhammad, July 1964, courtesy of Bruce Perry; W. D. Mohammed speech of Dec. 13, 1977, in Chicago; W. D. Mohammed speech of Nov. 19, 1978, in New Orleans, reprinted in W. D. Mohammed, "As the Light Shineth from the East" (Chicago: WDM Publishing, 1980).

16   "The Voodoo Cult": Erdmann Doane Beynon, "The Voodoo Cult Among Negro Migrants in Detroit," *American Journal of Sociology,* Vol. 43 (May 1938), pp. 894–907.

16   fn William Ming and Chauncey Eskridge: *Chicago Sun-Times,* May 21, 1958; int. Warith Deen Mohammed, Nov. 14, 1991. "I never saw a more flagrant violation of due process," Ming said of the Wallace Muhammad case, WP, Dec. 12, 1960.

16   cloistered and useless: Int. Imam Warith Deen Mohammed (Wallace Muhammad), Nov. 14, 1991.

16   home to his mother, Clara: Ibid.

16   Wallace Muhammad's purpose: Ibid.

17   "The corrupt hypocrites": Warith Deen Mohammed speech, Chicago Community Night, Dec. 13, 1977, author's files. Also *Chicago American,* Sept. 15, 1964.

17   two long letters of criticism: Written statement by Wallace Muhammad, undated, circa June 1964, courtesy of Bruce Perry.

17   four thousand Muslims gathered: Security reports on the Muslim convention dated Feb. 27, 1963, Red Squad File No. 589, pp. 150405–6, CHS.

17   Wallace refused to speak.: Int. Imam Warith Deen Mohammed (Wallace Muhammad), Nov. 14, 1991.

17   "one God": Q'uran Sura 112.

17   Malcolm defended Elijah's adaptations: Written statement by Wallace Muhammad, undated, circa June 1964, courtesy of Bruce Perry; wiretap summary of Malcolm X conversation of March 8, 1963, FMXNY-3435.

18   phone wires burned: Wiretap summaries in SAC, Chicago, to Director, dated March 11, 1963, FMXNY-3429; New York report dated May 16, 1963, FMX-60; and New York report dated Nov. 15, 1963, FMX-74, pp. cover-B–E.

18   Ethel Sharrieff told her father: Conversation of March 2, 1963, wiretap summaries in SAC, Chicago, to Director, dated March 11, 1963, FMXNY-3429.

18   Malcolm broach to Wallace: Malcolm X, *Autobiography,* p. 297; written statement by Wallace Muhammad, undated, circa June 1964, courtesy of Bruce Perry. Later, Wallace Muhammad and Malcolm X each claimed to have learned of the bastard children from the other.

18   on the lawn with their babies: Warith Deen Mohammed speech, Chicago Community Night, Dec. 13, 1977, author's files.

18   Clara, was dead to him: Written statement by Wallace Muhammad, undated, circa June 1964, courtesy of Bruce Perry.

18   Wallace scarcely knew: Int. Imam Warith Deen Mohammed (Wallace Muhammad), Nov. 14, 1991.

18   hiding for seven years: Elijah Muhammad Phoenix address of Dec. 1967, MS, Jan. 19, 1968. Also wiretap transcript of Aug. 18, 1960, FMXNY-1965; Muhammad, *Message to the Black Man,* p. 178ff; Bontemps and Conroy, *Anyplace,* p. 216ff; Lincoln, *Sounds of Struggle,* p. 55ff; Clegg, *An Original Man,* pp. 37–40, 77–90; Agieb Bilal, "The Honorable Elijah Muhammad: Leadership in the African Continuum," unpublished paper, 1991.

18   most notably in 1942: FBI agents first arrested Elijah Muhammad under the name Gulam Bogans on May 8, 1942, in Washington, FEM-NR. Returned to Chicago for trial on draft-evasion charges, he was rearrested there when found hiding in a rug, and gave a statement to FBI agents on Sept. 29, 1942, FEM-NR.

19   his anthem to Malcolm: Int. Imam Warith Deen Mohammed (Wallace Muhammad), Nov. 14, 1991.

19   Elijah Muhammad's bastard children: Cf. Bland to Belmont, May 20, 1960, FEM-79. For propaganda distribution, an attached "blind" memorandum (concealing FBI authorship) sarcastically announced the birth on March 29, 1960, of a "bouncing, beautiful, brown-eyed, brown-haired daughter" to Evelyn Williams, an "unmarried young secretary" to Elijah Muhammad. See also Clegg, *An Original Man,* pp. 184–89.

19   "was to be": SAC, Chicago, to JEH, April 22, 1968, FBNH-NR, p. 3.

19   including a Chicago judge: Ibid., p. 5.

19   two years' accumulation: FBI traffic on the children born to Muslim secretaries Lucille Karriem and Evelyn Williams begins as early as a May 20, 1960, memorandum from Bland to Belmont at FBI HQ, FEM-79, noting the birth of Williams's daughter in hiding on March 30, 1960, and recommending that the intelligence be used to discredit Elijah Muhammad.

19   "There was no indication": SAC, Chicago, to JEH, April 22, 1968, FBNH-NR, p. 3.

19   Chicago FBI office recommended: SAC, Chicago, to Director, March 11, 1963, FMXNY-3435, p. 6. The recommendation is essentially repeated a month later in SAC, Chicago, to Director, April 10, 1963, FMXNY-3506.

19   "a nasty letter": Wiretap conversation of March 15, 1963, FMXNY-3506.

19   "seeking, prodding, and prying": Wiretap conversation of March 11, 1963, FMXNY-3435.

19   "an addict to publicity": Wiretap conversation of March 25, 1963, FMX-74, p. cover-B.

19   "a spoiled child": Wiretap conversation of March 15, 1963, FMXNY-3506; also conversation of March 16, 1963, FMXNY-3506.

19   Elijah sometimes praised Malcolm: Wiretap conversation of March 5, 1963, FMXNY-3429, p. 5.

19   ridiculed him as a usurper: Wiretap conversation of March 26, 1963, FMXNY-3609; wiretap conversation of March 28, 1963, FMXNY-3506; wiretap conversation of March 5, 1963, FMX-60, p. cover-D; wiretap conversation of March 7, 1963, FMXNY-3429.

19   Muhammad predicted: Wiretap conversation of March 26, 1963, FMXNY-3609.

19   Malcolm did fly to Phoenix: Malcolm X, *Autobiography,* pp. 298–99.

2. Prophets in Chicago

21   introduced to Rabbi Abraham Heschel: Int. Marc Tanenbaum, Jan. 2, 1990, and Feb. 5, 1991.

21   descended from dynastic generations: Neusner, *To Grow in Wisdom,* p. 197ff; Rothschild, *Between God and Man,* p. 7.

21   "banished melancholy": Heschel, *The Earth,* p. 75.

21   "by how much spiritual substance": Ibid., p. 9.

21   Chicago Conference on Religion and Race: Reports preserved in Box 2, Series 7, NCCIJ Collection, Marquette University Archives. Also scattered papers in the King files, including "Minutes of the Planning Committee, September 17, 1962," A/SC35f25.

21   sharp-eyed professional jockeying: Int. Mathew Ahmann and Jerome Ernst, Feb. 12, 1991; int. Oscar Lee, Sept. 26, 1991; int. Marc Tanenbaum, Jan. 2, 1990, and Feb. 5, 1991; int. Albert Vorspan, Aug. 13, 1992.

22   outcast among his colleagues: Int. Marc Tanenbaum, Jan. 2, 1990, and Feb. 5, 1991; int. Sylvia Heschel, Feb. 2, 1991; int. Mark Loeb, Dec. 6, 1990; int. Susannah Heschel, Nov. 15, 1990; int. Balfour Brickner, Feb. 4, 1991.

22   "Intellectual evasion": Heschel, *Insecurity of Freedom,* pp. 217–18.

23   "Wisdom is like the sky": Ibid., p. 42.

23   ". . . the cult of youth": Ibid., p. 71.

23   a quest to reform the ancient teachings: Of the vast literature on the Vatican Council and the development of the statement "Nostra Aetate," see Vorgimler, *Documents of Vatican II;* Yzermans, *American Participation;* Oesterreicher, *Rediscovery of Judaism;* Rynne, *Letters from Vatican City;* Gilbert, *Vatican Council and the Jews.* Also int. John Oesterreicher, May 24, 1991; int. Thomas Stransky, Feb. 27, 1992; int. Marc Tanenbaum, Jan. 2, 1990, and Feb. 5, 1991.

23   consultations so secret: American Jewish Committee, "White Paper, 1964–65," pp. 26–27, AJC. Also Schmidt, *Augustino Bea,* pertinent passages translated by Thomas Stransky at Tantur library, Jerusalem, Feb. 27, 1992. Cardinal Bea's name is pronounced "*Bay-*ah."

23   staff heard whispers: Int. Thomas Stransky, Feb. 27, 1992.

23   "There has never been an age": Heschel to Bea, May 22, 1962, "Ecumenical Council—IAD" file, AJC.

23   consulted Jewish specialists: Int. Arnold Aronson, March 5, 1991.

24   "Religion and race": Ahmann, *Challenge to Religion,* p. 55ff.

24   "Eleven o'clock on Sunday": Ibid., p. 155ff.

24–26   King's resolve to gamble to he left Savannah for the Conference: Summary from Branch, *Parting, passim.*

26   flight into Chicago: Int. Leslie Dunbar, May 12, 1986.

27   Never again did Dunbar: Ibid.

27   Bureau's institutional animosity: Branch, *Parting,* esp. p. 403ff. Also Garrow, *The FBI and Martin,* pp. 54–59, 78–85; O'Reilly, *"Racial Matters,"* p. 125f.

28 "whom we know most favorably": DeLoach to Mohr, Jan. 15, 1963, FK-NR.

28 newspapers attacked King: Branch, *Parting,* pp. 681–82.

28 gained FBI officials a clue: Atlanta SAC to Dir., Jan. 15, 1963, FSC-NR.

28 "deceit, lies and treachery": DeLoach to Mohr, Jan. 15, 1963, FK-NR.

28 ecumenical leaders had been turned away: Mathew Ahmann, "Summary Report," Box 2, Series 7, NCCIJ Collection, Marquette University Archives. Also int. Mathew Ahmann and Jerome Ernst, Feb. 12, 1991; int. Oscar Lee, Sept. 26, 1991; CD, Dec. 28, 1962.

29 so disgusted with Jackson: Int. Oscar Lee, Sept. 26, 1991.

29 fn seal up the stone doors: Ibid. This story, commonly mentioned by pastors on both sides of the NBC split, is confirmed by visual inspection of Olivet Baptist Church in Chicago, and by its listing there on South 31st Street.

29 William Stringfellow stunned: *Chicago Sun-Times,* Jan. 15, 1963. Also numerous interviews including Albert Vorspan (who also served on Stringfellow's panel), Aug. 13, 1992; Metz Rollins, Dec. 13, 1991. "I feared for Bill's life," recalled Rev. Will D. Campbell (int. Will D. Campbell, Aug. 13, 1992), adding that Rabbi Heschel was puzzled by Stringfellow's additional comment that Americans had failed the race issue for lack of a proper baptism, meaning a rebirth to a wholly new outlook. "Why did he say that?" Heschel asked Campbell. "What if I said the issue is circumcision?"

29 advance text of Rev. Will D. Campbell: *Time,* Jan. 25, 1963, p. 66; int. Will D. Campbell, Aug. 13, 1992.

30 "It is too late for us": Ibid. Also *Chicago Tribune,* Jan. 16, 1963.

30 "our whole future as a nation": NYT, Jan. 15, 1963, p. 16.

30 handwritten additions reflected a raw edginess: Speech, "A Challenge to the Churches and Synagogues," Jan. 17, 1963, A/KS4. Also CD, Jan. 19, 1963, p. 1.

30 "I wonder why": *Chicago Daily News,* Jan. 16, 1963.

31 "The greatest heresy is despair": *Chicago Sun-Times,* Jan. 16, 1963. Also Ahmann, *Challenge to Religion,* p. 55ff.

31 "We all died": Heschel, *Echo of Eternity,* p. 112.

31 "Moralists of all ages": Heschel, *The Prophets,* Vol. 1, p. 204.

31 eager devotion of King: Int. Andrew Young, Oct. 26, 1991; int. C. T. Vivian, May 26, 1990.

31 recognized by W. E. B. Du Bois: In Du Bois, *Souls of Black Folk,* p. 216: ". . . the preacher is the most unique personality developed by the Negro on American soil."

31 "May the problem of race": Speech, "A Challenge to the Churches and Synagogues," Jan. 17, 1963, A/KS4.

31 Heschel quoted the same: Ahmann, *Challenge to Religion,* p. 70; reprinted in Heschel, *Insecurity of Freedom,* pp. 85–100.

31 to illustrate the emotive force: Heschel, *The Prophets,* Vol. 1, pp. 212–13.

31 "the voice that God has lent": Ibid., p. 5.

32 vowed to see more of each other: Int. Marc Tanenbaum, Jan. 2, 1990, and Feb. 5, 1991; int. Albert Vorspan, Aug. 13, 1992; int. Arnold Aronson, March 5, 1991.

32 "We just thought": *Chicago Sun-Times,* Feb. 13, 1963.

32 "doleful hand wringing": *Time,* Jan. 25, 1963, p. 66.

32 volunteer clergy resolved to continue: Int. Mathew Ahmann and Jerome Ernst, Feb. 12, 1991; int. Metz Rollins, Dec. 13, 1991.

32 "bring sanity back": Mathew Ahmann confidential report, Oct. 6, 1963, A/SC35f28.

3. LBJ in St. Augustine

33 Lyndon Johnson waved: *Florida Times-Union,* March 11, 1963, p. 1, March 12, 1963, p. 1; *Miami Herald,* March 12, 1963, p. 14A; Daily Diary of the Vice President, March 11, 1963, LBJ.

33 Don Pedro Menéndez de Avilés: Colburn, *Racial Change,* p. 13; Lyon, *Enterprise of Florida, passim;* int. Eugene Lyon, Dec. 10, 1992.

34 presence at Nombre de Dios: Lyon, *Enterprise of Florida,* p. 115.

34 exterminate an explorer's colony of French Huguenots: Running just ahead of the Spanish competition, Charles IX of France had sent two expeditions to build a surviving but hard-pressed French outpost at Fort Caroline, near the mouth of the present St. Johns River in Florida. Menéndez conquered Fort Caroline on September 20, 1565, and later executed two groups of straggling prisoners in numbers totaling some four hundred. Ibid., pp. 120–27.

34 five hundred African slaves: In December 1565 Menéndez asked King Philip for an additional one thousand slave licenses for use in Florida, but complicated reversals forced his return to Spain before he could pursue his plans. Ibid., pp. 136–37.

34 earliest documentary slave records: Lyon, *Richer Than We Thought,* pp. 75–76, 96–97.

34 more than fifty years before: The work of several historians, including Eugene Lyon, Paul Hoffman, and Jane Landers, indicates that Spaniards actually held African bondsmen on future U.S. territory even before Menéndez reached St. Augustine in 1565. Beginning with Ponce de León in 1513, expeditions by Spanish colonizers such as Lucas Vázquez de Ayllon (1526), Panfilo de Narváez (1528), and Hernando de Soto (1539) had royal permission to bring up to one hundred slaves. Vázquez de Ayllon brought eight slaves, some of whom staged a revolt in 1526—more than eighty years before the first English colonists landed at Jamestown in 1607. But the Spanish settlements earlier than St. Augustine did not survive and most demographic records perished with them. See Jane Landers, "Africans in the Land of Ayllon" in Cook, *Land of Ayllon,* pp. 105–23; Hoffman, *New Andalucía,* esp. pp. 60, 78, 82; Lyon, *Enterprise of Florida,* pp. 39, 54, 136–37, 195.

34   fn "Twenty Negars": e.g. Woodson, *Negro in Our History,* p. 21; Quarles, *Negro in the Making,* p. 33; Lincoln, *Negro Pilgrimage,* pp. 10–11; Jordan, *White Over Black,* p. 44; Rice, *Black Slavery,* pp. 52–53; Grant, *Black Protest,* pp. 7–17.

34   chartering Fort Mose: Jane Landers, "Gracia Real de Santa Teresa de Mose: A Free Black Town in Spanish Colonial Florida," *American Historical Review,* Spring 1990, pp. 9–30.

34   penalty of castration: Jordan, *White Over Black,* p. 155.

34   archevil haven: Religious passion inflamed the colonial competition between the English and Spanish, and it also complicated each side's attitude toward the subordinated peoples. As a general rule, Spaniards considered their idea of slavery less odious to Africans than English chattel slavery. On the other hand, they felt at a disadvantage in dealing with Native Americans, in part because to them the Protestant departure from the structured doctrine of the Catholic Church was so shocking as to seem somehow in league with the vague practices of the Indians. According to Lyon, *adelantado* Menéndez himself "was strongly convinced that Protestant heretics and American aboriginals held similar beliefs, probably Satanic in origin." Lyon, *Enterprise of Florida,* p. 42.

34   "Turnbull's niggers": Int. David Nolan, April 4, 1991; Gannon, *Florida: A Short History,* pp. 20–21.

35   polls showed Robert Ripley: Summers, *Official and Confidential,* p. 102.

35   faces instead of their backs: Int. Michael V. Gannon, April 2, 1991. As the priest-historian in charge of the St. Augustine mission, Gannon accompanied Archbishop Hurley to Rome for the first session of the Vatican Council in the fall of 1962.

35   "Fifty-five": Int. Michael V. Gannon, Dec. 12, 1992.

36   letter asking Johnson: Fulwood and Hawthorne to LBJ, Feb. 23, 1963, III-C-24, NAACP.

36   three formal readings: Int. Fannie Fulwood, April 6, 1991.

36   "no event in which I will participate": LBJ to Fulwood, March 7, 1963, David Colburn papers, UF.

36   chief aide to Florida Senator George Smathers: Int. Scott Peek, Dec. 10, 1992. Peek was administrative assistant to Smathers. Also int. Fannie Fulwood, April 6, 1991. Documentary references to the negotiations before LBJ's visit include the transcript of a March 12, 1963, meeting with the St. Augustine city manager, III-C-24, NAACP; Fulwood and Hawthorne to President Kennedy, May 4, 1963, Box 24, Lee White Papers, JFK; Colburn, *Racial Change,* pp. 32–33; Garrow, ed., *St. Augustine,* pp. 18–19.

36   a mob had punished: Garrow, ed., *St. Augustine,* p. 15.

37   Henry Thomas decided to apply: Int. Henry Thomas, March 14, 1991; Colburn, *Racial Change,* p. 28.

37   Henry Thomas had become: Branch, *Parting,* pp. 412–18, 472–84.

37   froze up inside: Int. Fannie Fulwood, April 6, 1991.

37   Roy Wilkins called: Garrow, ed., *St. Augustine,* p. 18.

38   $159 phone bill: Gloster Current (national director of branches, NAACP) to Robert Saunders (Florida field secretary), March 22, 1963, III-C-305, NAACP.

38   Reedy, true to his promise: Int. Fannie Fulwood, April 6, 1991; int. Katherine and Henry Twine, April 2, 1991.

38   beneath the Tojetti ceilings: Gannon, *Florida: A Short History,* p. 57.

39   treasurer to Smathers: Herbert E. Wolfe owned several banks and a construction company, among other holdings: Garrow, ed., *St. Augustine,* p. 12.

39   "I'm *eatin'* with 'em!": Int. Scott Peek, Dec. 10, 1992.

39   "Don't forget us": Garrow, ed., *St. Augustine,* pp. 17–18.

39   "St. Augustine Pledged": *Florida Times-Union,* March 12, 1963, pp. 1, 2, 21, 25.

39   "the local problem which existed": Scott Peek to George Reedy, March 13 and March 14, 1963, Box 226, Vice Presidential Papers, LBJ.

39   tape recorder on an empty table: Colburn, *Racial Change,* p. 33.

39–40   "would make the city" to "they should have the fortitude to say so": Transcript of "Informal Conference between City Manager Charles F. Barrier and Representatives of local branch of NAACP, held in office of city manager on March 12, 1963," III-C-24, NAACP.

40   deceived with false promises: Ibid. Also Eubanks and Hayling to Vice President Johnson, Aug. 3, 1963, cited in "Racial and Civil Disorders in St. Augustine," a Report of the Legislative Investigation Committee of the Florida Legislature, Feb. 1965, pp. 67–68, reprinted in Garrow, ed., *St. Augustine.* In its "Report on the Open Meeting in St. Augustine, Florida, August 16 [1963]," the Florida Advisory Committee to the U.S. Commission on Civil Rights concluded that "promises of meeting with the Negro leaders were violated immediately on his [LBJ's] departure"—Papers of Judge Brian Simplon, UF.

40   "Since St. Augustine": Fullerwood and Hawthorne to JFK, May 4, 1963, Box 24, Lee White Papers, JFK. The letter actually reads "it's [sic] inception."

40   Kennedy did not reply: On behalf of Fullerwood, Hayling wrote JFK's assistant press secretary Andrew Hatcher on May 26, pressing for an answer to the May 4 letter, but no response appears in the files. Box 24, Lee White Papers, JFK.

40   "defeats the very purpose": Garrow, ed., *St. Augustine,* p. 20. Shelley actually wrote "polarities," corrected here to "polarizes."

40   "People on the scene": Blind memorandum on St. Augustine, appended to an Aug. 8, 1963, letter to Wyatt Walker from Hobart Taylor, Jr., executive vice chairman of the President's Committee on Equal Employment Opportunity, A/KP20f40.

4. GAMBLERS IN LAW

41 Jones worked simultaneously: Cf. April 1963 correspondence between Jones and Melvin Wulf regarding the entry of the ACLU into the *Sullivan* case as an *amicus*, A/KP11f24.

41 servants to the Lippincott family: Branch, *Parting*, pp. 317–18; int. Clarence Jones, Nov. 22 and Nov. 25, 1983.

41 "When a gambler gets": *James v. Powell, Jr.*, Record on Appeal, Supreme Court, New York County Index No. 11333-1960, p. 267; NYT, April 4, 1963, p. 37.

42 "Cool Breeze, you can't": *James v. Powell, Jr.*, p. 253.

42 in the head with a hammer: Ibid., p. 130ff. On James's background, see also WP, Feb. 14, 1967, p. B11, together with W. Montague Cobb to Drew Pearson, Feb. 17, 1967, Box G260, Drew Pearson Papers, LBJ.

42 "Do I look like a fool to you?": *James v. Powell, Jr.*, Record on Appeal, Supreme Court, New York County Index No. 11333-1960, p. 267.

42 slipped into the courtroom with a whispered: Int. Charles McKinney, Jan. 21, 1992.

42 neither they nor Powell's closest aides: Ibid. Also int. Percy Sutton, Nov. 28, 1989; int. Livingstone Wingate, July 8, 1992.

42 opposing lawyer summoned Powell: NYT, April 4, 1963, p. 37.

42 crippled Jewish children: NYT, April 5, 1963, pp. 1, 20.

42 advertisement placed by friends: NYT, March 29, 1960, p. 25. On *New York Times v. Sullivan*, see Lewis, *Make No Law, passim*; Branch, *Parting*, pp. 289–96, 370–71.

43 damages of $500,000: Lewis, *Make No Law*, pp. 35, 151.

43 "I hold in my hand": Powell speech of Jan. 13, 1960, reprinted in the Feb. 18, 1965, *Congressional Record*, p. 3007.

43 "Louis the Gimp": Ibid.

43 "both numbers and narcotics": Powell speech of Feb. 25, 1960, reprinted in the Feb. 18, 1965, *Congressional Record*, p. 3013.

43 "pauperizing Harlem": Hamilton, *Adam Clayton Powell, Jr.*, p. 430.

43 all 212 New York police captains: Powell speech of Feb. 25, 1960, reprinted in the Feb. 18, 1965, *Congressional Record*, p. 3013.

43 "We have in our hands": Powell speech of Feb. 18, 1965, *Congressional Record*, p. 3035.

43 first salvos drew: In a notable exception, the *New York Post* did publish a series on police corruption in the rackets, beginning on Feb. 29, 1960. The team of reporters, headed by the pioneer Negro journalist at a major white news organization, Ted Poston, openly acknowledged Powell as a catalyst.

43 "All pads are due": Powell speech of Feb. 25, 1960, reprinted in the Feb. 18, 1965, *Congressional Record*, p. 3013.

43 only the quiet resignation: Powell speech of March 2, 1960, reprinted in the Feb. 18, 1965, *Congressional Record*, p. 3013ff.

43 "who lives luxuriously": Ibid.

43 reiterate the "bag" system: Powell speeches of Feb. 25 and March 2, 1960, ibid.

44 trapdoors of public scandal: Hamilton, *Adam Clayton Powell, Jr.*, pp. 434–45; Jacobs, *Freedom Minus One*, p. 116ff.

44 Supreme Court agreed to review: On January 7, 1963. Jacobs, *Freedom Minus One*, p. 112.

44 "a 66-year-old domestic": NYT, April 5, 1963, p. 20. Another newspaper rhapsodized over Esther James as a "good citizen" who fought a lonely battle against sinister forces, including Powell and the mob: *New York World Telegram*, April 5, 1963, p. 3.

44 "If you dance": Branch, *Parting*, p. 277.

44 no racial issues pressed: Lewis, *Make No Law*, p. 109.

44 King lawyers welcomed: Int. Clarence Jones, Nov. 22, 1983; int. Harry Wachtel, Oct. 27, 1983.

44 split off the newspaper: Ibid. Also Lewis, *Make No Law*, p. 43.

44 seize the property of the four preachers: Ibid. Also Branch, *Parting*, pp. 571, 580.

45 Lord, Day & Lord: Lewis, *Make No Law*, p. 43.

45 "the unfriendliest newspaper": Adam Clayton Powell speech of Feb. 18, 1965, in *Congressional Record* of same day, p. 3037.

45 detailed account on the front page: "Powell Assailed in House Speech" (by Rep. John Ashbrook), NYT, Feb. 27, 1963, p. 1.

45 Arthur Powers was shot: NYT, Oct. 21, 1964, p. 23.

45 "finger woman": Adam Clayton Powell speech of Feb. 18, 1965, in *Congressional Record* of same day, p. 3035.

45 "I am against numbers": NYT, Jan. 4, 1960, p. 9.

45 offended editors: Hamilton, *Adam Clayton Powell, Jr.*, p. 432.

45 "his notably racist attitudes": NYT, Jan. 26, 1960, p. 32.

46 possessed soul: Glenn T. Eskew in Garrow, *Birmingham*, pp. 13–62.

46 conviction from the 1961 Freedom Rides: Lewis, *Make No Law*, pp. 162–63.

46 Shuttlesworth had assured King: Branch, *Parting*, p. 691. Andrew Young recalled the vote of the ministers in a speech at Birmingham's Sixteenth Street Baptist Church, Nov. 15, 1992.

46 out of jail and back again: Branch, *Parting*, pp. 708–11, 725–31.

46 "I'm writing this letter": Int. Clarence Jones, Nov. 25, 1983.

47 "when the cup of endurance": "Letter from Birmingham City Jail" quotations from Washington, *Testament of Hope*, pp. 289–303.

47   addressed the eight Birmingham clergy in dozens of voices: Branch, *Parting*, pp. 734–45.
48   shockingly held kings and peasants: Heschel, *The Prophets*, Vol. 1, pp. 159–67.
48   the power of the appeal lay dormant: Branch, *Parting*, p. 744.
49   still another landmark Supreme Court case: *Walker v. City of Birmingham*. See Westin, *Trial of Martin Luther King, passim.*

5. To Vote in Mississippi: Advance by Retreat

50   Moses was not from Mississippi: Moses description from Branch, *Parting*, pp. 325–31, 492ff.
50   Doar sought out Moses: Branch, *Parting*, pp. 508–10.
50   clandestine tour of Mississippi: Ibid., pp. 401–11; John Doar speech, "The Work of the Civil Rights Division in Enforcing Voting Rights Under the Civil Rights Acts of 1957 and 1960," courtesy of John Doar.
51   crammed Moses and seventeen others: Charles McDew oral history, p. 82ff, CRDP/OH.
51   "We had, to put it mildly": Branch, *Parting*, p. 560.
51   "continuing problem": "Special Report Mississippi Field Secretary," dated Oct. 12, 1961, and cover memo from Gloster B. Current, NAACP Director of Branches, dated Oct. 31, 1961, III-A-253, NAACP.
51   Medgar Evers broke down: Salter, *Jackson, Mississippi*, p. 21; Evers, *For Us, the Living*, pp. 215–23; Silver, *Closed Society*, pp. 93–95; Lord, *Past That Would Not Die*, p. 66.
52   insisted that his own wife: Evers, *For Us, the Living*, p. 139.
52   "That's all right, son": Ibid., p. 225.
52   Vernon Dahmer (pronounced "*Day*-mer"): Sources include interviews with his widow, Ellie Dahmer, and numerous family, June 21, 1992; Vernon Dahmer, Jr., June 23, 1992; Alvin Dahmer, Jan. 12, 1993; Raylawni Young Branch, June 22, 1992; Hollis Watkins, June 22, 1992; Victoria Gray Adams, May 14, 1991; Lawrence Guyot, Feb. 1, 1991; Joyce Ladner, Feb. 22, 1991; J. C. Fairley, June 20, 1992; Rev. John Cameron, June 23, 1992; Rev. Robert Beech, Dec. 8, 1991; J. L. Martin, June 21, 1992. Also int. Hollis Watkins by Joe Sinsheimer, Feb. 13, 1985; Whitehead, *Attack on Terror*, p. 236ff; and the Vernon Dahmer research file, courtesy of the Southern Poverty Law Center.
52   collecting the eggs: Int. Alvin Dahmer, Jan. 12, 1993.
52   had not allowed a single Negro: *United States v. Lynd*, 301 F.2d 818 (1962), p. 821.
52   Dahmer lost his bank credit: Int. Dahmer family, June 21, 1992.
52   met secretly in the Dahmer living room: Ibid. Also int. Raylawni Young Branch, June 22, 1992.
53   that Dahmer be expelled from Shady Grove: Ibid. Also int. J. C. Fairley, June 20, 1992; int. Alvin Dahmer, Jan. 12, 1993. The Dahmers recall that those expelled with Vernon Dahmer were George Kelly (a cousin), Major Bourne (owner of the downtown Negro grocery), and Silas Newell.
53   Moses pleaded: Int. Hollis Watkins, June 22, 1992; int. Hollis Watkins by Joe Sinsheimer, Feb. 13, 1985; int. Dahmer family, June 21, 1992.
53   meeting of NAACP chapter presidents: Together with interview material from Moses, Hollis Watkins, and the Dahmer family, the rough dates fit best with an NAACP convention described in Salter, *Jackson, Mississippi*, pp. 34–35.
53   "I'll take them both": Background on the placement of Watkins and Hayes at the Dahmer farm from interviews with Robert P. Moses, Feb. 15, 1991; int. Dahmer family, June 21, 1992; int. Hollis Watkins, June 22, 1992, and Jan. 11, 1993.
53–54   workshops on nonviolence: Branch, *Parting*, pp. 143, 204–5, 260–64, 274–93.
54   Nash who sent: Ibid., pp. 424–25, 430–44.
54   Nashville trio stayed on: Zinn, *New Abolitionists*, p. 79; int. James Bevel, May 17, 1985.
54   shrewdly prosecuted Nash and Bevel: *Jet*, Dec. 21, 1961, pp. 6–7.
54   "Do you want to go": Int. Bernard Lafayette, May 29, 1990.
54   Bevel looked the part: Ibid. Also Branch, *Parting*, pp. 263–64, 559.
54   Nash, who had been raised: Int. Diane Nash, April 26, 1990.
55   clerics informed her: Ibid.; *Jet*, Jan. 11, 1962, p. 23.
55   awkward silences between them: Int. Bernard Lafayette, May 29, 1990; int. Robert P. Moses, Feb. 15, 1991.
55   haunted aspect to his constant self-examination: Moses discussed the problem of moral complicity and leadership in many interviews. Once, for instance, he halted painfully while recalling Louis Allen, the witness who would be murdered himself after coming forward with testimony that Herbert Lee had been murdered. "Yes," said Moses, "except that you're not sure that he [Allen] understood what was happening. And that's the problem. I guess my only feeling about this is that you're willing to go the distance, too, so everything that you're asking people to do, you're doing yourself. And it's got to be done." Int. Robert P. Moses, July 30, 1984.
55   "After the hunting": Zinn, *New Abolitionists*, p. 79.
55   Bevel persuaded Moses: Int. James Bevel, May 17, 1985; int. Robert P. Moses, Feb. 15, 1991.
55   oppression requires the participation of the oppressed: Recalled by Nash at Session No. 2 of the Trinity College SNCC Reunion, April 14–16, 1988, transcript courtesy of Jack Chatfield.
55   withdrew the appeal: Nash "message" from jail, April 30, 1962, A/SC123f43.
56   "This will be a black baby": *Washington Afro-American*, May 8, 1962, p. 1.
56   "You know, son": Int. James Bevel, May 17, 1985.
56   arranged to bring Nash: Lafayette remarks at Session No. 3, Part 1, of the Trinity College SNCC Reunion, April 14–16, 1988, transcript courtesy of Jack Chatfield; int. Bernard Lafayette, May 29, 1990.

56   tried to persuade Nash: Int. Diane Nash, Feb. 20, 1985; int. Andrew Young, Oct. 26, 1991. For the Albany movement generally: Branch, *Parting*, pp. 524–61, 601–32.

56   back to Amzie Moore's: Int. Diane Nash, April 26, 1990.

56   placebo organization called COFO: Forman, *Black Revolutionaries*, p. 288; Carson, *In Struggle*, p. 78; Watters, *Jacob's Ladder*, pp. 63–65; int. Wiley Branton, Sept. 28, 1983.

57   one of COFO's earliest church gatherings: Mills, *Fannie Lou Hamer*, p. 24.

57   Hamer had come to see: Zinn, *New Abolitionists*, p. 93.

57   arrested Moses again: Raines, *My Soul Is Rested*, pp. 271–73; SNCC booklet, *Mississippi: A Chronicle of Violence*, p. 9, A/SC16f15; Branch, *Parting*, pp. 634–36.

57   owner of the Marlow plantation: Ibid. Also Mills, *Fannie Lou Hamer*, pp. 36–39.

57   Nash fired off a letter: *Jet*, Sept. 27, 1962.

58   "Let's go, bulls!": Int. Dahmer family, June 21, 1992.

58   Dahmer regularly pressed: Int. Hollis Watkins, June 22, 1992.

58   long-awaited check was useless: Int. Hollis Watkins by Joe Sinsheimer, Feb. 13, 1985.

58   Dahmer's mother, Ellen Kelly: Int. Dahmer family, June 21, 1992.

59   forty acres, a cow: Int. Vernon Dahmer, Jr., June 23, 1992.

59   brothers married "out of the race": Ibid. Also int. Robert Beech, Dec. 8, 1991.

59   white boss among servants: Int. Hollis Watkins, June 22, 1992.

60   "You don't want to be": Int. Vernon Dahmer, Jr., June 23, 1992.

60   graveyard behind Shady Grove Baptist Church: Ibid. From visual inspection of the Shady Grove gravestones, as interpreted by Vernon Dahmer, Jr., and his relatives, the main line of the family lineage buried there runs as follows: Susan Kelly (July 3, 1842–May 23, 1924) was the slave mistress of the white planter Kelly and the mother of Ellen L. (Kelly) Dahmer (March 27, 1876–December 22, 1954), who married George W. Dahmer (December 10, 1871–December 25, 1949). The latter two became the parents of Vernon Dahmer (March 10, 1908–January 10, 1966), whose first two wives are buried near him: Warnie Dahmer Williams (January 9, 1910–December 29, 1975) and Ora Lee Dahmer (July 9, 1919–March 22, 1950).

60   first open meeting took place: Int. Hollis Watkins, June 22, 1992, and Jan. 11, 1993; int. Alvin Dahmer, Jan. 12, 1993.

60   "I turned the question around": Int. Hollis Watkins, June 22, 1992.

61   "Who will meet me tomorrow": Int. Victoria Gray (Adams), May 14, 1991.

61   Beauty Queen's first: Ibid.

61   Doar arrived in Hattiesburg: *United States v. Lynd*, 321 F.2d 26 (1963).

61   pell-mell witness selection: Int. John Doar, May 12, 1986; John Doar speech, "The Work of the Civil Rights Division in Enforcing Voting Rights Under the Civil Rights Acts of 1957 and 1960," pp. 11–12, courtesy of John Doar.

61   dismissed the discovery portion: Factual synopsis from *United States v. Lynd*, 301 F.2d 818 (1962).

61   "injunction pending appeal": Bass, *Unlikely Heroes*, pp. 218–20.

62   "belief in simple choices": Int. Victoria Gray (Adams), May 14, 1991.

62   every day in court next to Vernon: Int. J. C. Fairley, June 20, 1992; int. Dahmer family, June 21, 1992.

62   Riddell suffered a heart attack: Lord, *Past That Would Not Die*, p. 134.

62   sensational marathon case: Ibid, pp. 131–53.

62   cherry bombs from Mayes Hall: Silver, *Closed Society*, p. 178.

62   camera taped to his ankle: Int. J. C. Fairley, June 20, 1992.

63   "the negro is not nearly so bad off": *Jackson Clarion-Ledger*, Jan. 28, 1963, quoted in Silver, *Closed Society*, p. 95.

63   runaway yearling calf: Int. Hollis Watkins, June 22, 1992; int. Dahmer family, June 21, 1992.

63   minuscule total of twelve: CBS Reports, "Mississippi and the 15th Amendment," Sept. 26, 1962.

63   revive a project in Selma: Int. Bernard Lafayette, May 28, 1990; Chestnut, *Black in Selma*, pp. 148–50; Hearings, House Judiciary Subcommittee No. 5, May 28, 1963, p. 1276.

63   first original voting suit: Department of Justice news release, April 13, 1961, FDC-NR.

63   two hundred of fifteen thousand: Ibid.

63   honor roll of the brave: Int. John Doar, May 12, 1986.

63   veteran local stalwarts: On December 9, 1958, both Samuel and Amelia Boynton testified under oath about the history of their work to register Negro voters. U.S. Commission on Civil Rights, *Hearings* (1959), pp. 211–27.

64   leading Negroes were fearful: Int. Bruce Boynton, Aug. 8, 1990; int. Amelia Boynton Robinson, Aug. 7, 1990; int. Bernard Lafayette, May 28, 1990; Chestnut, *Black in Selma*, pp. 153–59.

64   provide boarding: The teacher, Margaret Moore, drowned in the mid-1960s while attending one of SCLC's citizenship retreats near Savannah. Int. Amelia Boynton Robinson, Aug. 7, 1990; int. Marie Foster, Aug. 8, 1990.

64   Foster and her brother: Ibid. Also int. Jean and Sullivan Jackson (Foster's sister-in-law and brother), May 27, 1990.

64   white Catholic priest: Int. Bernard Lafayette, May 28, 1990.

64   pocketful of pennies: Chestnut, *Black in Selma*, pp. 38–40.

65   Enmity festered: Ibid., pp. 161–63.

65   "That little nigger": Int. Rev. L. L. Anderson, May 27, 1990.

65   "That will be your mistake": Ibid.

65   Lincoln collided: Ibid. Also trial records of *Alabama v. Anderson*, Dallas County Circuit Court No. 8799, in Fred Gray Papers, King Archives.

65   still held him vulnerable: Int. Bernard Lafayette, May 28, 1990.

66   eight unarmed Petteways: Ibid.

66   "powerless to register": Watters, *Jacob's Ladder,* p. 65.

66   Fear shut Greenwood: Branch, *Parting,* pp. 633–36; int. James Moore, June 25, 1992; Forman, *Black Revolutionaries,* pp. 283–87.

66   no better next door in Sunflower: Int. Charles Cobb, Aug. 20, 1991.

66   "So that you had": *Story of Greenwood, Mississippi,* Folkways Record FD5593.

67   nearly a third of the whites: Hearings, House Judiciary Subcommittee No. 5, May 28, 1963, p. 1278.

67   terminated all food relief: Zinn, *New Abolitionists,* p. 86; Branch, *Parting,* p. 713.

67   Ivanhoe Donaldson entered the movement: Carson, *In Struggle,* pp. 79–80.

67   SNCC's first national fund-raising: Forman, *Black Revolutionaries,* p. 293.

67   Camel Pressing Shop: Int. June Johnson, April 9, 1992.

67   Bevel finally gained: "I have talked to most of the ministers about the use of the churches but none seem to be willing to involve themselves," Bevel wrote in January 1963. In the same report, Bevel predicted that the best chance for getting a Greenwood movement started lay in providing emergency food for the hungry. Bevel, "Mississippi Report SCLC Field Secretary," A/SC41f5.

67   Bevel obtained: Int. Hollis Watkins, June 21, 1992; "Report on meeting at Wesley Methodist Church," March 18, 1963, A/SC41f7.

67   80 percent by the estimate: Hearings, House Judiciary Subcommittee No. 5, May 28, 1963, p. 1260.

68   "This is why you have": Ibid., p. 1259.

68   "We killed two-month-old Indian babies": NYT, April 6, 1963, p. 20.

68   "The chances are that": Andrew Young to "Reverend and Mrs. James Bevel," Feb. 21, 1963, A/SC41f5.

68   "Are you from Greenwood?": Int. June Johnson, April 9, 1992.

69   more than six hundred sharecroppers: Zinn, *New Abolitionists,* p. 88.

69   "We just mean to register": *Story of Greenwood, Mississippi,* Folkways Record FD5593.

69   destroying four stores: Hearings, House Judiciary Subcommittee No. 5, May 28, 1963, p. 1285.

69   galvanized many sharecroppers: Branch, *Parting,* pp. 712–25.

69   on February 25 and 26: *Story of Greenwood, Mississippi,* Folkways Record FD5593.

69   federal staff investigator: Chester Relyea of the U.S. Civil Rights Commission was arrested at the Greenwood bus station when he arrived on March 15 to investigate the cutoff of surplus foods and the lunch programs in the local public schools. *New Orleans Times-Picayune,* March 21, 1963.

69   Kennedy himself pushed: Cf. RFK "Speak to me" note on Burke Marshall's memo to RFK dated March 7, 1963, Box 16, Burke Marshall Papers, JFK.

70   Medgar Evers reported: Evers monthly report dated March 6, 1963, III-H-155, NAACP.

70   cosmetic salve: Harris, *Dreams Die Hard,* pp. 37–38; Meier, *Black Protest Thought,* p. 334; Evers to Gloster Current, Dec. 24, 1962, and Current reply to Evers, Feb. 26, 1963, III-H-155, NAACP.

70   Evers pushed New York: Evers, *For Us, the Living,* p. 252; int. Myrlie Evers, March 13, 1989; int. Andrew Young, Oct. 26, 1991.

70   Ponder heard Bevel: Annell Ponder, "Greenwood Citizenship Report, March 1963," A/SC41f7.

70   Septima Clark: Clark, *Echo in My Soul;* Clark, *Ready from Within;* Branch, *Parting,* pp. 263–64, 381–82, 575–78, 654, 899; Septima Clark Oral History, 1983, HOH.

70   first church-based literacy classes: Annell Ponder, "Greenwood Citizenship Report, March 1963," A/SC41f7.

70   more than 150 sharecroppers: Ibid.

70   "Who is going to believe": *Greenwood Commonwealth,* March 20, 1963.

70   set fire to the COFO office: Hearings, House Judiciary Subcommittee No. 5, May 28, 1963, p. 1295.

71   all eight women: Annell Ponder, "Greenwood Citizenship Report, March 1963," A/SC41f7.

71   Moses made occasional remarks: *Story of Greenwood, Mississippi,* Folkways Record FD5593.

71   officers with guns: Zinn, *New Abolitionists,* pp. 91–92.

71   Sudden spasms: Forman, *Black Revolutionaries,* pp. 296–98; Branch, *Parting,* pp. 717–21.

71   Negroes scattered: Branch, *Parting,* pp. 719–20.

71   Cleveland Jordan half dragged: Ida Mae Holland eyewitness report dated March 31, 1963, A/SC41f7.

71   Medgar Evers earned thunderous: Medgar Evers special report dated April 1, 1963, III-H-155, NAACP.

71   "the court must decide": NYT, April 4, 1963, p. 10.

71   "(b) suit": Under the 1957 statute that applied to voting, the Justice Department filed civil suits under Section 1971(a), which prohibited discrimination, and under Section 1971(b), which prohibited intimidation of prospective voters. "We called them (a) suits and (b) suits," recalled John Doar. The (b) suits were more difficult, more controversial, and rarer. Int. John Doar, May 12, 1986.

72   any trace of euphoria: Branch, *Parting,* pp. 723–25.

72   vacuum of public order: Int. John Doar, Oct. 29, 1984.

72   point of rebellion: Int. John Doar, Oct. 25, 1983.

73   Johnson boldly told Moses: Int. June Johnson, April 9, 1992.

73   Greenwood supplied sixty: Forman, *Black Revolutionaries,* p. 305.

73   symptoms of nonviolent combat fatigue: Branch, *Parting,* pp. 732–34.

73   "It's still not clear": Forman, *Black Revolutionaries,* pp. 305–7.

74   Hamer signed up: Mills, *Fannie Lou Hamer,* p. 51; Annell Ponder, "Greenwood Citizenship Report, March 1963," A/SC41f7.

74   skeletal visage of Kennard: Kennard was released on January 28, 1963, as recorded in the *Hattiesburg American* of the next day. Research courtesy of Jan Hillegas.

74   what transfixed Victoria Gray: Int. Victoria Gray Adams, May 14, 1991.

74   hitched a ride alone: Int. Victoria Gray Adams, May 14, 1991.

6. Tremors: L.A. to Selma

75   Bevel was in Birmingham: Branch, *Parting,* p. 734ff.

75   Walker's tactical innovations: Ibid., p. 730.

76   Bevel showed a film: Int. James Bevel, May 16–17, 1985. The film was an NBC White Paper entitled *Nashville Sit-ins,* produced by Bob Young, who later produced the 1964 feature film on the movement era, *Nothing but a Man.*

77   not just the older teenagers: Argument over the use of children in demonstrations from Branch, *Parting,* pp. 747–55.

77   line of fifty teenagers: Ibid., pp. 756–802.

77   trampled the chain-link fence: Int. Andrew Young, Oct. 26, 1991.

78   "Now this 'male Negro' business": Testimony of Lee Logan, May 6, 1963, BTT, p. 718ff.

78   all-white jury was probably best: Int. Earl Broady, Nov. 4, 1990, and March 25, 1991.

79   begin to admit: Ibid.

79   For a month now: Jury selection in the Muslim trial began on April 8, 1963. The last verdicts were announced on June 14, 1963.

79   up to 250 armed deputies: ANP news release dated June 17, 1963, b384f8, Claude Barnet Papers, CHS.

79   "Your Honor": BTT, p. 723.

79   "might pull a Muslim": LAT, May 6, 1963.

79   "As a Muslim": BTT, p. 1303.

79   "Just for the record": BTT, p. 365.

79   Kuykendall was to remain: Int. Paul Kuykendall, Feb. 7, 1992; int. Jesse Brewer, June 13, 1991; int. Samuel Hunter, Feb. 6, 1992; int. Frank Tomlinson, Oct. 15, 1991.

80   fn "The average so-called Negro": Malcolm X interview on the radio program *At Random,* March 3, 1963, FMXNY-3434.

80   Muslim witnesses denied: BTT, *passim;* int. Wazir Muhammad (Randolph Sidle), March 27, 1991; int. Karim Muhammad (Troy Augustine) by Jonah Edelman, June 14, 1991.

80   "We are not sitting idly by": Branch, *Parting,* p. 778ff.

81   Zeno testified: BTT, pp. 1397–98.

81   no human being could endure: Ibid., pp. 2590–91.

81   admitted feeling resentment: (Defendant Nathaniel X. Rivers), ibid., p. 1867.

82   "Are you a registered": Int. Amelia Boynton Robinson, Aug. 7, 1990; int. Bernard Lafayette, May 28, 1990.

82   Lafayette canvassed: Int. Bernard Lafayette, May 28, 1990.

82   and other pastors refused: Ibid. Also Chestnut, *Black in Selma,* pp. 160–63.

82   "They don't feel disposed": Int. Rev. L. L. Anderson, May 27, 1990.

82   "I understand you call yourself": Ibid.

83   "No, no, brother pastor": Ibid.

83   Tuesday evening, May 14: Tabernacle mass meeting from Chestnut, *Black in Selma,* pp. 163–65; STJ, May 15, 1963; Forman, *Black Revolutionaries,* p. 318. Also int. Bernard Lafayette, May 28, 1990; int. Rev. L. L. Anderson, May 27, 1990; remarks of Bernard Lafayette at Session No. 3, Part 1, of the Trinity College SNCC Reunion, April 14–16, 1988, transcript courtesy of Jack Chatfield.

84   758 racial demonstrations: Branch, *Parting,* p. 825.

7. Marx in the White House

86   "I cannot condone": Branch, *Parting,* p. 761.

86   "extreme and extremely dangerous": AJ, May 10, 1963, p. 26.

86   "School children participating": Branch, *Parting,* p. 762.

86   "making a fool of himself": LAT, May 5, 1963.

86   "any man who puts": Lomax, *When the Word Is Given,* p. 85.

86   "You can't call it results": Malcolm X interview on WUST radio, May 12, 1963, FMX-64.

87   "Grievances of the Two": MS, June 21, 1963, p. 1.

87   more stories about race: Rough news comparisons drawn from *New York Times* index entries for "Negroes," "NATO," "TV and Radio," and "Malcolm X (Little)" as follows: 1962 NYT Index, pp. 582, 643–50, 709–15, 900–907; 1963 NYT Index, pp. 489, 535–59, 596–604, 774–80; 1964 NYT Index, pp. 592, 656–91, 750–58, 1000–1005.

87   nine per week: Muse, *American Negro Revolution,* p. 39.

87   "have moved out in front": *U.S. News & World Report,* July 29, 1963, quoted in ibid.

87   "doomed to founder": *National Review,* July 2, 1963, pp. 519–20.

87 "The Peace Corps has won": Bill Moyers to Shriver, May 15, 1963, Box 41, Moyers Papers, LBJ.

87 "You have me reeling": Ibid.; int. Sargent Shriver, June 29, 1993.

88 President Kennedy met privately: Branch, *Parting,* pp. 796–809.

88 "might tear up that paper agreement": White House meeting, May 12, 1963, Audiotape 86.2, JFK.

88 "We ought to have him": White House meeting, May 20, 1963, Audiotape 88.4, JFK.

89 chorus of Baldwin's choosing: Branch, *Parting,* pp. 809–13.

89 Kennedy marked Jones: Ibid., p. 812.

89 Kennedy hurled his conflicted energies: Burke Marshall Oral History, LBJ.

90 On May 29, Johnson: Transcript of the May 29, 1963, meeting of the President's Committee on Equal Employment Opportunity, office files of George Reedy, Container 7, LBJ.

90 " 'Why should we hire Negroes?' ": Branch, *Parting,* p. 807.

91 "Can I obtain from you immediately": Page 26, transcript of the May 29, 1963, meeting of the President's Committee on Equal Employment Opportunity, office files of George Reedy, Container 7, LBJ.

91 "period and paragraph": Ibid., p. 68.

91 Antonio Taylor of New Mexico: Ibid., p. 86.

91 magnified his humiliation: Edison Dictaphone Recording of LBJ-Sorensen conversation, June 3, 1963, p. 14, LBJ.

91 distinguished public appointees: The public appointees to the employment committee included United Auto Workers president Walter Reuther, industrialist Edgar Kaiser, Dean Francis B. Sayre of the Washington Cathedral, and Rabbi Jacob J. Weinstein of Temple KAM in Chicago. Rabbi Weinstein recorded his impressions of the tense meeting in a letter to his friend Arthur Goldberg, then the newest Supreme Court Justice, about the meeting. "For 4¹/₂ hours we really sweated it out as Lyndon Johnson and Robert Kennedy engaged in a sharp dialogue," wrote Weinstein, "the one defending the Committee against the other's sharp probing into its methods." Jacob J. Weinstein Papers, 14f3, CHS.

91–92 the Memorial Day address: Vice President's Daily Diary for Thursday, May 30, 1963, LBJ. Also programs, invitations, and memos in Statements, Box 80, LBJ.

92 berated his staff: Int. Horace Busby, Feb. 12, 1992.

92 "One hundred years ago": Statements, Box 80, LBJ.

92 To the end of his life: Int. Horace Busby, Feb. 12, 1992. Cf. "The President wanted you to have a copy of his 1963 Memorial Day speech...." Harry McPherson to Adam Clayton Powell, Dec. 26, 1968, White House Central File, Name File, LBJ.

92 Not once had he been consulted: Burke Marshall Oral History, LBJ.

92 briefing notes over the shoulder: Lee White Oral History, fifth interview, March 17, 1970, JFK. Also Lee White Oral History, Sept. 28, 1970, LBJ; int. Lee White, Dec. 13, 1983.

93 the Vice President wilted: White House meeting of June 1, 1963, Audiotape 90.3, JFK.

93 personal nemesis, Robert Kennedy: Johnson refers to his conversation with Kennedy in Edison Dictaphone recording of LBJ-Sorensen conversation, June 3, 1963, pp. 6–7, LBJ.

93 "absolutely poured out his heart": The assistant was Norbert Schlei, assistant attorney general, Office of Legal Counsel. Graham, *Civil Rights Era,* pp. 77–78. Also LBJ to Sorensen, June 10, 1963, with "personal and confidential" attachment, Box 30, Sorensen Papers, JFK.

93 "We got a little popgun": Edison Dictaphone recording of LBJ-Sorensen conversation, June 3, 1963, p. 14, LBJ.

94 "I know the risks": Ibid., p. 4.

94 "Every cruel and evil influence": Ibid., p. 9.

95 "They'll probably boo me off the platform": Ibid., p. 18.

95 "I'm not gonna watch the parade": Branch, *Parting,* p. 808.

95 "Re-Cap": Hamilton, *Adam Clayton Powell, Jr.,* pp. 361–62.

96 appearing together more frequently: For instance, Malcolm and Powell shared the platform with Dick Gregory at a rally for the Mississippi Relief Committee in Harlem, March 23, 1963, FMX-53; Malcolm preached at Powell's church on June 23, 1963, FMX-74, New York report dated Nov. 15, 1963, pp. 20–21.

96 Malcolm X, who did nurse ambitions: Perry, *Malcolm: A Life,* p. 297; Lomax, *When the Word Is Given,* p. 97.

96 "It's hard to tell": Perry, *Malcolm: A Life,* p. 304.

96 leadership vacuum among Washington's Negroes: WP, May 6, 1963, p. 1.

96 regularly lionized Powell: First noticed in print by reporter M. S. Handler in NYT, April 23, 1963, p. 20.

96 Malcolm X slowly disappear: In his autobiography, Malcolm recalled that he noticed his presence fading in *Muhammad Speaks* as early as 1962. Malcolm X, *Autobiography,* p. 292.

96 "new assertive mood": NYT, April 23, 1963, p. 20.

96 Handler managed to squeeze: Int. J. Anthony Lukas, June 10, 1990.

97 Malcolm X called Phoenix: Wiretap conversation of April 27, 1963, FMX-74, p. cover-C.

97 Parks attended a karate class: "A Negro Photographer Shoots from Inside the Black Muslims," *Life,* May 31, 1963.

97 "shows how to deal": Ibid., p. 25.

97 doing his best to delay: Wiretap conversation of May 13, 1963, FMX-74, p. cover-C.

97 "being built around Malcolm": Wiretap conversation of May 14, 1963, FMX-74, p. cover-D.

98 staring into the drawn revolvers: LAT, May 23, 1963; MS, June 7, 1963, p. 1.

98 "Code 6-M": Int. Jesse Brewer, June 13, 1991; int. Samuel Hunter, Feb. 6, 1992; int. Frank Tomlinson, Oct. 15, 1991.

98   Laughter exploded: BTT, pp. 2659–60.
98   "And I think you have never": BTT, p. 2910.
98   "they ought to take": Ibid., pp. 2928–29.
99   "Now, without going into": Ibid., p. 2946.
99   "I can't see an officer": Ibid., p. 2986.
99   "thrown their guns down": Ibid., p. 2962.
99   "admitted certain things": Wiretap conversation of May 28, 1963, FMXNY-3634. The interpretation presented here draws upon interviews with Benjamin Karim and Yusuf Shah about the state of relations between Malcolm X and Elijah Muhammad in mid-1963 and about Malcolm X's complex documentary aims in writing his letters.
99   long Stokes deliberation: LAT, June 5, 15, 17, 1963; *California Eagle,* June 20, 1963.
99   collapsed of a heart attack: LAT, June 6, 1963.
100   campaign against their own verdict: Int. Earl Broady, Nov. 4, 1990, and March 25, 1991; int. Jacquelyn Ames (juror), March 26, 1991; int. Josephine Byrne (juror), March 26, 1991; int. Maureen Dobratz (juror), March 26, 1991; *California Eagle,* Aug. 22, 1963, p. 1; MS, Sept. 13, 1963.
100   remained the leading story: Among many screaming, page-one headlines in MS were "Rips 'KKK in Cop Clothes!' " June 7, 1963, and "Prison for the Innocent! Muslims Framed to Whitewash the Guilty?" Aug. 30, 1963.
100   "It will take fire": MS, July 19, 1963.
100   discarded as a lecture prop: Int. Benjamin Karim, March 19, 1991.
100   later from his autobiography: Malcolm X, *Autobiography,* p. 394.
100    $150,000 in a week: Branch, *Parting,* p. 806.
100   a friend said movie stars: Wiretap conversation of 5:19 P.M., June 1, 1963, between Levison and "Antoinette," FLNY-9-185a.
100   "a feeling of nationalism": Wiretap conversation of 11:31 P.M., June 1, 1963, FLNY-9–185a.
100   On May 30, he sent a telegram: King to JFK, HU2, 5/9/63– 7/19/63, Box 363, WHCF, JFK.
100   "We need the President": Wiretap conversation of 11:31 P.M., June 1, 1963, FLNY-9–185a.
101   National NAACP officers: Branch, *Parting,* pp. 813–14.
101   suddenly by way of Jackson: Evers, *For Us, the Living,* pp. 270–82; Moody, *Coming of Age,* pp. 234–51; Salter, *Jackson, Mississippi,* pp. 132–53; Branch, *Parting,* pp. 814–16.
101   "This is the *biggest* thing": Salter, *Jackson, Mississippi,* p. 145.
101   "Jackson Police Jail 600": NYT, June 1, 1963, p. 1.
101   Evers collaborated by phone: King comment in wiretap conversation of 11:31 P.M., June 1, 1963, FLNY-9–185a. Also int. Myrlie Evers, March 13, 1989.
102   officers arrested Henderson: Int. Thelton Henderson, Jr., Feb. 25, 1994.
102   first arrest in nearly thirty years: Wilkins, *Standing Fast,* pp. 288–89; Salter, *Jackson, Mississippi,* pp. 154-58.
102   the *Times* noted: NYT, June 2, 1963, p. 70.
102   "We've baptized brother Wilkins!": Wiretap conversation of June 2, 1963, FLNY-9–186a, p. 3.
102   What seized King: Like King, some observers in the black press perceived the Wilkins arrest as an omen of change, e.g. "Is NAACP Leaving Courts for Front-Line Protest?," CD, June 8–14, 1963. Soon after, other journals declared that the Wilkins arrest was merely a feinted concession to the Jackson upheaval: "When NAACP leaders were asked why their demonstrations were called off, [Director of Branches Gloster] Current replied, 'Would you want to be a murderer?' " "NAACP Switches Tactics in Massive Miss. Rights Fight," *Jet,* June 20, 1963, pp. 8–9.
102   "We are on a breakthrough": Wiretap conversation of June 1, 1963, FLNY-9–185a.
102   "Roy will only act": Wiretap conversation of June 1, 1963, FLNY-9–185a.
102   called each other like teenagers: Wiretap conversations of June 2, 1963, FLNY-9–186a, and June 3, 1963, FLNY-7–441.

8. SUMMER FREEZE

104   King received: Lee White to MLK, June 1, 1963, stamped receipt dated June 3, A/KP14f4.
104   On June 7, the General Board: Findlay, *Church People in the Struggle,* pp. 3–4; NCC press release dated June 7, 1963, A/SN115f3.
104   Continuing Committee: Findlay, *Church People in the Struggle,* p. 32; int. Mathew Ahmann and Jerome Ernst, Feb. 12, 1991.
104   subterranean groundswell: Int. Robert Stone, June 3, 1993; int. Metz Rollins, Dec. 13, 1991.
104   committing $500,000: Findlay, *Church People in the Struggle,* p. 33.
104   "The world watches to see": "A Report of the President's Temporary Committee of Six on Race," approved by the General Board on June 7, 1963, A/SN115f3.
105   bypass the leadership: Int. Robert Stone, June 3, 1993; int. Metz Rollins, Dec. 13, 1991; int. Oscar Lee, Sept. 26, 1991. Nearly thirty years later, Lee remained wounded that the National Council brought in a fresh team led by whites with little experience in race relations. "It was a rough kind of a deal," he recalled.
105   only Negro on the six-hundred-member: Int. Oscar Lee, Sept. 26, 1991; int. Andrew Young, Oct. 26, 1991.
105   fn Yale Divinity School: Lee background from int. Oscar Lee, Sept. 26, 1991; Findlay, *Church People in the Struggle,* pp. 17–18.
105   "the real depth": Rev. Edler Hawkins, quoted in "Minutes, National Council of Churches, Commission on Religion and Race," June 28, 1963.

105   "Twenty Days Later": Ibid.
105   "to *commit* ourselves": "A Report of the President's Temporary Committee of Six on Race," approved by the General Board on June 7, 1963, A/SN115f3.
105   "What Have I Personally Done": STJ, June 9, 1963, cited in Chestnut, *Black in Selma*, p. 167.
106   Ponder did not arrive in Greenwood: COFO, *Mississippi Black Paper*, pp. 17–24; Mills, *Fannie Lou Hamer*, pp. 56–77; Branch, *Parting*, pp. 819–21.
106   Andrew Young interjected: Wiretap conversation of 12:01 A.M., June 10, 1963, FLNY-9–194.
106   Guyot volunteered: Int. Lawrence Guyot, Feb. 1, 1991.
106   from far away in Danville, Virginia: Forman, *Black Revolutionaries*, pp. 326–31; Lyon, *Memories*, pp. 62–69.
106   "beastly conduct": MLK to RFK, 12:35 P.M. EST, June 11, 1963, A/KP31f18.
106   was pressing the FBI to find out: Memo, C. A. Evans to Hoover, June 11, 1963, cited in Mills, *Fannie Lou Hamer*, p. 36.
106   "There was no violence": NYT, June 12, 1963, p. 1.
106–107   "Dr. King Denounces President": NYT, June 10, 1963, p. 1.
107   Kennedy decided spontaneously: Branch, *Parting*, p. 823; NYT, June 12, 1963, p. 1.
107   two-toned 1957 Chevrolet: Forman, *Black Revolutionaries*, pp. 321–22.
107   "No, Red, don't shoot!": Remarks of Bernard Lafayette at Session No. 3, Part 1, of the Trinity College SNCC Reunion, April 14–16, 1988, transcript courtesy of Jack Chatfield.
107   "Milk is for calves": Int. Bernard Lafayette, May 28, 1990.
108   "We are confronted primarily": NYT, June 12, 1963, p. 20.
108   a law student newly arrived: Mills, *Fannie Lou Hamer*, pp. 63–64. After finishing Yale Law School and working as an equal rights lawyer for nearly three decades, including service as chair of the Equal Employment Opportunity Commission under President Jimmy Carter, Eleanor Holmes Norton was elected in 1990 to the U.S. House of Representatives from the District of Columbia.
108   An argument broke out: Int. Andrew Young, Oct. 26, 1991; int. James Bevel, May 17, 1985; int. Dorothy Cotton, Nov. 19, 1992.
109   "I hold *you* responsible!": Int. June Johnson, April 9, 1992.
109   telegram from the White House: JFK to MLK, June 12, 1963, A/KP14f4.
110   "Deeply regret that I had overlooked": MLK to JFK, June 13, 1963, A/KP14f4.
110   trustees of Lovett School: The conflict over Coretta King's attempt to enroll Martin III at Lovett is reviewed in "Statement of the Executive Committee of the Episcopal Society for Cultural and Racial Unity on the Lovett School Situation" (drafted by Rev. John B. Morris), Sept. 1963, A/KP9f26.
110   sniped at King during the funeral: Branch, *Parting*, pp. 825–31.
110   "may intimidate a few": NYT, June 13, 1963, pp. 1, 13.
110   off-base segregation: Graham, *Civil Rights Era*, p. 86.
111   annex to Harlem Hospital: NYT, June 13, 1963, p. 1; NYT, June 14, 1963, p. 1.
111   In Philadelphia: Graham, *Civil Rights Era*, pp. 278, 528–29.
111   In St. Augustine, Florida: Colburn, *Racial Change*, pp. 33–35.
111   "I and others have armed": Jacksonville LHM entitled "Racial Situation, St. Augustine, Florida," June 19, 1963, FSA-NR.
111   "racial feelings amongst the Negroes": Ibid.
111   received orders to shoot: Jacksonville LHM entitled "Racial Situation, St. Augustine, Florida," June 20, 1963, FSA-NR.
111   fired a shotgun into Hayling's garage: Jacksonville teletypes to FBI headquarters, July 2, 1963, FSA-476 and FSA-477.
111   tiny Itta Bena: June 18 Itta Bena arrests from undated SNCC report entitled *Mississippi*, A/KP16f15, p. 15; also int. William McGee, June 25, 1992; "Report on the Release of 57 Prisoners in Mississippi," by John M. Pratt of the National Council of Churches, Aug. 23, 1963, NCC RG6, b47f31, POH.
112   "Californian Is Charged": *Jackson Clarion-Ledger*, June 24, 1963, reprinted in Silver, *Closed Society*, p. 30.
113   fn "I have sworn": Byron de la Beckwith, "Open Letter to All Episcopalians," *Jackson Daily News*, March 16, 1956, located and preserved in the papers of Rev. Edwin King, b8f387, Tougaloo.
113   Newspapers described Beckwith: *Jackson Clarion-Ledger*, June 24, 1963, p. 1.
113   courthouse on June 25: Undated SNCC report entitled *Mississippi*, A/KP16f15, p. 15; undated affidavit of Douglas MacArthur Cotton, A/MFDP10f1; int. Hollis Watkins, June 22, 1992.
113   grumbling against William McGee: Int. William McGee, June 25, 1992.
114   truck hauled them away: Undated affidavit of Douglas MacArthur Cotton, A/MFDP10f1; int. Hollis Watkins, June 22, 1992.
114   Rusk sent a cable: Rusk to "All American Diplomatic and Consular Posts," June 19, 1963, NSF b295, JFK. See also the critical reply of John Kenneth Galbraith, U.S. ambassador to India, in Galbraith to Rusk, June 20, 1963, NSF b295, JFK.
114   "We assume": O'Donnell to King, June 19, 1963, A/KP14f4.
114   King went to the summit: Branch, *Parting*, pp. 835–41.
114   weakened or reversed: Graham, *Civil Rights Era*, p. 85.
115   fn "Of course, the less": Ibid.
115   Robert Kennedy offered: NYT, June 27, 1963, p. 1.
115   nobody in Congress had been interested: Robert Kennedy Oral History by John Bartlow Martin, JFK.
115   "sort of death wish": Ibid., cited in Graham, *Civil Rights Era*, p. 127.
115   "overwhelming the whole program": Branch, *Parting*, pp. 827–28.

115   soar briefly again in Detroit: Ibid., pp. 842–43.
115   "The incident was attributed": CD, July 6, 1963, p. 10.
115   "did this unbecomming [sic] thing": Rev. James Early, Sr., to MLK, July 1, 1963, A/KP1f7.
115   fn "I think any effort": *New York Journal American*, July 1, 1963, p. 6, FMXNY-3713.
115   fn "growing bitterness": CD, July 10, 1963, p. 10.
116   King debated: Branch, *Parting*, pp. 844–45.
116   wound up in notorious Parchman: "Report on the Release of 57 Prisoners in Mississippi," by John M. Pratt of the National Council of Churches, Aug. 23, 1963, NCC RG6, b47f31, POH; report marked "From: Hollis Watkins in Parchman State Penitentiary," A/SN23f12; undated affidavit of Douglas MacArthur Cotton, A/MFDP10f1; int. Hollis Watkins, June 22, 1992.
116   fn James K. Vardaman: Oshinsky, *Worse Than Slavery*, pp. 85–106.
116   Guyot and Watkins found themselves: Int. Hollis Watkins, June 22, 1992.
117   filed three novel actions: Branch, *Parting*, p. 826.
117   nameless for six weeks: Ibid., p. 827.
117   movement itself did not care: Int. Hollis Watkins, June 22, 1992; int. William McGee, June 25, 1992.
117   hanging in handcuffs: "Report on the Release of 57 Prisoners in Mississippi," by John M. Pratt of the National Council of Churches, Aug. 23, 1963, NCC RG6, b47f31, POH; undated affidavit of Douglas MacArthur Cotton, A/MFDP10f1.
117   fn *Gates v. Collier:* Oshinsky, *Worse Than Slavery*, pp. 241–48.
117   let their wastes fall down: Int. Hollis Watkins, June 22, 1992.

9. Cavalry: Lowenstein and the Church

118   Allard Lowenstein had trekked: Lowenstein, *Brutal Mandate, passim;* Chafe, *Never Stop Running*, pp. 131–65.
118   "We will not soon forget": Lowenstein address to the United Nations Fourth Committee, Oct. 17, 1959, reprinted in Stone and Lowenstein, *Acts of Courage*, pp. 7–14.
119   fact-finding tour of Southern campuses: Jones to Bishop, April 4, 1974, FAL-77, p. 10. This FBI summary of intelligence on Lowenstein noted his activity in "the so-called civil rights movement," citing an account in the *New York Times* of March 20, 1960.
119   "teachings and philosophies": Ibid., p. 18.
119   plotted the heartache of Spanish: Chafe, *Never Stop Running*, pp. 14–15.
119   Adlai Stevenson twice visited: Stone and Lowenstein, *Acts of Courage*, pp. 234–35.
119   "an energetic young American": Department of State airgram from Madrid, Aug. 17, 1962, cited in New York FBI report on internal security, dated Sept. 27, 1962, FAL-23, pp. 2–6.
119   "made it clear": Ibid.
119   agents mostly chased: See generally the Lowenstein FBI file, FAL, Serials 7 through 50. The FBI investigation of Lowenstein under the Foreign Agents Registration Act remained open from the fall of 1961 through the summer of 1963, as summarized in Jones to Bishop, April 4, 1974, FAL-77, p. 4.
119   perturbed administrators of Stanford: San Francisco FBI office investigative report dated April 30, 1962, FAL-18.
119   single-handedly bowled over campus culture: Chafe, *Never Stop Running*, pp. 166–77.
120   "Last week was perhaps": Armin Rosencranz to Lowenstein, May 13, 1963, b8f289, Lowenstein Papers, UNC.
120   fn "Awe is more than an emotion": Stanford lectures published as Heschel, *Who Is Man?*, pp. 88, 115–17.
120   Lowenstein was across the country: Chafe, *Never Stop Running*, pp. 178–79.
120   "this extra one": Robert Spearman to Lowenstein, b32f347, Lowenstein Papers, UNC.
120   "the hostile peak": "N." to Lowenstein, June 14, 1963, on the stationery of the UNC Dean of Women, b32f292, Lowenstein Papers, UNC.
121   "Dear Chief": Lowenstein to Chief Albert J. Lituli [sic], March 22, 1963, Box 16, Lowenstein Papers, UNC.
121   "Dear Sir": Lowenstein to the President, Eastern Air Lines, June 28, 1963, Box 16, Lowenstein Papers, UNC.
121   "Dear Miss Hepburn": Lowenstein to Hepburn, Aug. 27, 1963, Box 16, Lowenstein Papers, UNC.
121   three meals with James Meredith: Lowenstein speech of Oct. 2, 1963, at Stanford, Tape No. 631002-S1-2, SUARC.
121   on July 4 introduced himself: Carson, *In Struggle*, pp. 96–97; Harris, *Dreams Die Hard*, pp. 30–31; Cagin and Dray, *We Are Not Afraid*, pp. 210–11; Chafe, *Never Stop Running*, pp. 180–82.
121   Rev. Edwin King had hurtled: Int. Edwin King, June 26, 1992. Also Salter, *Jackson, Mississippi*, pp. 132–39; Edwin King, "Growing Up in Mississippi in a Time of Change"; Silver, *Closed Society*, pp. 58–60; Findlay, *Church People in the Struggle*, p. 141; int. Edwin King, June 26, 1992.
121   fn turned away from Galloway Church: Silver, *Closed Society*, p. 59; int. Edwin King, June 26, 1992; Cunningham, *Agony at Galloway*, pp. 13–35.
121   lug nuts on his tires: Dennis Sweeney speech of Oct. 2, 1963, at Stanford, Tape No. 631002-S1-2, SUARC.
121   acknowledged some weeping confessions: *Jackson Clarion-Ledger,* June 1, 1963, p. 1.
122   gift books by Gandhi: Int. Edwin King, June 26, 1992.
122   northward into the Delta: Ibid. Also Aaron Henry to Lowenstein, July 13, 1963, b8f294, Lowenstein Papers, UNC.

122   "I am at present in the heart": King telegram to Hosea Williams, July 9, 1963, A/KP3f15.

122   "I'm Al Lowenstein": Cagin and Dray, *We Are Not Afraid*, p. 210.

122   Bob Dylan and Josh White: NYT, July 6, 1963, p. 7.

122   "holding out": Chafe, *Never Stop Running*, p. 181.

122   Moses remembered him: Int. Robert P. Moses, Aug. 10, 1983.

122   Moses confessed the paralysis: Int. Robert P. Moses by Anne Romaine, Sept. 1966, pp. 64–69, A/AR.

122   Africans withdrew into formal mourning: Chafe, *Never Stop Running*, p. 181.

123   From this seed grew: Ibid. Also int. Edwin King, June 26, 1992.

123   no small resistance: Cf. Moody, *Coming of Age*, p. 297.

123   "Across the chasm between white and nonwhite": Lowenstein, *Brutal Mandate*, p. 185.

123   "Dear Al, Bad news!": Bill [Edwards] to Lowenstein, July 21, 1963, Lowenstein Papers, UNC.

123   "Mississippi: A Foreign": Lowenstein speech of Oct. 2, 1963, reprinted in Stone and Lowenstein, *Acts of Courage*, pp. 22–36.

123   "we've come up with two ideas": Ibid. For a recorded version of the complete speech, see Tape No. 631002-S1-2, SUARC.

123   Robert Spike: Findlay, *Church People in the Struggle*, pp. 34–35; int. Jack Pratt, March 25, 1991; int. Bruce Hanson, Feb. 22, 1991.

123   "practically no interest in racial": Findlay, *Church People in the Struggle*, p. 191, n. 18.

124   Gwynn Oak Amusement Park: NYT, July 5, 1963, p. 1.

124   full-time chemist: Williams profile, AJ, Nov. 8, 1965; Hosea L. Williams, "History and Philosophy of the Southeastern Georgia Crusade for Voters," A/SC139f2; int. Hosea Williams, Oct. 29, 1991.

124   not board material: Int. Hosea Williams, Oct. 29, 1991.

124   became like a son: Ibid. Also int. Septima Clark, Dec. 17, 1983.

125   Savannah's historic Negro pulpits: Woodson, *History of the Negro Church*, p. 41ff.

125   trademark .38-caliber pistols: Lester Hankerson Oral History, Telfair Academy of Arts and Sciences, Savannah; int. Lester Hankerson, nd.

125   climbed upon Tomochichi's Rock: Int. Hosea Williams, Oct. 29, 1991; int. Willie Bolden, May 14, 1992; NYT, June 14, 1963, p. 16.

125   obscure Civil War ordinance: NYT, July 11, 1963, p. 1; SCLC press release dated Aug. 15, 1963, A/SC139f23.

125   hemorrhage of runaway slaves: For contemporary evidence of distress about runaway slaves from the Savannah slaveowners' point of view, see Myers, *Children of Pride*, esp. Vol. 4, pp. 151–74.

125   eleven white citizens: SCLC press release dated Aug. 15, 1963, A/SC139f23; WP, Sept 4, 1963, p. 6.

125   Spike landed in Savannah: Robert Spike report, "A Night of Watching," July 26, 1963, p. 4, NCC RG6, b48f13, POH.

126   "Two Negroes Shot": NYT, July 12, 1963, p. 8.

126   "Spike for introducing them": Int. Andrew Young, Oct. 26, 1991.

126   undercurrents within Negro Savannah: Ibid. Also int. W. W. Law, Dec. 17, 1983; int. Hosea Williams, Oct. 29, 1991; NYT, June 27, 1963, p. 20.

126   meetings at the Flamingo Club: Oral histories by Carolyn Barlow, Sidney Barnes, Henry "Trash" Brownlee, Rick Tuttle, and Andrew Young, Telfair Academy of Arts and Sciences, Savannah.

126   "It was largely the work": Speech of July 12, 1963, Tape No. BB0358, PRA.

126   "You think these white folks": Ibid.

127   "This is the first time": Robert Spike report, "A Night of Watching," July 26, 1963, p. 2, NCC RG6, b48f13, POH.

127   Young's first trip to jail: Int. Andrew Young, Oct. 26, 1991.

127   "I had the strongest feeling": Robert Spike report, "A Night of Watching," July 26, 1963, p. 2, NCC RG6, b48f13, POH.

127   first group of white emissaries: Ibid., p. 8. Also Findlay, *Church People in the Struggle*, p. 79.

127   "There was constant police surveillance": Spike, "Report of the Executive Director," Sept. 5, 1963, NCC RG6, b47f31, POH, pp. 1–2.

128    $10,000 bail grant: Ibid., p. 3.

128   came to Jack Pratt: Int. Jack Pratt, March 25, 1991.

128   Pratt rushed back to Mississippi: Jack Pratt, "Report on the Release of 57 Prisoners in Mississippi," Aug. 23, 1963, NCC RG6, b47f31. Also Pratt memo on bail project, Oct. 21, 1963, A/SN115f3; Pratt speech at Union Theological Seminary, Jan. 7, 1964, NCC RG6, b47f31, POH.

128   threatening to shoot the prisoners: Undated affidavit of Douglas MacArthur Cotton, A/MFDP10f1.

128   "Put that gun down!": Int. Jack Pratt, March 25, 1991.

128   welcoming celebration: Ibid. Also int. William McGee, June 25, 1992; int. Hollis Watkins, June 22, 1992.

129   Arterbery greeted him with deputies: Jack Pratt, "Report on the Release of 57 Prisoners in Mississippi," Aug. 23, 1963, NCC RG6, b47f31.

129   "Praise God!": Int. Jack Pratt, March 25, 1991.

10. Mirrors in Black and White

130   Watkins did not attend: Int. Hollis Watkins, June 22, 1992.

130   "Even the Federal Government": Gentile, *The March on Washington*, p. 160.

131 "The black man is the original man": Malcolm X remarks on the Jay Lawrence radio show, WNOR, Norfolk, Va., Aug. 22, 1963, FMXNY-3804.

131 he held court: Forman, *Black Revolutionaries*, p. 333; Gentile, *The March on Washington*, p. 162.

131 consumed by an offstage controversy: Forman, *Black Revolutionaries*, pp. 333–34; Gentile, *The March on Washington*, pp. 170–83; Branch, *Parting*, pp. 872–80.

131 Malcolm congratulated him: Int. John Lewis by Archie Allen, AAP.

131 "I am not condemning": Gentile, *The March on Washington*, p. 162.

131 preempting regularly scheduled: Branch, *Parting*, p. 881.

131 "it would be impossible to bring": *Meet the Press* transcript for the program of Aug. 25, 1963.

131 "its worst case of invasion jitters": *Life*, Aug. 23, 1963, p. 63.

131 President Kennedy's campaign: Branch, *Parting*, pp. 840–41, 872; Gentile, *The March on Washington*, pp. 127–29, 142–50; Reeves, *President Kennedy*, pp. 578–82.

132 fn National Football League: *Baltimore Sun*, Nov. 21, 1993, p. 9C.

132 1,700 extra correspondents: Gentile, *The March on Washington*, p. 201; also "March Gets Big Play in World Newspapers," WP, Aug. 30, 1963, p. 5.

132 fn "I would walk around": Gentile, *The March on Washington*, pp. 198–99.

132 including politicians who supported: Int. Harry McPherson, Sept. 24, 1991.

132 "White legs and Negro legs": *Life*, Sept. 6, 1963, p. 22.

132 "I'm so proud of my people.": Ibid., p. 21.

132 four march-related arrests: WP, Aug. 29, 1963, p. 27.

132 fn a dozen years before the dawn: Reid, *The Chip*, p. 144.

133 "Negro Gothic": *Life*, Sept. 6, 1963, p. 21.

133 "Beer drinkers especially": WP, Sept. 4, 1963, p. 17.

133 network management believed: *Newsweek*, Sept. 23, 1963, pp. 63–66.

134 Kennedy granted Cronkite: Reeves, *President Kennedy*, pp. 586–87.

134 fn "We are trying to do": Text of interview, WP, Sept. 3, 1963, p. 11.

134 "leisurely": NYT, Sept. 3, 1963, p. 67.

134 Japanese singers: Ibid.

134 fill a thirty-minute report: *Newsweek*, Sept. 23, 1963, pp. 63–66.

134 network itself showed signs: NYT, Sept. 3, 1963, p. 67.

134 "There comes a time": *American Revolution '63*, NBC News special aired Sept. 2, 1963, transcript excerpts courtesy of Lawrence W. Lichty, the Woodrow Wilson Center, Washington, D.C.

135 news and entertainment programs: Dates, *Split Image*, pp. 256–57, 307, 366–67, 378, 389.

135 "The Negro in America": *Newsweek*, July 29, 1963, pp. 15–34.

136 "What the White Man Thinks": *Newsweek*, Oct. 21, 1963, pp. 44–57.

136 Americus, Georgia, death case: Branch, *Parting*, pp. 864–66; also Pratt memo of Oct. 21, 1963, A/SN115f3; Abram, *Day Is Short*, pp. 139–40.

136 fed up with demonstrations: NYT, Nov. 1, 1963, p. 19.

136 "a shocked and silent audience": *Stanford Daily News*, Nov. 8, 1963, found in Lowenstein Papers, f32f365, UNC.

136 legal forays by lawyers: Int. Jack Pratt, March 25, 1991.

136 Hayling had deployed: Colburn, *Racial Change*, pp. 40–42; Hayling telegram to Roy Wilkins, July 23, 1963, III-C-305, NAACP; SAC, Jacksonville, to Director, July 25, 1963, FSA-686; "Report on the Open Meeting in St. Augustine, Florida, August 16," Florida Advisory Committee to the U.S. Commission on Civil Rights," Brian Simpson Papers, UF.

137 "seemed emotionally upset": SAC, Jacksonville, to Director, July 23, 1963, FSA-645.

137 "Florida is going to get": *Daytona Beach Morning Journal*, July 26, 1963.

137 "drowses today": NYT, July 29, 1963, p. 9.

137 locked up until December: Colburn, *Racial Change*, p. 42.

137 first large-scale demonstration: Ibid., p. 48; SAC, Jacksonville, to Director, Sept. 2, 1963, FSA-831.

137 dynamite obliterated: Branch, *Parting*, pp. 888–91.

138 "massacre of the innocents": NYT, Sept. 17, 1963, p. 26.

138 twenty previous bombings: NYT, Sept. 16, 1963, p. 26.

138 Mercer University: NYT, Sept. 17, 1963, p. 26.

138 fn repulsed Oni with force: Holmes, *Ashes for Breakfast*, pp. 13–17.

138 "we join you in mourning": *Baptists Today*, Aug. 26, 1993.

138 "I know I speak": WP, Sept. 17, 1963, p. 1.

138–39 verge of open racial warfare to "We are all victims": Branch, *Parting*, pp. 891–92.

139 heard the news: Garrow, *Bearing the Cross*, p. 292.

139 most unusual of the satellite movements: Int. Diane Nash, Feb. 20, 1985, and April 26, 1990; int. Richard Fernandez, Jan. 10, 1991; int. William Sloane Coffin, July 16, 1991; int. Harvey Cox, May 3, 1991, Nov. 15, 1993.

139 Clarence Jones had recruited: Int. Charles T. McKinney, Jan. 21, 1992.

139 Bevel and Nash raged: Branch, *Parting*, p. 893; int. Diane Nash, April 26, 1990.

139 She reached Birmingham: Diane Bevel, "Report, September 17–20, 1963," A/SC41f8.

140 place a funeral wreath: WP, Sept. 17, 1963, p. 1.

140 "Marching and drills": Diane Bevel, "Proposal for Action in Montgomery" [undated, Sept. 1963], A/SC41f8.

140 "There is an amazing democracy": King eulogy, A/KS5.

140 Nash was left behind: Diane Bevel, "Report, September 17–20, 1963," A/SC41f8. Also "John" to "Mary, Buntz, and Al," [undated, Sept. 1963], b9f303, Lowenstein Papers, UNC.

140   including Bob Moses: Diane Bevel, "Report, September 17–20, 1963," A/SC41f8.

141   Rev. Ed King of Tougaloo: Ibid. Also King to Lowenstein, Oct. 2, 1963, b9f297, Lowenstein Papers, UNC.

141   Nash pushed her way: Garrow, *Bearing the Cross,* pp. 294–95.

141   first duty of movement leaders: Int. Diane Nash, Feb. 20, 1985, and April 26, 1990.

141   Nash began to advocate: Garrow, *Bearing the Cross,* pp. 294–96, 678. In an interview, John Lewis later recalled that a Negro reporter from the *Washington Post* had overheard him discussing the Montgomery plan with Nash, and that the ensuing leak of the plan caused a "ruckus." Int. John Lewis by Archie Allen, Sept. 23, 1969, AAP.

141   Robert Hayling decided: Colburn, *Racial Change,* pp. 51–53.

141   He called local television stations: SAC, Jacksonville, to Director, Sept. 19, 1963, FSA-888.

141   Twine later insisted: Int. Henry Twine, April 2, 1991.

141   Hayling stopped indecisively: Int. Robert Hayling by David Colburn, Sept. 28, 1978, Colburn Papers, UF.

141   telltale NAACP sticker: *Jet,* Nov. 21, 1963, pp. 18-19.

141   marched their captives: *Miami Herald,* Sept. 21, 1963, p. 1.

141   ceremonial burning: Colburn, *Racial Change,* p. 51.

141   Rev. Connie Lynch: Ibid., pp. 5–8.

142   "Some of you say": Eyewitness account of Rev. Irvin Cheney, Jr., attached to NAACP report from Ruby Hurley to Gloster Current, Sept. 26, 1963, III-H-213, NAACP.

142   "burr-headed bastard": Colburn, *Racial Change,* p. 52.

142   electrifying cry: Cheney account, III-H-213, NAACP.

142   "the nigger who wants to be king": Colburn, *Racial Change,* p. 53.

142   women of the Klan: Hurley to Gloster Current, Sept. 26, 1963, III-H-213, NAACP.

142   "then sauntered casually": Cheney account, III-H-213, NAACP.

142   A shotgun blast: *Miami Herald,* Sept. 21, 1963, p. 1.

142   earliest FBI teletypes: SAC, Jacksonville, to Director, 11:49 P.M., Sept. 18, 1963, FSA-879.

143   jury convicted Hayling: *Jet,* Nov. 21, 1963, p. 18; Jan. 1965; Colburn, *Racial Change,* p. 53.

143   September 19 summit: Branch, *Parting,* pp. 893–94; Audiotape 112.1, JFK.

143   delegation of white leaders: Sept. 23 meeting from Branch, *Parting,* pp. 896–98; Audiotapes 112.6, 113.1, JFK.

144   "we came here, sir": Ibid.

144   "will help a great deal": King statement "outside White House," Sept. 19, 1963, A/KS5; NYT, Sept. 20, 1963, p. 1.

144   explicitly ruled out: NYT, Sept. 24, 1963, p. 1.

144   negotiators disappeared: *Newsweek,* Oct. 7, 1963, p. 40.

144   critics ridiculed King: Branch, *Parting,* pp. 898–901.

144   "I'm concerned about having you": Int. Thelton Henderson, Feb. 25, 1994.

144   fn Arrested three times: Ibid.

144   Lewis led carloads: Int. John Lewis by Archie Allen, Sept. 23, 1969, AAP.

144   daily demonstrations at Selma: *Jet,* Oct. 17, 1963, pp. 14–17, 20–22; NYT, Sept. 18, 1963, p. 24; NYT, Sept. 25, 1963, p. 32; NYT, Sept. 26, 1963, p. 29; Chestnut, *Black in Selma,* pp. 168–69.

145   King was in Richmond: BN, Sept. 25, 1963, p. 5.

145   endorsed variations of the Bevel-Nash: Ibid. Also NYT, Sept. 25, 1963, p. 33; *Jet,* Oct. 10, 1963, pp. 6–10, Oct. 24, 1963, pp. 14–19.

145   Walker huffily resigned: Branch, *Parting,* p. 900.

145   Powell flatly told: Ibid., p. 899; NYT, Sept. 28, 1963, p. 22.

145   "I was naive enough": King address of Sept. 27, 1963, A/KS5.

145   "Do I not destroy my enemies": King, *Strength to Love,* p. 53.

11. Against All Enemies

146   nuclear missiles by 1958: Ambrose, *Eisenhower: The President,* p. 456.

146   Eisenhower remarked: Ibid., p. 590.

146   thermonuclear bombs: Ibid., p. 494.

147   McNamara had disclosed: Shapley, *Promise and Power,* pp. 97–98; Reeves, *President Kennedy,* pp. 59–62.

147   remove Eisenhower's internal brakes: Shapley, *Promise and Power,* pp. 104–8.

147   "Those families which are not hit": Ibid., p. 118.

147   fn frontier electronics: Reid, *The Chip,* pp. 116–22.

147   fn mountains of plutonium waste: Cf. WP, Feb. 2, 1993, p. 4, Feb. 17, 1993, p. 4, March 3, 1993, p. 10, Nov. 17, 1993, p. 4.

147   forever virgins: Int. Victoria M. Murphy, Aug. 17–18, 1993.

147   "invites Soviet transgression": Reeves, *President Kennedy,* pp. 375–76, 428; Shapley, *Promise and Power,* pp. 169, 395; Schlesinger, *A Thousand Days,* p. 729.

147   psychological legacy: Schlesinger, *A Thousand Days,* pp. 759–60.

147   each of three strategic arms: Shapley, *Promise and Power,* pp. 194–95.

148   Technicians were installing: WP, Aug. 27, 1963, p. 1.

148   "to use whatever time remains": Reeves, *President Kennedy,* p. 551.

148   early mail ran: Ibid., p. 553.

148   expressed mild reservations: WP, Sept. 3, 1963, p. 11.

148   underground bomb tests: Reeves, *President Kennedy,* p. 594.

148   Ike at his Gettysburg farm: A religious appeal to Eisenhower had been recommended to Kennedy by Martin Luther King on August 28, during the White House meeting just after the March on Washington. According to the recording of the meeting, Kennedy first reacted negatively to the idea—apparently thinking that King himself wanted to make the approach, which Kennedy knew would make Eisenhower reject it. When King assured him otherwise, joking that Eisenhower "happens to be in the other denomination," Kennedy warmed to the notion, especially when Blake stepped forward to volunteer. This cooperative banter between Kennedy and King stands out in the historical record of a relationship that was generally formal and uneasy. Branch, *Parting,* pp. 883–86.

148   "The Republicans have a great": Kennedy-Blake meeting of Sept. 30, 1963, Audiotape 113.2, JFK.

148   Kennedy and FBI Director J. Edgar Hoover: Schlesinger, *Robert Kennedy,* pp. 286–89; Powers, *Secrecy and Power,* pp. 335, 353–61; Branch, *Parting,* pp. 402–3, 562–66, 678-79, 902–6.

149   plots to assassinate Fidel Castro: Schlesinger, *Robert Kennedy,* pp. 517–22; Reeves, *President Kennedy,* pp. 288-93; Branch, *Parting,* pp. 566–69.

149   Ellen Rometsch: Branch, *Parting,* pp. 911–14. Also Hoover to Tolson, 9:45 A.M., Oct. 28, 1963, FER42. Hoover placed a copy of this memo in his confidential files: President Johnson folder, Section 22, FHOC.

149   blackmail between branches: Nicholas Katzenbach, who in the fall of 1963 was deputy attorney general under Robert Kennedy, was not privy at the time to the Attorney General's dealings with the FBI over either the Rometsch investigation or the King wiretap. As he came to understand it from Kennedy, Katzenbach saw the Attorney General as feeling blackmailed by Hoover over an issue separate from the protection of President Kennedy's private life: that Hoover threatened to undermine the administration politically with leaks about King and Communism unless Kennedy approved the King wiretap to prove he had nothing to hide. Katzenbach Oral History, Oct. 8, 1969, JFK, pp. 61–62; int. Katzenbach, June 14, 1991.

150   toward installing wiretaps: Garrow, *The FBI and Martin,* pp. 62–66; Branch, *Parting,* pp. 852–56, 859–62.

150   "the most dangerous Negro of the future": Sullivan to Belmont, Aug. 30, 1963, FK-NR.

150   "We are launched on a course": Lodge to Rusk, Aug. 29, 1963, in Gravel, *Pentagon Papers,* Vol. 2, pp. 738–39.

150   Hoover ordered his technicians: Bland to Sullivan, Sept. 6, 1963, FK-207.

150   "This is obviously the only: Lodge to State, Sept. 13, 1963, quoted in Reeves, *President Kennedy,* p. 599.

150   expanded program of wiretaps: Powers, *Secrecy and Power,* pp. 377–79.

151   "engaged in a form of social revolution": Sullivan to Belmont, Sept. 25, 1963, quoted in Garrow, *The FBI and Martin,* p. 71.

151   "If this treaty fails": WP, Oct. 8, 1963, p. 2.

151   "we cannot remove the Nhus": Lodge to State, Oct. 7, 1963, quoted in Reeves, *President Kennedy,* pp. 618–19.

151   reports mentioned assassination: Lodge to State, Oct. 5, 1963, CAS 1445, and Lodge to Rusk, Oct. 5, 1963, CAS 34026, in Gravel, *Pentagon Papers,* Vol. 2, pp. 767–68; CIA station Saigon to CIA, Oct. 5, 1963, and CIA to Saigon station, Oct. 5, 1963, cited in Reeves, *President Kennedy,* p. 617.

151   "totally secure and fully deniable": Bundy to Lodge, Oct. 5, 1963, CAP 63560, in Gravel, *Pentagon Papers,* Vol. 2, pp. 766–67.

151   authorization to wiretap King: Hoover to RFK, Oct. 7, 1963, FK-250.

151   "If the conditions": WP, Oct. 8, 1963, p. 9.

151   October 7 was Freedom Day: Zinn, *New Abolitionists,* pp. 150–66; Forman, *Black Revolutionaries,* pp. 345–54; Chestnut, *Black in Selma,* pp. 168–70; Lyon, *Memories,* pp. 98–103; King, *Freedom Song,* pp. 216–22.

152   "You can't talk to us": Statement of Carver Neblett, A/SN94. Neblett and Avery Williams were the two SNCC volunteers arrested for trying to give sandwiches to the voter applicants.

152   Baldwin publicly called: NYT, Oct. 8, 1963, p. 37.

152   "I've become jaded": Zinn, *New Abolitionists,* p. 160; int. Thelton Henderson, Feb. 25, 1994.

152   "Nothing like this": Zinn, *New Abolitionists,* p. 165.

152   Amelia Boynton reached: Boynton to King, Oct. 8, 1963, A/KP21f10.

152   "I never thought it would happen": NYT, Oct. 13, 1963, p. 77.

152   Rivonia Treason Trial: NYT, Oct. 11, 1963, p. 1.

152   "For Diem and Nhu": Lodge to Rusk and Harriman, Oct. 10, 1963, and CIA assassination cables dated Oct. 9 and Oct. 14, all cited in Reeves, *President Kennedy,* pp. 620, 750.

153   arrival that afternoon: NYT, Oct. 11, 1963, p. 1.

153   next scheduled visitors: The Blaik and Royall visit was scheduled for 6:15 to 6:35 P.M., October 10, 1963, following the appointment of Soviet Foreign Minister Gromyko, Soviet Ambassador Dobrynin, Secretary of State Rusk, and U.S. Ambassador to Moscow Thompson: Appointments schedule, JFK. Newspaper reports said the visit actually lasted more than an hour: NYT, Oct. 11, 1963, p. 25; BN, Oct. 16, 1963, p. 1.

153   two young children bounded: Earl Blaik Oral History, JFK.

153   "bland, p.r. approach": Blaik to Marshall, Nov. 1, 1963, Box 18, Marshall Papers, JFK.

153   "Kennedy for King": Earl Blaik Oral History, JFK.

153   fell to talking football: Ibid. Also Blaik to RFK, Nov. 18, 1963, Box 18, Marshall Papers, JFK.

154   Kennedy signed the wiretap: Garrow, *The FBI and Martin,* pp. 72–73; Branch, *Parting,* pp. 906–9; RFK to Evans, Oct. 10, 1963, FK171; Evans to Belmont, Oct. 10, 1963, FK254.

154 "an unprincipled man": Charles D. Brennan, "Communism and the Negro Movement—A Current Analysis," Oct. 16, 1963, FBI File 100-3-116, Serial 416.

154 Kennedy personally demanded: Garrow, *The FBI and Martin*, pp. 74–76; Branch, *Parting*, p. 911.

154 all four telephone lines: Hoover to RFK, Oct. 18, 1963, cited in Garrow, *The FBI and Martin*, p. 74.

154 "still vacillating": Evans to Belmont, Oct. 21, 1963, FK259.

154 glumly recommended: Young wrote King that "...the Kennedys are trying to asssure the nation that they are still 'white,'" in Young to MLK, Oct. 21, 1963, A/KP3515.

154 wiretaps on Bayard Rustin: Baumgardner to Sullivan, Oct. 25, 1963, FR-NR; Garrow, *The FBI and Martin*, p. 77.

12. FRONTIERS ON EDGE: THE LAST MONTH

155 trouble over an automobile ride: Branch, *Parting*, p. 909. Also int. Burke Marshall, Sept. 26, 1984; Marshall to Rep. George Huddleston, Oct. 28 and Nov. 6, 1963, Box 18, Marshall Papers, JFK; NYT, Nov. 7, 1963, p. 30; WS, Nov. 7, 1963, p. 1; *NY Herald Tribune*, Nov. 8, 1963, p. 8.

155 King explained: Int. Thelton Henderson, Feb. 25, 1994.

155 fn Alabama officials effectively sabotaged: Marshall to RFK, Oct. 4, 1963, Box 3, Marshall Papers, JFK; Hoover to Tolson et al., Nov. 7, 1963, FK-NR; Hoover to Tolson et al., Nov. 7, 1963, FER-99; *Saturday Evening Post*, June 6, 1964, p. 18.

155 Two state grand juries: NYT, Nov. 14, 1963, p. 14.

155 "men high in the circles": WP, Nov. 14, 1963, p. 8.

156 "so much fuss": King statement of Nov. 6, 1963, A/KS5.

156 Moses convinced a reluctant: Joseph Sinsheimer, "The Freedom Vote of 1963: New Strategies of Racial Protest in Mississippi," *The Journal of Southern History*, Vol. 55, No. 2, May 1989, pp. 217–44.

156 "getting 200,000 Negroes": "Dear Friends" letter from SNCC office in Greenwood, Sept. 15, 1963, A/SC41f3.

156 Moses wrote out: Moses to Lowenstein, Oct. 18, 1963, Box 16, Lowenstein Papers, UNC. Lowenstein, who prized the commission in part because SNCC workers had been hesitant to accept white student volunteers, attached a typed copy to a handwritten note to friends: "Have you seen this document?" See also Carson, *In Struggle*, pp. 96–98; Harris, *Dreams Die Hard*, pp. 38–40; Sinsheimer, "The Freedom Vote," pp. 228–30.

156 obtained large contributions: Jay Goodlatte-Bass to Lowenstein, Oct. 29, 1963, enclosing a $5,000 contribution from the Council for United Civil Rights Leadership, which was led by philanthropist Stephen Currier, A/KP7f29.

156 Walter Reuther: Reuther to Lowenstein, Oct. 26, 1963, Lowenstein Papers, UNC.

156 "Dear Al": Graham to Lowenstein, Oct. 30, 1963, b9f299, Lowenstein Papers, UNC.

156 Lowenstein was arrested twice: "Summary of Events, October 22 Through October 28," b32f354, Lowenstein Papers, UNC; also Lowenstein speech, "Race Relations in Focus," circa Aug. 1964, b32f246, Lowenstein Papers.

156 "We all go through": Lowenstein to "Dear Ones," Oct. 29, 1963, Box 16, Lowenstein Papers, UNC.

156 "Any white Northerner": Remarks of Dennis Sweeney at Stanford, Oct. 2, 1963, Tape No. 631002-S1-2, SUARC.

156 first volunteer to reach Yazoo City: Statement by Yale junior Nelson A. Soltman, Oct. 24, 1963, b32f354, Lowenstein Papers, UNC.

157 dragged from bed to jail: "Summary of Events, October 22 Through October 28," b32f354, Lowenstein Papers, UNC.

157 "My experiences here": Kenneth Klotz to Senator Birch Bayh, Oct. 28 [misdated], 1963, b32f354, Lowenstein Papers, UNC.

157 beaten by an irate white taxi driver: Events of Oct. 30, 1963, as recorded in SNCC pamphlet, *Mississippi*, A/KP16f15, p. 17.

157 "a whirlwind": Remarks of editor Eileen Strelitz at a Stanford press conference, Nov. 7, 1963, Tape No. 631002-S1, SUARC.

157 Hattiesburg police chief: "Summary of Events, October 22 Through October 28," b32f354, Lowenstein Papers, UNC.

157 hefty collection left: Remarks of editor Eileen Strelitz at a Stanford press conference, Nov. 7, 1963, Tape No. 631002-S1, SUARC.

157 "Norman Thomas, bless his heart": Lowenstein to "Dear Ones," Oct. 29, 1963, Box 16, Lowenstein Papers, UNC.

157 "decided to confine my activities": Remarks of Hugh Smith at a Stanford press conference, Nov. 7, 1963, Tape No. 631002-S1, SUARC.

157 "cut the palaver": Thomas Powers, "A Chance Encounter," *Commonweal*, April 11, 1980, cited in Stone and Lowenstein, *Acts of Courage*, pp. 342–47.

157 two hundred recorded cases: Joseph Sinsheimer, "The Freedom Vote of 1963: New Strategies of Racial Protest in Mississippi," *The Journal of Southern History*, Vol. 55, No. 2, May 1989, p. 232; Bruce Payne items of Nov. 1 and 2, in SNCC pamphlet, *Mississippi*, A/KP16f15, p. 17; "Statement of Events in Natchez, Miss.—November 1 and 2, 1963," b32f354, Lowenstein Papers, UNC; "Violence and Intimidation Intensity," a Collegiate Press Service release dated Nov. 4, 1963, b32f357, Lowenstein Papers, UNC.

157 detained Bob Moses: "Statement on Events in Jackson, Miss.—November 1 and 2, 1963," b32f354, Lowenstein Papers, UNC.

158   "We're SNCC": Int. Charles Cobb, Aug. 20, 1991.
158   two weeks earlier in Selma: Ivanhoe Donaldson field report, Oct. 13–31, 1963, b14f747, Edwin King Papers, TOU.
158   "Morse was on the phone": Stan Newman (aide to Rep. William F. Ryan) to Lowenstein, Oct. 28, 1963, Lowenstein Papers, UNC.
158   Thomas did keep: Norman Thomas to Lowenstein, Oct. 29, 1963, b9f299, Lowenstein Papers, UNC.
158   novelty of Thomas: NYT, Nov. 1, 1963.
158   "A drive to get votes": WP, Nov. 3, 1963, p. 4.
158   Moses quietly praised: Joseph Sinsheimer, "The Freedom Vote of 1963: New Strategies of Racial Protest in Mississippi," *The Journal of Southern History,* Vol. 55, No. 2, May 1989, p. 241.
158   "This is the first time": Ibid.
158   more valuable as antennae: Lowenstein interview by Anne Romaine, March 1967, A/AR, pp. 119–20.
158   network reporters jostled: *Stanford Daily* clipping, Nov. 8, 1963, b32f365, Lowenstein Papers, UNC.
158   "Well, besides being shot": Transcript of press conference, Nov. 7, 1963, Tape No. 631002-S1, SUARC.
159   "a bond stronger than the Whiffenpoofs": *Yale Daily News* clipping circa Nov. 10, 1963, b32f365, Lowenstein Papers, UNC.
159   Vietnamese generals were launching: Gravel, *Pentagon Papers,* Vol. 2, pp. 264–70; Reeves, *President Kennedy,* pp. 635-52.
159   "will not call on you": Reeves, *President Kennedy,* p. 647.
159   "No Nhus is good news.": Ibid., p. 615.
159   "the ground in which": Ibid., p. 652.
159   hailed the coup: David Halberstam dispatch, "Saigon Coup Gives Americans Hope," NYT, Nov. 4, 1963, p. 1, cited in ibid., p. 651.
159   murders shook President Kennedy: Gravel, *Pentagon Papers,* Vol. 2, p. 270; Reeves, *President Kennedy,* p. 643.
159   troublesome letter from Senator Richard Russell: Garrow, *The FBI and Martin,* pp. 75–76; Belmont to Tolson, Nov. 1, 1963, 100-3-116-517, FK-NR; Evans to Belmont, Nov. 1, 1963, 100-3-116-518, FK-NR.
160   Hoover to force reconsideration: Cf. Evans to Belmont, Sept. 20, 1963, and Baumgardner to Sullivan, Sept. 26, 1963, FL-NR. Assistant Attorney General Burke Marshall had submitted for FBI clearance a draft memo setting forth the Justice Department's warnings to Martin Luther King about alleged Communist advisers. FBI officials assumed that its purpose was to establish a protective record of vigilance, and while grousing that it made the Attorney General look too good, decided to inform Marshall "that he should feel free, of course, to submit the memorandum as he drafted it."
160   Three more times: Evans to Belmont, Nov. 1, 1963, 100-3-116-518, FK-NR.
160   fn "We didn't need to be told": Belmont to Tolson, Nov. 1, 1963, 100-3-116-517, FK-NR.
161   Kennedy finally scrapped the revisions: Evans to Belmont, Nov. 1, 1963, 100-3-116-518, FK-NR.
161   Katzenbach was beaming: Ibid. Also int. Nicholas Katzenbach, Oct. 22, 1986, and June 14, 1991; Robert Kennedy Oral History, p. 684ff, JFK.
161   "You and I are a mile apart": Katzenbach Oral History, Oct. 8, 1969, JFK.
162   "magnified into proportions": Evans to Belmont, Nov. 1, 1963, 100-3-116-518, FK-NR.
162   "This shows wisdom": Hoover handwritten note on ibid.
162   six o'clock on Friday evening: The brief Russell meeting took place at 5:00 P.M., and the first cable on Diem's surrender reached the White House at 6:05 P.M. President Kennedy sent further instructions to Lodge at 8:47 P.M. that night. Evans to Belmont, Nov. 1, 1963, 100-3-116-518, FK-NR; Reeves, *President Kennedy,* pp. 647–48.
162   "In summary": Marshall to RFK with attached memo from John L. Murphy to Marshall, both Nov. 5, 1963, Box 3, Burke Marshall Papers, JFK.
162   careened through Lincolnville: Colburn, *Racial Change,* pp. 55–57.
162   fn "was the prime mover": Gloster B. Current to Robert W. Saunders, Dec. 6, 1963, among other correspondence on the removal of Hayling in III-C-305, NAACP. Current was responding specifically to a letter from the Florida field secretary, detailing efforts to remove Hayling: "It has been his influence that has promoted much of the resistance from other sources. However, I must admit, that he has also been the moving force that sparked St. Augustine into motion. We have already spoken with some of the key young people in the youth movement and they are now working with us. Earlier, they were committed to Dr. Hayling." Saunders to Current, Nov. 15, 1963, III-C-305, NAACP.
162   Republicans were said to be scarcer: Paul B. Johnson for Governor flyer entitled "There are ONLY 44 Real Republicans in Mississippi," b32f362, Lowenstein Papers, UNC.
162   "Kill the threat": Paul B. Johnson for Governor flyer entitled "Vote the Mississippi Democratic Victory Ballot," Lowenstein Papers, ibid. This flyer managed to invoke the language of Abraham Lincoln to support one-party white supremacy: "A house divided cannot stand. Your liberty, your traditional values and your way of life are at stake."
162   "a vicious two-party political system": Paul B. Johnson for Governor flyer entitled "Two-Party System . . . would be the end of our way of life!" Lowenstein Papers, ibid.
163   "They are treating my workers like niggers": Joseph Sinsheimer, "The Freedom Vote of 1963: New Strategies of Racial Protest in Mississippi," *The Journal of Southern History,* Vol. 55, No. 2, May 1989, p. 242.
163   No Republican had bothered to run: *Time,* Nov. 15, 1963, p. 18; WP, Nov. 7, 1963, p. 9.
163   "Your democracy is nothing": Malcolm X speech at CCNY, Nov. 7, 1963, Tape C173–74, SCRBC.

163   Muhammad had removed Malcolm: WP, Oct. 21, 1963, p. B1, FMX-73.

163   surprisingly barbed comments: Int. Abdulalim Shabazz (Lonnie Cross), March 14, 1991.

163   "Could be": Int. Yusuf Shah (Captain Joseph), Oct. 17, 1991.

163   Malcolm confided nothing: Int. Benjamin Karim, Aug. 31, 1991.

163   "You may take offense": Malcolm X speech at CCNY, Nov. 7, 1963, Tape C173–74, SCRBC.

164   Myles Horton: Sketch of Horton from Branch, *Parting*, pp. 121–22, 289–90.

164   Horton presided over: Memo and agenda for Greenville workshop of Nov. 11–17, 1963, A/SN111f16; "Names and Addresses" for COFO workshop dated Nov. 19, 1963, A/SN111f16.

164   up to two thousand of them: A Yale Law graduate who participated in the Greenville conference soon warned of "huge legal problems expected to arise during the coming summer. It is probable that a large group of students—perhaps as many as 2,000—many of whom would be white, will be coming into the state...." Oscar Chase to Jack Greenberg, Nov. 20, 1963, A/SN111f16.

164   considered the white volunteers more trouble: Int. Lawrence Guyot, Feb. 1, 1991; int. Charles Cobb, Aug. 29, 1991; int. Hollis Watkins, June 22, 1992.

164   as recorded by SNCC adviser: Zinn, *New Abolitionists*, pp. 186–89.

164   A straw vote late Friday: Int. Lawrence Guyot, Feb. 1, 1991; int. Charles Cobb, Aug. 29, 1991; remarks of Lawrence Guyot, Session No. 4 of the Trinity College SNCC Reunion, April 14–16, 1988, transcript courtesy of Jack Chatfield.

165   Moses received summary notice: Branton to Moses and Aaron Henry, Nov. 12, 1963, cited in Watters, *Jacob's Ladder*, pp. 213–14; Annell Ponder to Martin Luther King, Nov. 18, 1963, A/SN111f16.

165   Kennedy had an unseen hand: Courtney Evans reported that Theodore White met with the Attorney General and his press secretary, Ed Guthman, in New York on November 4 regarding White's *Life* article on Negroes, Martin Luther King, and Communism. Evans to Belmont, Nov. 5, 1963, FRFK-429.

165   assigned a Harvard honors: Int. Michael Sayer, June 25, 1992.

165   "Negroes, bursting out": Theodore H. White, "Rushing to a Showdown That No Law Can Chart," *Life*, Nov. 22, 1963, p. 102ff.

165   his second installment: Theodore H. White, "Power Structure, Integration, Militancy, Freedom Now!: The Angry U.S. Negro's Rallying Cries Are Confusing His Just and Urgent Cause," *Life*, Nov. 29, 1963, p. 78ff.

166   students in Ohio: *Jet*, Oct. 3, 1963, p. 48.

166   massive reeducation: NYT, Nov. 10, 1963, p. 80.

166   "not leading too rapidly": WP, Nov. 13, 1963, p. B5.

166   special section on intermarriage: WP, Nov. 12, 1963, p. 11.

166   Robert Kennedy's confidant: E. L. "Red" Holland to Edwin Guthman, Nov. 13, 1963, Ed Guthman private papers.

166   flew south to Florida: NYT, Nov. 19, 1963, p. 1.

166   national debt ceiling: *Chicago Tribune*, Nov. 8, 1963, p. 4; on budget, cf. *Newsweek*, Jan. 28, 1963, p. 19ff.

167   "While the Federal": NYT, Nov. 19, 1963, p. 29.

167   interval with Father Michael Gannon: Int. Michael Gannon, April 3, 1991, Dec. 10, 1992.

167   convention of the United Synagogue: The Proceedings of the Golden Jubilee Convention, the United Synagogue of America, Nov. 17–21 1963, Concord Hotel, Kiamesha Lake, N.Y., courtesy of the United Synagogue of America, New York.

167   Heschel introduced King: Ibid.

168   "Freedom is not some lavish dish": Ibid.

168   King added a passage: King address to Union of American Hebrew Congregations, 47th Biennial Banquet, Nov. 20, 1963, b14f27, Jacob Rothschild Papers, EU.

168   stopped over at Idlewild: Hoover to RFK, Nov. 26, 1963, FL-NR; Hoover to RFK, Nov. 26, 1963, FK-NR; NY LHM "Re: Communist Party, United States of America, Negro Question, Communist Influence in Racial Matters, Internal Security," Nov. 21, 1963, FJ-NR; SA [name deleted] to SAC, NY, Nov. 18, 1963, FJNY-246.

168   "I'm not going to let Martin": Branch, *Parting*, pp. 858–60.

168   had made awkward excuses: Wiretap transcripts of Sept. 16, Sept. 23, and Oct. 28, 1963, FLNY-9-292a, FLNY-7-553A, FLNY-7-588a.

168   "You know, I'm": Wiretap transcript of Oct. 8, 1963, FLNY-7-610a.

168   "Notwithstanding trying circumstances": Baumgardner to Sullivan, Nov. 25, 1963, FL-NR.

169   Word had leaked: NYT, Oct. 17, 1963, p. 1; A. M. Sonnabend to Members of Key Leadership Groups, Oct. 17, 1963, "Ecumenical Council IAD, July–Oct. 1963," AJC; Bracker to Marc Tanenbaum, Oct. 28, 1963, AJC.

169   three Patriarchs denounced: NYT, Nov. 19, 1963, p. 1; Yzermans, *American Participation*, pp. 572–77; Vorgimler, *Documents of Vatican II*, pp. 48–49.

169   "giving honorable mention": "AJC White Paper 1964–65," AJC, p. 64.

169   Bea rose to address: Bea, *The Church*, pp. 154–59.

169   seethed with conspiracy: Michael Novak, "Intrigue in the Council," *New Republic*, Jan. 11, 1964, pp. 10–11; "AJC White Paper 1964–65," AJC, p. 65–67.

169   "As your Eminence knows": Heschel to Bea, Nov. 22, 1963, AJC.

169   urged Heschel not to panic: Int. Thomas Stransky, Feb. 27, 1992.

169   "What is put off": Irving M. Engel confidential memorandum, Feb. 10, 1964, "AJC White Paper —IAD," AJC, p. 7.

169   inscription in the Piazza Cavour: Int. Thomas Stransky, Feb. 27, 1992.

169   even the boisterous young people: Int. John Oesterreicher, May 24, 1991.

13. GRIEF

173   banged through the double doors: Miller, *Lyndon,* p 384.
173   bowled over a waiter: Wicker, *On Press,* p. 116.
173   "moving across that crowd": Ibid.
173   Sarah Hughes cried tears: Miller, *Lyndon,* p.384.
173   just as Tom Wicker: Wicker, *On Press,* p. 118.
173   shoved Johnson at a trot: Johnson, *The Vantage Point,* p. 11.
173   amid clashing orders: Notes dictated by Cliff Carter aboard *Air Force One,* Nov. 22, 1963, Vice President's Daily Diary, LBJ.
173   carload of reporters: Wicker, *On Press,* p. 120. The first shot at the Kennedy motorcade occurred about 12:30 P.M. Dallas (Central) time. The announcement of President Kennedy's death was made from Parkland Hospital about 1:20 P.M. Johnson took the oath of office at about 2:38 P.M. Notes dictated by Marie Fehmer aboard *Air Force One,* November 22, 1963, Vice President's Daily Diary, LBJ; Manchester, *Glory and the Dream,* pp. 1231–32.
174   "I want them to see": Johnson, *White House Diary,* p. 6.
174   "Just ah, think, think, think": Dictabelt of telephone conversation between LBJ and Arthur Goldberg, 9:00 P.M., Nov. 22, 1963, LBJ.
174   He laid the crucifix: Int. Sargent Shriver, Feb. 21, 1991.
174   waxen face sealed: Schlesinger, *Robert Kennedy,* p. 658.
174   first business caller: PDD, Nov. 23, 1963, LBJ.
174   correct panicky errors: WP "Assassination Files," Nov. 15, 1993, p. 10.
174   "That's one angle": WP, "Assassination Files," Nov. 16, 1993, p. 9.
174   ten hours of television news: Manchester, *Glory and the Dream,* p. 1232.
174   Heller took his brief turn: "Notes on Meeting with President Johnson, 7:40 P.M., Saturday, November 23, 1963," Box 7, Heller Papers, LBJ.
175   slices of cherry-vanilla pie: "Notes on a Quick Meeting with the President and Other Leading Members of the Kennedy Family," Nov. 19, 1963, Box 6, Heller Papers, LBJ.
175   pilloried bankers: Ibid. Also "Confidential Notes on Meeting with the President," Oct. 21, 1963, Box 6, Heller Papers, 1963.
175   Heller's economists had pushed: "War on Poverty" monograph, Heller to the Secretary of Agriculture et al., Nov. 5, 1963, and Heller to Lampman, June 3, 1963, Legislative Background of EOA 1964, Box 1, Heller Papers, LBJ; Lemann, *The Promised Land,* pp. 129–35.
175   to offset the tax cut: Comments of William Capron, transcript of Brandeis University conference on "The Federal Government and Urban Poverty," June 1973, RFK Oral History series, pp. 138–45, JFK.
175   "Having mounted a dramatic program": Heller, "Confidential Notes on Meeting with the President, October 21, 1963, Box 6, Heller Papers, LBJ. Also Heller to JFK, June 29, 1963, ibid., in which Heller argues that, "The civil rights message covers a lot of the ground, but there may well be room for a broader program not linked to race."
175   "make sure that we're doing": "Notes on a Quick Meeting with the President and other Leading Members of the Kennedy Family," Nov. 19, 1963, Box 6, Heller Papers, LBJ.
175   fn gain him no votes: Reeves, *President Kennedy,* pp. 655–57.
175   "That's my kind of program": Lemann, *The Promised Land,* pp. 140–41.
175   "Human Conservation": Heller to Secretary of Agriculture et al., Nov. 5, 1963, Legislative Background of EOA 1964, Box 1, Heller Papers, LBJ.
175   "push ahead full-tilt": "Notes on Meeting with President Johnson, 7:40 P.M., Saturday, November 23, 1963," Box 7, Heller Papers, LBJ; Johnson, *The Vantage Point,* p. 71.
175   chew discarded grapefruit: McPherson, *Political Education,* p. 139. Johnson's numerous public references to his Cotulla experience include a speech in honor of Mexican President Adolfo López Mateos, Feb. 22, 1964, PPP, 1963–64, pp. 308–10.
175   fn "[The children] never seemed": LBJ address to a Joint Session of Congress, March 15, 1965, PPP, 1965, p. 281.
175   his proudest moment: See LBJ to John Carmody, Jan. 31, 1959, cited in Dallek, *Lone Star Rising,* p. 183.
175   lit up 90 percent: Caro, *Path to Power,* pp. 516–28.
175   make his point physically: "Notes on Meeting with President Johnson, 7:40 P.M., Saturday, November 23, 1963," Box 7, Heller Papers, LBJ.
176   Baxter urged his congregation: McPherson, *Political Education,* pp. 214–15; Harry McPherson, quoted in Miller, *Lyndon,* pp. 404–5.
176   first murder ever broadcast: Manchester, *Glory and the Dream,* p. 1233.
176   He began by flatly denying: John McCone, "Memorandum for the Record," Nov. 25, 1963, regarding meeting at 3:00 P.M., Nov. 24, 1963, of LBJ, Rusk, McNamara, Ball, Bundy, McCone, and Lodge, Meeting Notes File, Box 1, LBJ.
176   "Lodge said that we were": Ibid.
176   Lodge was overly optimistic: Ibid. Also Shapley, *Promise and Power,* pp. 291–92; reminiscence by Bill Moyers in *Saturday Review,* Nov. 11, 1967, p. 53.
176   cool toward Lodge: "Why did you send Lodge out there, for God's sake?" Johnson asked Senator J. William Fulbright. "I just think he's got things screwed up good, that's what I think." Dictabelt of telephone

conversation between LBJ and Fulbright, 7:01 P.M., Dec. 2, 1963, LBJ. Johnson also generally criticized Lodge and Ambassador Averell Harriman, one of the principal stateside advocates of the coup against Diem, in a conversation with National Security Adviser McGeorge Bundy: Dictabelt of telephone conversation between LBJ and Bundy, 5:55 P.M., Dec. 9, 1963, LBJ.

176 portrait hung: Miller, *Lyndon,* p. 425.

176 "We had a hand in killing him": Ibid.

177 "Whenever those rich people": Int. Horace Busby, Feb. 3, 1992.

177 "I need you a lot more": Dictabelt and transcript of telephone conversation between LBJ and Larry O'Brien, 4:04 P.M., Nov. 25, 1963, LBJ. The burial ceremony had ended at 3:34 P.M. (NYT, Nov. 26, 1963).

177 reversed Kennedy's intention: Dictabelt of telephone conversation among Bill Moyers, LBJ, and Theodore Sorensen, 10:10 P.M., Nov. 25, 1963, LBJ.

177 thanks to Martin Luther King: Dictabelt of telephone conversation between LBJ and MLK, 9:20 P.M., Nov. 25, 1963, LBJ.

177 "all these ambassadors": Dictabelt of telephone conversation between LBJ and Theodore Sorensen, 10:10 P.M., Nov. 25, 1963, LBJ.

177 Johnson snatched time: Miller, *Lyndon,* p. 411.

178 Senate aide from Texas: Dictabelt of telephone conversation between LBJ and Horace Busby, 1:25 P.M., Nov. 26, 1963, LBJ.

178 devices such as the parallel: NYT, Nov. 28, 1963, p. 20. The *Times* identified the device as the "chiasmus."

178 "not to turn about": Ibid.

178 "Heavens to Betsy": Ibid., p. 21.

178 by Johnson's count: Dictabelt of telephone conversation between LBJ and Adam Clayton Powell, 2:22 P.M., Nov. 27, 1963, LBJ.

178 "As soon as Lyndon Johnson": Miller, *Lyndon,* p. 414.

178 "Like everyone else": Lowenstein to "My dear Mr. President," Nov. 27, 1963, WHCF—Name File, LBJ.

178 Thanksgiving SNCC conference: Branch, *Parting,* p. 920; int. Betty Garman Robinson, Jan. 28, 1991.

178 wiped out the planned agenda: Int. Michael Sayer, June 25, 1992. Sayer remembered the scheduled members of Congress as Rep. Donald Rumsfeld (R-Ill.) and Rep. William F. Ryan (D-NY).

179 "the problem of overcoming fear": *Movement Soul,* Folkways Album FD5486.

179 marathon freedom songs: Ibid.

179 approached Moses to ask: Int. Robert Stone, June 3, 1993.

180 "the Negro groups as such": Lawrence F. O'Brien to LBJ, Nov. 29, 1963, Box 3, Henry Wilson Papers, LBJ.

180 "Say to the Republicans": Dictabelt of telephone conversation between LBJ and Robert Anderson, 1:30 P.M., Nov. 30, 1963, LBJ.

180 "I believe that we can": Dictabelt of telephone conversation between LBJ and Rep. Richard Bolling, 6:50 P.M., Dec. 2, 1963.

180 "God almighty": Dictabelt of telephone conversation between LBJ and Rep. Carl Albert, 11:15 A.M., Dec. 4, 1963, LBJ. Also dictabelt of telephone conversation between LBJ and Lawrence O'Brien, 6:08 P.M., Dec. 4, 1963, LBJ.

180 "would be very bad": Dictabelt of telephone conversation between LBJ and J. Edgar Hoover, 10:30 A.M., Nov. 25, 1963, LBJ.

180 fn "I don't have much influence": Ibid.

180 Hoover's true goal: Dictabelt of telephone conversation between LBJ and Senator Everett Dirksen, 11:40 A.M., Nov. 29, 1963, LBJ.

180 "the country would be": Dictabelt of telephone conversation between LBJ and Senator Richard Russell, 4:05 P.M., Nov. 29, 1963, LBJ.

181 "I couldn't serve on it": Dictabelt of telephone conversation between LBJ and Senator Richard Russell, 8:55 P.M., Nov. 29, 1963, LBJ.

181 "a similar bombardment": Ibid. Johnson told Russell that Warren had surrendered in tears after Johnson had tongue-lashed him as follows: "I think you can put on your uniform of World War I, fat as you are, and do anything you can to save one American life." Chief Justice Warren's similar but less graphic recollection is recorded in Miller, *Lyndon,* p. 423.

181 "a West Coast lawyer": Hoover memorandum for Tolson et al., 1:39 P.M., Nov. 29, 1963, Folder 92, FHOC.

182 "the proposed group": Ibid.

182 "In Florida and on Cape Cod": Brennan to Sullivan, Dec. 1, 1963, Folder 92, FHOC.

182 King preached on Thanksgiving: Good, *Trouble I've Seen,* pp. 17–21.

182 "If they hated him": Mays to MLK, Nov. 29, 1963, A/KP15f30.

182 he was wounded: Branch, *Parting,* p. 918.

182 campaign in Albany, Georgia: Ibid., pp. 731–32.

182 Katzenbach turn him down: Int. Nicholas Katzenbach, June 14, 1991.

182 "I trust that": RFK to MLK, Dec. 4, 1963, A/KP24f21.

183 "Is it well?": Good, *Trouble I've Seen,* pp. 18–20.

184 merchants along Jamaica Avenue: NYAN, Dec. 7, 1963, p. 29, FMXNY-3980.

184 Malcolm first repeated statements: Perry, *Malcolm,* pp. 239–40.

184   Elijah Muhammad sent out: Malcolm X, *The Autobiography*, p. 300; comments of Yusuf Shah (Captain Joseph) on "Malcolm X: Make It Plain," PBS documentary, *The American Experience*, 1994. Int. Abdulalim Shabazz (Lonnie X Cross), March 14, 1991.

184   wrote out in advance: Int. Benjamin Karim, March 19, 1991; Perry, *Malcolm*, p. 240.

184   "the chickens coming home to roost": Malcolm X, *The Autobiography*, p. 301.

184   "had the nerve to say it": NYT, Dec. 2, 1963, p. 21.

184   "speech in which he mocked": NYT, Dec. 5, 1963, p. 22.

185   Malcolm X called Muhammad: Wiretap transcript of conversation between Malcolm X and Elijah Muhammad, Dec. 4, 1963, FMXNY-3978, pp. 3–4.

185   "The nation still mourns": MS, Dec. 20, 1963, pp. 1, 3.

185   Kennedy deserved respect: Cf. wiretap transcripts of Muhammad's conversations with inquiring reporters, Dec. 5 and 6, 1963, FMXNY-3988, pp. 1–2, 5–6.

186   "my work is in accordance": Wiretap transcript of Elijah Muhammad conversation, Dec. 5, 1963, FMXNY-3992.

186   "just a little spanking": Wiretap transcript of Elijah Muhammad conversation with James Farmer, Dec. 5, 1963, FMXNY-3988, pp. 2–3. An FBI informant quoted Muhammad as saying that "if he [Malcolm X] sticks out his lip and starts popping off, he will get a worse beating the next time." FMXNY-3978, p. 7.

186   "the ruler": NYT, Dec. 5, 1963, p. 22.

186   Rumors of an impending split: Cf. Ted Poston article in *New York Post*, Dec. 5, 1963, p. 2.

186   extended the speaking ban: Perry, *Malcolm*, p. 242. Also wiretap transcript of conversation between Elijah Muhammad and Malcolm X, Dec. 4, 1963, FMXNY-3978, pp. 3–4.

186   dispatched letters to Captain Joseph: Wiretap transcript of conversation between Elijah Muhammad and Malcolm X, Dec. 7, 1963, in Report to Director from SAC, Phoenix, Dec. 13, 1963, FEM-NR.

186   block him physically: Perry, *Malcolm*, p. 242.

186   fashioned parables: Wiretap transcript of conference call featuring Elijah Muhammad and Malcolm X, Jan. 2, 1964, in Report to Director from SAC, Phoenix, Jan 23, 1964, FEM-NR. Also int. Abdulalim Shabazz (Lonnie X Cross), March 14, 1991; int. Benjamin Karim, March 19, 1991; int. Yusuf Shah (Captain Joseph), Oct. 17, 1991.

186   secured Elijah Muhammad's permission: Wiretap transcript of conversation between Elijah Muhammad and Malcolm X, Dec. 7, 1963, in Report to Director from SAC, Phoenix, Dec. 13, 1963, FEM-NR.

186   "I feel like": Press conference of 12:05 P.M., Dec. 7, 1963, PPP, pp. 34–38.

187   "I've never agreed": LBJ phone call with Walter Heller, Dec. 14, 1963, Audiotape K6312.08, LBJ.

187   "You destroyed me": Dictabelt of telephone conversation between LBJ and Senator Richard Russell, 12:55 P.M., Dec. 7, 1963, LBJ.

187   "I tried my best": Ibid. Russell was referring to a consultation by then Secretary of State John Foster Dulles with congressional leaders on April 2, 1954, over a desperate French request for American air strikes in Indochina to rescue the besieged colonial forces at Dien Bien Phu. The congressional leaders convinced Eisenhower, through Dulles, that the United States must not intervene without support from other European powers, which effectively prevented U.S. military intervention that year. Ambrose, *Eisenhower: The President*, p. 178; Gravel, ed., *Pentagon Papers*, Vol. 1, pp. 100–101; Dallek, *Lone Star Rising*, p. 444.

187   "I'm not going to cavil": Int. Jack Valenti, Feb. 25, 1991; Johnson, *The Vantage Point*, pp. 157–58; Stern, *Calculating Visions*, p. 162.

187   made peace with James Rowe: PDD, Dec. 1, 1963, LBJ; McPherson, *Political Education*, pp. 215–16.

187   facilitated young Congressman Johnson's: Roberts, *LBJ's Inner Circle*, pp. 175–76; Caro, *Path to Power*, pp. 451–59.

188   "Uncle Lyndon": Caro, *Path to Power*, p. 452.

188   maiden speech to the U.S. Senate: LBJ speech of March 9, 1949, *Congressional Record*, Vol. 95, Part 2, pp. 2402–2409; LBJ to James H. Rowe, March 15, 1949, cited in Monroe Billington, "Lyndon B. Johnson and Blacks: The Early Years," *Journal of Negro History*, Jan. 1977, p. 39; Dallek, *Lone Star Rising*, pp. 369–70.

188   "there won't be any Senate": Rowe to "Lyndon," April 29, 1954, LBJA-Selected Names, Box 32, LBJ.

188   patched that up, too: Rowe worked briefly for Senate Majority Leader Johnson in 1956. Dallek, *Lone Star Rising*, p. 493.

188   Rowe kept pushing candidate Johnson: Rowe to LBJ, Jan. 17, 1959, and Aug. 24, 1960, LBJA-Selected Names, Box 32, LBJ.

188   "Mogul emperor": Dallek, *Lone Star Rising*, p.587.

188   Johnson pulled rank: McPherson, *Political Education*, p. 216.

188   to the White House Arthur "Tex" Goldschmidt: PDD, Dec. 12, 1963, LBJ; oral histories of Arthur E. Goldschmidt and Elizabeth Wickenden, June 3, 1969, and Elizabeth Wickenden, Nov. 6, 1974, LBJ; Caro, *Means of Ascent*, p. 11.

188   called his hero: PDD, Dec. 1, 1963, LBJ.

188   Aubrey Williams: Miller, *Lyndon*, pp. 64–68; Durr, *Magic Circle*, pp. 99–100; Dallek, *Lone Star Rising*, pp. 125–46.

188   Williams was a political casualty: Durr, *Magic Circle*, pp. 246, 249.

188   segregationist boycott: Ibid., pp. 269, 291.

188   Louisiana police: Kinoy, *Rights on Trial*, pp. 213–30; Kunstler, *Deep in My Heart*, pp. 237–38; O'Reilly, *Racial Matters*, p. 181; *Dombrowski v. Eastland*, 387 U.S. 82 (1967).

189   Williams was in failing health: Bill Moyers to Lady Bird Johnson, Dec. 12, 1963, and Cliff Carter to Aubrey Williams, Dec. 12, 1963, LBJ. Aubrey Williams was buried on March 6, 1965, the day before the Bloody Sunday march in Selma.

189   "Put them to work!": Caro, *Path to Power,* pp. 341–68.

189   King protested: MLK telegram to RFK, Oct. 6, 1963, A/KP24f20; MLK statement issued Sunday, Oct. 6, 1963, A/KS5.

189   did sow dissension: Cf. Wiley Branton to MLK, Dec. 11, 1963, A/KP4f47. Branton wrote King that he had been contacted directly by Jack Rogers, counsel for the Louisiana Joint Legislative Committee on Un-American Activities, and told that King was "being duped by 'communists.'" Although Branton said he knew Rogers was trying to smear King, he nevertheless advised King that there were "things in the report which disturb me and which probably will disturb you...."

189   "sever any and all relationships": Jones to MLK, Nov. 26, 1963, A/Kp13f15.

189   "King is playing a crafty game": Aubrey Williams to Jim Dombrowski, Feb. 26, 1960, enclosed along with two others in ibid. In his letter, Williams aimed nastier barbs at what he saw as tactical clumsiness on the part of Ralph Abernathy: "Abernathy is a fool."

189   "Now interestingly enough": Interview MLK by Donald H. Smith, Nov. 29, 1963, Donald H. Smith tapes, tape 9, side 1, SHSW.

189   displayed blown-up reproductions: Branch, *Parting,* pp. 853–54.

190   Johnson never mentioned: Garrow, *Bearing the Cross,* p. 308; Lee White to LBJ, Dec. 3, 1963, ExHU2, Pr8-1/K, LBJ.

190   vulgar Nazi signs: *Jet,* Dec. 19, 1963, p. 32.

190   forty-three minutes: 11:37 A.M. until 12:20 P.M., PDD, Dec. 3, 1963, LBJ.

190   "Well, here's Dr. King": LBJ phone call with David McDonald, Dec. 2, 1963, audiotape KG312.17, LBJ.

190   King praised Johnson: NYT, Dec. 4, 1963, p. 1.

190   warnings still sounded: According to FBI wiretaps, Clarence Jones told King on December 13 that representatives of the federal government were pressuring SCLC to purge one of its attorneys representing civil rights demonstrators (probably Arthur Kinoy) as a security risk. New York LHM, Dec. 17, 1963, FSC-NR, FJ-NR.

190   "Red ties": Column by Robert S. Allen and Paul Scott in *Long Island Star Journal,* Nov. 25, 1963. King received a copy through New York friends. The FBI preserved a copy in its files, FJNY-258.

190   "horrifying," said King: Wiretap transcript of MLK–Clarence Jones conversation of Nov. 30, 1963, cited in SAC, New York, to Director, Dec. 4, 1963, with attached New York LHM, FK-NR.

190   telephone credit cards: "Office of the President" to "SCLC Credit Card Holders," Dec. 5, 1963, A/KP32f7.

190   lawyers were locked: Garrow, *Bearing the Cross,* pp. 308–9; Jack Greenberg to William Kunstler, Nov. 22, 1963, A/KP17f13; Kunstler to Greenberg, Nov. 27, 1963, and Kunstler to King et al., undated, A/KP31f19. Complaints by King's lawyers about Kunstler mentioned in wiretap intercepts summarized in New York LHMs of Dec. 10, 1963, and Dec. 18, 1963, FK-NR.

190   dentist who treated: Dr. Roy Bell to Walker, Dec. 19, 1963, and Walker to Bell, Dec. 19, 1963, A/KP4f18.

190   quitting for lack of a pay raise: Branch, *Parting,* pp. 898–900.

190   "I really have been": Young to Clark, Cotton, and King, Dec. 17, 1963, A/KP29f12.

191   scolded the preachers: Clark to King, Dec. 12, 1963, A/KP29f18. Clark advised King in her cover letter that her memo summarized verbal remarks made to Young and Cotton on Nov. 22. "When Kennedy was killed," she wrote, "I too, felt the guilt of silence and immediately sat down with pen in hand." At other times, Clark was generous, almost motherly, toward King. Early in November, she had turned down an offered pay raise, saying she could not accept it "and feel perfectly free inside." She advised King that she did not want to burden him: "A Civil Rights Organization and its leaders have too much to do to help white people mature and Negroes awaken." Clark to King, Nov. 4, 1963, A/SC3f24.

191   Under heavy pressure: The book revision is the major topic of conversation picked up on Stanley Levison's telephone tap between October 1963 and March 1964. FLNY-7 and FLNY-9, *passim.*

191   "This book": Wiretap log of Nov. 26, 1963, FLNY-7-617a.

191   "I've got to finish off": Wiretap log of Oct. 8, 1963, FLNY-7-610a.

191   "to interpret the direction of change": Jones to MLK and MLK to Joan Daves, Nov. 26, 1963, A/KP27f8.

191   "this is now much closer": Wiretap log of Feb. 6, 1964, FLNY-7-689a.

191   "the first major civil rights demonstration": NYT, Dec. 16, 1963, p. 17.

191   "glaring reality": ADW, Dec. 16. 1963, p. 1.

191   Lewis went to jail: Mary King, *Freedom Song,* p. 181.

191   told the booking officer: Ibid., p. 175.

191   "Almost daily into winter": *Jet,* Jan. 9, 1964, pp. 6–9; Lyon, *Memories of the Southern Civil Rights Movement,* pp. 124–29; Good, *Trouble I've Seen,* pp. 25–29; NYT, Dec. 22, 1963, p. 25; NYT, Dec. 23, 1963, p. 44.

192   straddling the conflict: Lewis, *King,* pp. 233–35.

192   Daddy King hounded: Good, *Trouble I've Seen,* pp. 29–31.

192   "a where do we go from here": Wiretap summary of Jones-MLK conversation of Dec. 17, 1963, in New York LHM dated Dec. 18, 1963, FK-NR, pp. 2–3.

192   FEDERAL BUILDING in Oxford: Mills, *This Little Light,* pp. 69–77.

192   agent explained the physical evidence: BW, Dec. 18, 1963, p. 3.

192   "Your name has not been called": Clark to Horton, Dec. 5, 1963, Series G-17, No. 4007, UNC.

193   Henry expressed a practical worry: Minutes, COFO staff meeting, 11:30 A.M., Dec. 15, 1963, A/SN111f16.

193   "You can be bigger": Int. Lawrence Guyot, Feb. 21, 1991.
193   "see his ass put in jail": Mendy Samstein, "On the Hattiesburg Situation," nd (circa Jan. 1964), A/SN98f24.
193   "I think that will be": Ibid.
193   "Are you strong enough": Int. Lawrence Guyot, Feb. 1, 1991.
193   grandiose scheme to import 100,000: Minutes, COFO staff meeting, 5:00 P.M., Dec. 15, 1963, A/SN111f16.
193   "You're going to get a lot of folks killed": Ibid.
194   debate resumed after Christmas: Minutes of SNCC Executive Committee meetings, Dec. 28–31, 1963, compiled by Jim Monsonis and Cathy Cade A/SN6.
194   fn "We have to be practical": Ibid., p. 15.
194   "Some of the whites": Ibid., p. 22.
194   "pushed by Al Lowenstein": Ibid., p. 28.
194   "intends to obtain": Ibid., p. 29–30.

14. High Councils

195   swaths of black crepe: Johnson, *White House Diary,* p. 19.
195   seven top FBI officials: Baumgardner to Sullivan, Dec. 19, 1963, FK-NR; Sullivan to Belmont, December 24, 1963, FK-NR; Garrow, *FBI and Martin,* pp. 102–4.
195   phony engineering company: Branch, *Parting,* p. 915; testimony of Arthur Murtaugh, Nov. 17, 1978, in Hearings of the House Select Committee on Assassinations, Vol. 6, pp. 99–100; int. Robert Nichols, May 29, 1984.
196   "placing a good-looking female plant": Garrow, *FBI and Martin,* p. 103.
196   repeated five times a first requirement: Sullivan to Belmont, Dec. 24, 1963, FK-NR.
196   "We are most interested": Garrow *FBI and Martin,* p. 104.
196   money was the root of evil: Int. Robert Nichols, May 29, 1984.
197   "pretty much agreed with Hegel": Ibid.
197   "so-called civil rights": Baumgardner to Sullivan, Jan. 8, 1964, FK-NR.
197   "We will, at the proper time": Sullivan to Belmont, Dec. 24, 1963, FK-NR.
197   "Man of the Year": *Time,* Jan. 3, 1964.
197   "the unchallenged voice of the Negro people": Ibid., p. 27.
197   "They had to dig deep in the garbage": O'Reilly, *Racial Matters,* p. 136.
197   "We here to get Martin Luther King": Director to SAC, Tampa, Jan. 13, 1964, FBI File No. 9-41768-2, FRW-NR.
198   Hoover suspended official courtesies: Director to SAC, Detroit, Nov. 27, 1963, FRW-NR. This order is recalled by the Atlanta office in SAC, Atlanta, to Director, Jan. 16, 1964, FRW-NR.
198   Roy Wilkins asked: SAC, New York, to Director and SAC, Tampa, Jan. 29, 1964, FRW-NR.
198   "diplomatically decline": Director to SAC, New York, Jan. 22, 1964, FRW-NR.
198   transformed the 1890 farmhouse: Johnson, *White House Diary,* p. 20.
198   high-powered showerheads: Valenti, *A Very Human President,* p. 89.
198   steaks into the shape of Texas: Dugger, *The Politician,* p. 426.
198   mating instincts of nearby cattle: E. Ernest Goldstein, "How LBJ Took the Bull by the Horns," *Amherst* alumni magazine, Winter 1985, p. 15.
198   postponed Christmas dinner: Johnson, *White House Diary,* pp. 20–21.
198   mounted on a bale of hay: NYT, Dec. 28, 1963, p. 1.
198   souvenir ashtrays: Johnson, *White House Diary,* p. 21.
198   swirled in hospitality bowls: Int. Victoria Murphy, Aug. 17, 1993.
198   Whenever Mrs. Johnson saw: Ibid.
199   *Jet* magazine mistakenly said: *Jet,* Dec. 19, 1963, pp. 6–10; *Jet,* Dec. 26, 1963, p. 14.
199   retrieved prints to prove: LBJ phone calls with Andrew Hatcher, Roy Wilkins, and Whitney Young, Dec. 23, 1963, Audiotape K6312.17, LBJ.
199   "quit cuttin' us up": LBJ phone call with Whitney Young, Jan. 6, 1964, Cit. 1197, Audiotape WH6401.06, LBJ.
199   "I had my picture made": LBJ phone call with Roy Wilkins, Dec. 23, 1963, Audiotape K6312.17, LBJ.
199   "I've done as much as I can": Dictabelt of telephone conversation between LBJ and *Washington Post* executive Katharine Graham, 11:10 A.M., Dec. 2, 1963, LBJ.
199   Johnson aggressively befriended him: Victoria McHugh (Murphy) Oral History, pp. 12–13, LBJ.
199   marathon poverty caucus: Johnson, *The Vantage Point,* pp. 73–75; Lemann, *The Promised Land,* pp. 143–45; int. Jack Valenti, Feb. 25, 1991; int. Horace Busby, Feb. 3, 1992.
199   "Why did you say that?": Int. Horace Busby, Feb. 3, 1992.
199   wartime editor of *The Daily Texan:* Roberts, *LBJ's Inner Circle,* pp. 88–91.
199   standoff over segregation: *Time,* Nov. 10, 1961, p. 50.
200   segregation at Forty Acres: E. Ernest Goldstein, "How LBJ Took the Bull by the Horns," *Amherst* alumni magazine, Winter 1985, pp. 12–17.
200   "the President of the United States integrated us": Ibid. Also Miller, *Lyndon,* pp. 445–46.
200   "What kind of fool would I be": Wiretap transcript of Elijah Muhammad–Louis X [Farrakhan] conversation, Dec. 31, 1963, FMXNY-4073, pp. 1–3.

201 "Any laborer or minister": Wiretap transcript of Elijah Muhammad–Isaiah X [Karriem] conversation, Dec. 31, 1963, FMXNY-4074, p. 2.

201 "I cannot understand": Wiretap transcript of conference call featuring Elijah Muhammad and Malcolm X, Jan. 2, 1964, in Report to Director from SAC, Phoenix, Jan 23, 1964, FEM-NR.

201 bought maternity clothes: Wiretap transcript of Elijah Muhammad telephone call, Jan. 3, 1964, in Report to Director from SAC, Phoenix, Jan. 23, 1964, FEM-NR, p. 5.

201 "in the nest": Wiretap transcript of Elijah Muhammad telephone call, Jan. 7, 1964, in Report to Director from SAC, Phoenix, Jan 27, 1964, FMXNY-4073, pp. 4–6.

201 $100 per month: Perry, *Malcolm,* pp. 230–32, 305–6.

201 "even if they move to": Wiretap transcript of Elijah Muhammad telephone call, Jan. 7, 1964, in Report to Director from SAC, Phoenix, Jan. 27, 1964, FMXNY-4073, p. 5.

201 told Captain Joseph: Wiretap transcript of Elijah Muhammad telephone call, Jan. 4, 1964, in Report to Director from SAC, Phoenix, Jan. 27, 1964, FMXNY-4073, p. 4. According to this intercept, Muhammad directed that Minister James X [Shabazz] of the Newark temple take over Malcolm's pulpit duties, while Captain Joseph was to enforce Malcolm's removal.

201 "Let my son know that": Wiretap transcript of Elijah Muhammad telephone call, Jan. 3, 1964, in Report to Director from SAC, Phoenix, Jan 23, 1964, FEM-NR, p. 6.

201 "I'm not through with Malcolm yet": Ibid., p. 5.

201 Malcolm appeared in Phoenix: Goldman, *Death and Life,* pp. 125–26; SAC, Phoenix, to Director, Jan. 16, 1964, FMXNY-4023.

201 layover in Washington: Int. Abdulalim Shabazz (Lonnie X Cross), March 14, 1991.

202 Lonnie X never saw him again: Ibid.

202 "Sometimes he speaks nice and good": Wiretap transcript of Elijah Muhammad telephone call, Jan. 9, 1964, in Report to Director from SAC, Phoenix, Jan. 27, 1964, FMXNY-4073, pp. 7–8.

202 another tape and a letter: SAC, Phoenix, to Director, Jan. 16, 1964, FMXNY-4023.

202 "When a man is falling": SAC, Phoenix, to Director, Jan. 22, 1964, FMXNY-4066.

202 escaped into an airport hotel room: SAC, New York, to Director, Feb. 12, 1964, reporting on an FBI interview with Malcolm X conducted Feb. 4, 1964, and notes (form 302) of that interview dated Feb. 5, 1964, both FMX-81.

202 enlisted young Alex: Int. Alex Haley, Dec. 4, 1990.

202 article vilifying Elijah Muhammad: Alex Haley, "Mr. Muhammad Speaks," *Reader's Digest,* March 1960, pp. 100–04.

202 interview Malcolm X: *Playboy,* May 1963, p. 53ff.

202 love of Shakespeare: Int. Alex Haley, Dec. 4, 1990.

202 Haley had no inkling: Ibid. Also Malcolm X, *The Autobiography,* p. 405.

203 "You have not converted": Malcolm X, *The Autobiography,* p. 406.

203 Malcolm flew to Miami: Perry, *Malcolm,* pp. 245–46.

203 strange informant report: SAC, Miami, to Director, Jan. 21, 1964, FMX-78.

203 dinner at the Rockland Palace: SAC, New York, to Director, Jan. 29, 1964, FMX-80; Dick Schaap, "The Challenger and the Muslims," *New York Herald Tribune,* Jan. 23, 1964, p. 1; "Cassius Clay Almost Says He's a Muslim," NYAN, Jan. 25, 1964, p. 1; *Jet,* Feb. 6, 1964, pp. 58–59.

203 first papal trip: NYT, Jan. 5 and 6, 1964, p. 1; *New York Herald Tribune,* Jan. 5, 6, and 7, 1964, p. 1.

203 Paul received Sargent Shriver: NYT, Jan. 6, 1964, p. 1.

203 Shriver asked for a papal blessing: Int. Sargent Shriver, Feb. 21, 1991.

203 Greek Archbishop Iakovos: Poulos, *A Breath of God,* pp. 30–31.

204 secret agent of reconciliation: Ibid., p. 105.

204 "He that would love life": 1 Peter 3:10–11 and Psalm 34:12–16, cited in Vorgimler, *Commentary on the Documents of Vatican II,* pp. 56–57.

204 closed conference in February: Ibid., p. 59.

204 oral argument in the *Sullivan* case: NYT, Jan. 7, 1964, p. 21, Jan. 8, 1964, p. 19.

204 Goldberg discreetly sent down: Int. Harry Wachtel, Oct. 27, 1983, and May 17, 1990.

204 Washington office of William Rogers: Int. William Rogers, June 11, 1984; int. Harry Wachtel, May 17, 1990.

205 A relative newcomer: Branch, *Parting,* pp. 581–83.

205 introduced the highly prized counsel: Int. Harry Wachtel, May 17, 1990; Gandhi Society press release dated June 5, 1963, announcing the agreement of William Rogers and Samuel Pierce to appear before the Supreme Court in the *Sullivan* case, Box 50, Folder 1263, Lowenstein Papers, UNC.

205 Wachtel opened with a harsh appraisal: Int. Harry Wachtel, May 17, 1990.

205 Rogers took issue with Wachtel: Ibid.

205 "I agree with you": Ibid.

206 "fantastic": Proceedings of the Supreme Court in Case No. 39, Jan. 6, 1964, p. 10.

206 Alabama law allowed: In addition to the case records themselves, the legal history of the *Sullivan* case may be found ably and amply explored in Anthony Lewis, *Make No Law.*

206 largest judgment of its kind: Ibid., p. 35.

206 too many racial references: Int. Harry Wachtel, May 17, 1990.

206 annoyed with Rogers: Int. William Rogers, June 11, 1984.

206 "a death penalty for any newspaper": Proceedings of the Supreme Court in Case No. 39, Jan. 6, 1964, p. 21.

206 $300 million in damages: Perry, *Malcolm,* p. 35.

207 installed microphone bugs in his room: Garrow, *FBI and Martin,* pp. 104–6; Garrow, *Bearing the*

Cross, p. 310; Sullivan to Belmont, Jan. 6, 1964, FK-NR; "Summary of Highly Sensitive Coverage," Nov. 27, 1964, FK-1024.

207   "I'm fucking for God!": Author's interviews with FBI officials.

207   "This will destroy the burrhead!": Garrow, *FBI and Martin,* p. 106.

207   "King is a 'tom cat' ": Hoover notation on Sullivan to Belmont, Jan. 27, 1964, FBI 100-3-116-792, cited in ibid., p. 107.

207   "It is believed that the submissions": Director to SAC, Atlanta, Jan. 7, 1964, FK-NR.

207   "to take [King] off his pedestal": Sullivan to Belmont, Jan. 8, 1964, FBI 77-56944-19, cited in Garrow, *FBI and Martin,* p. 105.

208   "recent income tax returns of King": Baumgardner to Sullivan, Jan. 8, 1964, FSC-NR.

208   "If this judgment is permitted to stand": NYT, Jan. 8, 1964, p. 8.

208   farewell luncheon at the Washington Hotel: Int. William Rogers, June 11, 1984.

208   he never dreamed: Ibid. Also Rogers speech entitled *"NY Times v. Sullivan*—Twenty Years Later," Waldorf-Astoria, March 8, 1984, text courtesy of William Rogers.

208   over the next nine weeks: Historical accounts of the Court deliberations over *Sullivan* appear in Lewis, *Make No Law, passim,* esp. pp. 164–82; Eisler, *A Justice for All,* pp. 228–36.

208   "Although the Sedition Law was never tested": Opinion of the Court, *New York Times Co. v. Sullivan,* 376 U.S. 254 (1964), p. 276.

208   "I considered, and now consider": Ibid.

209   " 'actual malice' ": Ibid., p. 280.

209   "the case of the individual petitioners": Ibid., p. 286.

209   fn literal disappearance: In his front-page story announcing the Court's decision in March of 1964, reporter Anthony Lewis surfaced the tense, unspoken realities that he and other close contemporaries *knew* dominated the proceedings: "The *Times* argued that the purpose and effect of these suits was to discourage coverage of the racial situation." In his book on *Sullivan* a generation later, however, Lewis more accurately summarized the actual written record: "The *Times* petition did not emphasize the racial issue that formed the context of the libel action." The careful, cumulative avoidance of race in the legal argument came soon to dominate interpretation, especially by those lacking firsthand experience. By the 1980s, teachers and students read the *Sullivan* decision as pure First Amendment law, and commonly missed the formative persecutions against Martin Luther King and the civil rights movement. NYT, March 9, 1964, p. 1; Lewis, *Make No Law,* p. 109.

209   "was apparently a man of some thin skin": Eisler, *A Justice for All,* p. 228.

209   FBI executives debated: Garrow, *FBI and Martin,* p. 106.

209   returned to headquarters: Ibid.

210   visit him on Saturday, January 18: NYT, Jan. 19, 1964, p. 1; Whalen and Whalen, *The Longest Debate,* pp. 94–5.

210   "without a word or a comma changed": "Notes on Meeting: President Johnson, Clarence Mitchell and Joe Rauh, January 21, 1964," Box 26, Rauh Papers, LOC.

210   "lengthy and fruitful discussion": NYT, Jan. 19, 1964, p. 42.

210   Black Mountain retreat: Garrow, *Bearing the Cross,* pp. 310–11; "Assignments for Black Mountain retreat," A/KP32f7; "Tentative Agenda for SCLC Retreat, Black Mountain, N.C., January 20–22, 1964," A/KP32f7; FBI documents, including New York LHM, Jan. 21, 1964, FR-NR.

210   Prime Minister Nehru justified: King, *Why We Can't Wait,* pp. 134–5.

210   accepted advice to straddle: Jones to MLK, Jan. 29, 1964, A/KP27f8; MLK to Hermine Popper, Feb. 3, 1964, A/KP18f14; Levison's comments to Hermine Popper of Jan. 27, 1964, cited in FLNY7-679a and New York LHM, Feb. 5, 1964, FSC-NR, p. 2.

211   "Bill of Rights for the Disadvantaged": King, *Why We Can't Wait,* p. 137ff.

211   Wachtel was watching: Int. Harry Wachtel, Oct. 27, 1983, and May 17, 1990.

211   agreed to have the recordings destroyed: Ibid. Also Jones to C. T. Vivian, Feb. 11, 1964, A/KP13f18.

211   Levison's candid appraisal: Int. Clarence Jones, Oct. 25, 1983, Nov. 28, 1989.

211   marketing plans for King's forthcoming book: Wiretap transcript of Levison-Daves conversation, Jan. 31, 1964, FLNY7-683a; wiretap transcript of Levison-Daves conversation, Feb. 14, 1964, FLNY-9-443.

211   winter-long struggle to hire more efficient: This is a running theme of wiretap intercepts FLNY7 and FLNY9. Also Jones to King, Abernathy, and Walker, Jan. 31, 1964, A/KP33f21.

211   "What are SCLC's basic aims": "Tentative Agenda for SCLC Retreat, Black Mountain, N.C., January 20–22, 1964."

212   fn "Whatever his greatness": *Time,* Jan. 3, 1964, p. 13.

212   fn "typical hatchet job": Wiretap of Jones-Levison conversations, 9:59 A.M., and 12:55 P.M., Jan. 3, 1964, FLNY9-401, 401a.

212   fn letter of thanks: MLK to Henry Luce, Jan. 16, 1964, A/KP23f35.

212   Walker wanted to target Atlanta: Garrow, *Bearing the Cross,* p. 310.

212   unfit to be dogcatcher: New York LHMs of Jan. 30 and March 10, 1964, FK-NR; int. Cleveland Robinson, Oct. 28, 1983.

212   closing down his March on Washington office: New York LHM, Jan. 28, 1964, FK-NR.

212   strategy of protest: Rustin, "From Protest to Politics: The Future of the Civil Rights Movement," *Commentary,* Feb. 1964, p. 31ff.

212   "If the boys can run you once": Int. Bayard Rustin, Sept. 24, 1984.

212   page at the North Carolina airport: Garrow, *Bearing the Cross,* p. 311.

212   Piedmont Airlines flight 45: Charlotte FBI report dated Jan. 24, 1964, FK-NR; *Jet,* Feb. 6, 1964, p. 4.

213   bomb would destroy the Macedonia Baptist: McGowan to Rosen, Jan. 26, 1964, FK-293.
213   four different callers had warned: SAC, Milwaukee, to Director, Jan. 29, 1964, FK-NR.
213   "No activities of interest developed.": Garrow, *FBI and Martin,* p. 107.

15. HATTIESBURG FREEDOM DAY

214   resistance where he least expected it: Int. Robert Stone, June 3, 1993.
214   Summoned to the White House: PDD, Dec. 9, 1963, LBJ.
214   Spike declined to have his commission: Robert Spike, "Report to the Commission on Religion and Race," Feb. 21, 1964, pp. 1, 4, NCC RG 6, b47f30, POH.
214   "I would say to you": Gov. Paul Johnson inaugural address, Jan. 21, 1964, WLBT-TV news tape 0139/D22, MDAH.
215   Spike sent him a telegram: NYT, Jan. 23, 1964, p. 19.
215   idea of Dr. Gayraud Wilmore: Int. J. Metz Rollins, Jr., Dec. 13, 1991; int. Gayraud Wilmore, May 14, 1992; int. Robert Stone, June 3, 1993.
215   1,300 Presbyterian missionaries: Smith, *From Colonialism to World Community,* p. 277.
215   Smith's name put a jolt: Int. J. Metz Rollins, Jr., Dec. 13, 1991; int. Gayraud Wilmore, May 14, 1992; int. Robert Stone, June 3, 1993.
215   fifty-one white faces and clerical collars: list of "Clergy Participation, Freedom Day, January 22, 1964, Hattiesburg, Mississippi," A/SN101f8.
215   St. Paul's AME: Int. Victoria Gray Adams, Sept. 9, 1994.
215   Ella Baker arrived: Zinn, *SNCC,* pp. 102–22; Dittmer, *Local People,* pp. 220–21.
216   "We're here to prod": Zinn, *SNCC,* p. 105.
216   "Immanuel Kant": Ibid., p. 106.
216   Smith wrote down one of Guyot's sentences: Smith, *From Colonialism to World Community,* p. 268.
216   conceal money in their shoes: Ibid., p. 265.
216   "the guts to march": Ibid., p. 263.
216   Pratt and the white reporters: Int. Jack Pratt, March 25, 1991.
216   Smith drew celebrity housing: Smith, *From Colonialism to World Community,* p. 265.
217   Daisy Harris: Int. Daisy Harris, June 25, 1994.
217   Victoria Gray announced: Int. Victoria Gray Adams, May 14, 1991.
217   "Oh, Lord Jesus": Zinn, *SNCC,* p. 109.
217   Main Street on Tuesday: Ibid., pp. 110–11. Also Von Hoffman, *Mississippi Notebook,* pp. 12–13; Lyon, *Memories of the Southern Civil Rights Movement,* pp. 130–33; *Jackson Daily News,* Jan. 23, 1964, p. 6.
217   "Well, we got to protect": Int. J. Metz Rollins, Jr., Dec. 13, 1991.
217   Guyot stared: Int. Lawrence Guyot, Feb. 1, 1991.
217   dawned on Jack Pratt: Int. Jack Pratt, March 25, 1991.
217   her legs went limp: Int. Daisy Harris, June 25, 1994.
217   pressed Sheriff Bud Gray: Zinn, *SNCC,* pp. 112–13.
218   prevailing thought was to spare: Int. James K. Dukes, June 23, 1992.
218   SNCC's communications office: Michael Sayer to Julian Bond, Jan. 15, 1964; Sayer, "Comments on the Hattiesburg freedom Day," nd, A/SN98f24.
218   large contingent of reporters: Von Hoffman, *Mississippi Notebook,* p. 12.
218   "In such situations": Smith, *From Colonialism to World Community,* p. 266.
218   annoyance focused on Bob Moses: Freedom Day accounts cited above. Also SNCC press release "via Walter Tillow," A/SN101f8; COFO "Hattiesburg Report," Jan. 1964, A/SN54f9, p. 2; SNCC "Chronology of Intimidation and Violence," A/KP16f15, p. 18.
218   "lone picket": Int. Michael Sayer, June 25, 1992.
219   Hamer belted out: Zinn, *SNCC,* p. 113.
219   "Try to sing 'America' ": Smith, *From Colonialism to World Community,* p. 266.
219   trial of Bob Moses: Zinn, *SNCC,* pp. 117–21; Notice of appeal filed by J. Robert Lunney on behalf of Moses, NCC RG6, b50f7, POH.
219   long cigarette holder: Int. Victoria Gray Adams, May 14, 1991.
219   "My dog's so mean": Von Hoffman, *Mississippi Notebook,* p. 13.
219   interpreted a fruit basket: Smith, *From Colonialism to World Community,* p. 275.
219   vintage bootleg whiskey: Int. Jack Pratt, March 25, 1991.
219   "Preachers gone astray": Int. Robert Castle, March 3, 1993; *Jackson Daily News,* Jan. 27, 1964.
219   cut slits in his shoes: Int. Robert Stone, June 1, 1993.
219   "grandpa nigger": Smith, *From Colonialism to World Community,* p. 268.
219   first batch of replacement clergy: "Hattiesburg Project/Second Week Participants," A/SN101f8.
219   Nine of them were arrested: COFO Hattiesburg report, A/SN54f9, pp. 2–3; NYT, March 10, 1964, p. 17.
219   twenty-one third-week successors: "Hattiesburg Project/Third Week Participants," A/SN101f8.
219   arrested Guyot: COFO Hattiesburg report. A/SN54f9, p. 2; *Jackson Daily News,* Jan. 29, 1964, Feb. 1, 1964; Smith, *From Colonialism to World Community,* pp. 270–73.
219   fired Victoria Gray's husband: Int. Victoria Gray Adams, May 14, 1991.
220   recognized on the picket lines: Pickets fired on the morning after Freedom Day included eighteen-year-old John Gould, a shoeshine boy at the Central Barber Shop. COFO Hattiesburg report, A/SN54f9, p. 4.
220   obtained a restraining order: Petition and writ in case No. 22688, *City of Hattiesburg v. Robert Moses.*

United Presbyterian Commission on Religion and Race, Episcopal Society for Cultural and Racial Unity, the Rabbinical Assembly of America et al., Chancery Court of Forrest County, Jan. 29, 1964, NCC RG6, b50f7, POH.

220   sixty pickets went to jail: NYT, April 19, 1964, p. 65.

220   "You asked what the point": Statement of Rev. Emil J. Hattoon, cited in SNCC pamphlet, "Hattiesburg Freedom Day, January 22, 1964," A/SN98f24.

220   Spike's shrewd vision: Int. Robert P. Moses, Feb. 25, 1991.

220   "Never ask in advance": Int. Jack Pratt, March 25, 1991; int. Bruce Hanson, Jan. 21 and Feb. 22, 1991.

220   after picket hours on January 24: Minutes of Hattiesburg SNCC meeting, Jan. 24, 1964, A/SN100f13.

221   Cotton said he would wind up doing: Ibid.

221   fn "We have an office": Rita Schwerner to Anne Braden, Jan. 23, 1964, b55f15, Braden Papers, SHSW.

221   fn had first submitted: Cagin and Dray, *We Are Not Afraid,* pp. 256–61.

221   Edwin King had submitted: Edwin King to COFO Staff Executive Committee, Jan. 16, 1964, b12f612, Edwin King Papers, TOU.

221   Guyot swapped places: SNCC press release of Feb. 1, 1964, A/SN101f8.

222   Moses had risen to point out: Int. Michael Sayer, June 25, 1992.

222   Aaron Henry called from Clarksdale: "Information Concerning the Killing of Louis Allen," Jan. 31, 1964, A/SN51f6.

222   reproaching himself for losing track: Int. Robert P. Moses, July 30, 1984.

222   "They are after him in Amite": Moses to Doar, Aug. 2, 1962, files of Civil Rights Division, U.S. Department of Justice.

222   Allen had witnessed the event: Branch, *Parting,* pp. 510–22.

222   " 'tip-off man' ": Undated news story about Charles B. Gordon of *McComb Enterprise-Journal,* A/SN51f6.

222   what grieving relatives told him: "Report Concerning the Louis Allen Case by Robert Moses," A/SN51f6.

222   tried more than once to leave Mississippi: Julian Bond, "Activism of the Late Mr. Allen," *New South,* March 1964, pp. 12–15; Testimony of Elizabeth Allen, June 8, 1964, reprinted in *Congressional Record,* June 16, 1964; Elizabeth Allen affidavit, reprinted in COFO, *Mississippi,* pp. 30–37; Branch, *Parting,* p. 921.

223   Allen dived headlong: Murder account from above Allen sources, esp. undated news story by Charles B. Gordon of *McComb Enterprise-Journal,* A/SN51f6.

223   stood at the murder site to tell: ADW, Feb. 19, 1964, p. 8; CD, Feb. 4, 1964, p. 1.

223   "Advise All Persons": Director to SAC, New Orleans, Feb. 3, 1964, FBI File No. 44-24466 (Louis Allen murder), Serial 2.

223   "the victim is not a registered voter": Rosen to Belmont, Feb. 3, 1964, FBI File No. 44-24466 (Louis Allen Murder), Serial 4. Also Rosen to Belmont, June 22, 1964, FBI File No. 44-24466 (Louis Allen murder), Serial 4. Also Rosen to Belmont, June 22, 1964, FBI File No. 44-24466 (Louis Allen Murder), Serial 15, p. 3.

223   "The mainspring in the McComb racial turmoil": Undated news story by Charles B. Gordon of *McComb Enterprise -Journal,* A/SN51f6.

223   overrode lingering scruples: Branch, *Parting,* p. 921; int. Robert P. Moses, Feb. 15, 1991.

223   "The Briar Patch": Twelve Southerners, *I'll Take My Stand,* pp. 246–64.

224   "It's the importance": Robert Penn Warren, "Two for SNCC," *Commentary,* Feb. 1965, pp. 38–42; Warren, *Who Speaks for the Negro?,* pp. 87–100.

224   "They'd let me vote": Int. Robert Stone, June 1, 1993.

16. AMBUSH

225   Sargent Shriver kept an appointment: PDD, Jan. 31, 1964, 4:50 P.M., LBJ.

225   "Well, Sarge, that's really": Int. Sargent Shriver, Feb. 21, 1991.

225   fn Johnson often caricatured: Int. Victoria Murphy, Aug. 17, 1993.

226   "I'm gonna announce": LBJ phone call with Sargent Shriver, 1:02 P.M., Feb. 1, 1964, Cit. 1804, Audiotape WH6402.01, LBJ; PDD, Feb. 1, 1964, LBJ.

226   Shriver in full panic: Int. Sargent Shriver, Feb. 21, 1991.

226   fended off a last frantic call: LBJ phone call with Sargent Shriver, 2:25 P.M., Feb. 1, 1964, Cit. 1807, Audiotape WH6402.01, LBJ.

226   test performances of the Redeye: Remarks of Adam Yarmolinsky at the Brandeis conference on "The Federal Government and Urban Poverty," June 1973, RFK Oral History Collection, p. 232ff, JFK; Adam Yarmolinsky Oral History, July 13, 1970, p. 5, LBJ.

226   announced the appointment: NYT, Feb. 2, 1964, p. 1.

226   explained to Shriver: LBJ and Bill Moyers phone call with Sargent Shriver, 6:04 P.M., Feb. 1, 1964, Cit. 1809, Audiotape WH6402.01, LBJ.

226   Frank Mankiewicz: Mankiewicz Oral History, LBJ.

226   Adam Yarmolinsky: Adam Yarmolinsky Oral History, pp. 5–10, LBJ.

226   "It will never fly": Ibid. Also Schlesinger, *Robert Kennedy,* p. 689; Moynihan, *Maximum Feasible Misunderstanding,* p. 82; remarks of Adam Yarmolinsky at the Brandeis conference on "The Federal Government and Urban Poverty," June 1973, RFK Oral History Collection, p. 234, JFK.

227   community action advocates: The most prominent advocates of community action were David Hackett and Richard Boone, who worked from the Kennedy Justice Department on the President's Committee on Juvenile Delinquency, and Paul N. Ylvisaker, a son and grandson of Lutheran theologians who veered away from his clerical ambitions to become an expert on urban poverty for the Ford Foundation. Their influence on the poverty program is reviewed in Moynihan, *Maximum Feasible Misunderstanding,* pp. 79–86; Lemann, *The Promised Land,* pp. 121–25, 145–55. For Ylvisaker's background and motivation, see his speech, "A Relevant Christ—But a Relevant Church?," Feb. 5, 1964, AFF.

227   mindful of what he could sell: Int. Sargent Shriver, Feb. 21, 1991.

227   Hyman Bookbinder called: Int. Hyman Bookbinder, March 21, 1964.

227   looked to Attorney General Robert Kennedy: David Hackett to Kenneth O'Donnell with attached RKF to LBJ, Jan. 16, 1964, Box 39, Moyers Papers, LBJ; Hackett to Lee White, Jan. 23, 1964, Box 33, Walinsky Papers, Senate Subject File 65–68, JFK; "The attack on Poverty Bill," nd, Box 41, Heller Papers, LBJ.

228   "Been to any good funerals": Schlesinger, *Robert Kennedy,* p. 661.

228   "The innocent suffer": Ibid., p. 666.

228   "the new fellow": Ibid., p. 681.

228   lost most feeling for politics: "What Will R.F.K. Do Next?," *Saturday Evening Post,* March 28, 1964, pp. 17–20.

228   trip to Indonesia: Schlesinger, *Robert Kennedy,* pp. 682–85; *Life,* Jan. 31, 1964, p. 33.

228   Kennedy was ambushed by House members: Evans to Belmont, Jan. 31, 1964, FK-299; Callahan to Mohr, Jan. 31, 1964, FK-302.

228   Hoover had disclosed to them: Hoover testimony before the Judiciary Subcommittee of House Appropriations, chaired by John Rooney (D.-N.Y.), Jan 29, 1964, pp. 274–313.

228   three-week spitting match: Aside from the Hoover testimony of Jan. 29, the main focus of contention was visits to the FBI and Justice Department by *Atlanta Journal* reporter Reese Cleghorn, who sought information on King. Burke Marshall and other Justice Department officials firmly believed that the FBI was leaking secret wiretap material about King to Cleghorn, which the Bureau indignantly denied. Justice officials pretended that their only motive for seeking to prevent publication of derogatory King material was to protect the FBI's confidential sources. FBI officials fumed that the department was really trying to cover up its own collusion with King and its failure to brand him a subversive. ("I asked [RFK Press Secretary Ed] Guthman if the 'Saturday Evening Post' intended to 'whitewash' King," wrote DeLoach.) Cleghorn's research visit to Washington on February 5 renewed the bureaucratic hostilities. See DeLoach to Mohr, Feb. 5, 1964, FK-NR; Evans to Belmont, Feb. 5, 1964, FK-300; Evans to Belmont, Feb. 6, 1964, FK-307; DeLoach to Mohr, Feb. 12, 1964, FK-303. Also int. Ed Guthman, June 25, 1984.

228   "I pointed out that": Ed Guthman, Memo to Files, re RFK-JEH conversation of 10:00 A.M., Feb. 5, 1964, private files of Ed Guthman.

228   "[Burke] Marshall is a liar": Hoover note on DeLoach to Hoover, Feb. 18, 1964, FK-315.

228   circulated this exact charge: Hoover note ("Marshall is a liar.") on Rosen to Belmont, Feb. 25, 1964, FK-317; Hoover note ("Marshall is still a liar.") on Rosen to Belmont, Feb. 26, 1964, FK-319.

228   "I stated just like that woman": Hoover to Tolson et al., 10:51 A.M., Feb. 5, 1964, FK-297.

228   "The hurt that others feel": Fred Dutton to RFK, April 3, 1964, Box 8, AG Papers, JFK.

229   fight over a cigarette butt: *Baltimore Sun,* Feb. 6, 1994, p. 19.

229   "the greatest composers since Beethoven": *Rolling Stone Rock Almanac,* p. 81.

229   celebrate their seventeenth birthday: Jones, *Great Expectations,* p. 73.

229   double to twenty million: Ibid., p. 68.

229   "the buyingest age group in history": *Time,* April 17, 1964, p. 100.

229   "Have Mercy, Baby": Deay, *Stairway to Heaven,* p. 75.

229   "I Got a Woman": Wolff, *You Send Me,* p. 117.

229   formula had registered: Deay, *Stairway to Heaven,* pp. 73–107.

229   fn imitative "cover" recordings: Guralnick, *Sweet Soul Music,* p. 192.

230   "ears tingled": *Rolling Stone Rock Almanac,* p. 85.

230   "although unkempt in one way": *U.S. News & World Report,* Feb. 24, 1964, p. 88.

230   bowled over even Sam Cooke: Wolff, *You Send Me,* pp. 293, 296, 306–7.

230   childhood friend Lou Rawls: Ibid., pp. 43–44, 247–49.

230   critics would uphold: Deay, *Stairway to Heaven,* p. 85; Guralnick, *Sweet Soul Music,* p. 46; Wolff, *You Send Me,* pp. 290–92, 351.

230   misfortune to perform: Wolff, *You Send Me,* p. 293.

230   "You guys ain't as dumb": Hauser, *Muhammad Ali,* p. 63.

230   pantomimed as mighty Tarzan: CDD, Feb. 19, 1964, p. 4.

230   trial for shooting Medgar Evers: Massengill, *Portrait of a Racist,* pp. 180–202.

230   "I believe in segregation": Ibid., p. 197.

230   "For the next fifteen years": Ibid., p. 166.

231   "Shooting at Night": *The Nation,* Feb. 24, 1964, p. 180.

231   Myrlie Evers, prepared: NYT, Feb. 8, 1964, p. 1.

231   "a victory for the law": Massengill, *Portrait of a Racist,* p. 201.

231   Barnett had strolled publicly: Ibid., p. 202; NYT, Feb. 8, 1964, p. 10.

231   Lowenstein to tell: Minutes of COFO Convention, Feb. 9, 1964, MSS 191, b1f3, SHSW.

231   allowed to use assumed names: Ibid.

231   ninety-five prospective jurors: *The Nation,* Feb. 24, 1964, p. 180.

231   Howard Smith's proposal: Feb. 8 debate generally from *Congressional Record–House,* Feb. 8, 1964, pp. 2577–84; Whalen and Whalen, *The Longest Debate,* pp. 115–18; Harrison, *On Account of Sex,* pp. 176–81; Graham, *The Civil Rights Era,* pp. 134–39.

231   "Now I am very serious": *Congressional Record–House*, Feb. 8, 1964, p. 2577.
232   Eleven of the twelve female: Harrison, *On Account of Sex*, p. 178.
232   "women were a second class sex": *Congressional Record–House*, Feb. 8, 1964, p. 2580.
232   "Unless this amendment": Ibid., p. 2583.
232   "I know this Congress": Ibid.
232   "pandemonium reigned": Whalen and Whalen, *The Longest Debate*, p. 117.
232   Katzenbach had warned: Graham, *The Civil Rights Era*, p. 136.
233   "after I leave the floor": *Congressional Record–House*, Feb. 8, 1964, p. 2581.
233   surprise amendment: The strange origins of the sex discrimination provision in the 1964 law would be recognized popularly some thirty years later. Cf. "Judge Smith's Unintended Victory for the Ladies," *Plain-Dealer* (Cleveland), Jan. 9, 1994, p. 9; "Racists for Feminism! The Odd History of the Civil Rights Bill," WP, Feb. 4, 1994, p. C5.
233   "the apples-and-bananas fallacy": Carl M. Brauer, "Women Activists, Southern Conservatives, and the Prohibition of Sex Discrimination in Title VII of the 1964 Civil Rights Act," *The Journal of Southern History*, Feb. 1983, p. 51.
233   "Smith outsmarted himself": Whalen and Whalen, *The Longest Debate*, p. 117.
234   "I sort of feel like": Ibid., p. 122.
234   "I'm proud of you": LBJ phone call with Carl Albert, 8:32 P.M., Feb. 10, 1964, Cit. 2015, Audiotape WH6402.13, LBJ.
234   "You reckon he wants": LBJ phone call with Pierre Salinger and Lawrence O'Brien, 8:37 P.M., Feb. 10, 1964, Cit. 2019, Audiotape WH6402.13, LBJ.
234   "they couldn't pee a drop": LBJ phone call with Nicholas Katzenbach, 9:45 P.M., Feb. 10, 1964, Cit. 2037, Audiotape WH6402.14, LBJ.
234   "Whatever you want": LBJ phone call with Robert Kennedy, 9:07 P.M., Feb. 10, 1964, Cit. 2034, Audiotape WH6402.14, LBJ.
234   most gratifying positive votes: Findlay, *Church People in the Struggle*, p. 54.
234   Equality Cookies: Whalen and Whalen, *The Longest Debate*, p. 122.
234   "Why are you still there?": Clarence Mitchell Oral History, p. 30, LBJ; Whalen and Whalen, *The Longest Debate*, p. 119; Miller, *Lyndon*, p. 448.

17. Spreading Poisons

235   shot the Hayling bulldog: Colburn, *Racial Change*, p. 58.
235   parents of the four: PC, Jan. 25, 1964, p. 1.
235   Fullerwood did not refer: Colburn, *Racial Change*, pp. 57–58; int. Fannie Fullerwood, April 6, 1991.
235   firebombed a car: Hartley, p. 33, in Garrow, ed., *St. Augustine*.
235   burned the home of Bungum Roberson: Garrow, *Bearing the Cross*, p. 317; int. Katherine and Henry Twine, April 2, 1991.
236   Four shotgun blasts: Colburn, *Racial Change*, p. 58; "Racial and Civil Disorders in St. Augustine," p. 5, in Garrow, ed., *St. Augustine*; ADW, Feb. 23, 1964, p. 1; PC, Feb. 22, 1964, p. 1; int. Robert Hayling by David Colburn, Sept. 28, 1978, Colburn Papers, UF.
236   phone call to Martin: Int. Stetson Kennedy, Nov. 2, 1994.
236   steered him to Rev. C. K. Steele: Ibid. Also Fairclough, *To Redeem*, p. 104.
236   patch up his feud: Hartley, p. 32, in Garrow, ed., *St. Augustine*.
236   no one made inquiries: *Jet*, March 5, 1964, p. 4; int. Robert Hayling by David Colburn, Sept. 28, 1978, Colburn Papers, UF.
236   "This is my last swing": *Jet*, March 5, 1964, pp. 4–5.
237   Cuban kamikaze pilots: Wannall to Sullivan, Feb. 20, 1964, and Hoover "Memorandum for Confidential Files," Feb. 26, 1964, Section 92, FHOC.
237   Johnson fussed privately: LBJ phone call with Robert McNamara, 3:29 P.M., Feb. 26, 1964, Cit. 2116, Audiotape WH6402.22, LBJ.
237   two bombs severed rail lines: NYT, Feb. 28, 1964, p. 1.
237   pounded the lectern: Ibid.
237   ordered J. Edgar Hoover: LBJ phone call with J. Edgar Hoover, 8:53 P.M., Feb. 25, 1964, Cit. 2223, Audiotape WH6402.23, LBJ. (Johnson began the call with a joke Hoover did not seem to appreciate: "What's the matter, you got this phone tapped?") Johnson also discussed the railroad bombs with Labor Secretary Willard Wirtz (Cit. 2220) and the kamikaze threat with Senator George Smathers (Cit. 2244).
237   team of thirty FBI agents; NYT, Feb. 29, 1964, p. 10.
237   massive federal-state investigation: NYT, March 1, 1964, p. 1.
237   "Confusion to the enemy.": Int. Michael Gannon, April 3, 1991.
238   Sullivan's team would arrest: Int. Joseph Sullivan, Feb. 3, 1991; NYT, March 13, 1964, p. 18.
238   he led a small caravan: Colburn, *Racial Change*, p. 61.
238   freedom march of ten thousand: Garrow, *Bearing the Cross*, p. 316; PC, March 14, 1964, p. 1; report by Very Rev. Robert W. Estill in *Church and Race*, a bulletin of the Episcopal Church Center, New York, March 1964, p. 13.
238   Vivian promptly visited: Int. C. T. Vivian, May 26, 1990; int. Henry and Katherine Twine, April 2, 1991.
238   offered to help recruit: Ibid.
238   "Spring Vacation is a time": Hayling "for the St. Augustine Chapter of the SCLC" to the Massachusetts chapter of the Southern Christian Leadership Conference, March 11, 1964, SAHS.

238   small network of clergy and theologians: Int. Harvey Cox, May 3, 1991, and Nov. 15, 1993; int. Paul Chapman, Nov. 4, 1994.

238   "I got his eyes": Int. Virgil Wood, Aug. 2, 1994.

238   supremely grateful to Daddy King: Ibid. Also int. Harvey Cox, May 3, 1991, and int. Paul Chapman, Nov. 4, 1994.

239   *"This is not a vacation"*: Florida Spring Project application for "Demonstrations in St. Augustine, Florida," SAHS.

239   capsule history: Int. Harvey Cox, May 3, 1991; "Oldest Bias in America," MS, April 10, 1964, p. 4.

239   Cox approached three prominent Episcopal bishops: Int. Harvey Cox, Nov. 15, 1993. Virgil Wood's core group of clergy in Boston needed new adult volunteers in St. Augustine for a peculiar, technical reason aside from their competing commitments to Easter demonstrations in North Carolina. Rev. John Harmon, treasurer of the new Massachusetts SCLC, was the son-in-law of Judge Elbert Tuttle, chief of the U.S. 5th Circuit Court of Appeals, and Tuttle had warned that if Harmon or his close associates got arrested within his jurisdiction, the chief judge might well have to recuse himself from the great host of critical civil rights cases before his court. Harmon, Breeden, Wood, and Paul Chapman—the officers of the Massachusetts SCLC—avoided appearances in the entire 5th District, which included St. Augustine. (Int. Paul Chapman, Nov. 4, 1994).

239   coax a courtesy invitation: Int. Esther J. Burgess, Nov. 7, 1994.

239   grumbling within their own households: Int. Paul Chapman, Nov. 4, 1994.

239   wives of all three bishops: Written reminiscence by Esther J. Burgess, courtesy of Esther J. Burgess.

239   "If you never see me again": Int. Esther J. Burgess, Nov. 7, 1994.

239   first elected Negro bishop: *The Witness*, Vol. 49, No. 14, April 9, 1964.

239   founder of Groton School: *St. Augustine Record*, Feb. 7, 1981.

239   hurry-up training: Int. Virgil Wood, Aug. 2, 1994.

239   Paul Johnson sponsored bills: NYT, April 12, 1964, p. 76.

239   new state troopers: NYT, April 2, 1964, p. 67.

239   "Thompson's Tank": *Newsweek*, Feb. 24, 1964.

240   met secretly in Brookhaven: Cagin and Dray, *We Are Not Afraid*, p. 325; Nelson, *Terror in the Night*, p. 26.

240   "Selfishness is the festive queen": Dillard, *Clear Burning*, p. 124.

240   "We are men who humbly submit": Ibid., p. 121.

240   "We are being deluged": Moses to Lowenstein, nd (circa Feb. 1964), b9f302, Lowenstein Papers, UNC.

240   sixty counties on a single night: Whitehead, *Attack on Terror*, p. 26.

240   "mushroomed toward ten thousand": Cagin and Dray, *We Are Not Afraid*, p. 325.

240   Hamer was distributing: Report by Tom Scarbrough, Investigator, Feb. 21, 1964, MSSC.

240   "not to give this group": Ibid.

240   curtail Tougaloo College: Johnston to Gov. Johnson, Lt. Gov. Carroll Gartin, and State Senator E. K. Collins, March 26, 1964, MSSC.

240   "a list of the trustees": Erle Johnston, Jr., to File, subject, "Tougaloo College," April 13, 1964, MSSC.

241   "we are in a position to guarantee": Johnston to Dr. W. A. Hotchkiss, April 17, 1964, MSSC. Wesley Hotchkiss, the Sovereignty Commission's target, was a senior official in the United Church of Christ. As mentor and employer to Andrew Young, Hotchkiss shepherded Martin Luther King's citizenship program and as mentor to Robert Spike and the new Commission on Religion and Race, he became a linchpin of national church support for Mississippi Freedom Summer. (Int. Andrew Young, Oct. 26, 1991.)

241   President Beittel submitted: Dittmer, *Local People*, pp. 234–36. Dittmer suggests more darkly that the CIA accomplished Beittel's removal through its connections with another Tougaloo trustee, president Barnaby Keeney of Brown University.

241   "We have put into action": Johnston to Herman Glazier, Office of the Governor, June 9, 1964, MSSC.

241   publisher William Loeb: Whalen and Whalen, *The Longest Debate*, p. 145.

241   "Don't Forget to Vote": *Manchester Union Leader*, March 5, 1964, p. 1.

241   "the Negro will gain the upper hand": Ibid.

241   "rolling into the Granite State": Ibid.

241   "ROAR APPROVAL OF BARRY": *Manchester Union Leader*, March 6, 1964, p. 1.

241   presented as "The Gipper": *Manchester Union Leader*, March 6, 1964, p. 11.

241   "A democracy cannot exist": Ibid.

242   "supported a statewide ballot initiative": Edwards, *Reagan*, p. 123.

242   harbinger of national backlash: *Time*, Sept. 25, 1964, p. 23; Totton J. Anderson and Eugene C. Lee, "The 1964 Election in California," *The Western Political Quarterly*, June 1965, pp. 451–74; G. V. Kennard, "Fair Housing Showdown in the West," *America*, Jan. 28, 1967, pp. 142–46.

242   "Every citizen must rise up": *California Eagle*, Feb. 20, 1964, p. 1.

242   personal inspection on March 6: Lesher, *George Wallace*, p. 274. A month later, after Wallace stunned the nation by gathering 264,000 votes in Wisconsin, the *New York Times* published a story about his haphazard campaign there on the spontaneous initiative of "Delores Herbstreith, a 34-year-old mother of three." NYT, April 12, 1964, p. 76.

242   "The Negroes are starting": Reinhold Niebuhr to Will Scarlett, Feb. 3, 1964, Box 33, RN.

242   half a million children stayed home: PC, Feb. 15, 1964, p. 3.

242   "alienates the friends": Norman Thomas to Allard Lowenstein, March 18, 1964, b3f307, Lowenstein Papers, UNC.

242   headquarters moved swiftly: Sizoo to Sullivan, Feb. 4, 1964, FR-77; SAC, New York, to Director, Feb. 5, 1964, FR-NR.

243   "the Negro people": *New York Daily News,* Feb. 6, 1964, p. 4.

243   "Rustin is now at the very least": SAC, New York, to Director, and NY LHM, March 2, 1964, FR-NR.

243   "a tremendous opportunity": SAC, New York, to Director, Feb. 7, 1964, FBI File No. 100-3-104-34, Serial 518. In March, Director Hoover notified his New York office that the Rustin wiretap suggested a parallel opening to develop "certain animosities" between Rustin and Wyatt Walker, who was leaving King's Atlanta staff to live in New York. He added that the Rustin-Walker rivalry offered "potential for Bureau exploitation in neutralizing the influence of Martin Luther King. . . ." Director to SAC, New York, March 19, 1964, FK-NR.

243   twenty-one incoming officers: Baumgardner to Sullivan, March 25, 1964, and May 8, 1964, both from the file on the National Council of Churches, FBI File No. 100-50869.

243   "widen the rift": Bland to Sullivan, Feb. 7, 1964, with attached anonymous press release, "The Rift Widens Between Elijah Muhammad and His Principal Lieutenant Malcolm X Little," FMX-NR.

243   fed directly into the *Chicago Defender:* CD, Feb. 11, 1964, p. 2. With candor rare among recipients of FBI leaks, the *Defender* acknowledged that its source was an "anonymous, alleged 'insider.'" The portions of the letter printed in the paper are slightly more sophisticated than the headquarters draft, suggesting that the text was improved by Muslim specialists in the Chicago FBI office.

243   "All the papers have it": Wiretap intercept of Feb. 11, 1964, in SAC, Chicago, to Director, Feb. 14, 1964, FMX-4092, p. 4.

243   evening of February 17: Int. Burke Marshall, Sept. 26, 1984, int. Cartha "Deke" DeLoach, June 1, 1984.

244   "who desperately wants to become Vice President": DeLoach to Hoover, Feb. 18, 1964, FK-315.

244   "Katzenbach did his dirt": Hoover's handwritten note, Ibid.

244   fn "excised Lee Harvey Oswald's name": Gentry, *J. Edgar Hoover,* p. 556.

244   Johnson fired two White House aides: DeLoach to Hoover, March 6 and March 9, 1964, Section 92, FHOC.

245   "We'll let Bobby and them": LBJ phone call with Ed Weisl, Sr., Feb. 5, 1964, Cit. 1901, Audiotape WH6402.07, LBJ.

245   Johnson personally supervised: Cf. LBJ phone call with political adviser Cliff Carter, Feb. 10, 1964, Cit. 2006, Audiotape WH6402.13; LBJ phone call with DNC chairman John Bailey, Feb. 11, 1964, Cit. 2047, Audiotape WH6402.14; LBJ phone call with Cliff Carter, Feb. 12, 1964, Cit. 2056, Audiotape WH6402.15, LBJ.

245   "my two bits": LBJ phone call with Cliff Carter, Richard McGuire, and Kenneth O'Donnell, Feb. 11, 1964, Cit. 2050, Audiotape WH6402.14. LBJ.

245   "it's gonna be a problem": Ibid.

245   "shocking indeed": Baumgardner to Sullivan, March 4, 1964, FK-312.

245   "We have not lost": CDD, March 11, 1964, p. 18.

245   "Drawbacks plagued each option.": Garrow, *Bearing the Cross,* pp. 314–16; int. James Bevel, May 17, 1985; int. Diane Nash, April 26, 1990.

246   fn received suspended sentences: NYT, March 10, 1964, p. 30; March 14, 1964, p. 19.

246   King broke away for: Garrow, *Bearing the Cross,* p. 316; SAC, New Haven, to Director, March 12, 1964, FK-NR.

246   Marquette had dropped: SAC, Milwaukee, to Director, March 9, 1964, FK-323.

246   commendation upon the agent: O'Reilly, *Racial Matters,* pp. 148–49.

246   another honorary degree: Baumgardner to Sullivan, April 2, 1964, FK-348.

246   "said if it were not": DeLoach to Mohr, April 8, 1964, FK-349.

246   Kennedy's body had not yet cooled: DeLoach to Hoover, March 6, 1964, Section 92, FHOC.

246   "I made no comment": Ibid.

246   Guthman peace feeler: Int. Edwin Guthman, June 25, 1984.

246   in the White House pool: PDD, March 9, 1964, LBJ.

246   "absolutely clean": Hoover file memo of 3:07 P.M., March 12, 1964, Section 92, FHOC; LBJ phone call with J. Edgar Hoover, March 12, 1964, Cit. 24912, Audiotape WH6403.09, LBJ.

246   batch of weekly reports: Garrow, *FBI and Martin,* p. 110.

246   second thoughts on hiring Bayard: Hoover to Walter Jenkins, March 9, 1964, FK-NR.

246   report on Paul Corbin: LBJ phone call with DeLoach, March 12, 1964, Cit. 2489, Audiotape WH6403.09, LBJ.

247   the Bureau's chief suspect: Hoover file memo of 4:34 P.M., March 9, 1964, Section 92, FHOC; LBJ phone call with Hoover, March 9, 1964, Cit. 2422, Audiotape WH6403.06, LBJ.

247   "I do *not* want anything on King": Hoover's handwritten note on DeLoach to Mohr, March 16, 1964, FK-320.

247   fn "I told Judge Smith": Ibid. DeLoach recorded that Ed Willis of Louisiana, then chairman of the House Committee on Un-American Activities, also sought permission to attack King with FBI materials.

247   his forthcoming poverty program: DeLoach to Mohr, "Re: President Johnson's 'Message on Poverty,'" March 10, 1964, Section 92, FHOC.

247   "The informality, yet quiet dignity": DeLoach to LBJ, March 16, 1964, WHCF, PR, Box 367, LBJ.

247   Court's announcement: NYT, March 10, 1964, p. 1.

247   "a bunch of niggers": NYT, March 9, 1964, p. 42. Cox's comments were made to John Doar of the U.S. Justice Department in the presence of *Times* correspondent Claude Sitton. Aaron Henry, Bob Moses,

David Dennis, and Edwin King soon tried to force Cox off civil rights cases because of demonstrated bias. Pleadings in the case were retained in King's files, A/SC14f23.

247   "so concerned about being": King oral history int. by Berl Bernhard, March 9, 1964, p. 9, JFK.
248   "They had me chained": Ibid., p. 14.
248   "They were very, very upset": Ibid., p. 40.
248   "I really think we saw": Ibid., p. 9, also p. 26.
248   "At this point": Ibid., p. 31.
249   "He's rather a psycho": RFK oral history int. by John Bartlow Martin, April 13, 1964, p. 195, JFK.
249   "a very dangerous organization": Ibid., p. 197.
249   "in every way": Ibid., pp. 191, 194.
249   agents had spotted Stanley Levison: SAC, Atlanta, teletype to Director and New York, March 10, 1964, FSC-NR.
249   made King send for Levison: Wiretap transcripts of telephone conversations between Stanley Levison and Clarence Jones, March 2, 1964, FLNY9-460a, and March 5, 1964, FLNY9-463a; also wiretap transcript of Stanley and Bea Levison, March 10, 1964, FLNY9-468a, and wiretap transcript of Stanley Levison and Roy Bennett, Feb. 29, 1964, FLNY9-458a.
249   starve to death: Wiretap transcript of telephone conversation between Stanley Levison and his brother, Roy Bennett, Feb. 27, 1964, FLNY7-710a.
249   labored over publishing conflicts: Wiretap transcripts of telephone conversations between Stanley Levison and King's literary agent, Joan Daves, Feb. 18, 1964, FLNY7-701a, and February 26, 1964, FLNY9-450a; also Daves to MLK on book rights, Feb. 19, 1964, A/KP27f9.
249   "It, of course": Baumgardner to Sullivan, March 20, 1964, FK-NR, regarding King's article "The Hammer of Civil Rights" in *The Nation*, March 9, 1964, pp. 230–34.
249   second bonanza of microphone surveillance: Garrow, *FBI and Martin*, pp. 108–9.
249   twenty-one reels of tape: "Summary—Highly Sensitive Coverage—Martin Luther King, Jr.," Nov. 27, 1964, FK-1024.
250   West Coast SCLC office: Int. Thomas Kilgore, Feb. 11, 1988.
250   not cried this time: Dora McDonald to MLK, Feb. 18, 1964, A/SC1f15.
250   professorship for King: Ibid.
250   could not and would not: Hoover sent a summary of the intercepted King material to Walter Jenkins on March 6, but waited until after his March 9 meeting with President Johnson to send the summary, dated March 4, to Kennedy. Brennan to Sullivan, April 18, 1968, FK-3388; Garrow, *FBI and Martin*, p. 110.
250   cipher without duties: RFK oral history int. by John Bartlow Martin, April 13, 1964, p. 195, JFK.
250   crueler, gratuitous sting: Garrow, *FBI and Martin*, p. 110.
250   "Look at her": Author's interviews with FBI officials.
250   "vilification of the late President": Hoover blind file memo of April 9, 1968, Section 24, FHOC.
250   "deep personal appreciation": RFK to MLK, June 5, 1964, A/KP24f22.

18. THE CREATION OF MUHAMMAD ALI

251   Harlem radio station WWRL: NYT, March 7, 1964, p. 15.
251   "That's political!": Int. Benjamin Karim, Aug. 31, 1991.
251   Malcolm had taken liberties: ADW, March 7, 1964, p. 1.
251   "I am honored": *New York Post*, March 9, 1964, p. 4; FMXNY-4149.
252   intercepted Malcolm on the Triborough Bridge: NY LHM of March 16, 1964, FMX-107.
252   Bible on the dashboard: Int. Benjamin Karim, March 19, 1991.
252   stood to lose money: Little more than half the fifteen thousand seats of the Miami Beach Civic Auditorium were filled, and promoter MacDonald wound up losing $363,000. *Sports Illustrated*, March 9, 1994, p. 24.
252   "Don't start hitting me": Houser, *Muhammad Ali*, p. 66.
252   hints of the truth already seeping: Cf. *New York Journal-American*, July 6, 1963, and Feb. 27, 1964 (FMXNY-4108); Dick Schaap, "The Challenger and the Muslims," *New York Herald Tribune*, Jan. 23, 1964, p. 1; "Cassius Clay Almost Says He's a Muslim," NYAN, Jan. 25, 1964 (FMXNY-4072); Dave Brady, "Clay Defends Muslim Policy, Says Integration Is Wrong," *Louisville Courier-Journal*, Feb. 3, 1964, p. II-3; *Miami Herald*, Feb. 7, 1964; *Louisville Courier-Journal*, Feb. 7, 1964, p. II-6; Hauser, *Muhammad Ali*, p. 66.
252   MacDonald briefly canceled the fight: Ali, *The Greatest*, pp. 102–15.
252   Clay's open association: George Plimpton, "Miami Notebook: Cassius Clay and Malcolm X," *Harper's*, June 1964, pp. 54–61.
252   three of fifty-eight ringside reporters: ADW, Feb. 26, 1964, p. 1.
252   flattened his previous three opponents: *Sports Illustrated*, Feb. 24, 1964, p. 18.
252   sent a feature writer: Hauser, *Muhammad Ali*, p. 69.
252   "heart attack": *Jet*, March 12, 1964, p. 40.
252   retreat into Malcolm X's motel room: *Sports Illustrated*, March 9, 1964, pp. 26–27; Perry, *Malcolm*, pp. 247–49; Hauser, *Muhammad Ali*, pp. 105–6.
252   Malcolm hosted singer Sam Cooke: SAC, Miami, to Director, March 9, 1964, FMX-89; New York report dated June 18, 1964, FMX-125. See also Wolff, *You Send Me*, pp. 295–96.
252   accompanied by Malcolm X: *Louisville Courier-Journal*, Feb. 27, 1964, p. 1.
252   "Are you a card-carrying": NYT, Feb. 27, 1964, p. 34.

252 "Followers of Allah": Hauser, *Muhammad Ali*, p. 82.

252 "Muslim Story Irks Cassius": *Louisville Courier-Journal*, Feb. 27, 1964, p. III-5.

253 stretched along South Wabash Avenue: Undercover police report, Feb. 27, 1964, RS, file No. 589, CHS.

253 "whipped the crowd of 4,000": NYT, Feb. 27, 1964, p. 23 (FMXNY-4229). The undercover officer in ibid. reported that the frenzied crowd leapt to its feet during the speech of Louis X, "and it took a few minutes to restore order so that the speaker could continue."

253 "I have been given": Goldman, *Death and Life*, p. 131.

253 Clay indeed was his follower: ADW, Feb. 28, 1964, p. 4; *Miami Herald,* Feb. 28, 1964, p. C1; undercover police report, Feb. 27, 1964, RS, file No. 589, CHS.

253 Clay at breakfast with Malcolm: *Sports Illustrated*, March 9, 1964, p. 54.

253 glowingly of his conversation: ADW, March 1, 1964, p. 5.

253 "A rooster crows": NYT, Feb. 28, 1964, p. 22.

253 stunned the sportswriters: Hauser, *Muhammad Ali*, pp. 83–84, 103–5.

253 fn "will mean more": *Sports Illustrated*, March 9, 1964, p. 57.

253 "I don't want to be": NYT, Feb. 28, 1964, p. 22.

253 "Malcolm X's Role": NYT, Feb. 26, 1964, p. 39.

254 "Now's the time": Int. Yusuf Shah (Captain Joseph) Oct. 17, 1991.

254 "Lukman X confessed the plot": Int. Benjamin Karim, March 19, 1991; Malcolm X, *The Autobiography*, pp. 308–9; Goldman, *Death and Life*, p. 130; Perry, *Malcolm*, p. 250; Karim, *Remembering Malcolm*, pp. 159–160.

254 Hotel Theresa on Sunday: NYT, March 2, 1964, p. 36.

254 "Man, it was really a letdown drag": *Jet*, March 20, 1964, pp. 50–57.

254 Clay might join him: CD, March 2, 1964, p. 10 (FMXNY-4133); Ted Poston, "Clay in Malcolm X's Corner in Black Muslim Power Fight," *New York Post,* March 3, 1964, p. 4.

254 "Malcolm X got more requests": *New York Post,* March 2, 1964, p. 48.

254 tour of the United Nations: NYT, March 5, 1964, p. 39; ADW, March 5, 1964, p. 7.

255 "I'm holding him down": Wiretap log of March 4, 1964, FMXNY-4105.

255 supply another Muslim escort: Ibid.

255 extended his suspension: Malcolm X television interview by Joe Durso, *The World at Ten*, NY Channel 13, March 9, 1964, transcribed in NY FBI memorandum dated April 10, 1964, FMXNY-4346, p. 4; NYAN, March 14, 1964, p. 1.

255 sent Minister Louis X: Wiretap conversation of March 9, 1964, transcribed in SAC, Phoenix, to Director, March 12, 1964, FEM-NR, p. 1.

255 "regardless of circumstances": Ibid.

255 Malcolm called reporters: NYT, March 9, 1964, p. 1; *New York Post,* March 9, 1964, p. 4.

255 "There can be no revolution": Ibid. Also CDD, March 10, 1964, p. 3.

255 "Debate on Civil Rights Bill": NYT, March 9, 1964, p. 1.

255 "Now It's a Negro Drive": *U.S. News & World Report*, March 30, 1964, p. 38.

256 "See, the mistake": Malcolm X interview by Joe Durso, *The World at Ten*, NY Channel 13, March 9, 1964, transcribed in NY FBI memorandum dated April 10, 1964, FMXNY-4346, p. 13.

256 "You don't just walk away": Wiretap transcript of Muhammad telephone interview, March 10, 1964, from SAC, Chicago, to Director, March 12, 1964, FMXNY-4120, p. 2.

256 "must give up everything he has": Wiretap transcript of telephone conversation, March 9, 1964, in SAC, Phoenix, Airtel to Director, March 12, 1964, FEM-NR, p. 2.

256 "preserve the faith": Wiretap transcript of telephone conversation, March 10, 1964, in SAC, Chicago, to Director, March 13, 1964, FMXNY-4236, p. 3.

256 "Joseph led a grim delegation": Int. Yusuf Shah (Captain Joseph), Oct. 17, 1991.

256 notarized letter: Wiretap transcript of telephone conversation, March 13, 1964, in SAC, Chicago, to Director, March 20, 1964, FMXNY-4246, pp. 1, 3.

256 personal sympathy for Malcolm: Int. Benjamin Karim, March 19, 1991.

256 press conference at the Tapestry Suite: NY LHM dated March 13, 1964, FMX-NR; NYT, March 13, 1964, p. 20; Breitman, ed., *Malcolm X Speaks*, pp. 18–22; Goldman, *Death and Life*, pp. 133–36.

257 "As of this minute": Breitman, ed., *Malcolm X Speaks*, p. 20.

257 "His Theme Now": *U.S. News & World Report*, March 23, 1964, p. 56.

257 "The Ominous Malcolm X": *Life*, March 20, 1964, p. 40.

257 "embittered racist": NYT, March 14, 1964, p. 22.

257 "Negroes Ponder Malcolm's": NYT, March 15, 1964, p. 46.

257 "It is regrettable": MLK statement dated March 16, 1964, A/KP15f16; MLK trip cited in ibid.

257 "Whom do you think you are kidding": NYAN, Dec. 14, 1963, p. 1.

257 Malcolm's provocative implication: Asked by Robinson why he had not gone to the funeral of Medgar Evers, Malcolm had replied in an open letter, "When I go to a Mississippi funeral, it won't be to attend the funeral of a black man!" CD, Dec. 7, 1963, p. 10.

258 Robinson charged: CD, Nov. 22, 1963, p. 10; *New York Herald Tribune*, April 26, 1964, p. 10.

258 Malcolm X cheerfully agreed: CD, Dec. 7, 1963, p. 10.

258 Russell praised Ali: "New Champ Cassius Clay," news release dated March 2, 1964, Box 106, Claude Bennett Papers, CHS; *Miami Herald*, Feb. 29, 1964.

258 "so intolerant, so narrow-minded": ADW, March 29, 1964, p. 8; *Jet*, April 9, 1964, p. 56.

258 Racial Relocation Commission: *Congressional Record,* March 16, 1964, pp. 5337–52.

258 disguised as journalists: SAC, New York, to Director, March 26, 1964, FMX-NR.

258   "I don't think I'm dumb enough": Goldman, *Death and Life,* p. 135.
259   agents identified only four: New York LHM, March 13, 1964, FMX-NR.
259   "You just don't buck Mr. Muhammad": Malcolm X, *The Autobiography,* p. 409.
259   readymade wife: "'Tis Rumored Clay May Marry Muhammad's Granddaughter," news release dated March 4, 1964, Box 106, Claude Bennett Papers, CHS; PC, March 7, 1964, p. 4; *California Eagle,* March 12, 1964, p. 1.
259   Assistant Minister Benjamin 2X: Int. Benjamin Karim, March 11, 1991, March 19, 1991, and Aug. 31, 1991; Goldman, *Death and Life,* pp. 59–60.
260   maintaining Benjamin 2X as a spy: Report of Captain Joseph–Elijah Muhammad conversation of March 24, 1964, in SAC, Chicago, to Director, March 26, 1964, FEM-NR, p. 5.
260   "weak ones": Ibid., pp. 2–3; SAC, Phoenix, to Director, March 27, 1964, p. 3.
260   "As far as being a leader": Wiretap transcript of March 17, 1964, in SAC, Chicago, to Director, March 20, 1964, FMXNY-4246, pp. 8–12.
260   "only when the white man": Boston LHM, April 3, 1964, FMX-NR, pp. 1–3; *Harvard Crimson,* March 19, 1964; *Boston Globe,* March 19, 1964.
261   "that no-good, long-legged Malcolm": SAC, Phoenix, to Director, March 23, 1964, FMX-NR.
261   cut the heads off hypocrites: Ibid.
261   file eviction papers: Wiretap transcript of March 24, 1964, conversation, in SAC, Chicago, report to Director dated March 26, 1964, pp. 2–6.
261   "Malcolm X Tells of Death Threat": NYAN, March 21, 1964, p. 50; PC, April 4, 1964, p. 1.
261   "Excuse me, brother minister" and temple dispute: Int. Benjamin Karim, March 19, 1991; int. Yusuf Shah (Captain Joseph), Oct. 17, 1991; int. Louis Omar, June 23, 1994.
262   foiled the attempted coup: Wiretap conversation of March 24, 1964, in SAC, Phoenix, to Director, March 27, 1964, FMXNY-4261, pp. 2–3.
262   Friday night at Madison Square Garden: Hauser, *Muhammad Ali,* pp. 102–5.
262   "As the Bureau can imagine": SAC, Chicago, to Director, March 25, 1964, FMX-NR, p. 2.
262   forty converts from Temple No. 7: Ibid.
262   some twenty-six: SAC, Phoenix, to Director, March 27, 1964, FMXNY-4261.
262   "I do not have a court": Report, SAC, Chicago, to Director, April 7, 1964, FMX-NR, p. 4.

19. SHAKY PULPITS

263   "I am from India": Cunningham, *Agony at Galloway,* p. 48.
263   "It is not un-Christian": Ibid., p. 5.
263   never mentioned integration: Ibid., pp. 68–69.
264   fn church lawyer Jack Pratt: Pratt memos of Jan. 15 and Feb. 20, 1964, A/ATb3; Kinoy, *Rights on Trial,* p. 212. Pratt's co-counsel was William Kunstler.
264   "tension so thick": Cunningham, *Agony at Galloway,* p. 20–21.
264   "so high you could": Ibid., p. 73.
264   cumulative emotional toll: Int. Edwin King, June 26, 1992.
264   public announcement of Freedom Summer: NYT, March 16, 1964, p. 26.
264   "Freedom Radio": Moses to Forman, Goldman, Wright, Spike, Lowenstein, Goff, and Moore, March 2, 1964, b32f369, Lowenstein Papers, UNC.
264   Everett Parker: Cole, *The Reluctant Regulators,* pp. 63–66; Parker testimony, May 1, 1967, Vol. 5, Docket No. 16663, records of the Federal Communications Commission, NA; int. Charles Firestone, Oct. 24, 1990; int. Everett C. Parker, Jan. 2, 1991, and May 23, 1991.
264   banned all advertisement: Cole, *The Reluctant Regulators,* p. 161.
264   request of Andrew Young: Int. Everett C. Parker, May 23, 1991; int. Andrew Young, Oct. 26, 1991.
265   7,186 minutes: Draft petition dated April 8, 1964, NCC RG 6, b50f9, POH.
265   petition for the FCC: The voluminous record of the WLBT challenge is preserved as Federal Communications Commission Docket No. 16663, NA. See especially appellant brief dated Nov. 16, 1967, Vol. 13.
265   nearly half the viewing audience: Ibid. Also NYT, April 16, 1964, p. 75.
265   recognized no standing: *Office of Communication of United Church of Christ v. F.C.C.,* 359 F2d 994 (1966), pp. 999–1000.
265   worth about $12 million: Int. Everett C. Parker, May 23, 1991.
265   Henry signed anyway: Ibid.
265   twenty-year legal odyssey: The pivotal 1969 decision revoking the WLBT broadcast license is *Office of Communication of United Church of Christ v. F.C.C.,* 425 F2d 543 (1969).
265   Tougaloo College dropped out: Affidavit of Edwin King, June 7, 1964, Vol. 1, Docket No. 16663, records of the Federal Communications Commission, NA.
266   Johnson gathered 150 leading ministers: NYT, March 26, 1964, p. 1.
266   "I wish you could have seen": LBJ, "Remarks to Members of the Southern Baptist Christian Leadership Seminar," March 25, 1964, PPP, pp. 418–21.
267   King issued a statement: NYT, March 26, 1964, p. 13.
267   Senator Wayne Morse: Whalen and Whalen, *The Longest Debate,* pp. 147–48.
267   121 civil rights measures: NYT, March 20, 1964, p. 19.
267   vote of 50–34: NYT, March 26, 1964, pp. 1, 10.
267   "We shall now begin": Whalen and Whalen, *The Longest Debate,* p. 147.

267   Malcolm X took a seat: *New York Journal-American*, March 27, 1964, p. 4.

267   gnawing at King of late: MLK interview by Robert Penn Warren, March 18, 1964, A/KS; slightly edited in Warren, *Who Speaks for the Negro?*, p. 219.

267   fn March 18 interview: Ibid.

268   "If there is a prolonged": *Washington Daily News*, March 27, 1964, p. 3.

268   left by a separate door: Ibid.

268   Benjamin 2X excitedly snapped: Int. Benjamin Karim, March 19, 1991.

268   hinting that he might join: *New York Journal-American*, March 27, 1964, p. 4.

268   "Now you're going": *Washington Daily News*, March 27, 1964, p. 3.

268   "I would go so far": MLK to Abram Eisenman, April 3, 1964, A/KP9f21.

268   "con game": Perry, *Malcolm*, p. 255.

268   Billy Graham's independent crusades: NYT, April 3, 1964, p. 23; *Jet*, April 16, 1964, p. 54; Goldman, *Death and Life*, p. 138.

269   Philbert X of Lansing: *Chicago Sun-Times*, March 27, 1964, p. 4; Perry, *Malcolm*, pp. 256–57; "Malcolm X: Make It Plain," PBS documentary *The American Experience*, 1994.

269   Philbert wept: Report, SAC, Chicago, to Director, April 7, 1964, FMX-NR, p. 4.

269   "with no congregation": FBI transcript of *Kup's Show* episode aired March 28, 1964, FMXNY-4348, p. 11.

269   Minister Wilfred X: *Chicago Sun-Times*, March 27, 1964, p. 4; "Malcolm X: Make It Plain," PBS documentary *The American Experience* (1994).

269   "what happened in 1935": Wiretap transcript of March 24, 1964, conversation, in SAC, Chicago, report to Director dated March 26, 1964, p. 4.

269   served court papers: Eviction papers filed in Queens Civil Court, March 31, 1964, SAC, New York to Director, April 20, 1964, FMX-96.

269   "If he did, he would be": Minister James Shabazz in MS, April 10, 1964, pp. 1, 3, 9.

269   "Malcolm's Treachery, Defection": MS, May 8, 1964, p. 13

269   suggestion of Captain Joseph: Int. Yusuf Shah (Captain Joseph), Oct. 17, 1991.

269   Malcolm's severed head: MS, April 10, 1964, p. 3.

269   money borrowed hastily: Malcolm X, *The Autobiography*, p. 317; Perry, *Malcolm*, p. 262.

269   one-way ticket to Cairo: Urgent Coded Teletype, New York to Director, April 14, 1964, FMX-101.

269   "get spiritual strength": NYAN, April 18, 1964, p. 1; New York LHM, April 20, 1964, FMX-NR.

269   lawyer, Percy Sutton: Sutton answered the suit on April 13, the day of Malcolm's departure, and asked for the first of several postponements that stretched into June. SAC, New York to Director, April 20, 1964, FMX-96; New York FBI report dated June 18, 1964, FMX-125, pp. 60–62; int. Percy Sutton, Nov. 28, 1989.

269   Robert Beech rode: Robert Beech to the author, March 3, 1991; int. Robert Beech, Dec. 8, 1991.

270   extension of the Hattiesburg Freedom Day: Unsigned proposal for "Freedom day—Leflore County, Mississippi—March 25, 1964," A/SN111f16.

270   Freedom Day alarms: ADW, March 22, 1964, p. 3; AC, April 1, 1964, p. 1; affidavits of John Mathews, Willis Wright, George R. Davis, Alice Hemingway, and Charlie Hills in "Case Studies of Intimidation," A/SN54f9; Dittmer, *Local People*, p. 224.

270   "long-term commitment to this stuff": Int. Robert Beech, Dec. 8, 1991.

271   "That's far enough": Statement of Van Bogard Dunn et al., April 2, 1964, b9f439, Edwin King Papers, TOU.

271   a $500 fine: Ibid., p. 4.

271   held fast against the bishops: NYT, March 30, 1964, p. 14; Cunningham, *Agony at Galloway*, pp. 55–56.

271   "They were wrong to come here": Cunningham, *Agony at Galloway*, p. 57.

271   World Service budget: Ibid., pp. 61–67.

271   "WLBT made no mention": Affidavit of Edwin King, June 4, 1964, Vol. 1, docket No. 16663, records of the Federal Communications Commission, NA.

271   Lowenstein spent much of Easter: Int. Allard Lowenstein by Anne Romaine, March 1967, pp. 127–29, A/AR; Lowenstein to Mendy Samstein, April 3, 1964, Box 16, Lowenstein Papers, UNC.

272   Forman nursed: Forman, *Black Revolutionaries*, pp. 88–90, 379–81; Chafe, *Never Stop Running*, pp. 188, 206.

272   parked Lowenstein at the airport: Int. Robert P. Moses, Feb. 15, 1991.

272   "more than a thousand": *Harvard Crimson*, Feb. 23, 1964.

272   "I apologize in advance": Frank to Lowenstein, Feb. 24, 1964, b9f306, Lowenstein Papers, UNC. In later years, Frank would be elected to the U.S. House of Representatives from Massachusetts.

272   "on Monday we will break": Ilene Strelitz to Lowenstein, Feb. 11, 1964, b9f306, Lowenstein Papers, UNC.

272   tour by Martin Luther King: Ibid. Also Wedin, Schoolnick, and Strelitz circular letter to Western colleges, Feb. 15, 1964, b32f368, Lowenstein Papers, UNC.

272   "It is our conviction": Moses letter to Wilkins, Farmer, King, Forman et al. as "Friends of Freedom in Mississippi," nd, (early April 1964), A/SN100f14.

272   vacillated over how to obtain: Discussion of "Zinn Proposal" in Minutes of the SNCC Executive Committee meeting, March 29, 1964, A/SN6, pp. 4–5.

272   proved ineffective and awkward: Ibid. Also, Minutes of May 15, 1964, "Meeting Following Atlanta CUCRL Meeting," A/SN7, p. 3.

273   asked King as a favor: Comments of Julian Bond in Minutes of the SNCC Executive Committee meeting, May 10, 1964 (mistakenly labeled April 10), A/SN6, pp. 5–6.

273 CORE had issued: Moses to Farmer, March 2, 1964, A/SN111f16.

273 NAACP registration drive: ADW, March 16, 1964, p. 1.

273 "to project SNCC's image": Comments of Courtland Cox in Minutes of the SNCC Executive Committee meeting, May 10, 1964 (mistakenly labeled April 10), A/SN6, p. 4.

273 resolved to fight back: Minutes of the SNCC Executive Committee meeting, March 29, 1964, A/SN6.

273 "don't think the same way": Comments of Betty Garman in ibid., p. 3.

273 welcomed the National Lawyers Guild: Minutes of the SNCC Executive Committee meeting, March 29, 1964, A/SN6, pp. 1–2.

273 Andrew Young promptly advised: Minutes of May 15, 1964, "Meeting Following Atlanta CUCRL Meeting," A/SN7, p. 1.

273 Gloster Current: Ibid.

273 took his worries to the FBI: O'Reilly, *Racial Matters,* pp. 181–82.

273 threatened to pull his lawyers: Ibid. Also Dittmer, *Local People,* p. 230.

273 Pratt seconded Greenberg: Int. Jack Pratt, March 25, 1991; Findlay, *Church People in the Struggle,* pp. 104, n. 40, 105, n. 42.

273 "deliberate link": Ibid. Also Dittmer, *Local People,* p. 230.

273 church objection weighed heavily: Int. Robert P. Moses, Feb. 15, 1991; int. Jack Pratt, March 25, 1991.

273 Spike had followed up: 1991; Findlay, *Church People in the Struggle,* pp. 84–85; int. Bruce Hanson, Feb. 22, 1991; Arthur Thomas to CORR staff, Feb. 7 and Feb. 19, 1964, A/ATb3; Bruce Hanson to "Presidents, Deans, and Religious Advisers…," April 16, 1964, RG6, b47f32, NCC, POH.

273 Lowenstein campaigned against the guild: Dittmer, *Local People,* pp. 233–34; Chafe, *Never Stop Running,* pp. 190–92.

274 how they were made: Int. Allard Lowenstein by Anne Romaine, March 1967, pp. 127–29, A/AR.

274 Moses finally asked: Int. Robert P. Moses, Feb. 15, 1991.

274 infuriated him to hear: Dittmer, *Local People,* p. 192.

274 Lowenstein hurried to New York: Harris, *Dreams Die Hard,* pp. 53–54.

274 "My roommates were positively awed": Ron Bass to Lowenstein, May 12, 1964, Lowenstein Papers, UNC.

274 Lowenstein inspired New York students: Cagin and Dray, *We Are Not Afraid,* p. 47.

275 fn "While it is somewhat": Ibid., p. 241.

275 "militancy should not be confused": Bruce Campbell to Lowenstein, May 4, 1964, Lowenstein Papers, UNC.

275 "It is fundamental to our role": Mike Lawler (of UNC, Chapel Hill) to Lowenstein, April 19, 1964, Lowenstein Papers, UNC. Also Lawler to Lowenstein, May 15, 1964, ibid.

275 bait for federal intervention: Richard Woodley, "It Will Be a Hot Summer in Mississippi," *The Reporter,* May 21, 1964, p. 23.

275 "as communicative as a colony": Ilene Strelitz to Lowenstein, May 11, 1964, Lowenstein Papers, UNC.

275 SNCC could not feed: Marian E. Wright to Lowenstein, May 9, 1964, b9f312, Lowenstein Papers, UNC.

275 Only $10,000: Comments of Betty Garman in Minutes of the SNCC Executive Committee meeting, May 10, 1964, (mistakenly labeled April 10), A/SN6, p. 2.

275 $5 cash to pay a plumber: Holt, *The Summer That Didn't End,* pp. 39–42.

275 Moses sometimes despaired: Ibid., pp. 157–59.

275 Lowenstein discontinued: Marian E. Wright to Lowenstein, May 9, 1964, b9f312, Lowenstein Papers, UNC.

276 mistrusted him as a manipulator: Int. Betty Garman Robinson, Jan. 29, 1991; int. Dorothy Miller (Zellner), Dec. 12, 1991; int. Michael Miller, June 24, 1994.

276 "human syllogism": Ilene Strelitz to Lowenstein, April 20, 1964, Lowenstein Papers, UNC.

276 "I admit it took me": Ibid.

276 "Where will you be": "Bob" to Lowenstein, undated ca. May 1964, Lowenstein Papers, UNC.

276 Sweeney was destined to become: Harris, *Dreams Die Hard,* pp. 292–326; Chafe, *Never Stop Running,* pp. 450–58.

276 "Please let me know": Sweeney handwritten note to Lowenstein on Sweeney to Harold Taylor, May 31, 1964, b32f368, Lowenstein Papers, UNC.

20. MARY PEABODY MEETS THE KLAN

277 greeted at the Jacksonville airport: "Witness at St. Augustine, Florida," by Esther J. Burgess, courtesy of Esther J. Burgess; int. Esther J. Burgess, Nov. 7, 1994; *The Witness,* April 9, 1964.

277 nearly seventy people had been jailed: Colburn, *Racial Change,* p. 65; *Boston Globe,* March 29, 1964, p. 8.

277 "I do not believe": Int. Hosea Williams, Oct. 29, 1991.

278 mass meeting at Zion: "Witness at St. Augustine, Florida," by Esther J. Burgess, courtesy of Esther J. Burgess; *Boston Globe,* March 30, 1964, p. 3.

278 far north as Gorham: PC, April 4, 1964, p. 2.

278 Burgess made sure that the fruit cup: "Witness at St. Augustine, Florida," by Esther J. Burgess, courtesy of Esther J. Burgess.

278 "How nice it is": *Boston Globe,* March 31, 1964, pp. 1–2.

279 five stayed on to face arrest: NYT, March 31, 1964, pp. 1–2.

279 "I have a higher loyalty to God": "Witness at St. Augustine, Florida," by Esther J. Burgess, courtesy of Esther J. Burgess.

279 leadership crisis was flashing: Int. Paul Chapman, Nov. 4, 1994; int. William Sloane Coffin, July 16, 1991.

279 beaten their colleague Paul Chapman: *Boston Globe,* March 30, 1964, p. 5; int. Paul Chapman, Nov. 4, 1994; Burke Marshall to MLK, April 13, 1964, responding to King's telegram of March 31 "with reference to the assault upon Reverend Paul Chapman," A/KP24f22.

279 talking Mary Peabody into jail: Int. William Sloane Coffin, July 16, 1991.

279 communion service at Trinity Episcopal: *Boston Globe,* April 1, 1964, pp. 1–2; *The Witness,* April 9, 1964; Hartley, "A Long, Hot Summer," pp. 35–36, and "Racial and Civil Disorders," pp. 7–8, in Garrow, ed., *St. Augustine.*

279 Hosea Williams drilled: NYT, April 1, 1964, pp. 1, 27; int. Hosea Williams, Oct. 29, 1991; int. Willie Bolden, May 14, 1992.

280 surrounded them with cattle prod: Ibid. Also Jacksonville teletype to Director, March 31, 1964, FSA-1264; Jacksonville LHM, "Racial Situation, St. Johns County, Florida," April 1, 1964, FSA-NR.

280 Coffin told Peabody: Int. William Sloane Coffin, July 16, 1991.

280 "Thank you, Endicott": *Boston Globe,* April 1, 1964, p. 2.

280 Hayling scoured Elk's Rest: Int. William Sloane Coffin, July 16, 1991.

280 Georgia Reed: Ibid. Also int. Georgia Reed, April 2, 1991.

281 Governor Bryant still thought: C. Farris Bryant, oral history of March 5, 1971, by Joe B. Frantz, pp. 28–30, LBJ.

281 trouble getting Walter Jenkins: Transcript of Feb. 14, 1964, telephone conversation between Walter Jenkins and Governor Bryant, Series 2, Box 2, Jenkins Papers, LBJ.

281 two hundred demonstrators filled: PC, April 11, 1964, pp. 1–2; *Florida Times-Union,* April 1, 1964, p. 28.

281 fifty-seven Negro women in a smaller cell: Judge's handwritten notes on testimony of April 2, 1964, in Bryan Simpson Papers, UF.

281 "every inch the Boston blueblood": *Boston Globe,* April 2, 1964, p. 2.

281 "a muted pink suit": NYT, April 1, 1964, p. 27.

281 "You look just like": Int. Katherine and Henry Twine, April 2, 1991.

281 Fifty reporters clamored: Colburn, *Racial Change,* p. 67.

281 stimulated demands: Director to SAC, Jacksonville, March 31, 1964, FSA-1256.

282 opening with the Golden Rule: Matthew 7:12. NYT, March 31, 1964, p. 1.

282 flanked by Sheriff Davis: NYT, April 1, 1964, p. 1.

282 Mudd would report nightly: Whalen and Whalen, *The Longest Debate,* pp. 149–51.

282 Emissaries from Walter Cronkite: *Florida Times-Union,* April 1, 1964, p. 28.

282 Prat flew south: Int. Jack Pratt March 25, 1991.

282 eighty-eight new demonstrators: Jacksonville teletype to Director, April 1, 1964, FSA-1267; NYT, April 2, 1964, p. 18; Jacksonville LHM, April 2, 1964, FSA-NR.

282 Yale professor Jacques Bossiere: *Boston Globe,* April 3, 1964, p. 3.

282 breakfast of hominy grits: *Boston Globe,* April 2, 1964, p. 4.

282 "I understand you're representing": Int. Jack Pratt, March 25, 1991.

282 "These bums will all be back": Kunstler, *Deep in My Heart,* p. 275.

283 Davis again blocked: Ibid., pp. 271–84.

283 shoving Kunstler and Pratt: Ibid. Also int. Jack Pratt, March 25, 1991.

283 whittling on the bench: Colburn, *Racial Change,* pp. 119–21.

283 "Somebody goes and sticks their head": Transcript of Findings by Judge Bryan Simpson, April 2, 1964, Bryan Simpson papers, p. 35, UF.

283 not about to second-guess: Ibid., p. 382.

283 new Supreme Court ruling: NYT, March 31, 1964, p. 1; Kunstler, *Deep in My Heart,* pp. 279–80.

283 Simpson extracted a promise: Order of April 3, 1964, in *David Robinson et al. v. State of Florida,* Bryan Simpson Papers, p. 46, UF.

283 mass meeting that night: Kunstler, *Deep in My Heart,* p. 283; int. Jack Pratt, March 25, 1991.

283 "I feel as if a wall were crumbling": NYT, April 3, 1964, p. 23.

283 "I have been so deeply inspired": *Boston Globe,* April 3, 1963, pp. 1, 8.

283 "Grandmother Peabody": Robert K. Massie, "Don't Tread on Grandmother Peabody," *Saturday Evening Post,* May 16, 1964, pp. 74–76; Colburn, *Racial Change,* p. 70.

284 "Protesters Fail": NYT, April 4, 1964, p. 1.

284 frustrated Hosea Williams: "Racial and Civil Disorders," pp. 35–36, in Garrow, ed., *St. Augustine;* int. Hosea Williams, Oct. 29, 1991.

284 "I consider myself": NYT, April 2, 1964, p. 18.

284 rebuttal appearance: Colburn, *Racial Change,* p. 70–71.

284 "Mrs. Peabody's Act": *Florida Times-Union,* May 21, 1964, p. 18.

284 wore a gun openly: Oral History of L. O. Davis and Virgil Stuart, Tape B75#1, SAHS.

284 forty-odd bodies: Ibid.

284 Davis campaigned aggressively: Colburn, *Racial Change,* pp. 70–73.

284 avoided the new white militiamen: Int. Josephine Bozard, April 6, 1991.

284 dealer fired the man summarily: Ibid. Also Oral History of L. O. Davis and Virgil Stuart, Tape B75#1, SAHS.

285   Sunday School teacher, Dr. Hardgrove Norris: Colburn, *Racial Change*, pp. 131–33; int. Josephine Bozard, April 6, 1991; int. Ramelle Petroglou, April 4, 1991; int. David Nolan and Page Edwards, April 4, 1991; tape-recorded interviews with Hardgrove Norris, courtesy of David Colburn. With Norris as the likely source, an investigating committee of the Florida legislature addpted the "catspaw" theory in 1965. "Racial and Civil Disorders," pp. 8, 81, in Garrow, ed., *St. Augustine.*

285   shut off church contributions: Colburn, *Racial Change*, p. 168.

285   detected socialist tendencies: Int. Page Edwards, April 4, 1991.

285   "any or all of us ministers": WCKT-TV, Miami, *Fountain of Dissent*, Part 2, aired May 16, 1964, PEA.

285   Bernard Lee reported: "We've got to do some organizing here," Lee said on April 3. Hartley, "A Long, Hot Summer," p. 38, in Garrow, ed., *St. Augustine.*

285   Another King representative: John L. Gibson. Colburn, *Racial Change*, pp. 74–75.

285   never missed a Hayling mass meeting: Int. Fannie Fulwood, April 6, 1991.

285   Internal NAACP reports: Cf. Robert Saunders to Ruby Hurley, May 8, 1964, III-C-305, p. 2, NAACP.

285   "King is now having to back down": Robert Saunders to Gloster Current, June 16, 1964, III-C-305, NAACP.

285   two-day annual meeting: "Minutes of the Semi-Annual Board Meeting," April 16–17, 1964, A/KP29f3; Garrow, *Bearing the Cross*, pp. 320–21.

285   James Bevel lobbied: Ibid. Also Bevel to MLK, "Nonviolent vs. Brinksmenship," nd (stamped April 13, 1964), A/KP28f5.

286   Wyatt Walker closed his lengthy review: "Minutes of the Semi-Annual Board Meeting," April 16–17, 1964, A/KP29f3.

286   King was losing touch: Int. Wyatt Tee Walker by Donald H. Smith, Dec. 1963, SHSW; int. Wyatt Tee Walker, Aug. 20, 1984.

286   "Walker agreed to reconnoiter": Colburn, *Racial Change*, pp. 75–76. Garrow, *Bearing the Cross*, p. 325.

286   "our operation appears to be raggedy": "wtw" to MLK, "Suggested approach and chronology for St Augustine," nd (May 1964), A/KP20f44.

21. WRESTLING WITH LEGENDS

288   news from Pierre Salinger: Int. Victoria Murphy, Aug. 17, 1993; Johnson, *White House Diary*, p. 96.

288   George Reedy was confined: Goldman, *Tragedy*, pp. 139–40.

288   first time in Reedy's long acquaintance: Int. George Reedy, May 8, 1991; Reed, *Lyndon B. Johnson*, p. 23.

288   "Now that we are": Ward, *The Rich Nations and the Poor Nations*, pp. 35, 153.

288   ongoing conversations with Ward: Int. George Reedy, May 8, 1991; int. Jack Valenti, Feb. 25, 1991; *Time*, Sept. 3, 1965, p. 19. Johnson may well have been introduced to Barbara Ward by his friends Arthur Goldschmidt and Elizabeth Wickenden, whose careers as economic development experts acquainted them with Ward and her husband, Sir Robert G. A. Jackson, who worked with Goldschmidt at the United Nations. Goldschmidt commended Ward's speeches to Johnson shortly after the assassination (Goldschmidt to LBJ, Dec. 30, 1963, Name File, Barbara Jackson, LBJ). Eric F. Goldman, the Princeton historian whom Johnson brought to the White House in place of Arthur Schlesinger, Jr., wrote an enthusiastic review of *The Rich Nations and the Poor Nations* for the *New York Times Book Review* (Feb. 25, 1962, p. 1).

288   Air Force jets transport her from Europe: Cyrus Vance to Jack Valenti, June 4, 1964, and Barbara Ward to Valenti, June 12, 1964, Valenti Papers, AC54-87, LBJ; Ward to "My dear Mr. President," July 5, 1964, Name File Barbara Jackson, LBJ.

289   cowboy who drove terrified correspondents: Evans, *Lyndon B. Johnson*, pp. 429–31.

289   Johnson protested: Ibid. Also Miller, *Lyndon*, pp. 456–57.

289   Journalists were remarking: Press conference of March 15, 1964, PPP, pp. 364–65; Wicker, *On Press*, pp. 123–28.

289   "going around with a prayer": LBJ phone call with Sargent Shriver, Jan. 1, 1964, Cit. 1116, Audiotape WH6401.01, LBJ.

289   "the whole damned Secret Service": LBJ phone call with Rufus Youngblood, Jan. 6, 1964, Cit. 1208, Audiotape WH6401.06, LBJ.

289   "Your damn Secret Service": LBJ phone call with James Rowley, May 13, 1964, Cit. 3442, Audiotape Wh6405.06, LBJ.

289   "I might make you stay at home": LBJ phone call with Robert Byrd, April 10, 1964, Cit. 2995, Audiotape Wh6404.08, LBJ.

289   "It is a kind of embarrassing": LBJ phone call with William Fulbright, April 29, 1964, Cit. 3186, Audiotape WH6404.15, LBJ.

289   "something new in Presidential TV": Eric F. Goldman to LBJ, March 4, 1964, WHCF-PR, Box 367, LBJ.

290   needed to develop his own slogan: Press conference of March 15, 1964, PPP, pp. 364–65; Wicker, *On Press*, pp. 367–68.

290   five thousand police: *Time*, May 1, 1964, p. 18.

290   "I felt sorry for them": NYT, April 23, 1964, p. 26. LBJ made similar remarks the next day at a White House news conference. NYT, April 24, 1964, p. 14.

290   "wide-eyed, hare-brained": *Time*, May 1, 1964, pp. 18, 22, 33.

290   "bearded and untidy": NYT, April 23, 1964, pp. 1, 26.
290   gaping faults within the fair: Caro, *The Power Broker,* pp. 1082–1114. For a sampling of reports, see *The Christian Century,* July 29, 1964, pp. 968–69, and Oct. 7, 1964, pp. 1128–1129; *Life,* May 1, 1964, p. 26ff, and Aug. 7, 1964, p. 81ff; *Newsweek,* Feb. 1, 1965, p. 61; *The New Yorker,* May 2, 1964, pp. 35–39; *Saturday Evening Post,* May 23, 1964, pp. 12–29; *Time,* June 5, 1964, pp. 40–52
290   "I prophesy peace": NYT, April 23, 1964, p. 26.
290   settled a debilitating strike: Ibid., p. 1.
290   up before dawn to gallop: Johnson, *White House Diary,* pp. 117–23.
290   fingers started bleeding: *Time,* May 1, 1964, p. 20.
291   Johnson strayed: Int. Victoria Murphy, Aug. 17–18, 1993; Victoria McHugh (Murphy) oral history of June 9, 1975, pp. 1–4, LBJ.
291   Mentioning his favorite author: Remarks in Pittsburgh to the League of Women Voters, April 24, 1964, PPP, p. 534.
291   Johnson tried out the phrase: Ibid., pp. 533–37. The previous day in Chicago, Johnson had used the phrase "great society" four times in a speech to the Democratic Club of Cook County: Ibid., pp. 527–32.
291   "evoke a nation of humane grandeur: Ward urgently summarized "the greatest vision of our society" in her concluding paragraphs: "Am I free if my brother is bound by hopeless poverty and ignorance? . . ." Ward, *The Rich Nations and the Poor Nations* pp. 158–59.
291   "no ceiling on his energy": *Time,* May 1, 1964, pp. 17–21.
291   "King explained himself": MLK to Height, Branton, Farmer, Lewis, Randolph, Wilkins, and Young, April 21, 1964, A/KP27f38.
291   Wallace won a third: "Midwest Jolted by Wallace Vote," NYT, April 9, 1964, p. 19.
291   fn "Civil Rights—A Grim Day": *Boston Globe,* April 8, 1964, p. 1. Also "North's First Rights Martyr Made in Bloody Cleveland," *Jet,* April 23, 1964, pp. 14–23. By coincidence, Malcolm X was in Cleveland on the day Klunder died. On a radio show, Malcolm said the Klunder death proved Elijah Muhammad's theory that whites would resist integration violently, making it impossible. FBI transcript of Malcolm X remarks on *Contact,* Radio KYW, Cleveland, April 7, 1964, FMXNY-4455.
291   published a special page: NYT, April 19, 1964, p. IV-13.
292   still wanted to hire Bayard Rustin: Garrow, *Bearing the Cross,* p. 320.
292   New York advisers worried: Int. Clarence Jones, Nov. 25, 1983; int. Harry Wachtel, May 17, 1990. The Rustin topic was overheard on the Levison and Jones wiretaps frequently through the winter and spring of 1964, with suspicions about Rustin and the socialists beginning in March. Cf. wiretap transcripts of March 11, 1964, FLNY-9-469a, and March 16, 1964, FLNY-7-728a.
292   theorist Max Shachtman: Max Shachtman oral history by Stephen Chodes, 1962, CU/OH; Isserman, *If I Had a Hammer,* pp. 34–69; "Trotsky's Orphans," *New Republic,* June 22, 1987, pp. 18–22.
292   Trotsky literary estate: "Hearing Before the State Department in the Matter of Application for a Passport for Mr. Max Shachtman, National Chairman, Independent Socialist League," Nov. 3, 1953, pp. 33–34, Box 73, Joseph Rauh Papers, LOC.
292   workshops at times included: Int. Michael Harrington, Aug. 31, 1983, and Oct. 27, 1983; int. Irving Howe, Nov. 28, 1983.
292   New York lawyers reported: Int. Clarence Jones, Nov. 25, 1983.
293   quibbled with Levison: Ibid. Also int. Harry Wachtel, May 17, 1990.
293   "You're doing the same thing": Int. Clarence Jones, Nov. 28, 1989.
293   "are beginning to infiltrate": WP, April 15, 1964, p. 23.
293   resisted the urgent counsel: NY LHM, April 22, 1964, FJ-NR; Baumgardner to Sullivan, April 23, 1964, FL-NR; Hoover to Walter Jenkins, April 27, 1964, FK-NR.
294   Marshall had listened: Baumgardner to Sullivan, April 26, 1964, FK-NR.
294   "Hoover Says Reds Exploit": NYT, April 22, 1964, p. 30.
294   Hoover, blocked by Robert Kennedy: Int. Edwin Guthman, June 25, 1984.
294   "the Alsop case": Yoder, *Joe Alsop's Cold War,* pp. 153–58; WP, April 13, 1995, p. C1.
294   King pushed his advisers: NY LHM, April 27, 1964, FK-NR.
294   fn "revolting"; NYT, April 22, 1964, p. 30.
294   "Rev. King's Icy Fury": *San Francisco Examiner,* April 24, 1964.
294   dictated the King statement: SAC, San Francisco, to Director, April 23, 1964, FK-NR.
294   "King mentioned the Director": Sullivan to Belmont, April 23, 1964, FK-352.
295   "It would be encouraging to us": King statement "in response to a recent article written by Mr. Joseph Alsop and Mr. J. Edgar Hoover's charge," April 23, 1964, p. 3, A/KS. King's lawyers wrote letters of rebuttal to newspapers: Eskridge to Eugene Patterson, April 24, 1964, and Eskridge to John Hay Whitney, April 24, 1964, A/SC9f35.
295   "we have utilized": Hoover "Confidential" letter to LBJ, April 10, 1964, answering LBJ to Hoover, April 8, 1964, HU2/ST1, FG 135-6, LBJ.
295   Sullivan placed an emergency call: Sullivan to Belmont, April 23, 1964, FK-3116.
295   arranged microphone bugs: Garrow, *FBI and Martin,* p. 115.
295   "I want to hit him hard": Ibid., p. 113.
295   "the rhythms of man": Harris, *Dream Die Hard,* p. 57.
295   "If we have any anchor": Moses speech of April 24, 1964, SUARC.
296   rose for a standing ovation: Harris, *Dreams Die Hard,* p. 57.
297   "All the colored folks": Holt, *The Summer That Didn't End,* p. 159.
297   candidacy for the U.S. Senate: "Negro Woman Qualifies for Mississippi Senate Seat," SNCC press release of April 10, 1964, A/SN101f8.

297   Kentucky college secured : Findlay, *Church People in the Struggle,* p. 85.

297   "It is unbelievably absurd": Jane Stembridge to Mary King, April 21, 1964, cited in Mary King, *Freedom Song,* pp. 369–70.

22. FILIBUSTERS

298   superimposed clock: Whalen and Whalen, *The Longest Debate,* p. 166.

298   vigil at the Lincoln Memorial: NYT, May 2, 1964; Findlay, *Church People in the Struggle,* pp. 55–56.

298   "unparalleled in the annals": NYT, April 10, 1964, p. 1; NYT, April 26, 1964, p. 45; NYT, April, 29, 1964, p. 1; WP, April 29, 1964, p. 1.

298   reverse "enslavement" of white people: Cf. Kilpatrick, "What a Southern Conservative Thinks," *Saturday Review,* April 25, 1964, pp. 15–18; "Maybe It's Time to Look at the Antislavery Amendment," *U.S. News & World Report,* May 11, 1964, pp. 82–84.

298   "How can any Christian": *Congressional Record–Senate,* April 29, 1964, pp. 9535–44.

299   "I turn around": LBJ phone call with Bill Moyers, April 28, 1964, Cit. 3171, Audiotape WH6404.14, LBJ.

299   Oscar Lee preached the first: Findlay, *Church People in the Struggle,* p. 55.

299   President Johnson received: NYT, April 30, 1964, p. 1.

299   "From the time": PPP, April 29, 1964, Item 301, pp. 588–89.

299   "my herdmen and your herdmen": Genesis 13:8.

299   fn "If you ever follow dogs": NYT, April 29, 1964, p. 43.

299   Northern Presbyterians elected: NYT, May 22, 1964, p. 1.

299   dissenting elders renewed: Address of Dr. James Findlay at University of Chicago School of Divinity, April 24, 1995.

299   Southern Baptists voted down: NYT, May 22, 1964, p. 20.

299   invite Rev. Henry Russell: NYT, April 26, 1964, p. 61.

300   compromise that reunited Methodists: Methodist history summarized for General Assembly, as recorded in *Daily Christian Advocate,* April 29, 1960, pp. 79–80, 104–6, May 1, 1964, pp. 141–46, May 2, 1964, pp. 238–39, May 7, 1964, pp. 486–88.

300   "I would like to remind": *Daily Christian Advocate,* May 2, 1964, p. 179.

300   tumultuous Pittsburgh assembly: Ibid., pp. 218–42; NYT, April 29, 1964, p. 29, May 2, 1964, p. 1.

300   driving white Methodists: *Daily Christian Advocate,* May 1, 1964, p. 167.

300   Lawson wept openly: Int. James Lawson, March 26, 1991.

300   marched around the Pittsburgh Civic Arena: Ibid. Also int. Edwin King, June 26, 1992; NYT, May 3, 1964, p. 78; PC, May 9, 1964, p. 1.

300   Russell told colleagues: Whalen and Whalen, *The Longest Debate,* p. 237.

300   "grassroots resistance": cited in Harold H. Martin, "George Wallace Shakes Up the Political Scene," *Saturday Evening Post,* May 9, 1964, p. 86.

300   "We have shaken the eyeteeth": Ibid., p. 85.

300   developed a stump speech: Lesher, *George Wallace,* pp. 261–65, 272–73, 297–98.

300   chortled over the discovery: Ibid., p. 262.

300   "Anybody here": Ibid., p. 290.

301   "they are building": Ibid., p. 292.

301   Dirksen hinted instead: Stern, *Calculating Visions,* p. 180.

301   "Oh, I was shameless": Miller, *Lyndon,* p. 451; Whalen and Whalen, *The Longest Debate,* p. 201.

301   "killed off a rapidly growing": Whalen and Whalen, *The Longest Debate,* p. 189.

301   Tennessee Democrats selected: NYT, April 3, 1964, p. 23.

301   "The Negro has been read out": NYT, May 3, 1964, p. 72.

302   King joined Fred Shuttlesworth: Funeral recording in the possession of Mrs. W. E. (Pinkie) Shortridge; int. Pinkie Shortridge, July 29, 1986.

302   short notice to Nashville: Ibid. Also *Nashville Banner,* May 1, 1964, p. 1; MS, May 22, 1964, pp. 1, 4–6; int. John Lewis by Archie Allen, pp. 120–22, AAP; ADW, April 30, 1964, p. 1.

302   escorted King into a mass meeting: *Gadsden Times,* May 4, 1964.

302   "Who Is My Neighbor?": Luke 10:29–37.

302   "Everybody within the sound of my voice": MLK sermon, "The Three Philosophies of Life," May 3, 1964, A/KS.

302   favorite parable of the rich man Dives: Branch, *Parting,* pp. 12, 705; Luke 16 19–31.

303   returned by way of Cincinnati: MLK to Harold DeWolf, May 1, 1964, A/KP4f27.

303   poverty tour from Ohio down through Tennessee: LBJ remarks in Cumberland, Md.; Athens, Ohio; Knoxville, Tenn.; Rocky Mount, N.C.; etc., PPP, 1964, pp. 640–51.

303   two newborn tiger cubs: Ivan Allen, Jr., Oral History, May 15, 1969, pp. 12–13, LBJ.

303   "my Georgia ancestors": LBJ remarks at the Dinkler Plaza Hotel, May 8, 1964, PPP, p. 649.

303   walking speed for fifteen miles: NYT, May 9, 1964, pp. 1, 13.

304   forty thousand people: PC, May 16, 1964, p. 4.

304   "I need two new hands!": LBJ phone call with Lawrence O'Brien, May 8, 1964, Cit. 3365, Audiotape WH6405,03, LBJ.

304   "a household word": LBJ "Remarks Honoring J. Edgar Hoover...," May 8, 1964, PPP, pp. 654–55.

304   DeWolf had fallen: Int. Harold DeWolf, May 9–10, 1983.

304   "to place my less": DeWolf to "Martin and Coretta," May 13, 1964, A/KP4f37.

304   offered Boston university: Ibid. Also int. Harold DeWolf, May 9–10, 1983; reference to Boston University offer in SCLC Executive Staff Meeting minutes of May 4, 1964, A/KP32f7.

305   Mays had refused: Int. Benjamin Mays, March 6, 1984.

305   sending Mays a thousand-dollar donation: MLK to Mays, May 15, 1964, A/KP.

305   "amazes me": Mays to MLK, May 18, 1964, A/KP.

305   Yoki's ballet recital: MLK to Harold DeWolf, May 1, 1964, A/KP4f27; DeWolf to "Martin and Coretta," May 13, 1964, A/KP4f37.

305   "Where is the direct action?": Transcript of *Face the Nation,* CBS Television Network, May 10, 1964, p. 15, A/KS.

306   DeLoach had pushed: Guthman, "Memo for the Files," May 8, 1964, Edwin Guthman private papers.

306   Guthman quickly sent the FBI: Int. Edwin Guthman, June 25, 1984.

306   "Obviously, Guthman is skeptical": DeLoach to Mohr, May 13, 1964, Edwin Guthman private papers.

306   "In the past few months": RFK to Hoover, May 12, 1964, cited in Powers, *Secrecy and Power,* p. 392.

306   Guthman and DeLoach would agree: Guthman, "Memo for the Files," May 18, 1964, Edwin Guthman private papers.

306   national debt ceiling: *Florida Times-Union,* May 21, 1964, p. 6.

306   Whitten's nettlesome demand: Henry H. Wilson to Larry O'Brien, May 26, 1964, Box 4, Henry Wilson Papers, LBJ.

306   first criminal contempt citation: Coleman, *Adam Clayton Powell,* p. 101.

306   revised anti-poverty legislation: "mf" to LBJ, May 26, 1964, regarding phone call from Rep. Carl Albert, WE9, Box 25, LBJ.

306   "a laundry list a yard long": LBJ phone call with Lawrence O'Brien, May 11, 1964, Cit. 3395, Audiotape WH6405.04, LBJ.

307   "The Communist Split": *Time,* April 26, 1964, pp. 26–30.

307   Nehru died: NYT, May 26, 1964, p. 1; LBJ Letter of May 27, 1964, PPP, p. 719.

307   "Mr. Johnson has left an indelible imprint": NYT, May 22, 1964, p. 1.

307   Six American soldiers: *Time,* May 22, 1964, p. 28.

307   cumulative U.S. death toll: McNamara, *In Retrospect,* p. 321; Ernest Gruening speech of March 10, 1964, *Congressional Record,* p. S-4864.

307   "Opposing forces are": *U.S. News & World Report,* March 23, 1964, pp. 50–52.

307   "Sorry About That": CBS Special Report, *Vietnam: The Deadly Decision,* aired April 1, 1964, tape No. T79:0039, MOB.

307   strategic imperative was clearer: President Johnson underscored and defined the geopolitical necessity of "an independent non-Communist South Vietnam" by accepting McNamara's top secret National Security Action Memorandum, NSAM-288, on March 17, 1964. (Nowhere did the eighteen-page document consider whether a democratic form of government was, could be, or even should be supported by the people of Vietnam.) Bundy to NSC, March 17, 1964, and RSM to LBJ, March 16, 1964, NS-NSAM, Boxes 3–7, LBJ.

307   "Loss of this area": CBS Special Report, *Vietnam: The Deadly Decision,* aired April 1, 1964, tape No. T79:0039, MOB.

308   defeated Barry Goldwater: "A Vote for our Man in Vietnam," *Life,* March 20, 1964.

308   holding aloft the arm: Shapley, *Promise and Power,* p. 297.

308   nearly assassinated McNamara: NYT, May 11, 1964, p. 1; *Time,* May 22, 1964, p. 28.

308   bulletproof cloaks: Ibid.

308   "tide of deterioration": McNamara, *In Retrospect,* p. 119.

308   "by still trying to jump": NYT, May 11, 1964, p. 7.

308   facing a new coup against Khanh: *Time,* April 24, 1964, p. 33.

308   four more regimes that year: McNamara, *In Retrospect,* p. 101.

308   assume more efficient direct command: Ibid., p. 118.

308   "mount a successful campaign": NYT, May 19, 1964, pp. 1–2.

308   "just milquetoast as it can be": LBJ phone call with McGeorge Bundy, 11:24 A.M., May 27, 1964, Cit. 3522, Audiotape WH6405.10, LBJ.

308   "What do you think": LBJ phone call with Richard Russell, 10:55 A.M., May 27, 1964, Cit. 3519a, Audiotape WH6405.10. LBJ.

310   soldiers massed along Race Street: *Time,* May 22, 1964, p. 24; *Life,* May 22, 1964, p. 46C; Lyon, *Memories of the Southern Civil Rights Movement,* pp. 136–41; Lesher, *George Wallace,* pp. 298–300.

310   longevity record: Whalen and Whalen, *The Longest Debate,* p. 179.

310   removing Roger Mudd: Ibid., p. 187.

310   Wallace won 43 percent: NYT, May 20, 1964, p. 1.

310   "I wish I had entered California": NYT, May 21, 1964, p. 25.

310   "Most distressing of all": Ibid., p. 34.

310   "Maryland's Vote Held Anti-Negro": Ibid., p. 1.

310   Michigan on May 22: NYT, May 23, 1964, p. 1; *Time,* May 29, 1964, p. 18.

311   "help build a society": PPP, May 22, 1964, pp. 704–7.

311   twenty test runs: Valenti to LBJ, Dec. 15, 1964, WE9, Box 25, LBJ.

311   "There were twenty-nine": Miller, *Lyndon,* p. 459.

23. PILGRIMS AND EMPTY PITCHERS

312   Malcolm X returned: Goldman, *Death and Life,* pp. 182–83.

312   new Sunni Muslim name: NYAN, May 9, 1964, p. 62.

312   his favorite film: Karim, *Remembering Malcolm,* p. 97.

312   Handler kept muttering: Malcolm X, *The Autobiography,* pp. 412–13.

312   "Malcolm X Pleased": NYT, May 8, 1964, p. 1.

312   "Malcolm Rejects Race Separation": NYT, May 24, 1964, p. 1.

312   revised opinions on Judaism: Ibid. Also, undated NYAN news article cited in NY FBI report of Jan. 1965, FMX-215, p. 97; Breitman, ed., *Malcolm X Speaks,* pp. 62–63.

313   fn "You don't have to be Jewish": Breitman, *Last Year,* pp. 98–99.

313   letters Malcolm had sent home: NYT, May 8, 1964, p. 1; Malcolm X, *The Autobiography,* pp. 338–42; Breitman, ed., *Malcolm X Speaks,* pp. 58–64; Farmer, *Lay Bare the Heart,* pp. 229–30; Goldman, *Death and Life,* pp. 168–69.

313   known of white Muslims: Perry, *Malcolm,* pp. 263–64.

313   discussed them in public: For example: "Many people think we judge the white man because he is white. No, our attitude toward the American white man isn't because he is white. You have many people in the Muslim world whose skin is white as the people of Europe and North America. We judge the American because of the deeds, the collective deeds that Americans have done against black people. . . ." FBI transcript of Malcolm X remarks on *Contact,* Radio KYW, Cleveland, April 7, 1964, FMXNY-4455, pp. 22–23.

313   "new, positive insights": NYT, May 8, 1964, p. 1.

313   Malcolm found himself snatched: Malcolm X, *The Autobiography,* p. 325.

313   detained as a questionable Muslim: Ibid. Malcolm described his detention May 23, 1964, on *Kup's Show* in Chicago: FBI transcript in SAC, Chicago, to Director, June 19, 1964, FMXNY-4599, pp. 39–41.

314   prayed for six solid hours: Perry, *Malcolm,* pp. 265–66.

314   interval of delight: Malcolm X, *The Autobiography,* pp. 318–60; Perry, *Malcolm,* p. 264.

314   "Chinese Ambassador and Mrs. Huang Hua": Malcolm X, *The Autobiography,* p. 357.

314   summer home of the late W. E. B. Du Bois: letter of Shirley Graham Du Bois in *Ghanaian Times,* May 19, 1964.

314   African Marxists pressed him: H. M. Basner column in *Ghanaian Times,* May 18, 1964, cited in Dept. of State Airgram No. A-625, Accra to State, May 24, 1964. Third Secretary Daniel A. Britz reported that Malcolm "created less of a stir than the Embassy had feared." Boasting that "President Nkrumah was made aware of the controversial nature of Malcolm X before the visit," Britz reported erroneously that Nkrumah refused to give Malcolm an audience.

314   Mayfield's argument: *Ghanaian Times,* May 19, 1964.

314   Nkrumah, shied away: Goldman, *Death and Life,* pp. 172–73.

314   Malcolm ran into Muhammad Ali: Perry, *Malcolm,* pp. 270–71; Goldman, *Death and Life,* p. 178.

314   hurt by this snub: Hauser, *Muhammad Ali,* p. 110.

314   "funny white robe": NYT, May 18, 1964; *New York Post,* May 18, 1964, p. 4.

314   "America needs to understand Islam": Malcolm X, *The Autobiography,* p. 340.

315   "True Islam removes racism": Breitman, ed., *Malcolm X Speaks,* p. 360.

315   "The American whites": NYAN, May 30, 1964, p. 49.

315   "Do we correctly understand": Perry, *Malcolm,* p. 271.

315   pacified a *Life* correspondent: Malcolm X, *The Autobiography,* p. 415.

315   Robert Penn Warren: Warren, *Who Speaks for the Negro?* pp. 244–67.

316   "There is something of that": Ibid., p. 266.

316   "pale, dull yellowish": Ibid., p. 255.

316   "I MUST BE HONEST": Malcolm X, *The Autobiography,* p. 364.

316   James 67X seethed: Perry, *Malcolm,* p. 268.

316   reveled in the new freedom: Int. Benjamin Karim, March 11, 1991, March 19, 1991, and Aug. 31, 1991.

316   gave way to aimlessness: Ibid. Also Goldman, *Death and Life,* pp. 170, 182.

316   presentation on yoga: FBI wiretap transcript of June 4, 1964, FMXNY-1-2, p. 1.

317   debate in the Civic Opera House: *Chicago Sun-Times,* May 17, 1964; Chicago LHM, May 25, 1964, FMXNY-4515.

317   bridge expert Oswald Jacoby: FBI transcript of *Kup's Show,* May 23, 1964, in SAC, Chicago, to Director, June 17, 1964, FMXNY-4599, pp. 28–29.

317   "your white nationalism": FBI transcript of *Dateline Chicago,* WMBQ-TV, May 31, 1964, in SAC, Chicago, to Director, June 19, 1964, FMXNY-4592, p. 2.

317   "I very much doubt": FBI transcript of *Kup's Show,* May 23, 1964, in SAC, Chicago, to Director, June 17, 1964, FMXNY-4599, p. 6.

317   "I want to settle the situation": NYAN, May 30, 1964, p. 1.

317   "if Allah pleases him": Wiretap transcript of May 8, 1964, in SAC, Chicago, to SAC, New York, May 21, 1964, FMXNY-4482, p. 3.

317   have no dealings with Malcolm: Cf. report on Muhammad's instruction of May 13, 1964, in SAC, Phoenix, to SAC, Chicago, June 16, 1964, FMXNY-4577.

317   all those Muslims being shunned: SAC, Newark, to Director, May 1, 1964, FMXNY-4433.

318   lived under siege within his own family: Malcolm X remarks on *Conversation Piece,* WEEI radio, Boston, June 12, 1964, in Boston FBI LHM of June 15, 1964, p. 2.

318   "Everyone that sees me": MS, June 5, 1964, p. 8, quoting Genesis 4:14.

318   "We had the best": Malcolm X, *The Autobiography*, p. 411.
319   "You know": Karim, *Remembering Malcolm*, p. 182.
319   dispatched James 67X to locate: FBI wiretap summary of June 4, 1964, in SAC, New York, to SAC, Chicago, July 20, 1964, FMXNY-4754, p. 2.
319   "Mister Muhammad will be brought to justice": FBI wiretap summary of June 5, 1964, SAC, New York, to Director, July 1, 1964, FMXNY-4674, p. 2; FBI wiretap transcript of June 5, 1964, FMXNY-1-3a.
319   finished the June 3 installation: SAC, New York, to Director, June 4, 1964, FMX-113.
319   "a trapeze artist": FBI wiretap transcript of June 4, 1964, FMXNY-1-2, pp. 5, 8.
320   "pumping these brothers with poison": Ibid., p. 12.
320   "I know how to do it": Ibid., p. 11.
320   "Just another effort": SAC, New York, to Director, FMX-126.
320   "the Director told Manchester": DeLoach to Mohr, June 4, 1964, FRFK-1536.
320   review of the National Council of Churches: Sullivan to Director, May 8, 1964, FNCC-1172.
320   From John Doar up through Burke: Doar to Marshall, May 19, 1964, Box 3, Marshall Papers, JFK.
320   "turn the students": Katzenbach to LBJ through Lee White, "Civil Rights—Misc.," Box 6, Lee White Papers, LBJ.
321   "to avoid as much as possible": Marshall to RFK, June 5, 1964, Box 3, Marshall Papers, JFK.
321   "spectacularly efficient": RFK to LBJ, June 5, 1964, ExHU2/ST24, FG135, LBJ.
321   meeting alone with President Johnson: Ibid. Also, Valenti, *A Very Human President*, pp. 98–100; LBJ phone call with Lee White, June 4, 1964, Cit. 3624, Audiotape WH6406.02, LBJ.
321   McNamara had just delivered: Gravel, ed., *Pentagon Papers*, Vol. 2, pp. 323–26; McNamara, *In Retrospect*, pp. 121–23.
321   "is obviously the most important problem": RFK to LBJ, cited in Schlesinger, *Robert Kennedy*, pp. 784–85.
321   bugs for King's room at the Sheraton: Bland to Sullivan, May 27, 1964, MLK folder, Section 24, FHOC.
321   King to rent a summer beach: SAC, Jacksonville, to Director, coded teletype of May 28, 1964, FSA-1366.
321   "Let Freedom Ring": Good, *Trouble I've Seen*, p. 76.
322   "You are proving": PC, June 6, 1964, pp. 1, 4.
322   Research Committee: FBI intercept of Wachtel-Jones conversation, May 21, 1964, in FJ-NR; Research Committee members listed in A/KP25f37.
322   Rustin urged King: New York LHM dated June 9, 1964, FSC-NR.
322   "is so deeply rooted": NYT, May 29, 1964, p. 10.
322   pledged to return: ADW, May 28, 1964, p. 1.
322   Williams considered Young: Int. Hosea Williams, Oct. 29, 1991; int. Andrew Young, Oct. 26, 1991.
322   peaceful march of four hundred: Colburn, *Racial Change*, pp. 80–81.
322   twice that number at St. Mary's Baptist: Judge Bryan Simpson, "Findings of Fact and Conclusions of Law," in *Young v. Davis*, No. 64-133-Civ-J, June 9, 1964, in Simpson Papers, p. 6, UF.
322   cleaning a shotgun: PC, June 6, 1964, p. 4.
322   Williams ambushed him from the pulpit: Int. Hosea Williams, Oct. 29, 1991; int. Andrew Young, Oct. 26, 1991; Young, *A Way Out of No Way*, p. 90.
323   "prettiest girl in this church": Int. Andrew Young, Oct. 26, 1991.
323   Virgil Stuart halted the line: Good, *Trouble I've Seen*, p. 80.
323   "We come before Thee": Ibid., p. 83.
323   down the cheeks of Andrew Young: Int. Willie Bolden, May 14, 1992.
323   Three hundred fifty people: Colburn, *Racial Change*, p. 82.
324   C. T. Vivian flinched: Int. C. T. Vivian, May 26, 1990.
324   Georgia Reed volunteered: Hartley, "A Long, Hot Summer," p. 47, in Garrow, ed., *St. Augustine*; int. Georgia Mae Reed, April 2, 1991.
324   fifteen local Negroes back to jail: *Florida Times-Union*, May 29, 1964.
324   250 whites amassed to defend: Jacksonville FBK LHM dated June 1, 1964, FSA-1353, pp. 1–2.
324   press photographers tried to capture: Good, *Trouble I've Seen*, pp. 88–89; Colburn, *Racial Change*, pp. 82–83.
324   "There's that nigger lover!": Judge Bryan Simpson, "Findings of Fact and Conclusions of Law," in *Young v. Davis*, No. 64-133-Civ-J, June 9, 1964, in Simpson Papers, pp. 8–9, UF.
324   "although some teen-age girls": Claude Sitton, "2 Hurt in Clash in St. Augustine," NYT, May 29, 1964.
325   "We are declaring martial law": Judge Bryan Simpson, "Findings of Fact and Conclusions of Law," in *Young v. Davis*, No. 64-133-Civ-J, June 9, 1964, in Simpson Papers, p. 12, UF.
325   bushwhackers had fired: Ibid. Also Good, *Trouble I've Seen*, p. 89; Garrow, *Bearing the Cross*, p. 327; Hartley, "A Long, Hot Summer," p. 45, in Garrow, ed., *St. Augustine*.
325   "loss of momentum": NYT, May 30, 1964, p. 14.
325   "continue our efforts": ADW, May 30, 1964, p. 1.
325   "We cannot in good conscience": MLK to LBJ, May 29, 1964 (from San Diego), A/KS.
325   eleven thousand in San Diego: San Diego LHM of June 6, 1964, FSC-NR.
325   he called Burke Marshall: Lee White file memo, June 1, 1964, HU2/St9, LG/St. Augustine, LBJ.
325   "hang a Negro": Jacksonville FBI LHM, June 1, 1964, FSA-1353, p. 7.
325   explicit death threat against King: MLK statement of June 5, 1964, A/KS; Garrow, *Bearing the Cross*, p. 328.

325 Coretta King complained bitterly: Garrow, *Bearing the Cross.*

325 permission to bug the premises: Jacksonville urgent teletype to Director, 10:12 P.M., May 28, 1964, FK-NR.

325 anonymous tipsters had publicized: Colburn, *Racial Change,* p. 83.

325 Bryant of Florida boasted: Lee White file memo, June 1, 1964, HU2/St9, LG/St. Augustine, LBJ.

326 "Be certain that we do not yield": Hoover's handwritten note on UPI news story of June 9, 1964, FK-384; Baumgardner to Sullivan, June 10, 1964, FK-NR.

326 Hoover asked his aides: Jones to DeLoach, June 5, 1964, FK-NR.

326 "unshirted hell": LBJ phone call with George Smathers, June 1, 1964, Cit. 3602, Audiotape WH6406.01, LBJ.

326 "Discussions should be begun": Dolan to Marshall, June 5, 1964, Box 7, Marshall Papers, JFK.

326 "I want to commend you": Pat Watters, "St. Augustine," *New South,* Sept. 1964, p. 11.

326 Simpson had asked for a courtesy moratorium: Kunstler, *Deep in My Heart,* pp. 289–95; int. Andrew Young, Oct. 26, 1991.

326 Georgia Reed testified: Hartley, "A Long, Hot Summer," p. 47, in Garrow, ed., *St. Augustine.*

327 "they were just a bunch of kids": Kunstler, *Deep in My Heart,* p. 290.

327 "Why that man's a convicted felon": Hartley, "A Long, Hot Summer," p. 47, in Garrow, ed., *St. Augustine.*

327 1959 moonshine trial: *Miami Herald,* June 14, 1964, p. 14; *Port Arthur* (Tex.) *News,* June 15, 1977, p. 17.

327 Simpson asked: Pat Watters, "St. Augustine," *New South,* Sept. 1964, p. 10. FBI officials, who briefed Simpson on ties between law enforcement and the Klan, ignored the Catholic-Klan technicalities and routinely referred to Manucy as the "Exalted Cyclops of the St. Augustine Klavern." (Garrow, *Bearing the Cross,* pp. 328–29; Jacksonville FBI LHM, June 1, 1964, FSA-1353, pp. 4–5; Rosen to Belmont, June 2, 1964, FSA-1364.)

327 baccalaureate address two days later: NYT, June 8, 1964, p. 22.

327 taking Coretta with him: Int. John Maguire, Sept. 15, 1990.

327 causing a fright: Ibid.

327 "long and difficult wilderness": King speech of June 7, 1964, A/KS6.

327 fn $67 in his government account: Moyers to Walter Jenkins, June 8, 1964, Box 39, Moyers Papers, LBJ.

327 first gentile to receive: NYT, June 8, 1964, p. 22.

24. BRUSHFIRES

328 arsonists set fire: McGowan to Rosen, May 30, 1964, FSA-1343; Jacksonville teletype to Director, June 8, 1964, FSA-1343; Jacksonville LHM of June 8, 1964, FSA-1380, p. 2.

328 King and his new Research Committee: Wachtel to Reddick, June 2, 1964, A/KP25f26.

328 calling Muslim women: FBI wiretap transcript of June 7, 1964, FMXNY-1-5a, pp. 1–3.

328 "You think the Messenger is that ruthless?": Ibid., p. 1.

328 "The Nation would even murder": New York FBI LHM, June 8, 1964, FMXNY-4536.

328 loyalist members stayed late: Ibid., p. 2.

329 "Just tell him he's as good as dead": FBI wiretap transcript of June 8, 1964, FMXNY-1-6, p. 1.

329 Wallace rushed him into a studio: Ibid., pp. 3–7; SAC, New York, to SACs, Phoenix, Chicago, and Director, June 8, 1964, FMXNY-4539; Perry, *Malcolm,* p. 288.

329 He alerted friends: SAC, New York, to Director, June 9, 1964, FMXNY-4540; FBI wiretap transcript of June 7, 1964, FMXNY-1-5a, p. 2.

329 citizens' hearing on Mississippi: Summary of June 8 hearing prepared by Judge Justine Polier, A/SN100f14; Dittmer, *Local People,* p. 239.

329 "It cannot be stated": COFO notice to members of the United States Congress, June 3, 1964, cited in Holt, *The Summer That Didn't End,* pp. 204–7.

329 "That is why": Elizabeth Allen testimony of June 8, 1964, reprinted in *Congressional Record,* June 16, 1964, photocopied in A/SN111f17, p. 5.

329 Hartman Turnbow testified: Ibid., pp. 6–7.

329 "Not only have I been": Ibid., pp. 3–4.

329 piled into a car and headed from Greenwood: Affidavit of Charles McLaurin, July 27, 1964, A/MFDP10f3.

330 admitted that he was a nigger: Ibid. Also affidavits of James Jones, James Black, and Samuel Block regarding incident of June 8, 1964, A/MFDP10f1.

330 ambushed three white magazine writers: United States Commission on Civil Rights, *Law Enforcement: A Report on Equal Protection in the South,* 1965, pp. 30–31.

330 novelist Joseph Heller and other sponsors: Harold Taylor, Robert Coles, Noel Day, Paul Goodman, Joseph Heller, Murray Kempton, Justine Polier, and Gresham Sykes to LBJ, June 11, 1964, A/SN100f14.

330 Roy Wilkins was candidly criticizing: Staff Meeting Minutes, June 9–11, 1964, A/SN7, p. 11.

330 "Oh, but you are all so American": Ed King, "SNCC and Dr. Lohia," *New South,* Summer 1971, pp. 57–62.

330 marathon at Frazier's Lounge: Staff Meeting Minutes, June 9–11, 1964, A/SN7; Mary King, *Freedom Song,* pp. 307–25.

330 "There used to be a bond": Staff Meeting Minutes, June 9–11, 1964, A/SN7, p. 1.

331 "No one can be rational": Ibid., p. 15; Mary King, *Freedom Song,* p. 314.

331   "Don't you see?": Mary King, *Freedom Song,* p. 324.
331   "To the extent that we think": Staff Meeting Minutes, June 9–11, 1964, A/SN7, p. 4.
331   "the controllable things": Mary King, *Freedom Song,* p. 318.
332   Moses later sent Stokely: Forman, *Black Revolutionaries,* p. 374.
332   "I am probably a dead man already": Perry, *Malcolm,* p. 288.
332   "certain information": SAC, New York, to Director and SACs, Chicago, Los Angeles, and Phoenix, June 9, 1964, FMXNY-4540.
332   vetoed airing the sex charges: SAC, New York, to SAC, Boston, June 11, 1964, FMXNY-4549; SAC, New York, to Director and SACs, Chicago, Los Angeles, and Phoenix, June 11, 1964, FMXNY-4552; SAC, New York, to Director, July 1, 1964, FMXNY-4674.
332   brawl outside the Philadelphia mosque: FBI wiretap transcript of June 11, 1964, FMXNY-1-9a, p. 2.
332   refuge in the Chicago FBI office: Chicago LHM of June 15, 1964, FMXNY-4568.
332   reverberations among the women: SAC, Chicago, to Director, June 16, 1964, FMXNY-4576.
332   "If we don't stop clowning": Intercept of conversation between Lottie Muhammad and her mother, Clara, June 12, 1964, in ibid., p. 3.
332   "the direction which my life should take": Young to Douglass and Hotchkiss, June 9, 1964, A/KP27f41.
332   council had just voted formally: NYT, June 6, 1964, p. 26.
333   Simpson terminated the ban: Judge Bryan Simpson, "Findings of Fact and Conclusions of Law," in *Young v. Davis,* No. 64-133-Civ-J, June 9, 1964, in Simpson Papers, UF; *Jacksonville Journal,* June 10, 1964, p. 10; Hartley, "A Long, Hot Summer," p. 49, in Garrow, ed., *St. Augustine.*
333   crisis from Alabama: NYT, June 10, 1964, p. 1.
333   dispatched James Bevel: UPI news story of June 9, 1964, FK-384.
333   "heard of this incident": LBJ phone call with Robert Kennedy, June 9, 1964, Cit. 3646, Audiotape WH6406.03, LBJ.
333   shot down over northern Laos: An April coup in Laos collapsed resistance to the Laotian Communists (Pathet Lao). Historian Robert Warner described a haphazard, "unreal quality" to the short-lived coup that precipitated the introduction of U.S. warplanes in Laos, almost as a distraction from the Johnson administration's secret, protracted debate about war options in neighboring Vietnam. "Under house arrest, the prime minister [Souvanna Phouma] appeared on the balcony of his official residence," wrote Warner. "The U.S. Ambassador, Leonard Under, shouted encouragement to him from the garden. Within hours the right-wing generals were quarreling with one another." Warner, *Back Fire,* pp. 136–38; Gravel, ed., *Pentagon Papers,* vol. 3, pp. 172–74, 180; Shapley, *Promise and Power,* p. 300.
333   notifying congressional leaders: LBJ phone call with Carl Albert, June 9, 1964, Cit. 3649, Audiotape WH6406.04, LBJ.
333   "too big a deal of it": LBJ phone call with Hubert Humphrey, June 9, 1964, Cit. 3653, Audiotape WH6406.04, LBJ.
333   "If they'll just quit advancing": LBJ phone call with Mike Mansfield, June 9, 1964, Cit. 3651, Audiotape WH6406.04, LBJ.
334   "If we're gonna stay": LBJ phone call with Robert McNamara, June 9, 1964, Cit. 3663, Audiotape WH6406.04, LBJ.
334   Marshall called Lee White: Lee White file memo, June 10, 1964, HU2/St9, LG/St. Augustine, LBJ.
334   SCLC sent a telegram: UPI news story of June 9, 1964, FK-384.
334   Clarence Jones orchestrated: Hoover to Walter Jenkins, June 10, 1964, FK-377.
334   threats against King were not a federal matter: Ibid., p. 2.
334   "Dr. King—this is the letter": Young, handwritten note on Young to Douglass and Hotchkiss, June 9, 1964, A/KP36f15.
334   took the Senate floor at 7:38 P.M.: Whalen and Whalen, *The Longest Debate,* p. 195.
334   "749 years ago next Monday": *Congressional Record,* June 9, 1964, p. S13188.
334   "when it comes to employment": Ibid., p. S13150.
334   "a woman of one race": Ibid., p. S13201.
335   Andrew Young walked again: Colburn, *Racial Change,* p. 90; Good, *Trouble I've Seen,* pp. 92–93.
335   watched Young rise slowly: Int. Willie Bolden, May 14, 1992; int. Andrew Young, Oct. 26, 1991; Young, *A Way Out of No Way,* pp. 90–94.
335   "The thud of the kicks": *Jacksonville Journal,* June 10, 1964, p. 10.
335   as Martin Luther King left Atlanta: King arrived in Jacksonville by plane and drove toward St. Augustine at 10:40 A.M., twenty minutes before the cloture vote began in Washington. SAC, Jacksonville, teletype to Director, FBI, June 10, 1964, FSA-1388.
335   "I have attempted to reach": *Congressional Record,* June 9, 1964, p. S13206.
336   "curse of Noah": Ibid., p. S13207 (from Genesis 9:25).
336   "thy cattle gender": Ibid. (from Leviticus 19:19).
336   "to do what I will": Ibid. (from Matthew 20:15).
336   "even in heaven": Ibid. (from 1 Peter 3:22).
336   "the verbiage of the Declaration": Ibid., p. S13208.
336   "If all men": Ibid. (from Matthew 25:1–13).
336   "from the garden of Mrs. Humphrey": Ibid., p. S13207.
336   "But the Scriptural": Ibid., p. S13208.
336   after fourteen hours: Whalen and Whalen, *The Longest Debate,* p. 197.
336   fn filibuster filled: Ibid., p. 200; Graham, *The Civil Rights Era,* p. 151.

336   Californian Clair Engle: NYT, June 11, 1964, p. 21.
336   "we voted cloture": PPP, June 10, 1964, pp. 762–65.
336   "Hello, hero": PDD, 6:30 P.M., June 10, 1964, LBJ.
336   Lynda Bird's hamburger party: Johnson, *White House Diary*, pp. 162–64.
337   "Open up some communication": LBJ phone call with Lee White, June 10, 1964, Cit. 3671, Audiotape WH6406.05, LBJ.
337   "planting political stories": Cf. LBJ phone call with George Reedy, June 9, 1964, Cit. 3647, Audiotape WH6406.04, LBJ.
337   "the nicest thing": LBJ phone call with Robert Kennedy, June 11, 1964, Cit. 3699, Audiotape WH6406.06, LBJ.
337   "do a little heavy thinking": LBJ phone call with Richard Russell, June 11, 1964, Cit. 3680-81, Audiotape WH6406.05, LBJ.
337   "magnificent drama taking place": MLK address of June 10, 1964 (misdated June 11, 1964), A/KS7.
338   repeat the 40 percent loss: Lee White memo of June 10, 1964, David Colburn Papers, UF.
338   White House brokered messages: Ibid. Also White to MLK and Robert Hayling, June 11, 1964, Gen. HU2/ST9, LBJ; Douglass Cater to LBJ, June 11, 1964, David Colburn Papers, UF; Carl Holman to William L. Taylor, June 11, 1964, David Colburn Papers, UF; Judge Bryan Simpson to Assistant Deputy Attorney General Joseph P. Dolan, June 11, 1964, Box 7, Burke Marshall Papers, JFK.
338   "The Governor said that he would talk": Lee White memo of June 10, 1964, David Colburn Papers, UF.
338   fn "we are not going": Mrs. Edwin Price to Simpson, June 10, 1964, Bryan Simpson Papers, UF.
338   fn "how does it feel": W. Forrest Taylor to Simpson, Aug. 20, 1964, Ibid.
338   fn "You S.O.B.": "A mad citizen" to Simpson, Sept. 8, 1964, Ibid.
339   King presented himself for lunch: CD, June 13–19, 1964, p. 1; PC, June 20, 1964, p. 1; *Jet*, June 25, 1964, pp. 14–19; *Miami Herald*, June 12, 1964, p. 1; Colburn, *Racial Change*, pp. 91–92.
339   arrests for breach of peace: SAC, Jacksonville, to Director, June 11, 1964, FSA-1404.
339   Klansmen dressed as women: *Jet*, June 25, 1964, p. 16.
339   "Had it not been": WMBR (Jacksonville) radio special, *St. Augustine, Florida*, Tape No. 64005-NWR, PEA.
339   brick borders from public flower beds: NYT, June 12, 1964.
339   told the FBI they wanted to move King: SAC, Jacksonville, to Director, June 12, 1964, FSA-1403.
339   "Medgar Evers was just": Hartley, "A Long, Hot Summer," p. 53, in Garrow, ed., *St. Augustine*.
339   inches from a German shepherd guard dog: *Miami Herald*, June 14, 1964, p. 14.
340   "can be mobilized": Reddick to MLK, June 19, 1964, A/KP20f5.
340   fn "He gave every hearer": Harold H. Martin, "George Wallace Shakes Up the Political Scene," *Saturday Evening Post*, May 9, 1964, p. 87.
340   "great personal strife": Brando to MLK, June 10, 1964, A/KP4f46.
340   "Dear Sy": MLK to Rabbi Israel S. Dresner, June 12, 1964, A/KP8f32.

25. JAIL MARCHES

343   On Friday, June 12: Jacksonville LHM dated June 15, 1964, FSA-1438; NYT, June 13, 1964, p. 21. (The *Times* referred to Williams, a relative newcomer to its news pages, as a Hispanic "Jose" instead of the correct "Hosea," perhaps because his name was commonly pronounced with only two syllables.)
343   "We're not gonna be put in chains": Good, *Trouble I've Seen*, p. 96.
343   whiff of legend about Stoner: Massengill, *Portrait of a Racist*, p. 10; Carter, *Politics of Rage*, pp. 164–65.
344   "You need to learn more": Stoner to Police Commissioner Stephen Kennedy, Aug. 6, 1959, FEM-NR.
344   specialized in anti-Jewish polemics: "Down with the Jews," a circular by Stoner dated April 30, 1946, is one of several documents attached to a 1964 investigative report solicited by Judge Bryan Simpson. Another is a *Miami Herald* editorial dated June 6, 1947, which attacks Stoner for mailing a pamphlet stating, "The Jews are too evil to be allowed to live." Bryan Simpson Papers, UF.
344   friend and fellow stump speaker: "Portrait of an Extremist," *Saturday Evening Post*, Aug. 22, 1964, pp. 80–83.
344   doctrines of Dr. Wesley Swift: Ibid. Also Massengill, *Portrait of a Racist*, pp. 214–17, 274–85.
344   inspire white supremacy: Massengill, *Portrait of a Racist*, pp. 9–10, 239.
344   "When they said that": Good, *Trouble I've Seen*, p. 96.
344   "The coons have been parading": NYT, June 12, 1964, p. 21.
344   Stoner led a double column: Colburn, *Racial Change*, p. 95.
345   "She'll Be Comin' 'Round the Mountain": Ibid. Also Good, *Trouble I've Seen*, pp. 97–98.
345   Slave Market on Saturday: Jacksonville teletype to Director, June 13, 1964, FSA-1402.
345   "I respect you": Smathers telegram to MLK, June 13, 1964, A/KP20f41.
345   White told King's staff: White memorandum for the files, June 13, 1964, Box 5, Lee White Papers, LBJ.
345   King delivered his Rip Van Winkle: NYT, June 15, 1964, p. 32.
345   arrest a Yale student: *Miami Herald*, June 15, 1964; Jacksonville LHM dated June 15, 1964, FSA-1438, p. 5.
345   "The gratitude of people": *Newsweek*, June 29, 1964, p. 26.
345   Yale's 263rd commencement: NYT, June 16, 1964, p. 34.

345   Sidney Poitier's home: New York LHM dated June 16, 1964, FMX-NR; Clarence Jones correlation summary dated Nov. 30, 1965, FJ-105, p. 4.

345   conceal his excitement: Int. Clarence Jones, Oct. 26, 1983; New York LHM dated June 16, 1964, FMX-NR.

345–46   He arrived at Poitier's: Boston LHM dated June 15, 1964, FMXNY-4565; Goldman, *Death and Life,* p. 195; Perry, *Malcolm,* p. 288.

346   Malcolm amplified his charges: Boston LHM dated June 15, 1964, FMXNY-4565, p. 8. When Lucille Karriem had fallen in love with a member of the Boston Temple, Malcolm explained, Captain Clarence X and Minister Louis had prevailed upon her during the Nation's premarital interrogation to confess the father of her children.

346   "brain trust": FBI wiretap of June 17, 1964, FMXNY-1-15a, pp. 2–3.

346   challenged Minister Louis: FBI wiretap of 12:02 A.M., June 14, 1964, FMXNY-1-12.

346   "Tell Minister Louis to stop": Karim, *Remembering Malcolm,* pp. 103–4.

346   "a few words": Wiretap summary of June 9, 1964, FMXNY-4636.

346   "going right after the whole thing": Wiretap summary of June 12, 1964, FMXNY-4636, p. 2.

346–47   crestfallen when Benjamin 2X arrived: Int. Benjamin Karim, March 19, 1991; Karim, *Remembering Malcolm,* pp. 183–84; *Saturday Evening Post,* Feb. 27, 1965, p. 29.

347   Benjamin could offer: Boston LHM dated June 18, 1964, FMXNY-4585, p. 1.

347   disaffected Muslims in the room: Boston LHM dated Aug. 7, 1964, FMXNY-4826; Boston LHM dated Sept. 16, 1964, FMXNY-4966, containing record of Aug. 26, 1964, int. of John Thimas, and Aug. 31, 1964, int. of Aubrey Barnette.

347   The chase began: Int. Benjamin Karim, March 19, 1991; Goldman, *Death and Life,* p. 194; Perry, *Malcolm,* p. 288.

348   "It was here": Boston LHM dated June 18, 1964, FMXNY-4585, p. 4.

348   Benjamin 2X returned: Wiretap log of June 14, 1964, FMXNY-1-12a.

348   delivered his bastardy speech: New York LHM dated June 15, 1964, FMXNY-4557.

348   "and talk some stuff": Wiretap log of June 15, 1964, 1:26 a.m., FMXNY-1-13.

348   thirty-two officers escorted: Goldman, *Death and Life,* pp. 195–98; Perry, *Malcolm,* pp. 290–93.

348   "just like the Boy Scouts": Int. Yusuf Shah (Captain Joseph), Oct. 17, 1991.

348   "cut him to pieces": Conversation of June 15 in wiretap summary dated June 24, 1964, FMXNY-4636.

348   "I found out that": *New York World Telegram,* June 18, 1964, p. 1.

348   "There is no people": *New York Herald Tribune,* June 16, 1964.

349   "Muslim Factions at War": NYAN, June 20, 1964, p. 1.

349   "Says Muhammad Brought Stork": *Philadelphia Tribune,* June 20, 1964, pp. 1, 24.

349   begged her favorite son: Clara Muhammad–Wallace Muhammad conversation of June 16 in wiretap summary dated June 18, 1964, FMXNY-4594.

349   Muslims carrying rifles: Goldman, *Death and Life,* p. 199; SAC, New York, to Director, June 16, 1964, FMX-116.

349   telephone dead at the house: Wiretap log of Malcolm X conversation, June 15, 1964, FMXNY-1-15a; NYAN, June 20, 1964, p. 1.

349   grace period of several months: Perry, *Malcolm,* p. 292.

349   Jackie Robinson had received: *Miami Herald,* June 17, 1964, p. 1; Jacksonville to Director, June 16, 1964, FSA-1445.

349   fifty-one demonstrators: Jacksonville LHM dated June 17, 1964, FSA-NR.

349   camera crew from Miami: WKCT-TV, Miami, *St. Augustine: Fountain of Dissent,* 1964, Part 3, PEA.

349   petitioned Burke Marshall: Jacksonville teletype to Director, June 15, 1964, FSA-1408.

350   staying at the Lincolnville home: Int. Henry and Katherine Twine, April 2, 1991.

350   eating figs off a tree: Int. Janie Jones Price, April 6, 1991.

350   "This is the old": Good, *Trouble I've Seen,* pp. 99–100.

350   lost twenty pounds: *Jacksonville Journal,* June 17, 1964, p. 4.

350   prepared the audience for a settlement: Jacksonville teletype to Director, June 16, 1964, FSA-1422.

350   "Thank you very kindly": WKCT-TV, Miami, *St. Augustine: Fountain of Dissent,* 1964, Part 3, PEA.

351   "How is St. Augustine?": LBJ phone call with Lee White, June 16, 1964, Cit. 3751, Audiotape WH6406.09, LBJ.

351   Ohio auditorium that night: Sutherland, *Letters from Mississippi,* pp. 5–6; Carson, *In Struggle,* p. 113; Rothschild, *Black and White,* p. 54; Cagin and Dray, *We Are Not Afraid,* pp. 29–33; Dittmer, *Local People,* pp. 242–44; int. Cleveland Sellers by William Link, May 10, 1989.

351   CBS television documentary: CBS Reports, *Mississippi and the Fifteenth Amendment,* aired Sept. 26, 1962.

351   SNCC members eyed them warily: Int. Charles Cobb, Aug. 29, 1991.

351   Drills in nonviolence: Cagin and Dray, *We Are Not Afraid,* p. 33; Blackstone, PBS documentary *Eyes on the Prize,* I, 5, *This is America? Mississippi: 1962–64,* aired Feb. 18, 1987.

351   "I met those SNCC": Evans, *Personal Politics,* p. 70.

351–52   Hollis Watkins could not bear it.": Int. Hollis Watkins, June 22, 1992.

352   ten stewards of Mount Zion and Cole beating: NYT, June 28, 1964, p. 47; Huie, *Three Lives,* pp. 84–89; Holt, *The Summer,* pp. 266–67; Whitehead, *Attack on Terror,* pp. 47–51; Mars, *Witness,* pp. 168–75; Dittmer, *Local People,* p. 247.

352   "Father, I stretch my hands to Thee": A Methodist martyrdom hymn attributed to Charles Wesley, 1707–88, revised in the 1930s by J. Jefferson Cleveland and Verolga Nix.

353   fn "We are asking": Moses to LBJ, June 14, 1964, A/SN100f14.

353   another COFO press release: COFO press release of June 17, 1964, A/SN100f14.

353   orchestrated letters to Washington: Form letter to LBJ dated June 17, 1964, A/SN10014; reply to Clarence J. Harris from Lee White, June 29, 1964, A/SN100f12.

353   "Although on the surface": Lee White to LBJ, June 17, 1964, Ex HU 2/ST 24, LBJ.

353   James Lawson addressed: Sutherland, *Letters from Mississippi,* pp. 29–30.

353   John Doar warned: McAdam, *Freedom Summer,* p. 67; Dittmer, *Local People,* p. 245.

353   Forman denounced: Int. John Doar, May 12, 1986; int. Robert P. Moses by Joseph Sinsheimer, Dec. 5, 1984; int. Robert P. Moses, Feb. 15, 1991; Sutherland, *Letters from Mississippi,* p. 12; Huie, *Three Lives,* p. 94.

353   as after the Freedom Rides in 1961: Branch, *Parting,* pp. 485–88.

353   "He is more or less the Jesus": Sutherland, *Letters from Mississippi,* p. 15.

353–54   "record our profound": Ibid., p. 36.

354   "for the ideal naive": Ibid., p. 18.

354   "keep your eyes open": William Hodes letter to "Family," June 22, 1964, William Hodes Files, SHSW.

354   Wednesday night, June 17: Jacksonville LHM dated June 18, 1964, FSA-NR.

354   retained his customary long-windedness: Int. Israel Dresner, July 31, 1991.

354   Williams suffered a ribbing: Int. Hosea Williams, Oct. 29, 1991.

354   Vivian led the rabbis: Jacksonville teletype to Director, June 18, 1964, FSA-1427; Jacksonville LHM dated June 19, 1964, FSA-NR; NYT, June 19, 1964, p. 1; Colburn, *Racial Change,* pp. 98–100.

354   "Hold me, baby, I'm scared": Good, *Trouble I've Seen,* p. 103.

355   "a study of the legitimate": *Florida Times-Union,* June 18, 1964, p. 22.

355   King had responded positively: MLK statement of June 17, 1964, A/KS; *Newsweek,* June 29, 1964, p. 26.

355   hoisted a Confederate flag: *Florida Times-Union,* June 21, 1964, p. 22.

355   "Racial harmony has existed": Presentment of St. Johns County Grand Jury, June 18, 1964, served upon MLK at 5:12 P.M., A/KP20f41.

355   "not only an impractical request": Handwritten statement on the back of ibid. Also Jacksonville teletype to Director, June 20, 1964, FSA-1429.

355   "our prayers and best wishes": Proceedings of the 75th Annual Convention of the Central Conference of American Rabbis, June 17–19, 1964, p. 230, AJA.

355   prisoners refused an order: Int. Balfour Brickner, Feb. 4, 1991; int. Israel Dresner, July 31, 1991; int. Murray Saltzman, Jan. 8, 1991.

356   "We shall not forget": "Why We Went: A Joint Letter from the Rabbis Arrested in St. Augustine," by Eugene Borowitz, Balfour Brickner, Israel Dresner, Daniel Fogel, Jerrold Goldstein, Joel Goor, Joseph Herzog, Norman Hirsh, Leon Jick, Richard Levy, Eugene Lipman, Michael Robinson, B. T. Rubenstein, Murray Saltzman, Allen Secher, Clyde T. Sills, and Albert Vorspan, AJA.

356   Nelson Mandela and six other: NYT, June 12, 1964, p. 12, June 25, 1964, p. 12; WP, Feb. 12, 1994, p. 13. The Nation of Islam's newspaper, *Muhammad Speaks,* published excerpts of Mandela's speeches to the court at his 1962 and 1964 trials. MS, July 17, 1964, pp. 12, 14.

356   Governor William Scranton: NYT, June 12, 1964, p. 1, June 13, 1964, p. 1.

356   Supreme Court required: NYT, June 16, 1964, p. 1; *Newsweek,* June 29, 1964, p. 22.

356   thirty-four roll call votes: Whalen and Whalen, *The Longest Debate,* p. 209.

356   "death scene arias": Ibid., p. 212.

356   Goldwater flew to a farm: NYT, June 19, 1964, p. 1.

356   fuming that Eisenhower: John Grenier int. by Jack Bass and Walter De Vries, A-9, No. 4007, UNC.

356–57   counsel of his legal advisers: Edwards, *Goldwater,* p. 239.

357   decisive majority of seventy-three: Whalen and Whalen, *The Longest Debate,* pp. 215–17.

357   retrieved copies of FBI surveillance photographs: Cf. SAC, New York, to Director, June 29, 1964, FK-NR, responding to Hoover's order of June 19, 1964.

357   "because of the occupations": Garrow, *FBI and Martin,* pp. 116–17.

357   followed Clarence Jones: Cf. handwritten surveillance logs for the last week of June 1964, FJNY-NR.

357   "the most pertinent": Director to SAC, New York, June 25, 1964, FR-NR.

357   "goes further to invest": PPP, LBJ statement of June 19, 1964, p. 787.

357   San Francisco crowd of thirty thousand: NYT, June 21, 1964, p. 1; *Newsweek,* June 29, 1964, p. 21.

357   fn "Well, he's got a lot": LBJ phone call with Robert Kennedy, June 20, 1964, Cit. 3800, Audiotape WH6406.12, LBJ.

357   "I have come to California": PPP, LBJ at Irvine, California, June 20, 1964, pp. 793–95.

357   "wealthy industrialists": Tom Wicker, in NYT, June 22, 1964, p. 18.

358   bar mitzvah party of young Lyle Peskin: PDD, "12:30 A.M. entry," June 21, 1964.

358   bowling over Howard Smith: O'Brien to LBJ, June 18, 1964, Box 3, Henry Wilson Papers, LBJ; Whalen and Whalen, *The Longest Debate,* pp. 218–20.

358   "Y'all want civil rights": LBJ phone call with House Minority Leader Charles Halleck, June 22, 1964, Cit. 3810, Audiotape WH6406.12, LBJ.

358   urged Roy Wilkins and Whitney Young: PDD, June 19, 1964.

358   "I'm just afraid": LBJ phone call with Roy Wilkins, June 19, 1964, Cit. 3791, Audiotape WH6406.11, LBJ.

359   "dawning of new hope": NYT, June 20, 1964, p. 12.

359   "niggers want to integrate": Colburn, *Racial Change,* p. 103.
359   waded into the Atlantic Ocean: Jacksonville LHM dated June 22, 1964, FSA-1452.
359   slugged to their knees: NYT, June 21, 1964, p. 69; int. Dorothy Cotton, July 6, 1983.
359   "I can't understand why any white": NYT, June 21, 1964, p. 68.
359   executive order: "State of Florida, Executive Department, Tallahassee, *Executive Order Number Two,*" signed by Governor Farris Bryant, June 20, 1964, Bryan Simpson Papers, UF.
359   edict further ensnarled: Colburn, *Racial Change,* p. 105.
359   Florida motorist came upon: *St. Petersburg Times,* June 28, 1964, p. 4.
359   Lines of black and white marchers: NYT, June 22, 1964, p. 16; Jacksonville LHM dated June 22, 1964, FSA-1452, pp. 3–4.
360   Chicago's Soldier Field: NYT, June 22, 1964, p. 16; *Jet,* July 9, 1964, pp. 22–25; ANP press release for June 22, 1964, b107f4, Claude Barnett Papers, CHS.
360   pitched the eighth perfect game: NYT, June 22, 1964, p. 1. Of the seven previous perfect games, two had occurred in 1880, before the pitching distance was lengthened from 45 feet to 60.5 feet, and a third from 1917 carried an asterisk because the original starting pitcher, Babe Ruth, gave up a walk before being ejected. Ruth's substitute, Ernie Shore, came on to record the required twenty-seven consecutive outs, beginning when the walked leadoff runner was caught stealing second.
360   President for Life: NYT, June 22, 1964, p. 12.
360   fn "The Catholic church": Very Reverend Monsignor John P. Burns to MLK, June 18, 1964, with (attached) Chancellor Irvine Nugent to Burns, quoting Archbishop Hurley, June 18, 1964, A/KP20f41.
360   King awakened his former professor: Int. Harold DeWolf, May 9, 1983.

26: Bogue Chitto Swamp

361   Louise Hermey of Drew: Cagin and Dray, *We Are Not Afraid,* pp. 34, 41–43; Dittmer, *Local People,* p. 248.
361   "we're all sitting here": Sutherland, *Letters from Mississippi,* pp. 25–26.
361   nestled within a cluster: Cagin and Dray, *We Are Not Afraid,* pp. 248, 255.
362   "felt a prickly sensation": Mary King, *Freedom Song,* p. 378.
362   spread through emergency networks: Ibid., pp. 378–82; Holt, *The Summer,* pp. 189–90; Farmer, *Lay Bare the Heart,* pp. 271-73; Cagin and Dray, *We Are Not Afraid,* pp. 318–19.
362   "We've had discussions all winter": Belfrage, *Freedom Summer,* p. 17.
362   Rita Schwerner appeared: Cagin and Dray, *We Are Not Afraid,* pp. 320–21.
363   "It suddenly became clear": Belfrage, *Freedom Summer,* p. 18.
363   Moses drifted into solitary: Ibid. Hampton, *Voices of Freedom,* p. 190; int. Dorothy Zellner, Dec. 12, 1991.
363   "You are not responsible": Int. Victoria Gray Adams, May 14, 1991.
363   Edwin King passed along: Cagin and Dray, *We Are Not Afraid,* p. 347; Mary King, *Freedom Song,* p. 382; Holt, *The Summer,* p. 190.
363   James Farmer got through: Lee White, memorandum to the files, June 23, 1964, Ex HU2/ST24, LBJ.
363   "Developments COFO": Thomas to Lowenstein, June 22, 1964, b9f315, Lowenstein Papers, UNC.
363   civic-minded local woman: Mars, *Witness,* pp. 84–86.
363   just after the local FBI agent: Cagin and Dray, *We Are Not Afraid,* pp. 322–23.
364   "If they're missing": NYT, June 23, 1964, p. 13.
364   led by an insurance executive: Mars, *Witness,* p. 92.
364   into the Turner Furniture Store: Reflections of Claude Sitton and Karl Fleming at the University of Mississippi symposium "Covering the South," April 3–5, 1987.
364   "I'll tell you what": Ibid.
364   "basic contribution to our": PPP, June 22, 1964, pp. 799–800.
364   At 5:20, he informed: Mary King, *Freedom Song,* pp. 383–84; Holt, *The Summer,* p. 192.
364   Marshall reached Robert Kennedy: Cagin and Dray, *We Are Not Afraid,* pp. 324–25.
364–65   Paul Good to "Just Sleeping": Good, *Trouble I've Seen,* pp. 107–13.
365   "3 in Rights Drive": NYT, June 23, 1964, p. 1.
365   escorted the Goodman parents: Mary King, *Freedom Song,* pp. 385–86.
365   Joachim Prinz: Prinz to Meyer Feldman, June 24, 1964, and Lee White to Juanita Roberts (for LBJ), June 26, 1964, Ex HU2/ST24, LBJ.
365   spotter planes: Holt, *The Summer,* pp. 192–93.
365   Johnson stuck to his breakneck schedule: PDD, June 23, 1964.
365   "Tell [McGeorge] Bundy to come on in.": PDD, 5:51 P.M., June 22, 1964.
365   Johnson told an impromptu: NYT, June 24, 1964, p. 1; PPP, June 23, 1964, pp. 802–8.
365   "I think it's the human": RFK phone call with Jack Valenti, 3:11 P.M., June 23, 1964, Cit. 3831, Audiotape WH6406.13, LBJ.
365   announcement that he would not run: NYT, June 24, 1964, p. 1.
365   "How old are these kids?": LBJ phone call with Nicholas Katzenbach, 3:35 P.M., June 23, 1964, Cit. 3832, Audiotape WH6406.13, LBJ.
365   Marshall suggested: LBJ phone call with Burke Marshall, 3:51 P.M., June 23, 1964, Cit. 3834, Audiotape WH6406.14, LBJ.
366   "Jim, we got three kids": LBJ phone call with James Eastland, 3:59 P.M., June 23, 1964, Cit. 3836, Audiotape WH6406.14, LBJ.

366 Proctor had roared: Whitehead, *Attack on Terror,* pp. 63–68; Cagin and Dray, *We Are Not Afraid,* pp. 338–40.

366 Sullivan had reviewed: Int. Joseph Sullivan, Feb. 3, 1991.

367 "I wanted you to know": LBJ phone call with J. Edgar Hoover, 4:05 P.M., June 23, 1964, Cit. 3837, Audiotape WH6406.14, LBJ.

367 five more phone calls: PDD, June 23, 1964. Hoover implied that the agents could not see through the car windows or open its doors to inspect for bodies. When Johnson impatiently asked "why in the hell they can't take a crowbar," Hoover improvised nervously. "Well, we've broken into the car," he said. "We got the crowbars there within I guess about a half hour ago. And uh, broke open the doors, which couldn't be opened any other way. And now they're … getting the particles on the inside of the car out, and preserving such that can be preserved." LBJ phone call with J. Edgar Hoover, 6:15 P.M., June 23, 1964, Cit. 3857, Audiotape WH6406.14, LBJ.

367 "offhand presumption": LBJ phone call with J. Edgar Hoover, 7:15 P.M., June 23, 1964, Cit. 3869, Audiotape WH6406.15, LBJ.

367 "expects 'em to turn up": LBJ phone call with James Eastland, 4:25 P.M., June 23, 1964, Cit. 3845, Audiotape WH6406.14, LBJ.

367 fn "You better comb": LBJ phone call with J. Edgar Hoover, 5:35 P.M., June 23, 1964, Cit. 3853, Audiotape WH6406.14, LBJ.

367 "every facility of the department": LBJ phone call with Robert McNamara, 5:44 P.M., June 23, 1964, Cit. 3855, Audiotape WH6406.14, LBJ; PDD, June 23, 1964.

367 COFO headquarters within thirty minutes: Holt, *The Summer,* p. 193; Mary King, *Freedom Song,* p. 387.

367 "The car has been found": Belfrage, *Freedom Summer,* p. 21.

367 Johnson conferred: PDD, 6:33 P.M. until 9:21 P.M., June 23, 1964; Burke Marshall Oral History, Oct. 28, 1968, LBJ; int. Burke Marshall, Sept. 26, 1984; int. John Doar, May 12, 1986; int. Nicholas Katzenbach, June 14, 1991; Cagin and Dray, *We Are Not Afraid,* p. 327.

368 "We got the ox in a ditch": LBJ phone call with Allen Dulles, 7:05 P.M., June 23, 1964, Cit. 3868, Audiotape WH6406.15, LBJ.

368 Robert Kennedy postponed: NYT, June 25, 1964, p. 1.

369 eliciting cries of amazement: Aaron Henry Oral History, Sept. 12, 1970, LBJ.

369 other federal buildings: Mary King, *Freedom Song,* p. 388.

369 "I have arrived safely": Prosecutive summary of Dec. 19, 1964, FMB-1613, p. 7.

369 Spike successfully implored: Ibid., p. 389; int. Robert P. Moses by Joseph Sinsheimer, Dec. 5, 1984.

369 Moses took a delegation: Stephan Bingham, "Mississippi Letter" of Feb. 15, 1965, p. 5, b32f367, Lowenstein Papers, UNC.

369 parried criticism: Int. Robert P. Moses, July 30, 1984.

369 "It is a dreadful thing to say": WP, June 29, 1964, cited in Cagin and Dray, *We Are Not Afraid,* p. 350.

369 caravan of movement cars: NYT, June 25, 1964, p. 1.

369 unproductive interview: Farmer, *Lay Bare the Heart,* pp. 272–76.

369 dramatic arrival of Allen Dulles: NYT, June 25, 1964, p. 1.

369 "Why can't the FBI": Cagin and Dray, *We Are Not Afraid,* p. 352.

369 At the Meridian airport: O'Reilly, *Racial Matters,* p. 165.

370 "Send him down there, too!": Int. Joseph Sullivan, Feb. 3, 1991; Whitehead, *Attack on Terror,* p. 75.

370 "take over the investigation": LBJ phone call with J. Edgar Hoover, 5:30 P.M., June 24, 1964, Cit. 3891, Audiotape WH6406.16, LBJ.

370 "in the very able hands": NYT, June 25, 1964, p. 18.

370 He received the private entreaties: NYT, June 26, 1964, pp. 1, 15.

370 briefings on Communist infiltration: Erle Johnston, Jr., to Gov. Paul Johnson, June 26, 1964, MSSC.

370 most reliably in Alabama: Memo on information "Received at 4:05 P.M., June 25, 1964," from Colonel Lingo, Alabama State Police, MSSC.

370 reverse conspiracy: Reports by Sovereignty Commission investigator A. L. Hopkins dated June 29 and July 3, 1964, MSSC.

370 "the manipulations of a soulless state": *Meridian Star,* June 26, 1964, p. 1, cited in Huie, *Three Lives,* pp. 128–29.

370 Rustin met with: Belfrage, *Freedom Summer,* p. 26.

371 "Then it happened": McAdam, *Freedom Summer,* p. 71.

371 baths in backyard tubs: Sutherland, *Letters from Mississippi,* p. 42.

371 "you feel the heat": Ibid., p. 39.

371 Ron Ridenhour turned up: NYT, June 25, 1964, p. 19, June 26, 1964, p. 14.

371 armed posse hijacked two volunteers: NYT, June 27, 1964, p. 10.

371 movement supporters flocked to Itta Bena: William Hodes letter to "folks," "evening" of June 25, 1964, William Hodes Files, SHSW.

372 far north as St. Louis: Int. William McGee, June 25, 1992.

372 mayor of Hollandale: Affidavit of Stokely Carmichael regarding events after 5:30 P.M., June 25, 1964, A/MFDP2f4.

372 Carmichael and Cobb continued: Affidavit of Stokely Carmichael regarding events after 10:30 P.M., June 25, 1964, A/MFDP2f4; affidavit of Charles Cobb regarding events after 10:30 P.M., June 25, 1964, A/MFDP2f4.

372 Cobb found himself pleading: Int. Charles Cobb, Aug. 20, 1991.

372 carefully prepared script: Int. Burke Marshall, Sept. 26, 1984; int. Nicholas Katzenbach, June 14, 1991.

372   sympathized with Hoover's complaint: Hoover memorandum of 1:15 P.M., June 26, 1964, regarding telephone call from Dulles and LBJ, FNCC-NR; Brennan to Sullivan re "Allen W. Dulles," June 29, 1964, FNCC-NR; "Briefing by Mr. Allen W. Dulles re His Trip to Mississippi for the President," June 26, 1964, Ex HU 2/ST 24, LBJ.

372–73   "ought to review the number of agents": LBJ phone call with Allen Dulles and J. Edgar Hoover, 1:17 P.M., June 26, 1964, Cit. 3921, Audiotape WH6406.17, LBJ.

373   FBI agents had arrested: NYT, June 27, 1964, p. 10.

373   "You dig it": William Hodes letter to "folks," June 26, 1964, William Hodes Files, SHSW.

373   "that horror-ridden state": NYT, June 27, 1964, p. 24.

373   So did John Doar: Int. John Doar, May 12, 1986.

373   Doar was hearing: Ibid.

374   "The kids are dead.": Belfrage, *Freedom Summer,* pp. 32–33.

374   He nearly begged: Sutherland, *Letters from Mississippi,* p. 31.

374   fn "We are fully committed": Moses statement, June 27, 1964, A/SN54f8.

374   untrained sympathizers stay out: Mary King, *Freedom Song,* p. 395.

374   rolled south from Ohio: Cagin and Dray, *We Are Not Afraid,* p. 353.

374   drag a fifty-mile stretch: NYT, June 28, 1964, p. 1.

27: BEACHHEADS

375   "Tell him I've sent eight helicopters": PDD, 12:24 P.M., June 25, 1964.

375   chronic Turkish-Greek violence: Ibid. NYT, June 26, 1964, p. 1; *Newsweek,* June 29, 1964, p. 28.

375   rescued John Herbers: NYT, June 23, 1964, p. 15.

375   Herbers moved on to Mississippi: NYT, June 26, 1964, p. 14.

375   Danish photographer: NYT, June 23, 1964, p. 15.

375   UPI reporter told FBI: Jacksonville LHM dated June 26, 1964, FSA-NR, pp. 1–2.

376   quartet of Boston University professors: Int. Harold DeWolf, May 9–10, 1983; int. Paul Deats, Aug. 1, 1984; int. Paul Deats by Larry Elswit, Jan. 13, 1993; Garrow, *Bearing the Cross,* pp. 334–35. Aside from Neil Richardson, DeWolf's colleagues were Paul Deats, professor of Christian social ethics, and Albert Beisel, professor of constitutional law.

376   six concrete blocks: Hartley, "A Long, Hot Summer," p. 65, in Garrow, ed., *St. Augustine.*

376   withdrawal on Thursday morning left DeWolf: Int. Harold DeWolf, May 9–10, 1983; int. Paul Deats, Aug. 1, 1984.

376   second wade-in of the day: NYT, June 26, 1964, p. 1; Fred Shuttlesworth Oral History, Nov. 19, 1969, A/OH.

376   Rev. Elizabeth Miller: "Report on St. Augustine, Florida," by Rev. Elizabeth J. Miller, A/KP20f43; PC, July 11, 1964, p. 2.

376   fn "I felt that we could not": PC, July 4, 1964, p. 3.

377   Walter Hamphshire of New Jersey: *Newsweek,* July 6, 1964, p. 16.

377   bleeding white fighter triggered: Colburn, *Racial Change,* p. 107.

377   "They didn't beat the niggers!": NYT, June 26, 1964, p. 14.

377   "blows struck by": Jacksonville LHM dated June 26, 1964, FSA-NR, p. 3.

377   five hundred segregationists rallied: Colburn, *Racial Change,* pp. 1–12. The FBI estimated four hundred in ibid.; *Newsweek* and the *New York Times* estimated eight hundred.

377   DeWolf was startled: Int. Harold DeWolf, May 10, 1983.

377   "bigger than the FBI": Jacksonville LHM dated June 22, 1964, FSA-1452, p. 5.

377   vest made from a Confederate flag: CDD (Gary edition), July 6, 1964, p. 1.

378   he worked the crowd: WMBR-Jacksonville, *St. Augustine, Florida,* Tape No. 64005, NWR, PEA; Larry Goodwin, "Anarchy in St. Augustine," *Harper's* magazine, Jan. 1965, p. 79; Colburn, *Racial Change,* p. 8.

378   "There they come!": Int. Harold DeWolf, May 10, 1983.

378   Shuttlesworth's nightly march: Hartley, "A Long, Hot Summer," pp. 67–68, in Garrow, ed., *St. Augustine;* Garrow, *Bearing the Cross,* pp. 334–35.

378   a pause: Colburn, *Racial Change,* p. 9.

378   "A number of Negro women": NYT, June 26, 1964, pp. 1, 14.

378   Frady was trampled: Ibid.; *Newsweek,* July 6, 1964, p. 16.

378   headlong into a parking meter: Fred Shuttlesworth Oral History, Nov. 19, 1969, A/OH.

378   Davis later conceded in court: PC, July 11, 1964, p. 2.

379   "seemed primarily interested": Jacksonville LHM dated June 26, 1964, FSA-NR, pp. 3–4.

379   Miller learned to recognize: "Report on St. Augustine, Florida," by Rev. Elizabeth J. Miller, A/KP20f43, p. 6.

379   "This is the worst night": NY LHM dated June 26, 1964, FSA-NR.

379   call the Goodman parents: Levison wiretap log of June 27, 1964, FLNY-9-577a.

379   encouraging Marshall to push: MLK to Marshall, June 24, 1964, A/KP24f22.

379   "a total absence of hand-clapping": Tobias Simon to Honorable Bryan Simpson, June 29, 1964, Simpson Papers, UF.

379   out-of-town truce talks: Garrow, *Bearing the Cross,* pp. 335–36; int. Harold DeWolf, May 9–10, 1983.

380   Simpson wedged himself tightly: NYT, June 27, 1964, p. 1; PC, July 11, 1964, p. 2.

380   dared Judge Simpson: Farris Bryant Oral History, March 5, 1971, pp. 31–32, LBJ.

380   "You have to be": FBI wiretap transcript of June 28, 1964, FMXNY-1-26, pp. 4–5.

380 filled the Harlem Armory: NYT, June 29, 1964, p. 1.
381 "if he is the leader": Goldman, *Death and Life*, p. 202.
381 "a lot of those fishes and freaks": Elijah Muhammad wiretap transcript of June 29, 1964, FMXNY-4843, p. 2.
381 Jones commended Malcolm's statement: New York LHM dated July 1, 1964, FMXNY-4669.
381 "7:08 P.M. Jones left": "Physical surveillance of Clarence B. Jones on 6/29/64" (two pages), FJNY-NR.
381 only ninety members: New York LHM dated July 2, 1964, FMXNY-4675.
381 "We will creep into Florida": *Jet*, July 16, 1964, pp. 18–19.
381 "If the federal government": SAC, New York, to Director, June 30, 1964, FMXNY-1-28; Malcolm X telegram to MLK, June 30, 1964, A/KP15f16.
381 Muhammad laughed when: Elijah Muhammad wiretap transcript of July 1, 1964, FMXNY-4843, pp. 3–4.
381 "He is dying a little": Elijah Muhammad wiretap transcript of June 29, 1964, FMXNY-4843, p. 3.
382 Bryant devised a blustering gambit: Garrow, *Bearing the Cross*, p. 337; Colburn, *Racial Change*, p. 109; Abernathy, *Walls Came Tumbling*, p. 293.
382 Lynch was rallying segregationists: Jacksonville to Director, July 1, 1964, FSA-1476.
382 fresh criminal charges: Ibid.
382 hastily composed statement: King handwritten statement nd (June 30, 1964), A/KS.
382 "If things go as they are expected": WMBR-Jacksonville, *St. Augustine, Florida,* Tape No. 64005, NWR, PEA.
382 Outside influences have created: Bishop West to Rev. Seymour, July 1, 1964, SAHS.
383 "people will think": Colburn, *Racial Change*, pp. 170–72.
383 "Either that or be converted": Notes of Trinity Parish Church vestry meeting, July 1, 1964, 4:30 P.M., Colburn Papers, UF.
383 transfer out of Florida: Colburn, *Racial Change*, p. 172.
383 "If they [Mississippi authorities] encourage": Katzenbach to LBJ, with cover notes to Lee White and George Reedy, July 1, 1964, Ex HU, Box 26, LBJ.
383–84 "Dear Lyndon": Aubrey Williams to LBJ, July 1, 1964, WHCF, Name File, LBJ.
384 "the correct one": LBJ to Aubrey Williams, July 14, 1964, Ex CO1/Southeast Asia, LBJ.
384 "poor ol' Herb Wolfe": LBJ phone call with George Smathers, July 1, 1964, Cit. 4106, Audiotape WH6407.01, LBJ.
384 gruff, savvy chain-smoker: Int. Victoria Murphy, Aug. 17, 1993.
384 pick up an early draft: PDD, July 1, 1964.
384 filed paternity suits: Perry, *Malcolm*, pp. 305–8.
384 "Things are pretty hot": Goldman, *Death and Life*, pp. 203–4.
384 "merely another effort on the part": Domestic Intelligence Division unsigned cover note to teletype dated July 4, 1964, FMX-126.
385 "she didn't want to hear": Wiretap summary of July 6, 1964, conversation in SAC, Chicago, to SAC, Buffalo, FMXNY-4845, pp. 1–2.
385 "she feels that they don't": Report of July 7, 1964, wiretap conversation in SAC, New York, to Director, July 8, 1964, FMXNY-4696.
385 members to get him: Chicago LHM dated July 10, 1964, FMXNY-4710, p. 6; SAC, New York, to Director, July 7, 1964, FMX-133; Malcolm X wiretap transcript of 2:03 A.M., July 5, 1964, FMXNY-1-33.
385 Sharrieff testified in open court: CDD, July 6, 1964, pp. 1, 8; CDD, July 9, 1964, p. 3.
385 "Uncle Wallace told me": CDD, July 8, 1964, p. 12.
385 rushed to the police and FBI: Statement of Hassan Sharrieff at 3rd District police station, dated June 23, 1964, plus two memos dated July 8, 1964, "Muslims—Chicago Branch," RS File No. 589, CHS; SAC, Chicago, to Director, July 10, 1964, FMXNY-4711; Chicago LHM dated July 10, 1964, FMXNY-4710; SAC, Chicago, to Director, July 23, 1964, FMXNY-4766, pp. 7–8.
385 "I know they are fanatics": CDD, July 8, 1964, p. 3.
385 "Often I would imagine": "In the Name of Allah, God, the Originator," manifesto by Wallace D. Muhammad, July 1964, from files of Gladys Towles Root, courtesy of Bruce Perry.
385 guided the Sinatra family: Perry, *Malcolm*, p. 306.
385 wide black sombrero: CD, July 14, 1964, p. 5.
385 "DENY PATERNITY SUITS": CDD, July 6, 1964, p. 1.
385 "False Charges Filed": *Chicago New Crusader*, July 11, 1964, p. 5.
385 "Negro Prostitutes Accuse": *Los Angeles Herald-Dispatch*, July 11, 1964, p. 1.
385 "injected with medicines": *Los Angeles Herald-Dispatch*, July 16, 1964, p. 3.
385 flew to Egypt: New York report dated Jan. 20, 1965, FMX-215, pp. 102–3.
385 majority of his remaining days: Karim, *Remembering Malcolm*, pp. 176–77.
386 "Malcolm X Flees": PC, July 11, 1964, p. 1.
386 "Malcolm X Flys to African Parley": *New York World Telegram*, July 10, 1964.
386 "said he intended": NYT, July 14, 1964.
386 "After a while in America": Malcolm X, *The Autobiography*, p. 370.

28. TESTING FREEDOM

387 swore in General Maxwell Taylor: NYT, July 3, 1964, p. 1.
387 "In a few minutes": Whalen and Whalen, *The Longest Debate*, p. 225.

387   "we are past the danger point": PDD, July 2, 1964.

387   lemon cake at a seventeenth-birthday: Johnson, *White House Diary*, p. 173.

388   "One hundred and eighty-eight": PPP, July 2, 1964, pp. 842–44.

388   seventy-two ceremonial pens: Whalen and Whalen, *The Longest Debate*, p. 227.

388   curtail street demonstrations: Lee White, "Memorandum to the Files," July 6, 1964, Ex LE/HU2, LBJ.

388   filed suit within the hour: *Heart of Atlanta Motel v. United States*, 379 U.S. 241 (1964); Graham, *Civil Rights Era*, p. 170.

388   fn "The photographs of Lester Maddox": Maddox, *Speaking Out*, p. 57.

388   "As long as it is there": Stern, *Calculating Visions*, p. 185.

388–89   rescued Hollywood actor Jack Palance: *Newsweek*, July 20, 1964, p. 32; AC, Aug. 7, 1994, p. M4.

389   "could cause a great deal": WLBT news film 2730/F1730, MDAH.

389   "Guess *she* will never": William Hodes to "Folks," July 3, 1964, William Hodes Files, SHSW.

389   Moses clung to movement policy: Sutherland, *Letters from Mississippi*, p. 62; int. Dorothy Zellner, Dec. 12, 1991.

389   Word reached Greenwood: "Grats to the St. Augustine businessmen, if they really do what they say they will." William Hodes to "Folks," July 3, 1964, William Hodes Files, SHSW.

389   Rev. Samuel Wells blessed: Int. Rev. Samuel B. Wells, July 9, 1985.

389   blue-ribbon NAACP delegation: July 6, 1964, p. 1, July 7, 1964, p. 20, July 8, 1964, p. 19; Dittmer, *Local People*, p. 276.

389   fn Robert E. Lee Hotel: Report of A. L. Hopkins, Investigator, July 9, 1964, MSSC; NYT, July 9, 1964, p. 16; Cagin and Dray, *We Are Not Afraid*, p. 379.

389   SCLC conference in Birmingham: Garrow, *Bearing the Cross*, p. 339; King statement of July 16, 1964, A/KS.

389   "White folks act like": Young to Septima Clark, July 9, 1964, A/SC154f4.

390   "I don't worry about a gun": Belfrage, *Freedom Summer*, p. 72.

390   nearly wept to hear himself: Holt, *The Summer*, p. 45.

390   no Negro in Greenwood would dare: William Hodes to "Folks," July 4, 1964, William Hodes Files, SHSW.

390   Silas McGhee: Belfrage, *Freedom Summer*, pp. 130–31; von Hoffman, *Mississippi Notebook*, pp. 106–8; Dittmer, *Local People*, p. 276; Payne, *Light of Freedom*, p. 210.

390   "Well, you wasn't nowhere": Int. Silas McGhee, June 26, 1992.

390   Lewis moved eastward to Selma: Garrow, *Protest at Selma*, p. 34; Jerry DeMuth, "Black Belt, Alabama," *The Commonweal*, Aug. 7, 1964, pp. 536–39.

391   "Would appreciate any mail": Mary Varela to Andrew Young, Jan. 24, 1964, and Andrew Young to Mary Varela, Jan. 30, 1964, A/SC134f8. Varela, who recruited six Northern students for a Selma Literacy Project, expressed similar apprehensions in a letter to James Forman of SNCC: "The post office as you know is the intelligence center (in addition to the phone company) for the posse etc. I was doing all right until someone slipped up and sent me a check from the office in a letterhead envelope." Varela to Forman, March 11, 1964, A/SN23f3.

391   introduced himself: Remarks of Silas Norman at Session No. 6 of the Trinity College SNCC Reunion, April 14–16, 1988, pp. 2–12, transcript courtesy of Jack Chatfield.

391   "There's niggers in the Wilby!": Chestnut, *Black in Selma*, p. 174.

391   deputies invaded behind tear gas: Jerry DeMuth, "Black Belt, Alabama," *The Commonweal*, Aug. 7, 1964, p. 537; NYT, July 6, 1964, p. 19.

391   Lewis led seventy aspiring voters: NYT, July 7, 1964, p. 20.

391   "The Negroes were marched": Ibid.

391   Hare issued an injunction: *Selma Times-Journal*, July 10, 1964, p. 1; Chestnut, *Black in Selma*, pp. 172–78.

391   "New Law Hoax, Fraud": *Selma Times-Journal*, July 5, 1964, p. 1.

391   "liberalism is destroying democracy": *Selma Times-Journal*, July 10, 1964, p. 1.

391   Harold DeWolf wrote Martin: DeWolf to "Martin and Coretta," July 3, 1964, A/KP8f24; Robert Dyal to Bill Moyers, July 29, 1964, WH Name File, Box 144, LBJ.

392   Klan marched on the night of July 4: Colburn, *Racial Change*, p. 111.

392   fishing off a bridge: NYT, July 6, 1964, p. 19.

392   Brock kept his word: Jacksonville FBI report dated July 24, 1964, FSA-NR, pp. 7–8.

392   "claiming that they were afraid": Lee White to LBJ, July 15, 1964, HU2/ST9, LG/St. Augustine, LBJ.

392   4th of July picnic: Int. Ellen Dahmer, Vernon Dahmer, Jr., et al., June 21, 1992; int. Lorne Cress-Love, June 25, 1994; int. Stanley Zibulsky, June 26, 1994.

392   Hattiesburg's Freedom Schools: Sandy Leigh to Bob Moses, "Report from Hattiesburg," July 8–14, 1964, A/SN98f24; Sutherland, *Letters from Mississippi*, pp. 90–117; Holt, *The Summer*, pp. 97–128; Rothschild, *Black and White*, pp. 93–121; Dittmer, *Local People*, pp. 257–61.

392   eight to eighty-two: Terri Shaw memo, "Re: Hattiesburg Project," July 7, 1964, A/SN98f24, p. 3.

393   how to teach movement history: Sutherland, *Letters from Mississippi*, p. 93.

393   teachers abandoned lectures: Int. Richard Kelly, June 25, 1994; int. Lorne Cress-Love, June 25, 1994; int. Stanley Zibulsky, June 26, 1994.

393   In Moss Point: Int. Lawrence Guyot, Feb. 1, 1991.

393   Stallworth fell wounded: Sutherland, *Letters from Mississippi*, pp. 119–21.

393   fn "sharing their terror with them": NYT, July 6, 1964, p. 19.

393   night riders bombed the group: *Los Angeles Herald-Dispatch*, July 25, 1964, p. 1; Harris, *Dreams Die*

Hard, pp. 60–63; Dittmer, *Local People,* pp. 266–68; Mary King, *Freedom Song,* p. 418; Payne, *Light of Freedom,* p. 223; int. Rev. Harry Bowie by Jack Bass and Walter De Vrie, March 31, 1974, Series A-98, Collection 4007, pp. 3–4, UNC.

393   arrested Rev. Robert Beech: Holt, *The Summer,* p. 214.

394   supervised the pilgrim clergy: Int. Robert Beech, Dec. 8, 1991; Holt, *The Summer,* p. 86.

394   Arthur Lelyveld: NYT, July 11, 1964, p. 22, July 13, 1964, p. 13; Sutherland, *Letters from Mississippi,* pp. 122–26; U.S. Commission on Civil Rights, *Law Enforcement,* p. 53. The injured summer volunteers were Lawrence Spears and David Owen, both of California.

394   drew suspended sentences: Tucker, *Mississippi from Within,* p. 110.

394   Freedom School with thirty-five students: Holt, *The Summer,* p. 217.

394   destruction of Mount Zion: Mount Zion Hill Baptist was burned July 17, 1964, Mount Vernon Missionary Baptist on July 22, and Rose Hill Baptist on July 24. Ibid. Also "Mississippi Bombings, Burnings Since June 16," A/SN36f6.

394   "75 students on the lawn": Sutherland, *Letters from Mississippi,* p. 104.

394   visiting white minister [Rev. Don McCord]: Von Hoffman, *Mississippi Notebook,* p. 71.

394   Malva and "Red" Heffner: Ibid., pp. 64–78; Good, *Trouble I've Seen,* p. 144; Harris, *Dreams Die Hard,* pp. 63–64; Mary King, *Freedom Song,* pp. 423–24; Dittmer, *Local People,* p. 305.

394   poisoned Falstaff, their dachshund: Von Hoffman, *Mississippi Notebook,* p. 78.

394   "When I'd go downtown": *Meridian Star,* Sept. 6, 1964, p. 1; Tucker, *Mississippi from Within,* pp. 122–23.

394   "I said, 'That's right' ": Belfrage, *Freedom Summer,* p. 142.

394   Greenwood's fourth Freedom Day: Ibid., pp. 142–70; Sutherland, *Letters from Mississippi,* pp. 174–76; Holt, *The Summer,* p. 217.

395   Silas McGhee watched: Int. Silas McGhee, June 26, 1992.

395   abduct him at gunpoint: Ibid.; U.S. Commission on Civil Rights, *Law Enforcement,* p. 44; Payne, *Light of Freedom,* pp. 211–12.

395   "James Bevel, the wonderful": William Hodes to "Folks," July 17, 1964, William Hodes Files, SHSW.

395   King returned to St. Augustine: Garrow, *Bearing the Cross,* pp. 340–41.

395   "The businessmen said before": King statement of July 16, 1964, A/KS.

396   surrounded Twine's car: "Racial and Civil Disorders in St. Augustine," Report of the Florida Legislative Investigation Committee, Feb. 1965, p. 46, in Garrow, ed., *St. Augustine.*

396   Twine crooked his elbow: Int. Katherine and Henry Twine, April 2, 1991.

396   fn "That ain't no trash out there": Ibid.

396   luxury integration: Ibid.

396   fn Galimore died: NYT, July 27, 1964, p. 1.

396   owner James Brock: Colburn, *Racial Change,* pp. 111–12; Jacksonville FBI report on James Brock dated July 24, 1964, FSA-NR, pp. 1–13.

396   Klansmen firebombed the Monson anyway: Ibid. Also *St. Augustine Record,* July 24, 1964, p. 1.

396   Pappy's Seafood Restaurant: SAC, Jacksonville, to Director, July 20, 1964, FSA-1515.

396   "We have gone too far": Hartley, "A Long, Hot Summer," pp. 70–71, in Garrow, ed., *St. Augustine.* (From St. Augustine, Hosea Williams wrote a letter asking for an extension of unpaid leave from his job as a chemist for the U.S. Department of Agriculture. Williams to Dr. F. O. Marzke, July 15, 1964, A/KP35f16.)

396   "It was a great moment": King statement of July 16, 1964, A/KS.

396–97   "profound and revolutionary changes": King statement before the Platform Committee of the Republican National Convention, July 7, 1964, A/KS.

397   bugged King's hotel room: Garrow, *FBI and Martin,* p. 117; FBI microphone surveillance summary dated Oct. 28, 1976, FSC-107.

397   adding four new wiretaps: Baumgardner to Sullivan, July 7, 1964, Folder 24, FHOC.

397   He arrived on July 10: Whitehead, *Attack on Terror,* pp. 93–98; DeLoach, *Hoover's FBI,* pp. 181–86.

397   God and the Ladies: Von Hoffman, *Mississippi Notebook,* p. 38.

397   "Hoover would not criticize": *Jackson Clarion-Ledger,* July 11, 1964, p. 1.

397   deployment merely fueled: Cagin and Dray, *We Are Not Afraid,* pp. 370–71.

398   "With so many FBI agents sleuthing": Tucker, *Mississippi from Within,* p. 49.

398   "Money is no object!": Int. Roy Moore, June 22, 1992.

398   empty files and dummy walls: Ibid. Also DeLoach, *Hoover's FBI,* p. 181; Ungar, *FBI,* p. 413.

398   Sullivan then delivered: Int. Joseph Sullivan, Feb. 3, 1991.

398   callers promised to shoot: Whitehead, *Attack on Terror,* p. 97; int. Cartha DeLoach, June 1, 1984.

398   "Hoover Leaves State": *Jackson Clarion-Ledger,* July 12, 1964, p. 1.

398   ninth church loss: Pleasant Plains Missionary Baptist Church in Browning, Mississippi, near Greenwood, was burned to the ground early on the morning of July 11. *Jet,* Oct. 7, 1964, p. 20; ADW, July 12, 1964, p. 1; "Mississippi Bombings, Burnings Since June 16," A/SN36f6.

398   calls from Walter Jenkins: DeLoach to Mohr, July 11, 1964, FLP-57.

398   bushwhacking in Georgia: Five memos from McGowan to Rosen, July 11, 1964, FLP-3, FLP-5, FLP-9, FLP-11, and FLP-12; Whitehead, *Attack on Terror,* pp. 310–11; *Jet,* July 30, 1964, p. 8.

398   two .12-gauge shotgun blasts: SAC, Atlanta, to Director, July 12, 1964, FLP-22.

398   Casper from vacation: Evans to Belmont, July 11, 1964, FLP-15.

398   reinforcements from Newark: Hyde to Mohr, July 13, 1964, FLP-33.

399   report for the White House: Hoover to Walter Jenkins "(BY COURIER SERVICE)," July 12, 1964, FLP-19.

399   "a substantial payment": McGowan to Rosen, July 12, 1964, FLP-10.

399   "Press vigorously": Note on Rosen to Belmont, July 13, 1964, FLP-16. Hoover wrote a similar instruction on Evans to Belmont, July 11, 1964, FLP-15.

399   Hoover called President Johnson: Hoover note on DeLoach to Mohr, July 11, 1964, FLP-57.

399   fisherman James Bowles: ANP release dated July 13, 1964, Box 107f5, Claude Barnett Papers, CHS.

399   badly decomposed lower body: Mars, *Witness,* p. 100; Cagin and Dray, *We Are Not Afraid,* pp. 371–72; McAdam, *Freedom Summer,* p. 103; Holt, *The Summer,* p. 216.

399   "FIND HEADLESS BODY": CDD, July 14, 1964, p. 1.

399   "That was a dastardly thing": LBJ phone call with RFK, 3:22 P.M., July 13, 1964, Cit. 4220, Audiotape WH6407.07, LBJ.

399   "No, that's not correct": LBJ phone call with J. Edgar Hoover, 3:34 P.M., July 13, 1964, Cit. 4221, Audiotape WH6407.07, LBJ.

399   disappearance seven weeks earlier: ADW, July 14, 1964, p. 1.

399   agents eventually arrested: Whitehead, *Attack on Terror,* pp. 98–100.

400   jostling across two states: Int. Joseph Sullivan, Feb. 3, 1991.

400   an exchange of letters: Hoover to Walter Jenkins and LBJ to Hoover, both July 13, 1964, Ex HU, Box 26, LBJ. (Cartha DeLoach, the White House liaison for the FBI, says he drafted both Hoover's report and Johnson's reply in this instance and many others. Int. Cartha DeLoach, June 1, 1984.)

29. THE COW PALACE REVOLT

401   "dime store New Deal": NYT, July 16, 1964, p. 17.

401   "begin to count on": Ambrose, *Eisenhower: The President,* p. 652.

401   Eisenhower himself stirred the passions: White, *The Making,* p. 199.

402   "Ike Struck Lowest Blow": NYAN, July 19, 1964, p. 4.

402   "well-dressed and well-mannered": White, *The Making,* p. 199.

402   "Hell, I don't want to talk": Edwards, *Goldwater,* p. 266.

402   "ugly tone": *Life,* July 24, 1964, pp. 15–18.

402   "reduce a once great party": NYT, July 16, 1964, p. 30.

402   Goldwater sought an audience: Edwards, *Goldwater,* pp. 276–78.

402   "By golly, that makes real sense": Ibid.

403   "stunningly total": *Newsweek,* July 27, 1964, p. 18.

403   "GOP Convention Spurns Negroes": *Cleveland Call and Post,* July 18, 1964, p. 1.

403   "Negro Delegates to GOP": Associated Negro Press release dated July 22, 1964, Box 107f6, Claude Barnett Papers, CHS.

403   "The Great Purge of Negroes": *Jet,* July 9, 1964, p. 10.

403   "GOP Negroes Washed Away": CD, July 16, 1964, p. 3.

403   George W. Lee of Memphis: Associated Negro Press release dated July 13, 1964, Box 107f5, Claude Barnett Papers, CHS; *Cleveland Call and Post,* July 18, 1964, p. 2.

403   "for the first time": PC, July 23, 1964, p. 4.

403   375 convention delegates: Carter, *Politics of Rage,* p. 219.

403   fn "The Georgia delegation": *Cleveland Call and Post,* July 18, 1964, p. 3.

403   "Cal. GOP/White Man's Party": *California Eagle,* June 11, 1964, p. 4.

403   fourteen of 1,308: *Cleveland Call and Post,* July 18, 1964, p. 1. The *Chicago Daily Defender* counted thirteen and later fifteen Negro delegates, while *Jet* reported "less than 10." *Jet,* July 16, 1964, p. 4.

404   "had been shoved": *Cleveland Call and Post,* July 18, 1964, p. 3. Also *Newsweek,* July 27, 1964, p. 21; ADW, July 23, 1964, p. 4.

404   setting his suit jacket on fire: Associated Negro Press release dated July 22, 1964, Box 107f6, Claude Barnett Papers, CHS; CDD, July 15, 1964, p. 12; PC, July 23, 1964, p. 3.

404   "I now believe I know": PC, July 23, 1964, p. 1.

404   "GOP Convention, 1964 Recalls Germany, 1933": CD, July 18, 1964, p. 1. *Jet* published a similar story: "Senator's Rise Is Compared to the Upshoot of Adolf Hitler." *Jet,* July 30, 1964, pp. 22–27.

404   "The Grand Old Party": CD, July 16, 1964, p. 4.

404   "Scranton on the Move": ADW, July 5, 1964, p. 1.

404   "stands to reason": ADW, July 16, 1964, p. 4.

404   "may have a stimulating effect": ADW, July 17, 1964, p. 4.

404   "useless for a Negro today": ADW, July 22, 1964, p. 4.

404   "I think we just gave the South": Lemann, *The Promised Land,* p. 183.

404   One alarmist feared: Henry Wilson, Jr., to Lawrence O'Brien, July 8 1964, Box 4, Henry Wilson, Jr., Papers, LBJ.

404   "for your lifetime and mine": Califano, *Triumph and Tragedy,* p. 55.

405   fully 80 percent: On final passage in the House, Republicans voted 136 yes and 35 no, Democrats 153 yes and 91 no. In the Senate, Republicans voted 27 yes and 6 (including Barry Goldwater) no, Democrats 46 yes and 21 no.

405   with Senator Goldwater on the roof: *Newsweek,* July 27, 1964, p. 19; Carter, *Politics of Rage,* pp. 220–22; Edwards, *Goldwater,* p. 242.

405   "Bobby Kennedy tearing around": *The Reporter,* Oct. 8, 1964, p. 27.

405   "Today we hear": Lesher, *George Wallace,* pp. 308–9.

30. King in Mississippi

407 contentious staff debates: Int. Andrew Young, Oct. 26, 1991; int. Hosea Williams, Oct. 29, 1991; int. James Bevel, Feb. 20, 1985.
407 new organizational chart: SCLC organizational chart, A/KP32f8.
407 Clark's scolding reminders: Clark to Young, July 12, 1964, A/SC154f4.
407 "There were many days": Young to Clark, July 20, 1964, A/SC154f4.
408 invitation from Bob Moses: COFO Executive Committee minutes of July 10, 1964, A/SC41f13; Annell Ponder to MLK, July 14, 1964, A/KP7f24; SCLC draft press release, nd, A/SC16f11; Forman, Moses, and Dennis to Ella Baker et al., July 13, 1964, A/MFDP23f3.
408 "a normal life": Garrow, *Bearing the Cross*, p. 341.
408 "It's a ticklish problem": LBJ phone call with RFK, 12:25 P.M., July 21, 1964, Cit. 4288, Audiotape WH6407.11, LBJ.
408 "Maybe you can put a quietus": LBJ phone call with J. Edgar Hoover, 1:06 P.M., July 21, 1964, Cit. 4295, Audiotape WH6407.11, LBJ.
409 "I understand someone there's threatening": LBJ phone call with J. Edgar Hoover, 12:40 P.M., July 21, 1964, Cit. 4291-2, Audiotape WH6407.11, LBJ.
409 "in front and in back of him": Ibid. Also Hoover memorandum for Tolson et al., 12:42 P.M., July 21, 1964, FK-NR.
409 suspicion in headquarters: Rosen to Belmont, July 21, 1964, FK-401.
409 Louisiana agents: Rosen to Belmont, July 23, 1964, FK-NR.
409 Wilmer Jones looked through holes: Mars, *Witness*, pp. 124–26; Whitehead, *Attack on Terror*, pp. 111–24; Cagin and Dray, *We Are Not Afraid*, pp. 391–93; int. Joseph Sullivan, Feb. 3, 1991.
410 "I happen to be a Christian": Calvin Trillin, "Letter from Jackson," *The New Yorker*, Aug. 29, 1964, pp. 86–91.
410 "I'm here on a twofold visit": Item 0130, Reel D21, WLBT Newsfilm Collection, MDAH.
410 "for Negroes there hardly seemed": Belfrage, *Freedom Summer*, p. 174.
410 "Gentlemen, I will be brief": NYT, July 22, 1964, p. 20.
411 Klan hate leaflets: *McComb Enterprise-Journal*, July 22, 1964, p. 1.
411 "the price of a good fifth of Scotch": Tucker, *Mississippi from Within*, p. 47.
411 "searing love": Belfrage, *Freedom Summer*, p. 177.
411 "De Lawd!": Clark, *Echo in My Soul*, p. 42.
411 harvesting attention: Int. Betty Garman Robinson, Jan. 29, 1991.
411 Moore posted agents: Rosen to Belmont, July 22, 1964, FK-415.
411 Eastland interrupted Senate debate: *Congressional Record*, July 22, 1964, pp. S16593–97.
411 "about as many Communists": UPI newswire, July 22, 1964, FK-Sub1.
411 Roy Moore was best known: Whitehead, *Attack on Terror*, p. 89.
411 broadcast by Walter Cronkite: McGowan to Rosen, July 22, 1964, FK-405.
411 stayed up past midnight: Rosen to Belmont, July 24, 1964, FK-416.
411–12 warning Coretta King: Sizoo to Sullivan, July 23, 1964, FK-406.
412 "all of those leaders": MLK speech of July 22, 1964, at the Jackson, Mississippi, Masonic Temple, A/KS.
412 a tepid response: Belfrage, *Freedom Summer*, pp. 175-77.
412 "EMERGENCY MEMORANDUM": Moses and FDP Coordinators to "All Field Staff and Voter Registration Volunteers," July 19, 1964, A/SN16f2.
412 King met Moses at Tougaloo: Itinerary for Mississippi tour, A/SC41f8, A/KP16f11; int. Edwin King, June 26, 1992.
413 tactical questions: Forman, Moses, and Dennis to Ella Baker et al., July 13, 1964, A/MFDP23f3.
413 "my obsession with Mississippi": Lowenstein speech at National Workshop on Race and Religion, summer 1964, b32f346, Lowenstein Papers, UNC.
413 Lowenstein peppered: Casey Hayden to Moses, "Notes on Conversation with Al Lowenstein," July 14, 1964, A/MFDP23f4.
413 "America needs at least one party": MLK statement, July 22, 1964, A/KS.
413 King appeared on television: Good, *Trouble I've Seen*, pp. 125–26.
413 King drove eastward in a caravan: Ibid. Also Cagin and Dray, *We Are Not Afraid*, pp. 380–81; Garrow, *Bearing the Cross*, p. 342; Tucker, *Mississippi from Within*, p. 46; int. Edwin King, June 26, 1992.
413 snack on a pickled pig's foot: Young, *Easy Burden*, p. 305; int. C. T. Vivian, May 26, 1990.
413 Rainey and Judge Leonard Warren: Rainey to Hoover, July 28, 1964, FK-423; Morell to DeLoach, Aug. 4, 1964, re Warren letter to Hoover dated July 28, 1964, FK-422. No charges were ever brought against Judge Warren in connection with the triple murder.
414 "a long line of Negro women": Hoover memorandum for Tolson et al., 3:08 P.M., July 16, 1964, FK-NR.
414 "cornpone evangelism": Good, *Trouble I've Seen*, p. 127.
414 Beatrice Cole recalled: Int. Edwin King, June 26, 1992.
415 Goldwater met alone for sixteen minutes: NYT, July 25, 1964, p. 1; *U.S. News & World Report*, Aug. 3, 1964, p. 4; PPP, transcript of July 24, 1964, news conference, pp. 887–92; Edwards, *Goldwater*, pp. 272–73; Stern, *Calculating Visions*, p. 196.
415 "launching pad": LBJ phone call with Nicholas Katzenbach, July 25, 1964, Cit. 4338, Audiotape WH6407.14, LBJ.
415 stripped to boxer shorts: Int. Edwin King, June 26, 1992.

415   arsoned during his visit: Mount Vernon Missionary Baptist Church, burned on the night of July 21–22, 1964, and Rose Hill Church, burned on July 24, 1964. "Mississippi Bombings, Burnings Since June 16," A/SN36f6. Also *Jet*, Oct. 7, 1964, p. 20.

415   return to the Leflore Theater: Sutherland, *Letters from Mississippi*, pp. 178–83; Dittmer, *Local People*, p. 278; Payne, *Light of Freedom*, pp. 211–12; affidavits of Silas McGhee, Robert Zellner, Dorothy Zellner, Judy Richardson, and Robert Weil, all July 1964, A/MFDP10f3.

415   "cursing and hollering and carrying on": Int. Silas McGhee, June 26, 1992.

415   "I'm not going to go into that": Affidavit of Robert Weil, July 30, 1964, A/MFDP10f3.

416   "Now (12:40 Atlanta)": "From Betty Garman in Greenwood/J. Bond," July 27, 1964, William Hodes Files, SHSW.

416   "When a man fights back": Belfrage, *Freedom Summer*, pp. 183–88.

416   assemble the county convention: Minutes of the Leflore County Convention, July 27, 1964, A/MFDP10f5.

31. Riot Politics

417   flashed into a ten-day crisis: Manchester, *Glory and the Dream*, p. 1249; Goldman, *Tragedy*, pp. 203–4; PC, Aug. 1, 1964, p. 1.

417   "You dirty niggers!": *Newsweek*, July 27, 1964, p. 34.

417   "a great deal of the Negro": Hobart Taylor, Jr., to LBJ, July 17, 1964, with attached notes from Jack Valenti to Lee White and from Bill Moyers to Jack Valenti, Ex HU 4/HU 4, Box 3, LBJ.

417   CORE workers organized: Farmer, *Freedom When*, pp. 27–28; Meier, *CORE*, pp. 302–3.

418   "I am prepared to be a Tom": Grant, *Black Protest*, pp. 349–56.

418   Farmer of CORE fared no better: Farmer, *Lay Bare the Heart*, pp. 279–85.

418   "Sending Bourke [sic] Marshall": Moyers to LBJ, July 20, 1964, Office of the President, Box 8, LBJ.

418   Johnson decided instead to announce: PPP, White House statement of July 21, 1964, pp. 876–77.

418   Thomas E. Dewey: Section 135, Parts 1 and 2, FHOC, *passim.*

418   Rockefeller disclosed: Hoover memo for Tolson et al., 1:35 P.M., July 21, 1964, FNR-NR.

418   Hoover relayed: Hoover memo for Tolson et al., 1:50 P.M., July 21, 1964, FNR-NR.

418   "to investigate the police lieutenant": Hoover memo for Tolson et al., 1:35 P.M., July 21, 1964, FNR-NR.

418   fn confessions to social workers: New York LHM dated July 24, 1964, headed "Lieutenant Thomas Gilligan/James Powell (Deceased)—Victim—Civil Rights," Section 135, Part 1, FHOC.

418   fn *Jet* magazine's eulogy: *Jet*, Aug. 6, 1964, pp. 12–19.

419   "Achilles heel": DeLoach to Hoover, Sept. 9, 1964, Section 135, Part 1, FHOC.

419   award-winning CBS documentary: CBS Television, *The Making of the President, 1964*, Tape No. 65043, PEA.

419   "strategy of domestic tranquility": White, *The Making*, p. 221.

419   "Starkly put": Ibid., p. 223.

419   fn "almost tomorrow in the eyes of history": Ibid., pp. 223–24.

419   "adolescent troops": Ibid., p. 241.

419   Malcolm X as a likely architect: Bland to Sullivan, Sept. 10, 1964, Section 135, Part 1, FHOC; Grant, *Black Protest*, p. 351.

420   "Has there been anything": Wiretap transcript of July 31, 1964, FMXNY-sub1-59a.

420   "a 'don't get involved' attitude": Sullivan to Belmont, "Racial Disorder, Rochester," Sept. 11, 1964, Section 135, Part 1, FHOC.

420   "lay the facts on the line": Hoover's handwritten note on ibid.

420   staging a general White House conference: DeLoach to Hoover, Sept. 9, 1964, Section 135, Part 1, FHOC.

420   "where there is an outside": Draft report for Dewey dated Sept. 18, 1964, Section 135, Part 2, FHOC, p. 14.

421   three times on one page: DeLoach to Mohr. Also Hoover memo for Tolson et al., 11:35 A.M., both Sept. 25, 1964, Section 135, Part 2, FHOC.

421   Dewey told Hoover: Hoover memo for Tolson et al., 11:47 A.M., Sept. 25, 1964, Section 135, Part 2, FHOC.

421   "greatly perturbed": DeLoach to Mohr, Sept. 22, 1964, Section 135, Part 2, FHOC.

421   "For some reason": Draft report for Dewey dated Sept. 18, 1964, Section 135, Part 2, FHOC, p. 2.

421   "F.B.I. Says Riots Had No Pattern": NYT, Sept. 27, 1964, p. 1.

421   Wilkins was pleasantly surprised: Wilkins, *Standing Fast*, p. 304.

421   Warren Commission made public: NYT, Sept. 28, 1964, p. 1.

421   Johnson invited Attorney General: White, *The Making*, p. 263.

422   "a big blowup": LBJ phone call with McGeorge Bundy, July 29, 1964, Cit. 4383-84, Audiotape WH6407.17, LBJ.

422   "My judgment is that": Ibid.

422   fn "I have Jack Valenti": LBJ phone call with John Connally, July 23, 1964, Cit. 4320-23, Audiotape WH6407.13, LBJ.

422   "If I can't offer": Ibid.

422   talked congenially: LBJ phone call with RFK, July 27, 1964, Cit. 4349, Audiotape WH6407.15, LBJ.

422   Kennedy's political energy: Guthman, *We Band of Brothers*, pp. 273–78; *Newsweek*, July 13, 1964, p. 34.

422 "that with him there died idealism": Guthman, *We Band of Brothers*, p. 274.
423 more than six hours on Tuesday: New York LHM dated July 30, 1964, FK-NR, p. 1.
423 "the undermuck of Harlem": White, *The Making*, p. 241.
423 "Wingate of course double-crossed Martin": Bayard Rustin Oral History by T. H. Baker, June 17, 1969, LBJ.
423 shuttled between the parties: Garrow, *Bearing the Cross*, p. 343; New York LHMs dated July 28, 1964, July 30, 1964, and Aug. 3, 1964, FK-NR.
423 "utterly unresponsive": MLK press statement of July 30, 1964, A/KS.
423 slander suit filed against him: NYT, April 13, 1965, p. 27, May 27, 1965, p. 48, June 3, 1965 ("Ill Negro Helped by Lieut. Gilligan"), p. 37.
423 "violent and futile disorder": Wilkins telegram to John Lewis, July 22, 1964, John Lewis Chronological File, AAP.
423 Wilkins proposed: Wilkins, *Standing Fast*, p. 304; Forman, *Black Revolutionaries*, p. 368; Garrow, *Bearing the Cross*, p. 343; int. James Farmer, Nov. 18, 1983.
424 "Negro Leaders Split": NYT, July 30 and July 31, 1964, p. 1.
424 Kennedy found himself listening: White, *The Making*, pp. 263–66; Evans and Novak, *Exercise of Power*, pp. 468–72; Valenti, *Very Human President*, pp. 113–15; Kearns, *Lyndon Johnson*, pp. 201–3; Guthman, *We Band of Brothers*, pp. 280–82; Clifford, *Counsel*, pp. 394–98. Kennedy dictated his version of the conversation, as preserved in Schlesinger, *Robert Kennedy*, pp. 711–15. President Johnson described his version immediately afterward in two phone calls: with Clark Clifford, 2:17 P.M., Cit. 4392-93, and with McGeorge Bundy, 2:30 pm, Cit. 4394-95, both July 29, 1964, Audiotape WH6407.18, LBJ.
424 "it would be unwise for our party": Johnson, *The Vantage Point*, pp. 576–77.
424 planned with Clark Clifford: LBJ phone call with Clark Clifford, 11:45 A.M., July 29, 1964, Cit. 4389, Audiotape WH6407.18, LBJ.
424 "courage and forthrightness": LBJ phone call with Clark Clifford, 2:17 P.M., July 29, 1964, Cit. 4392-93, Audiotape WH6407.18, LBJ.
425 "This is quite hopeful": LBJ phone call with McGeorge Bundy, 2:30 P.M., July 29, 1964, Cit. 4394-95, Audiotape WH6407.18, LBJ.
425 Kennedy declined suggestions: LBJ phone call with Clark Clifford, 8:21 P.M., July 29, 1964, Cit. 4409, Audiotape WH6407.19, LBJ.
425 "Any preferences or choices?": LBJ phone call with Kenneth O'Donnell, July 30, 1964, Cit. 4426, Audiotape WH6407.20, LBJ.
425 lasting desire to conceal: Even in his 1971 memoirs, Johnson presented Robert Kennedy as the incidental victim of a high-minded maxim that a president should separate electoral politics from good government. Johnson, *The Vantage Point*, pp. 98–100.
425 "his Adam's Apple": Schlesinger, *Robert Kennedy*, p. 714.
426 "drop to zero overnight": Johnson, *White House Diary*, pp. 186–87.

32. CRIME, WAR, AND FREEDOM SCHOOL

427 task force of eighty-three FBI agents: Callahan to Mohr, Aug. 18, 1964, FLP-217.
427 three double-barreled shotguns: SAC, Atlanta, to Director, July 14, 1964, FLP-113, p. 2.
427 they whipped Potts: SAC, Atlanta, to Director, July 13, 1964, FLP-113, pp. 9–10; SAC, Atlanta, to Director, July 15, 1964, FLP-52, p. 3.
427 Sims bludgeoned: SAC, Atlanta, to Director, July 13, 1964, FLP-113, pp. 5–6.
427 evidence seemed "sketchy": Atlanta FBI report dated July 22, 1964, FLP-115, p. 154.
427 Pollock frankly allowed: SAC, Atlanta, to Director, July 15, 1964, FLP-52, pp. 3–4.
428 11:30 P.M. and again at 12:20 A.M.: Atlanta FBI report dated July 22, 1964, FLP-115, pp. 151–55; SAC, Atlanta, to Director, July 13, 1964, FLP-113, pp. 6–9. The shooting victims were Alice Fair and John Clink.
428 4th of July rally: SAC, Atlanta, to Director, July 21, 1964, FLP-81; SAC, Atlanta, to Director, July 15, 1964, FLP-52, pp. 7–8; Lesher, *George Wallace*, p. 307.
428 refuge in Bob Walker's Drive-In: Atlanta FBI report dated July 22, 1964, FLP-115, pp. 148–50; Good, *Trouble I've Seen*, pp. 180–81.
428 run over by a passing freight train: SAC, Atlanta, to Director, July 15, 1964, FLP-52, p. 6; SAC, Atlanta, to Director, July 21, 1964, FLP-81, p. 1; AC, July 25, 1964, p. 1.
429 anonymous pedestrian as Melvin Reed: SAC, Atlanta, to Director, July 16, 1964, FLP-87, p. 5.
429 fifty small dents: Hoover to Walter Jenkins "BY COURIER SERVICE," July 12, 1964, FLP-19; Atlanta FBI report dated July 22, 1964, FLP-115, pp. 448–52.
429 Guest had finished only the first grade: Statement of Herbert Guest, Aug. 6, 1964, FLP-152.
429 mistrust within the Klan families: Report on July 15, 1964, of KKK Women's Auxiliary, in SAC, Atlanta, to Director, July 16, 1964, FLP-87, pp. 1–2; SAC, Atlanta, to Director, July 30, 1964, FLP-122; McGowan to Rosen, July 31, 1964, FLP-132.
429 Guest's thirty-seventh birthday: AC, Aug. 19, 1964, p. 1; SAC, Atlanta, to Director, Aug. 19, 1964, FLP-213; DeLoach to Mohr, Aug. 19, 1964, FLP-210.
430 whirlwind of gossip: Report of investigator A. L. Hopkins, Aug. 6, 1964, MSSC.
430 blitz was designed: Int. Joseph Sullivan, Feb. 3, 1991, July 26, 1996; Whitehead, *Attack on Terror*, pp. 127–28; Cagin and Dray, *We Are Not Afraid*, pp. 394–96.
430 "they think they know": LBJ phone call with Carl Sanders, Aug. 1, 1964, Cit. 4617-18, Audiotape WH6408.02, LBJ.

430   "in a case such as this": Rosen to Belmont, July 31, 1964, FMB-1191.
430   Half the globe away: On the August 2 Gulf of Tonkin incident, see Karnow, *Vietnam,* pp. 380–84; Johnson, *The Vantage Point,* pp. 112–13.
431   "hired personnel": Gravel, ed., *Pentagon Papers,* Vol. 3, p. 183.
431   "a pervasive infusion of Americans": Karnow, *Vietnam,* p. 361.
431   "the Vietnamese had some difficulty": Gravel, ed., *Pentagon Papers,* Vol. 3, p. 327.
431   "This is no drill": *Newsweek,* Aug. 17, 1964, p. 19.
432   Maxwell Taylor objected: Taylor, *Swords and Plowshares,* pp. 318–19; McNamara, *In Retrospect,* p. 131.
432   "make it look like": LBJ phone call with Robert Anderson, 9:46 A.M., Aug. 3, 1964, Cit. 4631-32, Audiotape WH6408.03, LBJ.
432   rumors that Jacqueline Kennedy: LBJ phone call with Robert McNamara, 10:20 A.M., Aug. 3, 1964, Cit. 4633, Audiotape WH6408.03, LBJ.
433   "not only with the objective": NYT, Aug. 4, 1964, p. 1.
433   tranquil White House schedule: PDD, Aug. 3, 1964.
433   at the Tallahassee airport: NYT, Aug. 3, 1964, p. 11; NYT, Aug. 4, 1964, p. 13.
433   Supreme Court sent: *Dresner et al. v. City of Tallahassee,* 375 U.S. 136.
433   Rudd sent them off: NYT, Aug. 5, 1964, p. 36; *Florida Times-Union,* Aug. 4, 1964, p. 3.
433   Robert McAfee Brown: "Pathfinding Protestants," *Newsweek,* May 25, 1962, pp. 84–86; "Catholics' Protestant," *Time,* Jan. 14, 1963, pp. 71–72.
433   white inmates more often reviled: Int. Robert McAfee Brown, July 17, 1991; int. Israel Dresner, July 31, 1991; int. Robert Stone, June 3, 1993.
433   "this ship could be attacked tonight": LBJ phone call with Robert McNamara, 9:43 A.M., Aug. 4, 1964, Cit. 4658, Audiotape WH6408.03, LBJ.
434   "two unidentified vessels": LBJ phone call with Robert McNamara, 10:53 A.M., Aug. 4, 1964, Cit. 4662, Audiotape WH6408.04, LBJ.
434   "as belligerents from first detection": Karnow, *Vietnam,* p. 384.
434   warnings of a trap: Gravel, ed., *Pentagon Papers,* Vol. 3, pp. 184–85.
434   prepare retaliatory airstrikes: Johnson, *The Vantage Point,* p. 114.
434   "many reported contacts": McNamara, *In Retrospect,* p. 133.
434   Sharp reassured: Ibid.
434   "Certain that original": Ibid.
434   sudden swarms of blowflies: MIBURN prosecutive summary, Dec. 19, 1964, FMB-1613, pp. 281–86; Whitehead, *Attack on Terror,* pp. 132–34; Cagin and Dray, *We Are Not Afraid,* pp. 397–99; DeLoach, *Hoover's FBI,* p. 189.
435   Admiral Sharp, had conceded: McNamara, *In Retrospect,* p. 134.
435   routed through the Pentagon: Gravel, ed., *Pentagon Papers,* Vol. 3, p. 185.
435   50-caliber shell fragment: McNamara, *In Retrospect,* p. 131.
435   "those dumb stupid sailors": Karnow, *Vietnam,* p. 390.
435   fn judgment of historian Stanley Karnow: Ibid., p. 389.
435   fn Tuesday attack never happened: McNamara, on a visit to Vietnam thirty-one years later, said he was "99 and 99-100ths percent sure it didn't occur." NYT, Nov. 10, 1995, p. 3.
435   fn "The U.S. ships blazed out": *Newsweek,* Aug. 17, 1964, p. 20.
435   fn "There was now plenty": *Life,* Aug. 14, 1964, p. 21.
435   "Some of our boys": Notes taken at leadership meeting on Aug. 4, 1964, Box 1, Meeting Notes File, LBJ.
436   authorization for airstrikes: McNamara, *In Retrospect,* p. 135.
436   at 8:01 Walter Jenkins: PDD, Aug. 4, 1964; LBJ phone call with Cartha DeLoach, Aug. 4, 1964, Cit. 4693, Audiotape WH6408.05, LBJ; Whitehead, *Attack on Terror,* pp. 135–36; DeLoach, *Hoover's FBI,* pp. 189–90; Cagin and Dray, *We Are Not Afraid,* p. 401.
436   fetched two men ashore: PDD, Aug. 4, 1964.
436   "a day of tension": Dan Rather, CBS, on *Presidential Address: The Tonkin Gulf Report,* Aug. 4, 1964, Tape T81:0368, MOB.
436   Everett Alvarez: Karnow, *Vietnam,* p. 388.
436   Seeger used movement songs: Sutherland, *Letters from Mississippi,* p. 189.
436   "From now on": Belfrage, *Freedom Summer,* pp. 192–93.
436   Price escorted a hearse caravan: MIBURN prosecutive summary, Dec. 19, 1964, FMB-1613, pp. 286, 378–85; *Newsweek,* Aug. 17, 1964, p. 28.
437   "We had to call Washington": Belfrage, *Freedom Summer,* p. 193.
437   Moses held aloft: Howard Zinn, *Vietnam: The Logic of Withdrawal,* cited in Zaroulis and Sullivan, *Who Spoke Up?,* p. 24.
437   "Lyndon Gives Navy": *Jackson Clarion-Ledger,* Aug. 4, 1964, p. 1.
437   Moses circled with questions: Int. Robert P. Moses, Feb. 15, 1991.
437   James Lackey: Lackey's prior statements summarized in SAC, Atlanta, to Director, July 30, 1964, FLP-122.
437   "I raised the roof": Statement of Loretta Lackey, Aug. 18, 1964, FLP-246.
437   "Sims and Myers kept insisting": Statement of James Lackey, Aug. 6, 1964, FLP-151.
437   Guest claimed a more passive role: Statement of Herbert Guest, Aug. 6, 1964, FLP-152.
437   on the arrest of Myers: Rosen to Belmont, Aug. 6, 1964, FLP-139.
437   Sanders issued a telling statement: NYT, Aug. 7, 1964, pp. 1, 13.

437   DeLoach and his supervisors: M. A. Jones to DeLoach, Aug. 7, 1964, FLP-142; DeLoach to Mohr, Aug. 7, 1964, FLP-149.

438   50,611 investigative miles: SAC, Atlanta, to Director, Aug. 12, 1964, FLP-178.

438   crippling *Screws* precedent: *Screws v. United States*, 325 U.S. 91; Branch, *Parting*, pp. 408–9; Rosen to Belmont, Aug. 6, 1964, FLP-151.

438   "I am going to kill me a nigger": Statement of James Lackey, Aug. 6, 1964, FLP-151.

438   "I think a soldier in uniform": LBJ phone call with Cartha DeLoach, Aug. 6, 1964, Cit. 4781, Audiotape WH6408.09, LBJ.

438   Moses had posted: "*Please Post* Re: Securing Justice Department Action," July 13, 1964, A/KP16:16.

438   statewide convention: Dittmer, *Local People*, pp. 281–82.

438   "Until the killing of a black": NYT, Aug. 7, 1964, p. 13.

439   church-issue hand fan: WLBT News footage of MFDP Convention, Aug. 6, 1964, Tape 0898/D19, MDAH.

439   Joseph Rauh explained: Rothschild, *Black and White*, pp. 66–68.

439   "When you have two": Good, *Trouble I've Seen*, p. 170.

439   "Bob Moses didn't seem so confident": Sutherland, *Letters from Mississippi*, p. 214.

439   "As things stand right now": Good, *Trouble I've Seen*, p. 171.

439   "open to *all* the people": Blackside, Inc. PBS series, *Eyes on the Prize*, I vol. 5, *Mississippi: Is This America?*

439   "Now this is not the kind": Good, *Trouble I've Seen*, p. 172.

440   "This was probably": Sutherland, *Letters from Mississippi*, p. 214.

440   "all of us here": Ibid., p. 215.

440   Evers refused to observe: Good, *Trouble I've Seen*, p. 171.

440   excluded most NAACP candidates: Dittmer, *Local People*, pp. 282–83.

440   fund-raising memorials: Betty Garman to Dave Dennis, Aug. 14, 1964, A/SN111f18.

440   follow-up autopsy: Int. Jack Pratt, March 25, 1991; Cagin and Dray, *We Are Not Afraid*, pp. 406–7.

440   "I have never witnessed": Dittmer, *Local People*, p. 183.

440   "No Evidence of Beating": NYT, Aug. 7, 1964, p. 13.

440   "Chaney Was Given a Brutal Beating": NYT, Aug. 8, 1964, p. 7.

441   "The police held up traffic": Sutherland, *Letters from Mississippi*, p. 191.

441   CORE's David Dennis: Blackside, Inc. PBS series, *Eyes on the Prize*, I vol. 5, *Mississippi: Is This America?* Also Cagin and Dray, *We Are Not Afraid*, pp. 409–10; Dittmer, *Local People*, pp. 283–84.

441   "blessed chaos": Holt, *The Summer*, pp. 116, 233.

441   fourth-grade sisters: Margaret, Alice, and Lillie Dwight were among the speakers honoring their former teachers, Stanley Zibulsky and Richard Kelley, at a thirty-year reunion of the St. John's United Methodist Freedom School, Hattiesburg, June 25, 1994.

441   fn "In this course of human events": Holt, *The Summer*, pp. 323–24.

441   education caucus proposed thirteen planks: Ibid., pp. 116–22.

442   fn detonated a 5-kiloton: NYT, Oct. 23, 1964, p. 2. Also NYT, Oct. 12, 1964, p. 23, Oct. 13, 1964, p. 86, Oct. 27, 1964, p. 77, Oct. 29, 1964, p. 70, Nov. 18, 1964, p. 30. "Officials refused to go ahead with the test until wind conditions were right," the *Times* reported on Oct. 23, "in view of the possibility that the explosion might crack the earth and permit radioactivity to escape.... On the surface of the blast site were a collection of instruments, a Confederate battle flag, and a small sign that read, 'The South Shall Rise Again.'"

442   delegates eventually voted down: Sutherland, *Letters from Mississippi*, p. 109.

442   "It was the single time": Dittmer, *Local People*, p. 260.

33. WHITE HOUSE ETIQUETTE

443   "I want to talk to him": PDD, Aug. 5, 1964.

443   Tonkin Gulf Resolution: Karnow, *Vietnam*, pp. 391–92; NYT, Aug. 7, 1964, p. 1, Aug. 8, 1964, p. 1.

443   Johnson congratulated Rusk: "MEMORANDUM FOR THE RECORD," Aug. 13, 1964, re 12:35 P.M. Aug. 10, 1964, meeting in Cabinet Room, McGeorge Bundy Office Files, b. 18-19, LBJ.

443   "did not wish to escalate": Ibid.

443   jeep under camouflage of ferns: *Life*, Aug. 21, 1964, cover, p. 26.

443   imposing a state of siege: Gravel, ed., *Pentagon Papers*, Vol. 2, p. 329.

444   "Khanh has a 50/50 chance": Gravel, ed., *Pentagon Papers*, Vol. 3, pp. 530–33.

444   ouster of Adam Yarmolinsky: Int. Sargent Shriver, Feb. 21, 1991; Lemann, *The Promised Land*, p. 157.

444   Yarmolinsky had spearheaded: Int. Robert McNamara, June 18, 1991.

444   bellwether symbol of controversy: "We seriously objected to Adam Yarmolinsky ... we knew something about his own background ... [wanted] to be sure that we had a person who was not controversial, who would not become controversial.... They did get rid of Mr. Yarmolinsky." Rep. L. H. Fountain (D.-N.C.) Oral History, July 15, 1969, pp. 16–17, LBJ.

444   "nothing to stop them": NYT, Aug. 6, 1964, p. 1.

444   "This is my blood": LBJ phone call with Carl Sanders, Aug. 1, 1964, Cit. 4617-18, Audiotape WH6408.02, LBJ.

444   "We've bled 'em to death": LBJ phone call with Walter Reuther, Aug. 1, 1964, Cit. 4624-25, Audiotape WH6408.03, LBJ.

444   "magic 200": LBJ phone call with Lawrence O'Brien, Aug. 5, 1964, Cit. 4766-67, Audiotape WH6408.08, LBJ.

444   scripted phone message to Louisiana: LBJ phone call with RFK, 12:00 P.M., Aug. 7, 1964, Cit. 4793, Audiotape WH6408.10, LBJ; LBJ phone call with Lee White, 4:15 P.M., Aug. 7, 1964, Cit. 4811, Audiotape WH6408.11, LBJ.

444   "it is my duty to enforce": LBJ phone call with John McKeithen, 4:50 P.M., Aug. 7, 1964, Cit. 4814, Audiotape WH6408.11, LBJ.

444   "Joe Rauh was on television": LBJ phone call with Bill Moyers, Aug. 7, 1964, Cit. 4815-18, Audiotape WH6408.12, LBJ.

444   Johnson knew: Cf. LBJ phone call with Rep. George Mahon of Texas, Aug. 6, 1964, Cit. 4770, Audiotape WH6408.08, LBJ. Mahon told Johnson: "Now this Adam Yarmanlisky [sic], whatever his name is, he is not an asset."

444   Shriver squirmed: Int. Sargent Shriver, Feb. 21, 1991.

444   From a phone in the hallway: Ibid. Also PPD, phone log, 3:00 P.M., Aug. 6, 1964.

445   established the War on Poverty: NYT, Aug. 7, 1964, p. 1.

445   "Well, we've just thrown you": Adam Yarmolinsky Oral History, July 13, 1970, pp. 17–19, LBJ. ("It was like a funeral in the offices when we heard Shriver had caved in," recalled one of Shriver's deputies at the poverty task force. Int. Hyman Bookbinder, March 21, 1991.)

445   "really had the gall": LBJ phone call with Bill Moyers, Aug. 7, 1964, Cit. 4815-18, Audiotape WH6408.12, LBJ.

445   McCone had disclosed: LBJ phone call with Robert McNamara, 12:46 P.M., Aug. 6, 1964, Cit. 4773, Audiotape WH6408.08, LBJ.

445   "This is a very delicate subject": LBJ phone call with Robert McNamara, 8:24 A.M., Aug. 8, 1964, Cit. 4819, Audiotape WH6408.12, LBJ.

445   Walter Jenkins reported: LBJ phone call with Walter Jenkins, 10:52 A.M., Aug. 8, 1964, Cit. 4821-24, Audiotape WH6408.13, LBJ.

445   reported sacrifice of Yarmolinsky: NYT, Aug. 7, 1964, p. 4, Aug. 8, 1964, p. 6.

445   "No, your thoughts are wrong": PPP, press conference of Aug. 8, 1964, at LBJ Ranch, p. 941.

445   "None of us is important": Califano, *Triumph and Tragedy,* p. 77.

446   "Service—3 Years Later": NYT, Aug. 8, 1964, p. 12, Aug. 7, 1964, p. 15.

446   prisoners were immensely relieved: Int. Robert McAfee Brown, July 17, 1991; int. Israel Dresner, July 31, 1991; int. Robert Stone, June 3, 1993.

446   two admitted pipe-beaters: Holt, *The Summer,* p. 233; NYT, Aug. 9, 1964, p. 21.

446   praised Judge Bryan Simpson: NYT, Aug. 6, 1964, p. 16; "Defense Fund Attorneys· Win St. Augustine, Fla. Victory," NAACP LDEF press release, Aug. 8, 1964, A/KP17f14.

446   grand jury undercut Simpson: "Further Presentment of Grand Jury," Aug. 5, 1964, A/KP20f42; Garrow, *Bearing the Cross,* p. 344.

446   "out of line": "Racial and Civil Disorders in St. Augustine," p. 48, in Garrow, ed., *St. Augustine.*

446   have the judge impeached: Colburn, *Racial Change,* pp. 131–35.

446   bouts of depression and letdown: Int. Katherine and Henry Twine, April 2, 1991. "Hayling was bitter," SCLC staff leader John Gibson told historian David Garrow. "He felt we'd dumped him." Garrow, *Bearing the Cross,* p. 685.

446   "On the surface": Hayling and Twine, "Dear Fellow Citizens," Sept. 22, 1964, A/SC139f10.

447   "terrific squabble": Wiretap conversation of Aug. 5, 1964, described in New York LHM dated Aug. 6, 1964, FK-NR.

447   "thinking now prevalent": Ibid.

447   for a lost passport: DeWolf to MLK, Aug. 9, 1964, A/KP4f37.

447   meeting with President Johnson: MLK to LBJ, Aug. 7, 1964, King Name File, LBJ, cited in Garrow, *Bearing the Cross,* p. 685.

447   pulpit appearance for Ralph Abernathy: MLK telegram to Dr. O. Clay Maxwell, Sr., Aug. 6, 1964, A/KP15f26.

447   services on Sunday, August 9: NYT, Aug. 10, 1964, p. 1.

447   "no leader outside of Harlem": NYT, Aug. 10, 1964, p. 15.

447   "The church must be reminded": "A Knock at Midnight," MLK sermon delivered Aug. 9, 1964, A/KS6.

447   Monday at Amherst: NYT, Aug. 11, 1964, p. 25.

447   long strategy meetings: King's calendar cleared seven hours, 11:00 A.M.–6:00 P.M., on Tuesday, Aug. 11, 1964: log, A/SC29.

447   Research Committee: Garrow, *Bearing the Cross,* pp. 332, 414–15; int. Harry Wachtel, Oct. 27, 1963.

447   proposed *Playboy* interview with King: Andrew Young to Alex Haley, Aug. 10, 1964, A/KP19f40.

447   fn Haley promised to donate: Alex Haley telegram to Dora McDonald, July 6, 1964, A/KP19f40.

447–48   reprimanding one of their own number: Jones to MLK, Aug. 24, 1964, A/KP13f23. "It upset Martin that I said that," recalled Jones of his complimentary references to Malcolm X. Int. Clarence Jones, Oct. 26, 1983.

448   Rustin undertook: Int. Clarence Jones, Jan. 26, 1984. Jones recalled that Rustin "just assumed the role of calling the White House." The available records indicate that Rustin acted in King's name, with an imprecise mix of maverick initiative and prior approval.

448   "Mr. Rustin told me very confidentially": Mary White to Valenti, 6:30 P.M., Aug. 11, 1964, PL1/ST24, Box 81, LBJ.

448 "If it looks like": Lee White to LBJ, Aug. 12, 1964, PL1/ST24, Box 81, LBJ.

448 awkward minuet continued: New York LHM dated Aug. 14, 1964, FR-NR; Garrow, *Bearing the Cross,* p. 345.

448 "King has made it so crystal clear": Lee White to LBJ, re "Conversation with Bayard Rustin," Aug. 13, 1964, PL1/ST24, Box 81, LBJ.

448 instructions from Johnson: PDD, phone log, Aug. 13, 1964; LBJ's handwritten note on Lee White to LBJ, Aug. 13, 1964, PL1/ST24, Box 81, LBJ.

448 "We'd have more damn wars": LBJ phone call with Walter Reuther, Aug. 17, 1964, Cit. 5003, Audiotape WH6408.27, LBJ.

448 "if we mess with the group": LBJ phone call with Hubert Humphrey, 11:05 A.M., Aug. 14, 1964, Cit. 4917-18, Audiotape WH6408.19, LBJ.

448 James Rowe to identify: LBJ phone call with James Rowe, Aug. 14, 1964, Cit. 4935, Audiotape WH6408.20, LBJ.

449 "panicky or desperate": LBJ phone call with Roy Wilkins, Aug. 15, 1964, Cit. 4940-41, Audiotape WH6408.21, LBJ.

449 fn "The motivation of King": Ibid.

449 "questionable people that met here": LBJ phone call with Walter Reuther, Aug. 17, 1964, Cit. 5003, Audiotape WH6408.27, LBJ.

449 "I did not detect any anger": Lee White to LBJ, Aug. 13, 1964, PL1/ST24, Box 81, LBJ.

449 tour in Holland: NYT, Aug. 16, 1964, p. 64.

449 "He won't be gone": LBJ phone call with Lee White, Aug. 13, 1964, Cit. 4912, Audiotape WH6408.19, LBJ.

449 Adickes gave in to six students: Int. Sandra Adickes, June 25, 1994. Adickes, a young teacher of four years' experience in New York City elementary schools, had been introduced to movement-style education in 1963 as a volunteer in Prince Edward County, Virginia, where public schools had been closed since 1959 to avoid integration. Smith, *Closed Their Schools, passim;* Branch, *Parting,* p. 413.

449 Herring arrived twenty minutes later: NYT, Aug. 15, 1964, p. 22; Holt, *The Summer,* p. 239. Mayor Pittman told reporters that routine inventory would be completed over the weekend, but he closed the library indefinitely when a second group of Freedom Schoolers presented themselves Monday morning. NYT, Aug. 19, 1964, p. 26.

449 "We have to serve the colored": *Adickes v. S. H. Kress & Co.,* 398 U.S. 144 (1970).

450 fn Harlan delivered: Ibid.

450 airstrip near Greenwood: Int. Harry Belafonte, March 6–7, 1985; Forman, *Black Revolutionaries,* p. 385.

450 Idella Craft achieved local fame: Int. James Moore, June 25, 1992.

451 "I am thirty-seven years old": Sutherland, *Letters from Mississippi,* pp. 183–84.

451 special beds and all-night sentries: Int. Dorothy Zellner, Dec. 12, 1991.

451 Poitier did calisthenics: Int. Harry Belafonte, March 6–7, 1985.

451 noise emptied Lula's Restaurant: Report labeled "Shooting of Silas McGhee, 8/15, 8:45 P.M.," William Hodes Files, SHSW; NYT, Aug. 16, 1964, p. 55; Payne, *Light of Freedom,* pp. 211–13.

451 McGhee himself reared up: Int. Silas McGhee, June 26, 1992.

452 Belfrage nervously ducked home: Belfrage, *Freedom Summer,* pp. 231–41.

452 parallel crises elsewhere: Holt, *The Summer,* pp. 241–42; "Mississippi Bombings, Burnings Since June 16," A/SN36f6.

452 Moses balanced his footing: Kasher, *Photographic History,* pp. 154–55.

452 renewed by telegram: Rustin to Lee White, Aug. 17, 1964, PL1/ST24, Box 81, LBJ.

452 White said the meeting was set: NY LHM dated Aug. 20, 1964, FR-NR.

452 Kennedy had sandwiched: Branch, *Parting,* pp. 834–35.

453 "He says the chances": Moyers to LBJ, Aug. 19, 1964, Ex PL1/ST24, LBJ.

453 intercept on King's guest home: King and his family were staying with Justine and Louis Smadbeck, friends of Coretta King. Garrow, *FBI and Martin,* p. 118; Coretta King, *My Life,* p. 251.

453 King and his allies: Garrow, *Bearing the Cross,* p. 346; NY LHM dated Aug. 20, 1964, FR-NR.

453 Johnson's entire purpose: Lee White to LBJ, "Notes for Meeting with Negro Leaders," Aug. 19, 1964, Ex HU2, PR8-1, Box 3, LBJ.

453 "Deke's information is that": Unsigned memo (from Lee White), Ex PL1/ST24, LBJ.

453 fifty-nine minutes: PDD, Aug. 19, 1964.

453 "regret that I am unable": MLK telegram to LBJ (dictated by Andrew Young), Aug. 19, 1964, A/KP27f7.

453–54 "The attached telegram": Lee White to LBJ, Aug. 19, 1964, Ex PL1/ST 24, Box 81, LBJ.

454 "whole life's work": LBJ phone call with George Reedy, 12:34 P.M., Aug. 19, 1964, Cit. 5030, Audiotape WH6408.28, LBJ.

454 direct statement or release: There were scattered small stories on the rumors, without citing the telegram, e.g., "LBJ Gets Negro Warning," WP, Aug. 20, 1964, p. 4.

454 their own peculiar crisis: "A check here at the Bureau fails to reflect that we knew anything about the cake." DeLoach to Mohr, Aug. 19, 1964, FLP-210. "The success of this technique was proven, inasmuch as Guest furnished damaging information." SAC, Atlanta, to Hoover, Aug. 1964, FLP-213.

454 Moses ended the three-day staff conference: NYT, Aug. 20, 1964, p. 1; Holt, *The Summer,* pp. 246–47.

454 "The end is tonight": NYT, Aug. 23, 1964, p. 85.

454 churches burned that night: NYT, Aug. 20, 1964, p. 13; "Mississippi Bombings, Burnings Since June 16," A/SN36f6.

454   "For so long as man": NYT, Aug. 21, 1964, p. 1; Goldman, *Tragedy*, pp. 223–24.

455   scapegoat Adam Yarmolinsky: Ibid. Yarmolinsky that very day was sending out job queries, complete with his résumé and letters of recommendation. Yarmolinsky to Earl C. Bolton (University of California, Berkeley) and Anne Ford (Houghton Mifflin), Aug. 20, 1964, Box 12, Yarmolinsky Papers, JFK.

455   President who fished from his pocket: WP, Aug. 21, 1964, p. 2; PDD, Aug. 20, 1964.

455   interviewed Stokely Carmichael: Correspondent Larry Grelman, *Mississippi Negro 1964*, WHWH-Princeton, Tape No. 64016 NWR, PEA.

34. A Dog in the Manger: The Atlantic City Compromise

456   Wallace hotly denounced: NYT, Aug. 22, 1964, p. 6; WP, Aug. 22, 1964, p. 5.

456   arranged by recent state law: NYT, Aug. 21, 1964, p. 1.

456   Gem Motel on Pacific: Dittmer, *Local People*, p. 286.

456   "a hymn-singing group": WP, Aug. 22, 1964, p. 4.

457   Schwerner's station wagon: Sellers, *River of No Return*, p. 108.

457   "IV. B. 2.": "Essential Legal Points for Briefing the Delegates," b16f740, Edwin King Papers, TOU.

457   Sweeney escorted: Harris, *Dreams Die Hard*, p. 71.

457   cautious sympathy: Int. Charles Cobb, Aug. 20, 1991.

457   panel of historians: NYT, Aug. 21, 1964, p. 12.

457   Saturday morning breakfast: Int. Mendy Samstein by Anne Romaine, Sept. 4, 1966, A/AR.

457   Democrats had resolved: NYT, June 28, 1964, p. 43.

457   "Joe, they've screwed you!": Mills, *This Little Light*, p. 116.

457   strategy needed cameras: Int. Joseph Rauh, Oct. 17, 1983.

457   "This is a helluva thing": LBJ phone call with Walter Jenkins, 8:30 P.M., Aug. 21, 1964, Cit. 5107, Audiotape WH6408.32, LBJ.

458   "I don't give a damn": LBJ phone call with Walter Reuther, 8:56 P.M., Aug. 21, 1964, Cit. 5112, Audiotape WH6408.32, LBJ.

458   "I never heard of it": LBJ phone call with Hubert Humphrey, 12:15 P.M., Aug. 25, 1964, Cit. 5181, Audiotape WH6408.36, LBJ.

458   "We have only an hour": WP, Aug. 23, 1964, pp. 1, 24.

458   "could seat a dozen dead dodos": "Brief Submitted by the Mississippi Freedom Democratic Party," prepared by Joseph L. Rauh, Jr., assisted by Eleanor K. Holmes and H. Miles Jaffee, Aug. 1964, p. 2.

458   "On them is the blood": WP, Aug. 23, 1964, p. 24.

458   "over one hundred ministers": NYT, Aug. 23, 1964, p. 81.

458   Rauh objected: Mills, *This Little Light*, p. 118.

458   "It was the 31st": Ibid., pp. 119–21.

459   Hamer vanished: Holt, *The Summer*, p. 169; Carson, *In Struggle*, p. 125; Dittmer, *Local People*, p. 288.

459   "We will return": Blackside, Inc. PBS series, *Eyes on the Prize*, I vol. 5, *Mississippi: Is This America?*

459   Johnson was hosting thirty: PDD, 2:30–5:25 P.M., Aug. 22, 1964.

459   Four strays: NYT, Aug. 23, 1964, p. 1.

459   calling for a general walkout: NYT, Aug. 25, 1964, p. 23.

460   "a very enjoyable": WP, Aug. 23, 1964, p. 1.

460   "Johnson Still Silent": Ibid.

460   stood in silent tribute: Ibid.

460   "I say to you that": MLK statement of Aug. 22, 1964, A/SC27f40.

460   "a political cross": WP, Aug. 23, 1964, p. 1.

460   "the party in Mississippi": Ibid., p. 26.

460–61   yanked FBI technicians out: Turner to Branigan, Aug. 23, 1964, FK-440.

461   room directly below: WP, Jan. 26, 1975, p. 1.

461   "Lyndon is way out of line": DeLoach, *Hoover's FBI*, p. 5.

461   DeLoach had thrown together: Garrow, *FBI and Martin*, pp. 118–19; O'Reilly, *Racial Matters*, pp. 186–87.

461   "to embarrass the President": H. N. Bassett to Callahan, Jan. 29, 1975, reprinted in Church, *Hearings Before the Select Committee*, p. 634.

461   supplied by NBC News: Ibid., p. 636.

461   Rustin was telling King: NY LHM dated Aug. 25, 1964, FK-NR, pp. 1–4.

461   "fall by the wayside": NY LHM dated Aug. 24, 1965, FR-NR.

461   Larry Still described: *Jet*, Sept. 3, 1964, pp. 22–26.

461   voices at the Gem Motel: Mills, *This Little Light*, p. 123.

461   "After the first Negro": Ibid., p. 120.

462   416 night telegrams: Burner, *Gently He Shall Lead*, p. 175.

462   "won the Boardwalk": Int. Joseph Rauh, Oct. 17, 1983.

462   "We won't take": WP, Aug. 23, 1964, p. 24.

462   twenty-six major credentials contests: MFDP brief, pp. 72–73. For discovering the Texas precedent, Rauh gave credit to his co-author and young legal assistant Eleanor K. Holmes (Norton), who would serve a generation later as U.S. representative from the District of Columbia. Int. Joseph Rauh, Oct. 17, 1983.

462   Texas case of 1944: Dugger, *The Politician*, pp. 137–38.

462   "The thing is out of hand now!": LBJ phone call with James Eastland, 6:21 P.M., Aug. 22, 1964, Cit. 5130, Audiotape WH6408.33, LBJ.

462   "to be perfectly frank": LBJ phone call with James Eastland, 7:10 P.M., Aug. 22, 1964, Cit. 5131, Audiotape WH6408.33, LBJ.

462   "People oughtn't to want": LBJ phone call with James Eastland, 12:02 P.M., Aug. 22, 1964, Cit. 5121, Audiotape WH6408.33, LBJ.

462   shutting off the cotton subsidy: LBJ phone call with James Eastland, 3:35 P.M., Aug. 22, 1964, Cit. 5133, Audiotape WH6408.33, LBJ.

462   best Eastland could secure: LBJ phone call with James Eastland, 4:56 P.M., Aug. 23, 1964, Cit. 5138, Audiotape WH6408.34, LBJ.

462   "I thought he was gonna procrastinate": LBJ phone call with Walter Jenkins, 3:58 P.M., Aug. 23, 1964, Cit. 5136, Audiotape WH6408.34, LBJ.

463   Mondale to head: Garrow, *Bearing the Cross,* p. 347.

463   exhausted recess toward dawn: NYT, Aug. 25, 1964, p. 23.

463   circular picket line: Ibid., p. 24; int. Dorothy Zellner, Dec. 12, 1991.

463   lobster feasts around open beach fires: *Life,* Sept. 4, 1964, pp. 20–28.

463   plunged on horseback: NYT, Aug. 23, 1964, p. 81.

463   "get lost in the business": LBJ phone call with Walter Reuther, 8:46 A.M., Aug. 24, 1964, Cit. 5140, Audiotape WH6408.34, LBJ.

463   "In the last few days": MLK to LBJ, Aug. 24, 1964, WHCF, Box 52, LBJ. An attached note from Paul Popple to Lee White reads, "I have sent the blue copy in to the President."

463   "trying to get me in it": LBJ phone call with Richard Russell, 11:10 A.M., Aug. 24, 1964, Cit. 5143, Audiotape WH6408.34, LBJ.

464   the Kennedy myth: Miller, *Lyndon,* pp. 472–74.

464   two much anticipated events: Schlesinger, *Robert Kennedy,* pp. 715–16; *Life,* Sept. 4, 1964, pp. 30–31.

464   mount surveillance of Kennedy: WP, Jan. 26, 1975, p. 1.

464   "refused to elaborate": Jones to DeLoach, Aug. 25, 1964, FRFK-1653.

464   "applause hit like thunder": Schlesinger, *Robert Kennedy,* p. 716.

464   "obviously another attempt": Jones to DeLoach, Aug. 24, 1964, FRFK-1686. On the *Washington Post* article of Aug. 23, 1964, entitled "Kennedy Top-Rated as Justice Boss," by reporter James Clayton, Hoover wrote, "What do we know of Clayton?"

464   "got a virus": Juanita Roberts to LBJ, Aug. 24, 1964, and Juanita Roberts to "Dorothy," March 1, 1965, Ex PL1/ST24, Box 81, LBJ.

465   into the Pageant Motel: NYT, Aug. 25, 1964, p. 23.

465   Humphrey passionately advocated: Int. Joseph Rauh by Anne Romaine, June 1967, A/AR, pp. 331–32.

465   direct and indirect orders: Cf. LBJ phone call with Hubert Humphrey, Aug. 14, 1964, Cit. 4917, Audiotape WH6408.19, LBJ: "Well, I left it up to you and Ken O'Donnell to handle this Mississippi thing."

465   fn "You better talk": LBJ phone call with Walter Reuther, Aug. 17, 1964, Cit. 5003, Audiotape WH6408.27, LBJ.

465   Humphrey protested: Mills, *This Little Light,* p. 125; Anne Romaine interviews with Joseph Rauh, Fannie Lou Hamer, Edwin King, Allard Lowenstein, Robert P. Moses, A/AR; int. Robert P. Moses, Oct. 11, 1983, March 13, 1988; Dittmer, *Local People,* p. 294.

465   "I walked into the lion's den": LBJ phone call with Hubert Humphrey and Walter Jenkins, Aug. 24, 1964, Cit. 5156-57, Audiotape WH6408.34, LBJ.

466   Lawrence and Joseph Rauh parried: Int. Joseph Rauh by Anne Romaine, June 1967, A/AR, pp. 333–35.

466   troubles over Alabama: NYT, Aug. 25, 1964, pp. 1, 23.

466   Connor of Birmingham: NYT, Sept. 6, 1964, p. 42.

466   "This is as embarrassing as all hell": NYT, Aug. 25, 1964, p. 23.

466   "he owes me $400": Comments of Bill Minor, reporter for the *New Orleans Times-Picayune,* at "Covering the South: A National Symposium on the Media and the Civil Rights Movement," University of Mississippi, April 1987.

466   Rauh had lost control: Int. Joseph Rauh, Oct. 17, 1983.

467   "so that it looks right": LBJ phone call with James Reston and Arthur Sulzberger, 7:16 P.M., Aug. 24, 1964, Cit. 5162-62, Audiotape WH6408.35, LBJ.

467   "They are just distressed": LBJ phone call with Walter Reuther, 8:25 P.M., Aug. 24, 1964, Cit. 5165, Audiotape WH6408.35, LBJ; PDD, Aug. 23–24, 1964.

467   550,000 automobile workers: NYT, Aug. 25, 1964, p. 14.

467   into Atlantic City before dawn: Dittmer, *Local People,* p. 294.

467   dinner off trays: PDD, Aug. 24, 1964.

467   fn plane to fetch the Steinbecks: LBJ phone call with John Steinbeck, Aug. 21, 1964, Cit. 5111, Audiotape WH6408.32, LBJ.

467   fn novelist had developed: Int. Jack Valenti, Feb. 25, 1991. Steinbeck posed forty-one questions about Johnson's taste and personality ("Of what is he afraid? ... Is he ever silly?"), and offered suggestions ranging from gestures ("Let him choose a favorite flower.... Meeting any one at all, let him take it from his button hole and present it") to speech delivery: "... by wrong emphasis and dull delivery, he missed most of the punch lines. He just spoke it off sync.... That's why I'd like to know if he can carry a tune. We know from his dancing that he has a good sense of rhythm."

In the summer of 1964, Steinbeck sent ideas to LBJ through Jack Valenti. He recommended that Johnson attack Goldwater ("This jack-ass is nuts") for suggesting that "the German soldier was superior to the American fighting man...." After the Tonkin Gulf incident, he recommended that the United States sink North Vietnamese ships as pirates. "What you call a thing is very important," Steinbeck advised.

Steinbeck, "Notes and questions for J.V. about LBJ," nd, AC 84-57, Valenti Papers, LBJ; Steinbeck to Jack Valenti, July 10, 1964, AC 84-57, Valenti Papers, LBJ; "Goldwater Interview with *Der Spiegel*," NYT, July 10, 1964; "Transcript of Unpublished Part of *Der Spiegel*'s Interview with Goldwater," NYT, July 11, 1964, p. 10; Moyers to LBJ, July 14, 1964, Box 8, Office of the President, LBJ; Steinbeck to Jack Valenti, Aug. 5, 1964, AC 84-57, Valenti Papers, LBJ.

467 "Full Fiery Throttle": *Life*, Sept. 4, 1964, pp. 20–21.

467 "I am not going to": Draft statements from Mrs. Johnson and Jack Valenti, Aug. 1964, Ex PL1/ST24, LBJ.

467 "Unbroken Harmony": NYT, Aug. 25, 1964, p. 1.

467 "every one of those big states": LBJ phone call with John Bailey, 9:22 A.M., Aug. 25, 1964, Cit. 5173-74, Audiotape WH6408.35, LBJ.

468 disclosed a new plan: LBJ phone call with A. W. Moursund, 10:05 A.M., Aug. 25, 1964, Cit. 5175, Audiotape WH6408.36, LBJ.

468 When George Reedy called: LBJ phone call with George Reedy, Aug. 25, 1964, Cit. 5176, Audiotape WH6408.36, LBJ.

468 fn "The times require leadership": Ibid.

468 "If anybody's entitled": LBJ phone call with Walter Jenkins, Aug. 25, 1964, Cit. 5177, Audiotape WH6408.36, LBJ.

468 "I do not remember hours": Johnson, *White House Diary*, p. 192. The Johnsons' cook, Zephyr Wright, was another family intimate who said she believed until the last minute that President Johnson would drop out of the 1964 race. Miller, *Lyndon*, p. 475.

468 decisive crunch: Dittmer, *Local People*, pp. 293–98; Burner, *Gently He Shall Lead*, pp. 180–84; Hampton, *Voices of Freedom*, pp. 200–202; Mills, *This Little Light*, pp. 126–28; NYT, Aug. 26, 1964, p. 1; WP, Aug. 26, 1964, p. 1.

468–69 wiretaps picked up frantic consultations: DeLoach to Walter Jenkins, "Morning Summary of Activities," Aug. 25, 1964, cited in U.S. Senate, *Hearings Before the Select Committee to Study Governmental Operations with Respect to Intelligence Activities*, vol. 6, pp. 714–17.

469 "The convention has decided": Int. Joseph Rauh by Anne Romaine, June 1967, A/AR; Joseph Rauh Oral History by Paige Mulhollan, July 30, 1969, LBJ; int. Joseph Rauh, Oct. 17, 1983.

469 terminate Rauh's employment: Ibid. Reuther told President Johnson of a similar threat four days earlier: "I talked to Joe Rauh, and I talked to him as seriously as I ever talked to any human being, and I said, 'Look, Joe, we've been friends for years, and you're our lawyer, and by God, if you don't work this thing out on a sensible, reasonable basis, then you and I are gonna part company, because I'm in the President's corner on this thing all the way.' " LBJ phone call with Walter Reuther, Aug. 21, 1964, Cit. 5112, Audiotape WH6408.32, LBJ.

469 "Your funding is on the line": Int. Robert P. Moses, Aug. 11, 1983; int. Joseph Rauh, Oct. 17, 1983.

469 2,316 to 2,318: WP, Aug. 26, 1964, p. 6.

469 Moses bridled: Int. Robert P. Moses, Aug. 11, 1983.

469 Edwin King suggested: Int. Edwin King, June 26, 1992.

470 "The President will not allow": Int. Edwin King by Anne Romaine, Nov. 1966, A/AR.

470 "You cheated!": Ibid. Also int. Robert P. Moses, Feb. 15, 1991.

470 "a white man hitting": Int. Joseph Rauh, Oct. 17, 1983.

470 Lawrence admitted: WP, Aug. 26, 1964, p. 6.

470 "actually raised his voice": Belfrage, *Freedom Summer*, p. 252.

471 "a wholesale walkout": LBJ phone call with Carl Sanders and John Connally, Cit. 5183-84, Audiotape WH6408.37, LBJ.

472 "Mississippi's debt": WP, Aug. 27, 1964, p. 2.

472 Rauh shed tears: Int. Joseph Rauh, Oct. 17, 1983.

472 vigil escalated swiftly: Belfrage, *Freedom Summer*, pp. 252–54.

472 helping to smuggle MFDP members: WP, Aug. 26, 1964, p. 6.

472 "I made about four": Sutherland, *Letters from Mississippi*, pp. 220–21.

472 only three of them: Fred Berger of Natchez, Randolph Holladay of Picayune, and Douglas Wynn of Greenville. Mills, *This Little Light*, p. 131.

472 fn "You're a patriot": LBJ phone call with Doug Wynn, Aug. 25, 1964, Cit. 5209, Audiotape WH6408.38, LBJ.

472 fn Klan death threats: LBJ phone call with Jack Valenti, Aug. 31, 1964, Cit. 5286, Audiotape WH6408.43, LBJ; LBJ phone call with Nicholas Katzenbach, Aug. 31, 1964, Cit. 5294, Audiotape WH6408.43, LBJ.

472 riots and demonstrations: LBJ phone call with Walter Jenkins, Aug. 25, 1964, Cit. 5210, Audiotape WH6408.38, LBJ.

472 Watson angrily ordered: Walter Adams to Walter Jenkins, Sept. 1, 1964, PL1/ST24, Box 81, LBJ.

473 Moses waved off: Dittmer, *Local People*, p. 299.

473 Reedy hesitantly answered a summons: Reedy, *Lyndon B. Johnson*, p. 55.

473 "By God, I'm gonna go": Int. George Reedy, May 8, 1991.

473 "the dumb bastards on your side": Int. Joseph Rauh, Oct. 17, 1983.

473 "I honestly don't care": Int. Joseph Rauh by Anne Romaine, June 1967, A/AR.

473 "You're a traitor": Forman, *Black Revolutionaries*, p. 392.

473 drunk in a bar: Int. Jack Pratt, March 25, 1991.

473 King delivered a speech: Int. Robert P. Moses, March 13, 1988. "King was neutral," said Moses. "He wasn't taking Bayard's position."

473 conflicted private advice: Int. Edwin King by Anne Romaine, Nov. 1966, A/AR.

474   "Moses could have been Socrates": Burner, *Gently He Shall Lead*, p. 187.

474   people back home were counting on them: Int. Victoria Gray Adams, May 14, 1991.

474   "When they got through": Dittmer, *Local People*, pp. 340–41.

474   "We didn't come": Carson, *In Struggle*, p. 126; Mills, *This Little Light*, p. 132.

474   Reuther's bracing news: PDD, 10:00 A.M.–11:20 A.M., Aug. 26, 1964.

474   agreement by Martin Luther King: Young, *Easy Burden*, p. 310.

474   "vast bulk": WP, Aug. 26, 1964, p. 1.

474   ducked three calls: PDD, Aug. 26, 1964.

474   spontaneous midday walk: Ibid. Goldman, *Tragedy*, pp. 249–50.

474   "One of them must now": CBS Television, *The Making of the President 1964*, Tape No. 65043 PST, PEA.

474–75   "We're going to nominate your boy": Humphrey, *The Education*, pp. 303–4.

475   scrambled the entire presidential entourage: Goldman, *Tragedy*, pp. 250–51.

475   a helicopter blade: Int. George Reedy, May 8, 1991.

475   unbroken wave of applause: Guthman, *We Band of Brothers*, p. 291; Schlesinger, *Robert Kennedy*, pp. 717–18.

475   "Party and nation": CBS Television, *The Making of the President 1964*, Tape No. 65043 PST, PEA.

475   strongly suspected aides: Int. George Reedy, May 8, 1991.

475   "quit because Mr. Johnson": NYT, Aug. 29, 1964, p. 6.

475   "I don't want to louse": LBJ phone call with George Reedy, Aug. 30, 1964, Cit. 5270, Audiotape WH6408.42, LBJ. Reedy first despaired about the leak of his "resignation" in a phone call with LBJ, Aug. 26, 1964, Cit. 5243, Audiotape WH6408.40, LBJ.

475   Deke DeLoach applied successfully: DeLoach to Mohr, Aug. 29, 1964, cited in Church, *Hearings Before the Select Committee*, pp. 624–30. On the memo Hoover wrote, "DeLoach should receive a meritorious award."

475   wearing black neck placards: Mills, *This Little Light*, p. 131.

475   Atlantic City a bitter turning point: Int. Robert P. Moses, Oct. 11, 1983, March 13, 1988, Feb. 15, 1991; also Dittmer, *Local People*, p. 362.

475   Hamer led farewell: Belfrage, *Freedom Summer*, pp. 255–56.

476   birthday celebration illuminated: Kasher, *Photographic History*, p. 158.

476   veered across the airfield: Miller, *Lyndon*, pp. 480–81; Graham, *Personal History*, pp. 360–67.

476   "We're going to Texas": Humphrey, *The Education*, p. 305.

476   "I looked ridiculous": Ibid., p. 307.

476   "Cousin Oriole, wake up!": PDD, Aug. 28, 1964.

35. "WE SEE THE GIANTS . . ."

477   twenty-three Coca-Cola signs: Good, *Trouble I've Seen*, pp. 175–93.

477   "There's no crime in Georgia": Ibid., p. 182.

477   Loretta Lackey sat mute: Rosen to Belmont, Sept. 2, 1964, FLP-261.

477   "Doctor, does that mean": Good, *Trouble I've Seen*, p. 185.

478   "my mind is boiling": Ibid., pp. 189–90.

478   preying carpetbaggers: SAC, Atlanta, to Director, Sept. 8, 1964, FLP-274, p. 4.

478   "Don't come back": NYT, Sept. 5, 1964, pp. 1, 9.

478   acquitted the defendants: Jack Nelson, "Backlash and Black Power: A Reporter's Reflections," *New South*, Winter 1967, p. 41.

478   state authorities aborted: Rosen to Belmont, Sept. 8, 1964, FLP-285.

478   "cost my good county": H. C. Echols to Hoover, Oct. 17, 1964, FLP-341.

478   J. Edgar Hoover replied: Hoover to H. C. Echols, Oct. 21, 1964, FLP-342.

478   "telephonically advised": Rosen to Belmont, Sept. 4, 1964, FLP-271.

478   notices on the Penn trial: Cf. Hoover instruction written on Atlanta teletype to Hoover dated Aug. 14, 1964, FLP-208.

478   "certain to raise speculation": Katzenbach to LBJ, Sept. 4, 1964, Ex HU2/ST 24, Box 27, LBJ.

478   President had publicly forecast: PPP, press conference of Aug. 8, 1964.

478   audience with Pope Paul VI: Cf. Archbishop Paul Hallinan (Atlanta) to Cardinal Cicognani, Andrew Young telegram to Cicognani, Hallinan to MLK, and Hallinan to Archbishop Martin O'Connor (Rome), all Sept. 4, 1964, A/KP12f17.

478   income tax trial in 1960: Branch, *Parting*, pp. 293–99, 308–11.

478   represented Elijah Muhammad: Int. Chauncey Eskridge, Feb. 22, 1985.

479   recent marriage: Ali married Sonji Roi of Gary, Indiana, on Aug. 14, 1964. NYT, Aug. 15, 1964, p. 17.

479   "is keeping up with MLK": Wiretap log reprinted in *United States v. Clay*, 430 F2d 165 (1970), p. 168.

479   Nearly five years later: Garrow, *FBI and Martin*, pp. 202, 282. On first discovery that Ali had been overheard on wiretaps, see NYT, Aug. 31, 1968, p. 21.

479   Hoover launched a crossfire: "Hoover Brands Negro Columnist as a 'Racist,' " *Miami Herald*, June 25, 1969, p. 3; Rowan, "It Is Time for J. Edgar Hoover to Go," *Washington Star*, June 15, 1969; Rowan, *Breaking the Barriers*, pp. 293–94; Hoover to Tolson, DeLoach, and Sullivan, June 24, 1964, FK-3613.

479   blamed the late Robert Kennedy: "Bobby Approved King Wiretap, FBI Says," *Miami Herald*, June 19, 1969, p. 1.

479 banished Special Agent Nichols: Int. Robert Nichols, May 29, 1984.

479 "end of innocence": Dittmer, *Local People*, p. 302.

479 "things could never be the same": Sellers, *River of No Return*, p. 111.

479 "Well, I'll give fifty years": Int. Robert P. Moses, Feb. 15, 1991.

479 "it never occurred to us": Mary King, *Freedom Song*, pp. 344–45.

479 Lewis called it a blow: Carson, *In Struggle*, p. 127. Also Forman, *Black Revolutionaries*, pp. 395–96.

479 "Who holds the power?" (emphasis added): Sherrod newsletter of Oct. 12, 1964, Union Theological Seminary, A/CS5f8, pp. 10–11.

480 SNCC had grown: Forman, *Black Revolutionaries*, pp. 423–24.

480 144 far-flung field organizers: Minutes, Executive Committee, Sept. 4, 1964, A/SN6.

480 $165,000 in one New York: Minutes, Executive Committee, Sept. 5, 1964, A/SN6.

480 "the problem is deeper": Minutes, Executive Committee, Sept. 4, 1964, A/SN6.

480 Moses faction and a Forman faction: Int. Robert P. Moses, Aug. 19, 1983, Feb. 15, 1991; int. Robert P. Moses by Joseph Sinsheimer, Dec. 5, 1984; Forman, *Black Revolutionaries*, pp. 411–33.

480 applications from more than a hundred: Minutes, Executive Committee, Sept. 5, 1964, p. 7, A/SN6.

480 guests for the Belafonte trip: Minutes, Executive Committee, Sept. 4, 1964, A/SN6.

481 eleven flew to Guinea: Ibid. Also Carson, *In Struggle*, p. 134; Neary, *Julian Bond*, p. 73.

481 Hamer's wide-eyed exclamations: Mills, *This Little Light*, pp. 134–36.

481 Belafonte rushed off: Ibid.; int. Harry Belafonte, March 6–7, 1985; Hampton, *Voices of Freedom*, pp. 204–6.

481 broke happily into tears: Jack O'Dell, "Like in Mississippi," *Freedomways*, 2nd Quarter, 1965, pp. 234–35.

481 with Belafonte presiding: Int. John Lewis by Archie Allen, Sept. 24, 1969, AAP.

481 "I realized on this trip": Forman, *Black Revolutionaries*, p. 409.

481 braided in cornrows: Mills, *This Little Light*, p. 137.

482 "sold about three million of you": Int. Matthew Jones by Archie Allen, Nov. 9, 1969, AAP.

482 all but two went home early: Forman, *Black Revolutionaries*, p. 411.

482 SNCC-style tour: "The Trip," report submitted by John Lewis and Donald Harris, Dec. 14, 1964, 14 pp., A/SC45f14.

482 Malcolm entranced them: Hampton, *Voices of Freedom*, p. 206; Carson, *In Struggle*, p. 135; int. John Lewis by Archie Allen, 1969, pp. 169–71, AAP.

482 Lewis visited the cabaret: Int. John Lewis by Archie Allen, Sept. 24, 1969, AAP.

482 press conference at Boston University: Tape recording and transcript of press conference, Sept. 11, 1964, BUK.

483 passed through the Berlin Wall: NYT, Sept. 13, 1964, p. 66; *Jet*, Sept. 24, 1964, p. 6.

483 "For the first time": MLK Berlin sermon of Sept. 13, 1964, A/KS6.

483 "like grasshoppers": Numbers 13:32–33.

483 Theological Seminary of Berlin: MLK to Bishop Otto Dibelius (thank-you letter), Sept. 28, 1964, A/KP12f3.

483 "It would be shocking indeed": Baumgardner to Sullivan, Aug. 31, 1964, FK-450.

484 Malone notified headquarters: Baumgardner to Sullivan, Sept. 8, 1964, FK-452; U.S. House of Representatives, *Hearings Before the Select Committee on Assassinations*, vol. VII, p. 257.

484 "drastically watered down": NYT, June 12, 1964, p. 1.

484 Behind closed doors: Vorgimler, ed., *Commentary*, pp. 59–65; "AJC White Paper, 1964–65," pp. 68–95, AJC; NYT, Sept. 4, 1964, p. 2.

484 "I am ready to go to Auschwitz": Heschel statement of Sept. 3, 1964, IAD, AJC.

484 fn Soloveitchik rejected: NYT, Aug. 16, 1964, p. 7.

484 entreaties that he not go: Int. Sylvia Heschel, Feb. 4, 1991; int. Marc Tanenbaum, Feb. 5, 1991.

484 protection from Rabbi Louis Finkelstein: Louis Finkelstein, "Three Meetings with Abraham Heschel," *America*, March 10, 1973, pp. 203–4.

484–85 plead face-to-face with Pope Paul VI: Moore, *Human and the Holy*, p. 13.

485 "*mostly* with words": Vorgimler, ed., *Commentary*, p. 105.

485 "*Magno cum dolore*": Ibid., p. 83.

485 "all peoples will address": NYT, Nov. 21, 1964, p. 9; int. John Oesterreicher, May 24, 1991.

485 "Who Crucified Christ?": The *Jerusalem Times*, cited in Vorgimler, ed., *Commentary*, p. 105.

485 SCLC office announced: "Martin Luther King to Meet with Pope Paul," SCLC press release dated Sept. 16, 1964, by Barbara Suarez, A/KS.

485 "to determine if there": Baumgardner to Sullivan, Sept. 17, 1964, FK-479, reprinted in U.S. House of Representatives, *Hearings Before the Select Committee on Assassinations*, vol. VII, pp. 257–58.

485 matched Hoover's longevity: Cf. "Monsignor Cicognani," *Commonweal*, Jan. 5, 1934, pp. 269–70.

485 Paul VI greeted MLK: *Rome Daily American*, Sept. 19, 1964, FK-463; NYT, Sept. 19, 1964, p. 3.

485 "I am amazed": Garrow, *FBI and Martin*, p. 121.

485 "a new and transparently disingenuous": Garrow, *FBI and Martin*, pp. 120–21.

486 dropped plans to attend: Wachtel to "My dear Martin," Oct. 2, 1964 (apologizing for failure to attend), A/KP25f27.

486 agents who knew Daddy King: Garrow, *FBI and Martin*, p. 120.

486 five hundred SCLC delegates: NYT, Sept. 30, 1964, p. 22.

486 "get program printed": Handwritten item No. 9 in MLK convention list headed "C.T.," A/KP31f8.

486 "send letter in my name": Handwritten item No. 2 in MLK convention list headed "Andy Young," A/KP31f8.

486   King himself issued: Handwritten "Executive Orders," A/KP31f8.
486   receipts of $626,000: Garrow, *Bearing the Cross*, p. 353.
486   leaving behind a suit jacket: Ritz Hotel general manager to MLK, Sept. 22, 1964, A/SC1f20; log, Research Committee meeting, A/SC29.
486   preached for Fred Shuttlesworth: MLK appointments log for Sept. 27, 1964, A/SC29; Shuttlesworth to MLK, date na, A/KP22f12.
486   begged off one engagement: MLK to Ted Brown, Sept. 25, 1964, A/KP3f17.
486   generally cordial reception: Intercepted comments by Bayard Rustin on Oct. 2, 1964, in FBI HQ blind memorandum of Oct. 6, 1964, FK-NR.
486   "extremely cooperative and reliable": SAC, Savannah to Director, Sept. 26, 1964, Section 24, FHOC.
486   dropped three bugging devices: Sizoo to Sullivan, Sept. 30, 1964, citing microphone surveillance request by Savannah SAC Edward L. Boyle, FSC-174.
486   well-placed physical surveillance: Savannah LHM dated Oct. 1, 1964, FSC-171.
486   segregationist bomb threat: Savannah LHM dated Oct. 1, 1964, FSC-181.
486   Eskridge established: Trust agreement dated and executed Sept. 29, 1964, by MLK, Eskridge, Shuttlesworth, Abernathy, and Archibald Carey, A/SC49f6.
487   his son might be a candidate: Minutes, SCLC board meeting of Sept. 30, 1964, A/KP29f4.
487   five hundred delegates: NYT, Oct. 2, 1964, p. 27.
487–89   "have our Valley Forges" to "battle is in our hands": Annual Report of MLK to the 8th Annual SCLC Convention, Savannah, Georgia, delivered Oct. 1, 1964, A/KS6; Garrow, *Bearing the Cross*, pp. 353–54.

36. MOVEMENTS UNBOUND

490   first run of sixty-three weeks: NYT, Sept. 1, 1964, p. 30.
490   "a benign infection": *The New Yorker*, Aug. 29, 1964, p. 14.
490   adoring youth riots: *Rolling Stone Rock Almanac*, pp. 90–92.
490   Chagall installed: NYT, Sept. 7, 1964, p. 21.
490   "steerable parachute": NYT, Aug. 23, 1964, p. 86.
490   "bothersome hump": NYT, Dec. 13, 1964, p. 86.
490   girl counting: Manchester, *Glory and the Dream*, p. 1260; Edwards, *Goldwater*, pp. 299–300.
491   40 percent more than Johnson: Edwards, *Goldwater*, p. 287.
491   using grim phrases: Ibid., p. 319.
491   "lobbing one into the men's room": Manchester, *Glory and the Dream*, p. 1260.
491   "The President and the Bomb": NYT, Sept. 9, 1964, p. 42.
491   relished tales of his grandfather: Rochlin, *Pioneer Jews*, pp. 127–31, 224–25.
491   unmentionable on any account: Cf. NYT, July 16, 1964, p. 17.
491   nose of Lincoln's bust: NYT, Aug. 20, 1964, p. 1.
492   "the more the federal government": NYT, Sept. 12, 1964, p. 10.
492   "to tell you what to print": NYT, Sept. 16, 1964, p. 12.
492   took the edge off: Good, *Trouble I've Seen*, pp. 210–11.
492   "an invisible silken curtain": Johnson, *White House Diary*, pp. 195–96.
492   rejected its last Republican: Cohodas, *Strom Thurmond*, p. 26.
492   outlaw fraternal orders: Woodward, *Strange Career*, p. 100.
492   hegemony produced 98 percent: Cohodas, *Strom Thurmond*, p. 37.
492   "will make a Czar of the President": Ibid., p. 333.
493   "go all the way and change parties": Ibid., p. 340.
493   "The Democratic Party": "Television Address of Senator Strom Thurmond to the People of South Carolina on the 1964 Presidential Race, September 16, 1964," *Congressional Record*, Sept. 17, 1964, pp. S22302–5.
493   distinctive new lapel pin: NYT, Sept. 18, 1964, p. 1.
493   minimized the switch: NYT, Sept. 17, 1964, p. 42.
493   Democratic chairman questioned: Columbia, South Carolina, *The State*, Sept. 17, 1964, pp. 1, 6.
493   Hollis Watkins claimed: Int. Hollis Watkins by Joseph Sinsheimer, Feb. 13, 1985; int. Hollis Watkins, June 21, 1992; int. Mike Sayer, June 25, 1992.
494   burned there in a single week: July 17–24, 1964, in "Mississippi Bombings, Burnings Since June 16," A/SN36f6.
494   conquered a pronounced stutter: Int. Mike Miller, June 24, 1994.
494   undiminished vigilante rampage: U.S. Commission on Civil Rights, *Law Enforcement*, pp. 30–35; Dittmer, *Local People*, pp. 305–7.
494   Festival of Football Queens: Heirich, *The Beginning*, p. 44.
494   picketed the *Oakland Tribune*: Viorst, *Fire in the Streets*, pp. 284–86.
494   twenty-six-foot-wide brick strip: Heirich, *The Beginning*, pp. 49–65.
495   "People grab whatever": Harris, *Dreams Die Hard*, pp. 79–80.
495   one with a punctured eardrum: Dittmer, *Local People*, pp. 306–7.
495   "We have jointly manned the tables": Heirich, *The Beginning*, p. 81.
495   "Let Savio speak": Ibid., pp. 90–93.
496   Savio's desire to be identified: Mike Miller to the author, Dec. 2, 1992.
496   chapters must confine themselves: Int. Mike Miller, June 24, 1994.

496 "let us try to avoid": "Rough Minutes of a Meeting Called by the National Council of Churches to Discuss the Mississippi Project," Sept. 18, 1964, A/SN115f3; Carson, *In Struggle,* p. 137.

497 neutral facilitators: Int. Jack Pratt, March 25, 1991.

497 transported Alyene Quin: Dittmer, *Local People,* pp. 307–8.

497 "when he doesn't even have a garage": Tucker, *Mississippi from Within,* p. 124; U.S. Commission on Civil Rights, *Law Enforcement,* pp. 33–35.

497 "argued strenuously": Lee White to Jack Valenti, "Request for Meeting with the President by McComb, Mississippi Bombing Victims," Sept. 23, 1964, HU2/ST24, Box 27, LBJ.

497 met with columnist Drew Pearson: Remarks on McComb by Bob Moses, Dennis Sweeney, and Mike Miller, at SNCC "West Coast Conference," Nov. 1964, Tape No. 239, A/JF.

497 "Do you think I would": Dittmer, *Local People,* p. 308.

497 "nothing in the history": *Jet,* Oct. 7, 1964, pp. 16–21.

497 two more bombings: Homes of Ardis Garner and Matthew Jackson. "Mississippi Bombings, Burnings Since June 16," A/SN36f6; MS, Nov. 20, 1964, pp. 12–13.

497 "criminal syndicalism": Harris, *Dreams Die Hard,* p. 80; NYT, Sept. 27, 1964, p. 41.

497 "They are coming through": Lee White to LBJ, Sept. 24, 1964, HU2/ST24, Box 27, LBJ.

497 several minutes with Johnson: PDD, Sept. 24, 1964.

498 "New Dulles Mission Urged": NYT, Sept. 26, 1964, p. 23.

498 yard of the Natchez mayor: "Mississippi Bombings, Burnings Since June 16," A/SN36f6.

498 "I never said they were good kids": Tucker, *Mississippi from Within,* p. 124.

498 eight hundred cases: Int. Roy Moore, June 22, 1992.

498 fn Moore's volunteers: Ibid.; Ungar, *FBI,* p. 204.

498 surfaced in a McComb newspaper: Dittmer, *Local People,* p. 309.

498 hauling one hundred: SAC, Jackson, to Director, Sept. 17, 1964, FMB-1170.

498 two grand juries dueled: SAC, Jackson, to Director, Sept. 18, 1964, FMB-1178.

498 "the most courageous sheriff": Mars, *Witness,* p. 129.

498 Barnett was the brother: Rosen to Belmont, Sept. 25, 1964, FMB-1227.

499 guarded even from his employers: Katzenbach pressed FBI officials to reveal how they had located the three bodies, fearing that extralegal methods such as wiretaps might "taint" evidence for the entire case. After a long bureaucratic struggle, the FBI acknowledged paying a confidential source for the location, but Sullivan refused to reveal the identity of the source to the Justice Department, fearing leaks and threats on the source's life. Cf. Rosen to Belmont, Sept. 16, 1964, FMB-NR; Rosen to [redacted], Sept. 17, 1964, FMB-1172; Rosen to Belmont, Sept. 21, 1964, FMB-NR.

499 "all of your agents": Whitehead, *Attack on Terror,* p. 172.

499 Katzenbach wired formal orders: Rosen to Belmont, Sept. 25, 1964, FMB-1226.

499 eight-point contingency plan: Ibid., pp. 2–3.

499 begged not to be called: Mars, *Witness,* pp. 134–40.

499 Sullivan cajoled witnesses: Int. Joseph Sullivan, Feb. 3, 1991.

499 Officer Wallace Miller: Whitehead, *Attack on Terror,* pp. 157–62; Cagin and Dray, *We Are Not Afraid,* pp. 429–31.

499 "If Wallace Miller": Int. Joseph Sullivan, Feb. 3, 1991.

499 outdone by a young street agent: Ibid.

499 "I've been expecting you": Vollers, *Ghosts of Mississippi,* pp. 220–21.

499 hundred dollars a week: Huie, *Three Lives,* p. 154.

499 forty pages of notes: Cagin and Dray, *We Are Not Afraid,* p. 434.

500 Sam Bowers quoted: Whitehead, *Attack on Terror,* pp. 175–76.

500 "Once we had Miller": Int. Joseph Sullivan, Feb. 3, 1991.

500 "the greatest repository": NYT, Sept. 28, 1964, p. 1.

500 Philadelphia riot police: NYT, Sept. 1, 1964, p. 1.

500 firebombs struck [the *Los Angeles Herald-Examiner*]: Cf. LAT, Aug. 20, 1964.

500 stomped them on a Sunday afternoon: Boston FBI report dated Sept. 16, 1964 (including Barnette statement of Sept. 2, 1964), FMXNY-4966; Aubrey Barnette with Edward Linn, "The Black Muslims Are a Fraud," *Saturday Evening Post,* Feb. 27, 1965.

500–501 Rev. Virgil Wood ran behind: Int. Virgil Wood, Aug. 2, 1994.

500–501 fn "Now the Black Muslims": *Kup's Show,* Feb. 27, 1965, transcript in Chicago FBI report of March 15, 1965, FMX-NR.

501 twenty-two people had heard Benjamin 2X: New York LHM dated Sept. 10, 1964, FMXNY-4946.

501 shutting down the wiretap: Assistant Attorney General J. Walter Yeagley to Hoover, Sept. 2, 1964, FMX-149; Hoover to SAC, New York, Oct. 2, 1964, FMX-155.

501 fn closing intercept: SAC, New York, to Director, Oct. 2, 1964, FMX-163, p. 7; SAC, New York, to Director, Oct. 3, 1964, FMX-159.

501 "does not have a hundred": SAC, Chicago, to Director, Sept. 8, 1964, FMX-NR.

501 "Other messengers like Moses": NYT, Aug. 28, 1964, p. 28.

501 "to be the strongest black man": *Chicago American,* Sept. 15, 1964; news clip in RS, File 589, CHS.

501 Philadelphia's Venango Ballroom: Philadelphia LHM dated Oct. 8, 1964, FMXNY-5036, pp. 1–9; int. Benjamin Karim, March 19, 1991.

502 Muslims should forget: Ibid. Also int. Warith D. Mohammed, Nov. 14, 1991.

502 Wallace knowingly launched: Chicago LHM dated Aug. 19, 1964, FMXNY-4880.

502 Peabody unexpectedly lost: NYT, Sept. 12, 1964, p. 10.

502 "everything on a silver platter": NYT, Sept. 21, 1964, p. 1.

502   one million people hailed: White, *The Making*, pp. 366–67; Miller, *Lyndon*, pp. 481–82; Valenti, *Very Human President*, pp. 160–61.

503   Berkeley students protested: Heirich, *The Beginning*, pp. 98–119.

503   "All right": Ibid., p. 118.

503   expeditions of five hundred: Viorst, *Fire in the Streets*, pp. 290–91.

503   "the Muslims pulled a car": FBI wiretap intercept reported in SAC, Phoenix, to SAC, Boston, Oct. 2, 1964, FMXNY-5010.

503   eventual conviction in January: Aubrey Barnette with Edward Linn, "The Black Muslims Are a Fraud," *Saturday Evening Post*, Feb. 27, 1965, p. 29.

503   DeLoach took a bulletin: Lee White to LBJ, Oct. 1, 1964, Ex HU2/ST24, LBJ.

504   editor hazarded: Dittmer, *Local People*, pp. 309–11.

504   "local officials are publicly": Lee White to LBJ, Sept. 30, 1964, w/ attached Katzenbach to LBJ, Sept. 28, 1964, Ex HU2/ST24, LBJ.

504   Four Episcopal ministers: NYT, Oct. 1, 1964, p. 32.

504   "Some were bombings by white people.": Ibid.

504   Dittmer later discounted: Dittmer, *Local People*, p. 310.

504   three Klansmen: NYT, Oct. 2, 1964, p. 27; speech of Gov. Paul Johnson, Oct. 1, 1964, WLBT news film 2770/F1800, MDAH; Whitehead, *Attack on Terror*, pp. 166–68; U.S. Commission on Civil Rights, *Law Enforcement*, pp. 37–39. The U.S. Civil Rights Commission reported that most of the weekly bombings were carried out by a Ku Klux Klan klavern called the South Pike Rifleman's Association, organized as an affiliate of the National Rifle Association in order to purchase arms and ammunition at discount. The klavern was known informally as the Wolf Pack.

504   King announced this news: NYT, Oct. 2, 1964, p. 27; *Jet*, Oct. 14, 1964, pp. 4–7.

504   fn transcripts of the McComb broadcasts: Vol. 9, FCC Case No. 16663, NA.

504   fn landmark 1969 decision: WLBT case summary, Cole and Ottinger, *Reluctant Regulators*, pp. 63–68.

504   Watkins soon released: Whitehead, *Attack on Terror*, pp. 169–71.

505   "blindness and indifference": Tucker, *Mississippi from Within*, p. 127.

505   Pearson sent bond money: "Running Summary of Incidents During the 'Freedom Vote' Campaign," pp. 89–90, A/KP7f26.

505   "Statement of Principles": Dittmer, *Local People*, p. 312.

505   "Judge Orders Secrecy": NYT, Oct. 3, 1964, p. 1.

505   fn first baby boom cohort: Jones, *Great Expectations*, pp. 70–73.

505   all Thursday night huge throngs: Heirich, *The Beginning*, pp. 129–44; Viorst, *Fire in the Streets*, pp. 291–92.

506   FBI agents arrested: Whitehead, *Attack on Terror*, p. 174.

506   "Violence Not Linked": NYT, Oct. 4, 1964, p. 1.

506   located Jimmy Jordan: Whitehead, *Attack on Terror*, p. 179.

506   Proctor petitioned: Int. Joseph Sullivan, Feb. 3, 1991.

506   "affiliations, the black-white problem": Anonymous, "Introduction: Semi-Introspective," paper for the Nov. 1964 Waveland conference, b1f11, A/CS.

506   "Why do we organize": Memo re "SNCC Staff Retreat," Oct. 1964, b1f11, A/SC.

506   "After the election": Memo "From Sherrod," ibid. It begins: "First of all, let us thank God for the wisdom of the pinched toe and the empty belly." It ends: "We were kids; now we're grown-up—almost. We still have a little time before the giant awakes. This may be the last time; I don't know."

506   "Well, shit on": Minutes, 5th District Meeting, Nov. 25, 1964, A/SN 100f13, p. 9.

506   "I have begun to split up": Anonymous, "Introduction: Semi-Introspective," paper for the Nov. 1964 Waveland conference, b1f11, A/CS.

506   "One reason guys fight": Minutes, 5th District Meeting, Nov. 25, 1964, A/SN 100f13, p. 9.

506   The internal contest was widely defined: Carson, *In Struggle*, pp. 138–42; Forman, *Black Revolutionaries*, pp. 411–37; Mary King, *Freedom Song*, pp. 437–74; Dittmer, *Local People*, pp. 315–37. At Waveland on Nov. 6, 1964, Forman was quoted as follows: "Someone has said there is a power struggle going on . . . ," in minutes, A/SN7.

506   Moses sat silent: Int. Robert P. Moses, Aug. 10, 1983, Feb. 15, 1991.

506   silent pantomime: Int. Mike Sayer, June 25, 1992.

507   "Moses is drinking": Poem by Mississippi volunteer Dov Green, quoted in Mary King, *Freedom Song*, pp. 441–42.

507   "Rivals are not enemies": Mike Miller to SNCC National Staff, Oct. 23, 1964, courtesy of Mike Miller.

507   "If we assign a quota": Anonymous, "Introduction: Semi-Introspective," paper for the Nov. 1964 Waveland conference, b1f11, A/CS.

507   "we really believe": Frank Smith, "Position Paper No. 1," b1f11, A/CS.

507   a prophetic paper, written anonymously: Mary King, *Freedom Song*, pp. 567–69.

507   "I was sure that we": Ibid., p. 439.

507   "the best way to keep someone": Harris, *Dreams Die Hard*, p. 88.

508   "tried to give equal weight": Forman, *Black Revolutionaries*, p. 418.

508   "the cities are our jungles": Bob Moses and Dennis Sweeney at SNCC "1st West Coast Conference," Stanford University, Nov. 1964, Tape No. 239, A/JF.

508–9   Proctor patiently visited to "Sir, I know just how you feel.": Statement of James Jordan, Nov. 5, 1964, and statement of Horace Doyle Barnette, Nov. 20, 1964, in prosecutive summary dated Dec. 19, 1964,

FMB-1613; Whitehead, *Attack on Terror*, p. 183; int. Joseph Sullivan, Feb. 3, 1991; Cagin and Dray, *We Are Not Afraid*, pp. 294, 393, 432–34.

37: LANDSLIDE

513   fn "I don't want you sneaking": Halberstam, *October 1964*, p. 55.
513   throat of a borrowed tuba: Ibid., p. 317.
513   Jenkins quietly submitted: *U.S. News & World Report*, Oct. 26, 1964, pp. 54–56; Clifford, *Counsel*, pp. 399–402.
514   "verbally caressed": Miller, *Lyndon*, p. 485.
514   On October 9: PDD, Oct. 9, 1964, LBJ.
514   "nonparticipation, but just short": WP, Oct. 10, 1964, p. 1.
514   "knows the sound of the wind": *New Orleans Times-Picayune*, Oct. 10, 1964, p. 2.
514   "I thought he had": "Remarks at a Fundraising Dinner in New Orleans," Oct. 9, 1964, pp. 1281–88, PPP.
514   " 'Nigger! Nigger! Nigger!' ": Johnson, *The Vantage Point*, p. 110; int. Horace Busby, Feb. 3, 1992.
515   "The audience gasped": Goldman, *Tragedy*, pp. 292–94.
515   "a physical thing": Valenti, *Very Human President*, p. 161.
515   climactic phrase was rendered: *Jet*, Oct. 22, 1964, p. 4; PPP, 1964, p. 1286; AJ, Oct. 10, 1964, p. 1.
515   "Nigra! Nigra! Nigra!": Miller, *Lyndon*, p. 485.
515   "Johnson Hits at Hatred": AJ, Oct. 10, 1964, p. 1.
515   "tired and negative": "BUZZ" (Horace Busby) to LBJ, nd, b10, Moyers Papers, LBJ.
515   "transparent exploitation of racism": NYT, Oct. 14, 1964, p. 20.
515   "Travail and torment": NYT, Oct. 4, 1964, p. 1.
515   confidential October reports: Larry O'Brien to LBJ, Oct. 6, 11, 20, and 23, 1964, Box 3, Henry Wilson Papers, LBJ.
515   "It is becoming more and more apparent": O'Brien to LBJ, Oct. 11, 1964, Box 3, Henry Wilson Papers, LBJ.
516   "Separate political structures": O'Brien notified Johnson that St. Augustine, Florida, was an extreme case in which racial conflict caused the existing white Democratic structure literally to dissolve, as "it has proved impossible to get a campaign chairman so far." O'Brien to LBJ, "Florida Organizational Meeting," Oct. 20, 1964, Box 3, Henry Wilson Papers, LBJ.
516   Powell was still bargaining: Hamilton, *Adam Clayton Powell*, pp. 438–39.
516   "we must see this is done": O'Brien to LBJ, Oct. 23, 1964, Box 3, Henry Wilson Papers, LBJ.
516   "look like Johnson has me": Bayard Rustin–Walter Fauntroy conversation of Oct. 17, 1964, cited in NY LHM dated Oct. 20, 1964, FK-NR.
516   King delivered four speeches: Garrow, *Bearing the Cross*, p. 354.
516   Dr. Asa Yancey: *Jet*, Oct. 29, 1964, p. 23.
516   King instructed his assistant: Int. Bernard Lee, June 19, 1985.
516   kept him off the board: Int. Benjamin Mays, March 6, 1984.
517   Hallinan appeared in person: Coretta King, *My Life*, p. 17; Young, *Easy Burden*, p. 313.
517   King chuckled: *Jet*, Oct. 29, 1964, pp. 14–21.
517   "a beautiful bright shining light of hope": Ibid., p. 21.
517   "the greatest of American ideals": RFK to MLK, Oct. 14, 1964, Box 21, RFK Senate Papers, JFK.
517   telegram warmly commending King: LBJ to MLK, 10:06 P.M., Oct. 16, 1964 (from aboard *Air Force One*), King Name File, LBJ.
517   hysteria over Walter Jenkins: NYT, Oct. 15, 1964, pp. 1, 31, Oct. 16, 1964, pp. 1, 20; Kearns, *Lyndon Johnson*, pp. 207–9; Goldman, *Tragedy*, pp. 295–98; Clifford, *Counsel*, pp. 401–2; Miller, *Lyndon*, pp. 486–87; DeLoach, *Hoover's FBI*, pp. 384–87.
517   "And if Lincoln abolished": PPP, LBJ speech of Oct. 15, 1964, p. 1343.
517   spotless personnel file: Califano, *Triumph and Tragedy*, pp. 19–20.
517   get-well flowers: NYT, Oct. 28, 1964, p. 34.
517   "top alley cat": Garrow, *FBI and Martin*, pp. 121–22; Powers, *Secrecy and Power*, p. 418; Summers, *Official and Confidential*, p. 357.
518   "No Evidence Is Uncovered": NYT, Oct. 23, 1964, p. 1.
518   "mysterious disease": Gentry, *J. Edgar Hoover*, pp. 580–81.
518   engulfed by the news: Manchester, *Glory and the Dream*, p. 1262.
518   South Vietnam's execution: NYT, Oct. 11, 1964, p. 12, Oct. 12, 1964, p. 3, Oct. 13, 1964, p. 1, Oct. 15, 1964, p. 12.
518   Mantle's eighteenth: Halberstam, *October 1964*, pp. 344–49.
518   "bound to be seriously detrimental": NYT, Oct. 15, 1964, p. 31.
518   never registered: NYT, Oct. 24, 1964, p. 13.
519   specialized tour: Int. Jack Pratt, March 25, 1991; Stern, *Calculating Visions*, pp. 213–14; *Jet*, Nov. 12, 1964, pp. 8–10; NYT, Oct. 30, 1964, p. 24; Bayard Rustin Oral History, June 17, 1969, LBJ.
519   Addison Junior High: Int. Jack Pratt, March 25, 1991.
519   "All of us have the privilege": MLK remarks of Oct. 22, 1964, Tape No. 62, A/KS.
520   quarrels festered: Int. Bernard Lee, June 19, 1985; int. Dora McDonald, Dec. 31, 1990; int. Andrew Young, Oct. 26, 1991; Bayard Rustin–A. J. Muste conversation of Oct. 15, 1964, cited in NY LHM dated Oct. 16, 1964, FK-NR; Young, *Easy Burden*, p. 320.

520 "Dr. King can't come": Int. Jack Pratt, March 25, 1991.

520 "Proposition 14 is sinful": Notes on Los Angeles speech of Oct. 27, 1964, A/KS6.

520 "the right of any person": *Time,* Sept. 25, 1964, p. 23; *Jet,* Oct. 22, 1964, pp. 58–61.

520 "This is a strange year": NYT editorial quoted in *California Eagle,* Oct. 1, 1964, p. 2.

520 Ronald Reagan emerged: Cannon, *Reagan,* pp. 13, 98–99.

520 repudiated just before it was broadcast: Edwards, *Goldwater,* pp. 329–37.

520 "Should Moses have told": Edwards, *Reagan,* pp. 235–46.

521 repeat national telecast: Ibid., pp. 77–80.

521 King tour rolled back: Garrow, *Bearing the Cross,* p. 357.

521 "Brother Goldwater has presented": *Baltimore Sun,* Nov. 7, 1964, p. 18.

521 Rustin as sideman: Baltimore LHM dated Nov. 2, 1964, FSC-NR.

521 Martin had no trouble: Poinsett, *Louis Martin,* pp. 146–47.

521 disavowed the leaflets: Baumgardner to Sullivan, Nov. 2, 1964, FK-511; *Baltimore Sun,* Nov. 3, 1964, p. 1; Cosman, ed., *Republican Politics,* p. 33.

521 "cater to the prurient curiosity": NYT, Oct. 30, 1964, p. 1.

521 defended the clergy: Ibid.

521 "I first learned": Miller, *Lyndon,* p. 489.

522 "God, I hate": PDD, Nov. 3, 1964, p. 2, LBJ.

522 helicopters grounded: PDD, Nov. 4, 1964, p. 3, LBJ.

522 Johnson overwhelmed Goldwater: White, *The Making,* Appendix A.

522 fn Roosevelt's record: Edwards, *Goldwater,* p. 338. For Nixon's 1972 result, see Haldeman, *Haldeman Diaries,* p. 532, or Ambrose, *Ruin and Recovery,* p. 11. In 1984, Ronald Reagan won 59 percent of the popular vote and a record 525 electoral votes.

522 forty-eight House seats: Cosman, ed., *Republican Politics,* p. 167.

522 keenest predictor of outcome: White, *The Making,* p. 304.

522 George Bush: *Time,* Oct. 16, 1964, p. 39.

522 "To the Negro": *Reporter,* Dec. 17, 1964, p. 20.

522 "White Backlash Doesn't Develop": NYT, Nov. 5, 1964, p. 1.

522 "Backlash proved only a flick": Goldman, *Tragedy,* p. 303.

522 "one-shot affair": WP, Nov. 5, 1964, p. 11.

523 Proposition 14 carried California: Lynn W. Eley and Thomas W. Casstevens, *The Politics of Fair-Housing Legislation.* San Francisco: Chandler Publishing Co., 1968, esp. pp. 261–84.

523 headed toward Supreme Court: *Reitman v. Mulkey,* 87 S. Ct. 1627 (1967).

523 "the most important civil rights case": Nathan Lewin to the Solicitor General, Jan. 9, 1967, Admin. Hist./Dept. of Justice, Vol. 7, Part xb[2], LBJ. If the Supreme Court upheld Proposition 14, warned Lewin, "it will doubtless throttle the last hopes for fair-housing legislation in this country." On May 29, 1967, the Court overturned Proposition 14 in a 5–4 decision, holding that it "involves the state in racial discrimination." By then, California governor Reagan advocated legislative repeal of the Rumford Act.

523 oppose the Voting Rights Act of 1965: Cannon, *Role of a Lifetime,* pp. 518–25.

523 "indisputable proof": Edwards, *Goldwater,* p. 344.

523 "a minority party indefinitely": Ibid.

523 "an end to a competitive": Ibid.

523 "problems likely to arise": Henry Wilson to Larry O'Brien, Nov. 25, 1964, Box 4, Henry Wilson Papers, 25pp., LBJ.

523 "based around the right to vote": NYT, Nov. 5, 1964, p. 1.

524 SCLC organization chart: Among papers for the SCLC executive staff meeting at the Gaston Motel in Birmingham, Nov. 12–13, 1964, A/KP32f8.

524 "never reach the point": Minutes, executive staff meeting, Nov. 12–13, 1964, A/KP32f8.

524 "the ontological need": Harry Boyte, "Dialogue—An Interpretation," presented at SCLC executive staff meeting, Nov. 12, 1964, A/KP32f8.

524 Bevel proposed Selma: Minutes, executive staff meeting, Nov. 10–12, 1964, A/KP32f8; Garrow, *Bearing the Cross,* pp. 358–59; int. C. T. Vivian, May 26, 1990.

524 bombardment of proposals: Hoover memos to Katzenbach, Moyers, Marshall, and Yeagley, all Nov. 6, 1964, FK-NR; New York LHM dated Nov. 10, 1964, FK-NR; Hoover cable to Legat London, Nov. 10, 1964, FK-517; blind memo headed "Martin Luther King, Jr.," dated Nov. 12, 1964, FK-521; New York LHM dated Nov. 18, 1964, FK-NR.

525 "loom large": New York LHM dated Nov. 24, 1964, FK-NR.

525 "peephole journalism": Raines, *My Soul,* pp. 407–8; int. Eugene Patterson, April 6, 1991.

525 "carries the seed": "Discerning the Signs of History," MLK sermon of Nov. 15, 1964, A/KS7.

525 New York's Abyssinian Baptist: Lewis, *King,* p. 256; MLK sermon of Nov. 15, 1964, A/KS7.

525 collection of $1,844.80: Powell to MLK, Nov. 16, 1964, A/KP19f45.

526 no King girlfriend: Int. Eugene Patterson, April 6, 1991.

526 "site of renewed SCLC activity": SAC, Miami, to Director and Mobile, Nov. 17, 1964, FSC-203X.

526 exclusively female reporters: Int. Sarah McLendon, July 2, 1997; int. Else Carper, July 2, 1997; int. Betty Beale, July 2, 1997; int. Frances Lewine, July 2, 1997; int. Mary McGrory, July 1, 1997; int. Helene Monberg, July 2, 1997; DeLoach, *Hoover's FBI,* pp. 203–4.

526 three times his allotted hour: Int. Cartha DeLoach, June 1, 1984; int. Sarah McLendon, July 2, 1997; Garrow, *FBI and Martin,* p. 122; DeLoach, *Hoover's FBI,* pp. 204–5; Stokes Committee, *Hearings,* Vol. 7, pp. 51–52.

526 "In view of King's attitude": Transcript printed in *U.S. News & World Report,* Nov. 30, 1964, pp. 56–58.

526   by Communist advisers: Robert Kennedy Oral History by Anthony Lewis, Dec. 4, 1964, p. 693, JFK; NYT, Nov. 20, 1964, p. 18.

526   "The girls": DeLoach testimony of Dec. 3, 1975, in Church Committee, *Hearings,* Vol. 6, p. 173.

527   "Hoover Assails Warren Findings": NYT, Nov. 19, 1964, p. 1.

527   "Blast at Police Corruption": WP, Nov. 19, 1964, p. 1.

527   Andrew Young knew: Young, *Easy Burden,* p. 315.

527   "While I resent": Baumgardner to Sullivan, Nov. 19, 1964, FK-537.

527   "drop the part": Ibid.

527   "I cannot conceive": NYT, Nov. 20, 1964, p. 1; Garrow, *Bearing the Cross,* p. 360.

527   Katzenbach walked into Hoover's office: Int. Nicholas Katzenbach, June 14, 1991.

527   "we solidly backed Dr. King": NYAN, Nov. 28, 1964, p. 1; PC, Nov. 28, 1964, p. 1; *Jet,* Dec. 3, 1964, pp. 6–8.

527   Wachtel and Rustin peppered: Int. Harry Wachtel, Oct. 27, 1983.

527   "What motivated such": MLK to Hoover, Nov. 19, 1964, FK-584.

528   Atlanta office compiled: Atlanta to Director, urgent teletype of 10:30 P.M., Nov. 19, 1964, FK-539.

528   "King kept the Agent waiting": Rosen to Belmont, Nov. 20, 1964, FK-581.

528   "is old and getting senile": Garrow, *FBI and Martin,* p. 125.

528   "further evidence": Ibid., p. 124.

528   "O.K. But I don't understand": Hoover note on Rosen to Belmont, Nov. 20, 1964, FK-581.

528   Propaganda operations expanded: Garrow, *FBI and Martin,* pp. 124–26; Powers, *Secrecy and Power,* p. 420. Among new efforts to discredit King with religious groups, DeLoach's public relations office supervised contacts with several leaders of the Baptist World Alliance, and Assistant Director, Domestic Intelligence Division, William Sullivan personally briefed a "horrified" Dr. Edwin Espy of the National Council of Churches. Jones to DeLoach, Dec. 8, 1964, FK-624; Sullivan to Belmont, Dec. 16, 1964, FK-636; Garrow, *FBI and Martin,* pp. 132–33; Findlay, *Church People,* pp. 87–88.

528   first new batch of anti-King material: Sullivan to Belmont, Nov. 22, 1964, FK-NR.

528   "a great liability": *"KING,* In view of your low grade...." Undated anonymous letter, Section 24, FHOC.

529   known as the suicide package: Garrow, *FBI and Martin,* pp. 125–26; Sullivan, *The Bureau,* p. 142. In 1978, the House Select Committee on Assassinations concluded of this letter, "The final paragraph clearly implied that suicide would be a suitable course of action for Dr. King...." Stokes Committee, *Final Report,* pp. 573–75. Since the letter became public, Hoover loyalists from the FBI have maintained stoutly that it was entirely the idea of Assistant Director William Sullivan, who later broke with Hoover and conspired during the Nixon years to replace the aged director. Killed in a 1977 hunting incident, Sullivan died an apostate to the Hoover era—expelled from the Society of Former FBI Agents and demonized as the scapegoat for its excesses. The House committee did not firmly resolve who approved the King suicide package within the FBI, but it did suggest with understated logic that the complexity of the mission, the traces of it in the files, and the climate of fury against King at the time all point to the operation as an institutional product. The question of responsibility remains a gray area of argument almost by nature of the secretive operation itself, somewhat like the issue of whether presidents "knew" or "approved" of assassination attempts by the CIA during the Cold War.

529   Joe Sullivan entered the fray: Int. Joseph Sullivan, Feb. 3, 1991.

529   patrolled the successful integration: NYT, Nov. 19, 1964, p. 1.

529   declined for the fourth and last time: U.S. Commission on Civil Rights, *Law Enforcement,* pp. 54–55.

529   two hundred reported intimidations: "Running Summary of Incidents During the 'Freedom Vote' Campaign, Oct. 18–Nov. 2, 1964," A/KP7f26; Harris, *Dreams Die Hard,* pp. 82–89.

529   Rumors buzzed the corridors: Int. Robert Scherrer, May 5, 1983, and Nov. 4, 1983; int. Lawrence Heim, March 21, 1991; Frederic Dannen, "The G-Man and the Hit Man," *The New Yorker,* Dec. 16, 1996, pp. 68–81.

529   "I only put Chaney's foot": Statement of Horace Doyle Barnette, Nov. 20, 1964, in prosecutive summary dated Dec. 19, 1964, FMB-1613, pp. 171–77.

530   "pressure groups that would crush": *Jet,* Dec. 10, 1964, pp. 6–7; Powers, *Secrecy and Power,* p. 420.

530   meeting at the Barbizon Hotel: Oates, *Let the Trumpet,* pp. 317–18; Schlesinger, *Robert Kennedy,* p. 392; int. Harry Wachtel, Oct. 27, 1983; int. Clarence Jones, Nov. 25, 1983; int. Cleveland Robinson, Oct. 28, 1983.

531   the day's late-breaking news: WLBT news broadcast of Nov. 25, 1964, Vol. 9, FCC Case No. 16663, NA; NYT, Nov. 26, 1964, p. 1; Mars, *Witness,* p. 140; Whitehead, *Attack on Terror,* p. 195. *U.S. News & World Report* reprinted the FBI's entire "King States/Facts" rebuttal, Dec. 7, 1964, pp. 46–47.

531   headquarters had inventoried: Blind memo of Nov. 27, 1964, headed "SUMMARY—HIGHLY SENSITIVE COVERAGE—MARTIN LUTHER KING, JR." and marked, "Route in Envelope," FK-1024.

531   Hoover decreed: Hoover handwritten note on DeLoach to Belmont, Dec. 2, 1964, appended to ibid.

531   occasional contact Roy Wilkins: Cf. DeLoach to Mohr, Feb. 25, 1960 (on DeLoach's meeting with Wilkins of Feb. 24), FRW-6; also, Jones to DeLoach, March 16, 1965 (summarizing the FBI's past contacts with Wilkins before a Gridiron Club dinner at which Hoover was to sit next to him), FRW-NR.

531   "I interrupted Wilkins": DeLoach to Mohr, Nov. 27, 1964, FRW-16.

531   "president of Morehouse College": Int. Cartha DeLoach, June 1, 1984.

531   "My dear Mr. President": Hoover to LBJ, Nov. 30, 1964, FRW-15.

531   "as they might feel a duty": Sizoo to Sullivan, Dec. 1, 1964, Section 24, FHOC.

531   correspondents acknowledged being pitched: Garrow, *FBI and Martin,* pp. 130–31; Fairclough, *To Redeem,* pp. 218–19; Theoharis and Cox, *The Boss,* pp. 356–57.

531   Katzenbach himself undertook: Int. Nicholas Katzenbach, June 14, 1991; int. Ed Guthman, June 25, 1984; Garrow, *FBI and Martin,* p. 127; Church Committee, *Hearings,* Vol. 6, p. 210.

532   fn "Their defense is always": Katzenbach Oral History by Larry J. Hackman, Oct. 8, 1969, JFK.

532   polls favored Hoover: Powers, *Secrecy and Power,* p. 421.

532   "have exercised their freedom of speech": PPP, LBJ press conference of Nov. 28, 1964, pp. 1611–20.

532   "the alleged reports of my being replaced": Hoover to June Winchell, Nov. 30, 1964, FBI File No. 62–31615, Serial 1230. Winchell, wife of ardently pro-Hoover columnist Walter Winchell, had sent Hoover a telegram of crisis support: "Johnson is quote disenchanted unquote. Oh dear God. Shades of the Roosevelt years, Alger Hiss, etc., etc., etc. Billy Sol, Baker, Jenkins. And Johnson is disenchanted? I am now for the first time frightened for this country."

532   "I'd rather have him inside": Powers, *Secrecy and Power,* p. 393.

533   personal response for Bradlee: Bradlee, *A Good Life,* pp. 271–72. Anthony Lewis refuted *Newsweek* in print, writing that "Hoover's position remains basically strong." NYT, Dec. 6, 1964, p. E4.

533   "If I had seriously proposed": Paul Clancy, "The Bureau and the Bureaus," *The Quill,* Feb. 1976, pp. 12–18. In 1970–71, Peter Lisagor of the *Chicago Sun-Times* talked at a reporters' lunch of resisting the tapes and other bait against King, then scoffed at the suggestion that he could have written about the FBI's bugging and propaganda operations themselves, saying it just was not done. He cited the fearful cult of Hoover, dependence on the FBI for other stories, and the questionable ethics of turning against a news source. (Author's personal recollection.)

533   Farmer reached King: Int. James Farmer, Nov. 18, 1983; Farmer, *Lay Bare the Heart,* pp. 268–71; Garrow, *FBI and Martin,* pp. 128–29.

533   "Let freedom ring!": Miller, *Voice of Deliverance,* pp. 146–47.

533   1953 field investigation: SAC, Chicago, to Director, July 31, 1953, and report of Special Agent Jesse Syme, Aug. 11, 1953, FAC-NR.

533   "a highly controversial colored lawyer": Jones to Nease, Oct. 20, 1958, FAC-56; Jones to DeLoach, Nov. 18, 1959, FAC-69.

533   "voluminous information": Jones to DeLoach, Nov. 19, 1959, FAC-72.

533   "associated with known or suspected": Jones to Nease, Oct. 20, 1958, FAC-56.

534   asked to meet Director Hoover: Jones to Nease, Aug. 21, 1958, FAC-53.

534   introduce his niece: Carey to Hoover, June 11, 1959, FAC-58.

534   grand-niece Liberty: Carey to Hoover, June 29, 1959, FAC-61.

534   "the Director was considerably embarrassed": DeLoach to Mohr, June 2, 1960, FAC-82.

534   fn "I cannot tell you how pleased": Carey to Hoover, Sept. 1, 1960, FAC-83.

534   "any time the Bureau or I": Hoover to Tolson et al., March 21, 1961, FAC-85.

534   Hoover put his own: Carey to Hoover, Nov. 19, 1959, FAC-70.

534   accommodation to power: Int. Andrew Young, Oct. 26, 1991.

534   lack of Negro agents: DeLoach to Mohr, June 2, 1960, FAC-82.

534   translated King's Hoover troubles: Carey wrote King a balanced letter of congratulations after he received the Nobel Prize: "It is my own opinion that Hoover has done some fine things in the civil rights field. . . . However, I thought his statement was in very poor taste and your statement was just magnificent. I stay proud of you. The Lord bless you." Carey to MLK, Dec. 11, 1964, A/KP5f13.

534   "I interrupted Dr. Young again": DeLoach to Mohr, Dec. 1, 1964, FK-570.

534   nervous but mannerly chat: Garrow, *FBI and Martin,* pp. 129–30; Garrow, *Bearing the Cross,* pp. 362–64; DeLoach, *Hoover's FBI,* pp. 208–11; Young, *Easy Burden,* pp. 318–19; Lewis, *King,* pp. 256–57; int. Andrew Young, Oct. 26, 1991; int. Cartha DeLoach, June 1, 1984.

535   King flinched: Drew Pearson, "Meeting with Hoover Amazes King," WP, Dec. 5, 1964.

535   negotiating intensely: Rosen to Belmont, Dec. 1, 1964, FMB-1413; Rosen to Belmont, Dec. 2, 1964, FMB-1414.

535   ten legal impediments: SAC, Jackson, to Director, Dec. 3, 1964, FMB-1420.

535   did not trust local officials: William H. Johnson, Jr., to Erle Johnston, Jr., Dec. 4, 1967, MSSC.

535   Sullivan pressed: Int. Joseph Sullivan, Feb. 3, 1991.

535   "indicated that King was calling the shots": SAC, Jackson, to Director, Dec. 3, 1964, FMB-1420.

535   command decision to proceed: Rosen to Belmont, Dec. 4, 1964, FMB-1427; Whitehead, *Attack on Terror,* pp. 197–202.

536   "In a small town like this": WP, Dec. 5, 1964, pp. 1, 17.

536   "the whole country is taking orders": Cagin and Dray, *We Are Not Afraid,* p. 436.

536   traveling party to grow: Oates, *Let the Trumpet,* p. 320; Young, *Easy Burden,* p. 321; Coretta King, *My Life,* pp. 18–19.

536   "I must commend": Whitehead, *Attack on Terror,* p. 202.

536   "a very dangerous organization": Robert Kennedy Oral History by John Bartlow Martin, March 1, 1964, pp. 195–97, JFK.

536   "Negroes' brains are twenty percent smaller": Robert Kennedy (with Burke Marshall) Oral History by Anthony Lewis, Dec. 4, 1964, p. 669.

536   "general criticism": Ibid., pp. 665–68.

536   "what I understand from Hoover's": Ibid., pp. 670–73.

537   fn "I said, 'Mr. King' ": *Time,* Dec. 14, 1970, p. 16. *Time* had published the tough-guy version as an inside news scoop on Aug. 17, 1970.

537   "I never really had any": Robert Kennedy (with Burke Marshall) Oral History by Anthony Lewis, Dec. 4, 1964, p. 682.

38: NOBEL PRIZE

538   packed for a summer trip: Goldman, *Death and Life*, p. 222.
538   stepped off a flight from Paris: New York LHM dated Nov. 25, 1964, FMX-183.
538   "felt foolish coming back": Malcolm X speech of Feb. 15, 1965, in Perry, *Last Speeches*, p. 116.
538   "coming back loaded": New York LHM dated Oct. 15, 1964, FMX-156, p. 4.
538   "Congolese Forced American Officials": NYT, Nov. 25, 1964, p. 1.
538–39   "President Johnson is responsible": New York LHM dated Nov. 25, 1964, FMX-183.
539   personal reunions: Perry, *Malcolm*, p. 331.
539   visited her in 1952: Ibid., p. 141.
539   Muhammad raged privately: Chicago LHM dated Nov. 18, 1964, FMX-181.
539   Captain Joseph to warn: *Chicago New Crusader*, Nov. 28, 1964; NYT, Nov. 8, 1964, p. 48.
539   beaten to death on the street: Clegg, *An Original Man*, p. 226; Perry, *Malcolm*, p. 341.
539   announcement to the Fruit: New York FBI report of Jan. 20, 1965, FMX-215, p. 69.
539   Hoover cabled: Director to Legat, London, Nov. 30, 1964, FMX-187.
539   To British audiences: Perry, *Malcolm*, p. 331.
539   "No matter how many bills pass": Malcolm X address of Dec. 3, 1964, in HQ LHM dated Jan. 11, 1965, FMX-209.
539   At Oxford University: "Cheers for Malcolm X at Oxford," *London Daily Telegraph*, Dec. 4, 1964.
539   C. L. R. James: Lincoln, *Sounds of Struggle*, p. 161.
539   told a London radio audience: *New York Courier*, Dec. 19, 1964.
539   "never could accept": PC, Dec. 5, 1964, p. 6.
539   first non-Anglican: Lewis, *King*, p. 259.
539   FBI surveillance agents: NY LHM dated Dec. 8, 1964, FMX-199.
540   "Mr. Malcolm, we hereby officially": Sharrieff telegram of Dec. 7, 1964, as printed in the *Chicago Crusader* of Dec. 12, 1964, and circulated to FBI HQ by Chicago LHM dated Dec. 15, 1964, FMX-NR.
540   "That was Elijah": Malcolm X speech of Feb. 15, 1965, in Perry, *Last Speeches*, p. 117.
540   Louis X of Boston called Malcolm: MS, Dec. 4, 1964, cited in Perry, *Malcolm*, p. 332, and Clegg, *An Original Man*, p. 226.
540   "Malcolm shall not escape": Ibid. Also Goldman, *Death and Life*, p. 247.
540   "Top Stories of '64": MS, Jan. 15, 1965, p. 15. That same issue also reprinted the March denunciation of Malcolm by his brother Philbert X.
540   acquittal in traffic court: Perry, *Malcolm*, p. 333.
540   "a friend of mine": "HARYOU Panel to Hear Malcolm X," NYAN, Dec. 17, 1964; news clip in FMX-NR.
540   "word is out": Int. Livingston Wingate, July 8, 1992. Wingate, who was director of HARYOU-ACT and a political ally of Adam Clayton Powell, recalled getting a panicked phone call: "I was late getting in the office that morning, and they called me: 'Wingate, get down here, get down here, get down here. Everybody's nervous. Malcolm's here, and they're thinking he may be shot at any moment.' "
540   to Oslo on December 8: "Schedule for Oslo Trip," A/KP12f67.
540   audience at the Royal Palace: Coretta King, *My Life*, pp. 24–25.
540   considerable tension: Int. Harry Wachtel, Oct. 27, 1983; int. Marian Logan, April 24, 1984; Garrow, *Bearing the Cross*, p. 366; Young, *Easy Burden*, p. 320.
540   "At least five other men": Porter cited in FBI HQ LHM dated Feb. 4, 1965, and Legat London to Director, Feb. 4, 1965, FR-NR.
540   drafting suggestions: Int. Harry Wachtel, Oct. 27, 1983.
541   own handwritten draft: Nobel Prize speech drafts, A/KP18f33 and A/KP12f67.
541   "I am mindful": Text of Nobel Prize acceptance, NYT, Dec. 11, 1964, pp. 1, 33.
541   never again submit: Coretta King, *My Life*, p. 25.
541   against the Norwegian protocol chief: Int. Bernard Lee, June 19, 1985; int. Andrew Young, Oct. 26, 1991; int. Dora McDonald, Dec. 31, 1990.
541   receipt of the gold: NYT, Dec. 11, 1964, p. 1; *Jet*, Dec. 24, 1964, pp. 18–21.
541   hearing that day in Mississippi: Cagin and Dray, *We Are Not Afraid*, p. 437; Mars, *Witness*, p. 148; Whitehead, *Attack on Terror*, pp. 204–5.
542   "We had hoped": Television transcript of King press conference, Dec. 10, 1964, A/KS.
542   spontaneous freedom songs: Young, *Easy Burden*, p. 321.
542   Juanita Abernathy swooned: NYT, Dec. 12, 1964, p. 18.
542   "some in King's inner circle": Cf. FBI wiretap transcript of phone call between Bayard Rustin and Stanley Levison, July 21, 1968. Rustin: "He [Abernathy] wants her [Juanita Abernathy] there, you know, to get a little limelight." Levison: "And what will happen is that she'll be ignored." Rustin: "And then it's going to be like it was up in Oslo, when she had a heart attack." FLNY-9-1738a, p. 5; int. Bernard Lee, June 19, 1985; int. Dora McDonald, Dec. 31, 1990.
542   fn "Will you help relieve": Eskridge to Greenberg, Dec. 28, 1964, A/SC9f37.
542   complained to Harry Wachtel: Int. Harry Wachtel, Oct. 27, 1983.
542   "toast to God": Coretta King, *My Life*, p. 27; Young, *Easy Burden*, p. 322; int. Bernard Lee, June 19, 1985; int. Harry Wachtel, Oct. 27, 1983.
542   carrying Viking torches: NYT, Dec. 12, 1964, p. 1.

542 "war is the most extreme": "Outline for Nobel Prize Lecture," Nobel Prize speech drafts, A/KP18f33 and A/KP12f67.

543 overran the Grand Hotel: Garrow, *Bearing the Cross*, pp. 366–67; Williams, *The King*, pp. 198–99; int. Harry Wachtel, Oct. 27, 1983.

543 danced in public: Coretta King, *My Life*, pp. 27–29.

543 "Only Martin's family": Garrow, *Bearing the Cross*, p. 366.

543 "Ralph's estrangement": Young, *Easy Burden*, p. 320. A brokenness between King and Abernathy persisted until Memphis in 1968, Bernard Lee would recall before his own death: "That's how serious it was." Int. Bernard Lee, June 19, 1985.

543 McNamara drew President Johnson: Gravel, ed., *Pentagon Papers*, Vol. 2, p. 422, Vol. 3, pp. 247–59.

544 *"Esquire* Magazine": Moyers to LBJ, Dec. 10, 1964, Box 10, Moyers Papers, LBJ.

544 fn "I remember the conversation well": Ibid.

544 nearly eight hundred students: NYT, Dec. 4, 1964, p. 1.

544 "We are told that the mob": Heirich, *The Beginning*, p. 239.

544 "helped destroy freedom": Ibid., p. 232.

544 faculty voted to support: Ibid., p. 241.

544 "Berkeley Protest Becomes a Ritual": NYT, Nov. 15, 1964, p. 49.

544 "beards and long hair": NYT, Dec. 3, 1964, p. 50.

544 Warner Brothers Studios agreed: Per agreement signed by DeLoach, Dec. 11, 1964, Section 3, FHOC.

544 stipulations for the show: ADIC, Los Angeles, to HQ, Feb. 1, 1973, Section 3, FHOC; int. Cartha DeLoach, June 1, 1984.

544 DeLoach himself grew weary: Ibid.

544 connect the undignified corpse: Wolff, *You Send Me*, pp. 1–6, 316–29.

545 gathered at the Chicago funeral: Ibid., pp. 331–32.

545 tragedy in the Negro press: *Jet*, Dec. 31, 1964, pp. 56–63; *Jet*, Jan. 31, 1965, p. 58; PC, Dec. 19, 1964, p. 1; A. S. "Doc" Young, "The Mysterious Death of Sam Cooke," five-part series in CDD, Jan. 1–4, 1965.

545 claimed to possess: CDD, Jan. 11, 1965, p. 12.

545 Maxwell Taylor dressed down: Gravel, ed., *Pentagon Papers*, Vol. 2, pp. 345–48.

545 "Generals acting greatly offended": Ibid., pp. 349–50; Karnow, *Vietnam*, pp. 398–99; NYT, Jan. 11, 1965, pp. 1, 3.

545 "drop him off": Baumgardner to Sullivan, Dec. 17, 1964, FR-NR.

545 told friends of the prostitute chases: Log of Rustin phone contact with Rachelle Horowitz and Tom Kahn, Dec. 16, 1964, in ibid. Also Garrow, *Bearing the Cross*, p. 366.

545 distress call on December 15: Report on Levison-Jones phone call in SAC, New York, to Director, Dec. 16, 1964, FK-633.

545 suddenly realized: Int. Clarence Jones, Jan. 16, 1984, and Aug. 18, 1986.

545 "I never want to see": Ibid.; Branch, *Parting*, p. 860.

546 "14 motion picture": NYT, Dec. 18, 1964, p. 37.

546 fn King recited the 1870: Ibid.

546 claimed a crowd of ten thousand: Int. Cleveland Robinson, Oct. 28, 1983. Robinson said he raised money for the rally from singer Sammy Davis, Jr., and that his biggest disappointment was that Lionel Hampton was not able to bring his band on short notice from Puerto Rico.

546 sit briefly with Malcolm X: Int. Andrew Young, Oct. 26, 1991; Young, *Easy Burden*, p. 325. (The Young memoir notes erroneously that the "well known photograph" of King and Malcolm was taken at this event.) Malcolm X referred to witnessing King's armory speech in an interview with reporter Claude Lewis. Gallen, *As They Knew Him*, p. 169.

546 In his speech: "Address to the Harlem Community Salute," Dec. 17, 1964, Tape No. 27, A/KS.

546 parable of the rich man Dives: Branch, *Parting*, pp. 12, 705.

547 stopped off at the White House: NYT, Dec. 19, 1964, p. 32; King statement to Washington reporters, Dec. 18, 1964, A/KS; Garrow, *Bearing the Cross*, p. 368.

547 to steer King off three: Lee White to LBJ, Dec. 18, 1964, Diary Back-up, Box 12, LBJ.

547 fn On the Nobel trip: NYT, Dec. 8, 1964, p. 53; King address in City Temple Hall, London, Dec. 7, 1964, A/KS; "King Advocates Congo Withdrawal," NYT, Dec. 14, 1964, p. 3. Among King's Nobel Prize papers is a note from Clarence Jones urging him to mention the 1960 Peace Prize won by Chief Albert Luthuli, in order to "forge a link or bond between the US Civil Rts Movement and the African (or So African) Liberation Movement." Nobel Prize speech drafts, A/KP18f33 and A/KP12f67.

547 fn introduction of television: NYT, Nov. 10, 1964, p. 1.

547 send them a copy: Lee White to MLK, Jan. 6, 1965, Diary Back-up, Box 12, LBJ.

547 Clark's son Ramsey: Ramsey Clark Oral History by H. T. Baker, March 21, 1969, LBJ.

547 "Now what's Georgia doing?": Juanita Roberts note, Diary Back-up, Box 12, LBJ.

547 retrieve Ralph and Juanita: PDD, Dec. 18, 1964, LBJ.

547 encountered Fannie Lou Hamer: Mills, *This Little Light*, pp. 140–44; Breitman, ed., *Malcolm X Speaks*, pp. 105–36; Malcolm X speech at the Williams Institutional Church, New York, Dec. 20, 1964, Audiotape C-185, SCRBC.

548 "I go for that": Ibid, p. 134.

548 fn "Malcolm Favors a Mau Mau in U.S.": NYT, Dec. 21, 1964, p. 20.

549 "I'm not interested": Gallen, *As They Knew Him*, pp. 171–73.

549 retained bruised memories: Summary of Clarence Jones–King phone call of December 21, 1964, in New York LHM dated Dec. 23, 1964, FK-NR.

549   paralyzed with dissension: Forman, *Black Revolutionaries,* pp. 411–40.
549   Moses was opposing: Int. Robert P. Moses, July 31, 1984, Feb. 15, 1991; int. Lawrence Guyot, Feb. 1, 1991.
549   withdrew from deliberations: Dittmer, *Local People,* pp. 324–37.
549   Guyot announced in Jackson: Informant report on MFDP meeting, Dec. 20, 1964, MSSC.
549   Ryan revealed: Kinoy, *Rights on Trial,* p. 271.
549   "the root cause of Mississippi injustices": MLK press release and "Dear Congressman" letter of Dec. 24, 1964, A/KS; MLK mass telegram dated Jan. 3, 1965, A/KP24f27.
549   Leon 4X Ameer: Goldman, *Death and Life,* pp. 249, 308; Perry, *Malcolm,* p. 341.
549   "It was he": Malcolm X speech of Feb. 15, 1965, in Perry, *Last Speeches,* pp. 136–37; Goldman, *Death and Life,* p. 414.
550   Atlantans were agitating: NYT, Dec. 29, 1964, p. 1.
550   fn annual goodwill dinner: Allen, *Mayor,* pp. 94–95.
550   first acknowledgment of controversy: "City's Leaders Express Cautious, Mixed Feelings," AC, Dec. 29, 1964, p. 2.
550   since the announcement: Benjamin Mays of Morehouse wrote Mayor Ivan Allen on the day of the Nobel announcement, suggesting that Atlanta give King some "official recognition." Mays to Allen, Oct. 15, 1964, A/KP15f31.
550   told family that he did not care: Coretta King, *My Life,* p. 32.
550   Abernathy was refusing: Int. Andrew Young, Oct. 26, 1991.
550   instructing the SCLC staff: Garrow, *Bearing the Cross,* p. 366.
550   overheard Coretta King worrying: Garrow, *FBI and Martin,* p. 133.
550   agent took notes: SAC, New York, to Director, Dec. 30, 1964, FMX-203. The New York FBI office also recorded Malcolm's appearance, but the verbatim transcript was not completed until January 14. "Remarks of Malcolm X on Les Crane Show on WABC-TV, Channel 7, 12/28/64," transcript prepared Jan. 14, 1965, FMXNY-5392.
550   by train to Philadelphia: Philadelphia LHM dated Jan. 19, 1965, FMX-NR, pp. 4–6.
550   Malcolm would be shot: SAC, Philadelphia, to Director, Dec. 29, 1964, FMXNY-5326.
550   forming an alliance: SAC, Boston, to Director, Dec. 30, 1964, FMXNY-5330.
551   Malcolm called home: SAC, Philadelphia, to Director, Dec. 30, 1964, FMXNY-5328.
551   Malcolm X received a delegation: Breitman, ed., *Malcolm X Speaks,* p. 137.
551   "Excuse me for raising": Ibid., p. 144.
551   "That's what split the Muslim movement": Breitman, *Last Year,* p. 17.

39: To the Valley: The Downward King

552   drive from Atlanta to Selma: Int. Ralph Abernathy, Nov. 19, 1984; Garrow, *Bearing the Cross,* p. 372.
552   joint quarters in the guest room: Int. Jean and Sullivan Jackson, May 27, 1990.
553   shared many ties: Ibid. Also int. Amelia Boynton Robinson, Aug. 9, 1990; int. Marie Foster, Aug. 8, 1990; int. L. L. Anderson, May 27, 1990; int. Bernard Lafayette, May 28, 1990.
553   Andrew Young moved: Int. Andrew Young, Oct. 26, 1991.
553   "forty colored ladies of Selma": Amelia Boynton to MLK, Nov. 30, 1963, A/KP21f10.
553   Hare's sweeping injunction: Fitts, *Selma,* p. 140; Garrow, *Protest at Selma,* p. 34.
553   King's scouts in Selma: Harry Boyte to R. T. Blackwell, "Report on Selma Visit Last Week," Dec. 14, 1964, A/SC146f8; int. C. T. Vivian, May 26, 1990.
554   fn "Segregation was not": Hampton and Fayer, *Voices,* p. 216.
554   Negro Elks Hall: Fitts, *Selma,* p. 140.
554   down to the control of Selma sidewalks: Fager, *Selma 1965,* pp. 5–6; Chestnut, *Black in Selma,* pp. 195–98.
554   "Dr. King Due": NYT, Jan. 1, 1965, p. 16; WP, Jan. 2, 1965, p. 2.
554   Friday night's Orange Bowl: Fager, *Selma 1965,* p. 4.
554–55   "Today marks the beginning": NYT, Jan. 3, 1964, p. 1; Fager, *Selma 1965,* pp. 10–11.
555   to open the 89th Congress: NYT, Jan. 5, 1965, p. 1.
555   "I'se de Mississippi": *Jet,* Jan. 21, 1965, pp. 14–17; NYT, Jan. 5, 1965, p. 17.
555   move to seat the five: Kinoy, *Rights on Trial,* pp. 272–75; Mills, *This Little Light,* pp. 152–54.
556   Bill Moyers replied carefully.: White House press briefing, 6:33 P.M., Jan. 4, 1965, "Legislative Background, Voting Rights Act of 1965," Box 1, LBJ.
556   fn "tried harder here": Garrow, *Protest at Selma,* p. 34.
556   Katzenbach wanted time: Int. Nicholas Katzenbach, June 14, 1991; Garrow, *Protest at Selma,* pp. 35–39.
556   constitutional amendment: Draft constitutional amendment dated Jan. 8, 1965, "Legislative Background, Voting Rights Act of 1965," Box 1, LBJ.
556   "the first continental union": NYT, Jan. 5, 1964, p. 16.
556   75 million viewers: Dave Waters to LBJ, Jan. 13, 1965, Box 367, WHCF-PR, LBJ.
556   Coretta King called: Garrow, *FBI and Martin,* pp. 133–34; Garrow, *Bearing the Cross,* pp. 372–74.
556   Abernathy was rushed in: Abernathy, *Walls Came Tumbling,* pp. 309–11, 472–73.
556   fn Andrew Young remembered: Young, *Easy Burden,* pp. 328–29.
557   interpretation was unanimous: Stokes Committee, *Staff Reports,* Book 3, pp. 158–61.
557   They were too rattled: Int. Harry Wachtel, Oct. 27, 1983, May 17, 1990; int. Bernard Lee, June 19, 1985.

557   "They are out to break me": Garrow, *FBI and Martin*, p. 134.

557   Eskridge was toughened: Int. Chauncey Eskridge, Feb. 20, 1985, Feb. 22, 1985; int. Yvonne Eskridge, Jan. 13, 1991.

557   relationship with Stanley Levison: Int. Harry Wachtel, Oct. 27, 1983, May 17, 1990.

558   Harvard's Memorial Church: NYT, Jan. 11, 1965, p. 27.

558   settled for DeLoach: Garrow, *FBI and Martin*, pp. 134–35; Young, *Easy Burden*, pp. 329–31; Abernathy, *Walls Came Tumbling*, pp. 311–12; Stokes Committee, Staff Reports, Book III, pp. 169–70.

558   "gloated to his superiors": Garrow, *Bearing the Cross*, p. 377.

558   spoke at Johns Hopkins: Log, A/SC29; Jan. 11, 1965, address on obsolete war, "Nonviolence or Nonexistence," A/KS7.

558   second Klan confession: NYT, Jan. 11, 1965, p. 1.

558   three Greenwood plumbers: NYT, Jan. 8, 1965, p. 32.

558   secretaries failed to appear: Clegg, *An Original Man*, p. 227.

558   instructions from Captain Joseph: Int. Yusuf Shah (Captain Joseph), Oct. 17, 1991.

558   shot Brown in the back: Goldman, *Death and Life*, p. 250; Perry, *Malcolm*, p. 341.

558   new alias: New York report dated Jan. 20, 1965, cover page A, FMX-215.

558   Bevel stunned: Fager, *Selma 1965*, p. 25.

559   first Selma youth rally: Mobile LHM dated Jan. 15, 1965, FDCA-275.

559   "If you can't vote": Webb and Nelson, *Selma*, p. 6.

559   block captains were elected: Bevel report to R. T. Blackwell, Jan. 12, 1965, A/SC146f8.

559   From a downtown storefront: Int. Diane Nash, Oct. 26, 1997.

559   tandem approach: Remarks by Silas Norman, Session No. 6, Trinity College SNCC reunion, 1988; int. Bernard Lafayette, May 28, 1990.

559   pitched their self-selected young newcomers: Ibid. Also int. Fay Bellamy, Oct. 29, 1991; int. Frank Soracco, Sept. 13, 1990; int. Charles Fager, Sept. 27, 1983; Charles Fager 1965 Oral History, Project Sough, SUARC.

559   "Things are starting to move": Soracco to "Dad and Ann," Jan. 9, 1965, courtesy of Frank and Sandy Soracco.

559   mass meeting at First Baptist: Mobile LHM dated Jan. 15, 1965, FDCA-275.

560   "I am trying to get over": MLK address of Jan. 14, 1965, Selma surveillance tape No. 7, BIR.

560   Johnson called King: PDD, Jan. 15, 1965, LBJ; "Contacts with Civil Rights Leaders, 1963–68," Legislative Background, Voting Rights Act of 1965, Box 1, LBJ; Garrow, *Bearing the Cross*, p. 382.

560   recruitments intensified: Staff notes, Jan. 14, 1965, A/SN7.

560   "students that refuse": Staff notes, Jan. 15, 1965, A/SN7.

560   continued negotiations: Garrow, *Protest at Selma*, p. 42.

560   "begging on my knees": Int. Sheriff Robert "Cotton" Nichols, May 28, 1990.

560   "Mrs. Anderson has so many": Staff notes, Jan. 16, 1965, A/SN7.

560   first skirmish: Fager, *Selma 1965*, pp. 26–29; STJ, Jan. 18, 1965, p. 1; Rosen to Belmont, Jan. 18, 1965, FDCA-275x7.

561   Robinson slugged him once: Paul Good, "States Rights Partisan Slugs Dr. King in Hotel," WP, Jan. 19, 1965, p. 1.

561   serious consternation in the Justice Department: Rosen to Belmont, Jan. 18, 1965, FDCA-275x10; SAC, Mobile, to Director, Jan. 18, 1965, FDCA-275x21.

561   "Commander! Commander!": Int. Sheriff Robert "Cotton" Nichols, May 28, 1990.

561   "rumblings of discontent": STJ, Jan. 19, 1965, p. 1.

561   "And charge 'em with what?": Raines, *My Soul*, pp. 214–17.

562   Clark ordered their arrest: NYT, Jan. 20, 1965, p. 1.

562   "Don't be scared": Webb and Nelson, *Selma*, p. 27.

562   "It was no surprise to me": Bevel address of Jan. 19, 1965, Selma surveillance tape No. 8, BIR.

562   "out of control": WP, Jan. 20, 1965, p. 1.

562   Wednesday in three waves: SAC, Mobile, to Director, Jan. 20, 1965, FDCA-275x26.

562   1.2 million: WP, April 6, 1992, pp. 1, 20.

562   frostbitten crowd: Reeves, *Profile of Power*, p. 35.

563   "the first Inauguration": *Jet*, Feb. 4, 1965, pp. 6–10.

563   Turnbow, who declared: Mary King, *Freedom Song*, pp. 352–53.

563   Johnson's telegram: LBJ telegram to MLK, Jan. 18, 1965, A/KP26f8.

563   "wrestles with all the time": Bromley Smith minutes, LBJ meeting with congressional leaders, Jan. 22, 1965, Box 18–19, McGeorge Bundy Office Files, LBJ.

563   fn "We are faced here": Taylor to LBJ, Jan. 6, 1965, quoted in McNamara, *In Retrospect*, pp. 165–66.

563   procession of teachers: Webb and Nelson, *Selma*, pp. 34–37; Fager, *Selma 1965*, pp. 36–40; Chestnut, *Black in Selma*, pp. 199–200; Young, *Easy Burden*, p. 349; Raines, *My Soul*, pp. 242–43; Hampton and Fayer, *Voices*, pp. 218–19; int. Amelia Boynton Robinson, Aug. 9, 1990; int. Marie Foster, Aug. 8, 1990.

564   3:24 P.M. Friday: Mobile LHM dated Jan. 29, 1965, FDCA-276, p. 1.

564   "three hundred Negro children": SAC, Mobile, to Director, Jan. 22, 1965, FDCA-267.

564   Reese declared: F. D. Reese Oral History of March 13, 1978, by Larry D. Vasser, Alabama Historical Commission, BIR. Twenty years later, Bernard Lee said the teachers' march "helped a heck of a lot more than people realized, because it settled the question of the legitimacy of the movement." Int. Bernard Lee, June 19, 1985.

564   speaking trip to Canada: Breitman, ed., *Malcolm X Speaks*, p. 216.

564   fought off a Friday night ambush: Goldman, *Death and Life*, p. 250.

565   "I saw the man knock him": Malcolm X, lecture of Jan. 24, 1965, in *Afro-American History*, p. 44.

565   "A very bad situation has set in": Ibid., p. 47; also Tape C-190, SCRBC.

565   issued a court order: TRO of Jan. 23, 1965, in *Amelia P. Boynton, James Gildersleeve, John Lewis, Hosea Williams, Louis Lloyd Anderson et al. v. James G. Clark, Jr., Sheriff of Dallas County, Alabama, et al.*, Civil Action No. 3559-65, text sent to FBI headquarters with SAC, Mobile, to Director, Jan. 23, 1965, FDCA-263. Judge Thomas wrote that the Boynton case covered issues "substantially similar" to the Justice Department's complaint filed the previous summer, *United States v. James G. Clark, Jr., Sheriff of Dallas County, et al.*, Civil Action No. 3438-64, which was still pending.

565   "segregationist judge": Bevel address of Jan. 24, 1965, cited in Mobile LHM dated Jan. 29, 1965, FDCA-276, p. 4.

565   authorities felt betrayed: Fager, *Selma 1965*, pp. 41–43.

565   specific tribes in Africa: Chestnut, *Black in Selma*, pp. 172–86.

566   "Y'all don't treat": Ibid., p. 186.

566   Baker ordered one dragged: SAC, Mobile, to Director, Jan. 25, 1965, FDCA-265.

566   one of the two women fired: Amelia Boynton to MLK, Nov. 30, 1963, A/KP21f10; Fager, *Selma 1965*, p. 45, Branch, *Parting*, pp. 921–22.

566   "I probably hit": *Jet*, Feb. 11, 1965, pp. 6–9.

566   mass meeting at Tabernacle: Mobile LHM dated Jan. 29, 1965, FDCA-276, p. 7.

566   "They are not just running": Bevel and Anderson remarks at mass meeting of Jan. 25, 1965, Selma surveillance tape No. 5, BIR.

567   "I have a psychological theory": King remarks at mass meeting of Jan. 25, 1965, Selma surveillance tapes Nos. 1–3, BIR.

567   "Is there no balm": Jeremiah 8:22.

567   "I don't believe in half": Abernathy remarks at mass meeting of Jan. 25, 1965, Selma surveillance tapes Nos. 4–5, BIR.

568   "People held their sides": Fager, *Selma 1965*, p. 46.

568   Baker ordered the arrest: SAC, Mobile, to Director, Jan. 26, 1965, FDCA-271; Garrow, *Protest at Selma*, p. 45.

568   Nobel Prize dinner: NYT, Jan. 28, 1965, p. 15; *Jet*, Feb. 11, 1965, pp. 26–28; Raines, *My Soul*, pp. 454–62; Allen, *Mayor*, pp. 95–99; Int. Eugene Patterson, April 6, 1991; Pomerantz, *Where Peachtree*, pp. 334–40; Allen, *Secret Formula*, pp. 337–39; Greene, *Temple Bombing*, pp. 414–25.

569   Sullivan made another clandestine plea: Garrow, *FBI and Martin*, pp. 135–36.

569   dispatch to the White House: Hoover to Moyers, Jan. 22, 1965, FK-756.

569   "We could get shot": Pomerantz, *Where Peachtree*, p. 338.

569   "You know how when": Raines, *My Soul*, p. 461.

569   McGill saluted King: Recorded tributes, Jan. 28 (sic), 1965, A/KS.

570   "To think that this": Greene, *Temple Bombing*, p. 422.

570   Rabbi Rothschild presented: Remarks of Jan. 27, 1965, Box 15, Item 16; 1965 recollections, "One Man's Meat," Box 15, Item 28; MLK to Rothschild, March 8, 1965, Box 6, Item 13; Hallinan to Rothschild, Feb. 5, 1965, Box 6, Item 14. All in Jacob Rothschild Papers, EU.

570   variations on his Nobel: MLK address of Jan. 27, 1965, A/KS. The benediction by Ralph Abernathy is preserved in A/SC59f12.

570   "Dear Boss": Pomerantz, *Where Peachtree*, p. 340.

570   next night's staff review: Garrow, *Protest at Selma*, p. 47.

570   fifty-seven Negro applicants: *Jet*, Feb. 11, 1965, p. 8.

570   to go to jail Monday: Garrow, *Bearing the Cross*, p. 382.

40: SAIGON, AUDUBON, AND SELMA

571   Huynh Thi Yen Phi: NYT, Jan. 27, 1964, p. 3.

571   "We are losing the war": Ibid., p. 1.

571   "sweated down two or three pair": Johnson, *White House Diary*, p. 232.

571   "a short but explosive": McNamara, *In Retrospect*, pp. 166–68. See also the related John T. McNaughton memo, Jan. 4, 1965, Doc. No. 247, in Gravel, ed., *Pentagon Papers*, Vol. 3, pp. 683–84.

572   Rusk narrowly disagreed: Rusk, *As I Saw It*, p. 447.

572   Taylor explored ways to overthrow: Karnow, *Vietnam*, pp. 399–400.

572   "still the best hope": Ibid.

572   "The current situation": McNamara, *In Retrospect*, p. 170.

572   make him the scapegoat: Taylor, *Swords and Plowshares*, pp. 332–35.

572   "No good general": Taylor to RFK, Feb. 11, 1965, Box 12, Corr: Personal 64–68, T65, RFK Senate Papers, JFK.

572   Malcolm X flew to Los Angeles: Perry, *Malcolm*, pp. 342–43; Goldman, *Death and Life*, pp. 250–51.

572   "If these cases aren't hurried": *Chicago Tribune*, Feb. 25, 1965, in File No. 589, RS, CHS; Los Angeles LHM dated Sept. 2, 1965, FMX-417.

573   meet him at the Statler Hilton: Los Angeles LHM dated Feb. 4, 1965, FMXNY-5526.

573   secretaries slipped out: LAT, Feb. 23, 1965, p. 1.

573   Malcolm X called his ally Wallace Muhammad: LAPD Intelligence Division to Chicago PD Intelligence Unit, Feb. 4, 1965, File No. 589, RS, CHS.

573   Wallace opposed the idea: Int. Ronald Shaheed, Sept. 24, 1997; int. Agieb Bilal, Nov. 18, 1994.

573   "They had gotten so insane": Malcolm X speech of Feb. 15, 1965, in Clark, ed., *Final Speeches*, p. 113.

573   through the basement baggage room: Los Angeles LHM dated Feb. 4, 1965, FMXNY-5526, p. 2.

573   Malcolm declared that the teaching: Ibid., pp. 3–4.

573   At Chicago's O'Hare Airport: Int. Thomas Decker, Nov. 27, 1991; SAC, Los Angeles, to Director, Feb. 4, 1965, FMXNY-5527.

573   Malcolm arranged a clandestine meeting: Perry, *Malcolm*, pp. 343–44; Chicago's *American*, Feb. 1965, in File No. 589, RS, CHS.

574   ten hours over three days: SAC, Chicago, to Director, Feb. 15, 1965, FMX-239; Director to SAC, New York, Feb. 17, 1965, FMX-228, p. 2.

574   Wallace said Malcolm's purpose: Int. Ronald Shaheed, Sept. 24, 1997; int. Agieb Bilal, Nov. 18, 1994.

574   forbidding him to receive Islamic material: WP, Nov. 8, 1963, p. 3.

574   proved that the Nation: Int. Thomas Decker, Nov. 27, 1991.

574   *Kup's Show:* Goldman, *Death and Life*, p. 251.

574   "I've gotten older": SAC, Chicago, to Director, Feb. 4, 1965, FMX-230.

574   departed the studios of WBKB-TV: SAC, Chicago, to Director, Jan. 31, 1965, FMX-216; *Chicago Sun-Times*, April 5, 1965.

575   astonished that the attackers: Int. Thomas Decker, Nov. 27, 1991.

575   fn *Cooper v. Pate: Chicago Tribune*, June 8, 1965; int. Thomas Decker, Nov. 26, 1991.

575   "nine or ten members": New York LHM dated Feb. 4, 1965, FMXNY-5528.

575   Newspapers reported his destination: The *Alabama Journal* of Jan. 28, 1965, said Malcolm was to visit Montgomery or Selma, and the *Tuskegee Grams* reported on Jan. 22, 1965, that he would visit Tuskegee on Feb. 3. SAC, Mobile, to Director, Jan. 29, 1965, FMX-NR.

575   He sent Eskridge secretly: Wiretap intercepts of Feb. 1, 6, and 8, 1965, in SAC, Phoenix, to Director, Feb. 11, 1965, FEM-NR.

575   King rallied volunteers: Mobile LHM dated Feb. 5, 1965, FDCA-324, pp. 1–3.

575   "I think this is most": King ABC news statement of Feb. 1, 1965 (misdated as Feb. 2), A/KS.

576   "At approximately 10:42": SAC, Mobile, to Director, Feb. 1, 1965, FDCA-288.

576   tactic designed to ensure: Fager, *Selma 1965*, p. 49.

576   "And he said": STJ, Feb. 1, 1965, p. 1.

576   Cheers erupted: Fager, *Selma 1965*, pp. 52–53.

576   Baker appealed to King: Int. Frank Soracco, Sept. 12–14, 1990, Oct. 21, 1997; int. Sheriff Robert "Cotton" Nichols, May 28, 1990.

577   "Dr. King and 770": NYT, Feb. 2, 1965, p. 1.

577   "520 More Seized": NYT, Feb. 3, 1965, p. 1.

577   "Sing one more freedom song": NYT, Feb. 4, 1965, p. 1.

577   "three hundred more in Selma": Ibid. Also, SAC, Mobile, to Director, Feb. 3, 1965, FDCA-290; SAC, Mobile, to Director, Feb. 3, 1965, FDCA-295.

577   King was settled with Abernathy: STJ, Feb. 3, 1965, p. 2.

577   Waldorf-Astoria stationery: MLK notes, "Do following . . . ," A/KP22f6; Garrow, *Bearing the Cross*, pp. 383–85.

577   Young called Clarence Jones: SAC, New York, to Director, Feb. 3, 1965, FK-790.

577   White advised President Johnson: White to LBJ, "Message from Dr. Martin Luther King," Feb. 3, 1965, EX HU2/ST1, LBJ.

577   "An alternative which King": Ibid.

577   Prathia Hall arrived: Notes of Feb. 4, 1965, headed "Miss Prathia Hall made this report last night," A/SN94.

578   "number 3 tubs": Ibid.

578   Disputes broke out: Fay Bellamy's minutes of the Thursday staff meeting, which she took just after escorting Malcolm X to Selma, reflect that some staff members blamed lazy or ideologically conservative NAACP staff lawyers from New York for job firings and jail conditions in Perry County. "I, Fay Bellamy, personally think the above idea is sort of ridiculous," she added to her minutes. "I must say that NAACP lawyers have been working their butts off with no play time in between." Staff meeting notes, Feb. 4, 1965, A/SN7.

578   three thousand students squeezed: Mobile LHM dated Feb. 8, 1965, FMX-237.

578   "some of its time getting peace": The *Campus Digest* (Tuskegee student newspaper), Feb. 13, 1965, p. 1; Clark, ed., *Final Speeches*, pp. 20–22.

578   "How is Viola?": Int. Fay Bellamy, Oct. 29, 1991.

578   arrive in Selma at 9:47: SAC, Mobile, to Director, Feb. 4, 1965, FDCA-306.

578   "Why are you here today?": Malcolm X press conference of Feb. 4, 1965, Selma surveillance tape No. 10, BIR.

578   a spokesman followed: STJ, Feb. 4, 1965, p. 1.

578   protracted staff debate: Int. Fay Bellamy, Oct. 29, 1991; int. Charles Fager, Sept. 27, 1983; int. Bernard Lafayette, May 28, 1990; int. Frank Soracco, Sept. 12–14, 1990; int. C. T. Vivian, May 26, 1990; *Jet*, March 11, 1965, pp. 28–30.

579   "I'm a field Negro": Clark, ed., *Final Speeches*, p. 27.

579   "I'm not intending": Ibid., p. 28.

579   Diane Nash Bevel came to sit with him: Int. Diane Nash, April 26, 1990, Oct. 26, 1997.

579   Malcolm told Coretta King: Hampton and Fayer, *Voices of Freedom*, pp. 221–22.

579   drove away at 12:40 P.M.: SAC, Mobile, to Director, Feb. 4, 1965, FDCA-306, p. 2.
579   "Segregation is the invention": "Notes—Feb. 1–5, 1965, MLK in jail," A/KP22f6.
579   refusing visits that day: *Washington Evening Star,* Feb. 5, 1965, p. 3.
579   "I should like to say": NYT, Feb. 5, 1965, pp. 1, 14; PPP, LBJ's thirty-seventh news conference, Feb. 4, 1965, pp. 131–39; Garrow, *Protest at Selma,* pp. 51–52.
579   Judge Thomas's latest federal: Fager, *Selma 1965,* p. 58; Garrow, *Bearing the Cross,* p. 385.
580   "call Jack tonight": "Notes—Feb. 1–5, 1965, MLK in jail," A/KP22f6.
580   audit that week: Francis A. Covington to Abernathy, Feb. 6, 1965, A/SC55f13.
580   fn FBI informant, James Harrison: Garrow, *FBI and Martin,* pp. 175–79, 201; Garrow, *Bearing the Cross,* pp. 468, 715.
580   Rustin had signed: Int. Bayard Rustin, Sept. 24, 1984; "Teachers' Groups Battle Over Dr. King's Support," *Philadelphia Bulletin,* Jan. 25, 1965; Patrick H. Hughes, Jr., to MLK, Jan. 24, 1965, A/KP19f28; MLK statement on "the collective bargaining election of Philadelphia teachers," Jan. 28, 1965, A/KS.
580   King hated jail: Int. Andrew Young, Oct. 26, 1991.
580   Vivian led a march: STJ, Feb. 5, 1965, p. 1.
580   second march of 450: Ibid. Also SAC, Mobile, to Director, Feb. 5, 1965, FDCA-314.
580   firing his revolver: NYT, Feb. 6, 1965, p. 10.
580   At 1:12 P.M.: Mobile LHM dated Feb. 12, 1965, FDCA-341, p. 2.
580   smudge of lipstick: NYT, Feb. 6, 1965, p. 10.
580   six members: Identified tentatively as Harry Wachtel, Bayard Rustin, Clarence Jones, Cleveland Robinson, Walter Fauntroy, and Michael Harrington. New York LHM dated Feb. 8, 1965, FR-NR. FBI surveillance agents confirmed seeing Rustin enter 575 Madison Avenue at 12:55 P.M. and "take the elevator to the fifth floor," where Wachtel's office was located. SAC, New York, to Director, Feb. 8, 1965, FR-NR, p. 3.
580   expressed dismay by telephone: Int. Harry Wachtel, Oct. 27, 1983, Nov. 29, 1983; int. Bayard Rustin, Sept. 24, 1984.
580   "THIS IS SELMA": NYT, Feb. 6, 1965, p. 15.
580   fifteen members of Congress: Garrow, *Bearing the Cross,* p. 384.
581   King was depressed: Int. Harry Wachtel, Oct. 27, 1983, Nov. 29, 1983; int. Bayard Rustin, Sept. 24, 1984; int. Clarence Jones, Nov. 25, 1983; int. Andrew Young, Oct. 26, 1991.
581   press conference for three o'clock: Mobile LHM dated Feb. 12, 1965, FDCA-341, pp. 2–3.
581   "Dr. King to Seek": NYT, Feb. 6, 1965, p. 1.
581   "Where the hell does he": Int. Lee White, Dec. 13, 1983, Dec. 3, 1991; int. Harry Wachtel, Oct. 27, 1983.
581   "grandstanding": Ibid.
581   Jones over an FBI wiretap: New York LHM dated Feb. 8, 1965, FK-NR, p. 5.
581   "strong recommendation": NYT, Feb. 7, 1965, p. 1.
581   a disaster near the mountain village of Pleiku: NYT, Feb. 7, 1965, p. 1; Karnow, *Vietnam,* pp. 427–428; McNamara, *In Retrospect,* pp. 170–71.
581   "is not behind us": Bromley Smith, "Summary Notes of 545th NSC Meeting," Feb. 6, 1965, Meeting Notes File, Box 1, LBJ.
582   overrode Mansfield: Ibid. Also William P. Bundy Oral History by Paige E. Mulhollan, May 26, 1969, pp. 7–12, LBJ.
582   "chronology of the crisis": NYT, Feb. 8, 1965, p. 14.
582   "hatless, tense and pale": Ibid.
582   Aboard *Air Force One:* Johnson, *Vantage Point,* p. 126; Gravel, *Pentagon Papers,* Vol. 3, pp. 308–15.
582   "*sustained reprisal* against the North": McGeorge Bundy, "A Policy of Sustained Reprisal," Feb. 7, 1965, Gravel, *Pentagon Papers,* Vol. 3, pp. 687–91.
582   rushed to catch up: SAC, Mobile, to Director, 12:43 A.M., Feb. 6, 1965, FDCA-320; SAC, Mobile, to Director, 2:01 P.M., Feb. 6, 1965, FDCA-311; NYT, Feb. 7, 1965, p. 44.
582   "hornet's nest": SAC, New York, to Director, Feb. 7, 1965, FK-852.
582   most Wachtel could wheedle: Int. Lee White, Dec. 13, 1983, Dec. 3, 1991; int. Harry Wachtel, Oct. 27, 1983.
582   Jones negotiated a press release: SAC, New York, to Director, Feb. 7, 1965, FK-857; Hoover to the Attorney General, Feb. 8, 1965, FDCA-389.
583   King released late Sunday: NYT, Feb. 7, 1976, p. 17.
583   White was recommending: Garrow, *Bearing the Cross,* pp. 386–87.
583   Bevel led fifty volunteers: SAC, Mobile, to Director, Feb. 8, 1965, FDCA-391.
583   sham reform: Fager, *Selma 1965,* pp. 59, 64.
583   three visiting whites: Ibid., p. 65.
583   "shaking with anger": NYT, Feb. 9, 1965, p. 17.
583   "Bevel was roughed up somewhat": STJ, Feb. 9, 1965, p. 2.
583   King urged citizens: Ibid., p. 1; NYT, Feb 9, 1965, p. 17.
583   Williams tried to convince: NYT, Feb. 10, 1965, p. 18.
583   gathered late Tuesday afternoon with Harry Wachtel: WS, Feb. 10, 1965, p. 1; CDD, Feb. 10, 1965, p. 1; SAC, New York, to Director, Feb. 8, 1965, FDCA-392.
583   Rauh submitted a rough draft: "Proposal submitted by Joseph Rauh," Legislative Background, Voting Rights Act of 1965, Box 1, LBJ.
583   King had kept silent as promised: Lee White to LBJ, Feb. 8, 1965, Legislative Background, Voting Rights Act of 1965, Box 1, LBJ.
583   anxious looks from Wachtel: Int. Harry Wachtel, Oct. 27, 1983.
584   "We can't forget": Transcript of Feb. 9, 1965, Congressional Briefings on Vietnam, Box 1, LBJ.

584   "the situation is by no means": Ibid.

584   "Bundy Gives an Optimistic": NYT, Feb. 9, 1965, p. 12.

584   Bundy emphasized: Karnow, *Vietnam*, p. 428; William P. Bundy Oral History by Paige E. Mulhollan, May 26, 1969, pp. 10–11, LBJ. Those privy to Bundy's occasional comments about the savagery of Vietcong terrorism faulted or admired his rare slips of patriotic emotion. "For example, John Macy was amazed at lunch yesterday to hear from McGeorge Bundy the nature of Viet Nam terrorism," Bill Moyers wrote Johnson that same day, recommending a candid speech on the war. "Two or three paragraphs by you on this subject, in some detail, would have considerable impact." Moyers to LBJ, Feb. 9, 1965, Box 10, Moyers Papers, LBJ.

584   White chased after Humphrey: Garrow, *Bearing the Cross*, p. 388; int. Harry Wachtel, Oct. 27, 1983.

584   statement drafted: "Suggested King Statement," Legislative Background, Voting Rights Act of 1965, Box 1, LBJ.

584   shaped front-page news: "President Promises Dr. King Vote Move," NYT, Feb. 10, 1965, p. 1; "Johnson Plans to Speed Rights Pace, King Says," WS, Feb. 10, 1965, p. 1; "President Given King Views on Vote Situation," STJ, Feb. 10, 1965, p. 2.

584   detained Malcolm X: Legat, Paris, to Director, Feb. 11, 1965, FMX-233.

585   "trouble the public order": *New York Herald Tribune*, European Edition, Feb. 10, 1965, FMX-235.

585   expressed shock: New York LHM dated Feb. 11, 1965, FMX234.

585   "absolutely unnoticed": Lecture at the London School of Economics, Feb. 10, 1965, in Clark, ed., *Final Speeches*, pp. 46–64; Tape C-190, side 2, SRBC.

586   "got it going": Ibid. Some portions of the tape are difficult to understand. Clark renders this phrase, "got it and gone."

586   By FBI count: SAC, Mobile, to Director, Feb. 10, 1965, FDCA-330.

586   "Let Our Parish Vote": Fager, *Selma 1965*, pp. 65–66.

586   "a ludicrous game": STJ, Feb. 10, 1965, p. 1.

586   Clark posted a rear guard: SAC, Mobile, to Director, Feb. 10, 1965, FDCA-330.

586   Some stopped to vomit.: Webb and Nelson, *Selma, Lord Selma*, pp. 66–67; *Time*, Feb. 19, 1965, p. 23.

586   Letha Mae Stover: NYT, April 28, 1965, p. 22.

586   meetings Wednesday night: SAC, Mobile, to Director, Feb. 19, 1965, FDCA-346.

586   "aware of our groans": MLK mass meeting remarks, Feb. 10, 1965, Selma surveillance tape No. 10, BIR.

586   midnight strategy session: King left Brown Chapel for the Torch Motel meeting at 10:54 P.M. SAC, Mobile, to Director, Feb. 19, 1965, FDCA-346.

586   King's pained recommendation: Fairclough, *To Redeem*, p. 238.

587   "Negroes Don't Know": MA, Feb. 9, 1965, p. 1.

587   "in order to get": Minutes, Feb. 10, 1965, "Wednesday night at the Torch Motel," A/SN7.

587   "no sense of political timing": Wiretap summary of MLK–Clarence Jones conversation, New York LHM dated Feb. 16, 1965, FMXNY-5586, pp. 2–4. Belafonte did arrange a truce meeting toward the end of April. CD, May 5, 1965, p. 4.

587   fn "tries to solve racial": WP, Feb. 7, 1965, p. E1.

587   fell hardest upon Diane Nash Bevel: Int. Diane Nash, Oct. 26, 1997; int. James Bevel, May 17, 1985; int. Bernard Lafayette, May 28, 1990; int. Andrew Young, Oct. 26, 1991; int. Bernard Lee, June 19, 1985; int. Charles Fager, Sept. 27, 1983; int. John Lewis, June 8, 1983; int. Hosea Williams, Oct. 29, 1991; int. Frank Soracco, Sept. 13, 1990.

588   "playing to a worldwide audience": STJ, Feb 11, 1965, p. 1.

588   "I'm human, too": Fager, *Selma 1965*, p. 67.

588   threatened to arrest Clark: Remarks of Charles Quinn at the University of Mississippi symposium, "Covering the South," April 3–5, 1987.

588   kill any students: Int. Sheriff Robert "Cotton" Nichols, May 28, 1990.

588   march four times larger: NYT, Feb. 12, 1965, p. 58.

588   shackled to a hospital bed: WP, Feb. 12, 1965, p. 2; *Chicago Tribune*, Feb. 12, 1965; NYT, Feb. 12, 1965, p. 58; int. Bernard Lafayette, May 28, 1990.

588   hounded the Justice Department: Mobile LHM dated Feb. 13, 1965, FDCA-335; int. Diane Nash, Oct. 26, 1997.

588   collapsed early that morning: NYT, Feb. 13, 1965, p. 1.

588   "Thus ended": Ibid., p. 17.

588   chapel pews of Gammon Theological Seminary to "Did he mean it": Int. Robert P. Moses, July 31, 1984; Forman, *The Making*, pp. 348–39; Sellers, *The River*, pp. 137–41; int. John Lewis by Archie Allen, pp. 184–85, AAP; int. Cleveland Sellers, Dec. 14, 1983; int. Kwame Toure (Stokely Carmichael), Jan. 31, 1984; int. Charles Cobb, Aug. 20, 1991; int. Fay Bellamy, Oct. 29, 1991; int. Michael Sayer, June 25, 1992; unsigned informant report headed, "Atlanta, Georgia/February 11–16, 1965," MSSC; Branch, *Parting*, pp. 325–28.

590   Malcolm X returned home: Malcolm X, *The Autobiography*, pp. 427–28.

590   fire alarm at 2:46 A.M.: New York LHM dated Feb. 16, 1965, FMX-246; NYT, Feb. 15, 1965, p. 1.

590   having hustled barefoot in underwear: Goldman, *Death and Life*, pp. 262–63; SAC, Detroit, to Director, Feb. 17, 1965, FMX-NR; Malcolm X speech of Feb. 15, 1965, in Clark, ed., *Final Speeches*, p. 135.

590   Qubilah complained: WP, June 3, 1997, p. 3.

590   "collection of $200": SAC, Detroit, to Director, Feb. 17, 1965, FMX-NR.

590   conspiracy theories: Nation of Islam officials charged that Malcolm firebombed the home to spite them, because they were on the verge of having him evicted from property owned by the Nation. (Under court order, Malcolm did vacate the badly damaged house four days later.) This allegation received scattered

support ranging from FBI reports and Malcolm's critics to a biographer. SAC, New York, to Director, Feb. 14, 1965, FMX-241; NYT, Feb. 19, 1965, p. 31; Clark, ed., *Final Speeches,* pp. 120, 195–99; Perry, *Malcolm,* pp. 351–56.

590 fn "I *know* he didn't": Int. Yusuf Shah (Captain Joseph), Oct. 17, 1991.

590 "Elijah Muhammad could stop": Malcolm X New York speech of Feb. 15, 1965, in Clark, ed., *Final Speeches,* p. 124.

590 "I have to straighten out": Malcolm X Detroit speech of Feb. 14, 1965, in ibid., p. 83.

590 "dropping bombs on dark-skinned people": Malcolm X Rochester speech of Feb. 16, 1965, in ibid., p. 150.

591 "Think of this": Malcolm X New York speech of Feb. 15, 1965, in ibid., p. 136.

591 "so complex that it was impossible": Malcolm X Rochester speech of Feb. 16, 1965, in ibid., p. 170.

591 talks at the Hotel Albert: Fager, *Selma 1965,* p. 69.

591 More than four hundred of these: SAC, Mobile, to Director, Feb. 15, 1965, FDCA-339.

591 "I filled out the form": NYT, Feb. 16, 1965, p. 18.

591 "about 150 Negroes were so inspired": Ibid.

591 Vivian tried to lead: Garrow, *Bearing the Cross,* pp. 390–91.

591 Nuns crowded around King: NYT, Feb. 17, 1965, p. 35.

592 addressed a voting rally: Ibid.

592 church in Lowndes County: SAC, Mobile, to Director, Feb. 15, 1965, FDCA-345; SAC, Mobile, to Director, Feb. 16, 1965, FDCA-351.

592 "The similarity will certainly shock you.": STJ, Feb. 16, 1965.

592 "the ultimate expression": "Sanity and Realism Must Come to Selma," STJ, Feb. 18, 1965, p. 1.

592 "Virus Fells King": CDD, Feb. 18, 1965, p. 1.

592 FBI wiretap picked up Ralph Abernathy: New York LHM dated Feb. 18, 1965, FK-NR. Abernathy appealed to Bayard Rustin, who obtained the money from Wachtel.

592 "Selma *still* isn't right!": Fager, *Selma 1965,* pp. 70–71. King stayed afterward for a strategy session, missing his flight to Atlanta. He stayed overnight at the Sullivan Jackson home in Selma, and left for home Thursday morning. SAC, Mobile, to Director, Feb. 18, 1965, FDCA-358.

592 fn "The naked boldness": Baumgardner to Sullivan, Feb. 18, 1965, FK-917.

592 irate sentiment prevailed: Fager, *Selma 1965,* pp. 72–73.

592 overflowed Mount Zion Baptist: Int. C. T. Vivian, May 26, 1990; int. Willie Bolden, May 14, 1992; Hampton and Fayer, *Voices,* pp. 222–23.

593 correspondents told their crews: Remarks of Charles Quinn and Richard Valeriani, at the University of Mississippi symposium, "Covering the South," April 3–5, 1987.

593 two abreast from Mount Zion: Garrow, *Bearing the Cross,* pp. 390–91; Fager, *Selma 1965,* pp. 72–74.

593 correspondents instantly sent crews: Remarks of Charles Quinn and Richard Valeriani, at the University of Mississippi symposium, "Covering the South," April 3–5, 1987.

593 "Negroes could be heard": NYT, Feb. 19, 1965, pp. 1, 29.

593 Fifty state troopers: Ibid. The *Selma Times-Journal* counted twenty-one state trooper cars at the scene. STJ, Feb. 19, 1965, pp. 1, 5.

593 bleeding into Mack's Cafe: Mount Zion sources from above, plus NYT, Feb. 20, 1965, p. 1, and affidavit of Cager Lee, Feb. 23, 1965, collected by the Inter-Citizens Committee of Birmingham, Alabama.

593 expelled one crippled customer: Affidavit of James Bell, Feb. 23, 1965.

593 cafe owner saw troopers: Affidavit of Normareen Shaw, Feb. 23, 1965.

593 shot him twice in the stomach: NYT, Feb. 20, 1965, p. 1; STJ, Feb. 19, 1965, p. 1; Fager, *Selma 1965,* p. 74; Hampton and Fayer, *Voices,* pp. 224–25; affidavit of Viola Jackson, Feb. 23, 1965; affidavit of Cager Lee, Feb. 23, 1965.

593 George Baker: Affidavit of George Baker, Feb. 26, 1965. Witnesses also charged that patrol cars chased down random Negroes far out of town. Affidavit of George Sawyer, Feb. 22, 1965 (attacked at Piggly Wiggly store); affidavit of John C. Lewis, Feb. 22, 1965 (stopped by state troopers outside Marion on his way home from work, left unconscious on the car seat).

593 "This situation can only": MLK to Katzenbach, Feb. 19, 1965, A/KP21f11.

593 Katzenbach replied: Katzenbach to MLK, Feb. 19, 1965, A/KP21f11. Katzenbach called J. Edgar Hoover the next morning, and was assured that an investigation was already under way. Hoover approved the same day a request by the Mobile SAC for six additional FBI agents in Selma. Hoover for Tolson et al., 9:52 A.M., Feb. 19, 1965, FCT-NR; Rosen to Belmont, Feb. 19, 1965, FDCA-440.

594 "a nightmare of State Police": Cited in Garrow, *Protest,* p. 62.

594 Jimmy Lee Jackson: *Jet,* March 18, 1965, pp. 14–19; Bullard, *Free at Last,* pp. 76–77.

594 Wilson Baker stopped him: Fager, *Selma 1965,* pp. 76–77.

594 relief of some terrified: Int. Frank Soracco, Sept. 13, 1990; int. L. L. Anderson, May 27, 1990.

594 "naming the places": *Congressional Record,* Feb. 18, 1965, p. H3037.

594 just lost an appeal: "High Court Refuses," NYT, Jan. 19, 1965, p. 19; "Judgment Against Powell Is Increased to $210,000," NYT, Feb. 12, 1965, p. 1.

594 no more respectful attention: NYT, Feb. 15, 1965, p. 26, Feb. 19, 1965, p. 1, March 1, 1965, p. 17.

594 Dirksen set the tone: *Congressional Record,* Feb. 18, 1965, p. S-3146ff; Frank Church Oral History dated Sept. 16, 1977, pp. 20–27, LBJ.

594 "these former colonial regions": *Congressional Record,* Feb. 17, 1965, pp. S-2869–89. Senator George McGovern of South Dakota delivered a similar speech the same day. Dirksen concentrated his attack on Church, most likely because of his seniority on the Foreign Relations Committee.

594 Johnson was hosting another: Transcript from tape, Feb. 18, 1965, Congressional Briefings on Vietnam, Box 1, LBJ.

594   As usual: Cf. transcript from tape, Feb. 18, 1965, Congressional Briefings on Vietnam, Box 1, pp. 16–17, LBJ. (LBJ: "They waked me the other morning at 1:30. I called the Situation Room, and they said the boys were off the deck. 'They're off, they're on their mission, they're on their way.' And at 3:30 I waked up without anybody calling me, and I called them and said, 'Where are my boys?' And they said, 'Well, they are all back but four....'")

595   "what's necessary to win that war": Transcript from tape, Feb. 18, 1965, Congressional Briefings on Vietnam, Box 1, p. 7, LBJ.

595   "choose up and the winner take it": Ibid., p. 14.

595   orders approved February 13: Gravel, *Pentagon Papers*, Vol. 3, p. 321.

595   arrested General Nguyen Khanh: Karnow, *Vietnam*, p. 401.

595   "Khanh Is Deposed": NYT, Feb. 19, 1965, p. 1.

595   Johnson announced that Head Start: Levitan, *Poor Law*, p. 136.

595   "in view of the disturbed situation": Gravel, *Pentagon Papers*, Vol. 3, pp. 324–25.

595   "condition of virtual non-government": Ibid., p. 323.

595   Taylor put Khanh on an airplane: Ibid., p. 325.

595   Final bomb clearance: The first sustained sorties were initiated for February 26, but a series of bad-weather days postponed them until March 2. Ibid., pp. 329–30. Also, Gravel, *Pentagon Papers*, Vol. 2, p. 354.

595   ROLLING THUNDER: Karnow, *Vietnam*, p. 340. The hymn, "How Great Thou Art," begins: "O Lord my God, when I in awesome wonder/Consider all the worlds Thy hands have made/I see the stars, I hear the rolling thunder/Thy power throughout the universe displayed."

595   "the United States had dropped": Ibid., p. 341.

595   first two American combat battalions: Gravel, *Pentagon Papers*, Vol. 2, p. 422, Vol. 3, pp. 389–90.

596   "Now I pray several times": mf [Marie Fehmer] to Buzz [Horace Busby], with LBJ dictation and *Christian Science Monitor* inquiry attached, Feb. 22, 1965, Box 52, Busby Papers, LBJ.

596   "The air was heavy": Int. Yusuf Shah (Captain Joseph), Oct. 17, 1991.

596   Harlem temple felt the fury: Barboza, *American Jihad*, pp. 150–51.

596   many distant captains: Goldman, *Death and Life*, p. 414.

596   Ali checked into the Americana: Ibid., p. 314.

596   Louis X of Boston presided: Magida, *Prophet of Rage*, p. 84.

596   knew of the pressures: Robert Lipsyte, "Other Muslims Fear for Lives," NYT, Feb. 22, 1965, p. 10.

596   made and canceled trips: Goldman, *Death and Life*, pp. 265–68.

596   "when I jump out and say": Remarks on the Stan Bernard *Contact* program, WINS Radio, New York, Feb. 18, 1965, in Clark, ed., *Final Speeches*, pp. 184–229. Still, Malcolm seized upon detailed new inquiries. When his fellow radio guest, Aubrey Barnette, told listeners of being stomped the previous August, Malcolm begged program host Bernard's indulgence to ask Barnette if he knew whether the defense lawyer for the attackers had been "retained by the Muslims in Boston or was he retained by the Chicago headquarters?" Barnette said Chicago, indicating that headquarters orchestrated even the aftermath of punishment.

596   "It's a time for martyrs now": *Life*, March 5, 1965, p. 28ff.

596   a secretary and four members: Goldman, *Death and Life*, pp. 409–19; Karim, *Remembering Malcolm*, pp. 191–93; int. Benjamin Karim, March 19, 1991; int. Yusuf Shah (Captain Joseph), Oct. 17, 1991; "Who Killed Malcolm X?", CBS *60 Minutes*, Jan. 17, 1982. Also (courtesy of William Kunstler) affidavit of Mujahid Abdul Halim (Talmadge X Hayer, alias Thomas Hagan), Feb. 25, 1978; affidavit of William M. Kunstler, Feb. 28, 1978; affidavit of William M. Kunstler, April 3, 1978; Petition for Writ of Habeas Corpus, Muhammad Abdul Aziz (Norman 3X Butler) and Khalil Islam (Thomas 15X Johnson), Dec. 31, 1979; int. William Kunstler, Dec. 13, 1991.

596   "Malcolm X paced backstage.": Goldman, *Death and Life*, pp. 268–75; Alex Haley epilogue in Malcolm X, *The Autobiography*, pp. 431–46; Perry, *Malcolm*, pp. 364–66; Karim, *Remembering Malcolm*, pp. 191–193; int. Benjamin Karim, March 19, 1991.

597   "Get your hand out": Ibid. Also SA [deleted] to SAC, New York, Feb. 21, 1965, FMXNY-5644; SAC, Philadelphia, to Director, Feb. 23, 1965, FMX-243; SAC, Philadelphia, to Director, Feb. 22, 1965, FMX-245; Bland to Sullivan, Feb. 22, 1965, FMX-259; Bland to Sullivan, Feb. 22, 1965, FMX-264; Baumgardner to Sullivan, Feb. 22, 1965, FMX-273; SAC, New York, to Director, Feb. 22, 1965, FMX-283; New York LHM dated March 12, 1965, FMX-360; New York report dated Sept. 8, 1965, FMX-418, pp. 4–9 *Baltimore Afro-American*, Feb. 27, 1965, p. 1.

597   "I am deeply saddened": MLK statement of Feb. 21, 1965, A/KP15f16.

597   On Monday in Selma: SAC, Mobile, to Director, 2:10 P.M., Feb. 22, 1965, FDCA-425; SAC, Mobile, to Director, 6:00 P.M., Feb. 22, 1965, FDCA-422; SAC, Mobile, to Director, 6:10 P.M., Feb. 22, 1965, FDCA-411; SAC, Mobile, to Director, 11:42 P.M., Feb. 22, 1965, FDCA-431.

597   "That is another matter": NYT, Feb. 23, 1965, p. 16.

597   Katzenbach called King: Garrow, *Bearing the Cross*, p. 392; CDD, Feb. 24, 1965, p. 5.

597   "absolute extinction of all": Fager, *Selma 1965*, p. 79.

597   private objective of city officials: FBI agents reported to headquarters that Mayor Smitherman was complaining to Governor Wallace that state troopers occupied Selma and Brown Chapel without a specific request from local authorities. SAC, Mobile, to Director, 6:00 P.M., Feb. 23, 1965, FDCA-422.

597   local citizens welcomed: NYT, Feb. 23, 1965, p. 16.

597   "Followers of Malcolm X": STJ, Feb. 22, 1965, p. 1. Elsewhere, the *Charlotte Observer* declared, "Black Nationalist Civil War Looms," and *U.S. News & World Report* exclaimed, "Now It's Negroes vs. Negroes in America's Racial Violence," in what writer Claude Clegg called "an exasperated tone." Cited in Clegg, *An Original Man*, p. 230.

597   Colonel Al Lingo: Branch, *Parting*, pp. 795–96, 891–93.

597   "baseless and irresponsible": Fager, *Selma 1965*, p. 80. The Alabama Senate toned down the wording of the original resolution, after some local news organizations protested the failure to protect reporters on the scene in Marion. STJ, Feb. 24, 1965, p. 1.

598   "twilight march": NYT, Feb. 24, 1965, p. 1.

598   press conference Wednesday: Transcript (from an FBI recording) of MLK press conference at Delta Air Lines Crown Room, LAX, Feb. 24, 1965, A/KS.

598   Christian Nationalist State Army: SAC, Los Angeles, to Director, 12:06 P.M., Feb. 24, 1965, FK-980; SAC, Los Angeles, to Director, 5:21 P.M., Feb. 24, 1965, FK-954.

598   dynamite thefts by fugitives: LAT, Feb. 27, 1965, p. 12.

598   guarding a theater on Sunset Boulevard: LAHE, Feb. 26, 1965, p. B1.

598   "the biggest hypocrite alive": J. Ann Williams, "Louis Lomas Unmasks Rev. King's Hypocrisy," LAHD, March 13, 1965, p. 1.

598   "pitifully wasted": "... He was a case history, as well as an extraordinary and twisted man, turning many true gifts to evil purpose.... He could not even come to terms with his fellow black extremists. The world he saw through those horn-rimmed glasses of his was distorted and dark. But he made it darker still with his exaltation of fanaticism.... It will take alertness and vigilance on the part of the police, especially in view of the ease with which lethal weapons are available, to make sure that violence is avoided." NYT, Feb. 22, 1965, p. 20.

598   "In Poland": "The murder of Malcolm X has made no great impact on world opinion. Malcolm himself is not generally being treated as a martyr, even in African and Asian areas sensitive to the American race problem." "World Pays Little Attention to Malcolm Slaying," NYT, Feb. 28, 1965, p. 74.

598   spilled in thousands: LAT, March 1, 1965, p. 5.

598   Bevel returned to Selma: STJ, Feb. 26, 1965, p. 1.

598   Rev. Lorenzo Harrison: NYT, March 1, 1965, p. 17.

599   Their marriage cracked: *Jet*, May 6, 1965, pp. 42–43; *Chicago Tribune*, April 6, 1965, April 12, 1969; int. Bernard Lafayette, May 28, 1990; int. Diane Nash, Oct. 26, 1997; int. James Bevel, Nov. 23, 1997.

599   "Oh, yeah.": Int. Bernard Lafayette, May 28, 1990.

599   "I tell you, the death": NYT, Feb. 27, 1965, p. 10.

599   pulled up two texts: Fager, *Selma 1965*, pp. 82–83; Hampton and Fayer, *Voices*, p. 226. Fager dates the Bevel sermon proposing the Montgomery march to Feb. 28, two days later than Roy Reed's account in the *Times*. It is possible that Bevel gave two sermons building upon the same ideas. The author has conflated the two accounts to the earlier date. David Garrow, in *Bearing the Cross*, p. 394, traces the idea of the Montgomery march to Marion activist Lucy Foster, on information from SCLC's James Orange.

599   "I must go see the king": Fager, *Selma 1965*, pp. 82–83.

599   "Be prepared to walk": NYT, Feb. 27, 1965, p. 10.

599   retained their life's pledge: Int. Diane Nash, Oct. 26, 1997.

599   500,000 nonregistered Negro voters: Garrow, *Protest at Selma*, pp. 7, 11, 20, 189.

599   telegram of condolence: "... While we did not always see eye to eye on methods to solve the race problem, I always had a deep affection for Malcolm and felt that he had the great ability to put his finger on the existence and root of the problem.... Always consider me a friend...." MLK telegram to "Mrs. Malcolm X," Feb. 26, 1965, A/KP15f16.

599   tiny march of twelve: Fager, *Selma 1965*, p. 84.

599   oppose the escalating war: Garrow, *Bearing the Cross*. p. 394.

600   "love will conquer hate": Webb and Nelson, *Selma, Lord Selma*, pp. 80–82.

600   "We will bring": NYT, March 2, 1965, p. 1.

Epilogue

601   appeared in dramatic submisson: Chicago's *American*, Feb. 25, 1965, p. 1, in FBI files as FMXNY-5705.

601   Malcolm's own brothers: Perry, *Malcolm*, pp. 375–77.

601   crowd of two thousand: Baumgardner to Sullivan, Feb. 27, 1965, FMX-NR.

601   "Put the light on him": Magida, *Prophet of Rage*, p. 90.

601   "I judged my father": Ibid., p. 89. Also, Goldman, *Death and Life*, p. 301; Clegg, *An Original Man*, p. 231.

601   baker, welder, painter: Employment history on Wallace D. Muhammad job application for Motorola, Inc., in file No. 589, RS, CHS; int. W. D. Mohammed (W. D. Muhammad), Nov. 14, 1991; Clegg, *An Original Man*, p. 245; "The Islam Connection," *Playboy*, May 1980, p. 201.

601   Doubleday canceled: Tim Warren, "The Rocky Road to Publication of Book on Malcolm X," *Baltimore Sun*, Nov. 16, 1992, p. D-1.

601   "understood, perhaps more profoundly": "An Eloquent Testament," NYT, Nov. 5, 1965, p. 35.

602   fn "shocked when former secretaries": I. F. Stone, *The New York Review of Books*, Nov. 11, 1965, pp. 3–5.

602   fifteen languages: Tim Warren, "The Rocky Road to Publication of Book on Malcolm X," *Baltimore Sun*, Nov. 16, 1992, p. D-1.

602   At the trial: Goldman, *Death and Life*, pp. 318–59.

602   Marks sentenced: SAC, New York, to Director, April 14, 1966, FMX-441.

602   conspiracy theories: cf. Farmer, *Lay Bare*, pp. 230–37; Breitman, *The Last Year*, pp. 141–52; Goldman, *Death and Life*, pp. 359–73.

602   spent decades: Int. Yusuf Shah (Captain Joseph), Oct. 17, 1991; int. Benjamin Karim, Aug. 31, 1991; Karim, *Remembering Malcolm*, pp. 192–93.

602 Police wrecked the Newark: *Jet,* Jan. 13, 1966, pp. 24–27.

602 "swindled": Magida, *Prophet of Rage,* p. 105.

602 a bank, a Learjet: Clegg, *An Original Man,* pp. 251–54.

602 filched $23,000 cash: Ibid., p. 261.

603 killed Hakim Jamal: Ibid., pp. 261–62,

603 Hamaas Abdul-Khaalis: Ibid., pp. 262–64; Goldman, *Death and Life,* pp. 433–34; interview of Kareem Abdul-Jabbar, in Barboza, *American Jihad,* pp. 213–22.

603 "Let this be a warning"; Magida, *Prophet of Rage,* pp. 97–98; Evanzz, *The Judas Factor,* p. 321.

603 murder of Minister James: Clegg, *An Original Man,* p. 262; Barboza, *American Jihad,* p. 115.

603 war among factions: Some NOI officials of that era assert that enforcers and officers took advantage of police intimidation to shake down drug dealers and deal drugs themselves, sometimes squabbling over a cut for the mosque. Int. Agieb Bilal, Nov. 6, 1990; int. Benjamin Karim, Aug. 31, 1991.

603 "Cut off their heads": Magida, *Prophet of Rage,* pp. 99–100.

603 "My son's got it right": W. D. Muhammad pamphlet, *As the Light Shineth From the East* (1980), pp. 143–46.

603 broken refrigerator door: Int. Agieb Bilal, March 19, 1991.

603 ministers swore fealty: MS, March 14, 1975, pp. 1–3.

603 "I was born for this mission": MS, March 21, 1975, p. 1.

603 "suspended" to "abolished": Goldman, *Death and Life,* pp. 434–36; Clegg, *An Original Man,* pp. 277–81.

603 "punch your teeth out": Barboza, *American Jihad,* pp. 94–104.

603 "What we should see": W. D. Muhammad taped address, November 1980.

603–4 "If he hadn't hurt me": W. D. Muhammad taped address, Chicago, Dec. 13, 1977.

604 "with fire in my ears": Int. Wazir Muhammad (Randolph X Sidle), March 27, 1991.

604 fn "recent behavior and attitude": LAT, March 3, 1965.

604 Farrakhan broke away: Clegg, *An Original Man,* pp. 281–82; Magida, *Prophet of Rage,* pp. 115–38.

604 reviving his sectarian doctrines: Farrakhan preserved Elijah's teachings on creation by Yacub, white devils, the "Mother ship," Allah as carnate being, and his elaborate numerologies, but he did allow members of the Nation to vote, beginning in 1984. Magida, *Prophet of Rage,* p. 145.

604 hire several of the deceased: Ibid., pp. 135–36.

604 entangled probate: Clegg, *An Original Man,* p. 279.

604 Joseph could not accept: Int. Yusuf Shah (Captain Joseph), Oct. 17, 1991; int. Agieb Bilal, Nov. 6, 1990.

604 Arthur X Coleman: Int. Nuri Salaam (Arthur X Coleman), April 10, 1991.

604 Hayer filed affidavits: Goldman, *Death and Life,* pp. 423–29; Barboza, *American Jihad,* p. 150; W. D. Muhammad taped address, November 1980; Karl Evanzz, "Deadly Crossroads," WP, Dec. 10, 1995, p. C3; int. William Kunstler, Dec. 13, 1991.

604 insulted American Jews: Magida, *Prophet of Rage,* pp. 139–72.

604 "Nothing that I wrote": Steven Barboza, "A Divided Legacy," *Emerge,* April 1992, p. 32. Continuing to speak ambiguously of the Malcolm X murder, Farrakhan told an interviewer in 1994, "I can't say that I approved and I really didn't disapprove." On Feb. 26, 1993, Farrakhan spoke of Malcolm's death to his NOI convention in Chicago: "I loved Elijah Muhammad enough so that I would kill you . . . yesterday, today, and tomorrow. We don't give a damn about no white man's laws when you attack what we love." Clegg, *An Original Man,* p. 251; Karl Evanzz, "Deadly Crossroads," WP, Dec. 10, 1995. p. C3.

604 Qubilah was charged: WP, Jan. 13, 1995, p. 1.

604 truce on the stage: "Farrakhan Seeks End of Rift with Shabazz/Apologizes for 'Hurt' but Denies Involvement in Malcolm X Death," WP, May 8, 1995, p. 1.

605 home fire that killed: NYT, June 2, 1997, p. 1; June 24, 1997, p. 1; Aug. 5, 1997, p. 1.

605 "one who bares his teeth"; W. D. Muhammad taped address, Chicago, Dec. 13, 1977.

605 "They shut themselves out": "Appeal to Minister Farrakhan," *Bilalian News,* April 28, 1978, p. 7.

605 "not even the Muslims": W. D. Mohammed (W. D. Muhammad) address, Washington, D.C., Nov. 18, 1990.

605 "The person wrapped up": Ibid.

605 Muslim American Society: W. D. Mohammed (W. D. Muhammad) address, East Rutherford, N.J., Aug. 30, 1997.

605 estimates of Muslims: Barboza, *American Jihad,* p. 9; WP, Sept. 5, 1994, p. D1; NYT, Aug. 28, 1995, p. 1; *Baltimore Sun,* Oct. 22, 1996, p. 13; *Chicago Tribune,* Aug. 28, 1997, p. 1.

605 goal was to win: Int. W. D. Mohammed (W. D. Muhammad), Nov. 14, 1991.

605 "All of us": Int. Yusuf Shah (Captain Joseph), Oct. 17, 1991.

605 Cager Lee of Marion: Ben Owens to Randolph Blackwell, Aug. 21, 1965, A/SC146f5.

606 All 1,144 applicants: John Doar, "The Work of the Civil Rights Division in Enforcing Voting Rights Under the Civil Rights Acts of 1957 and 1960," *Florida State University Law Review,* Fall 1997, p. 14.

606 jumped from 7 to 60 percent: Parker, *Black Votes Count,* pp. 29–30.

606 Watkins drove from Greenwood: Int. Hollis Watkins, June 22, 1992; int. Dennis and Bettie Dahmer, June 21, 1992.

606 Gray had signed out: Int. James K. Dukes, June 23, 1992.

606 Preachers repeated his announcement: Int. Ellie Dahmer, June 21, 1992; int. J. C. Fairley, June 20, 1992; Whitehead, *Attack on Terror,* p. 235.

606 two o'clock that night: Int. Ellie, Harold, Dennis, and Bettie Dahmer, June 22, 1992; *Hattiesburg American,* Jan. 10, 1966, p. 1; NYT, Jan. 11, 1966, p. 10; MS, Feb. 16, 1968; Whitehead, *Attack on Terror,* pp. 235–38; NYT, April 2, 1995, p. 18.

607   Martin arrived: Int. J. L. Martin, June 21, 1992.
607   two tires flattened: Whitehead, *Attack on Terror,* p. 238.
607   "They finally got me": Int. J. C. Fairley, June 20, 1992.
607   "I think I made a mistake": Int. Robert Beech, Dec. 8, 1991.
607   suffocated because hot smoke: *Hattiesburg American,* Jan. 11, 1966, p. 1, Jan. 13, 1966, p. 1; int. Ellie Dahmer, June 22, 1992.
607   Negroes nearly rioted: *Hattiesburg American,* Jan. 15, 1966, p. 1.
607   local whites banded: *Hattiesburg American,* Jan. 22, 1964, p. 1.
607   "Since the Negroes have equal": Ibid., p. 4.
607   white siblings were moved: Int. Vernon Dahmer, Jr., June 23, 1992.
607   movement quarrels: Int. J. C. Fairley, June 20, 1992; int. Robert Beech, Dec. 8, 1991; int. Ellie Dahmer, June 22, 1992.
607   "There has been no effort": Current to Beech, Feb. 4, 1966; Beech to Current, March 4, 1966; Current to Beech, March 11, 1966; Beech to Current, April 1, 1966. All box 3, A/AT.
607   Katzenbach announced: *Hattiesburg American,* Jan. 11, 1966, p. 1.
607   Johnson sent a telegram: LBJ to Mrs. Vernon Dahmer, 11:40 A.M. Jan. 11, 1966, Name File, LBJ.
608   "We all know": Parker, *Black Votes Count,* p. 47.
608   fn Thirteen state election laws: Ibid., pp. 37–39.
608   "I am very sorry": Affidavit of Devours Nix, Feb. 14, 1966, cited in Dillard, *Clearburning,* p. 182.
608   Bowers had violated an agreement: Statement to FBI by Lawrence Byrd, March 2, 1966, reprinted in Ibid., pp. 310–32; int. J. L. Martin, June 21, 1992.
608   Supreme Court had reinstated: SAC, Washington to Director, March 28, 1966, enclosing opinion written by Justice Potter Stewart in Case #65 Appellate, *U.S. vs. Herbert Guest et al.,* FLP-398; Whitehead, *Attack on Terror,* pp. 219–20, 258; Cagin and Dray, *We Are Not Afraid,* pp. 441–42.
608   "quite enthusiastic": DeLoach to Tolson, March 30, 1966, FLP-NR; Rosen to DeLoach, March 30, 1966, FLP-399.
608   defendants won acquittal: Rosen to DeLoach, June 16, 1966, FLP-475; Interesting Case Memorandum dated Nov. 1, 1968, pp. 13–14, FLP-NR.
608   "Sims went to Athens": SAC, Atlanta to Director, May 5, 1966, FLP-405; SAC, Atlanta to Director, May 12, 1966, FLP-421.
609   began serving the maximum: Interesting Case Memorandum dated Nov. 1, 1968, pp. 13–14, FLP-NR.
609   invalid for lack of black people: NYT, Feb. 21, 1967; Feb. 28, 1967, p. 40; March 1, 1967, p. 1.
609   Jackson's Temple Beth Israel: Nelson, *Terror,* pp. 29–32.
609   Price was confident: Cagin and Dray, *We Are Not Afraid,* p. 445.
609   the Meridian courtroom: Ibid., pp. 445–52; Whitehead, *Attack on Terror,* pp. 260–84.
609   November, bombs damaged: Ibid., pp. 65, 69–70.
609   constable who spot-checked: Nelson, *Terror,* pp. 79–80.
609   confession of Billy Roy Pitts: Whitehead, *Attack on Terror,* pp. 252–55. Aside from Pitts, Delmar Dennis, and Lawrence Byrd, Klan witnesses against Sam Bowers in the Dahmer case included T. Weber Rogers, who testified that he heard Bowers order the Dahmer murder. NYT, Jan. 23, 1969, p. 21.
610   Charles Wilson: Ibid., pp. 256–57; int. Charles Wilson, June 24, 1992.
610   grand jury indicted eleven: *Hattiesburg American,* Jan. 25, 1968, p. 1; *Time,* April 8, 1966, p. 27; NYT, Jan. 26, 1968, p. 17.
610   murder convictions at three trials: Whitehead, *Attack on Terror,* pp. 302–3; NYT, March 16, 1968, p. 17; July 20, 1968, p. 25; July 29, 1968, p. 18; Feb. 1, 1969.
610   fight or show chicken: Int. James Dukes, June 23, 1992.
610   jury deadlocked 11–1: *Hattiesburg American,* May 18, 1968, p. 1. In 1995, three former jurors stated that all twelve jurors voted "guilty" out loud, but that one juror consistently changed to "not guilty" on secret ballots. NYT, April 2, 1995, p. 18.
610   Bowers survived a second: NYT, Jan. 26, 1969, p. 1.
610   "Pitts 'Sings Again' ": *Hattiesburg American,* May 1, 1969, p. 1. Also, "Doctor Brings New Angle into Wilson Murder Trial/Says he believes state witness Pitts has a disease which would make him over-react," *Hattiesburg American,* July 27, 1968, p. 1.
610   secretly poisoned Dahmer: Int. J. L. Martin, June 23, 1992.
610   burned a store: Nelson, *Terror,* p. 106.
610   in May bombed: Ibid., pp. 120–24.
610   gravely wounded Thomas Tarrants: Ibid., pp. 17–22, 173–87; Whitehead, *Attack on Terror,* pp. 285–301. The shootout occurred when the waiting law enforcement team tried to arrest Tarrants and Ainsworth at the home targeted to be bombed. A policeman was shot in the heart, a bystander in the liver. Both survived.
610   Jack Nelson: Nelson, *Terror,* pp. 147–56, 189, 239–40. Nelson raised questions beyond the competency of the law enforcement work at the scene, including borderline entrapment and improper use of privately raised informant money. He quoted an FBI agent's statement that the Bureau responded more aggressively when the White Knights of the Klan began to target white victims: "Once the Jews were attacked, it was a different ball game. This wasn't just a local across-the-tracks case. It involved the whole United States." Other issues include the necessity, irony, or squalor of dealing with Alton Wayne Roberts (and his brother) after his conviction in the Neshoba County murders. Confessions and court testimony named him as the Klansman who took initiative to fire four of the five bullets that killed Chaney, Goodman, and Schwerner.
610   five-year toll: Marsh, *God's Long Summer,* p. 49; Nelson, *Terror,* pp. 11–13.
610   Charles Wilson served: NYT, Dec. 24, 1972.

611   paroled in 1978: Int. Dennis Dahmer, Nov. 14, 1997.

611   "When a priest sees": Charles Marsh, "Rendezvous with the Wizard," *Oxford American,* October–November 1996, p. 31.

611   Ellie Dahmer petitioned: NYT, May 27, 1994, p. B18; April 2, 1995, p. 18; int. Dennis Dahmer, Nov. 13, 1997.

611   drifted from Mississippi: Int. Bob Moses, Aug. 10, 1983.

611   Bevel sleeping in a bathtub: Int. Jean and Sullivan Jackson, May 27, 1990.

611   "I felt like I was praying": Int. Susannah Heschel, Nov. 15, 1990; int. Sylvia Heschel, Feb. 4, 1991.

611   drinking corn whiskey: Int. June Johnson, April 9, 1992.

611   "Use Mississippi not": Cagin and Dray, *We Are Not Afraid,* p. 439.

611   "Now I looked": Petras, ed., *We Accuse,* p. 151.

611   "sought out Al Lowenstein": Int. Bob Moses, July 30, 1984.

611   "Lowenstein brought Parris": Ibid. Also Chafe, *Never Stop Running,* pp. 218–20.

612   "I got angry": Int. Bob Moses, July 31, 1984.

612   "declare peace": Dellinger, *From Yale to Jail,* pp. 208–15.

612   conference in New Orleans: Int. Bob Moses, July 30, 1984.

612   safe to become Moses: Int. Bob Moses, July 31, 1984.

612   marriage collapsed: Ibid. Also, Burner, *And Gently He Shall Lead Them,* pp. 218–20.

612   fled underground to Canada: Cagin and Dray, *We Are Not Afraid,* pp. 452–53.

612   adopted by the children as "Uncle Bob": Int. Bob Moses, Feb. 15, 1991.

612   Moses panicked: Ibid.

612   granted him tacit asylum: Ibid.

612   feared he was dead: Int. Doris Moses, Jan. 8, 1993.

612   Moses told himself: Int. Bob Moses, Feb. 15, 1991.

613   Rauh wrote: Int. Joseph Rauh, Oct. 17, 1983.

613   Moses did not reply: Int. Bob Moses, Feb. 15, 1991.

613   "I felt that way": Remarks of Diane Nash, Session 2, Trinity College SNCC Conference, 1988.

613   Algebra Project: Dittmer, *Local People,* p. 432; "Mississippi Learning," *The New York Times Magazine,* Feb. 21, 1993, pp. 28–72.

Major Works Cited in Notes

Abram, Morris B. *The Day Is Short: An Autobiography*. Harcourt Brace Jovanovich, 1982.

Ahmann, Mathew. *Race: Challenge to Religion*. Henry Regnery Co., 1963.

Allen, Frederick. *Secret Formula: How Brilliant Marketing and Relentless Salesmanship Made Coca-Cola the Best-Known Product in the World*. HarperBusiness, 1994.

Allen, Ivan Jr., with Paul Hemphill. *Mayor: Notes on the Sixties*. Simon & Schuster, 1971.

Ambrose, Stephen E. *Eisenhower: The President*. Simon & Schuster, 1984.

———. *Nixon: Ruin and Recovery, 1973–1990*. Simon & Schuster, 1991.

Barboza, Steven. *American Jihad: Islam after Malcolm X*. Doubleday, 1994.

Bass, Jack. *Unlikely Heroes*. Simon & Schuster, 1981.

Bea, Augustin Cardinal. *The Church and the Jewish People*. Harper & Row, 1966.

Belfrage, Sally. *Freedom Summer*. Fawcett, 1966.

Bontemps, Arna, and Jack Conroy. *Anyplace But Here*. Hill and Wang, 1966.

Bradlee, Benjamin C. *A Good Life: Newspapering and Other Adventures*. Simon & Schuster, 1995.

Branch, Taylor. *Parting the Waters: America in the King Years, 1954–63*. Simon & Schuster, 1988.

Breitman, George. *The Last Year of Malcolm X*. Pathfinder Press, 1967.

———, ed. *Malcolm X Speaks*. Grove Press, 1965.

Bullard, Sara. *Free at Last: A History of the Civil Rights Movement and Those Who Died in the Struggle*. Oxford University Press, 1993.

Burner, Eric R. *And Gently He Shall Lead Them: Robert Parris Moses and Civil Rights in Mississippi*. New York University Press, 1994.

Cagin, Seth, and Philip Dray. *We Are Not Afraid: The Story of Goodman, Schwerner, and Chaney and the Civil Rights Campaign for Mississippi*. Macmillan, 1988.

Califano, Joseph A., Jr. *The Triumph and Tragedy of Lyndon Johnson*. Simon & Schuster, 1991.

Cannon, Lou. *Reagan*. Putnam, 1982.

———. *President Reagan: The Role of a Lifetime*. Simon & Schuster, 1991.

Caro, Robert A. *The Years of Lyndon Johnson: The Path to Power*. Alfred A. Knopf, 1982.

———. *The Means of Ascent*. Alfred A. Knopf, 1990.

Carson, Clayborne. *In Struggle: SNCC and the Black Awakening of the 1960s*. Harvard University Press, 1981.

Carter, Dan T. *The Politics of Rage: George Wallace, the Origins of the New Conservatism, and the Transformation of American Politics*. Simon & Schuster, 1995.

Chafe, William H. *Never Stop Running: Allard Lowenstein and the Struggle to Save American Liberalism*. Basic Books, 1993.

Chestnut, J. L., Jr., and Julia Cass. *Black in Selma*. Farrar, Straus & Giroux, 1990.

[Church Committee]. U.S. Senate. *Hearings Before the Select Committee to Study Governmental Operations with Respect to Intelligence Activities*. Vol. 6. Nov. 18, 19; Dec. 2, 3, 9, 10, 11, 1975. U.S. Government Printing Office, 1976.

———. *Supplementary Detailed Staff Reports on Intelligence Activities and the Rights of Americans, Book III, Final Report of the Select Committee to Study Governmental Operations with Respect to Intelligence Activities*. April 23, 1976. U.S. Government Printing Office, 1976.

Clark, Septima. *Echo in My Soul*. Dutton, 1962.

————. *Ready from Within: A First Person Narrative.* Edited with an introduction by Cynthia Stokes Brown. Trenton, N.J. Africa World Press, 1990.

Clark, Steve, ed. *Malcolm X: February 1965, The Final Speeches.* Pathfinder Press, 1992.

Clegg, Claude Andrew III. *An Original Man: The Life and Times of Elijah Muhammad.* St. Martin's Press, 1997.

Clifford, Clark, with Richard Holbrooke. *Counsel to the President: A Memoir.* Random House, 1991.

COFO (Council of Federated Organizations). *Mississippi Black Power.* Random House, 1965.

Cohodas, Nadine. *Strom Thurmond and the Politics of Southern Change.* Simon & Schuster, 1993.

Colburn, David R. *Racial Change and Community Crisis: St. Augustine.* Columbia University Press, 1985.

Cole, Barry. *The Reluctant Regulators: The FCC and the Broadcast Audience.* Addison-Wesley Co., 1978.

Coleman, Emmett. *Adam Clayton Powell.* Bee-Line Books, 1967.

Cone, James H. *Martin & Malcolm & America: A Dream or a Nightmare.* Orbis Books, 1991.

Cook, Jeannine, ed. *Columbus and the Land of Allyon: The Exploration & Settlement of the Southeast.* Lower Altamaha Historical Society, 1992.

Cosman, Bernard, and Robert J. Huckshorn, eds. *Republican Politics: The 1964 Campaign and Its Aftermath.* Praeger, 1968.

Cunningham, W. J. *Agony at Galloway: One Church's Struggle with Social Change.* University Press of Mississippi, 1980.

Dallek, Robert. *Lone Star Rising: Lyndon Johnson and his Times, 1908–1960.* Oxford University Press, 1991.

Dates, Jannette L., ed., and William Barlow, co-ed. *Split Image: African Americans in the Mass Media.* Howard University Press, 1990.

Deay, Davin, with Mary Neely. *Stairway to Heaven: The Spiritual Roots of Rock 'n' Roll.* Ballantine/Epiphany, 1986.

Dellinger, David. *From Yale to Jail: The Life Story of a Moral Dissenter.* Pantheon, 1993.

Dillard, W. O. Chet. *Clear Burning.* Persimmon Press, 1992.

Dittmer, John. *Local People: The Struggle for Civil Rights in Mississippi.* University of Illinois Press, 1994.

Du Bois, W. E. B. *The Souls of Black Folk.* New American Library, 1969.

Dugger, Ronnie. *The Politician.* Norton, 1982.

Durr, Virginia Foster. *Outside the Magic Circle.* University of Alabama Press, 1985.

Edwards, Lee. *Reagan. A Political Biography.* Viewpoint Books, 1967.

————. *Goldwater: The Man Who Made a Revolution.* Regnery, 1995.

Eisler, Kim Isaac. *A Justice for All: William J. Brennan, Jr., and the Decisions That Transformed America.* Simon & Schuster, 1993.

Evans, Sara. *Personal Politics.* Vintage, 1980.

Evers, Mrs. Medgar. *For Us, the Living.* Doubleday, 1967.

Fager, Charles E. *Selma 1965.* Beacon Press, 1985.

Fairclough, Adam. *To Redeem the Soul of America: The Southern Christian Leadership Conference and Martin Luther King, Jr.* University of Georgia Press, 1987.

Farmer, James. *Freedom—When?* Random House, 1965.

————. *Lay Bare the Heart.* Arbor House, 1985.

Findlay, James F., Jr. *Church People in the Struggle: The National Council of Churches and the Black Freedom Movement, 1950–1970.* Oxford University Press, 1993.

Forman, James. *The Making of Black Revolutionaries.* Macmillan, 1972.

Gallen, David, et al. *Malcolm X As They Knew Him.* Carroll & Graf, 1992.

Gannon, Michael V. *Florida: A Short History.* University of Florida Press, 1993.

Garrow, David. *Protest at Selma: Martin Luther King, Jr., and the Voting Rights Act of 1965.* Yale University Press, 1978.

————. *The FBI and Martin Luther King, Jr.* W. W. Norton, 1981.

————. *Bearing the Cross: Martin Luther King, Jr. and the Southern Christian Leadership Conference.* William Morrow, 1986.

————, ed. *Birmingham, Alabama, 1956–1963: The Black Struggle for Civil Rights.* Carlson Publishing, Inc., 1989.

————, ed. *St. Augustine, Florida, 1963–1964: Mass Protest and Racial Violence.* Carlson Publishing, 1989.

Gentile, Thomas. *March on Washington: August 28, 1963.* Dew Day Publications, Inc. 1983.

Gentry, Curt. J. *Edgar Hoover: The Man and the Secrets.* W. W. Norton, 1991.

Gilbert, Arthur. *The Vatican Council and the Jews.* The World Publishing Co., 1968.

Goldman, Peter. *The Death and Life of Malcolm X.* University of Illinois Press, 2nd, 1979.

Good, Paul. *The Trouble I've Seen: White Journalist/Black Movement.* Howard University Press, 1975.

Graham, Hugh Davis. *The Civil Rights Era: Origins and Development of National Policy.* Oxford University Press, 1990.

Grant, Joanne. *Black Protest: History, Documents and Analysis, 1619 to the Present.* Fawcett World Library, 1968.

Gravel, Mike, ed. *The Pentagon Papers: The Defense Department History of United States Decisionmaking on Vietnam.* Beacon Press, 1972.

Greene, Melissa Fay. *The Temple Bombing.* Addison-Wesley, 1996.

Guralnick, Peter. *Sweet Soul Music.* Harper & Row, 1986.

Guthman, Edwin. *We Band of Brothers.* Harper & Row, 1971.

Halberstam, David. *October 1964.* Villard Books, 1994.

Haldeman, H. R. *The Haldeman Diaries: Inside the Nixon White House.* Putnam, 1994.

Hamilton, Charles V. *Adam Clayton Powell, Jr.: The Political Biography of an American Dilemma.* Atheneum, 1991.

Hampton, Henry, and Steve Fayer. *Voices of Freedom: An Oral History of the Civil Rights Movement from the 1950s through the 1980s.* Bantam, 1991.

Harris, David. *Dreams Die Hard.* St. Martin's Press, 1982.

Harrison, Cynthia. *On Account of Sex: The Politics of Women's Issues, 1945–1968.* University of California Press, 1988.

Hauser, Thomas. *Muhammad Ali: His Life and Times*. Simon & Schuster, 1991.
Heirich, Max. *The Beginning: Berkeley, 1964*. Columbia University Press, 1968.
Heschel, Abraham J. *The Earth is the Lord's*. Farrar, Straus & Giroux, 1949.
———. *The Insecurity of Freedom*. Schocken Books, Inc., 1959.
———. *Who Is Man?* Stanford University Press, 1965.
———. *Israel: An Echo of Eternity*. Farrar, Straus & Giroux, 1967.
———. *The Prophets*. 2 vols. Harper & Row, 1969.
Hoffman, Paul E. *A New Andalucia and a Way to the Orient*. Louisiana State University Press, 1990.
Holmes, Thomas J., and Gainer E. Bryan, Jr. *Ashes for Breakfast: A Diary of Racism in an American Church*. The Judson Press, 1969.
Holt, Len. *The Summer That Didn't End*. Heinemann (London), 1966.
Huie, William Bradford. *3 Lives for Mississippi*. Signet, 1968.
Humphrey, Hubert H., edited by Norman Sherman. *The Education of a Public Man*. Doubleday, 1976.
Jacobs, Andy. *The Powell Affair: Freedom Minus One*. Bobbs-Merrill, Co. Inc., 1973.
Johnson, Lady Bird. *A White House Diary*. Holt, Rinehart and Winston, 1970.
Johnson, Lyndon B. *The Vantage Point*. Holt, Rinehart and Winston, 1971.
Jones, Landon, Y. *Great Expectations*. Coward McCann & Geoghegan, 1980.
Jordan, Winthrop D. *White over Black: American Attitudes Toward the Negro, 1550–1812*. University of North Carolina Press, 1968.
Karim, Benjamin, Peter Skutches and David Gallen. *Remembering Malcolm*. Carroll & Graf, 1992.
Karnow, Stanley. *Vietnam: A History*. Penguin, 1984.
Kasher, Steven. *The Civil Rights Movement: A Photographic History, 1954–68*. Abbeville Press, NY, 1996 .
Kearns, Doris. *Lyndon Johnson & the American Dream*. Harper & Row, 1976.
King, Coretta Scott. *My Life with Martin Luther King, Jr*. Holt, Rinehart & Winston, 1969.
King, Martin Luther, Jr. *Why We Can't Wait*. Signet, 1964.
King, Martin Luther, Jr. Edition 1982. *Strength to Love*. Harper & Row, 1964.
King, Mary. *Freedom Song*. William Morrow, 1987.
Kinoy, Arthur. *Rights on Trial: The Odyssey of a People's Lawyer*. Harvard University Press, 1983.
Kunstler, William M. *Deep In My Heart*. William Morrow, 1966.
Lemann, Nicholas. *The Promised Land: The Great Black Migration and How It Changed America*. Alfred A. Knopf, 1991.
Lesher, Stephan. *George Wallace: American Populist*. Addison-Wesley, 1994.
Levitan, Sara. *The Great Society's Poor Law*. Johns Hopkins University Press, 1969.
Lewis, Anthony. *Make No Law: The Sullivan Case and the First Amendment*. Random House, 1991.
Lewis, David L. *King: A Critical Biography* . University of Illinois Press, 1970, 1978.
Lincoln, C. Eric. *The Negro Pilgrimage in America*. Bantam Books, 1967.
———. *Sounds of Struggle*. William Morrow, 1967.
Lomax, Louis E. *When the Word Is Given: A Report on Elijah Muhammad, Malcolm X, and the Black Muslim World*. The World Publishing Co., 1963.
Lord, Walter. *The Past That Would Not Die*. Pocket, 1967.
Lowenstein, Allard K. *Brutal Mandate: A Journey to South West Africa*. Macmillan, 1962.
Lyon, Danny. *Memories of the Southern Civil Rights Movement*. Chapel Hill/Center for Documentary Studies, 1992.
Lyon, Eugene. *The Enterprise of Florida*. University of Florida Press, 1974.
Lyon, Eugene. *Richer Than We Thought: The Material Culture of Sixteenth-Century St. Augustine, El Escribano*. The St. Augustine Journal of History, 1992.
Maddox, Lester Garfield. *Speaking Out: The Autobiography of LGM*. Doubleday, 1975.
Magida, Arthur. *Prophet of Rage: A Life of Louis Farrakhan and His Nation*. Basic Books, 1996.
Malcolm X, and Alex Haley. *The Autobiography of Malcolm X*. Grove Press, 1964.
Manchester, William. *The Glory and the Dream: A Narrative History of America*. Little, Brown, 1973.
Mars, Florence. *Witness in Philadelphia*. Louisiana State University Press, 1977.
Marsh, Charles. *God's Long Summer*. Princeton University Press, 1997.
Massengill, Reed. *Portrait of a Racist: The Real Life of Byron De La Beckwith*. St. Martin's Press, 1996.
McAdam, Doug. *Freedom Summer*. Oxford University Press, 1988.
McNamara, Robert S. *In Retrospect: The Tragedy and Lessons of Vietnam*. Times Books, 1995.
McPherson, Harry. *A Political Education*. Houghton Mifflin, 1988.
Meier, August. *Black Protest Thought in the Twentieth Century*. Bobbs-Merrill, 1965, 1971.
Meier, August and Elliott Rudwick. *CORE: A Study in the Civil Rights Movement*. University of Illinois Press, 1973.
Miller, Keith. *Voice of Deliverance: The Language of Martin Luther King, Jr. and Its Sources*. The Free Press, 1992.
Miller, Merle. *Lyndon: An Oral Biography*. Ballantine, 1980.
Mills, Kay. *This Little Light of Mine: The Life of Fannie Lou Hamer*. Dutton, 1993.
Moody, Anne. *Coming of Age in Mississippi*. The Dial Press, 1968.
Moore, Donald J. *The Human and the Holy: The Spirituality of Abraham Joshua Heschel*. Fordham University Press, 1989.
Moynihan, Daniel P. *Maximum Feasible Misunderstanding: Community Action in the War on Poverty*. The Free Press, 1969.
Muhammad, Elijah. *Message to the Blackman in America*. Muhammad Mosque of Islam #2, 1965.
Muse, Benjamin. *The American Negro Revolution: From Nonviolence to Black Power, 1963–67*. University of Indiana Press, 1968.
Myers, Robert Manson. *The Children of Pride*. Popular Library, 1977.
Neary, John. *Julian Bond: Black Rebel*. William Morrow, 1971.

Nelson, Jack. *Terror in the Night: The Klan's Campaign Against the Jews.* Simon & Schuster, 1993.
Neusner, Jacob, and Noam M. M. Neusner, eds. *To Grow in Wisdom: An Anthology of Abraham Heschel.* Madison Books, 1990.
O'Reilly, Kenneth. *Racial Matters: The FBI's Secret File on Black America.* The Free Press, 1989.
Oates, Stephen B. *Let the Trumpet Sound: The Life of Martin Luther King, Jr.* Harper & Row, 1982.
Oesterreicher, John M. *The Rediscovery of Judaism.* Seton Hall University, 1971.
Oshinsky, David M. *"Worse Than Slavery": Parchman Farm and the Ordeal of Jim Crow Justice.* The Free Press, 1996.
Perry, Bruce. *Malcolm: A Life of the Man Who Changed Black America.* Station Hill Press, 1991.
———, ed. *Malcolm X: The Last Speeches.* Pathfinder Press, 1989.
Poinsett, Alex. *Walking with Presidents: Louis Martin and the Rise of Black Political Power.* Madison Books, 1997.
Pomerantz, Gary M. *Where Peachtree Meets Sweet Auburn: A Saga of Race and Family.* Penguin, 1997.
Poulos, George. *A Breath of God: A Biography of Archbishop Iakovos.* Holy Cross Orthodox Press, 1984.
Powers, Richard Gid. *Secrecy and Power: The Life of J. Edgar Hoover.* The Free Press, 1987.
Quarles, Benjamin. *The Negro in the Making of America.* Macmillan, 1969.
Raines, Howell. *My Soul Is Rested.* Bantam, 1977.
Reeves, Richard. *President Kennedy: Profile of Power.* Simon & Schuster, 1993.
Reid, T. R. *The Chip: How Two Americans Invented the Microchip & Launched a Revolution.* Simon & Schuster, 1984.
Rice, C. Duncan. *The Rise and Fall of Black Slavery.* Harper & Row, 1975.
Roberts, Charles Wesley. *LBJ's Inner Circle.* Delacorte Press, 1965.
Rochlin, Harriet and Fred. *Pioneer Jews: A New Life in the American West.* Houghton Mifflin, 1984.
Rothschild, Fritz A. *Between God and Man: An Interpretation of Judaism.* The Free Press, 1975.
Rothschild, Mary Aickin. *A Case of Black and White: Northern Volunteers and the Southern Freedom Summers, 1964–65.* Greenwood Press, 1982.
Rusk, Dean. *As I Saw It.* Norton, 1990.
Rynne, Xavier. *Letters From Vatican City.* Farrar, Straus & Co., 1963.
Salter, John R. Jr. *Jackson, Mississippi.* Exposition Press, 1979.
Schlesinger, Arthur M, Jr. *A Thousand Days: John F. Kennedy in the White House.* Fawcett, 1965.
———. *Robert Kennedy and His Times.* Ballantine, 1978.
Schmidt, Stephan. *Augustino Bea.* Rome: New City Editors Press, 1987.
Sellers, Cleveland, with Robert Terrell. *The River of No Return: The Autobiography of a Black Militant.* William Morrow, 1973.
Shapley, Deborah. *Promise and Power: The Life and Times of Robert McNamara.* Little, Brown, 1993.
Silver, James W. *Mississippi: The Closed Society.* Harcourt, Brace & World, 1963.
Smith, Bob. *They Closed Their Schools: Prince Edward County, Virginia, 1951–64.* University of North Carolina Press, 1965.
Smith, John Coventry. *From Colonialism to World Community: The Church's Pilgrimage.* The Geneva Press, Philadelphia, 1982.
Stern, Mark. *Calculating Visions: Kennedy, Johnson & Civil Rights.* Rutgers University Press, 1992.
[Stokes Committee]. U.S. House of Representatives. *Investigation of the Assassination of Martin Luther King, Jr. Hearings Before the Select Committee on Assassinations, Vol. vi, Nov. 17, 20, 21, 1978.* U.S. Government Printing Office, 1979.
———. Investigation of the Assassination of Martin Luther King, Jr. Hearings Before the Select Committee on Assassinations, Vol. vii, Nov. 27, 28, 29, 30, 1978. U.S. Government Printing Office, 1979.
Stone, Gregory, and Douglas Lowenstein. *Lowenstein: Acts of Courage and Belief* Harcourt Brace Jovanovich, 1983.
Sullivan, William. *The Bureau: My Thirty Years in Hoover's FBI.* W. W. Norton, 1979.
Summers, Anthony. *Official and Confidential: The Secret Life of J. Edgar Hoover.* G. P. Putnam's Sons, 1993.
Sutherland, Elizabeth. *Letters from Mississippi.* McGraw-Hill, 1965.
Taylor, Maxwell D. *Swords and Plowshares.* Norton, 1972.
Theoharis, Athan G. *The Boss: J. Edgar Hoover and the Great American Inquisition.* Temple University Press, 1988.
Tucker, Shirley. *Mississippi From Within.* Arco, 1965.
Ungar, Sanford J. *FBI: An Uncensored Look Behind the Walls.* Atlantic-Little, Brown, 1975.
Valenti, Jack. *A Very Human President.* Pocket, 1977.
Viorst, Milton. *Fire in the Streets.* Simon & Schuster, 1979.
Vollers, Maryanne. *Ghosts of Mississippi.* Little, Brown, 1995.
Von Hoffman, Nicholas. *Mississippi Notebook.* David White, 1964.
Vorgimler, Herbert, ed. *Commentary on the Documents of Vatican II.* Herder and Herder, 1969.
Warner, Roger. *Back Fire: The CIA's Secret War in Laos and Its Link to the War in Vietnam.* Simon & Schuster, 1995.
Warren, Robert Penn. *Who Speaks for the Negro?* Random House, 1965.
Washington, James M., ed. *A Testament of Hope: The Essential Writings of Martin Luther King.* Harper & Row, 1986.
Watters, Pat and Reese Cleghorn. *Climbing Jacob's Ladder: The Arrival of Negroes in Southern Politics.* Harcourt, Brace & World, 1967.
Webb, Sheyann & Rachel W. Nelson, as told to Frank Sikora. *Selma, Lord, Selma: Girlhood Memories of the Civil-Rights Days.* University of Alabama Press, 1980.
Whalen, Charles and Barbara. *The Longest Debate: A Legislative History of the 1964 Civil Rights Act.* Seven Locks Press, 1985.

White, Theodore H. *The Making of the President 1960.* Pocket, 1961.

Whitehead, Don. *Attack on Terror: The FBI Against the KKK in Mississippi.* Funk and Wagnalls, 1970.

Wicker, Tom. *On Press.* Viking, 1978.

Wilkins, Roy, with Tom Mathews. *Standing Fast: The Autobiography of Roy Wilkins.* The Viking Press, 1982.

Wolff, Daniel, with S. R. Crain, Clifton White, and G. David Tenenbaum. *You Send Me: The Life & Times of Sam Cooke.* William Morrow, 1995.

Woodson, Carter G. *The History of the Negro Church.* 2nd Ed., Associated Publishers, 1921.

———. *The Negro in Our History.* Associated Publishers, 1922.

Woodward, C. Vann. *The Strange Career of Jim Crow.* Oxford University Press, 1955, 1974.

Yoder, Edwin M., Jr. *Joe Alsop's Cold War: A Study of Journalistic Influence and Intrigue.* University of North Carolina Press, 1995.

Young, Andrew. *A Way Out of No Way: The Spiritual Memoirs of Andrew Young.* Thomas Nelson, 1994.

———. *An Easy Burden: The Civil Rights Movement and the Transformation of America.* HarperCollins, 1996.

Yzermans, Vincent A., ed. *American Participation in the Second Vatican Council.* Sheed and Ward, 1967.

Zaroulis, Nancy, and Gerald Sullivan. *Who Spoke Up? American Protest Against the War in Vietnam, 1963–75.* Doubleday & Co., 1984.

Zinn, Howard. *SNCC: The New Abolitionists.* 2nd Edition, Beacon Press, 1965.

Index